SALEM HEALTH

Psychology & Behavioral Health

SALEM HEALTH

Psychology & Behavioral Health

Volume 2

Comorbidity – Health psychology

Editor

Paul Moglia, PhD

South Nassau Communities Hospital

Oceanside, NY

Salem Press

A Division of EBSCO Information Services, Inc.

Ipswich, Massachusetts

GREY HOUSE PUBLISHING

∞The paper used in these volumes conforms to the American National Standard for Permanence of Paper for Printed Library Materials, Z39.48 1992 (R1997).

Some of the updated and revised essays in this work originally appeared in *Magill's Encyclopedia of Social Science: Psychology*, edited by Nancy A. Piotrowski, PhD (2003) and *Magill's Survey of Social Science: Psychology*, edited by Frank N. Magill (1993).

Publisher's Cataloging-In-Publication Data
(Prepared by The Donohue Group, Inc.)

Psychology & behavioral health / editor, Paul Moglia, PhD. – Fourth edition.

5 volumes : illustrations ; cm. -- (Salem health)

At head of title: Salem health.
Previously published as: Psychology & mental health.
Includes bibliographical references and index.
Contents: Volume 1. Ability tests-Community psychology -- volume 2. Comorbidity-Health psychology -- volume 3. Hearing-Parental alienation syndrome -- volume 4. Parenting styles-Sleep -- volume 5. Sleep apnea-Philip Zimbardo; Appendixes; Indexes.
ISBN: 978-1-61925-543-2 (5-volume set)
ISBN: 978-1-61925-810-5 (vol.1)
ISBN: 978-1-61925-811-2 (vol.2)
ISBN: 978-1-61925-812-9 (vol.3)
ISBN: 978-1-61925-813-6 (vol.4)
ISBN: 978-1-61925-814-3 (vol.5)

1. Psychology, Applied--Encyclopedias. 2. Mental health--Encyclopedias. 3. Mental illness--Encyclopedias. 4. Medicine and psychology--Encyclopedias. I. Moglia, Paul. II. Title: Psychology and behavioral health III. Title: Salem health IV. Series: Salem health (Pasadena, Calif.)

BF636 .P86 2015
150.3

First Printing
Printed in the United States of America

COMPLETE LIST OF CONTENTS

VOLUME 1

VOLUME 2

VOLUME 3

VOLUME 4

VOLUME 5

Comorbidity

DATE: 1980's forward
TYPE OF PSYCHOLOGY: Psychopathology

Comorbidity is defined as the co-occurrence of two or more psychiatric illnesses. Also known as dual or co-occurring disorders, comorbidity often refers to the presence of a serious mental disorder and a substance use disorder, but other disorders such as anxiety and bipolar disorders often co-occur. The symptoms of comorbidity are more complicated, and make diagnosis more difficult and present greater clinical challenges than those of either a psychiatric or substance use disorder alone.

KEY CONCEPTS
- Case management
- Co-occuring disorders
- Dual disorders
- Integrated treatment
- Risk factors
- Self-medication
- Serious mental disorder
- Substance use disorder

INTRODUCTION

People with primary psychiatric disorders have high rates of substance abuse and addictive disorders and vice versa. These clinical conditions are defined in the *Diagnostic and Statistical Manual of Mental Disorders: DSM* 5 (2013) of the American Psychiatric Association, which is the widely used nomenclature for mental disorders. In the fields of clinical psychology and psychiatry, the terms comorbidity or dual diagnosis, generally apply to the presence of one or more serious mental disorders (SMDs) and one or more substance use disorders (SUDs). However, comorbidity can also refer to the co-occurrence of two or more serious mental disorders such as personality disorders .

PREVALENCE

Substance use disorders and addictive disorders are the most common and clinically severe disorders that affect people with serious mental disorders, which include major depression, bipolar disorder, anxiety disorders, and schizophrenia. The Substance Abuse and Mental Health Services Administration reported in 2009 that almost 9 million adults in the United States have co-occurring mental and substance use disorders. Estimates of the percentages of people with both lifetime serious mental and substance use disorders vary among different studies. The Epidemiological Catchment Area Study, which involved structured psychiatric interviews with more than twenty thousand randomly selected participants, found that nearly half of those diagnosed with schizophrenia (48 percent) and more than half (56 percent) of those diagnosed with bipolar disorder had one or more substance use disorders.

CAUSES AND CONSEQUENCES

Significant research has been conducted to attempt to determine why serious mental and substance use disorders co-occur. Studies of close family members and twins have suggested an inherited susceptibility to serious mental and substance use disorders, and investigations are pointing to the potential for overlapping genetic vulnerabilities. A 2010 report from the National Institute on Drug Abuse (NIDA), a division of the US Department of Health and Human Services, indicated an individual's vulnerability to addiction is 40–60 percent genetic, and a more recent (2013) study in the journal Nature Genetics linked five major mental disorders—schizophrenia, bipolar disorder, major depressive disorder, autism spectrum disorders, and attention-deficit hyperactivity disorder (ADHD)—to the same genetic variations. Furthermore, specific areas of the brain, such as those that use the neurotransmitter dopamine are affected by addictive substances and are known to be involved in several mental illnesses such as schizophrenia and depression. NIDA also reported that individuals diagnosed with mood or anxiety disorders and antisocial syndromes, such as antisocial personality disorder and its childhood precursor conduct disorder, are almost twice as likely to suffer from substance use disorder. Conversely, those suffering from substance use disorder are about twice as likely to also suffer from mood and anxiety disorders. It is unknown whether substance use causes mental illness or if the presence of a serious mental illness contributes to substance use disorder.

Anecdotal evidence suggests that individuals with mental disorders such as anxiety or depression or with negative side effects from a psychopharmacological course of treatment use certain substances to self-medicate to alleviate their symptoms. For example, people with depressive disorders often choose drugs that have stimulating effects, such as cocaine or amphetamines. Conversely, people with anxiety-inducing disorders often choose drugs that have sedative effects, such as opiates or alcohol.

Research suggests that people who have a mental illness are hypersensitive to the effects of drugs and alcohol. Small amounts of drugs and alcohol in people with a mental illness, compared with individuals with no mental illness, are more likely to impair the person's performance in cognitive and motor tasks. Furthermore, small amounts of drugs and alcohol can result in more abuse and dependence problems, as well as other negative consequences, for mentally ill individuals than for those who are not mentally ill.

TREATMENT OPTIONS

Comorbid disorders differ from single disorders in their clinical courses and treatment protocols. Individuals with comorbidity are generally more difficult to diagnose and treat, primarily because of the similarities between the symptoms of substance use disorder and major mental illnesses. Individuals with comorbidity often experience a greater number of psychotic symptoms, require more specialized and intensive treatment, and have poorer treatment outcomes than those with only a serious mental or substance use disorder. People with dual diagnoses also have more difficulty accessing treatment. According to 2009 report from the Substance Abuse and Mental Health Services Administration, only 7.4 percent of individuals with co-occurring disorders receive treatment for both conditions with 55.8 percent receiving no treatment at all.

Treatment programs for people with serious mental or substance use disorders have historically been administered through separate systems with different criteria for client services and different training, education, and certification requirements for service providers. Individuals with comorbidity usually have participated in sequential treatment in which they are expected to be free of either their serious mental or substance use disorder before receiving treatment for the other disorder. Another option is for such individuals to receive parallel treatment, thus participating in both treatments simultaneously but with different practitioners who work at different agencies or clinics.

Sequential and parallel treatments have led to fragmented and ineffective care for people with dual diagnoses. Such treatments force them to navigate the mental health and substance abuse systems separately and to struggle with the disparate messages that they receive from each about treatment goals and pathways to recovery. For example, many drug treatment programs prohibit patients from taking psychiatric medications, the mainstay of care for people with serious mental illness.

Integrated treatments for co-occurring disorders are delivered by professionals who view both serious mental and substance use disorders as "primary" conditions, provide coordinated care for co-occurring disorders, and adhere to consistent and shared philosophies and treatment plans. The essential ingredients of integrated treatments for people with comorbidity include assertive outreach procedures; case management models; comprehensive services; shared decision making with staff, clients, and clients' families; progressive stages that engage clients in treatment and help them avoid relapses; team approaches to service delivery; long-term commitment to services; cross-training for program staff; and the use of self-help groups and psychopharmacological interventions.

Integrated treatment for co-occurring disorders is more effective than either sequential or parallel treatments. Studies have found that people with co-occurring disorders who are in integrated treatment programs have sustained remission rates from substance use that are two to four times higher than those in nonintegrated treatment programs. Other benefits of integrated treatment for comorbidity include longer retention in treatment, lower rates of victimization, and less time in the hospital. The treatment dropout rates of people with dual diagnoses are very high, owing to their low motivation, cognitive impairment, and disorganized lives. Therefore, clinicians in integrated programs concentrate their services in the community, aggressively bringing comprehensive services to clients rather than expecting clients to seek such services. Comprehensive services encompass all areas of clients' lives and are aimed at improving their potential for obtaining employment, having stable housing, and living independently.

Treatment plans are more readily accepted and adhered to when people with comorbidity—and their families—have a role in developing and modifying such plans. Moreover, systematic or stage-wise models to treatment recognize that clients must be engaged in services, be motivated to change, be helped to achieve abstinence, and be taught to prevent relapses from serious mental and substance use disorders. Medications for serious mental and substance use disorders are instrumental in reducing and managing symptoms. If left untreated or treated with nonintegrated approaches, co-occurring serious mental and substance use disorders usually become more severe and chronic. People with dual diagnoses need considerable time to recover. Hence, integrated programs take a long-term view of success with such patients.

People with comorbidity are common in both the mental health and substance abuse treatment systems and in the criminal justice system. They present significant challenges to treatment providers and place tremendous strain on resources. Patients with dual disorders suffer from a wide range of public health problems and are unlikely to recover without long-term care. Offenders with comorbid serious mental and substance use disorders are more likely to recidivate, engage in violent behaviors, and have infectious diseases. Integrated programs have the best chance of helping them achieve more satisfying and productive lives.

The War on Drugs in the United States has swelled the country's probation, jail, and prison populations with unprecedented numbers of drug-abusing and drug-dependent offenders, and has lead to the implementation and evaluation of numerous drug treatment programs in correctional settings. Lost in the emphasis on providing drug treatment to offenders, however, is the very high rates of comorbid psychiatric disorders. The lack of specific programs for offenders with co-occurring disorders has resulted in high rates of rearrests and reincarcerations and has increased the likelihood of violent behaviors within this population.

Although the nation's correctional populations continue to grow, adequate and well-designed treatment programs are needed more urgently than ever to address psychiatric comorbidities among offender populations. Despite high rates of psychiatric comorbidity among offender populations, drug treatment programs in criminal justice settings and the general community have concentrated on drug treatment and have failed to address psychiatric comorbidity adequately. Unfortunately for those with comorbidity, not enough effective programs are available to meet the demand for such care.

BIBLIOGRAPHY

Boden, Matthew Tyler, and Rudolf Moos. "Predictors of Substance Use Disorder treatment Outcomes Among Patients with Psychotic Disorders." *Schizophrenia Research* 146.1–3 (2013): 28–33. Print.

Drake, R. E., et al. "A Review of Integrated Mental Health and Substance Abuse Treatment for Patients with Dual Disorders." *Schizophrenia Bulletin* 24 (1998): 589–608. Print.

Epstein J., P. Barker, M. Vorburger, and C. Murtha. *Serious Mental Illness and Its Co-occurrence with Substance Use Disorders*, 2002. DHHS Publication No. SMA 04–3905, Analytic Series A-24. Rockville: Substance Abuse and Mental Health Services Administration, Office of Applied Studies, 2004. Print.

Hills, H. A. *Creating Effective Treatment Programs for Persons with Co-occurring Disorders in the Justice System*. Delmar: GAINS Center, 2000. Print.

Kessler, R. C., et al. "Lifetime Co-occurrence of DSM-III-R Alcohol Abuse and Dependence with Other Psychiatric Disorders in the National Comorbidity Survey." *Archives of General Psychiatry* 54 (1997): 313–21. Print.

Lee, S. Hong. "Genetic Relationship Between Five Psychiatric Disorders Estimated from Genome-Wide SNPs." Nature Genetics 45 (2013): 984–94. Print.

Mueser, K. T., R. E. Drake, and M. A. Wallach. "Dual Diagnosis: A Review of Etiological Theories." *Addictive Behaviors* 23 (1998): 717–34. Print.

National Institute on Drug Abuse. "Comorbidity: Addiction and Other Mental Illnesses." *Research Report Series* (2010). Print.

Arthur J. Lurigio

See Also: Alcohol dependence and abuse; Anxiety disorders; Bipolar disorder; Depression; Personality disorders; Schizophrenia: Background, types, and symptoms; Substance use disorders.

Complex experimental designs

Type of psychology: Psychological methodologies

Complex experimental designs in psychology research investigate the effects of two or more variables on an individual's behavior; when the effects of these variables combine to predict the behavior, rather than acting independently, this is called an interaction. Knowledge of interactions contributes to an ability to understand research observations.

Key Concepts

- Analysis of variance
- Experimental variable
- Main effect

- Statistical significance
- Subject variable

INTRODUCTION

Psychology seeks to predict and understand the behavior of individuals, whether humans or other animals. To produce general rules about individual behavior, its research methods usually involve making large numbers of observations of behavior of different individuals or of the same individual at different times.

At the simple level of design, psychological research measures a single behavior repeatedly and summarizes these observations—for example, describing the mean amount of practice needed to learn a task, the percentage of people who express a particular attitude, or the mean reaction time to answer a question. Such research can show what typically happens, but it does not predict when this behavior will occur, suggest how it can be altered, or explain what causes it.

At an intermediate level of design, research in psychology is concerned with how one measured characteristic or experience of an individual human or animal relates to some behavior of that same individual that the researcher is trying to predict or understand. In a post facto intermediate research design, the predictor variable is some quality or characteristic of the individual that already exists, called a subject variable. In an experimental intermediate research design, the predictor variable is some recent experience or current stimulus, called a manipulated variable, that the psychologist performing the research has selected and administered.

Behavior is called a variable because it can differ (or vary) among individuals or in the same individual at different times. Subject variables, such as gender, self-consciousness, age, and birth order, also differ among individuals and, in some cases, within the same individual over time. Manipulated variables include psychoactive drugs, persuasive arguments, sensory isolation, and psychotherapy. They vary in the sense that the researcher exposes different individuals, or the same individual at different times, to different levels or amounts of that treatment.

FACTORIAL RESEARCH DESIGNS

Complex (or factorial) research designs investigate how two or more predictor variables are related to the individual's behavior. An example would be studying how a number of subject variables, such as age, ethnicity, religion, gender, and intelligence test scores, all combine to predict political attitudes. In this case, one has a post facto complex research design. If the predictor variables are all manipulated by the experimenter—the amount of an administered drug varied, differing anxiety-inducing instructions given, and tasks of contrasting difficulties presented—then this is an experimental complex research design. The most common approach combines the measurement of subject variables with the manipulation of variables for the purpose of learning whether the effects of the manipulation have the same effects on all kinds of individuals. This is the mixed complex research design. An example of the latter design would be the measurement of gender and age followed by the manipulation of the kind of message used to persuade individuals about the importance of recycling waste; later, the individuals' recycling behavior would be observed.

In this last example, the three factors being measured to see if they are related to recycling behavior may yield between zero and seven statistically significant results from an analysis of variance of the data. An analysis of variance is defined as a statistical technique, commonly abbreviated as ANOVA, used in inferential statistics to determine which behaviors that are measured are related to differences in other variables. Of the significant results, three may be main effects, meaning that the differences in observed behavior occur for any of the variables when averaged across all levels of the other variables. Any effects that are not main effects are interactions, meaning that the effect on behavior of one or more variables may be affected by a change in another variable.

In other words, if one message was found to be more effective than the other for boys but not for girls, an interaction would be said to exist. The effect of the message on recycling behavior would not be the same for all people, but rather would depend on the gender of the listener. When such an interaction occurs, it can be said that the effect of one variable on the measured behavior depends on the level of the other variable.

In this three-factor example, there are four possible interactions. One of them is the three-way interaction, since there is a possibility that the behavior for each combination of the factors cannot be predicted merely by adding the independent main effects for each factor. This means that the three factors contribute to behavior in some manner such that they interact, so that they are not independent of one another. An example would be if one of the messages is less appealing to older girls than it is to younger girls, or to boys of any age. The other three possible interactions in this experiment are all possible pairings of the variables: gender and age, gender and message, and age and message.

VARYING RESEARCH FACTORS

Imagine the example given above concerning recycling first as a simple research design. In this case, measurement (in some carefully defined and described manner) of behavior alone might find that 15 percent of all people practice recycling. To learn more about the causes of recycling, one might shift to an experimental intermediate research design.

By measuring the effects of varying the message about recycling, one might find the results shown in the left panel of the figure that accompanies this essay. This shows that message B produced more recycling (24 percent) than did message A (17 percent).

One should be wary of such a conclusion, however, whether it is found in published research or in one's own investigations. The mixed complex research design can make further measurements on subject variables to see whether these findings are the same for all individuals, or whether there is some personal characteristic that predicts the effect of the manipulated variable.

The right panel of the figure shows what might be found if gender were measured as well. Because equal numbers of boys and girls were assigned to each group, the mean recycling for each message remains the same (24 percent for message B, and 17 percent for message A), but it can be seen that the effect of each message was very different, depending on the gender of the individual. Here an interaction, which was not evident in the simple or intermediate research designs, can be seen. It is an important interaction because it shows that the effect of the messages on recycling behavior is different, depending on whether the listener is a boy or a girl.

Now imagine that another subject variable, age, were to be measured. The children were grouped into two categories, ages six to ten and ages eleven to fourteen. Thus, there were four groups, differentiated by gender and age: younger girls, older girls, younger boys, and older boys. Keeping the numbers in each group equal, it might be found that there are no effects of age on which message influences recycling behavior except in the girls who heard message B. In this group, young girls showed 23 percent recycling and older girls 13 percent. Thus, there would be a three-way interaction, in which both gender and age were dependent on each other to determine the effect of the message on behavior.

PRACTICAL AND THEORETICAL APPLICATIONS

Psychological researchers want to know about such interaction effects for both practical and theoretical purposes. An example of a practical application might be environmentalists reading this research to learn how best to improve recycling by children. Whether through television commercials broadcast during programs with a known audience, or through messages in the schools, environmentalists can tailor the message that will be the most effective for a given audience.

Basic researchers are trying to develop theories to understand more general behavior, such as attitude change or motivational processes. These theories may become sophisticated enough to make predictions for practical purposes such as the recycling program mentioned here, or changing people's behavior in therapy. In the present example, the interactions observed may cause the researcher to look at the content of message B to attempt to understand why it was more effective for all boys and for younger girls but was rejected by older girls. If the researcher noted that the message used a popular cartoon action figure as a role model for recycling, then possibly it is only boys and younger girls who identify with that action figure.

From further reading in the field of developmental psychology, the researcher may hypothesize that older girls would identify more with romantic fictional characters, and so design a recycling message that would have more appeal to them. The test of this new message would be an example of how complex research designs work to build cumulatively on previous research to produce more precise practical applications and also to improve theories about the sources of individual behavior.

ANALYZING COMPLEX BEHAVIOR

Complex experimental designs were developed to answer detailed questions about individual behavior. Simple and intermediate research designs provide some information, but the experience of psychological researchers is that behavior is not simple. Behavior has multiple causes that do not always act independently of one another. Thus there is the necessity for complex research designs, advanced statistical techniques, and sophisticated theories.

These methods are used in a great many areas of research in psychology. Therefore, the individual who wishes to know, at a professional level, about the behavior of humans and other animals must be able to understand the reports of the psychologists who do this research. Others can learn about psychology at a more general level by relying on secondary accounts written for a broader audience. Much of this research depends on the statistical technique of analysis of variance. This is often performed by using a computer software package designed for this purpose. These statistical software packages are great labor savers; at the same time, however, they can mislead researchers into incorrect conclusions about behavior if they are not familiar with experimental methodology.

SUBJECT VERSUS MANIPULATED VARIABLES

It is especially important when drawing conclusions to discriminate between subject variables and manipulated variables. The reason is causality. Subject variables are measured after the fact (post facto) and consist of characteristics that the individual already possesses. Logically, subject variables cannot be assured to be part of a cause-and-effect connection with the behavior of interest. They may possibly be the cause—for example, a measured trait of anxiety may affect reactions to stress—but characteristics such as age and gender may instead be contributors to socialization, experiences, hormonal changes, or peer pressure. Other subject variables such as education or social class may be a result of behavior rather than its cause. When subject variables are found in research to be related to behavior, they may be a cause of that behavior, but the research does not provide evidence to justify that conclusion. Only manipulated variables—in a careful, controlled experiment—may be assumed to cause the behavior that they precede.

A RANGE OF BEHAVIORAL INFLUENCES

It is also important that the researcher remember that the variables selected represent only a few of the possible influences on behavior. In some cases, the subject variables are only related to more powerful variables yet to be discovered. For the example used here, it was suggested that gender and age were predictors of the most effective persuasive message. Perhaps what was most important was that these were approximate predictors of which individuals prefer action figures over romantic figures. An analysis of how the persuasive messages are working may find that the answer to a question such as "Which figures do you prefer for playing?" would be a much more accurate predictor of the behavior in this situation than the mere assumption that boys and girls separate along lines of gender in every preference and psychological process. Awareness of these and similar research refinements comes with experience and training.

BIBLIOGRAPHY

Edwards, Allen Louis. *Experimental Design in Psychological Research.* 5th ed. New York: Harper, 1985. Print.

Kirk, Roger E. *Experimental Design: Procedures for the Behavioral Sciences.* Thousand Oaks: Sage, 2013. Print.

Martin, David W. *Doing Psychology Experiments.* 7th ed. Belmont: Wadsworth, 2008. Print.

Myers, Jerome L. *Fundamentals of Experimental Design.* 3d ed. Boston: Allyn, 1979. Print.

Ryan, Thomas P. *Modern Experimental Design.* Hoboken: Wiley-Interscience, 2007. Print.

Schneider, Sandra L. *Experimental Design in the Behavioral and Social Sciences.* Los Angeles: Sage, 2013. Print.

Sprinthall, Richard C. *Basic Statistical Analysis.* 8th ed. Boston: Allyn, 2007. Print.

Vercruyssen, M., and Hal W. Hendrick. *Behavioral Research and Analysis: An Introduction to Statistics Within the Context of Experimental Design.* Boca Raton: CRC, 2012. Print.

Winer, B. J. *Statistical Principles in Experimental Design.* 3d ed. New York: McGraw, 1991. Print.

Roger A. Drake

SEE ALSO: Animal experimentation; Archival data; Case study methodologies; Data description; Experimental psychology; Experimentation: Ethics and participant rights; Experimentation: Independent, dependent, and control variables; Field experimentation; Hypothesis development and testing; Observational methods; Qualitative research; Quasi-experimental designs; Research ethics; Sampling; Scientific methods; Statistical significance tests; Survey research: Questionnaires and interviews; Within-subject experimental designs.

Computer and internet use and mental health

TYPE OF PSYCHOLOGY: Psychopathology; Psychological methodologies; Social psychology

Technologies such as computers and the Internet are ubiquitous in contemporary culture, providing means of valuable work and social interaction and facilitating advances in mental health. Concurrently, some individuals

have proven vulnerable to these technologies, developing or exacerbating physical and mental pathology.

Key Concepts

- Addiction
- Carpal tunnel syndrome
- Compulsion
- Negative reinforcement
- Taboo
- Telehealth
- Social networking

INTRODUCTION

Technologies such as the computer and Internet provide immense health and social benefits. They serve as means to distribute telehealth—support and information services related to health care. They allow for social support among individuals in geographically distanced communities through social networking, providing benefits such as reduced isolation and social commerce. Moreover, computers and the Internet provide means of entertainment, such as online social gaming environments; learning, by improving hand-eye coordination in games; and skill development, by facilitating new ways of solving problems or puzzles.

DISORDERS RELATED TO COMPUTER AND INTERNET USE

The benefits of computer and Internet use are juxtaposed with both the physical and psychological pathologies that may result from use. Excessive computer use can take a physical toll on a person, affecting the back, hands, and eyes. Strained muscles and back stiffness from remaining sedentary for extended periods of time are some examples of the detriments of computer and Internet use. Failure to take regular breaks can also result in problems such as eyestrain. Moreover, serious functional difficulties, such as carpal tunnel syndrome, may result. Carpal tunnel syndrome occurs when an individual's nerves are compressed—resulting in excruciating pain in the hands, wrists, and forearms—because of the way in which a person is positioned at the computer and the time spent in those positions. Furthermore, because of the increased pain and discomfort, these ailments can affect feelings of well-being and even result in surgeries, lost time at work, and pain disorders.

Excessive computer use can also lead to compulsive disorders. Individuals may use the Internet for sexual activity or may overuse social-networking or online-gaming sites. In these cases, individuals spending large amounts of time in these activities may experience problems in other areas of their lives. These may result from foregoing face-to-face interactions in favor of online interactions or from spending so much time on the computer that an inability to complete other work, social, or personal obligations and responsibilities occurs. This condition is similar to addiction, in which the person engages in the use of substances despite serious social or physical consequences. In such cases, individuals may feel a compulsion, or pressing drive to participate in the behavior that feels inescapable. Negative reinforcement, or feelings of relief experienced after participating in the behavior that bolsters continued practice of the behavior, also increases the likelihood that the activity will become a vice. When individuals get locked into destructive behavior patterns, the result may be other psychological maladies such as depression and anxiety or feelings of a lack of control. Sometimes, these addictions preclude the person from meeting basic living needs.

Finally, use of the computer and Internet to participate in socially taboo behavior, or behavior which is deemed socially inappropriate and destructive, can also have psychological ramifications. The anonymity of the Internet may allow participation in illegal behaviors such as child pornography, harming children and potentially fostering problems such as compulsions in the adult participants. Exposure of taboo behavior can lead to relationship problems, exacerbation of substance-related problems, depression, and even suicide.

BIBLIOGRAPHY

Bourne, Edmund, and Lorna Garano. *Coping with Anxiety: Ten Simple Ways to Relieve Anxiety, Fear, and Worry.* Oakland: New Harbinger, 2003. Print.

Carnes, Patrick, David L. Delmonico, Elizabeth Griffin, and Joseph Moriarity. *In the Shadows of the Net: Breaking Free from Compulsive Online Sexual Behavior.* 2d ed. Center City: Hazelden, 2007. Print.

Castronova, Edward. *Exodus to the Virtual World: How Online Fun Is Changing Reality.* New York: Palgrave, 2008. Print.

Kirmayer, Laurence J., Eugene Raikhel, and Sadeq Rahimi. "Cultures of the Internet: Identity, Community and Mental Health." *Transcultural Psychiatry* 50.2 (2013): 165–91. Print.

Montgomery, Frances H., et al. "Monitoring Student Internet Patterns: Big Brother or Promoting Mental Health?" *Jour. of Technology in Human Services* 31.1

(2013): 61–70. Print.

O'Donohue, William T., and Tamara Penix Sbraga. *The Sex Addiction Workbook: Proven Strategies to Help You Regain Control of Your Life*. Oakland: New Harbinger, 2004. Print.

Tam, Philip, and Garry Walter. "Problematic Internet Use in Childhood and Youth: Evolution of a 21st Century Affliction." *Australasian Psychiatry* 21.6 (2013): 533–36. Print.

Taylor, T. L. *Play Between Worlds: Exploring Online Game Culture*. Cambridge: MIT P, 2006. Print.

Turkle, Sherry. *Life on the Screen: Identity in the Age of the Internet*. New York: Simon, 1997. Print.

Willard, Nancy E., and Karen Steiner. *Cyberbullying and Cyberthreats: Responding to the Challenge of Online Social Aggression, Threats, and Distress*. 2d ed. Champaign: Research Press, 2007. Print.

Young, Kimberly S. *Caught in the Net: How to Recognize the Signs of Internet Addiction—and a Winning Strategy for Recovery.* New York: Wiley, 1998. Print.

Nancy A. Piotrowski

See Also: Addictive personality and behaviors; Child abuse; Depression; Gambling; Games and mental health; Internet psychology; Sexual behavior patterns; Social networks; Social support and mental health; Virtual reality.

Computer models of cognition

Type of psychology: Cognition

The nervous system is the basis for all cognitive and mental activity. The nervous system can be viewed as processing information received from the environment. Computer models of cognition based on the actual structure of the human nervous system show great promise for elucidating the relationship between cognition and the nervous system.

Key Concepts

- Architecture
- Natural intelligence
- Netware
- Neural network
- neurocomputer
- Parallel distributed processing
- Processing elements
- Training law
- Transfer function
- Weights

INTRODUCTION

Human cognition depends on the operation of the neural anatomy that forms the nervous system. Essentially, the brain is composed of some 100 billion neurons. Roger Penrose has divided the brain into three areas: primary, secondary, and tertiary. Each of these three areas has a sensory and motor component. The primary areas are the visual, olfactory, somatosensory, and motor areas. These areas handle the input and output functions of the brain. The secondary areas lie near the primary regions and process the input received by the primary areas. Plans of action are developed in the secondary areas, and these actions are translated into movements of the muscular system by the primary cortex. The tertiary area makes up the rest of the brain. The most complex, abstract, sophisticated, and subtle activity of the brain occurs here. Information from the different sensory areas is received, collected, integrated, and analyzed. As Penrose says, "memories are laid down, pictures of the outside world are constructed, general plans are conceived and executed, and speech is understood or formulated." Thus, information or stimulation from the environment is received or input at the primary sensory areas. This information is then processed in increasingly complex and sophisticated ways in the secondary and tertiary sensory areas. The processed sensory information is sent to the tertiary motor area in the form of a grand plan of action, and it is then refined into plans for specific actions at the secondary and primary motor regions.

MODELS OF INFORMATION PROCESSING

The question for psychologists to solve is how to represent or model this complex activity that is the basis for human thought and action in the three regions of the brain. The theory of information processing contends that human cognition can be successfully modeled by viewing the operation of the brain as analogous to the operation of a computer. Penrose observed that the brain presents itself as "a superb computing device." More specifically, Robert J. Baron stated:

> The fundamental assumption is that the brain is a computer. It is comprised of some 100 billion computational cells called neurons, which interact in a variety of ways. Neurons are organized into well defined and highly structured

computational networks called neural networks. Neural networks are the principal computational systems of the brain.

A field known as neurocomputing, or computational neuroscience, holds great promise for providing such a computer-based model. The particular kind of computer to be used is a neurocomputer, which is modeled on the actual structure or architecture of the brain. The unit of the neurocomputer is the processing element, or neurode, which corresponds to a biological neuron. The neurocomputer is constructed of many neurodes that are interconnected to one another to form a neural network. Each neurode can receive a number of inputs, either externally or from other neurodes, and each input has a weight or strength given to it. These weights are all summed, and a single output results. This output can then act as an input to other neurodes to which it is interconnected. If the output is excitatory, it will encourage firing of the interconnected neurodes; if the output is inhibitory, it will discourage firing of the interconnected neurodes. The neurocomputer processes all the inputs and outputs in a parallel manner (that is, all of the neurodes can potentially operate simultaneously). The software that runs the neurocomputer is called netware. The netware provides the interconnections between neurodes, how the neural network will react to the input it receives (training law), and how the input and output are related to each other (transfer function). Neurocomputers are drastically different from any other kind of computer because their architecture and operation are modeled after the human brain. Thus, neurocomputers can perform human functions, such as being taught to learn new behaviors. Maureen Caudill refers to these computers as being "naturally intelligent," as opposed to the serial computer used with "artificial intelligence."

Because neurocomputers are constructed as analogues of the human nervous system, they are particularly adept and useful for solving the kinds of problems that the human brain can solve. Conventional computers would have great difficulty solving these problems because they are constructed to perform certain kinds of tasks very quickly and efficiently (for example, processing large amounts of numbers very rapidly), tasks that the human brain cannot do nearly as well.

USES OF ARTIFICIAL INTELLIGENCE

In *Naturally Intelligent Systems* (1990), Caudill and Charles Butler discuss two applications of neurocomputers and neural networks, one in medicine and the other in finance.

A machine called the vectorcardiograph was found, in tests, to be able to detect heart problems better than cardiologists could. The usual electrocardiograph records signals received from up to twelve leads placed on different parts of the body. Each recording is made separately and in a particular sequential order. In contrast, the vectorcardiograph records signals from only three locations (front-back, head-foot, right-left), and it records all three sources of data simultaneously. This parallel processing of the information suits the vectorcardiograph very nicely to neural networks.

Essentially, the vectorcardiograph was trained in three stages to differentiate between normal and abnormal electrocardiograms, much as a human is trained to discriminate or distinguish between two stimuli. In the first stage, the system was trained to recognize all the normal cases presented to it and a portion of the abnormal cases presented to it. The input weights were then set at the appropriate values and training continued. In the second stage, the neural network was trained also to recognize all normal cases and a portion of the remaining abnormal cases. Again, the input weights were set at their appropriate values. The third stage of training commenced, and training continued until the system could recognize the remaining abnormal cases. The training set consisted of vectorcardiographs from 107 people, half of whom were judged to be normal and half abnormal. When the vectorcardiograph was presented with sixty-three new cases never before presented, it correctly diagnosed 97 percent of the normal and 90 percent of the abnormal cases. Trained clinicians were able to identify, respectively, 95 percent and 53 percent of the cases. The diagnostic capabilities of the vectorcardiograph demonstrate the capabilities and potentials of neural networks.

A neural network known as the Multiple Neural Network Learning System (MNNLS) can be trained to make decisions to accept or reject a mortgage application. The system uses twenty-five areas of information that are divided into four categories: cultural (credit rating, number of children, employment history); financial (income, debts); mortgage(amount, interest rate, duration); and property (age, appraised value, type).

The MNNLS is a system of nine separate neural networks that are divided into three different layers, with three networks in each area. Each layer is analogous to a panel of three experts. One expert in each of the three layers concerns itself only with financial information, the second only with cultural and mortgage information, and the third with all four categories. When presented with a mortgage application, the first layer attempts to arrive at a decision. If the three "experts" all agree, the mortgage is accepted or rejected; however, if one of the experts disagrees with another, then the application goes to the second layer of experts, and the same process is repeated. The MNNLS is useful because it is very efficient and accurate. It is efficient because it is able to process a wide variety of problems because the neural networks correspond to different experts. The first layer effectively handles simple decisions, whereas the second and third layers can handle increasingly difficult decisions. MNNLS agreed with decisions made by humans about 82 percent of the time. In those cases in which the MNNLS disagreed with the human decision, the MNNLS was in fact nearly always correct. This happens because the MNNLS is a neural network that insists on consensus of a panel of experts (that is, consensus between separate neural networks). It would be economically unfeasible to have a panel of humans evaluate mortgages; however, a single person evaluating applications is more likely to make a mistake than a panel of evaluators.

METAPHORS OF MODELING

Stephen J. Hanson and David J. Burr astutely observed that "the computer metaphor has had a profound and lasting effect on psychological modeling." The influence of the computer can be seen especially in its use in artificial intelligence and in computer metaphors of learning and memory, in which information is processed, encoded, stored, and retrieved from three distinct memory stores (sensory, short-term, and long-term memory). The particular computer that has been used as the metaphor of the human mind and cognition has been the digital or serial computer.

It eventually became apparent to cognitive scientists, however, that the digital computer is actually a poor analogy for the human mind, because this computer operates in a decidedly nonhuman way. For example, the digital computer operates much too fast—much faster than the human mind can process information. It also processes much more data than the human mind can process. If the software is sound, the digital computer is perfect and operates error-free. Human problem solving, on the other hand, is characterized by mistakes. The digital computer is not capable of autonomous learning. It does only what it is told to do by the program; it cannot teach itself new things, as can a human. The digital computer is very poor at pattern recognition tasks, such as identifying a human face, something an infant can do very rapidly. The digital computer provides no information about the underlying structure (the nervous system) that makes human cognition and information processing possible.

A number of cognitive scientists have argued that the fields of artificial intelligence and traditional cognitive science have reached dead ends because of their reliance on the digital computer analogy of the mind, which is limited and largely inaccurate. Cognitive science and neurophysiology are now striking out in a promising new direction by using neural networks and neurocomputers as the analogue of the human mind. The human mind is closely related to the human brain; many would argue that the mind is equivalent to the brain. Therefore, to study the mind and cognition, the researcher must build a computer that is modeled on the architecture of the brain. The neurocomputer is modeled on the human brain, and the digital computer is not.

Unlike digital computers, neurocomputers operate in a manner consistent with the operation of the human nervous system and human cognition. Neurocomputers provide a potentially promising way to understand cognition, as well as providing a productive connection and interrelationship with neurophysiology.

BIBLIOGRAPHY

Addyman, Caspar, and Robert M. French. "Computational Modeling in Cognitive Science: A Manifesto for Change." *Topics in Cognitive Science* 4.3 (2014): 332–41. Print.

Allman, William F. *Apprentices of Wonder: Inside the Neural Network Revolution*. New York: Bantam, 1990. Print.

Caudill, Maureen, and Charles Butler. *Naturally Intelligent Systems*. 3d ed. Cambridge, Mass.: MIT P, 1993. Print.

Coward, L. Andrew. *A System Architecture Approach to the Brain: From Neurons to Consciousness*. New York: Nova Biomedical, 2005. Print.

Frankish, Keith, and William M. Ramsey. The Cambridge *Handbook of Cognitive Science*. Cambridge: Cambridge UP, 2012. Print.

Friedenberg, Jay, and Gordon Silverman. *Cognitive Science: An Introduction to the Study of Mind*.

Thousand Oaks: Sage, 2006. Print.

Gill, Satinder, ed. Cognition, *Communication and Interaction: Transdisciplinary Perspectives on Interactive Technology.* New York: Springer, 2007. Print.

Hanson, Stephen J., and David J. Burr. "What Connectionist Models Learn: Learning and Representation in Connectionist Networks." *Behavioral and Brain Sciences* 13.3 (1990): 471–518. Print.

Harnish, Robert. *Minds, Brains, Computers: An Historical Introduction to Cognitive Science.* New York: Blackwell, 2002. Print.

Marsa, Linda. "Computer Model Mimics Infant Cognition." *Discover* Jan./Feb. 2012: 53. Print.

Penrose, Roger. *The Emperor's New Mind: Concerning Computers, Minds, and the Laws of Physics.* New York: Penguin, 1991. Print.

Stillings, Neil A., et al. *Cognitive Science: An Introduction.* Cambridge: MIT P, 1998. Print.

Laurence Miller

SEE ALSO: Artificial intelligence; Brain structure; Cognitive psychology; Computer and Internet use and mental health; Internet psychology; Neurons; Neuropsychology; Synaptic transmission.

Concept formation

TYPE OF PSYCHOLOGY: Cognition

To think and communicate about the endless objects, living things, and events in the world, a person simplifies those things by mentally grouping them and organizing them based on relationships and features they have in common. The process of constructing rules about how things go together is called concept formation, and it is a powerful mental tool.

KEY CONCEPTS

- Artificial concepts
- Concept
- Concept formation
- Fuzzy borders
- Natural concepts
- Prototype
- Stimulus materials

INTRODUCTION

Humans are faced with the task of making sense of a world that contains a seemingly endless array of unique objects and living things. To reduce this endless uniqueness to something that is mentally manageable, people form concepts. A concept can be defined as an abstract idea based on grouping objects or events according to their common properties. Concepts guide thoughts and behaviors, so it is important to understand both the nature of those concepts and how people construct them. Animals of all types also have the ability to form concepts. Animals form concepts at a much more fundamental level than humans, but they have been shown to differentiate among various colors and various geometric patterns, for example. Throughout its long history, research on concept formation has used animals, such as pigeons and rats, as well as human subjects.

In daily life, the term "concept" is used in a way that is different from the way in which psychologists use it. Whereas psychologists say that a concept exists when two or more things are grouped on the basis of a common feature or property of each, everyday language uses the term "concept" to refer to abstract ideas, such as the concept of "integrity," or to a mental picture in one's mind, for example, "I have a concept of how I want my room to look." The term is used here as psychologists use it. Psychologists also frequently use the word "category" as a synonym for "concept."

Psychologists have had to be innovative when designing experiments to study concept formation, because there is no way to observe the way in which people think or form concepts directly. The techniques vary from study to study, but subjects are typically asked to choose which of several items fits a particular concept.

The early researchers in the area, including Jerome Bruner, Jacqueline Goodnow, and George Austin, used materials in their experiments that have since been referred to as "artificial" stimuli or concepts, because they used geometric figures such as circles and squares of various sizes and shapes that were deliberately devised to have only a certain number of alterable characteristics or features. Years later, researchers such as Eleanor Rosch became interested in "natural" concepts, based on complex real-world objects, in which partial membership in a category is a possible alternative.

TECHNIQUES OF STUDY

In a typical study on artificial concept formation, a psychologist would construct visual patterns that would not normally be encountered in daily life. The patterns would be printed on cards to create the stimulus materials, or anything presented to a subject during the course of an experiment that requires that subject to make a response. These visual patterns would vary in terms of size, shape, number, or color, for example, and would be referred to as dimensions. Basically, a dimension is any changeable characteristic of the stimulus. A dimension can have two or more values, and the value is determined by the number of sizes, shapes, numbers, or colors being utilized.

In this example, each dimension can have three values. In other words, there would be objects of small, medium, and large size; circular, triangular, and square shapes; one, two, or three items; and purple, red, and green colors. Varying those dimensions and values, the particular stimulus patterns presented to the subject would be things such as two large green squares, three small red triangles, or perhaps one medium purple circle. The concept to be learned is selected by the researcher beforehand and is kept secret from the subject, because the subject must discover the concept. The concept might be something such as "purple triangles of any size and any number." Thus, in this case, the specific concept to be learned would be "purple and a triangle."

In a concept-formation task, the stimuli are usually presented to the subjects in one of two ways: the reception method or the selection method. In the reception technique, the subject is shown a single card and is asked to state whether that card displays the concept that the experimenter had in mind. The experimenter then tells the subject whether the response is correct or incorrect. The subject is then shown another card.

In the selection technique, by contrast, the entire set of cards is simultaneously displayed to the subject in one large array. The number of cards in the entire set is determined by the combination of all possible dimensions and values. The subject selects a particular card from the array, stating whether it displays the concept to be learned. Following each selection and judgment, the experimenter informs the subject about correctness.

USE OF RULES AND CATEGORIES

Some tasks require subjects to discover the values, the rule, or both. A rule tells how the values must be combined. The two most common kinds of rules are called conjunction and disjunction. The conjunction rule uses the word "and," as in "all figures that are both purple and triangles." Thus, a subject learning a concept involving the conjunction rule would learn to respond yes to all purple triangles and no to all other figures. The disjunction rule uses the word "or," as in "all figures that are purple or a triangle or both."

An important development in research on concepts involves natural concepts or real-life categories. Rosch pointed out that the artificial-concept learning tasks use materials unlike those encountered in the everyday world. Most concepts in the everyday world do not fall into neatly defined categories. Many have fuzzy borders—conceptual borders that appear ill defined and shift according to the context in which the category member occurs—that involve some uncertainty. For example, is a tomato a fruit or a vegetable? Rosch theorized that people decide whether an item belongs to a particular category by comparing that item with a prototype or best example for that category. An apple is highly prototypical of the fruit category, whereas a coconut is a less typical example.

MAKING SENSE OF THE ENVIRONMENT

If a person understands the concept of sunglasses, that individual can recognize something as a pair of sunglasses even though they may look different from all the other sunglasses the person has seen before. A new pair of sunglasses with iridium-coated lenses can be included within the concept because the pair has qualities that are common to the entire class of objects that people refer to as sunglasses. They have earpieces, they block out the sun to some degree, and they cover the eyes. Sunglasses belong to the even larger conceptual category of eyewear. Concepts such as eyewear, cookware, furniture, and vehicles are very useful. It would be impossible to think intelligently without the ability to form concepts. Without that ability, every time a person encountered something that was slightly different from other things, it would be necessary to learn about that object as if it were completely new.

A person would then primarily function instinctually because, according to Michael Eysenck, it would be impossible to relate prior learning to new situations. By applying concepts, a person can develop an immediate understanding of new objects or ideas, because they can be related to a general class of similar objects and ideas that are familiar. A person knows what to expect from an object, even when it is encountered for the first time. In this way, thinking beings save an amazing amount of work. Concepts reduce the complexity of the environment and eliminate the need to learn constantly.

IMPLICATIONS FOR EDUCATION

The development and refinement of some concepts take place over a long period of time. A person can have general concepts about some things, precise concepts about others, and also be in the process of refining vague concepts. In the course of life, a person's understanding of a particular concept develops and expands with additional experience, advanced training, and new information. Understanding this has ramifications for formal education. Much teaching is directed toward the development of concepts. In fact, it would be almost impossible to use the vast amount of mental information that is available to human beings to solve problems, make decisions, understand language, and communicate without the ability to simplify the world by means of conceptualization. One of the principal objectives of formal education is to allow students to formulate a hypothesis, or tentative guess, about how some attribute contributes to a concept. Students are then encouraged to test the hypothesis. If it is wrong, they can adopt a new hypothesis that incorporates different attributes or the same attributes but with different rules, based on feedback they receive from an instructor.

Researchers have identified a number of factors involved in concept learning that apply to the process of education. One factor is the number of attributes. It is easier to learn a concept if there are only one or two relevant attributes, rather than several. Another factor is salience. It is easier to learn a concept if the relevant attributes are salient, or obvious. A third factor is positive examples. People tend to make better use of positive examples, although it is sometimes helpful and even necessary to give some negative examples. For example, imagine teaching a young child the concept of "house cat" by using examples that are all positive. One shows the child pictures of a Persian, a Siamese, and a Russian Blue. From the viewpoint of a teacher, it is desirable to highlight or emphasize the relevant features of the concepts to make them salient, such as mentioning that the creatures in all the pictures have fur. The child learns to say "cat" to each picture. A teacher cannot, however, be certain which aspects of the pictures determine the child's response. For all the teacher knows, the child considers a picture of a cat to be another example of a "dog." For this reason, it is important to include relevant negative examples. In general, negative examples tend to be more useful in later stages of training.

ARTIFICIAL INTELLIGENCE

As science fiction becomes fact, it is becoming desirable to be able to "teach" computers how to form concepts. This type of investigation is conducted in the field of artificial intelligence. To develop artificial ways of duplicating human thought and intelligence, it is important to know how the thought process is accomplished by humans. Imagine a task in which a computer is asked to identify whether something is a triangle. A computer could be programmed to learn the concept, but it would take a very sophisticated program. In comparison, it is easy for humans to recognize immediately what constitutes a triangle, based on vast experience with other triangular objects. Concept formation in computers provides the foundation for the ability to recognize handwriting, fingerprints, speech, and many other things electronically.

One of the problems for computers is that, although some concepts are well defined, most are not: This is Rosch's point. In addition, human experience and context play an important role in concept formation, which poses difficulties for computers. Even more troublesome for a computer is the fact that many conceptual categories are based on human imagination. Because people have knowledge about the world and how it operates, they adjust their conceptual categories to fit reality. Unless computers have human knowledge and experience, their concepts will not be exactly like those of humans.

CONCEPT THEORIES

Throughout the history of the scientific study of concept formation, three main types of theories have become apparent. They are association theory, hypothesis-testing theory, and information-processing theory. In the associationistic view, the organism passively receives information from the environment. Each example of the concept that has yet to be learned provides the organism with an additional piece of information. In this way, relevant features are reinforced, whereas irrelevant features disappear. This approach requires nothing from the organism except a memory of previous examples. This approach was in vogue in the first half of the twentieth century. According to associationistic views, stimuli gradually become associated with some response by means of a complex form of discrimination learning. By means of discrimination learning, discriminable aspects of stimulus patterns are detected and labeled. Later modifications of association theory introduced the idea of mediation, assuming that concepts are formed because of an intervening step in the mind of the learner, which connects the stimuli with the response.

A second line of theory development, hypothesis testing, views the subject as an active participant in the process of concept learning. According to this line of thought, the organism always has some hypothesis regarding the unknown concept. Incoming information is used to check the current hypothesis and is used as the basis for modifying that hypothesis if it is incompatible with existing evidence. Eventually, the organism hits on the correct hypothesis and forms the concept. The research of Bruner, Goodnow, and Austin, which was first published in 1956, adhered to the view of the organism as an active hypothesis tester.

Finally, theories were developed that emphasized the information-processing nature of concept formation. These theories view the process in terms of a sequence of decisions made by the learner. The learner is seen as accepting external information, or stimuli, processing the information in a variety of ways, and producing some final response. One of the earliest attempts to produce an information-processing model for the learning of concepts was made by Earl Hunt in 1962.

BIBLIOGRAPHY

Bourne, Lyle E., Jr. *Human Conceptual Behavior.* 1966. Reprint. Boston: Allyn, 1970. Print.

Bourne, Lyle E., Jr., Roger L. Dominowski, and Elizabeth F. Loftus. *Cognitive Processes.* 2d ed. Englewood Cliffs: Prentice, 1986. Print.

Braisby, Nick, and Angus Gellatly. *Cognitive Psychology.* Oxford: Oxford UP, 2012. Print.

Bruner, Jerome S., Jacqueline J. Goodnow, and George A. Austin. *A Study of Thinking*. 5th ed. New Brunswick: Transaction, 2005. Print.

Eysenck, Michael W., and Mark T. Keane. *A Handbook of Cognitive Psychology.* 4th ed. Hillsdale: Lawrence, 1984. Print.

Hunt, Earl B. *Concept Learning: An Information Processing Problem.* 1962. Reprint. New York: Krieger, 1974. Print.

Quaranta, Mario. "Fuzzy Set Theory and Concepts: A Proposal for Concept Formation and Operationalization." *Comparative Sociology* 12.6 (2013): 785–820. Print.

Robinson-Riegler, Bridget, and Gregory Robinson-Riegler. *Cognitive Psychology: Applying the Science of the Mind.* Boston: Pearson, 2012. Print.

Rosch, Eleanor H. "Classification of Real-World Objects: Origins and Representation in Cognition." *Thinking: Readings in Cognitive Science*. Ed. P. N. Johnson-Laird and P. C. Wason. Cambridge: Cambridge UP, 1980. Print.

Stainton, Robert, ed. *Contemporary Debates in Cognitive Science.* Malden: Blackwell, 2006. Print.

Deborah R. McDonald

See Also: Cognitive psychology; Decision making; Learning; Logic and reasoning; Pattern recognition; Thought: Inferential; Thought: Study and measurement.

Conditioning

Type of psychology: Learning

Conditioning and learning are roughly synonymous terms. Both refer to changes in behavior resulting from experience, but conditioning has a more specific meaning and refers to changes in behavior that are the direct result of learning relationships between environmental events. Two types of relationships are studied by learning psychologists. The first involves learning the relationship between environmental events that consistently occur together. The second involves learning the environmental consequences of behavior. These two learning scenarios correspond to classical and operant conditioning respectively.

Key Concepts

- Behavioral approach
- Conditioned stimulus (CS)
- Conditioned response (CR)
- Contiguity
- Law of effect
- Operant response (R)
- Reinforcing stimulus (Sr)
- Schedules of reinforcement
- Shaping
- Unconditioned stimulus (US)
- Uncontitioned response (UR)

INTRODUCTION

Learning refers to any change in behavior or mental processes associated with experience. Traditionally psychologists interested in learning have taken a behavioral approach, which involves studying the relationship between environmental events and resulting behavioral changes in detail. Though the behavioral approach typically involves studying the behavior of nonhuman subjects in controlled laboratory environments, the results from behavioral research have often found wide application and use in human contexts. Since the early twentieth century, behavioral psychologists have extensively studied two primary forms of learning, classical and operant conditioning.

CLASSICAL CONDITIONING

Classical conditioning is also referred to as associative learning or Pavlovian conditioning, after its primary founder, the Russian physiologist Ivan Petrovich Pavlov. Pavlov's original studies involved examining digestion in dogs. The first step in digestion is salivation. Pavlov developed an experimental apparatus that allowed him to measure the amount of saliva the dog produced when presented with food. Dogs do not need to learn to salivate when food is given to them—that is an automatic, reflexive response. However, Pavlov noticed that, with experience, the dogs began to salivate before the food was presented, suggesting that new stimuli had acquired the ability to elicit the response. To examine this unexpected finding, Pavlov selected specific stimuli, which he systematically presented to the dog just before food was presented. The classic example is the ringing of a bell, but there was nothing special about the bell per se. Dogs do not salivate in response to a bell ringing under normal circumstances. What made the bell special was its systematic relationship to the delivery of food. Over time, the dogs began to salivate in response to the ringing of the bell even when the food was not presented. In other words, the dog learned to associate the bell with food so that the response (salivation) could be elicited by either stimulus.

In classical conditioning terminology, the food is the unconditioned stimulus (US). It is unconditioned (or unlearned) because the animal naturally responds to it before the experiment is begun. The sound of the bell ringing is referred to as the conditioned stimulus (CS). It is not naturally effective in eliciting salivation—learning is required in order for it to do so. Salivating in response to food presentation is referred to as the unconditioned response (UR) and salivating when the bell is rung is referred to as the conditioned response (CR). Though it would seem that saliva is saliva, it is important to differentiate the conditioned from the unconditioned response, because these responses are not always identical. More important, one is a natural, unlearned response (the UR) while the other requires specific learning experiences to occur (the CR).

Classical conditioning is not limited to dogs and salivation. Modern researchers examine classical conditioning in a variety of ways. What is important is the specific pairing of some novel stimulus (the CS) with a stimulus that already elicits the response (the US). One common experimental procedure examines eye-blink conditioning in rabbits, where a brief puff of air to the eye serves as the US and the measured response (UR) is blinking. A tone, a light, or some other initially ineffective stimulus serves as the CS. After many pairings in which the CS precedes the air puff, the rabbit will begin to blink in response to the CS in the absence of the air puff. Another common behavior that is studied in classical conditioning research is conditioned suppression. Here a CS is paired with an aversive US, such as a mild electric shock. Presentation of the shock disrupts whatever behavior the animal is engaged in at the time, and with appropriate pairing over time the CS comes to do so as well. A final example that many humans can relate to is taste-aversion learning. Here a specific taste (CS) is paired with a drug or procedure that causes the animal to feel ill (US). In the future, the animal will avoid consuming (CR) the taste (CS) associated with illness (US). Taste aversions illustrate the fact that all forms of conditioning are not created equal. To learn a conditioned eye-blink or salivation response requires many CS-US pairings, while taste aversions are often learned with only one pairing of the taste and illness.

UNDERLYING FACTORS

Psychologists have long studied the factors that are necessary and sufficient for producing classical conditioning. One important principle is contiguity, which refers to events occurring closely together in space or time. Classical conditioning is most effective when the CS and US are more contiguous, though precisely how closely together they must be presented depends on the type of classical conditioning observed. Taste-aversion conditioning, for example, will occur over much longer CS-US intervals than would be effective with other conditioning arrangements. Nevertheless, the sooner illness (US) follows taste (CS), the stronger the aversion (CR) will be.

Though seemingly necessary for classical conditioning, contiguity is not sufficient. A particularly clear demonstration of this fact is seen when the CS and US are presented at the exact same moment (a procedure called simultaneous conditioning). Though maximally contiguous, simultaneous conditioning is an extremely poor method for producing a CR. Furthermore, the order of presentation matters. If the US is presented before the CS rather than afterward, as is usually the case, then inhibitory conditioning will occur. Inhibitory conditioning is seen in experiments in which behavior can change in two directions. For example, with a conditioned suppression procedure, inhibitory conditioning is seen when the animal increases, rather than decreases, its ongoing behavior when the CS is presented.

These findings have led modern researchers to focus on the predictive relationship between the CS and the US in classical conditioning. An especially successful modern theory of classical conditioning, the Rescorla-Wagner Model, suggests that the CS acquires associative strength in direct proportion to how much information it provides about the upcoming US. In addition to providing a quantitative description of the way in which a CR is learned, the Rescorla-Wagner model has predicted a number of counterintuitive conditioning phenomena, such as blocking and overshadowing. Taken as a whole, the newer theoretical conceptions of classical conditioning tend to view the learning organism less as a passive recipient of environmental events than as an active analyzer of information.

Does classical conditioning account for any human behaviors? At first glance, these processes might seem a bit simplistic to account for human behaviors. However, some common human reactions are quite obviously the result of conditioning. For instance, nearly everyone who has had a cavity filled will cringe at the sound of a dentist's drill, because the sound of the drill (CS) has been paired in the past with the unpleasant experience of having one's teeth drilled (US). Cringing at the sound of the drill would be a conditioned response (CR). Psychologists have found evidence implicating classical conditioning in a variety of important human behaviors, from the emotional effects of advertising to the functioning of the immune system to the development of tolerance in drug addiction.

OPERANT CONDITIONING

At about the same time that Pavlov was conducting his experiments in Russia, an American psychologist named Edward L. Thorndike was examining a different form of learning that has come to be called instrumental or operant conditioning. Thorndike's original experiments involved placing cats in an apparatus he designed, which he called a puzzle box. A plate of food was placed outside the puzzle box, but the hungry cat was trapped inside. Thorndike designed the box so that the cat needed to make a particular response, such as moving a lever or pulling a cord, for a trap door to be released, allowing escape and access to the food outside. The amount of time it took the cat to make the appropriate response was measured. With repeated experience, Thorndike found that it took less and less time for the cat to make the appropriate response.

Operant conditioning is much different from Pavlov's classical conditioning. As was stated before, classical conditioning involves learning "what goes with what" in the environment. Learning the relationship changes behavior, though behavior does not change the environmental events themselves. Through experience, Pavlov's dogs began to salivate when the bell was rung because the bell predicted food. However, salivating (the CR) did not cause the food to be delivered. Thorndike's cats, on the other hand, received no food until the appropriate response was made. Through experience, the cats learned about the effects of their own behavior on environmental events. In other words, they learned the consequences of their own actions.

To describe these changes, Thorndike postulated the law of effect. According to the law of effect, in any given situation an animal may do a variety of things. The cat in the puzzle box could walk around, groom itself, meow, or engage in virtually any type of feline behavior. It could also make the operant response, the response necessary to escape the puzzle box and gain access to the food. Initially, the cat may engage in any of these behaviors and may produce the operant response simply by accident or chance. However, when the operant response occurs, escape from the box and access to the food follows. In operant conditioning terminology, food is the reinforcer (Sr, or reinforcing stimulus), and it serves to strengthen the operant response (R) that immediately preceded it. The next time the animal finds itself in the puzzle box, its tendency to produce the operant response will be a bit stronger as a consequence of the reinforcement. Once the response is made again, the animal gains access to the food again—which strengthens the response further. Over time, the operant response is strengthened, while other behaviors that may occur are not strengthened and thus drop away. So, with repeated experience, the amount of time that it takes for the animal to make the operant response declines.

SKINNERIAN CONDITIONING

In addition to changing the strength of responses, operant conditioning can be used to mold entirely new behaviors. This process is referred to as shaping, and it was described by American psychologist B. F. Skinner, who further developed the field of operant conditioning. Suppose that the experiment's objective was to train an animal, such as a laboratory rat, to press a lever. The rat could be given a piece of food (Sr) each time it pressed the lever (R), but it would probably be some considerable time before it would do so on its own. Lever pressing does not come naturally to rats. To speed up the process, the animal could be "shaped" by reinforcing successive approximations of lever-pressing behavior. The rat could be given a food pellet each time that it was in the vicinity of the lever. The law of effect predicts that the rat would spend more and more of its time near the lever as a consequence of reinforcement. Then the rat may be required to make some physical contact with the lever, but not necessarily press it, to be rewarded. The rat would make more and more contact with the lever as a result. Finally, the rat would be required to make the full response, pressing the lever, to get food. In many ways, shaping resembles the childhood game of selecting some object in the room without saying what it is and guiding guessers by saying "warmer" as they approach the object, and as they move away from it, saying nothing at all. Before long, the guessers will use the feedback to zero in on the selected object. In a similar manner, feedback in the form of positive reinforcement allows the rat to "zero in" on the operant response.

Skinner also examined situations in which reinforcement was not given for every individual response but was delivered according to various schedules of reinforcement. For example, the rat may be required to press the lever a total of five times (rather than once) to get the food pellet, or the reinforcing stimulus may be delivered only when a response occurs after a specified period of time. These scenarios correspond to ratio and interval schedules. Interval and ratio schedules can be either fixed, meaning that the exact same rule applies for the delivery of each individual reinforcement, or variable, meaning that the rule changes from reinforcer to reinforcer. For example, in a variable ratio-five schedule, a reward may be given after the first five responses, then after seven responses, then after three. On average, each five responses would be reinforced, but any particular reinforcement may require more or fewer responses.

To understand how large an impact varying the schedule of reinforcement can have on behavior, one might consider responding to a soda machine versus responding to a slot machine. In both cases the operant response is inserting money. However, the soda machine rewards (delivers a can of soda) according to a fixed-ratio schedule of reinforcement. Without reward, one will not persist very long in making the operant response to the soda machine. The slot machine, on the other hand, provides rewards (delivers a winning payout) on a variable-ratio schedule. It is not uncommon for people to empty out their pockets in front of a slot machine without receiving a single reinforcement.

SUPERSTITIOUS PIGEONS

As with classical conditioning, exactly what associations are learned in operant conditioning has been an important research question. For example, in a classic 1948 experiment, Skinner provided pigeons with food at regular intervals regardless of what they were doing at the time. Six of his eight pigeons developed stereotyped (consistent) patterns of behavior as a result of the experiment despite the fact that the pigeons' behavior was not really necessary. According to the law of effect, some behavior would be occurring just prior to food delivery, and this behavior would be strengthened simply by chance pairing with reinforcement. This would increase the strength of the response, making it more likely to occur when the next reward was delivered—strengthening the response still further. Ultimately, one behavior would dominate the pigeons' behavior in that experimental context. Skinner referred to this phenomenon as superstition. One need only observe the behavior of baseball players approaching the plate or basketball players lining up for a free-throw shot to see examples of superstition in human behavior.

Superstition again raises the issue of contiguity—simply presenting reinforcement soon after the response is made appears to strengthen it. However, later studies, especially a 1971 experiment conducted by J. E. R. Staddon and V. Simmelhag, suggested that it might not be quite that simple. Providing food rewards in superstition experiments changes a variety of responses, including natural behaviors related to the anticipation of food. In operant conditioning, animals are learning more than the simple contiguity of food and behavior; they are learning that their behavior (R) causes the delivery of food (Sr). Contiguity is important, but is not the whole story.

In addition, psychologists have explored the question "What makes a reinforcer reinforcing?" That is to say, is there some set of stimuli that will "work" to increase the behaviors they follow in every single circumstance? The answer is that there is not some set of rewards that will always increase behavior in all circumstances. David Premack was important in outlining the fact that reinforcement is a relative, rather than an absolute, thing. Specifically, Premack suggested that behaviors in which an organism is more likely to engage serve to reinforce behaviors in which they are less likely to engage. In a specific example, he examined children given the option of playing pinball or eating candy. Some children preferred pinball and spent more of their time playing the game than eating the candy. The opposite was true of other children. Those who preferred pinball would increase their candy-eating behavior (R) to gain access to the pinball machine (Sr). Those who preferred eating candy would increase their pinball-playing behavior (R) to gain access to candy (Sr). Behaviors that a child initially preferred were effective in reinforcing behaviors that the child was less likely to choose—but not the other way around.

NEGATIVE CONSEQUENCES

Positive or rewarding outcomes are not the only consequences that govern behavior. In many cases, people respond to avoid negative outcomes or stop responding when doing so produces unpleasant events. These situations correspond to the operant procedures of avoidance and punishment. Many psychologists have advocated using reinforcement rather than punishment to alter behavior, not because punishment is necessarily less effective in theory but because it is usually less effective in practice. For punishment to be effective, it should be (among other things) strong, immediate, and consistent. This can be difficult to accomplish in practice. In crime, for example, many offenses may have occurred without detection prior to the punished offense, so punishment is not certain. It is also likely that an individual's court hearing, not to mention his or her actual sentence, will be delayed by weeks or even months, so punishment is not immediate. First offenses are likely to be punished less harshly than repeated offenses, so punishment gradually increases in intensity. In the laboratory, such a situation would produce an animal that would be quite persistent in responding, despite punishment.

In addition, punishment can produce unwanted side effects, such as the suppression of other behaviors, aggression, and the learning of responses to avoid or minimize punishing consequences. Beyond this, punishment requires constant monitoring by an external authority, whereas reinforcement typically does not. For example, parents who want to punish a child for a dirty room must constantly inspect the room to determine its current state. The child certainly is not going to point out a dirty room that will cause punishment. On the other hand, if rewarded, the child will bring the clean room to the parents' attention. This is not to suggest that punishment should necessarily be abandoned as one tool for controlling behavior. Rather, the effectiveness of punishment, like reinforcement, can be predicted on the basis of laboratory results.

INTERACTIONS AND BIOLOGICAL CONSTRAINTS

Though the distinction between classical and operant conditioning is very clear in principle, it is not always so clear in practice. This makes sense if one considers real-life learning situations. In many circumstances events in the environment are associated (occur together) in a predictable fashion, and behavior will have consequences. This can be true in the laboratory as well, but carefully designed experiments can be conducted to separate out the impact of classical and operant conditioning on behavior.

In addition, the effectiveness of both classical and operant conditioning is influenced by biological factors. This can be seen both in the speed with which classically conditioned taste aversions (as compared with other CRs) are learned and in the stimulation of natural food-related behaviors in operant superstition experiments. Related findings have demonstrated that the effects of rewarding behavior can be influenced by biology in other ways that may disrupt the conditioning process. In an article published in 1961, Keller and Marian Breland described their difficulties in applying the principles of operant conditioning to their work as animal trainers in the entertainment industry. They found that when trained with food reinforcement, natural behaviors would often interfere with the trained operant response—a phenomenon they called instinctive drift. From a practical point of view, their research suggested that to be successful in animal training, one must select operant responses that do not compete with natural food-related behaviors. From a scientific point of view, their research suggested that biological tendencies must be taken into account in any complete description of conditioning processes.

APPLICATIONS OF CONDITIONING TECHNOLOGY

Beyond being interesting and important in its own right, conditioning research also serves as a valuable tool in the psychological exploration of other issues. In essence, conditioning technology provides a means for asking animals questions—a way to explore interesting cognitive processes such as memory, attention, reasoning, and concept formation under highly controlled laboratory conditions in less complex organisms.

Another area of research is the field of behavioral neuroscience, or psychobiology, a field that combines physiological and behavioral approaches to uncover the neurological mechanisms underlying behavior. For example, the impact of various medications and substances of abuse on behavior can be observed by administering drugs as reinforcing stimuli. It is interesting to note that animals will produce operant responses to receive the same drugs to which humans become addicted. However, in animals, the neurological mechanisms involved in developing addictions can be studied directly, using both behavioral and physiological experimental techniques in a way that would not be possible with human subjects, due to ethical considerations.

In addition, the principles of classical and operant conditioning have been used to solve human problems in a variety of educational and therapeutic settings, a strategy called applied behavior analysis. The principles of operant conditioning have been widely applied in settings in which some degree of control over human behavior is desirable. Token economies are situations in which specified behaviors, such as appropriate classroom behavior, are rewarded according to some schedule of reinforcement. The reinforcers are referred to as tokens because they need not have any rewarding value in and of themselves, but they can be exchanged for reinforcers at some later time. According to the principles of operant conditioning, people should increase the operant response to gain the reinforcers, and if the token economy is developed properly, that is exactly what occurs. If token economies sound rather familiar it is for good reason. Money is an extremely potent token reinforcer for most people, who perform operant responses (work) to receive token reinforcers (money) that can later be exchanged for primary reinforcers (such as food, clothing, shelter, or entertainment).

Finally, learning principles have been applied in clinical psychology in an effort to change maladaptive behaviors. Some examples include a procedure called systematic desensitization, in which the principles of classical conditioning are applied in an effort to treat phobias (irrational beliefs), and social skills training, in which operant conditioning is used to enhance communication and other interpersonal behaviors. These are only two examples of useful applications of conditioning technology to treat mental illness. Such applications suggest the need for ongoing research into basic conditioning mechanisms. We must fully understand conditioning principles to appropriately apply them in the effort to understand and improve the human condition.

BIBLIOGRAPHY

Domjan, Michael, and Barbara Burkhard. *The Principles of Learning and Behavior.* 5th ed. Belmont, Calif.: Wadsworth, 2006. Print.

Hock, Roger R. *Forty Studies that Changed Psychology: Explorations into the History of Psychological Research.* Upper Saddle River: Pearson, 2013. Print.

Lavond, David G., and Joseph E. Steinmetz. *Handbook of Classical Conditioning.* New York: Springer, 2003. Print.

Miltenberger, Raymond G. *Behavior Modification: Principles and Procedures.* Belmont: Wadsworth Cengage, 2012. Print.Ormrod, Jeanne Ellis. Human Learning. Boston: Prentice Hall, 2012. Print.

Robinson-Riegler, Gregory, and Bridget Robinson-Riegler. *Cognitive Psychology: Applying the Science of the Mind.* 3rd ed. Boston: Allyn & Bacon, 2012. Print.

Schwartz, Barry, ed. *Psychology of Learning: Readings in Behavior Theory.* New York: W. W. Norton, 1984. Print.

Skinner, B. F. *Beyond Freedom and Dignity.* 1971. Reprint. Indianapolis, Ind.: Hackett, 2002. Print.

Zentall, Thomas R., and Edward A. Wasserman. *The Oxford Handbook of Comparative Cognition.* 2nd rev. ed. Oxford: Oxford UP, 2012. Print.

Linda R. Tennison

See Also: Aversion therapy; Behaviorism; Habituation and sensitization; Implosion; Learned helplessness; Learning; Operant conditioning therapies; Pavlovian conditioning; Phobias; Reflexes; Systematic desensitization; Thorndike, Edward L.

Conduct disorder

TYPE OF PSYCHOLOGY: Psychopathology

Children with conduct disorder show a deficit in social behavior. They are overtly hostile, disobedient, physically and verbally aggressive, vengeful, and destructive toward the property of others. Many of these children are diagnosed with antisocial personality disorder in adulthood. Genetic and environmental factors appear to interact as causative factors in the development of the disorder.

KEY CONCEPTS

- Antisocial personality
- Cohesive family model
- Juvenile delinquency
- Oppositional defiant disorder
- self-perpetuating cycle

INTRODUCTION

Conduct disorder is a psychiatric disorder that is first diagnosed during childhood or adolescence. It is characterized by a continuing pattern of antisocial behaviors that violate the rights of other people. According to the Centers for Disease Control and Prevention in 2009, the prevalence of conduct disorder in the United States is believed to be around 3 to 10 percent of the child and adolescent population. It is four to five times more common in males than in females. Conduct disorder in adolescence is considered to have serious consequences for society, as it contributes to the high rate of criminal offenses found in that age category. Although many children and adolescents engage in antisocial acts, persons with conduct disorder engage in the behavior in a repetitious and persistent fashion.

Actions that are associated with conduct disorder include bullying, lying, fighting, temper tantrums, destruction of property, stealing, setting fires, cruelty to both animals and people, physical assaults, truancy, and sexual assault. Early signs of conduct disorder can involve excessive arguments with parents, stubbornness, refusing to cooperate with adults, substance abuse, and vandalism. The prognosis for conduct disorder is poor, as it may lead to adult criminal behavior and problems in occupational and marital roles. Many persons with conduct disorder become involved with illegal drugs and excessive alcohol use.

A key factor associated with long-term negative outcomes for the child is the level of aggression shown by the individual. A particularly negative sign for long-term prognosis is the commission of sexual assaults. Highly aggressive children tend to remain aggressive over time and typically develop an antisocial personality in adulthood. About 25 to 40 percent of children with a conduct disorder that began before the age of ten have been found to develop an antisocial personality in adulthood. As adults, these individuals have a lack of remorse for hurting, mistreating, or stealing from other people. They do not conform to social norms nor do they care about other people. The adult with an antisocial personality acts in an impulsive fashion with disregard for the rights of others.

Another psychiatric disorder, oppositional defiant disorder, often precedes the development of conduct disorder. Oppositional defiant disorder is defined by a pattern of negativistic, defiant, disobedient, and hostile behavior toward authority figures. This disorder begins around six years of age, while conduct disorder typically does not begin until age nine. The specific signs of oppositional defiant disorder, according to the American Psychiatric Association, include often losing one's temper, often arguing with adults, actively defying or refusing an adult's requests, deliberately annoying people, blaming others for mistakes, being easily annoyed by others, being often angry and resentful, and being spiteful. The behaviors need to be present for at least six months to make the diagnosis. Almost all children with conduct disorder show the signs of oppositional defiant disorder. Neither of these psychiatric disorders should be confused with juvenile delinquency, which is a legal term referring to violations of the law by minors.

DIAGNOSIS

According to the American Psychiatric Association, a diagnosis of conduct disorder is appropriate when a child shows a persistent and repetitive pattern of behavior in which the basic rights of others or societal norms and rules are violated. The pattern of behavior has to be shown in the following areas: aggression to people and animals, destruction of property, deceitfulness or theft, or serious violations of rules. Specific examples in these categories include intimidation of others, initiating physical fights, using weapons, stealing while confronting a victim, forcing someone into sexual activity, fire setting, deliberately destroying property, running away from home, and school truancy. The disturbances in behavior must cause significant impairment in social, academic, or occupational functioning. The pattern of misconduct must last for at least six months to warrant the diagnosis. Two types of conduct disorder are recognized. The childhood-onset type occurs when the disruptions take place before age ten. An adolescent-onset type is reserved for those persons who show the behavior after that age. Usually the early-onset type of conduct disorder is related to serious outcomes and long-term problems.

CAUSAL FACTORS

The development of a conduct disorder appears to be the result of a combination of genetic and environmental factors. A genetic predisposition toward low verbal intelligence, mild psychoneurological problems, and a difficult temperament appears to set the stage for an early onset of conduct disorder in childhood. A self-perpetuating cycle emerges in the families of children with conduct disorder. The young child's difficult temperament can lead to problems in parent-child bonding. The mild psychoneurological deficits may make it difficult for the child to attain self-control of impulsive behaviors. As the child interacts with the environment, a lack of parental bonding and difficulty in controlling impulses leads to poor social skills and rejection from others. By the time the child is school age, readiness has not been attained for that structured setting. Often, teachers cannot focus sufficient attention on the child to overcome the deficits in learning already experienced by the child. The cycle continues as disruptive behaviors grow in intensity in the new environments and further rejection takes place. Other children begin to exclude the aggressive and oppositional child with the conduct disorder, and this enhances the sense of isolation for that child. Soon the child is drawn to other children, typically older peers, who have already been isolated for their conduct problems. The child with conduct disorder may then seek companionship from peers who are antisocial. Associating with such individuals reinforces the disruptive behaviors. Rejection by parents, peers, and teachers leads these children toward continuing isolation and alienation. Antisocial acts against people and property escalate as the children with conduct disorders band together.

Researchers have noted that the family situation of children with conduct disorder is filled with conflict and disharmony. Family discord and hostility are commonly expressed between family members. Frequently, the parents have an unstable marital relationship and experience disturbed emotional expression. They do not provide the child with a consistent pattern of guidance, acceptance, or affection. The parents are ineffective in their parenting behavior and provide little effective supervision or discipline. Children in these households do not learn respect for authority, nor do they learn how to succeed academically. As the child grows older, the parents withdraw from the child as they become fearful of demanding anything from their son or daughter. Basically, the children in these home environments are trained by family members in an indirect fashion to have antisocial tendencies.

A negative home environment is a powerful factor in the development of children who become violent. Research has shown that the biological parents of children with conduct disorder have a high rate of antisocial tendencies and criminal records. Frustrating and unstructured home environments promote the development of an early-onset form of conduct disorder. Parents who are themselves antisocial provide inadequate models for healthy emotional growth. Children may find an environmental pull toward negative behaviors as they grow in a home environment that is frustrating and produces a sense of malaise. Negative environmental influences become greatest on the child with a genetic vulnerability and poor home situation.

TREATMENT OPTIONS

The focus for treatment is on the dysfunctional patterns of behavior found in the families of children with conduct disorder. One approach is called the cohesive family model of treatment. This method targets the ineffective parenting strategies found in these families. The child with conduct disorder has not been socialized to behave in socially accepted ways. Children learn to escape or avoid parental criticism by increasing their negative actions. When this happens, the parents show increasing amounts of anger, which serves as a model for the child to imitate. During treatment, cooperation from parents is needed to teach the most effective methods to control the child's negative actions. Behavioral techniques based on learning principles are used to train parents in parenting skills. Parents are taught to consistently accept and reward only positive behaviors shown by their children. The parents must learn to stop focusing their attention on the negative actions. Specific skills are taught so that parents learn how to establish appropriate rules for the child and implement appropriate consequences for breaking rules.

Children can be taught to improve their verbal skills as a way to enhance their participation in groups and educational settings. Problem-solving skills are promoted in the child so that problem behaviors can be identified and alternatives can be selected. Family therapy permits a therapist to witness inappropriate interactions between family members and suggest ways to effectively interact with one another. Approaches a therapist may use are structural family therapy (SFT) or solution-focused family therapy (SFFT).

In some cases, the child with a conduct disorder is removed from the home environment. Foster homes or institutional settings may be recommended as the last resort to stop the detrimental effects of the home setting on the child. The goal then becomes to intervene with the parents to teach effective parenting skills and then return the child when progress has been made. A problem with this strategy is that the child often perceives the foster home as an additional rejection by both parents and society. The new setting must have a pronounced atmosphere of acceptance to counteract this possible sense of rejection.

BIBLIOGRAPHY

Biederman, J., S. Farone, and R. Russell. "Is Childhood Oppositional Defiant Disorder a Precursor to Adolescent Conduct Disorder? Findings from a Four-Year Follow-up of Children with ADHD." *Child and Adolescent Psychiatry* 47 (1996): 1193–204. Print.

Bloomquist, Michael L., and Steven V. Schnell. *Helping Children with Aggression and Conduct Problems: Best Practices for Intervention.* New York: Guilford, 2005. Print.

Cadoret, R., L. Leve, and E. Devor. "Genetics and Aggressive Behavior." *Psychiatric Clinics of North America* 20 (1997): 301–22. Print.

Chamberlain, P., and J. Rosicky. "The Effectiveness of Family Therapy in the Treatment of Adolescents with Conduct Disorders and Delinquency." *Journal of Marital and Family Therapy* 21 (1995): 441–59. Print.

Eddy, J. Mark. *Conduct Disorders: The Latest Assessment and Treatment Strategies.* Sudbury: Jones and Bartlett, 2006. Print.

Frick, P. *Conduct Disorders and Severe Antisocial Behavior.* New York: Plenum, 1998. Print.

Grilo, C., D. Becker, and T. McGlashan. "Conduct Disorder, Substance Use Disorders, and Coexisting Conduct and Substance Use Disorders in Adolescent Inpatients." *American Journal of Psychiatry* 153 (1996): 914–20. Print.

Hindshaw, S., and C. Anderson. "Conduct and Oppositional Defiant Disorder." *In Child Psychopathology.* Eds. E. Mash and R. Barkley. New York: Guilford, 2003. Print.

Hollander Barbara Gottfried. *Conduct Disorder.* New York: Rosen, 2014. Print.

Kadzin, A. E. *Conduct Disorder in Childhood and Adolescence.* Newbury Park: Sage, 1995. Print.

Nelson, Michael, III, Audrey L. Nelson, Alfred Finch, Jr., and Kathleen Hart. *Conduct Disorders: A Practitioner's Guide to Comparative Treatments.* New York: Springer, 2006. Print.

Rende, Richard. *Psychosocial Interventions for Biologically Based Problems in Childhood and Adolescence.* Malden: Wiley, 2014. Print.

Thomas, Christopher R., and Kayla Pope. *The Origins of Antisocial Behavior: A Developmental Perspective.* New York: Oxford UP, 2013. Print.Tolan, Patrick H., and Bennett L. Leventhal, eds. Disruptive Behavior Disorders. New York: Springer, 2014. Print.

Frank J. Prerost

SEE ALSO: Antisocial personality disorder; Anxiety disorders; Attachment and bonding in infancy and childhood; Attention-deficit hyperactivity disorder; Bed-wetting; Child abuse; Childhood disorders; Children's mental health; Dyslexia; Family life: Children's issues; Father-child relationship; Impulse control disorders; Juvenile delinquency; Learning disorders; Misbehavior; Mother-child relationship; Parental alienation syndrome; Piaget, Jean; Prenatal physical development; Psychotherapy: Children; Schizophrenia: High-risk children; Separation and divorce: Children's issues; Sibling relationships; Sociopaths; Stepfamilies; Stuttering; Teenage suicide; Teenagers' mental health; Violence by children and teenagers.

Confidentiality

TYPE OF PSYCHOLOGY: Psychological methodologies; Psychotherapy

Confidentiality is a special state of protection designed to limit unauthorized disclosure of and ensure secrecy about certain types of relationships, communication, and other information.

KEY CONCEPTS

- Competency
- Consent

- Duty to protect
- Duty to warn
- Ethics
- Federal certificate of confidentiality
- Institutional review board

INTRODUCTION

Confidentiality is important to psychologists in both its legal meaning and its ethical meaning. The legal meaning covers relevant federal, state, and local laws that may affect how much confidentiality can or must be maintained by a mental health practitioner. Ethics refers to moral principles or values; ethically, psychologists may choose to disclose or refuse to disclose information. Such values may be in conflict with the law but in the best interest of the individual research participant, therapeutic client, consultant client, or other party whose information, data, or relationships to the psychologist are being protected.

When individuals enter into a professional relationship with a psychologist, the psychologist provides information to the individuals, informing them of the limits of confidentiality pertaining to their relationship. In research projects, this takes place during the consent process, when participants give permission and agree to participate in the project proposed. Typically, the consent process is overseen by an institutional review board, a group of individuals who ensure that the rights of participants are properly addressed and protected. In therapy, this takes place during the intake process, before treatment begins. In any case, an individual may always disclose personal information as he or she wishes.

Legally, professionals such as psychologists are not allowed to disclose protected information unless given permission to do so by the client. However, some exceptions to this general rule exist. One exception is when clients admit that they may commit harm to themselves. In this situation, the psychologist takes appropriate action to prevent any harm coming to the individuals. The obligation to do so is known as a duty to protect. A second exception is when clients admit that they may commit harm to another person. In this situation, the psychologist takes appropriate action to prevent harm coming to the individual identified as the target of harm. Typically this activity by the psychologist is understood as a duty to warn.

It should be noted though that even with these duties, the information shared is only that necessary to achieve the duties to protect or warn. In either situation, what is imperative is that the individuals entering into any agreements with the psychologist be competent. Competency refers to the legal fitness of the individual to make such a decision. This means the individual is mentally able to understand the consequences of the decision, can make a free choice in the decision, and is choosing to enact the decision.

IMPORTANCE

Confidentiality is an important protection for a number of reasons. First, confidentiality is important because it protects therapeutic clients, research participants, their private information, and their interests. Second, such protection allows free participation in therapeutic activities, research, and other programs without fear of having private information disclosed without permission. This encourages honesty and trust. Particularly for research endeavors, confidentiality maintains the integrity of the scientific work at hand by dissuading participants from altering their information so as to protect themselves, which could inadvertently damage the research.

Such concerns about confidentiality in research have led to the development of special certificates of confidentiality for government-funded research projects, such as those sponsored by the National Institutes of Health. With a federal certificate of confidentiality, data collected from an individual for the purpose of research are given special protection from forced disclosure (such as with a subpoena). The certificate allows study investigators and their research institutions to refuse to disclose identifying information about participants that could have adverse consequences for the participant if it were disclosed. Information protected could include name, address, identifying numbers such as a Social Security number, criminal history, fingerprints, voiceprints, photographs, history of mental health problems, alcohol or drug use history, human immunodeficiency virus (HIV) status, pregnancy termination, or other sensitive medical data, such as bodily tissues or genetic information. These protections allow participants to avoid potential consequences such as problems related to reputation, employability, financial standing, and insurability, among others. This protection extends to any type of proceeding (civil, legislative, administrative, or criminal), whether at the federal, state, or local level of government.

CONTEXT

In the United States, the Fourth Amendment to the Constitution asserts that people have a right to be secure in their persons, houses, papers, and effects and to be protected against searches and seizures that are unreasonable or not founded in probable cause. With events such as the terrorist attacks of September 11, 2001, in the United States, concerns over confidentiality and the protection of private information were heightened. Debate raged over the need to balance individual desire for privacy with a strong need for information to protect national security.

In this same context, there are increasing requests for information from marketing companies, health care management organizations, and even the government for the purpose of federally funded research. At the same time, technology is increasing to the point that information shared by one individual could affect that person's entire family across generations. For instance, one person providing genetic information about family history of illness could affect the ability of that individual's family members to be insured or to be eligible for certain benefits. Confidentiality therefore is likely to develop as a more complex legal and ethical issue over time, as its relevance to whole systems of people, not just individuals, is recognized.

BIBLIOGRAPHY

Alderman, Ellen, and Caroline Kennedy. *The Right to Privacy.* New York: Vintage, 1997. Print.

Crook, M. "The Risks of Absolute Medical Confidentiality." *Science & Engineering Ethics* 19.1 (2013): 107–22. Print.

Dennis, Jill Callahan. *Privacy and Confidentiality of Health Information.* San Francisco: Jossey-Bass, 2000. Print.

Givens, Beth, and the Privacy Rights Clearinghouse. *The Privacy Rights Handbook: How to Take Control of Your Personal Information.* New York: Harper, 1997. Print.

Kress, Victoria E., et al. "Informed Consent, Confidentiality, and Diagnosing: Ethical Guidelines for Counselor Practice." *Jour. of Mental Health Counseling* 35.1 (2013): 15–28. Print.

Rothstein, Mark A., ed. *Genetic Secrets: Protecting Privacy and Confidentiality in the Genetic Era.* New Haven: Yale UP, 2000. Print.

Smith, Robert Ellis, and Sangram Majumdar. *Ben Franklin's Web Site: Privacy and Curiosity from Plymouth Rock to the Internet.* Providence: Privacy Jour., 2004. Print.

Stimmel, Barbara. "The Conundrum of Confidentiality." *Canadian Jour. of Psychoanalysis* 21.1 (2013): 84–106. Print.

Nancy A. Piotrowski

See Also: Health insurance; Health maintenance organizations; Law and psychology; Mental health practitioners; Research ethics.

Consciousness

Type of psychology: Consciousness

Consciousness refers to a number of phenomena, including the waking state; experience; and the possession of any mental state. Self-consciousness includes proneness to embarrassment in social settings; the ability to detect one's own sensations and recall one's recent actions; self-recognition; awareness of awareness; and self-knowledge in the broadest sense.

Key Concepts

- Awareness
- Alternate state of conciousness
- Developmental aspects of conciousness
- Evolution of conciousness
- History of conciousness study

INTRODUCTION

Many scientists have ignored the phenomena associated with consciousness because they deem it inappropriate for empirical investigation. However, there is clear evidence that this position is changing. Researchers in the fields of psychology, neurobiology, philosophy, cognitive science, physics, medicine, anthropology, mathematics, molecular biology, and art are now addressing major issues relating to consciousness. These researchers are asking such questions as what constitutes consciousness, whether it is possible to explain subjective experience in physical terms, how scientific methods can best be applied to the study of consciousness, and the neural correlates of consciousness.

Moreover, new methods of brain imaging have helped clarify the nature and mechanisms of consciousness, leading to better understanding of the relationship between conscious and unconscious processes in perception, memory, learning, and other domains. These and other questions have led to a growing interest in consciousness studies, including investigations of properties of conscious experience in specific domains (such as vision, emotion, and metacognition) and a better understanding of disorders and unusual forms of consciousness as found in blindsight, synesthesia, and other syndromes.

HISTORY OF CONSCIOUSNESS STUDY

The definition of consciousness proposed by English philosopher John Locke—"the perception of what passes in a man's own mind"—has been that most generally accepted as a starting point in understanding the concept. Most of the philosophical discussions of consciousness, however, arose from the mind-body issues posed by the French philosopher and mathematician René Descartes. Descartes raised the essential questions that until recently dominated consciousness studies. He asked whether the mind, or consciousness, is independent of matter and whether consciousness is extended (physical) or unextended (nonphysical). He also inquired whether consciousness is determinative or determined. English philosophers such as Locke tended to reduce consciousness to physical sensations and the information they provide. European philosophers such as Gottfried Wilhelm Leibniz and Immanuel Kant, however, argued that consciousness had a more active role in perception.

The nineteenth century German educator Johann Friedrich Herbart had the greatest influence on thinking about consciousness. His ideas on states of consciousness and unconsciousness influenced the German psychologist and physiologist Gustav Theodor Fechner, as well as the ideas of Sigmund Freud on the nature of the unconscious.

The concept of consciousness has undergone significant changes since the nineteenth century, and the study of consciousness has undergone serious challenge as being unscientific or irrelevant to the real work of psychology. Nineteenth-century scholars had conflicting opinions about consciousness. It was either a mental stuff different from everyday material or a physical attribute like sensation. Sensation, along with movement, separates humans and other animals from nonsensate and immobile lower forms of life. Scholars viewed consciousness as different from unconsciousness, such as occurred in sleep or under anesthesia. Whatever the theory, these scholars generally employed the same method, that of introspection.

EXPERIMENTAL STUDY

It was the German psychologist Wilhelm Wundt who began the experimental study of consciousness in 1879 when he established his research laboratory. Wundt saw the task of psychology as the study of the structure of consciousness, which extended well beyond sensations and included feelings, images, memory, attention, duration, and movement. By the 1920s, however, behavioral psychology had become the major force in psychology. John B. Watson was the leader of this revolution. He wrote in 1913, "I believe that we can write a psychology and never use the terms consciousness, mental states, mind . . . imagery and the like." Between 1920 and 1950, consciousness was either neglected in psychology or treated as a historical curiosity. Behaviorist psychology led the way in rejecting mental states as appropriate objects for psychological study. The inconsistency of introspection as method made this rejection inevitable. Neurophysiologists also rejected consciousness as a mental state but allowed for the study of the biological underpinnings of consciousness. Thus, brain functioning became part of their study. The neural mechanisms of consciousness that allow an understanding between states of consciousness and the functions of the brain became an integral part of the scientific approach to consciousness. Brain waves—patterns of electrical activity—correlate with different levels of consciousness. These waves measure different levels of alertness. An electroencephalograph provides an objective means for measuring these phenomena.

Beginning in the late 1950s, however, interest in the subject of consciousness returned, specifically in those subjects and techniques relating to altered states of consciousness: sleep and dreams, meditation, biofeedback, hypnosis, and drug-induced states. When a physiological indicator for the dream state was found, a surge in sleep and dream research followed. The discovery of rapid eye movement (REM) helped to generate a renaissance in consciousness research. Thus, during the 1960s there was an increased search for "higher levels" of consciousness through meditation, resulting in a growing interest in the practices of Zen Buddhism and yoga from Eastern cultures.

This movement yielded such programs as Transcendental Meditation, and these self-directed procedures of physical relaxation and focused attention led to biofeedback techniques designed to bring body systems involving factors such as blood pressure or temperature under voluntary control. Researchers discovered that people could control their brain-wave patterns to some extent, especially the alpha rhythms generally associated with a relaxed, meditative state. Those people interested in consciousness and meditation established a number of "alpha training" programs.

Hypnosis and psychoactive drugs also received great attention in the 1960s. Lysergic acid diethylamide (LSD) was the most prominent of these drugs, along with mescaline. These drugs have a long association with religious ceremonies in non-Western cultures. Fascination with these altered states of consciousness led to an increased interest in research on consciousness. As the twentieth century progressed, the concept of consciousness began to come back into psychology. Developmental psychology, cognitive psychology, and the influence of cognitive philosophy each played a role in influencing the reintroduction of the concept, more sharply etched, into the mainstream of psychology.

JEAN PIAGET

Jean Piaget, the great developmental psychologist, viewed consciousness as central to psychological study. Therefore, he sought to find ways to make its study scientific. To do so, Piaget dealt in great detail with the meaning of the subject-object and mind-body problems. Piaget argued that consciousness is not simply a subjective phenomenon; if it were, it would be unacceptable for scientific psychology. Indeed, Piaget maintained that conscious phenomena play an important and distinctive role in human behavior. Moreover, he directed research to examine the way in which consciousness is formed, its origins, stages, and processes. Consciousness is not a secondary phenomenon, nor can psychologists reduce it to physiological phenomena. For Piaget, consciousness involves a constructed subjective awareness. It is a developmentally constructed process, not a product. It results from interaction with the environment, not from the environment's action on it: "[T]he process of becoming conscious of an action scheme transforms it into a concept; thus becoming conscious consists essentially in conceptualization."

There are two relationships necessary for the understanding of consciousness. The first is that of subject and object. The second is the relationship between cognitive activity and neural activity. Both are essential to getting at the process of cognition and its dynamic nature.

MEMORY AND ALTERED STATES

A variety of studies and experiments have explored the effects of certain variables on consciousness. For instance, it is important to ascertain the way in which variables that increase memorability in turn influence metamemory. Results have been inconsistent. However, it was found that when experimenters directed subjects to remember some items and forget others, there was an increase in recalling those items that experimenters were directed to remember. There was, nevertheless, no effect on the accuracy of what was remembered.

Sleep and dreams, hypnosis, and other altered states have provided another intriguing area of study for those interested in consciousness. The relationship of naps to alertness later in the day has proved of great interest to psychologists. In one study, nine healthy senior citizens, seventy-four to eighty-seven years of age, experienced nap and no-nap conditions in two studies each. Napping was for one and one-half hours, from 1:30 to 3:00 p.m. daily. The no-nap condition prohibited naps and encouraged activity in that period. Various tests were used to measure evening activity as well as record sleep. Aside from greater sleep in the twenty-four-hour period for those who had the ninety-minute nap, there was no difference on any other measure.

The threat simulation theory of dreaming holds that dreams have a biological function to protect the dream self. This dream self behaves in a defensive fashion. An empirical test of this theory confirmed the predictions and suggests that the theory has wide implications regarding the functions of consciousness.

The study of consciousness, then, has elucidated understanding of perception, memory, and action; created advances in artificial intelligence; and illustrated the philosophical basis of dissatisfaction with the dualistic separation of mind and body. Electrical correlates of states of consciousness have been discovered, as well as structures in the brainstem that regulate the sleep cycle. Other studies have looked at neural correlates in various states such as wakefulness, coma, the persistent vegetative state, the "locked-in" syndrome, akinetic mutism, and brain death. There are many other areas of consciousness in which neuroscience has made major advances.

An important problem neglected by neuroscientists is the problem of meaning. Neuroscientists are apt to assume that if they can see that a neuron's firing is roughly correlated with some aspect of the visual scene, such as an oriented line, then that firing must be part of the neural correlate of the seen line. However, it is necessary to explain how meaning can be expressed in neural terms as well as how the firing of neurons is connected to the perception of a face or person.

IMAGERY

Imagery is associated with memory, perception, and thought. Imagery occurs in all sensory modes. However, most work on imagery has neglected all but visual imagery. Concerns with imagery go back to the ancient Greek philosophers. Plato and Aristotle, for example, compared memory to a block of wax into which one's thoughts and perceptions stamp impressions. Aristotle gave imagery an important place in cognition and argued that people think in mental images. Early experimental psychologists, such as Wundt, carried on this notion of cognition.

Around 1901, Oswald Külpe and his students at the University of Würzburg in Germany challenged these assumptions. However, these experiments employed introspective techniques, which Wundt and others attacked as being inconclusive. The controversy led to a rejection of mental imagery, introspection, and the study of consciousness itself. In the twentieth century, a movement toward seeing language as the primary analytical tool and a rejection of the old dominance of imagery came into fashion. The phenomenology of French philosopher and writer Jean-Paul Sartre also led to a decline of interest in imagery.

A revival of research on imagery followed the cognitive science revolution of the 1960s and 1970s, contributing greatly to the rising scientific interest in mental representations. This revival stemmed from research on sensory deprivation and on hallucinogenic drugs. Studies in the role of imagery mnemonics also contributed to this reemergence of imagery studies.

CONCLUSION

As the concept of a direct, simple linkage between environment and behavior became unsatisfactory in the late twentieth century, the interest in altered states of consciousness helped spark new interest in consciousness. People are actively involved in their own behavior, not passive puppets of external forces. Environments, rewards, and punishments are not simply defined by their physical character. There are mental constructs involved in each of these. People organize their memories. They do not merely store them. Cognitive psychology, a new division of the field, has emerged to deal with these interests.

Thanks to the work of developmental psychologists such as Piaget, great attention is being given to the manner in which people understand, or perceive, the world at different ages. There are advances in the area of animal behavior stressing the importance of inherent characteristics that arise from the way in which a species has been shaped to respond adaptively to the environment. There has also been the emergence of humanistic psychologists, concerned with the importance of self-actualization and growth. Clinical and industrial psychology have demonstrated that a person's state of consciousness in terms of current feelings and thoughts is of obvious importance. Although the role of consciousness was often neglected in favor of unconscious needs and motivations, there are clear signs that researchers are interested in emphasizing once more the nature of states of consciousness.

BIBLIOGRAPHY

Balibar, Etienne, and Stella Sandford. *Identity and Difference: John Locke and the Invention of Consciousness*. Brooklyn: Berso, 2013. Print.

Brann, E. T. H. *The World of the Imagination: Sum and Substance*. Savage, Md.: Rowman & Littlefield, 1991. Print.

Carter, Rita. *Exploring Consciousness*. Berkeley: University of California Press, 2004. Print.

Chalmers, D. *The Conscious Mind: In Search of a Fundamental Theory*. New York: Oxford University Press, 1997. Print.

Friedenberg, Jay. *Visual Attention and Consciousness*. New York: Psychology P, 2013. Print.

Greenfield, S. A. *Journey to the Centers of the Mind*. New York: W. H. Freeman, 1995. Print.

Libet, B. *Neurophysiology of Consciousness: Selected Papers and New Essays by Benjamin Libet*. Boston: Birkhäuser, 1993. Print.

Pereira, Alfredo. *The Unity of Mind, Brain, and World: Current Perspectives on a Science of Consciousness*. New York: Cambridge UP, 2013. Print.

Ramachandran, V. S. *A Brief Tour of Human Consciousness: From Impostor Poodles to Purple Numbers*. New York: Pi Press, 2005. Print.

Schwitzgebel, Eric. *Perplexities of Consciousness*. Cambridge: MIT P, 2013. Print.

Weiskrantz, L. *Consciousness Lost and Found*. New York: Oxford University Press, 1997. Print.

Frank A. Salamone

See Also: Automaticity; Consciousness: Altered states; Dementia; Dissociative disorders; Dreams; Hallucinations; Hypnosis; Insomnia; Instinct theory; Meditation and relaxation; Reflexes; Synesthesia; Thought: Inferential; Thought: Study and measurement; Virtual reality; Watson, John B.

Consciousness
Altered states

TYPE OF PSYCHOLOGY: Consciousness

The investigation of altered states of consciousness began in psychology with the recognition that consciousness is not a fixed, unvarying state, but is in a continual state of flux. Consciousness can be altered by many chemical and nonchemical means, and there is some evidence to indicate that certain altered states are necessary for normal psychological functioning.

KEY CONCEPTS

- Biofeedback
- Circadian rhythm
- Electroencephalogram (EEG)
- Hypnagogic and hypnopompic states
- Hypnosis
- Meditation
- Psychoactive drugs
- Restricted environmental stimulation (RES)

INTRODUCTION

The great psychologist William James, in his 1890 textbook *The Principles of Psychology*, made the following now-famous observation regarding states of consciousness:

> Our normal waking consciousness, rational consciousness as we call it, is but one special type of consciousness, whilst all about it, parted from it by the filmiest of screens, there lie potential forms of consciousness entirely different.

James went on to say that the understanding of human psychological functioning would never be complete until these alternate states were addressed. Most psychologists would now acknowledge that a person's normal waking consciousness is readily subject to changes. These changes are referred to as "altered states of consciousness." What constitutes a genuine altered state and how many such states may exist are both subjects of some controversy.

States of consciousness have always been central to the attempt to understand human nature. For example, every society of which any record exists has possessed both chemical and nonchemical means of altering consciousness.

From a historical point of view, Sigmund Freud may have done more than any other theorist to stimulate interest in states of consciousness. Freud's psychoanalytic theory of personality held that there were three primary levels of consciousness: consciousness, preconsciousness, and unconsciousness. The conscious level includes mental activities of which one is unaware. The preconscious level consists of mental material of which one is currently unaware but that can be voluntarily recalled—roughly equivalent to memory. The unconscious level, which held the greatest interest for Freud, contains thoughts, feelings, memories, and drives that are blocked from awareness because they are unpleasant or arouse anxiety. In addition to his interest in these three levels of consciousness, Freud's interest in altered states at various points in his career was manifested in investigations of cocaine, hypnosis, and the analysis and interpretation of dreams.

In the early twentieth century, with the growth of behaviorism, which insisted that to be a science, psychology should confine itself to investigating only objective, observable behavior, the study of altered states of consciousness fell out of favor. Events in the larger culture during the 1960s and 1970s, however, helped stimulate interest in altered states within psychology. During this period, efforts to expand consciousness by means of drugs, meditation, Eastern religious practice, and new ways of relating to oneself and others led to the active study of altered states of consciousness. The attempts of psychologists to study altered states of experience will perhaps be viewed in the future as a landmark in the development of psychology as a science. The willingness of psychology to explore the novel realms that altered states represent may help to expand the understanding of both consciousness and reality.

VARIATIONS IN CONSCIOUSNESS

Physiological psychologist Karl Pribram lists the following states of consciousness:

- states of ordinary perceptual awareness
- states of self-consciousness
- dream states
- hypnagogic and hypnopompic states
- ecstatic states (such as the orgiastic experience)
- socially induced trance or trancelike states
- drug-induced states
- social role states
- linguistic states
- translational states

- ordinary transcendental states
- extraordinary transcendental states achieved by special techniques
- other extraordinary states (those that allow "extra-sensory awareness")
- meditational states
- dissociated states, as in the case of pathological multiple personality
- psychomotor states manifest in temporal-lobe epilepsies

To that list could be added the following additional states: sleep; the hyperalert state, characterized by increased vigilance while one is awake; the lethargic state, characterized by dulled, sluggish mental activity; states of hysteria, with intense feeling and overpowering emotion; regressive states, such as senility; daydreaming with rapidly occurring thoughts that bear little relation to the external environment; coma; sleep deprivation; sensory overload or deprivation; and prolonged strenuous exercise. This list is by no means exhaustive.

Some of these states clearly represent greater degrees of alteration of the "normal" consciousness than others. There is, however, no universal agreement on what constitutes the normal state of consciousness. Charles Tart and other authors have suggested that what is usually called "normal" consciousness is not a natural, given state, but a construction based mainly on cultural values and inputs. In any case, some altered states of consciousness are experienced on a daily basis by everyone, while others are much more rare and may require great effort or special circumstances to achieve.

INFLUENCES ON ALTERED CONSCIOUSNESS

Some alterations in conscious functions are induced by daily changes in biological rhythms. Bodily events that occur in roughly a twenty-four-hour cycle are referred to as "circadian rhythms," from the Latin *circa* ("about") and *dies* ("day"). It is thought that these cycles are created by natural events, such as the light-dark cycle, and by other cues in the daily routine, such as mealtimes. The sleep-wake cycle is the major circadian rhythm, but there are others, such as fluctuations in body temperature. This daily body-temperature cycle appears to be directly related to levels of mental activity. When all external cues are removed, circadian rhythms extend to about twenty-five hours. As a result of prolonged isolation, the cycle can become completely distorted, with periods of up to forty hours of waking followed by periods of up to twenty-two hours of sleep. When the change is gradual in this way, the individual has a distorted sense of time and believes that he or she is experiencing normal periods of sleep and waking. Abrupt changes in circadian rhythms, as when one crosses several time zones, are what lead to that sleepy, uncomfortable feeling known as "jet lag."

In addition to biological rhythms, there are other regular daily variations in consciousness. On the way to sleep each night, people enter a kind of twilight period known as the "hypnagogic state." The state of consciousness that is entered immediately before waking is called the "hypnopompic state." In both these states, one is partially asleep and partially continuing to process environmental stimuli. Both are characterized by vivid imagery, and many people have reported creative insight during these periods.

STAGES OF SLEEP

Sleep is not a unified state, but it consists of five distinct stages: one stage of rapid eye movement (REM) sleep and four stages of non–rapid eye movement (NREM) sleep. During a typical night's sleep, one moves in and out of these stages four or five times. REM sleep is primarily associated with periods of dreaming. Sleeping subjects awakened during a period of REM sleep report having just experienced a dream about 80 percent of the time, compared with fewer than 10 percent when NREM sleep is interrupted. Psychologists are still unclear on exactly why humans need to sleep, but the need for periods of REM sleep might be part of the reason. When sleeping subjects are deprived of REM sleep (and their NREM sleep is undisturbed), they often show many of the symptoms of not having slept at all. Also, when later given the opportunity for uninterrupted sleep, they spend a greater percentage of time in the REM stage, as if they were trying to make up for the lost REM sleep (this is referred to as the "REM-rebound effect"). The REM-rebound effect is lessened if the individual is encouraged to engage in an increased amount of daydreaming, which indicates a possible connection between day and night dreams.

PSYCHOACTIVE DRUGS

The use of psychoactive drugs is a common method for altering consciousness. These drugs are chemical substances that act on the brain to create psychological effects and are typically classified as depressants, stimulants, narcotics (opiates), hallucinogens, or antipsychotics. Several drugs, such as nicotine, caffeine, and alcohol, are so much a part of the lifestyle in modern society that users may not even think of them as drugs. The use of many psychoactive drugs can lead to physical or psychological dependence, or addiction, as the body or mind develops a physiological or psychological need for the drug. The body can also build up a tolerance for a drug, which means that higher and higher doses are necessary to produce the same effects. Once addiction has been established, discontinuing the use of the drug can lead to withdrawal symptoms, such as nausea, fever, convulsions, and hallucinations, among others, which can sometimes be fatal.

The type of altered state produced by a psychoactive drug depends on the class to which the drug belongs. Depressants, such as alcohol, barbiturates, and tranquilizers, depress central nervous system functioning and usually produce relaxation, anxiety reduction, and—eventually—sleep. Narcotics (opiates), such as heroin, morphine, and codeine, depress activity in some areas of the cortex but create excitation in others, producing feelings of euphoria and providing relief from pain. Stimulants, such as amphetamines, cocaine, caffeine, and nicotine, stimulate central nervous system activity, producing feelings of alertness and euphoria and lack of appetite. Hallucinogens, such as lysergic acid diethylamide (LSD), mescaline, and psilocybin, can produce hallucinations, delusions, exhilaration, and, in some cases, quasimystical experiences.

HYPNOSIS AND MEDITATION

Two popular nonchemical techniques for altering consciousness are hypnosis and meditation. Hypnosis was first discovered in the eighteenth century by Franz Mesmer, and its history has been full of controversy ever since. An altered state is induced in hypnosis by the suggestive instructions of the hypnotist, usually involving progressive relaxation. The hypnotized subject often appears to be asleep but remains alert inside, exhibiting varying degrees of responsiveness to the suggestions of the hypnotist. Research done in the 1840s by James Braid found that only about 10 percent of the population can enter the deepest hypnotic state; others may not be hypnotizable at all. The rest of the population can achieve some degree of hypnotic induction. Psychologists argue about whether hypnosis is a genuine altered state or simply a form of role playing.

There is less controversy regarding meditation as a true altered state. Since the mid-1960s, there has been extensive research on the physiological changes that occur during meditation. Some of the findings include a decrease in oxygen consumption during meditation , a cardiac output decrease, and slowing of the heart rate. During meditation, electroencephalogram (EEG) patterns are dominated by the alpha rhythm, which has been associated with relaxation. An EEG is a graphic recording of the electrical activity of brain waves. Researchers R. K. Wallace and Herbert Benson believed that there was sufficient physiological evidence to justify calling the meditative state a "fourth major state of consciousness" (along with waking, dreaming, and sleeping), which they termed a "wakeful, hypometabolic [reduced metabolic activity] state." Beginning meditators usually report feelings of relaxation and "ordinary thoughts," while advanced practitioners sometimes report transcendental experiences of "consciousness without content."

APPLICATIONS OF HYPNOSIS

Research on altered states of consciousness has led to many benefits. The analgesic properties of hypnosis were verified in research conducted by Ernest Hilgard at Stanford University. He found that hypnotic suggestion could be used to reduce or eliminate experimentally induced pain. Even though subjects were not consciously aware of the pain, Hilgard found that, with the right questions, he could uncover a "hidden observer," a dissociated aspect of the subject's conscious awareness that did monitor the feelings of pain. Hilgard reports that hypnotic relief from pain has been reported for the chronic pain of arthritis, nerve damage, migraine headaches, and cancer. For individuals who are unable to be anesthetized because of allergic reactions or fear of needles, hypnosis is often used as an effective substitute for the control of pain. It has been effectively applied in cases involving dental work, childbirth, burns, abdominal surgery, and spinal taps. Hypnotic suggestion has also been effective in reducing the nausea associated with cancer chemotherapy.

The use of hypnosis to recover forgotten memories is much more controversial. One dramatic phenomenon displayed with certain hypnotic subjects is age regression, in which the individual not only is able to recall vividly childhood memories but also seems to reenact behaviors from childhood, including body postures, voice, and handwriting characteristics of a given age. There is no way of knowing, however, whether this represents true recall or is simply a type of fantasy and role-playing. Hypnosis has also been used to enhance the memories of crime witnesses in court proceedings. There is evidence, however, that actual recall does not become more accurate and that the witness may be unintentionally influenced by the suggestions of the hypnotist, which could lead to inaccuracies and distortions in the "remembered" events. For this reason, courts in many states automatically disqualify testimony obtained by means of hypnosis.

BENEFITS OF MEDITATION

Research on the physiological effects of meditation led to the application of meditative techniques as a treatment to combat stress-related illnesses. Meditators have often experienced significant decreases in such problems as general anxiety, high blood pressure, alcoholism, drug addiction, insomnia, and other stress-related problems. Researchers have also found that the scores of meditators on various psychological tests have indicated general mental health, self-esteem, and social openness. Many psychologists argue, however, that these effects are not unique to meditation and can be produced by means of other relaxation techniques. Meditation researcher Robert Ornstein has suggested that the long-term practice of meditation may induce a relative shift in hemispheric dominance in the brain from the left hemisphere, which is associated with such linear processes as language and logical reasoning, to the right hemisphere, which is associated with nonlinear processes such as music perception and spatial reasoning. Consistent with this idea are findings that meditators are better on certain right-hemispheric tasks such as remembering musical tones but worse on verbal problem-solving tasks that involve the left hemisphere.

BIOFEEDBACK

Early research on advanced meditators in India indicated that they could exhibit control over what are normally autonomic processes in the body—for example, speeding up or slowing down the heart rate at will, stopping the heart for up to seventeen seconds, controlling blood flow to different areas of the body, and controlling brain-wave patterns at will. At first, these results were met with skepticism, but it is now known that humans and animals can learn to control previously involuntary processes by using a technique known as "biofeedback." Through biofeedback training, an individual who is connected to a special measuring device can monitor autonomic events such as blood pressure, skin temperature, and muscle tension. Having this information can allow the individual gradually to gain control over these autonomic processes. Biofeedback techniques have been applied to an enormous variety of clinical problems. EEG biofeedback, for example, has been used to train epileptics to emit brain-wave patterns that are incompatible with those that occur during brain seizures. Other disorders that have been successfully treated by means of biofeedback include cardiac disorders, high blood pressure, tension headaches, anxiety, and neuromuscular disorders such as cerebral palsy.

SENSORY DEPRIVATION

Other applications have grown out of research on altered states of consciousness produced by restricting sensory stimulation from the environment. Researchers in the 1950s completed extensive studies on the effects of prolonged sensory deprivation. Subjects placed in soundproof isolation chambers with translucent goggles to eliminate vision and padded arm tubes to minimize touch sensation often experienced negative psychological effects after about a day. Most subjects suffered from extreme boredom, slowed reaction time, and impaired problem-solving ability. Some subjects reacted to sensory deprivation by creating their own internally generated sights and sounds in the form of hallucinations. These results led to the institution of special procedures to help reduce the effects of sensory deprivation in certain occupations: for example, airline pilots on long night flights, astronauts living for prolonged periods in tiny space capsules, and individuals working in isolated weather stations. A controlled form of sensory deprivation known as "restricted environmental stimulation therapy (REST)" has been used to reduce the effects of overarousal and hyperactivity. REST sessions usually involve floating in heavily salted warm water in a dark, soundproof tank. Most subjects find this floating sensation very pleasant, and there have been many reports of long-term reductions in high blood pressure and other stress-related problems.

ARGUMENT FOR STATE-SPECIFIC SCIENCES

Although traditional scientific methods are poorly suited to the study of consciousness, many beneficial tools that can be used to measure the physiological correlation of altered states, such as the electroencephalograph, have been developed as an outgrowth of the study of states of consciousness.

Tart suggested the creation of state-specific sciences. In reaching this conclusion, he argues that any particular state of consciousness (including ordinary waking) is a semiarbitrary construction—a specialized tool that is useful for some things but not for others and that contains large numbers of structures shaped by a particular culture's value judgments. Thus, science is observation and conceptualization carried out within the highly selective framework provided by a culturally determined ordinary state of consciousness. Tart suggests that, since altered states of consciousness often represent radically different ways of organizing observations and reworking conceptualizations of the universe (including oneself), if the scientific method were applied to developing sciences within various states of consciousness, there would be sciences based on radically different perceptions, logics, and communications, and thus science as a whole would gain new perspectives that would complement the existing one.

Regardless of whether this suggestion is taken seriously, it is clear that the study of states of consciousness has achieved legitimacy in scientific psychology. The investigation so far has revealed that human consciousness is much more diverse and varied than many psychologists previously believed.

BIBLIOGRAPHY

A.D.A.M. Medical Encyclopedia. "Biofeedback." *Medline Plus.* US National Library of Medicine, 30 Oct. 2011. Web. 18 Feb. 2014.

"Brain Basics: Understanding Sleep." *National Institute of Neurological Disorders and Stroke.* National Institutes of Health, US Dept. of Health and Human Services, 5 Dec. 2013. Web. 18 Feb. 2014.

Cvetkovic, Dean, and Irena Cosic, eds. *States of Consciousness: Experimental Insights into Meditation, Waking, Sleep, and Dreams.* New York: Springer, 2011. Print.

Flannagan, Owen J. *Dreaming Souls: Sleep, Dreams, and the Evolution of the Mind.* New York: Oxford UP, 2001. Print.

Havens, Ronald A. *Self Hypnosis for Cosmic Consciousness: Achieving Altered States, Mystical Experiences, and Spiritual Enlightenment.* Bethel: Crown House, 2007. Print.

Hilgard, Ernest Ropiequet. *Divided Consciousness: Multiple Controls in Human Thought and Action. Expanded ed.* New York: Wiley, 1986. Print.

Hobson, J. Allan. *The Dream Drugstore: Chemically Altered States of Consciousness.* Cambridge: MIT P, 2002. Print.

Nash, Michael R., and Amanda J. Barnier, eds. *The Oxford Handbook of Hypnosis: Theory, Research, and Practice.* Oxford: Oxford UP, 2012. Print.

Ornstein, Robert Evan, ed. *The Nature of Human Consciousness.* San Francisco: Freeman, 1973. Print.

Ornstein, Robert Evan. *The Psychology of Consciousness.* 2nd rev. ed. New York: Penguin, 1986. Print.

Rock, Andrea. *The Mind at Night: The New Science of How and Why We Dream.* New York: Basic, 2005. Print.

Ward, Colleen A., ed. *Altered States of Consciousness and Mental Health: A Cross-Cultural Perspective.* Thousand Oaks: Sage, 1989. Print.

Wolman, Benjamin B., and Montague Ullman, ed. *Handbook of States of Consciousness.* New York: Van Nostrand Reinhold, 1986. Print.

Derived from: "Consciousness: Altered states." *Psychology and Mental Health.* Salem Press. 2009.

Oliver W. Hill, Jr.

See Also: Antianxiety medications; Antidepressant medications; Antipsychotic medications; Circadian rhythms; Consciousness; Dementia; Dissociative disorders; Dreams; Hallucinations; Hypnosis; Insomnia; James, William; Meditation and relaxation; Synesthesia; Thought: Inferential; Thought: Study and measurement; Virtual reality.

Constructivist psychology

Type of psychology: Psychotherapy

Constructivist psychology recognizes that people actively create the realities to which they respond. People organize their experience by actively constructing templates of meaning that help them interpret their past, negotiate their present, and anticipate their future.

Key Concepts

- Conversation
- Meanings
- Narratives
- Philosophy
- Psychotherapy

INTRODUCTION

One tenet of constructivist thought is that the narratives that people tell serve two functions. One, they are organizational, allowing people to account for the plot structure of their past. Two, they are anticipatory, orienting people toward a meaningful future. Our stories are who we are.

Another tenet of constructivist thought is that the nuances of people's construction of the world are what is important, not whether this construction is right or wrong. A constructivist emphasizes developing a viable, workable construction of people, things, and events, rather than an accurate representation of absolute reality. People can construct multiple meanings for the events in their lives, each meaning may help them to understand and respond creatively to their experience. The Journal of Constructivist Psychology, formerly the International Journal of Personal Construct Psychology, contains empirical research, conceptual analyses, critical reviews, and occasionally case studies that further explore aspects of constructivist psychology.

ROOTS

There is no single founder of constructivist psychology, but it has roots in philosophy. Some early contributors are the German philosopher Immanuel Kant, British psychologist Frederic C. Bartlett, and Swiss psychologist Jean Piaget Kant believed that experience and sensation were not passively written into a person, but rather that the mind is an active, form-giving structure that transforms and coordinates data into integrated thought. For example, a man may believe that all women are inferior to all men. At committee meetings, this man ignores women, devalues their contributions, and forgets that women made helpful suggestions or recommendations. This man has inadvertently constructed a world that fits his preconceived ideas.

Bartlett applied constructivist concepts in his investigations of human memory. In classical research on remembering, Bartlett maintained that memories were reconstructed out of bits and pieces of recollected information. For example, when people witness a crime, they do not store intact, unchangeable photographs of it. Rather, their impressions are ongoing and can be shaped by subsequent questioning, comments, and other information, such as what they read in the newspaper.

Piaget chronicled how children's cognitive schemas change as a function of maturation. Piaget documented how children do more than simply learn facts; they actually change the way they think as they mature. For example, a four-year-old will look at one set of ten pennies in a widely spaced row and believe that they are more pennies than a second set of fifteen closely spaced pennies, even though this child can count accurately. At age seven, in contrast, this same child will grasp that the pennies are unchanged by how closely they are packed together and will know that the second set contains more pennies.

PSYCHOTHERAPY

Seen through a constructivist lens, psychotherapy involves a quest for relatedness, connection, and mutuality of meaning in spite of uniqueness. The psychotherapist must join with the client to develop a refined map of the individual's often inarticulate constructions by focusing on personal meanings, the constructions of roles, and the relationship between client and therapist.

Constructivists distrust highly standardized procedures for modifying human behavior. Likewise, constructivists oppose applying universal categories of disorders that fail to capture the richness and subtlety of any given individual. For example, a constructivist would resist using a diagnosis of major depression because this dry category fails to convey any information about how the patient makes meaning out of life. Treatment or diagnostic manuals cannot accommodate the individual person or the specific relationship.

Further, constructivists resist viewing the therapist as an expert who makes the client more functional or adaptive. Rather, constructivists grant that therapist and client are both experts, and no one knows the client's world or experience better than the client. The constructivist recognizes that because the client's constructions are working fictions rather than established facts, they are amenable to alternative interpretations.

Because emotional adjustment is not simply a straightforward matter of making one's thoughts realistic and in line with the observable world, constructivist therapists draw the client's attention to troubling discrepancies between working models of self and world and of moment-to-moment experiencing. For example, the client views herself as calm and rational, yet she speaks in a pressured way, grips the chair strongly, and has a frown on her face, all of which suggest anger or another strong emotion. One goal is not to dispute negative emotions, but to intensively explore the emotions and extend her self-awareness in the direction of greater complexity and integration. Another goal is to develop new meanings. For example, the therapist might ask her to speak aloud in the critical voice of her conscience. As she angrily delineates shortcomings, she might realize the resemblance to her mother's criticisms. Therapy might help her synthesize her self-contempt and her need for comfort into a new self-acceptance.

Constructivist therapists who treat the entire family view therapy as a conversation whose goal is to alter the whole system. The therapist functions not as an expert who gives answers, but more as a conversation manager who promotes exchanges between family members that dissolve old problems by helping people talk about them in new ways and reach new perspectives.

In a constructivist view, human knowing is more than simply developing realistic mental maps of an external world. Rather, a person actively creates a narrative by binding past experiences and ongoing life events into meaningful units across time, themes, and persons.

BIBLIOGRAPHY

Gaines, Brian R. "Humans as Scientists: Scientists as Humans." *Jour. of Constructivist Psychology* 26.3 (2013): 210–17. Print.

Lyddon, William J. "Forms and Facets of Constructivist Psychology." *In Constructivism in Psychotherapy.* Ed. Robert A. Neimeyer and Michael J. Mahoney. Washington: American Psychological Association, 1999. Print.

Neimeyer, Greg J., ed. *Constructivist Assessment: A Casebook.* Newbury Park: Sage, 1993. Print.

Neimeyer, Robert A. "Constructivist Psychotherapies." *Encyclopedia of Psychology.* Washington: American Psychological Association, 2000. Print.

Neimeyer, Robert A., and Alan E. Stewart. "Constructivist and Narrative Psychotherapies." *Handbook of Psychological Change.* Ed. C. R. Snyder and Rick E. Ingram. New York: Wiley, 2000. Print.

Raskin, Jonathan D., and Sara K. Bridges, eds. *Constructivist Psychotherapy in the Real World.* New York: Pace University Press, 2008. Print.

Schweitzer, Jeffrey R. "Metaphor, Mapmaking, and Mair: Reliving a Poetics of Psychological Inquiry." *Jour. of Constructivist Psychology* 26.2 (2013): 149–56. Print.

Winter, David. "Personal Construct Psychology as a Way of Life." *Jour. of Constructivist Psychology* 26.1 (2013): 3–8. Print.

Lillian M. Range

See Also: Behavior therapy; Cognitive therapy; Emotions; Memory; Personality theory; Piaget, Jean.

Consumer psychology

Type of psychology: Cognition

Psychologists have investigated many aspects of consumer behavior; the ultimate goal of nearly all research on consumers is to understand how consumers obtain and process information and why they choose some goods and services and not others.

Key Concepts

- Attitude
- Behavioral intention
- Belief
- Compensatory rules
- Subjective norm

INTRODUCTION

The decision-making approach to understanding consumer behavior follows from the assumption that the consumer is someone who seeks and takes in information from numerous sources, processes it, and then makes a selection from a set of alternatives. A major proponent of this view is James R. Bettman. The essence of his theory, presented in *An Information Processing Theory of Consumer Choice* (1979), is an explanation of how consumers react to information—from advertisers, friends, family, salespeople, and so on. The theory integrates six components of information processing: limitations in the human capacity to process information; the motivation to move from some initial state to a desired state; attention to and perceptual encoding of information; the search for information from memory and the external environment, and the evaluation of this information; decision processes; and the effects of consumption and learning. All these components are related through the construct of choice. Put another way, one becomes motivated, pays attention, obtains and evaluates information, learns, and compares alternatives to reach a goal. Because of its comprehensive nature, Bettman's theory of consumer choice has been highly influential in the academic and marketing communities.

The information-processing and decision-making perspectives on consumer purchases stand in sharp contrast to an alternative view, called behavioral influence, which presumes that consumers respond directly to pressures of the environment and give little or no conscious thought to their purchases. There is some evidence that consumer purchase decisions can be influenced by factors (such as music) of which they are unaware. Hence, consumers can be influenced by factors that they cannot evaluate and weigh in a decision process. This raises special concerns about methods of protecting consumers.

Perhaps the most useful and enduring theory to explain consumer behavior is Martin Fishbein and Icek Ajzen's theory of reasoned action. This theory states that behavior results from an intention. For example, the purchasing of a product is a consequence of an intention to purchase that product. Thus, what is important to understand is how people form intentions. Consumers form intentions by taking into account two types of information. One is their overall evaluation of the product. The other is the subjective norms supporting purchase of the product. According to this theory, people plan to purchase a product if they evaluate it positively and believe that their purchase of it would be approved by those who are important to them. Because this theory emphasizes attitudes concerning a behavior toward an object and not only the object itself, it has successfully predicted many behaviors that attitudes alone could not.

In reality, the extent to which information is sought, evaluated, and weighed in a decision process on the part of a consumer depends greatly on the extent to which the consumer is involved in the process. The complexity of the decision process varies with consumer involvement. If the consumer is relatively uninvolved, the search for information is likely to be limited, with little evaluation of alternatives. With such routine decision making, there is little opportunity for the formation of attitudes toward the product—until after purchase or consumption. Involvement is thought to be a result of the personality of the consumer, the nature of the product, and characteristics of the situation. Consumers who are more self-confident, younger, more educated, or less experienced with the product category tend to engage in a more extensive information search. Consumers show greater information search for products with higher perceived financial, performance, social, or physical risk. Situational factors such as amount of time, quantity of product, or store alternatives also help determine the extent of information search.

The consumer's decision to buy involves two major components: what brand to buy and where to purchase it. The decision process used to purchase a product can be classified as either compensatory or noncompensatory. With a compensatory rule, only the overall evaluation is important. This means that high evaluations on one dimension can compensate for low ones on another. In contrast, a noncompensatory rule results in a product being eliminated if it falls below an acceptable level on one dimension, regardless of its standing on other dimensions.

The decision process has been monitored by a variety of techniques to learn whether compensatory or noncompensatory rules are being used. Another objective of studying the consumer-choice process is to learn how information is selected and used. Researchers have used eye-movement monitors, computerized information displays, and information boards to track the order and extent of information search. Research by cognitive psychologists has shown that people tend to compare products on a single attribute rather than forming overall evaluations of each product and then making comparisons. This points to the value of displaying information such as unit price or nutritional values, which facilitates comparisons across products.

THE DIFFICULTIES OF PREDICTION

The prediction of behavior on the basis of attitudes has always been complex. While it is true that people who have a positive attitude toward a product buy more of it than those who do not, other hypothesized links between attitudes and behavior simply do not hold. For example, lifestyle surveys have shown an increasing trend toward the belief that meal preparation should take as little time as possible. Yet during the same time period in which these surveys were conducted, sales of frozen pizza remained constant and sales of frozen dinners fell.

Along similar lines, attitudes toward advertisements do not necessarily correlate with attitudes toward the product being advertised, let alone with purchase of the product. Even a specific attitude may fail to predict behavior toward an object. To demonstrate this, one might ask a friend to describe her attitude toward a Mercedes or a Porsche and toward a Kia. The attitude of many people toward the former is far more favorable, but in reality they are less likely to purchase their preferred make of automobile.

One reason the theory of reasoned action has been successful is that it does not attempt to link attitudes to behaviors in general. Because of this, the prediction of specific behaviors toward "attitude objects" can be achieved. This theory can also be applied to changing specific behaviors. For example, if a person does not intend to engage in a safety practice, a traditional attitude-change approach would attempt to persuade the person of the value of the practice. Fishbein and Azjen's theory, however, suggests an alternative: persuading the person of the existence of subjective norms supporting the safety practice. This approach is not suggested by any other theoretical perspective on consumer behavior.

The debates about information and consumer decision making have had an impact on public policy and regulatory activities. William Wilkie identifies three concerns in the policy arena, all of them relating to the type, amount, and form of information that should be provided to consumers. First is the goal of providing consumers with complete information. Only by being fully informed can people spend their time, money, and effort in their best interest. Yet complete information may be impossible, and, even if it is available, the consumer may be unwilling or unable to process it all in decision making.

The second objective of public policy is to provide information that is "choice-neutral." Since the marketing community presents information that will favor particular brands, public policy provides balance with an emphasis on objective information. The last, and most difficult, public policy application concerns trade-offs between the freedom of marketers to control information dissemination and the costs and benefits of information to consumers. This is likely to remain a politically controversial matter.

An understanding of the decision rules used by consumers can be applied effectively in marketing. The use of noncompensatory rules is encouraged by product ratings of critical factors such as safety. It is easy to eliminate those brands that do not possess a certain rating or "seal of approval" from further consideration. Another application of this principle can be seen in attempts to create the belief that consideration of a particular attribute should dominate the choice process. By stressing price and only price, the marketer is in effect telling the consumer that no other attributes are relevant. No matter how competing brands may be evaluated on other attributes, they cannot compensate for inferior positions on the price dimension.

A good illustration of strategies to promote noncompensatory decision rules can be seen in the environmental movement. By focusing consumers on the environmental impact of their purchases, marketers prevent other attributes from being taken into consideration. Sometimes this can lead to the purchase of one product over another, as in the case of cloth rather than disposable diapers; or one brand of the product may be chosen over alternatives, as in the case of nonchlorine rather than chlorine bleach or a high- rather than a low-energy-efficient appliance. In the most extreme cases, noncompensatory rules in decision making can lead to "negative purchases": If all brands of tuna fish are obtained through techniques that kill dolphins, no brand is bought. Similarly, consumption of products with possible health hazards falls if a single dimension dominates information search and noncompensatory rules are used by consumers. No price reduction or rebate will induce one to purchase any brand if the product itself is judged unacceptable along the health dimension. One way of inhibiting such negative purchase decisions is to create ambiguity about the actual health hazards of the product or about information on product risks. With an overload of information that is difficult to process effectively, the consumer may become more reluctant to deem a product below the threshold necessary for purchase.

ADVERTISING AND CONSUMPTION

There have historically been three independent forces stimulating research on consumer behavior. One arises from the desire to influence consumers. Consumer decision-making research combines with advertising and marketing to create desires for products, preferences for brands, and patterns of consumption. An opposing force encouraging consumer behavior research is the desire to protect consumers; organizations committed to consumer rights have identified their own agendas for research on the decision-making processes of consumers. The third group interested in consumer behavior consists of scientists with a fundamental interest in human behavior as it occurs in the marketplace. The field on the whole is neutral with respect to the interests of consumers or those who wish to influence them.

The strong emphasis on decision making in the field of consumer psychology has, as in many areas in psychology, been encouraged by the cognitive revolution. Although researchers continue to recognize that people respond to affective and emotional appeals, they have become more attuned to consumers' conscious processing of information. This trend can be expected to continue. The need to gather and evaluate information will grow as products and services become more diverse and complex. Another reason that consumer psychology will continue to place an emphasis on decision making is consumers' demand for more complete and accurate information about goods and services.

One of the limitations of the cognitive theories of consumer decision making is that they typically fail to take into account differences between individuals and groups of people. Consumer psychology is likely to become increasingly concerned with market segmentation as the ability to understand the diverse needs of various groups develops. Further specialization of research on the aged and children as consumers is also predictable. Among emerging global trends is an increased interest in marketing to women around the world. The rise of Internet shopping has also made enormous changes in consumer behavior, diminishing the face-to-face interaction of consumer and salesperson and vastly increasing the ease of comparison shopping.

BIBLIOGRAPHY

Acuff, Daniel S. *What Kids Buy and Why.* New York: Free, 1999. Print.

Bettman, James R. *An Information Processing Theory of Consumer Choice.* Reading: Addison, 1979. Print.

Fenwick, Ian, and John A. Quelch, eds. *Consumer Behavior for Marketing Managers.* Boston: Allyn, 1984. Print.

Foxall, Gordon R. "Consumer Behavior Analysis: Behavioral Economics Meets the Marketplace." *Psychological Record* 63.2 (2013): 231–37. Print.

Graham, Judy F. *Critical Thinking in Consumer Behavior: Cases and Experiential Exercises.* Upper Saddle River: Pearson Education, 2004. Print.

Griskevicius, Vladas, and Douglas T. Kendrick. "Fundamental Motives: How Evolutionary Needs Influence Consumer Behavior." *Jour. of Consumer Psychology* 23.3 (2013): 372–86. Print.

Jacoby, Jacob, and Jerry C. Olson, eds. *Perceived Quality: How Consumers View Stores and Merchandise.* Lexington: Lexington Books, 1985. Print.

Solomon, Michael R., and Nancy J. Rabolt. *Consumer Behavior: In Fashion.* Upper Saddle River, N.J.: Prentice Hall, 2007. Print.

Wells, Victoria K., and Gordon R. Foxall. "Matching, Demand, Maximization, and Consumer Choice." *Psychological Record* 63.2 (2013): 239–57. Print.

Wilkie, William L. *Consumer Behavior.* 3d ed. New York: John Wiley & Sons, 1994. Print.

Janet A. Sniezek

See Also: Advertising; Attitude-behavior consistency; Attitude formation and change; Behavioral economics; Cognitive dissonance; Cognitive maps; Field experimentation; Group decision making; Motivation; Motivation: Intrinsic and extrinsic; Survey research: Questionnaires and interviews.

Cooperation, competition, and negotiation

Type of psychology: Social psychology

Cooperation, competition, and negotiation are social processes central to the functioning of a group. They influence the effectiveness of a group in making decisions, completing tasks, and resolving differences, and they have a major impact on interpersonal relationships among group members.

Key Concepts

- Competitive social situations
- Contriently interdependent goals
- Principled negotiation
- Prisoner's dilemma
- Social trap
- Strategic negotiation

INTRODUCTION

The terms "cooperation," "competition," and "negotiation" are fairly common words used to describe frequent interpersonal experiences. Most people can immediately draw to mind experiences of each type. These processes are of particular importance in the functioning of a group. Because a group is commonly defined by social scientists as two or more people exerting influence on one another, discussion of each term can be understood as describing a process among informal groups, such as friends, spouses, business partners, coworkers, and classmates, as well as more formally established groups, such as appointed or elected committees, boards of directors, faculty, and members of an organization.

When people cooperate with one another, it is assumed that members of the group have similar goals; when they compete with one another, it is assumed they have different (and often conflicting) goals. This distinction is illustrated in definitions offered by Morton Deutsch, a leading researcher in group processes. Deutsch suggested that in cooperative situations, goals are "contriently interdependent," which means simply that goal achievement by one group member facilitates goal achievement by other members. In competitive situations, goal achievement by one group member hinders goal achievement by other members. It is often under conditions of competition that the process of negotiation enters. Cooperation and competition (with resulting negotiation) are central factors influencing group characteristics such as cohesiveness, effectiveness, and interpersonal relationships.

SELF-INTEREST AND SOCIAL DILEMMAS

Researchers have been interested in studying behavior when long-term interests are served by cooperation but short-term interests are served by looking out for oneself. In fact, these dilemmas are frequently involved with issues threatening the future of society, such as waste recycling, pollution control, and the depletion of natural resources. The question left to answer is how one reconciles self-interest (for example, not spending money to fix the damaged pollution-control device on one's automobile) with societal well-being (the necessity of reducing pollutants).

Psychologists have used laboratory games to study such social dilemmas. Perhaps the most frequently used game is called the prisoner's dilemma. In this game, a subject (here named John) is one of two criminal suspects who have been working in tandem. The two subjects are being questioned separately by a district attorney (DA) about a crime that has been committed; both are guilty. The DA, however, has only enough evidence to convict both of a lesser crime. The DA offers each suspect a chance to confess. If John confesses and his cohort does not, John will be granted immunity and the DA will have enough evidence to convict his partner of the more serious offense. This is the best scenario for John but the worst for his partner. If the partner confesses and John does not, the partner is granted immunity and John receives the heavier sentence. This is the worst scenario for John but the best for his cohort. If neither confesses, each will receive a light sentence for the lesser crime; this is the second-best scenario for each individual but the best scenario for the overall partnership. Finally, if both confess, each will receive a moderate sentence for the lesser offense. This is the third-best scenario for each individual but a bad option for the partnership.

It has been found that, in the prisoner's dilemma, most people will confess, although not confessing is the most cooperative approach with one's partner; confession is considering self-interest first, even at the expense of one's partner. If John adopts only an individualistic perspective and does not worry about the collective good, confessing is the better strategy; after all, if his partner does not confess, then he is free. If the partner does confess, John will receive a moderate sentence rather than risking a severe sentence by not confessing.

There is, however, a catch in this situation: Both prisoners will think the same way; hence, both will receive a moderate sentence. If both had not confessed and, in a sense, cooperated with each other, both would receive a light sentence. By looking out for self-interest, both partners lose.

Variations of this dilemma have been developed around themes more relevant to the typical citizen, especially the college student (such as negotiation for bonus points in a course). Each variant of the game is structured so that each party is better off individually by not cooperating. However, if both parties do not cooperate, they end up worse off than if they had cooperated.

STRATEGIC NEGOTIATION

There are ways for people or groups to avoid such social traps, or situations in which, by both not cooperating, conflicting parties end up worse off than if they had cooperated.

One approach is to employ strategic negotiation, a reciprocal communication process in which parties with conflicting interests can examine specific issues and make, as well as consider, offers and counteroffers. Negotiation involves the ability to communicate, which may not always be available in situations of conflict (including some of the laboratory games employed by psychologists).

Sometimes negotiation is viewed solely as a process of protecting self-interests. Some people, often called hard bargainers, talk tough, even employing threatening tactics. The person who threatens to sue or claims that there is nothing to be negotiated would be an example of a hard bargainer. Soft bargainers, on the other hand, are willing to bend, even to the point of sacrificing self-interests. Such individuals often believe that their good-faith approach is a model for the other negotiator, thereby promoting reconciliation while still hoping for important concessions. In group settings, soft bargainers may be concerned about group cohesion and make concessions contrary to self-interest. The extent to which hard versus soft bargaining is effective is a complex matter, depending on many factors present in the negotiation process. Thus, it is neither easy nor necessarily accurate to claim that one technique is better than the other.

ELEMENTS OF EFFECTIVE NEGOTIATION

Despite the hard-bargaining tone of the title *Getting to Yes: Negotiating Agreement without Giving In* (1981; 3rd ed. 1991), the authors, Roger Fisher and William Ury, drawing on research as part of the Harvard Negotiation Project (a project dealing with all levels of conflict resolution, ranging from marital relationships to global disputes), promote what they call principled negotiation Their approach identifies four basic elements of effective negotiation and problem solving. First, they recommend that negotiators separate the people from the problem. By focusing on the problem rather than the intentions or motives of the people involved, participants are more likely to see themselves as working together, attacking the problem rather than each other. Second, the authors recommend that negotiators focus on interests by identifying underlying issues rather than by negotiating specific positions. They claim that position taking often obscures what the participants really want. Third, before trying to reach agreement, the negotiators should individually and collectively generate a variety of options, especially identifying options that may produce mutual gain. By adopting this strategy, the negotiation is transformed into a group problem-solving process. Finally, negotiators should insist that the eventual resolution be based on some objective criteria considered fair by both parties. The principled negotiator is thus neither hard nor soft, but is able to reach agreement without, as the title of the book says, giving in.

One of the key elements of Fisher and Ury's approach is the process of getting people to attack problems rather than each other, thus fostering a sense of cooperative teamwork. What is implied is that working cooperatively makes the task at hand more manageable and the negotiating process more enjoyable, with a more effective outcome resulting.

RESEARCH

A series of studies conducted by Deutsch during the 1940s and 1950s generally supports these assertions. Small groups of five people met over a five-week period, some working in cooperative situations, others in competitive situations. Members of the cooperative groups, where all group members would be equally rewarded for a combined effort, indicated that they liked their group and its individual members better, reacted more favorably to other members' contributions, and generally rated the overall experience higher than did members of competitive groups (in which group members were told that the amount and quality of their individual contributions to the task at hand would be rank ordered).

Later studies provide additional support demonstrating the superiority of cooperation. In one study, members of cooperative groups found the atmosphere more relaxing and felt greater freedom to contribute to the group process than did members of competitive groups. In general, it can be said without equivocation that interpersonal relationships are more positive in cooperative than in competitive group situations.

The question remains, however, whether cooperative groups are more effective in achieving goals or in making good decisions than are competitive groups. Results of several studies generally support, as expected, the notion that when group members coordinate their efforts, the outcome is more successful than when group members compete with one another. One study compared two groups of interviewers in a public employment agency. Interviewers in a cooperative atmosphere, in which interviewers worked together to place applicants in job settings, were more successful than interviewers in a more competitive atmosphere.

Is competition ever healthy in a group setting? Most of the research that stresses the advantages of a cooperative atmosphere has involved highly interdependent tasks. That is, to reach a goal, group members must rely on one another for success. Thus, it should not be surprising that teams in a sport that requires considerable teamwork (for example, basketball or volleyball) should perform better when players get along with one another. For sports in which teamwork is less important (for example, cross-country running or skiing), however, a sense of harmony among team members may be less beneficial, especially if recognition is provided on an individual basis. Therefore, although research has rarely documented advantages of a competitive atmosphere, there appear to be some conditions in which a sense of competition among group members is not particularly disruptive. The key is whether the task requires a highly interdependent effort among group members.

Some surprising sex differences have been found with regard to individual cooperation and competition, especially in laboratory studies involving games such as the prisoner's dilemma. While the traditional gender-role stereotype for women is to be cooperative and accommodating in an attempt to maintain harmony, research seems to indicate that women sometimes demonstrate a more competitive nature than men. One explanation of this finding is that women are more likely to make choices that are consistent with the interpersonal setting. If the interpersonal setting suggests competition (as it does in the prisoner's dilemma game), women compete at least as hard as men; if it suggests cooperation, women cooperate at least as much as men.

CONTRIBUTIONS OF DEUTSCH AND SHERIF

Much of the work on cooperation and competition must be credited to Deutsch's classic studies of the 1940s and 1950s. Deutsch's mentor was the respected social psychologist Kurt Lewin at the Massachusetts Institute of Technology. The relationship between Lewin and Deutsch was more than that of teacher and student. Lewin later founded the Commission on Community Interrelations. As a member of that commission, Deutsch was one of the first researchers to employ scientific methodology in studying societal effects of racially integrated housing. Undoubtedly, Lewin's work on leadership had a major impact on Deutsch. Just as Lewin's research suggested that leaders who facilitate a cooperative climate among group members in decision-making processes maximize group productivity and member satisfaction, Deutsch's research clearly stresses the superiority of a cooperative versus competitive intragroup atmosphere.

In the late 1950s, Muzafer Sherif also studied the comparative processes of competition and cooperation by creating such conditions in real-life settings. Sherif discovered that the social dynamics of preadolescent boys in a camp setting were very similar to patterns of group behavior among adults. Groups functioned well in a cooperative atmosphere, especially under conditions of intergroup competition. The most striking finding in Sherif's research was how the conflicting groups could overcome their differences when presented superordinate goals—that is, goals that were compelling for both groups but that could not be attained without the help of the other group.

REAL-LIFE APPLICATIONS

Cooperation is not always easily attained. Much of the research discussed, particularly regarding negotiation, suggests that the unbridled pursuit of self-interest is detrimental to the collective good. This may help explain why history is replete with examples of military escalation between opposing countries and why mutual disarmament is so difficult. One-sided disarmament leaves that side vulnerable to exploitation, which, from that side's perspective, is the worst predicament in which to be.

Research conducted on group processes, including research on cooperation, competition, and negotiation, may help people further understand such important real-life issues as how a board of directors can most efficiently run a corporation or what atmosphere is most conducive to good decision making—whether that decision is about a family vacation, a neighborhood plan to fight crime, or an international dispute. In an age of international tensions, interracial conflicts, labor-management disputes, and domestic friction, the study of group processes is crucial.

BIBLIOGRAPHY

Brewer, Marilynn B., and Masaki Yūki. *Culture and Group Processes.* Oxford: Oxford UP, 2013. eBook Collection (EBSCOhost). Web. 19 May 2014.

Fisher, Roger, and William Ury. *Getting to Yes: Negotiating Agreement without Giving In.* 3rd ed. London: Random, 1997. Print.

Harré, Rom, and Fathali M. Moghaddam. *The Psychology of Friendship and Enmity: Relationships in Love, Work, Politics, and War.* Santa Barbara: Praeger, 2013.

Jandt, Fred Edmund. *Win-Win Negotiating: Turning Conflict into Agreement.* New York: Wiley, 1987. Print.

Levine, John M. Group Processes. New York: Psychology, 2013. Print.

Pruitt, Dean G., and Sung Hee Kim. *Social Conflict: Escalation, Stalemate, and Settlement.* 3rd ed. Boston: McGraw, 2004. Print.

Sullivan, Brandon A., Mark Snyder, and John L. Sullivan, eds. *Cooperation: The Political Psychology of Effective Human Interaction.* Malden: Blackwell, 2008. Print.

Ury, William. *Getting Past No: Negotiating in Difficult Situations.* Rev. ed. New York: Bantam, 2007. Print.

Peter C. Hill

See Also: Affiliation and friendship; Altruism, cooperation, and empathy; Cooperative learning; Group decision making; Groups; Leadership; Parenting styles; Social identity theory; Social perception.

Cooperative learning

Type of psychology: Social psychology

Cooperative learning refers to a variety of ways in which individuals work together to produce or obtain some defined goal. Research supports the effectiveness of cooperative learning strategies in the areas of achievement, positive interactions with others, and self-esteem development.

Key Concepts
- Dyad
- Group investigation
- Student teams-achievement divisions (STAD)
- Task specialization
- Teams-games-tournament (TGT)

INTRODUCTION

Cooperative learning involves working in small groups toward some desired end. Groups, in and of themselves, do not have to be cooperative. Group members may compete for benefits, or an individual group member may assume all the responsibility for a group task. Neither of these group situations is cooperative. In cooperative learning, individuals depend on one another to receive benefits. Cooperative learning methods can be contrasted with competitive methods, which have individuals work against one another to reach a goal, and individualistic methods, which encourage each person to work toward a goal without regard for the performance or behaviors of others.

Informal group activities such as sharing ideas can be considered cooperative learning. Some psychologists believe that even simple cooperative interactions between individuals can be associated with enhanced cognitive and social development. Most of the research on cooperative learning, however, reflects a more formal, structured approach.

JIGSAW LEARNING TECHNIQUE

One of the first structured cooperative learning techniques, "jigsaw," was developed by social psychologist Elliot Aronson and his colleagues. Aronson envisioned an academic environment in which a heterogeneous mix of students could achieve success and learn to appreciate one another through equal-status contact. In jigsaw, students are placed in small groups that mix characteristics such as race, gender, and ability. The teacher assigns a common task, such as learning about Christopher Columbus, to the entire class. The assignment is broken down into subtopics. For example, the assignment on Columbus might include a review of Columbus's early life, information on his voyages, a description of life in and around North America when Columbus set sail, and a review of Columbus's later life. Each student in a group assumes responsibility for one of the subtopics of the assignment. Students then meet with members from other groups who share the same subtopic. At this point, students have formed new, specialized groups in which individuals with the same information can help one another master the subtopic. Afterward, the members of the specialized groups return to their original groups to teach the material they have mastered and to learn the information on the other subtopics from other group members. Achievement is measured by testing students individually on all the information for the assignment. Jigsaw also includes extensive team-building and communication-training activities.

USE OF GROUP REWARDS

Although Aronson and his colleagues had high expectations for the cognitive and social benefits of jigsaw, reviews of the effects have been mixed. Cooperative learning methods that have emphasized group rewards over the individual rewards associated with jigsaw have shown more consistent benefits for learners. For example, Robert Slavin and his colleagues at The Johns Hopkins University have developed several successful group-reward cooperative learning methods, including student teams-achievement divisions (STAD) Student teams-achievement divisions and teams-games-tournament (TGT).Teams-games-tournament In STAD the teacher presents a lesson and students study worksheets in small, heterogeneous groups. Afterward, students take individual quizzes. Group scores are computed based on how much each group member improves over previous performance; group scores are reported in a class newsletter. TGT differs by having group members compete against members of other teams with similar records of past performance; group scores are based on the competition.

Two techniques developed by other research teams, learning together and group investigation, also use group rewards. Learning together emphasizes the development of social skills such as trust, conflict resolution, and accurate communication. Students work together to complete a single piece of work and are rewarded for working cooperatively and for task performance. In group investigation, small groups of students choose topics from a unit that the class is studying. Group members then choose a subtopic for each member to investigate. Like jigsaw, group investigation uses task specialization—the dividing up of responsibility among group members for separate aspects of the group activity. Unlike jigsaw, in group investigation, group members work together to prepare a presentation for the entire class and are rewarded for group work.

BENEFITS

Taken together, the various cooperative learning methods illustrate that there are benefits to cooperative learning methods over traditional competitive or individualistic approaches to instruction. Cooperative learning is also credited with increasing positive social interactions. Researchers report greater interaction between members of different racial or ethnic groups, greater acceptance of mainstreamed students, and greater friendship among students. Teachers and students in cooperative classrooms report more positive attitudes toward school. Finally, students in cooperative learning studies often show increased levels of self-esteem.

IMPLICATIONS FOR EDUCATION

Because of the clear relevance of cooperative learning techniques for the education of children, cooperative strategies have been investigated in a number of long-term school projects. A good example is the Riverside Cooperative Learning Project. One part of the project involved training student teachers in cooperative learning techniques and evaluating the effects of the training on their students. Elementary school student teachers were randomly assigned to either a traditional classroom structure, a STAD-structured classroom, or a TGT-structured classroom. STAD was considered the purest example of cooperative learning in the study because TGT contains a competitive element; in that group, members compete against members of other groups to gain points for their own group (team). Thus, TGT is a combination of cooperation and competition. TGT is still considered to be more of a cooperative method than the traditional classroom, which is oriented toward competitive and individualistic activities.

The academic gains that students made under the three classroom structures varied in the Riverside project based on the race of the students. African American students made the greatest gains in the STAD classroom, the classroom considered to be the clearest example of cooperative learning. Students of European descent did best in the TGT(cooperative-competitive) classroom. Mexican American students made the greatest gains in the traditional classroom. These results are important because they add support to the belief that some of the racial differences that occur in performance in schools may be related to cultural preferences for one type of classroom structure over another.

In this study, the authors were surprised that the Mexican American students did not do better in the cooperative classrooms, since studies on ethnic differences suggest that Mexican American culture is oriented toward cooperation over competition. The Mexican American children in the Riverside project, however, were third-generation Americans with little knowledge of Spanish. Before the study began, they tested like the European American students in terms of cooperation; the African American students, on the other hand, tested higher than the Mexican American and the European American students on cooperation. Knowing which classroom structure will be best for a student is not as simple as determining the student's racial or ethnic heritage.

Classroom climate was more positive in the cooperative classrooms than in the traditional classrooms, particularly for the Mexican American and African American students. Cooperativeness was higher among students in cooperative classrooms, and students in cooperative classes were more democratic in choosing friends. Schools that want to emphasize social change, then, might prefer cooperative learning methods. Yet while cooperative techniques seemed better overall, the Riverside project also demonstrated that a variety of classroom structures may be necessary in schools to optimize performance for a majority of students.

EFFECTS IN THE WORKPLACE

Cooperative learning methods have also been investigated in laboratory studies with adult learners. Such studies are important for understanding the extent of the effects of cooperative learning methods and for evaluating whether these methods might be useful with older students and with materials that might be found in work environments. If the effects of cooperative methods on achievement transfer to work environments, employers might begin to train people differently and increase job performance. If the effects of cooperative methods on social interactions transfer to work environment, employers might improve organizational climates and also enhance job performance. Since the workforce is becoming more diversified, information on reactions to cooperative learning methods by different groups of people should be beneficial. A diversified environment also puts increased pressure on organizations to determine the best ways to get people to work together for increased productivity.

Preliminary studies on adults suggest that cooperative learning benefits can be obtained with dyads (a pair of persons working together on a task), that individual accountability and external rewards may not be as critical as they are in the school setting, and that personality differences and the type of material being learned may be more important.

CULTURAL AND ETHNIC CONSIDERATIONS

The topic of cooperation has been an important one for psychologists almost since the origins of psychology as a science in the late nineteenth century. John Dewey, a philosopher and educator who discussed the importance of cooperation in education, and Kurt Lewin, a psychologist who influenced the study of group dynamics in the 1940's, are both seminal figures in the study of cooperation. Most of the current research on structured cooperative methods, however, can be traced to studies in the 1970's. Some of those early researchers were particularly concerned with the changing demographic patterns in schools that made schools seem more heterogeneous than had been the case in the past. Civil rights legislation ordering desegregation contributed to changes in the makeup of some schools. Mainstreaming also added variety to the composition of classrooms. Around the same time, an increase in research on ethnicity seemed to indicate that cultural differences between groups that considered themselves to be disenfranchised (for example, African Americans and Mexican Americans) and the European American majority culture were not going to disappear. If anything, the nation was becoming more diverse, and the probability of intergroup conflict seemed even more likely if people did not learn to work together.

Some theoreticians also speculated that differences in achievement between different racial and ethnic groups might be related to clashes between cultural values and classroom structures. In essence, classroom structure might serve as a tool for discriminating against some potentially capable students. The traditional classroom atmosphere in the United States continues to be highly competitive and individualistic. Students compete for higher grades, often at the expense of others. Cooperation is for the most part discouraged because teachers are asked to evaluate the work of the individual for grades. Yet the increasing ethnic diversity of the United States means that better understanding of ethnic groups and procedures that enhance learning for as many students as possible are important considerations for educators and employers. If researchers and theoreticians of cooperative learning methods have addressed the cognitive, social, and personal effects of cooperative methods, they will be increasingly influential in a number of settings.

BIBLIOGRAPHY

Aronson, Elliot, et al. *The Jigsaw Classroom*. 2d ed. Reading, Mass.: Addison-Wesley, 1997. A classic in the field. Discusses the rationale for developing this cooperative learning method, explains the jigsaw technique in detail, and presents the research findings.

Gillies, Robyn M. *Cooperative Learning: Integrating Theory and Practice*. Newbury Park, Calif.: Sage Publications, 2007. Offers strategies for introducing cooperative learning into the classroom, with a focus on problem solving and classroom discussion. Includes information on the major research that supports this learning style.

Johnson, David W., and Roger T. Johnson. *Learning Together and Alone*. 5th ed. Boston: Allyn & Bacon, 1999. Aimed primarily at teachers. Contrasts cooperative, competitive, and individualistic learning methods and their appropriate uses.

Jolliffe, Wendy. *Cooperative Learning in the Classroom: Putting It into Practice*. Thousand Oaks, Calif.: Paul Chapman, 2007. An overview of cooperative learning methods, with suggestions on how to encourage students to work in pairs or in small groups

Kagan, S., et al. "Classroom Structural Bias: Impact of Cooperative and Competitive Classroom Structures on Cooperative and Competitive Individuals and Groups." In *Learning to Cooperate, Cooperating to Learn,* edited by Robert E. Slavin et al. New York: Plenum, 1985. Only for those who want more information about the Riverside project. The project is described, and graphs are interpreted for the reader.

Sharan, Shlomo, ed. A *Handbook of Cooperative Learning Methods.* Westport, Conn.: Praeger, 1999. Aimed at teachers, offers an array of cooperative learning techniques and commentary on their use in the classroom.

Slavin, Robert E. *Cooperative Learning: Theory and Research*. 2d ed. Boston: Allyn & Bacon, 2000. Reviews various cooperative learning methods, some in detail, and the cognitive, social, and personal benefits associated with cooperative learning.

__________. "Research on Cooperative Learning: Consensus and Controversy." *Educational Leadership* 47, no. 4 (1989/1990): 52-54. A very readable discussion of areas of agreement and disagreement in the field. Only one among a variety of articles in this issue by major theoreticians and teachers of cooperative learning methods.

Judith L. Gay

See Also: Cooperation, competition, and negotiation; Educational psychology; Learning; Prejudice reduction; Work motivation.

Coping
Chronic illness

Type of psychology: Stress

When people develop a chronic illness, their entire lives change. Efforts that are undertaken to counteract these increased demands are called coping endeavors. Different people behave differently under such duress. However, certain coping styles have better outcomes, such as maintaining a positive outlook or being optimistic, avoiding repressive coping, and obtaining social support.

Key Concepts
- Appraisal
- Crisis theory
- Emotion-focused coping
- Encounter
- Hardiness
- Optimism
- Problem-focused coping
- Retreat
- Shock
- Social support
- Transactional model

INTRODUCTION
In modern times, chronic illnesses are becoming increasingly common. In the twenty-first century, the leading causes of death in the United States are chronic diseases, as opposed to the beginning of the previous century, when infectious diseases were more rampant. Chronic illnesses are diseases that are long in duration, have multiple risk factors, have a long latency period, are usually noncontagious, cause greater and progressive functional impairment, and are generally incurable. Examples of common chronic illnesses include heart diseases (such as coronary heart disease and hypertension), cancers (malignant neoplasms), chronic obstructive lung diseases (bronchial asthma, emphysema, and chronic bronchitis), cerebrovascular diseases (stroke), diabetes mellitus, kidney diseases (end-stage renal disease and renal failure), musculoskeletal disorders (rheumatoid arthritis and osteoarthritis), chronic mental illnesses, neurological disorders (epilepsy, Alzheimer's disease, Parkinson's disease, and multiple sclerosis), and some of the results of accidents or injuries (traumatic brain injury, spinal cord injury, amputations, and burns). Dealing with these illnesses presents numerous challenges for patients and their family members and care providers. "Coping" is a term that is usually used to describe the process by which people manage demands in excess of the resources that are at their disposal. Therefore, in addition to medical treatment, management of chronic illnesses must address lifelong coping with these illnesses.

The interest in coping with chronic illnesses can be traced back to late 1960s, with the work of American physician Thomas Holmes and Richard Rahe, then a medical student, at the University of Washington. They constructed the Social Readjustment Rating Scale (SRRS) to assess the amount of stress to which an individual is exposed. Personal injuries or illnesses were rated as the sixth-most-important events in terms of their intensity in affecting one's life and increasing the chances of further illness in the subsequent year of life.

MODELS OF COPING
American psychologist Franklin Shontz, in his book *The Psychological Aspects of Physical Illness and Disability* (1975), described the phases of reaction to any illness. The first stage on being diagnosed with a chronic illness is what he described as the stage of shock, in which the person is in a bewildered state and behaves in an automatic fashion with a sense of detachment from all surroundings. In this stage, patients often describe themselves as observers rather than participants in what is happening around them. The second stage is the stage of encounter or reaction. In this stage, the person is feeling a sense of loss and has disorganized thinking. Emotions of grief, despair, and helplessness are common. In this stage, patients often describe the feeling of being overwhelmed by reality. The third stage is what Shontz calls retreat. In this stage, the feeling of denial becomes very strong, but this state cannot persist and the patient gradually begins to accept reality as the symptoms persist and functional impairments ensue.

In the 1980s, American psychologist Richard Lazarus, an emeritus professor at the University of California at

Berkeley, proposed the famous coping model called the transactional model. This model has also been applied widely in understanding coping with chronic illnesses. According to the transactional model, all stressful experiences, including chronic illnesses, are perceived as person-environment transactions. In these transactions, the person undergoes a four-stage assessment known as appraisal. When confronted with a diagnosis of chronic illness, the first stage is the primary appraisal of the event. In this stage, the patient internally determines the severity of the illness and whether he or she is in trouble. If the illness is perceived to be severe or threatening, has caused harm or loss in the past, or has affected someone known to the person, then the stage of secondary appraisal occurs. If, on the other hand, the illness is judged to be irrelevant or poses minimal threat, then stress does not develop and no further coping occurs. The secondary appraisal determines how much control one has over the illness. Based on this understanding, the individual ascertains what means of control are available. This is the stage known as coping. Finally, the fourth stage is the stage of reappraisal, in which the person determines whether the effects of illness have been negated.

According to the transactional model, there are two broad categories of coping. The first one is called problem-focused coping, and the second one is called emotion-focused coping. Problem-focused coping is based on one's capability to think about and alter the environmental event or situation. Examples of this strategy at the thought-process level include utilization of problem-solving skills, interpersonal conflict resolution, advice seeking, time management, goal setting, and gathering more information about what is causing one stress. Problem solving requires thinking through various solutions, evaluating the pros and cons of different solutions, and then implementing a solution that seems most advantageous to reduce the stress. Examples of this strategy at the behavioral or action level include activities such as joining a smoking-cessation program, complying with a prescribed medical treatment, adhering to a diabetic diet plan, or scheduling and prioritizing tasks for managing time.

In the emotion-focused strategy, the focus is inward and on altering the way one thinks or feels about a situation or an event. Examples of this strategy at the thought-process level include denying the existence of the stressful situation, freely expressing emotions, avoiding the stressful situation, making social comparisons, or minimizing (looking at the bright side of things). Examples of this strategy at the behavioral or action level include seeking social support to negate the influence of the stressful situation; using exercise, relaxation, or meditation; joining support groups; practicing religious rituals; and escaping through the use of alcohol and drugs.

CRISIS THEORY OF COPING

In the 1980s, American psychologist Rudolf Moos proposed the crisis theory to describe the factors that influence the crises of illnesses. He identified three types of factors that influence the coping process in illness. The first category of factors comprises the illness-related factors. The more severe the disease in terms of its threat, the harder is the coping. Examples of such severe threats include conditions such as burns that are likely to produce facial disfigurement, implantation of devices for excreting fecal or urinary wastes, or epileptic seizures. The second category of factors comprises background and personal factors. These factors include one's age, gender, social class, religious values, emotional maturity, and self-esteem. For example, men are often affected more if the illness threatens their ambition, vigor, or physical power, while children show greater resilience because of their relative naïveté and limited cognitive abilities. The third category of factors identified by Moos comprises physical and social environmental factors. Generally speaking, people who have more social support tend to cope better when compared to people who live alone and do not have many friends.

Moos proposed in his crisis theory that these three factors impinge on the coping process. The coping process begins with cognitive appraisal, in which the patient reflects on the meaning of the illness in his or her life. This leads to formulating a set of adaptive tasks. Moos identified three adaptive tasks for coping directly with the illness: dealing with the symptoms and functional impairment associated with the illness or injury, adjusting to the hospital environment or medical procedures, and developing relationships with care providers. He further identified four adaptive tasks as crucial for adapting to general psychosocial functioning: maintaining a sense of emotional balance and controlling negative affect; preserving a sense of mastery, competence, or self-image; sustaining meaningful relationships with friends and family; and preparing for a future of uncertainty. The family members or long-term care providers who work with such patients also undergo these seven adaptive processes and must make these adjustments for effective coping. These adaptive tasks usually result in specific coping strategies. Moos described the following coping strategies: denial, or minimizing the seriousness of the illness (which is sometimes helpful, especially in the earlier stages); seeking information; learning medical procedures (which is sometimes helpful for self-care, such as taking insulin shots); mastering adaptive tasks; recruiting family support; thinking about and discussing the future to decipher greater predictability; and finding a purpose in and positive impacts of the illness on one's life.

HEART DISEASES

Heart diseases or cardiovascular diseases have been the leading cause of death in the United States since the 1980s. Initial research on coping with heart disease was done on patients with myocardial infarction, or heart attack. The research focused mainly on the role played by denial, which is a defense mechanism, described by the famous Austrian neurologist

Sigmund Freud, who is also called the father of psychoanalysis. Researchers using the "denial scale" classified patients into "denying" and "nondenying" groups and studied the outcomes of recovery. It was found that denial played an important role in decreasing anxiety and even in reducing deaths in the early stages of heart attack recovery. However, during the later phases of recovery, denial added to noncompliance with medical care, decreased seeking of information about the disease, and increased the risk of recurrence of heart attack. Research comparing the specific role of repression (or denial) and sensitization to the presence of disease supports the importance of sensitization in improving the solicitation of information, social functioning, and outcomes through the reduction of complications.

Recent research on coping and heart diseases has broadened its focus, improved coping measurement tools, and studied several other dimensions of coping. The first of these dimensions is the comparison between problem-focused strategies and emotion-focused strategies as described by Lazarus. In general, it has been found that people who use a problem-focused coping strategy report better social and psychological adjustment following hospital discharge, and these approaches are beneficial in the long run for improving disease outcomes. Emotion-focused strategies have been found to be of some utility in the short term in decreasing distress but have not been found to be useful in the long term. Further, people using emotion-focused strategies have reported greater incidence of anxiety and depression as a result of the heart disease.

Another dimension of coping that researchers have studied pertains to optimism. American psychologist Charles S. Carver and his colleagues have found the beneficial effects of being optimistic when recovering from chronic heart disease. Similarly, researchers have found empirical evidence of what American psychologist Suzanne Kobasa described as hardiness, a term that comprises the trinity of control, commitment, and challenge, as being beneficial in improving psychosocial adjustment to heart disease and decreasing chances of anxiety and depression.

CANCERS

Cancers are a diverse group of diseases characterized by the uncontrolled growth and spread of abnormal cells in the body. At the start of the twenty-first century, cancers were the second leading cause of death in the United States. The lifetime probability of developing cancer was estimated at one in three, and it was estimated that cancers would soon be the leading cause of death and sickness. Cancers pose special challenges for coping, as these necessitate utilization of a wide range of coping options to deal with changing and often deteriorating functional abilities, medical challenges, treatment modalities (chemotherapy, surgery, and radiotherapy), and psychosocial reactions.

Like the earlier studies on coping with heart diseases, initial work on coping with cancers also focused on the role of defense mechanisms described by Freud. More recent research on coping and cancers has focused on personal disposition styles, coping strategies as described by Lazarus, and other special mechanisms. Results from disposition style studies suggest that internal locus of control and optimistic outlook are linked to lower levels of emotional distress and better psychological adaptation to cancer. On the other hand, avoidance or escapism has been associated with higher emotional distress. Problem-based coping strategies, as described by Lazarus, have also been found to be associated with better psychosocial adaptation to cancer. On the other hand, disengagement-oriented strategies such as wishful thinking, blaming oneself, and adopting a fatalistic or resigned attitude have been found to be associated with higher levels of emotional distress and worse psychosocial adaptation to cancer. Likewise, acceptance of the diagnosis of cancer and resignation to this fact have also been found to be associated with worse psychosocial outcomes. Other coping strategies such as freely expressing feelings, denial, and seeking religion have yielded equivocal results.

CEREBROVASCULAR DISEASES

In 2011, cerebrovascular disease (CVD) was the fourth leading cause of death in the United States and represented about 5 percent of deaths from all causes, according to the US Centers for Disease Control and Prevention (CDC). The most severe manifestation of CVD is stroke, with transient ischemic attack being a less severe clinically apparent variant. Stroke is a major cause of disability. Besides the usual generalized coping that goes with any chronic illness, coping with stroke specifically requires speech therapy, occupational therapy, and physiotherapy.

DIABETES

Diabetes mellitus is a disease in which the body is unable to sufficiently produce and/or properly use insulin, a hormone needed by the body to use glucose. The prevalence of this disorder has consistently risen in the United States, and as of 2013, it afflicted about 10 percent of the population, according to the American Diabetes Association. Besides the usual generalized coping that goes with any chronic illness, coping with diabetes specifically requires lifelong dietary changes, changes pertaining to physical activity patterns, and, in most cases, specific medicinal usage and compliance.

CHRONIC RESPIRATORY DISORDERS

Chronic lung diseases are a varied group of diseases that were, in 2011, identified as the third leading cause of death in the United States. According to the CDC, as of 2013, approximately fifteen million Americans reported being diagnosed with one of these disorders. The most common chronic respiratory disorders are asthma, emphysema, and chronic bronchitis. Besides the compliance to medical treatment and the usual generalized coping that goes with any chronic illness, coping with respiratory disorders entails gradual buildup of exercise stamina and effective management of stress through relaxation techniques, since many acute attacks are both exaggerated and precipitated by stress.

CHRONIC MUSCULOSKELETAL DISORDERS

Arthritis and musculoskeletal disorders were the most common causes of physical disability in the United States in 2013, affecting approximately 20 percent of the population, according to the CDC. Besides the usual generalized coping that goes with any chronic illness, these disorders require specific rehabilitative coping through physiotherapy, occupational therapy, and vocational rehabilitation.

CHRONIC MENTAL ILLNESSES

Poor and ineffective coping with stress often leads to persistent depression and anxiety. Besides these two common mental illnesses, other disorders such as schizophrenia, bipolar psychosis, variants of anxiety disorders, organic disorders (such as dementia and Alzheimer's disease), and other mental illnesses pose special coping challenges for patients and their family members. Besides the usual coping strategies, coping with mental disorders specifically involves long behavioral, psychological, and social challenges and therapies.

BIBLIOGRAPHY

Allen, Jon G. *Coping with Trauma*. 2d ed. Washington: American Psychiatric P, 2005. Print.

Clark, Cindy Dell. *In Sickness and in Play: Children Coping with Chronic Illness*. New Brunswick: Rutgers UP, 2003. Print.

Di Benedetto, Mirella, et al. "Co-Morbid Depression and Chronic Illness Related to Coping and Physical and Mental Health Status." *Psychology, Health & Medicine* 19.3 (2014): 253–62. Print.

Helgeson, Vicki S., and Kristin Mickelson. "Coping with Chronic Illness Among the Elderly: Maintaining Self-Esteem." *Behavior, Health, and Aging*. Ed. Stephen B. Manuck, Richard Jennings, Bruce S. Rabin, and Andrew Baum. Mahwah: Erlbaum, 2000. Print.

Livneh, Hanoch. "Psychosocial Adaptation to Cancer: The Role of Coping Strategies." *Journal of Rehabilitation* 66.2 (2000): 40–50. Print.

Livneh, Hanoch. "Psychosocial Adaptation to Heart Diseases: The Role of Coping Strategies. " *Journal of Rehabilitation* 65.3 (1999): 24–33. Print.

McCabe, Marita P., and Elodie J. O'Connor. "Why Are Some People with Neurological Illness More Resilient Than Others." *Psychology, Health & Medicine* 17.1 (2012): 17–34. Print.

Moos, Rudolf H., ed. *Coping with Life Crises: An Integrated Approach*. New York: Plenum, 1986. Print.

Nabors, Laura A., et al. "Factors Related to Caregiver State Anxiety and Coping with a Child's Chronic Illness." *Families, Systems & Health: The Jour. of Collaborative Family HealthCare* 31.2 (2013): 171–80. Print.

Romas, John A., and Manoj Sharma. *Practical Stress Management: A Comprehensive Workbook for Managing Change and Promoting Health.* 5th ed. San Francisco: Pearson/Benjamin Cummings, 2009. Print.

Manoj Sharma

SEE ALSO: Alzheimer's disease; Anxiety disorders; Assisted living; Biofeedback and relaxation; Cancer and mental health; Coping: Social support; Coping: Strategies; Coping: Terminal illness; Death and dying; Defense mechanisms; Depression; Hope and mental health; Hospice; Meditation and relaxation; Stress: Physiological responses; Stress-related diseases.

Coping
Social support

TYPE OF PSYCHOLOGY: Social psychology; Stress

Stress is a problem of modern society that everyone experiences at one time or another; people must develop ways to deal with stressful events or risk being overwhelmed by them. Social support, which means turning to other people for support in times of personal crises, is one of the most-often-used coping strategies.

KEY CONCEPTS
- Coping
- Resources
- Social comparison
- Social support
- Stress

INTRODUCTION

When there is a perceived discrepancy between environmental demands and one's ability to meet those demands, an individual is likely to feel stress. Stress has both psychological and physiological causes and effects. To continue to function in an adaptive way, everyone must learn to cope with stress. There are many ways to cope. At one extreme, some people avoid or deny the existence of stress. At the other extreme, some people seek out and directly confront the source of stress to overcome it. One of the most-often-used approaches in coping with stress is social support, which can be used on its own or combined with other coping strategies.

Social support has many meanings. Sometimes it is defined simply as information that one receives from others. This information could come from a variety of sources—from family, friends, coworkers, or even the family's faithful dog. For social scientists, social support is sometimes defined as the possibility of human interactions, and it can be measured by indicators such as marital status. In that case, it may be assumed that an individual who is married receives more social support than does one who is not married. This is often incorrect, however; there are many supportive relationships outside marriage—the parent-child relationship, for example. Sidney Cobb in 1976 indicated that social support should be viewed as the receipt of information that one is cared for, is valued, and belongs to a mutually supportive social network. Parent-child relationships, and many others, would thus be possible sources of social support. This multidimensional view of social support has gained acceptance. Research in the area of social support has found common themes related to the perception of outcomes of interactions among people. In this view, there are five major outcomes constituting social support: the perception of a positive emotion toward oneself from another; agreement with another person about one's beliefs or feelings; encouragement by another person to express one's beliefs or feelings in a nonthreatening environment; the receipt of needed goods or services; and confirmation that one does not have to face events alone, that others will be there when needed. Viewing social support in terms of the subjective perception of an interaction rather than as the opportunity to interact with another is a useful way to conceptualize social support.

The perception of social support serves an important function in maintaining a positive sense of well-being by enabling one to cope with and adapt to stress. It has been shown to have a positive effect on physical as well as mental health. For example, the prognosis for an individual recovering from a heart attack or coping with a diagnosis of cancer is better for those with a good network of sources of social support. Research has shown that people who are depressed tend to have fewer and less supportive relationships with family members, coworkers, and friends than those who are not depressed.

There are different theories regarding the relationship between social support and stress. Some psychologists believe that social support has a buffering effect, while others believe that social support has a direct effect on stress. According to the buffering-effect model, social support is important when one is faced with a stressor because it comes between the individual and the source of stress, and thus it protects the individual from the negative effects of the stressor. In this case, social support acts as a safety net in much the same way that a physical safety net protects the trapeze artist from injury during a fall; unless there is a fall, the net does not serve any function. In contrast, the direct-effect model contends that social support is important regardless of the presence of a stressor. In this case, social support is seen as providing a generally positive effect on the individual, which would incidentally provide the individual with resources that can be called into play when faced with stress. For example, experiencing positive interactions can boost one's self-esteem in general. The high self-esteem is incorporated into the individual's self-concept, whether or not the person is currently dealing with a stressful event. However, when faced with stress, the self-esteem would then provide the individual with confidence to engage in problem-solving techniques to overcome the stressor. There is evidence to support both suggested mechanisms for social support, and it is likely that social support has both a buffering and a direct effect.

Despite the evidence indicating that social support helps people cope with stress, some studies show a negative effect. It seems that there are different types of social support, and it is important to match the type of support provided to the type of support needed. Tangible support is the providing of material aid in the form of goods and services. It is often needed but rarely given. One of the few instances in which it is commonly offered is following a death in the family, when friends and neighbors may bring over casseroles so that the grieving family can eat nutritious meals. Long-term tangible support is more likely to come either from impersonal sources, such as community-supported welfare programs, or from the most intimate source, the immediate family. The intermediate social network, consisting of friends and neighbors, is not likely to provide long-term tangible support.

Informational support is offered more freely by sources at all levels. This form of support serves an educational function, providing information relevant to coping with a problem. An example would be telling people the proper authority to call when they have no heat in their apartments. The third form of social support is emotional support, which comes from the more intimate sources, one's family and close friends. This form of support involves expressing positive feelings toward an individual, acknowledging that person's worth, and accepting his or her expressions of beliefs and feelings.

A number of factors might influence whether social support is provided. One factor is the perception of the person needing help of the likelihood that the desired support would actually be provided. If a person believes that he or she will get the help that is needed, that person is more likely to seek out social support. Studies have shown that individuals who are reluctant to seek help are less likely to receive the support they desperately need. Another factor that can influence the likelihood that social support will be provided is the person who could provide the desired support. That person has to perceive that there is an actual need on the part of the person requesting help. The individual also has to determine whether he or she can provide the appropriate type of support. Finally, the person who needs help has to be willing to accept the offer of social support when it is made. It is important to remember that the receivers of social support are not the only potential beneficiaries of the interaction. Providers of social support can also benefit from the interaction. In fact, studies show that even young children have a need to be helpful to others, particularly people in their families.

SUPPORT SETTINGS

Social support is applied in a variety of settings, both informal and formal. Informal settings for social support include the sharing of one's problems with friends and family. For example, an advertising executive may be under pressure to put together a campaign for the company's biggest client, who is considering changing firms. Informational support may come from the executive's coworkers over lunch. She might explain to her coworkers the problems she is facing designing the program. The coworkers might have faced similar problems, and they could tell the executive what they did to cope with the problems when they were experiencing them. The coworkers might provide tangible support by volunteering their time to work together on the campaign. Emotional support is more likely to come from the executive's family when she describes her day over dinner. The family members need to convey their love and respect to the executive. In this case, they need to indicate that their regard for the person is not dependent on the success of any advertising account. It might be counterproductive for the spouse to express confidence in the executive's ability to develop a successful campaign; the executive may then feel under more pressure, because now she not only has to worry about keeping the account but also may worry about disillusioning her spouse and losing that important source of support. Members of social networks need to be careful that they provide the correct form of social support, because providing support that does not match the needs of the recipient may be harmful.

Social support is important not only in a work setting but in a personal setting as well. For example, a man who is trying to lose weight would benefit from emotional support from his family and friends who let him know that they care about him and support his decision to lose weight. When dieting gets difficult, loved ones might be tempted to tell the dieter that they think he is fine just the way he is. That is not supportive of his decision to lose weight, however, and it works against his success. Informational support can be provided by giving the dieter information about ingredients and methods of meal preparation. This kind of support can be provided by a variety of people; waiters are generally quite willing to discuss this subject with restaurant patrons to give the needed information for a wise choice from the menu. This kind of support is requested so often, in fact, that many restaurants include such information on the menus themselves—an example of social support that is community based. Tangible support for weight loss can come from a diet or exercise partner who embarks on a weight-loss program with the dieter; another example would be a friend who provides low-calorie meals for the dieter.

Another informal setting in which social support is increasingly being provided is on the Internet.There has been a proliferation of Internet news and support groups that provide both informational and emotional support to individuals facing a number of physical and mental illnesses including diabetes, cancer, acquired immunodeficiency syndrome (AIDS), and depression. The use of support groups by the elderly in particular, many of whom may have been socially isolated prior to their use of the Internet, has increased significantly.

FORMAL SUPPORT

These examples of situations in which people need social support can also be used to illustrate support in a formal setting. The executive who is undergoing stress might seek professional help from a counselor. A counseling situation takes place in a supportive environment and is generally focused on emotional support; however, some therapy situations can also provide informational and tangible support. Behavior therapy can be a source of informational support, such as when the executive is given homework assignments to identify what specific behaviors or thoughts are triggers for her stress. A clear identification of the trigger will aid in setting up a program to combat the stress. Sometimes people take part in group therapy settings, where a counselor works with several clients at the same time. Participants in the session become a tight social network that provides emotional, informational, and sometimes even tangible support. In this case, the executive might practice her presentation for the group, and the other members' critique might include new ideas or techniques that can be used to solve her problem. Constructive criticism of a presentation is a service that could be considered a form of tangible support, as well as informational and emotional support.

A dieter can get support in a formal setting by joining an organized group such as Weight Watchers or Overeaters Anonymous. Losing weight alone can be a difficult task, and research has demonstrated that successful weight reduction is more likely to occur in group settings. Emotional support comes from fellow dieters who understand exactly what the dieter is experiencing and accept him as he is. In this case, everyone has the same problem, so the dieter does not feel that he does not fit in to society. Informational support comes from the group leader, who helps set goals and explains what behaviors need to be modified to achieve those goals. It also comes from other group members, who share recipes and advice on how to combat challenges. Tangible support comes in the form of the low-calorie meals provided by some weight-control programs or of a bond with a group member who can become an exercise partner. Social support from groups of people with common problems has been found to be so helpful that the number of such support, or self-help, groups is growing enormously. These groups are being founded for people with a wide range of problems: rape victims, people with alcohol dependency, spouses of military personnel stationed in a war zone, parents of sudden infant death syndrome (SIDS) victims, and caregivers of individuals with physical or mental illnesses. Formal social support groups, in a sense, act as the extended family that may be absent in a modern, mobile society.

Because positive social support has been associated with improved mental and physical health and overall well-being, interventions designed to promote positive health behaviors and to reduce adverse health behaviors have been targeted for not only individuals at risk but also their social support networks, which can play a significant role in influencing an individual's behavior. For example, in the attempt to reduce drinking and driving among young people, advertisers have used slogans such as "Friends don't let friends drive drunk," hoping to encourage peers to support responsible drinking and the use of designated drivers. Physicians have also discovered that patients are more likely to comply with their advice if spouses and children are involved in the treatment regimen, because these patients are more likely to practice safe health behaviors and comply with treatment if they feel they have the support of family and friends. Thus, the concept of social support can be useful not only in helping individuals cope when faced with stressful events in both formal and informal settings but also in enlisting the cooperation of an individual's social support network to promote successful behavioral health change.

THEORIES OF SUPPORT

Social support is best understood in the context of social comparison theory, first presented by Leon Festinger in 1954. People have a need to be "correct," to do the right thing, and to behave in a socially appropriate manner. It is not always easy to determine the correct position to hold in different situations. For example, how does someone decide what to wear to a party? Often, an individual will call a friend who is also going to the party and ask what the friend is planning to wear. A person tends to make decisions in ambiguous situations by observing what other people are doing. In general, one feels comfortable when behaving, dressing, or thinking in a manner that is similar to those around one. A woman is likely to feel uncomfortable and underdressed if she wears a skirt and blouse to a party where everyone else is in formal attire. A skirt and blouse are perfectly acceptable articles of clothing for a woman and are no less functional at a party than a formal gown would be. She may have worn that outfit to a social gathering previously and felt perfectly comfortable. When everyone else is dressed differently, however, she feels that she stands out and therefore is not dressed correctly. Correctness is determined by majority standards. People learn by the process of socialization to conform to those around them. Social comparison is the process by which people learn norms, or social expectations, in different settings.

In the process of learning norms, one also learns the social benefits of conformity: acceptance by others. When an individual expresses an idea or behavior that is consistent with the ideas or behaviors of others, then the social group is comfortable around that person and permits that person to join the group. If that person deviates from the group norm, then that person may be ostracized by the group. This is the basis of peer pressure, which people learn to apply at a young age.

When people turn to others for informational social support, they often are looking for guidance to help fit in with a social norm—to do or think the right thing. Emotional social support tells one that one is like others and is valued and accepted by others. Tangible social support tells one that one's needs are acceptable and that other people will perform behaviors similar to one's own behavior to meet those needs. The goal of both social comparison and social support is to validate oneself by ensuring that one does not deviate from social expectations.

In an interesting experiment designed to test the role of social comparison in emotional reactions, subjects were asked to wait until it was their turn to participate in an experiment; the experiment was explained to some subjects in a way designed to create apprehension. Subjects were given the opportunity either to wait alone or to wait with others. Those who were made fearful tended to want to wait with others more than did subjects who were not made fearful. This preference demonstrated that fear creates a desire to affiliate. More important, however, subjects showed a preference to wait with others only if they were told that the others were waiting for the same experiment. In this context, it is easy to understand the growth of support groups for specific problems. When facing a stressful situation, people need to be around others who can really understand what they are going through—in other words, other people with the same problem. There is strength in numbers.

BIBLIOGRAPHY

Asbury, Trey, and Schawn Hall. "Facebook as a Mechanism for Social Support and Mental Health Wellness." *Psi Chi Jour. of Psychological Research* 18.3 (2013): 124–29. Print.

Bin Li, et al. "Positive Psychological Capital: A New Approach to Social Support and Subjective Well-Being." *Social Behavior & Personality: An International Jour.* 42.1 (2014): 135–44. Print.

Goldsmith, Daena J. *Communicating Social Support*. Cambridge: Cambridge University Press, 2008. Print.

Pierce, Gregory R., Barbara R. Saranson, and Irwin G. Saranson, eds. *Handbook of Social Support and the Family.* New York: Plenum, 1996. Print.

Sarason, Barbara R., Irwin G. Sarason, and Gregory R. Pierce, eds. *Social Support: An Interactional View.* New York: Wiley, 1990. Print.

Schaefer, C., J. C. Coyne, and R. S. Lazarus. "The Health-Related Functions of Social Support." *Journal of Behavioral Medicine* 4 (1981): 381–406. Print.

Silver, R., and C. Wortman. "Coping with Undesirable Life Events." *Human Helplessness.* Ed. Judy Garber and Martin E. P. Seligman. New York: Academic Press, 1980. Print.

Suls, Jerry. "Social Support, Interpersonal Relations, and Health: Benefits and Liabilities." *Social Psychology of Health and Illness.* Ed. Glenn S. Sanders and Jerry Suls. Malden: Blackwell, 2003. Print.

Uchino, Bert N. *Social Support and Physical Health: Understanding the Health Consequences of Relationships.* Cambridge: Yale UP, 2004. Print.

Vaux, Alan. *Social Support: Theory, Research, and Intervention.* New York: Praeger, 1988. Print.

Ze-Wei Ma, Peng Quan, and Tian Liu. "Mediating Effect of Social Support on the Relationship Between Self-Evaluation and Depression." *Social Behavior & Personality: An International Jour.* 42.2 (2014): 295–302. Print.

Barbara A. Brenner; updated by Leonie J. Brooks

SEE ALSO: Coping: Chronic illness; Coping: Strategies; Coping: Terminal illness; Health psychology; Self-help groups; Social perception; Social support and mental health; Stress: Behavioral and psychological responses; Stress-related diseases; Support groups.

Coping
Strategies

TYPE OF PSYCHOLOGY: Stress

In 1967, Psychological Abstracts first used coping as a separate entity, and since then more than ten thousand articles and books related to this concept have been published in psychology and health sciences. It is generally accepted that coping is the way in which people handle stress, and the term is usually used to denote the handling of more difficult stressful situations. Coping strategies are broadly classified in two types: problem focused and emotion focused.

KEY CONCEPTS

- Adaptation
- Appraisal
- Defense mechanisms
- Emotion-focused coping
- Hardiness
- Mastery
- Problem-focused coping
- Sense of coherence
- Social support
- Transactional model

INTRODUCTION

The word "cope" is derived from the Latin word *colpus*, meaning "to alter," and, as defined in Webster's Dictionary, is usually used in the psychological paradigm to denote "dealing with and attempting to overcome problems and difficulties." In psychology, the word "coping," in addition to this behavioral application, has been used as a broad heuristic in several other domains, including as a thought process, as a personality characteristic, and in social context.

The concept of coping can be traced back to the defense mechanisms described in the psychoanalytical model by the famous Austrian neurologist Sigmund Freud. Freud described several methods that a person's mind uses to protect itself: introjection, isolation, projection reversal, reaction formation, regression, repression, sublimation, turning against the self, and undoing. While defining all these terms is beyond the scope of the present discussion, it is worth noting that, according to Freud, mechanisms of defense are the devices that the mind uses in altering one's perception to situations disturbing the internal milieu or mental balance. He applied the concept in identifying sources of anxiety through free association.

One of Freud's associates, Austrian physician Alfred Adler, disagreed with Freud and described defense mechanisms as protective against external threats or challenges. Sigmund Freud's daughter, Anna Freud, herself a renowned psychologist, included both of these viewpoints and underscored the role of defense mechanisms as protective against both internal and external threats. She also extended the repertoire of defense mechanisms to include denial, intellectualization, ego restriction, and identification with the aggressor. Therefore, it appears that the concept of defense mechanisms was very similar to the present understanding of coping at the thought process level and preceded the concept of coping. However, psychologist Norma Haan, in her book *Coping and Defending* (1977), clearly distinguishes defense mechanisms from coping. She contends that coping is purposive and involves choices, while defense mechanisms are rigid and set. Coping, according to Haan, is more focused on the present, while defense mechanisms are premised on the past and distort the present.

Psychologist Robert White, in *Stress and Coping: An Anthology* (1991), contends that coping is derived from the larger biological concept of adaptation. The origin of all species is a result of adaptation mediated through the process of natural selection. This concept of adaptation is extended in the behavioral realm to include dealing with minor problems and frustrations, such as waiting in the grocery line, as well as more complex difficulties, such as dealing with the death of a spouse. In this context, coping is essentially an adaptation under more difficult conditions. White also talks about the term "mastery," which he contends is quite unpopular with psychologists because of its connotation with "superiority" and "winning and losing." However, mastery is another way of describing the concept of coping, whereby the anxiety or danger is mastered.

Perhaps the greatest impetus to the contemporary understanding of coping has come from the work of the American psychologist Richard Lazarus, an emeritus professor at the University of California at Berkeley, and his colleagues. Lazarus introduced the transactional model of stress and coping in his 1966 book *Psychological Stress and the Coping Process*. He elaborated this concept further in 1984 in the book *Stress, Appraisal, and Coping* (with coauthor Susan Folkman).

According to the transactional model, stressful experiences are perceived as person-environment transactions. In these transactions, the person undergoes a four-stage assessment known as appraisal. When confronted with any possible stressful situation, the first stage is the primary appraisal of the event. In this stage, based on one's previous experience, knowledge about oneself, and knowledge about the event, the person internally determines whether he or she is in trouble. If the event is perceived to be threatening or has caused harm or loss in the past, then the stage of secondary appraisal occurs. If, on the other hand, the event is judged to be irrelevant or poses no threat, then stress does not develop and no further coping is required. The secondary appraisal determines how much control one has over the situation or the event. Based on this understanding, the individual ascertains what means of control are available. This is the stage known as coping. Finally, the fourth stage is the stage of reappraisal, in which the person determines whether the original event or situation has been effectively negated. The primary focus of Lazarus's conceptualization of coping is on coping as an application of thought processes and behavioral efforts to combat demands that exceed a person's resources. The hallmarks of this conceptualization are its focus on the process of coping as opposed to personality traits; the importance of specific stressful situations in inducing coping as opposed to a general physiological response; and a lack of reference to the outcome (whether positive or negative), as opposed to the mastery concept, which emphasizes only the positive aspects.

COPING STRATEGIES

According to the transactional model, there are two broad categories of coping. The first one is called problem-focused coping, and the second one is called emotion-focused coping. Problem-focused coping is based on one's capability to think about and alter the environmental event or situation. Examples of this strategy at the thought-process level include utilization of problem-solving skills, interpersonal conflict resolution, advice seeking, time management, goal setting, and gathering more information about what is causing one stress. Problem solving requires thinking through various solutions, evaluating the pros and cons of different solutions, and then implementing a solution that seems most advantageous to reduce the stress. Examples of this strategy at the behavioral or action level include activities such as joining a smoking-cessation program, complying with a prescribed medical treatment, adhering to a diabetic diet plan, or scheduling and prioritizing tasks for managing time.

In the emotion-focused strategy, the focus is inward on altering the way one thinks or feels about a situation or an event. Examples of this strategy at the thought-process level include denying the existence of the stressful situation, freely expressing emotions, avoiding the stressful situation, making social comparisons, or minimizing (looking at the bright side of things). Examples of this strategy at the behavioral or action level include seeking social support to negate the influence of the stressful situation; using exercise, relaxation, or meditation; joining support groups; practicing religious rituals; and escaping through the use of alcohol and drugs.

Several predictive empirical studies done using this model have generally shown that problem-focused strategies are quite helpful for stressful events that can be changed, while emotion-focused strategies are more helpful for stressful events that cannot be changed.

Some of these coping strategies are healthy, such as applying problem-solving skills; some are neither inherently healthy nor unhealthy, such as practicing some religious rituals; and some are unhealthy or maladaptive, such as denying the existence of a stressful situation or escaping through the use of drugs.

Choice of coping strategy is influenced by the quantity and quality of available resources for coping that may be available to a person. These resources include knowledge (for example, knowledge of the functioning at a workplace), skills (such as analytical skills), attitudes (for example, self-efficacy or confidence in one's ability to perform a specific behavior), social resources (people with whom a person can exchange information), physical resources (health and stamina), material resources (money), and societal resources (policies and laws).

MEASUREMENT OF COPING STRATEGIES

Self-reported, paper-and-pencil tools are commonly used in measuring coping strategies. A popular assessment tool for measuring coping strategies is the Ways of Coping (WOC) Checklist developed by Lazarus and Folkman, which contains sixty-eight different items. These responses have been divided into eight categories: accepting of responsibility (such as criticizing or lecturing oneself), confrontational coping (expressing anger), distancing (trivializing the situation), escape avoidance (wishing that the situation would go away), planned problem solving (making a plan of action and following it), positive reappraisal (changing or growing as a person in a good way), seeking of social support (talking to someone to find out about more about the situation), and self-controlling (keeping feelings to oneself). A further revision of this scale, the Ways of Coping Checklist-Revised, contains a list of forty-two coping behaviors.

American psychologist Charles S. Carver and his colleagues have designed the Coping Orientations to Problems Experienced (COPE) scale. The COPE scale has twelve component scales for types of coping strategies that include acceptance, active coping, denial, disengagement, humor, planning, positive reframing, religion, restraint, social support, self-distraction, and suppression of competing activities. Carver has also designed and tested a brief version of the COPE scale for use with other large protocols that has been found to be efficacious. Other scales have been developed to measure the daily utilization of coping.

PERSONALITY TRAITS AND COPING

The relationship between personality trait characteristics and coping has been suggested and studied by several researchers. American psychologist Suzanne Kobasa, in her 1977 University of Chicago doctoral dissertation, studied the role of personality and coping. Specifically, she examined the characteristics of highly stressed people among those who remained healthy and those who did not manifest any illness following stressful times. She coined the term "hardiness" to depict the personality profile of people who remained healthy. Her research found three general characteristics of hardiness: the belief of control or the ability to influence the events of one's experience, commitment to activities in life or a feeling of deep involvement, and challenge to further development or anticipation of change.

Israeli medical sociologist Aaron Antonovsky described the concept of "sense of coherence," also related to personality traits, as being central to coping. He described three components as being representative of this concept: comprehensibility, meaningfulness, and manageability. Comprehensibility means that the person believes that the world around him or her is making some sense, there is some set structure, and there is some level of predictability. Manageability implies the faith that a person has in his or her ability to meet the various demands in life in one way or another. Meaningfulness implies the belief that whatever one does has a purpose in life. Antonovsky proposed that people who possess a higher sense of coherence tend to cope better in life.

Another personality characteristic that has been studied in relation to coping is optimism. Optimism is the tendency to look at the brighter side of things and to expect positive outcomes from one's actions. Research has shown that optimism improves effective coping. Carver and his colleagues studied the effects of optimism in patients suffering from breast cancer, heart rehabilitation patients, and people in other stressful situations and found the beneficial effect of optimism on coping.

American cardiologists Meyer Friedman and Ray Rosenman, in their observations of heart disease patients, described two types of personalities: Type A and Type B. People with type A behavior pattern are characterized by time urgency impatience, competitiveness, and hostility. Those with type B show the opposites of these characteristics, exemplified by no time urgency and being cooperative and patient in their disposition. Type A personalities have been found to demonstrate negative coping styles in terms of showing more negative physiological and psychological outcomes.

SOCIAL ENVIRONMENT AND COPING

Coping does not occur in vacuum. Most stressful situations entail involvement with people. Therefore, social environment influences stress and coping. Social environment can be conceptualized at a broader level as the social structure, and it can also be conceptualized in a specific, narrow way as close social relationships. The latter are often described as social support and depict the most common way researchers have studied the social relationship in the context of coping. The broader effect of social structure on coping is rather obvious. For example, a person on the higher rung of the social ladder would have access to greater resources and thus would be able to apply a variety of coping resources, while a person at the bottom of the social ladder, living in poverty, would have fewer resources at his or her disposal.

Social support has been conceptualized from different perspectives. American sociologist James House defined social support as the "aid and assistance that one receives through social relationships and interpersonal exchanges" and classified it into four types. The first is emotional social support, or the empathy, love, trust, and caring that one receives from others. The second kind is instrumental social support, or the tangible aid and service that one receives from others. The third type is informational social support, or the advice, suggestions, and information that one receives from others. The fourth type is appraisal social support, or the information that one receives for self-assessment. Social support has a direct effect on lowering stress levels and improving effective coping, as well as providing stress "buffering effects," or what statisticians call effect modulation. For example, a person undergoing stress may talk to a friend, who may provide a tangible aid to cope (direct effect), may modify the receiver's perception of the stressful event, or may enhance the receiver's belief that he or she can cope with the stressful event (buffering effect).

BIBLIOGRAPHY

Bloona, Richard, ed. *Coping with Stress in a Changing World.* 5th ed. New York: McGraw, 2011. Print.

Dewe, Philip. "Determinants of Coping: Some Alternative Explanations and Measurement Issues." *Psychological Reports* 88.3 (2001): 832–34. Print.

Eckenrode, John, ed. *The Social Context of Coping.* New York: Plenum, 1991. Print.

Field, Tiffany M., Philip M. McCabe, and Neil Schneiderman, eds. *Stress and Coping.* Hillsdale: Erlbaum, 1985. Print.

Lazarus, Richard S., and Susan Folkman. *Stress, Appraisal, and Coping.* New York: Springer, 2006. Print.

Monat, Alan, and Richard S. Lazarus, eds. *Stress and Coping: An Anthology.* 3rd ed. New York: Columbia UP, 1991. Print.

Rice, Virginia H., ed. *Handbook of Stress, Coping, and Health: Implications for Nursing Research, Theory, and Practice.* 2nd ed. Thousand Oaks: Sage, 2012. Print.

Robbins, Paul R. *Coping with Stress: Commonsense Strategies.* Jefferson: McFarland, 2007. Print.

Romas, John A., and Manoj Sharma. *Practical Stress Management: A Comprehensive Workbook for Managing Change and Promoting Health.* 6th ed. San Francisco: Pearson, 2013. Print.

Snyder, C. R., ed. *Coping: The Psychology of What Works.* New York: Oxford UP, 1999. Print.

Manoj Sharma

See Also: Adler, Alfred; Biofeedback and relaxation; Coping: Chronic illness; Coping: Social support; Coping: Terminal illness; Decision making; Fight-or-flight response; General adaptation syndrome; Hope and mental health; Meditation and relaxation; Problem-solving stages; Social support and mental health; Spirituality and mental health; Stress: Behavioral and psychological responses; Stress: Physiological responses; Stress: Theories; Support groups.

Coping
Terminal illness

Type of psychology: Cognition; Consciousness; Social psychology; Stress

Terminal illness is perceived as a catastrophic threat to the continued existence of the self, one's relationships, and all that is valued in this life. Successful coping depends on available medical, personal, social, and spiritual resources. The hospice movement has introduced a humane and holistic approach to the support of the dying, treats the family as the unit of care, and is an alternative to the traditional, medical model.

Key Concepts

- Death and dying
- Death anxiety
- International hospice movement
- Lazarus and Folkman model of coping
- Palliative care
- Religious reframing
- Self-help groups
- Stages of dying
- Terminal illness
- Thanatology

INTRODUCTION

A terminal illness cannot be cured and, therefore, is recognized by the person dying as a catastrophic threat to the self, to the individual's relationships, and to the body. In terms of the model of coping proposed by Richard Lazarus and Susan Folkman, death is the perceived threat or stressor causing stress and is evaluated by primary appraisal; the response or coping strategy depends on the person's secondary appraisal of available physical, psychological, social, and spiritual resources. The relationship between the perception of threat and the coping response is dynamic in that it changes over time. For example, the threat of death varies with physical or psychological deterioration and calls for changing strategies during the period of dying.

Anxiety and fear are typical of any crisis; however, when faced with the overwhelming crisis that death poses, a dying person is flooded with death anxiety or mortal fear of dying. Two classic views of death anxiety are Freudian and existential. Sigmund Freud believed that it was impossible to imagine one's own death and that "death anxiety" is really fear of something else, whereas the existentialists believe that awareness of mortality is a basic condition of human existence and is the source of death anxiety. In 1996, Adrian Tomer and Grafton Eliason offered a contemporary "regrets" model, where death anxiety is a function of how much one regrets not having accomplished what one had hoped to accomplish in light of the time left. A major criticism of their work is that achievement takes precedence over social relationships and other sources of meaning. In 2000, Robert J. Kastenbaum proposed an edge theory, where the response to extreme danger is distinct from the ordinary awareness of mortality. He suggested that death anxiety is the consequence of a heightened awareness of potential disaster at the edge of what is otherwise known to be relatively safe.

Thanatology, the study of death and dying, focuses on the needs of the terminally ill and their survivors. Some thanatologists distinguish between fear of the process of dying and fear of the unknown at death. For example, the Collett-Lester Scale, established in 1994, operationalizes these ideas by offering four subscales: death of self, death of others, dying of self, and dying of others. A major problem with studies of death anxiety is that researchers typically employ self-report questionnaires that measure conscious attitudes. In general, the construct validity of questionnaires is reduced when anxiety is confounded with unconscious denial or when death is confounded with dying.

HOSPICE AND PALLIATIVE CARE

From the beginning of the twentieth century until the 1970s, Americans with terminal illnesses usually died in hospitals. Medical treatment focused on pathology; control of pain with narcotics was limited, as most physicians were worried about consequent drug addiction. Efforts to save lives were machine-intensive and often painful. The psychological, social, and spiritual needs of the person were not as important as the heroic effort to preserve life at any cost. When Dame Cicely Saunders, a British nurse and physician, opened St. Christopher's Hospice in London in 1967, she introduced holistic reforms that treated both the dying person and his or her family and included regular administrations of morphine for the amelioration of pain. It was discovered that control of pain is better when dosing at regular intervals and that the total dosage may be less than if drugs are offered only in response to severe, acute pain. Saunders was a profound inspiration to the international hospice movement, as well as to the new field of palliative medicine. (The goal of palliative care is to relieve pain and symptoms and is different from traditional, curative care.)

Initially, hospices were based in hospitals; however, toward the end of the twentieth century, home-based care became common. A full-service program provides an interdisciplinary team of a physician, social worker, registered nurse, and pastor or counselor; round-the-clock care is available. Furthermore, after death, support services are offered to grieving families. In the United States, the National Hospice Reimbursement Act of 1983 offered financial support for full-service hospice care. A local hospice is an important coping resource for someone who chooses to forgo traditional medical treatment. It offers a means for preserving some control of the environment, as well as for maintaining personal dignity. Most important, a peaceful, pain-free death is possible.

STAGES OF DYING

About the time that the international hospice movement was gaining momentum, an important book titled *On Death and Dying* (1969) was published in America by the psychiatrist Elisabeth Kübler-Ross. She presented transcripts of interviews with dying patients who were struggling with common end-of-life concerns. What gripped American readers was her call for the treatment of dying people as human beings and her compelling, intellectual analysis of dying as a sequence of five stages: denial and isolation, anger, bargaining, depression, and acceptance. However, according to Robert J. Kastenbaum, there is no real empirical verification of her stage theory. Specifically, dying need not involve all stages and may not proceed in the sequence described by Kübler-Ross. Therapists point out that depression and anxiety are ever present but change in intensity—sometimes manageable, sometimes overwhelming. Although theoreticians argue about the scientific status of Kübler-Ross's stage theory, clinicians use her ideas to tailor therapeutic regimens depending on the current needs of their patients. One way to evaluate current status is in terms of how the patient is coping with various threats and challenges posed by dying.

The "stages" of dying may be thought of as emotion-focused coping behaviors for responding to death, a stressor that cannot be changed. In contrast, problem-focused coping behaviors are appropriate when an aspect of the stressor can be changed. When a dying mother is too weak to care for a child, she copes with the problem of her weakness by arranging for child care. When a husband is worried about the financial security of his wife, he draws up a will.

Denial is usually the first response to the shocking news of terminal illness. Denial of one's impending death is a way of coping with the threat of losing one's self and key relationships. The loss of one's self is characterized by the loss of what one values as personally defining. For example, death implies the ultimate loss of strength or of the capacity for meaningful work and ushers in a radical, unwanted change of self-concept. However, denial allows an acceptance of the facts at a slower, more manageable rate and is a way to cope emotionally with death anxiety.

Anger is a common venting response once denial is no longer consuming. (Other venting strategies include crying, yelling, sarcasm, and recklessness.) The private or public expression of anger is evidence that the person has moved beyond complete denial toward the recognition of death as a real threat.

Bargaining with fate or some higher power is a futile but common coping strategy, whereby the person tries desperately to restore body integrity and self-concept. The efforts are sometimes heroic, as when a person has accepted that he or she is dying but tries to maintain some version of prior meaningful activities. The scope is limited and the places may change, but relationships and activities critical to self-concept continue for as long as possible.

Depression is marked by sorrow, grief for current and future losses, and diminished pleasure. It is different from the anxiety that arises when a person fears that what is necessary for an intact self is jeopardized; in contrast, depression occurs when the dying person is certain that he or she has lost what is necessary. Depression is the most common psychological problem in palliative-care settings. However, when ordinary depression becomes major, the treatable condition is often unrecognized and patients suffer needless emotional pain. Minor depression, an expected coping behavior, may be adaptive, whereas major depression is maladaptive and requires medical intervention.

Acceptance of a terminal condition is viewed by many clinicians as a desired end-state because the possibility of a peaceful death comes with acceptance. The person has not given up emotionally but has reached a point of choosing not to struggle for survival. Therapists of various kinds interpret acceptance in the light of a particular worldview or theoretical paradigm. For example, the transpersonal counselor sees acceptance as evidence of an intrapsychic transformation of the self to a higher level of consciousness.

OTHER COPING STRATEGIES

Dying presents many threats and challenges, including psychological and spiritual distress, pain, exhaustion, loss of independence, loss of dignity, and abandonment. In addition to depression and anxiety, guilt is a response to believing that one must have been a bad person to deserve such a fate or that one risked one's health in a way that brought on the illness. Sometimes people feel guilty because of anger and sarcasm vented on hapless family members, friends, helpers, or a higher power. Thoughts of suicide may occur when depression is severe enough or if the pain is intolerable. Not all people suffer all these assaults, but each requires a strategy for coping.

It is not uncommon for friends and relatives to pull away from the dying person because of their own anxiety and discomfort. Witnessing the physical and emotional distress of a valued person poses a threat to successful, day-to-day management of mortal fears; one way to cope is by ignoring the dying. Unfortunately, physical or emotional distancing causes dreadful isolation and a sense of abandonment just when social support is most critically needed. The terminally ill in such a predicament may cope by turning to a pastoral counselor, therapist, self-help group, or local hospice.

Each type of therapist has a different focus. A psychoanalyst might encourage frank discussions of fears and anxieties. A cognitive behavioral therapist might focus on changing maladaptive behavior by modifying negative thought patterns. A humanistic-existentialist might encourage a life review to help consolidate the patient's perceptions of the meaning of life and as a way to say "good-bye." A transpersonal counselor might focus on facilitating a meaningful transformation of self in preparation for death. A primary goal of therapy of any kind with dying patients is to promote physical and psychological comfort. Often, the therapist is an advocate acting as a liaison between the patient and the hospice, hospital, family, or friends. The therapist may provide helpful psychoeducational interventions, such as alleviating distress about an upcoming medical procedure by informing the patient about the rationale for the procedure, the steps involved, the predictable side effects, and the prognosis or forecast for the outcome. When the therapist also educates the family, the quality of their support is enhanced, thereby improving the well-being of the patient.

SELF-HELP GROUPS

Self-help groups provide significant mutual support to the terminally ill and to those in mourning. They are available in professional and nonprofessional settings. They are usually composed of peers who are in a similar plight and who, therefore, are familiar with the depression, anxiety, and guilt associated with dying. Access to a new, primary group counteracts common feelings of alienation and victimization by offering the opportunity for meaningful social support and information. Mutual disclosure reduces feelings of isolation and abandonment by building a community of peers. Sharing successful strategies for coping with secondary losses triggered by terminal illness restores hope. (For example, group members may know how to cope with the disfigurement of mastectomy or with confinement to a wheelchair.) Group participants also encourage one another to be active partners in their own medical care. Unreliable patterns of communication and reluctance to talk about dying are common outside the group; however, group members talk to one another openly, thereby reducing the dismay associated with patronizing exchanges with doctors and nurses or the silence of family and friends.

RELIGIOUS AND SPIRITUAL COPING

Psychologists emphasize the ways in which adversity may be conquered or controlled, but not every stressor is controllable. Certainly, dying brings into sharp relief the fact that humans are ultimately powerless in the face of death. At the end of life, people often turn to religion or spirituality for answers as to the purpose of their lives, the reasons for suffering, the destination of their souls, the nature of the afterlife—whether a life everlasting exists. Coping theorists may reduce the function of religion to "terror management," but others believe that the experience of the sacred cannot be understood empirically and that religion is more than an elaborate coping mechanism.

The psychologist of religion Kenneth I. Pargament studied the relationship between religion and coping. He defined religion functionally in terms of a search for significance in the light of the sacred. He described a typical Christian belief system involving the event (in this case, death), the person, and the sacred. Core beliefs are that God is benevolent, the world is just or fair, and the person is good. Dying jeopardizes the balance of this belief system; to cope, people turn to religious reframing as a way of conserving the significance or value of their core beliefs. For example, people facing a seemingly pointless death reframe its significance—death becomes an opportunity for spiritual growth or enlightenment; this preserves the beliefs that the person is good and that God is benevolent. Others reframe the nature of the person as being sinful; otherwise, why does suffering exist? The result is that belief in a just world is preserved. Some reframe their beliefs regarding the sacred and consider God as punishing. However, several researchers have found that only a small proportion of people attribute their suffering to a vengeful, punishing God. Another way to reframe the nature of God is to reconsider his omnipotence. People may conclude that a loving God is constrained by forces in nature. This reframed belief preserves the idea that God is good.

Dying is not always the occasion for spiritual crisis; people of deep Christian faith find solace in their relationship with God or with their understanding of the transcendent. The psychiatrist Harold G. Koenig reports in *The Healing Power of Faith* (1999) that faith, prayer, meditation, and congregational support mitigate fear, hopelessness, and the experience of pain. For people committed to a Christian religious or spiritual belief system, God or spirit is a source of peace and hope while dying.

BIBLIOGRAPHY

Balk, David E. *Dealing with Dying, Death, and Grief During Adolescence*. New York: Routledge, 2014. Print.

Cook, Alicia Skinner, and Kevin Ann Oltjenbruns. *Dying and Grieving: Life Span and Family Perspectives*. 2nd ed. Fort Worth: Harcourt Brace, 1998. Print.

Kastenbaum, Robert J. *Death, Society, and Human Experience*. 11th ed. Boston: Pearson, 2014. Print.

Kessler, David. *The Needs of the Dying: A Guide for Bringing Hope, Comfort, and Love to Life's Final Chapter.* New York: Harper, 2007. Print.

Kübler-Ross, Elisabeth. *On Death and Dying*. 1969. Reprint. New York: Routledge, 2009. Print.

Lair, George S. *Counseling the Terminally Ill: Sharing the Journey.* Washington, DC: Taylor & Francis, 1996. Print.

Miller, Glen E. *Living Thoughtfully, Dying Well: A Doctor Explains How to Make Death a Natural Part of Life.* Harisonburg: Herald, 2014. Print.

Pargament, Kenneth I. *The Psychology of Religion and Coping: Theory, Research, and Practice*. New York: Guilford, 2001. Print.

Tanja Bekhuis

See Also: Coping: Chronic illness; Coping: Social support; Coping: Strategies; Death and dying; Depression; Health psychology; Hospice; Kübler-Ross, Elisabeth; Law and psychology; Stress: Behavioral and psychological responses; Stress-related diseases; Support groups.

Cosmetics and beauty

Type of psychology: Evolutionary; Social; Community

As early as ancient Egypt,both men and women have used cosmetics to enhance natural beauty and, evolutionary psychologists would claim, to simulate health. The popularity and social acceptability of cosmetic use have waxed and waned through the ages, dependent on its association with different social identities. In contemporary Western society, men do not generally wear makeup and women vary in use depending upon the normative expectations of their social class and the social event. To what extent cosmetic use is a deceptive signal of attractiveness and good health or an honest signal of social interest and identity is a matter of speculation.

Key Concepts

- Cosmetics
- Social class
- Social identity
- Status symbol
- Evolutionary psychology theory
- Sociocultural theory

Cosmetic use has been common practice for millennia. As such, this practice has been the focus of much instruction on the proper attitude toward cosmetic use, and attitudes have ranged from the ancient Egyptians' acceptance of cosmetics for both men and women to the ancient Romans complex view of cosmetic use, disapproving of it for men and skeptical of it for women. During the Renaissance, cosmetics were widely used by women. One controversial product of the time was belladonna, a tincture applied to the eyes to dilate the pupils. This could be considered an attractiveness enhancement or a deceptive signal of interest in the gazed upon individual. We know now this product was dangerous to the user and, at the time, it was regarded with suspicion by the authorities because of its deceptive nature.

During the Victorian era in the United States, respectable women did not wear makeup though foundation was considered acceptable to cover up freckles and brown spots and even the skin tone. Later, from the 1890s on, more makeup use by respectable women was considered acceptable. This ambivalence has been characteristic of attitudes toward cosmetic use throughout its history. Modern research shows the power of cosmetics relating to personal odor, manipulated by perfume, facial cosmetic use, and hair coloring and styling.

Research shows that certain odors serve as a positive for attractiveness, though some research shows this to be the case only when they are so faint as to be consciously undetectable. However, cosmetic techniques, such as perfume use, are somewhat puzzling phenomena.

Ancient peoples frequently used perfume and thought it would make them more appealing and pleasing to the gods of the society and, from a pragmatic modern view, to counteract the unpleasant odors of ancient cities. In modern times a number of studies relate the odor of the human body to differing attractiveness ratings. Therefore, perfume is an interesting aspect of the debate between evolutionary and sociocultural theorists about the relative importance of these factors in attractiveness. There is an impressive amount of research on how natural odors influence the perceived attractiveness of an individual. Men judging women are attracted to the natural odor that signals a histocompatibility complex complementing their own. Ovulating women in adult entertainment make more tips than when they are not ovulating. The scent of women who are naturally ovulating compared to women on the birth control pill may also lead to higher ratings of sexual attractiveness at the peak of ovulation. Given the evidence that natural scent is an attractiveness signal and the use of perfume tends to obscure that natural scent, perfume use is perplexing from an evolutionary psychology perspective.

In more recent years, perfume has transmuted from a material used to cover bad smells to a status symbol. One of the effects of widespread use may have been to broaden the range of potential suitors. If perfume use obscured the natural scent of the individual in a socially acceptable way, the natural scent of the individual would not be a filter screening out potentially undesirable mates. In this way perfume use may be likened to the widespread use of contraceptives, a practice by whichhumans shape behaviors to produce an outcome that may be most personally optimal but not most optimal for healthy species growth.

Like odor, hair color is also a variable people have chosen to manipulate. As a rare and therefore desirable characteristic, blonde hair has often been considered a beauty sign. Moreover, hair dye is often used to cover the signs of age signified by gray hair. Depending upon the social status of the individual and the zeitgeist, men and women have chosen to wear wigs or dye their hair to fit better with their social class or the one to which they aspire. Manipulation of hair by removal is a common human behavior that has served as a gender identity issue. Males typically wear head hair shorter than females, a characteristic that may be attributed to the ancient Roman army cutting long hair when found to provide a handle for enemies. In 17th century England, political parties were known by their haircuts. The roundheads (anti-royal and pro-Parliament) cut their hair very short and dressed plainly while the cavaliers (pro-royal and anti-Parliament) wore long hair and elaborate clothes. Hair style has been used to telegraph a variety of social identities including political leanings, sexual orientation, social class, and fashion awareness status. All these factors have been shown to affect beauty judgments.

Research shows that in the United States,a woman with makeup compared to one without is, depending on the judge, seen as roughly 30% more attractive. Similar research in France shows that the educational background (psychology, business, or aesthetics undergraduate students) of the judges and the age of the judged modulates this factor. The use of cosmetics seems to strike some judges as inappropriate for the social group to which the judge or target belongs.

How cosmetics causes this effect is somewhat controversial. Evolutionary psychologists would see cosmetic use as being effective in leading the cosmetic user to be regarded as healthier because cosmetics cover various imperfections and skin irregularities and allow the user to simulate a more healthful and symmetrical appearance. In earlier times facial cosmetics were seen as useful for covering up scars from accidents, acne, or smallpox infections. Sociocultural theorists argue that cosmetic use is an effective tool of impression management. As an aspect of being a member of specific social groups there is an expectation of a certain appearance in clothing, hair color and style, and makeup use. From a psychological perspective, the user is indicating an interest in being regarded as a more gendered, sexually desirable, aesthetically pleasing individual. Research suggests that a woman wearing makeup stimulates the same brain area (orbital frontal cortex) that is stimulated when viewing an attractive woman.

Moreover, it seems that there are two aspects of makeup use. One is to simulate a healthy appearance. The use of foundation and perhaps blush could serve that purpose. By concealing age spots and/or dark or light spots and evening out the complexion the individual appears to be healthier. Blush can be used to impart a "healthy glow" to the user's skin which also signals good health. These makeup uses are typically unobtrusive and do not serve as a detectable aspect of a made-up face. "Natural look" makeup serves this purpose, and some makeup lines specifically market this look..

Another aspect of makeup use is specific to various cultural activities. Expectations are associated with various activities including graduations, gymnastics, dances, weddings, name days, and so on. If one wants to be a full-fledged participant in those activities, or subcultures, one needs the makeup to match. There is a wealth of social psychological research that shows an important factor in interpersonal attraction is attractiveness of appearance and similarity. Cosmetics can serve both purposes.

Mainstream cultural membership can be seen as serving to indicate the most common look and boost attractiveness. The other use of makeup serves to indicate a type of subcultural identity. This includes any member of a subcultural group where makeup may serve as a status booster and a social identity factor. Ethnic subcultures such as African Americans, Hispanics, Asians, Caucasians, and Native Americans have different makeup markets and various cosmetics. For example, Native American makeup particularly includes tribal identification patterns. Athletes such as football, baseball, or lacrosse players may mark black stripes under their eyes purportedly to diminish the glare that may disrupt their play. Musicians, such as Kiss or Marilyn Manson, may wear makeup as a signature style and to show their rejection of mainstream gender expectations of males. The other subcultures listed are interested in maximizing attractiveness for a member of that subculture. Common American subcultures include goths, skinheads, emos, preps, bohemians, hackers, and punks. Members of these groups have a distinctive makeup style they are expected to display though the purpose may be to demonstrate membership in a subculture rather than enhance overall attractiveness.

One of the more unusual subcultures, the gyarus, originated in Japan and is instructive in deconstructing a subculture. This group mostly consists of girls in their teens and early twenties. The name, a Japanese transliteration of the English word for girl, comes from a 1970s brand of jeans known as gurl. Gyaru fashion has changed through the years but features include or have included a distinctive mode of talking which some have described as Japanese valley girl, with an emphasis on slang articulated in a particular way, a fashion choice that includes short skirts, minimal tops, tanned (now whitened) skin tone, blonde or neon hair, highly decorated nails, and noticeable amounts of makeup which feature dark eyeliner and fake eyelashes to make the eyes look bigger. Though music is not a priority for gyaru culture, members do a form of dance called para para.

While this is an example of a Japanese subculture, it captures the idea of defining characteristics of a subculture regardless of the society in which it exists. Therefore, to summarize cosmetics and beauty, cosmetics serve two purposes. One, the evolutionary psychology theorists would support its use to simulate a healthy appearance by covering up flaws in the person's appearance. The other, more sociocultural in nature, emphasizes the use

Photo: iStock

of cosmetics and other fashion choices such as clothing, hair style and removal, talk, and political attitudes, to establish a social identity. The increase in assortative mating where individuals most often choose those similar to themselves as life partners increases the value of information about the possible partner. The information on how a person has chosen to modify his or her appearance through cosmetic use is increasingly useful in choosing a compatible partner.

BIBLIOGRAPHY

Downing, S. (2012). *Beauty and cosmetics*: 1550-1950. Shire. This is a very short book covering the history of fashionable cosmetics by time period and social attitude. Not written by a scholar known for an interest in the makeup area but written in a scholarly manner.

Etcoff, N. (1999). *Survival of the prettiest*. New York, NY: Doubleday. An evolutionary psychology viewpoint on how beauty has been valued in women, written by a practicing psychologist. The author posits that appreciation for beauty is embedded in our genes and fashion is a status symbol but unrelated to beauty.

Lakoff, R., & Scherr, R. L. (1984). *Face value: The politics of beauty*. London, UK: Routledge & Keagan Paul. This book argues that the feminist view of beauty as power is a myth. The authors support the view that beauty is political and they caution that "women must learn the pitfalls of that form of political exchange." The writing is oriented toward the humanities.

Banner, L. W. (2006). *American beauty*. Los Angeles, CA: Figueroa Press. In this work, academic historian Lois Banner explores the history of beauty in the United States from the 19th through the 20th century. In contrast Survival of the Prettiest, Dr. Banner see beauty defined by desirable and specific physical features and fashion styles, both of which rapidly change.

Don R. Osborn

SEE ALSO: Aesthetics; Aesthetic preferences; Appearance; Consumers; Physical attractiveness; Self esteem.

Couples therapy

TYPE OF PSYCHOLOGY: Psychotherapy

Relationship distress represents one of the most common reasons that individuals seek psychological help in the United States. As a result, there is an increasing demand for treatment services that are both effective in altering destructive marital interactions and efficient in the use of the therapist's and clients' time.

KEY CONCEPTS

- Cross-complaining loop
- Domestic violence
- Operant conditioning
- Prevention programs
- Validation loop

INTRODUCTION

Traditionally, marriage vows have represented pledges of mutual love and enduring commitment. Since the 1960s, however, marital relationships have changed dramatically. In fact, while more than 90 percent of the United States population will marry at least once in their lifetime, the US Census Bureau estimated in 2009 that approximately 40 percent of all first marriages and approximately 60 percent of all second marriages end in divorce. Moreover, while the average first marriage in the United States will last approximately eight years, second marriages typically endure for approximately the same time period at 8.5 years. It appears that a repetitive pattern of marriage, distress, and divorce has become commonplace. Such a cycle often results in considerable pain and psychological turmoil for the couple, their family, and their friends. These statistics dramatically indicate the need for effective ways to help couples examine and reapproach their relationships before deciding whether to terminate them.

Interpersonal relationships are a highly complex yet important area of study and investigation. The decision to marry (or at least to commit to a serious intimate relationship) is clearly one of the most significant choices many people make in their lives. Fortunately, advances in couples therapy have led to increased knowledge about interpersonal relationships and methods for improving relationship satisfaction. These advances have been documented in the scientific literature, and they extend to the treatment of cohabitating partners, premarital couples, remarried partners, married and premarital same-sex couples, separating or divorced couples, and stepfamilies. Moreover, couples-based treatment programs have shown effectiveness in the treatment of depression, anxiety disorders, domestic violence, sexual dysfunction, and a host of other problems.

COMMUNICATION AND CONFLICT RESOLUTION

Often, partners who seek couples therapy or counseling have problems in two areas: communication and conflict resolution. These are the two major difficulties that most often lead to divorce. It has been shown that communication skills differentiate satisfied and dissatisfied couples more powerfully than any other factor. Indeed, communication difficulties are the most frequently cited complaint among partners reporting relationship distress.

Psychologist John M. Gottman, in *Marital Interaction: Experimental Investigations* (1979) and the co-written *A Couple's Guide to Communication* (1976), is one of many researchers who have highlighted the importance of communication problems within distressed relationships. Many characteristic differences between distressed and satisfied couples have been noted. Partners in distressed couples often misperceive well-intended statements from their partners, whereas satisfied couples are more likely to rate well-intended messages as positive; distressed partners also engage in fewer rewarding exchanges and more frequent punishing interactions than nondistressed couples. A partner in a distressed relationship is more immediately reactive to perceived negative behavior exhibited by his or her partner. There is generally a greater emphasis on negative communication strategies between distressed partners.

Distressed couples appear to be generally unskilled at generating positive change in their relationship. Gottman also reported that distressed couples are often ineffectual in their attempts to resolve conflicts. Whereas nondistressed couples employ "validation loops" during problem-solving exercises (one partner states the conflict and the other partner expresses agreement or support), distressed couples typically enter into repetitive, cross-complaining loops. These loops can be described as an interactional sequence wherein both individuals describe areas of dissatisfaction within the relationship yet fail to attend to their partners' issues. Moreover, as one spouse initiates aversive control tactics, the other spouse will typically reciprocate with similar behavior.

THERAPY FORMATS

Couples therapy attempts to alleviate distress, resolve conflicts, improve daily functioning, and prevent problems via an intensive focus on the couple as a unit and on each partner as an individual. Couples therapists are faced with a variety of choices regarding treatment format and therapeutic approach. Individual therapy focuses treatment on only one of the partners. Although generally discouraged by most practitioners, individual treatment of one partner can provide greater opportunities for the client to focus on his or her own thoughts, feelings, problems, and behaviors. Clients may feel less hesitant in sharing some details they would not want a spouse to hear, and individual treatment may encourage the client to take greater personal responsibility for problems and successes. In general, these advantages are outweighed by the difficulties encountered when treating relationship problems without both partners being present. In particular, interpersonal interactions are complex phenomena that need to be evaluated and treated with both partners present.

Concurrent therapy involves both partners being seen in treatment separately, either by the same therapist or by two separate but collaborating therapists. Advantages of the concurrent format include greater individual attention and opportunities to develop strategies to improve relationship skills by teaching each partner those techniques separately. Concurrent treatment, however, does not allow the therapist(s) to evaluate and treat the nature of the interpersonal difficulties with both partners present in the same room.

Conjoint format, on the other hand, involves both partners simultaneously in the therapy session. Conjoint treatment is widely used and generally recommended because it focuses intensively on the quality of the relationship, promotes dialogue between the couple, and can attend to the needs and goals of each partner as well as the needs and goals of the couple. The history of conjoint marital therapy begins, ironically, with Sigmund Freud's failures in this area. He believed firmly that it was counterproductive and dangerous for a therapist ever to treat more than one member of the same family. In fact, in 1912, after attempting to provide services simultaneously to a husband and wife, Freud concluded that he was at a complete loss about how to treat relationship problems within a couple. He also added that he had little faith in individual therapy for them.

Conjoint treatment is designed to focus intensively on the relationship to effect specific therapeutic change for that particular couple. Interventions can be tailor-made for the couple seeking treatment, regardless of the nature of the problem the couple describes (such as sexual relations, child rearing, or household responsibilities). Moreover, couples are constantly engaged in direct dialogue, which can foster improved understanding and resolution of conflict. As compared with other approaches, conjoint marital therapy can focus on each of the specific needs and goals of the individual couple.

Group couples treatment programs have received increased attention and have shown very good to excellent treatment success. Advantages of group treatment for couples include opportunities for direct assessment and intervention of the relationship within a setting that promotes greater opportunity for feedback and suggestions from other couples experiencing similar difficulties. In fact, group therapy may promote positive expectations through witnessing improvements among other couples as well as fostering a sense of cohesiveness among couples within the group. In the group format, each partner has the opportunity to develop improved communication and conflict resolution approaches by learning relationship skills via interaction with the therapist(s), his or her spouse, and other group members. In addition, the cost of individual, concurrent, and conjoint therapy, in terms of time as well as dollars, has prompted several researchers and clinicians to recommend group couples therapy.

THERAPEUTIC APPROACHES

There are numerous approaches to the treatment of relationship problems practiced in the United States. Psychodynamic therapy focuses attention on the unconscious needs and issues raised during an individual's childhood. Phenomenological therapists focus on the here-and-now experiences of being in a relationship and have developed a variety of creative therapeutic techniques. Systems therapists view interpersonal problems as being maintained by the nature of the relationship structure, patterns of communication, and family roles and rules.

Behavioral marital therapy, however, is the most thoroughly investigated approach within the couples therapy field. Starting from a focus on operant conditioning (a type of learning in which behaviors are altered primarily by the consequences that follow them— reinforcement or punishment), behavioral marital therapy includes a wide range of assessment and treatment strategies. The underlying assumption that best differentiates behavioral treatments for distressed couples from other approaches is that the two partners are viewed as ineffectual in their attempts to satisfy each other. Thus, the goal of therapy is to improve relationship satisfaction by creating a supportive environment in which the skills can be acquired. Behavioral marital therapy incorporates strategies designed to improve daily interactions, communication patterns, and problem-solving abilities and to examine and modify unreasonable expectations and faulty thinking styles.

BEHAVIORAL-EXCHANGE STRATEGIES

Psychologists Philip and Marcy Bornstein, in their book *Marital Therapy: A Behavioral-Communications Approach* (1986), described a sequential five-step procedure in the treatment of relationship dysfunction. These steps include intake interviewing, behavioral exchange strategies, communication skills acquisition, training in problem solving, and maintenance and generalization of treatment gains.

Intake interviewing is designed to accomplish three primary goals: development of a working relationship with the therapist, collection of assessment information, and implementation of initial therapeutic regimens. Because spouses entering treatment have often spent months, if not years, in conflict and distress, the intake procedure attempts to provide a unique opportunity to influence and assess the couple's relationship immediately. Because distressed couples often devote a considerable amount of time thinking about and engaging in discordant interpersonal interactions, it naturally follows that they will attempt to engage in unpleasant interactions during initial sessions. Information about current difficulties and concerns is clearly valuable, but improved communication skills and positive interactions appear to be of even greater merit early in treatment. Thus, couples are discouraged from engaging in cross-complaining loops and are encouraged to develop skills and implement homework procedures designed to enhance the relationship.

SKILL TRAINING

Building a positive working relationship between partners is viewed as essential in couples treatment programs. During training in behavioral exchange strategies, couples are aided in specifying and pinpointing behaviors that tend to promote increased harmony in their relationship. Couples engage in contracting and compromise activities to disrupt the downward spiral of their distressed relationship.

Training in communication skills focuses on practicing the basics of communication (such as respect, understanding, and sensitivity) and of positive principles of communication (timeliness, marital manners, specification, and "mind reading"), improving nonverbal behaviors, and learning "molecular" verbal behaviors (such as assertiveness and constructive agreement). Improved communication styles are fostered via a direct, active approach designed to identify, reinforce, and rehearse desirable patterns of interactions. Clients are generally provided with specific instructions and "practice periods" during sessions in which partners are encouraged to begin improving their interactional styles. It is common for these sessions to be audiotaped or videotaped to give couples specific feedback regarding their communication style.

Training in problem solving is intended to teach clients to negotiate and resolve conflicts in a mutually beneficial manner. Conflict resolution training focuses on learning, practicing, and experiencing effective problem-solving approaches. Couples receive specific instruction on systematic problem-solving approaches and are given homework assignments designed to improve problem-solving skills. Because the value of couples therapy lies in the improvement, maintenance, and use of positive interaction styles over time and across situations, treatment often aims to promote constructive procedures after the termination of active treatment. Thus, people are taught that it is generally easier to change oneself than one's partner, that positive interaction styles may be forgotten or unlearned if these strategies are not regularly practiced, and that new positive interactions can continue to develop in a variety of settings even as treatment ends.

COMPARATIVE RESEARCH

To highlight further the utility and effectiveness of behavioral-communications relationship therapy, Philip Bornstein, Laurie Wilson, and Gregory L. Wilson conducted an empirical investigation in 1988 comparing conjoint and behavioral-communications group therapy and group behavioral-communications therapies to a waiting-list control group (couples who were asked to wait two months prior to beginning treatment). Fifteen distressed couples were randomly assigned to experimental conditions and offered eight sessions of couples therapy. At the conclusion of treatment (as well as six months later), the couples in active treatment revealed significant alleviation of relationship distress. The conjoint and group couples revealed similar levels of improvement in communication skills, problem-solving abilities, and general relationship satisfaction. The waiting-list couples, on the other hand, revealed no improvement while they waited for treatment, indicating that relationship distress does not tend to improve simply as the result of the passage of time.

PREVENTION AND DISORDERS

Another line of couples research has focused on the utility of premarital intervention and distress- and divorce-prevention programs. Unlike treatment programs, prevention programs intervene before the development of relationship distress. Prevention efforts are focused on the future and typically involve the training of specific skills that are viewed as useful in preventing relationship distress. Three major approaches to premarital intervention include the Minnesota Couples Communication Program, Bernard Guerney's relationship enhancement approach, and the Premarital Relationship Enhancement Program. Research is generally supportive of the effectiveness of these programs in helping partners learn useful skills that translate into improved relationships for at least three to eight years following the program. In addition, some evidence indicates that the alarming divorce rate in the United States can be decreased if partners participate in prevention programs before marriage; prevention programs that emphasize communication and conflict-resolution skills seem most advantageous.

IMPROVING TREATMENT

Researchers and clinicians have witnessed large increases in the numbers of couples seeking treatment from therapists. The Bureau of Labor Statistics reported the employment rate for marriage and family therapists to grow an estimated 29 percent from 2012 to 2022, which is a much faster-than-average growth rate than is predicted in other occupations. As the demand for couples treatment increases, more time and effort is devoted to improving treatment methods. The behavioral approach has been shown to be highly effective in reducing relationship distress and preventing divorce; however, many believe that cognitive components such as causal attributions and expectations are strongly related to satisfaction in the relationship. Moreover, it has been argued that dysfunctional cognitions may interfere with both the establishment and maintenance of positive behavior change. Evidence has prompted some researchers and practitioners to advocate a more systematic inclusion of strategies of cognitive behavior therapy within the behavioral marital therapy framework. Specifically, it is possible that the combination of cognitive and behavioral approaches will demonstrate increased utility if the two treatments are presented together in a singular, integrated treatment intervention. Such treatment would afford couples the opportunity to benefit from either one or both of the complementary approaches, depending on their own unique needs, at any time during the course of treatment. Moreover, such an integration of cognitive and behavioral tactics would parallel effective approaches already employed with depressed or anxious clients.

BIBLIOGRAPHY

Beck, Aaron T. *Love Is Never Enough*. New York: Harper & Row, 1989. Print.

Bornstein, Philip H., and Marcy T. Bornstein. *Marital Therapy: A Behavioral-Communications Approach*. New York: Pergamon, 1986. Print.

Fruzzetti, Alan E. *The High Conflict Couple: A Dialectical Behavior Therapy Guide to Finding Peace, Intimacy, and Validation*. Oakland: New Harbinger, 2006. Print.

Gottman, John M., et al. *A Couple's Guide to Communication*. Champaign: Research Press, 1979. Print.

Gottman, Julie, and John M. Gottman. *Ten Principles for Doing Effective Couples Therapy*. New York: Norton, 2014. Print.

Gurman, A. S. *Casebook of Marital Therapy*. New York: Guilford, 1985. Print.

Gurman, A. S., and D. P. Kniskern. *Handbook of Family Therapy*. Vol. 2. New York: Brunner/Mazel, 1991. Print.

Hendrix, Harville. *Getting the Love You Want: A Guide for Couples*. New York: Holt, 2008. Print.

Hewison, David, Christopher Clulow, and Harriet Drake. *Couple Therapy for Depression: A Clinician's Guide to Integrative Practice*. New York: Oxford UP, 2014. Print.

Jacobson, Neil S., and A. S. Gurman, eds. *Clinical Handbook of Couple Therapy*. 4th ed. New York: Guilford, 2008. Print.

Jacobson, Neil S., and Gayla Margolin. *Marital Therapy: Strategies Based on Social Learning and Behavior Exchange Principles*. New York: Brunner/Mazel, 1979. Print.

Pitta, Patricia. *Solving Modern Family Dilemmas: An Assimilative Therapy Model*. New York: Routledge, 2014. Print.

Gregory L. Wilson

SEE ALSO: Behavioral family therapy; Cognitive behavior therapy; Gay, lesbian, bisexual, and transgender mental health; Group therapy; Midlife crisis; Psychotherapy: Effectiveness; Separation and divorce: Adult issues; Separation and divorce: Children's issues; Strategic family therapy.

Creative reminiscence

TYPE OF PSYCHOLOGY: Clinical; Counseling; Developmental; Psychotherapy

Creative reminiscence is a technique of psychotherapy that uses the psychology of memory to help explore, reflect, and construct the narratives that make us who we are. The technique is used primarily in written and oral psychotherapeutic discourse. Creative reminiscence can also employ various forms of artistic expression (e.g., dance, painting, music) that foster and portray memories. When memories are revealed we can gain insight into patterns of thought and feeling that create our narratives.

KEY CONCEPTS:

- Dynamic reminiscence
- Memory
- Metaphor
- mMetaphor, trauma
- Narrative paradigm

INTRODUCTION

Robert Butler, former Director of the Institute on Aging, was one of the first researchers to recognize the important role of reminiscence in human development. In his work with healthy older adults in the 1950s and 60s, he became aware of their reports of an internal process of reviewing and coming to terms with the past. Butler wrote what has become a classic in reminiscence psychology, "The Life Review: An Interpretation of Reminiscence in the Aged" (1963). He describes life review as a spontaneous personal process of recalling and evaluating one's life and making sense of the life one has lived. Butler theorizes that retellings represent a deep psychic urging toward a final reckoning. He goes on to note that life review is similar to the psychotherapeutic process in that a person reviews the past in order to understand the present. Useful in the process of creating a life review are such memorabilia as scrapbooks, family photo albums, letters, possessions, genealogies, and music.

While there is no clear consensus regarding the difference between reminiscence and life review, Butler and others conceptualize reminiscence as thinking and telling about the past, either as a solitary or communal act, thought out, written, or spoken, resulting most often in an improved sense of well-being. Life review is a similar process, but is more systematic and evaluative, a deliberate undertaking for the specific purpose of gaining insight and feeling better. More recent theorists have an openness to inconsistencies in recall and an acceptance of the narrative metaphor of self not as a static entity that can be objectively perceived but as one that evolves only as it is narrated. Thus, the memories generated in creative reminiscence not only reflect one's perception of a past self, but they help create change as the self evolves. Scholarly discussion, studies, and methods have surged since Butler's early work, with numerous applications of reminiscence to psychotherapy such as structured life review therapy, guided autobiography, integration of reminiscence with cognitive behavior therapy by examining history of cognitive distortions, reminiscence as a component of self-efficacy theory to fortify coping strategies with chronic illness, life review and evolving systems approach groups in prison, and coming to terms perspective in nursing homes.

Reminiscence is also prominent in the fringes of psychotherapeutic treatment. For example, Shaping Voices is an organization in Sussex, England, that provides cultural programs for people to recall shared memories and stories, often incorporating dance, music, photography, poetry, and drama with particular reference to reminiscence. The UK Alzheimer's Society has shown that packaging from past decades can be a powerful trigger to recall past experience in people with dementia, and Nestle UK & Ireland, who said they were inundated with requests from caregivers, introduced a "reminiscence pack" of items from their archive to create a nostalgic sensory experience. The pack consists of a board game, old photos, and labels and wrappers and can be downloaded free from the Internet. In the United States the late John Kunz, psychotherapist and author, founded the International Institute for Reminiscence and Life Review in 1995 which promotes research and practice of reminiscence and life review and helps preserve life reviews through DVDs and other media.

CREATIVE REMINISCENCE AND PSYCHOTHERAPY

All psychodynamic psychotherapies involve some type of reminiscence with the goal of helping people become aware of their histories and how they have learned particular thought or behavioral patterns that may contribute to present unhappiness. Sometimes people get stuck in the past and are burdened with such emotions as regret, grief, or unfulfilled dreams. Traditional therapies tend to focus on problematic experience and pathology, defining people in terms of illness and then attempting to "cure" them. In contrast, narrative therapy, usually associated with the work of Michael White and David Epston, is an approach to healing mental distress that emphasizes strengths and competencies, showing clients how to provide their own solutions. Rather than focusing on individual pathology or interpersonal troubles, narrative therapists help people review their life stories andsee how the details of their lives are social and personal constructions that are not rigid but evolve as stories change. The technique of creative reminiscence is compatible with the narrative approach to psychotherapy, with the emphasis on competence and mastery and revisioning one's history. The past provides one with a general sense of identity and guides one in imagining the future. Character evolves, and one can be part of that evolution by coming to terms with the past and paying attention to present purposes. With this understanding, reminiscence can be therapeutically future-oriented.

Sally Chandler and Ruth Ray conducted life-writing groups for an adult community in Detroit. They make the differentiation between fixed and dynamic reminiscence. Fixed reminiscence refers to the stories that tend not to change with each retelling. They sound well-rehearsed, as if the narrator has told them countless times, and the core meaning remains unchanged. Repetition in fixed reminiscence appears to set the stories in stone. Chandler and Ray refer to such reminiscences as frozen anecdotes. Fixed reminiscence can become ruminative and painful, particularly when what is remembered is traumatic. Dynamic reminiscence, on the other hand, is change-oriented. With reflection, the fixed can become dynamic, especially in the context of a group session in which others help in a shared reconstruction of the past. The function of the group is to help one tell a story, to evoke different remembered and remembering selves. Studies in reminiscence show that listeners shape what tellers tell. What one reminisces about one's life depends in part on who is listening and the relationship one has with the listener. A group of college alumna, for instance, who meet decades after graduation, may describe a shared experience, each in different ways from the other. Emotions one attributes to the past may sometimes arise from the way she or he feels in the present. It is also true that some memories may have vanished permanently, or perhaps one may be motivated by memories that are inaccurate. Through retelling the experience, some parts may be deemphasized and some highlighted, creating a dynamic landscape, depending on the listener. Thus, dynamic reminiscence is more like a painting than a photograph. This post-modern view does not claim a solipsistic existence in which there is no objective reality. Rather, it gives credence to the social construction of thought, consistent with what psychologist Jerome Bruner calls the narrative mode of thinking, with an openness to particulars rather than constructs about variables and classes.

HOW CREATIVE REMINISCENCE WORKS

The first step in creative reminiscence is becoming aware of life stories through memories. Soon after a psychotherapist meets a client, the two will construct a psychosocial history (i.e., factual information about the client's past, including date and place of birth, and information about past and present home life, e.g., family members, family structure, school performance, hobbies, significant illnesses, mood or thought problems, religious beliefs, substance abuse issues, sexual development, trauma, eating and sleeping). Creative reminiscence is the technique of therapeutic conversations that follows this history, the interpretations in which the client reflects on the past. In this sense, creative reminiscence seems synonymous with dynamic reminiscence. The former refers specifically to a therapeutic technique and the latter to a thought process. Creative reminiscence stirs up memory and creates new attempts to interpret the past. Creative reminiscence starts with the facts of a psychosocial history, and much more develops from that. What is important to the client's well-being and construction of a better life is not what exactly happened, but what exactly it means that something happened. The client's perception will be full of rich experience of everything he or she knew before and after what happened. While this distinction may seem obvious, it has far reaching therapeutic implications. For instance, a client may report a history of behavioral issues in childhood or mood instability in early adulthood. An unexplored categorization such as "oppositional defiant" or "borderline personality" does little to advance psychotherapeutic outcome.

Once stories are evident, metaphors can be created. For example, a young biracial man (BK) in a prison study had labeled himself as an "obese oddball" in childhood. His white father was absent, and with freckles and lighter skin than his dark mother and half siblings, BK felt different from the rest of his extended family. A narrative metaphor he found helpful was life is a battlefield. BK grew to have an adolescent preoccupation with mosh pit dancing as a way of making fierce physical contact while intoxicated in a socially accepted venue. Body slamming, or moshing, is the activity of aggressively hitting one's upper body against another person in a pit during a concert. BK felt the mosh pit provided a place for him to express his rage about feeling inadequate. He could go to the pit by himself and dance in the dark. At one concert,BK met drug dealers decided to "experiment." He came to realize that he was also self-medicating his depression. He began getting high on speed and cocaine and was pleased to see that he lost weight. With a slimmer body he wanted to try the rave scene. BK chose life is a playground as the metaphor for this part of his life. He recalled that his mother had described to him the disco scene from her youth. He thought the rave might be similar: a large community of youth getting together late at night and dancing to a continuous mix of loud electronic music and colorful strobes and laser lights. BK sold candy and sparkly jewelry at the raves from his knapsack and began to see how easy it was to sell drugs too. He made large amounts of money quickly. One morning around 8 a.m. BK was caught by the police as he was driving home after a rave with an array of drugs in his car. He received a four-year-sentence. Life as a battle for BK was a metaphor he thought he outgrew, but he came to realize, in a creative reminiscence group in prison, that he was in a losing battle, and that the playground metaphor was an escape for him and equally as destructive.

Recreating old stories loosens the hold they have. BK asked, repeatedly, in a therapeutic group setting of peers: Why am I an outcast because my missing father was irresponsible and left me looking like a stranger in my own home? Who defined my life as a battle? What makes escape into illegal physical pleasures a solution to my depression? Have my old stories outgrown their usefulness? Creative reminiscence of biographical knowledge helps one discover a self different from the one based on old stories. It is not a process of fact finding but of finding the context of the facts of one's life.

How does creative reminiscence work with trauma? Responses to trauma can include obsessive thinking, nightmares, flashbacks, and often seemingly random startle responses. Numerous researchers, including James Pennebaker at the University of Texas, have shown the therapeutic benefits of writing about trauma and that such writing can result in a significant decrease in the negative effects it caused. Writers are instructed to write freely and disregard grammar, punctuation, and spelling. The focus becomes not the traumatic event itself (fixed reminiscence)but one's feelings about the event (dynamic reminiscence). Unlike ordinary memories, traumatic memories tend to be stored as a disordered array of sensory perceptions and negative affect (emotion). Emotional expression, and writing in particular, appears to reduce negative affect by converting the chaotic thoughts and feelings into an organized, logical, and linguistic understanding of the traumatic event. Improvement has been noted on physiological measures, including immune system function. In the context of talk therapy, reminiscence of a bad experience can be validated by a therapist or group. When feelings about traumatic memories are validated and understood, they are less likely to become fixed in memory and less likely to generate obsessive rumination. In trauma work, the process of guiding creative reminiscence involves recognizing the initial damage and making the memories dynamic and open to change. This requires attention to and respect of a client's denial or non-reflection as a defense mechanism. The clinician must be more than well-meaning and understand the importance of timing of insight, not rushing clients to review events that may overwhelm them and recognizing that denial may be adaptive in early bereavement.

BACK TO THE FUTURE OF REMINISCENCE

In a recent article in the *International Journal of Reminiscence and Life Review*, Jeffrey Webster asks, "Is it time to reminisce about the future?" He discusses the perception of past and future intertwining and that both are infinite while the present is delimited. Moreover, both remembering the past and imagining the future have strong cognitive constructionist elements. For instance, recall of the past is sometimes distorted by needs, desires, and cognitive limitations, and memories are constructed within those distortions. This occurs with the future too which may be distorted by schemas, scripts, and prior knowledge. Furthermore, empirical findings show a common neurological network that is triggered by both recalling autobiographical memories as well as imagining future self scenarios. Webster describes the intimate links between memory of one's personal past and anticipated future. For example, reminiscing about a past dating experience may bring up thoughts about future similar activities such as meeting someone on an online dating site. Or while preparing for a blind date, one may conjure up a barrage of prior experiences: How anxious was I about meeting someone new? What did I do to prepare? How much time did I spend on that first date? Webster notes the advantage of mentally travelling in time from past experience to anticipated future. By constantly writing, revising, editing, and recounting our life stories as we age, evolving self narratives keep our experiences fresh and new.

BIBLIOGRAPHY

Chandler, S. & Ray, R. (2002). *New Meanings For Old Tales: A Discourse-Based Study of Reminiscence and Development in Late Life*. In J. Webster & B. Haight (Eds.). Critical advances in reminiscence work: From theory to application (76-94). New York, NY: Springer. These writers are trained in ethnography and textual analysis. They document their work with groups and note that fixed and dynamic reminiscence are not static categories, that a fixed reminiscence is always potentially reflective, and that a reflective story may at some point become a fixed piece.

Haber, D. (2006). "Life Review: Implementation, Theory, Research, and Therapy". *International Journal of Aging and Human Development*, 63(2), 153-171. Haber provides a history and discussion of the literature based on his review of about 600 abstracts and 140 publications. He notes the skills necessary to implement life review therapies and suggests training programs for certification.

Haight, B., & Haight, B. (2007). *The Handbook of Structured Life Review.* Baltimore, MD: Health Professions Press. This book is a practical manual involving eight one-hour life review sessions organized around Erik Erikson's developmental life stages.

Freeman, M. (2009). *Hindsight*. New York, NY: Oxford University Press. In his earlier work Freeman developed the concept of narrative foreclosure in which a person feels there is nothing to add to his or her life story and has no interest in looking for different interpretations. Hindsight is about the psychology of looking back, and Freeman provides an in-depth view into the nature of memory, narrative, and time.

McAdams, D. (2005). *The Redemptive Self*. New York, NY: Oxford University Press. Psychologist Dan McAdams has been researching and writing about narrative theory and therapy for more than twenty years. McAdams argues that adolescents create life stories based on childhood experience and that these stories help form identity throughout adulthood. He contributes to the theory of Erikson with his concept of generativity in old age, and he describes a particular generativity in Americans that is revealed in stories of redemption. Dr. McAdams is the Director of the Foley Center for the Study of Lives at Northwestern University, and the center's website www.sesp.northwestern.edu/foley/ is a rich source of information about narrative theory and therapy.

Tahir, L. (2005). "The Evolving Systems Approach and Narrative Therapy for Incarcerated Male Youth". In D.B. Wallace (Ed.). *Education, Arts, and Morality.* (85-101). New York, NY: Kluwer Academic. This study applies Gruber's evolving systems approach and narrative techniques to the study of disenfranchised young men who were taught to re-story their lives.

White, M. & Epston, D. (1990). *Narrative Means To Therapeutic Ends.* New York, NY: W.W. Norton. This is an early text on narrative therapy in which both authors provide interesting case examples of how people can learn to make stories of their lives, externalizing problems in order to look at them objectively.

Laura Tahir

See Also: Autobiographical memory; Creativity; Imagery; Imagination; Memory.

Creativity

Type of Psychology: Cognitive; Developmental; Neuropsychology; Social

Creativity can be defined as the ability to generate a novel idea or product. Creative people tend to be divergent thinkers, and tend to be open minded and interested in a wide variety of things. Creativity cannot be measured by standardized intelligence tests, although more recent theories of intelligence have acknowledged the importance of including creative thinking as a type of intelligence. There are tests that purport to measure creativity, the most popular being the Torrance Test of Creative Thinking (TTCT). In recent years, the link between creativity and mental illness has been explored, although research has not been able to establish causality between the two. Overall, more research needs to be done on creativity and the creative process so greater understandings can be established.

Key Concepts:

- Divergent thinking
- Multiple intelligences
- Sternberg's triarchic theory
- Positive psychology
- Torrance Test of Creative Thinking

INTRODUCTION

Creativity can be defined as the ability to generate novel ideas, as well as the ability to think in original ways. Creative individuals tend to see the "big picture," and can find connections amongst things that others cannot see. It can also be defined as the ability to come up with a unique approach to create a new product, whether it is a piece of music, a poem, a work of art, or a scientific theory. Many researchers feel that creative people are divergent thinkers, or individuals who can generate many ideas quickly in response to a single prompt. For example, divergent thinkers may be quickly able to think of new and unique uses for everyday items such as a spoon, a brick, or a pencil. Convergent thinkers, on the other hand, use only knowledge and logic to answer prompts or questions. Another aspect of creativity may be what is known as cognitive complexity. Cognitive complexity is having a preference for elaborate, intricate, complex stimuli and thinking patterns. Creative people on the whole tend to have a wider range of interests as compared to non-creative individuals. They tend to be more interested in the philosophical, abstract, and outside the box ideas.

Creativity tends to be a neglected research interest in the field of psychology, most likely because it is a difficult construct to operationally define or test. However, the latter half of the 1900's saw a resurgence of interest in creativity as a psychological construct, and now, a handful of psychological journals and handbooks directly deal with research on the science of creativity.

THE HISTORY OF CREATIVITY

Most all of the world's religious systems depend on a creation story, where one or more gods have the creative power to design the world. In Greek mythology, Zeus, fathered nine daughters, or "muses", each of whom represented a different domain of creative accomplishment (i.e., music, drama, comedy, and dance). Ancient Romans believed that each individual is born with a spirit who watched over an individual's creative talents. Many still see creativity as a "gift from the gods", or God Himself. This aspect of creativity may stunt research, for if creativity is considered a spiritual gift, it becomes difficult to scientifically explain it.

In the 1960's however, the emergence of the field of Humanistic Psychology brought new attention to creativity as a psychological construct. Humanistic Psychology focuses on the tenets of unconditional positive regard and unlimited human potentiality. Abraham Maslow, in his description of self-actualization, included creativity as part of the profile of a self-actualized person. To help formulate his theory, he studied the lives of several individuals he perceived as self-actualized. Most of those individuals were theorists, writers, and composers like Franz Joseph Haydn, Robert Browning, Albert Einstein, and Walt Whitman.

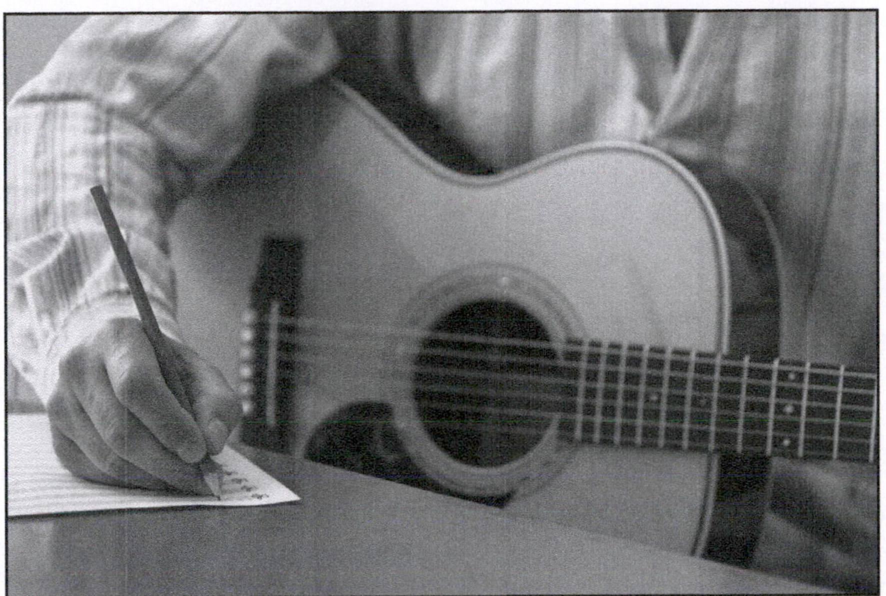

Photo: iStock

The introduction of the field of Positive Psychology in early 2000 by Martin Seligman created a space for continuation of scientific research on creativity. Positive Psychology can be considered a branch of Humanistic Psychology, and it's concentration is on how to create healthy, grateful, resilient, intrinsically motivated, and creative human beings. Positive psychology tends to decrease psychology's focus on psychopathology, and increases interest in the vitality of the individual.

CREATIVITY AND INTELLIGENCE

Most traditional intelligence tests measure convergent thinking rather than divergent thinking. Questions are asked, and there is usually one acceptable answer. Traits of creativity and traditional intelligence are not often paired together. However, in the 1980's, two intelligence theories were created that did view creativity as an essential part of intelligence. These two theories were Sternberg's *Triarchic Theory* (1988) and Gardner's *Theory of Multiple Intelligences* (1983). Sternberg's Triarchic Theory asserted that intelligence can be defined as how well an individual deals with environmental changes throughout their lifespan. Sternberg outlined that humans generally have three basic types of intelligence: analytic intelligence, creative intelligence, and practical intelligence. Analytic intelligence is generally measured by traditional IQ tests, and is focused on the solving of academic problems. Creative intelligence is the ability to use experience and existing knowledge to create new, "out of the box" solutions. Finally, practical intelligence focuses on everyday life situations, such as how to change a tire, or sew a button on a shirt.

Howard Gardner's Theory of Multiple Intelligences focuses on several types of intelligence, many of them creative types. Gardner believes that individuals learn and are smart in different ways, and that having multiple intelligences may allow for a broadened view of intelligence as a whole, both for the benefit of the educational system as well as overall society. Gardner's multiple intelligences include musical/rhythmic intelligence, visual spatial intelligence, verbal linguistic intelligence, logical mathematical intelligence, bodily kinesthetic intelligence, interpersonal intelligence, intrapersonal intelligence, and naturalistic intelligence. In recent years, he has also mentioned adding existential as well as moral intelligence to the list.

THE TORRANCE TEST OF CREATIVE THINKING (TTCT)

One of the most famous tests of creativity is the Torrance Test of Creative Thinking. Although the Torrance Test has been used mostly for testing gifted students, it can also be used to assist in individualizing instruction for students in schools, or as a tool for assessing and enhancing creativity. There are two basic Torrance Tests: the Figural Torrance Test of Creative Thinking, and the Verbal Torrance Test of Creative Thinking.

The Figural Torrance Test of Creative Thinking uses three picture-based exercises to measure fluency, elaboration, originality, resistance to premature closure, and abstractness of titles in individuals age 5 and up. The Figural TTCT also provides standardized scores for creative strengths such as emotional expressiveness, storytelling articulateness, unusual visualization, humor, imagery, and fantasy.

The Verbal TTCT uses six word-based exercises to asses fluency, flexibility, and originality. The Verbal TTCT includes five activities, entitled Ask and Guess, Product Improvement, Unusual Uses, Unusual Questions, and Just Suppose. The creator of the Torrance Tests, Ellis Paul Torrance, wanted the general testing environment for the TTCT to be fun and game like. Therefore, elimination of test anxiety and external stress during this test is important.

CREATIVITY AND MENTAL ILLNESS

There has been much talk in recent years about the perceived link between creative thought and mental illness, although science has not been able to verify or disprove the relationship. Although many famous creative people have been institutionalized and/or have suffered mental illness in their lifetimes (i.e.: Sylvia Plath, Irving Berlin, Georgia O'Keefe, Vincent Van Gogh), there have also been many artists, writers, poets, and scientists that have not suffered from mental illness. Ultimately, it is difficult to prove causality, although a review of research on the topic is presented below.

In 1987, Dr. Nancy Andreason tested 30 writers from the Iowa Writing Workshop, comparing them with 30 educationally matched control subjects. The experimental group of creative writers had significantly higher levels of bipolar disorder than did the control group. In 1995, A.M. Ludwig wrote a book examining the lives of over one thousand eminent individuals, finding a high level of mental illness in individuals involved in the creative professions. It is important to note that these studies have been criticized for their highly specialized samples, inconsistent methodologies, and overall subjectivity.

Neurologically, brain states between individuals in a creative versus a mentally ill state may actually be very similar. Creative thinking, manic depression, and schizophrenia both involve an unusually high level of frontal lobe activity, and atypical dopamine levels are seen in both schizophrenia and those who have high creative drive. However, this does not mean that creativity and mental illness are one in the same.

CONCLUSION

It becomes clear that creativity is tied to divergent thinking and openness of mind. It is also an important element of problem solving, wellbeing, and academic as well as everyday life success. However, more psychological and educational research is desperately needed in order to close the gap between assumptions and real scientific knowledge when it comes to creativity.

BIBLIOGRAPHY

Kim, K.H. (2006). "Can We Trust Creativity Tests? A Review of the Torrance Tests of Creative Thinking (TTCT)". *Creativity Research Journal*, 18, 3 – 14. An overview of the most used test to measure levels of creativity in both children and adults. Reviews pros and cons, as well as reliability and validity of the Figural TTCT as well as the Verbal TTCT.

Ludwig, A.M. (1995). *The Price of Greatness: Resolving the Creativity and Madness Controversy.* New York: Guilford Press. Focuses on the stories of 1000+ eminent scholars, writers, artists, and musicians. Ludwig's book is a classic on the perceived link between mental illness and creative thought.

Plucker, J.A., Beghetto, R. A. & Dow, G.T. (2004). "Why Isn't Creativity More Important To Educational Psychologists? Potentials, Pitfalls, and Future Directions In Creativity Research". *Educational Psychologist*, 39, 83-96. The authors of this article ponder why the field of creativity is still suffering from a dearth of research. They hypothesize that myths and stereotypes surrounding creativity halt thorough scientific inquiry. Plucker, Beghetto, and Dow also explore ideas regarding how to enhance research on creativity.

Pope, R. (2005). *Creativity: Theory, History, and Practice.* New York: Routledge. A thorough review of the history and theory of creativity. Discusses the myths surrounding creativity, and explores theories of creative process. Pope also examines the past, present and future of creativity as a whole.

Sussman, A. (2007). "Mental Illness and Creativity: A Neurological View Of The 'Tortured Artist' ". *Sanford Journal of Neuroscience*, 1. Retrieved from http://web.stanford.edu/group/co-sign/Sussman.pdf. Explores the similarities and differences of the brain states of those who are creative and those who are mentally ill.

Gina Riley

See Also: Idea production; Imagination; Innovation; Novel ideas; Thinking; Unique.

Creativity and intelligence

Type of psychology: cognitive, developmental, educational, neuropsychology,

The relationship between intelligence and creativity is a complex, unilateral dependency that exists between these two prized human attributes. It involves issues within adolescent and adult development, cognitive development and learning, and identifying, measuring and defining these. While most intelligent people are not unusually creative, those that are rarely have measured IQs under 120, the start of the "superior range." Though intelligence is not creativity, and having a great deal of intelligence does not imply great creative ability, creativity as evidenced in creative productivity does require a minimum of intellectual ability.

Key concepts

- Convergent thinking
- Creativity
- Divergent thinking
- Intelligence
- Intelligence quotient (IQ)
- Multiple intelligences

INTRODUCTION TO INTELLIGENCE

Humans have investigated the nature of intelligence for as long as there has been philosophy. Plato and Aristotle were fascinated with the concept of intelligence and its study continues today: how to define it, measure it, and of course for Americans, how to improve it. In the later part of the Twentieth Century, working independently, English anthropologist, Francis Galton and French neurologist, Jean-Martin Charcot laid the foundations for psychology's formal efforts to measure intelligence. Galton invented psychometrics, the principles and procedures used in testing and measurement, and differential psychology (the study of individual differences). Charcot bridged the relationship between physiological and psychological components of the human person. His student, Alfred Binet, became the most famous name in the history of the study of intelligence by inventing, at the French government's commission, a way to distinguish school children who should be placed in what today would be called special education. This work resulted in the Binet-Simon Test in 1905. This test is the basis for all intelligence testing that utilizes an intelligence quotient or IQ. University of Stanford psychologist, Lewis Terman expanded and refined Binet's work and produced the first "IQ test, the Stanford-Binet. Its current version tests intelligence in five areas: fluid reasoning, knowledge, quantitative reasoning, visual-spatial processing, and working memory.

With the current efforts in the research on intelligence, more complex definitions have been developed. Tufts University psychologist and psychometrician, Robert Sternberg has promoted a triarchic theory of intelligence: (1) analytical, the competence on academic tasks, the ability to deal with familiar problems, (2) creative, the ability to generate novel ideas to common situations, and (3) practical, the capability of dealing with everyday situations using one's own knowledge and experiences, having "street smarts." Sternberg further conceptualized that successful intelligence would encompass the person's ability to take advantage of his or her known strengths and at the same time to compensate for his or her personal weaknesses. Another huge advance in understanding intelligence was Harvard psychologist, Howard Gardner's work on multiple intelligences. These expand the intellectual domains IQ tests assess (verbal and mathematical reasoning, and to a lesser extent, visual-spatial reasoning and memory) to include linguistic, musical, logical-mathematical, spatial, bodily-kinesthetic, and personal intelligences.

These and other advances in the study of intelligence promote the concept that intelligence is a meaningful human attribute if it is "successful." Intelligent people are not those with high IQs, but those who are able to adapt to their environment and either modifying or accommodating to it as necessary. Successful intelligence implies a survival component and that meaning in people's lives is enhanced as a result of their thinking. Excellent grades, high IQ scores, and high income suggest the presence of high intelligence, but they do not guarantee its continued successful application. People who obtain fulfillment and enhance meaning in their world are the guarantors that high intelligence is present.

INTRODUCTION TO CREATIVITY

While creativity as a concept, ability, and process is viewed quite differently across cultures, its study within the branch of developmental psychology is largely Western in orientation and begins with the ancient Greeks who believed their novel discoveries, inventions, and ideas had relation to the preternatural and mysterious. They understood that their creative genius was manifest in their art, literature, drama, music, ship design, political processes, and military strategies. Later, Christians would relate invention of what was novel and practical as analogous to what they believed was the divine process of creation: as God created the universe and all within it, human beings were to create the new and novel from the material which God provided. Modern thought has shifted to emphasize creativity as a function of particular, perhaps peculiar, types of human thought, a type of thinking that most seem capable of in modest measure, but few are capable of in impressive measure.

Measuring creativity has brought about various definitions. Researchers have looked at the concept in various ways in an attempt to understand its complexity. Creativity researcher, C. W. Taylor in his seminal review of creativity investigations, categorized four main approaches to investigating creativity: (1) "creative-person" studies the characteristics and traits of creative people; what makes them different from most; (2) "creative-process" seeks to understand the operation under which creativity occurs including cognitive, emotional, and behavioral aspects; (3) "creative-environment" explores social climate and environmental variables that promote or inhibit the development of creative thoughts and products; and (4) creative-product" explores the end-products of the creative process and in what ways are they unusual, inventive, and useful. The presence of creative products always presumes the presence of creative people who originated them. This last approach emphasizes the ability to "outside the box" in ways that result in effective, successful change.

Another important dimension in considering individual intelligence and creative thought is social surroundings and personal history. The difference between intelligent people and intelligent, creative people is the latter's ability to formulate a new idea or response to the situation at hand. These creative individuals use their previous experiences, background, education, and cultural inheritance to make a difference that is of high quality and new. Because people are social and interactive, the wealth of this collective experience refines creative thinking and output. Innovation and ingenuity result when creative people are open to receiving, and then mentally manipulate and re-think, their interactive experiences. Creative people may isolate themselves to produce their work, but their isolation is preceded by necessary interactions and relationships. The end products, a new recipe, novel, dance movement, gadget, or synthesis of ideas then is brought back into the social arena for a greater good and use.

INTELLIGENCE AND CREATIVITY

Researchers have attempted to answer the question if it is necessary for creative people to be intelligent and for intelligent people to be creative. In general, studies show that intelligence, as measured as IQ, tends to be relatively stable over time, and creativity, while also generally stable, is more variable than verbal and mathematical reasoning, the aspects of intelligence IQ tests emphasize. Cognitive psychologist, J. P. Guilford and associates developed the concept of divergent thinking (DT) which is a matrix defined by 24 intellectual abilities, or "factors," that are involved in thinking creatively. These factors include fluency of thinking (ability to come up with a number of different solutions to a problem), flexibility of thinking (ability to simultaneously process the different possible solutions to a problem), originality (ability to come up with new ideas), sensitivity to problems and, figural and semantic elaboration (ability to process the details of an idea, whether through words or pictures). Their work remains the best attempt to quantitatively relate intelligence to creative thinking. Their research shows a direct positive correlation between DT scores and level of creativity at least until they studied highly creative individuals. Among this group, the correlations between DT skills and creative productivity markedly fell off. What seems apparent is that highly creative persons utilize abilities other than those 24 DT factors. The inherent problem in studying highly creative people is similar to establishing IQs for high IQ people. It is difficult to develop a test that can validly and reliably assess abilities in these highly gifted people whether highly intelligent, highly creative, or both.

Another paradoxical finding in research linking intelligence with creativity is that average to high average IQ persons often score higher on tests of creative ability than superior (120) IQ persons. Referred to as the "threshold theory of intelligence and creativity," it seems not that the more intelligent people are, the less creative aptitude they have, but that more intelligent people (again, as IQ-defined) rely more on their superior convergent thinking (CT), problem solving skills than others.

Intelligence and creativity remain extensively studied in terms of their individual natures and their relationship to each other. As researchers work to unite intelligence and creativity, it remains fundamentally clear that these are not unitary concepts that can be linearly related as both are fluidic, multidimensional capacities that converge in several spheres. Intelligence is necessary for creativity potential to exist and be realized in creative products, but it is not sufficient by itself to quicken the creative process. Some creative domains like painting, cooking, and graphic design, may require less convergent thinking ability than other creative domains like architecture, engineering, physics, and mathematics. As more researchers attempt to understand their complex relationship of intelligence and creativity, it has become apparent that more variables are involved and need consideration than are understood. It also remains to be seen if scientific research into these desired attributes will be intelligent and creative enough to fully reveal their relationship.

BIBLIOGRAPHY

Carter, Philip and Ken Russell, *More Psychometric Testing: 1000 New Ways to Assess Your Personality, Creativity, Intelligence, and Lateral Thinking*. This is a follow-up to their 2001 book, Psychometric Testing: 1000 Ways. It contained a series of self-administered inventories that assessed components of personality like confidence, broadmindedness, aggression, sensuality, and optimism. This work continues with constructs like coping under pressure, patience, need to control, and need to obsess with exercises to enhance lateral and creative thinking.

Csikszentmihalyi, Mihaly, *Creativity: Flow and the Psychology of Discovery and Invention*. New York: NY, HarperCollins, 1996. Despite the surname challenge for English readers, Csikszentmihalyi is one of the few outstanding thinkers and researchers on creativity, its relation to intelligence, and how they may be encouraged. This is a systematic analysis of the impact of creativity on various fields. He includes a chapter on ways to enhance personal creativity.

Diamond, Marian and Janet Hopson, *Magic Trees of the Mind: How to Nurture Your Child's Intelligence, Creativity, and Healthy Emotions from Birth through Adolescence*. New York: NY, Penguin Putnam, 1998. The authors take the results of brain studies and suggest approaches specific to the developmental stage of the child. They cogently demonstrate how intellectual growth is irrevocably linked to emotional health.

Gardner, Howard, *Intelligence Reframed: Multiple Intelligences for the 21st Century*. New York: NY, 1999. The 'father of multiple intelligences' persuasively reasons how the theory can be applied to classroom and workplace learning. He addresses critics of his earlier work who maintained that he failed to offer enough practical application as to how all the intelligence domains can be enhanced.

Michalko, Michael, *Cracking Creativity: The Secrets of Creative Genius*. Berkley, CA: Ten Speed Press, 2001. Through his review of highly creative, successful persons, he describes ways readers can apply techniques for enhancing their own creative thinking.

Paul Moglia, PhD and Faith Abalos-Merino

See Also: Correlation; Creativity; Innovation; Intelligence quotient.

Creativity
Assessment

Type of psychology: Intelligence and intelligence testing

Creativity is the ability to make something new that is widely valued. Various methods have been developed to assess this quality.

Key Concepts

- Big "C" versus little "c" creativity
- Convergent thinking
- Creativity
- Divergent thinking
- Flexibility
- Fluency
- Intelligence
- Originality
- Problem finding
- Problem solving

INTRODUCTION

The study of creativity has undergone many changes and developments, particularly since the early 1960s, and it has received recognition as a field in its own right. Creativity has traditionally been assessed via the finished products of the artist, musician, writer, poet, or inventor. The general consensus of the public has usually served as the final criterion of creativity. Any distinction between creativity and talent could be difficult to ascertain. The assessment of talent has usually been the province of people within a particular field. Musicians, artists, writers, and others in specific fields have assessed the skills of their students or protégés, either formally or informally; in some fields, specific tests do exist.

One generally accepted construct regarding creativity is divergent thinking. People who are considered creative seem to think in a more divergent mode. They see possibilities and options that are not perceived by most other people. If most people were to ask themselves the possible uses for a brick, they would probably list a few: to build a house, for example, or perhaps to use as a doorstop. Divergent thinkers may indicate that it could be used as a weapon, a hammer, a paperweight, a bookend, or a supportive device.

Commonly assessed components of divergent thinking include fluency, flexibility, elaboration, and originality. Fluency refers to the number of ideas that a person can generate to solve a given problem or produce a certain result. Flexibility is the ability to generate a number of different kinds of ideas. The amount of detail that one can supply for one's ideas is known as the amount of elaboration. Originality refers to the novelty or statistical infrequency of each idea. This concept has often been used as a synonym for creativity. If one person out of a hundred has an idea that no one else has, for example, that idea may be termed original. It might be strange, even bizarre, but it might also be positive.

Some theorists view creative thinking as a process or a series of stages. Finding a problem might be one stage, developing possible solutions would be another, and choosing a "best" solution would be another. Things may go wrong in any stage along the way. When difficulties are encountered, it is often effective to defer conscious thought for a period of time; often, this enables one to achieve a new insight into a problem. If one becomes fatigued, it is often best to rest and return to the problem when one is refreshed.

Some researchers have described different types of creativity. For example, Mihaly Csikszentmihalyi, in his 1997 book *Creativity: Flow and the Psychology of Discovery and Invention*, distinguished between everyday (little "c") creativity and extraordinary (big "C") creativity that transforms a domain. Little "c" creativity might be used to find a way to get to work faster, while big "C" creativity further develops a domain of knowledge or skill, often leading to eminence of the individual in that field. Other researchers have studied the relation between creativity and talent. Howard Gardner in 1993's *Creating Minds*, emphasized the role that specific aptitudes play in making something that is both new and valued. In his view, creativity can develop independently in one of eight "intelligences": linguistic, logical-mathematical, musical, spatial, bodily- kinesthetic, interpersonal, intrapersonal, and naturalistic. A creative writer (with linguistic intelligence) is not necessarily a creative musician, even if the writer also plays music.

Another aspect of creativity is validation. After one has created or invented something, one attempts to ascertain whether the idea, music, poem, or other creative endeavor truly has merit. The "test of time" is perhaps the ultimate element of validation. Sometimes an invention or creation is valued only for a time, then discarded; sometimes it is changed or improved on. On the other hand, works such as the symphonies of Wolfgang Amadeus Mozart, the plays of William Shakespeare, and the artwork of Leonardo da Vinci have stood the test of time and are still held in high esteem.

Intelligence has been thought to be an important aspect of creativity; a certain minimal amount of intelligence is certainly necessary. Mentally retarded people are, in general, not very creative. On the other hand, and more surprising, there are few people with very high intelligence quotient (IQ) scores who are creative. They appear to be preoccupied with finding the "right" answer; perhaps they naturally think more convergently. As previously noted, divergent thinking is a crucial aspect of creativity. If one is extremely intelligent, one may therefore need to make radical changes to think in divergent ways. Alternatively, intelligence as traditionally conceived and measured may not relate closely to domains (such as music or movement) where creativity emerges.

Personality has also been examined in terms of creativity. Research indicates that creative people seem to have a greater range of knowledge and interests than noncreative people. They seem to have an openness to new experience and have a willingness to try new types of things. They appear to value independence as well as complexity. A good sense of humor is also noted. The creative personality is persistent and is willing to take risks. Many creative people are seen to have high energy and activity levels. Organization and abstraction skills are well developed. Creative people are able to tolerate ambiguity better than less-creative people; they seem to function well in ill-defined settings or situations and employ fairly unusual problem-solving strategies.

SAMPLE ASSESSMENT PRACTICES

A number of tests have been developed that attempt to measure creativity in school-age children. E. Paul Torrance became a leading figure in the field of creativity in the 1950s. His tests of divergent thinking have been used and researched extensively. There are two parts to the Torrance Tests of Creative Thinking (published by the Scholastic Testing Service), a verbal section and a "figural" section. There are several subtests in each area. In the verbal test, seven activities must be performed, including asking, guessing causes, guessing consequences, product improvement, unusual uses, unusual questions, and "just suppose." In the figural realm, there are three activities: picture construction, picture completion, and circles. There are complete manuals for administrative, scoring, and illustrative purposes. A number of organizations offer computerized scoring services. Teachers or others who have not had special training are able to score the tests fairly reliably if they have invested the time to study the scoring guides carefully.

A test developed by Frank Williams, another researcher in the field of creativity, is the Exercises in Divergent Thinking and Divergent Feeling. The creative thinking part of the test offers a total score as well as subscores in fluency, flexibility, originality, and elaboration. On the creative feeling test, scores are offered on curiosity, imagination, complexity, and risk taking; again, a total score is offered. These tests represent the variables thought by Williams to be most important in creativity.

The parts of this test, in conjunction with the Williams scale, can help to identify children with creative potential. The Williams scale asks parents and teachers to rate children on a three-point scale in terms of their fluency, flexibility, originality, elaboration, curiosity, complexity, imagination, and risk taking. There are also four open-ended questions that allow parents and teachers to express specific concerns and offer salient information about the child. There is considerable specificity to the Williams scale, but there is also a ceiling effect in that some students can earn only a certain number of points; this may therefore give a limited vision of the test taker's skills and creative potential.

The Group Inventory for Finding Talent (GIFT), which allows children to rate their preferences for various activities, is also available. The GIFT has subscales for imagination, independence, and many interests. This test is computer-scored by the company rather than by the examiner or teacher. This test was developed by Gary Davis and Sylvia Rimm, two well-known experts in the field of gifted education. A major cross-cultural effort to study creative thinking was undertaken by Hans Jellen and Klaus Urban.Their test, the Test for Creative Thinking and Drawing Production (TCT-DP), was administered to subjects in eleven countries.

All these tests can help to discover creative potential in children, but few creativity researchers would advise that tests be used alone or argue that they are necessarily better predictors of creative potential than are alternative assessment techniques, such as expert judges' ratings of creative performances by children. One such alternative developed by Teresa Amabile is the consensual assessment technique, in which expert judges independently evaluate children's creative products. The assumption is that experts in a domain know what is creative when they see it. Other assessment alternatives offer more guidance by training judges to score products or portfolios according to subjective dimensions (such as aesthetic appeal or originality) or a scoring guide.

By adulthood, creativity has generally identified itself through a history of creative performances or products, so the problem of identifying creative talent is often not as acute as it was during the school years. Nevertheless, economic conditions may force a person to work at a job that provides no avenues or extra time to maximize creativity. Without help, some people may never find an outlet for their talents and skills. For this reason, adult personality assessments and interest inventories often include subscales that attempt to measure creativity, originality, or some similar construct. Scores on these measures can be used to develop self-understanding, find a suitable job placement, or increase work satisfaction.

DEVELOPING CREATIVITY

Everyone has some creative potential, but it may be difficult to discern exactly how much potential one has or in what field or domain it may lie. Creativity remains an elusive concept but one of great interest to many researchers; journals, conferences, and organizations are devoted to the subject.

Some psychologists and educators have been concerned with ways of enhancing creativity; one method is the idea of brainstorming. In this strategy, people offer ideas and suggestions regarding the clarification of or solution to a problem. All options are accepted, and no negativism is allowed; this enhances the climate of the group. Only later do the group members focus on which ideas are reasonable or possible. Some researchers have attempted to use behavioral reinforcement principles and procedures to promulgate creative responses; others have examined the effectiveness of creativity training.

Methods have focused on either short-term or long-term programs.

Creativity in the classroom is another area that has been of concern. Some educators have worried in particular that educational reform movements may ultimately stifle creativity in the classroom. Psychologists John Glover and Roger Bruning have offered suggestions for enhancing classroom creativity. Teachers, they suggest, should "try to find something positive in all ideas." Strange or unusual questions from students should not be discounted. Creativity should be rewarded systematically; it should also be expected. Creativity should be rewarded with extra credit when grades are given, and creative behaviors should be modeled by teachers. Teacher educator Alane Starko suggests in 2009's *Creativity in the Classroom: Schools of Curious Delight* that students be given the opportunity to find problems, rather than simply devising creative solutions. Content and lessons should expect students to question as well as answer, investigate as well as comprehend. Because creative people must ultimately identify new problems as well as provide new answers to problems, creativity must be investigated, assessed, and nurtured.

BIBLIOGRAPHY

Csikszentmihalyi, Mihaly. *Creativity: Flow and the Psychology of Discovery and Invention.* New York: Harper, 1997. Print.

Diliello, Trudy C., Jeffery D. Houghton, and David Dawley. "Narrowing the Creativity Gap: The Moderating Effects of Perceived Support for Creativity." *Jour. of Psychology* 145.3 (2011): 151–72. Print.

Fishkin, Anne S., Bonnie Cramond, and Paula Olszewski-Kubilius, eds. *Investigating Creativity in Youth: Research and Methods.* Cresskill: Hampton, 1999. Print.

Gardner, Howard. *Creating Minds.* New York: Basic, 1993. Print.

Kuan Chen Tsai, and S. Michelle Cox. "Business Students' Beliefs about Creativity." *Jour. of Business Studies Quarterly* 4.2 (2012): 1–10. Print.

Precourt, Geoffrey. "What We Know About Creativity." *Jour. of Advertising Research* 53.3 (2013): 238–39. Print.

Runco, Mark A., and Robert S. Albert, eds. *Theories of Creativity.* 2d ed. Cresskill: Hampton, 2001. Print.

Sawyer, R. Keith. *Explaining Creativity: The Science of Human Innovation..* New York: Oxford UP, 2006. Print.

Starko, Alane Jordan. *Creativity in the Classroom: Schools of Curious Delight.* New York: Routledge, 2009. Print.

Sternberg, Robert J. ed. *Handbook of Creativity.* New York: Cambridge UP, 2007. Print.

Michael J. Shaughnessy; updated by John F. Wakefield

SEE ALSO: Brief therapy; Community psychology; Coping: Strategies; Disaster psychology; Fear; Mood disorders; Stress: Behavioral and psychological responses; Stress: Physiological responses; Suicide.

Crisis intervention

DATE: 1940's forward
TYPE OF PSYCHOLOGY: Psychotherapy

Crisis intervention is a short-term approach to assisting individuals during times when their coping mechanisms are overtaxed. It may be employed at the scene of the crisis, or it may be a form of short-term therapy.

KEY CONCEPTS

- Coping skills
- Crisis situation
- Emergency response
- Hotline
- Stress response

INTRODUCTION

Crisis intervention theory was first developed in the 1940s by Erich Lindemann and later expanded on by Gerald Caplan. Lindemann developed this time-limited treatment after the Cocoanut Grove nightclub fire in Boston. After the fire, he witnessed both acute and delayed reactions of survivors and relatives of survivors. Lindemann discovered that people need to grieve after a tragedy. If the grieving process is impeded, negative outcomes are far more likely to develop. Caplan expanded on Lindemann's work in the 1960s and studied crisis points in people's lives.

A crisis can take many forms: a natural disaster, a criminal victimization, a medical emergency, bad news, or personal and family difficulties. A crisis can also occur when an individual receives unexpected information. There are some events, like a sudden death or illness, that will cause a crisis for most individuals. Some events, such as the terrorist attacks on September 11, 2001, are national and international crises. Generally speaking, any emotional, mental, physical, or behavioral stress can be perceived as a crisis; however, a stressful event does not necessarily lead to a crisis response. A crisis situation develops if the event exceeds the individual's perceived (not actual) coping skills.

RESPONSE TO EMERGENCIES

A crisis intervention response to emergencies and crisis intervention therapy differ, but in both, a variety of techniques are used in the short term to assist an individual dealing with a traumatic situation. A crisis intervention response may be necessary in a variety of situations from a suicide attempt to a hostage situation, to the aftermath of terrorist attacks. Generally this response involves law-enforcement personnel or other first responders (such as firefighters or paramedics) in some way.

Immediately on arrival at the scene, responders must identify the type of crisis and devise an intervention strategy based on the specific situation. The situation is first contained and controlled, and then it is diffused. Common crises are hostage situations, which often involve negotiating with the hostage taker or takers; barricade situations; and individuals threatening suicide.

Once any crisis has been resolved, whether successfully or not, debriefing will occur. How each member of the crisis team responded will be examined so that this knowledge can be used to improve future crisis responses. Crises can also have long-term effects on interventionists, which also must be addressed.

CRISIS HOTLINES

In the 1970s and 1980s, crisis hotlines began to be used as a method of assisting individuals in crisis. Individuals who call in crisis can receive very brief counseling. This may be appropriate for a person considering suicide or for someone who has recently been victimized. Hotlines can also provide information to callers, links to needed services, and educational outreach.

CRISIS INTERVENTION THERAPY

The purpose of crisis intervention therapy is to reduce emotional distress and to increase coping skills. The ultimate goal of crisis intervention is not just to return the individual to a prior functioning level but also to raise it. Crisis intervention presents the psychologist or mental health worker with unique opportunities because individuals are most open to change when they clearly see that previously used coping strategies are no longer working.

Individuals can seek treatment from psychologists and therapists in private practice. Most cities have rape crisis centers, centers for victims of violent crime, and women's health clinics where crisis counseling can be found. College and university campuses offer counseling services to students.

Children in crisis situations can be especially vulnerable because they have had fewer years to develop coping skills. Violence can occur in schools or within the home. School psychologists and social workers can help children deal with stress. When children are exposed to long-term stress through abuse or neglect at home, intervention may focus on the entire family and helping everyone develop better coping skills.

The therapist and client will meet to define the current problem and examine responses that have not worked. From that point, alternative responses will be discussed. A behavioral therapist may have the client rehearse new responses. In some cases, medication can also be used to lessen anxiety or depression and facilitate progression in therapy.

STRESS

Hans Selye conceptualized the stress response as a biological response that progressed through alarm, resistance, and exhaustion. Unremitting stress can result in a variety of physical disorders involving the cardiovascular system, gastrointestinal system, immunological response, and even skin conditions. Stress can also result in psychological disorders. In the short term, severe stress can result in the development of panic attacks and acute stress disorder. When stress continues over an extended period of time, post-traumatic stress disorder, mood disorders, sleep disorders, and a variety of other psychological disorders may arise.

BIBLIOGRAPHY

Dattilio, Frank M., and Arthur Freeman. *Cognitive-Behavioral Strategies in Crisis Intervention.* 3rd ed. New York: Guilford, 2010. Print.

Doherty, George. *Crisis Intervention Training for Disaster Workers: An Introduction.* Laramie, Wyo.: Rocky Mountain Disaster Mental Health Institute, 2007. Print.

Heath, Melissa Allen, and Dawn Sheen. *School-Based Crisis Intervention: Preparing All Personnel to Assist.* New York: Guilford, 2005. Print.

James, Richard K., and Burl E. Gilliland. *Crisis Intervention Strategies.* 7th edition. Belmont: Brooks/Cole, 2013. Print.

Loshak, Rosemary. *Out of the Mainstream: Helping the Children of Parents with a Mental Illness.* London: Routledge, 2013. Print.

Roberts, Albert R., and Kenneth R. Yeager. *Pocket Guide to Crisis Intervention.* New York: Oxford UP, 2009. Print.

Sandoval, Jonathan. *Crisis Counseling: Intervention and Prevention in the Schools.* New York: Routledge, 2013. Print.

Seeley, Karen M. *Therapy After Terror: 9/11, Psychotherapists, and Mental Health.* New York: Cambridge UP, 2008. Print.

Ayn Embar-Seddon O'Reilly and Allan D. Pass

SEE ALSO: Brief therapy; Community psychology; Coping: Strategies; Disaster psychology; Fear; Mood disorders; Stress: Behavioral and psychological responses; Stress: Physiological responses; Suicide.

Cross-cultural psychology

TYPE OF PSYCHOLOGY: Biological bases of behavior; Cognition; Developmental psychology; Multicultural psychology

Traditional views of psychology often ignored the role of culture in characterizing human behavior and thought. Researchers have since begun to appreciate the role of culture in psychology and recognize that culture and thought are often mutually interdependent.

KEY CONCEPTS

- Collectivistic cultures
- Dispositional factors
- Fundamental attribution error
- Individualistic cultures
- Religion
- Situational factors

INTRODUCTION

Cross-cultural psychology is a broad term for the scientific study of human behavior and mental or cognitive processes within different cultures. In general, this field addresses similarities and differences between cultures. According to the American social psychologists Richard Nisbett and Ara Norenzayan, the view that there are differences between cultures, at least in terms of cognitive processes, was not widely held in the twentieth century. Instead, most psychologists assumed that basic cognitive processes were universal—that the fundamental aspects of thinking and perceiving that involve attention, memory, learning, and reasoning operated in the same way among all cultures. Based on their research and that of other scholars, Nisbett and Norenzayan concluded that the basic processes of thinking and behavior are shaped by culture, although there are aspects of thinking and perceiving that may be innate (genetic or possessed at birth) and that limit or constrain the degree to which such shaping is possible.

HOW THINKING CONSTRAINS CULTURE

In the field of developmental psychology, there is much evidence to suggest that very young children have sets of basic building blocks that they use to understand human minds, important entities, and world events. These sets of building blocks are thought to be innate and domain specific (for example, one set helps children understand how other people think, and another set helps them understand the properties of objects). Evidently, they are common to all infants across cultures and limit the types of thinking about the world that can exist in any culture.

For example, the American developmental psychologist Elizabeth Spelke describes an experiment in which infants were shown a single toy animal placed on a stage. A curtain was lowered to hide or occlude the toy, and a second toy was shown to the infants and then placed behind the screen. Next, the screen was raised, revealing either both toys or only one of the toys. Infants looked longer at the single toy than the two toys. This finding shows that the infants were able to keep track of the two objects in their minds, even when the objects were hidden, and were surprised that one of the toys had disappeared. It also suggests that infants do not need to learn that objects do not spontaneously disappear. Related experiments by American developmental psychologist Renee Baillargeon show that without being taught, infants understand that objects cannot spontaneously appear, break apart, coalesce, or change size, shape, pattern, or color. This findings illustrate one of the basic building blocks of all cultures, the principle of persistence, which states that certain object changes are impossible.

Another type of thinking that may constrain cultures involves ideas about religion. American anthropologist and psychologist Pascal Boyer notes that religions share many similar beliefs across cultures—for example, the belief that something nonphysical, such as an invisible spirit, survives after a person's death and can be contacted by a select few individuals. These ideas arise from basic beliefs shared among cultures about physics, biology, and the mind.

HOW CULTURE SHAPES THINKING

Differences between cultures lead to different ways of thinking. Consider the differences between individualistic and collectivistic cultures. In an individualistic culture, people view themselves more as individuals and are taught to act independently, taking personal responsibility for their successes and failures. In a collectivistic culture, people view themselves more as members of groups and are taught to act interdependently, favoring the needs of the group over their own individual needs. The United States is an example of an individualistic culture, while most East Asian cultures are collectivistic.

These different cultural perspectives affect thinking in many ways. For example, one important finding in social psychology is the fundamental attribution error, which is the tendency to overestimate how much a person's behavior is due to dispositional factors and to underestimate how much it is due to situational factors. Dispositional factors refer to a person's internal characteristics, such as personality traits, abilities, and motives; situational factors refer to external causes. For example, students might explain that they did well on an exam because they are intelligent (a dispositional factor) or because the teacher gave an easy exam (a situational factor). Collectivistic cultures are less likely to make the fundamental attribution error than individualistic cultures. For example, cultural psychologists Michael Morris and Kaiping Peng examined newspaper reports of two mass murders and found that an American newspaper was more likely to describe the mass murders in terms of dispositional factors, such as a very bad temper, whereas a Chinese newspaper was more likely to focus on situational factors, such as isolation from the Chinese community due to having been recently fired.

Cultures arise in different geographical regions and environments, which can lead to important differences between cultures. One area of differences is the family structure. Most families across societies have parents who are monogamous (one man married to one woman). However, in some families, there is polygamy, which includes polyandry (one woman married to more than one man) and polygyny (one man married to more than one woman). According to American social psychologists Douglas Kenrick, Steven Neuberg, and Robert Cialdini, polygamy arises in cultures because of survival needs. For example, a polyandrous woman in Tibet may marry several men who are brothers because the harsh environment in the high Himalayan desert makes it difficult for a single man and woman to survive. The brothers in turn share the wife so that they can preserve the family estate from generation to generation. This family structure, which is called fraternal polyandry, appears to be driven by economic conditions originating from the environment.

BIBLIOGRAPHY

Berry, John W., et al. *Cross-Cultural Psychology: Research and Applications*. 3rd ed. Cambridge: Cambridge UP, 2011. Print.

Goldstein, Susan. *Cross-Cultural Explorations: Activities in Culture and Psychology. 2nd ed. Boston: Pearson, 2008. Print.*

Heine, Steven J. *Cultural Psychology.* 2nd ed. New York: Norton, 2012. Print.

Keith, Kenneth D., ed. *Cross-Cultural Psychology: Contemporary Themes and Perspectives.* Malden: Blackwell, 2011. Print.

Krumov, Krum, and Knud S. Larsen. *Cross-Cultural Psychology: Why Culture Matters.* Charlotte: Information Age, 2013. Print.

Laungani, Pittu D. *Understanding Cross-Cultural Psychology: Eastern and Western Perspectives.* Thousand Oaks: Sage, 2007. Print.

Matsumoto, David, and Fons J. R. van de Vijver, eds. *Cross-Cultural Research Methods in Psychology.* New York: Cambridge UP, 2011. Print.

Nisbett, Richard E. *The Geography of Thought: How Asians and Westerners Think Differently . . . and Why.* New York: Free, 2003. Print.

Shiraev, Eric B., and David A. Levy. *Cross-Cultural Psychology: Critical Thinking and Contemporary Applications.* 5th ed. Boston: Pearson, 2013. Print.

Edward J. Wisniewski and Jing Wu

See Also: Cultural competence; Culture and diagnosis; Culture-bound syndromes; Multicultural psychology; Religion and psychology.

Crowd behavior

TYPE OF PSYCHOLOGY: Social psychology

Crowd behavior is the study of how the behavior of people in groups differs from that of individuals. People in crowds often become much more focused on their social identity than on their individual identity. As a result, they are much more influenced by the norms of the group.

KEY CONCEPTS

- Bystander effect
- Deindividualism
- Diffusion of responsibility
- Social identity theory

INTRODUCTION

Crowds are groups of people who are together for short periods of time. The study of crowd behavior examines the actions that people in a crowd perform and how these actions differ from the behavior of individuals acting alone. Crowd behavior became a focus of scholarly thought in the late nineteenth and early twentieth centuries in reaction to social turmoil in western Europe. Italian criminologist Scipio Sighele was among the first to write about crowd behavior; French psychologist Gustave Le Bon, the founder of crowd psychology, formalized and popularized the concept with his book *The Crowd*, published in 1895. Le Bon's ideas reached a wide audience and are said to have influenced German dictator Adolf Hitler and Italian dictator Benito Mussolini. Because crowds have performed many senseless and destructive acts, both historically and in modern times, understanding crowd behavior remains extremely important for psychologists.

The term "crowd" refers to a wide spectrum of human gatherings, varying in their complexity and the intention with which people join them. Some crowds are casual ones in which people come together by happenstance, such as a group of pedestrians standing on a sidewalk. These tend to be simple, disorganized groups of people who do not know one another and will probably not see each other again. Other crowds are conventionalized; the people have all chosen a common activity, such as watching a parade or a sporting event, and express excitement in standard ways, such as cheering. Some crowds are purposive, choosing to be together for a common goal, such as a rally or political protest. These groups are often highly cohesive and highly organized.

Because crowds differ so much in their composition, organization, and purpose, there is also considerable variation in typical crowd behavior. Popular and scholarly attention has tended to focus on situations in which crowd behavior is considered problematic. In these situations, the crowd often has an unusual problem to solve rapidly—for example, how to respond to a hostile police force. The occurrence of riots and violence attests to the fact that these sorts of problems are not always solved constructively by crowds. It should be noted, however, that crowds are capable of behaving in positive ways as well.

UNDERLYING PSYCHOLOGICAL PROCESSES

Early theories of crowd behavior hypothesized that unruly crowds were made up of criminals or the mentally deficient. Proponents of this perspective assumed that crowd behavior could be explained by the individual personalities of people in the crowd and that certain kinds of people were more likely to be found in a crowd. Le Bon provided a more psychological analysis of crowd behavior, recognizing that even people of high intelligence could become members of an unruly crowd. He believed that crowds transform people, obliterating their normal abilities to be rational and putting them in a hypnotic, highly suggestible state. Le Bon disapproved of crowd behavior in all forms; consequently, in his book he painted an extremely negative picture of crowd behavior.

Modern social psychological research suggests that neither of these early viewpoints is a good description of the psychological forces underlying crowd behavior. Experimental research has determined that almost any individual could be influenced to behave in uncharacteristic ways under the right circumstances. Le Bon's perspective has also been greatly refined. Rather than relying on his concepts of mass hypnosis and loss of rationality, modern researchers draw primarily from social identity theory to help explain crowd behavior. Social identity theory, originally developed by European psychologists Henri Tajfel and John Turner in the 1970s, posits that individuals derive an important part of their sense of identity from the groups to which they belong. Groups such as one's family, school, or religion can all be positive sources of identity.

Under some circumstances, crowds can become a source of identity as well. A key psychological mechanism through which crowds become a source of identity is deindividuation, the loss of a person's inhibitions and sense of identity when he or she is in the presence of others. Crowds are especially likely to lead to deindividuation for a number of reasons. First, crowds cause individuals to feel less accountable for their actions; they are less likely to be singled out and feel less personally responsible for any act the crowd commits. Crowds also focus attention away from the self, so one's own values and internal standards become less influential. Thus, in line with social identity theory, deindividuation leads a person to become focused on social identity rather than individual identity. When social identity is important to a person, he or she becomes particularly susceptible to social influence. Group norms, or a group's standards and expectations regarding appropriate behavior, become especially significant, and the individual is likely to conform strictly to those norms. In the short time frame of many crowd gatherings, the norm becomes whatever everyone else is doing.

It should be noted, however, that being amid a group of people does not always lead one to become deindividuated, nor does it always lead to the ascendancy of social identity over individual identity. Often crowds do not engage in collective behavior at all. For example, on most city streets, pedestrians walking and milling about do not consider themselves to be part of a group and do not draw a sense of identity from the people around them.

Eugen Tarnow noted that these wide variations in the effect of crowds on individuals can be best understood by identifying two phases of a crowd: an individual phase and a conforming phase. During the individual phase, people move freely about. At these times, individuals are not particularly aware of their membership in a crowd and are not particularly influenced by those around them. In the conforming phase, however, individuals in a crowd are highly aware of the group of which they are a part, and they show high levels of conformity. During this phase, the group norms heavily influence each individual's behavior. Crowds typically alternate between these two phases, sometimes acting collectively, sometimes individually. For example, at a sporting event, fans are sometimes talking to their friends about topics of individual interest. However, when points are scored by the home team, the crowd responds collectively, as part of a social group. At these moments spectators are not responding as individuals but as members of a social group, "fans."

The behaviors that members of a crowd perform will thus depend on how strongly the crowd becomes a source of social identity and what behavioral norms become established among the group. Because these factors vary considerably from group to group, crowds cannot be characterized as wholly negative or uniformly simplistic, as Le Bon described them.

THE VIOLENT CROWD

Violent and destructive acts are among the most studied forms of crowd behavior. Many historical examples, from the French Revolution of 1789 to the Los Angeles riots of 1992, attest to the destructive power of crowds. However, a crowd of deindividuated people will not become violent unless a group norm of violence becomes established. In riots, for example, there is usually an identifiable precipitating event, such as one person smashing a window, that introduces a norm of violence. If a critical mass of people immediately follows suit, a riot ensues. Some other crowds, such as lynch mobs, have the norm of violence previously established by their culture or by the group's previous actions.

Further, there is some evidence to suggest that the way in which a crowd of people is viewed by authorities can escalate crowd conflicts. For example, in 1998, European psychologists Clifford Stott and Stephen Reicher interviewed police officers involved with controlling a riot in Great Britain. Their analysis revealed that while police officers recognize that crowds contain subgroups of more dangerous or less dangerous members, they tend to treat all group members as potentially dangerous. The police officers' negative expectations often translate into combative behavior toward all crowd members. By acting on their negative expectations, authority figures often elicit the very behaviors they hope to prevent, which often leads to increased violence and conflict escalation.

Much evidence suggests that there is a direct relationship between degree of deindividuation and the extremity of a crowd's actions. For example, in 1986, Brian Mullen examined newspaper accounts of sixty lynchings that occurred in the first half of the twentieth century. His analysis revealed that the more people present in the mob, the more violent and vicious the event. Similarly, Leon Mann found in his analysis of twenty-one cases of threatened suicides that crowds watching were more likely to engage in crowd baiting (encouraging the person to jump from a ledge or bridge) when crowds were large and when it was dark. On a more mundane level, sports players are more aggressive when wearing identical uniforms than when dressed in their own clothes. Any factor that increases anonymity seems to increase deindividuation and the power of social identity, thus also increasing the likelihood of extreme behavior.

In South Africa, psychological research on these phenomena has been presented in murder trials. People being tried for murder have argued that these psychological principles help explain their antisocial behavior. The use of psychological research findings for these purposes has sparked a great deal of controversy in the field.

THE APATHETIC CROWD

While crowds are most infamous for inciting people to rash action, sometimes crowds inhibit behavior. Research on helping behavior suggests that helping is much less likely to occur when there are many people watching. This well-established phenomenon, known as the bystander effect, was researched and described by American psychologists John Darley and Bibb Latané. In a typical experiment, participants overhear an "accident," such as someone falling off a ladder, and researchers observe whether participants go to help. Most people help when they are alone, but people are significantly less likely to help when they are with a crowd of other people. Darley and Latané argued that bystanders in a crowd experience a diffusion of responsibility—that is, each individual feels less personally responsible to act because each assumes that someone else will do so.

This phenomenon is exacerbated by the fact that in many situations, it is unclear whether an event is an emergency. For example, an adult dragging a screaming child out of a store could be a kidnapper making away with a child or a parent responding to a tantrum. Bystanders observe the reactions of others in the crowd to help them determine what the appropriate course of action is in an ambiguous situation. However, because the situation is ambiguous, typically each individual is equally confused and unsure. By waiting for someone else to act, bystanders convey the impression to others that they think nothing is wrong. Psychologists call this phenomenon pluralistic ignorance. People assume that even though others are behaving in exactly the same way as themselves (not acting), they are doing so for a different reason (knowing the situation is not an emergency). Thus, a social norm of inaction can also become established in a crowd.

THE PROSOCIAL CROWD

Despite the potential for great violence and destruction, most crowds that gather do so quite uneventfully. Further, sometimes crowd behavior is quite positive and prosocial. Research shows that sometimes deindividuation can lead to prosocial behavior. For example, nonviolent protests operate under an explicit norm of peaceful resistance and rarely lead to escalated violence on both sides. The power of prosocial norms was experimentally established in a 1979 study conducted by psychologists Robert Johnson and Leslie Downing. Johnson and Downing had participants dress in either nurses' apparel or a white robe and hood like those worn by the Ku Klux Klan. Some from each group had their individual identity made known, while the rest did not. All participants were then given the opportunity to deliver an electric shock to someone who had previously insulted them. Among participants wearing the robes, those who were not identified delivered higher shock levels than those who were. Presumably these people were deindividuated and thus more strongly influenced by the violent cue of their costume. Of those in nurses' uniforms, the opposite was observed. Unidentified, deindividuated participants gave much less intense shocks than identified participants did. They were also more strongly influenced by the cues around them, but in this case the cues promoted prosocial action.

BIBLIOGRAPHY

Borch, Christian. "Crowd Theory and the Management of Crowds: A Controversial Relationship." *Current Sociology* 61.5/6 (2013): 584–601. Print.

Borch, Christian. *The Politics of Crowds: An Alternative History of Sociology.* New York: Cambridge UP, 2012. Print.

Coleman, A. M. "Crowd Psychology in South African Murder Trials." *American Psychologist* 46.10 (1992): 1071–79. Print.

Drury, John, and Clifford Stott, eds. *Crowds in the 21st Century: Perspectives from Contemporary Social Science.* New York: Routledge, 2013. Print.

Gaskell, G., and R. Benewick, eds. *The Crowd in Contemporary Britain.* London: Sage, 1987. Print.

Le Bon, Gustave. *The Crowd: A Study of the Popular Mind.* London: Unwin, 1896. Print.

McPhail, Clark. *The Myth of the Madding Crowd.* New York: de Gruyter, 1991. Print.

Mann, L. "The Baiting Crowd in Episodes of Threatened Suicide." *Journal of Personality and Social Psychology* 41.4 (1981): 703–9. Print.

Reicher, S. *Crowd Behaviour.* Cambridge: Cambridge UP, 2008. Print.

Reicher, S. "'The Crowd' Century: Reconciling Practical Success with Theoretical Failure." *British Journal of Social Psychology* 35.4 (1996): 535–53. Print.

Surowiecki, James. *The Wisdom of Crowds*. New York: Anchor, 2005. Print.

Van Ginneken, Jaap. *Crowds, Psychology, and Politics, 1871–1899*. New York: Cambridge UP, 1992. Print.

Cythia McPherson Frantz

See Also: Bystander intervention; Community psychology; Group decision making; Group therapy; Groups; Social support and mental health.

Cultural competence

Type of psychology: All

Cultural competence is characterized by a set of skills and developmental experiences constituting an ongoing awareness of important differences among individuals from communities with different backgrounds related to biological, environmental, historical, political, psychological, religious, and other social aspects of heritage.

Key Concepts

- Bias
- Culture
- Ethnicity
- Norms
- Prejudice
- Racism

INTRODUCTION

When psychology is practiced, whether as a science or as a profession, it is practiced in a social and environmental context called culture. Culture is a characteristic of populations reflected in traditional beliefs, values, rituals, and other behaviors that are shared and transmitted from one generation to another. Culture is often thought of in terms of concepts such as ethnicity and norms. Ethnicity is generally described as a personal background characteristic connoting individual membership in a group that is defined by a common and distinctive linguistic, racial, national, and religious heritage. Norms are understood as the standard, average, or model behaviors, beliefs, or values people might have in a particular social grouping.

When psychologists speak of cultural competence, they are speaking about proper psychological practice that reflects an ongoing state of understanding, perceiving, and evaluating interactions among persons of differing cultural backgrounds. This can take place in therapeutic relationships, educational relationships, research endeavors, efforts to develop public policy, and even the way information is presented. These interactions also may take place among individuals, families, communities, institutions, and nations. As such, this means that cultural competence must extend to these other levels of understanding human behavior and interactions.

Cultural competence also involves awareness and knowledge that there are many types of differences based on culture. Such awareness might include the varying values and importance assigned to different holidays, personal traits, language, standards of dress, standards of beauty, and even cultural icons by members of a particular cultural group. Other important dimensions of culture include differences in terms of preferred behavior states, such as being active or passive, or the types of interpersonal values that are preferred, such as cooperation versus competition. Still others are found in terms of preferences for acquiring knowledge (through teaching, through experience, or both), how time is seen (as linear, as cyclical, or in terms of important events), and even for how reality is seen (objectively, subjectively, spiritually, or some combination of these ways of experiencing). This list is certainly incomplete, as cultures are constantly evolving. The things that make cultures distinct are dynamic in nature, and therefore achieving cultural competence is an ongoing process that requires constant self-awareness and self-evaluation.

IMPORTANCE

A good understanding of one's own culture and those of other individuals is important, as the points of interaction among cultures are where problems can develop. Bias, or an impartial or erroneous judgment or tendency to misperceive people or situations, may be activated by a lack of awareness of cultural issues. One familiar way cultural bias may present itself is through prejudice. Prejudice is a judgment based on a bias, and it is typically injurious or detrimental to the person misjudged and to the person doing the misjudging.

One particularly damaging type of prejudice that can result from a lack of cultural competence is racism, or prejudice based on race. Racism entails a belief that one's own race is superior to others. It is mostly associated with prejudice. Racism and prejudice may show up between individuals or groups, causing harm to one or both parties. However, racism may also show up not only at the level of individuals but also at the institutional level. For instance, some might call racial profiling an institutional form of racism. In health care, as an example, this might be evidenced in the form of individuals of a particular ethnic or cultural background being refused access to important health care services because of ill-informed beliefs about their need for such services, or it might develop because health care providers are not properly educated as to how different problems might present in culturally unique ways. Such a lack of identification would then result in a lack of referral for treatment services. The root cause of a lack of multicultural education at the point of identifying problems might be interpreted as a form of cultural incompetence at the individual and institutional levels. Some might go as far as to designate such consequences as a result of institutional racism. To some, this might seem an extreme judgment because the problems may result from a lack of awareness rather than deliberate discrimination, but this is at the heart of the concept of cultural competence: encouraging those in the social sciences and social services areas to always be on the alert for such potential problems.

CONTEXT

In 2012, the Pew Research Center projected that by the year 2050, changes in both immigration and birthrates among individuals of different cultural backgrounds will mean that just under half of US residents will be of a non-Hispanic white racial background. Global communications are also increasing, as more forms of media become available to a wider audience through the Internet, television, and radio. Additionally, definitions of culture extend beyond race and ethnicity; cultures can be defined in terms of characteristics such as age, gender, sexual orientation, and socioeconomic status. As a result, the concept of cultural competence is likely to grow in importance as interactions among diverse cultures are likely to increase and foster as many opportunities for miscommunication as communication. Given this, cultural knowledge must be incorporated into policy development that supports clear communication among culturally diverse populations.

BIBLIOGRAPHY

Berry, John W., et al. "Intercultural Communication and Training." *Cross-Cultural Psychology: Research and Applications*. 3rd ed. New York: Cambridge UP, 2011. 358–80. Print.

Bhui, Kamaldeep. "Cultural Competence: Models, Measures and Movements." *Elements of Culture and Mental Health: Critical Questions for Clinicians*. Ed. Bhui. London: Royal College of Psychiatrists, 2013. 83–84. Print.

Chryssochoou, Xenia. *Cultural Diversity: Its Social Psychology.* New York: Wiley-Blackwell, 2004. Print.

Diller, Jerry V. *Cultural Diversity: A Primer for the Human Services.* 5th ed. Belmont: Wadsworth, 2014. Print.

Kitayama, Shinobu, and Dov Cohen. *Handbook of Cultural Psychology.* New York: Guilford, 2010. Print.

Sue, Derald Wing, and David Sue. *Counseling the Culturally Diverse: Theory and Practice.* Hoboken: Wiley, 2013. Print.

Zofi, Yael S. *Communicating through a Global Lens: How to Broaden Your Perspective in a Cross Cultural World.* Ed. Susan Victor. New York: AIM Strategies, 2007. Print.

Nancy A. Piotrowski; updated by Sharon Wallace Stark

SEE ALSO: Clinical interviewing, testing, and observation; Cross-cultural psychology; Data description; Experimentation: Independent, dependent, and control variables; Multicultural psychology; Observational methods; Prejudice; Prejudice reduction; Racism; Research ethics; Sexism.

Culture and diagnosis

TYPE OF PSYCHOLOGY: Psychological methodologies; Psychopathology

Culture has been recognized as an increasingly important context for evaluating all normal and problematic human behavior. In the process of establishing diagnoses related to mental health conditions, full understanding of culture is imperative to avoid misdiagnosis and to properly understand the nature and functions of mental health symptoms.

KEY CONCEPTS

- Culture-bound syndrome
- Differential diagnosis
- Norms
- Nosology
- Symptom expression

INTRODUCTION

Medical diagnosis is a process of identifying information to determine the nature of a problem. In the study of mental disorders, the systems used to classify diagnoses evolve to accommodate newly generated knowledge. Nosology, or the study of systems of disease classification, facilitates expansion of existing diagnostic systems.

There are many nosological systems used to classify mental illnesses. The two major systems used worldwide are the *Diagnostic and Statistical Manual of Mental Disorders* (DSM) and the *International Classification of Diseases* (ICD). The DSM is an American system of diagnosis. The ICD, as the name indicates, is an international system of diagnosis. Both are used in many countries. Different systems exist to meet the needs of different cultures because behavioral norms vary from culture to culture. Oftentimes, one country may have a variety of cultural norms because of immigration. The DSM is used in many developed industrialized countries. There are, in essence, common social processes in these countries that make use of the DSM even outside the United States appropriate to those cultures.

However, any mental health nosological system is constantly affected by cultural variation. Individuals from different cultural groups—whether defined by country of origin, religion, language, race, or ethnicity—may show unique types of symptom expression (the way in which mental health problems are experienced, voiced, shown, or recognized). The presence of hallucinations, for example, may mean very different things from culture to culture depending on how, where, and when they are expressed. Health providers, therefore, must be familiar with cultural differences to accurately understand symptoms and their meanings. Further, good differential diagnosis—skills to discern one condition from another with similar symptoms—is necessary so that common cultural experiences are not misinterpreted as mental illness and, conversely, uncommon experiences are not misinterpreted as cultural when in fact they may be a sign of illness.

KEY ASPECTS

Good mental health care requires understanding of the cultural identity of the individual receiving treated. This includes how the person identifies with a cultural or ethnic group and the degree of involvement the person has with that group. Individual social and environmental circumstances are also important. Stress, day-to-day functioning, and the person's relationship to primary support groups, including religious networks, must be understood to see the person in context. Further, the roles support groups may play in helping a person with an illness are also important.

Practitioners must understand how an individual's cultural reference group explains any illness the person may have. This understanding is often called cultural competence. There may be specific words or phrases used to describe an illness, particular meaning to certain types of symptoms, theories to explain the causes, and preferences with regard to what kind of care to seek and how to seek it. Culture-bound syndromes—specific patterns of behavior that are recognized by local cultures as problematic and troubling—may also be present. These may or may not be linked to diagnosable problems, but they are recognized cultural experiences in specific locales. For example, susto, which afflicts indigenous people of Latin America, is an illness in which fright causes the soul to leave the body, resulting in symptoms such as sickness and unhappiness. Depending on how it manifests, it may also be associated with any number of conditions in the DSM or ICD, but it is a recognized experience among some Latino individuals in areas of Mexico and Central and South America.

The role of healer has varied meaning, social status, and expectations attached to it, depending on the culture in question. Specific types of healers may be more or less welcome depending on the specific problem and how it is understood. Sensitivity related to communication and language issues are also very important, as a language barrier may be a significant obstacle between a provider and client when trying to understand delicate personal experiences and issues.

Finally, cultural issues influence not only the diagnosis but also the process of care. All aspects of care need thorough examination to ensure they are appropriate. This can include proper selection of assessment tools in the person's preferred or first language; inclusion of different family members in work with the provider; and selection of culturally appropriate exercise, eating, social, or other mental health behaviors.

BIBLIOGRAPHY

Andary, Lena, and Yvonne Stolk. *Assessing Mental Health across Cultures*. Bowen Hills: Australian Academic P, 2008. Print.

Bhui, Kamaldeep, ed. *Elements of Culture and Mental Health: Critical Questions for Clinicians*. London: Royal College of Psychiatrists, 2013. Print.

Fernando, Suman. *Mental Health Worldwide: Culture, Globalization and Development*. New York: Macmillan, 2014. Print.

Garcia, Betty, and Anne Petrovich. *Strengthening the DSM: Incorporating Resilience and Cultural Competence*. New York: Springer, 2011. Print.

Helman, Cecil G. *Culture, Health, and Illness*. 5th ed. London: Hodder Education, 2007. Print.

Paniagua, Freddy A.. "Assessment and Diagnosis in a Cultural Context." *Culture and Therapeutic Process*. Ed. Mark M. Leach and Jamie D. Aten. New York: Routledge, 2010. Print.

Paniagua, Freddy A., and Ann-Marie Yamada, eds. *Handbook of Multicultural Mental Health: Assessment and Treatment of Diverse Populations*. 2nd ed. Oxford: Elsevier, 2013. Print.

Payer, Lynn. *Medicine and Culture*. Rev. ed. New York: Holt, 1996. Print.

Nancy A. Piotrowski

SEE ALSO: African Americans and mental health; Asian Americans/Pacific Islanders and mental health; Biracial heritage and mental health; Cultural competence; Culture-bound syndromes; Latinos and mental health; Multicultural psychology; Native Americans/Alaskan Natives and mental health; Prejudice; Prejudice reduction; Racism.

Culture-bound syndromes

DATE: 1960s onward
TYPE OF PSYCHOLOGY: Psychopathology

Culture-bound conditions are psychological disorders that are limited to certain cultures. Some may be culturally specific expressions of largely universal psychological disorders, whereas others may be distinct disorders in their own right. Debate persists on how best to integrate culture-bound syndromes into diagnostic practices.

KEY CONCEPTS
- Amok
- Etic-emic distinction
- Koro
- New cross-cultural psychiatry model
- Pathogenic-pathoplastic model
- Taijin-kyofusho

INTRODUCTION

In the late 1960s, the fields of psychology and psychiatry developed a particular interest in how cultural factors shape the manifestation of mental disorders. Before that time, some believed that mental disorders were largely universal in their underlying causes and expression. Several decades of cross-cultural research highlighted the limitations of this view by uncovering potentially important differences in the prevalence and expression of certain psychological conditions across the world.

MODELS

There are two major models of psychological disorders that are limited to certain cultures. The first, a pathogenic-pathoplastic model, presumes that mental disorders across the world are identical in their underlying causes (pathogenic effects) but are expressed differently depending on cultural factors (pathoplastic effects). According to this model, cultural influences do not create distinctly different disorders but merely shape the outward expression of existing disorders in culturally specific ways.

Harvard University's Arthur Kleinman and some other cultural anthropologists contended that this model underestimates the cultural relativity of mental disorders. In its place, Kleinman proposed the new cross-cultural psychiatry model, which maintains that many culture-bound syndromes are causally distinct conditions that bear no underlying commonalities to those in Western culture. According to this alternative model, non-Western disorders are not merely culturally specific variations of Western disorders.

In some ways, these competing models parallel the etic-emic distinction in cross-cultural psychology. As noted by University of Minnesota psychiatrist Joseph Westermeyer and others, the term "etic" refers to universal, cross-cultural phenomena that can occur in any cultural group. Conversely, the term "emic" refers to socially unique, intracultural perspectives that occur only within certain cultural groups. There is probably some validity to both perspectives. Some culture-bound syndromes may be similar to conditions in Western culture, whereas others may be largely or entirely distinct from these conditions.

EXAMPLES

Some culture-bound conditions appear to fit a pathogenic-pathoplastic model. For example, seal hunters in Greenland sometimes experience kayak angst, a condition marked by feelings of panic while alone at sea, along with an intense desire to return to land. Kayak angst appears to bear many similarities to the Western condition of panic disorder with agoraphobia and may be a culturally specific variant of this condition.

A culture-bound syndrome widespread among the Japanese is taijin-kyofusho, an anxiety disorder characterized by a fear of offending others, typically by one's appearance or body odor. Some authors have suggested that taijin-kyofusho is a culturally specific variant of the Western disorder of social phobia, a condition marked by a fear of placing oneself in situations that are potentially embarrassing or humiliating, such as speaking or performing in public. Interestingly, Japan tends to be more collectivist than most Western countries, meaning its citizens view themselves more as group members than individuals. In contrast, most Western countries tend to be more individualistic than Japan, meaning their citizens view themselves more as individuals than as group members. As a consequence, taijin-kyofusho may reflect the manifestation of social phobia in a culture that is highly sensitive to the feelings of others.

In contrast, other culture-bound conditions may be largely distinct from Western disorders and therefore difficult to accommodate within a pathogenic-pathoplastic model. In koro (genital retraction syndrome), a condition found primarily in southeast Asia and Africa, individuals believe their sexual organs (for example, the penis in men and breasts in women) are retracting, shrinking, or disappearing. Koro is associated with extreme anxiety and occasionally spreads in contagious epidemics marked by mass societal panic. Although koro bears some superficial similarities to the Western diagnosis of hypochondriasis, it is sufficiently different from any Western condition that it may be a distinctive disorder in its own right.

Another potential example is the Malaysian condition of amok. In amok, individuals, almost always men, react to a perceived insult by engaging in social withdrawal and intense brooding, followed by frenzied and uncontrolled violent behavior. Afflicted individuals, known as "pengamoks," often fall into a stupor after the episode and report memory loss for their aggressive actions. Although amok may be comparable in some ways to the sudden mass shootings occasionally observed in Western countries, such shootings are rarely triggered by only one perceived insult or associated with stupor following the episode. Amok, incidentally, is the origin of the colloquial phrase "running amok."

PSYCHIATRIC CLASSIFICATION

The fourth edition of the American Psychiatric Association's *Diagnostic and Statistical Manual of Mental Disorders* (DSM-IV) provided a list of twenty-five culture-bound syndromes, including taijin-kyofusho, koro, and amok. Appearing in an appendix of the fourth edition, this list was the first official attempt by the mental health community to recognize culture-bound syndromes as worthy of research and clinical attention. The 2000 text revision of the DSM-IV (the DSM-IV-TR) added an outline of issues and factors that clinicians should consider when making diagnoses for culturally diverse patients.

Nevertheless, some researchers criticized the DSM-IV's list of culture-bound syndromes. Some, like McGill University psychiatrists Lawrence J. Kirmayer and Eric Jarvis, argued that some of these "syndromes" are not genuine mental disorders but rather culturally specific explanations for psychological problems familiar to Western society. They cited the example of dhat, a culture-bound condition in the DSM-IV appendix that is prevalent in India, Pakistan, and neighboring countries. Dhat is commonly associated with anxiety, fatigue, and hypochondriacal worries about loss of semen. As Kirmayer and Jarvis observe, many or most individuals with dhat appear to suffer from depression, so dhat may merely be a culturally specific interpretation of depressive feelings.

Other critics charged that DSM-IV's list of culture-bound syndromes was marked by Western bias and that some well-established psychological conditions in Western culture are in fact culture bound. For example, based on a comprehensive review of the literature, Harvard University psychologist Pamela Keel and Michigan State University psychologist Kelly Klump argued persuasively that bulimia nervosa (often known simply as bulimia), an eating disorder often characterized by repeated cycles of binging and purging, is a culture-bound syndrome limited largely to Western culture. Indeed, the few non-Western countries in which bulimia has emerged, such as Japan, have been exposed widely to Western ideals of thinness in recent decades. In contrast, as Keel and Klump noted, anorexia nervosa (often known simply as anorexia) appears to be about equally prevalent in Western and non-Western countries.

For the fifth edition of the DSM (DSM-5), published in 2013, American Psychiatric Association sought to address some of these concerns. While the DSM-5 retains the list of culture-bound syndromes, along with their "idioms of distress" and explanations, in an appendix, it also integrate their symptoms throughout the manual as additions to existing classifications. For example, "offending others," a symptom of taijin-kyofusho, was listed under the diagnostic criteria for social anxiety disorder.

Another modification was the addition of an interview guide with questions about the patient's cultural, racial, ethnic, and religious heritage, which is intended to afford patients an opportunity to describe their condition in their own terms and help clinicians better interpret this information.

Mental health professionals are increasingly recognizing that psychological conditions are sometimes influenced by sociocultural context and that such context must be taken into account in their diagnoses. More research is needed to ascertain how best to classify culture-bound syndromes and integrate cultural influences into diagnostic practices.

BIBLIOGRAPHY

Aneshensel, Carol S., Alex Bierman, and Jo C. Phelan. *Handbook of the Sociology of Mental Health.* Dordrecht: Springer, 2013. Print.

Kirmayer, Lawrence J., and Eric Jarvis. "Cultural Psychiatry: From Museums of Exotica to the Global Agora." *Current Opinion in Psychiatry* 11.2 (1998): 183–89. Print.

Mezzich, Juan E., et al. "The Place of Culture in DSM-IV." *Journal of Nervous and Mental Disease* 187.8 (1999): 457–64. Print.

Murphy, Jane M. "Psychiatric Labeling in Cross-cultural Perspective." *Science* 191.2431 (1976): 1019–28. Print.

Paniagua, Freddy A.. "Assessment and Diagnosis in a Cultural Context." *Culture and Therapeutic Process.* Ed. Mark M. Leach and Jamie D. Aten. New York: Routledge, 2010. Print.

Paniagua, Freddy A., and Ann-Marie Yamada, eds. *Handbook of Multicultural Mental Health: Assessment and Treatment of Diverse Populations.* 2nd ed. Oxford: Elsevier, 2013. Print.

Simons, Ronald C., and Charles C. Hughes, eds. *The Culture-Bound Syndromes: Folk Illnesses of Psychiatric and Anthropological Interest.* Boston: Reidel, 1986. Print.

Sue, Derald Wing, and David Sue. *Counseling the Culturally Diverse: Theory and Practice.* Hoboken: Wiley, 2012. Print.

Tseng, Wen-Shing. "From Peculiar Psychiatric Disorders Through Culture-Bound Syndromes to Culture-Related Specific Syndromes." *Transcultural Psychiatry* 43.4 (2006): 554–76. Print.

Westermeyer, Joseph. "Psychiatric Diagnosis across Cultural Boundaries." *American Journal of Psychiatry* 142.7 (1985): 798–805. Print.

Scott O. Lilienfeld and April D. Thames

See Also: African Americans and mental health; Anorexia nervosa and bulimia nervosa; Anxiety disorders; Asian Americans/Pacific Islanders and mental health; Cross-cultural psychology; Culture and diagnosis; Depression; Eating disorders; Latinos and mental health; Multicultural psychology; Native Americans/Alaskan Natives and mental health; Phobias.

D

Data description

Type of psychology: Psychological methodologies

Data description refers to how the results from research studies are organized, summarized, and characterized statistically.

Key Concept
- Bar graph
- Frequency polygon
- Grouped frequency distributions
- Histogram
- Interquartile range
- Line graph
- Mean
- Median
- Mode
- Negatively skewed distributions
- Positively skewed distributions
- Range
- Semi-interquartile range
- Simple frequency distributions
- Standard deviation
- Variance

INTRODUCTION

Almost all research investigations involve studying a sample of individuals randomly selected from a population with the goal of applying what is learned from the sample to all the individuals who constitute the population. A critical part of this enterprise entails organizing, summarizing, and characterizing the data collected from the sample in meaningful ways. To accomplish this aim, researchers use statistical procedures and graphing techniques. Among these techniques are frequency distributions, measures of central tendency, and measures of variability. In addition, the numbers that constitute research data have different meanings. This is reflected in the scales of measurement to which numbers adhere.

SCALES OF MEASUREMENT

Not all numbers are created equal. Different numbers have different meanings and thus have different characteristics. For example, the number 24 on the back of a baseball player's jersey does not indicate that the player is twice as good as another player who wears the number 12. On the other hand, $24 does indicate twice as many dollars as $12. To differentiate these characteristics, one must understand the scale of measurement to which numbers adhere.

There are four scales of measurement. In ascending order, they are nominal, ordinal, interval, and ratio. Each scale has all the characteristics of the preceding scale plus one additional unique characteristic. Numbers that adhere to the nominal scale simply represent different categories or groups, such as the numbers 1 or 2 to indicate the gender of a research subject. The ordinal scale has the characteristic of different categories but also reflects relative magnitude or degree of measurement, such as ranking photographs from 1 to 5 based on their aesthetic qualities. Both features of separate categories and relative magnitude are reflected in the next scale, the interval scale, with the added characteristic that the distances between successive numbers on the scale are of equal interval. Temperatures on either the Celsius or Fahrenheit scale would be examples of an interval scale of measurement. Finally, numbers that adhere to the ratio scale of measurement reflect the three characteristics of the interval scale along with an absolute zero point, with a value of 0 representing the absence of the measurement. The variables, for example, of time, height, or body weight all would adhere to the ratio scale of measurement. In a research context, knowing the scale of measurement to which numbers adhere will have an impact on the type of statistical procedure used to analyze the data.

ORGANIZING DATA

At the completion of any research study, the data collected need to be organized and summarized in ways that allow the researcher to identify trends or other interesting consistencies in the results. One of the techniques for organizing and summarizing data, especially large sets of data, is the frequency distribution. Frequency distributions allow the researcher to tabulate the frequencies associated with specific response categories and also allow for the data to be summarized and characterized in a more manageable fashion. The organized frequency data are then presented in table form, with the response categories organized in ascending or descending order. Organizing the results in such a manner will facilitate making interpretations from and conclusions about the data.

Generally speaking, there are two types of frequency distribution: simple frequency distribution and grouped frequency distribution. These two types of frequency distribution are constructed identically, with one exception. The simple frequency distribution entails categorizing frequencies for each and every possible response category or score (symbolized as X), while grouped frequency distributions combine specific categories or specific scores into groups called class intervals. Grouping frequencies into class intervals has the advantage of making data sets with wide-ranging categories or scores easier to manage and thus easier to summarize. However, doing so does come with a price. By grouping categories or scores together, the researcher loses some specificity with regard to the number of frequencies associated with particular categories or scores.

Much information can be gleaned from a frequency distribution table. Apart from listing the scores or response categories and their frequencies (symbolized as f), frequency distributions often contain columns indicating the percentage of the total frequency each particular frequency represents (symbolized as % f), the cumulative frequency counts (symbolized as cum f) and their associated percents (symbolized as % cum f), the products of each pair of $f \times X$ terms (symbolized as fX), and the products of each pair of $f \times X^2$ terms (symbolized fX^2). Each of these two latter columns, along with the frequency column, is summed (indicated by the capital Greek letter Σ). These sums are then used in calculating the values of the mean and the standard deviation.

An example of the use of a frequency distribution can be seen in the case of a researcher interested in determining the frequencies with which heights (in inches) present in a sample of fifty subjects. (The number of subjects in a research study is indicated by N.) Each subject's height measurement might be presented in the simple frequency distribution in figure 1.

Organizing the data in this manner allows the researcher to make sense of the data by identifying the most frequent (65 inches) and least frequent (59 inches and 71 inches) height, along with the percentage of the total associated with each height category, and by recording the cumulative frequencies and their associated percentages. Moreover, by examining the values in the "f" column, the manner in which the heights are distributed over the various categories can be easily ascertained. In this distribution, for example, the greatest number of frequencies are associated with height categories that lie toward the middle range of scores, while very few frequencies are associated with heights that lie at either the upper or lower end of the range of height scores. This type of distribution is called a bell-shaped curve or a normal distribution and is often a characteristic of psychological and behavioral data.

MEASURES OF CENTRAL TENDENCY

Because research data represent large sets of numbers, it is desirable, in fact necessary, to summarize these data to facilitate making sense of them. In an attempt to accomplish this goal, researchers calculate summary statistics that provide one value whose purpose is to reflect the general characteristics of the data. The most frequently used summary statistics are called measures of central tendency, and they include the mean or arithmetic average, the median or middle point of the distribution, and the mode or most frequently encountered score in the distribution.

The calculations for the mean, median, and mode are quite simple. Adding all the scores together and dividing by the number of scores in the distribution obtains the mean. In the simple frequency distribution above, the sum of all the scores is indicated by ΣfX, while the number of scores is reflected in the Σf term. Thus, the mean for this set of data is 3,224 ÷ 50, or 64.48 inches. The median or middle point of this distribution of fifty scores lies somewhere between the twenty-fifth and twenty-sixth scores. Since this point in the distribution does not have an actual score associated with it, the convention is to estimate the value of this score by averaging the twenty-fifth and twenty-sixth scores. It just so happens that the twenty-fifth and twenty-sixth scores in the above distribution both have values of 64 inches, therefore making the median (64 + 64) ÷ 2, or 64 inches. Lastly, since the mode is the most frequently exhibited score in the distribution, its identification in the above simple frequency distribution is obtained by looking down the "f" column and determining the largest frequency and its associated height score. By doing so, the mode for this distribution is determined to be 65 inches.

The measures of central tendency are not only useful for using a single value to characterize large data sets but also helpful in identifying the shape of the distribution. For example, it is known that distributions whose mean, median, and mode values are all the same (or similar) most likely are normal distributions. A distribution whose mean value is larger than its median value is most likely to be positively skewed. Positively skewed distributions are those that have the majority of their frequencies toward the lower end of the range of scores. In contrast, when the median value of a distribution exceeds the mean value, then the majority of scores fall at the upper end of the range of scores and the distribution is described as being negatively skewed.

Of the three measures of central tendency, the mean is the most frequently used. However, the use of this statistic will depend on the shape of the distribution and the scale of measurement to which the scores adhere. The mean should be used when working with either interval or ratio data and also when the distribution is approximately normal and does not contain many excessively extreme scores at either end of the distribution. The last criterion is important because the presence of extreme scores in the distribution can severely distort the value of the mean. For this reason, government statistics that summarize income or house prices, for example, typically report median values. When the mean is inappropriate to use, the median is the statistic of choice, as long as the data adhere to either the ordinal, interval, or ratio scale. The mode can be used with any scale of measurement and is typically the statistic of choice with nominal data.

MEASURES OF VARIABILITY

Although measures of central tendency are useful statistics, they reflect only one aspect of the data. Another important feature of the data is the amount of spread or dispersion that exists among the scores. This dimension is reflected in another class of statistics called measures of variability. The most straightforward measure of variability is the range. (It should be noted that the range is not used with nominal data.) The range sample reflects how far apart two extreme scores in the distribution are from each other. In its simplest form, the range is calculated by subtracting the least value from the greatest value. In the height data in Figure 1, the range would equal 14 inches (that is, 72 inches minus 58 inches). A variant of the range is the interquartile range, and its calculation entails taking a difference between the scores that lie at the twenty-fifth and seventy-fifth percentiles. Again, using the height data, it can be seen in the "cum f" column that the scores that lie at the twenty-fifth and seventy-fifth percentiles are 66 and 63, respectively; thus the interquatile range would equal 3 inches. Another variant of the range is called the semi-interquartile range, and its calculation is the interquartile range divided by 2. For the height data, the semi-interquartile range would be 1.5 inches. The range, or one of its variants (typically the semi-interquartile range), is used as the measure of variability when the median is used as the measure of central tendency.

The utility of the ranges as measures of variability is quite limited, since their calculations involve using only two scores from the distribution. The variance and standard deviation, on the other hand, use all the scores in their calculations and thus are better measures, but they do require that the data fit either the interval or ratio scale of measurement. The variance is obtained by applying the following formula to the data: [ΣX2 – (ΣX)2 ÷ N)] ÷ N. Thus, the variance for the height data discussed above would be equal to [208,210 – (3,2242 ÷ 50)] ÷ 50 or 6.53 inches. (Note that a mathematically equivalent formula is [Σ(X – mean)2]÷ N]). The standard deviation is simply the square root of the variance, and its value would be 2.56 inches. Of these two measures of variability, the standard deviation is the one almost always used, and it is reported when the appropriate measure of central tendency is the mean.

The variance and standard deviation are important in a number of ways. First, the variance represents a measurement that reflects the average squared dispersion between each score and the mean of the distribution. (Note that mathematically, squaring the difference between the score and the mean when calculating the variance or standard deviation is necessary to avoid always obtaining a quotient of 0.) Second, the variance can be interpreted as an estimate of the margin of error when using the mean to predict the value of a randomly selected individual's score from the population. For example, based on the sample of fifty subjects presented in the frequency distribution above, the height of a randomly selected person from the population would be 64.48 ± 6.53 inches. Another example of a variance measure would be the margin of error that accompanies the results of most public opinion polls. Finally, the standard deviation is used in calculating a standardized score, also known as a z-score. A standardized score is equal to the squared difference between the score and the mean divided by the standard deviation (that is, z = (X – mean)2 ÷ standard deviation). Standardized scores are helpful in comparing the relative performance of scores that come from different populations and samples and are also used in determining various proportions of the population associated with different regions of the normal distributions. For example, 68.26 percent of the scores in a normal distribution will fall within ±1 z-score unit (or ±1 standard deviation unit) from the mean, while 95.44 percent will fall within ±2 z-score units (±2 standard deviation units).

GRAPHS

It has been said that a picture is worth a thousand words. This is also true when it comes to research data. Researchers often will present their data or summary statistics calculated from their data in graphic form. There are several ways to do this. Frequency data are often displayed via a frequency polygon, bar graph, or histogram. All three of these types of graphs plot the frequency data as a function of the score categories on a set of X,Y axes, as is illustrated in figures 2, 3, and 4.

Apart from the obvious differences in their look, these three graphs differ in another way. Frequencies associated with either the nominal or ordinal scale of measurement should be plotted using a bar graph, while data that reflect some quantifiable measurement (that is, quantitative data) can be plotted using either a frequency polygon or a histogram. It is the convention to use a frequency polygon, rather than a histogram, when there is a large range of scores to be plotted on the X-axis. Another important feature of frequency polygons is that the left- and right-hand sides of the curve are anchored to the X-axis. This is accomplished by starting the X-axis off with the score below the lowest score in the data set and ending the X-axis with the score above the highest score. There are no frequencies associated with these two X values, thus the curve is anchored to the X-axis.

Data derived from an experiment, on the other hand, are usually plotted using a line graph. A line graph typically plots the mean of some measure (called the dependent variable) as a function of the variables (called the independent variables) studied in the experiment. Also included in a line graph are T-bars that extend from the mean. The T-bars represent each plotted mean's measure of variability, often expressed in terms of ±1 standard deviation unit. Line graphs do, however, require that the data be derived from either an interval or ratio scale of measurement. Experimental data that are either ordinal or nominal in nature should be plotted using a bar graph.

The example of a line graph provided in figure 5(see page 540) presents fictitious data for illustration purposes. The relationship expressed in this graph is the effect of number of alcoholic drinks (one independent variable) on the number of words recalled (the dependent variable) in both male and female subjects (a second independent variable). The mean values for each of the eight groups of subjects are plotted along with their standard deviations, represented by the T-bars that extend upward and downward from each point in the graph. In this set of fictitious data, it can seen that, on average, female subjects were more adversely affected by either one or two alcoholic drinks, but showed the same degree of memory impairment as male subjects when three alcoholic drinks were administered.

INFERENTIAL STATISTICS

All the methods thus far described are descriptive in nature; that is, they simply describe, summarize, and illustrate the trends that exist in the data. Many other statistical procedures exist that enable researchers to make inferences about the population at large based on sample data. These procedures are referred to as inferential statistics. Essentially, the goal of all inferential statistics is to establish, within a specific probability of certainty, whether groups of subjects performed differently and whether these differences are attributable to the effects of the independent variable being studied in the investigation.

Inferential statistical tests fall into two broad categories, depending on whether two groups or more than two groups of subjects were studied. Further, each broad category is subdivided into two subcategories called parametric and nonparametric tests. Parametric tests are used when certain assumptions about the population from which the subjects were selected can be safely made (that is, the population is normally distributed and the population variances of the groups are similar), while nonparametric tests do not require that these assumptions are met. Analyzing research data with inferential statistical tests is a critical component of the scientific process that enables researchers to identify cause-and-effect relationships in nature.

BIBLIOGRAPHY

Bruning, James L., and B. L. Kintz. *Computational Handbook of Statistics*. 4th ed. New York: Longman, 1997. Print.

Hanneman, Robert, Augustine J. Kposowa, and Mark Riddle. *Basic Statistics for Social Research*. San Francisco: Jossey-Bass, 2013. Print.

Heiman, Gary W. *Basic Statistics for the Behavioral Sciences*. 5th ed. Boston: Houghton, 2006. Print.

Keppel, Geoffrey. *Design and Analysis: A Researcher's Handbook*. 5th ed. Englewood Cliffs: Prentice, 2007. Print.

Larson, Ron, and Elizabeth Farber. *Elementary Statistics: Picturing the World*. Boston: Pearson, 2012. Print.

Siegel, Sidney. *Nonparametric Statistics for the Behavioral Sciences*. 2d ed. New York: McGraw, 1988. Print.

Spatz, Chris. *Basic Statistics: Tales of Distributions*. 9th ed. Belmont: Wadsworth, 2008. Print.

Wheelan, Charles J. *Naked Statistics: Stripping the Dread from the Data*. New York: Norton, 2013. Print.

Anthony C. Santucci

See Also: Animal experimentation; Archival data; Case study methodologies; Complex experimental designs; Experimental psychology; Experimentation: Ethics and participant rights; Experimentation: Independent, dependent, and control variables; Field experimentation; Hypothesis development and testing; Observational methods; Qualitative research; Quasi-experimental designs; Sampling; Scientific methods; Statistical significance tests; Survey research: Questionnaires and interviews; Within-subject experimental designs.

Death and dying

Type of psychology: Clinical; Counseling; Cross-cultural; Developmental; Family; Social

Key Concepts

- Anticipatory depression
- Bereavement
- Depression
- Grief
- Mourning
- Reactive depression
- Thanatology
- Uncomplicated bereavement

Medicine determines that death has occurred by assessing bodily functions in either of two areas. Persons with irreversible cessation of respiration and circulation are dead; persons with irreversible cessation of ascertainable brain functions are also dead. There are standard procedures used to diagnose death, including simple observation, brain-stem reflex studies, and the use of confirmatory testing such as electrocardiography (ECG or EKG), electroencephalography (EEG), and arterial blood gas analysis (ABG). The particular circumstances—anticipated or unanticipated, observed or unobserved, the patient's age, drug or metabolic intoxication, or suspicion of hypothermia—will favor some procedures over others, but in all cases both cessation of functions and their irreversibility are required before death can be declared.

Between 60 and 75 percent of all people die from chronic terminal conditions. Therefore, except in sudden death (as in a fatal accident) or when there is no evidence of consciousness (as in a head injury which destroys cerebral functions while leaving brain-stem reflexive functions intact), dying is both a physical and a psychological process. In most cases, dying takes time, and the time allows patients to react to the reality of their own passing. Often, they react by becoming vigilant about bodily symptoms and any changes in them. They also anticipate changes that have yet to occur. For example, long before the terminal stages of illness become manifest, dying patients commonly fear physical pain, shortness of breath, invasive procedures, loneliness, becoming a burden to loved ones, losing decision-making authority, and facing the unknown of death itself.

As physical deterioration proceeds, all people cope by resorting to what has worked for them before: the unique means and mechanisms which have helped maintain a sense of self and personal stability. People seem to go through the process of dying much as they have gone through the process of living—with the more salient features of their personalities, whether good or bad, becoming sharper and more prominent. People seem to face death much as they have faced life.

Medicine has come to acknowledge that physicians should understand what it means to die. Indeed, while all persons should understand what their own deaths will mean, physicians must additionally understand how their dying patients find this meaning.

In 1969, psychiatrist Elisabeth Kübler-Ross published the landmark *On Death and Dying*, based on her work with two hundred terminally ill patients. Though the work of Kübler-Ross has been criticized for the nature of the stages described and whether or not every person experiences every stage, her model has retained enormous utility to those who work in the area of death and dying. Technologically driven, Western medicine had come to define its role as primarily dealing with extending life and thwarting death by defeating specific diseases. Too few physicians saw a role for themselves once the prognosis turned grave. In the decades that followed the publication of *On Death and Dying*, the profession has reaccepted that death and dying are part of life and that, while treating the dying may not mean extending the length of life, it can and should mean improving its quality.

Kübler-Ross provided a framework to explain how people cope with and adapt to the profound and terrible news that their illness is terminal. Although other physicians, psychologists, and thanatologists have shortened, expanded, and adapted her five stages of the dying process, neither the actual number of stages nor what they are specifically called is as important as the information and insight that any stage theory of dying yields. As with any human process, dying is complex, multifaceted, multidimensional, and polymorphic.

Well-intentioned, but misguided, professionals and family members may try to help move dying patients through each of the stages only to encounter active resentment or passive withdrawal. Patients, even dying patients, cannot be psychologically moved to where they are not ready to be. Rather than making the terminally ill die the "right" way, it is more respectful and helpful to understand any stage as a description of normal reactions to serious loss, and that these reactions normally vary among different individuals and also within the same individual over time. The reactions appear, disappear, and reappear in any order and in any combination. What the living must do is respect the unfolding of an adaptational schema which is the dying person's own. No one should presume to know how someone else should prepare for death.

COMPLICATIONS AND DISORDERS

Kübler-Ross defined five stages of grief. Denial is the first stage defined by Kübler-Ross, but it is also linked to shock and isolation. Whether the news is told outright or gradual self-realization occurs, most people react to the knowledge of their impending death with existential shock: Their whole selves recoil at the idea, and they say, in some fashion, "This cannot be happening to me." Broadly considered, denial is a complex cognitive-emotional capacity that enables temporary postponement of active, acute, but in some way detrimental, recognition of reality. In the dying process, this putting off of the truth prevents a person from being overwhelmed while promoting psychological survival. Denial plays an important stabilizing role, holding back more than could be otherwise managed while allowing the individual to marshal psychological resources and reserves. It enables patients to consider the possibility, even the inevitability, of death and then to put the consideration away so that they can pursue life in the ways that are still available. In this way, denial is truly a mechanism of defense.

Many other researchers, along with Kübler-Ross, report anger as the second stage of dying. The stage is also linked to rage, fury, envy, resentment, and loathing. When "This cannot be happening to me" becomes, "This is happening to me. There was no mistake," patients are beginning to replace denial with attempts to understand what is happening to and inside them. When they do, they often ask, "Why me?" Though it is an unanswerable question, the logic of the question is clear. People, to remain human, must try to make intelligible their experiences and reality. The asking of this question is an important feature of the way in which all dying persons adapt to and cope with the reality of death.

People react with anger when they lose something of value; they react with greater anger when something of value is taken away from them by someone or something. Rage and fury, in fact, are often more accurate descriptions of people's reactions to the loss of their own life than is anger. Anger is a difficult stage for professionals and loved ones, more so when the anger and rage are displaced and projected randomly into any corner of the patient's world. An unfortunate result is that caregivers often experience the anger as personal, and the caregivers" own feelings of guilt, shame, grief, and rejection can contribute to lessening contact with the dying person, which increases his or her sense of isolation.

Bargaining is Kübler-Ross's third stage, but it is also the one about which she wrote the least and the one that other thanatologists are most likely to leave unrepresented in their own models and stages of how people cope with dying. Nevertheless, it is a common phenomenon wherein dying people fall back on their faith, belief systems, or sense of the transcendent and the spiritual and try to make a deal—with god, life, fate, a higher power, or the universe. They ask for more time to help family members reconcile or to achieve something of importance. They may ask if they can simply attend their child's wedding or graduation or if they can see their first grandchild born. Then they will be ready to die; they will go willingly. Often, they mean that they will die without fighting death, if death can only be delayed or will delay itself.

At some point, when terminally ill individuals are faced with decisions about more procedures, tests, surgeries, or medications or when their thinness, weakness, or deterioration becomes impossible to ignore, the anger, rage, numbness, stoicism, and even humor will likely give way to depression, Kübler-Ross's fourth stage and the one reaction that all thanatologists include in their models of how people cope with dying.

The depression can take many forms, for indeed there are always many losses, and each loss individually or several losses collectively might need to be experienced and worked through. For example, dying parents might ask themselves who will take care of the children, get them through school, walk them down the aisle, or guide them through life. Children, even adult children who are parents themselves, may ask whether they can cope without their own parents. They wonder who will support and anchor them in times of distress, who will (or could) love, nurture, and nourish them the way that their parents did. Depression accompanies the realization that each role, each function, will never be performed again. Both the dying and those who love them mourn.

Much of the depression takes the form of anticipatory grieving, which often occurs both in the dying and in those who will be affected by their death. It is a part of the dying process experienced by the living, both terminal and nonterminal. Patients, family, and friends can psychologically anticipate what it will be like when the death does occur and what life will, and will not, be like afterward. The grieving begins while there is still life left to live.

Bereavement specialists generally agree that anticipatory grieving, when it occurs, seems to help people cope with what is a terrible and frightening loss. It is an adaptive psychological mechanism wherein emotional, mental, and existential stability are painfully maintained. When depression develops, not only in reaction to death but also in preparation for it, it seems to be a necessary part of how those who are left behind cope to survive the loss themselves. Those who advocate or advise cheering up or looking on the bright side are either unrealistic or unable to tolerate the sadness in themselves or others. The dying are in the process of losing everything and everyone they love. Cheering up does not help them; the advice to "be strong" only helps the "helpers" deny the truth of the dying experience.

Both preparatory and reactive depressions are frequently accompanied by unrealistic self-recrimination, shame, and guilt in the dying person. Those who are dying may judge themselves harshly and criticize themselves for the wrongs that they committed and for the good that they did not accomplish. They may judge themselves to be unattractive, unappealing, and repulsive because of how the illness and its treatment have affected them. These feelings and states of minds, which have nothing to do with the reality of the situation, are often amenable to the interventions of understanding and caring people. Financial and other obligations can be restructured and reassigned. Being forgiven and forgiving can help finish what was left undone.

Kübler-Ross's fifth stage, acceptance, is an intellectual and emotional coming to terms with death's reality, permanence, and inevitability. Ironically, it is manifested by diminished emotionality and interests and increased fatigue and inner (many would say spiritual) self-focus. It is a time without depression or anger. Envy of the healthy, the fear of losing all, and bargaining for another day or week are also absent. This final stage is often misunderstood. Some see it either as resignation and giving up or as achieving a happy serenity. Some think that acceptance is the goal of dying well and that all people are supposed to go through this stage. None of these viewpoints is accurate. Acceptance, when it does occur, comes from within the dying person. It is marked more by an emotional void and psychological detachment from people and things once held important and necessary and by an interest in some transcendental value (for the atheist) or god (for the theist). It has little to do with what others believe is important or "should" be done. It is when dying people become more intimate with themselves and appreciate their separateness from others more than at any other time.

EXISTENTIAL CONSIDERATIONS

Every person will eventually die, and the fact of death in each life is one that varies by culture in terms of its meaning. For some cultures, dying is seen as the ultimate difficulty for dying people and their loved ones. For other cultures, it is seen as not difficult at all, but more so like passing on to another realm of existence. In Western cultures, however, dying has very much become a medical process, and it is often a process filled with challenging questions. Patients ask questions that cannot be answered; families in despair and anger seek to find cause and sometimes to lay blame. It takes courage to be with individuals as they face their deaths, struggling to find meaning in the time that they have left. Given this, in Western medicine, a profession that prides itself on how well it intervenes to avoid outcomes like death, it takes courage to witness the process and struggle involved in death. Working with death also reminds professionals of their own inevitable death. Facing that fact inwardly, spiritually, and existentially also requires courage.

Cure and treatment become care and management in the dying. They should live relatively pain-free, be supported in accomplishing their goals, be respected, be involved in decision making as appropriate, be encouraged to function as fully as their illness allows, and be provided with others to whom control can comfortably and confidently be passed. The lack of a cure and the certainty of the end can intimidate health care providers, family members, and close friends. They may dread genuine encounters with those whose days are knowingly numbered. Yet the dying have the same rights to be helped as any of the living, and how a society assists them bears directly on the meaning that its members are willing to attach to their own lives.

Today, largely in response to what dying patients have told researchers, medicine recognizes its role to assist these patients in working toward an appropriate death. Caretakers must determine the optimum treatments, interventions, and conditions which will enable such a death to occur. For each terminally ill person, these should be unique and specific. Caretakers should respond to the patient's needs and priorities, at the patient's own pace and as much as possible following the patient's lead. For some dying patients, the goal is to remain as pain-free as is feasible and to feel as well as possible. For others, finishing whatever unfinished business remains becomes the priority. Making amends, forgiving and being forgiven, resolving old conflicts, and reconciling with one's self and others may be the most therapeutic and healing of interventions. Those who are to be bereaved fear the death of those they love. The dying fear the separation from all they know and love, but they fear as well the loss of autonomy, letting family and friends down, the pain and invasion of further treatment, disfigurement, dementia, loneliness, the unknown, becoming a burden, and the loss of dignity.

The English writer C. S. Lewis said that bereavement is the universal and integral part of the experience of loss. It requires effort, authenticity, mental and emotional work, a willingness to be afraid, and an openness to what is happening and what is going to happen. It requires an attitude that accepts, tolerates suffering, takes respite from the reality, reinvests in whatever life remains, and moves on. The only way to cope with dying or witnessing the dying of loved ones is by grieving through the pain, fear, loneliness, and loss of meaning. This process, which researcher Stephen Levine has likened to opening the heart in hell, is a viscous morass for most, and all people need to learn their own way through it and to have that learning respected. Healing begins with the first halting, unsteady, and frightening steps of genuine grief, which sometimes occur years before the "time of death" can be recorded.

BIBLIOGRAPHY

Becker, Ernest. *The Denial of Death.* New York: Free Press, 1997. Written by an anthropologist and philosopher, this is an erudite and insightful analysis and synthesis of the role that the fear of death plays in motivating human activity, society, and individual actions. A profound work.

Cook, Alicia Skinner, and Daniel S. Dworkin. *Helping the Bereaved: Therapeutic Interventions for Children, Adolescents, and Adults.* New York: Basic Books, 1992. Although not a self-help book, this work is useful to professionals and nonprofessionals alike as a review of the state of the art in grief therapy. Practical and readable. Of special interest for those becoming involved in grief counseling.

Corr, Charles A., Clyde M. Nabe, and Donna M. Corr. *Death and Dying, Life and Living.* 6th ed. Belmont, Calif.: Wadsworth/Cengage Learning, 2009. This book provides perspective on common issues associated with death and dying for family members and others affected by life-threatening circumstances.

Forman, Walter B., et al., eds. *Hospice and Palliative Care: Concepts and Practice.* 2d ed. Sudbury, Mass.: Jones and Bartlett, 2003. A text that examines the theoretical perspectives and practical information about hospice care. Other topics include community medical care, geriatric care, nursing care, pain management, research, counseling, and hospice management.

Kübler-Ross, Elisabeth, Ed. *Death: The Final Stage of Growth.* Reprint. New York: Simon & Schuster, 1997. A psychiatrist by training, Kübler-Ross brings together other researchers' views of how death provides the key to how human beings make meaning in their own personal worlds. Addresses practical concerns over how people express grief and accept the death of those close to them, and how they might prepare for their own inevitable ends.

Kushner, Harold. *When Bad Things Happen to Good People.* 20th anniversary ed. New York: Schocken Books, 2001. The first of Rabbi Kushner's works on finding meaning in one's life, it was originally his personal response to make intelligible the death of his own child. It has become a highly regarded reference for those who struggle with the meaning of pain, suffering, and death in their lives.

McFarlane, Rodger, and Philip Bashe. *The Complete Bedside Companion: No-Nonsense Advice on Caring for the Seriously Ill*. New York: Simon & Schuster, 1998. A comprehensive and practical guide to caregiving for patients with serious illnesses. The first section deals with the general needs of caring for the sick, while the second section covers specific illnesses in depth. Includes bibliographies and lists of support organizations.

Paul Moglial

See Also: Bereavement; Death attitudes;Grief; Life expectancy; Mortality.

Deception and lying

Type of psychology: Developmental psychology

Although universal and ubiquitous in human social interaction, deception and lying can become problematic and need to be treated as a psychological condition either when the patient is unable to differentiate between the truth and lying or when the behavior becomes pervasive.

Key Concepts

- Dissimulation
- Machiavellian intelligence
- Mythomania
- Polygraph
- Psuedologia fantastica
- Psychological deception
- Simulation

INTRODUCTION

Deception is an attempt to convince another person that false information is true. Also referred to as subterfuge or beguilement, deception always involves manipulation and is concerned with ideas such as concealment, propaganda, and distraction. Often it can be hard to differentiate deception from the unintentional dissemination of false information because people are often easily self-deceived. Dissimulation is a form of deception involving concealment such as camouflage, which is visual concealment and often used by the military, and disguise, in which a person pretends to be somebody else. Simulation is a form of deception involving mimicry, which is often unconscious. Fabrication involves objects that are not what they appear to be. One psychological study found that 90 percent of Americans admitted to being deceitful. Police officers go to great lengths to discover the truth and often, although it is not 100 percent accurate, turn to polygraph to determine if a suspect is lying by recording physiological responses to pertinent questions.

A lie, whether oral or written, is simply an untruthful statement. Typically, the person who tells the lie intends the other person to believe the false information is true. Lies are usually meant to preserve a secret, maintain a reputation, protect another's feelings, or avoid punishment. Although other forms of deception, such as disguises or forgeries, are not considered to be lies, the objective nevertheless remains the same. Lies can be categorized as bold-faced lies, white lies, fabrications, perjury, bluffing, misleading statements, exaggerations, or dissembling.

Studies in social psychology and developmental psychology point out that in human development, the capacity for lying is universal. Indeed, Machiavellian intelligence, defined as a common milestone in human development, occurs around the age of four. At this point, children begin to lie convincingly enough for adults to believe them. Before this, children have not developed the cognitive ability to grasp the concept that others do not see the world as they do and their attempts at lying are too outlandish to be believed. Although children may successfully lie, at this developmental stage, they have not yet developed the moral framework necessary to understand the consequences of lying and generally lie to avoid punishment.

The oath that requires witnesses in courtrooms to tell "the truth, the whole truth, and nothing but the truth" recognizes that people do indeed lie. It is only after they become mature and exposed to various forms of lying that children come to understand the concepts of deception and lying. Lying among children varies greatly, but by early adulthood, it becomes understood that in many manifestations, lying is a normal part of social interchange and is not problematic. However, psychiatrists and psychologists warn that deception and lying can become habitual or compulsive.

DECEPTION IN PSYCHOLOGY

Deception and lying can be symptoms of psychiatric conditions. Pseudologia fantastica is the term used by psychiatrists to define habitual or compulsive lying. Mythomania is a condition characterized by an excessive or abnormal propensity for exaggeration. Patients experiencing delusion cannot differentiate between the truth and lies, but pathological liars recognize that they are giving out false information. Pathological lying, which has an internal root cause, is persistent, and pathological liars generally create stories that contain elements of truth and present the teller in a positive light. It remains uncertain whether pathological liars have control over the lies they tell. Psychiatrists and psychologists point out that in the case of pathological lying, it is not the nature of the lies that is problematic but rather the mental state associated with the behavior, and that patients who communicate false information in a delusional state are not lying because they are not deliberately misleading.

Although deception and lying can be treated as psychiatric disorders, at times psychiatrists and psychologists practice deception and lying themselves, often in experimental settings. For instance, deception was used in the famous 1963 experiment by Yale psychologist Stanley Milgram to determine the willingness of people to obey an authority figure. Participants were told they were participating in an experiment on learning and memory. They were commanded to administer increasingly forceful electrical shocks when other subjects answered questions incorrectly. However, the other subjects were not actually being hurt.

In the first decade of the twenty-first century, psychologists and psychiatrists advised the military on how to use psychological deception or warfare in the wars in Afghanistan and Iraq. Psychological warfare is defined as using propaganda and other psychological techniques for the purpose of influencing the behavior of hostile foreign groups to achieve national objectives. Some of the psychological methods employed in interrogation techniques received a certain level of criticism from members of the public.

BIBLIOGRAPHY

Akhtar, Salman, and Henri Parens, eds. *Lying, Cheating, and Carrying On: Developmental, Clinical, and Sociocultural Aspects of Dishonesty and Deceit.* Lanham: Aronson, 2009. Print.

Ariely, Dan. *The (Honest) Truth about Dishonesty: How We Lie to Everyone—Especially Ourselves.* New York: Harper, 2012. Print

Ford, Charles V. *Lies! Lies! Lies! The Psychology of Deceit.* Washington: Amer. Psychiatric, 1996. Print.

Knapp, Mark L. *Lying and Deception in Human Interaction.* Boston: Allyn, 2008. Print.

Lee, Kang. "Little Liars: Development of Verbal Deception in Children." *Child Development Perspectives* 7.2 (2013): 91–96. Print.

Pettit, Michael. *The Science of Deception: Psychology and Commerce in America.* Chicago: U of Chicago P, 2013. Print.

Rogers, Richard, ed. *Clinical Assessment of Malingering and Deception.* 3rd ed. New York: Guilford, 2008. Print.

Smith, David Livingstone. *Why We Lie: The Evolutionary Roots of Deception and the Unconscious Mind.* New York: St. Martin's, 2004. Print.

Vrij, Aldert. *Detecting Lies and Deceit: Pitfalls and Opportunities.* 2nd ed. Chichester: Wiley, 2008. Print.

M. Casey Diana

SEE ALSO: Factitious disorders; Milgram experiment; Misbehavior; Munchausen syndrome and Munchausen syndrome by proxy; Research ethics; Repressed memories.

Decision making

TYPE OF PSYCHOLOGY: Cognition

Because decision making is such a common and important human activity, it appears in theories of behavior in nearly every area of psychology. Behavioral decision researchers have been able to explain a variety of behaviors in terms of the cognitive processes involved in making decisions..

KEY CONCEPT

- Descriptive theory
- Heuristic
- Normative theory
- Preference
- Rationality
- Utility

INTRODUCTION

Much of what people do, with the exceptions of reflexive and habitual behavior, results from the cognitive processes of deciding. Even a minor decision, such as whether to drive a car, take the bus, or walk to work, involves the coordination of many complex processes. In making this choice, one might take into consideration one's perception of the weather, guilt about contributing to air pollution, feeling of physical energy, goal of obtaining more exercise, memory of a recent bus trip, desire for company, or judged likelihood of working late. Even such a relatively minor decision can be difficult to make because there are numerous considerations, and some favor one alternative while remaining considerations favor other alternatives. In addition, the decision maker cannot know all relevant information, so there is uncertainty about the outcomes of important events.

A major goal of decision research is to understand the rules that people use in choosing from alternatives. This often means gaining insight into the decision processes that are used when no alternative is clearly preferred. To accomplish this, it is necessary to understand what is meant by a rule and to identify different potential rules for selecting one of a set of alternative courses of action. Some rules are heuristics, or strategies for simplifying choice that limit the evaluation of alternatives. Heuristics can be very efficient. In the transportation example above, if one used a heuristic, one might consider only the amount of time available for getting to work. Such a simplistic analysis of the problem can, however, lead to a poor decision. In other words, the employee might have more regrets after using this heuristic than would be the case if he or she had made a more careful analysis of the alternatives.

DECISION THEORIES

Decision theory has a long history of identifying normative procedures for decision making. These procedures tell people what rules they should follow in making decisions. A standard rule is to take into account two dimensions for each decision alternative: likelihood and utility. This principle, which is embodied in subjective expected utility theory, is intended to maximize the personal value of one's anticipated outcomes. A person may be given a choice between a 50 percent chance of winning $100 and a certain $2. The first alternative has an expected outcome of $50 (calculated by 50 percent of $100 = $50), since that is what one would expect to win on average if one played this game many times. The other alternative has an expected outcome of $2 (calculated by 100 percent of $2 = $2). Subjective expected utility theory indicates that one should choose the first alternative, the 50 percent chance of $100, because it has a higher expected outcome. This choice is called "rational" in the sense that it is the choice that is likely to maximize earnings.

The cognitive approach to decision making emphasizes an understanding of the ways in which various factors influence the choices that people make in reality, regardless of whether they follow normative principles. In contrast to the normative approach, the cognitive approach is focused on description of the actual processes that people use. A person may be given a 30 percent chance of $100 or a certain $20. Calculations based on likelihood and value dictate that one should choose the first alternative, since its anticipated outcome of $30 (30 percent of $100 = $30) is more than $20. Many people, however, simply do not want to take the risk of receiving nothing with the first alternative, preferring the security of knowing that they will receive $20 to the uncertainty of getting $100 or nothing. The possibility of an additional $10 is not worth the risk. This is not necessarily "irrational." As this example shows, normative decision theory cannot predict what many or even most people will choose. For this reason, psychologists have become increasingly interested in examining the processes that people actually use to make decisions.

ILLUSIONS AND HEURISTICS

Of particular interest in the cognitive approach to decision making are those factors that lead to miscalculations of likelihood or utility, since they will ultimately contribute to undesirable outcomes. Psychologists Amos Tversky and Daniel Kahneman revolutionized the field of decision making by identifying factors that contribute to poor decision making. Some of these may be called "cognitive illusions," because they lead a decision maker to a judgment that is in fact a distortion of reality. One type of judgment that is often affected by such illusions concerns likelihood estimation, the chance of an event leading to a particular outcome.

Another type of judgment that is susceptible to illusionary distortion is the estimation of quantity or frequency. In making these estimations, people often use heuristics. In a heuristic for estimating quantity called anchoring and adjustment, one takes any available number as an initial starting point or anchor and then adjusts it to arrive at an estimate. For example, one might predict tomorrow's temperature by taking today's temperature and adjusting downward for forthcoming rainfall. Although heuristics can be more efficient than the careful and comprehensive analysis of relevant information, they can also be misleading.

Illusions and heuristics can be detrimental to good decision making because they lead the decision maker to a distorted view of the problem and available alternatives. It is often possible to develop procedures for improving the decision-making process. Elaborate technologies have been developed to assist people in making decisions in nearly every area. Sometimes it is instructive, however, merely to understand the processes that people use and to know their limitations. It must be kept in mind that evaluating the quality of decisions is difficult. One reason for this difficulty is that some decisions that are made with great care, thought, and objectivity can still have disappointing outcomes, while luck can operate to bring favorable outcomes despite poor decision processes. The ultimate key to improving human judgment and decision making is research that integrates normative and descriptive theories.

EXPECTANCY, UTILITY, AND MOTIVATION

The principles of subjective expected utility theory have been applied in a wide variety of problem areas. A distinction between expectancy and utility can be quite useful. For example, two people who choose to continue to smoke may do so for different reasons. One may truly believe that he or she has a high chance of developing a serious disease such as lung cancer; however, that person may anticipate great medical advances and expect that lung cancer will be only a mild problem by the time he or she is diagnosed with it. Though the expectation of a negative outcome is high, the outcome is not particularly negative to this individual. Another person may be convinced that lung cancer will continue to be a painful, expensive, deadly disease within his or her lifetime. Despite the fact that this outcome has great negative utility for this person, he or she may continue to smoke due to an expectation that he or she will not develop lung cancer. Each of these individuals is influenced by different factors. Understanding how the decision to smoke or to quit is made can assist health advocates—and tobacco advertisers—in influencing these decisions.

One of the areas in which subjective expected utility principles have been highly influential is that of motivation. While early theories of motivation viewed behavior as the result of basic drives or personality traits, subsequent theories emphasized the ways in which people thought about their options. From this perspective, it is meaningless to label someone "unmotivated." Everyone is motivated, in the sense that all people have time and effort to give to activities. People choose how much time and effort to give to each of the various options open to them: work, leisure, and family activities. Employees who do little or no work do not necessarily lack "drive" or have flawed personalities. They have simply decided to spend their time and effort on other things. This does not excuse or overlook the workers' lack of productivity, but it does suggest methods to alter their lack of performance. The key is to understand how they judge the utilities of outcomes that result from working and their perceived likelihood of obtaining these outcomes by choosing to put time and effort into work activities. Thus, the study of decision making is important to organizational efforts to enhance productivity.

BIASES IN DECISION MAKING

In one sense, it is easy to observe instances of illusions and heuristics that lead to biases in decision making in real life. Bad decisions seem to be everywhere. As noted, however, decisions that turn out badly may sometimes result from badly made decisions. People are accustomed to judging the actions of others and will label them irrational if it appears that they are choosing alternatives with inferior outcomes for themselves. During the Persian Gulf War of 1991, the American media frequently concluded that Saddam Hussein was "irrational" because he chose not to withdraw from Kuwait by the United Nations deadline. Though it is tempting to label an enemy irrational, it is wise to keep in mind a serious problem in determining irrationality in a decision maker: it is exceedingly difficult to assess the utility of any alternative for the decision maker. By American standards, it would have been better for Iraqi forces to withdraw from Kuwait before suffering enormous loss of life and eventually being forced to withdraw anyway, so it seemed that Hussein could not possibly be evaluating the alternatives realistically. Either he did not understand the potential magnitude of the human and economic losses that would result from a failure to withdraw or he did not understand the virtual certainty of losing the war. Hussein may, however, have understood both perfectly and simply have attached different utilities to the outcomes anticipated from withdrawal versus war. Perhaps from Hussein's perspective, the loss of life could be offset easily by the opportunity to show himself to the Arab world as someone who stood up to the international community, if only briefly.

Scientific investigations of biases in decision making require that the investigator prove that a given alternative is superior to the one that is chosen by most people. This is often done by means of mathematics or statistics. In one demonstration of the representativeness bias, people are given a brief personality sketch of "Linda" and asked to determine how likely it is that Linda is a member of various categories. Most people tend to judge Linda as more likely to be a bank teller and a feminist than merely a bank teller. In fact, however, there must be at least as many bank tellers as there are feminist bank tellers, since the category "bank teller" will contain all feminist bank tellers as well as all nonfeminist bank tellers. The illusion comes from the erroneous conclusion that because Linda's personality traits represent both the occupation of a bank teller and the political perspective of a feminist, she is more likely to be both than one or the other. Research such as this helps to determine how people can jump to conclusions and misjudge someone. Overestimating the likelihood that a person belongs to two categories diminishes one's ability to estimate appropriately the expected utilities of alternatives for decisions about that person.

DECISIONS IN THE WORKPLACE AND DAILY LIFE

Numerous forces have come together to fuel the study of human decision making as a cognitive process. One of these is the coming of the information age. With the transition from a production economy to a service economy, workers are no longer seen as people who engage in only physical work; rather, workers at all levels deal with information and decisions. It is no longer possible to attribute all the difficulty of making decisions to insufficient information, as decision makers are often overloaded and overwhelmed by information. The real problem they face is knowing which information to select and how to integrate it into the decision-making process.

Within psychology, two areas of study that have had a great impact on behavioral decision making are perception and quantitative psychology. Both Kahneman and Tversky did extensive work in the area of perception before becoming interested in studying the cognitive processes in human judgment and decision making. Many other behavioral decision researchers began their studies in quantitative psychology or statistics. The primary objective in this area is to learn how to make decisions under uncertainty using the laws of probability. Because this is what people routinely face in the course of their work and daily lives, there are many intriguing parallels between statistics and behavioral decision making.

Advances in understanding the rationality of human decision making were furthered, ironically, by economic theories that assumed rationality on the part of human decision makers. Psychologists who conducted empirical studies of people had data to show that many choices that people make do not follow rational economic models. For example, standard economic theory predicts that people will choose the option that maximizes their own payoff. Yet people often prefer a plan that they deem fair to everyone over one that is financially superior for themselves. Behavioral decision theory attempts to understand the way in which people actually make decisions, not the way that formal models say that they should.

BIBLIOGRAPHY

Ariely, Dan. *Predictably Irrational: The Hidden Forces That Shape Our Decisions*. New York: Harper, 2008. Print.

Connolly, Terry, Hal R. Arkes, and Kenneth R. Hammond, eds. *Judgment and Decision Making: An Interdisciplinary Reader.* 2nd ed. New York: Cambridge UP, 2000. Print.

Del Missier, Fabio, Timo Mäntlyä, and Wändi Bruine de Bruin. "Decision-Making Competence, Executive Functioning, and General Cognitive Abilities." *Journal of Behavioral Decision Making* 25.4 (2012): 331–51. Print.

Dewberry, Chris, Marie Juanchich, and Sunitha Narendran. "Decision-Making Competence in Everyday Life: The Roles of General Cognitive Styles, Decision-Making Styles and Personality." *Personality and Individual Differences* 55.7 (2013): 783–88. Print.

Hastie, Reid, and Robyn M. Dawes. *Rational Choice in an Uncertain World: The Psychology of Judgement and Decision Making*. Thousand Oaks: Sage, 2010. Print.

Moore, Karen O., and Nancy P. Gonzalez, eds. *Handbook on Psychology of Decision-Making: New Research.* New York: Nova Sci., 2012. Print.

Pammi, V. S. Chandrasekhar, and Narayanan Srinivasan. *Decision Making: Neural and Behavioural Approaches.* Amsterdam: Elsevier, 2013. Print

Plous, Scott. *The Psychology of Judgment and Decision Making*. New York: McGraw, 1993. Print.

Russo, J. Edward, and Paul J. H. Schoemaker. *Decision Traps: The Ten Barriers to Brilliant Decision-Making and How to Overcome Them.* New York: Simon, 1990. Print.

Slovic, Paul, Sarah Lichtenstein, and Baruch Fischhoff. "Decision Making." *Stevens' Handbook of Experimental Psychology.* Ed. Richard C. Atkinson et al. 2nd ed. Vol. 2. New York: Wiley, 1988. 673–738. Print.

Tversky, Amos, and Daniel Kahneman. "Judgment under Uncertainty: Heuristics and Biases." *Science* 185.4157 (1974): 1124–31. Print.

Janet A. Sniezek

See Also: Artificial intelligence; Cognitive development: Jean Piaget; Cognitive maps; Computer models of cognition; Consumer psychology; Deductive reasoning; Group decision making; Inductive reasoning; Logic and reasoning; Problem-solving stages; Problem-solving strategies.

Deductive reasoning

Type of psychology: Cognition

Deductive reasoning is a type of logic that moves from the general to the specific to make a conclusion. It requires that the general facts be true for the conclusion to be true. Deductive reasoning is used in most sciences, mathematics, debating, and argumentative writing.

Key Concepts

- Fallacy
- Geometry
- Inductive reasoning
- Logic
- Syllogism

INTRODUCTION

Deductive reasoning is a method for analyzing a situation using general, proven facts to validate a more specific conclusion. The usual format for deductive reasoning is the syllogism, which is a logical argument with three statements: the major premise, the minor premise, and the conclusion Both the major premise and the minor premise must be true for the conclusion to be true.

Deductive reasoning starts with a known fact, such as "all fish have gills," to which is added a second statement of proven fact, such as "a barracuda is a fish." The third statement uses the first two to prove that "a barracuda has gills." Deductive reasoning requires that the first two statements be true. If one or both are false, then the third statement is also false. An example of this would be "all fish have gills; a dolphin is a fish; therefore a dolphin has gills." The conclusion is false because the minor premise is false: a dolphin is a mammal, not a fish, and it does not have gills.

Deductive reasoning and its counterpart, inductive reasoning, are part of the philosophy of logic. Logic is a way of presenting arguments and then demonstrating the proof of those arguments using deductive reasoning, inductive reasoning, or some other method. The philosophy of logic studies reasoning, probability, and arguments that lead to demonstrating the cause of an occurrence. In addition, logic includes the study of fallacies, validity, and paradoxes.

APPLICATIONS

Deductive reasoning is used in numerous different areas of study. Geometric theorems use known characteristics about an object to determine what it is. Debaters and analytical writers use deductive reasoning to support their positions; research studies use it to either prove or disprove the theory that they are testing. Sciences such as medicine, biology, chemistry, and meteorology use deductive reasoning as well. In medicine, signs and symptoms are first determined, and from them a diagnosis is made. Biology uses the characteristics of a creature to determine its classification. In chemistry, a solution is tested, and the results are then used to determine the chemicals that make up the solution. A meteorologist looks at cloud types, wind-flow position and direction (the jet stream), and weather in the area to forecast the weather for the future.

At times, what appears to be a logical conclusion based on deductive reasoning turns out to be incorrect. This faulty reasoning can occur because of illegitimate or irrelevant points, lack of information, or biased evidence. Some faulty reasoning is based on emotions or fear. Such an error in reasoning can happen when a medical patient has some of the symptoms of a disease but not all of them, or when the person's signs and symptoms are too general to make a correct diagnosis. If there is a strong need to make a diagnosis so that treatment can begin, a physician may be forced to evaluate the signs and symptoms that are available to make a diagnosis.

HISTORY

Deductive reasoning began in the Greek classical period, which dates from 600 to 300 BCE. It was developed and described by philosophers such as Aristotle, Thales, and Pythagoras, among others. Aristotle's writings on logic were the beginning of the use of the syllogism for the evaluation of judgments. During this period, examples of deductive reasoning included predicting the likelihood of crop success or failure and determining the accuracy of statements made by politicians.

BIBLIOGRAPHY

Baum, Robert. *Logic*. 4th ed. Fort Worth: Harcourt, 1996. Print.

Dutilh Novaes, Catarina. "A Dialogical Account of Deductive Reasoning as a Case Study for How Culture

Shapes Cognition." *Journal of Cognition and Culture* 13.5 (2013): 459–82. Print.

Evans, Jonathan St. B. T., and David E. Over. "Reasoning To and From Belief: Deduction and Induction Are Still Distinct." *Thinking & Reasoning* 19.3 (2013): 267–83. Print.

Lande, Nelson P. *Classical Logic and Its Rabbit-Holes: A First Course*. Indianapolis: Hackett, 2013. Print.

Pine, Ronald C. *Essential Logic: Basic Reasoning Skills for the Twenty-First Century.* New York: Oxford UP, 1996. Print.

Rips, Lance J. *The Psychology of Proof: Deductive Reasoning in Human Thinking*. Cambridge, Mass.: MIT P, 1994. Print.

Salmon, Merrilee H. *Introduction to Logic and Critical Thinking*. 6th ed. Boston: Wadsworth, 2012. Print.

Schaeken, Walter, et al., eds. *Deductive Reasoning and Strategies*. Mahwah: Erlbaum, 2000. Print.

Seay, Gary, and Susana Nuccetelli. *How to Think Logically.* 2nd ed. Boston: Pearson, 2012. Print.

Walton, Douglas. *Methods of Argumentation*. New York: Cambridge UP, 2013. Print.

Christine M. Carroll

See Also: Cognitive psychology; Decision making; Inductive reasoning; Logic and reasoning.

Defense mechanisms

Type of psychology: Consciousness; Emotion; Personality

Defense mechanisms are used to safeguard the individual from unbearable anxiety. They are part of normal development but can become problematic if overused.

Key Concepts

- Anxiety
- Denial
- Displacement
- Introjection
- Object relations theory
- Projection
- Reaction formation
- Repression
- Splitting
- Sublimation

INTRODUCTION

The concept of defense mechanisms was originally proposed in the early twentieth century by Sigmund Freud, the father of psychoanalysis, who described them as ways to protect a person from experiencing overwhelming anxiety by keeping unacceptable impulses and thoughts from coming into conscious awareness. Anxiety is an unpleasant state of emotional distress signaling impending danger and is quite difficult to tolerate. According to Freud, anxiety is experienced when there is internal conflict or conflict between the self and external reality. Defense mechanisms distort reality, allowing people to feel less anxious.

REPRESSION

Repression was considered by Freud to be the primary defense mechanism, operating unconsciously by pushing down anxiety-provoking ideas and wishes, thus blocking them from awareness. This process, which requires a constant use of psychic energy to prohibit these dangerous ideas from reaching the conscious level, is normal except when used to an extreme degree.

COMMON DEFENSE MECHANISMS

In 1946, Anna Freud expanded on her father's work in this area and elaborated on specific defense mechanisms that may be used by the ego to minimize anxiety. In addition to repression, the ego may use other defense mechanisms, such as denial, reaction formation, projection, introjection, displacement, or sublimation.

Denial is characterized by a refusal to believe in the reality of an event as an attempt to cope with an external threat. For example, a person may deny a spouse's illicit affair despite clear evidence or signs of its occurrence. Denial also operates when someone refuses to acknowledge addiction or a serious medical condition. This defense can be used adaptively when it helps a person remain positive in a situation in which there is no possibility of remedy, such as having a terminal illness.

Reaction formation is used when a person deals with anxiety-laden feelings by repressing those feelings and consciously emphasizing the opposite. It can often be detected when a response or behavior is overdone and disproportionate to the context. For example, an individual may display exaggerated love and affection to conceal feelings of intense hatred or dislike.

Another important defense mechanism is projection, in which unacceptable anxiety-provoking feelings, impulses, and desires are conveniently attributed to someone else. Often, projection allows a person to not acknowledge an undesirable aspect of the self, yet see this characteristic and even vehemently dislike it in another person. Paranoid people, for example, may project unacceptable feelings of dislike or hatred onto others, thus believing that others hate them and are untrustworthy and dangerous. In so doing, paranoid people do not have to acknowledge their own hateful feelings, which cause anxiety and perhaps guilt. Introjection works in the opposite way by taking in or incorporating desirable aspects of another person, which can help minimize anxiety and feelings of inadequacy.

The defense mechanism of displacement redirects unacceptable sexual and aggressive impulses to a substitute target that is much less threatening. A classic example is when a man frustrated with his supervisor comes home and kicks the dog in anger. Dangerous impulses are thus directed toward a person or object considered safe, and anxiety is reduced.

Sublimation, often considered to be a more mature defense mechanism, transforms the direct expression of the instinct into a higher, more socially acceptable and useful form. Whereas the other defense mechanisms benefit only the individual, sublimation has the potential to benefit both the individual and society. For example, artists may redirect sexual energy into creative outlets that provide personal pleasure and societal edification.

DEFENSES AND OBJECT RELATIONS THEORY

Object relations theory further develops Freud's ideas, emphasizing the importance of the inner world and its impact on relationships with objects (others). Melanie Klein, considered by many to be the most influential object relations theorist, expanded on Freud's instinct theory and stressed the importance of human contact and the relational aspect of early infantile development. Patterns of relating to others are developed in childhood and recur throughout life.

Based on her observations of young children, Klein proposed that defense mechanisms start in infancy, helping the infant cope with feelings of anxiety associated with this period of extreme vulnerability and helplessness. Introjection is the process of incorporating or taking in good and bad external objects. Good (gratifying) objects are introjected to protect against anxiety by providing a good aspect of the self. Bad (frustrating) objects are taken in as a way to gain control and to maintain the positive perception of the needed other. Projection refers to the process of getting rid of good and bad internal objects. Destructive impulses are projected outside, allowing the infant to seemingly get rid of persecutory bad feelings and maintain a sense of inner goodness. Good internal feelings can also be projected, allowing the infant to attribute goodness to others. Splitting keeps the bad and the good apart and initially helps the infant to develop without unbearable anxiety. With maturity, one is able to experience others with ambivalence, having both good and bad qualities, rather than as all good (idealized) or all bad (devalued).

BIBLIOGRAPHY

Burgo, Joseph. *Why Do I Do That? Psychological Defense Mechanisms and the Hidden Ways They Shape Our Lives.* Chapel Hill: New Rise, 2012. Print.

Delgado, Sergio V., and Jeffrey R. Strawn. *Difficult Psychiatric Consultations: An Integrated Approach.* Heidelberg: Springer, 2014. Print.

Feist, Jess, Gregory J. Feist, and Tomi-Ann Roberts. *Theories of Personality.* 8th ed. New York: McGraw, 2013. Print.

Flanagan, Laura Melano. "Object Relations Theory." *Inside Out and Outside In: Psychodynamic Clinical Theory and Psychopathology in Contemporary Multicultural Contexts.* Ed. Joan Berzoff, Flanagan, and Patricia Hertz. 3rd ed. Lanham: Rowman, 2011. 118–57. Print.

Freud, Anna. *The Ego and the Mechanisms of Defense.* Rev. ed. New York: International UP, 1974. Print.

Klein, Melanie, and Joan Riviere. *Love, Hate, and Reparation.* New York: Norton, 1964. Print.

Roth, Priscilla. "The Paranoid-Schizoid Position." *Kleinian Theory: A Contemporary Perspective.* Ed. Catalina Bronstein. Philadelphia: Whurr, 2001. 32–46. Print.

Sekiya, Hideko, et al. "Object Relations in Adolescence: A Comparison of Normal and Inpatient Adolescents." *Psychiatry and Clinical Neurosciences* 66.4 (2012): 270–75. Print.

Sweet, Alistair D. "The Automaton Self: Defensive Organisation, Psychodynamics and Treatment Approaches." *Psychodynamic Practice* 17.4 (2011): 387–402. Print.

Joanne Hedgespeth

See Also: Anxiety disorders; Denial; Ego defense mechanisms; Freud, Anna; Freud, Sigmund; Freudian psychology; Paranoia; Projection; Repressed memories.

Defense reactions
Species-specific

Type of psychology: Learning

All animal species employ maneuvers and deceptive tactics to protect themselves from conspecific competitors, predators, and parasites. These defensive reactions include alarm calls, flocking or herding, mimicry, bluffing, displays, and aggressive counterattacks. Defensive mechanisms vary from species to species, but some defensive tactics are common throughout the animal kingdom.

Key Concepts

- Alarm
- Competition
- Display
- Dominance hierarchy
- Flocking
- Mimicry
- Pheremone
- Predation
- Prey density
- Saturation

INTRODUCTION

All living organisms live within complicated food and energy webs in which energy is transferred from organism to organism through consumption. Plants convert energy from sunlight to manufacture organic nutrients. Herbivorous animals eat plants to obtain this energy, and carnivorous animals eat herbivores and other carnivores to obtain the same energy. Within an animal species, individuals compete with one another for available food and natural resources to survive; in the process, they establish dominance hierarchies in which dominant individuals overpower subordinates. Among different species, interactions occur that lead to predation (an interspecific interaction in which the individuals of one animal species hunt and kill members of another species for food), disease, and parasitism; in each case, one species is feeding on another species.

Intraspecific competition and interspecific predation and parasitism represent principal animal behaviors important to the evolution of life. Each species possesses an innate (instinctive) drive to survive and to continue the transmission of its deoxyribonucleic acid (DNA) in space and time. Within the food webs of the living environment, each species evolves specific adaptations for survival that enable it to carve out a particular habitat, or place to live, and niche, or occupation, in the environment. Because the food webs of life on Earth are circular, the evolution of competition and predation are necessary for life to continue. All species will become predators (hunters) of certain other species and will simultaneously be prey (the hunted) for certain different species.

LEARNED AND GENETIC ADAPTATIONS

To survive, each species possesses specific adaptations for hunting its prey and for defending itself from predators. Defensive mechanisms come in many different varieties. Some very effective defense mechanisms are highly conserved between different species; other defenses are unique to only one or a few species. Of these defenses, some are instinctive, occurring automatically because of biochemical changes within individual animals, whereas others are learned from environmental experiences. Learned defensive mechanisms are prevalent in highly social mammal and bird species.

Intraspecific competition occurs among individuals of a given population or group and among different populations or groups. Within a population, the social structure is either genetically or behaviorally conditioned to construct castes or dominance hierarchies in which dominant individuals are superior to more subordinate individuals. The social insects (such as ants, termites, bees, and wasps), whose behavior is almost exclusively genetic in nature, construct their societies, or hives, around castes that have specific jobs to perform. Such societies revolve around a central fertile queen, sterile female workers, and male drones. Workers are subdivided into several specializations, such as hunting for food and defending the hive. Soldier workers have specialized body structures for attacking intruders; furthermore, they release pheromones (hormonal attractants) from their bodies at the sign of danger to attract other soldier workers to the region of intrusion.

DOMINANCE HIERARCHIES

Within the highly social and intelligent mammal and bird species, populations either migrate in bands or groups or set up individual adjacent territories that are heavily defended by the owner. In either of these situations, learned dominance hierarchies are established in which stronger individuals outcompete weaker individuals, thereby establishing a "pecking order" (as it is called for chickens) of precisely ranked dominant individuals to progressively more subordinate individuals. The dominant individuals possess the best territory, the most food, and the most mates. The most dominant individuals also have the best protection from predators, because their territories are central and therefore are shielded by the territories of more subordinate individuals. Consequently, the most subordinate individuals have the worst territories, poor food, few if any mates, and poor protection from predators, which usually attack outskirt territories. These territories are maintained by constant fighting among males, especially during the breeding season. Males vocalize and present visual displays (visual dances or series of movements or gestures by individuals to communicate such things as dominance, aggression, and courtship to other individuals) to force their opponents to submit; submission is routine, and few encounters are fatal.

PREDATOR-PREY INTERACTIONS

In interspecific predator-prey interactions,the prey utilize a variety of quick-response defenses. One of the most common defenses is the flocking or herding defense. When a predator approaches a group of prey and is identified, the discovering prey individual announces danger by a vocalization (an alarm call), specific movement, or the release of chemical pheromones to warn the other members of the group. The prey group response is instantaneous, with all members contracting into a dense mass. A predator is less likely to succeed in capturing a prey individual during an attack on a compact group than when the prey individuals are scattered. Furthermore, the predator may sustain personal physical damage in an attack on a compact group, which easily could turn on the predator. Most predators are far more successful at capturing very young, old, or sickly individuals that are isolated or located at the poorly defended outskirts of a prey group. Some predators, such as hawks, falcons, and wolves, do make repeated passes at compact groups in sometimes successful attempts at panicking individuals and thereby scattering the group. Flocking behavior is a very effective defense that is utilized by bees, fish, tadpoles, most bird species, and most mammal species. Prey species usually utilize excellent vision, hearing, and sense of smell.

The dynamics of predator-prey interactions can be complicated, although numerous mathematical models of such relationships have been developed that enable researchers to make predictions concerning future interactions in natural populations. Predator-prey interactions are important for the stability and survival of both predator and prey populations. Without prey, predators would die; however, without predators, prey populations would grow unchecked until they exceeded the available resources in the environment, ending in a massive population crash in which many individuals would die. Such occurrences have been thoroughly documented in many species, including moose, deer, rabbit, and even human populations. Defensive mechanisms are important to all species to ensure the survival of enough members of each species population to reproduce and continue the transmission of the species' genetic information. Perfect defense, however, could be as detrimental to the population as no defense. Numerous mathematical ecologists have developed impressive models of animal population growth based on predator-prey interactions. Among the most famous models are those that were developed by Alfred Lotka and Vito Volterra, and they still are in use. Such models are of critical importance to the study of human overpopulation.

ANIMAL DEFENSE MECHANISMS

Other species-specific defense mechanisms include camouflage, mimicry (an inherited or behavioral defense phenomenon in which an individual of a species either looks dangerous to its predators or can exaggerate its appearance to fool a predator), predator saturation (a defensive mechanism in some animal species in which a prey animal population synchronizes its growth so that it becomes too large for predators to consume any significant fraction of the population), and long-term incubation. Most species have adaptations in skin and fur coloration to blend in with their particular environment. For example, albino hares and squirrels predominate in areas that have snow for a good portion of the year, whereas the same species in more temperate climates usually have a grayish-brown coloration. Zebras have a striped pattern that enables them to blend with tall grass; many mammalian predators (lions, wild dogs) are color blind. Some species (the chameleon, for example) can alter their body color to their background through biochemical changes in their skin. Some lizard species simply discard body parts, such as their tails, when captured by predators.

Müllerian mimicry is a phenomenon used by moths and butterflies to defend themselves from bird predators. A few butterfly species with bright orange-black wings are poisonous; several dozen nonpoisonous species have coevolved bright black and orange or yellow wings and are therefore less likely to be eaten, since birds learn avoidance very quickly from only a few encounters with the poisonous varieties. Some species of fish, birds, and mammals have short, rapid bursts of reproduction, so that their predators are overwhelmed, or saturated, by the high prey densities. In both of these instances, some prey are eaten. The thirteen- and seventeen-year periodic locust species of North America combat predation by burrowing underground for many years before surfacing and reproducing within only a few weeks.

IMPLICATIONS FOR HUMAN SOCIETY

The study of species-specific defensive reactions is of intense interest to animal behavior researchers. Research into such behavior enables them to understand how highly adaptive and elaborate defenses have evolved in animal species over the past five hundred million years. These studies also have potential impact on the psychology of human behavior. Humans are very territorial animals and exhibit considerable competitive behavior, including interpersonal conflicts and aggression. Consequently, defense mechanism studies are strongly applicable to the study of human conflict, social tensions, and warfare. Furthermore, species-specific defense mechanisms are also of interest to medicine, since humans, while being the apparently dominant species on Earth, are subject to predation, particularly from parasitic bacterial, fungal, and viral diseases.

The explosion of human technological growth during the past century has included medical advances that have eradicated many diseases that once were major killers of humans. Medicine has been a tremendous artificial defense mechanism developed by the intelligence of the human species. It has defeated dozens of bacterial, fungal, and viral predators and parasites of humans. Because of these advances, humans live longer and better lives, human birthrates have soared, and human death rates have declined; however, the elimination of human predators has produced some serious problems. One is overpopulation. The explosive human population growth is approaching the planet's carrying capacity (the available food and resources). Some areas of the world, most notably Asia and Africa, have already seen human overpopulation far above the carrying capacity; the result has been devastating famines and millions of deaths. Furthermore, medical science is taxed by the appearance of new mutated viral and bacterial predators to replace the eradicated ones. The human immunodeficiency virus (HIV), which causes acquired immunodeficiency syndrome (AIDS), is an example. Furthermore, certain diseases, such as cholera, are on the rise worldwide. Life on Earth is very homeostatic (self-regulatory); it contains mechanisms for keeping populations of all species in check.

Leaving the microscopic scale, humans and other primates defend themselves from competitors and very large predators in much the same fashion. Humans have territories that each territory-holder defends. Furthermore, several dominant males may group to attack intruders and other predators. There can be no doubt that such behavior has evolved into the large armies that different countries have amassed to defend their territorial borders. The structure of many such armies is somewhat reminiscent of mammalian dominance hierarchies. The frontline soldiers who face the brunt of an opponent's attack usually are individuals who are less equipped and trained. They are sometimes called "cannon fodder." Better-trained, more dominant individuals follow; they are more likely to survive hostile encounters with the enemy.

Species-specific defensive behaviors are also applicable to human behavior in terms of social and personal relationships. Complex human societies are rigidly structured along territorial lines, with laws to regulate the behaviors of individuals. Cross sections through American cities reveal the segregation of the poor from the middle class from the rich, and the segregation of black from white from Hispanic. Individuals in each of these groups construct physical, social, and legal barriers to defend themselves from competition from outsiders. With overpopulation and competition for resources, individuals and countries resort to mechanical weapons ranging from handguns to semiautomatic rifles to atomic bombs. Stress, inequality, and mistrust of others involve biological reactions that have evolved over hundreds of millions of years.

Each animal species on Earth has evolved through the endurance of predator-prey interactions. Understanding how species defend themselves can be of great importance in helping endangered species to survive and in controlling the overpopulations of species and the spread of disease. It also can help humankind to alleviate many of its own species' social problems.

UNDERSTANDING ECOSYSTEMS

The study of species-specific defense mechanisms is of considerable interest to animal behaviorists and psychologists because of their implications for human behavior. All animal behaviors can be influenced by endogenous (instinctive) or exogenous (environmental) factors. Endogenous behaviors include imprinting and biochemical changes within the body of the individual that enable one to recognize events or situations instantaneously for survival. Behaviors such as recognizing danger are critical for survival and therefore must be instinctive. Within the intelligent and highly social mammals and birds, a period of learning during infancy enables the development of exogenous behaviors from experiences in one's immediate environment. Such learned behaviors are of equal importance in such species.

The study of species-specific defensive reactions allows scientists to uncover the intricacies of species interactions within the environment. In any given ecosystem (such as a forest, grassland, ocean, or desert), populations of thousands of different species are linked by intricate food webs. The destruction of the environment or the extinction of any one species can have irreparable effects on all the other species within the ecosystem. The defensive mechanisms of most species can work only so well.

BIBLIOGRAPHY

Andrewartha, Herbert George. *Introduction to the Study of Animal Populations.* 2d ed. Chicago: U of Chicago P, 1971. Print.

Choi, Charles Q. "Bug vs. Superbug." *Scientific American* 309.2 (2013): 24. Print.

Forbes, Peter. "Masters of Disguise." *Scientific American* 304.5 (2011): 80–83. Print.

Klopfer, Peter H., and Jack P. Hailman. *An Introduction to Animal Behavior: Ethology's First Century.* 2d ed. Englewood Cliffs: Prentice-Hall, 1974. Print.

Krebs, Charles J. *Ecology: The Experimental Analysis of Distribution and Abundance.* 5th ed. Reading: Addison, 2000. Print.

Lorenz, Konrad. *On Aggression.* Translated by Marjorie Kerr Wilson. New York: Routledge, 2002. Print.

Manning, Aubrey, and Marian Stamp Dawkins. *An Introduction to Animal Behavior.* 5th ed. New York: Cambridge UP, 2006. Print.

Marras, Stefano. "Schooling Fish Under Attack Are Not All Equal: Some Lead, Others Follow." *PLoS ONE* 8.6 (2013): 1–7. Print.

Wilson, Edward O. *Sociobiology: The New Synthesis.* 1975. 25th anniversary ed. Cambridge, Mass.: Belknap Press of Harvard UP, 2000. Print

David Watson Hollar, Jr.

See Also: Animal experimentation; Defense mechanisms; Ethology; Imprinting; Instinct theory; Learning.

Dementia

Type of psychology: Biological bases of human behavior; Cognitive; Developmental; Neuropsychological, psychopathology

While the concept of dementia has become much more common since 1906, when Alois Alzheimer described the first case of Alzheimer's disease, behaviors indicative of dementia were apparent in history books dating back to ancient Rome and Greece. Aristotle, Plato, and Hippocrates all referred to mental decline that inevitably accompanied old age. In the second century B.C., Cicero indicated that dotage, a decline in mental functioning, was not typical of all older adults but rather occurred only in those who were weak and did not remain mentally active. The first known use of the term dementia was by Celsus in the first century A.D. By the 17th century, different forms of dementia were recognized, and attempts were being made to find a biological basis for them. In 1776, the year of the American Revolution, senile dementia was first recognized as a medical disorder characterized by loss of memory with advancing age. Over the next century, problems with the blood supply to the brain were implicated in dementia. By 1906, Alzheimer had indicated that there were neurofibrillary plaques and tangles present in the brains of some people with dementia. These people were the first identified to have Alzheimer's disease. Over the past century, Alzheimer's disease and various other forms of dementia have garnered much attention as they have been diagnosed much more commonly as life expectancy has increased.

Key Concepts

- Alzheimer's disease
- Frontal lobe
- Organic brain syndrome
- Presenile dementia
- Senile dementia
- Senility
- Vascular dementia

INTRODUCTION

The terms dementia, senile dementia, and senility are often used interchangeably. The common denominator of these terms is underlying organic brain syndrome that generally brings about decreased cognitive functioning and memory loss in a manner that is severe enough to interfere with everyday life functioning. By definition, dementia is characterized by problems in at least two areas of brain function. The underlying biological basis relating to changes within the brain was clearly identified by Alzheimer in 1906. Since that time, greater understanding of these biological changes has developed. With that understanding, it has become increasingly clear that various types of dementia exist and that these are distinguishable by the type of biological deterioration that occurs. The majority of dementia symptoms are common to multiple disorders. These symptoms initially include decreased cognitive functioning, faulty reasoning, and memory loss and progress to changes in personality, loss of communication skills, and inability to manage personal hygiene.

FORMS OF DEMENTIA

While dementia is generally defined as organic brain syndrome that results in decreased cognitive functioning and memory loss in a manner severe enough that it interferes with everyday functioning, it is truly not a single disorder. To date there have been more than fifty different conditions identified that result in dementia. Generally dementia has been seen in older adults and therefore has been considered to be a typical result of the aging process. There are, however, many forms of dementia that present at earlier ages, and dementia is now recognized as a pathological condition that develops independently of age. Alzheimer's disease is the most common form of dementia, currently accounting for more than 60% of all known cases of dementia. In this type of dementia there is a buildup of neurofibrillary plaque consisting of beta-amyloid and tangles made up of the protein tau within the forebrain. The second most common known cause of dementia is damage to the blood vessels that feed the brain resulting in the condition known as vascular dementia or vascular cognitive impairment. This type of dementia occurs most commonly as a result of a stroke or mini-stroke (multi-infarct dementia) or as a result of the buildup of amyloid plaque building up in the blood vessels supplying the brain. It is currently thought that dementia with Lewy bodies is the third leading cause of dementia. In this disorder, abnormal deposits of protein in the brain progressively interfere with functioning. In the case where there is more than one underlying biological problem contributing to the cognitive decline, the condition is known as mixed dementia. Recent studies suggest that mixed dementia is much more common than previously thought. Other disorders, such as Parkinson's disease, Huntington's disease, Wernicke-Korsakoff syndrome, and Creutzfeldt-Jakob disease will lead to symptoms of dementia when the underlying disorders have progressed significantly. Traumatic brain injury (TBI), as a result of sports like football or boxing or vehicular accidents, is often linked to the underlying cause of some dementias. While most types of dementia are not reversible, conditions such as thyroid disease, certain brain tumors, some forms of hydrocephalus, and severe depression may produce symptoms of dementia that will disappear when the underlying condition is treated.

SYMPTOMS OF DEMENTIA

The signs and symptoms of dementia generally relate to loss of higher order cognitive functioning. Initially one may notice minor problems with memory like forgetting names or phone numbers progressing to difficulty remembering names for common objects. It is often difficult at first to differentiate between so-called normal memory loss and early dementia. With dementia there tends to be a relatively rapid progression of the disorder unlike normal memory loss accompanying age. Another differentiating factor tends to be that individuals without dementia are aware that they are forgetting, whereas people with dementia are unaware that a problem exists. Soon after, memory loss is often accompanied by impaired reasoning and judgment. Ability to follow directions and communicate becomes problematic. Following these symptoms, individuals often have difficulty carrying out activities of daily living. Individuals with dementia may suddenly seem unconcerned with personal hygiene. They may become disoriented to time and place. They very commonly remember things and people from their distant past, often mistaking children or grandchildren for their own parents or siblings. They may wander away easily and lose their way even in familiar areas. Eventually, they may even develop difficulty in their motor skills, limiting their mobility.

DIAGNOSIS AND TREATMENT OF DEMENTIA

Because more than 50 causes of dementia exist, it is important to determine which form is presenting. While there is no known cure for the primary dementias, some treatments can slow progression. Some secondary dementias may in fact be reversible. Neuropsychological testing can help establish the diagnosis and underlying cause because there are many other health problems that mimic dementia including medication interactions, nutritional deficiencies, and electrolyte imbalances. Many of these other disorders can be easily treated if they are identified. Currently, there are many types of dementia that are considered to have diagnoses of exclusion only. This includes Alzheimer's disease, which can only truly be diagnosed by the identification of neurofibrillary plaques and tangles in a cerebral biopsy performed during autopsy. It is therefore important to rule out all other possible diagnoses before determining that one has Alzheimer's disease or other types of dementia that are truly identifiable only after the death of the patient. Initially, neuropsychological testing should be done in order to evaluate the individual's cognitive functioning. This examination includes tests of attention, intelligence, memory, and concept formation. Following this testing, a neurological evaluation is typically completed in order to explore muscle and nerve functioning throughout the body, allowing one to uncover sensory and motor problems. Lab tests are done in order to check for hormone levels, electrolytes, or the presence of infection among other ailments. Genetic testing may be performed to check for certain alleles, like the presence of ApoE4 on chromosome 19, which may be indicative of a tendency to develop Alzheimer's disease. CT scans, PET scans, or MRIs will typically be done in order to identify structural problems. In some cases, this assortment of medical tests will help lead to a diagnosis. In other instances, the diagnosis of dementia is tentatively made and only finalized upon autopsy. When a presumptive diagnosis of dementia is made, there are certain medications that have been used to slow the progression of symptoms. These include a variety of cholinesterase inhibitors (e.g., Aricept, Cognex, Exelon) along with drugs that block the glutamatergic system (e.g., Memantine). While these drugs do not stop or reverse the progression of the disease, there is a great deal of ongoing research to determine ways to successfully deal with the neurofibrillary plaques and tangles often found in dementia.

BIBLIOGRAPHY

Atkins, S. (2015). *Dementia for dummies.* Chichester, UK: Wiley. A straightforward, easy read dealing with the various forms of dementia and their causes and symptomatology, highlighting both similarities and differences.

Boiler, F. & Forbes, M.M. (1998). History of dementia and dementia in history: An overview. *Journal of the Neurological Sciences*, 158(2), 125-133. This article reviews a brief history of dementia dating back to ancient Greece and follows its progress to the present. The work of Alois Alzheimer is reviewed and connected to present day views on dementia. Attempts are made to predict future works on dementia based on progress to date.

Berchtold, N. C., & Cotman, C. W. (1998). Evolution in the conceptualization of dementia and Alzheimer's disease: Greco-Roman period to the 1960's. *Neurobiology of Aging*, 19(3), 173-189. This article presents an in-depth history of the field of dementia dating 2000 years ago. It highlights the progression of the disorder from the time when it was viewed as mental deterioration that occurred as one got older for some unexplainable reason to the present day where the biological basis of dementia is understood but the disorder is still not curable.

Fife, B. (2011). *Stop Alzheimer's now!: How to prevent and reverse dementia, Parkinson's, ALS, multiple sclerosis & other neurodegenerative disorders.* Colorado Springs, CO: Picadilly Books. This book is written for the layperson yet presents an in-depth description of the biological and chemical changes that take place in organic brain syndromes and related neuromuscular disorders. It presents ideas as to how one can cope with these disorders focusing on dietary changes that may slow the progression of the disorders.

McKhann, G. M., Knopman, D. S., Chertkow, H., Hyman, B. T., Jack, C. R., Kawas, C. H., ... Phelps, C. H. (2011). The diagnosis of dementia due to Alzheimer's disease: Recommendations from the National Institute on Aging-Alzheimer's Association workgroups on diagnostic guidelines for Alzheimer's disease. *Alzheimer's & Dementia,* 7, 263-269. This journal in its entirety focuses on dementia and Alzheimer's disease. In this article, the National Institute on Aging's revised guidelines related to the diagnosis of Alzheimer's disease are reviewed in depth.

Robin Kamienny Montvilo

See Also: Adulthoot; Aging; Alzheimer's disease; Attention; Memory; Motorskills; Senility; Visual perception.

Denial

Type of psychology: Cognition; Consciousness; Developmental psychology; Emotion; Motivation; Psychopathology; stress

Denial is a cognitive mechanism in which aspects of reality are kept out of conscious awareness. It can serve as a defense against painful emotions or result from neurological impairment. It has an important emotional function in managing trauma and in coping with severe physical illness, particularly cancer.

Key Concepts

- Alienation
- Anosdiaphoria
- Anosognosia
- Confabulation
- Disavowal
- Negation
- Repression

INTRODUCTION

The term "denial" originally described a psychological defense in which aspects of reality were kept out of a subject's consciousness. In the strict sense, the person who denies something acts as if it does not exist. For example, a person with cancer looks in the mirror at a large facial tumor, blandly claims to see nothing there, does not seek medical care, and does not attend to the wound.

TYPES OF DENIAL

Over time, the term has been broadened and refined, and related terms have been introduced. "Disavowal" is essentially a synonym, translated from Sigmund Freud's use of the German word Verleugnung. Denial and disavowal include internal emotions; for example, unacceptable anger toward a parent who died. There is also denial of the emotional meaning of external events, such as the failure by Jews in the Warsaw Ghetto to recognize the relevance to them posed by Nazi genocide in other areas, even as they recognized the facts of what was happening. One can deny personal relevance, urgency, danger, emotion, or information. In each example, the subject has an unconscious emotional motivation for not allowing something into awareness.

To some degree, all defenses help a person avoid awareness of some part of the self or external reality. To this extent, denial is the cornerstone of the ego's defensive functions. In denial, however, the excluded idea or feeling is not available to the subject in any form. In contrast, related ego defenses allow greater conscious and preconscious awareness of the avoided elements.

"Repression" is a related term for a psychological defense in which an emotionally charged fact is temporarily ignored and held out of consciousness but can emerge easily. For example, a student who knows he has bad grades on a report card may "forget" to bring home his school backpack containing the grades. However, he will be aware of a nagging feeling of something amiss and instantly remember that he has left it at school when questioned.

Similarly, "negation" refers to a defense in which a fact is allowed into consciousness but only in the negative. An example would be someone who states, "I'm not jealous. I really admire all that she has." By allowing the possibility of jealousy but negating one's connection to it, denial of the emotion is maintained. In contrast, in true denial the idea of jealousy could not be allowed in consciousness at all.

Denial functions to prevent the individual from becoming overwhelmed by the threatening aspects of a situation. If the emotional impact of something is too great, it is initially kept out of awareness. Patients diagnosed with a terminal illness often respond with denial when they first receive this news. After the destruction of the World Trade Center towers in 2001, some Americans denied the facts of the huge buildings' collapse into dust, maintaining hope of survivors being found far beyond what could be medically expected, to soften the impact of that magnitude of loss.

Denial can be adaptive or maladaptive. Adaptive denial allows a person to function in a situation of unavoidable pain or danger. Maladaptive denial worsens functioning because action is needed on the denied elements. For example, in Roberto Benigni's film *La Vita é Bella* (1997; *Life Is Beautiful,* 1998), a father and son are in a German concentration camp in World War II. The father translates German commands incorrectly for his son, making up a game in which they must do certain things truly demanded by the Germans to get a big prize. By denying the danger and the meaning of the subjugation they face, he protects his son from overwhelming fear, humiliation, and anger. His denial is also adaptive because his son is still able to function as he must to survive. Ultimately, however, the father's denial becomes maladaptive for him. He becomes too wrapped up in the story to accommodate a changing situation and makes mistakes that result in his death.

Common examples of adaptive denial include disavowal of one's eventual death or the degree of risk in daily behaviors such as driving a car. Common examples of maladaptive denial include a substance abuser's refusal to see a problem or a teenager's denial of the risk in experimental behavior. In empirical studies, for example, smokers rate the health risk of smoking, especially for themselves, lower than do nonsmokers.

NEUROLOGY OF DENIAL

Denial can also result from neurological impairment. Anosognosia is a phenomenon common to patients with right hemispheric stroke in which they fail to recognize (neglect) or seem indifferent to anything located to their left. This can be visual—objects held up, words, or their own body parts—as well as tactile or auditory. For example, they will not shave the left side of the face, will forget to wear a left shoe, or will read only "girl" if shown the word "schoolgirl." Alienation is an extreme version of this, in which patients fail to recognize their own body parts. Shown their left arm, they may say, "Yes, it is attached to my left shoulder, but it is not mine," or "That is your arm, doctor." They maintain this view even when confronted. For example, when asked, "Is this not your wedding ring on this hand?" they may answer, "Yes, doctor. Why are you wearing my ring?" Anosodiaphoria is a related syndrome in which the patient recognizes he or she is paralyzed but denies the emotional significance of the inability to move.

Denial and neglect of this type are most often associated with lesions of the right inferior parietal lobule, a brain area thought important in the circuitry of the general arousal response that allows people to attend to stimuli from the opposite side. The cingulate gyrus and right thalamus have also been associated with this deficit. That these lesions are part of more global self-awareness and arousal circuits, however, is demonstrated by the disease of Wernicke-Korsakoff syndrome. In Wernicke-Korsakoff syndrome, caused by alcoholism, there is no discrete brain lesion. The individual loses the ability to form new memories and will confabulate, that is, make up stories about his or her life and also make up answers to questions, while appearing to deny any awareness that the stories are not true. Anton's syndrome is another denial syndrome, associated with bilateral occipital blindness, in which the individual believes and acts as if he or she is not blind.

The use and consequences of denial in cancer patients have been extensively studied. The majority of the studies suggest that people with heavier use of denial as a personality trait have an increased risk of breast, melanoma, and other cancers. Such people show increased levels of physical stress, such as blood pressure changes, when confronted with disturbing stimuli, but they are more likely not to report feeling upset. Chronic stress such as this, particularly linked to anger, is likely connected to changes in immune function and other physical events that compromise tumor suppression. Such people also tend to delay going to the doctor for diagnosis and treatment, further worsening prognosis.

In contrast, patients who deny their emotional reactions while in the state of recent diagnosis of cancer tend to have complied with treatment and report less emotional distress when evaluated months later. Their denial helps them not be overwhelmed by the traumatic news that they have cancer. Thus it appears that, in cancer patients, denial as a reaction to an acute threat promotes physical and mental health, while denial as a general coping strategy does not.

HISTORY OF DENIAL

Psychoanalyst Sigmund Freud first described the concept of disavowal, or Verleugnung, in 1923, in developing his notions of infantile sexuality. He said that children see a little girl's lack of a penis but "disavow" this fact and believe they see one anyway. He believed children later accept that the girl lacks a penis but are traumatized by this awareness, which Freud linked to female penis envy and male castration anxiety. Freud described a similar disavowal in writing about the fetishist in 1927. He believed fetishists choose a fetishistic object to replace a penis and thereby deny female castration in external reality but also experience anxiety if the object is not available, showing internal awareness of castration.

Freud believed that all human capacity to say "no" was fueled by the death instinct. He linked denial to three other types of "saying no": projection, negation, and repression. Because disavowal most rejects external reality, however, he thought that it "split the ego" and was the first step toward psychosis. It was also the most extreme form of negation.

Anna Freud also wrote about denial as a basic defense that was normal in children but not in adults. René Spitz described a developmental course to the infant's ability to say no. He took the infant who closes his eyes or falls asleep in an intensely stimulating or upsetting environment as the prototype for later forms of denial. Head-shaking and hiding behind a parent are later forms of denial. Spitz thought that denial expressed in this way was the first abstract thought of the infant because it involves imagining an alternative option to the current reality. He also noted its positive role in promoting independence, both in infants and in adolescents. Contemporary theorists such as Theodore Dorpat and Charles Brenner have refined notions of the psychological mechanism of denial and its subtypes, and they have struggled to distinguish how it differs from and underlies other psychological defenses. Others have studied the effects of denial in different populations, such as cancer patients. In everyday clinical practice, psychoanalysts and psychologists work with individual patients to determine when denial must be broken through to promote the individual's self-acceptance and mental and physical health, and when denial should not be confronted to avoid overwhelming a person with painful feelings. In this ongoing work, the understanding of denial remains at the core of the understanding of human coping and defense.

BIBLIOGRAPHY

Becker, Ernest. *The Denial of Death.* London: Souvenir, 2011. Print.

Edelstein, E. L., D. L. Nathanson, and A. M. Stone, eds. *Denial: A Clarification of Concepts and Research.* New York: Plenum, 1989. Print.

Freud, Anna. *The Ego and the Mechanisms of Defense.* New York: International UP, 1974. Print.

Gillick, Muriel R. *The Denial of Aging: Perpetual Youth, Eternal Life, and Other Dangerous Fantasies.* Cambridge: Harvard UP, 2007. Print.

Heffernan, Margaret. *Willful Blindness: Why We Ignore the Obvious at our Peril.* New York: Walker, 2011. Print.

Kreitler, S. "Denial in Cancer Patients." *Cancer Investigation* 17.7 (1999): 514–34. Print.

Trivers, Robert. *The Folly of Fools: The Logic of Deceit and Self-Deception in Human Life.* New York: Basic, 2011. Print.

Zerubavel, Eviatar. *The Elephant in the Room: Silence and Denial in Everyday Life.* New York: Oxford UP, 2007. Print.

Elizabeth Haase

See Also: Cancer and mental health; Defense mechanisms; Ego defense mechanisms; Emotions; Freud, Anna; Freud, Sigmund; Freudian psychology; Guilt; Psychoanalytic psychology and personality: Sigmund Freud.

Depression

Type of psychology: Psychopathology

The study of depression has focused on biological underpinnings, cognitive concomitants, stress and coping style precursors, and interpersonal context.

Key Concepts

- Bipolar disorder
- Major depressive episode
- Manic episode
- Unipolar depression

INTRODUCTION

Almost everyone gets "down in the dumps" or has "the blues" sometimes. Feeling sad or dejected is clearly a normal part of the spectrum of human emotion. This situation is so common that a very important issue is how to separate a normal "blue" or "down" mood or emotion from an abnormal clinical state. Most clinicians use measures of intensity, severity, and duration of these emotions to separate the almost unavoidable human experience of sadness and dejection from clinical depression.

Depression is seen in all social classes, races, and ethnic groups. It is so pervasive that it has been called "the common cold of mental illness" in the popular press. It is approximately twice as common among women as it is among men. Depression is seen among all occupations, but it is most common among people in the arts and humanities. Famous individuals such as U.S. president Abraham Lincoln and British prime minister Winston Churchill had to cope with depression; Churchill called the affliction "the black dog." Beach Boy Brian Wilson, journalist Mike Wallace, actors Owen Wilson and Brooke Shields, and musicians Kurt Cobain and James Taylor were known to have bouts of serious depression.

Of all problems that are mentioned by patients at psychological and psychiatric clinics, some form of depression is most common. It is estimated that approximately 25 percent of women in the United States will experience at least one significant depression during their lives. Contrary to a popular misconception that depression is most common among the elderly, it is actually most common in twenty-five- to forty-four-year-olds. About 10 percent of the college population report moderate depression, and 5 percent report severe depression. Suicidal thoughts are common in depressive clients.

DSM-IV-TR CRITERIA FOR MAJOR DEPRESSION

Major Depressive Episode

Five or more of the following symptoms present during the same two-week period and representing a change from previous functioning:

- depressed mood or loss of interest or pleasure (at least one); does not include symptoms clearly due to a general medical condition, mood-incongruent delusions, or hallucinations
- depressed mood most of the day, nearly every day, as indicated by either subjective report or observation made by others; in children and adolescents, can be irritable mood
- markedly diminished interest or pleasure in all, or almost all, activities most of the day, nearly every day, as indicated by either subjective account or observation made by others
- significant weight loss (when not dieting) or weight gain or decrease/increase in appetite nearly every day; in children, consider failure to make expected weight gains
- insomnia or hypersomnia nearly every day
- psychomotor agitation or retardation nearly every day observable by others, not merely subjective feelings of restlessness or being slowed down
- fatigue or loss of energy nearly every day
- feelings of worthlessness or excessive or inappropriate guilt (which may be delusional) nearly every day, not merely self-reproach or guilt about being sick
- diminished ability to think or concentrate, or indecisiveness, nearly every day, either by subjective account or as observed by others
- recurrent thoughts of death (not just fear of dying), recurrent suicidal ideation without a specific plan, or suicide attempt or specific plan for committing suicide

Criteria for Mixed Episode not met

Symptoms cause clinically significant distress or impairment in social, occupational, or other important areas of functioning

Symptoms not due to direct physiological effects of a substance or general medical condition

Symptoms not better accounted for by bereavement, persist for longer than two months, or characterized by marked functional impairment, morbid preoccupation with worthlessness, suicidal ideation, psychotic symptoms, or psychomotor retardation

Major Depressive Disorder, Single Episode (DSM code 296.2x)

Presence of single Major Depressive Episode

Major Depressive Episode not better accounted for by Schizoaffective Disorder and not superimposed on Schizophrenia, Schizophreniform Disorder, Delusional Disorder, or Psychotic Disorder Not Otherwise Specified

No Manic Episodes, Mixed Episodes, or Hypomanic Episodes, unless all manic-like, mixed-like, or hypomanic-like episodes are substance- or treatment-induced or due to direct physiological effects of a general medical condition

Specify for current or most recent episode: Severity/ Psychotic/Remission Specifiers; Chronic; with Catatonic Features; with Melancholic Features; with Atypical Features; with Postpartum Onset

Major Depressive Disorder, Recurrent (DSM code 296.3x)

Presence of two or more Major Depressive Episodes; with an interval of at least two consecutive months in which criteria not met for Major Depressive Episode

Major Depressive Episodes not better accounted for by Schizoaffective Disorder and not superimposed on Schizophrenia, Schizophreniform Disorder, Delusional Disorder, or Psychotic Disorder Not Otherwise Specified

No Manic Episodes, Mixed Episodes, or Hypomanic Episodes, unless all manic-like, mixed-like, or hypomanic-like episodes are substance- or treatment-induced or due to direct physiological effects of a general medical condition

Specify for current or most recent episode: Severity/ Psychotic/Remission Specifiers; Chronic; with Catatonic Features; with Melancholic Features; with Atypical Features; with Postpartum Onset

Specify: Longitudinal Course Specifiers (with and Without Interepisode Recovery); with Seasonal Pattern

In long-term follow-up, it has been found that approximately 15 percent of depressed individuals eventually kill themselves. Alternatively viewed, approximately 60 percent of suicides are believed to be caused by depression or by depression in association with alcohol abuse. As has been vividly portrayed in the media, teenage suicide in the United States is increasing at an alarming rate.

The role of family or genetic factors in depression was addressed long ago by Robert Burton in *The Anatomy of Melancholy* (1621), in which he noted that the "inbred cause of melancholy is our temperature, in whole or part, which we receive from our parents" and "such as the temperature of the father is, such is the son's, and look what disease the father had when he begot him, his son will have after him." More than 350 years later, the role of family factors in depression was addressed in a major collaborative study in the United States. In what was called the National Institute of Mental Health Collaborative Study of the Psychobiology of Depression, a large number of standardized instruments were developed to assess prevalence and incidence of depression, life histories, psychosocial stressors, and outcome of depression. The family members of depressed persons were assessed along with the depressed individual. It was found that bipolar depression was largely confined to relatives of individuals with bipolar disorder. Unipolar depression, however, was common among relatives of both unipolar- and bipolar-depressed individuals. The different patterns of familial transmission for bipolar and unipolar disorders strengthen the general conviction that these two disorders should be kept distinct from each other.

One explanation for increased vulnerability to depression in close relatives of depressed individuals is an inherited deficiency in two key components of brain chemistry: norepinephrine and serotonin, both of which are neurotransmitters. If depressions could be reliably subtyped according to the primary neurotransmitter deficiency, the choice of antidepressant medication would logically follow. Research is conflicting, however, on whether there is one group of depressed individuals who are low in norepinephrine and normal in serotonin and another group of depressives who are low in serotonin and normal in norepinephrine. Future developments in the study of neurotransmitters may have practical implications for the matching of particular pharmacotherapy interventions with particular types of depression. Evidence does indicate that for many depressed patients, substantial alteration in neurotransmitter activity occurs during their depression. This altered activity may directly mediate many of the disturbing symptoms of depression.

COGNITIVE AND STRESS THEORIES

A different approach to understanding depression has been put forward by cognitive theorists. According to Aaron T. Beck, in *Cognitive Therapy and the Emotional Disorders* (1979), cognitive distortions cause many if not most of a person's depressed states. Three of the most important cognitive distortions are arbitrary inference, overgeneralization, and magnification and minimization. Arbitrary inference refers to the process of drawing a conclusion from a situation, event, or experience when there is no evidence to support the conclusion or when the conclusion is contrary to the evidence. For example, an individual concludes that his boss hates him because he seldom says positive things to him. Overgeneralization refers to an individual's pattern of drawing conclusions about his or her ability, performance, or worth based on a single incident. An example of overgeneralization is an individual concluding that she is worthless because she is unable to find her way to a particular address (even though she has numerous other exemplary skills). Magnification and minimization refer to errors in evaluation that are so gross as to constitute distortions. Magnification refers to the exaggeration of negative events; minimization refers to the underemphasis of positive events.

According to Beck, there are three important aspects of these distortions or depressive cognitions. First, they are automatic—that is, they occur without reflection or forethought. Second, they appear to be involuntary. Some patients indicate that these thoughts occur even though they have resolved not to have them. Third, the depressed person accepts these thoughts as plausible, even though others would clearly not view them in the same manner.

While there is ample empirical support for the association of depression and negative cognitive factors such as cognitive distortions, irrational beliefs, and negative statements about oneself, research that demonstrates the ability of cognitive variables to predict subsequent depression is just beginning. It appears that a cognitive vulnerability plays a role in symptom formation for at least some individuals and in the maintenance of ongoing episodes of depression for many, if not all, depressed persons.

Yet another approach to understanding depression focuses on stress and coping. James Coyne, in a 1991 article, suggests that depression may be understood as a failure to cope with ongoing life problems or stressors. It has been hypothesized that coping effectively with problems and stressors can lessen the impact of these problems and help prevent them from becoming chronic. Depressed patients show slower recovery if they display poor coping skills. Avoidance coping strategies appear to be particularly likely in depression and are one example of poor coping. Depressed persons also show elevated levels of emotion-focused coping strategies, such as wishful thinking, distancing, self-blame, and isolation. These strategies also tend to be ineffective. Although most forms of coping are impaired during an episode of depression, only self-isolation, an interpersonal avoidance strategy, appears to be an enduring coping style of persons vulnerable to depression. Thus, coping processes appear to change for the worse during an episode of depression, and poor coping helps to maintain the episode. In particular, depressed persons appear likely to avoid problem situations and to engage in strategies with a low likelihood of resulting in problem resolution or an enhanced sense of personal control.

Interpersonal approaches to understanding depression are related to stress and coping models but highlight the interpersonal environment as particularly important in depression. There is considerable evidence that low levels of social support are related to depression. Perhaps the relationship between social support and depression results from the fact that depressed persons do not seek social support; however, there is also evidence that poor social support leads to or maintains depressive symptomatology. In particular, evidence links the absence of close relationships with the development of depressive symptomatology. Accordingly, the work on general social support and depression can be seen as pointing in the direction of direct consideration of intimate relationships and their role in depression. Since the strongest family ties are usually in the marital relationship, it is natural to look to the marital relationship for particularly powerful opportunities to provide social support. Indeed, there is considerable evidence of an association between marital discord and depression. It had been expected by some that the association between marital discord and depression would be greater for women than men; however, it is generally equivalent between sexes when one looks across studies. Indeed, the risk of having a major depressive episode is approximately twenty-five times higher for both men and women if they are in a discordant marital relationship than if they are in a nondiscordant marital relationship.

TREATMENT METHODS

There are a number of ways to understand depression, and each approach appears to have something to offer. Given the distressing nature of depression, it is not surprising that these differing approaches have led in turn to several effective ways of treating depression.

Pharmacological interventions for unipolar depression have sometimes been held to normalize a genetically determined biochemical defect; the evidence, however, does not support this extreme biological characterization of unipolar depression. Yet neurotransmitters may directly mediate many of the behaviors affected in depression (for example, sleep, appetite, and pleasure), and neurotransmitter level and activity are disturbed as a concomitant of many episodes of depression. Hence, the use of antidepressant agents that influence neurotransmitter level or activity should be helpful in reducing or eliminating symptoms of depression even if the disturbance in neurotransmitter level or activity is itself the result of environmental or cognitive changes. In addition, there is considerable direct evidence that antidepressants can be useful in the treatment of depression in many cases. In controlled trials, both more recently developed and older forms of antidepressants provided improvement rates of 66 to 75 percent, in contrast to placebos, which showed improvement rates of 30 to 60 percent. Exactly for whom they will work, however, and exactly how or why they work are still not entirely clear.

A second effective approach to the treatment of depression can be found in cognitive therapy. It has become clear that altering cognitions and behavior in a cognitive behavioral format can relieve an ongoing episode of depression and may reduce the likelihood of relapse further than the use of psychopharmacology alone. Thus, cognitive processes are, at a minimum, reasonable targets of intervention in the treatment of many depressed patients. In addition, cognitive therapy appears to work well at decreasing depressive symptomatology even in the context of ongoing marital discord. Thus, for many depressed patients, interventions targeted at altering dysfunctional, negative automatic thoughts are likely to be useful.

Finally, interpersonal psychotherapy (IPT) Interpersonal psychotherapy has been developed by Gerald Klerman. This successful approach emphasizes abnormal grief, interpersonal disputes, role transitions, loss, and interpersonal deficits, as well as social and familial factors. Results of a large, multicenter collaborative study conducted by the National Institute of Mental Health (NIMH) indicated that IPT can work as well as antidepressant medication for many depressed patients. In addition, earlier research indicated that IPT can improve the social functioning of depressed patients in a manner not typically produced by antidepressant medications alone. Given the interpersonal problems that are often part of a depressive episode, these improvements in social functioning and interpersonal environment appear to be particularly important for depressed persons. In a related development, marital therapy has been tested as a treatment for depressed persons who are maritally discordant, and it appears to be successful.

FROM MELANCHOLY TO PROZAC

The identification of depression as a recognizable state has a very long history. Clinical depression was described as early as the eighth century b.c.e. in the biblical descriptions of Saul. During the fourth century b.c.e., Hippocrates coined the term "melancholy" to describe one of the three forms of mental illness he recognized. Later, Galen attempted to provide a biochemical explanation of melancholy based on the theory of "humors." Indeed, repeated descriptions and discussions of depression are present from classical times through the Middle Ages and into modern times.

The first comprehensive treatment of depression in English was provided by Timothy Bright's *Treatise of Melancholia* (1586). In 1621 Robert Burton provided his own major work on depression, *The Anatomy of Melancholy.* Most of the credit for developing the modern understanding of affective disorders, however, is given to Emil Kraepelin, a German psychiatrist. It was in Kraepelin's system that the term "depression" first assumed importance.

Since classical times, there has been debate about whether depression is best considered an illness or a response to an unhappy situation. Indeed, it is obvious to the most casual observer that sadness is a normal response to unhappy events. Even now, there is less than

DSM-IV-TR CRITERIA FOR DYSTHYMIC DISORDER (DSM CODE 300.4)

Depressed mood for most of the day, more days than not, indicated either by subjective account or observation by others, for least two years

In children or adolescents, mood can be irritable and duration must be at least one year

Presence, while depressed, of two or more of the following:

- poor appetite or overeating
- insomnia or hypersomnia
- low energy or fatigue
- low self-esteem
- poor concentration or difficulty making decisions
- feelings of hopelessness

During this two-year period (one year in children or adolescents), person has never been without symptoms for more than two months at a time

No Major Depressive Episodes during this two-year period (one year in children or adolescents)

Disturbance not better accounted for by chronic Major Depressive Disorder or Major Depressive Disorder, in Partial Remission

Previous Major Depressive Episode is possible, provided there was full remission (no significant signs or symptoms for two months) before development of Dysthymic Disorder

After initial two years (one year in children or adolescents) of Dysthymic Disorder, superimposed episodes of Major Depressive Disorder are possible; in that case, both diagnoses may be given when criteria are met for Major Depressive Episode

No Manic Episodes, Mixed Episodes, or Hypomanic Episodes

Criteria not met for Cyclothymic Disorder

Disturbance does not occur exclusively during the course of a chronic Psychotic Disorder, such as Schizophrenia or Delusional Disorder

Symptoms not due to direct physiological effects of a substance or general medical condition

Symptoms cause clinically significant distress or impairment in social, occupational, or other important areas of functioning

Specify: Early Onset (before age twenty-one) or Late Onset (age twenty-one or older)

Specify for most recent two years: with Atypical Features

DEPRESSION IN CHILDREN

Possible signs:

- frequent sadness, tearfulness or crying
- withdrawal from friends and activities
- lack of enthusiasm or motivation
- decreased energy level
- major changes in eating or sleeping habits
- increased irritability, agitation, anger or hostility
- frequent physical complaints such as headaches and stomachaches
- indecision or lack of concentration
- feelings of worthlessness or excessive guilt
- play that involves excessive aggression directed toward oneself or others or that involves persistently sad themes
- recurring thoughts of death and suicide or self-destructive behavior

complete agreement on when fluctuations in mood should be considered pathological and when they are within normal limits. To help resolve this problem, diagnostic criteria have been developed, and structured interview procedures are often used to determine whether a particular individual should be considered depressed.

In the American Psychiatric Association's *Diagnostic and Statistical Manual of Mental Disorders: DSM-IV-TR* (rev. 4th ed., 2000), a common diagnostic tool, unipolar depression is divided into the categories dysthymic disorder, major depressive disorder-single episode, and major depressive disorder-recurrent, while bipolar depression is divided into bipolar I disorder, bipolar II disorder, cyclothymic disorder, and bipolar disorder not otherwise specified (NOS). In most articles, the term "depression" refers to unipolar depression only. Because unipolar depression is much more common than bipolar depression, it is likely that it will continue to attract a larger share of research attention in the future.

Throughout history, models of depression have become increasingly sophisticated, progressing from Hippocrates' theory that depression was produced by an excess of black bile to modern biochemical, cognitive, coping, stress, and interpersonal models. In the future, even more sophisticated models of depression may provide guidance for the next great challenge facing clinical psychology: reversing the trend in Western societies toward ever-increasing rates of depression.

BIBLIOGRAPHY

Beach, Stephen R. H., E. E. Sandeen, and K. D. O'Leary. *Depression in Marriage*. New York: Guilford, 1990. Summarizes the literature on basic models of depression. Provides the basis for understanding the important role of marriage in the etiology, maintenance, and treatment of depression.

Beck, Aaron T. *Cognitive Therapy and the Emotional Disorders*. 1976. Reprint. London: Penguin, 1991. Clearly lays out the basics of the cognitive model of depression. An important start for those who wish to understand the cognitive approach more thoroughly.

Burns, David D. *Feeling Good: The New Mood Therapy*. Rev. ed. New York: William Morrow, 2002. Provides a very entertaining and accessible presentation of the cognitive approach to depression. Presents basic results and the basics of cognitive theory, as well as a practical set of suggestions for getting out of a depression.

Coyne, James C., ed. *Essential Papers on Depression*. New York: New York University Press, 1985. Includes representatives of every major theoretical position advanced between 1900 and 1985. Each selection is a classic presentation of an important perspective. This source will acquaint the reader with the opinions of major theorists in their own words.

Coyne, James C., and G. Downey. "Social Factors and Psychopathology: Stress, Social Support, and Coping Processes." *Annual Review of Psychology* 42 (1991): 401-426. This influential essay ties together stress and coping with interpersonal processes to provide a deeper understanding of the nature of depression. Also provides an account of advances in the way both depression and interpersonal processes related to depression may be studied.

Gordon, James. *Unstuck: Your Guide to the Seven-Stage Journey Out of Depression*. New York: Penguin Press, 2008. A psychiatrist trained at Harvard Medical School offers a program for getting out of depression that does not include taking medication.

Kleinman, Arthur, and Byron Good, eds. *Culture and Depression*. Berkeley: University of California Press, 1985. This exceptional volume examines the cross-cultural research on depression. Authors from anthropology, psychiatry, and psychology attempt to address the diversity that exists across cultures in the experience and expression of depression.

Paykel, Eugene S. *Handbook of Affective Disorders*. 2d ed. New York: Guilford, 1992. Provides comprehensive coverage of depression, mania, and anxiety in relation to depression. Includes detailed descriptions of symptoms, assessment procedures, epidemiology, and treatment procedures.

Solomon, Andrew. *The Noonday Demon: An Atlas of Depression*. New York: Charles Scribner's Sons, 2003. Solomon, who suffered serious depression himself, provides an insightful investigation of the subject from multiple perspectives of history, psychology, literature, psychopharmacology, law, and philosophy.

Stahl, Stephen M. *Essential Psychopharmacology of Depression and Bipolar Disorder.* New York: Cambridge University Press, 2000. Thorough coverage of the rapidly expanding options in drug treatments for depression.

Williams J. Mark G., John D. Teasdale, Zindel V. Segal, and Jon Kabat-Zinn. *The Mindful Way Through Depression: Freeing Yourself from Chronic Unhappiness.* New York: Guilford, 2007. The authors look at the reasons for depression and the negative thinking and self-doubt that plague those who suffer from it. They include of program of mindfulness techniques that offer relief from depression.

Stephen R. H. Beach

See Also: Abnormality: Biomedical models; Abnormality: Psychological models; Antidepressant medications; Bipolar disorder; Cognitive behavior therapy; Cognitive therapy; Coping: Social support; Drug therapies; Emotional expression; Emotions; Mood disorders; Psychopharmacology; Seasonal affective disorder; Suicide; Teenage suicide; Teenagers' mental health; Women's mental health.

Depth and motion perception

Type of psychology: Sensation and perception

Depth and motion perception are key aspects of visual perception. They aid in form recognition and play an important role in visually guided navigation..

Key Concepts

- Apparent motion
- Biological motion
- Corollary discharge theory
- Corresponding points
- Fusion
- Induced motion
- Monocular cues for depth
- Optic array
- Random-dot stereograms
- Stereopsis

INTRODUCTION

A person looking at the view from a high vantage point can easily perceive that some objects in the landscape below are closer than others. This visual discrimination appears to require no apparent skill; the information is contained in the light that enters the eyes after being reflected off the objects in question. This light is focused onto the back of the eyes by the cornea and the lens of the eye. Once it reaches the back of the eye, the light is reflected onto the two-dimensional surface of the retina and causes a variety of retinal cells to fire, yet the observer perceives the scene in three dimensions. Furthermore, in spite of the presence of two separate physical retinal images, only one visual object is perceived. These phenomena are so natural that they occasion no surprise; instead, people are surprised only if they have trouble determining depth or if they see double. Yet it is this natural phenomenon—single vision from two distinct retinal images—that is truly remarkable and requires an explanation.

PERCEPTION OF A SINGLE FUSED IMAGE

The process that results in one percept arising from two retinal images is known as fusion. The physiological hypothesis of fusion is founded on the structures and functions of the visual pathways and is supported by increasing amounts of neuroanatomical and neurophysiological evidence. It represents the mainstream of thought in physiological optics today. The phenomenon of fusion, then, is based on a relationship between points on the two retinas. For every point on the left retina, there is a corresponding point on the right retina. Corresponding points are the pairs of anatomical locations, one from each retina, that would overlap if one retina could be slid on top of the other. So, for example, if the foveae of the two eyes are both focused on the same object, A, the images in each eye cast by A are said to lie on corresponding points on the two retinas. Similarly, any other object producing images in the two eyes that are equidistant from the fovea in each eye is also said to be stimulating corresponding points. All these objects will be at about the same distance as A. This hypothesis states that corresponding points are anatomically connected and that these connections form a final common pathway, or fusion center. For sensory fusion to occur, the images not only must be located on corresponding retinal areas but also must be sufficiently similar in size, brightness, and sharpness to permit sensory unification.

SPECIFIC QUALITIES OF DEPTH PERCEPTION

Perception of depth is created by various depth cues that signify the three-dimensionality of a scene from the two-dimensional information on the retina. Many of these cues are monocular depth cues, meaning that they give information about depth in a scene even if the observer is using only one eye. The cues include overlap, shadowing, relative brightness, and aerial perspective. Visual experience in these cases depends on the transfer of light from an object in the real world to the eye of the observer. These cues depend on characteristic ways that light travels to the eye or interacts with the medium through which it passes. In other cases, size and object relations provide information about depth. These cues include relative size, familiar size, perspective, and texture gradients. Monocular depth cues are used by artists to create the impression of depth in their artwork. However, it is rare that a painting is mistaken for an actual scene, because there are some cues that cannot be used in pictures.

Some of these cues, such as motion parallax and optical expansion, involve changes in the pattern of retinal stimulation as a result of motion. Objects closer to a moving observer than the fixation point would appear to move much faster than those further away. In addition, certain cues for distance and depth arise from the physical structure of visual systems. These physiological cues to depth include convergence (the turning in of the eyes as objects approach the face) and binocular disparity.

The problem of how the third dimension is perceived has been a point of debate for many noted philosophers, especially the empiricists. It has been suggested that different angles of inclination of the eyes (convergence) and different degrees of blurring of the image and strain in the muscles of the lens (accommodation) are the primary cues. There is, however, another potentially important perceptual source of information about relative distance for animals with binocularly overlapping fields of vision: binocular or retinal disparity, which is based on the fact that the two eyes see from slightly different positions, creating two different views of the world. If the two eyes are focused on an object, A, the images in each eye cast by A are said to lie on corresponding points on the two retinas as described earlier. The images cast by a nearer or more distant object, B, will fall on noncorresponding or disparate points on the two retinas, and the amount or degree of disparity will depend on the differences in depth between A and B. Thus, if the brain can compute the degree of disparity, this will give precise information about the relative distances of objects in the world.

It is possible to manipulate binocular disparity under special viewing conditions to create a strong depth impression from two-dimensional pictures. If pairs of pictures are presented dichoptically to each eye, and each picture depicts what that eye would see if an actual object in depth were presented, a strong depth effect is achieved. The stereoscope, invented by Sir Charles Wheatstone in 1833, operates on this principle. Two photographs or drawings are made from two slightly different positions, the distance being the separation of the two eyes, approximately sixty-three millimeters. The stereoscope presents the left picture to the left eye and the right picture to the right eye so that they combine to produce a convincing three-dimensional image of the scene. Wheatstone was the first to realize that horizontally displaced pictures presented in this fashion produced stereopsis, or binocular depth perception.

Most stereoscopic pictures contain other depth information in addition to disparity. Monocular cues such as linear perspective, overlap, or relative size may contribute to the depth effect. Vision psychologist Béla Julesz, however, created the illusion of depth using only a stereoscope and random dot patterns that contained no depth information other than disparity. This effect can be achieved by first generating two identical random dot patterns with a computer and then shifting a subset of the dots horizontally on one of the patterns to create the disparity. When viewed monocularly, each pattern gives a homogeneously random impression without any global shape or contour; when the two views are combined in a stereoscope, the shifted dot pattern appears as a small square floating above the background. Thus, even with no other depth information present, retinal disparity can cause the perception of depth.

How does the brain use the disparity information provided by images that fall on noncorresponding positions on the retinas of the two eyes? There are many binocular neurons in a cat's visual cortex that are sensitive to small differences in retinal disparity. Monkeys also have these neurons, also called disparity-selective cells, of which there are several types. Tuned excitatory cells respond strongly to a single, very small disparity (usually near zero) and weakly to any other disparity. The tuning width of these cells along the dimension of disparity is very narrow. Tuned inhibitory cells respond well at all depths except on or near the fixation plane. Finally, near cells and far cells respond strongly to stimuli in front of or beyond the fixation plane, respectively, but little if at all to the opposite stimuli. There is a "functional architecture" for binocular disparity in the feline visual cortex, with horopter-coding cells located near the boundaries of ocular dominance columns and near and far cells predominating at the interior of the columns. These neurophysiological findings in cats and monkeys can be extrapolated to human depth perception as well.

A further question of interest is whether the neural streams that process stereopsis are associated with the parvocellular or the magnocellular layers of the lateral geniculate nucleus. Evidence in support of a parvocellular component to stereopsis has been reported. Monkeys with lesions in the parvocellular layers of the lateral geniculate nucleus showed disruptions in fixations of random-dot stereogram stimuli, particularly for fine dot arrays, while magnocellular lesions seemed to have little or no effect. This suggests that the parvocellular stream is needed to process stereopsis when the stimuli are presented in fine dot arrays, as in random-dot stereograms.

MOTION PERCEPTION

One essential quality that distinguishes animals from plants is the capacity for voluntary movement. Animals move to find mates, shelter, and food and to avoid being eaten themselves. However, the ability to move brings with it the requirement to sense movement, whether to guide one's progress through the world or to detect the movement of other mobile animals, such as approaching predators. For sighted animals, this means sensing movement in the retinal image.

The need to sense retinal motion as quickly as possible places great demands on the visual system. Movement is characterized by subtle but highly structured changes in retinal illumination over space and over time. To sense movement very early in processing, the visual system relies on specialized neural processes that make use of information about localized changes of image intensity over time, effectively isolating the parts of the image that contain movement. However, to code the direction of movement, this temporal change information must be combined with information about spatial change-intensity edges. Increases of intensity over time come from image regions with spatial edges that are, for example, bright on the left and dark on the right. Decreases over time are associated with edges of opposite contrast polarity. These space-time pairings signify motion from left to right. A reversal of polarity in either the temporal signal or the spatial signal would signify motion in the opposite direction.

The medial temporal area in the visual cortex is thought to be very important for motion perception because 90 percent of neurons in this area are directionally sensitive and damage to this area impairs one's ability to detect the direction of movement. How can the brain tell the difference between object motion and eye movement? Corollary discharge theory proposes that information about eye movement is provided by signals generated when the observer moves, or tries to move, his or her eyes. A motor signal travels from the brain to the eye muscles to move the eyes. The image moves across the retina and creates a sensory movement signal. If the sensory movement signal reaches the cortex, motion of the object is perceived. If only the eyes move, the corollary discharge signal, a copy of the motor signal, is transmitted to a hypothetical structure (the comparator) that receives both the corollary discharge signal and the sensory movement signal. This cancels the sensory movement signal so that object motion that does not really exist is not perceived. There is a growing body of psychophysical and physiological evidence supporting corollary discharge theory, but researchers still do not completely understand the processes involved.

Perception of movement can be determined by how things move relative to one another in the environment as well. James J. Gibson coined the term "optic array" to refer to the structure created by the surfaces, textures, and contours of the environment. He believed that what is important about the optic array is the way it changes when either an observer or something in the environment moves. A local disturbance in the optic array indicates that the object causing the disturbance is moving; a global disturbançe indicates that the observer is moving through the environment, which is stationary.

Perception of movement can even assist in the perception of three-dimensional forms. Several studies have demonstrated just how much information can be derived from biological movement. In these studies, actors were dressed in black and small lights were attached to several points on their bodies, including their wrists, elbows, shoulders, hips, and feet. Films were then made of the actors in a darkened room while they were performing various actions, such as walking, jumping, dancing, and lifting both a light and a heavy box. Even though observers who watched the films could only see a pattern of moving lights against a dark background, they could readily perceive the pattern as belonging to a human, could identify the behaviors in which they were engaged, and could even tell the actors' genders.

There are also instances in which the perception of movement exists even though no movement is actually occurring. A person who sits in a darkened room and watches two small lights that are alternately turned on and off perceives a single light moving back and forth between two different locations rather than two lights turning on and off at different times. This response, known as the phi phenomenon, is an example of apparent motion. Theater marquees and moving neon signs make use of this phenomenon. Instead of seeing images jumping from place to place, people perceive smooth movement in a particular direction. This ability to perceive movement across "empty space" was the basis for the creation of the first motion pictures in the late 1800s, and it may also explain some unidentified flying object (UFO) sightings related to flashing lights on radio towers. A related phenomenon, called induced motion, occurs when a person sitting in a train or bus feels that the vehicle has begun to move when actually the vehicle next to it has moved. The movement of one object induces the perception of movement in another object.

BIBLIOGRAPHY

Blake, Randolph, and Robert Sekuler. *Perception.* 5th ed. New York: McGraw, 2006. Print.

Bruce, Vicki, Patrick Green, and Mark A. Georgeson. *Visual Perception: Physiology, Psychology and Ecology.* 4th ed. New York: Psychology, 2003. Print.

Dörschner, Katja. "Image Motion and the Appearance of Objects." *Handbook of Experimental Phenomenology: Visual Perception of Shape, Space and Appearance.* Ed. Liliana Albertazzi. Malden: Wiley, 2013. 223–42. Print.

Gibson, James J. *The Ecological Approach to Visual Perception.* Hillsdale: Erlbaum, 1986. Print.

Goldstein, E. Bruce. *Sensation and Perception.* 9th ed. Belmont: Wadsworth, 2014. Print.

Gregory, R. L. *Eye and Brain: The Psychology of Seeing.* 5th ed. Princeton: Princeton UP, 1997. Print.

Howard, Ian P., and Brian J. Rogers, eds. *Perceiving in Depth.* 3 vols. New York: Oxford UP, 2012. Print.

Johansson, Gunnar. "Visual Motion Perception." *Scientific American* June 1975: 76–89. Print.

Julesz, Bela. *Foundations of Cyclopean Perception.* Cambridge: MIT P, 2006. Print.

Vishwanath, Dhanraj. "Visual Information in Surface and Depth Perception: Reconciling Pictures and Reality." *Perception beyond Inference: The Information Content of Visual Processes.* Ed. Liliana Albertazzi, Gert J. van Tonder, and Vishwanath. Cambridge: MIT P, 2010. 201–40. Print.

Wade, Nicholas J., and Michael T. Swanston. *Visual Perception: An Introduction.* 3rd ed. New York: Psychology, 2013. Print.

Cynthia O'Dell

See Also: Nearsightedness and farsightedness; Pattern recognition; Pattern vision; Sensation and perception; Senses; Vision: Brightness and contrast; Vision: Color; Visual system.

Despair

Type of psychology: Counseling; Clinical; Existential-humanistic; Psychopathology; Psychotherapy

Distorted thoughts and beliefs can result in despair and a sense of hopelessness, and that despair and hopelessness then determines how we look at the possibilities for our future. Our future then builds on distorted thoughts and beliefs that determine how we think, feel, and behave in the present. Fortunately, psychotherapeutic processes can stop the negative cycle of despair and lead to new possibilities for the future.

Key concepts

- Cognitive distortions + hopelessness = despair
- Cognitive restructuring
- Despair
- Existential despair
- Psychological despair
- Types of hopelessness

INTRODUCTION

Despair is a very common human feeling. It is typically thought of as a loss of hope and often the person experiencing it is unaware of it. Most people have experienced despair or have been on the verge of despair in response to difficult times in their lives. Typically, despair is a transient experience and dissipates as we move through difficulties such as the loss of a loved one, loss of a job, divorce, financial difficulties, relationship difficulties at work or in our personal lives, health issues, psychological difficulties, environmental challenges such as fires, floods, tornadoes, blizzards, hurricanes, or the impact of events locally, here in the U.S., or around the world.

Despair is a state of mind: the psychological and physical experience of giving up, feeling hopeless, feeling helpless, being despondent, desperate, exhausted, disheartened, resigned, and emotionally drained. Despair is also a state of mind in which a complete loss of hope drives a person to struggle against circumstances with disregard for the consequences. Despair, in fact, can often result from maladaptive resistance to dealing with life the way it just is. Reaching a despairing state of mind does not have to be sourced in a singular, significant, life-changing event. The resistance is often fueled by faulty thoughts and misconceptions called cognitive distortions. These distortions and beliefs can lead to single-mindedness that something is wrong with what happened and it should not be that way. Believing that things should not be this way is a "way of being" that often locks the mind in a state of hopelessness and futility therefore innervating the experience of despair.

Despair is an appropriate response to circumstances and usually diminishes and later dissipates once a person is willing to accept the reality of his or her circumstances and take appropriate actions to deal with the difficulties. However, for some appropriate actions are not taken over an extended period of time, and their resistance remains and despair deepens, impairing their ability to function, diminishing quality of life, and preventing them from moving forward with their goals and desires. In those cases, despair can lead to depression and, in extreme cases, suicide.

In some situations, despair is a resistance to being genuine and authentic. It is also an unwillingness to to strive toward something of purpose. Such despair is often seen in people who are talented, have unfulfilled dreams, and are emotionally paralyzed to take appropriate steps to actualize their potential. Such despair is called existential despair.

EXISTENTIAL DESPAIR

Existential despair does not come from the outside world. It arises from a deep sense of hopelessness within us that seems to have no cause. The more we notice our despair, the worse it becomes. It pervades every corner of our being. The total sense of hopelessness experienced seems impossible to overcome or to conceal or embrace. Some feel very ashamed, unlovable, and unattractive because of their sense of despair. Some cling desperately to a highly resistant, single-minded sense of self-sufficiency. They will not allow others to help which perpetuates and deepens a profound sense of hopelessness. They get caught up in a negative loop in which they feel despair and hopelessness about their despair and hopelessness. The person's emotions and actions are driven by cognitive distortions that lead to hopelessness and despair. Many situations in life can lead us to despair

UNDERSTANDING THE HOPELESSNESS OF DESPAIR

Despair is driven by hopelessness. There are many types of hopelessness humans experience. Recognizing the type of hopelessness one is experiencing is important in overcoming the hopeless that results in despair. *In Hope in the Age of Anxiety,* Anthony Scioli and Henry Biller define nine different types of hopelessness and offer strategies for overcoming them:

- The first type of hopelessness is due to feelings of alienation that can result in individuals feeling they are different than others and no longer feeling worthy of love. They may then close themselves off to protect themselves from more pain or rejection.
- Feelings of being forsaken or totally abandoned at a time of greatest need is another type of hopelessness.
- Feeling uninspired is especially difficult for underprivileged persons who have few good role models or opportunities for growth and can result in hopelessness.
- People feel powerlessness and hopeless when they feel their dreams and goals are being thwarted or crushed by other people or circumstances.
- Oppression is a type of hopelessness in which a person or groups of people are, in a cruel or unjust manner, burdened mentally and physically through adverse conditions or through provoked anxiety or fear.
- Limitedness is often experienced by people living in poverty or people with severe physical handicaps or crippling learning disabilities. Not only do they experience everyday survival as a struggle, but they also feel they will never be able to master things like other people do.
- Doom is a type of hopelessness individuals experience when they are weighed down by the despair that life is over. They believe they do not have what it takes to make it in the world or to

continue living if suffering from a serious, life-threatening illness.

- Hopelessness can result from captivity that is enforced by an individual or a group. Prisoners fall in this category as well as those who are held captive in a controlling, abusive relationship.
- Helplessness results from feeling exposed and vulnerable due to trauma or repeated exposure to uncontrollable stressors. Individuals no longer believe they are safe in the world.

COGNITIVE DISTORTIONS

Forms of hopelessness are usually fueled by cognitive distortions. Cognitive distortions are faulty assumptions and misconceptions that we are unaware of and are hidden from our view. We do not recognize them as a distortion but they are. Working with these faulty distortions then negatively influence our emotions and behaviors. Distortions include the following:

- All or nothing thinking
- Overgeneralization
- Mental filter
- Disqualifying the positive
- Jumping to conclusions
- Magnifying or minimizing (catastrophizing)
- Emotional reasoning
- Should statements
- Labeling and mislabeling
- Personalization
- Self-worth

Albert Ellis has written many books indicating that the main cognitive distortions can be traced back to certain types of irrational thinking. He has proposed an A-B-C paradigm that elucidates his theory. A is the activating event. Something happens that triggers the depression, despair, or other emotional state. B is the belief system that the individual has or employs. The belief system can be rational, logical, reasonable, sane, realistic, appropriate, or irrational, illogical, unreasonable, insane, inappropriate, or unrealistic. Often irrational thinking is linked to three key words: should, ought, or must. C is the consequence of the person's thinking, thought processes, or internal dialogue. If the person is thinking rationally and logically, he or she will feel appropriate emotional reactions. If the person is thinking illogically and unreasonably, he or she will feel deep depression or despair.

OVERCOMING HOPELESSNESS THAT LEADS TO DESPAIR

Understanding the psychological mechanisms that create despair can help resolve it quickly and result in appropriate actions that will assist someone getting "back on track" and on the road to coping and overcoming the concerns that have befallen him or her. There may often need to be extensive intervention on the part of psychiatric, mental health, and medical professionals to assist with people in the throes of alcohol, suicidal thoughts, homelessness, or chronic, life-ending medical conditions.

BIBLIOGRAPHY

Beck, A.T. (1967). *Depression: Causes and Treatment.* Philadelphia, PA: University of Pennsylvania Press.

Ellis, A. (1962). *Reason and Emotion In Psychotherapy.* New York, NY: Lyle Stuart.

Michael Shaughnessy and June Shepherd

SEE ALSO: Anxiety; Coping; Depression; Major depression.

Development

TYPE OF PSYCHOLOGY: Developmental psychology

Developmental theories allow psychologists to manage and understand the enormous body of data on behavioral development from infancy through old age. Theories of development focus on many different issues and derive from many perspectives and periods in history. All, however, are concerned with explaining stability and change in human behavior as individuals progress through their lives.

KEY CONCEPTS

- Behaviorism
- Emergent process
- Heuristic
- "Organic lamp" theory
- Psychodynamic theory

INTRODUCTION

Developmental theory has changed greatly over time. The theories of societies at various times in history have emphasized different aspects of development. The Puritans of the sixteenth and seventeenth centuries, for example, focused on the moral development of the child;

they believed that Original Sin was inherent in children and that children had to be sternly disciplined to make them morally acceptable. In contrast to this view was the developmental theory of the eighteenth century French philosopher Jean-Jacques Rousseau, who held that children were born good and were then morally corrupted by society. Sigmund Freud was interested in psychosexual development and in mental illness; his work therefore focused on these areas. John B. Watson, B. F. Skinner, and Albert Bandura worked during a period when the major impetus in psychology was the study of learning; not surprisingly, this was the focus of their work.

As developmental theorists worked intently within given areas, they often arrived at extreme positions, philosophically and scientifically. For example, some theorists focused on the biology of behavior; impressed by the importance of "nature" (genetic or other inherited sources) in development, they may have neglected "nurture" (learning and other resources received from the parents, world, and society). Others focused on societal and social learning effects and decided that nurture was the root of behavior; nature has often been relegated to subsidiary theoretical roles in physiological and anatomical development. Similar conflicts have arisen concerning developmental continuity or discontinuity, the relative activity or passivity of children in contributing to their own development, and a host of other issues in the field.

These extreme positions would at first appear to be damaging to the understanding of development; however, psychologists are now in a position to evaluate the extensive bodies of research conducted by adherents of the various theoretical positions. It has become evident that the truth, in general, lies somewhere in between. Some developmental functions proceed in a relatively stepwise fashion, as Jean Piaget or Freud would hold; others are much smoother and more continuous. Some development results largely from the child's rearing and learning; other behaviors appear to be largely biological. Some developmental phenomena are emergent processes (any process of behavior or development that was not necessarily inherent in or predictable from its original constituents) of the way in which the developing individual is organized, resulting from both nature and nurture in intricate, interactive patterns that are only beginning to be understood. These findings, and the therapeutic and educational applications that derive from them, are comprehensible only when viewed against the existing corpus of developmental theory. This corpus in turn owes its existence to the gradual construction and modification of developmental theories of the past.

THEORETICAL QUESTIONS AND PROPERTIES

Theoretical perspectives on development derive from a wide variety of viewpoints. Although there are numerous important theoretical issues in development, three questions are central for most theories. The first of these is the so-called nature-nurture question, concerning whether most behavioral development derives from genetics or from the environment. The second of these issues is the role of children in their own development: are children active contributors to their own development, or do they simply and passively react to the stimuli they encounter? Finally, there is the question of whether development is continuous or discontinuous: Does development proceed by a smooth accretion of knowledge and skills, or by stepwise, discrete developmental stages? Perspectives within developmental psychology represent very different views on these issues.

Useful developmental theories must possess three properties. They must be parsimonious, or as simple as possible to fit the available facts. They must be heuristically useful, generating new research and new knowledge. Finally, they must be falsifiable, or testable. A theory that cannot be tested can never be shown to be right or wrong. Developmental theories can be evaluated in terms of these three criteria.

PSYCHODYNAMIC THEORIES

Arguably, the oldest developmental theoretical formulation in use is the psychodynamic model, which gave rise to the work of Erik H. Erikson and Carl Jung, and has as its seminal example, the theory of Sigmund Freud. Freud's theory holds that all human behavior is energized by dynamic forces, many of which are consciously inaccessible to the individual. There are three parts to the personality in Freud's formulation: the id, which emerges first and consists of basic, primal drives; the ego, which finds realistic ways to gratify the desires of the id; and the superego, the individual's moral conscience, which develops from the ego. A primary energizing force for development is the libido, a psychosexual energy that invests itself in different aspects of life during the course of development. In the first year of life (Freud's oral stage), the libido is invested in gratification through oral behavior, including chewing and sucking. Between one and three years of age (the anal stage), the libido is invested in the anus, and the primary source of gratification has to do with toilet training. From three to six years, the libido becomes invested in the genitals; it is during this phallic stage that the child begins to achieve sexual identity. At about six years of age, the child enters latency, a period of relative psychosexual quiet, until the age of twelve years, when the genital stage emerges and normal sexual love becomes possible.

Freud's theory is a discontinuous theory, emphasizing stage-by-stage development. The theory also relies mainly on nature, as opposed to nurture; the various stages are held to occur across societies and with little reference to individual experience. The theory holds that children are active in their own development, meeting and resolving the conflicts that occur at each stage.

The success of psychodynamic theory has been questionable. Its parsimony is open to question: There are clearly simpler explanations of children's behavior. The falsifiability of these ideas is also highly questionable because the theories are quite self-contained and difficult to test. Psychodynamic theory, however, has proven enormously heuristic—that is, having the property of generating further research and theory. Hundreds of studies have set out to test these ideas, and these studies have significantly contributed to developmental knowledge.

BEHAVIORIST THEORIES

In contrast to psychodynamic theories, the behaviorist theories pioneered by John B. Watson and B. F. Skinner hold that development is a continuous process, without discrete stages, and that the developing child passively acquires and reflects knowledge. For behaviorists, development results from nurture, from experience, and from learning, rather than from nature. The most important extant behaviorist theory is the social learning theory of Albert Bandura, which holds that children learn by watching others around them and imitating others' actions. For example, Bandura demonstrated that children were far more inclined to commit violent acts (toward a toy) if someone else, particularly an adult, committed the acts first. The children were especially disposed to imitate if they perceived the acting individual as powerful or as rewarded for his or her violent actions.

ORGANIC LAMP THEORIES

The behaviorist theories are relatively parsimonious and heuristic. They are also testable, and it has been shown that, although many of the findings of the behaviorists have stood the test of time, there are developmental findings that do not fit this framework. To understand these findings, one must turn to the so-called organic lamp theories. This term comes from the fact that within these theories, children are seen as active contributors to their own development, and certain developmental processes are held to be "emergent": As fuel combusts to produce heat and light in a lamp, hereditary and environmental factors combine in development to produce new kinds of behavior. This framework was pioneered by Kurt Goldstein and Heinz Werner, but the most significant extant organic lamp theory is the cognitive development theory of Jean Piaget.

PIAGET'S CONTRIBUTIONS

Piaget's theory involves a discontinuous process of development in four major stages. The sensorimotor stage (birth to two years) is followed by the preoperational stage (two to seven years), the concrete operational stage (seven years to adolescence), and the formal operational stage (adolescence to adulthood). During the sensorimotor stage, the child's behavior is largely reflexive, lacking coherent conscious thought; the child learns that self and world are actually different, and that objects exist even when they are not visible. During the preoperational stage, the child learns to infer the perspectives of other people, learns language, and discovers various concepts for dealing with the physical world. In the concrete operational stage, the ability to reason increases, but children still cannot deal with abstract issues. Finally, in formal operations, abstract reasoning abilities develop. The differences among the four stages are qualitative differences, reflecting significant, discrete kinds of behavioral change.

Piaget's theory is not entirely accurate; it does not apply cross-culturally in many instances, and children may, under some experimental circumstances, function at a higher cognitive level than would be predicted by the theory. In addition, some aspects of development have been shown to be more continuous in their nature than Piaget's ideas would indicate. Yet Piaget's formulation is relatively parsimonious. The various aspects of the theory are readily testable and falsifiable, and the heuristic utility of these ideas has been enormous. This theory has probably been the most successful of the several extant perspectives, and it has contributed significantly to more recent advances in developmental theory. This progress includes the work of James J. Gibson, which emphasizes the active role of the organism, embedded in its environment, in the development of perceptual processes; the information-processing theories, which emphasize cognitive change; and the ethological or evolutionary model, which emphasizes the interplay of developmental processes, changing ecologies, and the course of organic evolution.

MODERN-DAY APPLICATIONS

Developmental theory has been important in virtually every branch of medicine and education. The psychoanalytic theories of Freud were the foundation of psychiatry and still form a central core for much of modern psychiatric practice. These theories are less emphasized in modern clinical psychology, but the work of Freud, Erikson, Jung, and later psychodynamicists is still employed in many areas of psychotherapy.

The behavioristic theories have proved useful in the study of children's learning for educational purposes, and they have considerable relevance for social development. An example is seen in the area of media violence. Bandura's work and other research stemming from social learning theory have repeatedly demonstrated that children tend to imitate violent acts that they see in real life or depicted on television and in other media, particularly if the individuals who commit these acts are perceived as powerful or as rewarded for their actions. Although this is disputed, especially by the media, most authorities are in agreement that excessive exposure to televised violence leads to real-world violence, largely through the mechanisms described by social learning theorists. Social learning theory has contributed significantly to an understanding of such topics as school violence, gang violence, and violent crime.

INTERPLAY OF NATURE VERSUS NURTURE

The organic lamp views have provided developmentalists with useful frameworks against which to understand the vast body of developmental data. Work within the Piagetian framework has shown that both nature and nurture contribute to successful development. One cannot, for example, create "superchildren" by providing preschoolers with college-level material. In general, they are simply not ready as organisms to cope with the abstract thinking required. On the other hand, the work of researchers on various Piagetian problems has shown that even very young children are capable of complex learning.

Organic lamp theory has demonstrated the powerful interplay between biological factors and the way in which children are reared. An example is seen in the treatment of Down syndrome, a chromosomal condition that results in mental retardation. The condition occurs when there are three chromosomes, rather than two, at the twenty-first locus. Clearly, this is a biological condition, and it was believed to be relatively impervious to interventions that come from the environment. It has now been shown, however, that children afflicted with Down syndrome develop much higher intelligence when reared in an intellectually stimulating environment, as opposed to the more sterile, clinical, determined environments typically employed in the past. The child's intellect is not entirely determined by biology; it is possible to ameliorate the biological effects of the syndrome by means of an environmental intervention. This type of complex interplay of hereditary and environmental factors is the hallmark of applied organic lamp theory.

The most important application of developmental theory generally, however, lies in its contribution to the improved understanding of human nature. Such an understanding has considerable real-world importance. For example, among other factors, an extreme faith in the nature side of the nature-nurture controversy led German dictator Adolf Hitler to the assumption that entire races were, by their nature, inferior and therefore should be exterminated. His actions, based on this belief, led to millions of human deaths during World War II. Thus, one can see that developmental theories, especially if inadequately understood, may have sweeping applications in the real world.

BIBLIOGRAPHY

Dowling, John E. *The Great Brain Debate: Nature or Nurture?* Princeton: Princeton UP, 2007. Print.

Gollin, Eugene S., ed. *Developmental Plasticity: Behavioral and Biological Aspects of Variations in Development*. New York: Academic Press, 1981. Print.

Lerner, Richard M. *On the Nature of Human Plasticity.* New York: Cambridge UP, 1984. Print.

Miller, Patricia H. *Theories of Developmental Psychology.* 4th ed. New York: Worth, 2002. Print.

Piaget, Jean. *Biology and Knowledge*. Chicago: U of Chicago P, 1971. Print.

Pickren, Wade E., Donald A. Dewsbury, and Michael Wertheimer. *Portraits of Pioneers in Developmental Psychology.* New York: Psychology Press, 2012. Print.

Revelle, Glenda. "Applying Developmental Theory and Research to the Creation of Educational Games." *New Directions for Child & Adolescent Development* 2013.139 (2013): 31–40. Print.

Shaffer, David Reed. *Developmental Psychology: Childhood and Adolescence*. 7th ed. Belmont:

Wadsworth, 2007. Print.
Siegler, Robert S. *Emerging Minds: The Process of Change in Children's Thinking.* New York: Oxford UP, 1998. Print.
Thompson, Dennis, John D. Hogan, and Philip M. Clark. *Developmental Psychology in Historical Perspective.* Malden: Wiley, 2012. Print.

Matthew J. Sharps

SEE ALSO: Adolescence: Cognitive skills; Aging: Cognitive changes; Attachment and bonding in infancy and childhood; Behaviorism; Cognitive development: Jean Piaget; Developmental methodologies; Developmental psychology; Ego psychology: Erik H. Erikson; Gender identity formation; Physical development: Environment versus genetics; Psychosexual development.

Developmental disabilities

TYPE OF PSYCHOLOGY: Developmental psychology

Developmental disabilities are conditions that result in substantial functional limitations. They manifest themselves in childhood and persist throughout the life span, requiring a continuum of medical, educational, and social services.

KEY CONCEPTS
- Activities of daily living (ADLs)
- Individual education plan (IEP)
- Individual family service plan (IFSP)
- Medically fragile
- Mental retardation
- Pervasive developmental disorder (PDD)

INTRODUCTION

The concept of developmental disabilities was first introduced in the Developmental Disabilities Services and Facilities Construction Act of 1970. Subsequently, the Developmental Disabilities Assistance and Bill of Rights Act of 1990 defined developmental disabilities. The term "developmental disability" means a severe, chronic disability of a person five years of age or older that is attributable to a mental or physical impairment or a combination of both. The disability must manifest itself before the person reaches the age of twenty-two and be expected to continue indefinitely. It results in substantial functional limitations in three or more areas of major life activity, including self-care, receptive and expressive language, learning, mobility, self-direction, capacity for independent living, and economic self-sufficiency. The inclusion of the requirement of substantial functional limitations in three or more major life areas forms the basis for provision of services to individuals with severe impairments.

The American Psychiatric Association does not use the term "developmental disabilities." However, it does identify pervasive developmental disorders (PDD) in its diagnostic manual. The description of these disorders and their manifestations in many ways overlaps the definition of developmental disabilities.

The terms "developmental disabilities" and "mental retardation" are often used as if they were synonymous. However, there are important distinctions as well as areas of overlap. The President's Committee on Mental Retardation uses the definition developed and utilized by the American Association on Mental Retardation and generally understood by the Arc-USA (a national organization for people with mental retardation and related developmental disabilities and their families). Developmental disabilities covers more disabilities than those encompassed under mental retardation. Developmental disabilities indicate severe and chronic disabilities, while mental retardation includes a large number of individuals functioning at the mild level of cognitive impairment who require little or no support in adulthood. However, mental retardation does account for 70 percent of the people who are developmentally disabled. The term "medically fragile" is sometimes used to describe those vulnerable individuals whose complex medical needs can seriously compromise their health status.

POSSIBLE CAUSES

There are a multitude of etiologies for developmental disabilities. The cause can be prenatal, perinatal, or postnatal. Risk factors for developmental disabilities can be biological, environmental, or a combination of both. Genetics plays a role in conditions, such as Tay-Sachs disease and other inborn errors of metabolism, Klinefelter's syndrome, Fragile X syndrome, and Down syndrome, that typically lead to developmental disability. Genetic causes may be chromosomal abnormalities, single gene defects, or multifactorial disorders. For example, autism appears to have a genetic component that interacts with developmental factors.

A number of conditions in the prenatal environment may increase the likelihood that a child will be born with the potential for a developmental disability. Fetal alcohol syndrome, for example, is completely preventable if pregnant women do not drink alcohol. Women who have sufficient amounts of folic acid in their diets reduce the risk of having a child with a neural tube defect that can result in a developmental disability.

Smoking during pregnancy, use of certain drugs such as cocaine or heroin, poor maternal nutrition, and extremes of maternal age greatly increase the chances of fetal brain damage or premature delivery and low birth weight. Babies with low birth weights are three times more likely than normal-weight babies to have developmental disabilities. Approximately 25 percent of very premature (twenty-seven weeks or earlier) infants have a severe developmental disability of some kind, according to Iris Lesser, director of the School-Age Unit at Yeshiva University's Children's Evaluation and Rehabilitation Center.

Children may later be at risk through environmental causes such as lead poisoning, inadequate nutrition, infections, nonstimulating environments, abuse, neglect, and traumatic brain injury.

DIAGNOSING DEVELOPMENTAL DISABILITIES

Developmental disabilities are defined in terms of what an individual can or cannot do rather than in terms of a clinical diagnosis. They affect the typical processes in a child's growth, particularly the maturation of the central nervous system. For this reason, early identification is important. The potential exists for an improved outcome if children are provided with education and habilitation. Prenatal diagnostic techniques may be appropriate for at-risk pregnancies. If a fetus is affected, the physician is better able to plan the delivery and prepare for special care during the newborn period.

Newborn screening is another way in which to identify conditions that can result in developmental disabilities if untreated. The Apgar test is administered by the medical staff in the delivery room at one minute, five minutes, and, if there are complications, at ten and fifteen minutes after birth. It measures the effects of various complications of labor and birth and determines the need for resuscitation. The test assesses physical responsiveness, development, and overall state of health using a scale of five items rated from 0 to 2. A low Apgar score at birth can signal the potential for a developmental disability.

Measurement of head circumference is a useful tool for predicting whether an infant is likely to have a neurodevelopmental impairment such as microcephaly. A blood test screening can be done for phenylketonuria (PKU), congenital hypothyroidism, galactosemia, maple syrup urine disease, homocystinuria, and biotinidase deficiency. Early detection of these conditions and appropriate intervention may reduce the severity of the resulting disability.

An older child can be referred to a developmental pediatrician for assessment of a developmental disability if the child has not attained expected age-appropriate developmental milestones, exhibits atypical development or behavior, or regresses to a previous level of development. Correcting for prematurity in developmental testing is necessary. An instrument commonly used is the Denver Developmental Screening Test. The more severely affected a child is, the clearer is the diagnosis, since an individual's failure to meet developmental milestones may represent a short-term problem that resolves over time as the child "catches up." Even readily identifiable indicators of potential disability do not always result in expected delays.

Related issues such as feeding, elimination, and cardiorespiratory problems; pressure sores; and infection control are also considered as part of the diagnosis. Screening for lead poisoning or psychological testing may be recommended.

At whatever age the person is referred, a multidisciplinary evaluation attempts to establish a baseline of the present level of performance, including both skills and deficits. Activities of daily living (ADLs) such as bathing, eating, and dressing are widely used in assessing this population. Needing assistance with ADLs becomes an important criterion for determining eligibility for public and private disability benefits. An appraisal is made of those deficits that can be remediated and those that require accommodation. The predictive accuracy of the diagnosis improves with the individual's age.

Language development is another predictor variable. Individuals with developmental disabilities may have little or no apparent intent to communicate and may not understand that they can affect their environment through communication.

Though developmental disabilities by definition are severe, it is possible that a child not previously identified could be detected by routine public school prekindergarten screening.

THE DEVELOPMENTALLY DISABLED POPULATION

The Administration for Intellectual and Developmental Disabilities of the United States Department of Health and Human Services estimates that there are four million Americans with developmental disabilities. Data specific to the incidence and prevalence of developmental disabilities are difficult to obtain because of the various etiologies present in this population. Conditions that often fall under the umbrella of developmental disability include mental retardation, autism spectrum disorders, epilepsy, spinal cord injury, sensory impairment, traumatic brain injury, and cerebral palsy.

Though developmental disabilities can be associated with neurological damage, many of the conditions resulting in a developmental disability do not result in lowered intellectual functioning. Persons with developmental disabilities are estimated to comprise 1.2 to 1.3 percent of the population. This percentage has risen markedly since the mid-1970s for two reasons: increased life span for older individuals with disabilities and a greater number of children and adolescents surviving conditions that previously would have been fatal. The number of children ages six to seventeen classified as having an autism spectrum disorder in public special education program rose from 22,664 in 1994 to 211,610 in 2006.

Between 200,000 and 500,000 people in the United States over the age of sixty may have some form of developmental disability. Some of these individuals present special problems as they age. Those with epilepsy appear to be at greater risk for osteoporosis, while those with Down syndrome seem to begin the aging process earlier than others.

TREATMENT OPTIONS

The person with a developmental disability needs a combination of interdisciplinary services that are individually planned and coordinated and of lifelong or extended duration throughout the life cycle. Because the causes and manifestations of developmental disabilities are so varied, each affected person is unique and requires an individualized approach to treatment and training. Each disability has specific needs that must be addressed and accommodations that must be provided.

When a defect has been identified prenatally, fetal treatment may be possible to prevent developmental disability. Some inborn errors of metabolism respond to vitamin therapy given to the mother. Bone marrow transplants and fetal surgery have also been performed.

Services for children from birth to two years old provide special education as well as access to specialists in the areas of speech and physical therapy, psychology, medicine, and nursing. Assistive technology, physical adaptations, and case management are also offered. Medical management, monitoring, and consultation may be the responsibility of a developmental pediatrician.

Early intervention may be home-based, or the child can be enrolled in a center with a low child-to-teacher ratio. In either case, an Individual Family Service Plan (IFSP) is developed that includes a statement of the child's present level of development; the family's concerns, priorities, and resources; major outcomes to be achieved; the specific early intervention services to be provided; identification of the coordinator responsible for implementing the plan; and procedures for transition to preschool.

Among the equipment used in treating the child may be positioning devices, wheelchairs, special car restraints, amplification devices, and ambulation aids. Some children may require gastronomy tubes, tracheostomy tubes, cardiorespiratory monitors, nasogastric tubes, ventilators, bladder catheters, splints, or casting. They may be placed on antiepileptic medication, antispasticity drugs, antireflux medications, antibiotics, respiratory medications, or medications to influence mood and behavior.

The Individuals with Disabilities Education Act mandates comprehensive educational services for children from three through twenty-one years of age. Services are offered in a continuum of settings that are individually determined. These settings may include hospitals, residential facilities, separate day schools, homes, and public schools. Children are ideally placed in what the law refers to as "the least restrictive environment." An Individualized Education Plan (IEP) replaces the IFSP.

ADLs are a prime focus of the educational program. The goal is to promote independence in such areas as eating, drinking, dressing, toileting, grooming, and tool use, which, in turn, fosters self-esteem.

Facilitating language acquisition and communicative intent are critical to any intervention program. Many developmentally disabled individuals will need numerous stimulus presentations before acquiring a rudimentary vocabulary. For those children who continue to be nonverbal, alternative communication systems such as sign language, use of pictures, and communication boards are introduced to enable communicative interaction. Computers with interface devices such as switches or touch-sensitive screens may be introduced to children with cerebral palsy.

Children with developmental disabilities exhibit challenging behaviors more often than typically developing children. After previously unrecognized medical conditions are ruled out as causes, positive behavioral supports at home and in school or traditional behavior management programs aim at producing comprehensive change in those challenging behaviors. Drugs that affect central nervous system function can also be helpful in treating disruptive behaviors.

Newer treatment approaches include neurodevelopmental therapy and sensory integration therapy. Neurodevelopmental therapy is widely used by physical and occupational therapists. It emphasizes sensorimotor experience to facilitate normal movement and posture in young developmentally disabled children with cerebral palsy or other related disorders. Sensory integration is a normal process in which the child's central nervous system organizes sensory feedback from the body and the environment and makes appropriate adaptive responses. Sensory integration therapy uses controlled sensory input to promote those adaptive responses.

Adults with developmental disabilities are living longer than ever before. Most have the ability to live happy, productive lives in their communities. One component of treatment is transition planning. The Developmental Disabilities Act of 1984 emphasizes the importance of employment of persons with developmental disabilities and offers guidelines for providing supported employment services. Other transition issues include sexuality, social integration, recreation, and community residential options. Medical and physical care plans are necessary since long-term consequences of therapeutic interventions may occur. Movement disorders can result from the prolonged use of neuroleptic medications, while bone demineralization may be secondary to the chronic use of certain anticonvulsants.

HISTORY OF TREATMENT

Services for people now referred to as having a developmental disability began in the United States in 1848 in Boston. The philosophy of early schools was to cure the "deviant." However, by 1877 a unidisciplinary medical model replaced the educational model and emphasized providing shelter and protection to this population. Later, the interest in Mendelian genetics led to a change in focus to protecting society from those whose disabilities were considered hereditary. By 1926, twenty-three states had laws requiring mandatory sterilization of the developmentally disabled on the books, and between 1925 and 1955 more than fifty thousand involuntary sterilizations occurred in the United States. In the 1950s, parents began to organize opportunities for individuals with developmental disabilities within public school systems.

Treatment evolved from the medical model to a multidisciplinary approach in which a physician consulted with members of other disciplines. Later, an interdisciplinary model emerged in which professionals from each discipline gathered together to discuss their individual assessments and decide jointly on a plan of care. More recently, a transdisciplinary approach has been developed in which professionals, along with the individual concerned and the family, work together equally to identify needs, plan care, implement interventions, and evaluate progress.

Though the term "developmental disabilities" was not used in it, PL 94-142, the Education for All Handicapped Children Act of 1975, mandated a free, appropriate, public education for children who could be considered developmentally disabled. The Education of the Handicapped Act Amendments of 1986 extended early identification and intervention services under the auspices of the public schools to identified children three to five years of age and those at risk for developmental disabilities. This legislation was reauthorized as the Individuals with Disabilities Education Act (IDEA) of 1990. Guarantees of equal protection under the law were extended to adults with developmental disabilities by the Americans with Disabilities Act (ADA) of 1990.

In 2008, President George W. Bush signed the ADA Amendments Act, which expanded the ADA definition of disability, increasing the number of people covered under the act's provisions.

The years since 1970 have been a period of remarkable growth and achievement in services for individuals with developmental disabilities. Cultural, legal, medical, and technological advances have occurred. Services now include protection and advocacy systems under the auspices of state councils on developmental disabilities; university centers involved in education, research, and direct service; training in self-determination; and family supports. At the heart of this growth has been a transformation from a system of services provided primarily in institutions to one provided primarily in local communities. There has been a movement away from segregation and toward integration following what has been called the principle of normalization.

BIBLIOGRAPHY

Batshaw, Mark L., ed. *Children with Disabilities*. 6th ed. Baltimore: Brookes, 2007. Print.

Copeland, Mildred E., and Judy R. Kimmel. *Evaluation and Management of Infants and Young Children with Developmental Disabilities*. Baltimore: Brookes, 1989. Print.

Dowrick, Peter W. "University-Affiliated Programs and Other National Resources." *Handbook of Developmental Disabilities*. Ed. Lisa A. Kurtz, Peter W. Dowrick, Susan E. Levy, and Mark L. Batshaw. Gaithersburg: Aspen, 1996. Print.

Jacobson, John W., James A. Mulick, and Johannes Rojahn eds. *Handbook of Intellectual and Developmental Disabilities*. New York: Springer, 2008. Print.

McLaughlin, P. J., and Paul Wehman, eds. *Mental Retardation and Developmental Disabilities*. Austin: Pro-Ed, 1996. Print.

Mirenda, Pat. "Revisiting the Mosaic of Supports Required for Including People with Severe Intellectual or Developmental Disabilities in their Communities." *AAC: Augmentative & Alternative Communication* 30.1 (2014): 19–27

Roth, Shirley P., and Joyce S. Morse, eds. *A Life-Span Approach to Nursing Care for Individuals with Developmental Disabilities*. Baltimore: Brookes, 1994. Print.

Shogren, Karrie A. "Core Concepts of Disability Policy, the Convention on the Rights of Persons With Disabilities, and Public Policy Research With Respect to Developmental Disabilities." *Jour. of Policy & Practice in Intellectual Disabilities* 11.1 (2014): 19–26. Print.

Williamson, Heather J., and Elizabeth A. Perkins. "Family Caregivers of Adults With Intellectual and Developmental Disabilities: Outcomes Associated With US Services and Supports." *Intellectual and Developmental Disabilities* 52.2 (2014): 147–59. Print.

Gabrielle Kowalski

SEE ALSO: Data description; Developmental psychology; Experimentation: Independent, dependent, and control variables; Scientific methods; Hypothesis development and testing; Observational methods.

Developmental methodologies

TYPE OF PSYCHOLOGY: Developmental psychology

Developmental methodologies describe how information about age-related changes in people's physical growth, thought, and behavior is collected and interpreted. Sound methodologies are essential for describing accurately the course of life-span development, comparing people with different environmental and biological backgrounds, predicting developmental patterns, and explaining the causes of positive and negative outcomes in development.

KEY CONCEPTS

- Cohort
- Control
- Generalizability
- Research designs
- Research methods

INTRODUCTION

Developmental methodologies have as their purpose the investigation of questions about age-related changes throughout the life span, and they include both a variety of research methods and the designs within which these methods are applied. The overarching framework for developmental methodologies is the scientific process. This process embodies systematic rules for testing hypotheses or ideas about human development under conditions in which the hypotheses may be supported or refuted. This process also requires that research be done in such a way that it can be observed, evaluated, and replicated by others.

Data collected through developmental methodologies can be characterized as descriptive, correlational, or experimental. Descriptive data simply describe a variable—for example, the average age of the adolescent growth spurt. Correlational data provide information on relationships between variables, such as the association between newborn size and the amount of smoking a mother did during pregnancy. Experimental data result from the careful manipulation of one variable to discover its effect on another, and only in experimental studies can cause-and-effect relationships among variables be inferred. For example, experimental studies demonstrate that training techniques can cause an improvement in the memory performance of persons in late adulthood.

RESEARCH CATEGORIES

Developmental research methods are commonly separated into three general categories. One of these categories is observational methods, in which researchers observe people as they go about their lives. The settings for such research can be homes, schools, playgrounds, nursing homes, and so on. Observational research may be quite subjective, as in diary studies in which the researcher writes down observations and impressions in a free-flowing manner. The extensive cognitive developmental model of Jean Piaget had its beginnings in hypotheses that emerged from diary studies of his children. On the other hand, observational research may be very rigorous and systematic; researchers carefully define what and how they will observe and record and then train data collectors before any formal observations are made. Videotaping of children's language samples, which are then carefully segmented and analyzed, is an example of this systematic approach.

The second category, self-report methods, is generally more intrusive than observational research. It involves asking questions of participants and may take the form of interviews, questionnaires, or standardized tests. Interviews may be free-flowing or highly structured, with predetermined questions and sequence. The famous studies of sexual behavior by Alfred Kinsey, for example, used carefully planned interview techniques. Questionnaires and standardized tests are usually structured with both questions and response categories provided. Questionnaires are often used to gather descriptive information such as size of family or educational level, as well as opinions on a variety of social issues. Standardized tests are used to assess a great variety of information, including measured intelligence, vocational interests, and self-concept.

The third category of developmental methods involves experimentation. Experimentation can occur in natural settings where individuals may not be aware that they are participating in research, such as in situational studies of children's moral behavior. It can also occur in laboratories where individuals may be unaware of their participation or fully aware of the artificiality of the setting and even the study's intent. Research using a complex apparatus to study newborn perception is one example of the former, while research using nonsense syllables in memory tasks to assess age differences in free recall is an example of the latter.

RESEARCH METHODS AND DESIGNS

Research methods can be compared according to their generalizability and their ability to control participants' selection, experiences, and responses. Generalizability refers to the extent to which research results are applicable to people beyond those who participated in the study. Generally, methods that are more intrusive and contrived provide the greatest opportunity for control—the extent to which a researcher can regulate who participates in a study, what the participants experience, and how the participants respond. Thus, laboratory experimentation often is associated with high levels of control. For the same reasons, however, questions are raised regarding the applicability to the real world of data collected in the artificiality of a laboratory. Thus, observation in natural settings is often associated with high levels of generalizability. Both control and generalizability are desirable and are sought in developmental research regardless of method.

To assess whether age-related changes exist, developmental research methods are applied within larger frameworks of research designs that require that data be collected at two or more points in developmental time. These designs permit inquiry into whether behavior is the result of maturational changes associated with age changes, such as the emergence of language in infancy; the effect of the immediate social context, such as a nation at war; or the effect of historical events which affected everyone born at about the same time (a group known as a cohort, a term which means an identifiable group of people that has a common association), such as growing up during the Great Depression. Two of the most common designs are cross-sectional and longitudinal designs. In cross-sectional designs, data are collected on different cohorts at the same time. These designs permit an examination of age differences in behavior; however, they cannot separate out the effects of different life experiences between cohorts. In longitudinal designs, data are collected on the same cohort a number of times. These designs permit an examination of developmental trends for individuals; however, they cannot separate out the effects of social change, since no comparison can be made to a group not experiencing the social context. An alternative to cross-sectional and longitudinal designs is sequential designs, in which data are collected on a number of cohorts a number of times. These designs are able to reveal the effects of age, cohort, and social context. Because of the difficulties of administering these complex designs and their expense, sequential designs are least often applied, even though they provide the most useful developmental information.

Regardless of the research methods or designs utilized, developmental methodologies must account for the complexity of human development. They must control for multiple variables, such as age, cohort, social context, socioeconomic class, gender, educational level, and family structure. They must take into account the culture of the participants, and they must protect against bias in formulating the research hypothesis, applying the methods, and interpreting the data collected.

Developmental methodologies are applicable to literally any developmental question, from conception to death. Resultant data permit description of current status, comparison between groups, prediction of developmental patterns, and explanation of the causes of developmental outcomes. Description, comparison, prediction, and explanation all contribute to a better understanding of development, which in turn permits the fostering of social settings that promote healthy development, as well as intervention to prevent potential developmental problems or to counter developmental problems already in existence.

NEWBORN RESEARCH

Research on the competencies of newborns provides one demonstration of the relationship between understanding and therapeutic intervention. Observational research of newborns and young infants indicates a cyclical relationship in infant attention when the infant is interfacing with a caregiver. This cycle is one of activation, discharge, and then recovery when the infant withdraws its attention. Caregivers who adjust their behavior to their infants' rhythms by entering into interaction when their infants are responsive and slackening off when their infants withdraw attention experience a greater amount of time in which the infant looks at them than do caregivers who either attempt to force their own rhythms on their infants or continuously bombard their infants with stimulation.

Psychologists are applying this understanding as part of an overall intervention program with premature infants who enter the world at risk for physical, social, and intellectual impairments. Premature newborns require greater stimulation than full-term newborns before they respond; however, they also are overwhelmed by a level of stimulation to which full-term newborns respond very positively. This narrow range of tolerance can disrupt the relationship between a parent and the premature infant. In experimental research, parents of premature newborns have been trained to imitate everything their infants do, and by so doing follow their infants' rhythms. This training helps parents remain within the narrow tolerance of their infants and increases the amount of positive interaction both experience. This, in turn, contributes positively to healthy social development of this high-risk group of infants.

TELEVISION STUDIES

Research on the developmental effects of television provides a demonstration of the relationship between understanding and influences on social policy. Beginning in the mid-1950s with a series of inquiries and hearings sponsored by a Senate subcommittee on juvenile delinquency, followed by a Surgeon General's report and associated Senate hearings in the early 1970s and a major National Institute of Mental Health report in the early 1980s, questions about the effect of violent programming on children have been raised in the public domain. Consequently, public efforts have emerged to control the amount and timing of violence on television and to regulate the number and content of television commercials targeted at children. Central to the national debate and social policies surrounding television content has been the application of developmental methodologies.

Significant research in this area emerged in the early 1960s with the now-classic Bobo doll studies of Stanford University psychologist Albert Bandura. In a series of experimental laboratory studies, nursery school children observed a variety of televised models behaving aggressively against an inflatable punching-bag clown. Later, when their play behavior was observed in a controlled setting, children clearly demonstrated imitation of specific aggressive behaviors they had viewed. Additional experimental laboratory studies have been conducted; however, they have been consistently criticized for their artificiality. Consequently, field experiments have emerged in which the experimental variables have been actual television programs, and the effects have been assessed on spontaneous behavior in natural settings, such as playgrounds.

Since experimental studies require systematic manipulating of variables for their effects to be observed, and since the manipulations of levels and types of aggression and other relevant variables such as home violence are either unethical or impractical, numerous correlational studies have also been conducted. Most of these have assessed the relationship between the amount of violence viewed and subsequent violent behavior, violent attitudes, or perceptions of violence in the real world. Many of these studies have applied longitudinal or sequential designs covering many years, including one longitudinal study that covered a span of twenty-two years from childhood into adulthood. These studies have controlled multiple variables including age, educational level, and initial level of aggressive behavior. Although not all studies have supported a causal link between television violence and aggressive behavior and attitudes, the large majority of laboratory experimental, field experimental, and correlational studies indicate that children do learn antisocial and aggressive behavior from televised violence and that some of them may directly imitate such behaviors. The effects depend on the characteristics of the viewers and the settings.

Not only have developmental methodologies been used after the fact to discover the effects of television programming, they also have been applied proactively to develop prosocial children's programming, and then to evaluate the effects of those prosocial programs on children's development. The program Sesame Street, for example, has as its foundation research into child development, attention, and learning. In fact, one of its objectives has been to act as an experimental variable, intervening into homes in which children are economically and educationally disadvantaged. Although researchers have had limited access to those high-risk homes, both experimental research and correlational longitudinal research support the effectiveness of Sesame Street in developing early academic skills, school readiness, positive attitudes toward school, and positive attitudes toward people of other races.

EVOLUTION OF RESEARCH

Today's developmental methodologies have their origins in the nineteenth century, with its advances in science and medicine, the emergence of the fields of psychology and psychoanalysis, and developments in measurement and statistics. Developmental psychological research and methodologies often emerged to deal with concrete social problems. With compulsory education bringing approximately three-quarters of all American children into classrooms at the beginning of the twentieth century, social concerns were focused primarily on child health, education, and social welfare. Consequently, the first major research into child intellectual, social, and emotional development also occurred during this period, and developmental psychology began to consolidate as a distinct discipline of psychology.

The universal draft of World War I required assessment of multitudes of older adolescent and young adult men with vast differences in education, health status, and social and emotional stability. Standardized testing became the tool to evaluate these men, and it has remained a major tool in developmental methodologies, as well as in other disciplines of psychology. Following the war, efforts to understand these individual differences led to the first major longitudinal studies, which were focused on descriptions of normative growth and predictions of developmental patterns; some of these studies have followed their participants and next generations for more than fifty years.

In the two decades following World War II, the baby boom and national anxiety over falling behind the Soviet Union in science and technology rekindled efforts dampened during the war years in the disciplines of developmental and educational psychology.

Of particular interest were methodologies in applied settings such as school classrooms, focused on learning and academic achievement. Also during this period, greater accessibility to computers permitted increases in the complexity of developmental research methods and designs, and of resultant data analyses. Complex sequential designs, intricate correlational techniques, and multiple-variable techniques became much more frequently used in research.

Heightened awareness of economic and social inequalities in the United States following the Civil Rights movement led to many carefully designed educational, health, social, and economic interventions into communities that were economically at risk. The interventions were part of developmental methodologies in which experimental, correlational, and descriptive data were collected longitudinally to assess their outcomes. Head Start educational programs are one prominent example.

In more recent decades, with changes in family structure, developmental methodologies have been applied to questions about single parenting, day care, and "latchkey" children. With substance abuse, developmental methodologies have been applied to questions about prenatal development in wombs of addicted mothers, postnatal development of infants born drug-addicted, and developmental intervention for drug-related disabilities in many of these infants. With more adults living longer and healthier lives, developmental methodologies have been applied to questions about learning and memory, self-esteem, and life satisfaction among persons in late adulthood. Clearly, developmental methodologies will continue to be relevant as long as people are motivated to understand and nurture healthy life-span development and to intervene into social problems.

BIBLIOGRAPHY

Laursen, Brett, and Todd D. Little. *Handbook of Developmental Research Methods*. New York: Guilford, 2012. Print.

Miller, Scott A. *Developmental Research Methods*. 3d ed. Thousand Oaks: Sage, 2007. Print.

Mukherji, Penny, and Deborah Albon. *Research Methods in Early Childhood: An Introductory Guide*. Los Angeles: SAGE, 2010. Print.

Mussen, Paul Henry, ed. *Handbook of Research Methods in Child Development*. New York: Wiley, 1960. Print.

Nielsen, Joyce McCarl, ed. *Feminist Research Methods: Exemplary Readings in the Social Sciences*. Boulder: Westview, 1990. Print.

Sears, Robert R. "Your Ancients Revisited: A History of Child Development." *Feminist Research Methods: Exemplary Readings in the Social Sciences*. Vol. 5. Ed. E. M. Hetherington. Chicago: U of Chicago P, 1975. Print.

Sommer, Barbara B., and Robert Sommer. *A Practical Guide to Behavioral Research: Tools and Techniques*. 5th ed. New York: Oxford UP, 2001. Print.

Thompson, Ross A. "Methods and Measures in Developmental Emotions Research: Some Assembly Required." *Jour. of Experimental Child Psychology* 110.2 (2011): 275–85. Print.

Triandis, H. C., and A. Heron, eds. Basic Methods. Vol. 4. *Handbook of Cross-Cultural Psychology: Developmental Psychology*. Boston: Allyn, 1981. Print.

Wolman, Benjamin B., ed. *Handbook of Developmental Psychology*. Englewood Cliffs: Prentice, 1982. Print.

Michael D. Roe

SEE ALSO: Data description; Developmental psychology; Experimentation: Independent, dependent, and control variables; Scientific methods; Hypothesis development and testing; Observational methods.

Developmental psychology

DATE: Late 1800's forward
TYPE OF PSYCHOLOGY: Developmental psychology

Developmental psychology studies developmental change and continuity over the human life span. This field has shifted from behaviorism to cognitive constructivism and has begun moving toward contextualism, as evidenced by changing conceptualization of human development, theories, and research methodology, and a move toward interdisciplinary endeavor.

KEY CONCEPTS

- Developmental design
- Developmental psychology
- Developmental science
- Developmental theory
- Worldview

INTRODUCTION

Developmental psychology examines human developmental change and continuity from conception to death. The field began with a focus on children, expanded coverage to adolescent development, and later came to include the adulthood period, in the end covering the entire life span.

Early Greek philosophers such as Plato and Aristotle, as well as French philosophers from the sixteenth and eighteenth centuries such as René Descartes and Jean-Jacques Rousseau, planted the seed for nativism, which holds that human ideas and behaviors are innate and that development evolves through maturation. Seventeenth century philosopher John Locke laid the foundation for behaviorism with his concept of *tabula rasa*, that life experience impresses its marks into a newborn's "blank slate." Naturalist Charles Darwin and physiologist William Preyer published their baby biographies in 1877 and 1882, respectively, signifying the beginning of modern child psychology. G. Stanley Hall, the father of developmental psychology, brought both theory and methodology to new levels with the publication of *Adolescence* (1904) and *Senescence* (1922).

The American Psychological Association (APA) established its first nineteen divisions before World War II, among which was Division 7: Developmental Psychology. In December, 1945, Division 20: Division on Maturity and Old Age was added to the list (renamed Division of Adult Development and Aging in 1970). Although this addition is organizationally separated from Division 7, it has contributed to the conceptual expansion of developmental psychology beyond childhood and adolescence. In May, 2008, the presidents of these two divisions started an initiative to encourage dialogue among all developmental psychologists to integrate conceptualization and measurement in the study of human development.

ISSUES AND ASSUMPTIONS

When studying what changes occur and why, developmental psychologists are traditionally concerned with the following issues: whether the developmental changes are continuous (gradual) or discontinuous (later stages being qualitatively different from earlier stages), whether the cause for change is genetic (nature/heredity) or environmental (nurture), whether people develop along the same path through the same stages (universality) in the same order (invariability) or the development is unique and specific to each individual, and whether the person plays an active or a passive role. Developmental psychologists agree on the following assumptions regarding human development:

- Development is a lifelong process—development goes on beyond childhood; earlier events bear consequences in later developments.
- Development involves both gains and losses at all ages—it is not all gains in formative years and all losses in older years.
- Plasticity (capacity to select, change, and reorganize to adjust or adapt to events or life conditions) remains throughout life—learning, adaptation, and reorganization are possible at all ages.
- Development is embedded in historical, cultural, and social contexts—development does not occur in a vacuum.
- Development is multidimensional, multidirectional, and multicausal—development occurs in different areas (biological, psychological, cognitive, social, emotional); varies in timing, pace, and directions (different paths); and is shaped by many factors (such as biological, social, sociocultural, and historical influences and personal history) and their interactions.
- Understanding development requires multiple disciplines—it requires the collective efforts of biologists, neuroscientists, psychologists, sociologists, anthropologists, and others to understand the complexity of human development.

Developmental psychologists study various aspects of human development, including its genetic or biological foundations and its role in physical and physiological, psychological, moral, emotional, and social or relational domains. They also study human bioecology, including the individual's biological, social or relational, natural and physical, societal and institutional, historical, and cultural contexts.

MAJOR DEVELOPMENTAL THEORIES

Developmental theories can be categorized according to the worldviews that they reflect. The selection of non-developmental theories by developmental psychologists to explain development also reflects their worldviews. Learning theories (such as John B. Watson's classical conditioning and B. F. Skinner's operant conditioning) represent the mechanistic worldview, which sees the world as objective and predictable. Behavioral changes can be determined by situational antecedents and reinforcement or punishment following the responses. The developing person is rather passive, like a machine responding to external stimulation and getting molded by the environment. Changes are continuous, and developmental paths and outcomes may differ, contingent on the specific environment, action, and consequence. Information-processing and computational models using the computer metaphor and neuralnetwork model to study cognitive development also belong to this category.

Many stage theories in developmental psychology reflect the organismic view, which believes in inherent organization, activity, and purposefulness. These theories hold that development goes through an invariable and universal sequence of stages, with later stages built on the outcomes of earlier stages. All stages are believed to be qualitatively different from one another. The person is seen as actively construing the reality through organization and functions while interacting with the environment. A classic example is Jean Piaget's theory of cognitive development. Sigmund Freud's psychosexual developmental theory, Erik H. Erikson's psychosocial developmental theory, Lawrence Kohlberg's theory of moral development, John Bowlby's ethological theory of attachment, William G. Perry, Jr.'s model of college students' intellectual development, Donald Super's theory of vocational development, Daniel Levinson's theory of adult development, and Elisabeth Kübler-Ross's stages in the dying process all exemplify thisworldview.

The contextualist worldview challenges the universality assumption in the organismic view and the simplistic determinism in the mechanistic view. Its major tenet is that development is not context-free. The earlier theoretical models took in contextual factors, although in a simpler form as compared with the later systems theories, which involve hierarchical systems with multiple interactions and integrations (fusion) at multiple levels. Lev Vygotsky's sociocultural theory illustrates the former, and Urie Bronfenbrenner's bioecological systems theory and Paul Baltes's life-span developmental theory and his selection, optimization, and compensation (SOC) model are examples of the latter.

Developmental theories also differ as to whether they regard development as driven by genetic forces through maturation or caused by environmental shaping through learning. Noam Chomsky's language theory represents nativism, and learning theories emphasize nurture. Most theories no longer create a split between nature and nurture; rather, interaction and bidirectional influences are accepted. Robert Plomin's perspectives on heredity environment relationships and Sandra Scarr and Kathleen McCartney's gene-environment correlations well demonstrate this understanding.

Another difference is seen in the domain-general versus domain-specific debate. The domain-general perspective believes in general cognitive competence that governs all cognitive performance. The domain-specific perspective argues for separate origins and developmental courses, as well as specific brain structures (faculties) for knowledge-based skills and abilities. Piaget's theory and Robbie Case's neo-Piagetian theory of cognitive development are domain general. Expertise studies and Howard E. Gardner's multiple intelligences have domainspecific assumptions.

RESEARCH

To study developmental changes, three variables are particularly relevant: age, cohort, and time of measurement. Age is the chronological age of the person, cohort refers to a group of people who were born in a certain year or in a specific period (such as a generation), and time of measurement means the time when data are collected. Brief descriptions of three categories of developmental designs follow.

Cross-Sectional Designs. A cross-sectional design involves at least two age groups measured once: for example, two groups of twenty-year-olds and fifty year-olds measured in 1990. Researchers want to learn about age differences, but age and cohort are confounded so that researchers are not able to know whether the differences observed are caused by people's different ages or their exposure to different historical events since they were born in different years.

Longitudinal Designs. A longitudinal design involves one group of people (a particular cohort) measured repeatedly over time: for example, one group of people aged fifteen interviewed in 1990 and then in 2000. There are three variations. Trend or time-lag designs involve people of the same age, but data collecting occurs in different years (for example, collecting data from graduating seniors every year to study the trends or changes in seniors' characteristics). Cohort longitudinal designs involve collecting data in different years from different samples selected from the same cohort (for example, collecting data from a baby-boomer sample in 2002 and from a new baby-boomer sample in 2007 to study the changes in the cohort). Panel longitudinal designs involve data collecting from the same group repeatedly over time (for example, the same people are interviewed every ten years to study changes). Longitudinal studies may reveal age-related changes over time, confounded with time of measurement. They are time-consuming and may suffer from the history effect (effects of irrelevant events that happened in the intervals between data-collecting points), attrition (loss of participants), and difficulty in generalizing the findings to different cohorts.

Sequential Designs. A sequential design combines cross-sectional and longitudinal components in that it follows several cohorts over time with multiple points of data collecting: for example, three age groups interviewed in 1990, 1995, and 2000. These studies are valuable because multiple comparisons can be made to figure out age differences, changes over time, developmental trends, and cohort effects.

Some developmental psychologists, especially those who are interested in skill development and domain-specific theories, use the microgenetic method to detail the developmental course of a particular skill (precursor, emerging, developing, or maturing). Other methods, such as systematic observations, caregivers' reports, and psychophysiological techniques (for example, electroencephalogram, or EEG, and functional magnetic resonance imaging, or fMRI) are very useful, especially when the people being studied have limited cognitive abilities.

The American Psychological Association (APA) has published "Ethical Principles of Psychologists and Code of Conduct" to guide all psychologists in conducting research and providing professional services. Developmental psychologists need to pay particular attention to ethical treatment of people who are legally incapable of giving informed consent or having difficulty understanding explanations (for example, young children and people with mental disabilities).

CHANGES AND PROSPECTS

The world has changed. People are living longer, and globalization is taking place. Cultural influences are crossing territorial boundaries, and workplaces are becoming diversified. Advancements in technology have created new modes of interaction and also made possible new ways of conducting research and analyzing data. Responding to these drastic changes, psychology is undergoing paradigmatic shifts from dichotomous to interactionist and to complex, dynamic, multilevel contextualist paradigms. A subdiscipline in psychology, developmental psychology has also exhibited this trend.

Extended life expectancy has made it necessary to study adulthood, especially middle and late adulthood. The life-span approach to developmental psychology requires building new theories for adult development and aging, developing new instruments appropriate for adults, and establishing norm references for adults. Research methods, both quantitative and qualitative, must address developmental questions (such as sequential designs and life interviews) and multilevel processes (such as changes in relationship units in structure and over time). Developmental psychologists must work with scientists in other disciplines such as sociology, gerontology, neuroscience, cultural psychology, and behavioral genetics. Through such endeavors, developmental psychology will benefit from mutual stimulation with developmental science and applied developmental psychology. In developmental science, whole-personoriented research focuses on the interplay of collective variables inside and outside the individual (mutual/bidirectional/reciprocal, contextual/dynamic interaction, and integration/fusion) and the relationships between earlier events and their resultant outcomes. Developmental scientists seek to identify parameter critical values that will signify a system's qualitative change when gradual, unstable, quantitative changes during phase transitions eventually reach and cross over the critical values. Variations and instabilities are particularly valued because they provide opportunities for selection and self-organization (true developmental changes). The shared interest in human development across the life span, developmental changes in contexts and over time, and interdisciplinary collaboration can be reciprocally beneficial to developmental psychology and developmental science, and to applied developmental psychology as well.

BIBLIOGRAPHY

Bornstein, Marc H., and Michael E. Lamb. *Developmental Science: An Advanced Textbook*. 5th ed. Mahwah, N.J.: Lawrence Erlbaum, 2005. Describes the history of developmental science, major positions and principles, theories, and applications.

Geary, David C. "Evolutionary Developmental Psychology: Current Status and Future Directions." *Developmental Review* 26 (2006): 113-119. Examines developmental psychology as a multidisciplinary field, with the evolutionary theory brought in, and discusses difficulties with multiple-level analysis and issues interesting to developmental scientists.

Miller, Joan G. "Essential Role of Culture in Developmental Psychology." *New Directions for Child and Adolescent Development* 109 (2005): 33-41. Discusses the essential role of culture in theory building and research methods in developmental psychology.

Miller, Patricia H. *Theories of Developmental Psychology*. New York: Worth, 2002. Reviews major developmental theories.

Pillemer, David B., and Harold W. Sheldon. *Developmental Psychology and Social Change*. New York: Cambridge University Press, 2005. Offers a sociohistorical perspective on the evolution of developmental psychology and examines how historical events, societal changes, and social policies have shaped the field's scope, focus, and research.

Plomin, Robert. *Development, Genetics, and Psychology*. Hillsdale, N.J.: Lawrence Erlbaum, 1986. Discusses the bidirectional interaction between heredity and environment.

Roberts, Maxwell J. *Integrating the Mind: Domain General Versus Domain Specific Processes in Higher Cognition*. Philadelphia: Psychology Press, 2007. Reviews the evidence provided by researchers in their debate on whether the mechanism for higher-order cognition is domain general or domain specific and integration is advocated.

Sigelman, Carol K., and Elizabeth A. Rider. *Life-Span Human Development*. 6th ed. Belmont, Calif.: Wadsworth Cengage Learning, 2009. Introduces the readers into the field of life-span human development.

Ling-Yi Zhou

See also: Behaviorism; Bronfenbrenner, Urie; Children's mental health; Cognitive development: Jean Piaget; Death and dying; Development; Developmental methodologies; Elders' mental health; Erikson, Erik H.; Freud, Sigmund; Hall, G. Stanley; Kohlberg, Lawrence; Kübler-Ross, Elisabeth; Men's mental health; Piaget, Jean; Research ethics; Skinner, B. F.; Teenagers' mental health; Watson, John B.; Women's mental health.

Dewey, John

Born: October 20, 1859, in Burlington, Vermont
Died: June 1, 1952, in New York, New York
Identity: American philosopher, psychologist, and social reformer
Type of psychology: Cognition; Learning; Sensation and perception

Dewey was the most influential American theorist of educational psychology in the twentieth century.

Raised in a family of modest means in Burlington, Vermont, John Dewey graduated from the University of Vermont in 1879. After teaching in high schools for three years, he did graduate study in philosophy and psychology at Johns Hopkins University. He worked for a year with G. Stanley Hall in one of the first American laboratories of psychology, but he was much more influenced by philosopher George S. Morris, whose abstract theories were inspired by Hegelian idealism. In 1884, he completed his doctoral dissertation, "The Psychology of Kant," and from then until his full retirement in 1939, he served as professor of philosophy and psychology successively at the University of Michigan, the University of Chicago, and Columbia University.

In his early articles on psychology, Dewey attacked the idea of mind-body dualism and attempted to reconcile Hegelian idealism with experimental psychology. He argued that psychology must begin with experience and that only afterward is it possible to isolate the relationships between subject and object. In the first edition of his textbook, *Psychology* (1887), he presented psychology as the study of how "absolute self-consciousness" is manifested in individual consciousness. Within a few years, however, in his revisions of the book, he moved away from this quasi-religious idealism and began to advocate a philosophy of evolutionary naturalism, emphasizing the adjustment of individuals to their environment. Influenced by William James and George Herbert Mead, he gradually accepted an instrumental form of pragmatism, considering "mental entities" as tools useful for an organism's survival and advancement.

Dewey's influential article "The Reflex Arc in Psychology," which appeared in the *Psychological Review* in 1896, is usually considered the beginning of functionalism in psychology. Unlike Edward Titchener, who took a structuralist and introspectionist approach, Dewey focused on how organisms adapt to changing environmental conditions. Rather than conceiving stimulus and response as separate events, he asserted that they were two aspects of a functional relationship, like links in a chain. Elected president of the American Psychological Association in 1899, Dewey used his presidential address, "Psychology and Social Practice," to emphasize the importance of social conditions to the development of the psyche. As he came to view psychology as a social science, his interests began to center on the construction of the character and habits of individuals and the reform of social institutions.

Except for *Human Nature and Conduct* (1922), Dewey's later works were not devoted to psychology proper, although all of his major works are relevant to psychological concerns and problems. His interests increasingly focused on social reform and the practical application of educational theory. Recognized as the leader of the progressive education movement, he emphasized problem solving, social development, and nonauthoritarian "child-centered" teaching. Because of these emphases, many admirers and critics have mistakenly interpreted Dewey as an opponent of adult direction, intellectual rigor, and the acquisition of knowledge.

BIBLIOGRAPHY

Campbell, James. *Understanding John Dewey: Nature and Cooperative Intelligence*. Chicago: Open Court, 1995. Recognized as the best one-volume discussion of Dewey's philosophical perspective within the context of social and intellectual history.

Dalton, Thomas Carlyle. *Becoming John Dewey.* Bloomington: Indiana University Press, 2002. A scholarly study of how Dewey's thought was influenced by a wide diversity of philosophers, psychologists, and natural scientists.

Hildebrand, David. *Dewey: Beginner's Guide.* Oxford, England: One World, 2008. Concise and critical analysis of Dewey's theories in ethics, functional psychology, pragmatism, and social reform.

Thomas Tandy Lewis

See Also: Children's mental health; Cognitive psychology; Educational psychology; Environmental psychology; James, William; Learning.

Diagnosis

Type of psychology: All

Diagnosis is a process whereby an assessor evaluates symptoms and signs of illness or abnormality to be able to determine the type of problem present. This can be done using interviews, observation, and formal testing instruments or procedures, including biological tests.

Key Concepts

- Assessment
- Associated features
- Course
- Criteria
- Differential diagnosis
- Interviewing
- Screening
- Signs
- Symptoms

INTRODUCTION

The word "diagnosis" is derived from two Greek roots: *dia*, which means "to distinguish," and *gnosis*, which means "knowledge." It is most often understood to be a static noun, but from the perspective of a psychologist or a person assessing an afflicted individual, it is seen as a process whereby one understands the condition of the affected person. Diagnosis is not a one-time event but is ongoing. For example, conditions may worsen over time or be complicated by other problems; therefore, diagnoses may shift. As such, continued assessment is very important to maintain an accurate diagnosis to facilitate effective treatment. When diagnoses shift, changes can be noted in terms of new or worsened signs (the observable indications of mental health problems) and symptoms (the problems reported by clients indicating their discomfort, notice of changes, or abnormality in their way of being). In many ways, the process of diagnosis has no discrete end but instead consists of different observation points in time when the progress of a disorder is evaluated.

SCREENING

The goal of diagnosis is to arrive at information that can be communicated and used to aid in treatment. In the United States, mental health diagnoses are typically based on the framework presented in the American Psychiatric Association's *Diagnostic and Statistical Manual of Mental Disorders* (DSM),which is updated periodically. In other parts of the world, the *International Classification of Diseases* (ICD) is used for similar purposes. The ICD is maintained cooperatively by professionals associated with the World Health Organization and updated regularly. To be diagnosed with a particular mental disorder by either of these systems, individuals go through a systematic evaluation to determine whether they satisfy the diagnostic criteria, or the conditions necessary to qualify for a disorder.

Often, the diagnostic process begins when individuals notice symptoms and seek the consultation of a professional. Alternatively, this process might be prompted by a significant other, such as a friend or family member, or even an employer or religious adviser, who notices a problem. Sometimes when individuals seek consultation for one problem, such as minor physical or mental health complaints, the assisting professionals may notice other symptoms that trigger investigation. At that time, the professional will begin a series of systematic inquiries, ruling possible conditions in and out of consideration, to determine how best to proceed with further diagnostic work. In some cases, a preliminary step called screening may be undertaken. Screening is a relatively brief procedure in which the signs and symptoms that have the highest association with specific mental health conditions are asked about to determine whether a more thorough evaluation is necessary.

Typically, at the conclusion of a screening a person is placed into one of two categories: possibly having the condition of concern or most likely not having the condition. Those individuals in the former category receive more thorough evaluations. Those who are judged as unlikely to have the condition do not receive more thorough evaluations immediately but instead may be invited to continue their own observations of symptoms or to begin another path of diagnostic inquiry.

For those performing the screening, the primary goal is to identify those individuals who may have a problem. It is also important, however, not to rule out individuals for further evaluation who might actually have the condition of concern but do not exhibit signs of it during the screening. In technical terms, the first group is known as true positives: individuals who are screened as likely to have the condition and who actually have it. The second group is known as false negatives: individuals who are screened as not having the condition but actually do have it.

Screening tests increase in their usefulness if they are not overly sensitive and do not produce too many false positives: people who screen positive but who actually do not have the condition. It is important to minimize false positives because some diagnostic procedures, such as magnetic resonance imaging (MRI), are expensive. Additionally, some diagnostic procedures can be invasive, such as injection dye procedures used to observe different organ systems in action. Minimizing false positives in screening saves money for health care providers but, more important, also saves potential pain, suffering, and anxiety for individual clients. Finally, screening also increases in usefulness when it can effectively identify true negatives: individuals who are screened as not having the problem and who in fact do not. The sooner these individuals are identified, the more quickly they can be referred onward to other professionals for evaluation or considered for other diagnostic possibilities.

ASSESSMENT

In general, screening is important because it is often brief, can be applied to a large number of people with little effort, saves expensive time on evaluation, and yet can efficiently identify individuals who may be most likely to have a formal mental health condition. The next step in a diagnostic workup after one is screened as positive is the process of assessment, a lengthier process in which detailed information about the patient's probable condition is gathered in a systematic way. Assessment procedures may include formal diagnostic interviewing, in which the psychologist or clinician asks a step-by-step series of questions to get a clear picture of what the symptoms are and how they developed. Interviewing can be used to assess not only the individual affected but also family members or significant others, as sometimes these individuals have valuable information related to the history or development of the symptoms. These informants can also be helpful if the individual is not able or willing to speak or to describe the condition.

Both screening and assessment procedures may also include the use of paper-and-pencil questionnaires, surveys, or checklists about symptoms. They also may include observation by the psychologist in interpersonal interactions or under certain other conditions and formal medical tests such as blood tests, urine toxicology, and tests of psychomotor performance. Usually the biggest differences between screenings and assessments are based on speed, cost, and the skill to do the work involved. Because assessment is more in-depth than screening, it is more expensive, takes longer, requires greater skill, and is also more intensive for both the evaluator and the individual undergoing assessment.

Overall, assessment procedures seek to reveal the course of the symptoms present or how they have changed over time. Assessment also seeks to show how the most prominent symptoms relate both to one another and to less prominent symptoms. This is particularly important to a process called differential diagnosis, in which disorders that may appear alike in some features are diagnostically separated from one another to determine if one or more conditions are present.

If, in the process of assessment, the number, severity, and duration of the individual's symptoms and signs meet the diagnostic criteria, or standards of required evidence to warrant a diagnosis, then a diagnosis is rendered. If the signs and symptoms are all present but fall short of the right number, severity, or duration, then the condition might be thought of as subclinical. This means that although the symptoms do not meet the formal criteria necessary to warrant a diagnosis, they are problematic and may still require some clinical observation and attention.

Finally, sometimes a client may have one disorder that is clearly present but also what might be called leftover symptoms that do not seem to fit. In some cases, these symptoms may be what are known as associated features, or symptoms associated with disorders but not part of the disorder in a formal diagnostic way. For example, many people who suffer from agoraphobia also experience symptoms of depression. In some cases, these individuals also qualify for a diagnosis of depression. In other cases, they are experiencing depressed mood as a consequence of having agoraphobia, and the depression is an associated feature. Once these aspects of a diagnosis are understood, the information can be put to use.

IMPORTANCE

Diagnoses are important because of the information that they convey, in facilitating effective communication among professionals, and in facilitating effective treatment planning. The diagnostic terminology of the DSM and ICD allows professionals to communicate clearly with one another about their clients' conditions.

This communication helps to direct clients to the proper treatment and also ensures continuity of care when clients switch treatment providers. For example, a client who is traveling or is outside his or her regular locale may need assistance and seek out another health care provider. The new provider would be greatly aided in helping the client by communication with the regular provider about the individual and his or her condition. A proper assignment could then be reached to create a useful treatment strategy.

On another level, standard diagnoses are useful because they allow for important communication between clinicians and researchers in psychology. This is most true when new symptoms are emerging and the need arises to develop new treatment strategies. When the mental health community uses the same language about signs and symptoms in the study of specific conditions, medical and psychological knowledge can advance much more efficiently.

More practically, diagnostic information is important to treatment because of the necessity to justify treatment financially. When a client meets formal diagnostic criteria for a disorder, the health care provider can administer services and justify the treatment to insurance agencies and others interested in the financial management of mental health problems. Diagnoses may also help such agencies to discover trends in which treatments work and where disorders tend to be developing (the focus of the field of epidemiology) or to recognize gaps in services, such as when people with certain disorders suddenly disappear from the mental health care system.

Even more important, however, standard diagnoses and thorough diagnostic procedures allow for good communication among professionals, their clients, and the families of those affected by mental illness. Communicating diagnostic information effectively to the client and family members or significant others is likely to help with the management of the problem. The better that all involved understand the symptoms and prognosis, the more likely everyone is to assist with treatment compliance. Further, it can be very helpful to families to learn that their loved ones have formal diagnoses. Mental health conditions can create chaos and misunderstanding, and improvements in relationships may occur if families and significant others are able to place problematic symptoms in perspective. Rather than attributing symptomatic behavior to personal irresponsibility or problems of character, family members and friends can see the symptoms as reflecting the illness. Although this understanding does not make everything perfect, it may help facilitate a more effective problem-solving strategy for the affected person and significant others.

CONTEXT

Diagnosis is a process most often associated with a visit to see a primary care physician, but primary care physicians are not the only ones who perform this work. Licensed and certified professionals of many types gather diagnostic information and render diagnoses. Psychiatrists and psychologists predominate in the area of mental health diagnoses, but social workers, educational counselors, substance use counselors, criminal justice workers, social service professionals, and those who work with the developmentally disabled also gather mental health diagnostic information and use it in their work.

Over time, the process of assessment has been separated from the actual diagnostic decision, so that assistants and helpers may be the ones gathering and organizing the symptom-related information to present it to the expert diagnostician who has the authority to render the diagnosis. This shift has occurred as a matter of financial necessity in many cases, as it is more expensive to use experts for time-intensive information gathering than it is to use such assistants. Increasing effort has also been focused on developing more accurate diagnostic screening and assessment instruments to the same end. If time can be saved on assessment by using screening, so that only likely cases receive full symptom assessment, then valuable medical resources will be saved. Further, if paper-and-pencil or other diagnostic procedures can be used to better describe symptoms in a standardized manner, then even the time of diagnostic assistants can be saved.

On one hand, such advances may allow more people to be treated in an efficient manner. On the other hand, some complain that people can go undiagnosed and consequently continue to suffer. This situation may be particularly likely for individuals who are not often included in the research on which the screening instruments are designed, such as women and minorities. Similarly, others suggest that these processes put too much paper between the client and the health care provider, creating barriers and weakening therapeutic relationships.

Considering cultural practices and understandings of the doctor-patient relationship is also important, as many cultural groups see the social nature of this relationship as a critical piece of the treatment interaction. While efficiency and saving money are important, recognition that those goals are culturally bound choices must be made. In contemporary society, culture is often a reason that speed and efficiency must be put on hold to truly do an accurate job with diagnosis; more and more culturally relevant pieces of information are used in diagnosis. The way a person expresses a disorder in one culture may differ from how a person from another culture expresses the same disorder. As such, diagnosticians must recognize cultural differences in terms of the way in which symptoms are experienced, expressed, and understood. For some, mental health disorders may be seen as expressions of underlying spiritual problems; for others, they may be seen as disharmonies among elements in the universe or environment; and for others, they may be seen as extensions of physical problems. Each of these perspectives is a valid way of understanding such conditions.

Culture is not limited to a client's race or ethnicity; it also varies by characteristics such as gender, age, sexual orientation, socioeconomic status, and locale. Increasingly, diagnosticians are forced to grapple with such diversity so as to improve diagnostic procedures and client care. Such characteristics are important to diagnosis not only because of differences in perspectives on illness but also because of differences in the prevalence of illnesses in various groups and how those groups may or may not respond to the treatments available. This distinction is particularly important when considering medical conditions that might be associated with psychological disorders. In some cases, medical problems may mimic psychiatric disorders; in other cases, they may mask such disorders. Because some disorders are more common in certain populations, knowledge of such differences is important to the process of differential diagnosis.

Culture is an important consideration in diagnosis because the information gathered is transmitted socially. Knowledge of diagnoses is exchanged among professionals, researchers, and clients and their families. Diagnoses have social meaning; some diagnoses can cause a person to be stigmatized. As crucial differences exist in the degree of stigmatization in different cultures, the delivery of such important mental health information deserves thoughtful consideration, good planning, and follow-up to ensure that all parties involved are properly informed.

Finally, knowledge is a moving target. Just as diagnosis may shift in an individual over time, the societal and scientific understanding of conditions may change because of new information. In the twenty-first century, the field of developmental psychopathology increasingly forces scientists studying psychopathology to reconsider models of etiology. Associations among conditions from childhood and adulthood are leading to new theories and questions that may ultimately affect screening, assessment, and diagnosis. For instance, some children who develop behavioral problems may grow up to develop any of a number of other mental health problems later in life. Therefore, better understanding of how such conditions happen may lead to earlier screening for adult problems in children and perhaps earlier and more effective treatments.

BIBLIOGRAPHY

American Psychiatric Association. *Diagnostic and Statistical Manual of Mental Disorders: DSM-IV-TR*. Rev. 4th ed. Washington, D.C.: Author, 2000. The standard text outlining the major mental health disorders diagnosed in the United States.

Beutler, Larry E., and Mary L. Malik. *Rethinking the DSM: A Psychological Perspective*. Washington, D.C.: American Psychological Association, 2002. Offers critique of the dominant diagnostic framework used in the United States, the *Diagnostic and Statistical Manual of Mental Disorders* (DSM).

Castillo, Richard J. *Culture and Mental Illness: A Client-Centered Approach*. Belmont, Calif.: Wadsworth, 1997. Discusses how cultural issues fit into the diagnostic process and the understanding of mental health and illness.

Seligman, Linda. *Diagnosis and Treatment Planning in Counseling*. 3d ed. New York: Plenum, 2004. Connections between diagnosis and treatment planning are highlighted in this text, with case examples for illustration.

Shea, Shawn Christopher. *Psychiatric Interviewing: The Art of Understanding—A Practical Guide for Psychiatrists, Psychologists, Counselors, Social Workers, and Other Mental Health Professionals*. 2d ed. Philadelphia: W. B. Saunders, 1998. The skills of interviewing as a means of establishing a therapeutic relationship and the basis for forming diagnostic impressions are reviewed from a perspective that is useful for a variety of mental health practitioners. Also allows nonprofessionals to see how interviewing is structured and leads to diagnoses.

Simeonsson, Rune J., and Susan L. Rosenthal, eds. *Psychological and Developmental Assessment: Children with Disabilities and Chronic Conditions*. New York:

Guilford Press, 2001. This text focuses on issues important to the diagnosis of mental health and other behavioral disorders in children.

Trzepacz, Paula T., and Robert W. Baker. *Psychiatric Mental Status Examination.* New York: Oxford University Press, 1993. The mental status examination is one of the foundations of any psychiatric diagnosis. This book describes these procedures for assessing the appearance, activity level, mood, speech, and other behavioral characteristics of individuals under evaluation.

Nancy A. Piotrowski

See Also: Assessment; Confidentiality; *Diagnostic and Statistical Manual of Mental Disorders* (DSM); International Classification of Diseases (ICD); Mental health practitioners; Mental illness: Historical concepts; Observational methods; Psychopathology; Sampling; Scientific methods; Survey research: Questionnaires and interviews.

Dialectical behavioral therapy

Type of psychology: Clinical; Counseling; Family; Psychopathology; Psychotherapy

Dialectical behavioral therapy (DBT) is a specific therapeutic approach focused on the treatment of overemotional disorders that include borderline personality disorder (BPD) and other conditions characterized by self-harming behaviors, recurrent suicidal thinking, and suicidal attempts.

Key Concepts

- Acceptance
- Borderline personality disorder.
- Dialectic
- Lability.

INTRODUCTION

In 1987, psychologist Marsha M. Linehan published her method for treating patients with borderline personality disorder (BPD), which she called dialectical behavioral therapy. Borderline personality disorder is one of more serious and treatment-resistant personality disorders, characterized by dysregulation of emotions (an inability to regulate and control emotional responses), as well as of thoughts, behaviors, and interpersonal relations, including how a person relates to the self. People with this personality configuration experience affective instability, difficulty managing their anger, random impulsivity, proclivity for self-harm, paranoia, extreme fear of abandonment, uncertainty about who they are, and chronic emotional emptiness.

Traditional treatments assumed that therapists could not avoid rejecting patients' self-destructive behaviors and attitudes. These approaches were change-oriented and, though well intentioned, frequently put the therapist at odds with the patient. In developing dialectical behavioral therapy, Linehan enumerated strategies that allowed therapists to accept patients where they were, promoting acceptance-oriented skills in addition to traditional change-oriented skills. An accepting attitude toward patients affirms the worldview inherent in their feelings, attitudes, thoughts, and behavior. It promotes the rectitude of patients' experiences and all aspects of their personal worlds. It also maintains that, however patients are being in the moment, it is the best that they are able to be at that time.

Underlying dialectical behavioral therapy is a constellation of worldviews that highlights the importance of dialectic and the acceptance of life as it is. Acceptance draws heavily from Zen principles; dialectic has its philosophical roots in the work of Immanuel Kant, Frederick Shelling, and, most of all, Georg Hegel. Dialectic is the synthesizing of point and counterpoint. For every stance or particular behavioral occurrence, there is an equally valid, but opposite, stance or occurrence. The therapist supports the patient's moving toward a healthier integration of these ostensibly irreconcilable positions. In practice, dialectical behavioral therapy strategies draw heavily from traditional cognitive and behavioral therapy techniques and process approaches well known in person-centered and emotion-focused therapies.

Before dialectical behavioral therapy, patients with borderline personality disorder were considered almost impossible to treat effectively beyond varying levels of therapeutic stabilization. People with borderline personality disorder are emotionally flammable and fragile, unable to reliably regulate their inner states, have conflict-ridden relationships, frequently consider suicide, and often engage in self-harming behaviors such as cutting. They were raised in and typically perpetuate an invalidating environment, a social environment that actively opposes acceptance of patients' perceptions, feelings, judgments, attitudes, and behaviors. This toxic climate perpetuates pervasive criticism, denigration, trivializing, and random social reinforcement. People in this environment are denied genuine attention, respect, understanding from others, and positive regard for who they are and what they are experiencing. Stress and perceived abandonment or rejection overwhelm the ability of people with borderline personality disorder to self-regulate, and they remain chronically, recurrently, emotionally vulnerable. Therapists were often frustrated (and sometimes intimidated) by these patients' volatility and high degree of risk. Dialectical behavioral therapy became a road map for therapists who trained in it.

HOW THE THERAPY WORKS

Patients who undertake dialectical behavioral therapy begin with "pretreatment," a series of psychotherapy sessions in which the therapist and patient establish a shared understanding of dialectical behavioral therapy's rationale, agreements about what each expects of the other, the levels of dialectical behavioral therapy interventions and treatment targets, and perhaps most important, the commitment to be in treatment. In pretreatment, patients agree to stay in therapy for a specified period, most commonly a year, to come to all therapy sessions, to come on time, to work toward ending all self-harming behaviors, to undertake interpersonal skills training, and to pay fees in a timely manner. Therapy is usually discontinued if four consecutive sessions are missed. Therapists promise to maintain their own ongoing and professionally supportive training, to be available for weekly sessions and phone consultations, to demonstrate positive regard and nonjudgmental attitudes, maintain confidentiality, and obtain additional consultation as would benefit the therapy.

LEVELS OF TREATMENT

Level I of treatment establishes a target hierarchy that includes reduction of self-harming behaviors such as cutting or burning oneself, of behaviors and barriers that interfere with treatment, and of behaviors that interfere with establishing a healthier quality of life. Patients at the early stages of dialectical behavioral therapy treatment are usually highly distressed, bordering on hopelessness, and at the mercy of the enigmatic flow of their own emotional surges. Self-injury, drug abuse, depression, and suicidal thinking are the norm at this state.

Level II begins when the skills developed in Level I are sufficient to contain self-harming patterns. The therapist begins to presumptively treat patients with post-traumatic stress interventions, as these enhance their ability to experience aversive emotions without being undone by them. As progress is made, other emotionally difficult, even overwhelming targets are identified. The emotional and psychological commitments to remaining in treatment at these early stages can result in patients' working against their goals, as in missing therapy appointments, showing up late, and not completing agreed-on homework; it can also result in psychological regression, wherein patients at Level II treatment exhibit Level I functioning (for example, burning or cutting themselves or engaging in other dangerous behaviors). Patients at these levels of care must be closely monitored. Once the functional goals of Level II are reliably sustained, the majority of patients leave treatment. They have expended a great effort at much personal cost to have gotten this far.

For patients proceeding to Level III, the targets of treatment are similar to those of typical psychotherapy in that they aim at reducing or eliminating behaviors that are not debilitating but interfere with experiencing ordinary pleasure, happiness, fulfillment, and personal meaning.

Level IV targets higher-order psychological values: a functional application of one's philosophy of person, integration, and the blending of spiritual elements with those of psychological self-actualization.

MODALITIES OF TREATMENT

Dialectical behavioral therapy uses four modes of treatment that are not commonly found together in other therapeutic approaches: group-skills training for patients, individual therapy for patients, telephone consultations between patients and therapists, and therapists' participation in an ongoing consultation team. Many of the ways borderline personality disorder patients regress are through perceived, and thus experienced, negative social interactions. These are most effectively worked through and improved by training in a group setting. Individual therapy is typically weekly and involves working toward the established and mutually agreed-on targets during pretreatment. Because the inner life of patients with borderline personality disorder can be so tumultuous, telephone consultations are routinely used to bolster patients and review how to apply the concepts and skills discussed in individual and group training. Because this is such a challenging patient population, the standard practice of dialectical behavioral therapy requires its practitioners to meet regularly with other dialectical behavior therapists for case presentation, honing of dialectical behavioral therapy therapeutic skills, and peer consultation.

FUTURE

Though Linehan focused her earlier work on patients with borderline personality disorder, and dialectical behavioral therapy is the therapy of first choice in their treatment, the principles and techniques have been applied to other often hard-to-treat patient groups such as those with eating disorders, bipolar disorder (in conjunction with targeted psychopharmacology), histrionic personality disorder, a history of sexual and violent assault, and a variety of diagnoses among the elderly. Though it requires a high degree of patient commitment and specific training that implies lifelong learning, it is the most powerful and effective intervention available to a patient group that had often been considered nearly impossible to treat effectively.

BIBLIOGRAPHY

Hanh, Thich Nhat. *The Miracle of Mindfulness: An Introduction to the Practice of Meditation*. New York: Houghton Mifflin, 2004. Nondenominational introduction to meditative techniques. Has many suggestions and exercises that provide a good focus for achieving peaceful acceptance of what are often tumultuous emotional states.

Linehan, Marsha M. *Skills Training Manual for Treating Borderline Personality Disorder*. New York: Guilford Press, 1993. The key work for learning how to deal with this patient group. Written for professionals, it is a comprehensive, integrated and invaluable resource, a true breakthrough work in the field of psychotherapy.

McKay, Matthew, Jeffrey C. Wood, and Jeffrey Brantley. *Dialectical Behavioral Therapy Workbook: Practical DBT Exercises for Learning Mindfulness, Interpersonal Effectiveness, Emotional Regulation, and Distress Tolerance*. New York: New Harbinger, 2007. Solid resource for those trying to cope with "overemotional conditions" such as borderline personality disorder. Is best used in conjunction with professional treatment.

Marra, Thomas. *Depressed and Anxious: The Dialectical Behavior Therapy Workbook for Overcoming Depression and Anxiety*. New York: New Harbinger, 2004. Great self-help work. Structured, focused, pertinent for helping people with high levels of depression or anxiety use dialectical behavior therapy themselves. Not a substitute for professional treatment.

Spradlin, Scott E. *Don't Let Your Emotions Run Your Life: How Dialectical Behavioral Therapy Can Put You in Control*. New York: New Harbinger, 2004. Deceptively simple workbook that has been largely well received by patients and psychologists. Practical help for those struggling with overemotional disorders. More effective as an adjunct to dialectical behavior therapy treatment.

Yudovsky, Stuart C. *Fatal Flaws: Navigating Destructive Relationships with People with Disorders of Personality and Character.* 4th ed. Washington, D.C.: American Psychiatric Association, 2005. Eloquent, easy-to-read, evidence-based, practical treatment for calming tumultuous interpersonal waters typical of borderline personality disorder.

Paul Moglia

See Also: Cognitive-behavioral therapy; Marsha Linehan; Personality disorders; Psychotherapy; Treatment.

Disability
Psychological impact

Type of psychology: Biological bases of human behavior; Clinical; Counseling; Developmental; Health; Rehabilitation; School

Disability is a phenomenon in our society that many of us may face in our lifetime. This could be attributed to a congenital condition, sudden accident, aging, or an age-related genetic disease. Disability is defined as a mental or physical impairment that substantially limits a person from completing a major life activity in an able-body environment. This could include, but is not limited to, breathing, thinking, learning, processing information, seeing, hearing, walking, talking, and engaging in recreational and social play, working. Additionally, an impairment may limit an individual because of societal attitudes (stigma and prejudice) regarding the specific condition (e.g.,HIV/AIDS in the early part of the epidemic in the 1980s). Examples of disability types are characterized as persons with perceptual disabilities which include learning, visual, and hearing impairments; illness-related conditions which incorporate diabetes, cancer, and AIDS; neurological conditions like cerebral palsy or multiple sclerosis; intellectual disabilities such as Down syndrome; psychiatric disabilities as witness in schizophrenia, bipolar disorder, or major depression; mobility-related disabilities such as quadriplegia; and environmental concerns as seen in asthma, allergies, and environmental toxins.

Key concepts

- Barrier free society
- Disability awareness
- Disability adjustment
- Barrier free society
- Psychological impact

INTRODUCTION

People have been defined by their ability to engage in society on many levels. Some of this engagement consists of having the ability to love a family and procreate, participate in recreational and social play, work , be involved in a nexus with a religious affiliation, participate fully in the community in which they reside, and so much more. Being diagnosed with a disability at birth or during childhood, young adulthood, middle life, or even senior years can greatly change the expectations of accomplishing some of these life goals. Thus, living with the label of disability can be an emotional and stressful endeavorand quite a psychological adjustment.

Currently, it is estimated that there are 51 million people in the United States with a defined disability (Annual Disability Compendium, 2010). A disability is characterized as a mental or physical impairment that substantially limits a person from completing a major life activity. In American society, individuals with disabilities face many societal barriers which prevent them from having full access to life activities. This could cause extreme psychological stress and hardship in such an individual. Thus, strong advocates lobbying for bills to be passed into law in order to protect these individuals and grant them the rights to engage in work activities, receive an adequate level of education, and access to social services within their local community were established.

Despite proactive legislation, the severity and type of the physical or mental disability can impact the level of participation an individual has in society. The psychological impact of disability surrounds the personal, psychological, environmental, societal, and economic aspects of the diagnosis of the disability. The personal impact involves the feelings experienced when initially diagnosed with a disability. They may experience initial shock, disbelief, denial, anger, reduced levels of self-esteem, depression, anxiety, fear of death, and grief as they mourn the loss of body functioning and status.

The person's psychological view of the disability is considered mostly in a negative light and may include a marked unacceptable conceptualization framework of the person's body status. Many are now placed into the sick role or a role of pity and charity attributed to the disability. This is a common view of the biomedical model of disability, where the disability is viewed as pathology that requires treatment. This view posits that the person who has the disability mustbe fixed. If unable to cure the disability, the person is then placed in the role of pity or charity because he or she is no longer viewed as having the able-bodied status and require care and assistance.

This person has lost able-bodied status and is now viewed as a non-contributor in society and, further, may require the intensive care and support of the society. The stigma and prejudice associated with the disability causes the person to feel psychological stress and develop a negative self-image. Thus, dealing with disability, depending on the person affected, is considered more an adaptation than an acceptance of the disability. True acceptance of the disability is a psychological journey that each person undertakes. This journey greatly depends on the type of disability and the quality of life after the diagnosis.

Diagnosis may cause an individual to call into question the meaning and purpose of life. It challenges one's values and life commitments, and an individual may try to find some significance to what happened. He or she may look at global meaning and situational meaning to assist with life salience.

The person may also wonder about his or her ability to deal with the effects of the disability and the impact of the disability on educational, occupational, familial, sexual, parenting, social, driving, political, religious, shopping, beauty, and exercise goals that the person had prior to the diagnosis. Can I still live a "normal" life despite my disability? Can I live in this environment despite having a disability? Can I work, have a family, or even engage in recreational activities despite having a disability? These questions often cause psychological stress.

DISABILITY AWARENESS

Disability awareness consists of environmental, societal, and economic factors. The environmental aspects associated with disability include barriers in the environmental structure. To fully comprehend disability awareness associated with environmental barriers, it is helpful to view the construct of disability as a more global perspective. To accomplish this task, we must use the social model of disability. This model focuses on power, resources, and unequal access for persons with disabilities. This model was developed in the United States during the 1960s and 1970s.

The model originated from the deinstitutionalization and independent living movements which were organized by individuals with more severe physical and mental disabilities. They wanted to live more freely in the community and be transferred out of the sick role fostered by state and city institutions. These individuals advocated for more involvement in decisions pertaining to their living arrangements in the community, relationships, employment needs, use of assistive technology, and the removal of environmental barriers.

They believed that the disability was not the problem. Rather, the problem was the environment that created architectural and attitudinal barriers that prevented a person with a disability from accessing the liberties that society offers others. What needed to change was a society that provided equal access to all persons. Persons needed to be considered temporarily able-bodied because anyone can become disabled in the future. This thinking would enable a society to have full access for all to benefit. This access includes retail services, technology and media, legislation, polling stations, education, employment, buildings, exits, restrooms, parking spots, transportation, and medical facilities to name a few.

The societal implications of disability originate from a long history of viewing the person with a disability as an inferior individual. From the 17th through the 19th centuries, mental illness was considered demon possession and/or the lack of religious belief. We can trace the mental health movement where individuals who had mental impairments were separated from those who did not. People with mental disabilities were placed into asylums where they were chained, beaten, sexually abused, denied food or water, neglected, and placed into isolation for displaying their symptomology. Some of these patients died from this deplorable care, and others survived hoping for a better outcome.

Doctor Philippe Pinel from France and Dr. Benjamin Rush from the United States were the first to treat patients with mental disabilities in revolutionary new ways. These physicians took off the chains from their patients. They dispensed respect, care,dignity, kindness, and true medical alternatives, and by listening to the patients, they achieved excellent results. They emphasized the value of careful observations, record keeping, and experimentation. They also applied objective scientific methods to the study and treatment of mental illness.

Dorothea Dix also became one of America's famous champions of the rights of persons with mental illness during the 19th century. She was a strong advocate and visited several hundred sites in the United States where persons with mental illness were incarcerated. As she visited, she collected data and used that information to successfully launch appeals for reform to both state and federal legislators. Finally, in 1860, her efforts were successful. She was able to procure state legislatures to appropriate funds to create new mental facilities that would provide humane treatment to patients with mental illness.

Finally, there are economic facets that can be attributed to disability. These facets are the economic cost of treating the disability, the economic hardship the disability might cause due to loss of employment, underemployment, or no employment opportunity because of workplace discrimination associated with the disability. Other economic challenges attributed to disability can be cost of housing and vehicle modifications related to the disability, cost of assistive technology, rehabilitation aids and devices, human assistants, and insurance.

DISABILITY ADJUSTMENT

As the person begins to adjust to the disability, the person needs to utilize a problem-focused coping framework. This involves developing appropriate problem-solving skills which assists the person in determining how to cope and what to do. This will help the person develop reaction steps that might be either to deal with the consequences of the disability or to ignore it. Next, the person will have to define a plan. This plan can incorporate the need for social support.

Social support is defined as the relationships that a person with a disability has in life in order to cope with the disability. These relationships have some meaning and sense of attachment for the person with a disability. There are three categories of social support:

1. social embeddedness which is a connection a person has to others in their environment,
2. perceived social support which is a person's cognitive appraisal of connections to others, and
3. enacted support which is the action conducted by others as they demonstrate their support of the person with the disability.

These types of support are demonstrated by emotional or physical care, material resources, and spiritual guidance. These types of support can be given by numerous sources such as family members, friends, clergy, medical service providers, and social service agencies.

In addition to developing support, they should also utilize medical and mental health interventions. Those with a disability must take a health-oriented, self-management approach when working with the consequences of the disability. They should define their vocational calling, seek employment opportunities, or obtain volunteer options. They must also accept their new body image as a beautiful person with a disability and define their self-worth as a good person with a disability. Persons with disabilities should utilize support groups, reference materials, and work toward an achievable inner acceptance and peace. Ultimately, they are responsible for ridding themselves of the rage, anger, and frustration attributed to the diagnosis of the disability.

A BARRIER FREE SOCIETY

While a person with disability may experience psychological distress, living in a barrier free society can aid the healing process. This means that the person with the disability is not faced with architectural and attitudinal barriers and can be explained by the environmental model of disability. This model examines the individual with the disability and the environment in which the individual lives. In this model, disability is characterized as the individual's acquirement of diverse achievements, functional skills, traits, and strengths, including biological and organic features. Advocates for this model believe that limitations, experienced as the result of a disability, are environmentally or socially based. Essentially, social barriers of people with disabilities consist of both physical inaccessibility and the perceptions and attitudes held by individuals without disabilities toward individuals with disabilities. Because of this problem, legislation such as the Americans with Disabilities Act Amendments Act of 2008 (PL 110-325), the Americans with Disabilities Act of 1990 (PL 101-336), the Individuals with Disabilities Education Act of 1990 (PL 101-476), and the Rehabilitation Act Amendments of 1992 (PL 102-569) were passed in hopes of leveling the playing field for persons with disabilities.

BIBLIOGRAPHY

Annual Disability Compendium Disability Statistics. Retrieved January 26, 2011, from the Disability Compendium Web site: http://www.disabilitycompendium.org/pdf/Compendium2010.pdf, 2010. This is an annual disability statistics manual which states the disability utilization rates including the number of persons in the United States with disabilities, social services utilization rates, employment, education, and recreational activities, It is an academic andcomprehensive look at disability statistics in the United States.

Hanjorgiris, W. F., & O'Neill, J. H. (2006)." Counseling People With Disabilities: A Sociocultural Minority Group Perspective". In C. C. Lee (Eds.), *Multicultural Issues in Counseling: New Approaches to Diversity* (319-343). Alexandria, VA: American Counseling Association. This is a systematic analysis of the impact of disability on clients with disabilities. This text is a good user's guide for counseling professionals who plan on working with members from this population.

McLennon, S. "Knowledge, Attitudes, and Skills Related to Disabilities Among Psychologists - Are We Competent To Practice In This Multicultural Domain?" (Doctoral Dissertation, Seton Hall University, 2012). Dissertation Abstracts International, 73, 11-B, E, 2013. This research investigation analyzes the professional competency areas needed for licensed psychologists in order for them to work effectively with clients with disabilities. This was a path analysis design that identified 22 variables needed for psychologists to master when working with this population.

Olkin, R. (2002). "Could You Hold The Door For Me? Including Disability In Diversity". *Cultural Diversity & Ethnic Minority Psychology*, 8(2), 130-137. This article is a pioneer review of disability in the field of psychology, and how most psychologists are lacking the skill-set needed to work effectively with this population. This article further states how disability issues are not commonly taught in graduate psychology programs and how disability is a psychological problem that most psychologists will encounter in their day-to-day practice with clients.

Peterson, D. (2008). "Disability In Counseling Psychology". In S, D. Brown & R, W Lent (, *Handbook of Counseling Psychology* (212-232). New York, NY: Wiley. This text examines the need for the aspect of disability to be considered a multicultural counseling domain area of interest in the field of psychology. This text helps psychologists understand the psychological implications of disability for patients with disabilities.

Rubin, S. E., and Roessler, R. T. (2008). *Foundations of Vocational Rehabilitation*. Austin, TX: Pro. Ed Process. This text is a comprehensive review of the historical perspective on disability in the United States; disability models designed and implemented; legislation enacted in the United States to help establish a barrier free society; the heroes and champions of the disability movement; and treatment interventions established to assist persons with disabilities to improve the quality of their lives.

Sharon McLennon Wier

See Also: Coping; Developmental disabilities; Marsha Linehan; Occupational therapy; Physical disabilities; Psychotherapy; Stress; Therapy.

Disaster psychology

Type of psychology: Emotion; Sensation and perception; Social psychology; Stress

Disaster psychology examines how emotional trauma can be assessed and treated during emergencies and investigates disaster-related conditions such as post-traumatic stress disorder..

Key Concepts

- Catastrophes
- Emergency
- Mass casulties
- Relief workers
- Shock
- Survivors
- Trauma
- Unpredictability
- Victims
- Witnesses

INTRODUCTION

Disaster psychology deals with the reactions and responses of victims and witnesses of natural and artificial catastrophes, such as earthquakes, tornadoes, hurricanes, airplane crashes, train wrecks, toxic spills, industrial accidents, fires, explosions, terrorism, and school shootings, which often involve mass casualties. In 2011, the American Red Cross (ARC) estimated that it responded to over 70,000 disasters requiring external emergency aid every year, ranging from single-home fires or floods to national catastrophes. In addition, international events such as the 2004 tsunami in Southeast Asia and the 2008 terrorist attacks in Mumbai, India, require the assistance of emergency workers from around the world.

Mental health professionals use their skills to help trauma survivors and relief workers cope with the drastic changes and shock associated with tragedies. Many mental health professionals consider disaster service a social responsibility. Even though people may not have obvious physical wounds, they usually suffer emotional pain. Disaster mental health personnel often serve as media contacts to educate the public about ways to resume normalcy.

Short-term crisis mental health services assess the psychological status of affected populations, provide grief counseling, and initiate individual and community recovery. They provide emotional support when relatives identify bodies at morgues. Volunteers help victims who temporarily suffer survivor guilt, anxiety, mood swings, sleep disturbances, social withdrawal, and depression by reassuring them that they are reacting normally to abnormal, unexpected, and overwhelming situations that have disrupted their lives and that their heightened emotions will eventually lessen.

Long-term disaster psychology recognizes how catastrophes can result in some participants having post-traumatic stress disorder and other delayed or chronic reactions such as nightmares and flashbacks, which are sometimes triggered by disaster anniversaries or sirens. Therapists also deal with disaster-related conditions such as substance abuse, irrational fears, and self-mutilation.

In addition to providing practical services, some disaster psychologists conduct research to develop more effective methods to help people during disasters. Procedures are developed to be compatible with varying coping styles for adults and children. Disaster psychologists often conduct workshops and conferences to teach techniques based on prior experiences to mental health relief workers, health professionals, and community leaders. Preparation and planning for future disasters is an important component of disaster psychology. Disaster mental health providers educate representatives of schools, municipalities, humanitarian organizations, and corporations about disaster readiness.

Disaster mental health professionals create educational materials to inform people about how to cope with disasters. Most disaster psychology literature addresses how disasters make people feel vulnerable and helpless and suggest practicing psychological skills to acquire some control during volatile situations. For example, after the September 11, 2001, terrorist attacks on the United States, many disaster psychological pamphlets emphasized how to keep in perspective the actual personal risks of unknown threats such as anthrax contamination and biological warfare.

HISTORICAL DEVELOPMENT

Mental health professionals developed disaster psychology methods based on medical triage techniques and practical experiences with disasters. Several notable disasters were crucial to establishing disaster mental health services. When 491 people died in Boston's Cocoanut Grove nightclub fire in 1942, Erich Lindemann investigated how survivors reacted emotionally. Disaster mental health authorities often cite Lindemann's trauma and stress study as the fundamental work addressing disaster crisis theory. Pioneers in this emerging field used studies of military and civilian reactions to war-related stress and anxiety.

In 1972, a dam collapse resulted in the flooding of Buffalo Creek in West Virginia, causing 125 deaths. Approximately five thousand people became homeless. When survivors sued the dam's owner, attorneys hired mental health consultants, who collected information about the psychological impact of the disaster on the community. This information was evaluated twenty years later, when investigators conducted a follow-up psychological study of survivors. The 1974 Disaster Relief Act stated that Federal Emergency Management Agency (FEMA) emergency funds could be used for mental health services. The Three Mile Island nuclear meltdown in 1979 revealed the need for mental health disaster services to be better coordinated and focused.

A decade later, the ARC emphasized that coordinated professional mental health response procedures comparable to medical health response plans were crucial. Often, ARC nurses who were not qualified to provide psychological services encountered disaster victims and relief workers in need of such help. The situation was exacerbated by the succession of major disasters in 1989: the Sioux City, Iowa, airplane crash in July; Hurricane Hugo in the Caribbean and southeastern United States in September; and the Loma Prieta earthquake in the San Francisco Bay area in October. Psychologists who assisted airplane crash survivors and victims' families suggested that the American Psychological Association (APA) work with the ARC to establish a national plan for the training of disaster mental health personnel.

Mental health teams were assigned to accompany ARC relief workers when Hurricane Hugo occurred. These volunteers were already exhausted when the San Francisco earthquake took place, but instead of returning home, relief personnel were asked to transfer to San Francisco. Unfamiliarity with inner-city and ethnic cultures, language barriers, and long-duration service assignments intensified relief workers' stress, and the need for mental health services for relief workers became apparent.

PROFESSIONAL ORGANIZATION

Although mental health professionals provided disaster services throughout the twentieth century, disaster psychology emerged as a professional field during the 1990s. In 1990, the APA financed a California Psychological Association disaster-response course, and the ARC assisted with the class. Tornadoes in Illinois in the spring of 1991 prompted the Illinois Psychological Association to respond to the ARC's request for mental health services. The first community request for disaster mental health services occurred after a tornado devastated Sherwood, North Dakota, in September 1991. Citizens sought help for their children in coping with the damage and casualties.

The ARC established the Disaster Mental Health (DMH) services by November 1991 and issued guidelines for training, certification, and service. Psychologists attending ARC disaster training began offering courses in their regions. The APA agreed to collaborate with the ARC the next month. Representatives of the APA and ARC decided that the APA's Disaster Response Network (DRN) would prepare psychologist volunteers to offer free mental health services to survivors and relief workers at disaster scenes. After Hurricane Andrew hit Florida in 1992, approximately two hundred DRN psychologists helped survivors with the ARC. The APA has established task forces to evaluate mental health responses to various catastrophes.

The APA sponsors a Committee on Psychiatric Dimensions of Disaster (CPDD), formed in 1993 after three years of development as a task force. Members of this committee supply educational information to help psychiatrists provide disaster-related services. The committee seeks to advance the field of disaster psychiatry through training and research to determine the optimum psychiatric treatment for disaster victims. Members distribute materials to district branches to aid local response to potential disaster situations. The American Psychiatric Association also posts information about disaster topics on its website (http://www.psych.org).

The APA's emergency-services and disaster-relief branch cooperates with other mental health groups and emergency services to prepare professionals to respond appropriately and effectively to psychological aspects of disasters. Multiorganization conferences in 1995 and 1996 clarified mental health professionals' roles during disasters and approved APA goals. Facing such challenges as 2005's Hurricane Katrina demonstrated the need for such coordinated efforts to aid victims.

Psychiatrists often feel limited by the ARC's prohibition of psychiatrists from prescribing medications while acting as ARC volunteers, and some mental health professionals formed local groups to intervene during disaster relief. Disaster Psychiatry Outreach (DPO) was established after the 1998 Swissair Flight 111 crash as an effort to provide better disaster mental health services in the New York City vicinity. Most DPO volunteers are qualified to prescribe medications for survivors and their families. Ethical and legal concerns specific to disaster mental health services provided by any source include abandonment of victims and solicitation of patients.

DISASTER PROCEDURES

At a disaster scene, mental health professionals aid medical emergency workers in identifying people who are behaving irrationally. Disaster psychologists help people deal with injuries or losses of family members and homes. Specific emotional issues might include disfigurement, loss of body parts, or exposure to grotesque scenes. Psychologists soothe disaster victims undergoing sudden surgical procedures.

Most disaster survivors and relief workers are resilient to permanent emotional damage. Volunteers advise people who seem likely to suffer psychiatric disorders due to the disaster to seek professional treatment. People in denial who ignore disaster-induced psychological damage can develop disorders such as post-traumatic stress disorder (PTSD), which can have a detrimental effect on social and professional interactions. The fourth edition of the APA's *Diagnostic and Statistical Manual of Mental Disorders* (1994, DSM-IV) was the first to classify acute stress disorder (ASD), which has symptoms resembling PTSD but lasts only a few days to several weeks within one month of trauma. ASD is distinguished from PTSD by the presence of dissociative symptoms beginning either during the disaster or soon after.

Disaster mental health professionals introduce new methods, such as critical incident stress management (CISM) and critical incident stress debriefing (CISD), based on experiences and research. CISM was created to help emergency personnel who undergo stages of demobilization, defusing, debriefing, and education. Debriefing helps people voice their experiences and often provides group support from colleagues. Relief workers immersed in such stressful situations as recovering bodies often seek counseling. Twenty percent of the 1995 Oklahoma City bombing emergency workers received psychological attention. After the September 11, 2001, terrorist attacks, counselors reported that approximately two thousand emergency workers sought their services.

Research topics include evaluation of how PTSD is related to disasters or how heroes react to public attention, disaster-stimulated life changes such as marriage or divorce, stress reactions of secondary victims who are not directly affected by disasters, and variables such as gender, religious affiliation, and ethnicity. Children, adolescents, and elderly victims have unique needs during and after disasters. Other possible research groups include the homeless, the disabled, and people who are medically or mentally ill at the time of the disaster. Researchers use computer and technological advances to enhance studies of data and model disaster scenarios.

Internationally, academic programs, symposiums, and conferences explore disaster-related mental health topics. The University of South Dakota's Disaster Mental Health Institute (http://www.usd.edu/arts-and-sciences/psychology/disaster-mental-health-institute/) offers a comprehensive curriculum of undergraduate and graduate disaster psychology courses to train ARC-approved disaster mental health personnel.

BIBLIOGRAPHY

Austin, Linda S., ed. *Responding to Disaster: A Guide for Mental Health Professionals*. Washington: Amer. Psychiatric, 1992. Print.

Everly, George S., Jr., and Jeffrey T. Mitchell. *Critical Incident Stress Management (CISM): A New Era and Standard of Care in Crisis Intervention*. 2nd ed. Ellicot City: Chevron, 1999. Print.

Fullerton, Carol S., and Robert J. Ursano, eds. *Posttraumatic Stress Disorder: Acute and Long-Term Responses to Trauma and Disaster.* Washington: Amer. Psychiatric, 1997. Print.

Gist, Richard, and Bernard Lubin, eds. *Response to Disaster: Psychosocial, Community, and Ecological Approaches*. Philadelphia: Brunner, 1999. Print.

Greenstone, James L. *The Elements of Disaster Psychology: Managing Psychosocial Trauma; An Integrated Approach to Force Protection and Acute*

Care. Springfield: Thomas, 2008. Print.
Jacobs, Gerard A. "The Development of a National Plan for Disaster Mental Health." *Professional Psychology: Research and Practice* 26.6 (1995): 543–49. Print.
Norwood, Ann E., Robert J. Ursano, and Carol S. Fullerton. "Disaster Psychiatry: Principles and Practice." *Psychiatric Quarterly* 71.3 (2000): 207–26. Print.
Luber, Marilyn, ed. *Implementing EMDR Early Mental Health Interventions for Man-Made and Natural Disasters: Models, Scripted Protocols and Summary Sheets.* New York: Springer, 2014. Print.
Raphael, Beverley, and John P. Wilson, eds. *Psychological Debriefing: Theory, Practice and Evidence.* New York: Cambridge UP, 2000. Print.
Roeder, Larry W., ed. *Issues of Gender and Sexual Orientation in Humanitarian Emergencies: Risks and Risk Reduction.* New York: Springer, 2014. Print.
Somasundaram, Daya. *Scarred Communities: Psychosocial Impact of Man-Made and Natural Disasters on Sri Lankan Society.* New Delhi: SAGE, 2014. Print.
Ursano, Robert J., Brian G. McCaughey, and Carol S. Fullerton, eds. *Individual and Community Responses to Trauma and Disaster: The Structure of Human Chaos.* New York: Cambridge UP, 1994. Print.
Wilson, John P., and Catherine So-kum Tang, eds. *Cross-Cultural Assessment of Psychological Trauma and PTSD.* New York: Springer, 2007. Print.
Zaumseil, Manfred, et al., eds. *Cultural Psychology of Coping with Disasters: The Case of an Earthquake in Java, Indonesia.* New York: Springer, 2014. Print.

Elizabeth D. Schafer

See Also: American Psychiatric Association; American Psychological Association; Anxiety disorders; Clinical interviewing, testing, and observation; Community psychology; Coping: Social support; Cross-cultural psychology; Cultural competence; Death and dying; Depression; Emotions; General adaptation syndrome; Health psychology; Internet psychology; Media psychology; Mental health practitioners; Post-traumatic stress disorder; Psychology: Fields of specialization; Stress: Behavioral and psychological responses; Stress: Physiological responses; Stress-related diseases; Support groups.

Discipline

Type of psychology: Biological bases of human behavior, Cognition, Development, Social

It's called grit, and it is the one factor that predicts success more than any other. According to psychologist Angela Ducksworth who addressed an audience on the topic during a recent Ted Talk, "Grit is passion and perseverance for very long-term goals. Grit is having stamina. Grit is sticking with your future, day in, day out, not just for the week, not just for the month, but for years, and working really hard to make that future a reality. Grit is living life like it's a marathon, not a sprint."

Key Concepts

- Decision-depletion
- Discipline
- Ego depletion
- Grit
- Self-control
- Willpower

INTRODUCTION

Dietary restrictions aside, which would you prefer, a cookie right now or two cookies later on?

In a now famous test of willpower school children faced that very question. In 1970 Walter Mischel tested nursery school children's ability to delay gratification. In his experiment children sat alone in a room without distractions while a marshmallow sat on a table in front of them. The children were told that they could eat the marshmallow immediately but if they waited until after the adult left the room and then returned in a short while (15 minutes) they could have a second marshmallow. The children could also ring a bell to summon the adult before they returned and then consume the treat immediately and relinquish the reward. Of the more than 600 school children tested, most attempted to delay gratification for a second treat but only a third were successful at waiting the full 15 minutes for the reward of the second marshmallow.

The ability to use willpower and exercise self-control in the short term for the sake of long-term goals is now considered the most critical factor in predicting who will be successful in any arena. Ducksworth led a team of psychologists that studied a variety of people in many different settings from military cadets to high school students at risk for dropping out to salespeople and national spelling bee competitors. The single question: in each of these different settings who is most likely to succeed? The greatest predictor for success over and above good looks, health, family income, standardized test scores, and even intelligence was grit.

SELF-CONTROL IS LIKE A MUSCLE

Muscles are the ropes that mobilize the pulleys of our joints and power our skeletal structure. They respond to the brain in both voluntary and involuntary ways. Without muscles one would be completely immobile, unable to blink, walk, or even breathe and pump blood throughout our veins. According to Baumeister, a prominent researcher on the topic, self-control is like a muscle in a number of important respects. First, much like a muscle, self-control is depleted after use. A trainer in a health gym will prescribe exercising a group of muscles to exhaustion. The trainer will also prescribe rest periods between exercise sessions so the muscles can develop and grow. Once a muscle has been broken down to be used for energy the body needs some period of time to rebuild it. This is also the case with self-control. After exercising self-control a person's willpower is depleted temporarily making it more difficult for him or her to resist additional temptations.

Second, self-control is like a muscle because the more it is used the stronger it eventually becomes. Depending on nutrition, body type, and frequency of training, improvements in physical strength and stamina are inevitable with a consistent regimen. This is also the case with the "self-control muscle." Essentially, the well of discipline a person draws from whenever he or she resists a temptation is emptied in the short term but fills to greater capacity over time.

Third, self-control is like a muscle because people have some control over how the energy is expended. People can be more stringent in how they regulate their resources when future demands may tax their willpower. In essence, people know how and when to "keep some in the tank" or conserve their energy for later, more difficult tasks. Indeed, a group of researchers found that people would curtail current performance to a greater degree when they expected to have to exert self-control later on. Similarly, an athlete who is fatigued but still has some energy reserves can persevere and mount a major effort at an important moment during competition.

Extending the analogy further, acquiring self-control in one arena can grant discipline in other areas not related to the one in which self-control has been exercised. For example, smokers who quit remained abstinent for a longer period when they had worked to strengthen their self-control in other areas. This is also similar to physical and athletic ability; an athlete who is transitioning from one sport to another is likely to have an easier time acquiring the skills of the new sport than a person who has never played sports at all. Even without experience in a new sport, an athlete has acquired some general set of useful skills such as strength, flexibility, and kinesthetic awareness.

Lastly, self-control is like a muscle because it requires fuel in order to operate. In the human body food is converted into glucose to supply the body with fuel for everyday activities. Glucose is also brain fuel providing neurotransmitters with the energy to properly function. Discipline appears tied to glucose levels in the brain; after exerting self-control glucose levels drop. This can be resolved fairly easily by consuming food to restore glucose levels. For someone whose self-control reserve is depleted, performance on additional tests of self-control are higher when glucose supply has been replenished.

MAKING DECISIONS DEPLETES SELF CONTROL RESERVES

When people have used their stores of willpower and energy to exert self-control their subsequently reduced state is known as ego depletion. Ego depletion is associated with many different activities. For example, controlling one's thoughts, managing one's emotions, refusing to act on unwanted impulses, and focusing attention are all acts of self-control. Managing one's personal impression, dealing with difficult people, and overcoming poor behavior from someone close such as a spouse or child are also ego-depleting. Behaviors like overeating, overspending, aggression, and sexual impulses are affected by one's level of self-control resources. Furthermore, studies have shown that ego depletion is correlated with domestic violence, prejudice, cheating and/or stealing, exacerbated pre-menstrual syndrome, reduced diplomatic ability, and worse performance on tasks requiring intelligence and mental effort. Willpower, therefore, is an all-purpose mechanism used for everything from treating people kindly to acting within the confines of the law to sticking to a dietary regimen. When there is something at stake, such as an imminent monetary reward, people are more likely to push through states of ego depletion. Ego depletion can be counteracted with humor and other positive emotions. It can also be dealt with by making implementation plans, that is "if – then" conditions, when faced with a taxing situation. For example, "If she offers me a piece of cake, then I will just eat two bites and say I'm full."

LIFESTYLE CHOICES

Many successful people credit some of their success to limiting the number of choices they must make in a day. What is it that Barack Obama and Mark Zuckerberg have in common? Despite few apparent similarities between the two men they have both made a lifestyle choice that makes their difficult jobs a bit easier to execute. That is, they both wear the same outfit every day. The founder of Facebook has been criticized for his uninspiring and not entirely professional attire which consists of a t-shirt and blue jeans every day, a uniform he dons whether he meets with developers or board members. However, he has shrewdly eliminated one less decision that many people agonize over at least once every day. Similarly, President Obama says he wears the same thing every day, either a blue or a gray suit, because, he reports, that is one less decision he has to make enabling him to make the important decisions involved with governing the nation. Albert Einstein and Steve Jobs also reportedly adopted the same strategy of choosing a monotonous wardrobe in order to get more done in a day. Other highly successful people report automating certain aspects of their lives, such as having the same thing for lunch every day, to enable them to preserve the necessary mental resources to deal with important issues they face daily.

MILITARY STYLE DISCIPLINE

The military spends the bulk of a recruit's early training instilling discipline with all-consuming tactics that govern everything from attire and meals to sleep schedules and clothing. According to one journalist turned intelligence officer, "Basic training is the doorway to the military. Civilians enter, and soldiers come out." The security of a nation depends on soldiers' ability to be in a certain place at an appointed time without fail, carry out orders, and maintain the appropriate physical condition for combat. The military cannot take the chance that a person will put his or her own needs above that of what is required for duty. Indeed, a person may be ultimately required to sacrifice health and life and would not be expected to do this if he or she is unable to sacrifice a morning of sleep or an extra piece of cake.

Taking this approach to the extreme the military assumes that new recruits have no discipline whatsoever and immediately thrusts the individual into a set of rigorous training mechanisms known as basic training. It includes everything the future soldier needs to know for daily life in the military. In addition to the very demanding physical challenges meant to cultivate a high level of fitness, recruits also learn how to properly address ranked officers, clean and maintain personal items and equipment, and function within a chain of command. A successful recruit is one who is in excellent physical condition and who is mentally able to accommodate a variety of circumstances and challenges.

The military also works to instill a sense of pride in caring for one's possessions and appearance. This extends to a strong focus on how cadets carry themselves, how their clothes and gear are cared for; shoes must be shined and particular details of the uniform must be strictly adhered to. Bouncing a quarter off the bed and a neat living environment indicates a crisp and well-organized soldier. The difference between life and death means knowing where equipment is and that it is functioning properly in the heat of the moment. An individual who cannot be bothered to care for his things or appearance is likely to be sloppy in other arenas as well.

CAN SELF-CONTROL BE TAUGHT OR LEARNED?

Aside from the portion of the population that aspires to military careers, discipline is warranted in most other arenas as well. Long-term substantive success in the workplace, in health and fitness, and in interpersonal relationships all require restraint and deferring immediate gratification in service of a higher, and ultimately more rewarding, set of goals and achievements. It thus behooves families, corporations, and even high school guidance counselors to craft guidelines and support measures that enable its members to learn greater degrees of self-control. In fact, some regimens have been found to increase self-control. People are less depleted by self-control tasks after a two-week period of monitoring their posture and improving it whenever they notice it is sloppy or monitoring and recording everything they eat. Strictly adhering to a rigorous exercise program for a period of two months vastly increased participants' ability to exert self-control and avoid pleasurable, distracting stimuli to maintain focus on laborious tasks. Furthermore, those who adhered to the exercise regimen improved in self-control in areas of their life outside of the laboratory unrelated to physical fitness. Namely, they were better able to regulate their consumption of alcohol, cigarettes, and caffeine and more likely to perform daily household chores and to study rather than watch television.

MARSHMALLOWS REVISITED

So what became of those children who were actually able to wait the full amount of time to receive the reward of the second marshmallow? Research showed that these children when reviewed 18 to 20 years later had scored higher than average on the SAT and were judged to be much more competent than their peers.

BIBLIOGRAPHY

Baumeister, R.F. (2012). Self-control – The moral muscle. The Psychologist, 25(2), 112-115.

Baumeister, R.F., Fohs, K.D., & Tice, D.M. (2007). The strength model of self control. Current Directions in Psychological Science, 6(16), 351-355.

Jacquelyn Berry

See Also: Authoritarian; Authoritative; Childhood development; Childrearing; Child relations; Parent child relations; Parenting; Parenting styles.

Dissociative disorders

Date: 1990s forward

Type of psychology: Psychopathology

Dissociative disorders are characterized by a disruption in consciousness that is most often caused by a self-defense against trauma. These disorders fall into four major types: dissociative amnesia, dissociative identity disorder, and depersonalization/derealization disorder. Treatments for dissociative disorders usually focus on revealing the underlying trauma or stressors producing the dissociative symptoms.

Key Concepts

- Amnesia
- Confabulation
- Dissociation
- Fugue
- Identity disorder

INTRODUCTION

According to the classification system in the *Diagnostic and Statistical Manual of Mental Disorders: DSM-V* (5th ed., 2013), which is published by the American Psychiatric Association, dissociative disorders can be divided into three major types that share the underlying process of dissociation. When some people are faced with unusual stress from a traumatic event, they cannot cope with the situation and experience overwhelming levels of anxiety. To escape the anxiety, they may experience dissociation as a defensive reaction. Dissociation involves the splitting of the event from the conscious mind so that the stressor or trauma is not remembered. Consequently, these people may experience a loss of memory about the trauma, which enables them to escape the emotional distress. Dissociation has often been associated with such traumatic events as combat, rape, incest, natural disasters, and accidents. Without the memory of the trauma in the conscious mind, a person can avoid the emotional turmoil and anxiety that normally would be present.

Dissociative disorders emerge when the dissociation becomes extreme and begins to negatively affect everyday functioning. The split in consciousness can affect a person's integration of thoughts and feelings while influencing how the individual acts toward others. Some people with dissociative disorders develop conflicting images of themselves or form actual coexisting personalities.

The DSM-V presents the diagnostic criteria for three major types of dissociative disorders: dissociative amnesia, dissociative identity disorder, and depersonalization/derealization disorder. Dissociative fugue, a fourth subtype listed in previous editions of the DSM, has now been combined with dissociative amnesia.

The most common dissociative symptom is amnesia, which can be found in most of the dissociative disorders. The DSM-V identifies dissociative amnesia as one of the dissociative disorders. This diagnosis is made when the dissociation is limited to amnesia and does not involve other symptoms. The person with dissociative amnesia is unable to remember information, and this memory loss cannot be explained as mere forgetfulness. The memory loss usually involves a traumatic event. A specific trauma, such as an accident, is the precipitating event for the amnesia and is associated with painful emotions and psychological turmoil. Most often the amnesia has an abrupt onset and the memory loss is apparent to the person with amnesia. However, the person with amnesia usually shows a lack of concern about or appears indifferent to this loss of memory. The lack of concern or indifference stems from the fact that the amnesia prevents the person from experiencing emotional upset or anxiety as a result of undergoing a stressful event. The dissociation serves as a protective device to retain emotional stability. The DSM-V describes several forms of dissociative amnesia, including localized amnesia with loss of memory of a specific situation, generalized amnesia with loss of memory of an entire lifetime of experiences, and selective amnesia with only partial loss of memory. An interesting aspect of dissociative amnesia is the person's attempt to adapt to the memory loss. Some individuals begin to create false information or false memories to hide the loss in memory caused by the amnesia. This process is termed confabulation.

Fugue is a variant of dissociative amnesia in which those with memory loss travel away from their homes, leave their jobs, and take on new activities. The onset of the fugue occurs very suddenly. This type of amnesia is considered to be fairly rare and takes place in response to unusual stressors such as war or natural disasters. When a dissociative fugue begins, the person usually wanders far from home. The wandering and amnesia can last for several days or even months but most often last only for a brief period of time. Amnesia is present during the dissociative fugue, but the person is unaware of the memory loss. It is only when the dissociative fugue disappears that the person is again aware of events preceding the onset of the disorder.

IDENTITY DISORDER

Dissociative identity disorder is commonly referred to as multiple personality disorder. The person with dissociative identity disorder has at least two distinct personalities that repeatedly take over the individual's actions. The number of personalities varies for people with the disorder, but the number usually ranges from five to ten distinct personalities that can emerge at any given time. Usually one personality is dominant and is termed the host, and the other secondary personalities are called alters. The movement from one personality to another is usually sudden and can be dramatic. It is common for each personality to be unaware of or to have amnesia about the existence of the other personalities. Memories of events that took place when one personality is present usually remain with only that personality. However, in many cases, one personality has knowledge of all of the alter personalities, or there is superficial awareness among all the personalities. The personalities that emerge in dissociative identity disorder can be either male or female, can differ in ethnicity, and can have dissimilar ages. The different personalities typically show different traits or characteristics, such as one alter being extroverted and another shy and introverted. In casual conversation, the different personalities do not usually seem unusual or strange in their behavior or manner. It is often only through lengthy interactions or clinical interviews with mental health professionals that the different personalities become apparent. The exact cause of dissociative identity disorder is not clear, but people with the disorder usually have experienced a traumatic event in childhood. The most common childhood traumas are physical or sexual abuse, including incest.

DEPERSONALIZATION AND DEREALIZATION

Depersonalization disorder is characterized by the symptom of people experiencing recurrent alterations in their perceptions. People's perception of the physical environment may change so that it seems unreal or strange. This change in perception is known as derealization. When derealization takes place, people report that everything seems different, as if they have entered a dream state. Depersonalization is the sensation or perception that the person's body or personal self has become strange or different. Both internal feelings and external perceptions become changed, so that the person feels estranged or alienated. A person may have the sensation that part of the body have changed in size or shape. Some specific symptoms of depersonalization include hemidepersonalization, in which the person feels that one half of the body has changed or is unreal; doubling, in which a person feels himself or herself to be outside the body; and double orientation, which is having the sensation of being in two places at the same time. A person with depersonalization/derealization disorder may experience symptoms of either depersonalization or derealization, or may experience both.

The symptoms of depersonalization usually occur quickly and afflict mostly young adults. Although the causes of this disorder are not exactly known, it has been found that it develops after periods of extreme stress, or after an experience of extreme anxiety.

OTHER DISSOCIATIVE CONDITIONS

Beyond the three major types of dissociative disorders, the DSM-V includes two diagnoses for dissociative conditions which do not fall under any of those categories, other specified dissociative disorder and unspecified dissociative disorder. Other specified dissociative disorders include chronic symptoms of more than one dissociative disorder, identity issues as a result of brainwashing or torture, and short-term dissociative reactions to stressful events. Unspecified dissociative disorder (like its predecessor in the DSM-IV, Dissociative Disorder—Not Otherwise Specified) is a diagnosis used when a patient experiences dissociative symptoms but does not fully meet the criteria for any existing dissociative disorder, or when the clinician has insufficient information to determine which specific diagnosis would best fit the patient.

PATIENT DEMOGRAPHICS

Dissociative amnesia is fairly common and appears to occur more often in women than in men. The incidence of dissociative amnesia varies depending on the prevalence of traumatic events such as natural disasters and combat situations. The majority of cases are initially identified in emergency departments of hospitals.

Dissociative identity disorder has been found to be most common in adolescence and young adulthood, with most diagnoses made around the age of thirty. Women have most often been diagnosed with the disorder, which is considered to be a fairly rare disorder. The professional community has engaged in extensive debate about the prevalence of the disorder in the general population. Some professionals dispute the validity of the diagnosis.

Depersonalization/derealization disorder is most often seen in women and is usually diagnosed during young adulthood or adolescence. According to the DSM-V, 95% of those who experience symptoms of this disorder do so prior to the age of 25. There are insufficient scientific studies to establish the prevalence of the disorder in the general population.

TREATMENT OPTIONS

Treatments for dissociative disorders usually focus on the underlying trauma or source of anxiety that triggered the dissociative symptoms. In dissociative amnesia, the treatment tries to reveal the lost memories through extensive psychiatric interviewing, drug-assisted interviews to overcome the memory blocks, and hypnosis. The most common drugs used to assist in the recovery of lost memories are the barbiturates and the benzodiazepines. After forgotten memories are retrieved, the person receives psychotherapy to help cope with the associated anxiety of the memory.

The treatment process for dissociative identity disorder is directed toward discovering the childhood traumatic event that began the development of alternative personalities. The psychotherapy for this disorder is usually a long-term process as the various personalities need to be assessed and eventually integrated into the host personality. The therapist needs to eventually work with the personality that recalls the trauma that triggered the dissociation to overcome the anxiety associated with the event. The person must come to terms with the early childhood trauma and begin to give up the various alters that have helped to manage the anxiety and other negative emotions that were created from the childhood experience. The childhood traumas associated with dissociative identity disorder involve serious violations of basic trust and security. For example, the child who is sexually abused or is the target of incest experiences the extreme betrayal of the nurturing and security that a parent should provide. The different characteristics of the various personalities develop over time to cope with that basic betrayal.

The treatment for the depersonalization disorder has a different focus. There is little scientific evidence regarding the best approach for treatment. Many of the persons with this disorder eventually receive psychotherapy and some psychoactive medication. Most often antianxiety medications such as the benzodiazepines are used to help control the patient's apprehensions and worries.

BIBLIOGRAPHY

Coons, Peter. "The Dissociative Disorders: Rarely Considered and Underdiagnosed." *Psychiatric Clinics of North America* 21 (1998): 637–648. Print.

Cronin, Elisabeth, Bethany L. Brand, and Jonathan F. Mattanah. "The Impact of the Therapeutic Alliance on Treatment Outcome in Patients with Dissociative Disorders." *European Journal of Psychotraumatology* 5 (2014): n. pag. European Journal of Psychotraumatology. Coaction, 6 Mar. 2014. Web. 18 Apr. 2014.

Evren, C., and E. Daibudak. "Temperament, Character, and Dissociation Among Detoxified Male Inpatients with Alcohol Dependency." *Journal of Clinical Psychology* 64 (2008): 717–727. Print.

Jans, T., et al. "Long-Term Outcome and Prognosis of Dissociative Disorder with Onset in Childhood or Adolescence." *Child and Adolescent Psychiatry and Mental Health* 23 (July, 2008): 19. Print.

Klanecky, A., et al. "Child Sexual Abuse, Dissociation, and Alcohol: Implications of Chemical Dissociation via Blackouts Among College Women." *American Journal of Drug and Alcohol Abuse* 34 (2008): 277–284. Print.

Kon, L., and E. Glisky. "Interidentity Memory Transfer in Dissociative Identity Disorder." *Journal of Abnormal*

Psychology 117 (Aug. 2008): 686–692. Print.
Myrick, Amie C. et al. "An Exploration of Young Adults' Progress in Treatment for Dissociative Disorder." *Journal of Trauma & Dissociation* 13.5 (2012): 582–95. Print.
Spiegel, David et al. "Dissociative Disorders in DSM-5." *Depression and Anxiety* 28.9 (2011): 824–52. Print.

Frank J. Prerost

See Also: Amnesia and fugue; Antianxiety medications; Anxiety disorders; Child abuse; Coping: Strategies; Defense mechanisms; Ego defense mechanisms; Forgetting and forgetfulness; Multiple personality; Psychotherapy: Effectiveness; Psychotherapy: Goals and techniques; Repressed memories; Schizophrenia: Background, types, and symptoms; Stress: Behavioral and psychological responses

Dix, Dorothea

Born: April 4, 1802, in Hampden, Maine
Died: July 17, 1887, in Trenton, New Jersey
Identity: American social reformer
Type of psychology: Emotion; Motivation

Dix was a pioneer in the reform of conditions for housing and treating the mentally ill.

Dorothea (originally Dorothy) Dix was born in a small village on the Massachusetts frontier, then part of Maine. Alienated from her family, she ran away to live with her grandmother in Boston at age twelve and, by fourteen, had opened the first of several schools. Influenced by her father's Methodist evangelicalism and a growing circle of Boston Unitarians, she hoped to influence the young through moral education, teaching, and providing an example of rigorous self-control (especially repression of emotion), self-sacrifice, and social activism. She published her first educational book, *Conversations on Common Things,* in 1824.

In 1841 she viewed for the first time the treatment of the mentally ill, often chained in poorhouses and jails with inadequate food, clothing, and sanitation. She then made her life's work the establishment of institutions where her principles of moral education could be used to reintroduce the mentally ill to society. Beginning in Massachusetts, she toured facilities throughout eastern, midwestern, and southern states and wrote "memorials" to legislators. She became the most successful political lobbyist of her time. Her proposal to grant millions of acres of public land to states for the establishment of mental institutions was passed by Congress in 1854 but vetoed by President Franklin Pierce. Her activities led to the funding of thirty-two mental hospitals as well as other institutions, and, during her travels abroad between 1854 and 1856, she played a major role in changing European attitudes. She published *Remarks on Prisons and Prison Discipline in the United States* in 1845; her other publications included "memorials" on prisons and the mentally ill, collections of hymns and moral tales for children, and meditations.

Her fame led to her appointment as Superintendent of Union Army Nurses at the outbreak of the Civil War; her strict standards and independence created enemies among nurses and government officials, and her authority was undermined. After the war, despite failing health, she attempted to continue her activities. She eventually settled in a private suite in the state hospital in Trenton, New Jersey, the first hospital built through her efforts. She died there in 1887.

BIBLIOGRAPHY

Brown, Thomas J. *Dorothea Dix: New England Reformer.* Cambridge, Mass.: Harvard University Press, 1998. Brown examines legends of family abuse and alcoholism in Dix biographies, explores Dix's life in terms of her dual roles as conservative Victorian lady and social activist, and presents a detailed account of her activities as congressional lobbyist and international reformer.
Gollaher, David. *Voice for the Mad: The Life of Dorothea Dix.* New York: Free Press, 1995. General biography with a detailed account of Dix's activities in individual states.
Herstek, Amy Paulson. *Dorothea Dix: Crusader for the Mentally Ill.* Berkeley Heights, N.J.: Enslow, 2001. Simply written general biography in the Historical American Biographies series; contains a chronology of major events in Dix's life and a brief bibliography.

Betty Richardson

See Also: Educational psychology; Mental illness: Historical concepts; Moral development; Psychology: History.

Dog psychology

Type of psychology: Animal behavorial; Cognitive; Comparative

Dog psychology is a rapidly expanding field that uses scientific methods to study all aspects of dog behavior and mental functions. Whereas earlier studies used dogs to uncover principles of learned behavior that apply to all species, recent studies are more likely to highlight differences in cognition between dogs and other animals, especially as they pertain to their interactions with humans. Dog psychology is also concerned with the origin and treatment of problem behaviors in dogs.

Key Concepts

- Dominance
- Personality
- Reinforcement
- Scientific method
- Sensitive or critical period
- Sensory system
- Separation anxiety

INTRODUCTION

Dog psychology asks many of the same fundamental questions about dog behavior that psychologists have asked about human behavior. How do dogs perceive and think about the world? How do they learn and what do they remember? How are their interactions with their physical and social environments shaped by biology, evolution, and experience? Do dogs have personalities? Why do some dogs exhibit symptoms of distress and how should clinical problems in dogs like anxiety, excessive fear, and compulsive behavior be treated? All of these questions are motivated by a desire to understand dog behavior in terms of underlying mental processes and internal states.

The approach used to answer these questions about dog behavior is based on scientific methodology, the same approach used to study human behavior. Theories are formulated, specific hypotheses are developed and tested through observation and experiment, the findings are interpreted with the support of statistical analyses, and the original theories are subsequently refined, amended or, occasionally, abandoned.

Historically, dogs were important in studies of the general principles of learned behavior. Ivan Pavlov's seminal studies of classically conditioned salivation in dogs laid the foundation for our understanding of how human behavior can be changed by experience and for the development of treatments for addiction and phobias that are in use today. In the 1950s and 1960s, John Paul Scott and John L. Fuller used five representative dog breeds to examine the role of heredity in the development of behavior. Although the use of dogs as model systems continues today, contemporary research reflects a broader interest in dogs and their relationship to humans, including their comparatively superior sensitivity to human communicative cues.

SENSING THE WORLD

Dogs acquire information about their environment using the same sensory modalities that humans use but, because of structural differences in their sensory systems, the quality of their perceptual experiences is not identical. Understanding the sensory systems of dogs and any breed influences is crucial for developing appropriate stimuli for studying other aspects of dog psychology. Most research has focused on vision, hearing, and olfaction.

In both dogs and humans, vision depends on two types of retinal photoreceptors, cones and rods. Differences in the properties, number, distribution, and wiring of these receptors account for the dichromatic color vision of dogs, their superior vision in dim light, and their poorer visual acuity in bright light. In addition, whereas humans have forward-oriented eyes, dogs have eyes that are positioned more laterally giving them a wider field of view but a narrower field of binocular vision.

Color vision is dependent on cone receptors. Normal human color vision is trichromatic but a study of just three dogs revealed only two classes of cone photopigment: one that responds maximally to a wavelength of 555 nm (perceived as yellowish) and another that responds maximally to 429 - 435 nm (perceived as bluish). Thus, the blue-yellow color vision of dogs is most similar to that of a human deuteranope, a person with red-green color blindness. Night vision, which is rod dependent, is three to four times more sensitive in dogs than in humans and is aided by a sheet of light-reflecting cells, the tapetum lucidum, located at the back of the dog's eye.

Dogs do not see as clearly in daylight as humans do. They lack a well-defined fovea populated by cone receptors mapped onto retinal ganglion cells in a one-to-one ratio. Instead, their retinal ganglion cells receive inputs from several receptors and form a horizontally elongated oval-shaped area, the visual streak. The intensity of the visual streak is correlated with skull length and appears least pronounced and more circular in shape in flat-faced (brachycephalic) dog breeds. It has been suggested that this change which is also accompanied by more frontally located eyes may improve perception of human faces.

Hearing research has shown that dogs detect not only frequencies in the range audible to the human ear but high (ultrasonic) frequencies that are inaudible to humans. In general, dogs hear frequencies up to 45 kHz, well above the upper limit of about 20 kHz for human hearing. To date, research has not found breed-related differences in basic hearing ability. Audiograms for four dogs, each representing a different breed, were found to be quite similar despite considerable differences in their body size, the area of their tympanic membrane, the distance between their ears, and the shape of their pinnae (upright or floppy).

Dogs have a remarkable ability to detect scents and have been trained to report the presence of odors from narcotics, explosives, and cancers at concentrations that are imperceptible to humans. Sniffing draws the odor molecules into the dog's nose where they come into contact with the receptors on the olfactory epithelium. These neural signals are then decoded by the olfactory bulb in the brain. Even the smallest dog has tens of millions more receptors, a more expansive olfactory epithelium, and a substantially larger olfactory bulb than a human does. Dogs also pump fluid containing scent molecules into their vomeronasal organ, a structure that humans do not have. This system is used in the processing of social odors or pheromones.

COGNITION

Cognition studies encompass a wide range of topics including knowledge of object properties and the physical world, learning about events and consequences, the nature and duration of memory, communication, and problem solving. Whereas some areas have more than a hundred year history of research, others have been examined only very recently in dogs.

Learning through association was famously demonstrated in Pavlov's studies of conditioned salivation in dogs which showed that a previously neutral stimulus comes to elicit a new response, salivation, following its repeated pairing with food which automatically elicits salivation. Dogs were also subjects in Edward Thorndike's classic puzzle box experiments, better known for using cats, which led him to formulate the law of effect in 1898 to explain how reward and punishment altered instrumental behavior. These approaches to learning in animals dominated psychology for many decades, although not without criticism. In the late 1960s, experiments revealed that Pavlovian conditioned responses depended upon the CS-US contingency and contributed to the contemporary view that only surprising or unpredicted events stimulate associative learning. In the 1980s, experiments demonstrated that instrumental behavior was sensitive to a change in the value of its consequences and corroborated the viability of a goal-directed rather than strictly habit-based analysis of instrumental learning.

Dog training methods have been heavily influenced by the study of learning in experimental psychology. Studies have begun to assess the relative effectiveness and psychological impact of fear-based approaches including correction procedures and negative reinforcement such as constructional aggression treatment (CAT), reward-based approaches including shaping and clicker training, and social methods that use modeling or observational techniques such as the do-as-I-do method.

One of the fastest growing areas of cognition research examines dogs' use of human-given cues, such as pointing, bowing, or head turning, to solve a problem. In a typical set-up, food has been hidden in one of two identical containers and a human helps the dog choose by pointing towards the baited container. Studies have shown that dogs outperform wolves, horses, and primates on these tasks and that their ability to use human attentional state and referential signaling is present early in development. Several hypotheses have been considered to explain the superior performance of dogs on these tasks including selection of this trait during domestication, an effect of cohabitation with humans, and associative learning.

Studies of cognitive development have examined what puppies know about the physical world using techniques similar to those used with human infants such as searching for an object that has disappeared from view. Cognition research with elderly dogs has been important in recognizing a syndrome that is similar to Alzheimer's disease. The symptoms in dogs, which include disorientation, disruption of activity and sleep, and poor performance on memory tests, are associated with pathogenic changes in the brain and may be improved through an antioxidant rich diet and selegiline, a monoamine oxidase inhibitor.

SOCIAL BEHAVIOR

Dogs have long been regarded as having evolved from a wolf ancestor although the how, when, and where remain in dispute. Traditionally, they been characterized as pack animals equipped with wolf-like instincts to protect their members, defend resources, and vie for alpha status in the pack hierarchy. Current research, however, recognizes the limitations inherent in using wolf behavior to comprehend dog social behavior. Issues that have received substantial attention in the research literature are the socialization period, intraspecific communication, and dominance.

The concept of a critical or sensitive period is common in psychology. It implies a window of limited duration for appropriate experiences to lay the groundwork for normal development. The optimal window for social bonding in dogs extends from 3 weeks to at least12 weeks, before fear of novelty overrides their inclination to approach social stimuli. Evidence of the importance of early socialization comes from several sources. Livestock guarding dogs, like the Maremma, instinctively protect sheep from predation if raised with lambs as young puppies. In the Bar Harbor studies of the 1950s and 1960s, puppies were raised under varying conditions of social impoverishment; those reared with minimal human contact later feared people. Such findings suggest that puppies should be given some exposure to the types of environments and stimuli they will likely encounter as adults.

Dogs use a number of facial, postural, and vocal expressions to signal their emotional state. For example, a relaxed open mouth and a loosely wagging tail indicate a friendly disposition and invite approach whereas a wrinkled muzzle with bared teeth, raised hackles, and a stiff, erect tail state the opposite. Selective and designer breeding, however, have created communication handicaps as the capacity for displaying visual signals is diminished by drastic morphological alterations in some breeds. Recent research on vocalization has shown that dogs and humans can correctly identify the emotional contexts associated with barks and growls. While the expression of these signals is largely innate, some evidence from studies of play suggests that their meaning may be learned.

Dominant and submissive are labels used to denote the social status of individuals in a pack. Behavioral displays associated with dominance include confident approach, raised tail, eye contact, mounting, laying a paw across another dog's back, raised leg urination, ground scratching and overmarking. In contrast, during an interaction with a dominant dog, submissive dogs keep their tails low or tucked between their legs, avert their gaze, lick the mouth of the dominant dog, roll on their backs, and dribble urine. Many of these signals are commonly directed towards human members of the dog's pack. The method of dominance reduction for resolving problem behaviors including aggression has been deemed unsafe. Moreover, research has questioned the original assumptions about wolf social behavior on which dominance reduction was based.

INDIVIDUAL DIFFERENCES

Dog psychology is also concerned with explaining how and why dogs behave differently from each other. For example, the aim of personality research is to characterize individual differences among dogs that are stable over time and have the power to predict patterns of behavior across a range of situations. The aim of clinical research is to identify the etiology, diagnosis, and treatment of psychological disorders that can severely compromise a dog's quality of life. Additionally, personality and clinical research on dogs may be undertaken because of the potential insights such studies may yield for our understanding of human behavior, particularly from the perspectives of genetics and pharmacology.

A popular approach to personality research in animals is based on the five factor theory of human personality. For dogs, the four relevant traits to be measured are active-inactive, affectionate-aggressive, anxious-calm, and intelligent-stupid. Personality profiles are derived from questionnaires completed by dog owners or from observations of dogs in natural or contrived situations. Personality profiling may be useful for early assessment of the suitability of puppies for future service work. One study used foster-owner ratings of German shepherd puppies on the Canine Behavior Assessment and Research Questionnaire (C-BARQ) which consists of questions about the frequency and severity of various behaviors. Three months later, the puppies were given a temperament test which quantifies reactions to various stimuli and social situations and is used by the Swedish military to determine suitability for military service. Statistical analyses revealed that C-BARQ scores predicted behavior on the temperament test. Puppy screening is in place for protection and detection work in law enforcement and for training as seeing-eye dogs, hearing dogs, medical alert and response dogs, and therapy and assistance dogs.

There is substantial research on three clinical issues in dogs: aggression, compulsive behavior, and separation anxiety. Aggression toward humans and other animals is a leading cause of canine euthanasia or relinquishment to a shelter. Aggressive behavior has been attributed to a number of factors including inadequate socialization, learning, brain serotonin imbalance, and genetics. Hypothyroidism has also been linked to aggressive behavior in dogs with one study finding thyroid problems in 60 percent of aggressive dogs. Dog-bite victims tend to be children and the elderly and they are most likely to be bitten by a familiar dog.

Symptoms of compulsive behavior may include excessive licking of paws, flank or blanket sucking, tail or shadow chasing, and fly catching. Breed predispositions have been documented and treatment usually involves pharmacotherapy. The stress of confinement and lack of exercise, common in a shelter environment, can also induce stereotypical behavior in which affected dogs repetitively rebound off the kennel walls, spin in circles, or pace.

Separation anxiety is a well-documented behavior characterized by vocalization distress, destruction especially toward barriers such as doors and windows, panting and drooling, pacing and inappropriate elimination. Symptoms usually peak within 20 minutes of owner departure. No single predisposing factor has been identified although dogs with a history of multiple owners, shelter exposure, premature weaning, or severe illness in puppyhood may be most at risk. Behavior modification alone or combined with pharmacotherapy is an effective treatment in many cases.

BIBLIOGRAPHY

Bradshaw, J. (2011). *Dog Sense.* New York, NY: Basic Books. Covers the history and behavior of dogs from the perspective of an anthrozoologist. Includes chapters on smell, emotion, training, and problems with pedigrees.

Dodman, N. H. (1996). *The Dog Who Loved Too Much: Tales, Treatments and The Psychology Of Dogs.* Bantam. Collection of case studies of psychological issues and their behavioral and pharmacological treatment by a veterinary behaviorist. Excellent chapter on separation anxiety.

McConnell, P. B. (2002). *The Other End Of The Leash.* New York, N.: Ballantine Books. Engaging account of body language in dogs and human-dog communication faux-pas by a zoologist and certified applied animal behaviorist. Excellent discussion on dominance.

Miklosi, A. (2007). *Dog Behavior, Evolution and Cognition.* New York, NY: Oxford University Press. Comprehensive review of the science of dog behavior by one of the leading researchers in the field.

Ruth M. Colwill

SEE ALSO: Animal behavior; Animal ethology; Comparative psychology; Dogs; Interspecies interaction.

Dolphin psychology

TYPE OF PSYCHOLOGY: Comparative; Cognitive; Developmental; Experimental; Social psychology

It is clear that dolphins, as well as many mammals, can be trained to portray a behavior when given certain conditioned stimuli. But how much deeper and through what situations and conditions can their intellectual abilities apply? Observations and experiments are unlocking the cognitive abilities of the cetacean mind. Tests on self-awareness, ability to comprehend complex sentences and inferential reasoning skills provide insights into the psychology of the dolphin brain. By studying these complex processes, we gain understanding of how non-human intelligent species, like dolphins, mental processes truly work.

KEY CONCEPTS

- Body awareness
- Inferential reasoning
- Joint attention
- Mirror self-recognition
- Signature whistles
- Theory of mind

INTRODUCTION

Animal cognition researchers utilize a ratio of body size to brain size called the encephalization quotient, or EQ. Because larger animals would ordinarily have larger brains and small animals smaller brains, the EQ is universally used to identify species where the ratio is suggestive of disproportionately large brains for an animal's typical size. Wherever the EQ is high, scientists infer superior intelligence. While humans have the largest EQ, many species of cetaceans, the family group to which dolphins, porpoises, and whales belong, have high EQs.

The common bottlenose dolphin, tursiops truncatus, is perhaps of greatest interest because it has evolved an unparalleled brain mass relative to its body size. While humans have an EQ of 7.0, bottlenose dolphins, along with four other delphinidae (dolphin) species, have EQs ranging from approximately 4.1 to 5.0; these are ratios significantly greater than those found in any of the anthropoid apes. Of the delphinidae, the bottlenose brain is of special interest because the cerebral cortex, where thought processes occur, has the most convoluted and circuitous pattern of any animal, including humans. This area is a blood-rich, highly oxygen-dependent, and highly complex brain formation which invites scientific inquiry. It is clear to scientists that bottlenose dolphins think. What is intriguing is that there may be particular, individual dimensions of thought, the way certain incoming data is processed, for example, that may exceed human capacity.

DOLPHIN COMMUNICATION

Dolphins are known for their remarkable social adaptations. They make many associations with each other throughout their lifetime in social groups, called pods. Dolphins display what researchers call a fission-fusion society, meaning that dolphins leave social groups and temporarily join other ones. This creates the need to communicate with potentially new pods or reunite with previous ones. In order to make these connections and address one another, dolphins have developed ways of identifying themselves and others. This labeling is what scientists have termed signature whistles. Signature whistles are individual specific calls that are emitted during separation as well as introduction to new individuals. This adaptation to make connections and social bonds has helped dolphins thrive throughout their evolutionary history.

By one year old, calves have developed signature whistles that will remain generally stable throughout their lives. In order to develop signature whistles, calves must learn to use another's whistles and model theirs accordingly. One study done on six calves in Sarasota Bay gave evidence that calves may learn to modify signature whistles of dolphins they seldom associate with in their communities rather than dolphins with whom they have strong associations. This makes sense because it differentiates the types of signature whistles in one area and helps identifying others to be more salient. Thus, calves display the ability of vocal learning. This ability evidences that dolphins hold a mental representation that is coupled with the whistle given.

The ability to identify other individuals by signature whistles is a novel adaptation, and studying pods over time can show their ability of long-term social recognition. A study by Jason Bruck suggested that dolphins can hold mental representations of signature whistles of other dolphins for up to 15 and sometimes 20 years, despite the amount of time they were associated. The ability of long-term recognition could potentially help dolphins recognize other individuals and help with admitting new members to groups within their fission-fusion society.

Comprehension, reasoning and manipulation

Much of what is known about dolphin's comprehensive abilities comes from the ground-breaking research of Louis Herman. He conducted multiple studies to explore a dolphin's range of inferential reasoning. Dolphins can learn certain signals for different objects and can even learn inverse sentence structures for as many as five items. When given the signaled instructions such as left, basket, right, ball, in, Herman demonstrated that dolphins can understand to put the ball on their right into the basket on the left. If the instructions ask to do things that are not possible, for example, if an object is not present or if the syntactic structure is not comprehensible, dolphins will reject the request and continue to wait for a semantically sound request. This shows the dolphins' ability for rational reasoning and responding.

Herman also showed that dolphins can manipulate their environments to create the ability to respond to requests. For example, one dolphin named Akeakamai was given the instruction to swim through the hoop, but it was located on the bottom of her pool. So she spontaneously manipulated the hoop by bringing it upright and swimming though it. Akeakamai also spontaneously manipulated her environment when she was told to fetch multiple items. Instead of bringing them back one at a time she balanced the items with different parts of her bodies in order to bring a group of them back at once. This spontaneous manipulation provided evidence that dolphins can think outside given instructions and effectively and efficiently respond.

Dolphins can also understand the ability to create things. Elele, another dolphin Herman studied, was able to understand the concept of creating and when given the signal came up with 72 spontaneous behaviors over her 144 trials. Thirty-eight of those behaviors were never seen or exhibited before and thus independent of the possibilities of mimicking another dolphin's behaviors or being taught. Elele made them up, illustrating that dolphins have the ability to invent things in their own mind and display their ideas.

JOINT ATTENTION

Due to the dolphin's social nature, researchers wondered if they could understand some of the fundamental skills of human social cognition. Following a gaze is a skill infants can learn by 15 months of age, foreshadowing the comprehension of joint attention. Put simply, it is following the direction someone is looking. It is then followed by understanding and adopting the point for the purpose of directing the receiver's attention to something one desires or pointing as a means to simply share something one found of interest. Although dolphins evolutionarily cannot point, it has been found through experiments that they can understand the idea of the point and gaze without previous exposure. One experiment by marine researcher Alain Tschudin tested six dolphins who had never been exposed to pointing. A red bucket and a white container lid were placed to the left and right of each dolphin and then each was given a hand signal to fetch it. The informant only used right hand signals to point to the right and cross body signals to point to objects on the left. The goal was to determine if they could comprehend what object the informant was directing them toward. Over 12 test trials, three dolphins were able to perform above chance in touching the correct object and the other six reached significance by their 18th trial. Thus, evidence suggests that dolphins can readily understand a dynamic pointing gesture. To test head gazing cues, Tschudin used the same set up and instead of pointing used his head to show the dolphins where the object was. In the first 12 trials, two of the dolphins performed above chance and with continued trials two more were above chance. However, the point and head gaze were both dynamic signals meaning that the movement of the arm or head could have potentially been interpreted by the dolphin as a direction on where to go and not the point or gaze itself. Pack and Herman wanted to test if dolphins could understand the static point so they conducted an experiment in which objects were placed around the dolphin and a first informant gave a signal for an action with no destination object. Then a screen raised and the informant maintained a stationary point. Both dolphins tested were virtually errorless in interpreting the signals, supporting the belief that dolphins can understand dynamic and static cues. Another marine mammal researcher, Mark Xitco,wanted to see if dolphins could create their own cues to make a referential indication toward an object. For six months dolphins Toby and Bob were exposed to SCUBA divers who had an underwater keyboard to communicate certain goal objects or areas in which these objects were. Things like toys or food were placed in clear containers in which the dolphin would need the assistance of a tool or human to open. Spontaneously, the dolphins fixed themselves in front of containers and using their rostrums, or their mouth area, began a signal at the object. This behavior only occurred if divers were present so it can be interpreted as the dolphins' version of pointing. Not only is it intriguing that they were able to spontaneously adopt this referencing of objects but simultaneously the dolphins were observed to monitor the diver's attentional condition. Monitoring was defined as Toby and Bob following the divers with their heads while keeping their body positioned toward the goal object. It occurred when divers were far from the dolphin or the object was far, not when the dolphin and diver were close. Monitoring shows that the dolphin is waiting for the attention of

Photo: iStock

the diver and can actually infer the diver's attention. This theory-of-mind capability, the idea that one can interpret the mental state of another, can be explored in a follow-up study by Xitco et. al. Dolphins were notably able to employ monitoring and pointing behaviors when the diver was face forward. Dolphins may use body position and the direction someone is looking to infer where his or her attention is focused. Not only can dolphins understand human points but they can also instinctively devise their own mechanisms for drawing attention to desired items. Strong evidence suggests that this pointing is referential because it is much more likely to occur in the presence of a diver who is face toward the dolphin and thereby inferring where the diver's attention is according to body positioning. This ability to think outside of one's self and attribute mental states to others is evidence of a dolphin's consciousness. Awareness of one's own existence was once thought of as a strictly human trait and separated us from all other animals. This level of consciousness portrays some physical understanding that one is the author of one's body and actions areunder one's own control. To demostrate that dolphins have a sense of body awareness, Herman conducted an experiment in which one dolphin, Elele, had to use nine different parts of her body to carry out different directions given. She succeeded 90% of the time in showing different body parts and 68% of the time using different body parts to complete tasks never presented to her before. Furthermore, there is evidence that she can recognize some ownership and agency over her body and how it moves and has a sense of her own body-image. Never before was she exposed to having labels for each body part. By her ability to incorporate and move her body in different ways to complete tasks, she exhibited an awareness of her own body parts and perhaps a conscious perception that she has control of them. Diana Reiss and Lori Marino also explored dolphin consciousness in the ability to recognize their mirror-images as themselves. During training sessions, two dolphins at the New York Aquarium were under three conditions: marked, sham-marked (touched but no mark left behind) or not handled during training sessions. After each training session the amount of time of release and investigation of their body in a mirror was significantly greater when they had felt the mark, or sham-mark than when not being handled at all. They did not display any social behaviors toward the mirror, like other animals do under the belief it is another animal. But instead for a significant amount of the trials, their first action was a self-directed behavior in order to view the marking. When the mirror was present and uncovered, dolphins spent more time than in any other of the conditions in the experiment. Thus, during a sham-mark trial, when the dolphin realized it was not marked, it would be more likely to stop its self directed behaviors. Although dolphin self-awareness requires deeper investigation there is evidence that they can recognize themselves in mirrors and can align their bodies as a means to investigate certain areas of it.

BIBLIOGRAPHY

Herman, L. (2010). "What Laboratory Research Has Told Us About Dolphin Cognition". *International Journal of Comparative Psychology*, 23(3), 310-330. Herman goes into more detail about dolphins' ability to understand, reason, and manipulate their environment in a series of different studies conducted at the University of Hawaii and The Dolphin Institute, U.S.A. He demonstrates their cognitive abilities in a variety of different settings and makes inferences.

Reiss, D. (2011). *The Dolphin In The Mirror: Exploring Dolphins Minds and Saving Dolphin Lives*. Boston, MA: Houghton Mifflin Harcourt. A memoir of Diana Reiss based on her years of cetacean research and activism that explores the dolphin's mental processes as a means to prompt better protection laws for dolphins.

Reynolds, J., Wells, R., & Eide, S. (2000). *The Bottlenose Dolphin: Biology and Conservation*. Gainesville, FL: University Press of Florida. An exploration of the many different aspects of dolphins' lives to demonstrate their intelligence seen in everyday abilities. It also outlines the current arguments about controversial conservation practices.

Briana F. Moglia

See Also: Animal behavior; Animal ethology; Comparative psychology; Dolphins; Interspecies interaction; Mammals.

Domestic violence

Type of psychology: Psychopathology

Domestic violence refers to all forms of abuse that occur within families, including child abuse, elder abuse, and spouse abuse. The term came into common usage in the 1970's to emphasize wife abuse. Domestic violence (wife abuse) is explained by several psychologically based theories that in turn propose different solutions.

Key Concepts

- Battered woman syndrome
- Cycle of violence
- Domestic violence
- Family systems theory
- Feminist psychological theory
- Learning theory
- Post-traumatic stress disorder
- Psychoanalytic theory
- Systems theory
- Wife abuse

INTRODUCTION

Domestic violence is difficult to measure since there are no agreed-on standards as to what it is. In addition, most domestic violence occurs in private, and victims are reluctant to report it because of shame and fear of reprisal. Its scope is also difficult to determine, and society's reluctance to acknowledge it results in only estimates of the number of rapes, robberies, and assaults committed by family members and other relatives, such as spouses, former spouses, children, parents, boyfriends, and girlfriends.

In the 1970's, publicity about domestic violence, and more specifically wife abuse, made the public aware that many women did not live in peace and security in their own homes. Through the usage of the terms "abuse," "woman abuse," "battering," "partner abuse," "spouse abuse," "intimate violence," "family violence" and "relationship violence," feminists made the public aware of the problem. As a result of the publicity, women were identified as the most likely victims of domestic violence.

The selection of a name for the behavior will have implications for treatment choices. In addition, the term "domestic violence" removes the issue from a societal perspective, which condones, reinforces, and perpetuates the problem. Domestic violence minimizes the role of gender and places the relationship in the dominant spot. As a result, the choice of a name offers varying perspectives, which differentially view the persons involved, the nature of the problem, and possible solutions.

Abused women in a domestic violence situation are confronted with several types of abuse, namely economic abuse, physical abuse, psychological/emotional abuse, and sexual abuse. Economic abuse results when the financial resources to which a woman is legally entitled are not accessible to her. Examples of economic abuse include being prevented from seeking employment even if qualified to do so, as well as being denied access to needed education, which would aid the woman in securing better employment.

Physical abuse is the major way that men control the behavior of women. Abused women have likened psychological or emotional abuse to brainwashing. Little research has been done on this type of abuse because it is difficult to record. The abused woman is terrorized, isolated, and undermined by her abuser. Psychological or emotional abuse allows men to avoid the legal effects of physical abuse, since they can frighten women without touching them. Five common emotional abuse methods include isolation, humiliation and degradation, "crazy-making" behavior, threats to harm the woman and those she loves, and suicidal and homicidal threats.

Sexual violence was reported by 33 percent to 59 percent of the battered women in a study by Angela Browne published in 1987. Since 1992, it has been legal in all fifty states for a woman to charge her husband with rape. Historically, rape was thought of as intercourse forced on someone other than the wife of the accused. As a result, a woman could not legally accuse her husband of rape.

POSSIBLE CAUSES

Four theories, each of which has a psychological basis, attempt to explain wife abuse. Each of the theories has a unique perspective regarding the causes of wife abuse. The four theories are family systems theory, feminist psychological theory, learning theory, and psychoanalytic theory.

The first theory, family systems theory, includes the application of systems theory to all current family therapy approaches. Systems theory stresses mutual influences and reciprocal relationships between the individual members and the whole, as well as vice versa. In family systems theory, abuse is seen as a feature of the relationship between the abused wife and her husband. Underlying the abusive behavior, both the abused wife and her husband have a frail sense of self. When they marry or establish a relationship, a battering routine or system unfolds. Several factors lead the man to have a drive for power and control over the woman. These factors include social conditions, the need for control, intimacy fears, and lack of awareness of his own conflicts regarding dependency. The abused woman, in turn, has a limited range of coping behaviors, dependency conflicts, a history of childhood family violence, and other psychosocial traits that are similar to those of the man. Change is prevented from occurring, and the dysfunctional interpersonal behavior patterns continue as a result of the unwritten expectations that control these behaviors. Change is blocked by the use of violent behavior.

The second theory, feminist psychological theory, is based on the work of American feminist psychologist Lenore Walker.Walker, Lenore She believes that the behaviors of abused women are coping behaviorsCopingdomestic violence developed as a result of living in a brutal environment.

Walker first theorized the concept of learned helplessness as used in relation to abused women. The abused woman can do nothing to stop the violence. The woman's chief concern is survival. However, survival comes with consequences. Several of the consequences include passively giving in to her abuser, becoming an observer of her own abuse through the process of disassociation, and waiting for days to seek medical care because she may distort the reality of the abuse. In addition, women's helplessness is reinforced by society in two ways. First, women learn to respond passively to abuse through gender role socialization. Second, women's ability to control their lives is thwarted through the interrelated effects of sexism, discrimination, and poverty.

Walker has described a cycle of violence that unfolds in the individual relationship. The woman yields to the batterer's demands in the first stage to keep small episodes from increasing. However, over time these small episodes increase and accumulate. The woman also begins to withdraw from family and friends because she does not want them to know what is going on as the family tension increases. As time passes, the woman withdraws from the batterer as well, because she realizes that her efforts to prevent further development of the violence are futile. The batterer, in turn, becomes more and more angry because he fears that he is losing control of his wife. He then explodes, in the second stage. The third stage quickly follows; the batterer is characterized as being placid and there is a pause in the abusive behaviors. The man promises the woman that he will change, brings her gifts, and is extremely regretful. He changes back into the man she originally loved and is at his most defenseless state.

To explain the behaviors of women who have been frequently abused, Walker developed the theory of the battered woman syndrome,Battered woman syndrome which she sees as a variant of post-traumatic stress disorder (PTSD). The key behaviors of anxiety, cognitive distortion, and depression can on one hand help a woman to survive her abuse. On the other hand, they can interfere with her ability to change her life situation by using appropriate methods.

The third theory is learning theory, incorporating both social learning theory and cognitive behavioral therapy. Social learning theorists stress the occurrence of modeling and the reinforcements received for abusive behavior. Cognitive behavioral theorists stress the internalization of beliefs that support abusive behavior. Boys may internalize the belief that they should be in charge by learning abusive behaviors from male role models, ranging from their fathers to media stars. Girls internalize the belief that they are helpless and weak, by learning passively from their role models. Later adult behaviors are hindered by the earlier learned behaviors and internalized messages.

The fourth theory, psychoanalytic theory, focuses on intrapersonal pathology.Intrapersonal pathology Abused women and abusing men feel that early life experiences shape the particular pathological personality. The battered woman develops beliefs and behaviors that are dysfunctional in adulthood, although they are based in childhood experiences with cruel persons. The women do not resist the abuse. They submit to the abuse because they fear offending the stronger male and also because they think of themselves as deserving abuse. The women choose abusive men and may even touch off the abusive behavior, because of their strong feelings of worthlessness. Passive-aggressive, psychopathic, obsessive-compulsive, paranoid, and sadistic are some of the labels given to violent men who have experienced severe and traumatic childhood abuse episodes. Men learn that violence gets them what they want and also allows them to feel good about themselves, in spite of their childhood experiences of abuse both as victims and as observers.

DIAGNOSING DOMESTIC VIOLENCE

Six factors have been identified as increasing a woman's chances of being in an abusive relationship: age, alcohol use, childhood experience with violence, race, relationship status, and socioeconomic factors.

A person's risk of being abused or being an abuser increases among adolescents. Research has discovered high levels of abuse among dating couples. However, the rate of violence among dating couples falls below that of couples who are married or cohabitating if controlled for age.

Clinical samples in which women are asked to describe their husbands' drinking patterns have provided the basis for the opinion that men beat their wives when they are drunk. Researchers have found that from 35 to 93 percent of abusers are problem drinkers. Better controlled studies have found that in only 25 percent of the cases was either partner drinking at the time of the abuse.Alcohol dependence and abusedomestic violence

Individuals are more likely to be an abused woman or an abusive man if they were abused as a child. It is less clear that a relationship exists between witnessing wife abuse as a child and experiencing it as an adult. Researchers have found that men are more likely to become adult abusers if they observed domestic violence as boys. The data are inconclusive regarding a woman's chance of being abused if she observes domestic violence as a child. Men who observed domestic violence between their parents are three times more likely to abuse their wives. Sons of the most violent parents have a rate of wife abuse 1,000 percent greater than sons of nonviolent parents.

African American and Latino families have above-average rates of wife abuse. Abuse rates for African Americans are four times the rate of white Americans and twice the rate of other minorities. There are twice as many Latina women abused as non-Latina white women. Socioeconomic statusSocioeconomic factors can explain these differences. According to data from a 1980 survey, African Americans earning $6,000 to $11,999 annually (approximately 40 percent of all African American respondents) had higher rates of wife abuse than comparably earning white Americans, while they had lower rates than white Americans in all other socioeconomic levels. When age, economic deprivation, and urban residence are controlled, then the differences between Latina and non-Latina white Americans vanish.

Legally married couples have half the amount of violence as cohabitating couples. It is felt that cohabitating couples may allow conflict to escalate because they are less invested in the relationship, more likely to struggle over autonomy and control issues, and more isolated from their social networks.

Domestic violence is more common in families with fewer economic resources, though it is found in all socioeconomic levels. Higher rates of wife abuse have been found in families where the man works in a blue-collar job or is unemployed or underemployed and the family lives at the poverty level.

THE ABUSED POPULATION

Male partners severely assault more than 1.5 million married and cohabitating women each year. Of women treated in hospital emergency rooms, 22 percent to 35 percent are there because of symptoms related to abuse. Approximately 20 percent to 25 percent of all women are abused at least once by a male partner. Victims of boyfriends tend to be young (sixteen to twenty-four years old), while victims of current or former spouses are likely to be older (twenty to thirty-four years old). Women in families with incomes over $50,000 are four times less likely to be abused than are women in families with annual incomes of less than $20,000.

TREATMENT OPTIONS

The four theories of domestic abuse also provide several treatment options for the psychologist.

Family systems theory prescribes marital counseling-Couples therapydomestic violence to bring about change in the marital system and to identify dysfunctional patterns. Partners are each responsible for changing the way they relate to each other and for the specific behaviors that contribute to the violence.

Walker describes three levels of intervention in terms of feminist psychological theory. Primary prevention changes the social conditions that directly and indirectly contribute to the abuse of women. Examples would include eliminating rigid gender role socialization and reducing levels of violence in society. Secondary intervention encourages women to take control of their lives and to break the cycle of violence. Examples include crisis hot lines as well as financial and legal assistance. A shelter where the women will slowly regain their ability to make decisions for themselves and where they will be safe is an example of tertiary intervention. At this level, women have been totally victimized and are unable to act on their own.

Learning theory stresses that the partners be given opportunities to learn and be rewarded for a new range of actions and underlying beliefs. It is felt that intervention should teach the partners how they have learned and been rewarded for their present behaviors. As a result, the intervention moves beyond a pathological framework. Other approaches, mainly from a cognitive behavioral perspective, strive to change dysfunctional thoughts, teach new behaviors, and eliminate the abuse. This approach works with couples and with abusive men in a group.

Psychoanalytic theory stresses long-term, corrective, individual psychotherapy. The end result of the therapy would be to help the abused woman to break the cycle of violence. She would learn to avoid choosing men who re-create her familiar and unhappy childhood by their violent behavior.

HISTORY OF TREATMENT

Domination of women by men has a long history. Early Roman law gave men absolute power over their wives. However, it is not clear if they had the power to put their wives to death. Physical force was their chief means of control. As the Roman Empire declined, men's right to control women continued to be supported by church doctrine.

The "rule of thumb" was born in English common law, which stated that men had the right to beat their wives as long as the weapon they used was "a rod no bigger than their thumb." Early U.S. judicial decisions supported the right of men to beat their wives. The government's hands-off policy and the legal sanction to a husband's right to control the behavior of his wife were the two major impacts of the court rulings. The first wave of feminists in the nineteenth century briefly exposed the existence of wife abuse and made some efforts to criminalize it. This state of affairs continued until the 1970's, when the second wave of feminism exposed the public to the abuse that many women experienced in their own homes. The battered women's movement identified two key concerns: first, to create a society that no longer accepted domestic violence and, second, to provide safe, supportive shelter for all women who were abused.

BIBLIOGRAPHY

Abrahams, Hilary. *Supporting Women After Domestic Violence: Loss, Trauma, and Recovery*. London: Jessica Kingsley, 2007. A guide for helping women after they have left an abusive relationship. It explains why women feel grief, anger, and confusion in these circumstances and how they can regain a positive sense of self-esteem.

Ammerman, Robert T., and Michel Hersen, eds. *Assessment of Family Violence: A Clinical and Legal Sourcebook*. 2d ed. New York: John Wiley & Sons, 1999. Leading figures in the field of family violence review the research and examine strategies and measures relevant to assessment of the problem. They also comment on treatment planning and legal requirements. Other areas of concern include epidemological models, intervention planning, and standards of practice.

Browne, Angela. *When Battered Women Kill*. New York: Free Press, 1989. A study based on interviews with 250 physically abused women, forty-two of whom had killed their batterers, shows how "romantic idealism" drives the early stages of the abusive relationship. Obsessive "love" continues along with the abuser's need to physically control the woman. In addition, coping and survival strategies of the battered women are presented.

Buttell, Frederick P. "Moral Development Among Court-Ordered Batterers: Evaluating the Impact of Treatment." *Research on Social Work Practice* 11, no. 1 (2001): 93-107. Court-ordered participants in a cognitive behavioral group treatment program for batterers were studied regarding changing their levels of moral reasoning. The control group consisted of thirty-two adult men with an average age of thirty-two years, 84 percent of them African American, who were ordered into a standard group treatment program. The major finding was that the current treatment program was ineffectual in changing batterers' moral reasoning.

Goetting, Ann. *Getting Out: Life Stories of Women Who Left Abusive Men*. New York: Columbia University Press, 1999. Sixteen women shared their stories with the author, who organized them into seven categories, including women of privileged backgrounds, children, two-timing batterers, family and friends to the rescue, shelter life, positive workings of the system, and the impacts of loss and death. A very readable book.

Gondolf, Edward W., and Robert J. White. "Batterer Program Participants Who Repeatedly Reassault: Psychopathic Tendencies and Other Disorders." *Journal of Interpersonal Violence* 16, no. 4 (2001): 361-380. Psychopathic tendencies were studied in 580 men from four batterers' programs. The men had assaulted their partners many times in spite of arrests for domestic violence and being referred to batterer counseling programs. The major conclusion was that men who had abused their partners many times were no more likely to have a psychopathic disorder than other men.

Jackson, Nicky Ali. *Encyclopedia of Domestic Violence*. New York: Routledge, 2007. Leading scholars in the field of domestic violence research contributed to this resource, outlining the traditional as well as the breakthrough issues in this complicated problem. Includes a discussion on what impact different cultures and religions have on domestic violence. Alphabetically arranged.

Jones, Loring, Margaret Hughes, and Ulrike Unterstaller. "Post-traumatic Stress Disorder (PTSD) in Victims of Domestic Violence: A Review of the Research." *Trauma Violence and Abuse* 2, no. 2 (2001): 99-119. An analysis of data from the literature focusing on the interplay between post-traumatic stress disorder and being a battered woman. The authors identified three major objectives of the study as well as seven major findings, chief of which is that PTSD symptoms are consistent with the symptoms of battered women.

Krishman, Satya P., Judith C. Hilbert, and Dawn Van Leeuwen. "Domestic Violence and Help-Seeking Behaviors Among Rural Women: Results from a Shelter-Based Study." *Family and Community Health* 24, no. 1 (2001): 28-38. A study conducted on a sample of predominantly Hispanic women living in rural communities that focused on their help-seeking behaviors, including those at a rural domestic violence shelter. One major finding was that a high percentage of the Hispanic subjects had thought about and/or attempted suicide.

Pellauer, Mary. "Lutheran Theology Facing Sexual and Domestic Violence." *Journal of Religion and Abuse* 2, no. 2 (2000): 3-48. The author argues that Martin Luther was theologically ambivalent on the issues of wife battering and child abuse and seemed to be confused between the ideas of sexuality and sexual violence. She ends her essay with a review of the themes for a Lutheran response to domestic violence, as well as making several recommendations for action based on further analysis of Luther's writings and teachings.

Smith, Darcy M., and Joseph Donnelly. "Adolescent Dating Violence: A Multi-systemic Approach of Enhancing Awareness in Educators, Parents, and Society." *Journal of Prevention and Intervention in the Community* 21, no. 1 (2001): 53-64. Mental health professionals have hesitated to report that adolescents are the fastest-growing at-risk segment of the population. One in eight high school students and one in five college students will be involved in abusive relationships. In 1993, six hundred teenage girls were murdered by their boyfriends. Useful prevention and treatment strategies are also presented.

Walker, Lenore E. *The Battered Woman Syndrome*. 2d ed. New York: Springer, 2000. A readable volume in which the author reports the results of a research project to identify key psychological and sociological factors that make up the battered woman syndrome. In addition, she tested eight specific theories about battered women and also gathered relevant data about battered women.

Carol A. Heintzelman

SEE ALSO: African Americans and mental health; Aggression; Aggression: Reduction and control; Anger; Battered woman syndrome; Child abuse; Codependency; Family life: Adult issues; Family life: Children's issues; Latinos and mental health; Rape and sexual assault; Separation and divorce: Adult issues; Separation and divorce: Children's issues; Violence and sexuality in the media; Violence by children and teenagers.

Down syndrome

TYPE OF PSYCHOLOGY: Psychopathology

Down syndrome, a congenital condition linked to a specific chromosomal error, has received significant attention from physicians and other health professionals, educators, psychologists and other providers of human services, and researchers from a variety of disciplines. Early identification and intervention, special education, vocational education, and supportive services in adulthood contribute to an increasingly favorable prognosis for persons with this condition.

KEY CONCEPTS

- Chromosome 21
- Mosaicism
- Nondysjunction
- Translocation
- Trisomy 21

INTRODUCTION

Down syndrome (DS) is a clinical condition present at birth that is characterized by certain distinctive physical features, varying degrees of delay in different developmental domains, and specific genetic abnormalities. At least three genetic errors have been identified as forming the basis of the syndrome. Trisomy 21, characterized by an extra chromosome 21 in every cell, is the most common condition (95 percent) and is known as nondysjunction. In 3 to 4 percent of Down syndrome cases, a portion of chromosome 21 has undergone translocation to another chromosome, usually chromosome 14, resulting in a partial trisomy 21, known as Robertsonian translocation. Mosaicism, the rarest type (1 percent), is distinguished by a mixture of cells, some of which have an extra chromosome 21, whereas others are normal (including immature red blood cells). The first two types tend to be similar with respect to physical features and degree of intellectual limitation. Those who have a mosaic type tend to have a milder form of the condition.

The condition was first identified as a clinical entity in 1866 by an English physician, John Langdon Down, who described its characteristic features. Because of a superficial physical resemblance between people who had these features and Mongolians, Down labeled the syndrome "mongolism," and those who had it "mongols" or "mongoloids." These labels persisted until the latter half of the twentieth century, when "Down syndrome" became the preferred designation.

Many physical features have been ascribed to Down syndrome, but the most common characteristics are a face that looks round when viewed from the front but appears flat in profile; brachycephaly or a slightly flattened back of the head; eyes that slant slightly upward, with prominent epicanthic folds; a short, broad neck; thin lips and a mouth cavity slightly smaller than average while the tongue is slightly larger; hands that tend to be broad, with short fingers, of which the littlest sometimes has only one joint instead of the usual two and may be slightly curved toward the other fingers (clinodactyly), and the palm may have only one crease going across it or two creases that may extend right across it; feet that tend to be stubby, with a wide space between the first and second toes, where a short crease on the sole begins; hypotonia or low muscle tone, so that limbs and necks are often floppy; and weak reflexes.

Slower than average development that may result in developmental deficits is characteristic of persons with Down syndrome. The extent of developmental delay varies among individuals and within the same individual across different developmental domains. Among individuals, the degree of the developmental lag or deficit is influenced by the type of Down syndrome and by environmental factors. Within the same individual, the highest levels of development are usually attained in the physical or social domains, while the lowest tends to be in language.

ASSOCIATED FEATURES AND DISORDERS

Down syndrome is often associated with mental retardation.Mental retardation Studies of intellectual development in people with Down syndrome before the 1900's reported that for individuals with Down syndrome, intelligence quotient (IQ) scores fell within the "idiot" or, in current terminology, "profound mental retardation" range. During the first half of the twentieth century, similar studies found that 50 to 75 percent of persons with Down syndrome had IQ scores ranging from 20 to 50; the average IQ score was 20 to 35, indicative of severe mental retardation. Those early studies recruited their samples mainly from institutions. Subsequent studies that drew their samples from the entire population yielded higher IQ scores. The majority of children and adults with Down syndrome had IQ scores falling within 30 to 50, with the group average between 40 and 50, classifiable as moderately retarded. Studies in the 1960's found that 5 to 10 percent of older children and adults with Down syndrome had IQ scores indicative of mild mental retardation and were considered "educable." By the mid-1970's, studies included former participants in early intervention programs and as much as 33 to 50 percent of older children and adults with Down syndrome attained IQ scores in the mild mental retardation range. Some had IQ scores within the dull-normal range, and a few had scores in the normal range.

Many infants with Down syndrome (40 to 50 percent) are born with congenital heart disease. Lower proportions have congenital anomalies of the gastrointestinal tract (5 to 12 percent) or congenital cataracts (3 percent). In childhood, some start having convulsive seizures (8 percent). About 15 to 20 percent of adults with Down syndrome, in some cases people in their thirties, exhibit what seem to be clinical signs of Alzheimer's disease.

PREVALENCE

Down syndrome occurs approximately once in 700 to 1,100 births. It is found in all ethnic groups. Slightly more male than female children have received this diagnosis, for reasons yet unknown. Children with Down syndrome have been born to women of any age. Two-thirds are born to mothers under age thirty-five and one-fifth of all children with Down syndrome are born to mothers under age twenty-five. Although there is some evidence that having a father of an advanced age may increase the risk of Down syndrome, the primary risk of having a child with the syndrome is associated with the mother's age at the time of conception, particularly after the age of thirty-five.

ETIOLOGY

John Langdon Down thought that the syndrome he had identified was caused by a reversion to a primitive Mongolian ethnic stock. This etiological hypothesis was repudiated by his son, Reginald Down, also a physician. The hypothesis that Down syndrome might be caused by a chromosomal abnormality was first advanced in 1932 but was not confirmed until 1959, with the discovery of an extra chromosome 21 in children with Down syndrome by Jerome Lejeune and, independently, Patricia Jacobs. Later, geneticists found other chromosomal abnormalities, translocation and mosaicism, in children who had

Down syndrome. In all forms of Down syndrome, faulty cell division accounts for the chromosomal error.

The molecular basis of Down syndrome resulting from trisomy remains uncertain. Translocation of the portion of chromosome 21 in partial trisomy has allowed geneticists to identify the specific region in which overexpression of genetic information results in Down syndrome. However, as many as two hundred or more genes are encoded in that region. Several genes in particular have been suspected, including those that regulate heart and skeletal development, as well as genes involved in regulation of deoxyribonucleic acid (DNA) replication.

PRENATAL SCREENING AND DIAGNOSIS

Prenatal screening for Down syndrome can be done using a combination of either three or four tests. The triple test includes tests for alpha-feroprotein (AFP), estriol, and human chorionic gonadotropin (hCG). These three tests together with a test for inhibin make up the quad test. Approximately 60 to 80 percent of fetuses with Down syndrome can be identified through either the triple or the quad test and consideration of the mother's age.

The most commonly used techniques in prenatal diagnosis of Down syndrome are amniocentesis, chorionic villus sampling (CVS), and ultrasonography. Compared with amniocentesis, CVS can be performed much earlier in pregnancy and produces results more quickly because chromosomal studies can be performed immediately. Studies show that the risk associated with CVS is slightly but not significantly greater than that of amniocentesis. The latest technique, developed in the 1990's, is fluorescent in situ hybridization (FISH).

Appropriate caution is needed in prenatal diagnosis of Down syndrome because certain techniques may involve some risk to the mother or fetus. Siegfried M. Pueschel states that prenatal diagnosis is indicated when screening tests reveal that AFP and estriol levels are low and hCG and inhibin levels are significantly increased; the mother is age thirty-five or older; the father is about age fifty or older; the couple has a child with Down syndrome or another chromosomal abnormality; the parent has a balanced chromosome translocation; or the parent has a chromosome disorder.

COURSE OF THE DISORDER

Many studies have reported a decrease in IQ of individuals with Down syndrome with increasing age. This does not imply that intellectual development has stopped or reversed its course. According to researcher Cliff Cunningham, the IQ decline is an artifact of how IQ is calculated. Some studies suggest that people with Down syndrome who have higher IQ scores continue to develop intellectually well into their twenties and possibly up to their late thirties. Those with much lower IQ scores reach a plateau much earlier and their intelligence remains in the severe mental retardation range.

Research has shown that children with Down syndrome go through the same steps in language acquisition and acquire the same linguistic structures or language rules as normally developing children, but they do so at a slower pace. Also, periods when their progress occurs at a near normal rate (around four to seven years of age) are followed by periods when very little progress occurs. After spending years at this developmental plateau, Down syndrome children may experience growth in linguistic structures again in late adolescence. Because children and adolescents with Down syndrome seem unable consistently to maintain and apply the linguistic rules that they have already acquired, their ultimate language levels are low. Within this population, there are variations in rate of development and in the ultimate level of language attainment associated with differences in general intelligence, environment, and other factors. There is also variability in development within different language domains. Receptive vocabulary tends to be greater than expressive vocabulary. There are longer delays in development of language production than in language comprehension, and in acquisition of syntax compared with acquisition of lexical or vocabulary skills. Last, some evidence suggests that in children with Down syndrome, the understanding of language use in social interaction and communication may be greater than that suggested by their actual levels of grammatical development, and that they use nonverbal behaviors to augment their verbal communications. Despite the slow progress and somewhat low levels of ultimate attainment, the language of persons with Down syndrome is meaningful, relevant, and communicative.

Soon after birth, infants with Down syndrome are able to engage in reciprocal interactions with their parents by using social signaling behaviors such as smiling, eye contact, and vocalization. These social behaviors emerge with only minor delays and distortions. There are individual differences among infants and parents in their abilities to enter into these early social interactions. Parental differences in resilience (that is, in coming to terms emotionally with having an infant who has Down syndrome) imply differences in readiness for reciprocal social interactions with their infants. In general, the development of infant-mother attachment in children with Down syndrome follows the same sequence observed in normally developing children but proceeds at a slower rate.

Similarly, the social skillsSocial interactions of children with Down syndrome emerge in the same sequence but lag behind those of their peers without the condition. This is evident in the development of mutual gaze behavior, social play, and communication skills. Although this lag can affect peer relations, it has been noted that mutual social and language adaptation can take place between children with and without Down syndrome, leading to more social interactions. In adolescence and adulthood, persons with Down syndrome may have fewer friends than they would like and interact with those they have less frequently than their peers without Down syndrome. This is partly from lack of opportunity, since they depend on parents and other adults to take them to places and events that promote friendship development. Often, their friendships are restricted to others with Down syndrome and people whom they encounter at school and at work. Many refer to people with whom they have professional relationships (such as social workers) as friends.

TREATMENT AND PROGNOSIS

There are no effective medical interventions that can "cure" Down syndrome. Still, comprehensive, high-quality medical care from birth onward remains essential to promote the physical growth and development and to maintain the health of this population. Research has shown that cognitive, linguistic, and social development of young children with Down syndrome can be improved significantly through early identification and intervention, including physical and speech therapy. For older children, adolescents, and adults in this population, special education, vocational training, and supportive services in adulthood have produced marked increases in educational, occupational, and social skills, and in overall adaptation to the community. Family involvement is an essential ingredient for the success of these various approaches.

Home-rearing, parent advocacy, public policies and programs that provide an array of services including special education, and supportive communities have markedly improved the outcomes for this population. Increasingly, more adults with Down syndrome are able to attain self-sufficiency or partial self-sufficiency, to hold jobs or work in sheltered workshops, to live independently or in group homes, and, in general, to live as well-functioning members of their communities.

BIBLIOGRAPHY

Cicchetti, Dante, and Marjorie Beeghly, eds. *Children with Down Syndrome: A Developmental Perspective*. New York: Cambridge University Press, 1990. Written for graduate students and professionals interested in the development of children with Down syndrome, this book provides an in-depth treatment of theory and research on the topic.

Evans-Martin, F. Fay. *Down Syndrome*. New York: Chelsea House, 2008. Looks at the genetic basis for Down syndrome, health issues, interventions, and treatments.

Firthel, Richard A., ed. *Focus on Medical Genetics and Down's Syndrome Research*. New York: Nova Biomedical Books, 2007. Collection of essays that hone in on the genetic basis for Down syndrome and what the science means for treatment.

Skallerup, Susan, ed. *Babies with Down Syndrome: A New Parents' Guide*. Bethesda, Md.: Woodbine House, 2008. This up-to-date work on parenting a Down syndrome baby includes contributions from the medical field and the perspectives of parents.

Soper, Kathryn Lynard. *Gifts: Mothers Reflect on How Children with Down Syndrome Enrich Their Lives*. Bethesda, Md.: Woodbine House, 2007. The book is a collection of personal recollections by mothers who have given birth to children with Down syndrome.

Felicisima C. Serafica; updated by Richard Adler

See Also: Abnormality: Biomedical models; Developmental disabilities; Genetics and mental health; Intelligence; Intelligence quotient (IQ); Language; Mental retardation; Physical development: Environment versus genetics; Prenatal physical development.

Dreams

Type of psychology: Cognition; Consciousness

Dreams are the series of images, thoughts, and feelings that occur in the mind of the sleeping person. Dreams are usually confused with waking reality while they are occurring. Distinctive neurological phenomena are associ-

ated with the production of dreams, and diverse psychological experiences are conveyed in dreaming.

Key Concepts

- D-sleep
- Latent content
- Manifest content
- NREM sleep
- REM sleep
- S-sleep
- Sleep mentation

INTRODUCTION

Humans spend roughly one-third of their lives sleeping, and laboratory research indicates that about a quarter of the sleep period is filled with dreaming. Thus, if a person lives seventy-five years, he or she will spend more than eight of those years dreaming. People throughout the millennia have pondered the meaning of those years of dreaming, and their answers have ranged from useless fictions to psychological insights to the mark of God.

Some of the earliest known writings were about dreams. *The Epic of Gilgameš*, written around 3500 BCE, contains the first recorded dream interpretation. An Egyptian document dating to the Twelfth Dynasty (1991–1786 BCE) called the Chester Beatty Papyrus, after its discoverer, presented a system for interpreting dreams. The biblical book of Genesis, attributed to Moses, who is said to have lived between 1446 and 1406 BCE, records a dream of Abimelech (a contemporary of Abraham and Sarah) from a period that appears to antedate the Twelfth Dynasty. Artemidorus Daldianus (ca. second century CE) provided a comprehensive summary of ancient thinking on dreams in his famous book, *Oneirocritica* (The interpretation of dreams).

To better understand dreaming, it must be distinguished from other altered states of consciousness. If the person is fully awake and perceives episodes departing from natural reality, the person is said to have experienced a vision. Experiencing an unintended perceptual distortion is more properly called a hallucination. A daydream is a purposeful distortion of reality. In the twilight realm of dreamlike imagery occurring just before falling asleep or just before becoming fully awake, hypnagogic or hypnopompic reverie, respectively, are said to occur. Dreams occur only in the third state of consciousness—being fully asleep. Another distinction is needed to differentiate between the two types of psychological phenomena that occur when a person is in this third realm of consciousness. Dreams have the attributes of imagery, temporality (time sequence), confusion with reality, and plot (an episode played out). Those subjective experiences that occur during sleep and are lacking in these attributes can be labeled as "sleep mentation."

TYPES OF DREAMS

Just as there are different types of dreamlike experiences, there are different kinds of dreams. Although there will be shortcomings in any effort toward classifying dreams, some approximate distinctions can be made in regard to sleep stage, affect (feelings and emotions), reality orientation, and dream origin.

When people fall asleep, brain activity changes throughout the night in cycles of approximately 90 to 110 minutes. Research with the electroencephalograph (which records electrical activity) has demonstrated a sequence of four stages of sleep occurring in these cycles. The first two stages are called D-sleep (desynchronized EEG), which constitutes essential psychological rest—consolidation of memories and processing of thoughts and emotions. The other two stages, which constitute S-sleep (synchronized EEG), are necessary for recuperation from the day's physical activity—physical rest. S-sleep usually disappears during the second half of a night's sleep. Dreaming occurs in both S-sleep and D-sleep but is much more likely to occur in D-sleep.

A further distinction in the physiology of sleep is pertinent to the type of dreaming activity likely to occur. During stage-one sleep, there are often accompanying rapid eye movements (REM) that are not found in other stages of sleep. Researchers often distinguish between REM sleep, where these ocular movements occur, and non-REM (NREM) sleep, in which there is an absence of these eye movements. When people are aroused from REM sleep, they report dreams a majority of the time—roughly 80 percent—as opposed to a minority of the time—perhaps 20 percent—with NREM sleep. Furthermore, REM dreams tend to have more emotion, greater vividness, more of a plot, a greater fantastical quality, and episodes that are more likely to be recalled and with greater clarity. According to the French National Institute of Health and Medical Research, greater wakefulness during the night and higher frequency of dreaming are linked with more frequent dream recall.

The prevalence of affect in dreams is linked with people's styles of daydreaming. Those whose daydreams are of a positive, uplifting quality tend to experience the greatest amount of pleasant emotionality in their dreams. People whose daydreams reflect a lot of anxiety, guilt, and negative themes experience more unpleasant dreams. While most dreams are generally unemotional in content, when there are affective overtones, negative emotions predominate about two-thirds of the time. Unpleasant dreams can be categorized into three types. Common nightmares occur in REM sleep and are caused by many factors, such as unpleasant circumstances in life, daily stresses, or traumatic experiences. Common themes are being chased, falling, or reliving an aversive event. Night terrors are most likely to occur in stage-four sleep and are characterized by sudden wakening, terror-stricken reactions, and disorientation that can last several minutes. Night terrors are rarely recollected. A 2014 study by researchers at the University of Warwick, England, finds that frequent nightmares and night terrors in children may be associated with psychotic experiences in adolescence. An extreme life-threatening event can lead to posttraumatic stress disorder (PTSD). Recurring PTSD nightmares, unlike other nightmares and night terrors, are repetitive nightmares in which the sufferer continues to relive the traumatic event. Furthermore, PTSD nightmares can occur in any stage of sleep. Dreams are also involved in REM sleep behavior disorder, in which a sleeping person acts out what he or she is experiencing in REM sleep. Some research suggests this condition may be linked to the development of dementia with Lewy bodies in older men.

DREAMS AND REALITY

The reality level of dreams varies in terms of time orientation and level of consciousness. Regarding time orientation, dreams earlier in the night contain more themes dealing with the distant past—such as childhood for an adult—while dreams closer toward waking up tend to be richer in content and have more present themes—such as a current concern. The future is emphasized in oneiromancy, the belief that dreams are prophetic and can warn the dreamer of events to come. A famous biblical story exemplifies this: Joseph foretold seven years of plenty followed by seven years of famine after hearing about Pharaoh's dream of seven fat cows devoured by seven lean cows.

The unconscious mind contains material that is rarely accessible or completely inaccessible to awareness. The personal unconscious may resurrect dream images of experiences that a person normally cannot voluntarily recall. For example, a woman may dream about kindergarten classmates about whom she could not remember anything while awake. The psychologist Carl Jung proposed that dreams could sometimes include material from the collective unconscious—a repository of shared human memories. Thus, a dream in which evil is represented by a snake may reflect a common human inclination to regard snakes as dangerous.

When waking reality rather than unconscious thoughts intrude on dreaming, lucid dreams occur. Lucid dreams are characterized by the dreamer's awareness in the dream that he or she is dreaming. Stephen LaBerge's research has revealed that lucid dreams occur only in REM sleep and that people can be trained to experience lucidity, whereby they can exercise some degree of control over the content of their dreams. Such explorers of dreams have been called "oneironauts."

ORIGINS AND SIGNIFICANCE

Theories about the origins of dreams can be divided into two main categories: naturalistic and supernaturalistic. Proponents of naturalistic theories of dreaming believe that dreams result from either physiological activities or psychological processes. Aristotle was one of the first people to offer a physiological explanation for dreams. His basic thesis was that dreams are the afterimages of sensory experiences. A modern physiological approach to dreaming was put forth in the 1970s by J. Allan Hobson and Robert McCarley. According to their activation-synthesis theory, emotional and visual areas of the brain are activated during REM sleep, and the newly alerted frontal lobe tries to make sense of this information plus any other sensory or physiological activity that may be occurring at that time. The result is that ongoing activity is synthesized (combined) into a dream plot. For example, a man enters REM sleep and pleasant memories of playing in band during school are evoked. Meanwhile, the steam pipes in his bedroom are banging. The result is a dream in which he is watching a band parade by with the booming of bass drums ringing in his ears. Hobson does not believe that, apart from fostering recent memories, dreams have any psychological significance.

Plato believed that dreams do have psychological significance and can reveal something about the character of people. More recent ideas about the psychological origins of dreams can be divided into symbolic approaches that emphasize the hidden meanings of dreams and cognitive perspectives that stress that dreaming is simply another type of thinking and that no deep, hidden motives are contained in that thinking. The most famous symbolic approach to dreaming was presented by Sigmund Freud in his book *Die Traumdeutung* (1900; *The Interpretation of Dreams*, 1913). For Freud, the actual dream content is meaningless. It hides the true meaning of the dream, which must be interpreted. David Foulkes, in Dreaming: *A Cognitive-Psychological Analysis* (1985), proposed a contrary perspective. His cognitive approach to dreaming states that dreams are as they are remembered and that it is meaningless to search for deep meanings. Foulkes proposes that randomly activated memories during sleep are organized into a comprehensible dream by a "dream-production system."

The final category of dreams represents the most ancient explanation—dreams may have a supernatural origin. Often connected with the supernatural approach is the belief that deities or supernatural beings can visit a person in a dream and heal that person of physical illnesses. This belief is called "dream incubation" and was widely practiced by the ancient Greeks beginning around the sixth century BCE. Several hundred temples were dedicated to helping believers practice this art. Spiritual healing, not physical healing, is the theme presented in the numerous references to dreaming in the Bible: more than one hundred verses in nearly twenty chapters. The Bible presents a balanced picture of the origins of dreams. God speaks through dreams to Abimelech in the first book of the Old Testament (Genesis 20:6) and to Joseph in the first book of the New Testament (Matthew 1:20). However, Solomon (Ecclesiastes 5:7) and Jeremiah (23:25–32) warn that many dreams do not have a divine origin.

DREAM CONTENT

Dream content varies depending on the stage of sleep and time of night. Research has also revealed that characteristics of the dreamer and environmental factors can influence the nature of dreams.

Three human characteristics that influence dreams are age, gender, and personality. It has been found that children are more likely to report dreams (probably because they experience more REM sleep) and their dreams are reported to have more emotional content, particularly nightmarish themes. Elderly people report more death themes in their dreams. Male dreams have more sexual and aggressive content than female dreams, which have more themes dealing with home and family. Women report that they dream of their mothers and babies more when they are pregnant. Introverts report more dreams and with greater detail than extroverts. Psychotic individuals (those with severe mental disorders), depressed people, and those whose occupations are in the creative arts (such as musicians, painters, and novelists) report more nightmares. Schizophrenics and severely depressed people provide shorter dream reports than those of better mental health. It is also reported that depressed people dream of the past more than those who are not depressed.

Environmental factors occurring before and during sleep can shape the content of dreams. What people experience prior to falling asleep can show up in dreams in blatant, subtle, or symbolic forms. People watching movies that evoke strong emotions tend to have highly emotional dreams. In fact, the greater the emotionality of a daily event, the greater the probability that the event will occur in a dream during the subsequent sleep period. Those who are wrestling mentally with a problem often dream about that problem. Some have even reported that the solutions to their problems occurred during the course of dreaming. The German physiologist Otto Loewi's Nobel Prize–winning research with a frog's nerve was inspired by a dream he had. Sometimes events during the day show up in a compensatory form in dreams. Thus, those deprived of food, shelter, friends, or other desirables report an increased likelihood of dreaming about those deprivations at night.

Events occurring during sleep can be integrated into the dream plot as well. External stimuli such as temperature changes, light flashes, and various sounds can be detected by the sleeping person's senses and then become part of the dream. However, research indicates that sensory information is only infrequently assimilated into dreams. Internal stimulation from physiological activities occurring during sleep may have a greater chance of influencing the nature of dreams. Dreams about needing to find a bathroom may be caused in part by a full bladder. Similarly, nighttime activation of the vestibular system (which controls the sense of balance), the premotor cortex (which initiates movements), and the locus coeruleus (which plays a role in inhibiting muscles during sleep so that dreams are not acted out) perhaps can stimulate the production of dreams about falling, chasing, or being unable to move, respectively.

DREAM INTERPRETATION

There is a profusion of books about dream interpretation offering many different, and often contradictory, approaches to the subject. With so many different ideas about what dreams mean, it is difficult to know which approach is more likely to be successful.

A few principles increase the probability that a dream interpretation approach will be valid. First, the more dream content recalled, the better the opportunity to understand its meaning. Most people remember only bits and pieces of their dreams, and serious efforts to interpret dreams require serious efforts by people to remember their dreams. Second, the more a theme recurs in a series of dreams, the greater the likelihood that the theme is significant. Dream repetition also helps in interpretation: Content from one dream may be a clue to the meaning of other dreams. Finally, the focus of dream interpretation should be the dreamer, not the dream. To understand the dream, one must spend time and effort in knowing the dreamer.

There are many scholarly approaches to dream interpretation. Three theories are particularly noteworthy due to their influence on the thinking of other scholars and their utility for clinical application. Each perspective emphasizes a different side of the meaning of dreams.

Freud proposed that dreams are complementary to waking life. His basic thesis was that many wishes, thoughts, and feelings are censored in waking consciousness due to their unsuitability for public expression and are subsequently pushed down into the unconscious. This unconscious material bypasses censorship in dreaming by a process in which the hidden, "true" meaning of the dream, the latent content, is presented in a disguised form, the manifest content. The manifest content is the actual content of the dream that is recalled. To interpret a dream requires working through the symbolism and various disguises of the manifest content to get to the true meaning of the dream residing in the latent content. For example, Jane's manifest content is a dream in which she blows out candles that surround a gray-headed man. The candles might symbolize knowledge and the gray-headed man may represent her father. The latent content is that Jane resents her father's frequent and interfering advice. Thus, blowing out the candles represents Jane's desire to put an end to her father's meddling.

Jung proposed that dreams could be understood at different levels of analysis and that the essential purpose of dreams was compensatory. By compensatory, Jung meant that dreams balance the mind by compensating for what is lacking in the way a person is living life. For example, the timid Christian who is afraid to speak up for his or her beliefs with atheistic colleagues dreams of being a bold and eloquent evangelist. Jung believed that four levels of analysis could be used to help dreamers gain insight into their dreams. His general rule guiding the use of these levels is that recourse to analysis at deeper levels of consciousness is only warranted if the dream cannot be adequately understood from a more surface level of examination. To illustrate, a man has a dream in which he steps into a pile of manure. At the conscious level of analysis, it may be that he is dreaming about a recent experience—no need to posit symbolic interpretations. Looking into his personal unconscious, an image from his childhood may be evoked. Recourse to the cultural level of consciousness would examine what manure symbolizes in his culture. It could be a good sign for a farmer in an agrarian world, but a bad sign for a politician in an industrialized society. In some cases, it may be necessary to look at the dream from the perspective of the collective unconscious. Manure might be an ancient, universal image that symbolizes fertility. Could the man be questioning whether or not he wants to be a father?

Zygmunt Piotrowski developed a theory of dream interpretation based on psychological projection. For Piotrowski, in a dream about another person, that person may actually represent a facet of the dreamer's own mind. The more the dream figure is like the dreamer and the closer the proximity between the figure and the dreamer in the dream, the greater the likelihood the dreamer is projecting himself or herself (seeing in others what is really in the self) into that dream figure. For instance, a woman may dream she is walking with her closest friend but that friend is ignoring everything she is saying to her. An interpretation according to Piotrowski's system could be that the dreamer is actually dealing with the fact that she is not a good listener.

Dreams may be complementary, compensatory, or projective, useless fictions or avenues of insight, products of the brain or a touch from God. Many credible answers have been proposed, but it is hard to believe that there is a single explanation for every instance of dreaming. Perhaps the best answer is that dreams reveal many different things about many different dreamers—biologically, psychologically, socially, and spiritually.

BIBLIOGRAPHY

"Brain Basics: Understanding Sleep." *National Institute of Neurological Disorders and Stroke.* National Institutes of Health, US Dept. of Health and Human Services, 5 Dec. 2013. Web. 27 Mar. 2014.

Dement, William C. *The Promise of Sleep.* New York: Dell, 2000. Print.

Farthing, G. W. *The Psychology of Consciousness.* New York: Penguin, 1996. Print.

Freud, Sigmund. *The Interpretation of Dreams.* Trans. Joyce Crick. Ed. Ritchie Robertson. New York: Oxford UP, 2008. Print.

Hall, James A. *Patterns of Dreaming.* Boston: Shambhala, 1991. Print.

Hobson, J. Allan. *Dreaming: An Introduction to the Science of Sleep.* New York: Oxford UP, 2005. Print.

Kallmyer, J. D. *Dreams: Hearing the Voice of God through Dreams, Visions, and the Prophetic Word.* Harre de Grace: Moriah, 1998. Print.

Lusty, Natalya, and Helen Groth. *Dreams and Modernity: A Cultural History.* New York: Routledge, 2013. Print.

Pagel, James F. *Dream Science: Exploring the Forms of Consciousness.*Oxford: Academic, 2014. Print.

Rock, Andrea. *The Mind at Night: The New Science of How and Why We Dream.* New York: Basic, 2009. Digital file.

Rosen, Marvin. *Sleep and Dreaming.* Philadelphia: Chelsea House, 2006.

Schenk, Carlos H. "Sleep and Parasomnias." *National Sleep Foundation.* National Sleep Foundation, 2013. Web. 27 Mar. 2014.

West, Marcus. *Understanding Dreams in Clinical Practice.* London: Karnac, 2011. Print.

Paul J. Chara, Jr.

See Also: Analytical psychology: Carl Jung; Archetypes and the collective unconscious; Consciousness: Altered states; Freud, Sigmund; Freudian psychology; Hallucinations; Insomnia; Jung, Carl; Jungian psychology; Psychoanalytic psychology and personality: Sigmund Freud; Sleep.

Drive theory

Type of psychology: Motivation

A drive is a state influenced by an animal's need; the animal is motivated to reduce tension or to seek a goal. Drive theory is concerned with the nature of the internal forces that compel an animal's behavior..

Key Concepts

- Drive
- Drive reduction
- Law of effect
- Need
- Reinforcement

INTRODUCTION

One goal of science is to understand, predict, or manipulate natural events. A scientist may start by observing an event of interest and measuring it as precisely as possible to detect any changes. In experimental research, scientists systematically manipulate various other events to see whether the event of interest also changes. In survey research, different events are measured to see whether they vary with the event of interest. Understanding is achieved when the relationship between the event of interest (the dependent variable) and other events (independent variables) is established. One can then predict or manipulate the event of interest. A theory provides a guideline to organize the variables into a system based on common properties. To a psychologist, the dependent variable is the behavior of all animals and humans, and the independent variables (also called determinants) may be any other variable related to behaviors. Psychological research aims to discover the determinants of a certain behavior, some of which are motivational variables. The field of motivation examines why a particular behavior occurs, why it is so strong, and why it is so persistent.

A drive is a process related to the source of behavioral energy originating from within the body that is created by disturbances in homeostasis (a state of systemic equilibrium). A homeostatic imbalance creates a state of need for certain stimuli from the environment that can restore the balance. For example, abnormal body temperature and hyperosmolality of the body fluid (electrolyte concentration outside cells that is higher than that of the intracellular fluid, resulting in cell dehydration) are disturbances in homeostasis. The homeostatic balance can be restored through two means: physiological and behavioral. Physiological means such as vasodilation, sweating, and panting serve to reduce body temperature, while concentration of electrolytes in the urine by the kidneys reduces hyperosmolality. Behavioral means such as taking off clothes, turning on an air conditioner, and drinking cold liquid lower body temperature; drinking water would also result in reduction of hyperosmolality. One may examine a case of homeostatic imbalance in detail to illustrate how the two means function to restore the balance.

When the body fluid volume is reduced (hypovolemia) because of loss of blood or of body fluid due to intense sweating, the body responds immediately by vasoconstriction, reducing urine volume (through vasopressin release), and conserving sodium (through aldosterone release). Those are physiological means that will restore the blood pressure and prevent circulatory failure. Eventually, however, the body must get back the lost fluid from the environment via behavior (seeking water and drinking) to achieve long-lasting homeostasis. The physiological means are immediate and effective, but they are only stopgap measures. Behavior is the means by which the animal interacts with its environment to get back the lost resource.

DRIVE, REINFORCEMENT, AND LEARNING

The concept of drives is very important to the theories of Clark L. Hull, a neo-behaviorist. According to Hull, a drive has at least two distinct functions as far as behavioral activation is concerned: without drives there could be no reinforcement and thus no learning, because drive reduction is the reinforcement; and without drives there could be no response, for a drive activates behavioral potentials into performance. Drive theory maintains that a state named "drive," or D, is a necessary condition for behavior to occur, but D is not the same as the bodily need. D determines how strongly and persistently a behavior will occur; it connects the need with the behavior. This distinction between need and drive is necessary because while the state of need serves as the source of behavior, the intensity of behavior is not always related to the intensity of need. Need can be defined as a state of an organism attributable to deprivation of a biological or psychological requirement, related to a disturbance in the homeostatic state.

There are cases in which the need increases but behavior does not, or in which the need remains but behavior is no longer manifested. Prolonged deprivation, for example, may not result in a linear or proportional increase in behavior. A water-deprived animal may stop drinking even before cellular dehydration is restored to the normal state; the behavior is changing independent of homeostatic imbalance. Cessation of behavior is seen as being attributable to drive reduction.

Hull uses D to symbolize drive and sHr (H is commonly used to denote this, for convenience) to symbolize a habit that consists of an acquired relationship between stimulus (S) and response (R). It represents a memory of experience in which certain environmental stimuli and responses were followed by a reward. An effective reward establishes an S-R relationship; the effect is termed reinforcement. One example of an H would be an experience of maze stimuli and running that led to food. H is a behavioral potential, not a behavior. Food deprivation induces a need state that can be physiologically defined; then D will energize H into behavior. The need increases monotonically with hours of deprivation, but D increases only up to three days without food. A simplified version of the Hullian formula for a behavior would be "behavior = HD," or "performance = behavioral potential energizer." The formula indicates that learning, via establishing behavioral potential, and D, via energizing the potential, are both necessary for performance to occur. This is a multiplicative relationship; that is, when either H or D is zero, a specific performance cannot occur.

ROLE OF FREUD'S "ID"

In his psychoanalytical approach to behavioral energy, Sigmund Freud proposed that psychic energy is the source of human behaviors. The id is the reservoir of instinctual energy presumed to derive directly from the somatic processes. This energy is unorganized, illogical, and timeless, knowing "no values, no good or evil, no morality," according to Freud in 1933. The id operates according to the pleasure principle, using the primary process to discharge its energy as soon as possible, with no regard for reality. When the discharge is hindered by reality, however, the ego handles the situation according to the reality principle, using a secondary process to pursue realistic gratification. The ego mediates between the id on one hand and reality on the other.

Freud thus conceptualized the id to be the energy source and the ego to manage behavior in terms of reality. Learning is manifested in the way the ego manages behavior for gratification under the restriction of the environment and the superego. In this model, the drive is seen as the energizer of behavior. The similarity between the Freudian and Hullian concepts of drive is obvious. Food deprivation would generate homeostatic imbalance, which is the somatic process, and the need, which is similar to the energy of the id. The organism cannot obtain immediate gratification because of environmental constraints on acquiring food, so behavior is generated to negotiate with the environment. Drive is much like the ego, since it energizes the behavioral potentials into behaviors to seek reality gratification, which is equivalent to drive reduction. The concept of pleasure and behavioral changes commonly appears in various theories that incorporate a subtle influence of Freudian thought.

DEPRIVATION AND INCENTIVE MOTIVES

In one classic experiment, Carl J. Warden studied the persistence of behavior as a function of various sources, including the strength of a drive, using an apparatus called a Columbia obstruction box. He demonstrated that a rat without food would cross an electrified grid to reach a goal box that held food. When the rat was immediately brought back from the goal box to the start box, it would cross the grid again and again. The number of grid crossings was positively related to the number of days without food for up to three days. From the fourth day without food, however, the number of crossings slowly decreased. When baby rats were placed in the goal box, a mother rat would cross the grid repeatedly. When a male or female rat was placed in the goal box, a rat of the opposite sex would cross repeatedly. The number of crossings by the male rat was positively related to the duration it spent without a female companion.

These animals were all manifesting the effect of different drives: hunger, maternal instinct, and sex. It was shown that the maternal drive was associated with the greatest number of crossings (twenty-two times in twenty minutes), followed by thirst (twenty times), hunger (seventeen), female sex drive (fourteen), male sex drive (thirteen), and exploration (six). Warden demonstrated that various internal forces, created by deprivation and hormonal state, and external forces, created by different goal objects, together determine the grid-crossing behavior. The level of deprivation induces drive motivation; the reward in the goal box induces incentive motivation. In this example, the focus is on drive motivation.

If one were to place a well-trained rat into a maze, it might or might not run to the goal box. Whether it would run, how fast it would run, and how well (in terms of errors) it would run would depend on whether the subject were food deprived. With food deprivation, the well-trained rat would run to the goal box with few errors. If it had just been fed, it would not run; it would simply wander, sniff at the corner, and go to sleep. The environmental stimulus (the maze) is the same; the rat's behavior is different because the internal force—the drive created by food deprivation—is different. A need state produces D, and D triggers behavior. The behavior that will occur is determined jointly by the past experience of learning, which is termed H, and by stimuli, S, from the environment. An inexperienced rat, without the H of maze running, will behave differently from a well-trained rat in a maze. D is an intervening variable: It connects need and behavior, so one must consider both the source (need) and the consequence (behavior) to define D. When D is zero, there will be no maze running, no matter how well trained the rat is. On the other hand, if there is no H (training), the proper maze-running behavior will not occur, no matter how hungry the rat is. An animal must be exposed to a maze when hungry to learn to negotiate the various turns on the way to the goal box containing food. Without food deprivation (and the resultant D), the animal would not perform even if it could; one cannot tell whether an animal has the knowledge to run the maze until one introduces a D variable. H is a potential of behavior, and D makes the potential into the observable reality of performance. Motivation turns a behavior on.

These ideas can be applied to countless real-life examples. If a person is not very good at playing tennis (has a low H), for example, no matter how motivated (high D) he or she is, that person will not be able to beat a friend who is an expert at the game. If a person is very good at tennis (high H) but does not feel like playing (low D), perhaps because of a lack of sleep, he or she will not perform well. The same situation would apply to taking a test, delivering a speech, or running a marathon.

PUZZLE-BOX LEARNING

In another experiment involving drive, Edward L. Thorndike put a cat into a puzzle box. The cat attempted to get out via various behaviors (mewing, scratching, and so on). By chance, it stepped on a plate that resulted in the door opening, allowing the cat to escape. The cat was repeatedly returned to the box, and soon it would escape right away by stepping on the plate; other, useless behaviors were no longer manifested. The source of D in this case was the anxiety induced by confinement in the box, which could be measured by various physiological changes, such as heart rate and hormonal levels. Escaping makes the anxiety disappear, and D is reduced. D reduction results in an increase in the probability that the behavior immediately preceding it (stepping on the plate) will recur. Thorndike describes this puzzle-box learning as trial and error, implying a blind attempt at various means of escape until one happens to work. He states that a "satisfying effect" will create repetition, calling this the law of effect; the essence of the satisfying effect appears to be drive reduction. A five-stage learning cycle, then, consists of need, drive, behavior, drive reduction, and behavior repetition.

CENTRAL MOTIVE STATE

The question of how a habit (H) is formed and how it is stored in the brain is a lively research topic in the psychobiology of learning, memory, and cognition, as well as in neuropsychology, which deals with learning deficit and loss of memory. Drive and reinforcement are important variables that determine whether learning will succeed and whether past learning will be manifested as behaviors. Research on hunger and thirst forms one subfield of psychobiology.

If D is the common energizer of various behaviors, then all sources of D—hunger, thirst, sex, mothering, exploration—should have something in common physiologically. The so-called central motive state is hypothesized to be such a state. It is known that arousal is common to the sources of D. Research involves biological delineation of the sources of D; researchers are studying the mechanisms of hunger, for example. There has been insufficient attention paid to the physiological processes by which hunger may motivate various behaviors and by which drive reduction would serve as a reinforcement in learning. Extreme lack of motivation can be seen in some depressed and psychotic patients, which results in both a lack of new learning and a lack of manifesting what is already known. The neuronal substrates of this "lack of energy" represent one problem under investigation in the area of drive and motivation.

BIBLIOGRAPHY

Amsel, Abram. *Mechanisms of Adaptive Behavior: Clark Hull's Theoretical Papers, with Commentary.* New York: Columbia UP, 1984. Print.

Bolles, Robert C. *Theory of Motivation.* 2nd ed. New York: Harper, 1975. Print.

Deckers, Lambert. *Motivation: Biological, Psychological, and Environmental.* 4th ed. Boston: Pearson, 2014. Print.

Freud, Sigmund. *New Introductory Lectures on Psychoanalysis.* New York: Norton, 1933. Print.

Hull, Clark L. Principles of Behavior. New York: Appleton, 1943. Print.

Miller, Neal. *Learning, Motivation, and Their Physiological Mechanisms.* New Brunswick: Aldine, 2007. Print.

Petri, Herbert L., and John M. Govern. *Motivation: Theory, Research, and Applications.* 6th ed. Belmont: Wadsworth, 2013. Print.

Pfaff, Donald W., ed. *The Physiological Mechanisms of Motivation.* New York: Springer, 1982. Print.

Reeve, Johnmarshall. *Understanding Motivation and Emotion.* 5th ed. Hoboken: Wiley, 2009. Print.

Ryan, Richard M., ed. *The Oxford Handbook of Human Motivation.* New York: Oxford UP, 2012. Print.

Stellar, James R., and Eliot Stellar. *The Neurobiology of Motivation and Reward.* New York: Springer, 1985. Print.

Warden, Carl John. *Animal Motivation: Experimental Studies on the Albino Rat.* New York: Columbia UP, 1931. Print.

Sigmund Hsiao

See Also: Hull, Clark L.; Hunger; Incentive motivation; Instinct theory; Motivation; Motivation: Intrinsic and extrinsic; Sex hormones and motivation; Thirst.

Drug therapies

Date: 1950s forward

Type of psychology: Biological bases of behavior; Psychopathology; Psychotherapy

Psychotropic drugs have revolutionized the treatment of mental illness. Many disorders, including anxiety, depression, and schizophrenia, may be treated effectively with these modern drugs. However, the use of psychotropic drugs has created new problems, both for individuals and for society.

Key Concepts

- Antianxiety drugs
- Antidepressant drugs
- Antipsychotics
- Mood stabilizers
- Neurotransmitters
- Psychopharmacology
- Psychostimulants
- Psychotropic

INTRODUCTION

Before 1950, no truly effective drug therapies existed for mental illness. Physicians treated mentally ill patients with a combination of physical restraints, bloodletting, sedation, starvation, electric shock, and other minimally effective therapies. They used some drugs for treatment, including alcohol and opium, primarily to calm agitated patients. Interest in drug therapy in the early twentieth century was high, based on the rapidly increasing body of chemical knowledge developed during the late nineteenth century. Researchers in the first half of the twentieth century experimented with insulin, marijuana, antihistamines, and lithium, with varying success. The term psychopharmacology, the study of drugs for the treatment of mental illness, dates to 1920.

In 1951, a French scientist, Paul Charpentier, synthesized chlorpromazine (Thorazine) for use in reducing surgical patients' anxiety and preventing shock during surgery. Physicians noted its calming effect and began to use it in psychiatry. Previously agitated patients with schizophrenia become calmer, their thoughts became less chaotic, and they became less irritable. Chlorpromazine was truly the first effective psychotropic drug (that is, a drug exerting an effect on the mind) and is still used.

The discovery of chlorpromazine ushered in a new era in the treatment of psychiatric illness. Pharmaceutical companies have developed and introduced dozens of new psychotropic drugs. Many long-term psychiatric treatment facilities have closed, and psychiatrists have released the vast majority of their patients into community-based mental health care. Patients with mental health problems are treated on an outpatient basis, with brief hospitalizations for stabilization in some cases. Treatment goals are no longer simply to sedate patients or to protect them and others from harm but rather to provide them with significant relief from their symptoms and to help them function productively in society. As scientific knowledge about the brain and its function increases, researchers are able to create drugs targeting increasingly specific areas of the brain, leading to fewer adverse side effects.

This psychotherapeutic drug revolution has had some negative consequences, however. Drug side effects range from annoying to life threatening. Community mental health treatment centers have not grown in number or received funding sufficient to meet the needs of all the patients released from long-term care facilities. Many mentally ill patients have fallen through the cracks of community-based care and live on the streets or in shelters for the homeless. In addition, some physicians and patients have come to expect a "pill for every ill" and fail to use other, equally or more effective treatment methodologies. The majority of prescriptions for psychotropic drugs are written by generalist physicians rather than by psychiatrists, raising concerns about excessive or inappropriate prescribing. Some people abuse these drugs, either by taking their medications in excess of the amount prescribed for them or by obtaining them illicitly. Studies have shown that prescription drug abuse causes more injuries and deaths than abuse of all illicit drugs combined. Feminist scholars have pointed out that physicians tend to prescribe psychotropic drugs more readily for women than for men.

Despite the negative effects, psychotropic drugs are extremely important in the provision of health care, not only for those people traditionally thought of as mentally ill but also for people with chronic pain, serious medical illness, and loss and grief, and those who have experienced traumatic events.

HOW PSYCHOTROPIC DRUGS WORK

To understand how these mind-affecting drugs work, it is necessary to understand a little of how the brain works. The brain is made up primarily of neurons (nerve cells) that form circuits controlling thoughts, emotions, physical activities, and basic life functions. These nerve cells do not actually touch one another but are separated by a gap called a synapse. An electrical impulse moves along the neuron. When it reaches the end, it stimulates the release of chemicals called neurotransmitters into the synapse. These chemicals then fit into receptors on the next neuron and affect its electrical impulse. The neurotransmitters act by either causing the release of the electric impulse or inhibiting it so the neuron does not fire. Any neurotransmitter left in the synapse is then reabsorbed into the original neuron. This process is called reuptake.

Problems can arise in one of two ways: either too much or too little neurotransmission. Too much transmission may occur when the neuron fires in the absence of a stimulus or when too many neurotransmitters attach to the receptors on the far side of the synapse (the postsynaptic receptors). Too little transmission can occur when too few neurotransmitters attach to these postsynaptic receptors. The primary neurotransmitters involved in mental illnesses and their treatment are dopamine, serotonin (5-HT), norepinephrine, and gamma-aminobutyric acid (GABA).

ANTIDEPRESSANT DRUGS

Some scientists believe that depression is caused by insufficient norepinephrine, serotonin, or dopamine in the synapse. Others theorize that depression has to do with the number and sensitivity of postsynaptic receptors involved in the neuron's response. Drugs for the treatment of depression fall into four major classes: the monoamine oxidase inhibitors (MAOIs), the tricyclic antidepressants, the selective serotonin reuptake inhibitors (SSRIs), and atypical antidepressants. None of these drugs is addictive, although patients need to be weaned from them slowly to avoid rebound depression or other adverse effects.

MAOIs were the first modern antidepressants. Monoamine oxidase is an enzyme that breaks down serotonin, norepinephrine, and dopamine. Inhibiting the enzyme increases the supply of these neurotransmitters. MAOI drugs available in the United States include phenelzine (Nardil) and tranylcypromine (Parnate). These drugs are not used as commonly as are the other antidepressants, mostly because of their side effects. However, they are used when other treatments for depression fail. In addition, they may be used to treat narcolepsy, phobias, anxiety, and Parkinson's disease. Common side effects include drowsiness, fatigue, dry mouth, and dizziness. They may also cause orthostatic hypotension (a drop in blood pressure when arising) and sexual dysfunction. Most important, the MAOIs interact with tyramine-containing foods, such as hard cheese, red wine, and smoked or pickled fish. Consuming these foods along with an MAOI can cause a hypertensive crisis in which the patient's blood pressure rises to potentially deadly levels. Patients taking MAOIs must also avoid other drugs that stimulate the nervous system to avoid blood pressure emergencies.

The tricyclic antidepressants were introduced in 1958. They all inhibit the reuptake of neurotransmitters but differ in which one is involved. Some affect primarily serotonin, some norepinephrine, and some work equally on both. Tricyclics available in the United States include amitriptyline (Elavil), imipramine (Tofranil), doxepin (Sinequan, Adapin), desipramine (Norpramin), nortriptyline (Pamelor, Aventyl), amoxapine (Asendin), protriptyline (Vivactil), and clomipramine (Anafranil). Primarily used for depression, these drugs may also be helpful in the treatment of bed-wetting, agoraphobia (fear of being out in the open) with panic attacks, obsessive-compulsive disorder, chronic pain, nerve pain, and migraine headaches. An important treatment issue is that it takes two to three weeks of drug therapy before the depressed patient feels much improvement in mood and energy. During this time, the side effects tend to be the most bothersome, leading patients to abandon the treatment before it becomes effective. Another important treatment issue is that tricyclic antidepressants are highly lethal in overdose. Common side effects include dry mouth, blurred vision, constipation, urinary retention, orthostatic hypotension, weight gain, sexual dysfunction, cardiac problems, and jaundice. Some of the tricyclics are highly sedating and so may be useful in patients who are having difficulty sleeping. On the other hand, a patient who is already feeling sluggish and sleepy may benefit from a tricyclic that is less sedating. Any antidepressant may precipitate mania or hypomania in a patient with a predisposition to bipolar disorder. Elderly patients may be at increased risk for falls or confusion and memory impairment when taking tricyclics and should be started on very low doses if a tricyclic is indicated.

The newer selective SSRIs have several advantages over the tricyclics: They are much less lethal in overdose, are far safer in the elderly, and do not cause weight gain. They work, as the name implies, by decreasing serotonin reuptake, thereby increasing the amount of neurotransmitter available at the synapse. Like the tricyclics, SSRIs may need to be taken for several weeks before a patient notices significant improvement in mood and energy level. SSRIs available in the United States include fluoxetine (Prozac), sertraline (Zoloft), fluvoxamine (Luvox), paroxetine (Paxil), trazodone (Desyrel), nafazodone (Serzone), and venlafaxine (Effexor). In addition to depression, the SSRIs are used for treatment of bulimia nervosa and obsessive-compulsive disorder. Possible side effects include nausea, diarrhea, nervousness, insomnia, anxiety, and sexual dysfunction.

Other drugs used in the treatment of depression, known collectively as atypical antidepressants, include mianserin (Tolvon), maprotiline (Ludiomil), and bupropion (Wellbutrin). The mechanisms by which these drugs work are not clear, but they may be useful in patients for whom the other antidepressants do not work or are contraindicated.

MOOD STABILIZERS

Some patients who have depression also have episodes of elevated mood and erratic, uncontrolled behavior. These patients are diagnosed with bipolar disorder, formerly known as manic-depression. The underlying cause for this disorder is unknown, but there is a strong genetic predisposition. Evidence suggests it is due to overactivity of the neurotransmitters. Treatment for bipolar disorder consists of mood-stabilizing drugs. These drugs control not only the "highs" but also the episodes of depression.

Lithium is a naturally occurring mineral that was observed to calm agitated behavior as long ago as in ancient Egypt. Its usefulness as a mood stabilizer was first scientifically established in the 1940s, and it was approved in 1970 for use in the United States. It is effective not only in stabilizing the mood during a manic episode but also in the prevention of future episodes. A significant problem with the use of lithium is that the dose at which it becomes effective is quite close to the dose that produces toxicity, characterized by drowsiness, blurred vision, staggering, confusion, irregular heartbeat, seizures, and coma. Patients taking lithium must therefore have blood drawn on a regular basis to determine drug levels. Patients who have poor kidney function should not take lithium because it is excreted primarily through the urine. Lithium's side effects include nausea, diarrhea, tremor of the hands, dry mouth, and frequent urination.

Drugs usually used for the treatment of seizures may also help stabilize mood in bipolar patients, usually at lower doses than would be used for seizure control. These include carbamazepine (Tegretol), divalproex sodium (Depakote), gabapentin (Neurontin), lamotrigine (Lamictal), and topiramate (Topamax). It is believed that these drugs increase the amount of GABA at the synapse. GABA has a calming or inhibitory effect on the neurons. Side effects of these medications include dizziness, nausea, headaches, and visual changes.

PSYCHOSTIMULANTS

Attention-deficit hyperactivity disorder (ADHD) is found in both children and adults. Children with ADHD have difficulties at school because of impulsivity and inattention. The underlying cause of ADHD is extremely complex, and the ways in which drugs used to treat it work are equally complex. The most successful treatments are with psychostimulants, drugs that stimulate the central nervous system. Drug therapy is most effective when combined with behavioral treatments. The most commonly used psychostimulant is methylphenidate (marketed in varying formulations as Concerta, Daytrana, Metadate, Methylin, and Ritalin), but amphetamines are sometimes used as well. Formerly, depressed patients were treated with amphetamines and similar compounds; occasionally this use is still found. These stimulant drugs do improve school performance; however, they may cause growth retardation in both height and weight. They may also cause insomnia and nervousness. These drugs may be abused, leading ultimately to addiction, paranoia, and severe depression during withdrawal.

ANTIANXIETY DRUGS

Antianxiety drugs or anxiolytics are central nervous system depressants. Many of these drugs, in higher doses, are also used as sedative-hypnotics, or calming and sleep-inducing drugs. They seem to act by enhancing the effect of GABA in the brain. The earliest of these depressant drugs included chloroform, chloral hydrate, and paraldehyde, and they were used for anesthesia and for sedation.

Barbiturates were introduced in Germany in 1862 and were widely used for treatment of anxiety and sleep problems until the 1960s. Barbiturates are still available today, including pentobarbital (Nembutal), secobarbital (Seconal), amobarbital (Amytal Sodium), and phenobarbital (Solfoton, Luminal). Their major adverse effect is respiratory depression, particularly when used in combination with alcohol, another central nervous system depressant. With the advent of the safer benzodiazepines, use of the barbiturates has declined steadily.

Benzodiazepines are used for two major problems: anxiety and insomnia. Anxiety disorders appropriate for this kind of treatment include generalized anxiety disorder, panic disorder, obsessive-compulsive disorder, phobic disorder, and dissociative disorder. The benzodiazepines commonly used for anxiety include alprazolam (Xanax), chlordiazepoxide (Librium), clonazepam (Klonopin), clorazepate (Tranxene), diazepam (Valium), lorazepam (Ativan), and oxazepam (Serax). For most of these disorders, however, behavioral, cognitive, group, and social therapy, or one of these therapies plus medication, are more effective than medication alone. Benzodiazepines used for insomnia include estazolam (Prosom), flurazepam (Dalmane), midazolam (Versed), quazepam (Doral), temazepam (Restoril), and triazolam (Halcion). Benzodiazepines may also be used to prevent the development of delirium tremens during alcohol withdrawal. Patients become tolerant to the effects of these drugs, meaning they have the potential for physical dependency and addiction. In addition, benzodiazepines interact with many other drugs, including alcohol. Their use should be limited to brief periods of time, particularly in the treatment of insomnia. Long-term treatment for anxiety should be monitored carefully by the health care provider. Elderly people are more likely to suffer adverse effects (such as confusion or falls) from benzodiazepine use.

Another drug developed for treatment of anxiety is buspirone (Buspar). Propranolol (Inderal) and atenolol (Tenormin), usually used to treat high blood pressure, are useful in treating stage fright or performance anxiety, and clonidine (Catapres), another blood pressure medication, is successfully used in treatment of anxiety. Nonbenzodiazepine sleep agents include zolpidem (Ambien) and zaleplon (Sonata).

ANTIPSYCHOTIC DRUGS

Formerly known as major tranquilizers or neuroleptics, the antipsychotic drugs have revolutionized the treatment of schizophrenia and other psychoses. The underlying cause of psychosis is not known, but it is thought to be related to the neurotransmitter dopamine. Most of the antipsychotics block the dopamine receptors in the brain. The older antipsychotic drugs, some of which are no longer on the market, include chlorpromazine (Thorazine), thioridazine (Mellaril), perphenazine (Trilafon), trifluoperazine (Stelazine), fluphenazine (Prolixin), thiothixene (Navane), and haloperidol (Haldol). These older drugs treat the so-called positive symptoms of schizophrenia—hallucinations and delusions—but they have little effect on the negative symptoms, which include withdrawal, poor interpersonal relationships, and slowing of the body's movement. They also have multiple serious side effects, including severe muscle spasm, tremor, rigidity, shuffling gait, stupor, fever, difficulty speaking, blood pressure changes, restlessness, and involuntary movements of the face, trunk, arms, and legs. Some of these are treatable using other drugs, but some are neither treatable nor reversible. In an effort to overcome these problems, newer antipsychotics have been developed. The first of these was clozapine (Clozaril), which was successful in treating about one-third of the patients who did not respond to other antipsychotic drugs. Although it has fewer of the serious side effects listed above, a small percentage of patients experience a severe drop in the white blood cells, which puts them at risk for serious infection. For this reason, patients on clozapine must participate in frequent blood tests. Other newer antipsychotics include risperidone (Risperdal), olanzapine (Zyprexa), and quetiapine (Seroquel). In addition to fewer of the serious side effects, the newer antipsychotics seem to have some effect on the negative symptoms.

BIBLIOGRAPHY

Breggin, Peter R., and David Cohen. *Your Drug May Be Your Problem: How and Why to Stop Taking Psychiatric Drugs*. Rev. ed. Philadelphia: DaCapo, 2007. Print.

Drummond, Edward H. *The Complete Guide to Psychiatric Drugs: Straight Talk for Best Results*. Rev. ed. Hoboken: Wiley, 2006. Print.

Gorman, Jack M. *Essential Guide to Psychiatric Drugs*. 4th ed. New York: St. Martin's, 2007. Print.

Herzberg, David. *Happy Pills in America: From Miltown to Prozac*. Baltimore: Johns Hopkins UP, 2008. Print.

Kramer, Peter D. *Listening to Prozac: A Psychiatrist Explores Antidepressant Drugs and the Remaking of the Self*. New York: Penguin, 1997. Print.

Labbate, Lawrence A., et al. *Handbook of Psychiatric Drug Therapy*. 6th ed. Philadelphia: Lippincott, 2012. Print.

Ritter, Lois A., and Shirley Manly Lampkin. *Community Mental Health*. Sudbury: Jones, 2012. Print.

Shiloh, Roni, et al. *Atlas of Psychiatric Pharmacotherapy*. 2nd ed. Boca Raton: Taylor, 2013. Print.

Stahl, Stephen M. *Stahl's Essential Psychopharmacology: Neuroscientific Basis and Practical Applications*. 3d ed. New York: Cambridge UP, 2008. Print.

Rebecca Lovell Scott

See Also: Antianxiety medications; Antidepressant medications; Antipsychotic medications; Anxiety disorders; Attention-deficit hyperactivity disorder; Bed-wetting; Bipolar disorder; Caffeine and mental health; Depression; Hormones and behavior; Insomnia; Mood disorders; Mood stabilizer medications; Narcolepsy; Neurotransmitters; Obsessive-compulsive disorder; Pain management; Personality disorders; Placebo effect; Psychopharmacology; Schizophrenia: Background, types, and symptoms; Sleep; Stimulant medications.

DSM-5

Type of psychology: Clinical; Abnormal; Counseling; Neuroscience

The current classification system of psychiatric illnesses is known as the Diagnostic and Statistical Manual of Mental Disorders (DSM-5), which is published by the American Psychiatric Association (APA). Psychiatrists and other mental health specialists use the DSM-5 to understand the overall and specific nature of mental illnesses. The DSM-5 is the authoritative handbook for research and statistical (epidemiological/public health) analyses; in other words, it serves as a template to estimate the incidence (new cases) and prevalence (existing cases) of mental disorders in the general population. Most important, the DSM-5 provides common terminology and criteria to standardize the assessment and diagnosis of mental illnesses in a variety of clinical settings.

Key Concepts

- Psychiatry
- Nomenclature

- Diagnosis
- Mental disorders
- Mental status examination

INTRODUCTION

Mental illnesses are purportedly the result of abnormalities in brain structure and functioning. People are predisposed to symptoms of mental illnesses by unknown combinations of genetic predispositions (nature) and environmental and life experiences (nurture) that trigger inherited or acquired vulnerabilities to express symptoms (self-reported distress) and signs (observable indicators) of these diseases. As reflected in the DSM-5, psychiatric disorders can afflict children and the elderly, men and women, and people of all races, ethnicities, and nationalities.

Mental illnesses are disturbances that affect people's thoughts, feelings, and behaviors. According to the DSM-5, the overarching definition of mental disorders consists of three elements: distress (the occurrence of emotional pain and suffering), impairment or dysfunction (the inability to perform in school and work and to engage in healthy social relationships and activities), and comportment (the failure to adhere to widely accepted [culturally normative] expectations of behaviors that are operative in a particular place and time). The third element recognizes that symptoms of mental illnesses can be experienced, interpreted, and expressed in culturally specific ways.

Diagnosis is the first step in treating any disease, illness, or infection. However, unlike other medical problems, mental illnesses can rarely be identified or ruled out with objective tests (e.g., blood tests, brain imaging, or biopsies). To determine the causes, onset, course, and prognosis of psychiatric disorders, mental health providers must rely on patients' self-reported psychiatric histories, mental status examinations (lengthy interviews), and observations of patients' behaviors that might indicate signs of mental illnesses. This evaluation process must be performed systematically to achieve consistent and accurate diagnoses. The DSM-5 affords clinicians the structure and guidelines needed to arrive at diagnoses that are widely accepted and understood by members of the profession and reimbursable through insurance coverage.

PRECURSORS TO THE DSM

The origins of the DSM-5 can be traced to the 1840s when the U.S. Census Bureau attempted to count the number of patients in public psychiatric hospitals. The superintendent of one such hospital and a pioneer of modern psychiatry, Isaac Ray, spoke to fellow psychiatrists at a professional conference where he called for the formulation of a national system to measure mental illnesses (naming, classifying, and recording) thereby capturing the nature and extent of hospitalized patients' conditions. The first *Statistical Manual for Psychiatric Diseases* was compiled in 1933 by the Medico-Psychological Association (MPA) and was adopted by the American Neurological Association. This manual was revised several times from 1933 to 1952, the same year the APA published the first edition of the DSM.

DSM-I AND DSM-II

The DSM-I was written by psychiatrists who were mostly followers of Sigmund Freud and who adopted the theories of psychoanalysis as a model to explain, describe, and treat mental illnesses. In the DSM-I, the causes of psychiatric disorders (called "reactions") were attributed to internal conflicts that arose in childhood and were primarily of a sexually repressive nature. The DSM-I included 106 disorders and incorporated terminology and classification schemes from the nosology of the MPA and the general categories of mental disorders identified by the U.S. Army/Veterans Association. The psychoanalytic orientation continued to dominate the DSM-II, which was published in 1968. This second edition strived to achieve greater consistency with the World Health Organization's (WHO) *International Classification of Diseases* (ICD). The DSM-II included 182 disorders.

Several studies showed that DSM-based language for diagnosing psychiatric illnesses produced unreliable clinical findings. When presented with the same case materials or videotaped reenactments of patient interviews, different psychiatrists arrived at different diagnoses based on the descriptions of mental illnesses in the DSM-I and the DSM-II. Researchers also began to question the usefulness and validity of diagnostic categories, as well as the reification of these illnesses. In other words, unlike other types of medical illnesses, psychiatric disorders were not amenable to objective confirmatory evidence to verify diagnoses (e.g., blood tests and MRI findings); nonetheless, they were and are considered "real" diseases with different causes and definitive treatments. Concerns about the reliability and validity of the DSM-II led to a sea change in the field of psychiatry – the eponymous neo-Kraepelinian revolution – that drove the next edition of the DSM.

Known as the father of "scientific" psychiatric diagnoses, Emil Kraepelin was a late 19th, early 20th century physician who practiced in Germany. He argued that mental illnesses were genetically determined brain anomalies that should be treated with medical remedies. A keen observer and cataloger of symptom patterns, he studied and logged the apparent causes, onsets, courses, and prognoses of large numbers of patients under his care and supervision. Through these observations, he discovered commonalities in symptoms which he organized into discernible groupings of mental disorders. Kraepelin essentially created the first diagnostic nomenclature in the field of psychiatry. In particular, Kraepelin was noted for his differentiations among the three most serious psychiatric illnesses: schizophrenia (formerly known as dementia praecox), bipolar disorder (formerly known as manic depression), and major depression (formerly known as melancholia). These disorders are still considered major categories of serious mental illnesses.

DSM-III

Published in 1980, the DSM-III fundamentally changed the procedures for defining, categorizing, and diagnosing mental illnesses. Unlike its predecessors, the DSM-III eschewed the psychoanalytic orientation of earlier editions and replaced them with a more scientific methodology predicated on quantifiable symptoms and behaviors and specific diagnostic criteria. The DSM-III also introduced a multi-axial diagnostic system: Axis I (clinical disorders), Axis II (personality disorders and developmental disabilities), Axis III (medical conditions), Axis IV (psychosocial and environmental problems), and Axis V (Global Assessment of Functioning Scale). This edition of the DSM was heavily influenced by a group of psychiatrists at Washington University in St. Louis who established research diagnostic criteria, referred to as the Feighner Criteria, for 14 categories of mental illnesses, including schizophrenia, antisocial personality disorder, and anxiety disorder. The publication of these criteria became the basis for constructing the DSM-III and revising the ICD manual. The DSM-III included 265 disorders. All subsequent editions of the DSM have replicated the framework of the DSM-III.

DSM-IV

After the implementation of the DSM-III, inconsistencies were found in the descriptions of diagnostic categories and within those categories, and the diagnostic criteria were deemed unclear. To correct these problems, the APA convened a workgroup to revise the DSM-III. The outcome of this workgroup's activities included several modifications that were published as the DSM-III-R (revised) in 1987. In 1994, the DSM-IV was published following a six year effort that involved more than 1,000 professionals from several organizations. These professionals reviewed scientific studies to create an empirical platform to modify and update the manual. The DSM-IV-TR (text revision), published in 2000, included new diagnostic categoriesand recodified diagnostic criteria sets and 297 disorders.

DSM-5

After more than six years of expert meetings and field tests, the DSM-5 was released in 2013. The switch from Roman to Arabic numerals facilitated the labeling of subsequent editions (DSM-5.1, 5.2) and reflected the organic and dynamic nature of the manual. Heralded as a paradigm shift in psychiatric diagnoses, the newest edition promised major, but produced mostly moderate, changes to the previous volume. Mimicking its two immediate predecessors, modifications were instituted as the result of a consultative process that involved discussions of diagnostic experts, public debates and presentations, professional and academic journal articles, and national field tests of new diagnostic categories and criteria. Specifically, the DSM-5 revision process involved a task force and six study groups that addressed a number of essential diagnostic issues (e.g., gender and culture differences that affect psychiatric evaluations). In addition, 13 workgroups were formed to study disorders through literature reviews and submit proposals for new or reconstituted diagnostic criteria.

The DSM-5 is organized into three major sections. The first section, DSM Basics contains an overview of the manual and instructions on its use. The second section, Diagnostic Criteria and Codes, describes the diagnostic categories and enumerates diagnostic codes for medical and insurance records, criteria, subtypes when applicable (e.g., brief psychotic disorder, social anxiety disorder), and disease specifiers (e.g., early onset, chronic). The third section, Emerging Measures and Models, suggests areas for further research and discussion, contains a glossary of terms, and posits an alternative model to diagnose and classify personality disorders, which are enduring patterns of emotional experiences and expressions that adversely affect interpersonal relationships and undermine other areas of functioning. Compared to other types of psychiatric illnesses, personality disorders can be considered as "who patients are" rather than "what patients have." Therefore, these conditions can be quite difficult to treat.

Section 2 is the heart of the manual; it outlines the more than 300 psychiatric illnesses contained in the DSM-5 and stipulates guidelines for rendering a diagnosis for each. In order to arrive at a more precise diagnosis, this section also differentiates each diagnosis from cognate conditions and rules out other psychiatric illnesses or medical causes that could account for symptoms. The chapters are roughly organized from disorders most likely to be diagnosed in childhood to those most likely to be diagnosed in later stages of life. As with the DSM-III and the DSM-IV, each diagnosis is accompanied by a set of diagnostic criteria.

A certain number of these criteria must be met for a diagnosis to be selected. Furthermore, most diagnoses provide clinicians with specifiers that guide a more nuanced and detailed assessment of patients who meet the requisite number of diagnostic criteria. Finally, clinicians can rate the gravity of symptoms on a scale from mild to severe. The complete listing of the DSM-5 chapters is as follows:

- Neurodevelopmental Disorders
- Schizophrenia Spectrum and Other Psychotic Disorders
- Bipolar and Related Disorders
- Depressive Disorders
- Anxiety Disorders
- Obsessive-Compulsive and Related Disorders
- Trauma- and Stressor-Related Disorders
- Dissociative Disorders
- Somatic Symptom and Related Disorders
- Feeding and Eating Disorders
- Elimination Disorders
- Sleep-Wake Disorders
- Sexual Dysfunctions
- Gender Dysphoria
- Disruptive, Impulse Control, and Conduct Disorders
- Substance Use and Addictive Disorders
- Neurocognitive Disorders
- Personality Disorders
- Paraphilic Disorders
- Other Disorders

As an example, major depressive disorder consists of nine diagnostic criteria such as depressed mood, loss of pleasure in previously enjoyable activities or experiences, problems with appetite or sleep, and diminished energy. To receive a diagnosis of major depressive disorder, an individual must present with either depressed mood or loss of pleasure as well as four or more of the other diagnostic criteria. In addition, these symptoms must persist for a period of 2 weeks and be unexplained by the effects of substances or other medical conditions. As with other disorders in the DSM-5, the symptoms of depression can be mild, moderate, or severe. Symptoms can also be accompanied by psychotic features (i.e., hallucinations [false perceptions] and delusions [false beliefs]) or melancholic features (e.g., significant loss of appetite and weight loss and excessive and inappropriate guilt)

DIFFERENCES BETWEEN DSM-IV-TR AND DSM-5

The DSM-5 differs from the DSM-IV-TR in several ways. For example, the chapter in the DSM-IV-TR that focused on "Disorders Usually First Diagnosed in Infancy, Childhood, or Adolescence" was deleted, allowing the DSM-5 to recognize that such problems can appear throughout the life course. Additionally, the multi-axial diagnostic system was removed. The diagnoses subsumed under Axis II became separate diagnostic entities (e.g., personality disorders). Axis III and Axis IV were replaced by embedding medical, psychosocial, and contextual features within the diagnostic categories. Axis V was supplanted by the recommended use of the WHO Disability Assessment Schedule, which is included with other recommended but not prescribed assessment measures in Section 3 of the manual.

Other changes focused on specific diagnoses. For example, the subtypes of schizophrenia were eliminated because of acknowledged shortcomings in their validity and reliability. The diagnosis of "mental retardation" was changed to "intellectual developmental disorder" and its severity is now evaluated largely on the basis of adaptive functioning. The diagnosis of autism was also changed to autism spectrum disorder to acknowledge the multifariousness of the condition (i.e., not a single disorder) and variations in symptom severity. Asperger's disorder was eliminated as a stand-alone diagnosis and is now considered a manifestation of autism spectrum disorder. The diagnosis of hypochondriasis was renamed illness anxiety disorder and amended to consider the presence of somatic symptoms among those afflicted.

The distinction between substance abuse and dependence was also replaced by a single diagnostic category, substance-related disorders, with combined criteria and severity specifiers that more closely match the clinical presentations of these problems. The bereavement exclusion was removed from the diagnosis of major depression to acknowledge that these experiences are difficult to disentangle and that bereavement can trigger major depression among the bereft. The following enumerate the 17 disorders that were added to the DSM-5:

- Social (pragmatic) communication disorder
- Disruptive mood dysregulation disorder
- Premenstrual dysphoric disorder
- Hoarding disorder
- Caffeine withdrawal
- Cannabis withdrawal
- Excoriation (skin-picking) disorder
- Binge eating disorder
- Rapid eye movement sleep behavior disorder
- Restless legs syndrome
- Major neurocognitive disorder with Lewy body disease
- Mild neurocognitive disorder
- Disinhibited Social Engagement Disorder
- Central sleep apnea
- Sleep-related hypoventilation
- Gender dysphoria
- Gambling disorders

These 17 disorders were predicated on consensus panel debates, literature reviews, and field testing. Other conditions were discussed and relegated to the DSM-5 appendix because current evidence warranted that they be subjected to continued discussion and research. These conditions lacked the level of clinical or research support needed to reach the threshold of a bona fide diagnostic entity (e.g., attenuated psychosis disorder, Internet use gaming disorder, and non-suicidal self-injury). Still other conditions were rejected for inclusion with no further considerations recommended (e.g., anxious depression, hypersexual disorder, and sensory processing disorder).

BIBLIOGRAPHY

American Psychiatric Association. (2013). *Diagnostic and Statistical Manual of Mental Disorders* 5th Edition (DSM-5). Washington, DC: Author. More than ten years in the making, this volume is considered by many to be the definitive, authoritative guidebook for psychiatric diagnoses. Divided into three major sections and a detailed appendix, the book is a treatise on the diagnoses of mental illness and is of interest to mental health professionals of all backgrounds and for use in every clinical setting. Contains highly detailed descriptions of each diagnostic category as well as criteria for rendering primary and differential diagnoses.

Barnhill, J. W. (Ed.). (2013). *DSM-5: Clinical Cases*. Arlington, VA: American Psychiatric Publishing. This book encompasses a rich collection of engaging case studies of patients in every major DSM-5 diagnostic category. The case narratives also educate readers about the contextualization of psychiatric diagnoses as well as diagnostic features and subtleties based on gender, age, and cultural variations.

First, M. B. (2013). *Handbook of Differential Diagnoses*. Arlington, VA: American Psychiatric Publishing. Written by one of the leading psychiatrists in the United States, this hefty volume is designed for the sophisticated reader interested in learning both the science and art of diagnostic precision. The book contains several diagnostic approaches and algorithms for gathering and interpreting the information gleaned from psychiatric histories and mental status examination.

Morrison, J. (2013). *DSM-5 Made Easy: The Clinicians Guide To Diagnosis*. New York, NY: Guilford Press. This book provides simple and elucidative descriptions of each of the major diagnostic categories in the DSM-5. Delivered in a highly accessible style, every chapter has synoptic definitions, essential features, and case vignettes to help the reader apply diagnostic criteria to actual cases.

Sadock, B.J., Sadock, V. A., & Ruiz, P. (2014). *Synopsis Of Psychiatry* (11th ed.). Philadelphia, PA: Wolters Kluwer. This tome was first published in 1972 and covers the waterfront in terms of historical, clinical, and research knowledge in the field of psychiatry. With more than 30 chapters and 1,400 pages of densely written material, this book is easily the most comprehensive ever written about psychiatric theories and practices.

Arthur J. Lurigio

See Also: APA; Classification; Diagnosis; Mental disorders

DSM-5: Controversies

Type of psychology: Biological bases of human behavior; Clinical; Counseling; Developmental; Neuropsychology, Personality; Psychopathology; Psychotherapy

Behavioral and mental disorders afflict many people in the United States and throughout the world. A leading cause of disability, these disorders strike individuals of all ages and at every income level. Typically arising in adolescence and early adulthood, behavioral and mental disorders often prevent sufferers from fulfilling their employment, educational, and personal aspirations. In general, these disorders affect how people think, feel, and behave and are highly variable in onset, severity, course, and prognosis. The first step in treating psychiatric and psychological disorders is proper assessment and diagnosis. Diagnoses focus psychiatrists, psychologists and allied behavioral health professionals in the selection of treatments, medications and other interventions for effectively alleviating the symptoms. Psychiatric and psychological disorders are detailed in the American Psychiatric Association's (APA's) Diagnostic and Statistical Manual of Mental Disorders (DSM), presently in its 5th edition. Known as DSM-5, the manual was released in 2013 after more than 10 years of review, debate, and field-testing. During its evolution and initial implementation, DSM-5 was seriously criticized from a variety of quarters, including prominent psychiatrists and psychologists who participated in the creation of previous editions of the DSM. These criticisms pointed to DSM-5's developmental flaws and dubious usefulness as the diagnostic guidebook in psychiatry, psychology, and allied behavioral health clinical specialties.

Key concepts

- Diagnosis
- Mental disorders
- Measurement validity and reliability
- Nomenclature
- Psychiatry

INTRODUCTION

Documented throughout recorded history, mental illnesses (today, more appropriately referred to as disorders) have been attributed to various causes, such as demonic possession and an imbalance in bodily fluids known as the four humors: black bile, yellow bile, phlegm, and blood. The presence of too much or too little of any of these humors was believed to cause the symptoms of mental illnesses as well as account for differences in people's native temperaments. For example, too much black bile was purported to cause depression, whereas too much yellow bile was purported to cause irritability and agitation. To treat the superfluity of these biles, physicians employed herbal remedies, emetics (vomit-inducing substances), and bloodletting (cutting and leeching). As this example illustrates, even in ancient times, "psychiatric" diagnosis (imbalance in humors) dictated the selection of treatments (e.g., blood-letting).

Current views about the causes of psychiatric and psychological disorders concentrate on the structure and function of the brain, emphasizing the connections among neurons, which are the cells that transmit signals to one another through an electro-chemical process (neurotransmission). Estimates suggest that the brain consists of 100 billion neurons with 100 trillion interconnections. The connections occur at gaps between the cells called synapses. Signals are transmitted through the synaptic passage of neurochemicals that either excite or inhibit the adjacent cells, depending on the nature of the neurotransmitter, the amount of neurotransmitter released or already in the synapse, and the state of the receptor cell, which receives the signal.

Psychiatric/psychological symptoms (self-reported complaints) and signs (observable behaviors) are likely the result of problems in the wiring of neural circuits, which contain groups of neurons that regularly stimulate one another with neurotransmitters, thereby forming lasting connections. Unknown disruptions in these interconnections seemingly cause mental disorders, which are a product of both genetic predispositions and life experiences. The field of psychiatry, a branch of medical science and practice, rests on the notion that disorders in the DSM are brain diseases. In accordance with standard medical protocols, the treatment of any disease is predicated on identifying the defining characteristics of the disease (assessment), discerning the commonalities among those characteristics, which form a syndrome, and then naming them (diagnosis) by placing them in a pre-established (diagnostic) category that contains a criterion-based description of the malady. DSM-5 provides those descriptions, but its legitimacy as a medical compendium has been intensely scrutinized.

HISTORY OF DSM-I TO DSM-IV-TR

The DSM-5 is the prevailing repository or catalogue of psychiatric and psychological disorders. The manual contains the nomenclature of mental illnesses, which is the system that places and organizes such diseases into classes or categories. The DSM-5 creates a standard language for understanding the common characteristics of mental disorders and grouping them in accordance with their shared diagnostic features. The categorizations in DSM-5 were derived from reviews of studies and the consensus of panels of experts.

The first edition of the DSM (DSM-I) was published in 1952. The manual referred to diseases as "reactions" and elucidated them by using concepts and terminology that were drawn from the psychoanalytic theories of Sigmund Freud and his followers (e.g., Adolph Meyer), which provided a framework for describing, explaining, and treating the symptoms of mental illnesses. The term "reaction" denoted that environmental stressors could precipitate mental illnesses. The psychodynamic approach underscores the importance of early childhood experiences in the formation of the adult psyche and explains the origins of mental illnesses mostly in terms of repressed sexual urges and conflicts. The DSM-I contained 106 disorders that were divided into three broad categories: neurotic (anxious and depressed), psychotic (severe detachment from reality), and character disorders (enduring maladaptive styles of interacting with others and perceiving the world).

The DSM-II was released in 1968, maintaining the psychodynamic orientation of its predecessor and expanding to 182 disorders. It featured a section on childhood disorders, such as hyperkinetic reaction, the precursor to Attention Deficit Hyperactivity Disorder (ADHD), which appears in later editions of the DSM. In addition, the DSM-II included a section on sexual deviations (e.g., exhibitionism, transvestism, and homosexuality). Homosexuality became one of the first, and most, controversial diagnoses in the DSM, revealing the somewhat arbitrary, "political," and subjective nature of the diagnostic entities and criteria selected for the manual—a limitation that also applies to DSM-5. Following an outpouring of protests from gay rights' activists, a specially formed APA committee decided that homosexuality failed to meet the requirements necessary to be considered a definitive mental disorder and was removed from the seventh printing of the DSM-II.

The publication of the DSM-III in 1980 heralded a new era of psychiatric/psychological diagnoses by specifying sets of criteria for the diagnosis of each mental disorder. The psychodynamic orientation was removed and replaced with a more scientific and systematic methodology for rendering diagnoses. The manual expanded to 265 diagnoses and revolutionized the field of psychiatry by moving toward a brain disease model of the causes and treatments of mental illnesses. This change became particularly important after a series of studies demonstrated the low reliability among diagnosticians in psychiatry. Field trials were performed to test the diagnostic integrity of the disorders and the manual was organized into a multi-axial system, I through V: Clinical Disorders; Personality Disorders and Mental Retardation; General Medical Conditions; Psychosocial and Environmental Stressors; and Global Assessment of Functioning. The DSM-IV was published in 1994, with 279 disorders, and was revised in 2000 (DSM-IV-TR). The manual remained true to the multi-axial system and the sets of diagnostic criteria used for diagnoses.

THE DSM-5

Released in 2013, the DSM-5 appeared on the behavioral health world scene with considerable fanfare. Added to the DSM-IV-TR were 15 new diagnoses. In addition, the fifth edition dropped a few diagnoses, reconceptualized others, and subsumed several under other diagnostic categories. The DSM-5 consists of approximately 300 psychiatric disorders described within 20 major diagnostic categories that are arranged in the manual somewhat in the order in which they appear in the life course, including, for example, neurodevelopmental disorders (e.g., intellectual development disorder), depressive disorders (e.g., major depressive disorder), anxiety disorders (e.g., specific phobia), sleep-wake disorders (e.g., insomnia disorder), personality disorders (e.g., paranoid personality disorders), and neurocognitive disorders (e.g., delirium).

The DSM-5 has been roundly criticized by venerable members of the psychiatric and psychology guilds, some of whom were the principal architects of previous editions (most notably psychiatrists Spitzer and Francis), as well as the usual detractors and decriers of the field of psychiatry (e.g., Scientologists). Indeed, many of the brickbats hurled at the manual also were directed explicitly and implicitly at the profession of psychiatry itself, which overcame its flagging reputation with the publication of the DSM-III as noted above. These criticisms and controversies can be structured into four themes: Over-Reaching, Lack of Inclusiveness, Diagnostic Inflation and Invalidity, Conflicts of Interest, and Field Testing Challenges.

OVER-REACHING

The earliest discussions of the DSM-5 foretold of an empirically based system of classification that would be built on a foundation of neuroscience, more precisely identifying the causes of mental illnesses through brain imaging and other techniques for studying and visualizing the living brain. Brain imaging technology has advanced dramatically over the past 25 years, allowing scientists to obtain in-depth, multi-layered pictures of the brain's structures and to measure levels of activity in different brain areas in response to different stimuli. These breakthroughs have yielded considerable data on substance use disorders. For example, scientists know which general areas of the brain are affected (and altered) by the use of drugs and which are involved in drug cravings. However, for most other mental disorders, rather than directly viewing or confirming patients' diseases with objective tests and visual evidence, psychiatrists actually can only infer the presence of such illnesses by talking with their patients and observing their behaviors.

Neuroscientists have found little evidence to help locate the neural epicenters for severe mental illness, such as autism, schizophrenia, and bipolar disorder. The use of such research to construct and validate mental illnesses never came to fruition in the DSM-5 due to the insufficient knowledge of the brain's structures and its precise mechanisms or functions. In addition, the promise that the manual could be used to prevent psychiatric diseases through early detection and prophylactic treatment was also never fulfilled. The fields of psychiatry and psychology are limited by both the complexity of the brain as well as the disconnection between current brain imaging tools and knowledge about psychiatric diagnoses.

The impreciseness of the DSM's discrete diagnostic categories, noted below, spurred considerable discussion about the use of dimensions rather than groupings to capture psychiatric disorders. In the psychiatric arena, the difference between "normal" and "abnormal" can be difficult to distinguish, especially in the many gray areas of symptomology. Whether a person has a "mentally illness" or not is often a question of degree instead of kind (i.e., differences on dimensions and not between categories, respectively). Dimensions communicate more information about the specific symptoms and signs of mental illnesses and can be used more readily to document changes in the progression of disorders. Despite its purported benefits, the creation of a dimensional (ratings on a continuum) system to replace the categorical (groupings based on criteria) system in DSM-5 never materialized. Nonetheless, a hypothetical dimensional system as it pertains to personality disorders can be found in the appendix of the manual.

LACK OF INCLUSIVENESS

The construction of the DSM-5 was the most public in the manual's history. The American Psychiatric Association (APA) created a website that updated drafts of the manual and its integral components. Other websites and blogs cropped up as the content unfolded. Despite the public nature of the new nomenclature as it progressed through several iterations, many complaints arose about the closed decision-making protocols that led to the deletion and elimination of some diagnostic categories as well as the expansion and contraction of others. Members of the workgroups were compelled to sign confidentiality agreements that prohibited them from discussing their deliberations beyond the memberships of these tightly knit work groups. Furthermore, the APA conspicuously excluded previous members of the APA task forces that created the DSM-III and the DSM-IV. The APA also erected legal barriers to protect the intellectual property of the manual and the "DSM" copyright. People who built their own websites to share concerns about the evolution of the manual were threatened with legal action and barred from using "DSM" in the naming of their web domains.

DIAGNOSTIC INVALIDITY AND INFLATION

As noted above, the diagnostic categories of the DSM are largely descriptive groupings with fuzzy boundaries that contain overlapping criteria, permitting only poor distinctions between and among diagnoses. Research and clinical practices have suggested that comorbidities are common in the general population. Many people meet the diagnostic criteria for one or more psychiatric illnesses in part because many symptoms, especially the core manifestations of disorders (e.g., anxiety and depression), are shared among psychiatric categories and can lead to more than one diagnosis. The blurred contours between diagnostic categories also contribute to the difficulties inherent in the identification of clear-cut or differential diagnoses.

The DSM's listing of "disorders" can be misleading about the present state of knowledge in psychiatry. Many of these disorders are behavioral manifestations or clusters of symptoms with no organic or physical etiology to support a diagnosis and no external or objective tests to confirm their existence as noted earlier. The categories of the DSM-5 are descriptive and definitional only, lacking biomarkers, genetic causes, and prescriptions for treatments, which are absent from definitions of the mental disorders in the DSM-5. In other words, psychiatrists are still really treating "the mind" and not "the brain." The National Institute of Mental Health, the British Psychological Society, and the American Counseling Association have all openly decried the lack of validity in the DSM-5 and suggested instead the adoption of the psychiatric categories in the World Health Organization's *International Classification of Diseases-11* or the continued use of the DSM-IV-TR.

Direct-to-consumer advertising campaigns for antidepressants and other psychopharmaceutical agents have encouraged the simplistic view that mental illnesses are caused by biochemical imbalances that can be treated consistently and effectively by psychiatric medications. Although this perspective helps to destigmatize mental illnesses, it rests on shaky scientific grounds. Still unknown are the pathogeneses of mental illnesses and the mechanisms by which psychiatric drugs act on the brain. Moreover, normal responses to life's challenges, such as occasional bouts of sadness and insomnia as well as natural variations in human characteristics such as shyness, distractibility, and low energy are being more frequently diagnosed as mental illnesses, eventuating in diagnostic inflation and prescription fervor, which appears to be the case with autism, bipolar disorder, and ADHD.

The largest groups of consumers of psychiatric drugs are mostly healthy people rather than those with the most severe mental illnesses, who are also often uninsured, have limited access to care, and rely on sparsely funded public psychiatric services. Critics of the DSM-5 contend that drug companies have taken advantage of the market by promoting the aforementioned idea that everyday problems in living actually constitute psychiatric disorders caused by biochemical imbalances that can be corrected by medications. For example, numerous experts have attacked the creators of the DSM-5 for removing the "bereavement exclusion" from the current edition. This modification fails to recognize that the "normal" reaction to loss includes many of the symptoms of major depressive disorder and therefore does not constitute a "mental illness" among the bereft.

CONFLICTS OF INTEREST

The pharmaceutical companies have been the major impetus behind the creation of the DSM-III through the DSM-5 as well as the shaping of their various diagnostic categories and criteria. The motivation to cultivate new diagnostic entities in order to expand their markets for products and profits has often superseded the imperative to use scientific evidence as the polestar for selecting the best diagnoses and treatments for psychiatric illnesses. The pharmaceutical industry generates approximately 84 billion dollars in annual sales. To maintain these profits, drug companies invested substantial dollars into sponsoring psychiatric conferences, subventing the APA, and marketing drugs directly to consumers and psychiatrists.

Drug sale representatives offer psychiatrists' incentives (e.g., paid trips to conferences, speaking engagement fees), to prescribe their company's medications. Psychiatrists lend their names to clinical trials that demonstrate the effectiveness of the industry's drugs and accept drug company funds to support their own academic research. They also accept substantial consulting income to act as the drug companies' "opinion leaders" who present "objective" evidence in favor of prescribing the industry's latest psychiatric medications. In one the most egregious examples of conflict of interest, Johnson and Johnson awarded hundreds of thousands of dollars to a Harvard-based research center overseen by influential child psychiatrist Joseph Biederman. Investigations found that he accepted money for the center in order to help expand sales of the company's psychiatric drugs for use in children. In doing so, he promoted the diagnosis of pediatric bipolar disorder, which burgeoned during mid-1990s. The diagnosis has since been seriously questioned and largely replaced by Disruptive Mood Dysregulation Disorder in the DSM-5.

CHALLENGES WITH FIELD TESTING

To their credit, the developers of the DSM-5 engaged in an ambitious effort to field-test the revised criteria for its diagnostic categories by enlisting mental health professionals and asking them to solicit the cooperation of their patients. The protocols for collecting these data were quite complicated and time-consuming. Furthermore, the solicitation of clinicians came after the potential shortcomings and delayed releases of the DSM-5 had been highlighted in many public venues. As a result, far fewer professionals and their patients participated in the trials than anticipated, yielding a much smaller and less representative sample for the vetting of the new manual. In addition, levels of diagnostic agreement (consistency) for new or revised diagnostic categories were much lower than the scientific standard for even some of the most common mental disorders. Poor reliability in the field further eroded confidence in the DSM-5.

BIBLIOGRAPHY

American Psychiatric Association. (2013). *The Diagnostic and Statistical Manual of Mental Disorders* 5th Edition (DSM-5). Washington, DC: Author. More than ten years in the making, this volume is the definitive, authoritative guidebook for psychiatric diagnoses. Divided into three major sections and a detailed appendix, the book is a treatise on the diagnoses of mental illnesses and is of interest to mental health professionals of all backgrounds and for use in every clinical setting. Contains highly detailed descriptions of each diagnostic category as well as criteria for rendering primary and differential diagnoses.

Greenberg, G. (2013). *The Book Of Woe: The DSM-5 and The Unmaking Of Psychiatry.* New York: Penguin. A journalist and practicing clinical psychologist, Dr. Greenberg alternates between scientific elucidation and biting satire, which is aimed at the American Psychiatric Association and the pharmaceutical industry. He critiques them mostly for leading the field of psychiatry down the profit-driven pathway of over-diagnoses and the medicalization of everyday problems. This engaging book is full of colorful exchanges with critics on both sides of the DSM divide.

Horwitz, A V., & Jerome C. Wakefield, J.C. (2013). *All We Have To Fear: Psychiatry's Transformation Of Natural Anxieties Into Mental Disorders.* New York: Oxford University Press. The book traces the meaning and treatment of anxiety throughout the ages, exploring the validity of current DSM descriptions of anxiety disorders. The authors discuss theoretical models and research findings in an attempt to illuminate the true nature and extent of anxiety—both normal and pathological—and question the over-diagnoses of such disorders without being dismissive about their real existence and distressful consequences.

Paris, J., & Phillips, J. (Eds.). (2013). *Making The DSM-5: Concepts and Controversies.* New York: Springer. An edited volume, containing 11 chapters written by leading psychiatrists, psychologists, and sociologists, examines incisively the creation and implementation of the most recent edition of the DSM. Chapters address the lengthy and often fitful revision process as well as the suggested changes that were never incorporated into the final version. Major questions about the validity of the manual's diagnostic categories are raised throughout the book as well as concerns about the philosophical underpinnings and the practical utility of the diagnostic process itself.

Arthur J. Lurigio

See Also: APA; Diagnosis; Diagnostic and Statistical Manual of Mental Disorders; Mental disorders.

Dysgraphia

Type of psychology: Biological bases of human behavior; Clinical; Counseling; Developmental; Neuropsychological; School

Dysgraphia is a neurodevelopmental learning disorder which is manifested by significant difficulty in many aspects of writing. Letter formation, spatial organization, and spelling may be negatively impacted. Properly sequencing letters in words and words in sentences may be extremely difficult. Reversals, inversions, and transpositions of letters are common. The ability to generate letters from memory without a model may be impaired. Written work is often illegible.

Key Concepts:

- Fine motor dysfunction
- Grapho-motor control
- Learning disabilities
- Reversals, inversions, and transpositions
- Written expression

INTRODUCTION

The term dysgraphia was derived from Greek with "dys" meaning impaired and "graphia" meaning written by hand. This disorder, considered one of many different types of learning disabilities, is usually initially diagnosed when children first begin writing, most often in kindergarten or first grade. Researchers report that the disorder is more common in boys than girls. If milder forms of the disorder are included it can affect as many as 15 to 20% of children. Typically any tasks requiring fine motor skill, such as cutting, tracing, copying, and of course writing, are extremely difficult and frustrating.

Fine motor skills, which is the ability to control movements of smaller muscles such as those needed for writing and speaking, normally develop slowly over time. However, in some children these skills are delayed or develop so slowly that they impede the ability to meet normal school demands. Because this disorder specifically interferes in the child's ability to produce written work, it is highly visible to the child, teachers, and classmates, often resulting in loss of self-esteem and sometimes leading to a sense of failure and giving up. Writing is often extremely laborious and sometimes painful and consequently avoided and disdained. Learning how to properly hold a writing implement and the paper at the same time is more than many children with this issue can handle.

PRESENTATION

Dysgraphia is considered to involve three aspects: a motor component, a visual-spatial component, and a processing component. The most common motoric presentation of dysgraphia is very malformed letters so that writing is often illegible. The child is often simply unable to generate the precise finger movements required to produce legible letters. Sharp angles and changes of direction are particularly challenging. Other fine motor tasks such as tying shoes, closing buttons or snaps, and zippering may also present challenges.

The visual-spatial difficulties common in children with dysgraphia are most typically manifested in letters that appear to float off the line or collide with other letters. Spacing between letters and words is very difficult. Reversals (where letters are written backward or as if seen through a mirror), inversions (where letters are written upside down), and transpositions (where letters or words are in the wrong order) are also frequent signs of visual-spatial problems. Often these problems are not limited to writing but may appear in many additional tasks that demand good visual-spatial skills such as keeping a desk neat and organized, keeping papers in a folder, or putting needed materials away so that they can be easily retrieved.

Processing problems may be manifested by poor grammar and syntax in writing, leaving words out altogether and incoherently organizing sentences and paragraphs. These issues are often more closely related to language processing and expression than fine motor weakness.

INTERVENTIONS

Interventions to address the difficulties presented in dysgraphia fall into two categories: remediation and accommodation. Efforts to remediate often include exercises to improve fine motor strength and control. Clay play, finger exercises, stirring, mixing, threading, and beading can be helpful. Pencil mazes that slowly progress from very easy with extremely wide borders to difficult with much narrower borders can slowly improve pencil control. Connecting the dots, cutting, and tracing are also beneficial. Practicing writing letters in the air with very large movements and progressively reducing the size of the movements is often very productive. Initially, writing should be very large so as to reduce the demands for precise motor movements of the fingers. A great deal of repetition is often required to assist children to overlearn letter formation so that they can eventually concentrate on the content of their writing rather than on the mechanical aspects of forming letters. The specialized assistance of an occupational therapist is often necessary to offer some children a very individualized approach.

There are many accommodations available that can be of great assistance in helping children with dysgraphia. Special pencil grips and other writing implements can relieve discomfort and offer more control. Writing paper with extra large spacing and raised guide lines makes it easier to avoid floating and colliding letters and words. Teaching children to use their thumbs or other spacers between words can greatly improve intelligibility. An alphabet should always be available so that children can check, as often as necessary, to see how letters look so that they do not have to rely on memory. Computers offer a wonderful way for children with dysgraphia to produce work that looks great, is easy to edit, and can readily be checked for grammar and spelling. They should be taught typing skills as early as possible. Modern dictation programs even remove the need for typing. Some children may require additional time to complete assignments and to take tests. Some may even need a scribe for longer test responses.

With understanding, remediation, and appropriate accommodations, children with dysgraphia can be happy and successful. Most aspects of adult life, with a few exceptions, do not require well developed fine motor control. Word processing software and voice recognition software have greatly reduced the limitations of those with dysgraphia and, often in adulthood, dysgraphia is being relegated to little more than a nuisance.

BIBLIOGRAPHY

Diagnose and Treat Dysgraphia: Specific Learning Disability in Writing. Suite101.com www.suite101.com/content/dysgraphia-a46051#ixzz1LDarkNek. This website reprints a very informative newsletter about dysgraphia for parents and family who would like to learn more about symptoms and interventions.

Eide, B., & Eide, F. (2006). *The Mislabeled Child: How Understanding Your Child's Unique Learning Can Open The Door To Success.* New York, NY: Hyperion. This book is a very good overview of many types of learning issues including dysgraphia. It presents a readily understandable discussion of brain processes and learning styles and differences.

Painter, H. (2013). *Dysgraphia: Your Essential Guide.* New York, NY: HGP Industries. This is a brief primer for families regarding essentials about dysgraphia.

Sutherland, J. (2012). *Dysgraphia: Causes, Connections and Cures.* North Charleston, SC: Createspace. A very optimistic presentation of the etiology and treatment of dysgraphia for families and professionals alike.

What is Dysgraphia? ncld.org This website hosted by the National Center for Learning Disabilities offers charts with warning signs for dysgraphia by age from very young children through adolescence and adulthood. An extensive list of interventions is also offered by age.

Molly E. Sweetland and Elizabeth Rothstein

SEE ALSO: Fine motor skills; Handwriting; Physical therapy; Spatial perception; Spelling.

Dyslexia

TYPE OF PSYCHOLOGY: Language

Dyslexia is often defined as severe reading disability in children of otherwise average or above-average intelligence; it is thought to be caused by neuropsychological problems. Dyslexia frustrates afflicted children, damages their self-image, produces grave maladjustment in many cases, and decreases their adult contributions to society.

KEY CONCEPTS

- Auditory dyslexia
- Brain dysfunction
- Computed tomography (CT) scan
- Dysgraphia
- Electroencephalogram (EEG)
- Imprinting
- Kinesthetic imprinting
- Phonology
- Self-image
- Visual dyslexia

INTRODUCTION

The ability to read quickly and well is essential for success in modern industrialized societies. Several researchers, including Robert E. Valett, have pointed out that an individual must acquire considerable basic cognitive and perceptual-linguistic skills to learn to read. First, it is necessary to learn to focus one's attention, to concentrate, to follow directions, and to understand the language spoken in daily life. Next, it is essential to develop auditory and visual memory with sequencing ability, word-decoding skills, a facility for structural-contextual language analysis, the ability to interpret the written language, a useful vocabulary that expands as needed, and speed in scanning and interpreting written language. Valett has noted that these skills are taught in all good developmental reading programs.

Dyslexia may make it difficult to distinguish letters and words that are mirror images of each other. Yet 20 to 25 percent of the population of the United States and many other industrialized societies, people who otherwise possess at least average intelligence, cannot develop good reading skills. Many such people are viewed as suffering from a neurological disorder called dyslexia, a term that was first introduced by a German ophthalmologist, Rudolph Berlin,Berlin, Rudolph in the nineteenth century. Berlin meant it to designate all those individuals who possessed an average or above-average performance intelligence quotient (IQ) but who could not read adequately because of an inability to process language symbols. Others reported children who could see perfectly well but who acted as though they were blind to the written language. For example, they could see a bird flying but were unable to identify the word "bird" written in a sentence.

Although the problem has been redefined many times over the ensuing years, the modern definition of dyslexia is still fairly close to Berlin's definition. The American Psychiatric Association's *Diagnostic and Statistical Manual of Mental Disorders: DSM-IV-TR* (rev. 4th ed., 2000) labels this condition "reading disorder" and defines it as reading achievement substantially below that expected given chronological age, measured intelligence, and age-appropriate education that interferes significantly with academic achievement or activities of daily living requiring reading skills.

BRAIN DEVELOPMENT

Two basic explanations have evolved for dyslexia. Many physicians propose that it is caused by either brain dam-

DSM-IV-TR CRITERIA FOR READING DISORDER (DSM CODE 315.00)

Reading achievement, as measured by individually administered standardized tests of reading accuracy or comprehension, substantially below that expected given chronological age, measured intelligence, and age-appropriate education

Disorder interferes significantly with academic achievement or activities of daily living requiring reading skills

If a sensory deficit is present, reading difficulties exceed those usually associated with it

age or brain dysfunction. Evolution of the problem is attributed to accident, to disease, or to faults in body chemistry. Diagnosis is made by the use of electroencephalograms (EEGs), computed tomography (CT) scans, and other related technology. After such evaluation, medication is often used to diminish hyperactivity and nervousness, and physical training procedures called patterning are used as tools to counter the neurological defects.

In contrast, many special educators and other related researchers believe that the problem is one of dormant, immature, or undeveloped learning centers in the brain. The proponents of this concept encourage the correction of dyslexic problems by emphasized teaching of specific reading skills to appropriate individuals. Although such experts also agree that the use of appropriate medication can be of value, they lend most of their efforts to curing the problem by a process called imprinting,Imprinting which essentially trains the dyslexic patient through use of often-repeated, exaggerated language drills.

Another interesting point of view is the idea that dyslexia may be at least partly the fault of the written languages of the Western world. Rudolph F. WagnerWagner, Rudolph F. has pointed out that children in Japan exhibit an incidence of dyslexia that is less than 1 percent. One explanation for this, say Wagner and others, is that the languages of the Western world require reading from left to right. This characteristic is absent in Japanese—possibly, they suggest, making it easier to learn.

Several experts, among them Dale R. Jordan,Jordan, Dale R. recognize three types of dyslexia. The most common type—and the one most often identified as dyslexia—is visual dyslexia: the lack of ability to translate observed written or printed language into meaningful terms. The major difficulty here is that afflicted people see certain letters backward or upside down. The result is that, to them, a written sentence is a jumble of letters whose accurate translation may require five times as much time as would be needed by an unafflicted person.

AUDITORY DYSLEXIA AND DYSGRAPHIA

The other two problems viewed as dyslexia are auditory dyslexia and dysgraphia. Auditory dyslexia is the inability to perceive individual sounds of spoken language. Despite having normal hearing, auditory dyslexics are deaf to the differences between certain vowel or consonant sounds; what they cannot hear, they cannot write. Dysgraphia is the inability to write legibly. The basis for this problem is a lack of the hand-eye coordination required to write legibly.

Usually, a child who suffers from visual dyslexia also exhibits elements of auditory dyslexia. This complicates the issue of teaching such a student, because only one type of dyslexic symptom can be treated at a time. Also, dyslexia appears to be a sex-linked disorder; three to four times as many boys have it as do girls. In all cases, early diagnosis and treatment of dyslexia are essential to its eventual correction. For example, if treatment begins before the third grade, there is an 80 percent probability that dyslexia can be corrected. When dyslexia remains undiscovered until the fifth grade, this probability is halved. If treatment does not begin until the seventh grade, the probability of successful treatment is only 3 to 5 percent.

ASSESSMENT METHODS AND TREATMENT

Preliminary identification of the dyslexic child often can be made from symptoms that include poor written schoolwork, easy distractibility, clumsiness, poor coordination and spatial orientation, confused writing and/or spelling, and poor left-right orientation. Because nondyslexic children can also show many of these symptoms, the second step of such identification is the use of written tests designed to pick out dyslexic children. These include the Peabody Individual Achievement Test, the Halstead-Reitan Neuropsychological Test Battery, and the SOYBAR Criterion Tests. Many more personalized tests are also available.

Once conclusive identification of a dyslexic child has been made, it becomes possible to begin a corrective treatment program. Most such programs are carried out by special-education teachers in school resource rooms, in special classes limited to children with reading disabilities, and in schools that specialize in treating the disorder.

One often-cited method is that of Grace Fernald, which utilizes kinesthetic imprinting, based on a combination of "language experience" and tactile stimulation. In this popular method, the child relates a spontaneous story to the teacher, who transcribes it. Next, each word unknown to the child is written down by the teacher, and the child traces its letters over and over until he or she can write that word without using the model. Each word learned becomes part of the child's word file. A large number of stories are handled this way. Many variants of the method are in use. Though it is quite slow, many anecdotal reports praise its results. (Despite this, Donald K. Routh pointed out in 1987 that the method had never been subjected to a rigorous, controlled study of its efficacy.)

A second common method utilized by special educators is the Orton-Gillingham-Stillman method, developed in a collaboration by teachers Anna Gillingham and Essie Stillman and the pediatric neurologist Samuel T. Orton. The method evolved from Orton's conceptualization of language as developing from a sequence of processes in the nervous system that end in unilateral control by the left cerebral hemisphere. He proposed that dyslexia arises from conflicts, which need to be corrected, between this hemisphere and the right cerebral hemisphere, usually involved in the handling of nonverbal, pictorial, and spatial stimuli.

Consequently, the method used is multisensory and kinesthetic, like Fernald's; however, it begins with the teaching of individual letters and phonemes, and progresses to dealing with syllables, words, and sentences. Children taught by this method are drilled systematically to imprint a mastery of phonics and the sounding out of unknown written words. They are encouraged to learn how the elements of written language look, how they sound, how it feels to pronounce them, and how it feels to write them down. Routh has pointed out that the Orton-Gillingham-Stillman method is as laborious as that of Fernald. It is widely used and appreciated, however, and believed to work well.

Another method that merits brief discussion is the use of therapeutic drugs in the treatment of dyslexia. Most physicians and educators propose the use of these drugs as a useful adjunct to the training of dyslexic children who are easily distracted and restless or who have low morale because of embarrassment resulting from

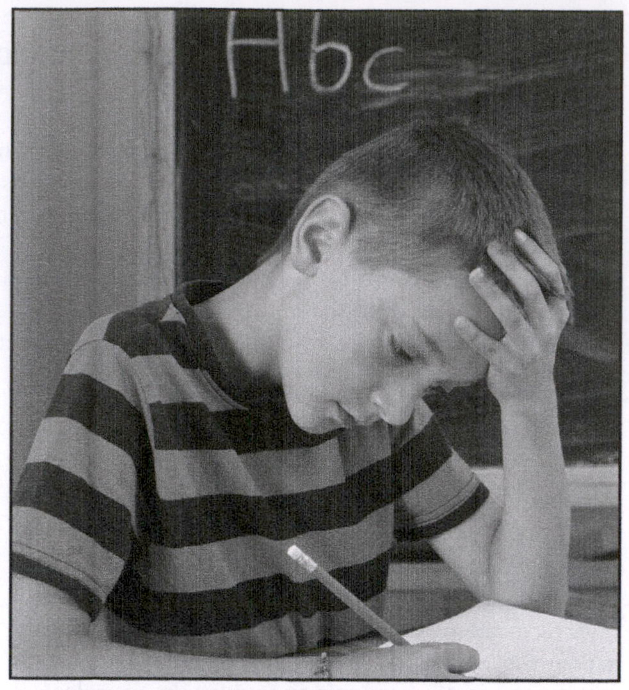

Photo: iStock

peer pressure. The drugs used most often are the amphetamine Dexedrine and methylphenidate (Ritalin).

These stimulants, taken in appropriate doses, lengthen the time period during which some dyslexic children function well in the classroom and also produce feelings of self-confidence. Side effects of overdose, however, include lost appetite, nausea, nervousness, and sleeplessness. Furthermore, there is the potential problem of drug abuse. Despite this, numerous sources (including both Valett and Jordan) indicate that stimulant benefits far outweigh any possible risks when the drugs are utilized carefully and under close medical supervision. Other, less dependable therapies sometimes attempted include special diets and the use of vitamins and minerals.

One other important aspect of the treatment of dyslexia is good parental emotional support, which helps children cope with their problems and with peer pressure. Useful aspects of this support include a positive attitude toward the afflicted child; appropriate home help for the child that complements efforts undertaken at school; encouragement and praise for achievements, without recrimination when repeated mistakes are made; and good interaction with special-education teachers assigned to a child.

RESEARCH

The identification of dyslexia more than one hundred years ago, which resulted from the endeavors of the German physician Berlin and of W. A. Morgan, in England, launched efforts to find a cure for this unfortunate disorder. In 1917, the Scottish eye surgeon James Hinshelwood published a book on dyslexia, which he viewed as being a hereditary problem, and the phenomenon became better known to physicians. Attempts at educating dyslexics, as recommended by Hinshelwood and other physicians, were highly individualized until the endeavors of Orton and coworkers and of Fernald led to more standardized and soon widely used methods.

Furthermore, with the development of a more complete understanding of the brain and its many functions, better counseling facilities, and the conceptualization and actualization of both parent-child and parent-counselor interactions, the prognosis for successful dyslexic training has improved significantly. Also, a number of extensive studies of dyslexic children have been carried out and have identified dyslexia as a complex syndrome composed of numerous associated behavioral dysfunctions related to visual-motor brain immaturity. These include poor memory for details, easy distractibility, poor motor skills, letter and word reversal, and the inability to distinguish between important elements of the spoken language.

A particularly extensive and useful study was carried out by Edith Klasen and described in her book *The Syndrome of Specific Dyslexia: With Special Consideration of Its Physiological, Psychological, Testpsychological, and Social Correlates* (1972). The Klasen study identified the role of psychoanalytical interventions in the treatment of some dyslexic subjects, and it pointed out that environmental and socioeconomic factors contribute relatively little to the occurrence of dyslexia but affect the outcomes of its treatment.

It is the endeavors of special educationSpecial education that have made the greatest inroads into treatment of dyslexia. Further advances in the area will undoubtedly be made, as the science of the mind grows and diversifies and as the contributions of the psychologist, physician, physiologist, and special educator mesh together more effectively.

BIBLIOGRAPHY

Hoien, Torliev, and Ingvar Lundberg. *Dyslexia: From Theory to Intervention.* Norwell, Mass.: Kluwer, 2000. Presents European research in the causes and treatment of dyslexia, much of it presented in English for the first time.

Nicolson, Roderick I., and Angela Fawcett. *Dyslexia, Learning, and the Brain.* Cambridge, Mass.: MIT Press, 2008. Leading dyslexia researchers theorize that the source of this disability may be rooted in the procedural learning system, in the cortical and subcortical regions of the brain.

Reid, Gavin. *Dyslexia: A Practitioner's Handbook.* 4th ed. New York: John Wiley & Sons, 2008. A review of dyslexia research and teaching practices for educators. Includes a review of resources for classroom strategies.

Reid, Gavin, and Janice Wearmouth. Dyslexia and Literacy: An Introduction to Theory and Practice. New York: John Wiley & Sons, 2002. Covers recent theoretical and practical approaches to dyslexia in both psychological and pedagogical contexts.

Snowling, Margaret J. *Dyslexia: A Cognitive Developmental* Perspective. 2d ed. New York: Basil Blackwell, 2000. Covers many aspects of dyslexia, including its identification, associated cognitive defects, the basis for development of language skills, and the importance of phonology. In addition, it contains many references.

West, Thomas G. *In the Mind's Eye: Visual Thinkers, Gifted People with Dyslexia and Other Learning Difficulties, Computer Images, and the Ironies of Creativity.* Updated ed. Amherst, N.Y.: Prometheus Press, 1997. Argues that the rise of computer technology favors visual over verbal thinkers, decreasing the difficulties faced by dyslexics and others with verbal learning disorders.

Sanford S. Singer

See Also: Attention; Brain damage; Brain structure; Language; Learning disorders; Peabody Individual Achievement Test (PIAT)

Dysphonia

Type of psychology: Biological bases of human behavior; Clinical; Counseling; Developmental; Neuropsychological; School

Voicing is produced when the lungs, diaphragm, abdominal and chest muscles, and ribs create airflow that is pushed through the larynx. In the larynx, the vocal folds vibrate and create a tone. This tone is then passed through the throat, oral cavity, and nasal cavity, where the tone is adapted to produce different speech sounds. A distur-

bance in the anatomy or physiology of the vocal folds within the laryngeal cavity causes dysphonia, or voice disorder. Dysphonia may be caused by masses on the vocal folds, changes in the consistency of the vocal folds, or changes in the way the vocal folds move. These changes in vocal fold anatomy and physiology become evident through vocal quality.

Key Concepts

- Adduction and abduction
- Phonation
- Vocal misuse and abuse
- Vocal nodules
- Vocal polyps

BACKGROUND

A voice is created when air from the lungs pushes through the vibrating vocal folds in the larynx and up through the nose and mouth. Any disorder or abnormality in this process is known as dysphonia. Dysphonia may occur in both children and adults. However, voice disorders occur more often in adult females and professionals who frequently use their voice in loud environments such as teachers, coaches, actors, and singers.

The larynx and vocal folds serve a variety of speech and nonspeech functions. The vocal folds adduct, or close, to protect the airway when swallowing. The vocal folds must abduct, or open, in order for air to flow from the lungs and up through the nose and mouth. The vocal folds may quickly adduct and then abduct to protect the airway from foreign materials by coughing. Finally, the vocal folds vibrate at varying speeds and frequencies to produce voicing necessary for speech. A disturbance in the ability for the vocal folds to adduct and abduct will result in an inability to appropriately produce sounds for speech and manifest in dysphonia.

ETIOLOGY

The most common cause of dysphonia is vocal misuse and abuse. Laryngitis, or an inflammation of the larynx, may result from vocal abuse. A virus such as a cold or flu, allergies, bacterial infections, or acid reflux may cause laryngitis.

Vocal misuse and abuse can lead to masses such as nodules or polyps to form on one or both vocal folds. Vocal fold nodules are callous-like tissue formations on the outer layer of the vocal folds. They arise from excessive yelling, screaming, or coughing. Nodules often decrease in size or disappear completely with vocal rest. However, surgical intervention can be necessary if nodules remain.

In the same way, polyps are also caused by vocal misuse and abuse. Polyps are blister-like masses that appear on one or both vocal folds. Most polyps are larger than nodules and may require surgical intervention.

Biological factors such as neuromuscular diseases and neoplastic growths impact vocal fold function as well and can lead to dysphonia. Malignant and benign neoplastic growths or tumors present in a similar fashion as a polyp or nodule and may cause pain during phonation. Degenerative diseases such as Parkinson's disease and dysarthria can lead to weak or paralyzed vocal folds. As the vocal folds weaken or paralyze, they are unable to make contact to produce vibrations needed to formulate a tone.

PRESENTATION

Voice disorders present themselves in the way a speaker's voice sounds to a listener. Changes to the vocal folds can cause the speaker to produce a lower pitch. Masses on the vocal folds prevent the complete closure that is necessary for phonation. The resulting spaces between vocal folds cause air to pass through and produce a breathy vocal quality. These masses may also lead to irregular vocal fold movements and result in a hoarse voice. Diseases that cause stiffness of the vocal folds will require the speaker to use more effort and pressure when pushing air from the lungs and will manifest in a strident, witch-like vocal quality. This increase in pressure can also cause abrupt initiations in speech. A change in the structure of the vocal folds, either by mass or stiffness, may also cause intermittent voice breaks or aphonia.

TREATMENT

Courses of treatment for dysphonia are largely dependent on the source of the problem. There are three major types of intervention for voice disorders: injections, voice therapy, and surgery. Unilateral vocal fold paralysis may be treated by collagen or TeflonTM injections to the paralyzed vocal fold. Injections to the site of immobility will not aid in vocal fold movement but will increase the mass of the vocal fold and allow the functioning vocal fold to make contact for phonation.

Voice therapy with a speech-language pathologist is the least invasive method of treatment for dysphonia. Voice therapy techniques vary based on diagnosis and symptoms but in general will aim to minimize symptoms of dysphonia and implement techniques for appropriate voice production. This form of intervention may also involve lifestyle changes such as periods of vocal rest, decreasing overuse of voice, decreasing excessive throat clearing, eliminating smoking, reducing alcohol intake, and increasing fluid intake.

Surgical intervention is typically the course taken when vocal rest and voice therapy are unsuccessful. Intervention may be recommended in order to remove a mass or tissue, repair laryngeal anatomy, or to reposition the vocal folds.

BIBLIOGRAPHY

Colton, R.H., Casper, J.K., and Leonard, R. (1996). *Understanding Voice Problems* (3rded.). Philadelphia, PA: Lippincott Williams & Wilkins.This book provides details on normal voice production and outlines a variety of voice disorders. Includes videos for better understanding of the vocal mechanism.

VoiceMatters.net: A community Designed for People Affected by Vocal Disorders. http://www.voicematters.net/ This website provides information about dysphonia as well as access to support groups and forums to communicate with other group members.

Voice Disorders. Retrieved from http://www.asha.org/public/speech/disorders/voice/ This website gives a basic overview of voice disorders and access to the American Speech-Language-Hearing Association database of practicing speech-language pathologists.

Molly E. Sweetland and Elizabeth Rothstein

See Also: Functional dysphonia; Organic dysphonia; Phonation; Speech; Speech therapy; Vocal organs; Vocology; Voice.

E

Eating disorders

Type of psychology: Psychopathology

Eating disorders include a group of eating and weight disturbances, including anorexia nervosa, bulimia nervosa, and binge eating disorder, associated with underlying psychological problems.

Key Concepts

- Anorexia nervosa
- Binge eating disorder
- Bulimia nervosa
- Eating disorder
- Obesity

INTRODUCTION

Eating disorders were identified as early as ancient Rome, when banqueters gorged themselves, then induced vomiting. Some of the early female Christian saints were anorexic. However, eating disorders only emerged as an area of social and medical concern in the second half of the twentieth century.

Persons with eating disorders have a distorted body image and unrealistic ideas about weight. Although they are found primarily among young, middle- to upper-middle-class, well-educated Caucasian women, Gender differenceseating disorderseating disorders increasingly affect and may be overlooked in men, older women, and persons of color. No single factor appears to be the cause of eating disorders, with social, cultural, psychological, genetic, biological, and physical factors all playing a part. Treatment may include hospitalization for nutritional monitoring and for stabilization in persons with serious medical complications or who are at risk for suicide. Regardless of the setting, treatment is best carried out by a multidisciplinary team, including a primary care physician or psychiatrist, a psychotherapist, a nutritionist, and, if appropriate, a family therapist.

Eating disorders are best thought of as problems involving body weight and distorted body image on a continuum of severity. The most serious is anorexia nervosa, a disorder characterized by weight loss greater than or equal to 15 percent of the body weight normal for the person's height and age. Bulimia nervosa is usually found in persons of normal weight and is characterized by consumption of large amounts of food followed by self-induced vomiting, purging with diuretics or laxatives, or excessive exercise. Binge eating disorder, found usually in persons with some degree of overweight, is characterized by the consumption of large amounts of food without associated vomiting or purging. Other, milder, forms of eating disorders are at the least serious end of the continuum. Obesity may or may not be part of this continuum, depending on the presence or absence of underlying psychological problems. About one-third of obese persons have binge eating disorder.

POPULATION AT RISK

Women constitute 90 percent of people diagnosed with eating disorders—eight million adolescent and young adult women in the United States alone. The majority of these are Caucasian (95 percent) and from middle- to upper-middle-class backgrounds. Research in the latter part of the twentieth century indicated that adolescent and young adult women were most likely to be affected; however, these disorders are now found in girls as young as nine and in older women. By the end of the twentieth century, eating disorders were also increasingly identified in women from other ethnic and socioeconomic groups. These disorders are most likely underreported in men and seem to affect gay men disproportionately. Also at risk are men with certain professions or avocations such as jockeys, dancers, body builders, and wrestlers, in which weight and body shape are an issue.

CAUSES OF EATING DISORDERS

No single cause has been identified for eating disorders. However, it is important to note that nearly all eating disorders begin with dieting to lose weight. Because these disorders are found almost exclusively in the developed world, where food is plentiful and where thinness in women is idealized, it appears that social and cultural factors are important contributors. Some theorists believe that cultural values of independence and personal autonomy rather than interdependence and the importance of human relationships contribute to eating pathology. Still others point to the changing and contradictory societal expectations about the roles of women as a contributing factor.

Studies suggest a genetic predisposition to eating disorders, particularly in those persons who engage in binge eating and purging behaviors. Their family histories typically include higher than expected numbers of persons with mood disorders and substance abuse disorders problems. Dysfunctions in the pathways for the substances that transmit messages in the brain, the neurotransmitters, are thought to play a role in the development and maintenance of eating disorders, although these dysfunctions are not sufficient to explain the entire problem by themselves. The psychological theories about the causes of eating disorders postulate that individuals with underlying feelings of powerlessness or personal inadequacy attempt to cope by becoming preoccupied with their body's shape and size. Finally, the incidence of sexual abuse is higher among persons with eating disorders, particularly bulimia nervosa, than among those in the general population.

Eating disorders seem to develop in three stages. Stage 1 involves the period from the time a child is conceived until the onset of a particular behavior that precipitates the eating disorder. During this stage, individual psychological, personal, and physical factors, plus family, social, and cultural factors, place the person at increased risk. Individual risk factors include a personal history of depression, low self-esteem, perfectionism, an eagerness to please others, obesity, and physical or sexual abuse. Family risk factors include a family member with an eating disorder or a mood disorder and excessive familial concern for appearance and weight. Social and cultural issues include emphasis on the cultural ideal of excessive thinness, leading to dissatisfaction with the body and dieting for weight loss. Young women who are dancers, runners, skaters, gymnasts, and the like may be particularly susceptible to this kind of cultural pressure.

Stage 2 involves the factors that precipitate the eating disorder. Some identified precipitating factors include onset of puberty, leaving home, new relationships, death of a relative, illness, adverse comments about weight and body appearance, fear of maturation, the struggle for autonomy during the midteen years, and identity conflicts.

Stage 3 involves the factors that perpetuate the eating disorder. These can be cognitive distortions, interpersonal events, or biological changes related to starvation.

ASSOCIATED MEDICAL PROBLEMS

Women with anorexia nervosa stop menstruating. Anorexics may also have abdominal pain, constipation, and increased urination. The heart rate may be slow or irregular. Many develop downy, dark body hair (lanugo) over normally hairless areas. They may have bloating after eating and swelling of the feet and lower legs. Low levels of potassium and sodium and other imbalances in the body's electrolytes can lead to cardiac arrest, kidney failure, weakness, confusion, poor memory, disordered thinking, and mood swings. The death rate for anorexics is high: About 5 percent will die within eight years of being diagnosed and 20 percent within twenty years.

Self-induced vomiting can lead to erosion of tooth enamel, gum abscesses, and swelling of the parotid glands in front of the ear and over the angle of the jaw. About one-third of women with bulimia have abnormal changes in their menstrual cycles. Some bulimics consume so much food in such a short period of time that their stomachs rupture. More than 75 percent of these individuals die. Use of ipecac and laxatives can lead to heart damage. Symptoms include chest pain, skipped heartbeats, and fainting, and these heart problems can lead to death. In addition, bulimics are at increased risk for ulcers of the stomach and small intestine and for inflammation of the pancreas.

One commonly overlooked problem is the female athletic triad,Athletes, eating disorders a combination of disordered eating, loss of menstruation, and osteoporosis. This can lead to fractures and permanent loss of bone minerals.

ANOREXIA NERVOSA

The diagnosis of Anorexia nervosa is made for persons who have lost 15 percent or more of the body weight that is considered normal for their height and age and who have an intense and irrational fear of gaining weight. Even with extreme weight loss, anorexics perceive themselves as overweight. Their attitude toward food and weight control becomes obsessive and they frequently develop bizarre or ritualistic behaviors around food, such as chewing each bite a specific number of times. Anorexics minimize the seriousness of their weight loss and are highly resistant to treatment.

The two basic types of anorexia nervosa are the restricting type and the binge eating/purging type. The restricting type is characterized by an extremely limited diet, often without carbohydrates or fats. This may be accompanied by excessive exercising or hyperactivity.

Up to half of anorexics eventually lose control over their severely restricted dieting and begin to engage in binge eating. They then induce vomiting, use diuretics or laxatives, or exercise excessively to control their weight. People who are in the binge eating/purging group are at greater risk for medical complications.

As the weight loss in either type reaches starvation proportions, anorexics become more and more preoccupied with food; they may hoard food or steal. They also experience sleep abnormalities, loss of interest in sex, and poor concentration and attention. In addition, they slowly restrict their social contacts and become more and more socially isolated. In general, anorexics of the binge eating/purging type are likely to have problems with impulse control and may engage in substance abuse, excessive spending, sexual promiscuity, and other forms of compulsive behavior. This group is also more likely to attempt suicide or to hurt themselves than others with eating disorders.

BULIMIA NERVOSA

Persons who have Bulimia nervosa are similar in behavior to the subset of anorexics who binge and purge, but they tend to maintain their weight at or near normal for their age and height. They intermittently have an overwhelming urge to eat, usually associated with a period of anxiety or depression, and can consume as many as 15,000 calories in a relatively short period of time, typically one to two hours. Binge foods are usually high calorie and easy to digest, such as ice cream. The binge eating provides a sense of numbing of the anxiety or relief from the depression. Failing to recognize that they are full, bulimics eventually stop eating because of abdominal pain, nausea, being interrupted, or some other non-hunger-related reason. At that point, psychological stress again increases as they reflect on the amount they have eaten. Most bulimics then induce vomiting, but some use laxatives, diuretics, severe food restriction, fasting, or excessive exercise to avoid gaining weight.

Bulimics tend to be secretive, binge eating and purging when alone. These episodes may occur only a few times a week or as often as several times a day. As with binge eating/purging anorexics, bulimics are likely to abuse alcohol and other drugs, make suicidal gestures, and engage in other kinds of impulsive behavior such as shoplifting. Because of the electrolyte imbalances and other adverse consequences of repeated vomiting or the use of laxatives or diuretics, bulimics are at risk for multiple serious medical complications which, if uncorrected, can lead to death.

BINGE EATING DISORDER

The American Psychiatric Association has developed provisional criteria for Binge eating disorder to study this disorder more completely. The criteria include compulsive and excessive eating at least twice a week for six months without self-induced vomiting, purging, or excessive exercise. That is, binge eating disorder is bulimia nervosa without the compensatory weight-loss mechanisms. For this reason, most binge eaters are slightly to significantly overweight. In addition to the eating problems, many binge eaters experience relationship problems and have a history of depression or other psychiatric disorders.

OTHER EATING DISORDERS

Anorexia and bulimia nervosa and binge eating disorder have strict diagnostic criteria set forth by the American Psychiatric Association. However, these three do not cover the entire spectrum of disordered eating patterns. Those people who induce vomiting after consuming only a small amount of food, for example, or those who chew large amounts of food and spit it out rather than swallow it, do not fit the diagnosis of bulimia. For such persons, a diagnosis of "eating disorder, not otherwise specified" is used.

PREVALENCE OF EATING DISORDERS

Anorexia nervosa is the rarest of the eating disorders, affecting fewer than 1 percent of adolescent and young women (that is, women ages thirteen to twenty-five) and a tiny proportion of young men. Bulimia nervosa, on the other hand, affects up to 3 percent of teenage and young adult women and about 0.2 percent of men. Even more of this age group, probably 5 percent, suffer from binge eating disorder. In obese patients, fully one-third meet the criteria for this disorder. Binge eating is the most common eating disorder in men, although more women actually have this disorder. Eating disorders, not otherwise specified, are even more common.

TREATMENT

Treatment of persons with eating disorders can take place in an inpatient or an outpatient setting. Hospitalization is indicated for patients with severe malnutrition, serious medical complications, an increased risk of suicide, and those who are unable to care for themselves or have failed outpatient treatment.

The first step in the treatment of anorexics must be restoring their body weight. This may require hospitalization. A system of carefully structured rewards for weight gain is often successful. For example, the gain of a target amount of weight may be tied to being allowed to go outside or having visits from friends. Once the anorexic is nutritionally stabilized, individual, family, Cognitive behavior therapyeating disorderscognitive behavior, and other therapies are indicated to address issues specific to the individual.

The first step in the treatment of bulimics is a comprehensive medical evaluation. Bulimics are less likely than anorexics to require hospitalization. As with anorexia nervosa, treatment includes individual, family, and cognitive behavior therapies. In addition, group therapy may be helpful. Cognitive behavior therapies are effective in the treatment of bulimia nervosa. Patients are taught to recognize and analyze cues that trigger the binge-purge cycle. Once analyzed, they are taught to reframe these thoughts, feelings, and beliefs to more adaptive and less destructive ones, thus altering the cycle.

Outpatient care should be carefully coordinated among a multidisciplinary team: an experienced health care practitioner to monitor the patient's medical condition, a therapist to address psychological and emotional issues, a family therapist to deal with control and other issues within the family, and a nutritionist to develop and monitor a sensible meal plan.

Medications may be a helpful adjunct in some cases, particularly in those eating-disordered patients who have an additional psychiatric diagnosis such as major depression or obsessive-compulsive disorder. Simply gaining weight usually improves mood in anorexics, but antidepressants (particularly the selective serotonin-reuptake inhibitors or SSRIs) may help not only with depression but also with the obsessive-compulsive aspects of the anorexic's relationship with food.

Several different antidepressants (including monoamine oxidase inhibitors, the tricyclics amitriptyline and desipramine, and high-dose fluoxetine, an SSRI) are associated with fewer episodes of binge eating and purging in bulimic patients, in addition to treating anxiety and depression. These drugs have not been studied extensively in the treatment of binge eating disorder, however.

PREVENTION OF EATING DISORDERS

Prevention measures should include education about normal body weight for height and techniques used in advertising and the media to promote an unrealistic body image. Parents, teachers, coaches, and health care providers all play a role in prevention. Parents, coaches, and teachers need to be educated about the messages they give to growing children about bodies, body development, and weight. In addition, they need to be aware of early signs of risk. Health care providers need to include screening for eating disorders as a routine part of care. Specific indicators include dieting for weight loss associated with unrealistic weight goals, criticism of the body, social isolation, cessation of menses, and evidence of vomiting or laxative or diuretic use.

BIBLIOGRAPHY

Arenson, Gloria. *A Substance Called Food*. 2d ed. Boston: McGraw-Hill, 1989. Presents a variety of perspectives on eating, including the physiological and the transpersonal. Particularly useful in providing self-help advice and treatment modalities. Examines the compulsiveness of food addiction and sees behavior modification as a means of addressing the addictive behavior.

Battegay, Raymond. *The Hunger Diseases*. Northvale, N.J.: Jason Aronson, 1997. Addresses the emotional hunger that, the author contends, underlies all eating disorders, from anorexia to obesity.

Bruch, Hilde. *The Golden Cage: The Enigma of Anorexia Nervosa*. Reprint. Cambridge, Mass.: Harvard University Press, 2001. A classic work by a pioneer in the field of eating disorders. Portrays the development of anorexia nervosa as an attempt by a young woman to attain a sense of control and identity. Discusses the etiology and treatment of anorexia from a modified psychoanalytic perspective.

Brumberg, Joan J. *Fasting Girls: The History of Anorexia Nervosa*. Rev. ed. New York: Vintage, 2000. Outlines the history of anorexia nervosa. Examines the syndrome from multiple perspectives while leaning toward a cultural and feminist perspective. A well-researched and very readable work.

Fairburn, Christopher G. *Cognitive Behavior Therapy and Eating Disorders*. New York: Guilford Press, 2008. This treatment guide offers information on eating disorders that cover a range of severity, even those that may fall outside the usual diagnoses. Especially helpful to clinicians treating those suffering from eating disorders.

Gordon, Richard. Eating Disorders: Anatomy of a Social Epidemic. 2d rev. ed. New York: Blackwell, 2000. A survey of clinical practice in dealing with eating disorders, as well as thorough coverage of their history and social context.

Gura, Trisha. *Lying in Weight: The Hidden Epidemic of Eating Disorders in Adult Women.* New York: Harper, 2008. Science writer Gura contends that the figure for those with an eating disorder—25 to 30 million—is woefully short. Millions more, she claims, have "subthreshold" eating disorders, those that do not rise to the standard set by the American Psychiatric Association's Diagnostic and Statistical Manual of Mental Disorders. While these girls may be dangerously obsessed with their bodies and exercise excessively, doctors often overlook their problem.

Hirschmann, Jane R., and Carol H. Munter. *When Women Stop Hating Their Bodies: Freeing Yourself from Food and Weight Obsessions.* New York: Fawcett, 1997. A follow-up to the authors' Overcoming Overeating (1988), reviews the psychological basis for compulsive eating and provides alternative strategies to persons who have an addictive relationship with food. Presents convincing arguments against dieting and proposes that self-acceptance, physical activity, and health are more appropriate long-term solutions to the problem of overeating.

Martin, Courtney E. *Perfect Girls, Starving Daughters: The Frightening New Normalcy of Hating Your Body.* New York: Free Press, 2008. Using more than one hundred interviews with women and girls from ages nine to twenty-nine, the writer concludes that perfection is the goal for them all, especially in their bodies. Includes coverage of such topics as the role fathers play in influencing their daughter's self-esteem, athletes' eating disorders, and the depiction of women in hip-hop.

Sacker, Ira M., and Marc A. Zimmerman. *Dying to Be Thin: Understanding and Defeating Anorexia Nervosa and Bulimia.* Updated ed. New York: Warner Books, 2001. A practical approach, written by two medical doctors, to understanding the sources and causes of eating disorders and how to overcome them. Includes a guide to resources, treatment clinics, and support groups.

Schwartz, Hillel. *Never Satisfied: A Cultural History of Diets, Fantasies, and Fat.* New York: Anchor Books, 1990. Schwartz, a historian, looks at diets and eating from the perspective of American social and cultural history. Begins with the first weight watchers, in the early nineteenth century; examines how "shared fictions" about the body fit with various reducing methods and fads in different eras.

Rebecca Lovell Scott

See Also: Anorexia nervosa and bulimia nervosa; Antidepressant medications; Anxiety disorders; Body dysmorphic disorder; Depression; Hunger; Obesity; Obsessive-compulsive disorder; Teenagers' mental health.

Ebbinghaus, Hermann

Born: January 24, 1850
Died: February 26, 1909
Identity: German psychologist
Birthplace: Barmen, Prussia (now in Germany)
Place of death: Halle, Germany
Type of psychology: Learning; Memory

Ebbinghaus was a pioneer in studying learning and memory using scientific principles.

Hermann Ebbinghaus grew up in the small town of Barmen, located on the verdant banks of the Wupper River in northwestern Germany. After a brief stint in the Prussian army, he completed his doctoral studies in philosophy at the University of Bonn in 1873. Soon after completing his education, Ebbinghaus took up residence in Berlin and eventually traveled in France and England for several years. While in England, Ebbinghaus read *Elemente der psychophysik* (1860; *Elements of Psychophysics*, 1966) by Gustav Theodor Fechner, which many believe had a profound impact in shaping his approach to studying memory.

In 1879, Ebbinghaus began a series of experiments in learning and memory that involved using himself as the only research participant. At that time, the prevailing method for studying cognition was through introspection, which was popularized by the eminent psychologist, Wilhelm Wundt. Ebbinghaus chose to study memory from a radically different perspective. He used scientific methods borrowed from the natural sciences, which involved the use of statistics and mathematical formulas to explain performance.

To circumvent problems that common words posed for memory experiments, Ebbinghaus created his own stimuli, which he called nonsense syllables. These were three-letter syllables made up of a consonant-vowel-consonant, such as SOP or BEV. Ebbinghaus conducted hundreds of experiments in which he would require himself to rehearse a list of nonsense syllables to the point where he could write them down, in their proper order, with perfect accuracy. After a time delay, he attempted to relearn a list, keeping track of the number of rehearsals needed to regain 100 percent accuracy. He then made a calculation, referred to as the method of savings, which was based on the difference between the number of rehearsals needed for the initial learning and the second go-around.

Ebbinghaus published the results of his memory experiments in *Über das gedächtnis: Untersuchurgen zur experimentellen Psychologie* (1885; *Memory: A Contribution to Experimental Psychology,* 1913). Attention was drawn to his forgetting curve, which indicated most forgetting was not a linear function. Instead, the majority of forgetting occurs during the first few hours and then gradually declines over the next several days and weeks.

BIBLIOGRAPHY

Boneau, Alan. "Hermann Ebbinghaus: On the Road to Progress or Down the Garden Path?" In Vol. 3 of **Portraits of Pioneers in Psychology,** edited by Gregory Kimble and Michael Wertheimer. Washington, D.C.: American Psychological Association, 1998. Print.

Halpern, Sue. *Can't Remember What I Forgot: The Good News from the Front Lines of Memory Research.* New York: Crown, 2013. Print.

Howes, Mary. *Human Memory: Structures and Images.* Thousand Oaks, Calif.: Sage Publications, 2007. Print.

Neath, Ian, and Aimee Surprenant. *Human Memory.* 2d ed. Belmont, Calif.: Wadsworth/Thomson Learning, 2003. Print.

Rey, Amandine Eve, Benoit Riou, and Rémy Versace. "Demonstration of an Ebbinghaus Illusion at a Memory Level: Manipulation of the Memory Size and Not the Perceptual Size." *Experimental Psychology* (2014): PsycARTICLES. Web. 24 Apr. 2014.

Whitman, R. Douglas. *Cognition.* Hoboken: Wiley, 2011. Print.

Wozniak, Robert. *Classics in Psychology, 1855-1914: Historical Essays.* Bristol, England: Thoemmes Press, 1999. Print.

Bryan C. Auday

See Also: Cognitive psychology; Experimental psychology; Learning; Memory; Memory: Empirical studies; Scientific methods.

Ecological psychology

Date: 1990's forward

Type of psychology: Consciousness; Psychotherapy; Social psychology

Ecological psychology is a fast-emerging field that includes emphases on how to effectively promote conservation and sustainability, how to cultivate a therapeutic relationship between person and world, and how to understand the interconnectedness of person-world.

Key Concepts

- Conservation
- Deep ecology
- Ecopsychology
- Environmental psychology
- Holism
- Nonduality
- Sustainability

INTRODUCTION

Respected scientific organizations have been warning of pending and even imminent ecological disasters in their publications. Exemplary among these are the Intergovernmental Panel on Climate Change, established by the United Nations (*Climate Change* 2013, 2008), the National Research Council of the US National Academy of Sciences and the Royal Society ("Understanding and Responding to Climate Change," 2014), the international Union of Concerned Scientists ("How to Avoid Dangerous Climate Change," 2007), and the Worldwatch Institute (*State of the World 2013: Is Sustainability Still Possible?*, 2013). Such conclusions have even been heralded in the popular media, for example by Al Gore in his 2006 book and film *An Inconvenient Truth,* for which he won the Nobel Prize.

Problems cited include global climate change caused by greenhouse gases; weakening of plant and aquatic life by acid rain; the destruction of the ozone layer by chlorofluorocarbons (CFCs); the chemical pollution of soil and groundwater and, increasingly, even oceans; the consequences of deforestation for global warming and depletion of oxygen; the exhaustion and destruction of fisheries and other habitats; and the consequent species extinction and reduction in planetary biodiversity.

The field of ecology, or environmentalism, arose over the last third of the twentieth century to solve these problems before they become cataclysmic. Psychologists have joined this quest, forming an interdisciplinary approach that brings psychological expertise to ecological issues. This collaboration was formed on the basis of several different aims, with the result that the field has divided into branches pursuing a variety of goals. The primary impetus driving the rapid growth of this collaboration was the simple recognition that environmental problems are caused by human action. Once environmental destruction was linked to human behavior, the attitudes, thoughts, and beliefs underlying those behaviors became a subject of great interest. That interest soon led to the realization that the dynamics of these behavior-guiding attitudes are the least understood aspect of these problems and therefore solving the environmental crisis requires addressing its underlying human basis, a project for which psychology is uniquely situated.

DEVELOPMENTS

The field of ecological psychology has just begun to coalesce and is still defining itself—even naming itself—so no univocally accepted tasks or even labels yet exist. Support for particular developments emerges and changes quickly. Nevertheless, it appears the field has attained three major branches, with a conservation, therapeutic, and holistic focus. Each direction offers richly innovative prospects that will probably become increasingly significant.

THE CONSERVATION FOCUS

Conservation, the largest of these emphases, is devoted to researching the attitudes, beliefs, and behaviors that contribute to the environmental crises and to discovering how to change them to effectively promote the key conservation actions: reduce, reuse, and recycle. Before psychology's involvement, most efforts to bring about such behavioral change were simply information-intensive mass media advertising campaigns to promote greater participation in sustainable living. These campaigns made little use of psychological research or expertise and were generally ineffective.

The involvement of psychological researchers led to clarification of the roles of beliefs and assumptions in environmentally relevant behaviors. Among these findings are the effects of cognitive presuppositions and perceptual biases on the persuasive efficacy of warnings of environmental consequences, on assessments about risk, and on judgments and prejudgments about relative cost-benefit issues. Such research shows how these presuppositions and biases lead to misjudgments that ultimately culminate in choices and behaviors that undermine conservation. Common biases include, for example, failing to include the indirect costs in considering the environmentally destructive potential of one's actions and unduly discounting the significance of the long-term consequences by overrating the importance of the short-term consequences. As research proceeds, a variety of controversies are emerging, which are yet to be resolved. Among these debates are the relative importance for behavioral change of shifting a person's values and beliefs versus altering the behavioral contexts in which a person operates, and the relative impact of individual versus corporate actions in worsening environmental problems.

Among many prominent researchers in this area are George Howard, Paul Stern, Stuart Oskamp, and Doug McKenzie-Mohr. More typically called "environmental psychology," the focus of this branch is the least controversial and so is already widely accepted by mainstream psychology. For example, American Psychologist, the flagship journal of the American Psychological Association (APA) often publishes related articles and dedicated a special issue in May–June 2011 to global climate change and psychology's role in dealing with it. In addition, the association's initiative on what it termed "society's grand challenges" includes a segment devoted specifically to global climate change. Other examples of the scope of this branch include such publications as the *Journal of Environmental Psychology,* Robert B. Bechtel's *Handbook of Environmental Psychology* (2003), and *The Oxford Handbook of Environmental and Conservation Psychology* (2012).

THE THERAPEUTIC FOCUS

The second major branch of ecological psychology emphasizes the therapeutic value of the relationship of the person with the natural world. This focus, sometimes called "ecotherapy," extends beyond mainstream psychotherapy and draws heavily from work in humanistic psychology. It is based on understanding the importance of a person's relationship with the natural world for the individual's psychological well-being. Ecotherapy holds that a deficiency in the person-world relationship can make a person psychologically dysfunctional and that enhancement of this relationship may improve an individual's psychological deficiencies.

Features of the natural world that facilitate mental health include awe, harmony, balance, aliveness, at-homeness, and openness. Research has shown that deepening a person's relationship with the natural world can result in the relief of a wide range of psychopathological symptoms, including anxieties, depressions, addictions, and violence. In addition to benefiting people with mental health problems, a therapeutic connection with the natural world has been found to provide many generally beneficial psychological changes, such as empowerment, inner peace, aliveness, compassion, decreased fatigue, mental clarity, enhancement of creativity, relaxation, stress reduction, restoration of well-being, and relief of alienation. Such work with more psychologically healthy people is sometimes called "ecoeducation." Research has begun to explore the benefits of a therapeutic relationship with nature for healthy child and adolescent development.

Researchers in this branch develop, apply, and assess practices designed to enhance the quality of a person's relationship with the natural world, with the idea of developing a repertoire of effective modalities. These usually take the form of specific sets of exercises intended to train or enhance a person's capacity for more deeply, fully, and openly sensing specific features of the natural world. Often these exercises are undertaken during extended stays outdoors in wilderness settings. Some practices are also borrowed from indigenous cultures whose relationships with the natural world are not as altered by the artifices of modern life in the more industrialized world. For example, some practices include a "vision quest" component, in which a portion of the person's time in the wilderness is spent alone, with the aim of discovering a significant insight. Sometimes, therapeutic goals are achieved by the enactment of a reciprocal interaction, in which one is both "nurtured by" the earth and "nurturing of" earth.

Among the most prominent innovators in this branch are Michael Cohen, founder of the Institute of Global Education and the director of Project Nature Connect; John Davis and Steven Foster, directors of the School of Lost Borders; Laura Sewell; Paul Shepherd; and Howard Clinebell. Universities that offer programs in ecological psychology, such as Naropa University, City University of New York, the Institute of Global Education, and John F. Kennedy University, , tend to emphasize this area.

THE HOLISTIC FOCUS

In contrast with the other two branches, both of which are applied in one way or another, the third branch represents "deep" ecological psychology: a fundamental inquiry into the foundational meanings and significance of the relationship between humans and nature. The holistic focus aims at nothing less than the study of the depletion and restoration of the fullness of the human spirit by healing the disconnection of person and world. This radical ontological inquiry typically takes the name ecopsychology and aligns with the movement within environmentalism known as deep ecology as formulated by Arne Naess in his article in *Deep Ecology for the Twenty-First Century* (1995), edited by George Sessions. It also draws from developments in contemporary physics that emphasize a systems approach or wholeness perspective. Two physicists have contributed greatly: Fritjof Capra, founder of the Center for Ecoliteracy and author of *The Hidden Connections: Integrating the Biological, Cognitive, and Social Dimensions of Life into a Science of Sustainability* (2002), and David Bohm, the author of *Wholeness and the Implicate Order* (1981).

As the most radical approach, this holistic focus is the least established within traditional psychology; it tends to draw support mainly from phenomenological and transpersonal psychologists. Its basic premises, increasingly demonstrated by research, are the interconnectedness of all aspects of the world within a reciprocal and synergistic whole and the value of experiencing this holism as a way to overcome the dualistic perspective that disconnects humans from nature, an alienation in which nature is seen as a sort of storehouse of commodities to be exploited. This alternative holistic vision has a breadth and depth that extends to offering and receiving implications from spiritual traditions, especially the more explicitly nondualistic ones. These have most commonly been the Native American, Wiccan, and Buddhist traditions, although they have increasing involved Christianity as well.

Longstanding leaders are Theodore Roszak, the founder of the Ecopsychology Institute at California State, Hayward, who coined the term "ecopsychology"; Ralph Metzner, the founder of the Green Earth Foundation; and Joanna Macy, a Buddhist activist and ecofeminist. Scholars of note include Elizabeth Roberts, Andy Fisher, Warwick Fox, Mary Gomes, and Allen Kanner. Many organizations, including the International Community of Ecopsychology, have formed to support this work.

BIBLIOGRAPHY

Clayton, Susan D., ed. *The Oxford Handbook of Environmental and Conservation Psychology.* New York: Oxford UP, 2012. Print.

Fisher, Andy. *Radical Ecopsychology: Psychology in the Service of Life.* 2nd ed. Albany: State U of New York P, 2013. Print.

Gardner, Gerald, and Paul C. Stern. *Environmental Problems and Human Behavior.* 2nd ed. Boston: Pearson, 2002. Print.

Howard, George S. *Ecological Psychology: Creating a More Earth-Friendly Human Nature.* Notre Dame: U of Notre Dame P, 1997. Print.

Metzner, Ralph. *Green Psychology: Transforming Our Relationship to the Earth.* Rochester: Inner Traditions, 1999. Print.

Roszak, Theodore, Mary Gomes, and Allen Kanner, eds. *Ecopsychology.* San Francisco: Sierra Club, 1995. Print.

Sewell, Laura. *Sight and Sensibility: The Ecopsychology of Perception.* Los Angeles: Tarcher, 1999. Print.

Winter, Deborah D. *Ecological Psychology: Healing the Split between Planet and Self.* Mahwah: Erlbaum, 2003. Print.

Winter, Deborah D., and Susan M. Koger. *The Psychology of Environmental Problems: Psychology for Sustainability.* New York: Psychology, 2011. Digital file.

Christopher M. Aanstoos

See Also: Attitude formation and change; Cognitive behavior therapy; Environmental factors and mental health; Environmental psychology; Environmental toxicology and mental health.

Educational psychology

Type of psychology: Learning

Educational psychology is a diverse and dynamic discipline aimed at facilitating human learning through effective instruction.

Key Concepts

- Cognitive skill induction
- Educational task
- Far transfer
- Interactive models
- Metacognition
- Near transfer
- Problem solving

INTRODUCTION

Teaching methods is a complex undertaking involving decision making at many levels as well as a diversity of skills. From kindergarten to college, teachers are involved in designing curricula, planning lessons, selecting texts, evaluating the products of learning, and monitoring a full range of action within the classroom. The choices are many, and effective teaching demands additional expertise in terms of the delivery of instruction. Indeed, the teacher functions both as a theorist, objectively analyzing the situation of learning and methods of instruction, and as a practitioner, in the more spontaneous delivery of instruction in an attempt to inspire young minds.

Teaching is the deliberate facilitation of learning; learning is a relatively permanent change in behavior or the gaining of a new perspective on or insight into a problem. Learning may take place without teaching. For example, children seem to acquire language without specific instruction. Teaching, on the other hand, may or may not be effective in stimulating learning. It is the goal of educational psychology to facilitate effective instruction to foster human learning.

Educational psychology, a diverse scientific discipline, attempts to apply psychological principles to understand, predict, and influence classroom learning. Just as teaching and learning are ongoing processes, so is educational psychology an evolving enterprise. Researchers search for dependable answers to many practical educational questions. They ask which teaching methods are most effective, as well as which methods work best for particular students. They examine whether grades are effective motivators (and again, for which students they are effective). They look at whether holding a student back a grade has positive or negative effects on subsequent performance. Research in educational psychology is often inconclusive because of the complexity of the questions, discrepancies in terminology, and/or faulty methodologies. For this reason, research is replicated; sound educational practice is based on well-supported trends. Educational psychology is a continually developing discipline, integrating theoretical perspectives with practical concerns.

LEARNING MODELS

In 1979, James Jenkins devised an interactive model for learning researchers that can be used as a guide to understanding classroom learning in terms of both personal and environmental (outside the person) factors. This tetrahedral model posits that learning is influenced by four types of variables: characteristics of the learner (beliefs, skills, energy level, and so on), characteristics of the teacher(voice, gender, attitude), criterion of evaluation (for example, whether the work is for a grade), and characteristics of the task (such as whether it is written or verbal, and whether it is timed). The interplay of these four types of variables affects the quality of learning. In helping a child who apparently has difficulty with mathematics, a teacher familiar with the principles of the tetrahedral model might consider interventions such as changing the type of tests (timed tests might not be fair to some learners), changing the grading system, or even changing the lessons to include visual or diagrammatic materials to explain math principles. Often the solution focuses on changing the learner, who is perhaps the hardest to change. Jenkins's model also serves as a framework for understanding how educational psychology is applied to classroom learning situations.

Student learning is complex, as are the variables that affect it. Learner and teacher characteristics, for example, include a variety of attributes. Some are stable or constant (sex, race, or ability). Others are consistent or generally stable, changing little over time or situation, such as attitudes, beliefs, and learning styles. Some learner and teacher attributes are unstable and likely to change, such as the level of arousal, anxiety, or mood. It is the more consistent variables that affect learning in general, are more easily measured, and are investigated more frequently. Among the most recently researched variables are perceptions of learners—about specific tasks, self, or others—which can be experimentally changed through a process of reorientation or instruction. Such variables are often found to affect students' willingness to engage or to persist, and consequently to affect their school achievement. Along similar lines, the investigation of students' metacognition, or their management of their own thought processes, has inspired the development of effective remedial reading programs and revitalized instruction of study skills.

Other research on instruction in cognitive skills has focused on interventions to teach thinking, either through stand-alone programs (such as a course in philosophy or a unit on how to make valid inferences), instruction in processing skills in the context of subject matter teaming (such as measuring in science or problem-solving strategies in math), or instruction in problem solving during an authentic task, such as a computer simulation (of pioneer travel, for example) or a project (such as a scientific experiment). Results generally suggest that regardless of which of the three approaches is used, cognitive skill instruction is effective only if skills are taught explicitly and if skill assessment tasks are similar to tasks used in training (near transfer). Generalization of effects to distantly related assessment tasks (far transfer) diminishes with the degree of characteristics shared between assessment and training tasks.

APPLIED RESEARCH

In a 1972 study investigating how college students learn, Gordon Pask and others differentiated holistic approaches and serialistic learning styles. Using a "teach-back" procedure, Pask had students create fictitious zoological taxonomies and then teach those classifications back to the experimenter. Serialists were characterized as remembering information in terms of lengthy strings of data. That is, bits of information were related sequentially and in a linear, step-by-step fashion. The serial style relies on memorization. Holists, on the other hand, remembered in terms of hierarchical relations, imaging the entire system of facts or principles in a more general manner; they focused on the big picture and fit details in later. The holistic strategy was related to what Pask called "comprehension learning," with the serialist orientation reflective of "operational learning" (focusing on details and procedures). Pask also found that teaching materials could be structured in either a holistic (meaningful) or serialistic (memorization) fashion and were most effective when matched to the student's corresponding learning style.

In addition to investigating learner characteristics, researchers in educational psychology have explored how it is that teacher characteristics affect student learning. In particular, teachers' motivational beliefs, a fairly consistent variable, have been linked to teaching behaviors. In 1984, Carole Ames and Russell Ames identified three systems of teacher motivation based on specific values held by teachers that result in different perceptions, motivations, and teaching strategies. In the ability evaluative system,Ability evaluative system teachers tend to maintain their notions of self-worth by protecting their own positive notions of their ability. That is, teachers see their personal value as contingent on students' success.

This results in blaming the student for failure and crediting themselves when students are successful. In the second system, the moral responsibility system, teachers primarily are concerned with the pupil. The resulting behaviors are the opposite of those associated with the ability evaluative orientation: blaming self for failures and crediting the student for success. In the task mastery condition, the task is of primary importance rather than a teacher's self-image. The focus is on accomplishing educational goals and fostering competence. Thus, from an interactionist perspective, teachers' beliefs about learning and about themselves are an integral part of the learning process.

The characteristics of the task are the third major type of variable affecting classroom learning and are a primary area of concern for researchers. Attributes of the task might include the type of task: aural or visual, motor or verbal, comprehension or memorization, self-instructional or teacher-assisted. A major development in the area of self-instruction as related to learning tasks has been computer-aided instruction. In 1983, educational psychologists James Kulik, Robert Bangert, and George Williams reviewed numerous studies regarding the use of computers for instructional purposes in sixth- to twelfth-grade classrooms. They found that there were moderate benefits in terms of improvement on examinations and in reducing the amount of time needed for learning. Also, children taught with computers developed more positive attitudes toward computers than those who were taught in the traditional manner.

Finally, the type of evaluation has an effect on classroom learning. Perhaps the most common type of student evaluation is grading, assigning letter or number ratings to reflect the quality of student work. Although grades may be intended to function as incentives or motivators to encourage students to perform, it is unlikely that they do so. In a 2000 study, Robert Slavin found that grades are used for three primary functions: evaluation, feedback, and incentives. As a result, grades function as less-than-ideal motivators. Also, grades are given too infrequently for young children to see any relationship between their daily work and a grade received weeks later. Grades may be effective incentives for older students, however; studies comparing college students in graded-versus-ungraded classes have found that grades do function as an incentive.

PHILOSOPHICAL ROOTS AND CONTEMPORARY MODELS

Educational psychology draws on many resources to form well-grounded models. The philosophical roots of educational psychology lie in the early twentieth century work of William James and John Dewey. Both were scholars who shared a concern for the application of psychological principles in the classroom. James described the teacher's role as that of developing good habits and productive thinking in the student. Dewey, on the other hand, called for the transformation of education in terms of expanding the curriculum to include the needs of an increasingly industrial society. Dewey saw schools as agents of social change.

As time progressed, psychology developed as a social science, and two major conceptions of learning were spawned: the Gestalt model and behaviorism. In the Gestalt view, learning is defined as a change in the perceptual process, or as understanding a problem in a new way—insight. In contrast, the behavioral view rests on the assumption of stimulus substitution: Existing responses became associated with new stimuli through the process of conditioning. The emphasis is on observed relationships—behaviors. Behaviorism had a profound influence on American education, in terms of both instruction and classroom management. For example, "time out,"Time-out or removing a child from the stimuli of the existing environment to a quiet and boring place, has been used as a form of punishment.

Since 1975, cognitive psychology, with its emphasis on the processes of learning, has dominated the instructional scene. The advent of computer technology offered a model of information processing, and advances in military technology demanded that researchers consider how it is that humans carry out decision-making processes. More specifically, it was wondered how learners attend to, organize, store, and retrieve information. In a 2001 study, Margaret Gredler cited three reasons for increased emphasis on cognitive processes: Behaviorism was too limited in explaining human activity, learners had come to be viewed as active manipulators rather than as passive recipients of knowledge, and learners were viewed as interacting with environments. Prominent instructional models based on cognitive theory include Jerome Bruner's discovery learning, emphasizing the teacher's role in creating situations in which students can learn on their own, and, in contrast, David Ausubel's reception learning, which focuses on teacher-structured learning in the form of well-organized lessons. From an interactive perspective, discovery learning empowers the learner by positing the teacher as a facilitator, whereas reception learning empowers the teacher in controlling the learning situation. Finally, a model of teaming and teaching originating in Lev Vygotsky's cultural-historical theory of development emphasizes the development of a child's cognition through interaction with an adult who both models a skill and verbally mediates the child's encounter with the task until the child achieves independence at the task. From an interactive perspective, Vygotsky's model might be seen to empower both teacher and learner in turn.

BIBLIOGRAPHY

Gredler, Margaret E. *Learning and Instruction.* 6th ed. Upper Saddle River, N.J.: Merrill-Pearson, 2009. Gredler discusses the functions of learning theory as it applies to instruction, the history of the development of educational psychology, and seven contemporary views on learning and instruction. The presentation is concise and appropriate for secondary and college students.

Schmeck, Ronald R., ed. *Learning Strategies and Learning Styles.* New York: Plenum, 1988. Offers a timely selection of popular thinking on student learning styles based on a variety of methodologies. Included are neuropsychological, cognitive, and affective perspectives. Well suited for college students as well as professionals.

Slavin, Robert E. *Educational Psychology.* 9th ed. Upper Saddle River, N.J.: Merrill-Pearson, 2009. Slavin offers a practical look at effective classroom practice based on recent research findings. The college-level text illustrates how research may directly affect classroom practice.

Snowman, Jack, Robert F. Biehler, and Curtis Bank. *Psychology Applied to Teaching.* 12th ed. Boston: Houghton Mifflin, 2009. A well-researched and timely look at classroom learning, this text emphasizes practical applications with real classroom situations. Especially useful for future teachers in secondary or college levels.

Ellen Lavelle; updated by John F. Wakefield

See Also: Cognitive development: Jean Piaget; Cognitive maps; Concept formation; Cooperative learning; Dewey, John; James, William; Learning; Piaget, Jean; Prejudice reduction; Teaching methods.

Ego defense mechanisms

Type of psychology: Emotion; Personality; Psychopathology; Psychotherapy

The concept of ego defense mechanisms, originally a central feature of Sigmund Freud's psychoanalytic theory, came to be incorporated into the general body of knowledge in the fields of psychology and psychiatry during the last half of the twentieth century. Ego defenses protect people from being overwhelmed by strong emotion and are crucial for psychological survival. However, when used maladaptively, they can result in the formation of psychiatric symptoms and psychopathology..

Key Concept

- Adaptation
- Anxiety
- Conflict
- Psychoanalysis
- Psychopathology
- Repression
- Suppression

INTRODUCTION

Ego defense mechanisms are complex, largely unconscious mental processes that protect people from becoming overwhelmed by strong emotions. Defense mechanisms protect the mind and nervous system just as the immune system protects the body, and they are essential for healthy functioning and adaptation. However, when they are used maladaptively, psychiatric symptoms can develop and result in psychopathology.

At birth, only rudimentary defenses are in place, so infants require substantial protection from external sources (caretakers) to prevent them from becoming overwhelmed by internal and environmental stresses. Over the course of childhood and continuing into adulthood, increasingly complex defense mechanisms develop and are added to an individual's defense repertoire. As a result, each individual forms a personal defense system from which to automatically draw when emotions threaten to become too stressful. Some defenses work better in certain situations than others, so optimal adaptation in life is related to having more mature defenses, as well as flexibility in using them.

HISTORY

The phenomenon of defense mechanisms was not recognized until it was identified in the last decade of the 1800s by Sigmund Freud, the Austrian founder of psychoanalysis. Freud described defense mechanisms as discrete processes for managing emotion and instincts, but for more than twenty years, he interchangeably used the general term "defense" and the term for one specific defense mechanism, "repression," which resulted in considerable confusion among his readers. In 1936, Freud clarified that there were many defensive operations used by the ego and referred to a book his daughter, Anna Freud, a famous psychoanalyst in her own right, had just written, entitled *Das Ich und die Abwehrmechanismen* (1936; *The Ego and the Mechanisms of Defense*, 1937). Building on this work, other researchers have since described additional defense mechanisms and have elucidated their roles as adaptive processes.

ANXIETY

In his seminal work, Sigmund Freud focused primarily on defense mechanisms in their role of protecting the ego from anxiety resulting from internal conflicts. A conflict is caused when two or more equally powerful influences cannot be satisfied at the same time. It is resolved when one of the influences prevails, but this often leads to frustration because one or more of the other goals is thwarted. Most internal conflicts involve the interactions of the id, ego, and superego. For example, one may have a strong id impulse to overeat, but one's superego may exert an equally powerful influence to remain thin. Thus, the sight of food may cause one to feel anxious without knowing why, because this conflict may be buried in the unconscious.

Conflicts may be either conscious or unconscious; according to Freud, all conflicts are accompanied by anxiety. Anxiety is an unpleasant emotional response that signals impending danger. It is anticipation of danger to be experienced in the future. Only the ego can feel anxiety, and this anxiety can be unbearable. It can occur in the absence of any objective external threat; even when a real threat exists, the emotional reaction is often much greater than warranted. For example, speaking in front of an audience is, in the real sense, not dangerous, but it can cause extreme anxiety in some people. Frequently, the threat that causes anxiety is unconscious, and the person may not be aware of the source.

Anxiety is a signal to take action, so it is both adaptive and self-regulating. That is, when faced with anxiety, the ego automatically attempts to reduce it, which at the same time should reduce the potential danger. In this regard, fear and anxiety are similar. For example, if a person is attacked, the person can fight the attacker or run away. In both cases, the danger will be removed and the fear will subside. Since one of the main functions of the ego is to maintain survival, its typical response is to take actions that will protect itself and the organism. The ego responds in a defensive manner to all types of anxiety, no matter what their source. In the example above, the mode of reducing fear is overt—that is, it is easily observable whether the person fights or runs away. In other situations, the actions taken by the ego to protect itself are said to be covert, which means they are not directly observable. These covert actions of protecting the ego from anxiety are called ego defense mechanisms. According to Freud, they operate at an unconscious level.

REPRESSION

Freud was especially interested in the process of repression, which begins when the ego fully separates itself from the id but probably does not become fully operational until the phallic psychosexual stage of development. In repression, the ego blocks or diverts any ideas, thoughts, feelings, or urges that it finds unacceptable or anxiety producing. For example, a person might have a desire to have sex with his or her boss or teacher, but if this wish is totally unacceptable to the superego, it can be repressed into the unconscious. Allowing this wish to become conscious would result in punishment from the person's superego in the form of guilt, anxiety, or shame. To avoid this psychological response, the ego prevents the idea from ever becoming conscious. Although there is no memory of this impulse, it is never destroyed; in fact, it maintains all of its energy, remaining immediately under the level of awareness with the potential to surface at any time. Because of this, the person may feel ill at ease or anxious but has no awareness concerning the origin of this distress. Furthermore, the repressed energy continues to seek expression, and it often escapes in a disguised form.

The most important disguised forms of repressed material are neurotic symptoms. According to Freud, repressed energy must be released if the organism is to remain healthy. As the ego puts more and more effort into repressing unacceptable drives, it becomes weaker; sooner or later, something has to give in. Symptoms serve as a compromise, because they allow the repressed ideas to be expressed indirectly in a disguised form without arousing anxiety. The symptoms may be either psychological or physical. Physical symptoms are sometimes called conversion reactions because the energy associated with the original repressed idea is converted into physical symptoms such as paralysis or even blindness, which are attributable to psychological causes rather than any real organic impairment. Thus, Freud delineated the manner in which repression can become maladaptive and result in psychopathology, a conceptualization that was extremely innovative for its time.

Freud hit on the notion of repression when he noticed that his patients were resisting his attempts to help them. In this sense, repression is intimately linked to resistance. According to Freud, when he was using hypnosis to treat his patients, this resistance was hidden; however, as soon as the technique of free association replaced hypnosis, resistance was clearly evident, and psychoanalysis was born.

Freud's concept of repression (which he first called "defense") appeared in print in 1894. At that time, most of his patients were women who were suffering from an emotional disorder that was then called hysteria. Freud believed that hysteria was caused primarily by the repression of sexual impulses and that it could be cured by means of a "talking" therapy. At the time, it was a giant leap for psychology, because the prevailing viewpoint of the nineteenth century was that emotional disorders were caused by organic or physical factors. Freud's theory emphasized a psychological cause and cure for emotional disorders, opening a new area of exploration and setting the stage for clinical psychology and psychiatry.

POST-FREUDIAN THEORIES

Freud wrote about various defense mechanisms in a number of his works, but his daughter, Anna Freud, is credited with bringing them all together in her book *The Ego and the Mechanisms of Defense*. In it, she describes the original nine defense mechanisms—repression, regression, undoing, isolation, turning against self, reaction formation, reversal, projection, and introjection—and also adds sublimation and displacement. Over the years, other defense mechanisms, such as denial, rationalization, identification, intellectualization, and idealization, were added. New knowledge was added as well, including the importance of defense with regard to other emotions, such as anger, and the differences between defenses due to the ages at which they first develop, as seen in Joseph Sandler and Anna Freud's book *The Analysis of Defense: The Ego and the Mechanisms of Defense Revisited* (1985).

In 1977, George E. Vaillant, a professor of psychiatry at Harvard University, published *Adaptation to Life*, a landmark study on the mental health and adaptation of a highly select group of male college graduates over a thirty-five-year period of adulthood. In his book, Vaillant documents important shifts in defensive styles during adult development, and he also demonstrates that individual differences in the types of defenses used were dramatically related to variance between the best and worst outcomes, especially with regard to measures of social, occupational, and psychological adjustment. Vaillant believed that there were innumerable defenses, but he selected eighteen of what he thought were the most salient mechanisms and organized them into four levels according to their hypothesized maturity and importance with regard to the development of psychopathology:

- Level 1: Psychotic Mechanisms (delusional projection, denial of external reality, and distortion)
- Level 2: Immature Mechanisms (projection, schizoid fantasy or withdrawal, hypochondriasis, passive-aggressive behavior, and acting out)
- Level 3: Neurotic Defenses (intellectualization, repression, displacement, reaction formation, dissociation)
- Level 4: Mature Mechanisms (altruism, humor, suppression, anticipation, sublimation)

Level 1 defenses were noted as common in childhood prior to age five, in dreams of healthy individuals at all ages, and in psychotic types of psychopathology. Level 2 mechanisms were common in healthy children between the ages of three and fifteen and in some types of adult psychopathology, such as severe depression and personality disorders. Level 3 defenses were deemed common in healthy people of all ages after the age of three, in mastering acute adult stress, and in neurotic disorders. Level 4 defenses were listed as common in healthy individuals from age twelve on.

With regard to the study participants, Vaillant found that as adolescents, they were twice as likely to use immature defenses as mature ones, but by middle life, they were four times as likely to use mature defenses rather than immature ones. This developmental shift was not equally obtained by everyone, however. Rather, the thirty men with the best outcomes (termed "generative") had virtually stopped using immature mechanisms by midlife, with roughly equal use of neurotic and mature defenses.

The men with the worst outcomes (termed "perpetual boys"), on the other hand, failed to show any significant shift in defenses after adolescence. Thus, Vaillant demonstrated that ego development, including maturation of defense mechanisms, was distinct from physical maturation as well as from cognitive or intellectual development and that the level of defense maturation was directly related to life adjustment.

Vaillant was especially struck by the importance of suppression as an adaptive defense mechanism. He defined suppression as the conscious or subconscious decision to deliberately postpone attending to conscious conflicts or impulses without avoiding them. This mechanism allows individuals to effectively cope with stress when it is optimal to do so. Vaillant delineated the evolution of this defense as beginning with denial before age five, followed by repression from five to adolescence, with suppression emerging during late adolescence and adulthood when defense maturation is optimal.

Thus, Vaillant helped to better delineate the relationship between the healthy and adaptive need for ego defense mechanisms and the psychopathological outcomes that occur when they are used maladaptively. Moreover, he demonstrated that their development over time is part of the maturation process. Unfortunately, this study involved a highly select group of men and no women, so generalizations to the larger population are difficult to make.

APPLICATIONS OF DEFENSE MECHANISMS

In spite of the difficulty with generalization, the body of information regarding defenses underscores the importance of teaching children and adolescents to use increasingly mature mechanisms. Research has shown that this can be done effectively with social and emotional literacy programs, for example, in school classrooms. This application primarily involves prevention and has been growing in use since about 1990.

Applications regarding interventions with individuals showing maladaptive defense use, on the other hand, have been used much longer than prevention. Sigmund Freud developed psychoanalysis at the turn of the twentieth century with this in mind, and other forms of psychotherapy have since evolved that also embrace the importance of defense mechanisms in the development of psychopathology.

One example from psychoanalytic theory provides an illustration of how complex this topic really is. Freud believed that many neurotic symptoms are associated with the sex drive. For example, a man with an unusually strong superego may repress all sexual impulses. Through the process of reaction formation, these impulses may be converted into compulsive hand washing. According to psychoanalytic theory, the symptoms serve as a substitute for the sexual gratification that he is not allowed to obtain in real life. This is an unconscious process, and the man has no idea of the connection between the symptoms and his sex drive. When a person's behavior is dominated by defense mechanisms, or when symptoms become severe, there may be a need for psychotherapy. The goal of therapy is not to eliminate defense mechanisms but rather to strengthen the ego so that it uses more mature processes and can respond to conflicts in a more adaptive and productive manner.

One of the objectives of psychoanalytic therapy is to uncover repressed material that is responsible for the unconscious conflicts or symptoms, which in turn facilitate the development of suppression. In a sense, people relive their lives in the therapy room so the conflict can be traced to its origin. To help the patient do this, the psychoanalyst uses two major techniques within the important context of the therapeutic relationship. The first is called free association. This involves having the patient talk about anything and everything that enters his or her mind, no matter how trivial or embarrassing it may be. This technique is based on the idea that thoughts and ideas do not enter one's mind accidentally. There is usually an important reason for their appearance, and eventually thoughts that are related to the conflict are revealed. The second technique is interpretation, which can involve analyzing dreams, actions, feelings of the patient for the analyst, and so on. Freud was especially interested in dreams, the "royal road to the unconscious." During sleep, ego defense mechanisms are weakened; therefore, many unconscious conflicts or desires may emerge—although still in a disguised form that needs to be interpreted by the therapist.

Although brief interventions can sometimes help people cope better with life's stresses, therapy usually takes a long time, because maturation is generally a slow and complex process. Repression is especially difficult, because once material is repressed, the ego sets up a counterforce that prevents it from becoming conscious in the future. This counterforce is called resistance. It is responsible for a person unconsciously resisting treatment, as removing the symptoms only serves to return the ego to the original anxiety-producing conflict.

In the example above, once the resistance is overcome, the therapist may determine that the compulsive hand-washing behavior is rooted in an unresolved Oedipus complex. In this case, the man's sexual attraction to his mother was repressed, and eventually all sexual impulses were treated in the same way. Giving careful consideration to timing, the therapist voices an interpretation, which is the method by which the unconscious meaning of a person's thoughts, behaviors, or symptoms is divulged. One interpretation is not enough to cure the patient, but a slow process of "working through," which involves many interpretations and reinterpretations, finally leads to insight. This last step occurs when a person fully understands and accepts the unconscious meaning of his or her thoughts and behaviors; at this point, the symptoms often disappear.

EXAMPLES OF SELECTED DEFENSE MECHANISMS

Regression involves reducing anxiety or other strong feelings by attempting to return to an earlier and less stressful stage of development and engaging in the immature behavior or thinking characteristic of that stage. The most basic type of regression is sleep, which occupies most of the time of infants. For example, in response to an anxiety-producing test, a person might sleep through the alarm and thus miss the test (and avoid anxiety). Other examples of regression are a child engaging in thumb sucking when a new sibling is born and an adult engaging in smoking, both of which have their roots in the oral stage of infancy. Regression is one of the first defense mechanisms to emerge, beginning in the first year of life.

Projection is when one first represses one's own unacceptable or dangerous impulses, attitudes, or behaviors and then assigns them to other persons. For example, a person may blame others for his or her failures. Freud believed that this occurs unconsciously, but some modern psychoanalysts believe that it can occur consciously as well. An example would be a married man with an unconscious desire to have an affair accusing his wife of having done so.

Denial occurs when the ego does not acknowledge anxiety-producing reality. For example, a person may not "see" that his or her marriage is falling apart and may behave as if nothing is wrong; a good student may "forget" that he or she failed a test in school. A form of psychotic denial is the example of a woman who continued to sleep with her husband's corpse for several days after he had died.

Rationalization occurs when the ego tries to excuse itself logically from blame for unacceptable behaviors. For example, a student declares that he or she failed a test because roommates kept him or her up the night before, or a person gets drunk because he or she had such a "tough day" at the office.

Isolation is the process that separates unpleasant memories from emotions that were once connected to them. In this case, the ideas remain, but only in isolated form. For example, one might vividly remember a childhood situation of being spanked by one's father but not recall the intense negative feelings one had toward him at that time because such feelings would be painful. This defense mechanism probably begins to emerge in the anal psychosexual stage, but it fully develops between ages three and five.

Introjection is also called identification. It involves modeling or incorporating the qualities of another person, such as one's parents or teachers. Sometimes people do this with people that they fear; by doing so, the fear associated with them is reduced. Anna Freud calls this "identification with the aggressor." For example, little boys identify with their fathers to reduce the castration anxiety associated with the Oedipus complex. As a result, boys adopt the social, moral, and cultural values of the father, all of which become incorporated into the superego.

Reaction formation occurs when a person expresses a repressed unconscious impulse by its directly opposite behavior. Hate may be replaced by love, or attraction by repulsion. The original feeling is not lost, but it does not become conscious. For example, a reaction formation to strong sexual impulses may be celibacy, or a parent who unconsciously hates his or her child may "smother" it by being overly protective. Reaction formation is another defense mechanism that is closely related to repression.

Sublimation involves channeling the power of instincts and emotions into scientific or artistic endeavors such as writing books, building cities, doing research, or landing a person on the moon. Freud believed that sublimation was especially important for building culture and society.

SUMMARY

Defense mechanisms were initially discovered and studied in terms of their role in psychiatric symptom formation when used maladaptively. Unfortunately, this led many people to believe that defense mechanisms themselves were dysfunctional, which is not true. As Vaillant and others have shown, defenses are necessary for adaptation, survival, and happiness, but some are more effective for different stages of life than others, and maturational shifts in the development of ego defenses can have profound effects on social, emotional, and occupational adjustment.

On the positive side, Freud's conceptualization of defense mechanisms led directly to his formulation of psychoanalysis, which was the first major personality theory and treatment method in psychology. Virtually all personality theories and treatment methods since then have been directly or indirectly influenced by the notions of defense and resistance. In addition, the concept of defense mechanisms has become an important part of Western language and culture.

BIBLIOGRAPHY

Appignanesi, Richard. *Freud for Beginners.* Illus. Oscar Zarate. New York: Writer and Readers, 1994. Print.

Beresford, Thomas P. *Psychological Adaptive Mechanisms: Ego Defense Recognition in Practice and Research.* New York: Oxford UP, 2012. Print. Diehl, Manfred, et al. "Change in Coping and Defense Mechanisms across Adulthood: Longitudinal Findings in a Eurpoean American Sample." Developmental Psychology 50.2 (2014): 634–48. Print.

Freud, Anna. *The Ego and the Mechanisms of Defense.* New York: International UP, 1974. Print.

Freud, Sigmund. *The Standard Edition of the Complete Psychological Works of Sigmund Freud.* Ed. James Strachey. 24 vols. London: Hogarth, 1953–74. Print.

Metzger, Jesse A. "Adaptive Defense Mechanisms: Function and Transcendence." *Journal of Clinical Psychology* 70.5 (2014): 478–88. Print.

Perry, J. Christopher. "Anomalies and Specific Functions in the Clinical Identification of Defense Mechanisms." *Journal of Clinical Psychology* 70.5 (2014): 406–18. Print.

Sandler, Joseph, and Anna Freud. *The Analysis of Defense: The Ego and the Mechanisms of Defense Revisited.* New York: International UP, 1985. Print.

Thurschwell, Pam. *Sigmund Freud.* 2nd ed. London: Routledge, 2009. Print.

Vaillant, George E. *Adaptation to Life: How the Best and the Brightest Came of Age.* Cambridge: Harvard UP, 1985. Print.

Salvatore Cullari; updated by Carol A. Kusché

SEE ALSO: Abnormality: Psychological models; Anxiety disorders; Consciousness; Defense mechanisms; Dreams; Ego, superego, and id; Psychoanalysis; Psychoanalytic psychology; Psychoanalytic psychology and personality: Sigmund Freud; Psychosexual development.

Ego psychology
Erik H. Erikson

DATE: Late 1930s forward
TYPE OF PSYCHOLOGY: Personality

Ego psychology, pioneered by Heinz Hartmann, Erik H. Erikson, Erich Fromm, Harry Stack Sullivan, and Karen Horney, provided a significant new reformation to the personality theory of Freudian psychoanalysis. Erikson's theory of the growth of the ego throughout the life cycle provided an especially important contribution to this movement.

KEY CONCEPTS
- Ego
- Id
- Psychoanalysis
- Psychosocial
- Unconcious

INTRODUCTION

Ego psychology emerged in the late 1930s as a reform movement within psychoanalysis. Psychoanalysis, as developed by Sigmund Freud in the previous three decades, was an innovative approach to understanding psychological life. Freud developed the methodology and vocabulary to focus on the meaningfulness of lived experience. For Freud, the true meaning of an experience was largely unconscious. Dreams, slips of the tongue or pen, and symptoms provided examples of such unconscious layers of meaning. In psychoanalytic terminology, beneath the level of the conscious ego, there is an unconscious substructure (the id). Freud used the metaphor of an iceberg to relate these two levels, indicating that the conscious level is analogous to the small, visible tip of an iceberg that shows above the water, whereas the unconscious level is like its large, underwater, invisible mass. The ego, this small surface level of the personality, "manages" one's relations with the world beyond the psyche. The id, in contrast, is "intrapsychic" in the sense that it is not in a relation with the "outer" world beyond the psyche. Rather, the id draws its energy from the biological energy of the instinctual body (such as instincts for sex and aggression). In this traditional psychoanalytic theory, then, the conscious level of the person is rooted in, and motivated by, an unconscious level, as psychological life is ultimately rooted in biological forces.

Freudian psychoanalysis advanced psychology by legitimating the study of the meaningfulness of human actions, but it did so at the price of conceiving of conscious, worldly experience as being only a surface, subtended by unconscious, biological forces, mechanisms cut off from worldly involvement. By the late 1930s, some psychoanalysts had concluded this was too steep a price to pay. The first to formulate these objections systematically was Heinz Hartmann, whose writings between 1939 and 1950 advanced the argument for the autonomy of the ego as a structure of the personality independent of the domination of the unconscious id. It was Hartmann who gave to this protest movement the name "ego psychology."

In the next generation of analysts, this movement found its most articulate voices: Erich Fromm, Harry Stack Sullivan, Karen Horney, and Erik H. Erikson. Writing from the 1940's through the 1980's, all contributed independently, with their own particular genius, to a perspective that grants to the ego a status much more significant than its role in Freudian psychoanalysis. For them, it is people's relations with the world (and not their subterranean biological energy) that is the most important aspect of their psychological life. For this reason, these psychologists have also sometimes been known as the "social" or "interpersonal" analysts. While all four have unquestionably earned their enduring international reputations, Erikson became the most well known, on account of his formulation of a powerful and comprehensive developmental theory to account for the growth of the ego throughout life. Freud had asserted that the ego was a weak aspect of the personality, whereas Hartmann posited a strong ego. However, there are wide individual differences in ego strength. Erikson demonstrated how ego strength emerges across stages of a person's development and showed that its particular growth depends on the quality, at each stage, of a person's relations with the world and with other people.

ERIKSON'S SHIFT TO THE PSYCHOSOCIAL LEVEL

Freud had also sketched a developmental theory for psychoanalysis. Built on his view of the primacy of the intrapsychic id and its bodily source of energy, this theory focused on psychosexual development. For Freud, "sexual" means more than the usual notion of genital sexuality; it is a more general dynamic expression of bodily energy that manifests itself in different forms at different developmental stages. The adult (genital) stage of sexuality, reached at puberty, is the culmination and completion of one's psychosexual development. Preceding that development, Freud saw four pregenital stages of psychosexual development: the oral stage, the anal stage, the phallic stage, and the latency stage. Hence, for this theory of psychosexual development, each stage is centralized as a stage by a particular expression of sexual or erogenous energy. In each stage there is a particular mode of the bodying forth of this energy as desire, manifested by the unique bodily zone that becomes the erogenous zone of that specific stage. It is seen as erogenous because of that bodily zone's capacity to be especially susceptible to stimulation or arousal, such that it becomes the prime source of bodily satisfaction and pleasure at that stage.

Erikson concluded that this psychosexual level was a valid but incomplete portrait of development. More than other proponents of ego psychology, he sought to work with Freud's emphasis on the bodily zones while striving to include that vision within a larger, more encompassing framework. Erikson theorized that each bodily mode correlated with a psychological modality, one that implicated the person's developing ego relations with the world. In particular, he emphasized one's relations with other people as the most important "profile" of the world. He saw the psychosexual meaning of the various bodily zones grounded by changes in the person's social existence at each stage. For that reason, Erikson named his approach a theory of psychosocial development and argued that the growth of the ego could not be reduced to changes in bodily energies. He demonstrated how the psychosexual dimension always implied a key human relation at the heart of each stage, and so the interpersonal could not be reduced to some intrapsychic cause but was itself the basis for the actual development of that stage.

The significance of this shift from the psychosexual level of development to the psychosocial one was enormous, but it can best be appreciated in the context of its depiction of each of the particular stages. One other impact was also strikingly noteworthy. Whereas Freud's theory of psychosexual development saw the process as coming to an end with the person's arrival at the genital stage (with puberty), Erikson realized that the growth of the ego in psychosocial development does not end there but continues in subsequent stages throughout the person's life. In that way, he also transformed developmental psychology from its origins as merely a child psychology into a truly life-span psychology, a revision that became widely accepted.

STAGES OF DEVELOPMENT

Erikson specified eight stages of psychosocial development over the course of the life cycle. He saw these unfolding not in a linear sense but epigenetically, that is, in such a way that each stage builds on those that came before. The first four of these stages are those of childhood, and here Erikson accepts Freud's delineation but adds a psychosocial dimension to each.

The first stage of development (roughly the first year of life) Freud termed the oral stage, naming it (as he did with each) after that region of the body seen to be the erogenous zone of that stage. For Freud, the baby's psychosexuality expresses itself primarily through the erogenous power of the mouth and lips. Certainly babies' tendency to mouth almost anything they can get hold of would indicate a certain erotic appeal of orality at this time.

However, for Erikson, this bodily expression is not the foundational one. Rather, orality is a wider theme. The essence of this oral pleasure is the satisfaction of "taking in" the world. Such taking in is not restricted to the mouth. Babies take in with their eyes, their ears, their fingers—in every way possible. Orality, as taking in, is not merely a bodily zone, but a psychological modality of relating to the world. This world-relation also implicates another person. For a quite helpless baby to be able to get or take in, there must be another there giving (typically a parent). This psychological modality, in other words, is already essentially and profoundly interpersonal. As a result, it is the quality of this interpersonal relationship with the "mothering ones" that will provide the basis of the baby's growth at this stage. If the parents (as the face of the world) are dependably there for the baby, the baby will come to be able to count on their omnipresent beneficence.

With such experience, the baby develops a sense of "basic trust"—Erikson's term for the ego growth of this first stage. Basic trust implies a certain relation with the world: specifically, one in which the person can relax and take his or her own ongoingness for granted. Once trust is gained, such a person can face the uncertainties to come with the secure confidence that, whatever may happen, he or she will be fine. In contrast, if the baby does not encounter a trustworthy world at this stage, he or she will be unable to develop this core sense of basic trust. The baby will, instead, be overwhelmed by the experience of "basic mistrust"—the anxiety that accompanies the lurking, ever-present possibility of threat, that edge of anonymous malevolence. Then, full openness to the world is always constricted by the need for the self-preservation of the ego.

Freud identified the second psychosexual stage (roughly the period from age one to three) as the anal stage, on account of the pleasure available by the new ability of the child to control eliminative functioning—what is colloquially called toilet training. Here again Erikson reexamined this bodily mode and discovered, at the heart of it, a psychosocial dynamic. The issue of control in mastering the processes of elimination involves two kinds of action: retention (of feces or urine) until one gets to the toilet and then elimination (once one is at the toilet).

Erikson recognized that this interplay between retention and elimination is more than merely the organ mode of sphincter control. Rather, it manifests a more basic psychological modality: the interplay between holding on and letting go. It is not only with regard to the eliminative functions that this dynamic gets played out in this stage. Most important, it is in the social arena, with one's parents, that toddlers grow this new capacity to exercise control. Even toilet training itself is an exquisitely interpersonal interaction of the child with the parental "trainers."

It is not only toilet training that distinguishes children's quest for control at this stage. In many ways the child is now striving for a new encounter with others. Securely grounded now by the sense of basic trust gained in the previous stage, children are ready to move from a relationship of dependence to one of independence. Even being able to stand up on their own two feet evinces this new relationship. From a newfound delight in the power of speaking the word "no!" to the appearance of strong preferences in everything from clothes to food, and most evidently in their emotional reactions to the denial of these preferences, toddlers are asserting a declaration of independence. Though the consequent contest of wills with the parents can be difficult, ultimately the child learns both to have autonomy and to recognize its social limits. This growth of autonomy is the key gain of this second stage, as the ego grasps its radical independence from the minds or control of others. If the child does not have the opportunity to develop this experience, the consequence would be to develop a crippling sense of shame and self-doubt instead.

The third stage of psychosexual development (ages three through six) is Freud's phallic stage, because the child's sexual organs become the erogenous zone at this time. Freud did not mean to imply that children experience their sexuality in the sense of adult, genital sexuality; there is no experience of orgasms and no interest in intercourse at this time. Rather, for Freud, the sex organs become erogenous on account of their power to differentiate gender. Hence, the classic psychoanalytic themes of penis envy and castration anxiety are rooted in this stage, as well as the Oedipal conflict—children's imaginal working out of their now gender-based relations with their parents.

For Erikson, it is not the genitals as bodily organs that are the source of such anxiety or envy. Rather, they symbolize social roles. As a result, in a sexist culture, it would be no wonder that a girl may envy the greater psychosocial status enjoyed by the boy. Correlatively, the boy would experience the anxiety of losing his newfound gender-based potency. Here again, Erikson finds a profound interpersonal dynamic at work. This new positing of oneself is not done only in the child's fantasy life. The ego at this stage is growing new capacities to engage the world: the ability to use language, more fine locomotor activity, and the power of the imagination. Through these developing capacities, children can thrust themselves forth with a new sense of purpose. On the secure basis of trust and autonomy, they can now include initiative in their world relations, supported by their parents as encouraging prototypes. On the other hand, the parents can so stigmatize such projects of initiative that children may instead become convinced that they manifest their badness. In such cases, feelings of guilt can overwhelm their sense of initiative, as they become crippled by guilt not only for what they have done but also for who they are as initiating beings.

Freud identified the fourth psychosexual stage as the latency stage (ages seven to twelve) because psychosexuality was not manifest at that time. It had become latent, or driven underground, by the conclusion of the Oedipal conflict. For Freud, psychosexual development is arrested at this stage and must await the eruption of puberty to get it started again. Erikson sees in this stage a positive growth in the child's ego. Once more, changes in psychosocial relations lead the way. The child goes off to school, and to a wider world beyond the immediate family circle, to encounter the world beyond the imaginal realm: a place in which actual accomplishments await the application of actual skills. Rather than being satisfied with imagining hitting a home run, the child now strives to actually hit the ball. It is, in other words, a time for the development of skills, techniques, and competencies that will enable one to succeed at real-world events. Sports, games, school, bicycling, camping, collecting things, taking care of pets, art, music, even doing chores now offer children arenas to test their growing capacity to learn the ways of the world.

At the heart of this learning process are teachers, not only professionals but also learned others of many kinds. The child becomes a student to many experts, from coaches to Cub Scout leaders to the older boy next door who already knows about computers. Even sports heroes or characters in books, with whom the child has no personal contact, can emerge as profoundly valuable teachers, opening the world and showing the way to mastery of it. This is what Erikson means by a sense of industry, which is for him the key egoic gain of this stage. If children's efforts are not encouraged and cultivated, however, they can instead find their industrious tendency overwhelmed by a sense of inferiority and inadequacy.

PSYCHOSOCIAL STAGES OF LATER CHILDHOOD

It is when the child arrives at Freud's fifth stage that the psychosexual and psychosocial theories must part from their previous chronological company. Freud's fifth stage is the genital stage: the completion of psychosexual development. With puberty, the person attains the same capacities and erogenous orientation as an adult and thus becomes as mature, psychosexually speaking, as any adult. For Erikson's theory, however, the onset of puberty does not mark the completion of psychosocial development, which continues throughout life, but only its next stage: adolescence (ages twelve to twenty-one). Once more, the changing bodily zone implicates a changing social existence, for puberty is more than a merely chemical or hormonal change. More than the body, it is the whole person who is transformed by this flood of new issues and possibilities. This eruption provokes questions that had been taken for granted before. "Who am I becoming? Who am I to be?" appear, in small and large ways. The new adolescent must confront such new questions when on a date, at a party, or even when deciding what to wear to school that day. In other words, the adolescent ego has now developed a self-reflective loop, in which its own identity is now taken as an issue to be formed, a task that it must resolve for itself.

The formation of ego-identity can be an especially acute challenge in contemporary culture, where the traditional embeddedness in extended families and communities is too often no longer available to provide the network of identifications with which to resolve these questions. Instead, adolescent peer groups become the key psychosocial relationship for this stage. These reference groups offer the adolescent the prospect of trying on a new identity by embracing certain subgroup values, norms, and perspectives. This experimental phase is an acting "as if"—as if the person were who he or she is trying to be.

Optimally, adolescents will have the latitude to assume and discard prospective identities within the fluidity of what Erikson called a psychosocial moratorium—a time-out from having to bear the same weight of consequences for their choices that an adult would. For example, a girl pledging a lifetime commitment to a boyfriend at thirteen does not in fact entail the same level of commitment that a marriage would; nor does deciding to major in accounting on arriving at college actually bind one to follow through with a lifetime career as an accountant. With sufficient opportunity to explore and try out various tentative choices, adolescents will, optimally, conclude this stage by arriving at a more clarified sense of their own values and sense of direction. If this is not achieved, adolescents will either be left with a feeling of identity diffusion or have prematurely foreclosed on a possible identity that does not fit.

PSYCHOSOCIAL STAGES OF ADULTHOOD

Beyond adolescence, Erikson also identified three psychosocial stages of adulthood: early adulthood, middle age, and old age. The first, roughly the period of one's twenties and thirties, begins with the person's moving out from under the insulating protection of the adolescent psychosocial moratorium. One's choices (of marriage, career, family) cease to be "as if"; they are now profoundly real commitments with long-term impact. Making such commitments is not only a momentary event (such as saying "I do") but also requires devoting oneself to living an ongoing and open-ended history. This new situation inaugurates the next psychosocial development, which Erikson names the crisis of intimacy versus isolation. Intimacy here has a broader range than its typical connotation of sexual relations: It encompasses the capacity to relate to another with fullness and mutuality. To be fully open with and to another person entails obvious risks—of being misunderstood or rejected—but with it comes the enormous gain of true love. To experience the closeness, sharing, and valuing of the other without boundaries is the hallmark of an infinite relationship (infinite, that is, not necessarily in duration but in depth). The relationship with a loved other is the evident psychosocial context of this growth. If it does not occur, then the early adult will come to experience instead a deep sense of isolation and loneliness. This consequence can accrue either through the failure to enter into a relationship or through the failure, within a relationship, to achieve intimacy. Some of the most terrible afflictions of isolation at this stage are within those marriages so lacking in intimacy that the couple are essentially isolated even though living together.

Beginning around age forty, a further stage of adult psychosocial development begins: middle age. The situation has once again changed. People are no longer merely starting out on their adulthood but have by now achieved a place in the adult world. Typically, if they are going to have a family, they have got it by now; if a career, they are well launched by now. Indeed, middle age, the period from forty to sixty-five, marks the attainment of the height of a person's worldly powers and responsibilities. Whatever worldly mountain one is going to climb in this lifetime, it is during middle age that one gets as high up it as one will go. The arrival at this new position opens the door to the next stage of development. Now the psychosocial growth will involve one's social relations with the next generation, centered on the issue of generativity versus stagnation. The long plateau of middle age offers the opportunity to become helpful to those who follow that upward climb. These are, most immediately, one's own children, but they also include the next generation in the community, on the job, in the profession, in the whole human family. The middle-aged adult is in the position of being the teacher, the mentor, the instituter, the creator, the producer—the generator. Having arrived at the peak of one's own mountain one no longer need be so concerned about placating someone else and so is able now to fully be oneself. To be an original, the middle-aged adult can also originate in the truest sense: to give of oneself to those who, following along behind, need that help. In this way, the person grows the specific ego-strength of care: an extending of oneself to others in an asymmetric way, giving without expectation of an equal return, precisely because one can. The failure to grow in this way results in stagnation—the disillusioned boredom of a life going nowhere. Some middle-aged adults, trying futilely to ward off this gnawing feeling of stagnation, hide behind desperate efforts of self-absorption, what Erikson called "treating oneself as one's one and only child."

By the late sixties, a variety of changes mark the onset of the final stage of psychosocial development: old age. Retirement, becoming a grandparent, declining health, and even the increasingly frequent death of one's own age-mates, all precipitate a new issue into the forefront: one's own mortality. While people at every age know they are mortal, this knowledge has no particular impact on one's life when one is younger because it is then so easily overlooked. In contrast, by old age, this knowledge of one's mortality is now woven into the very fabric of one's everyday life, in a way that it can no longer be evaded by imagining it postponed until some distant, abstract future.

Contemporary American society tends to avoid really confronting one's being-toward-death. Some psychologists have gone so far as to say that death has replaced sex as the primary cultural taboo, hidden in hospital rooms and code words ("passed on," "put to sleep," "expired"). Fearing death, people find it hard to grow old. If one is not available to the growth opportunities of this stage, one is likely to sink instead into despair—a feeling of regret over a life not lived. Often even one's despair cannot be faced and is then hidden beneath feelings of disgust and bitterness: a self-contempt turned outward against the world.

Erikson points out that this final stage of life offers the opportunity for the ultimate growth of the ego. To embrace one's mortality fully allows one to stand open-eyed at the edge of one's life, a perspective from which it becomes possible to really see one's life as a whole. One can then see, and own, one's life as one's own responsibility, admitting of no substitutes. It is this holistic vision of one's life that Erikson calls integrity: the full integration of the personality. It is in this vision that people can actually realize that their own lives are also integrated with life as a whole, in a seamless web of interconnections. Thus, the ego finally finds its ultimate, transpersonal home within the whole of being. It is this perspective that opens the door to wisdom, the final growth.

BIBLIOGRAPHY

Burston, Daniel. *Erik Erikson and the American Psyche: Ego, Ethics, and Evolution.* Lanham: Aronson, 2007. Print.

Coles, Robert. Erik H. *Erikson: The Growth of His Work.* New York: Da Capo, 1987. Print.

Coles, Robert, ed. *The Erik Erikson Reader.* New York: Norton, 2001. Print.

Erikson, Erik H. *Childhood and Society.* Rev. ed. New York: Norton, 1995. Print.

Erikson, Erik H. *Gandhi's Truth.* New York: Norton, 1993. Print.

Erikson, Erik H. *Identity and the Life Cycle.* New York: Norton, 1980. Print.

Erikson, Erik H. *The Life Cycle Completed.* Extended version. New York: Norton, 1998. Print.

Friedman, Lawrence. *Identity's Architect: A Biography of Erik H. Erikson.* Cambridge: Harvard UP, 2000. Print.

Hartmann, Heinz. *Essays on Ego Psychology.* New York: International UP, 1965. Print.

Stevens, Richard. *Erik Erikson: Exploring the Life Cycle, Identity, and Psychohistory.* New York: Macmillan, 2008. Print.

Yankelovich, Daniel, and William Barrett. *Ego and Instinct.* New York: Vintage, 1971. Print.

Christopher M. Aanstoos

See Also: Defense mechanisms; Developmental psychology; Ego defense mechanisms; Ego, superego, and id; Erikson, Erik H.; Oedipus complex; Penis envy; Personality theory; Psychoanalytic psychology; Psychoanalytic psychology and personality: Sigmund Freud; Psychosexual development.

Ego, superego, and id

Type of psychology: Personality

The ego, superego, and id are the three components of personality structure, according to Sigmund Freud. These hypothetical, interacting structures are used to explain human behavior.

Key Concepts

- Conscience
- Instincts
- Introjection
- Pleasure principle
- Primary process
- Reality principle
- Secondary process

INTRODUCTION

The ego, superego, and id are terms used by the father of psychoanalysis, Austrian Sigmund Freud, personality theory to describe the three components in the structural model of personality. He developed and wrote about this model in his classic work *Das Ich und das Es* (1923; *The Ego and the Id*, 1926).

Prior to the structural model, Freud's focus was on understanding and differentiating conscious and unconscious processes. He came to realize that an additional model was needed to further elucidate the working of the mind and to describe the special functions that parts of the mind utilize. The structural model is not a replacement for his topographical model (unconscious and conscious), but rather it complements his previous work.

Freud's structural model proposes that the personality has a definite structure, with three interacting components called the id, ego, and superego. The id is present from birth and is essentially a psychical representation of instincts or passions. The ego represents reason and thoughtful deliberation, while the superego represents the morals of society and ideal aspirations. These components are hypothetical and are not located in a specific region of the brain. Since Freud's initial background and work were biologically based, this represented a major shift toward a more psychological understanding of human behavior.

ID

The id is present at birth, is totally unconscious, and contains everything inherited at birth, especially the innate instincts or impulses. The purpose of the id is to satisfy one's innate urges. Freud theorized that the id operates according to the pleasure principle, seeking immediate gratification of wishes and a reduction of pain and tension. Since the id is infantile and primitive by nature, it attempts to satisfy its desires by what Freud termed primary process. This means that the id is illogical, asocial, impulsive, and demanding. Primary process means that there is action or discharge without thought or delay. There is no consideration of reality or the needs of others.

The id is instinctual and the source of all energy and passions. Freud proposed two classes of instincts: the sexual instincts, or eros, and the destructive instincts, or thanatos. Eros includes humans' drives for self-preservation and the preservation of the species through sexuality. These instincts are life affirming, seeking development and renewal. In direct contrast, thanatos opposes life and seeks to bring about death and destruction. Freud viewed the death instinct (thanatos) as a desire to return to an earlier, inorganic state with an absence of undesired stimulation. Both classes of instincts can be directed inward toward the self or outward toward others. Eros and thanatos are typically fused (combined) together, thus modifying the potential destructiveness of thanatos.

EGO

The ego, according to Freud, is the component of the mind that is able to adapt to the demands of the external environment. The ego develops from the id and learns about the external world through the senses. As the child interacts with the world, the ego gains important perceptual and cognitive abilities.

Freud proposed that the ego operates according to the reality principle, replacing the id's uninhibited search for gratification with thoughts and behaviors that take into account the conditions of real life and the needs of others. The ego uses a secondary process, a higher level of mental functioning, including intelligent reasoning and problem-solving skills, to mediate between the demands of the id, superego, and external reality. The ego therefore functions as the executive component of personality structure. The ego exercises delay and restraint in meeting the unrealistic demands of the id's impulses. It considers how pleasure can be obtained without bringing harm to the self or others.

The metaphor of a horse and rider was used by Freud to describe the relationship between the ego and the id. The horse represents the power and strength of the id, while the rider (ego) attempts to guide the horse in an appropriate direction.

After Freud's death, his daughter Anna and others focused their study on ego functioning in the personality. Ego psychology is a term used to describe the study of the ego and its role in adaptation and development.

SUPEREGO

Freud used the term superego, commonly referred to as conscience, to describe the third component of personality structure. The conscience is formed by the moral influences of parents and society, including rules and standards of conduct. It serves as the judge of what is right and wrong and can be quite harsh and perfectionistic.

The superego develops as children identify with parents and authority figures. Freud believed that the superego forms by an introjection (a process of taking inside or incorporating) of the values of the parents. It is interesting to note that this concept served as precursor to object relations theorists, who pay close attention to relationships between internal objects and external relationships. The superego, as an internal object, takes over the initial role of the parents by giving the ego orders, judging, and threatening it with punishments. Guilt feelings result when behavior does not live up to the expectations of the superego.

INTEGRATION OF ID, EGO, AND SUPEREGO

Freud theorized there would always be some conflict between the urges of the id, the morality of the superego, and the pressures of reality. The ego, as mediator, strives to fulfill the id impulses in a reasonable way while conforming to the superego's moral standards. Impulsive, reckless behavior results when the id is too dominant, whereas a dominant superego leads to a loss of normal pleasure as impulses are too restricted.

BIBLIOGRAPHY

Brenner, Charles. *An Elementary Textbook of Psychoanalysis*. Rev. ed. New York: Anchor, 1994. Print.

Diamond, Michael J., and Christopher Christian. *The Second Century of Psychoanalysis: Evolving Perspectives on Therapeutic Action*. London: Karnac, 2011. Print.

Elisha, Perrin. *The Conscious Body: A Psychoanalytic Exploration of the Body in Therapy.* Washington: American Psychological Association, 2011. Print.

Freud, Sigmund. *The Ego and the Id*. LaVergne: Pacific, 2011. Print.

Gay, Peter. *Freud: A Life for Our Time*. New York: Norton, 2006. Print.

Greenberg, Jay R., and Stephen A. Mitchell. *Object Relations in Psychoanalytic Theory.* Cambridge: Harvard UP, 2003. Print.

Webster, Jamieson. *The Life and Death of Psychoanalysis: On Unconscious Desire and Its Sublimation*. London: Karmac, 2011. Print.

Joanne Hedgespeth

See Also: Defense mechanisms; Denial; Ego defense mechanisms; Ego psychology: Erik H. Erikson; Emotions; Freud, Sigmund; Freudian psychology; Moral development; Oedipus complex; Penis envy; Personality theory; Psychoanalytic psychology and personality: Sigmund Freud; Psychosexual development; Self; Women's psychology: Sigmund Freud.

Elder abuse

Date: 1970s forward
Type of psychology: Biological bases of behavior; Cognition; Developmental psychology; Emotion; Psychopathology; Social psychology; Stress

With the increase in the geriatric population of the United States, elder abuse is a growing public health concern. Therefore, increased awareness of elder abuse, identification of its signs and symptoms, and prevention initiatives are imperative.

Key Concepts

- Caregiver neglect
- Emotional and psychological abuse
- Financial abuse
- Physical abuse
- Self-neglect
- Sexual abuse

INTRODUCTION

Elder abuse is the physical, emotional, or psychological injury or risk of injury; financial exploitation; or neglect in providing basic needs of an older adult. Although there is no universally accepted definition of old age, generally sixty or sixty-five years is considered the beginning of old age. Older Americans are the fastest growing population in the United States. According to the US Census Bureau, individuals sixty-five years of age and older made up more than 13 percent of the US population in 2012; that number is expected to increase to more than 20 percent by 2050, according to estimates by the US Department of Health and Human Services' Administration on Aging. As more responsibility is placed on family members to care for aging relatives, elder abuse is likely to increase as well.

Elder abuse usually constitutes repetitive acts of commission or omission that threaten the health and welfare of an older adult. Elder abuse does not receive the same recognition as child abuse and spousal violence and is often underreported or not reported at all. As such, the number of abused elders is probably highly underestimated. Victims often do not report abuse because they are embarrassed, fearful of repercussions by their caregivers, and likely to harbor feelings of guilt if they report their only source of shelter, support, and care.

Because so few people report elder abuse, it is important for health care providers to identify and know their obligations to report such abuse. In 1981, Congress proposed legislation to establish a national center on elder abuse, but the bill never reached the floor of Congress. In 1989, it was reintroduced as an amendment to the Older Americans Act, and elder abuse was finally recognized in federal legislation.

TYPES OF ABUSE

Physical abuse is the deliberate infliction of physical pain or injury. Examples include slapping, punching, bruising, or restraining. Psychological abuse is the infliction of mental or emotional anguish. Examples include verbal insults, humiliation, or threats. Financial exploitation is using the resources of an elderly person without consent. Examples include writing checks without permission and stealing money. Neglect is failure of a caretaker to provide basic needs to prevent physical harm, mental anguish, or illness. Examples include withholding nourishment, ignoring cleanliness, and neglecting physical needs. Self-neglect occurs when an elderly person compromises his or her health and safety by refusing assistance in care. Examples include refusing to eat and refusing needed medications. Sexual abuse is any unwanted sexual behavior. Examples include inappropriate touching and rape.

POSSIBLE CAUSES

Risks for elder abuse are divided into four major categories: physical and mental impairment of the victim, caregiver stress, transgenerational violence, and abuser psychopathology. Impairment of a dependent elder and a family history of violence and substance abuse are also identified as causes for elder abuse.

Though studies do not relate the victim's level of frailty to abuse, physical and mental impairment indirectly increase the risk of abuse because the victims are unable to leave an abusive environment or effectively defend themselves.

Caregiver stress may result in acting out anger toward the elderly person. Stress factors contributing to such outbursts may be related to the victim as well as to the caregiver and include alcohol or drug abuse, employment issues, low income, increased risk of falls, incontinence, verbal or physical aggression, and poor caregiving skills caused by a lack of knowledge about how to care for the elderly.

Transgenerational violence supports the premise that abuse is a learned behavior passed between generations. As such, a child who was abused by a parent may be abusive to the parent on becoming the caregiver. Domestic violence can persist throughout the life span and does not necessarily stop in old age.

Abuser psychopathology relates elder abuse to substance abuse and addiction, personality and mental disorders, and dementia. Risk factors for elder abuse as identified by the American Medical Association include living with the abuser, dementia, social isolation, and mental illness as well as alcohol or drug use by the caregiver. Other theories that have been used to explain elder abuse are exchange theory, which proposes dependencies between a victim and a perpetrator related to reactions and responses that continue into adulthood; social learning theory, which proposes that abuse is learned; and political economic theory, which proposes that the challenges faced by elders leave them in poverty and take away their importance in community life. Political economic theory addresses the marginalization of elders in society.

PREVENTION

Every state in the United States defines elder abuse, has passed elder abuse prevention laws, and employs some form of an elder abuse reporting system. Unfortunately, laws and the definition of abuse are inconsistent among states. Adult Protective Services (APS) are available in every state but provide assistance only when the victim agrees or is rendered mentally incapable to make decisions by the courts. Education about what constitutes abuse and neglect needs to be clear. Additionally, an understanding that abusive behavior in any form is never acceptable needs to be established. Finally, information about counseling for caregivers should be available so they know that services and support exist for them when they require it. Educating the public and raising public awareness of the extent of elder abuse are effective ways to prevent elder abuse. Increased social services to provide support for caregivers, respite care and counseling for family, and information about social issues that are triggers for abuse can be instrumental in preventing abuse. Developing an understanding of the risk factors for elder abuse and its signs and symptoms are also crucial in preventing cases of elder abuse.

Psychology Today offers some tips for older adults to keep them safe from abuse. These tips include maintaining a social life, remaining in touch with friends after moving in with a relative, asking a friend to check in weekly, and inviting friends to visit often. Older adults are also encouraged to make new friends and participate in community activities. They should check their own mail, report instances in which mail is intercepted, and have their own telephones. They should keep track of their belongings and make others aware that they know where everything should be. Older adults should attend to their personal needs as much as possible and keep appointments with doctors and dentists and other planned activities. They should maintain financial control and have Social Security or pension checks deposited directly to a personal bank account. Older adults should obtain legal advice about possible future disability, wills, property, powers of attorney, guardianships, or conservatorships. They should keep records, accounts, and property available for trusted people to manage affairs when they no longer can. They should not live with a person who exhibits violent behavior or alcohol or drug abuse. They should not leave their homes unattended for lengths of time or leave signs that they are not home, such as notes on the door. Instead, they should notify the police when they will be away. Older adults should not leave cash, jewelry, or other valuables in nonsecure locations. They should not accept personal care in return for the transfer or assignments of property unless a lawyer, advocate, or trusted person acts as a witness. They should not sign documents unless someone they trust has reviewed it and should not allow anyone to keep details of their finances or property management from them.

DIAGNOSIS AND SCREENING

Elder abuse often goes undetected because its signs and symptoms may be missed or victims may deny that injuries are a result of abuse. Symptoms may be mistaken for dementia, or caregivers may explain them to others in that way. Because elder abuse can present itself in many different ways, injuries must be evaluated based on the victim's general health and psychosocial environment. If elder abuse is diagnosed, then the victim's safety must be ensured while respecting his or her autonomy and independence. Some alerts for suspected abuse include bruises and lacerations; broken or fractured bones, untreated injuries in various stages of healing; sprains, dislocations, and internal injuries; medication overdoses or underutilization of prescribed drugs; a victim's report of being hit, kicked, or mistreated; a sudden change in behavior, such as agitation, depression, or withdrawal; dehydration or malnutrition; untreated bedsores and poor hygiene; untreated health problems; unsafe or unclean living conditions; and a caregiver's refusal of visitors.

Besides the physical signs of abuse, there are a variety of assessment tools for screening for elder abuse. Health care providers should screen patients who are sixty years of age and older for abuse at least annually. Some questions that the American Medical Association suggests should be asked are the following:

Has anyone at home ever hurt you?

Has anyone ever touched you without your consent?

Has anyone taken anything that was yours without asking?

Has anyone ever threatened you?

Have you ever signed any documents that you didn't understand or you didn't want to sign?

Are you afraid of anyone at home?

Are you alone a lot?

Has anyone ever failed to help you take care of yourself when you needed help?

REPORTING ABUSE

Area Agency on Aging, the county Department of Social Services, and Adult Protective Services are agencies that investigate elder abuse and neglect. State ombudsman's offices are instrumental in investigating and identifying elder abuse in long-term-care facilities. Once abuse or neglect is confirmed, protection services are mobilized. If the victim is mentally competent, then the victim must agree to accept the assistance. Alternately, the victim must be deemed by the courts to be mentally incapable of making decisions before assistance is mobilized.

All people share responsibility for reporting suspected cases of elder abuse. Professionals such as social workers, police officers, teachers, physicians, nurses, and those who provide services to the elderly are required by law to report suspected cases of elder abuse. One resource for reporting is the Eldercare Locator Hotline at (800) 677-1116. Calls are directed to a local agency for assistance. If 911 is called for suspected elder abuse, then the local police will intervene.

BIBLIOGRAPHY

"Elder abuse." *HelpGuide.org*. http://www.helpguide.org/mental/.

"Elder or dependent abuse." *Psychology Today*. http://www.psychologytoday.com/conditions/.

Hall, Barbara, and Terry Scragg, eds. *Social Work with Older People: Approaches to Person-Centered Practice*. New York: McGraw-Hill, 2012. Print.

Heath, J. M., F. A. Kobylarz, and M. Brown. "Interventions from Home-Based Geriatric Assessments of Adult Protective Service Clients Suffering Elder Mistreatment." *Journal of American Geriatric Society* 53 (2005): 1538–42. Print.

Koenig, R. J., and C. R. DeGuerre. "The Legal and Governmental Response to Domestic Elder Abuse." *Clinical Geriatric Medicine* 21.2 (2005): 383–98. Print.

Murray, Christine E., and Kelly N. Graves. *Responding to Family Violence: A Comprehensive, Research-Based Guide for Therapists.* New York: Routledge, 2013. Print.

Phelan, Amanda, ed. *International Perspectives on Elder Abuse.* New York: Routledge, 2013. Print.

"Projected Future Growth of the Older Population." *Administration on Aging.* Dept. of Health and Human Services, n.d. Web. 15 May 2014.

Quinn, K., and H. Zielke. "Elder Abuse, and Exploitation: Policy Issues." *Clinical Geriatric Medicine* 21.2 (2005): 449–57. Print.

Sellas, Monique, and Laurel Krouse. "Elder Abuse Overview." http://emedicine.medscape.com/article/.

"USA." United States Census Bureau. US Dept. of Commerce, 27 Mar. 2014. Web. 15 May 2014.

Sharon Wallace Stark

SEE ALSO: Ageism; Aggression; Aggression: Reduction and control; Aging: Cognitive changes; Aging: Physical changes; Alzheimer's disease; Anger; Assisted living; Battered person syndrome; Child abuse; Codependency; Dementia; Family life: Adult issues; Father-child relationship; Homelessness: Psychological causes and effects; Hospice; Impulse control disorders; Memory; Mother-child relationship; Rape and sexual assault; Risk assessment; Violence: Psychological causes and effects.

Elders' mental health

TYPE OF PSYCHOLOGY: Cognition; Emotion; Memory; Personality; Social psychology; Stress

Dementia, which is characterized by symptoms such as delirium, depression, and delusions, is the most common mental health problem among the elderly. Alzheimer's disease is the most prevalent form of dementia.

KEY CONCEPTS

- Alzheimer's disease
- Amyloid plaques
- Bipolar disorder
- Delirium
- Delusions
- Dementia
- Depression
- Electroencephalogram (EEG)
- Neurofibrillary tangles
- Senile psychosis

INTRODUCTION

According to the American Psychological Association, by 2012 an estimated 20 percent of elderly Americans had some form of mental illness, although much of this illness goes undiagnosed and untreated because many of the elderly are reluctant to seek the professional help that might alleviate their conditions. Medicare benefits for conditions relating to mental illness are often less generous than those for physical disorders. Therefore, elderly people, especially those who are financially constrained, are unwilling and often unable to pay for the treatment that could offer them relief from the mental problems they are experiencing.

The elderly population in the United States is growing exponentially and is expected to continue that growth throughout the twenty-first century. According to the US Census Bureau, individuals sixty-five years of age and older made up more than 13 percent of the US population in 2012; that number is expected to increase to more than 20 percent by 2050, according to estimates by the US Department of Health and Human Services' Administration on Aging. Not only will the number of people aged sixty-five or older continue to grow, but also, with advanced medical breakthroughs, many of them are expected to survive for two or more additional decades, leading active lives and enjoying reasonably good health into their eighties or nineties. Nevertheless, it is anticipated that millions of these people will have some form of mental illness.

COMMON MENTAL DISORDERS

The most common mental disorder that affects elderly Americans is dementia, with such accompanying conditions as delirium, depression, and psychosis. Many elderly individuals and their families overlook the symptoms of dementia, especially those that develop gradually. Often obvious symptoms are attributed to the normal aging process. Sometimes obvious symptoms are ignored by friends or family members in the hope that they will diminish or disappear. In the minds of many people, a degree of shame is still associated with any mental disorder, which leads them to deny even obvious symptoms.

Throughout history, many elderly individuals have exhibited eccentric behaviors and were forgetful. However, life expectancy was such that few people survived beyond their fiftieth year, and truly elderly people were seldom encountered. Their eccentricities could be shrugged off as being normal developments in the aging process. In medical circles, these behaviors were often identified as manifestations of senile psychosis.

In 1906, however, Alois Alzheimer, a German pathologist and neurologist, presented a case study of a fifty-seven-year-old woman, Auguste D., whose symptoms were classic symptoms of what has come to be called Alzheimer's disease. Following this patient's death, Alzheimer studied samples excised from her brain and found amyloid plaques, or accumulations of dark protein, in the brain's cortex and hippocampus. In his microscopic examinations of Augusta D.'s brain tissue, he found twisted tendrils of very fine fibers that he called neurofibrillary tangles. He concluded that these tangles were at the heart of this patient's mental disorder.

Alzheimer's disease, named after this pioneering physician, is the most prevalent type of dementia found in elderly patients. To date, the causes of this disease have not been identified definitively. It is known that those with Alzheimer's often survive for five to twenty years following the onset of the disease and that their conditions usually become progressively worse. Many Alzheimer's patients die from causes related to the disease.

NORMAL AGING VERSUS DEMENTIA

Symptoms that suggest dementia may occur in elderly people who are not experiencing dementia as such. As the aging process accelerates in people over the age of sixty-five, most of them experience a decrease in their sensory abilities, with declines in vision, hearing, touch, taste, and smell. Also, many of the elderly use prescription drugs that may interact adversely with one another, causing severe behavioral changes. Physicians are well advised to obtain lists of all the medications, including over-the-counter drugs, taken by their patients.

Among the most significant behavioral changes observed among the elderly is a decrease in memory, both short-term and long-term. In people with Alzheimer's disease, one of the first symptoms observed is a loss in short-term memory. Therefore, if older people show evidence that their short-term memory is failing, those who observe them might leap to the conclusion that they are in the early stages of Alzheimer's. However, even some perfectly healthy people are forgetful. Absentmindedness occurs among people of all ages and may be the result of many factors other than dementia.

Another symptom of dementia is a tendency to respond to questions inappropriately or to give answers that do not make sense. Among the elderly, however, deficits in hearing can cause people to misconstrue questions. Therefore, if an elderly person answers questions inappropriately, it may suggest an auditory deficit rather than dementia.

Visual and auditory deficiencies can result in older people's misinterpreting situations and reacting to them in ways that seem strange to those caring for them. Also, the elderly person in question might be living in a context quite different from the one that a caregiver perceives, so that conclusions reached based on the caregiver's observations may be inaccurate. It is important to view the behaviors of the elderly realistically within the actual contexts in which they live and function.

Some behaviors that younger people exhibit may intensify as they age. This is often a normal part of aging. People who have typically been rigid and suspicious in their early years may find that such tendencies increase substantially as they age, but such an increase does not categorically indicate dementia. However, if such behaviors turn to unhealthy or obsessive paranoia, dementia may account for the change.

As the motor abilities of older people decrease, often as a result of factors such as arthritis or reduced blood flow to the brain, they may walk with difficulty and seem to be disoriented, even though they may be performing quite appropriately given the total context of the situation in which they find themselves. They may also become confused or lost in unfamiliar surroundings, but this is not a clear indication of dementia. However, if they cannot find their way in familiar surroundings, dementia may be suspected.

When dealing with the elderly, misdiagnoses of dementia are common. They must be regarded as questionable if they are based on information that has been obtained solely through observation. Neurological testing and sophisticated procedures such as magnetic resonance imaging (MRI) provide more reliable diagnoses.

DEMENTIA

Dementia usually involves the loss of memory, particularly short-term memory, although in advanced cases, long-term memory may also be compromised. Those with dementia often have problems with language, most frequently being unable to bring forth the words they need to express themselves. This tendency may come and go as blood flow to the brain waxes and wanes.

One of the most devastating symptoms of dementia, one usually suggestive of Alzheimer's disease, is an inability to recognize the people and objects with which patients have been most familiar. Individuals may be unable to recognize their spouses. Patients may touch objects, such as hammers or screwdrivers, but be unable to determine how they function. They also may be unable to attach names to such objects.

People with dementia often have difficulty carrying out the motor functions that most people take for granted, but this is not a categorical indication of dementia because physical incapacities such as the joint pain that accompanies arthritis may severely limit the motor skills of those with this condition. Adverse drug interactions may also account for a decline in motor skills.

DELIRIUM

Delirium is an acute state of mental confusion marked by difficulty in focusing, sustaining thoughts, and shifting attention. Patients may misconstrue the statements and actions of others, often reacting to them with great suspicion. Those experiencing delirium may have difficulty sleeping and may be physically disturbed and restless, resulting in dramatic swings in their moods.

The judgment of such people is often impaired, and efforts to alter such misjudgments may elicit anger from them. They may also experience either significantly increased or decreased motor activity. If these symptoms manifest themselves suddenly or fluctuate over short periods of time, the person may be experiencing delirium.

A reliable diagnosis of delirium can be made by having an electroencephalogram (EEG) performed on the patient. If an EEG reveals a marked decrease in cerebral activity, delirium is likely to be the cause. When such a diagnosis is made, the condition may be treated with medications that can reduce the symptoms.

MANIFESTATIONS OF PSYCHOSIS

Various forms of psychosis may afflict the elderly. The most common occur in the elderly with schizophrenia or bipolar disorder. Among elderly patients diagnosed with schizophrenia or bipolar disorder, many may also have delirium or dementia.

Schizophrenia, a chronic brain disorder, is characterized by hallucinations and delusional thinking or behavior. Although schizophrenia is rare among people over the age of sixty-five, it can be a very disturbing and potentially dangerous condition. Most people with schizophrenia develop it in the second or third decade of life, but some are first diagnosed between the ages of forty and sixty-five, and others are diagnosed after reaching the age of sixty-five. Late-onset schizophrenia-like psychosis is more common in women and is characterized by paranoia, brain structure abnormalities, and cognitive deterioration. A family history of schizophrenia and a history of early childhood problems are usually absent. Schizophrenia differs from Alzheimer's disease in that hallucinations tend to be auditory rather than visual, delusions tend toward the bizarre, and patients usually recognize their caregivers. Elderly people who have schizophrenia are usually treated with antipsychotic medications. Psychosocial treatment such as cognitive behavior therapy and social skills training can also be helpful.

Bipolar disorder causes significant and often sudden mood swings in which patients fluctuate from the depressive state to the manic state, which sometimes reaches psychosis. Manic periods are characterized by heightened mood (irritability or euphoria), grandiosity, decreased sleep, and, in severe cases, a loss of touch with reality. Depression is a universal condition and is perfectly normal in most people, particularly if it has an identifiable cause such as loss of a job or financial difficulties. In such cases, once the cause is removed or controlled, the depression usually moderates. However, those with bipolar disorder, like the clinically depressed, are depressed for no apparent reason. They experience down moods that may be so pervasive that they can lead to such drastic outcomes as suicide, which is a major cause of death among those over the age of sixty-five. Bipolar disorder is most commonly treated with mood-stabilizing drugs such as lithium.

CLINICAL DEPRESSION

The elderly are more subject to depression than is the general population, partly because they are at a point in their lives when their spouses and close friends are dying, leaving the survivors feeling isolated and hopeless. This factor is combined with the physical deterioration that is part of aging. The diagnosis of severe, or clinical, depression is sometimes difficult because many people will not admit that they are depressed. Men experiencing deep depression may view such feelings as unmanly. Women who fight depression are often less skillful than men at masking their depression. Those dealing with them must understand various nuances that may suggest the condition.

Among these nuances, one of the most common is hypochondria. People who are basically healthy and organically sound may experience imaginary ills that are, to them, quite real. Overworked physicians may simply dismiss such patients because they cannot find anything wrong with them. A sensitive physician, however, will probe deeply enough to find the real cause of the patient's hypochondria and will avoid treating it medicinally until the basic causes have been uncovered.

Various behaviors provide the clues that signal a patient's depression. Among the most common of these are severe declines in self-image, often accompanied by dramatic decreases or increases in appetite; loss of interest in sex; difficulty in concentrating; loss of memory; reduction of motor skills; and significant declines in energy levels. People entering a depressive state may experience substantial gains or losses in weight. The clinically depressed may have seemingly unjustified feelings of guilt. They may experience physical manifestations such as a tightness in the chest or unexplained difficulty in breathing. They may also harbor thoughts of suicide and may have gone so far as to plan or to have attempted suicide.

Depression in the elderly can be treated with medications, but also can be dealt with successfully in many cases by making changes in lifestyle, such as becoming more actively involved socially. Seeing films and plays with friends and then discussing what they have seen or playing board games or card games can be a useful therapy for some elderly people. Many older people benefit greatly from participating in book clubs.

Nutrition exercise are also major components in maintaining the mental health of the elderly, who should eat three well-balanced meals a day and consume at least five portions of fresh vegetables and fruits daily. The elderly should limit their intake of alcohol and refrain from smoking. Regular activities such as walking, cycling, swimming, water aerobics, or yoga can help restore flexibility to aging joints and, if engaged in judiciously, can prolong one's active life. Exercise and proper nutrition often do more to control depression than any medication can.

BIBLIOGRAPHY

Barker, L. Randol, and Philip D. Zieve, eds. *Principles of Ambulatory Medicine*. 7th ed. Philadelphia: Lippincott, 2007. Print.

Brody, Claire M., and Vicki G. Semel, eds. *Strategies for Therapy with the Elderly: Living with Hope and Meaning*. 2d ed. New York: Springer, 2006. Print.

Budson, Andrew E., and Neil W. Kowall. *The Handbook of Alzheimer's Disease and Other Dementias*. Chichester: Wiley, 2014. Print.

Capezuti, Elizabeth A., et al., eds. *The Encyclopedia of Elder Care*. 3rd ed. New York: Springer, 2014. Print.

Evans, Sandra, and Jane Garner, eds. *Talking over the Years: A Handbook of Dynamic Psychotherapy with Older Adults*. New York: Brunner-Routledge, 2004. Print.

Levine, Robert V. *Defying Dementia: Understanding and Preventing Alzheimer's and Related Disorders*. Westport: Praeger, 2006. Print.

"Mental and Behavioral Health and Older Americans." *American Psychological Association*. APA, 2014. Web. 15 May 2014.

Mondimore, Francis Mark. *Bipolar Disorder: A Guide for Patients and Their Families*. 2d ed. Baltimore: Johns Hopkins UP, 2006. Print.

"Projected Future Growth of the Older Population." *Administration on Aging. Dept. of Health and Human Services*, n.d. Web. 15 May 2014.

Rosenberg, Jessica, and Samuel J. Rosenberg, eds. *Community Mental Health: Challenges for the 21st Century*. 2nd ed. New York: Routledge, 2013. Print.

Sabbagh, Marwan Noel. *The Alzheimer's Answer: Reduce Your Risk and Keep Your Brain Healthy*. Hoboken: Wiley, 2008. Print.

Tallis, Raymond C., and Howard M. Fillit, eds. *Brocklehurst's Textbook of Geriatric Medicine and Gerontology*. 6th ed. London: Churchill, 2003. Print.

"USA." United States Census Bureau. US Dept. of Commerce, 27 Mar. 2014. Web. 15 May 2014.

Wetherell, Julie Loebach, and Dilip V. Jeste. "Older Adults with Schizophrenia: Patients Are Living Longer and Gaining Researchers' Attention." *Elder Care* 3.2 (2003): 8–11. Print.

R. Baird Shuman

See Also: Ageism; Aging: Cognitive changes; Aging: Physical changes; Aging: Theories; Alzheimer's disease; Antidepressant medications; Antipsychotic medications; Assisted living;

Bipolar disorder; Death and dying; Dementia; Depression; Elder abuse; Forgetting and forgetfulness; Hallucinations; Hospice; Memory; Mood disorders; Mood stabilizer medications; Personality disorders; Psychotic disorders; Schizophrenia: Background, types, and symptoms; Suicide.

Electronic media and psychological impact

Type of psychology: Clinical; Consumer; Counseling; Developmental; Media; Social

Electronic media have the potential to transform the way individuals and groups communicate. These media vary across many factors including the types of communication signals (facial expressions, head nods, voice modulation), their chronemic timing (synchronous or asynchronous), and their ability to provide feedback and behavioral confirmation. These characteristics can be both advantageous and disadvantageous as compared to face-to-face communication.

Key Concepts

- Anonymous communication
- Computer-mediated communication
- Electronic media
- Hyperpersonal communication
- Social networking
- Synchronous vs. asynchronous communication

INTRODUCTION

Technological advances have spawned new and diverse ways that individuals can communicate with each other. These media vary in their capacity to communicate messages, the amount and quality of the information they can convey, the synchronicity of the interaction (that is communicating at the same time or asynchronously), and the anonymity of the participants. Of concern is how well electronic media can convey the breadth, depth, and nuances of communication like humor, emotion, trust, and credibility. Face-to-face (FTF) communication is considered the standard because it allows the exchange of a wide range of information that facilitates the ability to convey and interpret the meaning of a message, its veracity, as well as critical information about the sender including interest level, credibility, attitudinal similarity, and affinity. Communication across other types of media like written letters, text messages, and email varies in the amount of information that can be expressed by the sender and gleaned from the message by the receiver. As such, researchers have been interested in how these alternate ways of communicating influence the quality of the interaction, its efficiency, the development of interpersonal bonds, and the resulting outcomes (such as decision quality, negotiation profit). Early theorists believed that non-FTF forms of communication were impoverished compared to FTF. They lacked key elements and led to poor quality communication and social interactions. More recent developments recognize both the social benefits and drawbacks that electronic media pose for communication.

THEORETICAL PERSPECTIVES

Social Presence Theories. Early theories focused on the negative impact of media on communication and social interaction. Short, Williams, and Christie developed the social presence theory of media prior to the widespread use of personal computers, Internet access, and the cell phone revolution. Social presence was the degree to which a communication medium created a warm, close, interpersonal rapport between communicators. Media such as telephone and written communication were believed to create the perception of less presence than face-to-face communication because they involved interpersonal interaction that was less intimate, less immediate, and colder. Rodney Wellens extended this to computer-mediated communication and focused on the concept of psychological distance. Electronic forms of communication such as email, electronic chat, and message boards were hypothesized to have narrower bandwidths. Bandwidth referred to the ability of the medium to allow the exchange of a wide range of information during the conversation. The assumption was that greater information exchange led to warmer and higher quality interactions. Narrow bandwidth media resulted in reduced information exchange and difficulties developing close interpersonal bonds. Consequently, narrow bandwidth media were believed to lead to less effective communication and to have a negative impact on outcomes and interpersonal relationships. Supporting the social presence theory, Kiesler, Siegel, and McGuire found that individuals using narrow bandwidth media engaged in more disinhibited behavior (referred to as flaming behavior) including swearing, name calling, and hostile comments than those communicating FTF.

Media Richness Theory. Daft and Lengel proposed media richness theory to describe how media varied from one another. Richness refers to the number of information cues and quality of those cues that can be conveyed. Richer media convey more cues including the content of the verbal message, vocal cues, nonverbal cues, feedback information, and status cues. The verbal message refers to the content of the message being exchanged. Vocal cues include the speed of speech, pitch, and variations in speech patterns such as an increase in volume or hesitation. Nonverbal cues include eye contact, smiling, and hand gestures used when talking. Feedback can be conveyed through head nods, and utterances of agreement indicate understanding and reception of information. Status and power can be conveyed through symbolic actions such as sitting at the head of the table or through style of dress. In contrast, anonymity of participants can remove status cues and lead to greater equalization of participation. Richness is a function of the medium. Media that lack or block more cues are considered impoverished media. Ones that allow the exchange of more cues, like FTF, are considered richer media. Because richer media allow for greater information exchange, they are expected to result in higher quality interactions, better communication, and better outcomes.

Social Influence Theory. Social influence theory proposed that the effect of media on communication resulted because interaction, its interpretation, and its meaning are socially constructed among participants. Thus feelings of presence or distance are not solely a function of the communication medium used but are affected by the people as they interact, their perceptions, and their engagement with one another. Social influence theory emphasizes the basic need humans have to establish interpersonal relationships. Some relationships develop quickly, while others take more time to grow and flourish. In these interactions, we form impressions of others, exchange information, and assess whether we have an affinity/attraction for continuing the relationship. Information is exchanged through a give and take process which involves asking questions and revealing information through self-disclosure. People are motivated to develop relationships regardless of the medium used to communicate. Although missing cues, electronic forms of communication and text based messages can still produce strong interpersonal bonds, but they may take longer to develop. When cues are missing, communicators will adapt to whatever cues are available.

Social Identity Model of Deindividuation Effects (SIDE). The SIDE model recognizes that people develop identities that are both personal and social. The identity that becomes most salient will depend on the the expectations and goals of individuals and groups involved in the interaction. Immersion in a group leads to depersonalization, a shift from a personal identity to a group identity. Instead of predicting disinhibited behavior when a group identity becomes salient, the theory predicts that depersonalization will result in individuals adhering more closely to the norms and standards of their most salient identities. Salient identities provide communicators with information and expectations about the type, quantity, and quality of knowledge and personal details that should be shared.

Media vary in the extent to which individuals can feel anonymous. Anonymity can have varying effects. Anonymity changes the relative salience of personal versus social identities. When group categorizations become more salient, individuals may strive to represent themselves as ideal group members and more

Photo: iStock

strongly adhere to perceived group norms and values. Alternatively, anonymity may make the personal identity more salient increasing the individual's adherence to his or her own personal goals and values.

When information is missing, individuals might apply self-stereotypes to other group members and generalize their own beliefs and characteristics to "in-group members." Greater affinity for so called "in-group" members will result because without detailed information, the person assumes that the anonymous group members share similar views and interests. This perceived similarity increases the individual's willingness to share information and to trust the anonymous other.

Anonymity can also lead to less adherence to group norms. The lack of identity can increase behaviors that go against group norms. When interacting with members of a disliked or unsympathetic group, an individual may be more likely to feel less committed to group norms and to express his or her own opinions, values, and ideals.

Anonymity in electronic forms of communication also allows individuals to be strategic in their communications. They can present a certain image by highlighting certain aspects of their identity while downplaying other aspects. Facebook is a good example. Some people post only about the fun and interesting activities they engage in, while leaving out the mundane, boring, and perhaps more negative aspects of their daily lives.

Hyperpersonal Theory. Walther proposed the hyperpersonal theory of communication media because results of studies showed that sometimes less rich media were advantageous and sometimes they led to poorer outcomes. This theory was derived from the theoretical bases of the SIDE theory and social influence theory.

Hyperpersonal theory suggests that media can vary in how personal individuals feel using a medium and that these feelings can be beneficial and increase the effectiveness of the communication or can be disadvantageous. In less rich media, where there are fewer cues, individuals may be more likely to develop positive impressions of group members from social groups that they positively identify with and develop close, trusting relationships quickly. Anonymity in this case will build strong interpersonal bonds and likely lead to communication using electronic media (like texting or email) that is as effective as or possibly more effective than FTF communication. In the case where individuals are not identifiable and their values diverge from those of the group, they may be more willing to share their ideas and viewpoints using restricted media due to increased feelings of anonymity. This more candid sharing of information can lead to improved group decision making and represents an advantage of less rich media. In using less rich media, individuals will adapt their communication by using alternate types of cues. Essentially, hyperpersonal theory suggests that the social impact of electronic media can be both advantageous as well as detrimental. The outcome is dependent on the context and the people within the context.

Media Naturalness Theory. Media naturalness theory was proposed by Ned Kock and takes an evolutionary, Darwinian perspective on electronic media. Kock suggested that over evolutionary history, the human brain has evolved to communicate FTF. Newer forms of communication represent aspects of the environment to which humans must adapt. These forms represent obstacles that need to be overcome. Communication naturalness is comparative to FTF communication and is based on five characteristics: 1) co-location (our ability see and hear each other), 2) synchronicity, 3) the medium's ability to allow facial expressions to be conveyed and observed, 4) the medium's ability to allow body language to be conveyed and observed, and 5) the medium's ability to allow speech qualities to be conveyed and observed. In communication, there are often redundancies and some cues are not necessarily needed to communicate the message, the meaning, or the interpretation. Communication fluency (ease of understanding, speed of encoding and decoding the message, reduction in interpretation and message reception errors) varies with regard to the cognitive effort required to interpret the message. Cognitive effort is a function of the ambiguity of the message, the complexity of the message including the number of extraneous cues, and the amount of physiological arousal (excitement and pleasure) communicators experience in the context. Complex or ambiguous information will require cognitive effort to filter unnecessary components and interpret meaning. If the interaction requires individuals to search for or integrate information from a variety of sources, this can increase the cognitive effort required and decrease perceptions of media naturalness. In terms of naturalness, speech appears to be a more important cue than facial expressions and body language.

To make up for the lack of media naturalness, individuals can engage in compensatory adaptation which is a means of compensating for missing information or disfluency. Emoticons are one example of compensatory adaptation. In emails and text messages, a smiley face can be used to indicate that a person is joking. A language of abbreviations in text messaging (e.g., LOL – laughing out loud) allows the quick and easy communication of phrases without the need for typing the whole thought. Many cell phone text-messaging applications suggest words and phrases based on just a few typed letters. These innovations, however, can also lead to disfluency, for example auto correction errors that substitute the wrong word or even an embarrassing one. To the degree that individuals have to put effort into compensatory adaptation, the quality of the interaction may suffer, as well as their satisfaction with the relationship.

Media Synchronicity Theory. The final theory to be considered is media synchronicity theory (Dennis & Valacich, 1999), which suggests that communicators match media to their communication needs. The idea is that the goals of individuals and/or groups will determine the effectiveness of the medium used for communication. Matching the media to the need will reduce the detrimental effects of media and improve the quality of communications.

APPLICATIONS

Why do we need to understand how media influence communication, interpersonal bonds, and resultant outcomes? Technology is not going away. People are engaging in social interaction on computers, smart phones, and tablets. For many individuals from recent generations, such as those in the millennial (1984-1994) and digital native (1995-present) generations, mediated communication (e.g., texting, email, and the use of social networking) has always been part of how they communicate and connect with friends. People connect through social networking like Facebook, LinkedIn, and SnapChat. They talk to one another using video chat like Skype and Facetime. They interact in virtual worlds like the World of Warcraft and Second Life using avatar representations of themselves. They search for jobs and potential dates online. People shop and conduct business online. Telecommuting allows individuals to work remotely and creates the need for managers to supervise remotely. Students and workers can seek learning and training opportunities online. Distance learning programs allow course content to be delivered through electronic forms of communication. Massive Open Online Courses (MOOCs) have the potential to change radically the nature of higher education. Even corporate training has been transformed by mediated communication. Organizations with global workforces rely on a variety of mediated training approaches such as webinars, collaborative electronic meetings, and mlearning (i.e., mobile learning) modules presented on smart phones or tablets The types of computer-mediated communication technologies are growing and evolving and have important implications for our everyday lives.

ONLINE SOCIAL SUPPORT AND PROSOCIAL BEHAVIOR

People seek social support online to deal with a variety of stressors in their lives. For example, people connect through social media after a disaster, following job loss, and when facing a serious illness. They seek information and to connect with others who are faced with similar experiences sharing strategies for coping. The research evidence shows that this type of online support can have many positive effects.

Electronic media can enhance prosocial and helping behavior. Social networking can be used to rally support and help for a person in a time of need. Viral electronic media campaigns can be used to successfully raise funds for charities and recognize the positive contributions of individuals.

Electronic media also can lead to power equalization and greater participation of members of under-represented groups. Women negotiators using electronic mediated communication were more likely to adopt the assertive negotiation style often used by male negotiators.

ONLINE DATING

Online dating sites have become a popular way for individuals to meet romantic and sexual partners. Theories of the psychological impact of electronic media can provide insight into how people may respond differently in an online versus a FTF dating context. Hyperpersonal theory suggests that because online dating interactions have sparse cues, people may "fill in the blanks" and assume they have a lot more in common with virtual strangers than FTF strangers. Virtual daters may be more likely to idealize their online partners than FTF daters. When creating an online dating profile individuals might be more likely to strategically exclude information and present themselves in a flattering light. Whitty discussed the need for online daters to create a balance between an attractive version of the self and the real self. Online daters may be prone to disclose too much or too soon. Often online dating relationships progress from online contact to speaking on the phone to meeting in person. Strategic self-presentation and the potential for outright deception in online dating can have important implications for personal safety and the probability of long-term relationship success.

ONLINE AGGRESSION, CYBER BULLYING, AND PUBLIC SHAMING

The potential for electronic mediated interactions to lead to greater disinhibited behavior and more depersonalization means that electronic forms of communication may lead to aggressive online behavior. Virtual negotiators engaged in more hostile behavior than FTF negotiators. There is growing interest in the phenomenon of cyber bullying which occurs when individuals post comments, photos, images, videos, or other electronic messages that are meant to ridicule or embarrass another person. Electronic media often lead to greater perceived distance between the target and the bully. Targets become faceless and dehumanized. Bullies experience less empathy and engagement with the target and are removed from the potential for direct personal confrontation. Targets of aggression are readily available and access is 24/7. Cyber insults and ridicule can be broadcast with little effort to a large number of people almost instantaneously. Often victims of cyber bullying feel isolated and experience ostracism in a powerful way.

Ronson (2015) described the devastation experienced by individuals who have been publicly shamed using social media like Facebook and Twitter. Ill-considered tweets and posts that may be perceived as violating social norms can lead to a maelstrom of attacks and public criticism. Tens of thousands of individuals can jump on the bandwagon. Incidents of public shaming can take a great personal and financial toll on the shamed individual including loss of job, trauma, depression, and condemnation from family and friends.

Theories of the psychological impact of electronic media have important implications for understanding who is likely to engage in online aggression like cyber bullying, virtual rape, hate language, cyber stalking, and public shaming and the conditions that are likely to lead to mob rule.

As electronic forms of communication change the way people interact and behave, they have important implications for everyday life.

BIBLIOGRAPHY

Amichai-Hamburger, Y. (2013). *The Social Net: Understanding our Online Behavior.* Oxford, UK: Oxford University Press. A collection of articles from leading scholars focused on the social aspects of our online lives.

Baym, N. (2010) *Personal Connections In The Digital Age.* Malden, MA: Polity Press. This book describes how we connect through online media.

Bircheier, Z., Dietz-Uhler, B., & Stasser, G. (Eds.) (2011). *Strategic Uses Of Social Technology: An Interactive Perspective Of Social Psychology.* Cambridge, UK: Cambridge University Press. This edited volume examines the social psychological theories and research on computer-supported social interaction.

Daft, R. L., & Lengel, R. H. (1984). "Information Richness: A New Approach To Managerial Behavior and Organization Design". In B. M. Staw & L. L. Cummings (Eds.), *Research in Organizational Behavior* (pp. 191-233). Greenwich: JAI Press. This article lays out the information richness model.

Kiesler, S., Siegel, J., & McGuire, T. W. (1984). "Social Psychological Aspects Of Computer-Mediated Communication. *American Psychologist,* 39(10), 1123-1134. doi:10.1037/0003-066X.39.10.1123doi:10.1016/j.im.2008.12.002 Early article that describes the increase in disinhibited behavior in computer-mediated communication.

Kock, N. (2012). "Media Naturalness Theory: Human Evolution and Behaviour Towards Electronic Communication Technologies". In S. C. Roberts (Ed.), *Applied Evolutionary Psychology* (pp. 381-398). New York, NY: Oxford University Press. Presents an evolutionary perspective on the impact of electronic communication media.

Ronson, J. (2015). *So You've Been Publicly Shamed.* New York, NY: Riverhead Books.

Short, J. A., Williams, E., & Christie, B. (1976). *The Social Psychology Of Telecommunications.* London, UK: John Wiley & Sons. An early look at how means of communicating vary in social presence.

Stuhlmacher, A. F., & Citera, M. (2005). "Hostile Behavior and Profit In Virtual Negotiation: A Meta-Analysis". *Journal of Business and Psychology,* 20(1), 69-93. doi:10.1007/s10869-005-6984-y This is a quantitative review of the social psychological implications of electronic communication media on negotiation.

Walther, J. B. (2011). "Theories Of Computer-Mediated Communication and Interpersonal Relations". In M. L. Knapp & J. A. Daly (Eds.), *The Handbook Of Interpersonal Communication* (4th ed., pp. 443-479). Thousand Oaks, CA: Sage. An excellent review of the effects of the major theories of electronic media.

Maryalice Citera

See Also: Adolescent development; Interpersonal interaction; Media; Self concept; Social media; Technology.

Elimination disorders

Type of psychology: Psychopathology; Social psychology; Stress

Elimination disorders, in which a person urinates or defecates in inappropriate places after the age that toilet training should have occurred, affect a significant number of children. These embarrassing events can separate a child from his or her peer group and stunt proper psychological growth.

Key Concepts

- Encopresis
- Enuresis
- Fecal incontinence
- Nocturnal enuresis

INTRODUCTION

The *Diagnostic and Statistical Manual of Mental Disorders: DSM-5* (5th ed., 2013) defines elimination disorders—encopresis and enuresis—as the excretion of feces or urine, respectively, in areas other than those deemed socially acceptable, such as the toilet. For a psychiatrist to give this diagnosis, a child must experience at least one such elimination per month (encopresis) or two per week (enuresis) for a minimum of three consecutive months—or, in the case of enuresis, "clinically significant distress or impairment in social, academic (occupational) or other important areas of functioning"—once the child has reached the age at which proper waste disposal is considered a normal developmental skill. In general, children who suffer from elimination disorders do not have control of their bodily functions; therefore, the disorders are often considered the result of a physical condition or abnormality. However, children who do have rectal and bladder control will occasionally discharge urine or fecal matter voluntarily. This is usually an indication of an underlying psychological problem that requires thorough psychiatric evaluation.

The Society of Pediatric Psychology (SPP) has reported that an estimated 1.6 to 4 percent of children under ten years old suffer from encopresis, also known as fecal incontinence, with a higher prevalence among boys than girls. While the condition affects a significant number of children aged three and under, by adolescence fewer than 1 percent of the age group suffers from the affliction. Encopresis is often caused by constipation. In this case, a parent or caregiver will notice fecal leakage in a child's diaper or underwear. Constipation occurs because of a blockage in the rectum. Over time, the impacted fecal matter may dull the nerve endings in the rectum, further hindering a child from recognizing when a bowel movement is imminent. Almost all children in Western, industrialized countries are able to control their bowels by age five. Therefore, a child who suffers from encopresis after his or her fifth birthday may be subject to embarrassment, ridicule, or punishment within the context of a school environment. This situation can adversely affect the child's psyche, causing residual damage and potential future psychiatric disorders.

During a child's toddler years, enuresis, the inappropriate discharge of urine, is considered a normal aspect of development. In fact, enuresis is not considered a valid diagnosis for any child under five years old. If the activity persists into school-age years, it is considered a disorder; by age six, according to the SPP, approximately 25 percent of boys and 15 percent of girls still experience enuresis, usually in the form of bed-wetting. Nocturnal enuresis is the most common form of the disorder, approximately three times more prevalent than diurnal, or daytime, enuresis, and is the least embarrassing because it usually occurs separate from the scrutiny of the peer group. Diurnal enuresis is more common among girls than boys and may result from a physiological condition, physical stress such as laughter or athletic activity, or simply the child being preoccupied with other matters or reluctant to use available restrooms. As with encopresis, enuresis during daytime hours can cause embarrassment, which in turn can be damaging psychologically.

PSYCHOLOGICAL ISSUES RELATED TO ELIMINATION DISORDERS

Evidence suggests that certain psychological issues, while not the primary causes of the problem, may predispose a child to either encopresis or enuresis. Conversely, psychological issues often arise because a child suffers from elimination disorders. If a child is intentionally engaging in inappropriate defecation or urination, he or she may have additional behavioral problems or may be reacting to some new stress in his or her life. Also, a child may use voluntary elimination as a symbolic gesture of anger toward a parent or guardian. Evidence also indicates that children who have been sexually abused suffer from elimination disorders at higher rates than do children who have not been abused, though an elimination disorder is not by itself a sufficient indication of abuse. In such a case, the child's defecation or urination may be intentional but is most likely a subconscious reaction to the abuse.

Aftereffects of elimination disorders suggest a link between the problem and lingering psychological and psychiatric issues. Apart from the initial embarrassment and shame, sufferers may experience longer-term and more serious problems. A 2009 study by Shreeram et al. found that children who suffered from attention-deficit hyperactivity disorder (ADHD) were more likely to experience enuresis than those of the same age who did not. In general, mental disorders have a greater likelihood of surfacing in people who had enuresis as children, though whether enuresis is more likely to be an early indication or a precipitating factor is unknown.

MEDICAL AND PSYCHOLOGICAL TREATMENT

Before undertaking medical or psychological treatment, a professional must determine whether the disorder in question is primary, occurring in a child who has yet to be properly toilet trained, or secondary, occurring after a significant period in which the child displayed proper toilet training. A child with a secondary disorder might have emotional issues requiring further diagnostic psychiatric evaluation. On the other hand, a child with encopresis might only need to be taught proper etiquette, undergo a change in food consumption, or start a regimen of scheduled bathroom breaks. A child who suffers from nocturnal enuresis might be assigned "bell and pad" therapy, which involves sleeping on a pad that provides electronic notification when elimination has occurred; using this method, the child will eventually wake before urinating in bed. Drugs such as imipramine are available for enuresis, but relapse often occurs once the child has been weaned off the medication. Regardless of the degree to which a child experiences elimination disorders, all treatment should be administered with understanding, patience, and emotional sympathy while considering the long-term psychological well-being of the individual.

BIBLIOGRAPHY

Christophersen, Edward R., and Patrick C. Friman. *Elimination Disorders in Children and Adolescents.* Cambridge: Hogrefe, 2010. Print.

Frances, Allen. *Essentials of Psychiatric Diagnosis: Responding to the Challenge of DSM-5.* New York: Guilford, 2013. Print.

Marsh, Eric J., and Russell A. Barkley, eds. *Child Psychopathology.* 3rd ed. New York: Guilford, 2014. Print.

Reichenberg, Lourie W. *DSM-5 Essentials: The Savvy Clinician's Guide to the Changes in Criteria.* Hoboken: Wiley, 2014. Print.

Sadock, Benjamin J., Virginia A. Sadock, and Harold I. Kaplan. *Kaplan and Sadock's Concise Textbook of Clinical Psychiatry.* 3rd ed. Philadelphia: Lippincott, 2008. Print.

Seligman, Linda, and Lourie W. Reichenberg. *Selecting Effective Treatments: A Comprehensive, Systematic Guide to Treating Mental Disorders.* 4th ed. Hoboken: Wiley, 2014.

Shreeram, Srirangam, et al. "Prevalence of Enuresis and Its Association with Attention-Deficit/Hyperactivity Disorder among US Children: Results from a Nationally Representative Study." *Journal of the American Academy of Child and Adolescent Psychiatry* 48.1 (2009): 35–41. Print.

von Gontard, Alexander. "The Impact of DSM-5 and Guidelines for Assessment and Treatment of Elimination Disorders." *Supp. to European Child and Adolescent Psychiatry* 22.1 (2013): S61–67. Print.

Waller, Raymond J. *Fostering Children and Adolescent Mental Health in the Classroom.* Thousand Oaks: Sage, 2006. Print.

Christopher Rager

SEE ALSO: Bed-wetting; Behavior therapy; Childhood disorders; Children's mental health; Conditioning; Development; Psychotherapy: Children; Self-esteem; Sensation and perception; Sleep.

Ellis, Albert

BORN: September 27, 1913
DIED: July 24, 2007
IDENTITY: American psychotherapist, theorist, and trainer of therapists
BIRTHPLACE: Pittsburgh, Pennsylvania
PLACE OF DEATH: New York, New York
TYPE OF PSYCHOLOGY: Psychotherapy

Ellis created, developed, and promoted rational emotive behavioral therapy. Because he developed this efficient, easy-to-learn method, he is widely recognized as the founder of cognitive behavioral therapy.

Albert Ellis received his master's degree in clinical psychology in 1943 and his doctorate in 1947, both from Columbia University. After six years of practicing psychoanalysis, which he found inefficient, he developed rational emotive therapy, later renamed rational emotive behavior therapy (REBT). In 1959, he founded the nonprofit Albert Ellis Institute, from which he offered individual and group therapy, public presentations, and training for therapists. After his important early books (*A Guide to Rational Living* in 1961 and *Reason and Emotion in Psychotherapy* in 1962), Ellis also wrote voluminously on REBT.

REBT holds that people have two opposing types of beliefs: rational (contributing to their happiness and achievement of goals) and irrational (leading to self-defeat and dysfunctional behavior). Irrational beliefs fall into three categories: demands about the self ("I must always perform well and be approved of by significant people"); demands about others ("You must always treat me considerately"); and demands about life and the world ("Life must always be the way I want it and not too difficult").

REBT's principal technique is its ABC's, a way of analyzing the client's difficulties. "A" is the adverse or activating event that is retarding the client's goals. "B" is the client's belief (often irrational) about the event. "C" is the consequence (perhaps discomfort, anxiety, or procrastination) of the client's belief. The therapist disputes, through questions and challenges, the client's rigid, irrational beliefs so that they may be changed to less disturbing and absolute preferences.

Ellis received awards for distinguished contributions from the American Psychological Association, the American Counseling Association, and the Association for the Advancement of Behavior Therapy. Joseph Yankura and Windy Dryden sum up his influence by stating, "Ellis has not merely invented a widely practiced system of psychotherapy, he has created a philosophy of living which has the potential to help many human beings to lead happier, healthier and more productive lives."

BIBLIOGRAPHY

Albert Ellis Institute. http://www.rebt.org/

Bernard, Michael E., et al. "Albert Ellis: Unsung Hero of Positive Psychology." *Journal of Positive Psychology* 5.4 (2010): 302–10. Print.

Dryden, Windy, and Raymond DiGuiseppe. *A Primer on Rational-Emotive Therapy.* Champaign: Research, 2003. Print.

Ellis, Albert. *All Out! An Autobiography.* Amherst: Prometheus, 2008. Print.

Ellis, Albert. "Being a Therapist." *Psychiatric Times* 29.9 (2012): 7. Print.

Epstein, Robert. "The Prince of Reason: An Interview with Albert Ellis." *Psychology Today* 34.1 (2001): 66–76. Print.

Yankura, Joseph, and Windy Dryden. *Albert Ellis.* London: Sage, 1994. Print.

Glenn Ellen Starr Stilling

See Also: Cognitive therapy; Rational emotive therapy.

Emotional abuse

Type of psychology: Clinical; Counseling; Developmental; Psychopathology; Psychotherapy

All abuse is about power and control, and the abuser uses tactics to exert power and control over his or her victims. Emotional abuse is any kind of non-physical abuse imposed from one person to another. Victims of emotional abuse are subjected to repeated threats, manipulation, intimidation, and isolation that cause them to feel anxiety, fear, self-blame, and worthlessness. They can become convinced that no one else cares or wants them. Frequently they stay in abusive situations because they believe they have nowhere else to go. In contrast to physical violence, emotional violence is not easily identified because it is not readily evident. Emotional abuse can sometimes predict physical violence.

Key Concepts

- Abuse.
- Cycle of violence
- Interpersonal violence (IPV).
- Violence

INTRODUCTION

Emotional abuse is a form of interpersonal violence that encompasses all forms of non-physical violence and distress caused through non-verbal and verbal actions. Emotional abuse is deliberate and manipulative and is a method of control. It often occurs in conjunction with other types of abuse, but it may also occur in isolation. Like other types of abuse, emotional abuse most often affects those with the least power and resources.

Emotional abusers have a need to dominate and feel in charge of their victims. Threatening or coercive tactics like intimidation, humiliation, harassment, embarrassment, social isolation, verbal assaults, insults, threats, financial control, work restrictions, and disregard for victims' needs are all means to exert power and control over them.

Occasional abusive behavior does not intimate an abusive relationship, but the frequency and duration of emotional abuse episodes and the actions that lead up to emotional abuse determine if it is an ongoing pattern of abuse. Whether obvious or subtle, emotional abuse eventually results in victims feeling powerless, hurt, angry, worthless, and afraid.

Abusers choose who they will abuse. They do not threaten or abuse everyone; they abuse those closest to them. Abusers choose when to abuse. It is planned. In public, abusers may do well keeping themselves in control. Their outbursts of abusive behavior are conserved for private altercations. Abuse is not a random act of loss of control; abusers can and do stop when it is to their benefit.

Emotional abusers often struggle with the same emotions as their victims. Frequently, abusers were victims of emotional abuse that caused them to feel the same sense of powerlessness, hurt, fear, and anger. Consequently, offenders generally seek people who are helpless or who do not acknowledge their own feelings, perceptions, or viewpoints which then allows abusers to feel securely in control of their victims.

Tactics of emotional abuse ensure abusers maintain control of their victims. Such tactics include the following: isolation from family and friends that increases victims' dependence on their abuser; threats of personal harm, harm to loved ones, or self-harm that keep victims fearful to leave; intimidation with acts of aggression like destroying personal property, facial and physical gestures, harming pets, or displaying weapons that insinuate violent repercussions to make victims conform to the wishes of their abuser; and humiliation, verbal criticism, name-calling, shaming, and public insults that destroy self-esteem and leave victims powerless and controlled.

Eventually, victims of emotional abuse lose all sense of self. Emotional abuse is often longer lasting than physical abuse because it is a gradual destruction of victims' confidence and sense of self-worth. Victims may be fearful to talk to anyone about the abuse because they have been convinced by their abuser that no one will believe them or they are threatened with severe consequences if they do. Though physical injuries mend over time, emotional injuries can impact victims for a lifetime.

Victims' perceptions of their situation become unrealistic. They may not acknowledge or recognize the emotional abuse, and they develop coping mechanisms like denial and minimization of their abuse as means to accommodate for it. Victims' reports of emotional abuse reveal that their abusers controlled the company they kept, where they went, when they made family contact. They also threatened to take their children. Women, especially, reported that they were made to feel ashamed, belittled, or humiliated by their abuser.

Emotional abuse, like other forms of abuse, occurs in cycles. There are three phases in the cycle of violence: Phase I -Tension building phase, Phase II - Violence phase, and Phase III- Honeymoon phase. Over time the cycle of violence may change as the honeymoon phase shortens, and the tension and violence phases increase. A decision to leave an abusive situation takes time and even repeated episodes of abuse before victims can leave. The amount of time depends on a victim's insecurities and concerns for others in the immediate environment who may feel the repercussions of a victim's leaving.

Phase I, or the Tension building phase, is when the abuser is extremely demanding, critical and moody, becomes more controlling, and makes threats. Money issues, children, or work are common triggers. The victim minimizes the problem in an effort to control the situation, withdraws as tension builds, and may attempt to pacify the abuser by giving in. As the tension intensifies, the victim has less and less control or ability to mollify the situation as it transitions into Phase II.

Phase II, or the Violence phase finds the abuser spiraling out of control as he or she feels control over the victim dwindling. The abuser's threats increase, tension peaks, and physical or extreme emotional abuse follows. The violent incident is unpredictable, because it is not the victim's behavior that triggers it. It is usually triggered by an external event or the abuser's emotional state of mind. The abuser blames the victim for making "it" happen. The victim has lost control altogether and is helpless during this escalation. Sometimes victims instigate Phase II to "get it over with" so they gain some control again.

Phase III, or the Honeymoon phase, brings about a transformation in the abuser who is now remorseful, apologetic, and showers the victim with attention, expressions of love, and promises that "it" will never happen again as he or she manipulates the victim into forgiveness and draws the victim back into the relationship. Though confused, the victim often feels guilty and responsible for the incident, minimizes it, and forgives the abuser.

RISK FACTORS

Research regarding risk factors for emotional abuse is limited. Some general, identified risk factors for emotional abuse include lower socio-economic status, anger, fear, physical or mental disability, dependence, authoritarianism, low self-esteem, personality disorders, marital conflict, isolation, substance abuse, cognitive decline, and discrepancies between partners' education and occupation levels.

Risk factors for being an abuser include having problems controlling temper, extreme jealousy, fear of abandonment, history of being abused, unrealistic expectations of relationship, antisocial personality, risk taking personality, irresponsibility for own actions, animal cruelty, threats of violence, low self-esteem, relationship codependence, compulsiveness, substance abuse, personality disorder, and power and control issues.

Risk factors for being a victim of abuse include having low self-esteem, intense need for affection, history of being abused, substance abuser parents, codependence, depression, isolation, substance abuse, difficulty expressing emotions, validation of self through relationship, and selflessness. The majority of identified victims are women; however, men have been emotionally abused in both domestic and institutional settings.

SIGNS AND SYMPTOMS

Generally, people who are in abusive relationships are afraid or fearful of their partners, conform to whatever their partners want, let their partners know their every move, are contacted frequently by their partners when they are out with them, comment on their partners jealousy and temper, have imposed restrictions regarding contact with family and friends, have restricted access to transportation and money, experience very low self-esteem, and are withdrawn, depressed, anxious, or suicidal.

Emotionally abused children frequently have compromised psychological, social, and moral development, are usually aggressive, exhibit antisocial behaviors, act older than their age, are unhappy, frightened and distressed, are low achievers, frequently miss school, have poor academic performance, experience difficulty making friends, have impaired ability to feel and express emotions, show signs of physical neglect, and may complain of vague physical symptoms.

Adults who were emotionally abused as children are more likely to have difficulty establishing relationships, misinterpret social cues and others behaviors, and experience mental health problems.

Abusers humiliate, chastise, publicly mock, demean opinions, ideas, suggestions, or needs of their victims, trivialize victims' successes and accomplishments, control finances and how money is spent, stress mistakes victims may make, show no empathy for their victims, deny or blame victims for their abusive behaviors, problems, and difficulties, believe they are never wrong, are intolerant of perceived lack of respect, and use manipulative or threatening tactics (sulk, withdraw, body language, facial expressions, play victim) to punish victims or force them to comply.

CONSEQUENCES

Emotional abuse not only can result in psychological issues, but it can also cause physical issues like frequent headaches or back, leg, and stomach problems. Long-term effects of emotional abuse can lead to depression, anxiety, posttraumatic stress disorder, and difficulties in interpersonal relationships. Sadly, it also continues the cycle of abuse, as many abused individuals become abusers themselves.

TREATMENT AND PREVENTION

Without intervention, frequency and severity of abuse usually increase over time. Treatment depends on the dynamics of the abuse. Abuse resulting from family dysfunction may benefit from access to appropriate community services like nurse and social worker home visits to provide help to change behaviors or prevent abuse in high-risk families.

Abuse resulting from mental illness, substance abuse, or physical disabilities may benefit from social services and professional mental health interventions. Separating victims and their abusers may be necessary to secure victims' safety and wellbeing. Leaving the environment is essential if there is any indication that abuse is escalating or physical violence may follow. Counseling for both abusers and victims of abuse can provide channels for discussion and mitigating solutions to end the cycle of violence.

Leaving an abusive relationship can be difficult and dangerous. Having a place to go for protection, help, and support is important. Usually such places are with family or friends. However, if they are not available, then local shelters or other organizations that provide assistance for safely leaving an abusive relationship should be sought. For emergency situations resources include the following:

911 for all emergencies

The National Domestic Violence Hotline: 1.800.799. SAFE (7233)

National Child Abuse Hotline: 1-800-4-A-CHILD (2-24453)

BIBLIOGRAPHY

Krumins, G. (2011). *The Detrimental Effects Of Emotional Abuse*. Bloomington, IN:Author House. The author describes her personal experience as a victim of emotional abuse, how to identify, understand, manage, and heal from the experience, and what authorities, communities, families, and friends should know to assist.

O'Hagen, K. (2006). *Identifying Emotional and Psychological Abuse: A Guide For Childcare Professionals*. McGraw-Hill. The author identifies emotional and psychological development and abuse among children and adolescents that are highlighted in case studies that provide information about how to assess their emotional and psychological wellbeing.

Testa, A. (2007). *The Bully In Your Relationship: Stop Emotional Abuse and Get The Love You Deserve*. McGraw-Hill. The author provides a guide to identifying types of bullies and victims of bullies and taking action to change through work that rebuilds victims' power and control regarding bullying relationships.

Sharon W. Stark

SEE ALSO: Abuse; Emotional regulation; Personality disorder; Trauma; Victimization.

Emotional expression

TYPE OF PSYCHOLOGY: Emotion

Emotional expression includes both facial expressions and body movements that accompany the internal experience of emotion and that clearly serve to communicate that emotion to others. Influenced by the work of Charles Darwin, psychologists have long regarded the communication of emotion as an important function with survival value for the species.

KEY CONCEPTS

- Decoding
- Emotion
- Encoding
- Nonverbal communication

INTRODUCTION

The study of human emotion is a complex endeavor. It is complex in part because emotion is not a single event or process but is, instead, a collection of discrete events and processes. Humans experience a vast array of emotions, and each of those emotions consists of several components—the physiological changes that occur, the nonverbal communication of the emotion, and the subjective or felt experience. The topic of emotional communication or expression includes two related aspects: encoding (the expression of emotion) and decoding (the perception and reading of cues that signify an emotion).

Nonverbal forms of expression play an integral role in the complex human communication system. Examples of emotional expression by nonverbal means are easy to find. For example, if irritated, people may tense their bodies, press their lips together, and gesture with their eyebrows. With an averted glance or a prolonged stare, a person can communicate intimacy, anger, submission, or dominance.

In his now-classic 1872 *book The Expression of the Emotions in Man and Animals*, Charles Darwin argues that many nonverbal communication patterns, specifically emotional expressions, are inherited and that they evolved because they had survival value. He focuses primarily on the expression of emotion through specific changes in the appearance of the face and argues that the primary function of emotional expression is to inform others about one's internal state and, therefore, to inform them of how one is likely to behave. For example, when enraged, individuals commonly grimace and bare their teeth; the observer's perception of that anger suggests that the individual may behave aggressively. Frequently, such an expression (and the appropriate perception on the part of the target) results in the retreat of the target, thus avoiding an actual fight. For social animals who live in groups, such as humans, this rapid communication of internal states is highly adaptive.

THE UNIVERSAL AND THE SPECIFIC

If emotional expressions are a product of evolution and are, therefore, shared by all members of the species, their production and their interpretation should be universal. Cross-cultural research supports the universality of certain facial expressions. People in various cultures agree on how to convey a given emotion and how to convey it most intensely. The universal expression of anger, for example, involves a flushed face, brows lowered and drawn together, flared nostrils, a clenched jaw, and bared teeth. Several researchers have also shown that people from a variety of countries, including the United States, Japan, Brazil, and others, as well as people from several preliterate tribal groups who have had no previous contact with the Western world, have little difficulty identifying the emotions of happiness, anger, sadness, disgust, fear, and surprise, as exhibited in photographs or videotapes of members of their own cultures and of other cultures. Thus, both the encoding and decoding of certain emotional expressions are the same for people all over the world, regardless of culture, language, or educational background.

This universality, however, does not preclude the possibility that certain aspects of emotional expression may be learned. In fact, strong cultural (learned) differences can be found in the intensity and frequency with which certain emotions are expressed and in the situations that elicit certain emotions. For example, in cultures that encourage individuality, as in Western Europe and North America, emotional displays are often intense and prolonged. People express their emotions openly. In Asian and other cultures that emphasize social connections and interdependence, emotions such as sympathy, respect, and shame are more common than in the West, and people in such cultures rarely, and then only briefly, display negative emotions that might disrupt a peaceful group environment. Additional evidence for the role of learning in emotional expression is provided by research suggesting that women express emotions more intensely than men, who tend to hide their expressions to some degree.

People of different cultures also vary in their use of certain other forms of nonverbal cues to express emotion. That is, individual cultures have developed additional signals of emotion that are shared only within those cultures. For example, the psychologist Otto Klineberg reported in 1938 that Chinese literature was filled with examples of emotional expression that would easily be misunderstood by members of the Western world. Such examples include clapping one's hands when worried or disappointed, sticking out one's tongue to express surprise, and scratching one's ears and cheeks to express happiness.

DECODING EXPRESSIONS

The human ability to decode or interpret emotional expressions is, like the expression itself, also partly learned. Evidence for this can be found in the reactions of infants to novel situations and novel toys. Under such circumstances, infants frequently check their mother's facial expressions before approaching or avoiding the novel toy. If she looks happy or relaxed, the infant generally will approach; if she looks frightened, the infant will try to avoid the new situation or will approach the mother. Additional support is found in research that suggests that women are generally better at detecting emotional undercurrents and at detecting emotion from visual information only (such as facial expressions presented in pictures or in silent films) than men are. Such individual differences are probably the result of gender socialization, with girls socialized to be more sensitive to the feelings of others.

The term "facial expression" is commonly defined as a motor response resulting from an emotional state. That is, the facial expression is believed to be a consequence of the emotion. This is the position implied by most of the theory and research in the area. Yet with regard to the role of the expressive component in the experience of emotion, there is another possibility. Some researchers have suggested that facial expressions not only communicate but also regulate emotion. For example, Darwin wrote that "the free expression by outward signs of an emotion intensifies it. . . . On the other hand, the repression, as far as possible, of all outward signs, softens our emotions." This statement clearly suggests that the outward expression of emotion can either amplify or attenuate the intensity of the emotional experience. Support for this hypothesis is now readily available.

FINE-TUNING INTERPRETATION

As more is learned about the subtle changes in facial expression and body movements that are associated with specific emotions, the behavior of individuals in specific situations may be interpreted more accurately. For example, therapists can observe more closely the facial expression changes in their patients, thereby gaining access to emotional reactions that their patients may not discuss openly.

Several researchers have already reported that close scrutiny of changes in facial expression among patients during interviews supports the notion that many expression changes occur too quickly for easy detection. E. A. Haggard and F. S. Isaacs, for example, while searching for indications of nonverbal communication between therapist and patient, ran filmed interactions at slow motion and noticed that the expression of the patient's face sometimes changed dramatically within a few frames of the film. These changes were not observable when the film was run at regular speed. Furthermore, these subtle changes appeared to take place at key points during the interview. For example, although the patient's detectable expression included a smile when discussing a "friend," closer inspection of the film suggested that the patient actually exhibited the subtle facial changes associated with the expression of anger during the conversation. These "micromomentary" expressions are believed to reveal actual emotional states that are condensed in time because of repression.

Advanced technology allows researchers to measure subtle facial changes in other ways as well. For example, when a person is given mild emotional stimuli, electrodes attached to facial muscles can detect hidden reactions. Thus, although a person's face might not look any different, voltage changes on the skin may reveal micromuscular smiles or frowns underneath; perhaps this procedure will even result in a new approach to lie detection.

In addition to the work being done to develop an understanding of the normal but subtle changes associated with various emotions under normal circumstances, several researchers have looked at how emotional expressions change under abnormal circumstances. For example, the weightlessness experienced by astronauts results in the movement of body fluids toward the upper body, causing their faces to become puffy. Under these circumstances, a reliance on facial expressions for emotional information might increase the risk of misunderstanding. Thus, a full understanding of such changes is necessary for individuals likely to find themselves in such situations.

Nonverbal forms of emotional communication also play an important role in the normal development of the human infant. For example, the facial expressions of both infants and caregivers are important in the development of the attachment relationship. That is, the facial expressions of infants indicate to caregivers the infants' emotional states. Infants' expressions tell much about how they are "feeling" and thus allow adults to respond appropriately. Furthermore, the early signs of emotional expression in infants are events that clearly contribute to the development of the relationship between infant and caregiver. For example, the infant's first smile is typically interpreted in a personal way by the caregiver and is responded to with a returned smile and increased interaction on the part of the caregiver, thus resulting in a positive interaction sequence. Evidence of the first smile also leads to increased attempts by the caregiver to elicit smiling at other times, thus giving the caregiver a new topic with which to engage the infant in social interaction.

BODY LANGUAGE THROUGH TIME

Throughout history, humankind has acknowledged the existence of discrete emotions and has exhibited acceptance and understanding of the public aspect of emotions—the expressive movements that characterize each individual emotion. For example, sad (tragic) and happy (comic) facial masks were worn by actors during ancient times to portray the emotional tone of their characters and were correctly perceived by audiences. Similarly, today, in the theater and in everyday life, people accept the notion that the face has a real and definite function in communicating feelings or emotions; people automatically search the face of the speaker, studying facial expressions, to understand more fully what is being communicated in any interpersonal interaction.

Several well-known scientists of the nineteenth century and early scientific psychologists of the twentieth century acknowledged the importance of emotion and emotional expression. It was during the late nineteenth century that Darwin paved the way for theory and research on the facial patterns in emotion. In the early twentieth century, Wilhelm Wundt, the father of psychology, assumed that the face was the chief means of emotional expression. Thus the topic of emotion was considered a topic worthy of scientific investigation during the early years of psychology.

When behaviorism took over as the dominant psychological theory of the twentieth century, however, emotion, as well as all other topics that included "subjective" components, was forced out of the laboratory and out of the range of scientific study. During psychology's period of strong behavioristic orientation (the 1930s through the 1950s), most general theories of behavior and most major personality theories ignored emotion altogether or dealt with it only as a vague, global entity or process of little importance. There was very little scientific investigation into the existence of separate emotions, and therefore there was very little attention paid to the existence of discrete facial patterns for the communication of emotion. This overall lack of interest in facial patterns by behavioral scientists had little influence on common wisdom; people in general have maintained the age-old position that the patterns exist and that they have specific emotional significance.

As theories of emotion began to appear in the scientific literature, and as the potential importance of emotional expressions was considered, the question of innate versus learned facial patterns of emotional expression was addressed. For a substantial period of time, the dominant view was that there were no invariable patterns of expression. It was not until publication of the work of Silvan Tomkins, Carroll Izard, Paul Ekman, and other investigators during the 1960s that conclusive evidence for the existence of universal facial patterns in emotional expression was provided, confirming for science what people have always known. Since then, significant advances have been made in understanding the facial musculature changes associated with the expression of individual emotions and in understanding the development of the ability to interpret those facial musculature changes. It is, moreover, likely that significant advances will continue to be made in the identification of subtle changes in emotional expression and in understanding the important role of such facial patterns in interpersonal communication.

BIBLIOGRAPHY

Argyle, Michael. *Bodily Communication*. 2nd ed. New York: Routledge, 2013. Digital file.

Atkinson, R. L., R. C. Atkinson, E. E. Smith, and D. J. Bem. *Hilgard's Introduction to Psychology*. 13th ed. Fort Worth: Harcourt, 2000. Print.

Beattie, Geoffrey. *Visible Thought: The New Psychology of Body Language*. New York: Routledge, 2014. Digital file.

Darwin, Charles. *The Expression of the Emotions in Man and Animals*. Ed. Paul Ekman. 4th ed. New York: Oxford UP, 2009. Print.

Ekman, Paul. *Darwin and Facial Expression*. Cambridge: Malor, 2006. Print.

Izard, Carroll E. *The Face of Emotion*. 1971. Rpt. New York: Irvington, 1993. Print.

Izard, Carroll E. *Human Emotions*. New York: Plenum, 1977. Print.

Izard, Carroll E.. *Measuring Emotions in Infants and Children*. New York: Cambridge UP, 1986. Print.

Myers, David G. *Psychology*. 8th ed. New York: Worth, 2007. Print.

Scherer, K. R. *Facets of Emotion: Recent Research*. New York: Psychology, 2013. Print.

Wortman, Camille B., and Elizabeth F. Loftus. *Psychology*. 5th ed. New York: McGraw-Hill, 1999. Print.

Loretta A. Rieser-Danner

See Also: Anger; Denial; Emotional intelligence; Emotions; Facial feedback; Guilt; Jealousy; Love; Nonverbal communication.

Emotional intelligence (EI)

Date: 1980's forward

Type of psychology: Emotion; Intelligence and intelligence testing

Emotional intelligence is often referred to as a skill, ability, competency, and even a personality trait. Its definition, therefore, is constantly changing and somewhat controversial.

Key Concepts

- Emotion
- Emotional control
- Intelligence
- Multiple intelligences
- Self-awareness

INTRODUCTION

The concept of emotional intelligence is relatively new to the field of psychology. The ideas and concepts that are now referred to as emotional intelligence first came to be in the 1980's, when Howard E. Gardner first proposed his theory of multiple intelligences. The term "emotional intelligence" was introduced by Peter Salovey and John Mayer in a 1990 research paper. In 1995, the publication of Daniel Goleman's *Emotional Intelligence: Why It Can Matter More Than IQ* popularized the concept. Three common models of emotional intelligence have been developed: the ability-based model (Mayer and Salovey's four-branch model based on emotional skills and abilities), the mixed model (Goleman's model based on skills and competencies), and the trait model (based on personality traits). Because of the differences that exist among the three models and because the field is growing at such a rapid pace, a standardized definition of emotional intelligence has yet to emerge. Although not agreed on by researchers in the field, two common definitions of emotional intelligence are the ability to monitor the feelings and emotions of the self and of others and to use this information to guide one's behaviors, and the ability to identify and control emotions in oneself and in others.

MEASUREMENT AND ASSESSMENT

Several tools have been developed to assess emotional intelligence. The two most prominent tools are the Mayer-Salovey-Caruso Emotional Intelligence Test (MSCEIT) and the Emotional Competence Inventory (ECI). The MSCEIT is a self-report test, consisting of 141 items based on the four-branch abilities model of emotional intelligence. It measures abilities on each of the four branches, then computes a separate score for each branch and an overall emotional intelligence score. The test includes eight tasks that measure the four branches of emotional intelligence as defined by Mayer, Salovey, and David R. Caruso. These four branches of abilities, listed from most basic to most complex, are as follows: perceive emotions, use emotions to facilitate thought, understand emotions, and manage emotions. The ECI is based on Goleman's mixed model of emotional intelligence. It is a 360-degree survey that assesses emotional intelligence (EI) by asking the person and multiple raters to answer questions about the person's behavior. The test measures eighteen competencies that fall under the four dimensions of emotional intelligence as identified by the mixed model approach. The four dimensions are self-awareness, self-management, social awareness, and relationship management. The competencies measured in the ECI are said to be learned capabilities, and because of this, individuals can work on and further develop each of the four emotional intelligence dimensions.

TRAINING AND APPLICATION

Since its inception, the concept of emotional intelligence has been used in a wide variety of contexts to help people live more successfully. Although some of the first contexts in which emotional intelligence was used focused on worker productivity and satisfaction, the concept has since been applied successfully in a broad range of areas.

One of the areas in which emotional intelligence has proven to be very helpful is in relationship training. Emotional intelligence, by its nature, has a strong focus on empathy and on understanding the ways in which emotions influence people. When people are able to combine a sense of how their own emotions can guide or derail them with a developed awareness of how others feel, they are equipped to navigate the complexities of relationships across many situations. Emotional intelligence has also been applied in structuring educational settings for students, teachers, and parents. Curricula have been designed that incorporate appropriate emotional modeling, helping children regulate their emotions and connecting emotional experience to learning. Training children in the classroom in social and emotional skills has been shown to increase academic performance by 11 percentile points and to reduce conduct problems and aggression by 9 percent.

Emotional intelligence has also been widely used in skills training for supervisors and managers. In one randomized, controlled study with corporate executives, people who received training in emotional intelligence competencies were superior to the no-intervention control group in measures of social awareness, relationship management, self-management, and self-awareness, as reported by bosses, peers, and employees.

BIBLIOGRAPHY

Cherniss, Cary, and Mitchel Adler. *Promoting Emotional Intelligence in Organizations*. Alexandria, Va.: American Society and Training and Development, 2000. The authors provide a twenty-two-step process for developing and implementing emotional intelligence training within organizations. The book contains case studies and examples of both contemporary and past emotional intelligence training programs conducted within organizations.

Goleman, Daniel. *Emotional Intelligence: Why It Can Matter More than IQ*. New York: Bantam Books, 1995. The author explains why a high intelligence quotient (IQ) is no guarantee of success in the business world. The book details the five crucial skills of emotional intelligence and shows how they can determine people's lives in various ways. Goleman reports on studies of human biology and neuroscience that back up his claims that increasing one's emotional intelligence can improve one's life.

Mayer, John D., Peter Salovey, and Marc A. Brackett. *Emotional Intelligence: Key Reading on the Mayer and Salovey Model*. Port Chester, N.Y.: Dude, 2004. This book contains a collection of chapters and articles that introduce the emotional intelligence ability model as created by Mayer and Salovey. The book focuses on the theory, measurement, and application of the ability model.

Murphy, Kevin R., ed. *A Critique of Emotional Intelligence: What Are the Problems and How Can They Be Fixed?* Mahwah, N.J.: Lawrence Erlbaum, 2006. Includes contributions from both proponents and opponents of emotional intelligence and an essay on the measurement and definition of the concept.

Zeidner, Moshe, Gerald Matthews, and Richard D. Roberts. *What We Know About Emotional Intelligence: How It Affects Learning, Work, Relationships, and Our Mental Health.* Cambridge, Mass.: MIT Press, 2009. Examines all facets of emotional intelligence, including how it is developed and measured. Discusses how it relates to work and school.

Jeremy Wicks, Steven Nakisher, and Laurence Grimm

See Also: Emotional expression; Emotions; Intelligence; Intelligence quotient (IQ); Intelligence tests; Multiple intelligences; Personality rating scales.

Emotions

Type of psychology: Cognition; Consciousness; Emotion

Emotions refer to mental and physiological states associated with a wide variety of feelings, such as happiness, sadness, fear, and disgust. They play a central role in the lives of humans and other animals. Research on emotions has expanded into many fields, providing a wide range of perspectives.

Key Concepts

- Appraisal theories
- Basic emotions
- Cannon-Bard theory
- Cross-cultural differences
- Dialect theory
- James-Lange theory

INTRODUCTION

Over the centuries, philosophers, psychologists, and other scholars have debated the nature of emotions, offering a wide range of perspectives and theories. This debate addresses many issues, including basic questions such as why people have emotions and what their function is. Advances in neuroscience have led scientists to attempt to determine the parts of the brain involved in experiencing emotions. Child developmental psychologists address how young children understand others' emotions, and cognitive psychologists examine how emotion affects memory. Anthropologists and social psychologists investigate whether there are cultural differences in how people experience emotions.

REASONS FOR EMOTIONS

According to the English naturalist Charles Darwin and his theory of evolution, one reason people have emotions is because of natural selection. Emotions exist because they enhance the chance of surviving and reproducing. For example, when a deer senses another animal, it reacts with fear and freezes. This reduces its chance of being attacked because animals usually attack in response to motion. When a person freezes in response to a car whizzing by, the fear response may act to save the person's life. More generally, Dutch psychologist Nico Fridja suggests that emotions are a response to situations in which people need to do something. For example, a negative emotion suggests that something is wrong in the immediate situation and that the person must act to change the situation.

Expressions of emotions also play an important role in communicating information to others. Most people learn to read the expressions of others, infer their emotions, and monitor their behavior as a result. For example, if a person is arguing with someone who begins to raise his or her upper eyelids and show an open, "square" mouth revealing teeth (signs of aggression), then it may be time to end the argument. Nonhuman animals also communicate with emotional expressions, as documented by Darwin. For example, American psychologist Robert Plutchik described a common expression of a cat who has encountered an animal such as a threatening dog. The cat opens its incisors, pulls back its ears, erects the hair on its body, arches its back, and hisses. This expression indicates a mixture of fear and anger, signaling that it may attack the dog and making the cat look larger and more ferocious. As a result, the cat's emotional expression has adaptive value, as it decreases the chance of its being attacked, which increases the cat's chances of survival and reproduction. This type of emotional expression is shown by many species of animals. Plutchik notes that humans display a similar emotional expression, in which an increase in apparent size is achieved by expansion of the chest, thrusting the head forward, standing more erect, and sometimes by erection of the hair.

Despite these positive aspects of emotions, a large body of research suggests that emotions interfere with rational decision making by affecting people's thinking and motivation. However, American psychologists Douglas Medin and Arthur Markman note that some research suggests that emotions play a positive role in decision making. As an example, they describe the research of Portuguese neurologist Antonio Damasio, who suggests that anticipatory somatic feedback (for example, skin conductance response) is necessary for good decision making. He and his colleagues studied patients with damage to their prefrontal cortex (the part of the brain that plays an important role in reasoning, memory, and decision making). These patients, unlike people without such damage, never develop anticipatory skin conductance responses when evaluating risky decisions.

Damasio and his colleagues gave a gambling task to these patients. They were allowed to choose cards from four decks, A, B, C, and D. Choosing either deck A or B resulted in winning one hundred points. However, choosing either deck C or D resulted in winning only fifty points. (Points were converted into play money.) However, every once in a while, the selection of any deck would result in a loss (with deck A or B yielding a loss twice as great as deck C or D). Over the course of the gambling task, choosing from decks C and D yielded more points than choosing from decks A and B. Normal patients were initially attracted to the large number of points provided by decks A and B, but after experiencing "punishments," they tended to choose from decks C and D, which provided more points in the long term (over the course of the gambling task). However, patients with prefrontal damage tended to choose from decks A and B more often than from decks C and D. Further studies revealed that prefrontal patients performed poorly on these gambling tasks because they were not sensitive to anticipatory somatic feedback. Furthermore, the prefrontal patients had normal intelligence quotients (IQs) and should have been able to figure out the relative likelihood of the wins and losses in the different decks. Markman and Medin concluded that while emotion may sometimes hinder the making of rational choices, emotions are also sometimes important in correctly evaluating those choices.

DEFINING EMOTIONS

By trying to understand the differences between emotions and similar concepts such as moods, sensations, temperament, and surprise, researchers can obtain a better understanding of emotions. For example, American psychologist Jeff Larsen and his colleagues suggest that moods tend to be enduring and diffuse, whereas emotions tend to be short-lived and directed at particular objects or situations. English clinical psychologists Mick Power and Tim Dagleish also suggest that moods influence emotions. For instance, a father in a happy mood might not become angry toward his child for dropping her ice-cream cone. However, if the father was in an angry mood, he might become angry.

Temperament is more enduring than either emotions or moods, as it is a personality characteristic or trait of a person. Therefore, an angry type of person may become easily upset in many situations in which a happy person would not become upset. Researchers have argued that surprise is not an emotion. For example, American psychologists Andrew Ortony and Terence Turner note that emotions are characterized by valenced states (positive or negative feelings). However, they point out that surprise is not defined by a valenced state: A person can be surprised about winning a huge prize (a positive feeling), or surprised about the failure of his or her brand-new car to start in the morning (a negative feeling), or be surprised by some highly improbable but personally irrelevant fact such as that all the members of some committee, by chance, share the same birthday (a neutral feeling).

BASIC EMOTIONS

Many theories of emotions assume that a small set of basic or fundamental emotions exist. Ortony and Turner suggest a number of reasons why this might be true. Some emotions appear to exist in all cultures and in some nonhuman animals. They also seem universally recognizable by characteristic facial expressions. There might also be a set of basic emotions with biological functions that are particularly important to the survival of the individual and of the species. Finally, some researchers believe that there may be many emotions. If there is a small set of basic emotions, then researchers may be able to understand the larger set of emotions by using the basic emotions as building blocks for constructing nonbasic emotions.

As evidence for the existence of basic emotions, Power and Dagleish cite American psychologist Paul Ekman, who noted that every proponent of the existence of basic emotions who has conducted investigations has obtained evidence for six basic emotions: happiness, surprise, fear, sadness, anger, and disgust (though Ortony and others argue that surprise is not an emotion). They also note that Ekman and his colleagues have shown that different cultures label emotions in the same way. A study authored by Rachael E. Jack, Oliver G. B. Garrod, and Philippe G. Schyns and published in the January 2014 issue of *Current Biology*, narrowed the scope of basic emotion to just four, finding that the differentiation between fear and surprise, and anger and disgust is likely more social than biological, proposing a revised list of basic emotions: happiness, sadness, surprise/fear, and anger/disgust.

The claim that there are basic emotions is still a controversial and complicated issue. American psychologist Gerald Clore and Ortony argue that contrary to traditional views, emotions do not have clear boundaries or distinctive properties that allow them to be straightforwardly identified. For example, they do not have distinctive facial expressions or physiological states. Emotions do involve facial expressions, psychophysiology, and brain structures, but these properties are not sufficient to characterize basic emotions such as anger or fear. Instead, emotions are more variable.

SIMILARITIES AND DIFFERENCES AMONG CULTURES

Scholars are divided on whether emotions are universal or whether they differ across cultures. Defenders of the universalist approach claim that emotions are the product of human evolution and are part of humans' biological hardware (for example, Ekman and Plutchik). Therefore, cultures have similar experiences and expressions of certain basic emotions. Ekman found his six basic emotions—happiness, sadness, anger, fear, disgust, and surprise—to be universal. In contrast, the cultural relativist approach suggests that experience and expressions of emotions vary considerably and may even be socially constructed. Defenders of this view argue that all emotions are the product of a person's culture. Social values and cultural beliefs can affect how people express their emotions. Therefore, people in different cultures may have different emotional experiences and reactions to similar social situations.

Researchers have examined how cultural values and beliefs influence emotions. The influential Dutch writer Geert Hofstede developed a set of four dimensions that characterize cultures. The dimension of individualism reflects the extent to which a culture is individualistic or collectivistic. An individualistic culture tends to socialize its members to think of themselves as individuals and to give priority to their personal goals (for example, the culture of the United States). A collectivistic culture tends to socialize its members to think of themselves as members of the larger group and to place the group's concerns before their own (for example, the cultures of China, Japan, and Korea). Power distance reflects the extent to which members of a culture accept unequal distributions of power within institutions and organizations. Uncertainty avoidance reflects the degree to which members share beliefs and build institutions that protect them from discomfort and fear of ambiguous situations. Masculinity characterizes how much the culture values stereotypical masculine qualities (such as financial awards) rather than feminine qualities (such as caring for others).

Canadian psychologist Ulrich Schimmack found differences in how some cultures recognize emotions. For example, individualistic cultures were better at recognizing facial expressions of happiness than collectivistic cultures (though it is not clear why). Cultures high in uncertainty avoidance were less accurate at identifying fear. Schimmack suggests that this finding supports American psychologist David Matsumoto's hypothesis that cultures high in uncertainty avoidance have formed institutions to minimize fear, which may explain why they have difficulty identifying fear compared with cultures that are not high in uncertainty avoidance.

Some research suggests that there are both universal and cultural differences in recognizing and communicating emotions. When people were asked to identify emotions in other people, they were always able to outperform anyone making random guesses; however, Hillary Elfenbein and Nalini Ambady found that they were more accurate at identifying emotions when the emotions were expressed by members of their own culture rather than by members of a different culture. These researchers concluded that expressions of emotions are largely universal, but the subtle differences that exist across cultures challenge effective communication. For example, they suggested that people visiting a different country often intuit that their basic communication signals tend to be misinterpreted more often by people of a different country than people of their own.

On the basis of these and other findings, Elfenbein and Ambady developed the dialect theory of emotional expressions. The theory proposes that people's culture shapes their emotional expressions in a way that creates subtle differences in their appearance compared with the appearances of people from other cultures. Cultural differences in emotional expression also result from display rules—informal nonverbal rules about socially acceptable ways to use and control expressions. For example, most American women are likely to cry if a loved one dies in a war; however, Ekman reported that samurai women would smile rather than cry so as to conform to a display rule that women should hide distress and show joy in public.

THEORIES OF HOW EMOTIONS ARE EXPERIENCED

Many theories of emotions have been proposed. Almost all the theories in the last few centuries have been influenced by the work of philosophers such as Aristotle, Baruch Spinoza, and William Lyons. Some of the theories have been particularly influential in the study of emotion. The James-Lange theory of emotion was independently developed by two nineteenth century scholars, William James and Carl Lange. It states that as a response to experiences in a particular situation, the autonomic nervous system produces physiological changes such as muscle tension, increase in heart rate, perspiration, and dryness of the mouth. Emotions are feelings that come about as the result of these physiological changes. For example, a person who starts crying infers that he or she is sad because of the crying, and not the other way around. To most people this view of emotions is counterintuitive and goes against common sense.

The James-Lange theory was challenged in the 1920s by the physiologists Walter Bradford Cannon and Philip Bard. The Cannon-Bard theory of emotion suggested that emotions cause physiological change (a view that is opposite of the James-Lange theory). For example, if a person sees a strange man outside the window late at night, that person might experience the emotion of fear, which causes physiological changes such as trembling and sweating.

Perhaps the most important theory of emotions is appraisal theory, of which there are a number of variations. An important assumption shared by all appraisal theories is that the experience of an emotion is the result of how people interpret, evaluate, or appraise a particular situation. Put more simply, people decide to feel an emotion after interpreting or explaining what just happened. Differences in how people appraise the same situation can lead them to experience different emotions. For example, if an average skier and an expert skier are skiing down a mountain and come on a very steep slope, the expert skier interprets the upcoming situation as an exciting challenge and consequently experiences happiness. However, the average skier, who lacks the skill to tackle such a slope, interprets the situation as being dangerous and experiences fear. Also, the mental processes that a person uses to appraise a situation need not be slow, deliberate, or conscious. Appraisal of a situation and its resulting emotion can occur rapidly and unconsciously.

Psychologists Clore and Ortony have proposed an appraisal theory that involves two kinds of mental processes: a relatively slow reasoning process and a faster associative process. These processes serve different adaptive functions. The associative process prepares a person for a developing situation (such as hearing a loud animal noise). It is based on responses such as reflexes, release of adrenalin, and so on, that according to Clore and Ortony often get the emotional process started. The reasoning process is similar to the mental processes of other appraisal theories.

BIBLIOGRAPHY

Ekman, Paul, and Wallace V. Friesen. *Unmasking the Face: A Guide to Recognizing Emotions from Facial Cues.* Englewood Cliffs: Prentice Hall, 1975. Print.

Jack, Rachael E., Oliver G. B. Garrod, and Philippe G. Schyns. "Dynamic Facial Expressions of Emotion Transmit an Evolving Hierarchy of Signals over Time." *Current Biology* 24.2 (2014): 187–92. Print.

Lewis, Michael, Jeanette M. Haviland-Jones, and Lisa Feldman Barrett, eds. *Handbook of Emotions.* 3d ed. New York: Guilford, 2008. Print.

Ortony, Andrew, Gerald L. Clore, and Allan Collins. *The Cognitive Structure of Emotions.* New York: Cambridge UP, 1988. Print.

Plutchik, Robert. *Emotions and Life: Perspectives from Psychology, Biology, and Evolution.* Washington: American Psychological Association, 2003. Print.

Power, Mick J., and Tim Dalgleish. *Cognition and Emotion: From Order to Disorder.* Hove: Psychology Press, 2008. Print.

Sieb, Richard. "The Emergence of Emotions." *Activitas Nervosa Superior* 55.4 (2013): 115–45. Print. Wassmann, Claudia. "'Picturesque Incisiveness': Explaining the Celebrity of James's Theory of Emotion." Jour. of the History of the Behavioral Sciences 50.2 (2014): 166–88. Print.

Edward J. Wisniewski and Jing Wu

See Also: Anger; Cross-cultural psychology; Emotional expression; Emotional intelligence; Fear; Fight-or-flight response; Love; Mood disorders.

Encoding

Type of psychology: Memory

Encoding strategies include both intentional and unintentional processes that are used to improve memory performance. Encoding refers to the ways information gets put into memory. Encoding specificity is a theory of memory encoding that predicts that any cue that is present at the time of encoding will serve as an effective cue for retrieval of that memory event.

Key Concept

- Cue
- Encoding
- Retrieval
- Storage
- Target word

INTRODUCTION

Most people find it easy to remember certain events from the past, such as the best vacation they ever had. They would remember their age and the most interesting things they saw or did at that time, even if the events occurred years before. If people could not remember events in their lives, they would have no personal history, skills, or talents. Fortunately, humans are able to take information from the world and store it in a mental representation that allows them to use that past information in a current situation. This ability is a function of the way the human memory

The memory system records events as they occur; this process is called encoding. The information is stored in a memory trace until it is needed. A memory trace remains in storage until a cue (a specific clue that triggers a memory) for that memory occurs, at which time the memory will be retrieved from long-term storage and outputted for use.

SHORT-TERM AND LONG-TERM MEMORY

In the model that is often used to illustrate memory systems, information comes into the memory system and is then transported to short-term memory (STM), where it is held for both further encoding into, and interaction with, long-term memory (LTM). There are different encoding strategies for information, depending on whether it is to be used by STM or LTM. Some encoding strategies are unintentional, but others can be used purposefully to increase memory abilities.

One of the characteristics of STM is that it can only store five to nine items, and these items remain in STM for only about eighteen seconds. Thus, information processed in STM must either be encoded into LTM or be lost from the system. If, for example, one needs the information of a telephone number, one probably will repeat the number until one can dial. This is known as a rehearsal strategy, and it serves to make the information available until one uses it.

One way of overcoming the capacity limitations of STM is by an encoding strategy called chunking: A group of items are chunked into meaningful units, which allows STM to hold more information and to be aided by LTM. For example, if one were asked to remember the letters FCTIIIBWAABM by rehearsing the letters, one would not easily remember the sequence. If, however, one were asked to remember the same letters arranged as FBI CIA TWA IBM, one would have no trouble recalling the sequence. The letters are chunked into four meaningful units that are small enough for STM and can be encoded into LTM because of their meaningfulness.

Another encoding strategy is the use of imagery. To remember a list of items, one makes a visual image of the items. For example, if one is to remember the pair of words dog and ribbon, one might make an image of the dog with a big red ribbon on its tail. Imagery is similar to another encoding strategy called elaboration. This, like imagery, adds details to an event and gives it more meaning so that it is more easily remembered. For example, given directions to a concert, one might start thinking about the time one walked down Main Street. By adding these details, one elaborates on the event and increases one's memory. Elaboration is something that people do automatically, because memory is organized so that one event triggers memories of other events. If one hears the word dog, one automatically begins to retrieve things that one knows about dogs.

Another encoding strategy is called organization. This process groups items into larger categories of relatedness. For example, given a list of words to remember, such as dog, knife, rose, cat, horse, fork, daisy, spoon, and pansy, one would likely remember the words in three categories: flowers, utensils, and animals. This could be an intentional encoding strategy, and it aids memory because the retrieval (the process of getting information from the memory system) of the larger category also activates all the members of that category that are associated with it.

ASSOCIATED CUES

The theory proposed by Endel Tulving called encoding specificity contradicts organizational encoding. Tulving proposes that any cue present and specifically encoded at the time of study will serve as an effective cue for retrieval, even over cues that would seem to be more likely to trigger the memory. For example, in 1971 Tulving and D. M. Thompson gave subjects a list of word pairs to remember. One group was given a list of word pairs that were strong associates of each other, such as hot-cold. The other list had words that were weakly associated with each other, such as blow-cold. Later, at a test session, the first word was given as a cue, and subjects were asked to fill in the second target word. Each group was given both strong and weak associated cues. It might seem likely that given the cue hot-______, one would think of the target word cold even if one had been given the weakly associated pair of blow-cold at the time of study; however, this was not what happened. Subjects given the cue word blow at study could not recall cold when given hot as a cue but did very well when given their original cue word, blow. In other words, whatever cue word was encoded at the time of study was the best cue for retrieval of the target word at test regardless of how weakly or strongly associated the cue and target words were. Therefore, Tulving predicted that whatever cues are specifically encoded at the time of the event are the best cues for memory at the time of testing. Thus, encoding specificity can be extended to any context cues specific to the memory event. This includes the subject's mood or surroundings.

IMPORTANCE OF CONTEXT

Sometimes the information that is encoded into the memory event is related to the context or surroundings of that event; instead of a word cue, the environment at the time of encoding can be a cue for retrieval. For example, in 1975, Duncan Godden and Alan Baddeley found that memory was better if subjects were asked to remember something in the same physical environment in which they previously had learned the material. They had subjects study a list of words on shore and a list of words underwater. If the list was learned underwater, memory was better if the recall test was also underwater rather than on shore, and vice versa. They concluded that the context provided additional cues for memory.

These context effects have also been demonstrated to include a person's mood at the time of encoding, known as state-dependent effects. For example, in 1978 Gordon Bower hypnotized subjects into either a positive or negative emotional state and tested their memory for material when they were in the same and different emotional states. Students who were in congruent states of mind at study and test sessions had greater memory than students in different states of mind at study and test. Again, the contextual cues that were associated with a particular state of mind were present at both encoding and retrieval and served to aid recall by being specifically encoded with the event.

Thus, if one wants to increase one's memory skills, the more types of encoding strategies one uses, the better one will be able to remember. In addition, it is important to remember that using the same cues for both study and test sessions will also result in better performance. Therefore, one might try to do some studying in the same room where one will be taking a test.

EVOLUTION OF RESEARCH

Cognitive psychology encompasses the study of all the functions of the human mind, including thinking, problem solving, reasoning, attention, consciousness, and processing information. It is considered a relatively new field of psychology, although its roots go back to the work of early psychologists in the late nineteenth and early twentieth centuries; in a sense they go back even further, to the philosophers of centuries past. In the late 1800s, both the renowned psychologist William James and Sigmund Freud, the founder of psychoanalysis, wrote about aspects of consciousness and attention. In the same time period, Hermann Ebbinghaus began studying verbal learning and memory, while Wilhelm Wundt attempted to research the structure of the mind with his method of introspection.

Another significant contribution to cognitive psychology began in 1904, when Ivan Petrovich Pavlov proposed his principles of conditioned learning. This led the way for further study into the learning processes of humans and animals; learning became considered to be an overt action, not a process of the mind. Thus, John B. Watson proposed in 1913 that behavior was the only suitable topic for psychology to study, and the processes of the mind became a taboo subject for many years.

It was not until World War II that cognitive psychology again became a legitimate topic for research. This occurred because the topic of human error became an important question for the military: pilots' lives could be saved if more could be known about perception and actions. Researchers were employed to determine how decisions were made and to study the importance of attentional processes on performance. From this an entire field of study emerged, and the study of encoding strategies developed as a by-product of studying other processes of the memory system, such as attention, forgetting, and effective retrieval cues.

In the same time frame, the computer emerged; these areas of psychology were formulated in terms of an information-processing model of human memory. In other words, to understand the way memory systems work, a theoretical model of the brain was based on the computer. In 1968, Richard Atkinson and Richard Shiffrin suggested a model of memory that consisted of three memory stores, each with its own characteristics and functions. This consisted of the sensory register, the short-term memory, and the long-term memory. This information-processing model made the concepts of codes, storage capacity, trace duration, and retrieval failures an area of research. In studying these concepts, researchers discovered new topics of interest.

Research into encoding strategies is concerned with which elements of the environment are selected for encoding and how people can use this information to improve memory performance. The cue environment that is encoded is a topic of great interest, as it can aid performance if it can be predicted. Such components of the cue environment as gestures and emotions that are all encoded below the level of awareness are only beginning to be studied, and they should lead to a much better understanding of how to improve memory.

BIBLIOGRAPHY

Anderson, J. R. *Cognitive Psychology and Its Implications*. 6th ed. New York: Worth, 2005. Print.

Dehn, Milton J. *Working Memory and Academic Learning: Assessment and Intervention*. New York: Wiley, 2008. Print.

Ellis, Henry C., and Reed R. Hunt. *Fundamentals of Human Memory and Cognition*. 4th ed. Dubuque: Brown, 1989. Print.

Eysenck, Michael W., and Mark T. Keane. *Cognitive Psychology*. 6th ed. New York: Psychology, 2013. Print.

Greene, Robert L. *Human Memory: Paradigms and Paradoxes*. New York: Psychology, 2014. Print.

Groome, David, et al. *An Introduction to Cognitive Psychology: Processes and Disorders*. 2nd ed. New York: Psychology, 2013. Digital file.

Schwartz, Barry, and Dan Reisberg. *Learning and Memory*. New York: Norton, 1991. Print.

Smith, Frank. *Comprehension and Learning: A Conceptual Framework for Teachers*. New York: Holt, 1975. Print.

Tulving, Endel. *Elements of Episodic Memory*. London: Oxford UP, 2008. Print.

Donna Frick-Horbury

See Also: Artificial intelligence; Brain structure; Ebbinghaus, Hermann; Freud, Sigmund; Forgetting and forgetfulness; James, William; Long-term memory; Memory; Memory: Animal research; Memory: Empirical studies; Memory: Physiology; Memory: Sensory; Memory storage; Short-term memory.

Endocrine system and behavior

Type of psychology: Biological bases of behavior

Behavior, by definition, includes physiological events that are responses to internal and external stimuli; the endocrine system, through the action of hormones and in cooperation with the nervous system, plays a necessary role in bringing about these reactions in animals and humans.

Key Concepts

- Adrenal glands
- Biopsychology
- Ethology
- Hormone
- Hypothalamus
- Pituitary gland

INTRODUCTION

People have suspected that substances in the body contribute to behavior for a long time. During the fifth century bce., Hippocrates suggested in his humoral theory, that personality was determined by four body fluids: phlegm, black bile, yellow bile, and blood. The dominance of one of the fluids was associated with a specific behavior pattern, and a proportionate distribution of the fluids resulted in a balanced personality. This theory has contributed terms such as "phlegmatic," "bilious," and "good-humored" to describe personality types and states of mind.

Aristotle is reported to have performed castration experiments on both fowl and men to alter behavior. He believed that something produced by the testes caused typically male behavior. Several nineteenth century researchers continued the study of the connection between the testes and male reproductive behavior. In 1849, Arnold Adolphe Berthold implanted testes into the abdomens of castrated cockerels. Successful transplantation restored typical "male" behaviors such as crowing and combativeness.

During the late nineteenth and early twentieth centuries, knowledge of behavior and its causes increased. The science of ethology, which focuses on animal behavior, came into existence. In the early 1900s, John B. Watson founded a branch of psychology that became known as behavior science. This area of psychology concentrated on human behavioral studies. Eventually, ethology and behavior science contributed to biopsychology, also known as psychobiology, or biological psychology, a branch of psychology that analyzes data from neurosciences, genetics, endocrinology, and physiology in the quest for biological explanations of behavior, thoughts, and feelings. Biopsychology embraces several subdivisions. Physiological psychology focuses on nervous system and endocrine system research. Psychopharmacology specializes in the effects of drugs on the nervous system and, ultimately, on behavior. The development of therapeutic drugs is a goal of this discipline. The neuropsychologist studies the effects of brain damage on behavior. Psychophysiology differs from physiological psychology in that the psychophysiologist uses only human subjects while the physiological psychologist experiments on laboratory animals. Early research in physiological psychology focused on the nervous system, but it soon became evident that the endocrine system also influenced behavior and that the two systems were integrated and had coordinated effects on behavior. The classic endocrine system consists of ductless glands that produce chemical substances called hormones. The hormones elicit physiological responses, either locally or at some distant target site. When acting at a distance, the hormones travel to the site by way of the circulatory system.

Hans Selye, a Canadian scientist, proposed a direct connection between the endocrine system and behavior. In 1946, he described physiological events that were triggered by stress. This set of bodily changes became known as the general adaptation syndrome. The syndrome involved the mobilization of the autonomic nervous system, the adrenal glands, and the anterior lobe of the pituitary.

As research continued, data on the role of the endocrine system in determining behavior began to accumulate. Researchers continue to look to the endocrine system to provide clues about the causes of psychiatric diseases and the efficacy of hormone therapy in treating the diseases, as well as in altering behavior patterns.

INVERTEBRATES

Among most invertebrates (animals without backbones), endocrine glands are not in evidence. There is, however, an invertebrate endocrine system. Specialized cells known as neurosecretory cells serve as endocrine tissue. The cells, which resemble neurons (the functional cells of the nervous system) are hormone producers. In invertebrate animals such as the hydra and planaria, the secretions (hormones) of the neurosecretory cells seem to influence growth and may be the underlying cause of the tremendous powers of regeneration possessed by the animals. There are indications that the development of sexuality, the laying of eggs, and the release of sperm may be under hormonal control in these animals. Attempts to establish the link between hormones and invertebrate behavior when the hormones are produced by neurosecretory cells have inherent problems. A historic method of studying hormone influence involves removal of the secreting organ, which causes a hormone deficit. Changes in physiology, behavior, or both are observed. Utilization of this method was complicated by the difficulty in removing all the functioning neurosecretory cells. Modern gene deletion or knockout technologies, which can remove a hormone or its receptor from a single tissue as well the whole animal, allow a more thorough assessment of the effects of hormone deficit.

Hormone effects are observable and measurable in the more developed invertebrates such as the Arthropoda. Studies carried out on insects and crustaceans indicate the presence of both neurosecretory cells and endocrine glands. Among the behaviors and activities controlled by the hormones released from either the cells or the glands are molting, sexual differentiation, sexual behavior, water balance, and diapause. Because arthropods are encased in an outer skeletal structure, it is necessary for the animals to shed their outer structure to grow. During the growth years, the animals go through cycles of shedding the outer skeleton (molting), growing, and reforming an outer coat. There is evidence that insects are under hormonal control when they enter a state of diapause, or arrested behavior in adverse times.

VERTEBRATES

All vertebrates (animals with backbones) have a well-developed and highly organized endocrine system. The classic endocrine system consists of the pituitary, the pineal, the thyroid, the thymus, the pancreas, a pair of adrenals (each adrenal acts as two glands—the adrenal cortex produces unique hormones and functions independently of the adrenal medulla), a pair of parathyroids, and a pair of ovaries or testes. Most tissues in the body produce hormones that help the central nervous system integrate needs and function of the organism. Adipose tissue hormones signal the level of stored energy to the brain, which determines the satiety or hunger necessary to maintain energy stores. Endocrine tissue in the gastrointestinal tract readies the system for the digestive process. During a pregnancy, the placental tissue assumes an endocrine function. Although the kidneys do not produce a hormone directly, they release an enzyme that converts a blood protein into a hormone that stimulates red blood cell production.

All vertebrates have a pituitary. The pituitary is a small, round organ found at the base of the brain. This major endocrine gland interacts with the hypothalamus of the nervous system. Together they modulate many behaviors. The hypothalamus monitors physiological status by receiving neural input and hormone signals from many peripheral tissues. In turn, the hypothalamus signals the pituitary by either neural impulse or chemical messengers called neurotransmitters. The pituitary responds by releasing into the peripheral blood circulation, or stopping release, of pituitary hormones that will have an effect on peripheral physiology to alter the physiological event and influence behavior. The endocrine system exerts its effects by binding to cellular receptors that in turn regulate intracellular biochemistry such as metabolism and gene expression. The human endocrine system is typical of vertebrate endocrine systems and their effect on behavior, although more complex, as reflected by a more complex human system. For example, melanocyte-stimulating hormones, which are generated by the anterior lobe of the pituitary, greatly increase skin pigmentation in amphibians. This creates a protective coloration. In humans, certain types of melanocyte-stimulating hormones may darken the skin, especially in certain hormonal conditions as those found in pregnancy. However, the melanocyte-stimulating hormones are not the cause for racial skin tone variation. Other melanocyte-stimulating hormones affect appetite and sexual arousal. There are enough similarities among human and animal endocrine functions and effects, however, to warrant the use of data from both ethology and human behavioral studies in determining the biological bases for behavior.

INFLUENCE ON REPRODUCTIVE BEHAVIOR

The influence of the endocrine system on behavior has been studied on many levels. Much of the work has been done on animals. There is, however, a growing body of information on hormonal effects on a variety of human behaviors, including reproductive and developmental behavior, reaction to stress, learning, and memory. Studies carried out in reproductive and developmental biology on both animal and human subjects have substantiated the belief that hormones influence mating behavior, developmental events including sexual differentiation, and female and male sexuality.

Castration experiments have linked the testes with a male mating behavior pattern in animals. The sexually active adult male aggressively seeks and attempts to mount the female whether she is receptive or not. The castrated male retains the ability to mount a female but loses the aggressiveness and persistence of the normal male's pursuit. The castrated animal may assume more submissive female behavior and even engage in homosexual encounters. Normally, the release of reproductive hormones in the male is noncyclic, whereas in the female it is cyclic. Castrated animals begin to exhibit the female, cyclic pattern of hormone release. The hormonal influence is confirmed by administering androgens (male hormones) to the castrated animals. Male mating behavior and the noncyclic release of hormones returns.

The presence of male hormones has an effect on the female cycle and sexual receptivity. Pheromones are substances secreted on the body of one individual that influence the behavior of another. These chemical messengers function during mate attraction, territoriality, and episodes of fear. Their existence and functions are well documented throughout the animal kingdom, especially among insects and mammals. In experiments using rats, it was shown that the pheromones act in conjunction with male hormones in bringing the female rat to a state of receptivity. The urine of noncastrated males contains androgens. When a male is introduced into a cage of sexually inactive females, the male sends off chemical signals by way of pheromones and the androgen-containing urine. The result is the accelerated onset of estrus, or sexual receptivity, on the part of the females. Castrated males produce pheromones but do not have androgens in their urine. When castrated males are introduced into a cage of inactive females, the estrous cycle is not affected.

Female mammals, with the exception of monkeys, apes, and humans, also experience estrus. Under hormonal control, the female is receptive to the male once or twice a year, when her eggs are available for fertilization. This period of receptivity is known as the estrous phase, or heat. Research shows that the particular female hormone that induces estrus is progesterone.

HORMONAL INFLUENCES

The work done by researchers in developing contraceptives clarified the role of hormones in the functioning of the human female reproductive system. The system operates in a monthly cycle, during which ovarian and uterine changes occur under hormonal control. These hormones do not affect the woman's receptivity, which is not limited to fertile periods. Progesterone has effects on the nervous system and may be responsible for changes in mood or behavior.

Testosterone derivatives known as anabolic steroids are illegally used by some athletes in an attempt to increase muscularity, strength, and performance. Although both sexes do experience the desired effects, long-term, high-dosage usage has undesirable consequences. This is particularly true in women, who begin to exhibit a deepening of the voice, a male body shape, and increased body and facial hair. Both men and women can become sterile. Psychotic behaviors and states such as depression and anger have been recorded.

Developmental biologists indicate that hormones exert their influence as early as six or seven weeks into embryonic development. At this point, undifferentiated tissue with the potential of developing into either a female or a male reproductive system will develop into a male system in the presence of testosterone and into a female system in its absence. There is some evidence that the embryonic hormones have an effect on the developing brain, producing either a male or female brain. Functionally, this may account for the cyclic activity of female reproductive hormones and the noncyclic activity of male hormones. A few anatomical differences between male and female brains have been observed in both rats and humans. In the hypothalamus of the brain, there are cell bodies called nuclei. In rats and in humans, these nuclei are larger in males than in females.

Learning and memory can be experimentally affected by hormones. Experiments reveal that chemicals that resemble adrenocorticotropic hormone (ACTH) can extend the memory time of rats. Rats, stimulated by electric shock and provided with an avoidance possibility such as moving into another chamber of a cage or climbing a pole in the center of the cage, were administered ACTH-like molecules. The treated rats were able to remember the appropriate reaction to the stimulus for a longer period of time. In other experiments, rats in a maze were administered vasopressin, a posterior pituitary hormone, which increased their frequency in selecting the correct pathway through the maze.

The effect of vasopressin on human memory is not as clearly defined. There have been positive results with schizophrenic patients and patients with alcohol-induced amnesia. In these cases, memory has been enhanced to a limited degree. There is no evidence that learning and memory in humans will be greatly improved by the administration of vasopressin.

Hormones can also effect changes in eating and sleeping behavior. As the prevalence of obesity continues to grow, the physiological psychologist will be challenged to address integrated approaches. Sleeping disorders are also increasing in prevalence and can affect mood, behavior, and quality of life. As more traditional approaches to illness fail to achieve optimal health, understanding neuroendocrinology will become an important foundation to build effective interventions.

BIBLIOGRAPHY

Brennan, James F. *History and Systems of Psychology.* 6th ed. Upper Saddle River, N.J.: Prentice Hall, 2003. Print.

Carlson, Neil R. *Physiology of Behavior.* 11th ed. Upper Saddle River: Pearson Education, 2013. Print.

Drickamer, Lee C., Stephen H. Vessey, and Elizabeth Jakob. *Animal Behavior.* 5th ed. New York: McGraw-Hill, 2002. Print.

Goodman, H. Maurice. *Basic Medical Endocrinology.* 3d ed. San Diego, Calif.: American Elsevier, 2004. Print.

Kostyo, Jack L., and H. Maurice Goodman. "The Endocrine System." *In Handbook of Physiology.* New York: Oxford University Press, 1999. Print.

Lovallo, William R. "Do Low Levels of Stress Reactivity Signal Poor States of Health?" *Biological Psychology* 86.2 (2011): 121–28. Print.

Norris, David O. *Vertebrate Endocrinology.* 4th ed. Boston: Elsevier Academic Press, 2007. Print.

Pinel, John P. J. *Biopsychology*. 7th ed. Boston: Allyn & Bacon, 2008. Print.

Wadhwa, Pathik D. "The Contribution of Maternal Stress to Preterm Birth: Issues and Considerations." *Clinics in Perinatology* 38.3 (2011): 351–84. Print.

Rosemary Scheirer;
updated by Karen Chapman-Novakofski

See Also: Adrenal gland; Emotions; General adaptation syndrome; Gonads; Hormones and behavior; Memory: Animal research; Pituitary gland; Sex hormones and motivation; Stress: Physiological responses; Thyroid gland.

Endorphins

Type of psychology: Biological bases of behavior

Endorphins are naturally occurring chemicals in the brains of both vertebrates and invertebrates. They aid in pain relief, inhibit defensive behaviors such as fleeing and hiding, and are part of the brain's reinforcement system.

Key Concepts
- Addiction
- Analgesic effect
- Endogenous opioids
- Neurotransmitters
- Opiates
- Periaqueductal gray matter
- Placebo effect
- Stress

INTRODUCTION

The term "endorphin" means "endogenous, morphine-like substance." These naturally produced chemicals were discovered after researchers in the 1970s found that the opiate drugs morphine and heroin could physically bind to brain tissue. This binding occurred at neurochemical receptor sites on certain brain cells. Researchers began looking for the chemical that normally used these receptor sites, and soon discovered endorphins and their sister chemicals, the enkephalins. Collectively, these chemicals are referred to as endogenous opioids (opioid means opium-like). All are peptides, which consist of at least two amino acids linked together, and are often called opiate peptides. (Note that proteins, the body's building blocks, consist of multiple peptides.) Some endogenous opioids function as neurotransmitters for communication between brain cells. Others function less for the communication of a specific message and more as modulators of a neuron's response to yet other neurotransmitters.

The endorphins and other opioids are important because of their role in controlling pain, which has long been of interest to the medical profession. Morphine, which chemically resembles the endorphins, was one of the first painkillers known to humankind. It is the active component of opium, and its effects have been recognized for centuries. Morphine is still widely used clinically for treating pain. Unfortunately, morphine is addictive and produces unpleasant withdrawal symptoms. Also, the body develops a tolerance to morphine so that ever-increasing doses are needed to control pain. Many other effective pain relievers have similar problems. The discovery of endorphins and enkephalins has provided hope that scientists will one day be able to control pain without fear of addiction or withdrawal symptoms after the treatment with the painkiller ends.

BETA ENDORPHINS, ENKEPHALINS, AND DYNORPHINS

Endogenous opioids include alpha, beta, gamma, and delta endorphins; leucine and methionine enkephalin; dynorphins; and endomorphins. Most of these interact with three major subtypes of opioid receptors: mu, delta, and kappa. Of the endogenous opioids themselves, the beta-endorphins, the enkephalins, and the dynorphins have been most widely studied. The endorphins are the largest molecules in the endogenous opioid family, at about thirty amino acids long, while the enkephalins are shortest at about five amino acids long. Beta-endorphin and the dynorphins are more potent than the enkephalins and last longer in the body. Enkephalins are typically neurotransmitters, substances released by neurons that cause another nerve, muscle, or gland to respond to a given stimulus, of the brain and spinal cord. Though, weaker than endorphins, enkephalins are still considerably stronger and longer lasting than morphine.

The three primary types of endogenous opioids are distributed somewhat differently in the brain and spinal cord. The enkephalins and dynorphins are found primarily in the dorsal horn of the spinal cord, which receives incoming information, such as pain, from the body, and in the periaqueductal gray matter, which is part of the midbrain. Activation of the periaqueductal gray matter is clearly associated with analgesia for pain without affecting the person's response to other touch-related sensations such as pressure and temperature. This area receives input from the frontal lobe, amygdala, and hypothalamus, structures involved in emotional expression, and projects to circuits in the brainstem that are involved with pain regulation. The periaqueductal gray matter also plays a role in species-specific behaviors such as predation and self-defense. Beta-endorphin is found most commonly in the hypothalamus, which projects to many other areas of the brain, including areas where enkephalins and dynorphins are found. Beta-endorphins in the brain are released in response to unpleasant stimuli entering the brain. In the spinal cord, they are released in response to impulses relayed from the brain to peripheral muscles.

The most widely studied effect of endogenous opioids such as the endorphins is their ability to block painful stimuli (the analgesic effect). However, they have been associated with many other physiological activities, including thermoregulation, appetite, emotion, memory, lipolysis, regulation of bowel movements, reproduction, and pleasurable experiences. They produce their effects by binding to target cells at receptor sites, which are protein structures of a particular size, shape, and chemical charge that can be activated only by specific chemicals. The receptor sites for the opioid peptides are the same ones that bind morphine, which allows the drug to produce effects similar to those produced by endogenous opioids.

MECHANISM AND EFFECTS

The endorphins and other endogenous opioids appear to be inhibitory in nature. Activation of the opioid system increases inhibition in brain areas such as the periaqueductal gray matter, which in turn decreases the input the brain receives from the peripheral nervous system and the spinal cord. Thus, painful stimuli are blocked from reaching the upper brain. Morphine works the same way.

Although their effects are powerful, the endorphins and other endogenous opioids are typically found only in very low concentrations in nervous tissue. Because of this, most opioid research has been conducted in animals, in which cellular effects and injections into specific cells can be achieved. Animals, however, are unable to describe any feelings that might be produced. In humans, endorphins have generally been studied through plasma levels or cerebrospinal fluid levels.

Endorphins and other endogenous opioids are released in humans under conditions of physical or psychological stress. The physical stress most closely associated with an increase in plasma endorphin levels is aerobic exercise, especially running, although levels typically return to normal within thirty minutes to an hour after cessation of exercise. The endorphins are generally credited with decreased sensitivity to pain in athletes who suffer physical injury. They may also explain why some runners experience a feeling of well-being after prolonged, strenuous exercise.

ADDICTION AND THE PLACEBO EFFECT

The explanation for morphine addiction may also lie with opioids like the endorphins. Because morphine and the endorphins bind to the same receptors on cell membranes, the theory suggests that morphine, when available, occupies some of the receptor sites while the endorphins occupy the rest. This shuts down pain sensitivity. However, morphine and the other opiate drugs are exogenous (from outside) substances and are not as readily available to the individual as the endogenous opioids.

Furthermore, in patients to whom morphine is supplied, the natural circulating levels of the opioid enkephalins appear to decrease. Once enkephalin levels fall, the receptor sites to which they had been bound are no longer occupied, and pain stimuli can reach the brain. The increase in pain signals individuals to seek relief, and because they cannot increase their own endogenous opioids, they may take drugs such as morphine instead. This decrease in the circulation of natural opioids after morphine treatment may explain the phenomenon of drug craving and may partially explain morphine's withdrawal effects.

Endogenous opioids are even involved in addictions to other substances, most notably alcohol. Alcohol appears to trigger the release of endogenous opioids, which produces some of the reinforcing effects of alcohol. Plus, abstinence from alcohol increases the numbers of certain opioid receptors in a brain structure called the nucleus accumbens, which is involved in reinforcement. The increase in opioid receptors caused by alcohol abstinence is associated with an increased craving for alcohol.

Endorphins also appear to be involved in the placebo effect. Patients who receive sugar in place of typical analgesics and are told they will feel better soon, often do experience an improvement in their condition. Research shows that the improvement brought about by a placebo can sometimes be blocked by injections of naloxone, which inhibits endogenous opioids. The belief that an analgesic will work apparently triggers the release of endogenous opioids and actually produces some pain relief, at least in some individuals.

ROLE OF STRESS AND EXERCISE

Studies show that both animals and humans become less sensitive to painful stimuli while under stress. In humans, many instances have been described in which individuals experienced the severe stress of an injury without even being aware of the injury, or, if aware, without feeling the pain. For example, wounded soldiers sometimes claim to experience no pain from serious injuries, and sometimes even feel a sense of detachment or curiosity when viewing their wounds. Similarly, people show decreased pain sensitivity when engaged in the pleasant, but physically stressful, act of sexual intercourse. Much of this analgesic effect appears to be mediated by endogenous opioid release in the brain in response to pain. Drugs that block opioid receptors in the brain generally eliminate the decrease in pain sensitivity brought on by stressful events. Psychologically, this makes good sense. Pain is a warning to stay away from dangerous stimuli, but in individuals already fighting for their lives, pain is more of a distraction than an aid. For sexual intercourse, some experience of pain often occurs with the pleasure, but a species would not survive if the pain overcomes the reproductive drive.

Mood also can apparently be influenced by levels of endogenous opioids in the brain. Some badly injured people describe their mood as serene and accepting of the situation. More common experiences can alter mood in similar ways. One example is the athlete doing aerobic exercise. Strenuous exercise leads to physiological changes very similar to a stress reaction. Intense exercise, like that seen in long-distance running, can induce increases in naturally occurring opioids. Runners tested after a long run typically show elevated endorphin levels. Not only do they experience less pain, which is almost certainly an endorphin effect, but they sometimes experience a feeling of elation called the runner's high.

Some scientists attribute the runner's high to elevated endorphin levels. However, although endorphin levels remain elevated for only thirty minutes after a long run, the runner's mood typically remains positive for far longer, indicating that factors other than endorphins, such as other brain chemicals and the psychological sense of accomplishment, probably play a role. Still, dedicated runners and others who regularly do aerobic exercise often describe a sense of loss when unable to run or exercise. Some researchers have suggested that this need to exercise resembles a form of exercise addiction and that the sense of loss can be seen as withdrawal from the person's own endorphins. Exercise has even proven successful as a treatment for mildly depressed individuals, although whether this effect involves the endogenous opioids is unclear.

ANIMAL RESEARCH

The best known effects of the endogenous opioids are their ability to induce analgesia and to reinforce behavior. However, other effects have also been observed. Many of these have been seen primarily in animals, and have not been clearly identified in humans. For example, rats injected with endogenous opioids during memory tasks generally show impaired performance. Rats show increased physical activity with low doses of endorphins but generally show decreased activity with higher doses. Rats also experience increased grooming tendencies and increased sexual arousal after treatment with opiate peptides, and the suckling behavior of rat pups is associated with elevated opioid levels.

Other animals also experience changes in behavior after administration of endogenous opioids. Young chicks isolated from their mother or from other young chicks normally give loud distress cries. This behavior decreases after endorphin administration, and similar effects have been seen in guinea pigs and dogs. Goldfish show increased schooling behavior when treated with endorphins, and wild, white-crowned sparrows increase feeding behavior when given endorphin injections, which may reflect a decrease in their stress response to being captured. Undoubtedly, other behavioral effects of endogenous opioids will be identified in animals in the future, and it is likely that correlates will be found for many of these behaviors in humans.

HISTORY OF OPIATE STUDIES

During the early 1970s, the US government declared a war on drugs. Federal money was made available to study the effects of drugs and the basis of drug addiction. The opiates, particularly heroin, were included in the targeted drug groups. It was theorized at the time that if the opiates had an effect on the brain, they must be operating on receptors. Some of these opiate-like receptors were isolated in 1973 at the Johns Hopkins University School of Medicine by Solomon H. Snyder and Candace Pert. The presence of natural opioid receptors in humans suggested the existence of endogenously occurring opiate-like substances, and the first such endogenous opioids were isolated and identified in 1973. It soon became clear that the existence of endogenous opioids such as the endorphins and enkephalins would revolutionize theories about the role of natural brain chemistry in drug addiction. It was not understood until much later how many other behaviors would also involve natural brain opioids.

The endogenous opioids remain a major area of study in neuroscience. A complete understanding of such phenomena as pain, stress, eating, addiction, reinforcement, sexual pleasure, and many other behaviors will require a more complete knowledge of the endorphins, enkephalins, dynorphins, and other endogenous opiate-like substances. The promise is great for developing better pain relievers and better treatments for stress and drug addiction. It remains to be seen whether the ability of these substances to alter mood will be a danger or a boon.

BIBLIOGRAPHY

Carlson, Neil R. *Physiology of Behavior.* 11th ed. Boston: Allyn, 2012. Print.

Freye, Enno. *Opioids in Medicine.* New York: Springer, 2008. Print.

Gellman, Marc D., and J. Rick Turner. *Encyclopedia of Behavioral Medicine.* New York: Springer, 2013. Print.

Goldberg, Jeff. *Anatomy of a Scientific Discovery.* 25th anniversary ed. New York: Skyhorse, 2013. Print.

Lopez, Shane J. *The Encyclopedia of Positive Psychology.* Malden: Wiley, 2009. Print.

Meyer, Jerrold S., and Linda F. Quenzer. *Psychopharmacology: Drugs, the Brain, and Behavior.* Sunderland: Sinauer, 2005. Print.

Pasternak, Gavril W. *The Opiate Receptors.* New York: Humana, 2010. eBook Collection (EBSCOhost). Web. 20 May 2014.

Stannard, Cathy, Michael Coupe, and Tony Pickering. *Opioids in Non-Cancer Pain.* New York: Oxford UP, 2007. Print.

Annette O'Connor; updated by Charles A. Gramlich

SEE ALSO: Biofeedback and relaxation; Exercise and mental health; Meditation and relaxation; Nervous system; Neurons; Neurotransmitters; Pain; Pain management; Psychopharmacology; Stress: Physiological responses; Substance use disorders; Synaptic transmission.

Environmental factors and mental health

TYPE OF PSYCHOLOGY: Biological bases of behavior; Developmental psychology; Emotion; Social psychology; Stress

A person's immediate physical environment can be a source of satisfaction or a source of stress, anxiety, and fear. Most environmental stressors tend to be minor but chronic, and often their severity becomes major only when environmental variables shift. As a result, environmental stressors tend only to be as serious in their consequences as those affected by their outcomes are vulnerable.

KEY CONCEPTS

- Natural conditions
- Post-traumatic stress disorder
- Seasonal affective disorder
- Social conditions
- Stress reactions
- Trauma

INTRODUCTION

People's behavior is a partial by-product of their life experiences in interacting with the physical environment. Environmental stressors—whether events or forces—may result in reactions that influence behavior and mental health. Individuals under environmental stress seek to maintain a state in which they are comfortable both physiologically and psychologically. As the living environment places stress on people, their adaptation and coping are driven by both physical and psychological stress reactions. If the stresses become a severe irritant due to chronic exposure and a failure to adapt, both physical and mental health may suffer.

Although specific environmental factors have not been shown to cause specific mental health conditions, many environmental factors are thought to cause stressful situations that induce latent neuroses or exacerbate existing ones, often resulting in damaging behaviors and mental issues. The effects of environmental factors on neurotic or organic mental illness are difficult to assess because intense life experiences linked to the environment are often associated with situations that in and of themselves involve stress and fear. Though considerable anecdotal evidence exists, no definitive evidence demonstrates that environmental factors induce either neurotic or psychotic illness. However, statistical evidence indicates that the rate of admissions to hospitals for certain mental health issues increases during or after exposure to certain environmental stressors.

STRESS

Stress is the key component in understanding the relationship between environmental factors and mental health. Those in imposing environmental conditions experience stress, which makes adjustments necessary. Individuals seek to maintain a state in which they feel safe and comfortable. Environmental traumas and disasters, whether natural or human induced, occur in many forms. They produce feelings of terror, vulnerability, helplessness, uncertainty, loss of control, and threat to life, and create climates of short-term and long-term anticipatory stress regarding possible, probable, and imagined risks. Trauma suffered due to environmental stressors often creates the highest levels of anxiety and fear because it destroys the expectations of safety and trust that people have in their living environment. Even if an environmental stressor is dramatic and clearly evident, individuals vary in their assessment of and reaction to the threat. When environmental stressors endure over time, a person's assessment of threats and risks becomes an ongoing process and can result in chronic stress to vulnerable, high-risk individuals, culminating in physiological and psychological impact.

When individuals are exposed to an environmental stressor, their bodies first respond by initiating coping mechanisms, generally preparing the body for fight or flight, and triggering physiological changes driven by the adrenal-cortical system. If the stress is repeated or extended for a long period of time, the individual may become exhausted to the point where adaptive reserves are depleted and both physical and mental breakdowns begin to occur. However, a person's physical and mental reactions to environmental stressors are directly linked to the individual's distinct perceptions of vulnerability and subsequent ability to either adapt or accept the conditions. Ultimately, anyone who has been physically stressed by severe environmental conditions and experiences psychological issues to the extent that the past trauma interferes in his or her daily life may be diagnosed as suffering from an environmentally induced mental disorder.

Environmental factors considered linked to mental health issues fall into two categories: natural and social conditions. Natural conditions include specific environmental stressors such as the number of hours of daylight, meteorological conditions, and natural disasters. Social conditions involve factors such as crowding, crime, war, living and working space, and noise. Much of the psychological concern about the links between environmental stressors and mental health are directed exclusively toward understanding and treating the aftermath of traumatic events. However, it is important to understand that while human behavior resulting from the trauma of stressful environmental conditions may lead to mental disorders, this is not solely a psychological phenomenon but is usually a direct result of physiological conditions stressing the body.

NATURAL CONDITIONS

Some relationship appears to exist between mental well-being and meteorological variables: Fluctuations in atmospheric conditions are often correlated to changes in people's mental health. Changes in the weather seem to have strong effects on mood in general and depressive states in particular; with the most recognized association being a combination of high temperatures, low barometric pressure, and cloud cover. Psychiatrists recognize that some people suffer from seasonal affective disorder (SAD). Seasonal affective disorder is a group of depressive symptoms occurring in late autumn and winter and seeming to retreat in spring. The disorder is predominate in women living in higher latitudes and is linked to a shortage of sunlight. The counterbalance to seasonal affective disorder is that statistically more psychiatric emergencies occur on sunny, humid, hot days. Although sunshine seems to improve mood, excessive heat and humidity bring on irritating stresses, increasing levels of aggression. In certain geographic regions, wind is believed to be the cause of symptoms of mental illness. The Santa Ana and Chinook winds of North America, Foehn and Sirocco winds of Europe and North Africa, and Sharav wind of Israel are routinely linked to depression, nervousness, higher neuroticism, and violent crimes. Levels of sunshine, changes in temperature, and exposure to winds all result from changes in barometric pressure. Anecdotal evidence suggests a correlation between lower barometric pressures and increased cases of depression and suicide.

Environmental disasters are severe stressors that throw lives into chaos and fill survivors with terror of the unexpected and fear of loss, injury, or death. Individuals exposed to traumatic environmental events such as hurricanes, earthquakes, tornadoes, dust storms, volcanic eruptions, floods, tsunamis, firestorms, landslides, and avalanches have an increased exposure to a wide range of fear-inducing cues. The elements of trauma exposure—including threats to life, physical injury, exposure to grotesque sights, the collapse of social identity, loss of property and familiar environments, and violent and sudden death of loved ones, witnessed or not—may result in cases of both acute and post-traumatic stress disorders. In many instances, post-disaster stress disorders are intensified by manifestations of religious fears devoid of factual connection to the event.

SOCIAL CONDITIONS

Social conditions attributed to producing environmental stressors and resulting mental health issues involve the actions and perceived intentions of other people. Human-made disasters, failed social experiments, politics, military conflicts, and intolerance can all lead to environmental stressors affecting a population's psychology. In an attempt to limit certain human-induced environmental stressors, the fields of environmental psychology and environmental design have been developed. Environmental psychology suggests that one's living environment and its context can to a great extent provide an explanation for personal behaviors. The fundamental theories of environmental design suggest that people have an inherent need for personal space and territory and that specific aspects of constructed physical environments such as dimensions, open space, crowding, color, and landscape are all environmental stressors affecting an individual's sense of well-being and in turn affecting mental health. Research suggests that the design of living environments matters and has significant and demonstrable effects on behavior and psychological health. Living environments induce or reduce annoyances, which in turn establish the amount of stress with which an individual's coping and adaptive abilities must deal. Failure to adapt or cope leads to additional stress and frustrations that may eventually lead to certain psychopathological symptoms: This pathology is largely connected to the person's method of coping.

More than half the people on Earth live in cities. These urban environments are all characterized by increased population density, which is a strong environmental stressor, resulting in pollution, noise, fear of crime, and crowding. These urban stressors appear to affect mental health in some people, but they do occur equally across all cultures or urban settings. High population density is associated with a lack of physical space, pollution, a lack of certain resources, the close proximity of others, physical and social incivilities, and often uncontrolled interaction with strangers. For some people, living in an environment rife with continuous physical irritations and unregulated interactions causes cognitive and social overload. Such overload often results in heightened frustration, anxiety, and discomfort, which in turn may result in diminished mental health.

If pollution of any kind is continuous and creates ongoing physiological stresses, it could ultimately result in biological responses leading to the development of clinically identifiable mental health symptoms. As with all types of pollutants, noise is a physical irritant. Though numerous studies suggest relationships between exposure to high levels of occupational noise and the development of neurosis and between the presence of environmental noise and mental health, no definitive evidence exists that noise can induce neurotic or psychotic illness. Anecdotal evidence does suggest exposure to excessive noise may result in a variety of negative biological responses.

The main stressor resulting from living in an environment in which crime is likely is fear. Fear of crime and its associated violence can become chronic and intrusive and can increase the sense of helplessness among people, raising anxiety to the point that it compromises lifestyle. Those who have been victims of crime, especially violent crimes, may develop acute or post-traumatic stress disorders, or phobias.

The oldest social condition that is an environmental stressor is war. As with certain crimes, war is an intentional act of violence, and its main component as an environmental stressor is purpose-driven fear. The trauma to which both combatants and noncombatants are exposed during war is similar to the trauma of a devastating natural disaster—terror of the unexpected, sudden death, loss, horrific visual stimuli, disassociation, dislocation, and panic. Unlike the short-term initial shock and stress of most natural disasters, the environmental stressors of war may last continuously for years, subjecting victims to extensive periods of constant physiological and psychological pressure. The study of mental health issues in both surviving civilians and soldiers of wars has resulted in the acknowledgment, understanding, and diagnosis of acute and post-traumatic stress disorders and development of appropriate treatments.

BIBLIOGRAPHY

Fullerton, C. S., and R. J. Ursano, eds. *Post-traumatic Stress Disorder: Acute and Long-Term Responses to*

Trauma and Disaster. Washington, D.C.: American Psychiatric Press, 1997. Defines post-traumatic stress as a complex interaction between environment, biology, and mind, and suggests that trauma is always a catalyst for life change and adjustment.

Kopec, D. *Environmental Psychology for Design*. Chicago: Fairchild, 2006. Deals with the historical context of human habitation and how the fields of design and architecture integrate with environmental psychology in a meaningful and helpful way.

Leach, J. *Survival Psychology*. New York: New York University Press, 1994. Discusses the psychological consequences of survival and recovery from environmental and human-made disasters, addressing both victims' and rescuers' emotional and psychological behaviors over time.

Ursano, R. J., et al. *Individual and Community Responses to Trauma and Disaster: The Structure of Human Chaos*. New York: Cambridge University Press, 1994. Deals with the issues of preparedness, prevention, and care through psychiatric interventions involving civilian and military workers and survivors of natural and human-made disasters.

Van der Kolk, B. A., et al. *Traumatic Stress: The Effects of Overwhelming Experience on Mind, Body, and Society*. New York: Guilford Press, 1996. This critical analysis of the study of psychological trauma, including aspects of the psychological, emotional, biological, developmental, cultural, and historical research of traumatic stress, is scientifically and medically authoritative. Includes in-depth bibliographies.

Williams, S. W. *Environment and Mental Health*. New York: John Wiley & Sons, 1994. Reflects contemporary research in the field of environmental psychology with a focus on the physical rather than social environment. Derived from: "Environmental factors and mental health." Psychology and Mental Health. Salem Press. 2009.

Randall L. Milstein

See Also: Anxiety disorders; Coping: Strategies; Disaster psychology; Ecological psychology; Environmental psychology; Environmental toxicology and mental health; Fear; Fight-or-flight response; Generalized anxiety disorder; Stress: Behavioral and psychological responses; Stress: Physiological responses; Stress-related diseases.

Environmental psychology

Type of psychology: Biological bases of behavior; Social psychology; Stress

Environmental psychology examines the relations between the physical (natural or artificial) environment, or the context, and human behavior and experience. The discipline has proved valuable for understanding individual, social, and societal processes.

Key Concepts

- Cognitive map
- Context
- Crowding
- Environment
- Environmental cognition
- Environmental stressor
- Personal space
- Privacy
- Proxemics
- Territoriality

INTRODUCTION

Environmental psychology is concerned with the relationships between the physical environment—both natural and artificial—and human behavior and experiences. The term environment is best defined as the total set of circumstances by which one is surrounded, including physical, interpersonal, and sociocultural aspects. This can include where one goes to school, works, has a home, or lives.

In the field's early stages, it proved valuable for understanding the relationships between the physical environment and individual processes, such as the interpretation of information from the environment; social processes, such as the sharing and division of space; and societal processes, which are usually identified with key settings in society, such as school, work, home, and urban environments. The field expanded to include considerations of formal theories that attempted to explain person-environment relationships; cultural differences affecting such relationships; and practical applications aimed at improving person-environment interactions, such as designing better environments and encouraging the management of natural resources through energy conservation and recycling. Subfields of interest include environmental health, environmental ecology, the use of art in the environment and its psychological impact, urban and city planning, and environmental design.

AREAS OF RESEARCH

Research examining the relations between the physical environment and individual processes has traditionally focused primarily on three areas. One encompasses environmental perception, or the ways people take in information from their environment, and environmental cognition, or how people organize this information in their heads. A second area involves the ways people feel about and evaluate aspects of the physical environment. This includes both individual impressions, such as personal descriptions, preferences, and emotional responses (termed environmental appraisal), and collective impressions of places by expert groups (environmental assessment). A third area is the environmental aspects of personality, which looks at the ways characteristic patterns of behavior and experience influence people's transactions with the physical environment.

Studies have demonstrated that environmental perception is enhanced if the physical environment is novel, complex, surprising, or incongruous. Environmental cognition has been shown to be associated with life stage: In 1973, Roger A. Hart and Gary T. Moore demonstrated that as children age, their mental organization of the physical environment (their cognitive map) becomes less egocentric, then more projective (thinking of settings from various physical vantage points), and finally more abstract (thinking of settings through the use of abstract concepts such as coordinates and directions). Research on person-oriented environmental appraisals and place- or policy-oriented environmental assessments has focused primarily on the scenic quality of natural settings but has expanded to include a variety of physical contexts—urban air quality and nursing homes, for example. Studies on environmental aspects of personality have indicated that traditional personality variables may explain some aspects of person-environment relationships. Compared with reserved individuals, outgoing individuals rated landscapes as more serene and beautiful. People with an internal sense of control over their lives have been shown to prefer buildings within the classical architectural style, while those believing their lives to be influenced by powerful others or by fate prefer the romantic style.

PROXEMICS

Researchers in environmental psychology have extensively studied four areas in particular: personal space, territoriality, crowding, and privacy. These four areas compose proxemics, a field concerned with the ways in which individuals and groups deal with space as a limited resource and structure their activities accordingly. Personal space is the area surrounding a person's body, as if there were invisible boundaries, into which intruders may not come without causing discomfort. This space has been shown to be larger for men, variable for disturbed individuals, smaller in situations of attraction or cooperation, and larger in situations involving stigma or unequal status. Studies of territoriality have typically shown that men are more territorial than women and that occupying one's own territory is related to perceived control.

Research on crowding has distinguished between density, an objective measure of the number of individuals per unit area, and crowding, an individual's subjective perception of spatial restriction. Prolonged, high indoor density acts as an environmental stressor, often impairing health, affecting blood pressure and other cardiac functions; performance of complex tasks; and social interaction, causing increased aggression, withdrawal, and lack of cooperation. Privacy refers to the selective control of access to one's self or one's group. Studies have shown that private preferences, expectations, values, and behaviors vary from person to person and from occasion to occasion.

CONTEXT-SPECIFIC SOCIETAL RESEARCH

Research on the relationship between the physical environment and societal processes has concentrated on living at home, learning in the classroom, and functioning in the workplace. Each of these environments involves many perceptions, activities, and attitudes. The home environment can include one's residence, neighborhood, and city; living there may include such varied activities as shopping, relaxing, waiting for the bus, deciding who really owns the bathroom, preparing for potential disasters, and moving.

Researchers have applied many of the individual and social processes described above in the specific contexts of the home, city, school, and workplace. For example, research has shown that neighborhood satisfaction is related to the absence of environmental stressors (such as noise, pollution, and ugliness), although some individuals seem able to adapt to at least some of these stressors. Climate has been shown, at the urban level, to influence prosocial and antisocial behavior slightly; high temperatures seem to increase aggression, while comfortable temperatures increase the desire to help. Studies at schools have shown that classroom characteristics such as high noise and density levels may be associated with numerous difficulties—including decreased learning, participation, and classroom interaction—and may cause negative feelings about school.

PERSON-ENVIRONMENT THEORIES

Complementing the array of empirical studies are attempts at both theoretical and practical application. The theoretical applications have tried to provide integrative theories for the field—that is, for person-environment functioning more generally. A major theoretical point accepted by most investigators has been that the environment is composed not only of physical aspects but also of interpersonal and sociocultural aspects. To make sense of the field's varied theoretical applications, psychologists Irwin Altman and Barbara Rogoff have used the philosopher Stephen C. Pepper's four worldviews to organize theories of person-environment functioning.

In formist, or trait, approaches to person-environment relations, the focus is on individuals or psychological processes as self-contained entities, with environments playing supplementary or secondary roles. For example, an investigator adhering to this type of approach might study how traditional personality characteristics (such as the locus of control) affect environmental appraisal.

In mechanistic, or interactional, approaches, the focus is on person, group, or setting qualities as independently defined and influencing one another in causal fashions. Environmental factors are usually treated as causal influences on psychological functioning. For example, an investigator working from this type of approach might employ specific learning techniques to understand and then to decrease littering.

In organismic approaches, the emphasis is on dynamic and holistic systems, with complex reciprocal influences between person and environment components. For example, a researcher with this type of approach might study the development of individuals' cognitive maps across the life span.

Finally, in contextual, or transactional, approaches, the focus is on the changing relations among aspects of persons and of environments, which together compose holistic entities. An investigator might attempt to illustrate how descriptions of homes reflect inseparable confluences of psychological and environmental experiences.

DESIGNING OPTIMAL ENVIRONMENTS

Environmental psychology has also increasingly become concerned with practical applications such as optimizing person-environment relations. Such applications have included recommendations for the actual design of more fitting environments. For example, Barbara B. Brown and Altman have demonstrated that residential dwellings with real and symbolic barriers, which communicate a strong sense of territoriality—are less likely to be burglarized than residences lacking such barriers. Harry Heft has reviewed the work on prolonged high indoor density on children and found it to be associated with difficulties in visual and auditory discrimination, object permanence, and language development. M. Powell Lawton designed a nursing home that successfully enhanced patients' perceptual and social transactions with the environment.

INTERVENTION PROGRAMS

Research on environmental stress, at both the individual and societal levels, has generated intervention programs to decrease technological risk and to encourage the management and preservation of natural resources. For example, Jack Demick and his collaborators from Hiroshima University analyzed cultural differences in the impact of governmental legislation: Whereas the Japanese value group adherence to legislation as a whole, Americans value individuality and personal expression. These differences were then employed in the design of differential programs to enhance the use of automobile safety belts. Appeals to national pride were used in Japan; freedom of choice was emphasized in the United States. Other related programs include decreasing such environmental problems as air pollution, litter, and homelessness and increasing such processes as energy conservation and recycling. Robert Gifford's Environmental Psychology: Principles and Practice (2007) reviews many of the major applied programs in these and related areas.

CONTRIBUTIONS OF BRUNSWIK AND LEWIN

Historically, the first stirrings of environmental psychology occurred in the 1940s. This was followed by increased activity in the 1950s. The field grew significantly throughout the 1960s and into the 1970s. The movement in each of these decades is perhaps summarized best through the work of its pioneering researchers.

In the 1930s, psychologist Egon Brunswik, born in Budapest and trained in Vienna, immigrated to the United States. Initially focusing on the process of perception, he expanded his ideas to make three contributions to the field that became environmental psychology: He was one of the first to call for a more detailed analysis of the ways in which physical environmental factors affect behavior; he advocated the use of more varied environmental stimuli in psychological research than was typically the case; and he coined the term environmental psychology in 1934.

A psychologist who made more of a contribution than Brunswik was Kurt Lewin. Born in Prussia and trained in Germany, he also immigrated to the United States. He was extremely influential for several reasons. First, his work on field theory in the 1940s was the first to give significant attention to the molar physical environment; his original notion that behavior is a joint function of the interaction between person and environment became a basic premise of modern psychology. Second, he influenced many students, among them Roger Barker and Herbert Wright. In the 1950s, Barker and Wright developed ecological psychology, in which they studied behavior settings, small ecological units enclosing everyday human behavior (such as the restaurant or the pharmacy) with both physical-spatial and social aspects. Ecological psychology is often credited as the forerunner of environmental psychology.

REAL-WORLD FOCUS

Environmental psychology emerged in the 1960s as a problem-focused field, responding to practical questions posed by architects and planners about real-world design decisions. The shift from basic laboratory research to work on real-world applications was perhaps also expedited by changing societal realities related to the US involvement in the Vietnam War. This real-world focus was subsequently reinforced by environmental events such as the 1979 nuclear accident at Three Mile Island in Pennsylvania.

The movement into the real world, and its accompanying focus on the real-life functioning of individuals, highlighted, for the field of psychology as a whole, the need to take the environmental context into account in all theories and research on human behavior and experience. Although various subfields of psychology, such as developmental psychology, have acknowledged the importance of context, environmental psychology strongly reinforced this idea by providing a unique perspective on all psychological processes. Context will continue to be a driving force behind psychology's renewed commitment to understanding individuals' real-world functioning in all of its complexity.

An interesting shift that may expand environmental psychology in new ways in the twenty-first century is the effect of the Internet. Similarly, the presence and expansion of virtual environments essentially becoming real-world functioning spaces may also expand this field in new ways. Environmental psychology not only focuses on societal efficiency and functioning but also increasingly examines things such as the perception and evaluation of natural and engineered landscapes, cognitive mapping and special cognition, environmental risks and hazards perception, tourism and leisure behavior in relation to physical settings, psychological attachment and identity as related to places, and even the broader consequences of human interaction on the environment. As human populations continue to expand in number, the importance of this field will increase because of its relevance for all these aspects of twenty-first-century life.

BIBLIOGRAPHY

Bechtel, Robert, and Arza Churchman, eds. *Handbook of Environmental Psychology.* New York: Wiley, 2008. Print.

Clayton, Susan D., ed. *The Oxford Handbook of Environmental and Conservation Psychology.* New York: Oxford UP, 2012. Print.

Downs, Roger M., and David Stea, eds. *Image and Environment: Cognitive Mapping and Spatial Behavior.* Chicago: Aldine, 1973. Print.

Gifford, Robert. *Environmental Psychology: Principles and Practice.* 4th ed. Boston: Optimal, 2007. Print.

Hall, Edward Twitchell. *The Hidden Dimension.* 1966. Reprint. New York: Anchor, 1990. Print.

Holahan, Charles J. *Environmental Psychology.* New York: Random, 1982. Print.

Kopec, David Alan. *Environmental Psychology for Design.* 2nd ed. New York: Fairchild, 2012. Print.

Proshansky, Harold M., William H. Ittelson, and Leanne G. Rivlin, eds. *Environmental Psychology: People and Their Physical Settings.* 2d ed. New York: Holt, 1976. Print.

Saegert, S., and G. H. Winkel. "Environmental Psychology." *Annual Review of Psychology* Volume 41. Palo Alto: Annual Reviews, 1990. Print.

Steg, Linda, Agnes E. Van den Berg, and Judith I. M. de Groot, eds. *Environmental Psychology: An Introduction.*

Malden: Wiley, 2013. Print.

Stokols, Daniel, and Irwin Altman, eds. *Handbook of Environmental Psychology.* Malabar: Krieger, 1991. Print.

Wapner, S., and J. Demick. "Development of Experience and Action: Levels of Integration in Human Functioning." *Theories of the Evolution of Knowing.* Ed. Gary Greenberg and Ethel Tobach. Hillsdale: Erlbaum, 1990. Print.

Jack Demick; updated by Nancy A. Piotrowski

See Also: Cognitive maps; Coping: Strategies; Crowd behavior; Defense reactions: Species-specific; Field theory: Kurt Lewin; Health psychology; Stress: Behavioral and psychological responses; Stress: Physiological responses; Stress: Theories.

Environmental toxicology and mental health

Type of psychology: Cognition; Consciousness; Developmental psychology; Learning; Memory; Sensation and perception

The environment contains toxic chemicals and substances that have been found to cause neurological problems in people, particularly children. Some of the most problematic substances are lead and organic compounds found in herbicides, fungicides, and pesticides.

Key Concepts

- Bioaccumulation
- Biomagnification
- Fine eye-hand coordination
- Fungicide
- Herbicide
- Motor ability
- Pesticide

INTRODUCTION

Toxins in the environment—most notably, organic compounds used in herbicides, fungicides, and pesticides—have been found to affect the motor ability, cognition, and aggression levels of children. One pioneering study of Yaqui children in northwestern Mexico found profound behavioral differences when children who had been exposed were compared with a control group of similar ethnic background in a nearby location whose environment did not contain high levels of the same chemicals. Other substances, such as lead (in paint or soil) at levels of fewer than five hundred parts per million, also can cause neurological problems when ingested by young children, even as airborne dust.

THE YAQUIS AND PESTICIDE CONTAMINATION

A landmark study of the effect of toxic chemicals on the mental health of children involved two groups of Yaquis, an indigenous farming people who live and work in and near the Yaqui Valley in Sonora, Mexico. After World War II, a lack of water and financing forced the Yaquis off their farms in the valley. They leased their lands to outsiders, mainly corporate farmers, who were heavy users of pesticides, herbicides, and fungicides. These chemicals were applied by aerial spraying, by tractor, and by hand, bringing widespread contamination of land, water, and people in the Yaqui Valley.

About the same time, valley farm operations became mechanized, and irrigation and transport systems were established. Farming became big business. Yaqui families living in the foothills moved into the valley for employment, and some valley residents moved into the foothills to maintain family farms under local ownership.

Typically two crops per year were planted in the valley, and pesticides were applied as many as forty-five times per crop. Between 1959 and 1990, thirty-three different compounds were used for the control of cotton pests alone. Multiple organophosphate and organochlorine mixtures as well as pyrethroids were used. Specific compounds include dichloro-diphenyl-trichloroethane (DDT), dieldrin, endosulfan, endrin, heptachlor, and parathion-methyl. Organochlorines, which accumulate most often in body fat, are especially dangerous because of biomagnification (also known as "bioaccumulation"). In biomagnification, the effects of organochlorines increase in nearly exponential fashion up the food chain. As recently as 1986, 163 different pesticide formulations were sold in the southern region of Sonora. Substances banned in the United States, such as lindane and endrin, are readily available to farmers living in the Mexican part of the valley.

Contamination of the human population in the Yaqui Valley has been documented, with women's breast milk, after one month of lactation, found to contain levels of lindane, heptachlor, benzene hexachloride, aldrin, and endrin that were all above limits set by the Food and Agricultural Organization of the United Nations. In 1990, high levels of several pesticides were found in the cord blood of newborns and in the breast milk of Yaqui Valley residents.

In the valley, pesticide use was widespread and continued throughout the year, with little governmental control. Household insect sprays were applied daily in the lowland homes. By contrast, in the foothills, residents usually did not use synthetic pesticides or herbicides on their small farms. They maintained traditional methods of pest control in their gardens and usually killed insects in their homes by swatting them. Most of these people were exposed to pesticides only when the government sprayed DDT each spring to control malaria.

SPECIFIC EFFECTS OF ORGANIC PESTICIDES

In addition to producing physiological symptoms (burns on skin, loss of fingernails, rashes, and death in some cases), the chemicals used in the Yaqui Valley affected the motor skills, growth, and development of children living there. During the 1990s, Elizabeth Guillette, an anthropologist and research scientist at the University of Arizona, studied the affect of pesticide exposure on Yaqui children. Guillette's studies confirmed local observations that exposure to pesticides had a serious affect on the children's health, including their physical and mental development. Hers was the first study to examine neurobehavioral affects, including cognition, memory, and motor ability, in children exposed to pesticides.

In Guillette's study, the behavior of children living in the valley who were regularly exposed to many synthetic chemicals was compared with that of children living in the foothills, where pesticide use was largely avoided. The study selected two groups of four- and five-year-old Yaqui children who resided in the Yaqui Valley of northwestern Mexico. These children shared similar genetic backgrounds, diets, water-mineral contents, cultural patterns, and social behaviors. Guillette adapted a series of motor and cognitive tests into simple games the children could play, including hopping, ball catching, and picture drawing.

Before her study, Guillette had assumed that differences between the two groups would be subtle. Instead, she was shocked. According to an account by Jon R. Luoma, writing in Mother Jones, the lowland children had much greater difficulty catching a ball or dropping a raisin into a bottle cap—both tests of hand-eye coordination. They also showed less physical stamina. The most striking differences were revealed in the children's drawings of people. Pictures created by the foothill children were recognizable as people. The lowland children's drawings were infantile scribbles. The lowland youngsters were still exhibiting some motor problems, particularly with balance. Guillette found that the exposed children also demonstrated decreases in stamina, gross and fine eye-hand coordination, and thirty-minute memory.

Children who had experienced prolonged exposure to pesticides also became more violent. Guillette said she noticed that exposed Yaqui children often would walk by somebody else and strike the person without apparent provocation. The children who had been routinely exposed to chemicals became easily upset or angry after their parents made minor corrective comments. These behaviors were not noted in the foothills children. Valley children also appeared less creative in their play. They roamed an area aimlessly or swam in irrigation canals with minimal group interaction. Often, they sat in groups and did nothing. Foothill children, by contrast, were always busy and interacting with each other when engaged in group play.

Guillette concluded that toxins in the environment had placed the children of the agricultural area of the Yaqui Valley at a disadvantage for participating in normal childhood activities. In a follow up two years after her initial study, Guillette observed improvements in the children's drawings, although those of the lowland children were far less detailed, and lowland children exhibited ongoing difficulties with balance. Whether these effects would remain as the children grew into adulthood was not known.

According to psychology researchers Sue Koger and Deborah Winter, pesticide exposure may also be a risk factor for autism, conduct disorder, schizophrenia, and Parkinson's disease.

NEUROLOGICAL EFFECTS OF TOXIC METALS

Lead exposure is most dangerous to children under the age of six because their bodies are developing rapidly. It can damage brain function and the nervous system and also contribute to physiological problems, such as hearing loss and stunted growth. The most common pathway for lead to enter children's bodies is not ingestion of paint chips (very few children eat paint) but through routine hand-to-mouth contact with lead dust during painting or other remodeling of home interiors. In 1978, the Consumer Product Safety Commission banned paint containing more than six hundred parts per million of lead. However, lead is still used in roadway paint and by the military as a paint additive to accelerate drying, increase durability, maintain appearance, and repel destructive moisture. It can also be found in plumbing and in some dishes and glassware.

Toxicity due to lead exposure can affect any organ system in the human body. No standard for entirely safe exposure to lead exists, so any known exposure should be avoided.

Some studies indicate that lead poisoning can influence behavior, especially in children, contributing to juvenile delinquency and violent crime, although questions have been raised regarding whether the lead itself actually causes such behavior. Exposure to lead, especially at high levels, can produce coma, convulsions, hyperirritability, and stupor, sometimes leading to death. Lead exposure, even at low levels if maintained for months or years, can impede intelligence. Other symptoms of prolonged exposure include poor attention span, muscular tremor, and loss of memory. The younger a child, the greater the danger. Because the brains of younger children are still developing, they are afflicted with neurological problems from lead at lower levels than older children and adults.

If exposed to lead late in life, adults may experience many of the same symptoms as children, although they can tolerate a higher level of exposure without evident ill effects. Lead exposure in adults can cause decreased libido, mood changes, headache, lower cognitive performance, impeded hand dexterity, and delayed reaction time, decreased visual motor performance, dizziness, fatigue, and forgetfulness. Attention-deficit hyperactivity disorder (ADHD) may be caused by lead exposure, especially in childhood and adolescence. Some of lead's neurological effects, including ADHD, may persist into adulthood, even after the source of exposure has been removed.

Because of lead's toxicity, cities that contain closed smelters have been declared Environmental Protection Agency Superfund sites. In one such city, Omaha, Nebraska, lead toxicity has been detected in the soil at least five miles from a former smelter site on the Missouri River at the city's eastern border.

Mercury has long been known to cause neurological damage. In the Minamata Bay mercury poisoning, a Japanese manufacturing company dumped mercury-containing waste from the late 1950s to early 1970s into the nearby bay, which accumulated the seafood consumed by the local population. Those with so-called Minamata disease suffered brain lesions, paralysis, loss of speech, sight, or sound, tremors, and cognitive impairment, which had the most marked affects on patients who were fetuses and young children at the time. Studies conducted in the early 2000s found that pre- or postnatal mercury exposure was associated with learning disabilities, attention disorders, and reduced IQ. Mercury bioaccumulation in seafood continues to be a problem in Japan and elsewhere. Exposure can also come from broken thermometers, barometers, thermostats, or fluorescent light bulbs containing mercury, as well as cosmetic products.

Aluminum may be linked to dementia in older adults. Other metals with known toxicities include arsenic, cadmium, copper, iron, lithium, manganese, and thallium.

BIBLIOGRAPHY

Bellinger, David C. "Cognitive Disorders: Toxic Exposure." *Psychopathology of Childhood and Adolescence: A Neuropsychological Approach*. Ed. Andrew S. Davis. New York: Springer, 2013. 729–43. Print.

Guillette, Elizabeth A., et al. "An Anthropological Approach to the Evaluation of Preschool Children Exposed to Pesticides in Mexico." *Environmental Health Perspectives* 106.6 (1998): 347–53. Print.

Johansen, Bruce E. *The Dirty Dozen: Toxic Chemicals and the Earth's Future*. Westport: Praeger, 2003. Print.

Koger, Susan M., and Deborah Du Nann Winter. "Neuropsychology of Toxic Exposures." *The Psychology Of Environmental Problems: Psychology for Sustainability*. 3rd ed. New York: Psychology, 2010. Print.

Luoma, Jon R. "System Failure: The Chemical Revolution Has Ushered in a World of Changes. Many of Them, It's Becoming Clear, Are in Our Bodies." *Mother Jones*. Mother Jones and the Foundation for National Progress, July–Aug. 1999. Web. 6 Mar. 2014.

Nriagu, Jerome O. *Encyclopedia of Environmental Health*. Amsterdam: Elsevier Science, 2011. Print.

Oliff, Heather S. "Metal Toxicity: Your Brain under Siege." *Health Library*. EBSCO Information Services, 8 Jan. 2013. Web. 27 Mar. 2014.

"Parkinson's Disease: Hope through Research." *National Institute of Neurological Disorders and Stroke*. National Institutes of Health, US Dept. of Health and Human Services, 13 Mar. 2014. Web. 27 Mar. 2014.

Raloff, J. "Picturing Pesticides' Impacts on Kids." *Science News* 153.23 (1998): 358. Print.

"Statement of Angel Valencia, Yoemem Tekia Foundation, Tucson, Arizona POPs Negotiations, March 23, 2000." *Native News* 27 Mar. 2000: n. pag. Print.

Bruce E. Johansen

See Also: Abnormality: Biomedical models; Aggression; Children's mental health; Developmental disabilities; Ecological psychology; Environmental factors and mental health; Environmental psychology; Motor development.

Erikson, Erik H.

Born: June 15, 1902, in Frankfurt am Main, Germany
Died: May 12, 1994, in Harwich, Massachusetts
Identity: German-born American developmental psychoanalyst
Type of psychology: Developmental psychology

Erikson was an innovator of the psychosocial theory of human development, who emphasized developmental change throughout the human life cycle through a series of eight developmental stages.

Erik H. Erikson was born in west-central Germany. His mother, a single parent, married Erik's pediatrician, Theodor Homburger, when Erik was three. Erikson took his stepfather's name and remained Erik Homburger throughout his childhood and into early adulthood. The details of his birth were kept secret, an aspect of Erikson's life that influenced his work.

The twenty-five-year-old Erikson acquired a position in Vienna as an art teacher at a private school that was founded by Anna Freud, daughter of Sigmund Freud, the father of psychoanalysis. With her encouragement, Erikson graduated from the Vienna Psychoanalytic Institute in 1933, where he studied under Sigmund Freud. That same year, Erikson moved to the United States, obtained a teaching position at the Harvard Medical School, and became the first child analyst in Boston, Massachusetts. He officially changed his name to Erik H. Erikson on receiving his American citizenship. After leaving Harvard, he taught at Yale, and later at the University of California at Berkeley.

Erikson was interested in the influence of society and culture on child development. To help formulate his theories, he studied groups of Native American children in the United States. Through these studies he was able to correlate personality growth with parental and societal values. This research formed the basis for *Childhood and Society* (1950), which includes the "eight stages of psychosocial development,"Psychosocial development theory for which Erikson is best known.

Erikson emphasized developmental change throughout the human life cycle. He claimed that human beings develop through eight distinctive psychological stages spread over their entire life cycle. He further stated that each stage had a certain set of "crises" that must be resolved before moving on to the next stage. He believed that humans must complete each stage in successive order before entering the next, and that failure to successfully complete earlier stages could hinder their potential success in later stages.

Erikson's later studies centered on personal human development and social history. It was these psychohistorical studies that won him a Pulitzer Prize and National Book Award in 1969 for *Ghandi's Truth: On the Origin of Militant Nonviolence*.

After his formal retirement in 1970, Erikson continued to lecture and write essays and books. Following a brief illness, he died in 1994 in Harwich, Massachusetts, at the age of ninety-one.Erikson, Erik H.

BIBLIOGRAPHY

Bloland, Sue Erikson. *In the Shadow of Fame: A Memoir by the Daughter of Erik H. Erikson*. New York: Penguin, 2006. The daughter of Erikson, herself a psychotherapist and a faculty member at the Manhattan Institute for Psychoanalysis, recounts her life with her father, who was in private a complex and insecure man and in public a renowned thinker and seeker of fame.

Friedman, Lawrence Jacob. *Identity's Architect: A Biography of Erik H. Erikson*. Cambridge, Mass.: Harvard University Press, 2000. A meticulous biography by historian Friedman, who worked with Erikson and his wife in the years immediately preceding Erikson's death in 1994.

Stevens, Richard. *Erik Erikson: Exploring the Life Cycle, Identity, and Psychohistory*. New York: Palgrave Macmillan, 2008. Analyzes the work of Erikson and explains his contributions to the understanding of childhood and the life cycle.

Jack Carter

See Also: Developmental psychology; Ego psychology: Erik H. Erikson; Identity crises; Midlife crisis; Personality theory.

Ethology

Type of psychology: Origin and definition of psychology

Ethology, the study of animal behavior, is concerned with the adaptive significance of behavior and the physiological, genetic, and psychological basis of behavioral responses in the animal kingdom; ethology emphasizes the importance of heredity and evolutionary factors in the study of behavior.

Key Concepts

- Adaptation
- Conditioning
- Imprinting
- Innate
- Instinct
- Natural selection
- Stimulus

INTRODUCTION

Ethology, from the Greek *ethos* ("behavior" or "manner"), is the study of animal behavior. It is concerned primarily with the accurate description and rigorous experimental evaluation of animals' behavior under natural conditions. Unlike the field of behaviorism, which traditionally emphasized the sole importance of the environment on behavior, ethology also recognizes the genetic and physiological mechanisms that regulate behavioral processes. Ethologists operate under the primary assumption that much of behavior is hereditary and thus strongly influenced by the forces of natural selection. Natural selection is the process of differential survival and reproduction that leads to heritable characteristics that are best suited for a particular environment.

In their search for a common, unifying explanation of behavioral processes, ethologists have sought to address three specific issues: the accurate, nonanthropomorphic description of behavior under natural conditions; the underlying mechanisms that regulate and control behavior; and the adaptive significance of various behavior patterns.

DESCRIPTIVE APPROACH

In its earliest stages, ethology was characterized by a highly descriptive approach. Early ethologists were concerned primarily with accurate and objective accounts of behavior. Behavior, however, unlike other aspects of an organism's biology (such as morphology or physiology), was a difficult and elusive thing to characterize and thus required careful, unbiased approaches to understanding the ways in which animals responded to stimuli in their environment. Konrad Lorenz, one of the early founders of the field, insisted that the only way to study behavior was to make objective observations under completely natural field conditions. This approach, most evident in his classic studies on aggression and imprinting (the innate behavioral attachment that a young animal forms with another individual such as its mother, with food, or with an object during a brief critical period shortly after birth), greatly enhanced understanding of communication in the animal kingdom. In contrast to Lorenz's very subjective approach, the rigorous field experiments of Nikolaas Tinbergen and Karl von Frisch were similar to those that later would characterize modern ethology.

The classic work of all three of these early ethologists helped demonstrate how an animal's sensory limitations and capabilities can shape its behavior. For example, in a series of classic learning experiments, von Frisch convincingly documented the unusual visual capabilities of the honeybee. He first trained honeybees to forage at small glass dishes of sugar water and then, by attaching different visual cues to each dish, provided the animals with an opportunity to learn where to forage through the simple process of association. From these elegant but simple experiments, he found that bees locate and remember foraging sites by the use of specific colors, ultraviolet cues, and polarized light, a discovery that revolutionized the way in which humans view the sensory capabilities of animals.

MECHANISTIC BEHAVIOR

With the classic work of Lorenz, Tinbergen, and von Frisch came an increasing appreciation for the ways in which physiological limitations define behavioral differences between species. This awareness eventually gave way to a mechanistic approach to behavior, in which ethologists sought to determine how internal factors such as physiology, development, and genetics regulate and control behavior. The physiologically oriented ethologists, for example, focused on the influence of neuronal pathways and sensory organs on behavior. They were concerned with topics such as the control of feeding in insects, echolocation in bats, electric field detection in fish, and infrared detection in snakes. Similarly, neurobiologists attempted to show how behavioral changes are linked to modifications in the function of nerves and neuronal pathways. By observing the response of individual nerves, neurobiologists can observe changes that occur in the nerves when an animal modifies its behavior in response to some stimulus. In a similar way, they can show how learning and behavior are affected when specific nerve fibers are experimentally cut or removed.

ADAPTIVE BEHAVIOR

The third and perhaps most significant area in ethology is that which deals with the evolutionary (adaptive) significance of behavior. Since the seminal work of Charles Darwin, ethologists have maintained that a species' behavior is controlled largely by its genes. Darwin argued that an animal's behavior was no different from any other phenotypic characteristic (physical expression of the genes) in that it was heritable and therefore subject to the same kinds of selective processes that lead to evolutionary change among organisms. He considered instinctual (or innate) behavior a tremendous adaptation that frees some organisms from the risky and sometimes costly business of trial-and-error learning. At the same time, he recognized the adaptive plasticity that accompanies the more complex behaviors that involve various degrees of learning.

Both Lorenz and Tinbergen also recognized the importance of evolutionary questions in behavior, but Tinbergen was the first to put such hypotheses to rigorous experimental tests. In a classic experiment on the evolutionary significance of spines in sticklebacks, he tested predation rates by pike on several species of these fish. He found predation rates to be lowest on the three-spined stickleback (a conspicuous species with large horizontal spines), moderate on the more cryptic ten-spined stickleback (which possesses ten smaller vertical spines on its dorsal surface), and highest for unarmored minnows.

MECHANISMS OF HEREDITY

More recently, behavioral geneticists have shown that much of learning, and of behavior in general, is intimately tied to mechanisms of heredity. The results of hybridization experiments and artificial breeding programs, as well as studies on human twins separated at birth, clearly demonstrate a strong genetic influence on behavior. In fact, it has been well documented that many animals (including both invertebrates and vertebrates) are genetically programmed (or have a genetic predisposition) to learn only specific kinds of behaviors. Such is the case for song learning in birds.

Thus, ethology places tremendous importance on the evolutionary history of an organism. It emphasizes the adaptive significance of the various types of behaviors, and it assumes that an animal's behavior is constrained largely by its genetic and evolutionary background.

LEARNING PROCESS RESEARCH

The field of ethology has contributed markedly to the understanding of several psychological and behavioral phenomena. One such area is the learning process. Learning is defined as any modification in behavior (other than that caused by maturation, fatigue, or injury) that is directed by previous experience.

The early experiments of the behaviorist psychologists on conditioning (the behavioral association that results from the reinforcement of a response with a stimulus) led to the notion that all behavior is learned. Traditionally, behaviorists maintained that all complex behaviors are learned by means of either classical or operant conditioning. Classical conditioning, first demonstrated by the Russian psychologist Ivan Petrovich Pavlov, is a form of associative learning in which an animal responds to an unrelated, novel stimulus after it is repeatedly paired with a more relevant stimulus. Operant conditioning, also a form of associative learning, occurs when an animal learns by manipulating some part of its environment (for example, the animal might ring a bell to receive a reward). This form of learning usually improves with experience and is therefore referred to as trial-and-error learning.

The primary objective of the approaches employed by the early behaviorists was to eliminate or control as many variables as possible and thereby remove any uncertainty about the factors that may influence the learning process. These approaches were especially successful at identifying the external mechanisms responsible for learning. Such techniques focused only on the input (stimulus) and output (response) of an experiment, however, and consequently deemphasized the importance of proximate mechanisms such as physiology and genetics. In addition, these approaches generally ignored the evolutionary considerations that ethologists considered so fundamental to the study of behavior.

INNATE BEHAVIOR

In contrast, studies by the early ethologists suggested that much of behavior was dominated by innate processes that were constrained by the physiological and genetic design of the organism. Lorenz and Tinbergen, for example, demonstrated that many behavioral responses in the animal kingdom are fixed or stereotyped (instinctive) and are often elicited by simple environmental stimuli. They referred to such responses as fixed action patterns and to the stimuli that triggered them as sign stimuli.

The egg-rolling behavior of the greylag goose is perhaps one of the most widely cited examples of this kind of innate behavior. When one of these ground-nesting birds notices an egg outside its nest, it stands, walks to the egg, extends its bill in a very characteristic manner, and proceeds to roll the egg back to the nest. Although at first glance this may seem to represent a simple learned response, Lorenz and Tinbergen found this to be a highly ritualized behavior that was initiated by a very specific environmental stimulus. Through a series of clever experiments, Tinbergen showed that this behavior could be elicited by an egglike object (a ball) or even any object with a convex surface (a bottle or can), and that objects larger than eggs caused a more vigorous (supernormal) response. He also found that once the behavior was initiated, it always ran to completion. In other words, even when the egg was removed, the goose would continue with the motions as if it were returning the egg to the nest.

This and countless other examples of very ritualized behaviors, such as the avoidance response of ducklings to hawk models, the imprinting of young vertebrates on their mothers, the aggressive displays of male stickleback fish to the red bellies of other males, and the various courtship displays of a wide range of species, led early ethologists to conclude that much of behavior is governed by instinct.

These opposing views of ethologists and behaviorist psychologists eventually led to the misconception that learned behavior is governed entirely by the animal's environment, whereas instinct is completely controlled by the genes. It is now widely accepted, however, that nearly all forms of behavior and learning involve certain degrees of both processes. Countless studies, for example, have demonstrated that numerous animals are genetically programmed to learn only certain behaviors. In contrast, it has been shown that instinct need not be completely fixed, but instead can be modified with experience.

SOCIOBIOLOGY

A second area of ethology that has received much attention from a variety of behavioral researchers and in some cases has sparked considerable controversy is sociobiology. In the early 1970s, Edward O. Wilson and Robert Trivers of Harvard University initiated a new area of behavioral research when they began their investigations of the evolutionary basis of social behavior in animals. Their attention focused on the evolutionary enigma presented by altruistic behaviors—acts that one organism performs (often at its own expense) to benefit another. Examples include alarm calls in the presence of a predator and nest-helping behavior. The most extreme cases of such behavior are found in those insect societies in which only a few individuals reproduce and others work to maintain the colony. Through careful experimentation and observation, it was soon determined that such unselfish behaviors are directed toward related individuals and that such behaviors probably evolve because they promote the survival of other individuals who also possess the genes for those same altruistic acts.

Although they initially sparked much debate, studies of the evolutionary basis for social behavior eventually strengthened the ethologists' long-held notion that much of behavior is coded in the genes.

RESEARCH DEBATES

Although ethology had its beginnings with the work of Darwin and other early naturalists, it was von Frisch, Lorenz, and Tinbergen who conducted the first formal ethological studies and who received a joint Nobel Prize for their pioneering work in 1973. Their approach represented a considerable departure from that of behaviorist psychologists, and the differences between the two fields sparked a heated debate during the 1950s and 1960s, often referred to as the nature-versus-nurture controversy. Although this debate eventually led to the decline and virtual demise of behaviorism, it also helped shape modern ethology into a rigorous biological discipline that now holds a compatible niche within the realm of psychology.

Although the early ethologists argued that behaviorists treated their study organisms as "black-boxes" and ignored the genetic, physiological, and evolutionary backgrounds of their subjects, the behaviorists leveled several criticisms in return. In addition to their disbelief in the genetic control of behavior, they were most critical of the methodological approaches employed by ethologists. In contrast with the rigorously controlled laboratory experiments of psychologists, in which blind observers (observers unaware of the experimenters' hypotheses or experimental design) were often used to collect data, behaviorists held that early ethologists conducted nearly all their studies under natural conditions without any regard for experimental control. In addition, their observations were often highly subjective and almost never quantified. Even when attempts were made to quantify the behavior, they never involved the rigorous statistical and analytical techniques of the behaviorists.

Furthermore, although the early ethologists argued that much of behavior is shaped by evolution and constrained by an organism's physiological hardware, little evidence was initially available to support these contentions. Behaviorists, for example, held that ethologists often observed a behavior and casually assigned some adaptive significance to it without testing such evolutionary hypotheses.

These criticisms forced early ethologists to improve their approaches to data collection, experimental design, and data analysis, and as their approaches to the study of behavior were strengthened, so were their original hypotheses about the underlying control of behavior. Thus, as ethologists gained ground, behaviorism began to fall out of favor with most of the scientific community.

The basic views of early ethologists are still well preserved in all prominent areas of ethological research. In fact, the work of nearly all modern ethologists can best be characterized by the two basic sets of questions they seek to answer: the "how questions," concerning underlying proximate causes, and the "why questions," concerning ultimate causes (or evolutionary bases). The first of these is pursued by traditional ethologists and neurobiologists, while the latter is primarily the realm of behavioral ethologists. The fields of ethology and comparative psychology have begun to complement each other, and, increasingly, researchers from the two areas are merging their efforts on a diversity of research topics.

BIBLIOGRAPHY

Alcock, John. *Animal Behavior: An Evolutionary Approach*. 8th ed. Sunderland: Sinauer Associates, 2005. Print.

Burkhardt, Richard W. *Patterns of Behavior: Konrad Lorenz, Niko Tinbergen, and the Founding of Ethology*. Chicago: U of Chicago P, 2005. Print.

Eibl-Eibesfeldt, Irenaus. *Human Ethology.* New Brunswick: Aldine Transaction, 2007. Print.

Fisher, Arthur. "Sociobiology: A New Synthesis Comes of Age." *Mosaic* 22 (1991): 2–9. Print.

Gould, James L. *Ethology: The Mechanisms and Evolution of Behavior.* New York: Norton, 1982. Print.

Grier, James W. *Biology of Animal Behavior*. 2nd ed. New York: McGraw-Hill, 1992. Print.

Hötzel, Maria José, and Luiz Carlos Pinheiro Machado Filho, eds. *Applied Ethology.* Wageningen: Wageningen, 2013. Print.

Krebs, J. R., and N. B. Davies. *An Introduction to Behavioral Ecology.* 2nd ed. Oxford: Blackwell, 1991. Print.

McFarland, David, ed. *The Oxford Companion to Animal Behavior*. Rev. ed. New York: Oxford UP, 1987. Print.

Manning, Aubrey, and Marian Stamp Dawkins. *An Introduction to Animal Behavior.* 5th ed. New York: Cambridge UP, 2006. Print.

Plaisance, Kathryn S., and Thomas A. C. Reydon, eds. *Philosophy of Behavioral Biology.* New York: Springer, 2012. Print.

Raven, Peter H., and George B. Johnson. *Biology.* 7th ed. New York: McGraw-Hill, 2005. Print.

Ristau, Carolyn A., ed. *Cognitive Ethology: The Minds of Other Animals*. New York: Psychology, 2014. Print.

Michael A. Steele

See Also: Animal experimentation; Behaviorism; Habituation and sensitization; Imprinting; Learning; Reflexes.

Evolutionary psychology

Date: 1960s forward

Type of psychology: Biological bases of behavior

Evolutionary psychologists study the human brain and mind with the assumption that these are designed to produce behavior that was adaptive for human ancestors. Evolutionary psychologists believe that humans need to understand the origin of their mental processes to understand how they work and, therefore, how they might modify them to the advantage of their mental, psychological, and social health..

Key Concepts

- Attachment
- Emotion
- Evolution
- Language
- Perception
- Personality
- Sensation
- Sex differences
- Stereotypes

INTRODUCTION

Humans share with other mammals basic behaviors, motivations, and emotions, but only humans can reflect on and discuss their behaviors, motivations, and emotions, and only humans can influence the behaviors, motivations, and emotions of others through such abstract concepts as appeals to duty, religion, laws, blackmail, promises, and lies. Like other psychologists, evolutionary psychologists study the brain structures and mental functions that underlie these capacities. Unlike other psychologists, evolutionary psychologists begin with the assumption that human mental capacities evolved through natural selection the same way that human bodies did—that is, that the brain circuitry and processes underlying thought and behavior exist because they somehow helped human ancestors to survive and reproduce. It is this perspective, rather than research topics or methodology, that differentiates evolutionary psychology from other fields and approaches in psychology.

Arguing from this perspective, evolutionary psychologists have suggested that the aspects of brain and behavior that consistently conferred the greatest advantages on human ancestors are those that are most likely to now be automatic—that is, subconscious or instinctive.

People do not need to be aware of how they avoid large moving objects, for example, as long as they can do it. The corollary line of reasoning is that those aspects of brain and behavior that are now the most automatic are likely to be those that had the greatest and most consistent advantages in the past. For this reason, it is the instinctive and automatic behaviors, as well as the subconscious bases of thoughts and feelings, that have received the most attention from evolutionary psychologists.

SENSATION, PERCEPTION, AND HEDONIC PREFERENCES

Certain important aspects of the behavior of the physical world seem to be innately wired into, or easily acquired by, the human brain. Babies experience anxiety about steep drop-offs as soon as they can see them, without having to learn by experiencing a fall. They also flinch or move away from objects that are getting larger on a projection screen and therefore appear to be coming toward them. Although babies cannot count or do math, they very quickly appreciate such fundamental concepts as length, mass, speed, and gravity, as well as the concepts of more and less and larger and smaller. They typically acquire an easy grasp of one of the most abstract concepts of all: time.

Humans also exhibit innate preferences for things that were "good" for human ancestors and a dislike of things that were "bad." People naturally like sweet foods that provide them with the necessary glucose for their calorie-hungry brains and salty foods that provide them with the minerals to run their neuronal sodium-pump, yet they have to acquire (and may never acquire) a taste for bitter and foul-smelling foods, which signal their brains that the substance may contain toxins. The human brain also automatically causes people to develop intense aversions to foods that were ingested several hours before becoming ill. Even in cases when a person consciously knows that it was not that food that actually caused the sickness, the very thought of that item may cause nausea ten years after an illness.

Humans are also wired for other kinds of "taste." Children around the world prefer parklike landscapes that provide plenty of water and trees and forms of play that provide exercise, strengthen muscles, and increase physical coordination. Adults admire the beautiful faces and shapely bodies of the young, healthy, and disease-free—those who are the safest friends and most profitable mates. In sum, experiences of pain or disgust signal that something is potentially dangerous and is to be avoided; experiences of pleasure or admiration signal safety or opportunity and encourage a person to approach.

EMOTION, MOTIVATION, AND ATTACHMENT

Important emotions, too, appear early in life, without having to be learned. These so-called primary emotions include fear, anger, happiness, sadness, surprise, and disgust. Like tastes, emotions serve as signals to alert the conscious awareness about important stimuli, but they also serve as signals to others. The facial expressions that accompany primary emotions are performed consistently across cultures, even in children blind from birth. People instinctively understand the facial expressions signifying emotion and pay special attention when they see them.

Perhaps the most important emotion for survival and reproduction is the attachment that develops between an infant and its mother. Human infants are completely dependent on parental care and, even after weaning, require intensive investment and supervision. It is thus in the interest of both mother and child that a close bond form between them, to keep the child from wandering away and to keep the mother motivated to address the constant demands of her offspring. Infants can recognize their mother's voice and smell soon after birth and, as soon as their eyes are able to focus, can recognize—and show preference for—her face. Once they are old enough to crawl, babies develop an intense desire to be within sight of their mother and, when temporarily separated, experience and communicate great distress. Mothers, reciprocally, develop an intense attachment to their children, and they, too, experience distress on separation.

Other social emotions also motivate people to repeat mutually beneficial interactions and to avoid people who might take advantage of them. Guilt and shame are cross-cultural universals that indicate disgust toward one's own behavior and signal to others that one is unlikely to repeat the "rotten" behavior; allegiance and sympathy signal a willingness to help allies when in need; and vengeance and hatred warn those who have harmed someone that they endanger themselves if they approach again.

PERSONALITY, SEX DIFFERENCES, AND SOCIAL RELATIONS

Predicting other people's behavior is important, so any aspect of a person that is consistent and can help a person to predict accurately becomes worthy of attention. One source of predictability derives from consistent personality differences between the sexes. Boys and men around the world are, on average, more physically aggressive, more competitive, more impulsive, and more risk-prone than girls and women, who are, on average, more nurturant, more empathetic, more cooperative, and more harm-avoidant than boys and men. These differences have impacts on social behavior across the life span, influencing patterns of early childhood play, courtship, parenting, career choice, and participation in warfare, crime, and other high-risk activities.

In addition to sex differences, there are two major dimensions of personality that seem of particular importance: dominance/submissiveness and friendliness/hostility. As with tastes and emotions, one's assessment of another person's personality seems to highlight "good/safe" versus "bad/dangerous" and signals to approach or avoid, respectively. It seems that people attend to personality to determine who is likely to be a friend, to be trustworthy, and to be helpful, versus who is likely to hurt, to betray, and to take advantage.

In fact, it might have been the need to predict how other people might respond that led to human beings' great intelligence. Like other social species, humans constantly monitor the statuses of those around them: who is fighting, who is having sex, who is popular, who is not. Compared with other animals, however, humans have taken this kind of mental tracking to a level that is quite complex: a man can think about what a friend might think if his sister told him that she heard that he knew that his girlfriend had heard a rumor that he was seeing someone else but that he had not told him . . . and so on. Such multilevel cogitation requires a great deal of long-term and short-term memory, as well as an extensive ability to manipulate concepts and scenarios.

LEARNING, LANGUAGE, AND THINKING

Given humans' great intellectual capacity, evolutionary psychologists do not claim that all knowledge is inborn—it is obvious that humans acquire much information through learning. Nonetheless, evolutionary psychologists note that certain types of information are more easily learned than others.

Language, for example, is a kind of complex and abstract knowledge that comes as second nature to very young children. Across all cultures and languages, children progress through regular stages of language development, acquiring the ability to both understand and produce grammatical speech (or, in the case of deaf children, visual signs). At their peak, children actually acquire several new words an hour. Most adults, on the other hand, have to work extremely hard to acquire a second or third language, and it is exceedingly difficult to teach even the smartest computers and robots how to understand elementary forms of speech. Language is an example of a highly specialized kind of learning that is prewired into the human brain; it is acquired quickly during a critical period of brain development, and once achieved, it is never forgotten.

Similarly, humans readily develop mental stereotypes that, once acquired, are difficult or impossible to disregard. Stereotypes are, basically, abstract generalizations that arise from the subconscious integration of personal and vicarious experience. Like tastes, emotions, and attention to personality, the automatic generation of stereotypes helps a person to respond quickly and appropriately to new stimuli without wasting precious time assessing each nuance of each situation encountered each new minute of every day.

APPLIED EVOLUTIONARY PSYCHOLOGY

Evolutionary psychologists do not claim that behavior that was once adaptive is necessarily still adaptive, nor that behavior that has evolved is unchangeable. For example, while stereotypes were designed to work to a person's advantage, the experiences that now go into one's mental computations include not only real experiences but also thousands of images from movies, newspapers, and television. As a result, stereotypes reflect not necessarily reality and true experience but rather the biases of the society at large, often amplified in the make-believe world of Hollywood. Taking an evolutionary approach to psychology suggests that although people will continue to create stereotypes, by changing or monitoring media coverage, increasing exposure to positive images, or broadcasting the voices of the unheard, the content of stereotypes could be changed. Like other approaches to psychology, evolutionary psychology has practical implications that can help people to understand—and improve—the human condition.

BIBLIOGRAPHY

Baron-Cohen, S., ed. *The Maladapted Mind*. Hove: Psychology, 1999. Print.

Buss, David M. *Evolutionary Psychology: The New Science of the Mind*. 3d ed. Boston: Pearson, 2008. Print.

Campbell, Anne. *A Mind of Her Own: The Evolutionary Psychology of Women*. 2nd ed. New York: Oxford UP, 2013. Print.

Crawford, C., and D. L. Krebs, eds. *Handbook of Evolutionary Psychology: Ideas, Issues, and Applications*. Mahwah: Erlbaum, 1998. Print.

Damasio, Antonio R. *Descartes' Error: Emotion, Reason, and the Human Brain*. 1994. Rpt. New York: Penguin, 2005. Print.

Frank, R. H. *Passions Within Reason: The Strategic Role of the Emotions*. New York: Norton, 1990. Print.

Gaulin, S. J. C., and D. H. McBurney. *Psychology: An Evolutionary Approach*. Upper Saddle River: Prentice Hall, 2001. Print.

MacDonald, K. B., ed. *Sociobiological Perspectives on Human Development*. New York: Springer-Verlag, 1988. Print.

Mealey, L. *Sex Differences: Developmental and Evolutionary Strategies*. San Diego: Academic, 2000. Print.

Okami, Paul. *Psychology: Contemporary Perspectives*. New York: Oxford UP, 2013. Print.

Pinker, Steven. *The Language Instinct*. London: Bloomsbury, 2008. Print.

Scheibel, A. B., and J. W. Schopf, eds. *The Origin and Evolution of Intelligence*. Boston: Jones, 1997. Print.

Workman, Lance, and Will Reader. *Evolutionary Psychology*. New York: Cambridge UP, 2014. Print.

Linda Mealey

See Also: Aggression; Attachment and bonding in infancy and childhood; Cognitive psychology; Developmental psychology; Emotions; Father-child relationship; Gender differences; Intelligence; Language; Learning; Mother-child relationship; Motivation; Social perception.

Executive functions

Type of psychology: Neuropsychology; Developmental

Executive function is a name for a combination of mental processes that help us execute actions and reach goals. Among executive functions are impulse control, judgment, mental flexibility, planning and organization, reasoning, and problem solving. Often, attention and working memory are included under the umbrella of executive functions as well, but they may receive their own title. Executive functions mostly reside in the frontal lobe of the human brain and damage to this area may significantly impair social, professional, and cognitive functioning.

Key Concepts

- Dysexecutive syndrome
- Frontal lobe
- Inhibition
- Mental flexibility
- Personality
- Planning and organization
- Reasoning

INTRODUCTION

In the past several decades, interest in understanding the brain has grown. Our understanding of human brain anatomy and functions has increased from considering the brain to be a useless organ by ancient Egyptians to today's realization that brain structures are absolutely vital. Ancient Greeks considered the brain to be the center of the soul. Franz Joseph Gall, a neuroanatomist who worked in the 18th and 19th centuries pioneered the concept that various behavioral and personality functions are localized in different areas of the brain. He believed that personality was directly related to features and structures within the brain and claimed that by the shape of one's skull he could determine personality and cognitive profile. Gall's study was called phrenology. According to Gall, the qualities of "veneration," and "self-esteem" were located around the top of one's brain, what we now call the somatosensory cortex and the primary motor cortex. However, today we know that phrenological descriptions of function localization were simplistic and erroneous. Nevertheless, the underlying concept of localization of cognitive, executive, motor, and emotional functions has been confirmed.

Alexander R. Luria, a Soviet psychologist, is known throughout the scientific world for his neuropsychology work in the 20th century. He greatly contributed to the study of brain function localization through his work with war-related head injuries after World War II. By studying how brain damage changed emotions, behavior, and cognition, he contributed to the knowledge of localization of executive function. With development of neuroimaging, pharmacology, and psychological and medical sciences in the last 50 years, understanding of the brain has grown exponentially.

DEFINITIONS

Put simply, executive functions are functions of our brain. They are used to connect past experience with present action, inhibit inappropriate impulses, make decisions and solve problems, plan, organize, strategize, and manage time and space. Executive functions consist of the capacities that allow us to successfully engage in purposeful, independent, and self-directed behaviors. Executive functions are what allow us to deal with novelty and ambiguity of situations. Executive functions allow us to answer questions of "how" and "when" (e.g., When will you do this? How much do you know?). Even if other cognitive functions are impaired (e.g., memory), a person with intact executive functions can still function independently and find ways to compensate for the loss of other functions. For example, if a person has memory problems, by using her intact executive functions she may be able to set up alarms, use calendars and organizers, and ask for the help of family and friends in order to complete her goals. Thus, she will problem solve and find a way to compensate for her cognitive deficits.

Impairment of executive functions impacts all areas of a person's functioning: social relationships, problem-solving and decision-making strategies, approaching of novel tasks, plans for future actions, and monitoring of one's own performance. Motivation and ability to initiate new behavior, such as starting a day or cooking a meal, are also under the umbrella of executive functions. Persons with deficient executive functions will often lack self-direction and need to be told what to do in order to complete a task. Because patients with deficient executive function often lack motivation and awareness of their deficits, it is very challenging to treat them because they do not recognize their need for treatment.

Self-control, self-awareness, goal-directedness, and emotional regulation, which are personality characteristics, also belong to the domain of executive functions. Imagine a student who is unable to sit still, blurts out inappropriate comments in class, cannot check for errors and correct them, and is unable to control their mood. These behaviors point to problems with executive functions.

Mental flexibility, or ability to shift cognitive set, is also an executive function and a base for other skills and abilities. We use this ability when we change from one language to another in a single conversation or when we try to do some work while watching a newscast. Mental flexibility can also be seen as a component of abstract reasoning when trying to connect two seemingly distant concepts such as a tiger and a fox. Mental rigidity and concreteness of thought often occurs with impairment of executive function.

ANATOMY OF EXECUTIVE FUNCTIONS

It is difficult to discuss executive function without mentioning one of the largest lobes of the human brain, the frontal lobe. While today it is the most studied area of the cortex, it remains the least known. The frontal lobe is the area of the neocortex which is located in the front of our brain and is about one third of the entire human cortex. Executive function is mostly housed in the prefrontal cortex, or a front-facing area of the brain. One of the famous cases of frontal lobe damage was described more than 100 years ago. Prior to his injury, Phineas Cage was a family-loving, good-natured, honest man by all accounts. After an injury to the prefrontal cortex, he became fitful, indulged in profanity, and demonstrated poor judgment. This personality change is an example of the results of frontal lobe damage. Similar difficulties may be caused by events such as brain injury, stroke, lesion, tumor, schizophrenia, substance additions, and aging.

Diffuse damage to prefrontal cortex may produce some of the behaviors that reveal executive function deficits. For example, environmental dependency occurs when a person responds to the environment without consideration for appropriateness of his response to this situation. A patient will sexually respond to a nurse that smiled at him. Utilization behavior is the opposite of goal-oriented behavior. Tangentiality and circumloquaciousness (excessive wordiness) are symptoms of executive function deficit which reflect disinhibition and inability to selectively attend to relevant aspects of one's environment. Autonoetic awareness refers to self-awareness and autobiographical continuum which enables humans to determine their future goals based on the past experiences and outcomes. When this ability is damaged, an individual is unable to regulate her behavior and reference her behaviors to past experiences.

Three major structures of the frontal lobe are associated with executive function and particular frontal syndromes. These structures of the cortex are dorsolateral prefrontal cortex, orbitofrontal (also called limbic orbitofrontal) cortex, and medial frontal cortex. Damage to any of these areas presents a somewhat different clinical picture and reflects personality and behavioral change after the trauma or other type of damage to the corresponding cortical area.

Damage to the dorsolateral prefrontal cortex causes dorsolateral prefrontal syndrome, or dysexecutive syndrome. This syndrome is associated with the damage to the upper part of the prefrontal cortex. An individual who suffers this condition will show poor memory for event sequence and deficient problem-solving and reasoning skills. While the person may be able to name similarities between two concepts, he may not be able to generate new ideas (e.g., all possible uses for a brick). The patient is unable to understand the depth and extent of his deficits and has poor self-awareness which significantly impedes efforts of caretakers to assist such a patient.

Damage to the orbitofrontal area, the lower part of the frontal lobe, will lead to disinhibited syndrome (also known as orbitofrontal or pseudopsychopathic). As the name suggests, a person with this condition will appear to lack empathy and judgment. An individual may seem self-involved, impulsive, disinhibited (sexually, socially, etc.), and emotionally dysregulated. Family members may complain that the person has become uncaring and egotistical. Often patients with such frontal lobe damage will do almost anything to attain their desired goal (e.g., drink, gamble, become promiscuous). People with this condition tend to be hyperverbal and present with poor attention though memory may remain intact. Unlike true psychopathy, these patients may express remorse when their behavior is confronted.

Medial frontal syndrome (also akinetic or apathetic) is caused by damage to the medial frontal cortex, an area of the frontal lobe located between the two hemispheres. Damage to this cortex is notable for lack of movement, lethargy, lack of spontaneity in initiating behavior, and decreased arousal. Individuals with this syndrome lack insight into their condition and do not appreciate the extent of their deficits. Their memory for the past and inability to learn and remember new information are severely disrupted. Individuals with this syndrome lack interest or express no concern about loved ones and friends, whom they loved before the trauma to the brain occurred. Persons with this syndrome will appear dull and unmotivated.

ASSESSMENT AND REHABILITATION OF EXECUTIVE FUNCTION

Assessment of deficits in executive function may be performed through integrative approach involving several domains. Assessment starts with a clinical interview of the patient and/or his caregivers to estimate the extent to which the patient's emotions, behavior, and relationships have changed. The following topics are usually discussed: activity level, emotional responsiveness, social functioning, personality, attention, reasoning, judgment, and memory.

To measure the degree of the damage, an objective assessment is then conducted. Neuropsychologists usually perform standardized tests that target areas of executive function. A whole discipline of psychometrics is dedicated to developing tests and assessment methods to measure brain functioning. And finally, behavioral observations remain an extremely important part of the diagnosis. Nevertheless, because executive functions are involved in so many other processes and are so numerous, it is often challenging to capture them.

Treatment recommendations are offered after the diagnosis is made and etiology of the problem(s) determined. There are a few difficulties in remediation of executive functions. First, because it is difficult to capture these functions and quantify them, assessment of extent of the damage may be difficult. Theoretical basis on which to build interventions has been lacking. Second, because damage to the prefrontal cortex may cause a multitude of cognitive and behavioral symptoms, the goals of the rehabilitative interventions may be hard to establish and prioritize. Third, many people with damage to the prefrontal cortex exhibit low motivation, low self-awareness, and mood dysregulation, and it is difficult to involve these patients in the remediation process. However, some guidelines have been developed over time.

The basic principle of cognitive remediation is "if you don't use it, you lose it." It is easy to imagine how one's muscles and bones strengthen as a result of a consistent and challenging exercise regimen. The same idea is applied in cognitive remediation. If an individual trains skills and abilities, her mind will stay strong. Some of the prefrontal cortex exercises may involve continuous performance of one task while viewing varying images (i.e., multitasking) or problem solving and decision making in real or made-up novel or ambiguous situations. The level of difficulty should approach the level of one's cognitive and intellectual functioning. In order for the remediation of executive function to be effective, the caregiver must make the tasks personally relevant, multimodal, and somewhat challenging for the patient. Mindfulness training has been recently praised for improving attention, goal-directed behavior, and self-regulation. Psychotherapy helps individuals verbally process emotions and thought and exercise the ability to see life situations from different angles. It is helpful in developing mental flexibility, empathy, and self-awareness.

Furthermore, emerging literature is addressing psychotropic medication that helps remediate some executive deficits. Because the frontal lobe carries multiple dopaminergic pathways, dopaminergic agonists have been shown to be helpful in treatment of some of executive function deficits.

Assessment and remediation of executive function remain new and exciting areas of psychology and neurology and require more research and attention.

BIBLIOGRAPHY

Barkley, R. A. (2012). *Executive Functions: What They Are, How They Work, and Why They Evolved.* New York, NY: Guilford Press. This book provides a good overview of executive functions and their purpose and evolution.

Goldberg, E. (2009). *The New Executive Brain: Frontal Lobes In A Complex World.* London, UK: Oxford University Press. Discusses how executive functions mature and age, how damage affects behavior and emotions, and how one undertakes rehabilitating deficits in executive function.

Luria, A. R. (1976). *The Working Brain: An Introduction To Neuropsychology* (B. Haigh, Trans.). New York, NY: Penguin Books. This work reflects observational approach to neuropsychological syndromes, including those of executive functions. Luria was one of the founders of this discipline and his contribution is summarized in this book.

Schoenbuerg, M. R., & Scott, J. G. (Eds.). (2011). *The Little Black Book Of Neuropsychology: A Syndrome-Based Approach.* New York, NY: Springer. An introduction to neuropsychology that devotes several chapters to brain anatomy, executive functions, and affect.

Hannah L. Geller

SEE ALSO: Cognition; Cognitive control; Cognitive impairment; Neuropsychology; Neuroscience; Planning; Problem solving; Reasoning; Working memory.

Exercise addiction

TYPE OF PSYCHOLOGY: Addiction; Clinical; Counseling; Family; Psychopathology; Psychotherapy; Social

Regular exercise is a healthy way for people to stay in shape and decrease risk for many life-threatening diseases. However, in today's thin obsessed society people are now more than ever becoming addicted to working out. The Center for Disease Control (CDC) has recommendations for adults between the ages of 18 and 64, and many people in today's society exceed these recommendations, becoming addicted to working out.

KEY CONCEPTS

- Disorder
- Dysmorphia
- Physical fitness
- Thinspiration addiction

INTRODUCTION

While exercise addiction is not explicitly included in the new *Diagnostic and Statistical Manual of Mental Disorders* (DSM-5), it can be found under behavior addiction in the addictive disorder section. In the DSM-5 a behavior addiction is loosely defined as a person's behavior becoming obsessive, compulsive, and/or dysfunctional in a person's life. In today's world, the media is obsessed with body image which puts pressure on both males and females to obtain often unrealistic standards. When people decide they want to lose weight they often look to popular diets or fad fitness classes to get the results they want in the fastest way possible. Often, these trends are not the safest or healthiest ways to go about losing weight because people will plateau or get bored; however, there are some people who become consumed with the idea of having the "perfect" figure that these fitness trends promote. While working out consistently may not appear to be a bad thing, when it interferes with a person's daily life because he or she feels the need to work out for more than two hours every day, it becomes a problem. Another issue with exercise addiction is that people often cut calories while they are working out, leading to many physical issues. Finally, one of the biggest and arguably scariest parts of exercise addiction is that because working out is seen as a healthy lifestyle choice, many people do not realize it is a problem.

SOCIETY EXPECTATIONS AND WEIGHT LOSS

In the past decade weight loss shows have taken television by storm. Whether it is The Biggest Loser or Extreme Weight Loss there are many shows that encourage people to lose weight and demonstrate safe and effective ways to achieve weight loss goals. Along with television shows, the media is generally obsessed with body image. From the covers of celebrity gossip magazines showing perfect "bikini bodies" to news shows discussing whether or not it should be expected that women lose baby weight immediately, we are constantly saturated with the idea of being thin. While the Internet is a great source of inspiration for losing weight and researching effective diet and fitness plans, it can also cause people to form unrealistic body goals. The creation of thinspo or thinspiration was created to inspire other women to lose weight and become thin. Often, these pictures show women who have body mass indexes lower than what is considered to be in the normal range. By promoting images of unhealthy women, thinspiration further perpetuates the unobtainable ideal of being skinny rather than healthy which can lead to exercise addiction.

EXERCISE ADDICTION

Typical exercise guidelines. According to the CDC, the average 18-64 year old should use the following as guidelines for living a healthy, active lifestyle: two hours and 30 minutes of moderate intensity aerobic activity every week and two or more days of muscle strengthening activities. Or, adults can do one hour and 15 minutes of vigorous intensity aerobic activity every week and muscle strengthening activities on two or more days. Or, adults in that age range can do an equivalent mix of moderate and vigorous intensity aerobic activity and muscle strengthening activities on two or more days a week.

Exercise Addiction. While this seems like a lot to do during a given work week, people who have an addiction to exercise often work out to a much higher extent than CDC guidelines and allow working out to dictate their lives. Their exercise typically interferes with social, work, and family activities. Because exercise is seen as positive and it is possible to work out more than the CDC suggests without becoming addicted, it is often difficult to diagnose exercise addiction. While it is difficult to diagnose, there are a few signs that signal when exercising moves from a healthy habit to the realm of addiction.

Signs of exercise addiction. One of the first signs is that the amount of exercise is actually harmful to an individual. For example, if a person is working out four hours a day and is not consuming enough calories so as to provide enough fuel for his or her body, the caloric deficit can lead to stress fractures or other injury. Another sign of exercise addiction is that the person seems in a bad mood if he or she does not work out. If a person relies on the euphoric feeling after a work out to be happy, chances are high that he or she has an exercise addiction. One of the biggest red flags for people should be if a person is exercising through an injury or medical condition. While there are some forms of exercise that people may do if injured, there are others that raise concern. For example, if a person had major surgery and is out the next day trying to go for a run or lift weights it would be safe to suggest talking to him or her about a potential addiction to exercise.

CAUSES OF EXERCISE ADDICTION

While exercise addiction can occur due to a number of factors, one of the most commonly held beliefs is that people become addicted to the euphoric feeling after a workout. When a person pushes him or herself hard at the gym, endorphins are released causing a euphoric feeling. Similar to drug addiction, people want to continue to feel this good which leads to them working out more so that they experience euphoria. Again mirroring drug addiction people who work out and are in good shape will have to work out harder and increase the frequency and length of their workouts in order to feel this euphoric feeling. Because people believe that what they are doing is healthy, many do not consider their behavior as being an addiction. Rather they perceive it as something healthy.

Another important component of exercise addiction is body dysmorphia. Often, people suffering from exercise addiction also struggle with seeing a distorted vision of their bodies when they look in the mirror. People who suffer from body dysmorphic disorder typically see themselves as being fat or larger than they are which leads to excessive exercise. It is important to note that often people who suffer from both body dysmorphic disorder and exercise addiction become angry, hostile, or defensive when someone suggests they have a problem.

SOURCES OF SUPPORT

Because exercise addiction is identified as being similar to any other kind of substance abuse disorder, the treatment is also similar. Group therapy, individual counseling, and, in severe cases, inpatient facilities are used to help treat the addiction. In treatment, issues surrounding body image are discussed and explored, helping the client find ways to deal with his or her insecurities in a healthy way. Along with professional help, it is important that the person suffering from an exercise addiction feels supported by his or her friends, family, and other loved ones.

BIBLIOGRAPHY

How much physical activity do adults need? (2014, March 3). Retrieved October 28, 2014. Good resource to find out what kind and how much physical activity is recommended for the average adult.

Landolfi, E. (2012). "Exercise Addiction". *Sports Medicine*, 43, 111-119. Retrieved October 27, 2014, from http://ovidsp.tx.ovid.com.ezp-prod1.hul.harvard.edu/sp-3.13.1a Provides an overview of exercise addiction, its signs, and strategies for overcoming it.

Wichmann, S., & Martin, D.R. (1992). "Exercise Excess: Treating Patients Addicted To Fitness". *Physiological Sports Medicine*, 20, 193–200. Discusses professional treatment of clients with exercise addiction.

Lauren Ruvo

SEE ALSO: Addiction; Athletics; Exercise; Fitness; Self esteem; Self perception; Sports.

Exercise and mental health

TYPE OF PSYCHOLOGY: Biological bases of behavior; Developmental psychology; Psychopathology; Psychotherapy; Stress

Exercise is a behavior that affects both physical and mental well-being. It is well known as a practice for maintaining physical health. Though it is less well known for its impact on mental health, exercise can significantly improve mood, alertness, and feelings of well-being while decreasing fatigue, tension, stress, and depressed mood.

KEY CONCEPTS

- Compensatory behavior
- Compulsions
- Endorphins
- Negative reinforcement
- Positive reinforcement
- Rituals

INTRODUCTION

Physical exercise affects mental health by releasing endorphins, or hormones that put the body in a pleasurable state. As such, exercise may be naturally reinforcing because endorphins may serve as a positive reinforcer.

Often, doctors and specialists recommend an exercise regimen as part of a treatment program for conditions related to anxiety, depression, and stress reduction. Additionally, regular exercise can also affect conditions exacerbated by stress by helping to reduce stress. Headaches, pain disorders, fibromyalgia, chronic fatigue, and conditions such as diabetes may benefit from stress reduction in this regard. Stress reduction also may result from social bonding associated with exercise, including pairs or team sports or even simply walking or running with a friend. Additionally, direct effects on body fat, blood pressure, weight, and flexibility, among other physical aspects of health, also combine to make exercise beneficial for these conditions.

Mental health and exercise also are primary topics of sports psychology, an area of psychology that focuses on how mental state can affect athletic performance. Practitioners of sports psychology use numerous techniques to facilitate improved performance and persistence. Using visual imagery to see oneself performing successfully is one example of sports psychology. Another technique involves using positive self-statements to facilitate expectations of successful performance. Many times athletes and others participating in sports or other exercise activities may experience reductions in performance that may be accompanied by thoughts or beliefs that can cause or exacerbate poor performance. Therefore, approaches encouraging positive self-statements, ways of reshaping beliefs to support performance improvement, can be extraordinarily beneficial.

DISORDERS RELATED TO EXERCISE

Though exercise has many physical and mental health benefits, it can also be associated with varying mental health problems. Some individuals may have extreme concerns about weight, as found in the condition of anorexia nervosa, and may engage in excessive exercise. If a person is driven by fears of fatness, exercise may function as a compulsion, a behavior performed to reduce the fear and anxiety. Unfortunately, the reduction of these uncomfortable feelings about fatness can be negatively reinforcing, meaning that the reduction in anxiety serves as a benefit to encourage more and more exercise. Unlike positive reinforcement, or stimuli that increase behaviors, negative reinforcement works by removal of stimuli, in this case, reducing the fear and reinforcing the exercise. These compulsive patterns may develop into rituals. When the ritual is pathological, its interruption can further trigger anxiety, which then may help to further build the compulsion to follow through with the exercise rituals.

Similarly, individuals with bulimia nervosa may engage in exercise as a compensatory behavior for other problematic behaviors such as binge eating. Binge eating can trigger fears of a lack of control and fatness; the exercise behavior may be used to compensate for the overeating. Exercise is seen as a means of regaining control.

Individuals with body dysmorphic disorder, a condition in which a person has very serious concerns about how some aspect of a body part looks, may also engage in excessive exercise. Desire to affect the body, such as to gain control over its appearance, may also be related to compulsive exercise.

Remarkably, even when a person is warned of the deleterious effects of excessive exercise that may result from body-fat levels that are too low and a dysregulated hormone system, the person will still feel driven to exercise. These are conditions in which the benefits of exercise do not objectively outweigh the risks; however, the person is unable to see this. In reality, individuals must recognize the value of moderation even in exercise. Healthy exercise that supports mental health is beneficial behavior that outweighs the negative effects of exercise.

BIBLIOGRAPHY

Bassuk, Shari S., Timothy S. Church, JoAnn E. Manson. "Why Exercise Works Magic." *Scientific American* 309.2 (2013): 74–79. Print.

Bourne, Edmund J., and Lorna Garano. *Coping with Anxiety: Ten Simple Ways to Relieve Anxiety, Fear, and Worry.* Oakland: New Harbinger, 2003. Print.

Cox, Richard. *Sports Psychology: Concepts and Applications.* Columbus: McGraw, 2006. Print.

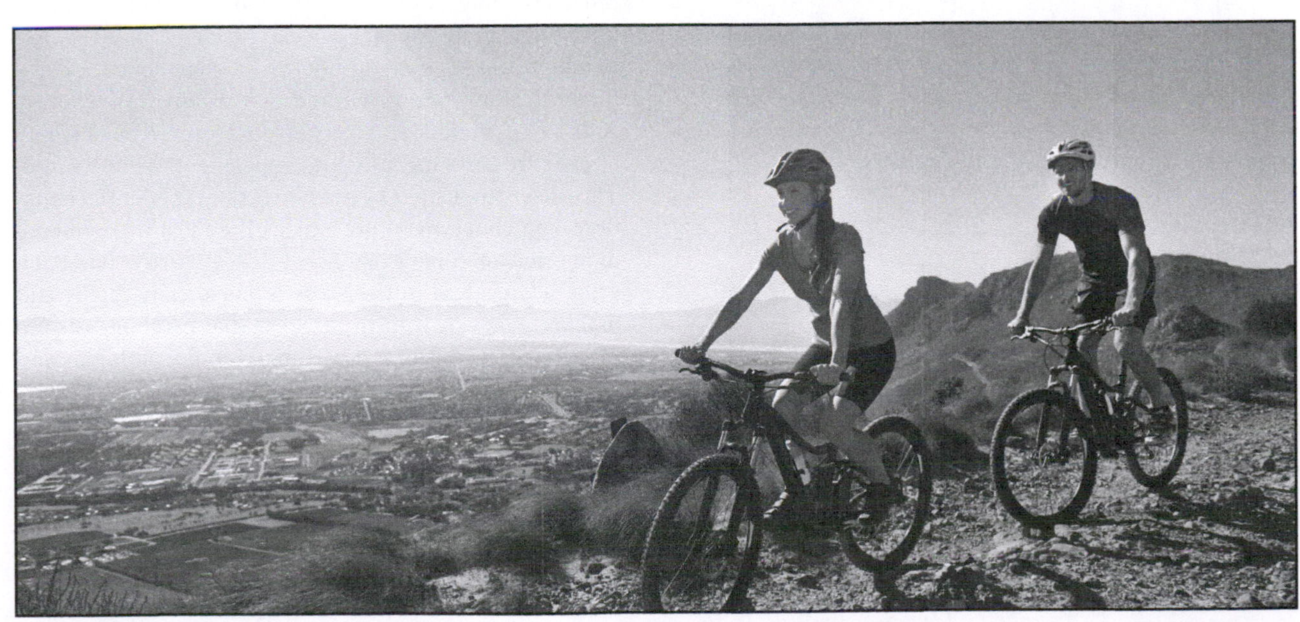

Photo: iStock

Friedman, Peachy. *Diary of an Exercise Addict*. Guilford: Pequot, 2008. Print.

Gregg, Jennifer A., Glenn M. Callaghan, and Steven C. Hayes. *Diabetes Lifestyle Book: Facing Your Fears and Making Changes for a Long and Healthy Life*. Oakland: New Harbinger, 2008. Print.

Malcolm, Estelle, et al. "The Impact of Exercise Projects to Promote Mental Wellbeing." *Jour. of Mental Health* 22.6 (2013): 519–27. Print.

Powers, Pauline S., and Ron Thompson. *The Exercise Balance: What's Too Much, What's Too Little, What's Just Right for You!* Carlsbad: Gurze, 2008. Print.

Szabo, Attila. "Acute Psychological Benefits of Exercise: Reconsideration of the Placebo Effect." *Jour. of Mental Health* 22.5 (2013): 449–55. Print.

Nancy A. Piotrowski

See Also: Anorexia nervosa and bulimia nervosa; Body dysmorphic disorder; Depression; Meditation and relaxation; Men's mental health; Pain management; Self-esteem; Sports psychology; Stress: Theories; Women's mental health.

Existential psychology

Type of psychology: Personality

Existential analysis, derived from the insights of existential philosophy, offers a powerful portrait of the fundamental dilemmas of human living. It stresses the individual's freedom to make choices responsibly and to live life authentically according to those choices.

Key Concepts

- Absurdity
- Authenticity
- Being-in-the-world
- Existential analysis
- Inauthenticity

INTRODUCTION

Existential psychology was inspired by the original insights of the philosophy of existentialism. By examining situations of great horror (such as the concentration camps of the Nazis) and of great beauty or joy (such as a father seeing his little girl happily skipping down the sidewalk), existentialism posited that human existence is without absolutes: There are no limits either to human cruelty or to human love. Existentialism removes all presuppositions, abstractions, and universal rules. It attacks the conformity and complacency caused by the illusion that a human is only a predetermined cog in a completely ordered, mechanical universe.

Modern culture can be alienating, with its huge bureaucratic and technological structures that do not recognize one's concrete existence. In spite of the pervasiveness of this alienation, existentialism holds that the possibility of existing as an authentic individual is never lost. Existentialism depicts the "absurdity" (the sense that there is no inherent basis for conferring meaning to life) of the lack of preestablished systems of meaning, but it rejects the artificiality of schemes that try to account for meaning as somehow produced by systems "out there," beyond the individual. Instead, existentialism returns to concretely lived situations as the birthplace of whatever meaning may be found in life. In that sense, life is an adventure that unfolds as one lives it. As William Barrett has said, "Life is not handed to us on a platter but involves our own act of self-determination."

Mainstream psychology has not, for the most part, addressed this existentialist outlook. Instead, it has borrowed from natural science the viewpoint that human life is essentially mechanistic and causally determined—that personal life can be reduced to a bundle of drives, stimuli, or biochemical reactions. The problem with those approaches, notes existential psychologist Rollo May, is that "the man disappears; we can no longer find 'the one' to whom this or that experience has happened." Thus, the crucial innovation offered by existential psychology is its aim to understand the personal, experienced reality of one's free and meaningful involvement in one's world. This is accomplished by analyzing the experiential situations and concerns of persons as the most fundamental dimension of their existence. This approach has been especially evident in the areas of personality theory and psychotherapy. It is in those areas that psychologists are most directly confronted with real human problems and are therefore unable to settle for abstract laboratory experiments as a basis for knowledge.

EMERGENCE OF STUDY

Psychologists began to turn to existentialism in the 1940s. The pioneers of existential analysis were psychoanalysts originally influenced by the ideas of Sigmund Freud. As analysts, they already stood outside mainstream experimental psychology and so were not as influenced by its presumptions. Furthermore, as therapists, their overriding purpose was to assist people who were experiencing real distress, anxiety, and conflict. Abstract theories and dogmas about stimuli and responses were more easily recognized as insufficient in that context, and an approach that focused on patients' actual existence was welcome.

The first practitioners were the Swiss psychiatrists Ludwig Binswanger and Medard Boss, whose early writings date from the late 1940s. They were inspired by the existential philosophy of Martin Heidegger's key book *Sein und Zeit* (1927; *Being and Time*, 1962). They believed that analysis needed to be broadened beyond the limits that Freud had established. In place of Freud's psychoanalysis—the aim of which was to understand an interior mental apparatus—they developed existential analysis, with the aim of understanding the person's existence, that is, the person's "being-in-the-world."

This term, developed by Heidegger, was meant by its hyphens to indicate that the relation of person and world is not merely one of the person being located "in" the world (as a pencil is located in a drawer). Rather, the person is always "worlded" in the sense that one's existence is a network of meaningful involvements—relationships that are specifically and uniquely one's own. Heidegger had called this the "care" structure, and he saw it as the very core of what it means to be a human being: that people care and that the people, places, and things with which one is involved inevitably matter.

Being-in-the-world as involvement is revealed by the ways in which such basic dimensions of the world as time and space are experienced. Time is not lived as a clock would record it, in equal minutes and hours. Rather, some hours drag on and on, whereas others zip by, depending on one's involvements. Similarly, the space of a strange place looms differently when it has become familiar. Even one's own body reflects this understanding of existence as being-in-the-world. A great variety of symptoms, from cold feet to high blood pressure, disclose one's involvements, as do gestures, both habitual and spontaneous.

Other continental European psychiatrists who advanced the development of existential psychology include Karl Jaspers, Eugene Minkowski, Henri Ey, Erwin Straus, Frederik Jacobus Buytendijk, and Viktor Frankl. In England, R. D. Laing, a brilliant young psychiatrist originally influenced by the British "object relations" school of psychoanalysis, developed an existential account of schizophrenic persons, beginning around 1960. He sought to show "that it was far more possible than is generally supposed to understand people diagnosed as psychotic." He proceeded to do so by examining their "existential context." In books such as *The Divided Self: An Existential Study in Sanity and Madness* (1965), Laing attempted to unravel the mystery of schizophrenic speaking and symptoms by revealing how their apparently nonsensical quality does have a sense when seen in terms of the person's own experience of the totality of his or her relationships and existence.

Existential analysis came to the United States at the end of the 1950s mainly through the influence of May, who introduced the writings of the European analysts. May provided both a scholarly background to the approach and an examination of its role in psychotherapy. His later books, such as *Man's Search for Himself* (1953), *Psychology and the Human Dilemma* (1967), and *Love and Will* (1969), did much to popularize existential psychology in the United States without trivializing its philosophical depth.

APPRECIATING PERSONHOOD

Existential therapists, such as May, have generally argued that they are not seeking to establish a new type of therapy with new techniques. Rather, they have developed a different approach, one that can be used with any specific therapeutic system. They developed a different way for the therapist to "be present" for the patient or client. This distinctive way of being present is well illustrated in Laing's therapeutic work; it hinges on the type of relationship that exists between the therapist and the patient. Laing pointed out the difference between two ways of relating to a patient: as a biochemical organism (and a diseased organism at that) or as a person. He cited, as an example, the difference between listening to another's speaking as evidence of certain neurological processes and trying to understand what the person is talking about. When a therapist sees a patient as an "it," the therapist cannot really understand that patient's desire, fear, hope, or despair. Seeing the patient as a person, however, implies seeing the patient "as responsible, as capable of choice, in short, as a self-acting agent."

This undiluted respect for the personhood of the patient is well exhibited in Laing's work with schizophrenic persons. In place of the usual medical model, Laing offered them a "hospital" in the original sense of that word: a place of refuge, of shelter and rest for a traveler. Their experience was respected there, however different it appeared. They were allowed to complete their journey through madness, accompanied by another person (Laing) who was always respectful that it was real.

May similarly asserted that "the central task and responsibility of the therapist is to seek to understand the patient as a being and as being-in-his-world." That understanding does not deny the validity of any psychodynamic insights; rather, it holds that any such dynamics "can be understood only in the context of the structure of existence of the person." Indeed, the very aim of existential therapy is to help the patient experience his or her existence as real. What makes it possible for the patient to change, said May, is ultimately this experience of being treated, in the moment, as the real person that the person is. That is why existential therapy emphasizes a sense of reality and concreteness above a set of techniques.

BEING-IN-THE-WORLD DILEMMAS

While each person's reality is unique, there are certain basic dilemmas that arise by virtue of one's being-in-the-world. Because existence is fundamentally a relationship with a world, the givens of existing provide what Irvin D. Yalom has called the "ultimate concerns of life." He has identified four: death, freedom, existential isolation, and meaninglessness. Yalom notes that the confrontation with any of these existential issues can become a serious conflict for a person. Specifically, to the extent that a person begins to become aware of these conflicts without yet facing them fully, that person will experience anxiety and so will seek to defend against the experience by turning away from the underlying concern. The task of the existential therapist is to use that experience of anxiety as a clue to help the patient find a way back to the ultimate concern and then, by fully facing it, discover the positive transformation it offers for authentic living. The first two of these ultimate concerns, death and freedom, can serve as illustrative examples.

The first of these conflicts is that one's life will end in death even though one wishes it could continue. Death therefore holds a terror that may leave one anxious. One may even try to evade any awareness of death, living as though one would live forever. For the existential therapist, however, this awareness of death can be used to propel the patient to live his or her life authentically. Because life's preciousness is most evident when one is aware that one will lose it, becoming authentically aware of one's mortality can give one a powerful commitment not to waste one's life. In that sense, the anxiety of trying to evade death can be turned around and transformed into a clue to help patients discover what it is that they would be most anxious about dying without having experienced.

The second of these conflicts has to do with freedom. Though it seems to be a positive value, realizing one's freedom fully can be terrifying, for it entails accepting responsibility for one's life. One is responsible for actualizing one's own true self. Experiences such as anxiety, guilt, and despair reveal the dilemma of trying to hide from oneself the fact that one was not willing to be true to oneself. They then provide the basic clue by which the patient can uncover the self.

ROOTS OF EXISTENTIALISM

Existentialism arose in the mid-nineteenth century with Søren Kierkegaard. He opposed the Hegelian philosophy dominant during his time with the criticism that its formalism and abstractness omitted the individual. He insisted that the existing person was the most basic starting point for philosophy, that the authentic acceptance of being an individual is the basic task of one's life, and that "the purpose of life is to be the self which one truly is." Through analyses of such experiences as passion and commitment, Kierkegaard showed the important truths of subjective life.

At the beginning of the twentieth century, Edmund Husserl established phenomenology as a philosophical method by which to investigate actual experience. This provided a powerful boost to existentialism, especially evident in Heidegger's subsequent analysis of the "care structure" as the meaning of being human. The next developments in existentialism arose in France, during and immediately after World War II. In a country occupied by the Nazis for five years, people who worked in the French Resistance movement became intimately acquainted with their own mortality. Death awaited around every corner; one never could know that this day was not the last. Such direct experience had a powerful impact on the French existential philosophers who participated in the Resistance movement, of whom Jean-Paul Sartre , Albert Camus, Simone de Beauvoir, and Maurice Merleau-Ponty are the best known.

While Merleau-Ponty wrote books of particular relevance for a psychology of perception and behavior, it was Sartre who most fully depicted the foibles of human life that are relevant to the psychotherapist. In philosophical books such as *L'Être et le néant* (1943; *Being and Nothingness*, 1956), as well as in plays and novels, Sartre lucidly revealed the ways people dodge rather than face their own freedom and their own responsibility to choose. For him, this living as if one were not really free (inauthentic living) was "bad faith." Sartre contrasted his "existential analysis" of phenomena such as bad faith with the Freudian psychoanalysis of the unconscious. In doing so, he replaced Freud's conceptions of a theoretical construct (the unconscious) with descriptions of experiences of living inauthentically.

These developments in France led to a burst of expanded interest in existentialism throughout the 1950s, in both Europe and the United States. By the 1960s, many new books, journals, and even graduate programs began to emphasize existential philosophy and psychology. Graduate programs that focused on existential psychology appeared at Duquesne University, West Georgia College, and Sonoma State University.

Existentialism became one of the primary sources of inspiration for an alternative to the dominant psychoanalytic and behavioristic psychologies that began to gather momentum in the 1960s under the name " humanistic psychology." By offering the perspective that people's experiences of their own situations are vitally important to an understanding of their behavior, this view posed a central challenge to mainstream experimental psychology. This existential insight did not sway most psychologists, however; instead, the rise of cognitive psychology in the 1970s and 1980s established a new paradigm. It, too, offered the key notion that a person's involvement was crucial to understanding behavior, but cognitive psychology defined that involvement in terms of a computational model: The person "takes in" the world by "processing information." That model preserved the mechanistic assumption so important to mainstream psychology—the very assumption that existential psychology most decisively disputed. As a result, existential psychology remains a lively critic on psychology's periphery rather than being an equal partner with more traditional approaches.

BIBLIOGRAPHY

Boss, Medard. *Psychoanalysis and Daseinsanalysis.* New York: Da Capo, 1982. Print.

Diamond, Stephen A. "What Is Existential Psychotherapy?" *Psychology Today.* Sussex, 21 Jan. 2011. Web. 19 May 2014.

Frankl, Viktor Emil. *Man's Search for Meaning.* New York: Washington Square, 2006.Print.

Frankl, Viktor Emil. *Man's Search for Ultimate Meaning.* Cambridge: Perseus, 2000. Print.

Jacobsen, Bo. *Invitation to Existential Psychology: A Psychology for the Unique Human Being and Its Applications in Therapy.* Hoboken: Wiley, 2008. Print.

Laing, Ronald David. *The Divided Self: An Existential Study in Sanity and Madness.* 1965. Rpt. New York: Routledge, 2001. Print.

May, Rollo. *The Discovery of Being.* 1983. Rpt. New York: Norton, 1994. Print.

May, Rollo, Ernest Angel, and Henri F. Ellenberger, eds. *Existence.* 1958. Rpt. Northvale: Aronson, 1995. Print.

Russo-Netzer, Pninit, and Alexander Batthyany. *Meaning in Positive and Existential Psychology.* New York: Springer, 2014. eBook Collection (EBSCOhost). Web. 19 May 2014. Print.

Valle, Ronald S., and Steen Halling, eds. Existential-Phenomenological Perspectives in Psychology. New York: Plenum, 1989. Print.

Welsh, Talia. *The Child as Natural Phenomenologist: Primal and Primary Experience in Merleau-Ponty's Psychology.* Evanston: Northwestern UP, 2013. Print.

Yalom, Irvin D. *Existential Psychotherapy.* New York: Basic , 1980. Print.

Christopher M. Aanstoos

See Also: Gestalt therapy; Humanistic psychology; May, Rollo; Person-centered therapy; Personality theory; Self-actualization; Social psychological models: Erich Fromm; Yalom, Irvin D.

Experimental psychology

Date: 1879 forward

Type of psychology: Psychological methodologies

Experimental psychology is a broad term that covers research in the various areas within psychology. Research is classified as either applied or basic, depending on whether it is being conducted to solve problems directly or to further academic knowledge. There are certain qualifications for research based on the scientific method, and research designs are classified as either descriptive or experimental depending on the amount of control present, which will affect the types of conclusions that can be drawn. Within experimental research, variables are classified as independent, dependent, or extraneous.

Key Concepts

- Basic and applied research
- Dependent variable
- Descriptive research

- Extraneous variable
- Functionalism
- Independent variable
- Operationism
- Structuralism

INTRODUCTION

Wilhelm Wundt founded the field of psychology, which he termed "experimental psychology," on establishing his lab at the University of Leipzig in Germany in 1879. Wundt was the first to identify psychology as a separate science, on par with the natural sciences such as biology, physics, and chemistry. Wundt himself was trained as a physiologist and philosopher, and the methods he used in both of those disciplines combined to give structure to the new field. The role of experimental psychology at its founding was to answer philosophical questions using scientific methods. Wundt defined consciousness as the appropriate subject matter for experimentation and devised methods such as introspection (reporting on inner experiences by the subjective observer) to study the activity and structures of the mind (the basis for the school of thought later termed structuralism). Wundt was responsible for removing psychology from the metaphysical realm, providing conclusive evidence that the mind could be studied scientifically. This profoundly affected the development of psychology in the years following, establishing an emphasis on the importance of scientific research methods.

Over the first century of its existence and beyond, psychology came to be defined as the scientific study of consciousness, emotions, and behavior, and experimental psychology is no longer the only type. There now are many other subfields in psychology, such as clinical psychology, social psychology, and developmental psychology, but experimental methods still underlie most of them because that is how knowledge is accumulated in each area. Experimental psychology itself has expanded to include both basic and applied research.

BASIC AND APPLIED RESEARCH

Basic research, the kind that Wundt himself conducted, is undertaken for the purpose of advancing scientific knowledge, even if the knowledge gained is not directly relevant to improving the lives of individuals. This type of research is more likely to take place in laboratory settings, often on university campuses, using undergraduate students or specially bred lab animals as experimental subjects. These settings do not approximate the natural environment, permitting factors that could interfere with interpretation of the results to be controlled or eliminated, making conclusions more accurate. Examples of basic research include studying animal behavior, examining the perceptual abilities of humans, or determining the factors contributing to aggressive behavior.

Basic research was the only type of research conducted in experimental psychology until the first decade of the twentieth century, when applied psychology was introduced through the American school of thought termed Functionalism. It was at this time that psychologists began being interested not only in how the mind works but also in how the mind works to help individuals interact with their environment. Most of the newer research involved conducting research with humans in their natural environment. For example, school psychologists were trying to find effective tests so that students could be taught at the appropriate levels (the first intelligence tests) and to identify how behavioral problems in the school or home could be controlled. Researchers also were trying to determine the factors that would increase efficiency and satisfaction in the workplace. In addition to these scenarios, researchers now attempt to solve such problems as finding effective ways to teach children with developmental disabilities, identifying new therapy techniques for those with psychological disorders, and developing strategies to increase healthy behaviors such as exercise and decrease unhealthy behaviors such as drug abuse. Applied research results tend to be more generalizable to others, but the relative lack of control sometimes limits the conclusions that can be drawn based on the results, so caution must be taken when recommending procedures from experiments.

THE SCIENTIFIC METHOD

The methods used for conducting either basic or applied research in experimental psychology are essentially the same as for conducting research in any other science. The first step in the process is identifying a research problem, a question that can be answered by appealing to evidence. Next will be a search for a theory, a general statement that integrates many observations from various research studies and is testable. From the theory is formed a hypothesis, a more precise version of the theory that is a specific prediction about the relationship between the variables in the research being conducted. At this point, the research is designed, which involves decisions about how many and what type of participants will be used, where the research will be conducted, the measurement procedures to be developed, and so on. After the relevant data are collected, they must be analyzed visually or statistically. This allows the drawing of conclusions about the findings, which are communicated to others in the form of presentation or publication. The research process is circular, in that the more questions that are answered the more new questions arise, and that is how science advances. There are key characteristics that must be present for good scientific research. Objectivity means that research must be free from bias. Data are to be collected, analyzed, interpreted, and reported objectively so that others are free to draw their own conclusions, even if they are different from those of the researchers. Control of factors that may affect the results of the research is necessary if those factors are not the specific ones being studied. For example, control for the effects of gender can be accomplished by ensuring that research samples include approximately the same number of males and females, unless the researcher is interested in looking for potential gender differences in behavior. In that case, the researcher would still want to control for factors such as age, education, or other characteristics that might be relevant. Control allows researchers to be more confident about the accuracy of their conclusions.

Operationism involves defining the variables to be studied in terms of the way they are measured. Many different operational definitions are possible for a particular concept such as aggression or love, and the results of research studies that use different operational definitions when combined provide more complete knowledge than if only one operational definition were used. Finally, replication is a key part of the research process because the aim of science is to accept only knowledge that has been verified by others. This requirement that results be replicable helps prevent bias and furthers objectivity.

DESCRIPTIVE VERSUS EXPERIMENTAL RESEARCH

Descriptive research is conducted to describe and predict behavior. Often these results are useful on their own, or such studies provide information to be used in future, more controlled, experiments. It can include archival research, an analysis of existing records of behavior, case studies, in-depth analysis of one or a few individuals, naturalistic observation, monitoring the behavior of subjects in their natural environment, or survey research in which individuals report on their own behavior. Descriptive research also includes correlational research, which examines relationships between variables that cannot be manipulated (such as gender, family background, or other personal characteristics that are not changeable). Correlational studies make it possible to predict changes in one variable based on observing changes in another, but as in all descriptive research, it is impossible to know whether or not changes in one variable caused the observed changes in another, so the conclusions to be drawn are limited.

The only type of research that can explain the causes of behavior is true experimental research, because that is the only type of research in which variables can be manipulated to see the observed effects on behavior. The variable that is manipulated is called the independent variable, and the variable that is measured to see the effects of the manipulation is called the dependent variable. Independent variables can be manipulated by measuring the effects of their presence versus absence (for instance, how reaction times differ when alcohol is consumed), their degree (how reaction times change as more alcohol is consumed), or their type (reaction times when alcohol is consumed as compared to when caffeine is consumed). Dependent variables are measured in terms of their latency (how long it takes for a response to occur) or duration (how long a response lasts), force (how strong the response is), rate or frequency (how often a response occurs within a period of time), or accuracy (the correctness of the response). There can be one or more each of the independent and dependent variables in any experiment, although having more variables increases the complexity of the analysis of the results. Every other variable that is present that could have an effect on the dependent variable in addition to the independent variable is considered an extraneous variable. These must be controlled (kept constant) or eliminated so that the researcher can be sure that changes in the dependent variable are due only to changes in the independent variable.

BIBLIOGRAPHY

Christensen, Larry. *Experimental Methodology.* 10th ed. Boston: Allyn, 2007. Print.

Jahoda, Gustav. "Critical Comments on Experimental, Discursive, and General Social Psychology." *Jour. for the Theory of Social Behaviour* 43.3 (2013): 341–60. Print.

Kantowitz, Barry H., David G. Elmes, and Henry L. Roediger III. *Experimental Psychology: Understanding Psychological Research.* 9th ed. Belmont: Wadsworth, 2009. Print.

Lundin, Robert W. *Theories and Systems of Psychology.* 5th ed. Lexington: Heath, 1996. Print.

Myers, Anne, and Christine H. Hansen. *Experimental Psychology.* Belmont: Thomson, 2012. Print.

Myers, David G. *Exploring Psychology.* 7th ed. New York: Worth, 2008. Print.

Rose, Anne C. "Animal Tales: Observations of the Emotions in American Experimental Psychology, 1890–1940." *Jour. of the History of the Behavioral Sciences* 48.4 (2012): 301–17. Print.

Smith, Randolph A., and Stephen F. Davis. *The Psychologist as Detective: An Introduction to Conducting Research in Psychology*. 5th ed. Upper Saddle River: Prentice, 2009. Print.

April Michele Williams

SEE ALSO: Animal experimentation; Archival data; Behaviorism; Case study methodologies; Complex experimental designs; Data description; Experimental psychology; Experimentation: Ethics and participant rights; Experimentation: Independent, dependent, and control variables; Field experimentation; Hypothesis development and testing; Observational methods; Qualitative research; Quasi-experimental designs; Research ethics; Sampling; Scientific methods; Statistical significance tests; Survey research: Questionnaires and interviews; Within-subject experimental designs.

Experimentation
Ethics and participant rights

DATE: 1960s forward

TYPE OF PSYCHOLOGY: Psychological methodologies

One of the tasks of government is to protect people from exploitation and abuse, including potential abuse by unethical researchers. American society has instituted several levels of control over research, thus ensuring that experimental ethics reflect the ethics of society at large. Still, few ethical decisions are easy, and many remain controversial.

KEY CONCEPTS
- Anonymity
- Clinical trials
- Informed consent
- Macroallocation issues
- Participant debriefing
- Placebo condition
- Professional ethics
- Right to privacy

INTRODUCTION
A primary task of government is to protect people from exploitation. Since scientists are sometimes in a position to take advantage of others and have occasionally done so, there is a role for government to regulate research to prevent exploitation of research participants. On the other hand, excessive regulation can stifle innovation; if scientists are not allowed to try new (and perhaps risky) experimental techniques, science will not progress, and neither will human understanding. This puts government in a difficult position: since research topics, scientific methodology, and public attitudes are continuously changing, it would be impossible to write a single law or set of laws defining which research topics and methods are acceptable and which are not. As soon as such a law were written, it would be out of date or incomplete.

INSTITUTIONAL REVIEW BOARDS
The United States Congress has decided to deal with this issue of research ethics by letting local communities determine what research with human participants is and is not appropriate according to contemporary local standards. Today, each institution conducting research must have a committee called an institutional review board (IRB) consisting of a minimum of five members, all of whom belong to the local community. To ensure that the committee is kept up to date on current human research methodologies, the IRB membership must include at least one scientist. At least one member must represent the general public and have no official or unofficial relationship with the institution where the research is taking place. A single person may fill multiple roles, and IRBs are also required to ensure that the board consists of both men and women and includes representatives with a variety of professions.

Each IRB is required to review written proposals for all local research on human participants before that research can begin. At most large institutions, the IRB has enough staffing to break into subcommittees to review proposals from different areas. It is the job of the IRB to ensure that unethical research is screened out before it starts. Government agencies that fund research projects will not consider a proposal until it has been approved by the local IRB, and if research is conducted at an institution without IRB approval, the government can withhold all funds to that institution, even funds unrelated to the research.

INFORMED CONSENT

To evaluate all aspects of a proposed research project, the IRB must have sufficient information about the recruitment of participants, the methods of the study, the procedures that will be followed, and the qualifications of the researchers. The IRB also requires that proposals include a copy of the informed consent contract that each potential participant will receive. This contract allows potential participants to see, in writing, a list of all possible physical or psychological risks that might occur as a result of participation in the project. People cannot be coerced or threatened into signing the form, and the form must also tell participants that even if they agree to begin the research study, they may quit at any time for any reason. Informed consent contracts must be written in nontechnical prose that can be understood by any potential participant; it is generally recommended that contracts use vocabulary consistent with an eighth-grade education.

Except for the file holding the signed contracts between the researcher and the participants, names of participants generally do not appear anywhere in the database or in the final written documents describing the study results. Data are coded without using names, and in the informed consent contract, participants are assured of the complete anonymity of their responses or test results unless there are special circumstances that require otherwise. If researchers intend to use information in any way that may threaten participants' privacy, this issue needs to be presented clearly in the informed consent contract before the study begins.

DECEPTION

Occasionally in psychology researchers use a form of deception by telling the participants that the study is about one thing when it really is about something else. Although it usually is considered unethical to lie to participants, deception is sometimes necessary, because participants may behave differently when they know what aspect of their behavior is being watched. (This is called a demand characteristic of the experimental setting.) More people will probably act helpful, for example, when they know that a study is about helpfulness. A researcher studying helpfulness thus might tell participants that they are going to be involved in a study of, say, reading. Participants are then asked to wait in a room until they are each called into the test room. When the first name is called, a person may get up and trip on his or her way out of the room. In actuality, the person who was called was really the experimenter's assistant (although none of the participants knows that), and the real point of the research is to see how many of the participants get up to help the person who fell down. In situations such as this, where demand characteristics would be likely, IRBs will allow deception to be used as long as the deception is not severe and the researchers debrief participants at the end by explaining what was really occurring. After deception is used, experimenters must be careful to make sure that participants do not leave the study feeling angry at having been "tricked"; ideally, they should leave feeling satisfaction for having contributed to science.

Even when participants have not been deceived, researchers are required to give an oral or written debriefing at the end of the study. Researchers are also obliged to ensure that participants can get help if they do experience any negative effects from their participation in the research. Ultimately, if a participant feels that he or she was somehow harmed or abused by the researcher or the research project, a civil suit can be filed in an attempt to claim compensation. Since participants are explicitly told that they can drop out of a study at any time for any reason, however, such long-term negative feelings should be extremely rare.

SPECIAL ISSUES IN CLINICAL TRIALS

Clinical psychology is perhaps the most difficult area in which to make ethical research decisions. One potential problem in clinical research that is usually not relevant for other research settings is that of getting truly informed consent from the participants. The participants of clinical research are selected specifically because they meet the criteria for some mental disorder. By making sure that participants meet the relevant criteria, researchers ensure that their study results will be relevant to the population who suffers from the disorder; on the other hand, depending on the disorder being studied, it may be that the participants are not capable of giving informed consent. A person who suffers from disordered thinking (as with schizophrenics) or dementia (as with Alzheimer's disease patients) or is otherwise mentally handicapped cannot be truly "informed." In the cases of individuals who have been declared incompetent by the courts, a designated guardian can give informed consent for participation in a research study. There are also cases, however, of participants being legally competent yet not capable of truly understanding the consequences of what they read. Authority figures, including doctors and psychologists, can have a dramatic power over people; that power is likely to be even stronger for someone who is not in full control of his or her life, who has specifically sought help from others, and who is trusting that others have his or her best interests in mind.

Another concern about clinical research is the susceptibility of participants to potential psychological damage. The typical response of research participants is positive: they feel they are getting special attention and respond with healthy increases in self-esteem and well-being. A few, however, may end up feeling worse; for example, if they feel no immediate gain from the treatment, they may label themselves as "incurable" and give up, leading to a self-fulfilling prophecy.

A third concern in clinical research regards the use of control or placebo treatments. Good research designs always include both a treatment group and a control group. When there is no control group, changes in the treatment group may be attributed to the treatment when in fact they may have been caused by the passage of time or by the fact that participants were getting special attention while in the study. Although control groups are necessary to ensure that research results are interpreted correctly, the dilemma that arises in clinical research is that it may be unethical to assign people to a control group if they need some kind of intervention. One way of dealing with this dilemma is to give all participants some form of treatment and to compare the different treatment outcomes to one another rather than to a no-treatment group. This works well when there is already a known treatment with positive effects. Not only are there no participants who are denied treatment; the new treatment can be tested to see if it is better than the old one, not only if it is better than nothing. Sometimes, if there is no standard treatment for comparison, participants assigned to the control group are put on a "waiting list" for the treatment; their progress without treatment is then compared with that of participants who are getting treatment right away. To some extent, this mimics what happens in nonresearch settings, as people sometimes must wait for therapy, drug abuse counseling, and so on. On the other hand, in nonresearch settings, those who get assigned to waiting lists are likely to be those in less critical need, whereas in research, assignment to treatment and nontreatment groups must be random. Assigning the most critical cases to the treatment group would bias the study's outcome, yet assigning participants randomly may be perceived as putting research needs ahead of clients' needs.

THE MILGRAM STUDIES

Concern about potential abuse of research participants arose in the 1960s, in response to publicity following a series of studies by Stanley Milgram at Yale University. Milgram was interested in finding out how physicians who had devoted their lives to helping people were so easily able to hurt and even kill others (in the name of science) in experiments in Nazi concentration camps.

In Milgram's now-famous experiment, each participant was paired with one of Milgram's colleagues but was told that this partner was another volunteer. Then each participant, both real and pretend, drew a slip of paper assigning him or her to the role of either "teacher" or "learner." Actually, both slips always said "teacher," but the assistants pretended that theirs said "learner"; this way, the real participants were always assigned the role of teachers. Milgram then showed participants an apparatus that supposedly delivered shocks; teachers, on one side of a partition, were instructed to deliver a shock to the learner on the other side whenever a mistake was made on a word-pairing task. The apparatus actually did not deliver shocks, but the learners pretended that it did; as the experiment continued and the teachers were instructed to give larger and larger shocks, the learners gave more and more extreme responses. At a certain point, the learners started pounding on the partition, demanding to be released; eventually, they feigned a heart attack.

When Milgram designed this study, he asked psychiatrists and psychologists what percentage of people they thought would continue as teachers in this experiment; the typical response was about 0.1 percent. What Milgram found, however, was that two-thirds of the participants continued to deliver shocks to the learner even after the learner had apparently collapsed. The participants were clearly upset; they repeatedly expressed concern that someone should check on the learner. Milgram would simply reply that although the shocks were painful, they would not cause permanent damage, and the teacher should continue. In spite of their concern and distress, most participants obeyed.

Milgram's results revealed much about the power of authority; participants obeyed the authority figure (Milgram) even against their own moral judgment. These results help explain the abominable behavior of Nazi physicians, as well as other acts of violence committed by normal people who were simply doing what they were told. Ironically, although Milgram's study was so valuable, he was accused of abusing his own participants by "forcing" them to continue the experiment even when they were clearly upset. Critics also claimed that Milgram's study might have permanently damaged his participants' self-esteem. Although interviews with the participants showed that this was not true—they generally reported learning much about themselves and about human nature—media discussions and reenactments of the study led the public to believe that many of Milgram's participants had been permanently harmed. Thus began the discussion of experimental ethics that ultimately led to the system of regulation in force today.

BIBLIOGRAPHY

American Psychological Association. "Ethical Principles of Psychologists and Code of Conduct." http://www.apa.org/ethics/code2002.html.

Boyce, Nell. "Knowing Their Own Minds." *New Scientist* 20 June 1998: 20–21. Print.

Creswell, John W. *Research Design: Qualitative, Quantitative, and Mixed Methods Approaches.* Thousand Oaks: Sage, 2014. Print.

Garner, Mark, Claire Wagner, and Barbara Kawulich, eds. *Teaching Research Methods in the Social Sciences.* Burlington: Ashgate, 2012. Digital file.

Penslar, Robin L. *Research Ethics: Cases and Materials.* Bloomington: Indiana UP, 1995. Print.

Perry, Gina. *Behind the Shock Machine: The Untold Story of the Notorious Milgram Psychology Experiments.* New York: New, 2013. Print.

Rothman, K. J., and K. B. Michels. "The Continuing Unethical Use of Placebo Controls." *New England Journal of Medicine* 331.6 (1994): 394–98. Print.

Sales, Bruce D., and Susan Folkman, eds. *Ethics in Research with Human Participants.* Washington: American Psychological Association, 2005. Print.

Sieber, Joan E. *Planning Ethically Responsible Research: A Guide for Students and Internal Review Boards.* Newbury Park: Sage, 1995. Print.

Slife, Brent, ed. *Taking Sides: Clashing Views on Controversial Psychological Issues.* 13th ed. Guilford: Dushkin, 2004. Print.

Linda Mealey

See Also: Animal experimentation; Case study methodologies; Experimentation: Independent, dependent, and control variables; Field experimentation; Observational methods; Qualitative research; Research ethics; Survey research: Questionnaires and interviews.

Experimentation
Independent, dependent, and control variables

Type of psychology: Psychological methodologies

The scientific method involves the testing of hypotheses through the objective collection of data. The experiment is an important method of data collection in which the researcher systematically controls multiple factors to determine the extent to which changes in one variable cause changes in another variable. Only the experimental method can reveal cause-effect relationships between the variables of interest.

Key Concepts

- Control group
- Control variables
- Dependent variable
- Ecological validity
- Experiment
- Field experiment
- Hypothesis
- Independent variable
- Random assignment

INTRODUCTION

Psychology is typically defined as the science of behavior and cognition and is considered a research-oriented discipline, not unlike biology, chemistry, and physics. To appreciate the role of experimentation in psychology, it is useful to view it in the context of the general scientific method employed by psychologists in conducting their research. This scientific method may be described as a four-step sequence starting with identifying a problem and forming a hypothesis. The problem must be one suitable for scientific inquiry—that is, questions concerning values, such as whether rural life is "better" than city life, are more appropriate for philosophical debate than scientific investigation. Questions better suited to the scientific method are those that can be answered through the objective collection of facts—for example, "Are children who are neglected by their parents more likely to do poorly in school than children who are well treated?" The hypothesis is the tentative guess, or the prediction regarding the question's answer, and is based on other relevant research and existing theory. The second step, and the one with which this article is primarily concerned, is the collection of data (facts) to test the accuracy of the hypothesis. Any one of a number of methods might be employed, including simple observation, survey, or experimentation. The third step is to make sense of the facts that have been accumulated by subjecting them to careful analysis; the fourth step is to share any significant findings with the scientific community.

RESEARCH APPROACHES

In considering step two, the collection of data, it seems that people often mistakenly use the words research and experiment interchangeably. A student might ask whether an experiment has been done on a particular topic when, in fact, the student really wants to know if any kind of research has been conducted in that area. All experiments are examples of research, but not all research is experimental. Research that is nonexperimental in nature might be either descriptive or correlational.

Descriptive research is nearly self-explanatory; it occurs when the researcher wants merely to characterize the behaviors of an individual or, more likely, a group. For example, one might want to survey the students of a high school to ascertain the level of alcohol use (alcohol use might be described in terms of average ounces consumed per student per week). One might also spend considerable time observing individuals who have a particular condition, such as infantile autism. A thorough description of their typical behaviors could be useful for someone investigating the cause of this disorder. Descriptive research can be extremely valuable, but it is not useful when researchers want to investigate the relationship between two or more variables (things that vary or quantities that may have different values).

In a correlational study, the researcher measures how strongly the variables are related or the degree to which one variable predicts another variable. A researcher who is interested in the relationship between exposure to violence on television (variable one) and aggressive behavior (variable two) in a group of elementary school children could administer a survey asking the children how much violent television they view and then rank the subjects from high to low levels of this variable. The researcher could similarly interview the school staff and rank the children according to their aggressive behavior. A statistic called a correlation coefficient might then be computed, revealing how the two variables are related and the strength of that relationship.

CAUSE AND EFFECT

Correlational studies are not uncommon in psychological research. Often, however, a researcher wants even more specific information about the relationships among variables—in particular, about whether one variable causes a change in another variable. In such a situation, experimental research is warranted. This drawback of the correlational approach—its inability to establish causal relationships—is worth considering for a moment. In the hypothetical study described above, the researcher may find that viewing considerable television violence predicts high levels of aggressive behavior, yet she cannot conclude that these viewing habits cause the aggressiveness. After all, it is entirely possible that aggressiveness, caused by some unknown factor, prompts a preference for violent television. That is, the causal direction is unknown; viewing television violence may cause aggressiveness, but the inverse (that aggressiveness causes the watching of violent television programs) is also feasible.

As this is a crucial point, one final illustration is warranted. What if, at a certain Rocky Mountain university, a correlational study has established that high levels of snowfall predict low examination scores? One should not conclude that something about the chemical composition of snow impairs the learning process. The correlation may be real and highly predictive, but the causal culprit may be some other factor. Perhaps, as snowfall increases, so does the incidence of illness, and it is this variable that is causally related to exam scores. Maybe, as snowfall increases, the likelihood of students using their study time for skiing also increases.

Experimentation is a powerful research method because it alone can reveal cause-effect relationships. In an experiment, the researcher does not merely measure the naturally occurring relationships between variables for the purpose of predicting one from the other; rather, he or she systematically manipulates the values of one variable and measures the effect, if any, that is produced in a second variable. The variable that is manipulated is known as the independent variable; the other variable, the behavior in question, is called the dependent variable (any change in it depends on the manipulation of the independent variable). Experimental research is characterized by a desire for control on the part of the researcher. Control of the independent variable and control over extraneous variables are both wanted. That is, there is a desire to eliminate or hold constant the factors, known as control variables, other than the independent variable that might influence the dependent variable. If adequate control is achieved, the researcher may be confident that it was, in fact, the manipulation of the independent variable that produced the change in the dependent variable.

CONTROL GROUPS

Returning to the relationship between television viewing habits and aggressive behavior in children, suppose that correlational evidence indicates that high levels of the former variable predict high levels of the latter. Now the researcher wants to test the hypothesis that there is a cause-effect relationship between the two variables. She decides to manipulate exposure to television violence (the independent variable) to see what effect might be produced in the aggressiveness of her subjects (the dependent variable). She might choose two levels of the independent variable and have twenty children watch fifteen minutes of a violent detective show while another twenty children are subjected to thirty minutes of the same show.

If an objective rating of playground aggressiveness later reveals more hostility in the thirty-minute group than in the fifteen-minute group, she still cannot be confident that higher levels of television violence cause higher levels of aggressive behavior. More information is needed, especially with regard to issues of control. To begin with, how does the researcher know that it is the violent content of the program that is promoting aggressiveness? Perhaps it is the case that the more time they spend watching television, regardless of subject matter, the more aggressive children become.

This study needs a control group: a group of subjects identical to the experimental subjects with the exception that they do not experience the independent variable. In fact, two control groups might be employed, one that watches fifteen minutes and another that watches thirty minutes of nonviolent programming. The control groups serve as a basis against which the behavior of the experimental groups can be compared. If it is found that the two control groups aggress to the same extent, and to a lesser extent than the experimental groups, the researcher can be more confident that violent programming promotes relatively higher levels of aggressiveness.

The experimenter also needs to be sure that the children in the thirty-minute experimental group were not naturally more aggressive to begin with. One need not be too concerned with this possibility if one randomly assigns subjects to the experimental and control groups. There are certainly individual differences among subjects in factors such as personality and intelligence, but with random assignment (a technique for creating groups of subjects across which individual differences will be evenly dispersed) one can be reasonably sure that those individual differences are evenly dispersed among the experimental and control groups.

SUBJECT VARIABLES

The experimenter might want to control or hold constant other variables. Perhaps she suspects that age, social class, ethnicity, and gender could also influence the children's aggressiveness. She might want to make sure that these subject variables are eliminated by either choosing subjects who are alike in these ways or by making sure that the groups are balanced for these factors (for example, equal numbers of boys and girls in each group). There are numerous other extraneous variables that might concern the researcher, including the time of day when the children participate, the length of time between television viewing and the assessment of aggressiveness, the children's diets, the children's family structures (single or dual parents, siblings or only child), and the disciplinary styles used in the homes. Resource limitations prevent every extraneous variable from being controlled, yet the more control, the more confident the experimenter can be of the cause-effect relationship between the independent and dependent variables.

INFLUENCE OF REWARDS

One more example of experimental research, this one nonhypothetical, will further illustrate the application of this methodology. In 1973, Mark Lepper, David Greene, and Richard Nisbett tested the hypothesis that when people are offered external rewards for performing activities that are naturally enjoyable, their interest in these activities declines. The participants in the study were nursery school children who had already demonstrated a fondness for coloring with marking pens; this was their preferred activity when given an opportunity for free play. The children were randomly assigned to one of three groups. The first group was told previously that they would receive a "good player award" if they would play with the pens when later given the opportunity. Group two received the same reward but without advance notice; they were surprised by the reward. The last group of children was the control group; they were neither rewarded nor told to expect a reward.

The researchers reasoned that the first group of children, having played with the pens to receive a reward, would now perceive their natural interest in this activity as lower than before the study. Indeed, when all groups were later allowed a free play opportunity, it was observed that the "expected reward" group spent significantly less time than the other groups in this previously enjoyable activity. Lepper and his colleagues, then, experimentally supported their hypothesis and reported evidence that reward causes interest in a previously pleasurable behavior to decline. This research has implications for instructors; they should carefully consider the kinds of behavior they reward (with gold stars, lavish praise, high grades, and so on) as they may, ironically, be producing less of the desired behavior. An academic activity that is enjoyable play for a child may become tedious work when a reward system is attached to it.

CRITICISMS

Although most would agree that the birth of psychology as a science took place in Leipzig, Germany, in 1879, when Wilhelm Wundt established the first laboratory for studying psychological phenomena, there is no clear record of the first use of experimentation. Regardless, there is no disputing the attraction that this method of research has had for many psychologists, who clearly recognize the usefulness of the experiment in investigating potential causal relationships between variables. Hence, experimentation is employed widely across the subfields of psychology, including developmental, cognitive, physiological, clinical, industrial, and social psychology.

This is not to say that all psychologists are completely satisfied with experimental research. It has been argued that an insidious catch-22 exists in some experimental research that limits its usefulness. The argument goes like this: experimenters are motivated to control rigorously the conditions of their studies and the relevant extraneous variables. To gain such control, they often conduct experiments in a laboratory setting. Therefore, subjects are often observed in an artificial environment, engaged in behaviors that are so controlled as to be unnatural, and they clearly know they are being observed—which may further alter their behavior. Such research is said to be lacking in ecological validity or applicability to "real-life" behavior. It may show how subjects behave in a unique laboratory procedure, but it tells little about psychological phenomena as displayed in everyday life. The catch-22, then, is that experimenters desire control to establish that the independent variable is producing a change in the dependent variable, and the more such control, the better; however, the more control, the more risk that the research may be ecologically invalid.

FIELD EXPERIMENTS

Most psychologists are sensitive to issues of ecological validity and take pains to make their laboratory procedures as naturalistic as possible. Additionally, much research is conducted outside the laboratory in what are known as field experiments. In such studies, the subjects are unobtrusively observed (perhaps by a confederate of the researcher who would not attract their notice) in natural settings such as classroom, playground, or workplace. Field experiments, then, represent a compromise in that there is bound to be less control than is obtainable in a laboratory, yet the behaviors observed are likely to be natural. Such naturalistic experimentation is likely to continue to increase in the future.

Although experimentation is only one of many methods available to psychologists, it fills a particular need, and that need is not likely to decline in the foreseeable future. In trying to understand the complex relationships among the many variables that affect the way people think and act, experimentation makes a valuable contribution: It is the one methodology available that can reveal unambiguous cause-effect relationships.

BIBLIOGRAPHY

Barber, Theodore Xenophon. *Pitfalls in Human Research.* New York: Pergamon, 1985. Print.

Carlson, Neil R. *Psychology: The Science of Behavior.* 6th ed. Boston: Allyn, 2007. Print.

Coolican, Hugh. *Research Methods and Statistics in Psychology*. 6th ed. New York: Psychology, 2014. Print.

Hearst, Eliot, ed. *The First Century of Experimental Psychology*. Hillsdale: Erlbaum, 1979. Print.

Schweigert, Wendy A. *Research Methods in Psychology: A Handbook*. 3rd ed. Long Grove: Waveland, 2012. Print.

Shaughnessy, John J., and Eugene B. Zechmeister. *Research Methods in Psychology.* 8th ed. New York: McGraw-Hill, 2009. Print.

Stern, Paul C., and Linda Kalof. *Evaluating Social Science Research.* 2nd ed. New York: Oxford UP, 1996. Print.

Walsh, Richard T. G., Thomas Teo, and Angelina Baydala. *A Critical History and Philosophy of Psychology.* New York: Cambridge UP, 2014. Print.

Mark B. Alcorn

SEE ALSO: Animal experimentation; Complex experimental designs; Data description; Hypothesis development and testing; Qualitative research; Quasiexperimental designs; Research ethics; Sampling; Scientific methods; Statistical significance tests; Within-subject experimental designs.

Eye movement desensitization and reprocessing (EMDR)

Type of psychology: Biological bases of human behavior; Clinical; Counseling; Family; Health; Psychopathology; Psychotherapy

Eye movement desensitization and reprocessing (EMDR) is an exposure therapy discovered in 1987 by Dr. Francine Shapiro. It was discovered "by accident" while walking in the park, according to her own account. Since that time, the technique has been heavily researched with veterans suffering from combat related posttraumatic stress disorder (PTSD) as well as other clinical populations. In addition, EMDR is utilized to help clients struggling with non-PTSD conditions including phobias, performance anxiety, social anxiety, and coping skills for medical and terminal illness and bereavement

Key Concepts:

- Desensitization
- Exposure
- Posttraumatic stress disorder
- Psychosomatic
- SUDS score

EMDR has become a first-line treatment for many clinicians to help clients overcome the devastating symptoms of PTSD. This is due to the rapid results often achieved in eliminating symptoms common to PTSD, such as nightmares, flashbacks, blackouts, rage, dissociation, exaggerated startled response, anxiety, depression, and avoidance of details reminiscent of the traumatic event. Sometimes use of EMDR is able to erase the image or memory completely. Considered an intervention with rapid results, EMDR reprocessing is often achieved in fewer than 30 minutes. In fact, session preparation often takes longer than the amount of time required for EMDR to reprocess the trauma.

APPLICATION

Because EMDR is an exposure-oriented therapy, the client must be willing and able to conjure and confront images and memories of the trauma. Images and memories are usually self-generated, but external cues may also be used to trigger memories. If the client is not able to tolerate a discussion about or unable to conjure an image of traumatic material, EMDR is contraindicated. In other words, EMDR is not an effective treatment for vague or repressed memories. Two main criteria determine whether the client is likely to benefit from EMDR: 1) the level of clarity and 2) the level of emotional disturbance the memory causes. If the traumatic memory is disturbing but not clear, EMDR's effectiveness is drastically reduced. The client must remember at least some important details of the trauma so that the memories can be reprocessed.

The second criterion is that the internal or external images are disturbing enough to the client that intense psychosomatic reactions are elicited. Common psychosomatic reactions include muscle tension, tightness in one's chest, butterflies in the stomach, clenching of fists and/or jaw, palpitations, sweating, dizziness, nausea, and crying. These psychosomatic reactions are often accompanied by feelings of intense fear, anger, helplessness, and horror. In other words, EMDR is most effective when traumatic memories are very clear and very disturbing. At the beginning of a treatment, clients will often say something like, "This happened twenty-five years ago, but I remember it like it was yesterday."

HOW EMDR WORKS

Although there is some controversy about why EMDR works, most agree that it involves bilateral brain stimulation which catalyzes emotional healing. This can be achieved through eye movements back and forth, alternating auditory pulsations, or tapping on the client's knees in a pitter-patter fashion. The left side of the brain is responsible for rational thinking and language, while the right side of the brain is thought to be associated with images, creativity, and feelings. A hallmark feature of PTSD is that the person experiences a disconnected reality between what they know to be true intellectually versus how they feel about themselves or the world emotionally. For example, a woman who was raped may understand intellectually that it was not her fault yet she may experience feelings of guilt or shame as though she were responsible for the incident. This is an example of a disconnection between the left brain and right brain. The left-right brain disconnection often results in a distorted, negative sense of self, and EMDR helps desensitize and reprocess trauma so that the right brain (feeling) defers to the left brain (rational).Thus the person experiences the memory according to rational reality as opposed to irrational feelings. During the course of a single session, the client may start the session sobbing uncontrollably about a traumatic event and after the session may say something like, "What happened to me was unfortunate, but it doesn't mean I have to walk around in fear anymore." When EMDR is successful, the shift in perspective is rapid and dramatic.

PROCEDURE

Use of EMDR is straightforward. The first step is to obtain a detailed description of the traumatic event with special emphasis on the image or snapshot that best represents the most painful part. It is usually easy for the client to identify the worst part, because it is often the subject of nightmares, flashbacks, or details that they most want to avoid. Once the targeted snapshot is identified, the client is asked to rate the snapshot on a scale of 0-10. The client's ability to rate their experience is vitally important because the clinician is dependent on the client's self reporting to verify the effectiveness of the treatment. This is known as the Subjective Unit of Disturbance Scale (SUDS); 0 represents no disturbance while 10 represents the most disturbing thing the client can imagine. At the beginning of the treatment session, a baseline SUDS score is taken. Periodically, the SUDS scores are recorded to determine whether EMDR is decreasing the client's level of disturbance associated with the trauma. Each set of eye movements lasts approximately one to two minutes. This process is repeated until the SUDS score decreases to 1 or 0.

In addition to the SUDS level, prior to starting desensitization, a detailed description of the incident is obtained. Then the client is asked what negative self concept is associated with the memory. This elicits the distortion which will be reprocessed by EMDR. For example, if we use EMDR for an incident where a person was robbed at gunpoint, the client is asked, "What negative self idea is associated with seeing the robber pointing a gun in your face?" The client will usually say something like "I'm dead!" As EMDR treatment progresses, the clinician checks between sets of eye movements to see whether anything has shifted in terms of the disturbing image (e.g., a gun pointed at the client's face) or the client's feelings associated with the image. Usually, the image becomes increasingly unclear, and the client reports that the incident feels more like a movie than his or her own life experience (desensitization).

In addition to a baseline SUDS score, a detailed description of the traumatic event, and negative, distorted self statements, EMDR preparation includes asking clients about their emotions and body sensations elicited by the trauma. The most common emotions reported are fear, anger, sadness, and helplessness. The most common bodily sensations are tight chest and/or jaw, heart palpitations, difficulty breathing, crying, butterflies in the stomach, and dizziness. After each set of eye movements, emotional and somatic symptoms are assessed. Typically, there is a direct relationship between the clarity of the image and the level of emotional and bodily discomfort.

The final part of the EMDR preparation is the creation of a "safe place." This is a happy scene or memory where the client can retreat if the disturbing images become too intense to tolerate. Even though it is useful for clients to know they can stop EMDR at any time, the safe place is rarely utilized. As noted above, EMDR preparation often takes longer than the actual treatment.

In summary, the client gives a detailed account of the trauma. A baseline SUDS score is recorded as well as the negative self statement and the related bodily sensations and emotions. The client is asked to focus on the disturbing image and then asked to open his or her eyes. A clinician then waves fingers in front of the client's field of vision, and he or she follows back and forth while keeping the head still. Each set of eye movements lasts about one to two minutes. Between sets, the client takes a deep breath and is asked to assess the clarity and level of disturbance of the traumatic image, as well as any changes to emotional and somatic status. This process is repeated until the SUDS score decreases to 1 or 0.

CONCLUSION

EMDR is an extremely useful image oriented exposure treatment that rapidly desensitizes and reprocesses traumatic memories and other anxiety-based irrational thoughts. EMDR requires that the traumatic memory is clear and disturbing and that the client can tolerate a discussion about it. Often, by the end of the brief treatment, the client feels relaxed and is unable to visualize the disturbing image any longer.

It should be noted that although EMDR is simple to understand conceptually, the client should pursue treatment only from licensed behavioral health professionals who are properly trained by groups like the EMDR Institute.

BIBLIOGRAPHY

Shapiro, F. (1995). *Eye movement desensitization and reprocessing: Basic principles, protocols, and procedures.* New York, NY: Guilford.This book is geared towards clinicians, giving a historical and theoretical background of the technique and providing the standard protocol in detail.

Shapiro, F., & Silk Forrest, M. (1997). *EMDR: The Breakthrough Therapy For Overcoming Anxiety, Stress and Trauma*. New York, NY: Harper Collins. This book is written for laypeople to give a taste of EMDR treatment and what disorders it may be useful in treating.

Grand, D. (2001). *Emotional Healing At Warp Speed: The Power of EMDR*. New York, NY: Crown Publishing Group. This book is written by an experienced EMDR practitioner and trainer. It is easy reading for the general population interested in an expert therapist's inspiring anecdotes.

www.emdr.com This is the homepage for the EMDR Institute. It includes a wealth of information about EMDR research and development as well as a description of the numerous humanitarian projects that practitioners are involved with. There are also pages that provide products, answers to frequently asked questions, and a list of EMDR certified clinicians by zip code.

Adam Lynn

See Also: Eye movement; Francine Shapiro; Post traumatic stress disorder. Psychotherapy; Therapy; Trauma; Treatment.

Eyewitness testimony

Type of psychology: Memory

In the study of memory and eyewitness testimony, knowledge of the factors that affect memory is applied to evaluate the ability of a witness to an event to recall details of the event and to recognize participants in the event. This knowledge is often applied to witnesses of a crime in regard to identifying the perpetrator.

Key Concepts

- Encoding
- Perception
- Recall
- Recognition
- Retrieval
- Storage

INTRODUCTION

Knowledge of how the memory process operates has been applied to the analysis of eyewitness testimony to assess the likelihood that a witness is correct in making an identification. The task of eyewitness identification depends on the three stages of the memory process: encoding, storage, and retrieval. The last stage, retrieval, can be divided into two parts: recall and recognition. Each of these stages is subject to the influence of several factors that may contribute to error in the process.

ENCODING

Encoding is the stage of acquiring information. In the case of eyewitness identification, it is the sighting of a person during an event. The circumstances of the event will affect the ability of a person to encode information, including the facial appearance of another person. A short period of viewing time, poor lighting, greater distance, and an obtuse angle of view will reduce the observer's ability to acquire information about appearance. Any distractions present will reduce the attention paid to the face of the person and reduce the facial information encoded. If there are other people present, they serve as distractions. If a weapon is present, it attracts the attention of the observer and reduces the attention to faces. This phenomenon is called the weapons effect. If the weapon is used in a threatening manner, it will be likely to attract even more attention and further reduce the encoding of facial detail. Highly salient features of the face may dominate the encoding of the face. For example, a prominent scar may attract attention and reduce the attention to other facial details. When this happens, the witness may easily mistake another person with a similar scar for the original person, even though other features are different. Only information that is encoded can be retained and retrieved later, so the encoding stage sets the limits for later identification.

Once information is encoded, it must be stored until it is retrieved for use. One is not constantly aware of the information one has; such information is held in storage until one retrieves it. The brain holds information by some electrochemical process. It is not known exactly how it works, but it is clear that the storage stage of memory is not passive and inert like a videotape. Memories can change while they are stored. The memory may change in two ways: it may fade, or it may be distorted. Information fades away over time. This effect of time on memory is one of the oldest findings in the field of psychology, documented by Hermann Ebbinghaus in 1885. His findings indicate that memory fades rapidly at first and continues to fade over time at a reducing rate. This fading could be evidenced by loss of details or a less accurate recall of details. Sometimes witnesses may still believe that they recall a face, but the memory has really changed so that their identification is inaccurate.

The other major factor affecting memory during the storage period is interference. Events that occur during the storage period may change the memory without the awareness of the witness. A witness may be exposed to information after an event and, without knowing it, incorporate that information into the memory of the event. One example of this type of effect is called unconscious transference. This occurs when a person seen in one setting is remembered as having been in another. Sometimes a witness will mistakenly identify someone seen in another setting as the one who committed a crime. The witness has, without knowing it, transferred the memory of the face of the innocent person into the crime memory.

The third stage of memory is retrieval. Witnesses may be asked to retrieve information by either recall or recognition. Giving a description of a person is an example of free recall. There are no external stimuli from which to select; witnesses simply retrieve whatever information they can. In the case of recognition, the witness is asked to identify someone from a photograph, in person, or from a group of photographs (a photo lineup) or a group of people (a live lineup). Sometimes lineups are videotaped. Recall may be distorted by suggestive questions or nonverbal cues. Elizabeth F. Loftus reported in her 1979 book Eyewitness Testimony that when people were asked, "How tall was the basketball player?" their descriptions averaged seventy-nine inches. When they were asked, "How short was the basketball player?" they estimated sixty-nine inches. This ten-inch difference was caused simply by the change in the wording of the question.

The accuracy of a witness's recognition in lineup situations can be greatly affected by the nature of the lineup. If a witness is asked to identify a person from a single photograph or a one-person lineup, there is a possibility of error attributable to the witness's expectation that this must be the person or the police would not produce the person. In multiple-choice lineups, the similarity of the alternative choices to the suspect is the major determinant of error. If only one or two people in the lineup are similar to the original description of a suspect, a witness really has few choices, and the result is similar to the single-choice lineup. Witnesses may sometimes select a person in a lineup who is similar to the one seen or who looks familiar for some other reason.

EYEWITNESSES AND THE JUSTICE SYSTEM

In some cases, the only evidence against a person accused of a crime is an identification by an eyewitness. In their 1973 book *Wrongful Imprisonment: Mistaken Convictions and Their Consequences,* Ruth Brandon and Christie Davies describe seventy cases in which an incorrect identification by an eyewitness led to a conviction. In 1973, after conducting his own study of the subject, New York surrogate court judge Nathan Sobel concluded that incorrect eyewitness identification led to more miscarriages of justice than all other factors combined. Because of the serious consequences of an incorrect identification and the possibility that misidentifications frequently occur, psychologists have applied their expertise in memory to the study of the factors that would affect the accuracy of eyewitness identification.

Loftus has reported a case of eyewitness testimony that illustrates one of the most important applications of the field, a criminal trial. The background to the trial began on October 12, 1977, at approximately 8:30 in the evening. Two men entered a liquor store in Watsonville, California. The first man stood directly across from a young male clerk and pointed a gun at him, demanding all the money. The second man stood four or five feet away, pointing a gun at an older clerk, who stood behind the first clerk. The first robber demanded the money from the cash register and the clerks' wallets. As the young clerk turned to replace his wallet, he heard a shot and dove to the floor. When he looked up, the first robber was almost out the door, and the second robber stood in the doorway smiling; the older clerk lay dead on the floor. As soon as the robbers left, the young clerk hit the alarm. A security guard responded immediately, and the clerk, in a state of shock, could only say, "Two men, one with a mustache, two men, one with a mustache."

The clerk was interviewed by police the next day, and he described one robber as a male Mexican, thirty-two to thirty-seven years old, about five feet, ten inches tall, 175 to 180 pounds, with black collar-length, unkempt hair. A composite drawing was made. During the next week, the clerk viewed two live lineups and a large set of black-and-white photographs. Two of the photographs were of a man named José Garcia. The clerk said that one of them looked similar to the robber. About a week later, the clerk viewed the set of photographs again and again said one of them was similar to the robber. Another week went by, and the clerk was shown a different set of color photographs. He picked out Garcia as "the guy; I wouldn't forget the face." Three days later, the clerk picked a man from a live lineup whose voice sounded like the robber. This man was an innocent police officer, so the clerk went back to the color photographs and said that Garcia was definitely the murderer.

Garcia was arrested and charged with murder and robbery. He was thirty-nine years old; he was five feet, ten inches tall, and he weighed 242 pounds. He spoke with a heavy Spanish accent and had tattoos lining both arms; his left hand was deformed from a sawblade accident.

Loftus was hired by the defense to testify about the factors that might cause the eyewitness to be inaccurate. After she was sworn in, her qualifications as an expert in eyewitness memory were presented to the court. The prosecution argued that the data from experiments only allowed general conclusions and not conclusions about the eyewitness in this case, and that experiments were not performed on real-life crimes. The judge ruled that the testimony would be heard by the jury. Through a long series of questions, the defense attorney attempted to bring before the jury the factors from the psychological research that are known to affect the ability of an eyewitness to make a correct identification. Some of the factors Loftus mentioned were the storage interval (there were several weeks between the crime and an identification), the high stress level of the witness during encoding, the possibility that the weapon used in the crime may have created a weapons focus, and the possibility that the viewing of pictures of the suspect several times before making an identification could have allowed for unconscious transference to occur.

The jury, after hearing Loftus's expert testimony, was unable to reach a verdict. The defendant was tried again a few weeks later; the process was repeated, and again the jury could not reach a verdict, so the defendant was set free. Interviews with the jury indicated that they valued the expert testimony of Loftus in their deliberations; nine were for acquittal and three were for conviction.

THE SCIENCE OF TESTIMONY

In 1900, French psychologist Alfred Binet (later famous for the development of intelligence testing) argued for the creation of a practical science of testimony. German psychologist William Stern was publishing studies of eyewitness testimony as early as 1902. In 1903, Stern testified in German courts of law as an expert on eyewitness testimony. Beginning in 1909, American psychologist Guy Montrose Whipple began a four-year series of articles in *Psychological Bulletin* in which he translated and interpreted European work on the subject as well as presenting his own.

Although it appeared that the field was ready to develop rapidly, it did not. Probably because most psychologists of the time focused more on theoretical issues than on applied problems and because the early psychologists working on eyewitness testimony were criticized for overgeneralization, the explosion of research on eyewitness testimony did not occur until the 1970s. Ulric Neisser, n his book *Cognition and Reality: Principles and Implications of Cognitive Psychology* (1976) and later in *Memory Observed: Remembering in Natural Contexts* (1982), presented the view that the advances in understanding human memory and social perception called for a new emphasis on observations made in a natural context. The majority of the research on memory applied to eyewitness testimony has been carried out since then.

Modern research has developed a large database on variables that affect the accuracy of an eyewitness, as well as on such issues as the best way to interrogate a witness, how to construct fair lineups, and how to help witnesses remember more accurately. A major topic of the 1980s and 1990s was the usefulness and appropriateness of the testimony of psychological experts in court proceedings. Some judges do not allow psychologists to testify about eyewitness reliability; however, other judges do allow such testimony. Psychologists disagree on whether this testimony serves a good purpose. It is clear that if testimony is given, the psychologist cannot say whether a given witness is correct or not. The psychologist may provide the jury members with information that can help them to evaluate the eyewitness testimony better. There may be scientific data about the circumstances of the case being tried that jurors do not know. Telling the jurors about the data can give them a better basis for evaluating the credibility of a witness. This can lead to improvement of the judicial process by more often convicting the guilty as well as saving the innocent.

BIBLIOGRAPHY

Ainsworth, Peter B. *Psychology, Law, and Eyewitness Testimony.* New York: Wiley, 1999. Print.

Greene, Robert L. *Human Memory: Paradigms and Paradoxes.* New York: Psychology, 2014. Print.

Lindsay, R. C. L., et al., eds. *The Handbook of Eyewitness Psychology.* New York: Psychology, 2012. Digital file.

Loftus, Elizabeth F. *Eyewitness Testimony.* Rpt. 4th ed. Newark: LexisNexis, 2007. Print.

McCloskey, Michael, Howard Egeth, and Judith McKenna. "The Experimental Psychologist in Court: The Ethics of Expert Testimony." *Law and Human Behavior* 10.1–2 (1986): 1–13. Print.

Thompson, Charles P., et al. *Eyewitness Memory: Theoretical and Applied Perspectives*. New York: Psychology, 2014. Digital file.

Wells, Gary L., and Elizabeth F. Loftus, eds. *Eyewitness Testimony: Psychological Perspectives*. New York: Cambridge UP, 1987. Print.

Wrightsman, Lawrence S. "Crime Investigation: Eyewitnesses." *Psychology and the Legal System*. 6th ed. Belmont: Wadsworth, 2007. Print.

Yarmey, A. Daniel. *The Psychology of Eyewitness Testimony.* New York: Free, 1979. Print.

Gary T. Long

See Also: Ebbinghaus, Hermann; Encoding; Forgetting and forgetfulness; Law and psychology; Long-term memory; Memory; Memory: Empirical studies; Memory storage; Short-term memory; Social schemata; Social perception.

Eysenck, Hans

Born: March 4, 1916
Died: September 4, 1997
Identity: German-born British research psychologist
Birthplace: Berlin, Germany
Place of death: London, England
Type of psychology: Personality; Psychological methodologies; Social psychology

Eysenck was best known for his theory of human personality.

Hans Eysenck was born in Berlin during World War I. His parents divorced when he was only two. As a result, his maternal grandmother reared him. When the Nazis came to power, Eysenck, a Jewish sympathizer, left Germany at the age of eighteen, seeking exile in France and then England.

Studying at the University of London, Eysenck earned a bachelor's degree in psychology in 1938. With Sir Cyril Burt as his graduate adviser, Eysenck earned a doctorate in psychology in 1940. During World War II, he served as a psychologist at the Mill Hill Emergency Hospital, doing research on the reliability of psychiatric diagnoses. His findings made him antagonistic toward mainstream clinical psychology for the rest of his life.

After the war, Eysenck taught at the University of London and founded the psychological department at the newly formed Institute of Psychiatry. He was promoted to a professor of psychology in 1955. His research ranged from personality and intelligence to behavioral genetics and from social attitudes to behavior therapy.

In 1964, he published *Crime and Punishment*, in which he suggested that criminals had failed to develop conditioned moral and social responses. He published *Smoking, Health, and Personality* in 1965 and suggested that lung cancer was due to an underlying emotional disorder rather than to smoking. His very controversial book *Race, Intelligence, and Education* was released in 1971. Based on data he had accumulated, it stated that intelligence quotient (IQ) scores were persistently lower among African Americans in comparison to white Americans. During a lecture in London, Eysenck was kicked and punched by students because of the content of this book. In 1981, he and Leon Kamin wrote *The Intelligence Controversy*. Eysenck tried to reduce the list of human personality traits to the smallest number of trait clusters. Common to the majority of trait systems are variables related to emotional stability, energy level, dominance, and sociability. Eysenck reduced the trait names to three higher-order factors: introversion-extroversion, neuroticism, and psychoticism. He attempted to explore the biological roots of each factor. He also founded and edited the journal *Personality and Individual Differences*.

Eysenck was a prolific writer, publishing seventy-five books and 1,050 articles. He was awarded the American Psychological Association's Distinguished Scientific Award in 1988, a United States Presidential Citation for Scientific Contribution in 1993, and the American Psychological Association's William James Fellow Award in 1994 and its Centennial Award for Distinguished Contributions to Clinical Psychology in 1996.

BIBLIOGRAPHY

Dana, Richard Henry, ed. *Handbook of Cross-Cultural and Multicultural Personality Assessment*. Hillsdale: Erlbaum, 2000. Print.

Eysenck, Hans. *Rebel With a Cause: The Autobiography of Hans Eysenck*. Rev. and expanded ed. New Brunswick: Transaction, 1997. Print.

Inman, Sally, Martin Buck, and Helena Burke, eds. *Assessing Personal and Social Development: Measuring the Unmeasurable*. London: Falmer, 1999. Print.

Shrout, Patrick E., and Susan T. Fiske, eds. *Personality Research, Methods, and Theory.* Hillsdale: Erlbaum, 1995. Print.

Alvin K. Benson

See Also: Intelligence quotient (IQ); Introverts and extroverts; Personality theory; Race and intelligence.

F

Facial feedback

Type of psychology: Emotion

The facial feedback theory of emotion concerns the relationship between emotional experience and facial expression. The theory argues that emotional experience (feelings) can be managed by producing different or opposite facial expressions. It also suggests that people do not experience emotions directly; instead, they infer or "read" their emotions from the expressions that appear on their faces.

Key Concepts
- Emotional experience
- Expressive behavior
- Self-perception processes
- Self-regulatory mechanisms

INTRODUCTION

The purpose of facial expressions has been a topic of interest to writers, poets, philosophers, and social scientists for centuries. Some scientists have suggested that facial expressions are simply the external manifestations of internal emotional states (sometimes referred to as affective states); that is, they play a role in emotional expression. Others claim that facial expressions are designed to communicate information about how people are feeling to other people. Still others have argued that facial expressions are the data on which people base decisions about the emotions they themselves may be experiencing. This latter idea is the foundation of the facial feedback theories of emotion.

FACIAL FEEDBACK THEORIES

In the early 1970s, psychologists first confirmed Charles Darwin's speculations, advanced in the 1870s, that a set of basic human facial expressions is innate and constant across cultures. Since then, researchers have sought to understand the function and significance of facial expressions in the production and experience of emotion. This search has led to the formulation of theories about the role of facial expressions in emotional experience, of which the facial feedback theories are one subset. Although there are several variants of the central theme, all facial feedback theories share three defining characteristics. First, all hold that the experience of naturally occurring emotions (such as anger or fear) can be managed by producing different or opposite facial expressions. In other words, if a person feels sad and "puts on a happy face," the experience of sadness will be reduced. Second, all these theories argue that in the absence of a naturally occurring emotion, self-generated facial expressions can produce their corresponding internal emotional states. In other words, even though a person may not feel sad, smiling will make that person feel happy. Finally, all the theories share a belief that internal emotional states are not experienced directly but are instead mediated by some sort of mechanism involving feedback from the skin or the muscles of the face (hence the term "feedback" in the name). Put simply, this means that the specific configuration of people's facial muscles tells them that they are experiencing a particular emotion. If people's faces display smiles, the particular arrangement of the muscles involved in smiling "tells" them that they are happy.

An example that was first offered by nineteenth-century psychologist William James may help clarify how facial (and other bodily) feedback is thought to lead to emotional experience. A woman encounters a growling bear in the woods. On noticing the bear, her heartbeat increases, her body secretes adrenaline (epinephrine), her face tenses in fear, and she runs away. Does she first notice she is afraid and then respond by fleeing from the bear, or does she flee first and then decide that she must have been afraid because she made a terrified facial expression? The latter idea explains the woman's behavior in terms of a feedback theory of emotional experience.

THEORETICAL VARIATIONS

Because they seem to suggest a process that is at odds with most people's intuitions, facial feedback theories have had a long and controversial history in social psychology. Their origins can be traced at least as far back as Darwin and James, and some social scientists have noted that the ideas embodied in facial feedback theories can be found in the writings of Homer and William Shakespeare. In *The Expression of the Emotions in Man and Animals* (1872), Darwin claimed that freely expressing an emotion would intensify its experience, whereas repressing or dampening the expression of an emotion would tend to reduce its effects. James echoed a similar idea in the second volume of *The Principles of Psychology* (1890). James's ideas, coupled with similar ideas offered independently by Danish physician Carl Lange, led to one of the earliest feedback theories, the James-Lange theory.

More recently, psychologist Silvan Tomkinsand social psychologists Carroll Izard, James Laird, John Lanzetta, and their colleagues have each proposed similar theories implicating facial expressions in the experience of emotions. Although they all differ in regard to the exact mechanism through which facial expressions produce or manage emotional experiences, all are collectively referred to as facial feedback theories. For example, the idea that facial expressions are emotions (or that being aware of one's facial expression is essentially the same as being aware of an emotion) is attributable to Tomkins. He argued that sensory receptors in the skin of the face provide information on the status of facial expressions that trigger emotional experiences from memory. The somewhat different idea that facial expressions are used (through self-perception processes) to infer an emotional state is based on the work of Laird. Laird argued that when people are unsure of what emotion they may be experiencing, they use attributional and self-perception processes to work backward, deciding that "if I am smiling, I must be happy."

EXPERIMENTS

Numerous social psychological experiments have supported the role of facial expressions in the production and regulation of emotions as predicted by the facial feedback theories. One of the propositions of facial feedback theories is that in the presence of naturally occurring emotions such as disgust or delight, generating an opposite facial expression should have the effect of reducing the intensity of the original emotional experience. In contrast, exaggerating a spontaneous facial expression should have the effect of enhancing the intensity of the original emotional experience. Psychologist Robert Kraut examined this proposition in an experiment in which subjects sniffed a set of substances with characteristically unpleasant, neutral, and pleasant odors. Subjects then rated how pleasant each odor was. The substances Kraut used ranged from pyridine and butyric acid (both of which have a disgusting odor) through water (a neutral odor) to vanilla, wintergreen, and tangerine (all of which are very pleasant smelling to most people). In addition to smelling and rating the odors spontaneously, the subjects were sometimes instructed to pose a facial expression of delight or disgust when sniffing the odors, irrespective of the odor's actual pleasantness. Kraut found a strong effect for posing the different facial expressions. Consistent with the first proposition of facial feedback theories, when subjects posed a delighted expression, they rated all the odors as more pleasant smelling than when they rated the odors after reacting to them spontaneously. In contrast, and consistent with the facial feedback hypothesis, when subjects posed a disgusted expression, they rated all the odors as less pleasant smelling than when they rated the odors after reacting to them spontaneously. The results of Kraut's experiment suggest that the proverbial wisdom of "putting on a happy face" when a person feels sad may contain more than a little truth.

A second proposition of the facial feedback theories is that in the absence of naturally occurring emotions, generating a facial expression should have the effect of producing the corresponding emotional experience. In an early experiment, Laird examined just this proposition. He covertly manipulated college students' facial muscles to produce a frown while attaching electrodes to their faces. In other words, as part of an experiment in which brain-wave recordings were supposedly being made, Laird told subjects to contract or relax various facial muscles. These instructions had the net effect of producing frowns without the subjects knowing that they were frowning. These subjects subsequently reported that they felt angry. Other students' facial muscles were arranged into smiles. These subjects reported feeling happy and rated cartoons to be funnier than did control subjects. These studies have been criticized, however, because subjects might have been aware that their faces were being arranged into frowns and smiles and may have been responding to experimental demand characteristics.

In a different study, social psychologists Fritz Strack, Lenny Martin, and Sabina Stepper had subjects rate cartoons while holding pens in their mouths. Some of these subjects clenched the end of a pen in their teeth, which models the facial muscle actions of smiling. Other subjects pursed the end of a pen in their lips, which models the facial muscle actions of frowning. According to these psychologists, these tasks model smiling and frowning more subtly than did Laird's manipulations. Consistent with facial feedback theory predictions, Strack and his colleagues found that the induced smilers rated the cartoons as being funnier than did the induced frowners.

RELATIONSHIP TO BIOFEEDBACK

Although facial feedback theories are concerned primarily with the effects of facial expressions on emotional experience, many of them acknowledge that facial expressions are not the only bodily cues that can produce or manage emotional experiences. For example, psychologists have found that people's physical posture (slumping versus sitting erect) affected their performance on a task. Similarly, a number of studies have shown that biofeedback techniques can be used to reduce anxiety and stress. When using biofeedback, people concentrate their attention on some internal event, such as breathing rate, pulse rate, or heartbeat, and consciously try to manage the event. With practice, biofeedback techniques have produced some surprising results.

Perhaps one of the most exciting potential applications for facial feedback theories is in clinical therapy settings. Izard has suggested that manipulation of facial expression can be used in a manner similar to biofeedback to help people cope with and overcome adverse emotional responses to situations and events. Although this application has not yet been put to the test, it could well become an important technique for use with such psychological problems as phobias, anxiety disorders, panic disorders, and depression.

CONTROVERSIES

Facial feedback theories of emotion are, as they have been since they were first suggested, surrounded by controversy. Facial feedback theories have received considerable attention from psychologists and psychophysiologists. They have attracted staunch supporters as well as vehement critics. Part of the controversy may be attributable to the theories' counterintuitive nature; they seem to fly in the face of common sense. On the other hand, proverbial wisdom suggests that at least some aspects of facial feedback theories make intuitive sense. Another part of the controversy has resulted from the difficulty of demonstrating the phenomenon in the laboratory. Although numerous studies have supported the facial feedback hypothesis, many have also failed to support it. In fact, two summaries of research related to facial feedback theories reached opposite conclusions concerning how well the available research has actually supported the theories.

As facial feedback research continues, a number of questions about the role of facial expressions (and other bodily movements) in the production and regulation of emotional experience remain unanswered. For example, what is the exact mechanism through which facial (and bodily) expressions produce and regulate emotion? Is it sensory feedback from the facial muscles and skin, unmediated by thinking, that affects emotional experience, as James, Darwin, Tomkins, and Izard have suggested? Is it sensory feedback mediated by self-perception processes, as Laird has proposed? Is it caused by some other, as-yet-unspecified mechanism? These questions will be important focuses of future research on the facial feedback theories.

In addition, a number of newer approaches to and formulations of facial feedback theories have been offered. One of the most intriguing is psychologist Robert Zajonc and colleagues' vascular theory of facial efference. According to this formulation, facial expressions produce their effects on emotion not through sensory feedback from the muscles and skin but through changes in the volume of blood that reaches the brain. Expanding on a model originally proposed by Israel Waynbaum at the beginning of the twentieth century, Zajonc proposes that the facial muscles regulate the amount of blood that reaches and helps cool the brain. He and his colleagues have shown, for example, that changes in brain temperature are related to changes in emotional experience and that changes in facial expressions affect brain temperature. This seemingly improbable theory has received some experimental support and promises to maintain interest in facial feedback theories. Along more practical lines, Izard's suggestions for using facial feedback as a therapeutic tool may provide an alternative technique for managing specific psychological problems. Because of the interest in human self-regulatory mechanisms within social psychology, facial feedback theories and their successors will undoubtedly receive additional theoretical and empirical attention. The future holds considerable promise for advances in understanding the true relationship between facial expressions and the emotions they represent.

BIBLIOGRAPHY

Buck, Ross. *The Communication of Emotion*. New York: Guilford, 1984. Print.

Darwin, Charles. *The Expression of the Emotions in Man and Animals*. Ed. Paul Ekman. 4th ed. New York: Oxford UP, 2009. Print.

Ekman, Paul, ed. *Darwin and Facial Expression: A Century of Research in Review*. Cambridge: Major Books, 2006. Print.

Finzi, Eric. *The Face of Emotion: How Botox Affects Our Moods and Relationships*. New York: Palgrave, 2013. Print.

Fiske, Susan T., and Shelley E. Taylor. *Social Cognition*. Boston: McGraw-Hill, 2008. Print.

Izard, Carroll E. *The Face of Emotion*. 1971. Rpt. New York: Irvington, 1993. Print.

Izard, Carroll E. "Facial Expressions and the Regulation of Emotions." *Journal of Personality and Social Psychology* 58.3 (1990): 487–98. Print.

Knapp, Mark L., and John A. Daly, eds. *The Sage Handbook of Interpersonal Communication*. Thousand Oaks: Sage, 2011. Print.

LaFrance, Marianne. *Why Smile: The Science behind Facial Expressions*. New York: Norton, 2011. Print.

Tomkins, Silvan Solomon. *The Positive Affects*. New York: Springer, 2008. Print.

John H. Fleming

See Also: Autism; Biofeedback and relaxation; Emotional expression; Emotional intelligence; Emotions; Nervous system; Neuropsychology; Nonverbal communication; Self-perception theory; Social perception.

Factitious disorders

Date: 2000 forward

Type of psychology: Psychopathology

Factitious disorders involve situations in which a person intentionally produces the signs and symptoms of a medical illness or psychiatric disorder to receive medical care. They are considered to be psychiatric conditions. The motivation of the person to appear ill is due to internal needs, and they are fully aware that their symptoms are fabrications.

Key Concepts

- Malingering
- Munchausen syndrome
- Munchausen syndrome by proxy
- Pseudologia fantastica
- Secondary gain
- Serial hospitalization

INTRODUCTION

People with factitious disorders attempt to produce or fabricate the signs and symptoms of medical and mental disorders to assume the role of a patient. They do not actually have these medical or mental disorders and are quite aware that they do not. They voluntarily fabricate an illness to become a patient but are not trying to achieve some secondary gain such as avoiding work responsibilities, obtaining money, or escaping from a particular duty. Factitious disorders share some similarities with Malingeringmalingering, which also involves the intentional production of symptoms associated with medical and mental disorders. However, the goal of malingering is to achieve some external reward such as worker's compensation, insurance money, or special accommodations, while factitious disorder involves only internal needs.

Many people with factitious disorder seek to be hospitalized and often experience serial hospitalizations. If staff at one medical facility discovers that the person has intentionally fabricated the symptoms of a particular disease, the person seeks medical care at a different hospital. The person with a factitious disorder commonly seeks unnecessary surgeries, medications, and physical procedures.

THOSE AFFECTED

The prevalence of factitious disorder in the general population is unknown. Hospital and medical professionals seldom record the diagnosis in discharge records because the person may voluntarily leave the facility once the deception is discovered or suspected. Although officially the disorder appears to be fairly rare, its incidence may be underestimated because numerous cases may not receive a formal diagnosis. The disorder seems to be more common among those who work in the health care industry than among people in other occupations. Women are diagnosed more frequently than men and tend to show severe manifestations of the intentional fabrication of illness.

DIAGNOSIS

Factitious disorders are one of the psychiatric disorders described in the *Diagnostic and Statistical Manual of Mental Disorders: DSM-IV-TR* (rev. 4th ed., 2000) published by the American Psychiatric Association. There are three forms of factitious disorder: predominantly psychological signs and symptoms, predominantly physical signs and symptoms, and combined psychological and physical signs and symptoms. Three central features of factitious disorders are an intentional fabrication of symptoms, a desire to assume the sick role, and a lack of external rewards for assuming that role. Munchausen syndrome is the most severe form of factitious disorder. Developing elaborate stories around a medical condition and traveling significant distances to gain medical treatments are common characteristics of this syndrome.

To make a diagnosis, the medical professional must go through a process of exclusion to determine that the signs and symptoms are not due to a true medical or psychiatric illness. This process requires careful examination of all reported signs and symptoms of illness. Typically, a psychiatrist becomes involved with the case to consider the existence of a factitious disorder.

DIAGNOSTIC TYPES

One type of factitious disorder has predominantly psychological signs and symptoms. In this type, the person intentionally makes up symptoms that suggest a particular psychiatric disorder. The person wanting to become a psychiatric patient is often treated with psychoactive medications and psychotherapy until the true nature of the patient's condition is discovered. These individuals present a false history suggestive of the psychiatric disorder that they are pretending to have. Pseudologia fantasticaPseudologia fantastica is often found in this type of factitious disorder and is characterized by colorful fantasies that add an element of drama to the individual's life history. It is believed that the stories become additionally dramatic to gain the attention of health care professionals.

A second type of factitious disorder is associated with predominantly physical signs and symptoms. Munchausen syndrome most often takes this form. People with this type of the disorder describe to medical professionals a diverse grouping of physical complaints that are suggestive of medical illness. The person voluntarily seeks to have numerous medical tests and procedures, including hospitalizations. Serial hospitalizations often take place as the person moves from hospital to hospital seeking medical care. The person with this type of factitious disorder is adept at presenting symptoms and signs of illness in a manner that is very convincing to the medical professional. Those with factitious disorder are very knowledgeable about diseases and illnesses and can deceive medical professionals about their true intentions. In some cases, the person manages to contaminate blood, urine, or fecal samples taken for medical tests to become a patient. Once a person achieves the goal of hospitalization, demands for additional medical tests and even surgery are common. As suspicions grow about the person's true intentions, the individual commonly threatens litigation and complains of incompetence among the medical caregivers.

The third type of factitious disorder is associated with a combination of psychological and physical signs and symptoms. People presenting with both forms of signs and symptoms can be particularly difficult to accurately diagnose. It is necessary for the medical professional to exclude a wide variety of both medical and mental disorders before diagnosis of factitious disorder can be made.

Factitious disorder by proxy is a condition in which a person, usually an adult, intentionally produces signs and symptoms of physical illness in another person, usually a child. This diagnosis is also known as Munchausen syndrome by proxy. As the adult caretaker makes the child appear to be ill, he or she can indirectly assume the role of a sick person. The adult usually seeks hospitalization of the child through

DSM-IV-TR CRITERIA FOR FACTITIOUS DISORDER

Intentional production or feigning of physical or psychological symptoms

The motivation for the behavior is to assume the sick role

External incentives for the behavior are absent

Code Based on Type

300.16 with Predominantly Psychological Signs and Symptoms

- If psychological signs and symptoms predominate in the clinical presentation

With Predominantly Physical Signs and Symptoms

- If physical signs and symptoms predominate in the clinical presentation

With Combined Psychological and Physical Signs and Symptoms

- If both psychological and physical signs and symptoms are present but neither predominates in the clinical presentation the fabrication of a false medical history, contaminating blood or urine samples, or causing injury to the child that may indicate illness or disease. For example, an adult caretaker may produce blood through pinpricks in the skin folds of a child or block the breathing of the child to produce evidence of respiratory distress.

POSSIBLE CAUSES

Attempts at explaining the causes of factitious disorder have focused on psychodynamics. This type of explanation tries to identify childhood experiences that negatively affected development and produced internal worries and concerns that later motivate adult actions. When reviewing the histories of patients who have been diagnosed with factitious disorder, it is common to find evidence of early parental rejection, neglect, or abuse. As adults, these patients evaluate their parents as cold and not nurturing. Many of these patients have also experienced hospitalizations in childhood that served as respites from the deprived home environments. Some experts think that persons with factitious disorder learned at an early age that medical personnel are caring, nurturing individuals. Consequently, the goal of receiving medical care and hospitalization has the intent of forming a positive nurturing bond that was absent in the patient's childhood.

An additional proposed psychodynamic cause of factitious disorder relates to the goal of being subjected to uncomfortable medical procedures and surgeries. Factitious disorder patients may believe that they caused their parents to reject them during their childhoods. They view the discomfort and pain of unnecessary medical procedures as a welcome punishment for causing the rejection.

LONG-TERM CONSEQUENCES

There are some exceptions, but the majority of cases of factitious disorder begin in young adulthood. It is common that the first manifestations of the disorder follow a real need for the individual or a close relative to be hospitalized. Typically, there are additional stressors in the person's life that may include some significant losses. There usually is a process in which the person studies the signs and symptoms of medical and mental illnesses and becomes familiar with a number of disease states. Responding to the internal needs of finding a satisfying relationship or punishing the self for childhood abandonment or rejection, the individual seeks care from a nurturing medical professional. The person's expansive knowledge about medical illness permits the escalation toward hospitalization and eventual serial hospitalizations.

Factitious disorder has a poor prognosis for change and often has a negative impact on occupational responsibilities. Many patients with this disorder experience economic strain and chaotic lifestyles. These patients often obtain numerous forms of identification to avoid detection and move from location to location. In general, the person with factitious disorder lacks a network of friends or social supports.

TREATMENT OPTIONS

No specific treatments have been found to be consistently effective in the treatment of factitious disorders. Psychotherapy is usually offered as a treatment strategy, but the patient with factitious disorder rarely seeks to be cured. Often the patient with factitious disorder seeks medical care for false medical or mental conditions but refuses treatment for the real factitious disorder. As a result, treatment efforts have focused on identifying the disorder as soon as possible after the person enters the medical care system in an attempt to prevent unnecessary treatment, diagnostic tests, and hospitalization. Once medical personnel discover that a hospitalized person has a factitious disorder, they usually respond with anger and resentment because they feel betrayed by the patient's lies and deceit.

Whenever a person with factitious disorder by proxy has been identified, there are a number of important considerations. Using a child as a means to gain medical treatments is a form of child abuse, and the legal system must become involved. The appropriate child protective service must be informed to protect the child and prevent any possible abuse or injury. If the child remains with the parent with factitious disorder by proxy, the child's welfare must be carefully monitored for an extended period.

BIBLIOGRAPHY

Eastwood, S., et al. "Management of Factitious Disorders: A Systematic Review." *Psychotherapy and Psychosomatics* 77 (2008): 209-218. An excellent source for information on the treatments for factitious disorder. The authors discuss the importance of establishing an evidence-based approach in treating this disorder.

Ehrlich, S., et al. "Factitious Disorder in Children and Adolescents: A Retrospective Study." *Psychosomatics* 49 (September, 2008): 392-398. To gain an understanding of the prevalence of factitious disorder, the authors completed a retrospective review of medical services to children and adolescents.

Eisendrath, S., et al. "Factitious Disorders: Potential Litigation Risks for Plastic Surgeons." *Annals of Plastic Surgery* 60 (January, 2008): 64-69. Many people with factitious disorders present with self-inflicted wounds that often require the medical attention of plastic surgeons. However, they often intentionally cause problems during the healing process. This is a useful source of information that demonstrates how these patients are problems for medical caregivers.

Sanders, M., and B. Bursch. "Forensic Assessment of Illness Falsification, Munchausen by Proxy, and Factitious Disorder." *Child Mistreatment* 7 (2002): 112-130. A good discussion of the importance of identifying factitious disorder by proxy to safeguard children. The evidence needed for a child abuse investigation is discussed.

Shaw, R., et al. "Factitious Disorder by Proxy: Pediatric Condition Falsification." *Harvard Review of Psychiatry* 16 (July, 2008): 215-224. This excellent review of the various manifestations of factitious disorder by proxy includes information on the identification and treatment of the disorder.

Frank J. Prerost

See Also: Child abuse; Deception and lying; Family life: Children's issues; Mother-child relationship; Munchausen syndrome and Munchausen syndrome by proxy.

Families and behavioral addictions

Type of psychology: Behavioral addictions

Addictions that involve social, observable behaviors but that do not involve abuse or dependence upon chemicals like alcohol, nicotine, prescription medications, or illicit drugs like marijuana, heroin, and cocaine. The dynamics and features that characterize chemical addiction (e.g., inability to maintain self-control, preoccupation with satiating urges, experiencing anxiety and panic in the face of not being able to satisfy urges, and substantial negative impact and consequences in other areas of one's life) also occur in behavioral addiction, but without individuals physically ingesting a substance that promotes the addictive response. While a behaviorally-addicted person can also have a simultaneous chemical addiction, these are understood as separate addictions even though treatment modalities overlap substantially. The most common occurring behavioral addictions involve food, pornography, video gaming, internet social networking, gambling (the addiction most studied), shopping, serial relationships, kleptomania, and exercise.

Key Concepts

- Denial and avoidance
- Enabling addictive behavior
- How wide spread

INTRODUCTION

While behavioral addictions are well accepted as serious mental and behavioral health problems today, this historically was not the case. Mental health and substance abuse specialists were slow to recognize the addictive properties found in behavioral addictions for several reasons. First, the behaviors are often those most people routinely engage in—such as shopping. The activities themselves are usually ordinary, everyday, "normal," and common. There is nothing inherently addictive about them. Second, some behavioral addictions that are not as ordinary (e.g., pornography) occurring privately, hidden from public view. Performed in secret, people who are addicted are unseen and unchallenged. Others are simply unaware. No one knew how badly the behaviors had gotten. Third, there was a general lack of awareness that such activities could become addicting in the same way that alcohol, cocaine, or prescription pain or anti-anxiety medications could. Even today, specialists do not agree that behavioral addictions are real addictions.

As more of the underlying characteristics of addiction are better understood, , more accurate recognition, reporting and intervention of behavioral addictions has occurred. Physicians, health care providers, educational and work place personnel, friends and family members are today more likely to express concern and push the idea that there is a serious problem here. While varying sources estimate the prevalence of behavioral addictions differently, most addiction specialists conservatively assume one in ten families has a behaviorally-addicted family member with some specialists believing the prevalence is as high as one family in three.

FAMILIES AND CAUSES

Chemical addictions run in families. Having one family member addicted to chemicals increases the likelihood fourfold that a "first order relative," a parent or sibling, will develop a chemical addiction over his or her lifespan. Behavioral addictions run in families as well, though it is unclear how much more likely a family member will develop a behavioral addiction when a first order relation is addicted to a specific behavior.

The connections between one behaviorally-addicted family member promoting a similar addiction in another family member are complex and poorly understood. Similarly, how particular family climates promot (or for that matter discourage) behavioral addiction is also not fully understood. The first, and most fundamental connection, is family-shared biology and genetics. The response in the brain's pleasure centers tends to be similar in genetically-related individuals. The enjoyment the video gaming addict gets will be similar among his family members even if the particular source of enjoyment (e.g., addictive catalogue shopping rather than video gaming) is different. The intensity of the reward and its recurrent allure will be similar. But, family genes do not cause addiction. As many as three-quarters of families with a behaviorally-addicted family member do not have a second addicted member. The genetic contribution lies in the "degree of likelihood" each family member shares for developing addiction, not that they will develop the addiction. The strength of the tendency to become addicted is largely shared though the outcomes (being addicted to gambling as a primary force in one's life or merely enjoying gambling as a pastime) are not necessarily the same. One is not destined to become addicted if a sibling or parent has become addicted. A second connection lies in what family members are exposed to and learn to imitate or react to. A straightforward example would be how children learn to imitate their parents. If a single mother suffers from a relational addiction in which she serially dates men regardless of the psychological health of these relationships, her daughters could learn that their value and sense of safety, security, and meaning is dependent on always being in a relationship. Though it could take years for the addictive properties of this behavior to develop in her daughters, the chances that they eventually will are increased. Her daughters see and experience the emotional anxiety and panic their mother exhibits when there is not an active, current dating relationship. Even if they do not have the language to describe what their mother is doing, they notice their mother's pattern and learn how to manipulate themselves and others to ensure they are part of a relationship. Even when daughters understand the self-destructive pattern their mother is enduring (and putting her children through), they learn that having a relationship, even a bad one, prevents feelings of insecurity and insignificance that could come if they are not in a relationship. So, their addictive pattern of incessant serial dating begins.

FAMILIES AND CONTINUATION

Though behavioral addictions are maladaptive and harmful to addicts and the families they live in, the addictions persist because the families' way of functioning. As much as the family may want the addiction to stop and as much suffering as the addicted member causes, the family responds as a unit in ways that end up supporting the addictive behaviors. Thus, the behaviors continue. While on the face of it, this dynamic seems contrary to the family's and its individual member's good, it demonstrates the powerful emotional need within families to hold together for their survival, that no members can be lost. Families achieve this through maintaining a psychic balance, what social psychology describes as homeostasis: the drive within a family to keep itself going, to keep what is, is, regardless of how harmful certain family patterns (e.g., abuse, neglect, addiction) are.

As the family realizes there is a problematic behavior, for example, one member's addiction to food, it responds initially with efforts to correct the problem. But, usually families are woefully inadequate to control a member's overeating let alone his or her addictive eating. As the family experiences repetitive failures, its emotional life becomes threatened, causing members to react to the addict in ways that createsemotional chaos within the family. Members become preoccupied with the addict's food consumption, where he or she is getting the food, where it is hidden, and how much is consumed. This preoccupation involves everyone in the family with the well-intentioned, but unsuccessful, goal of getting the addict to eat normally.

It's often the case that family members do not speak openly about the presence of addition within the family. Addiction becomes the family's secret. And, as a secret, it cannot be effectively addressed. The addict reacts, in turn, to their heightened concern and scrutiny, and since the addiction must be fed, he or she reacts against the family's efforts to help. These reactions take a variety of predictable forms: (1) Angrily denying the problem, thereby intimidating members to mind their own business and leave the addict alone; (2) Avoiding family encounters and becoming less visible, often in the guise of being too busy to participate in family activities like meals and spending large blocks of time at work, school, or in one's room. Meals can then be eaten alone or, at least not in the presence of family; (3) Helplessly proclaiming guilt and shame while vowing to get help or promising to try harder. Often, the addict begs everyone to leave him or her alone. In this setting, a confluence of negative emotional winds blows in all directions. Blame goes back and forth: Who really cares? Who is really selfish? Who really understands the addicted member? Who among the members will take a stand? This emotional riptide wreaks havoc within each member and within the system as a whole, and the emotional disconnection within the family grows.

FAMILIES AND TREATMENT

Just as families are typically central to successful treatment of chemical and substance abuse, they are usually central to successful treatment of behavioral addiction. First, open acknowledgement that the problemhas reached the stage of addiction, allows the addiction to be treated. In the early stages of treatment, or recovery, families are often confronted by the behaviorally-addicted member's denial that there is a problem, that the problem is as bad as members say, that the addict can control it, or that the behavior is anyone else's business. The addicted video gamer will likely argue the benefits to his many hours of his compulsive playing: It de-stresses him. He enjoys it. He has friends online who play as much as he does and he enjoys their comradeship. He is not bothering anybody. It falls to the family to honestly confront both the addict and no less itself, and how it has unintentionally enabled the addiction to continue. Family members need to recognize and openly declare what they used to do that allowed the addiction to continue and that they will no longer support the behavior. Love the addict; hate the addiction. Family members need to get help for themselves because it is inherently difficult to disengage from a loved one in trouble. They need to assume a position of full support for helping the addict getting help and of zero support for anything the addict does that does not promote recovery.

BIBLIOGRAPHY

American Academy of Child & Adolescent Psychiatry, "Facts for Families". *American Academy of Child & Adolescent Psychiatry,* Washington, DC, 2011. The Academy publishes this series, free for single print copies and able to be downloaded, as informational and response guides for parents and families facing a variety of real-world issues within families including behavioral addictions.

Bradshaw, John. *On the Family: A New Way of Creating Solid Self-Esteem.* Deerfield Beach, FL: Health Communications Inc., 1996. Based on his popular and still available public television series, Bradshaw remains one of the best introductions to understanding families are systems with dynamic, reactive energies. He explains in clear, insightful language the family's role in supporting on-going problematic and addictive behaviors in an individual family member.

Carnes, Patrick. *Don't Call It Love: Recovery from Sexual Addiction.* Bantam Books, New York, NY, 1991. Doctor Carnes discusses 11 behavioral types as well as presenting a three-year program of recovery that involves partners and children within a family-addiction context. Argues, somewhat controversially, that partners of sex addicts are their mirror images and have played enabling roles. Provides a program for recovery and family and partner healing.

Hayes, Steven and Levin, Michael. *Mindfulness and Acceptance for Addictive Behaviors: Applying Contextual CBT to Substance Abuse and Behavioral Addictions.* New Harbinger Books, Oakland, CA, 2010. First author, Dr. Steven Hayes is a pioneer in the application of mindfulness in treatment of substance abuse and addictions in general. This highly readable work is focused on helping the read apply this approach to any of a variety of behavioral addictions.

Mitchell, John. *How to Understand and Overcome Addiction Issues (Behavioral Issues).* Mitchellpublishing101@yahoo.com, 2010. Kindle edition available from Amazon Digital Services. A prolific self-help writer, Mitchell describes warning signs, family and individual denial, and practical advice about how behavioral addictions can be successfully managed.

National Institute on Drug Addiction, *NIDA Notes*, The National Institute of Drug Abuse, Washington, DC, 2011. The Notes is the Institute's major vehicle for relaying research findings to the field in a timely manner. It covers the areas of treatment and prevention research, epidemiology, neuroscience, behavioral research, health services research, and AIDS. The publication reports on advances in the drug abuse field, identifies resources, promotes an exchange of information, and seeks to improve communication among clinicians, researchers, administrators, and policymakers. The Institute publishes Notes bimonthly and it is free to the public and geared to the lay audience.

Sheppard, Kay, *From the First Bite: A Complete Guide to the Recovery from Food Addiction*. Health Communications, Inc., Deerfield Beach, CA, 2000. Warmly written for the person struggling with compulsive overeating, provides dietary guides that the whole family can participate in. Persuasively makes the case that food must be treated the way chemical addiction is treated.

WEB SITES OF INTEREST

Addiction and Recovery
http://www.netplaces.com/addiction-recovery

National Institute on Drug Abuse
http://www.nida.nih.gov

Substance Abuse and Mental Health Services Administration
http://www.samhsa.gov

Paul Moglia, and Eugenia F. Moglia

See Also: Addiction; Behavior; Childrearing; Emotional regulation; Family; Family dynamics; Response inhibition; Self control.

Families and substance abuse

Type of psychology: Addiction; Clinical; Counseling; Family; Health; Psychopathology; Psychotherapy; Social

Substance abuse refers to the over-indulgence in or excessive, chronic use of substances or chemicals to which one develops a physical, habitual, and/or psychological addiction. Technically, abuse and addiction are not exact equivalents. Abuse can refer to a one-time excessive use of substances that produces undesired consequences like a hang-over after a night of heavy drinking. Addiction refers to the development of an involuntary drive or need to satisfy the urges that not ingesting the substance produce. Drug, chemical, and substance dependency refers to one's physical dependency on the presence of the drug in one's system that without which, the person experiences withdrawal which can range in severity but is usually difficult and is one addicts work hard to avoid.

Key Concepts

- Drug abuse/addiction.
- Substance abuse

CAUSES

Initial substance and chemical use is almost always voluntary; the person decides to consume or not consume, and if consume, how much. The person is in charge of the choices he or she makes. Continued, frequent choices over prolonged time periods to take the drug produces chemical and structural changes in the brain that result in involuntary, compulsively-driven needs to acquire the drug again and again. This compromises the functioning of the areas of the brain involved in the inhibition of drives. The urge is never more than temporarily satisfied. There is much less, if any, volitional choice involved. The person is not in control; the substances are. What starts as innocent experiences of recreation, relaxation, excitement, social bonding, or isolated escape from life's challenges, becomes a driven need to constantly satisfy and resupply, so that monstrously powerful urges can be quieted, albeit always temporarily. Users are now abusers and abusers become addicts of the substances they are taking.

Substance abuse can theoretically involve any chemical, but more usually refers to commonly used and legal substances like tobacco (people become addicted to the nicotine in tobacco) and coffee or tea (people become addicted to the caffeine in coffee beans or tea leaves) to not-readily obtainable, illegal chemicals like cocaine, heroin, or marijuana, to (increasingly so in our culture) medicinal chemicals that legally require physician prescriptions to obtain as in anti-anxiety medicines or pain medications. While these substances are chemically quite varied, they all produce the same overt response in the abuser/addict: an unrelenting need to achieve the next altered state of consciousness, be it a "high," sleepiness, or excitability. Satisfying the need becomes more a priority than fulfilling responsibilities with family, friends, or at work. The addicts become emotionally cut off from family and friends regardless of how physically close they are. Addiction and the quest to satiate the next urge control their mental state. Those struggling with addiction often have repeated legal troubles and frequently use substances in dangerous situations (e.g., driving under the influence). The ability to resist the impulse to take the drug overtakes users' self-control and they are left helpless, and sadly beyond the help that their families can typically provide.

RISK FACTORS

While vulnerability to substance addiction can come about for many reasons, the most common involve a prior history of substance abuse in one's family, which is dually suggestive of (1) being exposed to and learning how to use substances (i.e., imitative, learned behavior) and (2) a genetic predisposition for responding more strongly to drugs than might be true for the average person, who is more than less likely raised in a family free of substance and chemical abuse. Geneticists are moving closer to identifying several genes and gene clusters which promote a much stronger pleasure response than is typical in the average person. Neuroscientists, similarly, are increasing their focus on relatively small, even tiny, areas of the brain that become highly excitable in addicted persons when drugs are introduced. Having a family history where a first order relative is chemically addicted and having a genetic loading for an unusually pleasurable response to drugs help explain why one in four families has one or more members who either abuses drugs or is addicted to drugs. This extrapolates to one out of two families having to cope in a major way with a relation or close friend who abuses or is addicted to drugs.

In addition to just having a first order relative who struggles with substances making it more likely than is true for the average person that he or she will develop addictive disease, having a behavioral or mental problem or illness, even common ones like anxiety and depression, also increases the odds that one will succumb to addictive disease. Through no choice of their own, but those who were neglected or abused as children, are also more likely to abuse and become addicted to chemicals. Research also shows that even the delivery system employed, that is, how the drugs are ingested puts someone on a faster tract to addiction with snorting or intravenous injection being the most dangerous.

IMPACT ON THE FAMILY

People, whatever their level of inherent predisposition for addictive disease, never start out intending to become addicts. People use substances to change an emotional state, to either enhance a state of feeling good or combat a state of feeling bad. Use easily becomes frequent use, frequent use increases the odds that use progresses to abuse; episodes of abuse, in turn, increase—and almost

Photo: iStock

guarantee—the odds that addiction will become the person's state of mind and being. They live the life of addictive preoccupation to the diminution of everything else—every value, every good deed, every responsibility, and every relationship. Athletes lose focus and drive, managers lose oversight of workers, mothers lose their ability to mother.

Having a substance abusing member in a family has long lasting, deleterious effects that bleeds families from the energy, bonds, and mutual nurturance that characterize what makes families more than groups of people who are more or less biologically related. The social dynamic in families is that each member reacts to all other members. Mothers react to spouses and their children. Fathers react to spouses and their children. Children react to each parent and each other sibling. This mesh of reactions results in a long term, developmentally progressive, complex social system that has its own life cycle. Having a member with a drug problem affects everyone else profoundly and usually in one of three ways. Paradoxically, members can respond in more than one of these ways at the same time. The most prevalent (and almost universally this is every members initial response) is to stay engaged with the substance abuser, to advise, counsel, support, reason with, show disappointment in, while seeking the promise of abstinence and reform. This understandable response by family members who love and are committed to each other is horribly ineffective, but nonetheless may last for decades. Engagement produces depression and hopelessness in the family which produce guilt and shame in the abuser. The pain of the guilt and shame, ironically, is more than the abuser can withstand and the negative emotions drive them back to the substance or chemical that they know will change this horrible feeling they have about themselves, albeit, again, always just for now.

The second most prevalent response, confrontation, usually arises sometime after the addiction is accepted as a real problem in the member and a real problem for the family. Confrontational responses generally have rapid onset with a short half-life. Most people cannot sustain high levels of intense anger and outrage indefinitely. The addict often recoils in the face of such an emotional onslaught and will nervously try to avoid the drug or at least not get caught taking the drug. Inevitably, because there is no specific treatment of the addictive disease, its remission is brief and when it surfaces again, it will again be met by the outrage of the offended family members. And the addict responds as before, recycling the pattern.

The third response, collaboration, moves family members away from being unwitting contributors to the problem they are trying to help their addicted member solve. It involves recognizing that, in the face of this disease, the family has become infected and diseased itself with its symptoms manifested in a long and varied series of unhelpful, maladaptive, dysfunctional responses that in one way or another fruitlessly and frustratingly attempt the impossible: remove the cause of the addiction, try to control the addiction, and find a cure for the addiction. While the term, engagement, suggests it would be otherwise, engagement initially requires the emotional and psychological detachment from the addict and his or her disease. Genetic loading and family history notwithstanding, the family (often slowly) comes to understand it did not cause the disease, it cannot (and has never been able to) control the disease, and it certainly cannot cure the disease.

TREATMENT FOR FAMILIES

Because of the intensity of emotions (good and bad) families have for its members, it is almost impossible for families to have an engaged response without outside guidance, direction, and support. Help for families coping with addicted members is wide-ranging. It can be grass roots groups like Al-anon, Nar-anon and other 12-step programs. Families can utilize a range of licensed behavioral health care professionals who specialize in substance abuse treatment. They can also turn to substance addiction treatment centers or programs, or even utilize the surgical-like treatment of addiction interventionists who facilitate addicts going into typically residential treatment centers.

Even if the addict refuses treatment, the family itself requires it. It must save itself. Often members will employ a strategy of emotional or physical avoidance. This denial parallels the way addicts themselves deny that they have a problem. These family non-addicts deny by avoiding, ignoring or absenting themselves from the families' daily life and special events. Other family members cry despairingly, blame themselves, plead and beg for reform, but secretly harbor their loss of hope: their son, daughter, brother, sister, father, mother—whoever it is, cannot be saved. Self-pity, hatred, resentment, guilt, and anger become the emotional winds of chaos wreaking havoc with normative family life which, while never perfect, should usually be health-promoting, protective, and positive for its members. In a poignant and sad ironic turn of events, these powerful and dangerous emotions become the drugs that intoxicate and ruin the functional life within the family. In families with addiction-diseased members, the family itself cannot be healthy until it works on itself (not the addict) to become healthy.

Just as families have primary ways of reacting to their drug abusing members, they also have fairly predictable developmental stages in reacting to them. In the beginning, as addicts behavior becomes harder to hide with drug seeking behavior spiraling away from their control, families begin to notice something is wrong. They feel concerned and worried and begin genuine attempts to look out for the troubled members' welfare. Families ask, remark, comment, suggest, and obtain promises of reduced or controlled use. Families may not leave the substances accessible or may search addicts' secret stashes. When these efforts don't work, frustrated families and annoyed addicts enter a kind of dance with each other. Families may either back away from watching or deny there is addictive disease in their midst (It is after all a hard thing to face.) or defensively insist the addiction is not really as bad as it seems. It couldn't be, never in our family. The addict will keep step with either approach. Families will protect, make excuses, and try to carry on their normal life. Slowly, as these efforts only prolong the addiction and delay treatment, families experience extreme emotional dissonance and inner self-doubt. Families become confused about whether they are tolerating addiction, enabling addiction, or just protecting itself. At this stage, families are well infected with the disease and no genuine happiness or health is now possible unless they get treatment independent of what the members who are addicted do. At this stage, peace of mind is only in memory.

For addicts, substance (and alcohol) addictions are 100% treatable diseases. As families accept that one of their own is a substance abuser, they can finally begin to make real changes. This critical turning point brings families to the fork in the road of either becoming obsessed with the addict's treatment or committed to treatment for themselves. For most families, the treatment of choice will be a family-centered, 12-step based program such as Al-anon or Nar-anon. They may amplify their own treatment meeting with a mental health specialist, skilled at recognizing early common dysfunctional family responses. As the family tends to its own health, it in fact gets healthier and, health by example can be a tremendous motivator to the addicted family member. With the right kind of help, healing can take place and the family can start to return to a normal way of life.

In addition to being an example of those invested in their own recovery, families can be huge catalysts for aiding the addicts' treatment and recovery processes. Families' response must be that there is nothing they will not do to support addicts' recovery, and there is nothing they will do to delay or interfere with it. Any communication from the addicted member that is not about his or her treatment and getting well is simply white noise. The words are meaningless. The addict's voice is the sound of one hand clapping. Families' roles here are critical; their everyday reactions will either promote health or enable disease. Though they may never have abused substances themselves, families with addicted family members must accept that they are coping with more than the substance abuse habits of an individual member. They are facing and must overcome what is a family disease and must get help accordingly.

BIBLIOGRAPHY

American Academy of Child & Adolescent Psychiatry, "Facts for Families". *American Academy of Child & Adolescent Psychiatry,* Washington, DC, 2011. The Academy publishes this series, free for single print copies and able to be downloaded, as informational and response guides for parents and families facing a variety of real-world issues within families facing substance abuse and chemical addictions.

Barnard, Marina. *Drug Addiction and Families.* The author, a senior research fellow at the Centre for Drug Misuse Research at the University of Glasgow, she has written extensively on the contributory role family environments can play in the development of substance "misuse," and how families can respond effectively. Philadelphia, PA: Jessica Kingsley Publishers, 2007.

Bradshaw, John. *On the Family: A New Way of Creating Solid Self-Esteem.* Deerfield Beach, FL: Health Communications Inc., 1996. Based on his popular and still available public television series, Bradshaw remains one of the best introductions to understanding families are systems with dynamic, reactive energies. He explains in clear, insightful language the family's role in supporting on-going problematic and addictive behaviors in an individual family member.

Congers, Beverly. *Addict in the Family: Stories of Loss, Hope, and Recovery.* Deerfield Beach: FL: Health Communications Inc., 2003. Generally regarded as a realistic yet inspirational read, includes real-life perspectives from family members coping with loved-ones addiction including the need for self-care.

Friel, John C. and Friel Linda D. *Adult Children Secrets of Dysfunctional Families: Secrets of Dysfunctional Families.*

Deerfield Beach, FL: Health Communications Inc., 1988. Based in large measure on their extensive clinical experience with families coping with substance abuse, the authors discuss how family dynamics within particular family systems promote conditions that foster substance abuse but also other mental and emotional health issues including childhood trauma.

Hayes, Steven and Levin, Michael. *Mindfulness and Acceptance for Addictive Behaviors: Applying Contextual CBT to Substance Abuse and Behavioral Addictions.* New Harbinger Books, Oakland, CA, 2010. First author, Dr. Steven Hayes is a pioneer in the application of mindfulness in treatment of substance abuse and addictions in general. This highly readable work is focused on helping the reader apply this approach to substance abuse and a variety of behavioral addictions.

Mitchell, John. *How to Understand and Overcome Addiction Issues (Behavioral Issues).* Mitchellpublishing101@yahoo.com,_2010. Kindle edition available from Amazon Digital Services. A prolific self-help writer, Mitchell describes warning signs, family and individual denial, and practical advice about how substance abuse affects families and how they can respond effectively.

National Institute on Drug Addiction, *NIDA Notes*, The National Institute of Drug Abuse, Washington, DC, 2011. The Notes is the Institute's major vehicle for relaying research findings to the field in a timely manner. It covers the areas of treatment and prevention research, epidemiology, neuroscience, behavioral research, health services research, and AIDS. The publication reports on advances in the drug abuse field, identifies resources, promotes an exchange of information, and seeks to improve communication among clinicians, researchers, administrators, and policymakers. The Institute publishes Notes bimonthly and it is free to the public and geared to the lay audience.

WEB SITES OF INTEREST

Addiction and Recovery
http://www.netplaces.com/addiction-recovery
National Institute on Drug Abuse
http://www.nida.nih.gov
Substance Abuse and Mental Health Services Administration
http://www.samhsa.gov

Eugenia F. Moglia and Paul Moglia

See Also: Addiction; Childrearing; Divorce; Dysfunction; Family relations; Family therapy; Relationships.

Family dynamics

Type of psychology: Clinical; Counseling; Developmental; Family; Social

In today's ever changing, fast paced world, the one thing that remains of constant importance is family. Modern families come in many different forms and while they may look different to outsiders, they all end up being an important part of the members' lives. The dynamics within each different family type has also evolved as society has become more accepting of different lifestyles.

Key Concepts

- Adoption
- Extended family
- Nuclear family
- Older parents
- Single parent family
- Stepfamilies
- Young parents

INTRODUCTION

The concept of family and what it means to be a part of a family is highly subjective and deserving of discussion. While the idea of family has evolved over time, the importance of family has remained constant. The nuclear family has always been deemed to be the "norm"; however, as society has become more accepting of different lifestyles, this idea has changed. There are older and younger parent families, single parent families, extended families, stepfamilies, and families who have adopted. Within these different types of families comes are different dynamics which form a family's unique identity. People often equate family in the media to the definition of a normal family; however, currently what is normal is highly subjective. For some families normal is to have a stepmother raise the children while the biological dad is at work whereas other families might find this abnormal and frown upon this practice. There is no right or wrong way to be a family; however, it is important to discuss the various family dynamics most commonly accepted in today's society so that we can deepen our understanding of those from different backgrounds than us.

NUCLEAR FAMILY

The nuclear family is most commonly considered an immediate family consisting of a mom, dad, and children. Research suggests that this definition is no longer applicable in the case of same-sex parent families; however, because there are still two parents without any children from previous marriages, this definition has merely evolved, not disappeared. The nuclear family definition has not been the only shift; the idea of family as a source of financial support has developed into an emotional-supportive centered relationship. The shift to a more emotional-supportive relationship has allowed families the opportunity to shape their relationships based on their feelings rather than what they are able to do for each other, facilitating deeper relationships.

Another change to the nuclear family is that people are living longer. Because of the increase in longevity, research suggests the importance of maintaining the emotional bond between generations. Another aspect relating to longevity is that many people are waiting to have children until later in life, after 35, thus resulting in older parents. Having older parents can often be scary for children. They voice concern that their parents may not be around for very long; however, this is typically a childhood worry that is outgrown.

Young parents can also be a part of the nuclear family. Young parents tend to be teen parents who decide to marry when they find out they are pregnant or they can be parents who decide to marry at a relatively young age.

SINGLE PARENT FAMILY

Single parent families emerged as a family form in the 1970s. Before then, very few American families identified themselves as single parent households. Often, people assume single parent families are caused by one of the parents leaving; however, this is not always the case. Sometimes, single parent families arise after the death of a spouse. The widow or widower may not choose to remarry or even date, creating a single parent household. It is also common for single parent families to be the decision of the mother to not involve the biological father for various reasons. While not as common, single parent families can also occur after an unmarried person decides he or she wants to adopt a child.

EXTENDED FAMILY

Extended family in the most literal sense refers to family members outside of the nuclear family. As mentioned in the nuclear family, it is important to maintain relationships across generations because people are living longer, making it easier for these bonds to develop into meaningful relationships. Sometimes, extended family members will move back in to the home of a nuclear family member.

Often, these extended family members will be able to offer insight into the family life that parents might have a difficult time objectively doing. For example, a grandparent might be able to shed light on a situation for his or her grandchild after a big fight with Mom or Dad.

Aside from being an extension of the nuclear family, extended family can play a crucial role in the case of an emergency (e.g., death of both parents) or some other disruption to the nuclear family (e.g., drug or alcohol abuse). In these instances, grandparents may intervene and offer to raise their grandchildren. Sometimes, these situations lead to adoption while other times it is a temporary arrangement. This is dependent on many factors including but not limited to the age of the child.

Within different cultures it is also necessary to note that extended families play a big role in daily life. For example, within the black community, extended family is incredibly important and often seen as central to a child's healthy development.

STEPFAMILIES

Stepfamilies are often referred to as blended families. Stepfamilies on the surface appear to be straightforward, occurring when two people marry and blend their preexisting families, typically from at least one previous marriage. Within these families the stepparent, stepchild, and biological parent interact as one unit. Often, this merging of two families goes well; however, often there is a degree of hostility between the stepparent and stepchild. This hostility may lead to the stepchild only talking to his or her biological parent and making the stepparent feel excluded from the relationship. This phenomenon is referred to as triangulation.

There are often cases when the families blend and both parents have children from previous marriages. In these instances it is very important for the blending to go smoothly so that there can be a feeling of solidarity amongst all parties involved. Stepchildren might not get along with their stepparent's children. If the parents are constantly speaking to each other about various issues arising within the family and children do not feel comfortable speaking to their stepparent about whatever situation may arise, it can lead to discomfort, hostility, and other negative feelings within the stepfamily unit.

ADOPTION

Families who decide to adopt make a decision to care for a child who is not biologically their own. When choosing to bring an adopted child into their home it is important for parents to take into consideration the child's history as well as the expectations the couple will have for this child.

Sometimes, parents who have biological children of their own prior to adopting will have the same expectations for the newly adopted child, but because there are many factors at hand (e.g., race, culture, environment), it is impossible to hold children to any preexisting standard.

Within adoption are many variations. One type of adoption is open adoption where the adopted children are able to have a relationship with their biological parents. The second type of adoption is the closed adoption which does not allow the adopted child access to his or her biological parents.

Adoption can also occur in same-sex families. The same issues can arise in these instances, but it is important to note that same-sex parents often adopt all of their children which does not create preexisting expectations..

BIBLIOGRAPHY

Bengtson, V. L. (2001). "Beyond The Nuclear Family: The Increasing Importance of Multigenerational Bonds". *Journal of Marriage and Family,* 63, 1–16. Bengston discusses the importance of multigenerational involvement as the nuclear family evolves.

Hanson, S., & Sporakowski, M. (1986). "Single Parent Families". *Family Relations*, 35(1), 3-8. This article discusses the rise of the nuclear family and how it has evolved into the single parent family. Makes the case that both family forms are still alive but have changed.

Berry, M., Barth, R.P., Cavazos Dylla, D.J., & Needell, B. (1998). "The Role Of Open Adoption In The Adjustment Of Adopted Children and Their Families. *Children and Youth Services Review*, 20, 151-171. Discussseshow open adoption is no longer as prevalent as it once was mainly because of the various problems it has caused for many adopted children and their adoptive parents. This article is very helpful in discussing the many ways in which adoption can be challenging but also incredibly rewarding.

Roberts, S. (2010, March 19). Extended Family Households Are On Rise. *New York Times*, A12(L). Extended family living with the nuclear family is on the rise as people continue living longer. The discussion centers on what this means for the extended family as well as the various reasons why more extended family members are feeling the need to move in with their children and grandchildren.

Speer, R. B., & Trees, A. R. (2007). "The Push and Pull Of Stepfamily Life: The Contribution Of Stepchildren's Autonomy and Connection-Seeking Behaviors To Role Development In Stepfamilies". *Communication Studies*, 58(4), 377-394. Within stepfamilies is often a lot of resistance against the stepparent/stepchild relationship due to the newness of the situation. Often, the stepchild relies on his or her biological parent and wants him or her to talk to the stepparent about whatever problems may arise. Also covers the importance of creating a strong stepparent/stepchild bond.

Lauren Ruvo

See Also: Childrearing; Divorce; Dysfunction; Family relations; Family therapy; Relationships.

Family life
Adult issues

Type of psychology: Developmental psychology

Family life provides one of the most important venues for adult psychological growth. Families provide context, opportunities, and support for rich development of the adult stages of intimacy, generativity, and personality integration. When families are psychologically healthy, these stages lead to the development of the capacity for love, caring, and wisdom.

Key Concepts

- Generativity
- Intimacy
- Life structure
- Personality integration
- Psychosocial development

INTRODUCTION

People develop psychologically throughout the life cycle, including the three stages of adulthood identified by Erik Erikson: early adulthood, middle adulthood, and later adulthood. Each stage is initiated by situationally new challenges and results in the growth of a new psychological capacity. Family life can provide the love and support needed to adapt to the changing demands of each phase in the life cycle.

Adults, unlike children, have membership in two families: the family of origin and the family they form as adults. Although both are influential, for healthy adults it is the family they create that will exert the most significant impact on their adult psychological development.

THE FAMILY IN EARLY ADULTHOOD

A new family begins when a couple agrees to support each other's physical, social, emotional, and spiritual well-being. In contrast to the experimental nature of adolescent relationships, an adult partnership requires a deep sense of commitment, an open-ended investment of oneself in a shared history. This committed relationship provides the context for the development of intimacy, the key requisite for psychosocial development in early adulthood. Intimacy is being authentically available for reciprocal, boundless connecting with an other in mutuality.

Intimacy means being in one's own space while also in a shared space. It is not a loss of oneself but a sharing that transforms one's own self. The two members of an intimate couple do not merge into each other. Such submergence is a sign of a dependent relationship and the loss of oneself. In contrast, healthy intimacy affords a quality of emergence, as the members become more fully themselves. One can be as unconstrained in the presence of the other as when one is by oneself. When intimacy is successfully achieved, the result is the development of a new psychological strength. The unique new strength of this stage is what Erikson calls simply "love."

Such openness and commitment entail many risks, not only of committing oneself inappropriately but also of being misunderstood or rejected. However, if adults do not develop intimacy, they will, over time, feel an increasing sense of isolation: cut off from deep human connection, lonely, without anyone with whom to share their deepest selves, even if married. They will retreat psychologically to a regressive reliving of earlier conflicts and to using others in self-centered ways.

The birth of a child marks the second milestone in the family life cycle, as the couple adds the role of parent into their lives. Parents must set aside many of their own needs to take care of a very dependent baby. Certain aspects of self will be neglected as this new role becomes central for the development of the parental self. New parents sacrifice sleep, free time, and time alone as a couple. They may also experience increased financial pressure. Moreover, caring for a baby is a significant responsibility, and new parents are often insecure about their parenting skills. If the couple, or one spouse, have difficulty adapting to their role as parents, their relationship as a couple may become strained. On the other hand, sharing in the care of children offers a profound context for deepening the sense of mutuality between the couple.

Children's early years are characterized by intense caregiving by the parents, who play a formative role as ideal prototypes internalized by the child's emerging sense of itself as an independent ego. When children reach the latency stage (around age six) and start school, yet another milestone in the parent-child relation emerges. Children now spend much of their time away from home, and the parents must adapt to this change. Their children will now be taught by others—teachers, coaches, friends—beyond the family circle. Increasingly, parents have the opportunity to become the joyful "witnesses" of their children becoming their own persons with their own networks of world relations and burgeoning interests and competencies.

The beginning of school can also prompt a change in the parents' schedule. If one parent had stayed at home to raise the child, that parent now typically enters or reenters the workforce beyond the home or attends college. While such a change brings added income, it also decreases homemaking time and can introduce new stresses on family life, especially if these changes are not anticipated and agreed on by both parents.

THE FAMILY IN MIDDLE ADULTHOOD

The family undergoes another major reorganization when the child reaches adolescence, the transition between dependent child and independent adult. Parents need to allow their adolescent gradually increasing independence and responsibility, so the child can increasingly rely on his or her own internal resources for emotional support and authority. What the adolescent seeks now is a different form of the parental relation: what psychologist Terri Apter characterizes as validation rather than interference. This step is not usually smooth; parents and adolescents often experience confusing power struggles as they negotiate their new roles. Adolescents may behave angrily and rebelliously or withdraw into their world of friends. This behavior can be stressful for the whole family, but it serves a function. Emotional and physical distance from their parents allows adolescents an opportunity to begin to see themselves for who they are apart from their family and allows them to develop their own support system independent of the family. That all this takes place while adolescents are still under the care of their parents makes it psychologically difficult but provides a valuable buffering for adolescents' forays beyond the family.

A particularly exemplary context for this change is adolescents' sexual maturation. Adolescents attain adult sexual capacity before attaining the social status of adults, introducing a disjuncture between these two dimensions of their development. On one hand, they are already adults (sexually speaking), but on the other hand they are not yet adults (societally speaking). Adolescents need to understand their sexuality and learn to socialize with the other gender while postponing fully adult enactment of their sexual capacities.

A successful resolution of this phase results in a mutual liking and respect between parents and their adolescent children, and the readiness of both for the adolescent to leave home, on internal and external levels. For parents, the experience of their adolescents' leaving home must be integrated and a changed relationship with them established. Next, without children at home, the parents must reconfigure who they are for each other, now that their long-standing role as mutual caretakers of children will no longer define their lives together. Issues that had been embedded within the parenting roles may make this adjustment extremely difficult. For those, male or female, who derived their identity from parenting, the ending of this role can result in a disorienting loss of self. For those parents who have been extremely involved in their children's lives as a way of avoiding marital problems, these issues will now become more obtrusive and may lead to divorce.

Rediscovering themselves as a couple apart from children can be distressing or joyful, but it will be a time for major modifications, not only of the couple's relation with each other but also of their entire life structure. New interests, jointly and individually, can now emerge, as their creativity is no longer tied to procreation. Previously neglected aspects of self now need to be balanced within a larger self-understanding. A more encompassing form of generativity becomes available as adult caring now transcends taking care of one's children and can extend to one's community, to one's profession, and to the next generation. Otherwise, adults risk becoming self-absorbed, treating themselves as their "one and only baby." With that comes stagnation, as life appears to be ever more disillusioning and boring.

THE FAMILY IN LATER ADULTHOOD

Another milestone for both husband and wife is retirement. Retirees may experience a loss of their sense of purpose, self-esteem, and contact with a broader group of adults. Those who worked primarily taking care of the home may experience an intrusion on their responsibilities and sense of privacy when the now-retired spouse has no particular place to go each morning. A successful adjustment to retirement is marked by taking pleasure in the increased company of the other, a discovery of mutually pleasing activities, and sufficient time alone to pursue individual interests and friendships.

Becoming a grandparent is another major development of older adulthood. When their children have children, parents usually experience a sense of pride and completion. First, their own child has grown into a responsible adult and become a parent, and another generation of their family has begun. Second, spending time with grandchildren may be a renewing experience for grandparents, especially if they primarily spend their time with older people. Third, grandparenting evokes memories of one's own parenting that can lead to making peace with one's own children regarding residual resentments and regrets from their parent-child relationship.

An aging adult's relationship with his or her child also changes in other ways at this time. It often becomes a relationship between equals, rather than between parent and child. A new dimension of friendship develops in their relationship, as one's adult children now become sources of authority and support.

A major concern of older adults is the loss of physical or cognitive functioning, requiring greater dependence. When one spouse can no longer do some of the things her or she used to, a healthy adjustment would include the ill spouse coming to accept this new dependence and the partner accommodating to these new responsibilities. Such optimal development will result in a heightened sense of intimacy, trust, and commitment. Disability in older adulthood may also transform parent-child relationships, with the children now assuming the role of caretaker.

The next phase of family life, widowhood (or, less commonly, widowerhood), is characterized by completing the mourning process, assuming roles formerly assumed by the other, and a renewed interest in people and activities. This process entails absorbing the shock of the other no longer being present and the accompanying feelings, which typically include anger, sadness, fear, relief, or guilt. When one's partner dies, it is a time to review the marriage and to acknowledge what was and what was not. Husbands or wives may find themselves unable to accept the other's death. If so, they may become embittered or depressed. This happens especially if there was some major unresolved conflict in the marriage or if there was a personal dysfunction that interfered with functioning emotionally, physically, or financially on one's own.

Old age is not only about loss. A life well lived now nearing its end affords a momentous positive growth opportunity as well: a uniquely insightful perspective from which to see one's life as one's own. As author Betty Friedan has pointed out, to "own" one's life, and so take full responsibility for it, enables the person to embrace it as a whole, in which every thread fits perfectly within an unbroken tapestry that admits of no substitutes. This vantage point opens a profound gratitude for one's family and for one's place in the family of life itself. This final growth is what Erikson meant by the term "integrity" and what is now more often referred to as "personality integration." With this sense of completion comes true wisdom and deep spiritual joy.

BIBLIOGRAPHY

Apter, Terri. *Altered Loves: Mothers and Daughters during Adolescence*. New York: Fawcett Columbine, 1991. Print.

Erikson, Erik H. *The Life Cycle Completed: A Review.* New York: Norton, 1982. Print.

Friedan, Betty. *The Fountain of Age*. New York: Simon, 2006. Print.

Lareau, Annette. *Unequal Childhoods: Class, Race, and Family Life*. 2nd ed. Berkeley: U of California P, 2011. Print.

Levinson, Daniel J., et al. *The Seasons of a Man's Life.* New York: Ballantine, 1988. Print.

Levinson, Daniel J., et al. *The Seasons of a Woman's Life.* New York: Ballantine, 1997. Print.

Malone, Thomas, and Patrick Malone. *The Art of Intimacy*. New York: Simon, 1992. Print.

Salmon, Catherine A., and Todd K. Shackelford, eds. *Family Relationships: An Evolutionary Perspective.* New York: Oxford UP, 2007. Print.

Scarf, Maggie. *Intimate Partners: Patterns in Love and Marriage.* New York: Ballantine, 2008. Print.

Washbourn, Penelope. *Becoming Woman: The Quest for Wholeness in Female Experience*. New York: Harper, 1979. Print.

Williams, Brian K., Stacey C. Sawyer, and Carl M. Wahlstrom. *Marriages, Families, and Intimate Relationships: A Practical Introduction.* 3rd ed. Boston: Allyn, 2012. Print.

Yablonsky, Lewis. *Fathers and Sons*. New York: Gardner, 1991. Print.

Christopher M. Aanstoos and Judi Garland

See Also: Behavioral family therapy; Couples therapy; Family life: Children's issues; Elder abuse; Family systems theory; Father-child relationship; Mother-child relationship; Parental alienation syndrome; Parenting styles; Retirement; Separation and divorce: Adult issues; Separation and divorce: Children's issues; Stepfamilies; Strategic family therapy; Teenagers' mental health.

Family life
Children's issues

Type of psychology: Developmental psychology

Children's issues in family life are a function of the cognitive, emotional, physical, linguistic, and social aspects of the child's development. Issues facing children in the family change as the child grows. Most families go through stages of development dependent on the issues with which the child is dealing. These stages contain common characteristics.

Key Concepts

- Authority stage
- Departure stage
- Family development stage theory
- Image making stage
- Interdependent stage
- Interpretive stage
- Nurturing stage

INTRODUCTION

Childhood is a time of rapid development and change. The family adjusts to these changes daily as the child develops physically, cognitively, socially, and emotionally. Families pass through several separate developmental stages as children are growing up. Perhaps the best known is the eight-stage model outlined in 1948 in the *Report of the Committee on the Dynamics of Family Interaction* written by Evelyn Millis Duvall, secretary of the National Conference on Family Relations, and Reuben

Hill, a sociologist at Iowa State College. This theory of family development focuses on group processes that resemble the aging and maturation of individuals. Briefly, those eight stages are the following:

- married couples (no children)
- childbearing families (oldest child aged birth to thirty months)
- families with preschool children (oldest child aged two and a half to six years)
- families with schoolchildren (oldest child aged six to thirteen years)
- families with teenagers (oldest child aged thirteen to twenty years)
- families launching young adults (beginning when the oldest child leaves home and ending when the youngest child leaves home)
- middle-aged parents (beginning with the "empty nest" and ending at the start of retirement)
- aging family members (beginning with the spouses' retirements and ending at their deaths)

This eight-stage model was published in many textbooks for decades. It provided the base for many more stage models, some of which were created to correct what scholars called flaws in the original model. Although the number of stages varies widely, from two to twenty-four, these theories nevertheless present structures that must be dealt with. Early stage theories had structures that effectively issued rules about what constituted a family task in a particular stage and how it could be deemed accomplished. Complaints about such structures promoted new stage theories that had more flexible definitions and offered transition periods between stages. The most modern of the stage theories also provide for families going through stages out of order or repeating stages due to remarriage.

Modern versions also combine family development stage theory with concepts from systems theory to better reflect how change is processed in families. In surveying the diverse family forms in American society, it is hard to defend the use of traditional stage theories. After all, if a stage theory outlines normative stages, then a family that does not follow it might be labeled nonnormative or abnormal. Family development stage theories do give a common-sense lexicon for describing families. For example, protection, safety, and health are the typical concerns of the people living in the family with infants and toddlers. Using these terms quickly identifies what is on the family's mind.

CONTEMPORARY STAGES OF PARENTHOOD

In the early 1980s, Ellen Galinsky, the president and cofounder of Families and Work Institute, a Manhattan-based nonprofit organization that conducts research on the changing family, took a creative approach to stage theory. She looked at family life from the parent's perspective and developed a six-stage model that described parent development. The image-making stage occurs during pregnancy, when parents form and reform images of the upcoming birth and the changes they anticipate. This is a period of preparation. In the nurturing stage, parents compare image and actual experience during the time from the baby's birth to the toddler's first use of the word "no" (about age eighteen to twenty-four months). This is a period of attachment and also of questioning. Parents may question their priorities and also how they spend their time. The authority stage occurs when the child is between two years and four to five years, when parents decide what kind of authority to be. This is a period of developing and setting rules, as well as enforcing them. The interpretive stage stretches from the child's preschool years to the approach to adolescence; this stage has the task of interpretation. In this period, parents interpret their own self-concepts as well as their children's. Parents also are concerned with interpreting the world to their children. The interdependent stage occurs during the child's teen years, when families revisit some of the issues of the authority stage but find new solutions to them as parents form a new relationship with their almost-adult child. The final stage, the departure stage, is when children leave home and parents evaluate not just their offspring's leave-taking but also the whole of their parenting experience. During each of these stages of parenthood, the child is developing emotionally, cognitively, socially, and physically.

CHILD DEVELOPMENT WITHIN FAMILY STAGES

Child development during the image-making stage of parenthood involves the development of the fetus in utero. This translates into the importance of good prenatal care for the mother. During the nurturing stage of parenthood, from the child's birth to eighteen to twenty-four months, families go through numerous transitions. Much of the infant's day involves activities such as feeding, diapering, and holding. This is the time for parents or caregivers to provide opportunities for the infant to interact naturally with the environment. Parents need to respond to the infant's interests and abilities and to create a healthy and challenging environment that will promote physical, mental, social, and emotional growth.

New research on infant brain development confirms the importance of loving and protecting children. An infant's experiences during the first three years of life shape both learning and behavior. Everyday moments, such as feeding a child while lovingly gazing into his or her eyes, provide nourishment for the child's brain as well as for the body. During the nurturing stage of family life, the interaction between parent and child stimulates brain growth and development.

In traditional family development theory, the preschool level is stage 3 or the authority stage of parenthood. Determined by the age of the oldest child, preschool refers to children two and a half to six years of age. A preschooler's main developmental task is self-mastery. It is with high awareness that the preschooler experiments with expanding language and abilities. During this stage, parents' growing awareness of power issues and their control of children result in the family working through developing and setting rules. Important parental tasks for this age include providing attention and security for the child, encouraging his or her development in all areas, meeting the preschooler's needs, maintaining active involvement in all areas of the preschooler's life, setting definite behavior boundaries for the child, and providing him or her with consistent responses and discipline. As a time of great change, the preschooler stage presents many new challenges for the family.

Parental attachment continues to build during these years, although secure children will explore on their own and utilize their parents as a safety net. Children will move away from their parents to explore for extended periods of time but will still watch the parent for encouragement and security. Passive experiences such as watching videos and television are not as stimulating for preschoolers as interactions with parents, caretakers, and positive age-appropriate peers. Interactive experiences that stimulate (without overwhelming) the brain will build neural connections. The growing preschooler needs exposure to new and novel experiences that are not frightening or overwhelming. Noises such as loud music, bass drum beats, or gunfire are negative experiences for the developing brain. Fear and lack of security create changes in brain chemistry that can affect the child's temperament, behavior, and ability to learn social skills and to interpret social cues.

The interpretive stage stretches from children's preschool years to their approach to adolescence. In this period, parents interpret their own self-concepts as well as those of their children. Parents also are concerned with interpreting the world to their children. The school-aged child's life becomes group centered during this stage. Group influence is inevitable in modern society. Few families are so isolated that their children do not have contact with other youth. Group influence is usually positive. Although parents often worry about peer pressure having a negative effect on their children (mistakenly thinking that it is something that occurs only during adolescence), the positive side of the issue is peer support. As children develop friendships and form social groups, they learn lessons of loyalty, kindness, fairness, and cooperation.

The fifth stage of parenthood is the stage during the child's teen years, when families revisit some of the issues of the authority stage but find new solutions as parents form a new relationship with their almost-adult child. The parent role shifts from leader to partner. Partnership does not imply increased time together, however. During the junior high and high school years, parents and teens spend less time together. For some parents, the drop in shared activity feels like rejection. For others, it is a relief. Still others report that they spend just as much time in family activity, but at arm's length from their children. As teens seek to form an identity, they almost always look for ways to be separate from their families. Autonomy can be achieved by making decisions on their own. Privacy may entail what looks like secrecy to the family.

The teen is an individual who is in a transitional stage. This may mean that the parent's role can become more that of a consultant or adviser. As direct caretaking is reduced, the parent also must make adjustment. Confusion may develop, however, when the teen occasionally demands a return to direct care.

When children leave home during the departure stage, parents evaluate not just their offspring's leave-taking but also the whole of their parenting experience. For most families in this stage, the launch is of primary importance. It is the time when younger family members take on adult responsibilities, typically by moving, taking employment, or marrying. Going away to college may be a launching, either full or partial, and as a result some families consider the age of eighteen or nineteen to be the start of adulthood. By most standards, Americans consider a launch to be appropriate before young adults reach their mid-twenties.

BIBLIOGRAPHY

Arnold, Catharine. *Child Development and Learning, Two to Five Years: Georgia's Story*. Newbury Park: Sage, 1999. Print.

Berk, Laura E. *Child Development*. 9th ed. Boston: Allyn & Bacon, 2013. Print.

Berman, Phyllis W., and Frank A. Pedersen, eds. *Men's Transitions to Parenthood: Longitudinal Studies of Early Family Experience*. New York: Lawrence Erlbaum, 2014. Print.

Berns, Roberta. *Child, Family, School, Community: Socialization and Support*. 8th ed. Belmont: Wadsworth, 2013. Print.

Galinsky, Ellen. *The Six Stages of Parenthood*. Cambridge: Perseus, 1989. Print.

Keenan, Thomas. *An Introduction to Child Development*. 2nd ed. Newbury Park: Sage, 2010. Print.

Siegel, Daniel J. *Brainstorm: The Power and Purpose of the Teenage Brain*. New York: Penguin, 2013. Print.

Sutherland, Peter A. *Cognitive Development Today: Piaget and His Critics*. Newbury Park: Sage, 1992. Print.

White, James A. *Dynamics of Family Development: A Theoretical Perspective*. New York: Guilford, 1991. Print.

Shelley A. Jackson

See Also: Behavioral family therapy; Children's mental health; Family life: Adult issues; Family systems theory; Father-child relationship; Mother-child relationship; Parental alienation syndrome; Parenting styles; Separation and divorce: Adult issues; Separation and divorce: Children's issues; Sibling relationships; Stepfamilies; Strategic family therapy.

Family systems theory

Date: 1950s forward

Type of psychology: Personality; Psychotherapy

Family systems theory grew out of the fields of psychoanalysis and developmental psychology. There are several different types of family therapy, all stemming from family systems theory. Family systems theory explores relationships between family members, familial multigenerational behavioral patterns, and how families work together.

Key Concepts

- Boundaries
- Bowen family systems theory
- Circular causality
- Coalition
- Differentiation
- Enmeshment
- Family homeostasis
- Family rules
- Genogram
- Human validation process model
- Joining
- Multigenerational patterns
- Quid pro quo
- Redundancy principle
- Structural family therapy
- Symmetrical and complementary relationships
- Triangles
- Unbalancing

INTRODUCTION

Family systems theory developed from several prominent influences during the 1950s. These influences include general systems theory (GST), psychoanalysis, developmental psychology, and the disruption of family relationships during World War II (and their subsequent rebuilding). Austrian-born biologist Ludwig von Bertalanffy developed general systems theory, which later influenced the development of family systems theory. Von Bertalanffy examined scientific and social phenomena holistically (exploring the whole) as opposed to using a reductionist or mechanistic approach (emphasizing the parts). In other words, he explored how parts of an organization or system interact and connect with one another to form a holistic working system.

American psychiatrist Murray Bowen is one of the foundational theorists of family systems theory. Bowen was born in the small town of Waverly, Tennessee. He was the oldest of five children and frequently had difficult relationships with his family members. Bowen readily drew on his own problematic family experiences in developing his systemic view of families. Bowen believed that the primary source of human emotional experience is the extended family unit. He believed that family members are emotionally interdependent and functional in reciprocal relationships with one another. Bowen's family therapy is often referred to as Bowen family systems theory or Bowenian therapy.

Argentine psychiatrist and family therapist Salvador Minuchin is another foundational family theorist. Minuchin examined the structure of the family and the way the family system interrelates. He believes that the way in which a family deals with stressors indicates whether a family system is functional or dysfunctional. He especially explored how family members developed appropriate social boundaries with one another. Minuchin pioneered such techniques as joining, whereby the family therapist enters into the family system and joins it so that it can be positively restructured or so that the family system can be a catalyst for positive change. Minuchin is credited with developing structural family therapy. He continues his work in family therapy through the Minuchin Center for Family Therapy.

American psychotherapist Jay Haley was also an influential figure in founding family therapy. He was the founding editor of the family therapy journal *Family Process*, and he significantly contributed to and shaped the empirical study of psychotherapy and family systems theory. He is credited with coining the term "strategic therapy" to describe a new type of family therapy, which differs from Bowenian family therapy. He worked with Minuchin and was involved in the evolution of structural family therapy.

American Virginia Satir is also credited with significantly shaping the family therapy movement. Satir studied how self-esteem develops in families and influences interpersonal relationships and relationship choices. For example, she asserted that in choosing romantic partners, individuals often choose a partner who matches their level of self-esteem, low or high. She called her system the human validation process model and incorporated humanism (a philosophy that affirms the dignity and worth of all people) and existentialism (a philosophy that focuses on the holistic experiences of an individual—thinking, feeling, and sensing) into her family systems work. She was often criticized for her humanistic focus by other family therapists. Although Satir made important contributions to the family therapy field, she eventually stopped doing family therapy because she was not embraced by her family therapy colleagues.

THEORETICAL OVERVIEW

In general, all family theorists subscribe to some basic beliefs. One significant belief is that the family is an interconnected unit or system wherein the actions of one family member affect all members in the family system. Family systems theory examines the organization, structure, and complexity of families and familial relationships. Family theorists explore patterns in families over generations, which in Bowen's family therapy is known as the multigenerational transmission process. An example of a multigenerational pattern might be if a grandfather, a father, and his son are all alcoholics. The substance abuse experienced in this family over generations would be considered a multigenerational pattern. Most family theorists also explore family members' emotional, social, and psychological boundaries with one another. Minuchin's work with families frequently focused on familial boundaries. Boundaries are respectful limits or social rules that govern the development and maintenance of interpersonal relationships. In family systems theory, healthy interpersonal boundaries permit appropriate degrees of emotional intimacy between two people. Families with few boundaries may be considered enmeshed or so deeply involved with one another that individual family members have difficulty establishing individual identities separate from their families. Family therapists often examine healthy and unhealthy boundaries within a family system.

Although family systems theory does explore past family history within a family system, its focus is primarily on the present. Family systems therapy can be done with individuals, couples, or the entire family. Families can be broken down into subsystems, which are often organized hierarchically, by gender or by generation. Family therapists explore relationship patterns among familial subsystems as well as how these subsystems affect the entire family unit. The two most popular forms of family systems therapy are Bowen family systems therapy and structural family therapy.

The Bowen family systems theory explores how individual family members differentiate themselves from their families of origin. The differentiation process is how individuals can remain a member of a family system and still be a separate individual, emotionally and psychologically. Bowen also explored relationship alliances in families, called triangles. Triangles are the basic building blocks of an emotional system and begin with a relationship alliance between two people. Bowen believed that when there is tension or stress in the relationship between these two people, a third person or thing is brought in to relieve this tension. This is known as triangulation, where two individuals are on the inside and another is on the outside of the relationship. For example, if a married couple is having difficulty with each other, they may focus on their children instead of confronting the problems within their marriage. Another example of triangulation is if the couple introduces their children into their marital conflicts so that the couple does not have to face their problems with one another. Bowen frequently drew family diagrams to examine relational patterns, identify family members, and highlight important family history and events. These diagrams are known as genograms and are still considered an important technique in family therapy.

At the heart of Bowen's work was his idea that within the nuclear family, relationships are shaped by how family members deal with anxiety within (and outside) the family. When families experience stress, members sometimes draw closer to one another or distance themselves. He describes the distancing as an emotional cutoff. Sometimes individuals who experience high levels of family conflict may cut themselves off from family members when they become adolescents or adults.

Minuchin's structural family therapy (SFT) differs from Bowen's family therapy in that Minuchin focused more on the social contexts in which families exist and the structure of families. Structural family therapy has its own unique terminology. Minuchin formally introduced the concept of exploring family subsystems. He stresses the exploration of boundaries within the family system in structural family therapy. Minuchin believes that family relationships are frequently organized by power hierarchies. For example, in a nuclear family, the parents may have the most power. This is usually considered an appropriate family structure. Healthy families show some flexibility in boundaries over time. For example, when young children become adolescents, they are usually allowed more freedom in making decisions than they were as children. However, dysfunctional families tend to be inflexible and unchanging over time. Minuchin believed that dysfunctional families develop inappropriate coalitions (alliances) among familial subsystems, which disrupt appropriate family hierarchies or subsystems. An example of this would be if a mother and daughter align themselves against the father. In such a case, Minuchin's goal would be to restructure the family system so that the mother and father develop a healthy coalition, which would rebalance the family system. In doing so, the appropriate hierarchy between parents and children is maintained. Minuchin would use the technique of joining or becoming a part of the family system so that it can be restructured.

Structural family therapy restructures families by unbalancing the current family system. Minuchin would often intentionally cause the family conflict and upheaval, which requires the family to change. In family therapy sessions, Minuchin would frequently isolate family coalitions from one another (either physically in the room or by asking family members to leave the room), deliberately break family rules, or have some family members watch other members in session, from behind a two-way mirror. These interventions were specifically designed to restructure unhealthy family patterns into more healthy ones.

Some key concepts of structural family therapy include family rules, family homeostasis, quid pro quo, the redundancy principle, symmetrical and complementary relationships, and circular causality. A structural family therapist would examine the covert and overt rules that govern the family. Minuchin believed that it was critical to understand a family's rules so that the therapist can then join the family system. Families tend to remain in the same pattern of functioning over time unless challenged to change. This is known as homeostasis. When structural family therapists unbalance a family system, they disrupt homeostasis. This is disruptive for families but allows them to be restructured. Family members often treat one another in the ways in which they are treated. This is known as quid pro quo. Families behave in repetitive ways over time (redundancy principle). Structural family therapy describes relationships between family members in terms of power. Symmetrical relationships occur between equals (mother-father), and complementary relationships occur between unequals (parent-child). Finally, the idea that events are interconnected and that behaviors are caused by multiple factors is known as circular causality. Structural family therapy is considered brief therapy (about ten sessions). It focuses on what needs to be changed and what solutions the family has already tried.

TREATMENT SUCCESS

Almost all family therapy is based on family systems theory. Family therapy has been successfully used with several different clinical populations, including families with members who have substance abuse issues, anorexia, schizophrenia, developmental delays, autism, and mood disorders. Family therapy is also successful with nonclinical populations and helps families adjust to changes, crises, and other problematic issues that develop within them. Family therapy is frequently considered the treatment of choice for these sorts of issues. Family therapy has expanded its focus from the nuclear family to explore nontraditional families, such as those with stepparents, stepsisters, and stepbrothers.

African American family therapist Nancy Boyd-Franklin has criticized traditional family therapy approaches that did not incorporate cultural sensitively within their treatment frameworks. Training of family therapists has come to incorporate multicultural family therapy approaches, which emphasize understanding how culture and ethnicity influence concepts such as differentiation, the multigenerational transmission process, and other traditional family therapy concepts. Boyd-Franklin highlighted the necessity of incorporating woman-led (single-mother) families and families in which extended family members are as important as the nuclear family into family therapy treatment frameworks. Some family therapists are also trained to work with families in which there are one or two gay parents.

BIBLIOGRAPHY

Bregman, Ona Cohn, and Charles M. White. *Bringing Systems Thinking to Life: Expanding the Horizons for Bowen Family Systems Theory*. New York: Routledge, 2011. Print.

Bowen, M. *Family Therapy in Clinical Practice.* Northvale: Aronson, 1968. Print.

Boyd-Franklin, N., and B. Hafer Bry. *Reaching Out in Family Therapy: Home-Based, School, and Community Interventions.* New York: Guilford, 2001. Print.

Haley, J. *Problem-Solving Therapy.* 2d ed. San Francisco: Jossey, 1991. Print.

MacKay, Linda. "Trauma and Bowen Family Systems Theory: Working with Adults Who were Abused as Children." *Australian & New Zealand Journal of Family Therapy* 33.3 (2012): 232–41. Print.

Minuchin, Salvador. *Families and Family Therapy.* London: Routledge, 1993. Print.

Nichols, Michael P. *The Essentials of Family Therapy.* 6th ed. Boston: Pearson, 2014. Print.

Satir, V., J. Banmen, J. Gerber, and M. Gomori. *Satir Model: Family Therapy and Beyond.* Palo Alto: Science and Behavioral, 1991. Print.

Steinglass, P. "A Systems View of Family Interaction and Psychopathology." *Family Interaction and Psychopathology.* Ed. T. Jacob. New York: Plenum, 1987. Print.

Whitchurch, G., and L. Constantine. "Systems Theory." *Sourcebook of Family Theories and Methods: A Contextual Approach*. Ed. P. Boss, et al. New York: Plenum, 1993. Print.

Katherine M. Helm

See Also: Couples therapy; Family life: Adult issues; Family life: Children's issues; Father-child relationship; Group therapy; Humanistic psychology; Mother-child relationship; Multicultural psychology; Satir, Virginia.

Father-child relationship

Type of psychology: Developmental psychology

Father-child relationships have increasingly been the subject of studies, and fathers have become well documented as major influences on children's development. In general, there are more similarities than differences between fathers and mothers with regard to what constitutes good parenting and the factors that promote positive relationships with children. Fathers who show warmth, nurturance, and age-appropriate structure tend to have children who are well adjusted.

Key Concepts

- Behavioral parent training
- Fathers
- Mothers
- Parenting styles
- Risk factors

INTRODUCTION

Cultural conceptions of fatherhood changed and expanded in the last part of the twentieth century; the role of the father has shifted from a distant or peripheral figure to a central and importance presence in children's lives. According to a 2013 survey conducted by the US Census Bureau, about 62 percent of children under the age of eighteen live with both their biological father and mother. An additional 4 percent live within families with a stepfather or an adoptive father, and 4 percent are raised by single fathers. Given that the majority of children have a father or father figure in their lives, the father-child relationship is important to examine.

Substantial progress has been made in the field, with increasing attention paid to understanding fatherhood and the factors related to a father's being involved in his children's lives. At the same time, fewer studies have examined father-child relationships compared with mother-child relationships, and little is known about variations in fathering across cultures and across ethnic groups within the United States. Moreover, research on paternal influences on children or father-child relationships has focused more on normal developmental processes than on abnormal developmental processes.

NORMAL DEVELOPMENT

Experts agree that fathers make an important contribution to children's development. Although the quantity of fathers' involvement and the style of their interactions with children differ from mothers' involvement with children, the processes involved in positive father-child relationships closely resemble those in positive mother-child relationships.

Studies have shown that involvement of fathers, particularly among dual-career couples, has been increasing gradually. Overall, fathers still spend less time with children than mothers do, and this pattern is evident regardless of the age of the child and regardless of the way that involvement is defined (for example, direct time spent in face-to-face interactions, availability or accessibility to the child, responsibility for the child, or managing family tasks). Also, fathers spend more time with their infants and toddlers than with their older children and adolescents. Although cultural images may portray fathers as avoiding infants and getting more involved with children when they are old enough to participate in shared interests such as sports, a number of studies have documented that fathers' time with children tends to be greatest during infancy and decreases with age. These patterns are also found with mothers and reflect the amount of direct caretaking that is required for infants and young children, needs that decrease over time as children become more independent and self-sufficient, and spend more time outside the home.

Research has also documented some stylistic differences in the ways fathers and mothers interact with their children. In particular, fathers in the United States spend a greater proportion of their time with children in play activities and engage in more tactile, physically stimulating play than mothers do. Mothers tend to engage in more toy-mediated play, role-play, and verbal, didactic play (such as storytelling) than fathers do. This difference is neither good nor bad.

Interestingly, although the amount of time spent with children can affect father-child relationships, it does not appear to be as important as the quality of the time that is spent with children. That is, if a father (or mother) spends large amounts of time with the child but is not sufficiently engaged with the child (for example, they are on the phone or responding to e-mail during much of the time), then the child is less likely to benefit than a child who experiences slightly less time with parents but higher quality time with parents (for example, full attention and positive engagement during parent-child interactions). Therefore, it is important for both fathers and mothers to reflect on the quality of the time they spend with their children rather than just the quantity.

Similarly, the lower level of involvement of fathers does not imply that fathers are less competent than mothers in parenting. Overall, the evidence suggests that fathers are equally capable of caring for children and children are equally likely to form secure attachment relationships with them. Indeed, the factors that constitute good parenting and contribute to positive relationships with children are the same regardless of the parent's gender. Specifically, authoritative parenting in both fathers and mothers is associated with healthy outcomes for children. Authoritative parenting is characterized by parents who set clear and consistent guidelines, structure, and standards for children's behavior, while also being warm and supportive. Their expectations for their child are reasonable and age-appropriate, monitoring their behavior but granting and encouraging increased autonomy as the child matures. They are nurturing, caring, and responsive, and their relationships with their children are marked by open communication, acceptance, and affection. Children tend to show the best emotional and behavioral functioning in the context of this parenting style.

FATHERS AND CULTURAL VARIATION

It is important to keep in mind that most of the research on fathers and father-child relationships has been based primarily on Western, Euro-American, middle-class, two-parent families. Therefore, it remains unclear whether these patterns can be generalized across cultures and ethnic groups. Some cross-cultural research, for example, indicates that fathers in Taiwan, India, Thailand, and the Aka Pygmies of Africa rarely engage in physical play with children, suggesting that mother-father differences in play styles may be culture-bound. Fathers in Japan, China, and South Korea are less likely to display an authoritative parenting style and spend less time with children than fathers in Western cultures, yet the majority of children in these cultures report close relationships with their fathers. The dearth of comparative studies leaves many questions about cultural variation in fathering yet unanswered.

Demographic changes in the United States have also fueled interest in possible variation across ethnic groups and other subgroups within the nation. According to the 2010 US Census, 36 percent of the US population belongs to an ethnic minority group. Similarly, children raised by primary-caregiving fathers, single fathers, stepfathers, and gay fathers have increased in recent decades, and yet these families remain underrepresented in studies on father-child relationships. More studies are needed to better understand the diversity in father-child relationships.

ABNORMAL DEVELOPMENT

In general, the father-child relationship is at risk when the father, the child, or both exhibit elevated levels of psychological symptoms or dysfunction. Parental psychological dysfunction tends to be reliably correlated with child adjustment problems, and there is evidence for intergenerational influence on many types of psychopathology. At the same time, it is important to note that research on fathers and children with psychological problems is much more limited than that of normal father-child relationships, and most researchers point to a complex interaction of biological, parenting, and sociocultural factors in explaining abnormal development.

Research that examines the adjustment of children of psychologically distressed fathers has produced a relatively consistent set of findings. Regardless of the type of psychological disturbance the father is experiencing (whether it is depression, substance abuse, or schizophrenia), children of psychologically distressed fathers tend to have poorer outcomes than do children of psychologically healthy fathers. However, the specific outcomes for these children may vary. Sometimes the children exhibit the same problems as their fathers (for example, a child whose father has a depressive disorder may also exhibit problems with depression), while other children may display a different set of problems from those of their fathers (for example, a child of an alcoholic father may show severe conduct problems). These problems are exacerbated by, or may come by way of, impaired parenting demonstrated by fathers with psychological problems. For example, depressed fathers are often unable to properly supervise children, may withdraw, or become more coercive and discipline children ineffectively, thereby putting children at risk for maladjustment. Moreover, research indicates that children of parents with psychological distress tend to experience multiple risk factors, and each risk factor may present an additive effect. In other words, children's risk for maladjustment becomes magnified when, in addition to parental psychopathology, there are other risk factors in the child's life, such as interparental conflict, poverty, abuse, or neglect.

A related line of research compares fathers of psychologically distressed children with fathers of psychologically healthy children. Less clear patterns have emerged using this approach, depending on the specific disorder that the child is experiencing. For example, although fathers of children with severe conduct problems tend to show significantly higher rates of psychopathology than fathers of well-functioning children, there tend to be few meaningful differences between fathers of children with attention-deficit hyperactivity disorder (ADHD) and fathers of children without ADHD.

Taken together, the relationship between fathers and children's psychological distress is evident, and the processes involved are complex and multifaceted. There are clear linkages between troubled fathers and troubled children for some psychological problems, and the linkages are strengthened when children are exposed to other risk factors such as interparental conflict and poverty. However, given that the relationship may not be as clear-cut for other psychological problems, more research is needed to help elucidate the interrelations and processes at play.

FATHERS AND TREATMENT

Parents are not always included in treatment or therapy for children's maladjustment, and fathers are much less likely to be included than mothers are. This gendered pattern is found to be consistent regardless of family constellation and the age of the child. Some attribute this finding to mothers taking on greater responsibility for their children overall and being more proactive about getting involved when their children experience troubles. Other researchers point out that in many cases, mothers are the only ones invited to therapy, exposing a tendency among both professionals and nonprofessionals to blame mothers rather than fathers for children's emotional and behavioral problems and, at the same time, privilege mothers over fathers in their ability to help children. This pattern is less salient for therapists and counselors who have received extensive family therapy training and those who value equality within the family.

Some evidence suggests that fathers can be helpful and that better long-term effects can be achieved when fathers are included in children's treatment or therapy. Studies of children with externalizing disorders or conduct problems, for example, find that when both fathers and mothers (versus mothers alone) are involved in behavioral parent training, children show significant maintenance of treatment gains. Noticeable increases can be found in the healthy communication patterns between the parents when fathers are involved in treatment. This may help decrease interparental conflict (such as arguing and fighting) that might be exacerbating the child's problems. Other studies have found that behavioral parent training is effective in helping decrease oppositional or conduct problems in children regardless of whether it is the father or the mother who is involved in treatment. Therefore, although there is general empirical support to encourage the inclusion of fathers in treatment, it is likely that the effectiveness of father involvement may depend on the particular familial context and a variety of other interrelated factors, including the type and severity of the presenting problem, the type of therapy, and the dynamics of the parties involved.

In summary, fathers matter. Children can benefit from positive relationships with fathers, just as they benefit from positive mother-child relationships. Although there may be some interesting differences between fathers and mothers, the similarities are more prevalent. Providing children with ample love, warmth, and quality time, as well as maintaining an authoritative parenting style, contributes to the well-being of young children, older children, and adolescents alike. Still, the field of studying fatherhood is relatively young, and more research is needed to better understand the diversity in fathering and father-child relationships.

BIBLIOGRAPHY

Booth, A., and A. C. Crouter, eds. *Men in Families: When Do They Get Involved? What Difference Does It Make?* Mahwah: Erlbaum, 1998. Print.

Lamb, M. E., ed. *The Role of the Father in Child Development*. 5th ed. New York: Wiley, 2010. eBook Collection (EBSCOhost). Web. 20 May 2014.

Marsiglio, W., ed. *Fatherhood: Contemporary Theory, Research, and Social Policy.* Thousand Oaks: Sage, 1995. Print.

Omi, Yasuhiro. *Lives and Relationships: Culture in Transitions between Social Roles.* Charlotte: Information Age, 2013. eBook Collection (EBSCOhost). Web. 20 May 2014.

Parke, R. D. "Fathers and Families." *Handbook of Parenting*. Ed. M. H. Bornstein. 2nd ed. Mahwah: Erlbaum, 2002. Print.

Parke, R. D. "Fathers, Families, and the Future: A Plethora of Plausible Predictions." *Merrill-Palmer Quarterly* 50.4 (2004): 456–70. Print.

Parker, Kim, and Wendy Wang. "Modern Parenthood: Roles of Moms and Dads Converge as They Balance Work and Family." *Pew Research: Social and Demographic Trends Project*. Pew Research Center, 14 Mar. 2013. Web. 20 May 2014.

Pattnaik, Jyotsna. *Father Involvement in Young Children's Lives: A Global Analysis*. Dordrecht: Springer, 2013. eBook Collection (EBSCOhost). Web. 20 May 2014.

Phares, V. *Fathers and Developmental Psychopathology*. New York: Wiley, 1996. Print.

Phares, V.. *"Poppa" Psychology: The Role of Fathers in Children's Mental Well-Being*. Westport: Greenwood, 1999. Print.

Pleck, J. H. "Why Could Father Involvement Benefit Children? Theoretical Perspectives." *Applied Developmental Science*. Special Issue: Fatherhood 11.4 (2007): 196–202. Print.

Tamis-Lemonda, C. A., and N. Cabrera, eds. *Handbook of Father Involvement: Multidisciplinary Perspectives*. 2nd ed. New York: Routledge, 2002. Print.

Vicky Phares; updated by Grace E. Cho

See Also: Elder abuse; Mother-child relationship; Parental alienation syndrome; Parenting styles; Separation and divorce: Adult issues; Separation and divorce: Children's issues.

Fear

Type of psychology: Emotion; Motivation

Fear is an unpleasant emotion that occurs in response to an immediate and identifiable threat, usually of an external nature. It includes physiological elements such as increased heart rate and muscular tension, behaviors such as running or hiding, and hormonal changes such as the release of epinephrine. Fear is adaptive, preparing individuals for immediate danger.

Key Concepts

- Amygdala
- Autonomic nervous system
- Conditioned emotional reaction
- Fight-or-flight response
- Primary versus secondary emotion
- Stress hormone

INTRODUCTION

All emotions have three components, behavioral, autonomic, and hormonal, which are synchronized during the emotional experience. For fear, the behavioral component consists of visible reactions of the face and body. A person's immediate facial response to a threatening stimulus involves a widening of the eyes and either the stretching of the lips horizontally or the actual opening of the mouth. Pupils dilate, and nostrils flare. With intense threats, the muscles tremble. Breathing rate increases, the skin pales, and sweating occurs. Frightened individuals usually throw their arms up and flinch away from the fearful stimulus. The hair often stands up on their bodies, particularly on the arms and head, in a process called piloerection. Urination or defecation may occur. Frightened individuals often emit inarticulate cries that seem almost reflexive. Depending on the closeness of the threatening stimulus and how long the experience lasts, these reactions may be followed by hiding, fleeing, or, if individuals find themselves trapped, fighting in desperate and uncontrolled panic. In rare cases, individuals can die while experiencing intense fear, usually because of cardiac arrhythmias. The fear response, in general, is often called the fight-or-flight response.

Charles Darwin argued in *The Expression of the Emotions in Man and Animals* (1872) that the physical expression of fear and the other emotions in humans was innate and had evolved from the way earlier animal species demonstrated similar emotions. As evidence, he argued that the facial expressions for various emotions were nearly identical in humans from all cultures and that similar physical responses and facial expressions occurred in most mammalian species. Later research has supported Darwin's hypothesis, suggesting that the behavioral expression of emotions is largely inherited. This does not mean that innate emotional tendencies cannot be modified through experience and practice. Most people recognize the behaviors associated with emotions such as fear, and many can fake them to a greater or lesser extent.

Many of the behavioral effects of fear, such as sweating and piloerection, are controlled by activation of the autonomic nervous system, which contains the sympathetic and parasympathetic branches, and is part of the peripheral nervous system. The autonomic system also produces internal reactions to fear. Heart rate and blood pressure increase. Blood flow increases to the muscles, while simultaneously decreasing to internal organs such as the stomach and intestines. The saliva glands reduce their output, and the mouth becomes dry. At the same time, stress hormones are released in the body. These include epinephrine, often called adrenaline, and cortisol, a type of natural steroid. Epinephrine increases glucose metabolism to make energy available to the body's cells and increases blood flow to the muscles. Cortisol promotes energy availability, increases blood flow, and increases alertness. It promotes blood clotting and healing should an injury occur.

LEARNED FEARS

Fear is an innate response of most complex nervous systems and was considered by John B. Watson, the founder of behaviorism, to be one of the three basic emotions, along with rage and love. Innately, fear is first activated in an organism by exposure to painful stimuli or such experiences as loud noises or heights. However, fear can be associated with specific objects or situations through learning. Watson and Rosalie Rayner, Watson's graduate assistant, illustrated this in a 1920 study known as the Little Albert study. The researchers exposed an eleven-month-old infant known as Albert B. to a white rat and a loud noise simultaneously. Albert quickly developed a fear of the rat, which illustrates classical conditioning. It is often said that Albert developed a phobia of white rats. Certainly, Albert developed a conditioned emotional reaction (CER), a learned emotional response to an object or situation. Phobias are believed to be examples of CERs.

Interestingly, conditioned fears develop more easily to some stimuli than to others. For example, fear of spiders and snakes is much more common than fear of automobiles or guns, even though deaths from guns and automobile accidents are more frequent in the modern world than deaths from spider or snake bites. Many researchers believe this is evidence of an evolutionary preparedness in learned fears. Cars and guns did not exist during the early evolution of the human species, but human ancestors had much to fear from snakes and other animals and from such experiences as falling from a high place or being caught in the open. The common dangers facing early humankind may have shaped humans genetically so that the species is more prone to some fears than others.

NEURAL INTEGRATION OF EMOTIONAL COMPONENTS

The primary brain structure for controlling and integrating the three components of emotion is the amygdala, an almond-shaped collection (nucleus) of neurons in the brain's limbic system. The amygdala contains a dozen subregions and is often called the amygdaloid complex. It is involved in both processing emotions and learning about emotional situations, especially for fear and anger. Several amygdaloid areas process fear. For example, the physical brain changes that accompany classically conditioned CERs appear to occur in the amygdala's lateral nucleus. However, the primary amygdaloid structure involved in fear is the central nucleus, which gets direct input from the lateral nucleus and is particularly responsive to aversive stimuli. Stimulation of the central nucleus in animals with drugs or electrical current triggers all three components of the fight-or-flight response. Creating a lesion in the central nucleus in animals abolishes learned fear responses; the animal becomes calmer when handled and shows lower levels of stress-related hormones. Isolation of the central nucleus by severing its inputs produces the same effects. The central nucleus directs fear responses by activating brain structures that manage heart rate, blood pressure, hormone release, and other emotional reactions.

Studies of the human amygdala generally report similar results to those seen in animals. Stimulation of the human amygdala in patients undergoing evaluation for brain surgery causes the emotion of fear. Lesions of the amygdala, as can occur with injuries or when damaged tissue is removed, make it harder for people to acquire CERs, and they are less likely to remember strongly emotional events. Studies have shown that activity increases in the amygdala when people perceive negative events, such as seeing a film about an automobile accident, or even while hearing threatening words such as slaughter or mutilate. Amygdala damage impairs people's ability to recognize facial expressions of fear and to recognize "scary" music, even while recognition of happy or sad music is unaffected.

FEELING AND COGNITION IN EMOTION

In experiencing emotions such as fear, more occurs than just physical responses of the body and hormonal system. There are subjective feelings and thought processes (cognitions) accompanying the emotion. The relationship between the physical responses, the feelings, and the cognitions has posed problems for psychologists because subjective phenomena are difficult to measure in humans and almost impossible to study in animals. One early theory that tried to explain the relationship between the physical and feeling aspects was the James-Lange theory. William James and Carl Lange, two psychologists working independently in the late 1800s, each concluded that the physical responses of emotions, such as the increased heart rate and dry mouth of fear, occur immediately after perception of a stimulus, and these physical responses cause the subjective feeling. Research generally supports the James-Lange theory for fear. Patients with spinal cord injuries that prevent brain recognition of the body's autonomic response to a fearful (or angry) stimulus often report less intense emotional feelings. Also, merely simulating the facial expressions of emotions activates elements of the autonomic nervous system and can produce some feeling aspects of emotion. Still other evidence suggests that cognitions, in particular, can also influence physiological states, such as those activated during fear. A strange noise in the house late at night triggers the fight-or-flight system, but the emotion immediately dissipates when the cat is identified as the cause.

A useful way to examine emotions is to consider primary versus secondary emotions. Fear is a primary emotion. It is an evolved and adaptive physiological response that occurs automatically in response to particular sensory stimulations such as loud sounds. The fear response produces a cascade of bodily reactions that help individuals deal with immediate threats. The amygdala is intimately involved in this process. Conscious awareness of the emotion either occurs parallel to the physiological response or follows it. Secondary emotions are more complex and generally begin in higher levels of the brain, particularly the prefrontal cortex, which is involved in planning and organizing behaviors. Secondary emotions, such as anxiety and shame, are acquired through learned experience and involve complex cognitions. However, they also activate the amygdala and the physiological mechanisms of emotion.

Consider anxiety, a secondary emotion related to fear. Anxiety is more about an expectation of threat than about immediate danger. It arises primarily from learned experiences and cognitive evaluations of a situation. For example, someone who drinks too much at a wedding and has a bad experience may develop anxiety when invited to another wedding. The anxiety is based on a cognitive expectation of what could go wrong. The anxiety activates some autonomic and hormonal elements of the fear response, although to a lesser degree than an actual threatening stimulus. If this mild anxiety helps the person avoid further bad experiences at weddings, perhaps by not drinking, then the anxiety has been adaptive and will eventually disappear. Unfortunately, while genuinely fearful situations usually arise and then terminate quickly, learned anxieties can become chronic and produce long-term activation of the fight-or-flight response. This results in the physically damaging effects of long-term stress. As an example, long-term activation of the amygdala's central nucleus can produce gastric ulcers in animals and probably has similar effects in humans. As negative physical effects are occurring, anxious people also experience negative moods, agitated thoughts, and a sense of losing control. Although they may not have immediate urges to physically hide or flee, they try to escape mentally by avoiding the anxiety-provoking situation or by distracting themselves from the negative thoughts. Thus, the normally adaptive mechanisms of the fear response become tied to maladaptive anxiety, which may develop into anxiety disorders such as phobia or panic disorder.

BIBLIOGRAPHY

Blanchard, Robert J., et al., eds. *Handbook of Anxiety and Fear*. Oxford: Academic, 2011. Digital file.

Butcher, James N., Susan Mineka, and Jill M. Hooley. "Panic, Anxiety, and Their Disorders." *Abnormal Psychology.* 13th ed. Boston: Allyn, 2006. Print.

Carlson, Neil R. "Emotion." *Physiology of Behavior*. 9th ed. Boston: Allyn, 2007. Print.

Freeman, Daniel, and Jason Freeman. *Anxiety: A Very Short Introduction*. Oxford: Oxford UP, 2012. Print.

Johnson, Steven. "Emotions and the Brain: Fear." *Discover Magazine* 1 Mar. 2003. Print.

Laird, James D. *Feelings: The Perception of Self*. New York: Oxford UP, 2007. Print.

LeDoux, Joseph. *The Emotional Brain*. New York: Simon, 1998. Print.

Plamper, Jan, and Benjamin Lazier, eds. *Fear: Across the Disciplines*. Pittsburgh: U of Pittsburgh P, 2012. Print.

Watson, J. B., and R. Rayner. "Conditioned Emotional Reactions." *Journal of Experimental Psychology* 3 (1920): 1–14. Print.

Zillmer, Eric A., Mary V. Spiers, and William Culbertson. "Higher Functional Systems." *Principles of Neuropsychology.* 2nd ed. Belmont: Wadsworth, 2007. Print.

Charles A. Gramlich

SEE ALSO: Adrenal gland; Antianxiety medications; Anxiety disorders; Aversion therapy; Conditioning; Defense mechanisms; Defense reactions: Speciesspecific; Emotional expression; Emotions; Endocrine system; Endorphins; Fight-or-flight response; General adaptation syndrome; Generalized anxiety disorder; Genetics and mental health; Instinct theory; Little Albert study; Panic attacks; Phobias; Stress: Behavioral and psychological responses; Stress: Physiological responses.

10.3331/Psychology_RS_65784

Femininity

TYPE OF PSYCHOLOGY: Developmental psychology

Femininity describes the qualities, formed by cultural and historical changes, perceived as feminine ideals to which all women at a specific time and place should aspire. Resistance or attempts to conform can be disastrous.

KEY CONCEPTS

- Feminine ideal
- Feminine stereotypes
- Femininity constructions
- Feminism
- Gender roles

INTRODUCTION

Femininity is a construct influenced by cultural attitudes and shaped by historical and ideological forces. However, unlike masculinity, in which boys become detached from their mothers and feminine influences and learn to be men, femininity results from both nature and nurture, as little girls usually derive their first feminine ideas from their mothers. Patriarchal social structure has been dominant throughout history, with specific places and times adhering to different ideas of femininity. Despite the fact that some countries have been deemed more feminine than others, the dominant male power structure is usually in effect. Women's ideas about their own femininity develop within and in response to a system of male dominance.

While feminism seeks the social, economic, and political equality of women and men, femininity describes qualities associated with being female. Traditionally, these qualities have been viewed as weakness, passivity, and submissiveness. Research indicates that from the earliest societies into the twentieth century, feminine gender roles were specifically different from masculine roles, with the weight of that tradition increasing year by year. A clear influence on American ideas of femininity in the twentieth century was the nineteenth-century Victorian distinction between the public and private spheres. The domain for most women at that time was the home; the love and devotion with which they ministered their duties to husband and family constituted a feminine ideal. Women were praised for the gentle and refined manner in which they nurtured and guided their families, thus becoming "angels" in their homes.

However, in the late nineteenth and early twentieth centuries, the New Woman began to undertake activities in the public sphere, including education, jobs, and the freedom to pursue, even in the face of condemnation, her idea of femininity. In the 1920s, women called flappers continued an assault on society's conservative feminine ideal by wearing shorter skirts, bobbing their hair, wearing makeup, and participating in somewhat scandalous activities. With the passage of time, ideas of femininity became even more contradictory. Feminine icons in the 1930s films, playing to a mostly female audience, depicted a silky, slender sexuality that represented a shift in ideal femininity. Moreover, during World War II, with men fighting abroad, the picture of Rosie the Riveter cheerfully assured citizens of the United States that women's femininity would not prevent them from doing a man's job. In the twenty-first-century United States, historical gender roles continue to influence society even as many women defy them and seek to define what femininity means to them as individuals.

STATUS

Further complicating the feminine ideal for women is the bombardment of images in advertising, films, popular music, the fashion industry, books, television, and magazines. Each one imparts to women the femininity required to attract men or to be a superb mother. Also, feminine stereotypes of extreme dimensions of body height and thinness—largely unattainable—strongly influence women, often having a dramatic effect on a woman's body image and causing some women to diet rigorously and even develop serious eating disorders. Beauty products have presumed a connection with femininity and, along with the fashion industry, have redefined the concept. Cosmetics and the latest fashion advertisements assure women that using such products will make them beautiful, stylish, and ultrafeminine. Tanning lotions and beds, piercings, implants, cosmetic surgeries, and feminine hygiene products are all proclaimed as necessities for an ideal femininity. These products cost women hefty sums of money and present health risks from infections, chemical reactions, botched surgeries, and cancer.

In considering the effects of femininity on feminism or vice versa, some women claim feminism, which includes struggling desperately to be successful in the business world, has been detrimental. Some argue that women with families, determined to "do it all," or at least prove their worth to the world, who put in long hours at work and even longer hours at home after work experience burnout and a hardness that keeps any desire for femininity at bay. Some women, perhaps with less invested in feminism, see no contradiction between feminism and femininity, insisting that femininity is actually a form of empowerment. Others, however, including author Laura Kipnis, view the two as incompatible. She reasons that as the radical, strident devotees of the women's movement of the 1970s moved into the 1980s, the movement began to lose steam and fall away from the mainstream. Feminists retreated to academic settings and publishing, leaving the remainder of women susceptible to the appeals of advertising. While feminism is an attempt to gain equality with men, femininity seeks an advantage for women by relying on their "ideal" female qualities to attract and influence men. In other words, feminism remained less important to most women than their own femininity.

BIBLIOGRAPHY

Barry, Kathleen, and Daniel Walkowitz. *Femininity in Flight: A History of Flight Attendants*. Durham: Duke UP, 2007. Print.

Blaise, Mindy. *Playing It Straight: Uncovering Gender Discourse in the Early Childhood Classroom*. New York: Routledge, 2012. Digital file.

Driscoll, Catherine. *Girls: Feminine Adolescence in Popular Culture and Cultural Theory*. New York: Columbia UP, 2013. Digital file.

Friedan, Betty. *The Feminine Mystique*. New York: Norton, 2001. Print.

Mac an Ghaill, Maírtín, and Chris Haywood. *Gender, Culture, and Society: Contemporary Femininities and Masculinities*. New York: Palgrave, 2007. Print.

Mead, Margaret. *Male and Female*. New York: HarperPerennial, 2001. Print.

Milestone, Katie, and Anneke Meyer. *Gender and Popular Culture*. Malden: Polity, 2012. Print.

Wolf, Naomi. *The Beauty Myth: How Images of Beauty Are Used Against Women*. New York: HarperPerennial, 2002. Print.

Mary Hurd

See Also: Anorexia nervosa and bulimia nervosa; Battered woman syndrome; Eating disorders; Feminist psychotherapy; Gender differences; Gender roles and gender role conflicts; Masculinity; Sexism; Women's mental health.

Feminist psychotherapy

Type of psychology: Psychotherapy

Feminist psychotherapy integrates feminist philosophy with principles of counseling and therapy. It promotes consciousness raising and awareness, fosters egalitarian therapist-client relationships, focuses on the ways in which personal problems are influenced by social forces and sexism, encourages individuals to acknowledge and act on their strengths, and emphasizes the importance of both personal change and social change.

Key Concepts

- Consciousness raising
- Equality
- Feminist analysis
- Gender bias
- Gender-role analysis
- Informed choice
- Personal as political

INTRODUCTION

Feminists are people who advocate political, social, and economic equality between women and men. Feminist therapy is much more difficult to define, because interpretations of feminist therapy depend on the particular feminist philosophy and therapeutic orientation that a therapist adopts. At the most basic level, feminist psychotherapy involves the integration of feminist principles with psychotherapeutic practices, but the nature of this combination takes many forms. A wide range of psychotherapies may be employed or combined in feminist psychotherapy, excluding those that are gender biased.

An assumption underlying feminist psychotherapy is that personal behavior and social expectations are interwoven in an intricate, complex manner. Problems are shaped by social and cultural environments that limit choices or encourage individuals to see themselves in restricted ways. Psychological conflicts are not viewed as personal deficits; they often arise from efforts to cope with or survive unjust or oppressive environmental conditions. When problems are viewed solely as internal conflicts or symptoms that need to be removed, women learn to feel responsible for and guilty about pain that is promoted or reinforced by inequality or gender-role expectations. The personal is considered political in the sense that personal change should be connected to social change that allows all people to meet their goals effectively.

ROOTS AND INFLUENCES

Feminist psychotherapy emerged during the women's movement of the 1970s in response to traditional mental health practices that contributed to an unequal, oppressive environment for women. Phyllis Chesler, in *Women and Madness* (1972), charged that women were diagnosed for both underconforming and overconforming to gender-role stereotypes and that the higher treatment and hospitalization rates of women were related to sexist mental health practices. Feminists within the mental health field noted that the goals, psychological theories, and practices of psychotherapists were based on masculine criteria of psychological health, encouraged hierarchical relationships between therapists and clients, and promoted adjustment to traditional, stereotyped roles for women. Feminist psychotherapy became a method for counteracting these negative influences.

The consciousness-raising groups associated with the feminist movement also influenced feminist psychotherapy. These groups provided women with an increasing awareness of sexism and its impact on personal lives and choices. Women reported therapeutic benefits of consciousness raising, including increased feelings of self-esteem and autonomy, awareness of commonalities between women, an expanded ability to express strong feelings such as anger, and an awareness of the ways in which sociopolitical forces influence the female experience. Feminist psychotherapists incorporated many elements of consciousness-raising groups into their work, and the group practice of feminist therapy has remained important.

ROLE OF THERAPY

Feminist psychotherapy began as a strong reaction against traditional therapy rather than as a particular form of therapy; however, feminist therapists have also transformed mainstream therapies by applying feminist perspectives. Feminist therapists have also developed personality theories that value women on their own terms rather than viewing them as diverging from the male norm. During the early 1970s, the feminist movement and feminist therapy did not adequately consider the needs of women of color and the combined impact of racism and sexism. Subsequent efforts have focused on acknowledging the diversity of women's lives and increasing the sensitivity of feminist practices to these complexities. Feminist therapy has also extended to counseling men and emphasizes the importance of integrating relationship and achievement needs, increasing the capacity for intimacy, creating mutual, collaborative relationships, and learning noncoercive problem-solving methods.

Feminist psychotherapists are often critical of the standard diagnostic criteria adopted by psychiatry and psychology and outlined in the American Psychiatric Association's Diagnostic and Statistical Manual of Mental Disorders. They believe that these categories have highly judgmental qualities and are based on a medical model that implies that psychological problems are lodged primarily within the person; such categorization may lead to blaming victims rather than solving the social problems that contribute to these personal problems.

The therapist-client relationship in feminist psychotherapy is based on egalitarian values. Therapists inform clients about their orientation and goals and attempt to demystify the counseling experience. Clients are encouraged to take on the attitude of a consumer and to ask questions of the therapist to ensure that they receive what they need from the therapy. Although feminist therapists work toward equalizing the balance of power, they also recognize that, because of their professional skills and the special status given to helping professionals, the relationship will not be fully equal. Clients are seen as their own best experts, as competent and powerful, and as capable of making productive choices.

THERAPEUTIC GOALS AND TECHNIQUES

The goals of feminist psychotherapy emphasize the importance of healthy, self-chosen change, rather than adjustment to status quo definitions of mental health. Consciousness raising about sexism in society is a central feature of feminist therapy, and clients are encouraged to understand the role of socialization and culture in shaping their lives. Because women are frequently socialized to define themselves according to expectations of significant others, feminist therapy emphasizes the importance of self-nurturing behaviors and defining one's own identity. In addition, since women are frequently taught to use covert, indirect forms of influence and communication in relationships, special emphasis is placed on learning direct, constructive, assertive forms of expression. Finally, it is hoped that as clients meet personal goals, they will become interested in working toward social change that will benefit all women and thus, indirectly, all people.

Although many forms of therapy can be integrated with feminist therapy, certain techniques are associated with feminist psychotherapy. Through gender-role analysis, clients are encouraged to examine their own gender-role behaviors and attitudes and choose alternatives to behaviors that are not productive for them. Gender-role analysis helps people identify how they learned from their culture the behaviors and emotions that are expected of them as "normal" women or men and to consider other ways of fulfilling their potential as competent persons. In addition, feminist analysis, or social analysis, is used to convey information about the sociocultural barriers that limit the development of women. This analysis may focus on the ways in which job discrimination, sexual harassment, stereotypes, or poverty may contribute to personal problems, and it helps clients understand the ways in which the environment limits their potential. Insight into these power structures decreases their damaging effects because clients recognize that they are not to blame for many of the problems they experience. In feminist analysis, clients are encouraged to separate internal causes of problems from external ones. When clients are able to distinguish between these factors, they feel greater freedom and commitment to make active, constructive changes within their own lives and within their environments.

Two additional techniques are the expression of anger and therapist self-disclosure. The recognition of sexism and oppression in society may lead to intense anger, and the healthy expression of emotion within a safe, mutual relationship is considered essential. Because women are frequently socialized to express only "soft" emotions, they may not have a vocabulary with which to express anger or may fear its destructive qualities. Techniques that help individuals express strong emotion in healthy, constructive ways contribute to their confidence. Finally, appropriate self-disclosure on the part of the therapist is an important tool because it decreases a client's feelings of aloneness and models the healthy expression of issues and feelings. The human qualities of the therapist help motivate and empower the client.

ROLE IN ANALYZING DEPRESSION

Feminist psychotherapy provides an alternative to traditional psychotherapy. The differences between a feminist approach and a traditional approach to problems can be illustrated by the discussion of depression in women. From a traditional perspective, depression is often viewed as resulting from biological vulnerabilities, faulty thinking patterns, skills deficits, or a depressive personality style. Psychotherapy focuses on removing the symptom and alleviating suffering so that the client can readjust to her living environment. A feminist perspective does not ignore personal factors and vulnerabilities, but it goes beyond them to examine the ways in which depression is associated with women's limited access to power and with other environmental factors.

The American Psychological Association National Task Force on Women and Depression has reported that women are significantly more likely to experience depression than men and that the interpersonal violence, poverty, and discrimination that women face contribute to these higher rates. Multiple roles, inequities in division of labor at home, the presence of young children in the home, and expectations that women will define themselves in terms of others contribute to suppressed anger and frustration and may lead to depression. In feminist therapy, the therapist and client identify and understand these factors, practice healthy ways of expressing suppressed emotion, focus on ways the client can define herself on her own terms, and establish ways of altering the environment so that the client can reach her potential.

ROLE IN MEDIATING VIOLENCE

Therapy for survivors of violence, such as rape, battering, or incest, is an important application of feminist psychotherapy. Gender-biased attitudes that were based on Sigmund Freud's view of women have promoted psychological myths and encouraged blaming the victim by suggesting that women are inherently masochistic and gain pleasure through experiencing pain. Other cultural attitudes contribute to notions that women's personal flaws lead to abuse, that sexual violence is caused by women's seductiveness, that women precipitate battering incidents through verbal provocation, and that women tend to remain in violent relationships. Many survivors of violence, having absorbed these negative cultural myths, struggle with low self-esteem and suffer in secrecy. Feminist therapists help clients talk about and deal with the intense feelings of shame and guilt that are fostered by myths about sexual and interpersonal violence. They validate women's experiences and acknowledge the painful circumstances, such as poverty or limited resources, that contribute to their pain. Feminist psychotherapists help women place blame outside themselves and deal with the anger that must be expressed toward perpetrators and a social system that condones violence against women. Providing support and a safe physical environment are also crucial components of feminist intervention. Finally, many survivors of violence experience further healing and empowerment by helping other women. They may become advocates on behalf of other women, engage in political efforts to establish new programs, or become involved in peer-counseling activities in a crisis center.

GROUP WORK

Group work is another component of feminist therapy. Groups enable individuals to decrease their isolation from other women, construct mutual support systems, and validate one another's strengths. When group members share experiences, the similarities of their concerns are often striking, and they become aware that broader social issues are often mistakenly identified as individual problems. Groups help counter the negative aspects of socialization that encourage women to adopt passive roles; they provide a safe environment in which members can practice new skills, develop confidence, and make new choices. The original feminist therapy groups were modeled after the consciousness-raising groups of the 1970s. Specialized feminist therapy groups deal with many issues, such as eating disorders, self-esteem concerns, or incest and abuse issues.

CONTRIBUTIONS TO PSYCHOLOGY

Feminist therapy not only is a distinct entity but also seeks to transform mainstream psychological practice. For example, because of the efforts of feminist psychologists, the American Psychological Association adopted the "Principles Concerning the Counseling and Therapy of Women," a document recommending that counselors and therapists become knowledgeable about and seek training in women's issues, use skills that will facilitate women's development, and work toward eliminating gender bias within institutions and individuals. Feminist therapists continue to work toward heightening the sensitivity of all therapists to women's concerns.

BIBLIOGRAPHY

Ballou, Mary, Marcia Hill, and Carolyn West, eds. *Feminist Therapy Theory and Practice: A Contemporary Perspective*. New York: Springer, 2008. Print.

Bograd, Michele, ed. *Feminist Approaches for Men in Family Therapy.* New York: Routledge, 2013. Print.

Brown, Laura S. *Subversive Dialogues: Theory in Feminist Therapy.* New York: Basic, 1994. Print.

Chesler, Phyllis. *Women and Madness.* Rev. ed. New York: Palgrave, 2005. Print.

Enns, Carolyn Zerbe. *Feminist Theories and Feminist Psychotherapies: Origins, Themes, Variations.* 2nd ed. New York: Haworth, 2004. Print.

Enns, Carolyn Zerbe, and Elizabeth Nutt Williams, eds. *The Oxford Handbook of Feminist Counseling* Psychology. New York: Oxford UP, 2013. Print.

Hill, Marcia, and Mary Ballou, eds. *The Foundation and Future of Feminist Therapy.* New York: Routledge, 2011. Print.

Silverstein, Louise B., and Thelma Jean Goodrich, eds. *Feminist Family Therapy: Empowerment in Social Context.* Washington: American Psychological Association, 2003. Print.

Carolyn Zerbe Enns

See Also: Abnormality: Psychological models; Depression; Femininity; Gender differences; Gender identity formation; Gender roles and gender role conflicts; Psychotherapy: Historical approaches; Women's mental health; Women's psychology: Carol Gilligan; Women's psychology: Karen Horney; Women's psychology: Sigmund Freud.

Fetishes

Type of psychology: Learning

Sexual fetishes are intense sexual fixations on an inanimate object or body part generally regarded as asexual to the point where the individual cannot be aroused without the object or normal sexual and societal functioning is affected.

Key Concepts

- Association
- Aversive conditioning
- Classical conditioning
- Imprinting
- Paraphilia
- Response
- Sexual fetishism
- Stimulus
- Transitional object

INTRODUCTION

One definition of fetish is an object, often created by people, believed to have magical or supernatural powers. In the late fifteenth century, Europeans wore charms or amulets described as fetishes. However, in modern psychology, a fetish is an inanimate object or body part that is the subject of intense sexual fantasies or urges and is necessary for the individual to obtain sexual satisfaction. As a paraphilia (a sexual deviation or perversion), fetishism requires the fetishist's attention to be focused not on the sexual partner but in a depersonalized manner on the object.

Fetishes are usually divided into two groups: form fetishes, in which the form and shape of the object (such as a pair of shoes or boots) are of utmost importance for arousal, and media fetishes, in which great significance is attached to the material (such as leather or lace) from which the fetish is made. Common fetishes include a person clad in black garters, stockings, and high-heeled shoes; a swatch of fabric, possibly soft or silky; and an object that has been worn. Fetish objects include corsets, diapers, gloves, rubber, spandex, furry items, and food. Typical fetish body parts are feet, legs, hair, and navels. Some fetishists are aroused by infantilism, pregnancy, or amputated limbs.

CAUSES AND TREATMENTS

The term sexual fetishism was coined by French psychiatrist Alfred Binet, whose most famous accomplishment was the development of a standardized test for intelligence. Binet described sexual fetishism as an individual's sexual attraction to a nonhuman object and offered his theory of associations to explain it. He believed fetishism to result from the accidental pairing of sexual sensation with an object that thereafter would be an object of arousal; however, he never explained clearly how this pairing could last a lifetime.

Another theory regarding fetishism was advanced in the 1950s by Donald Winnicott, who pursued the belief that fetishism may have originated in childhood, with a small cuddly object given by a mother to her infant child. This object, known as a transitional object, recalled the mother and assumed a huge significance in the child's life, particularly in the mother's absence. Winnicott reasoned that because the object brought the pleasant mother-child relationship to mind, it may have become a fetish object in the child's adult life.

Efforts to explain sexual fetishism recalled classical conditioning, advanced by Russian physiologist Ivan

Petrovich Pavlov in the early 1900s. In his study of digestion, for which he was awarded a Nobel Prize, he noticed that his dogs began to salivate when the attendant who regularly fed them entered the room. After a bell was repeatedly rung just before the attendant brought the food, the dogs soon began to salivate at the sound of the bell. This form of conditioning, in which the neutral stimulus (bell) is substituted for the unconditioned stimulus (food), results in a conditioned response (salivation).

Although classical conditioning seemed to be a plausible explanation for fetishism, it failed to mesh with Binet's idea that an initial pairing of sensation with the object would continue throughout the individual's life. One theory concerning the genesis of fetishism included imprinting, in which a young child fixes its attention on the first person in its experience and establishes a lifelong behavior pattern. Another theory was directed toward adolescence and conditioning associated with masturbation.

One modern theory arises from the fact that more men, historically, have been fetishists than women. It has been put forward that men, if influenced by their mothers, may feel shame or guilt when confronted by their own desires. Therefore, if dogged by these feelings, men might prefer to focus on an object or body part, rather than risk rejection or failure with a sexual partner.

Treatment or control of fetishism usually involves counseling, hypnosis, and prescription medications. Behavioral conditioning, usually aversive conditioning, is frequently used in the treatment of paraphiliacs. Negative stimuli such as thoughts of pain, foul odors, or "inappropriate images" are administered during moments of arousal and are designed to produce an association of pain with fetishism, eventually causing a painful response to fetishistic desires.

BIBLIOGRAPHY

Barlow, David H., ed. *The Oxford Handbook of Clinical Psychology*. New York: Oxford UP, 2014. Print.

Laws, D. Richard, and William T. O'Donohue, eds. *Sexual Deviance: Theory, Assessment, and Treatment*. 2nd ed. New York: Guilford, 2008. Print.

Lehmiller, Justin J. *The Psychology of Human Sexuality*. Malden: Wiley, 2014. Print.

Penny, James. *The World of Perversion: Psychoanalysis and the Impossible Absolute of Desire*. Albany: State U of New York P, 2006. Print.

Ray, William J. *Abnormal Psychology: Neuroscience Perspectives on Human Behavior and Experience*. Thousand Oaks: Sage, 2015. Print.

Rowland, David L., and Luca Incrocci, eds. *Handbook of Sexual and Gender Identity Disorders*. Hoboken: Wiley, 2008. Print.

Warwick, Linda L., and Lesley Bolton. *The Everything Psychology Book: Explore the Human Psyche and Understand Why We Do the Things We Do*. Cincinnati: Adams Media, 2004. Print.

Wolf, Theta H. *Alfred Binet*. Chicago: U of Chicago P, 1973. Print.

Mary Hurd

SEE ALSO: Abnormality: Psychological models; Aversion therapy; Binet, Alfred; Conditioning; Depersonalization; Imprinting; Pavlov, Ivan Petrovich; Sexual variants and paraphilias.

Field experimentation

TYPE OF PSYCHOLOGY: Psychological methodologies

Field experimentation comprises a variety of techniques to study people or other organisms within their natural environments; typically it involves observing, recording, tracking, and interviewing subjects to produce an in-depth study written as a narrative.

KEY CONCEPTS

- Covert research
- Field notes
- Hawthorne effect
- Inductive research
- Laboratory research
- Naturalistic observation
- Nonparticipant observer
- Participant observer

INTRODUCTION

As an alternative to studying behavior in the sometimes restricted and sterile confines of the laboratory, scientists can turn to field experimentation as a method of finding out how people or other organisms interact with their natural environment. As the term field experimentation implies, genuine science is being conducted; however, the research takes place in the context of the places where the subjects normally live, work, and play. Instead of removing subjects from their normal surroundings and placing them in artificial situations, a field researcher attempts to study behaviors as they occur spontaneously in the real world.

EVOLUTION OF PRACTICE

Royce Singleton Jr., Bruce Straits, Margaret Straits, and Ronald McAllister, in their book *Approaches to Social Research* (1988), make the point that field experimentation procedures were used long before the techniques were recognized by the scientific community. The authors also state there is a consensus that anthropologists—followed shortly thereafter by sociologists—first developed and then legitimized this approach to research. Anthropologist Franz Boas and sociologist Robert Park were among the early pioneers of field research during the late nineteenth century and the beginning of the twentieth century. Boas was noted for his research in cultural anthropology. He emphasized the importance of circumventing one's Western cultural biases by living in another culture for an extended time and acquiring that culture's perspective. On the other hand, Park, who taught for a number of years at the University of Chicago, was influential in encouraging students to use the city as an alternative laboratory—studying people where they lived.

Field experimentation grew out of a need to seek answers to questions that could not be brought into a laboratory setting. Foreign cultures, complex social relationships, and secretive sects are examples of the phenomena that lend themselves to this method. Laboratory research—research in which phenomena are studied in an artificial setting with rigorous procedures in place to control for outside influences—might be seen as a hindrance to understanding dynamic human behavior. An alternative method needed to be found, and field research filled this vacuum.

Early in its development, field experimentation used data-collection procedures that almost entirely consisted of informal notes. A long narrative describing a sequence of behaviors would not have been uncommon. There has been a gradual move toward the use of more "objective" techniques such as standardized rating scales, behavioral checklists, and structured surveys. These methods were created to quantify better the observations being made. Once the behaviors could be quantified (that is, once specific behaviors could be assigned numbers), they could be subjected to the same statistical analyses used by laboratory experimenters. This improved approach to data collection helped field experimentation methods play a significant role in the social and behavioral sciences.

ADVANTAGES

Studying people in their natural environments can yield a number of advantages over more traditional laboratory research methods. For example, it has been found that when subjects are aware that they are being studied, their actions sometimes differ from their actions when they are unaware that they are being observed. This phenomenon is known as the Hawthorne effect. A field study can avoid the Hawthorne effect by enabling the researcher to go "undercover" and study the subjects without their being aware that a study is going on. A field study helps ensure that genuine, rather than contrived, behaviors will emerge.

Another advantage of the field experimentation method is that it lends itself to the study of complex behaviors, such as relationships among family members, that would be too difficult to simulate in a laboratory setting. Another important strength is that the researcher can maintain the interaction between the subject and the setting in which the subject lives or works. Under this set of circumstances, the field study is the method most preferred. In addition, there are some instances in which time does not allow the researcher to bring the phenomena under study into the laboratory. Such instances include those associated with natural disasters or national calamities. For example, a researcher might want to study the psychological reactions of people who have lost their homes in a hurricane. Since it would be imperative to begin collecting data immediately, taking the time to develop a comprehensive survey or to identify and eventually test the important variables in a more controlled setting would jeopardize the data collection of this dynamic, rapidly changing situation.

DISADVANTAGES

Conducting a field experiment does not come without its share of disadvantages. First, there are many topics worthy of study that are too difficult to stage outside the well-controlled confines of a laboratory. Studying memory loss or the processes involved in solving a complex algebra problem are examples of these kinds of topics. Second, some researchers argue that because so many uncontrolled outside influences are present in a field study, it is difficult, if not impossible, to understand causal relationships among the behaviors being studied. Third, field research is particularly susceptible to the biases of the researcher while the data are being collected. Since data collection is typically less standardized and formal than in other methodologies, it is possible that the researcher may be unaware that observations that support the researcher's hypothesis may be recorded and given more attention than behaviors that go contrary to the researcher's beliefs. Some of the research published by anthropologist Margaret Mead during the 1920s, for example, has been called into question for this reason by other researchers who have reached different conclusions.

TECHNIQUES

Field experimentation usually entails going into a naturalistic setting to collect data that can be used to generate research questions. The researcher will take such information, begin to organize it, and try to draw some general conclusions from it. This process, referred to as inductive research, occurs when data are first collected and then used to formulate general principles. Thus, field research differs from many other kinds of research methodologies. Field research begins with a broad theory, then sets out to test specific aspects of the theory to see if the data support it.

Field experimentation represents a variety of strategies for studying behavior. One specific technique involves a researcher who goes into the field and chooses to identify herself or himself to the subjects; the researcher also becomes actively involved in the group's activities. The researcher has become a participant observer. An example of this method would be a person who wanted to study a violent inner-city gang. The researcher might approach the gang's leadership, then identify himself or herself and give reasons for studying the group. The researcher would also participate in the gang's meetings and other activities. Perhaps a better approach, in this situation, would be to do everything described except participating in the group's activities, especially if the gang's activities were illegal or harmful to others. In that case, the researcher, who revealed his or her true identity to the group yet chose to play a passive, inactive role from a distance, would be considered a "nonparticipant observer."

An equally important field study technique involves concealing the identity of the researcher from the group that is being studied. In a classic study by John Howard Griffin described in the book *Black Like Me* (1962), Griffin colored his skin to take on the appearance of a black man. He then traveled throughout the American South, documenting his experiences, especially those involving race discrimination. This kind of activity is called covert research.

Conducting research in the field does not prevent the researcher from manipulating or altering the environment. In fact, it is a rather common occurrence for the "field" to be contrived. For example, a study on altruism might be designed for field experimentation. A scenario would be designed to discover what kind of person would come to the assistance of someone in need. The "need" could be helping to fix a flat tire or helping a lost child find his or her mother. In either case, since both scenarios occur infrequently in the real world and would be difficult to study, the setting would need to be staged. The ability to stage events opens the possibility of studying a variety of phenomena in a convenient context.

FIVE STEPS OF FIELD EXPERIMENTATION

Five steps need to be completed in field experimentation. First, an appropriate field must be selected. This is a crucial decision, because the quality of the research hinges on the vitality of the data collected. Second, specific methods and techniques (for example, nonparticipant observation) must be developed to ensure that the behaviors the experimenter wants to observe can occur. In addition, an attempt must be made to eliminate outside influences that might bias the research. Third, the data must be collected. Fourth, the data must be organized, analyzed, and interpreted. The fifth and final step is to report the study within an appropriate format, which might be either a journal article or a book. To show how these steps are implemented and how field experimentation can contribute to scientific knowledge, two examples will be explored in detail.

CULTURAL PERCEPTIONS OF TIME

In his article "The Pace of Life," published in *American Scientist* (1990), Robert Levine attempted to understand how different cultures perceived time. In his opinion, attitudes toward time could affect a society's pace of life and ultimately might lead to detrimental health problems for its members. Levine chose to collect data from the largest city in six different countries: Japan, Taiwan, Indonesia, Italy, England, and the United States. To gauge the general pace of life, he chose to study three unique indicators: the accuracy of outdoor bank clocks, the average time it took pedestrians to walk a distance of 100 feet (about 30.5 meters), and the time needed for a postal clerk to complete a transaction that entailed selling stamps and returning some change. None of these measures relies on subjective evaluations of the pace of life by the person collecting the data. Levine preferred these particular "objective" measures over a survey approach, which might have required subjects to respond to how they "feel" about the pace of life. He was more interested in direct measures of behavior as indicators of pace.

Standardized techniques were employed while collecting the data to ensure that the pace-of-life indicators would be measured fairly. For example, walking speed would not be measured if it were raining outside. Levine chose a covert approach, since he did not want subjects to be aware that they were in a study, thus eliminating any Hawthorne effect. In addition, both participant and nonparticipant observations were made. Measuring walking speed some distance away from a subject would be an example of nonparticipant observation. On the other hand, the purchasing of stamps on the part of the experimenter was an example of the participant observer technique.

The data were collected primarily by Levine's students, who visited the countries. The data were then analyzed via basic statistical procedures. The study revealed that Japan had the fastest pace of life of the six countries, scoring the highest on all three measures. The United States came in with the second-fastest pace, followed by England; Indonesia was last, having the slowest walkers and the most inaccurate clocks.

Levine extended this research by looking at associations between the pace of life and both psychological and physical health. He found that the tempo of a society is significantly related to the prevalence of heart disease. In fact, the time-related variables often turned out to be better predictors of heart disease than psychological measures that identify high-energy behaviors in individuals. He concluded that a person who chooses to live in a fast-paced city should take necessary precautions to keep from becoming a time-urgent person. Living in a busy and stressful city can lead to unhealthy behaviors such as smoking and poor eating habits.

PSYCHOLOGICAL LABELS

In another field study, which came to be known as the Rosenhan experiment, David L. Rosenhan studied mental health professionals' ability to distinguish the "sane" from the "insane." Rosenhan later published the research in the article "On Being Sane in Insane Places" in 1973. He sent eight psychologically stable individuals to twelve different mental institutions to find out if they would be admitted as patients. Each "pseudopatient" went to an institution with an assumed name and a false occupation; this was necessary because three of the pseudopatients were psychologists and one was a psychiatrist, and they might be treated differently from other patients. The pseudopatients told the admitting staff that they had been hearing voices that appeared to say the words "hollow," "empty," and "thud." All pseudopatients were admitted and diagnosed as schizophrenic or manic-depressive. From the moment the pseudopatients gained entrance into the institutions, they began to act in a completely normal manner.

Rosenhan's study used both covert and participant observation techniques to collect the data. Field notes (the recorded behaviors and observations that make up the data of the field study) concerning the behavior of staff members were taken on a daily basis. Although Rosenhan was shocked that all of his assistants (as well as himself) were admitted, he was even more dismayed that the pseudopatients' "insanity" was never questioned by the staff. When the pseudopatients were observed writing their field notes, the behavior was interpreted by many of the staff members as paranoid and secretive.

The pseudopatients were released from the hospital between seven and fifty-two days later. Field studies, as this example indicates, can be filled with risks. None of the pseudopatients truly expected to be admitted, let alone having to stay an average of nineteen days in the hospital before the mental health professionals declared them well enough to be released. Rosenhan's study was significant because it underscored the problem of distinguishing the normal from the abnormal with conventional diagnostic procedures. Rosenhan applied the results of this study to the broader issue of psychological labels. He pointed out that categorizing an individual with a particular mental illness can be misleading and in many instances harmful. Rosenhan's pseudopatients were discharged with the label " schizophrenia in remission"—that is, according to the mental health workers, they had been relieved of their insanity, although perhaps only temporarily.

BIBLIOGRAPHY

Baker, Therese L. *Doing Social Research.* 3rd ed. New York: McGraw-Hill, 1999. Print.

Berg, Bruce Lawrence. *Qualitative Research Methods for the Social Sciences.* 7th ed. Boston: Allyn, 2009. Print.

Griffin, John Howard. *Black Like Me.* New York: New Amer. Lib., 2003. Print.

Levine, Robert V. "The Pace of Life." *American Scientist* 78 (1990): 450–59. Print.

Mehl, Matthias R., and Tamlin S. Conner, eds. *Handbook of Research Methods for Studying Daily Life*. New York: Guilford, 2012. Print.

Reason, Peter, and Hilary Bradbury. *Handbook of Action Research: Participative Inquiry and Practice*. Thousand Oaks: Sage, 2001. Print.

Reis, Harry T., and Charles M. Judd, eds. *Handbook of Research Methods in Social and Personality Psychology*. 2nd ed. New York: Cambridge UP, 2014. Print.

Rosenhan, David L. "On Being Sane in Insane Places." *Science* 179 (1973): 250–58. Print.

Singleton, Royce, Jr., Bruce C. Straits, M. M. Straits, and Ronald J. McAllister. *Approaches to Social Research*. 4th ed. New York: Oxford UP, 2005. Print.

Swingle, Paul, ed. *Social Psychology in Natural Settings: A Reader in Field Experimentation*. New Brunswick: Aldine Transaction, 2007. Print.

Teele, Dawn Langan, ed. *Field Experiments and Their Critics: Essays on the Uses and Abuses of Experimentation in the Social Sciences*. New Haven: Yale UP, 2014. Print.

Bryan C. Auday

SEE ALSO: Case study methodologies; Data description; Experimentation: Ethics and participant rights; Hypothesis development and testing; Observational methods; Qualitative research; Research ethics; Survey research: Questionnaires and interviews.

Field theory
Kurt Lewin

TYPE OF PSYCHOLOGY: Personality

Kurt Lewin's field theory maintains that behavior is a function of the life space, or psychological reality, of the individual. Individuals are motivated to reduce tensions that arise in this life space. Lewin's theory can be used to understand a wide range of everyday behavior and to suggest strategies for addressing social problems such as the reduction of prejudice and the resolution of social conflicts.

KEY CONCEPTS
- Life space
- Locomotion
- Quasi-stationary equilibrium
- Region of life space
- Tension

INTRODUCTION

Kurt Lewin was a theorist of everyday life. His field theory attempts to explain people's everyday behavior, such as how a waiter remembers an order, what determines the morale and productivity of a work group, what causes intergroup prejudice, how a child encounters a new environment, or why people eat the foods they do.

For Lewin, what determines everyday behavior is the life space of the individual. The life space represents the psychological reality of the individual; it is the totality of all psychological facts and social forces that influence an individual at a given time and place. For example, the life space of a child entering a novel domain is, for the most part, undifferentiated and thus results in exploration on the part of the child. On the other hand, the life space of an employee at work may be well differentiated and populated with demands from the employer to produce more goods, from coworkers to follow a production norm, and from home for more income. There might, additionally, be physical needs to slow down.

EVOLUTION OF LEWIN'S THEORY

Field theory was born on the battlefields of World War I. Lewin served as a soldier in the German army. His first published article was titled "The War Landscape," and it described the battlefield in terms of life space. The soldier's needs determined how the landscape was to be perceived. When the soldier was miles from the front, the peaceful landscape seemed to stretch endlessly on all sides without direction. As the war front approached, the landscape took on direction, and peaceful objects such as rocks and trees became elements of battle, such as weapons and places to hide.

After the war, Lewin took an academic appointment at the Psychological Institute of Berlin, where he served on the faculty with Gestalt psychologists Wolfgang Köhler and Max Wertheimer. While at the institute, Lewin further developed his field theory and conducted the first program of experimental social psychological research exploring topics such as memory for interrupted tasks, level of aspiration, and anger. His work derived as much from field theory as it did from his curiosity about the social world. For example, research on memory for interrupted tasks began when he and his students wondered why a waiter could remember their rather lengthy order but would forget it immediately after the food was served. In field theory terms, noncompleted tasks (such as the waiter's recall before delivering the order) were recalled better because they maintained a tension for completion compared to completed tasks, for which this tension is resolved.

As the Nazi Party rose to power in Germany, Lewin correctly perceived that his own Jewish life space and that of his family were becoming progressively more threatened and intolerable. Like many Jewish intellectuals of the time, Lewin emigrated to the United States; he obtained a number of visiting appointments until he established the Center for Group Dynamics at the Massachusetts Institute of Technology in 1944. Lewin's American research was much more applied than his work in Europe, and it concentrated particularly on social problems such as prejudice and intergroup conflict—perhaps as a result of his own experience of prejudice as a Jew in Germany.

Before his early death in 1947, Lewin helped train the first generation of American students interested in experimental social psychology, including such notables as Leon Festinger, Harold Kelley, Stanley Schachter, and Morton Deutsch. As a result, Lewin's intellectual legacy pervades the field of experimental social psychology. Lewinian social psychologists continue to carry on his research legacy by investigating topics of long-standing interest to Lewin, such as prejudice, achievement, organizational behavior, social cognition, and the reduction of cognitive tensions or dissonance, and by attempting to explain how individuals construe their environments and how those environments affect behavior.

LIFE SPACE REGIONS

The concept of life space is usually divided into two parts: person and environment. These two parts can be differentiated further into regions. A region is any major part of the life space that can be distinguished from other parts and is separated by more or less permeable boundaries. For example, regions differentiated within the person might consist of needs, goals, hopes, and aspirations of the individual, whereas the differentiation of the environment might consist of profession, family, friendships, social norms, and taboos.

Locomotion, or behavior and change in the life space, is determined by the differentiation of regions in the life space and by the forces for change emanating from each region. Often, in any given life space, there are opposing or conflicting forces. For example, the boss may want to increase productivity as much as possible, whereas coworkers may seek to limit production to levels obtainable by all workers. According to Lewin, these tensions, or opposing social forces, provide the motivation for behavior and change in the life space. Tension can be resolved by any number of activities, including reconfiguring the life space either physically (for example, getting a new job) or mentally (for example, devaluing either the boss's or coworkers' opinions); performing a substitute task that symbolically reduces tension (for example, performing different tasks of value to the boss); or finding the "quasi-stationary equilibrium," or position where all opposing forces are equal in strength (for example, performing at a level between boss's and coworkers' recommendations).

COMPARISON WITH BEHAVIORISM AND PSYCHOANALYSIS

It is useful to compare Lewin's field theory with the two other major theories of the time: behaviorism and psychoanalysis. Lewin's field theory can be summarized by the equation B = f(P,E), or, "behavior is a function of person and environment." In other words, behavior is function of the life space of a total environment as perceived by the individual. In psychoanalytic thought, behavior is a function of the history of the individual. For example, past childhood experience is supposed to have a direct impact on current psychological processes. In contrast, Lewin's theory is ahistorical. Although the individual's past may influence that person's approach and construal of the psychological field, its influence is only indirect, as behavior is a function of the current and immediate life space.

Lewin's field theory differs from behaviorism on at least two key dimensions. First, Lewin emphasized the subjectivity of the psychological field. To predict and understand behavior successfully, a therapist needs to describe the situation from the viewpoint of the individual whose behavior is under consideration, not from the viewpoint of an observer. Second, Lewin's theory emphasizes that behavior must be understood as a function of the life space or situation as a whole. In other words, behavior is motivated by the multitude of often interdependent forces affecting an individual, as opposed to one or two salient rewards or reinforcers that may be present.

ROLE IN SOCIAL CHANGE

Lewin's field theory has had many applications, particularly in the area of social change. Lewin's approach to solving social problems was first to specify, in as much detail as possible, the life space of the individual involved. Next, he would identify the social forces affecting the individual. Finally, Lewin would experiment with changing these social forces or adding new ones to enact social change. Two applications of field theory performed by Lewin and his associates serve as good examples. One deals with changing food preferences, and the other with the reduction of intergroup conflicts and prejudice.

During World War II, there was a shortage of meat, an important protein source, in the United States. As part of the war effort, Lewin was assigned the task of convincing Americans to eat sweetbreads—certain organ meats, which many Americans find unappetizing—to maintain protein levels. Lewin began by first describing the consumption channel, or how food reaches a family's table. At the time, housewives obtained food from either a garden or a grocery store and then moved it to the table by purchasing it, transporting it home, storing it in an icebox or pantry, and then preparing it. At each step, Lewin identified forces that prevented the gatekeeper—in this case, the housewife—from serving sweetbreads. Such forces might have included the belief that family members would not eat sweetbreads, inexperience with the selection and preparation of sweetbreads, or inherently distasteful aspects of the food.

In attempting to remove and redirect these forces, Lewin experimented with two approaches, one successful and the other not. In the unsuccessful case, Lewin presented housewives with a lecture detailing the problems of nutrition during the war and stating ways of overcoming obstacles in serving sweetbreads; he discussed ways to prepare sweetbreads, provided recipes, and indicated that other women had successfully served sweetbreads for their families with little complaint. Only 3 percent of the housewives hearing this lecture served sweetbreads. From Lewin's perspective, such a lecture was ineffective because it did not involve the audience and arouse the level of tension needed to produce change. Lewin's second method was a group discussion. The housewives were asked to discuss how they could persuade "housewives like themselves" to serve sweetbreads. This led to a discussion of the obstacles that the housewife might encounter, along with ways of overcoming these obstacles (just as in the lecture). Such a discussion was effective because it created tension for the housewife: "I just told everyone why they should and how they could eat sweetbreads, and I am not currently serving them myself." After this group discussion, 32 percent (an almost elevenfold increase) of the housewives involved served sweetbreads.

CONFLICT AND PREJUDICE

Lewin approached the problems of intergroup conflict and racial prejudice by describing the life spaces of the members of the conflicting parties. For example, Lewin saw the life space of many minority group members (such as religious and racial minorities) as full of obstacles and barriers that restrict movement in the life space. The life space of the majority member often consigned the minority member to a small and rigidly bounded region (for example, a ghetto). By isolating minority group members, majority group members can develop unrealistic perceptions or stereotypes of the out-group. Such life spaces are very likely to result in intergroup conflict.

The field theory analysis of racial prejudice suggests that one way to reduce intergroup conflict is to remove obstacles and increase the permeability of intergroup barriers. In the later part of his career, Lewin established the Commission on Community Interrelations as a vehicle for discovering ways of removing intergroup barriers. Lewin and his colleagues discovered some of the following successful techniques for promoting intergroup harmony: enacting laws that immediately removed barriers, such as racial quotas limiting the number of Jews who could attend certain universities; immediate hiring of blacks as sales personnel, thereby increasing the permeability of intergroup boundaries by making contact between group members more likely; responding directly to racial slurs with a calm appeal based on American traditions and democracy to provide a countervailing force to the slur; promoting meetings of warring groups in a friendly atmosphere as a means of breaking down group boundaries; and immediately integrating housing as a successful way of promoting racial harmony.

BIBLIOGRAPHY

Deaux, Kay, and Mark Snyder, eds. *The Oxford Handbook of Personality and Social Psychology.* New York: Oxford UP, 2012. Print.

De Rivera, Joseph, comp. *Field Theory as Human-Science: Contributions of Lewin's Berlin Group.* New York: Gardner, 1976. Print.

Fligstein, Neil, and Doug McAdam. *A Theory of Fields.* New York: Oxford UP, 2012. Print.

Hewstone, Miles, Wolfgang Stroebe, and Klaus Jonas, eds. *An Introduction to Social Psychology.* 5th ed. Chichester: Wiley, 2012. Print.

Lewin, Kurt. *A Dynamic Theory of Personality.* New York: McGraw-Hill, 1935. Print.

Lewin, Kurt. "Group Decision and Social Change." *Readings in Social Psychology.* Ed. Theodore M. Newcomb and Eugene L. Hartley. New York: Holt, 1947. Print.

Lewin, Kurt. *Resolving Social Conflicts; and, Field Theory in Social Science.* Washington: American Psychological Association, 1997. Print.

Marrow, Alfred Jay. *The Practical Theorist: The Life and Work of Kurt Lewin.* New York: Basic, 1969. Print.

Perecman, Ellen, and Sara R. Curran. *A Handbook for Social Science Field Research: Essays and Bibliographic Sources on Research Design and Methods.* Thousand Oaks: Sage, 2006. Print.

Wheelan, Susan A., Emmy A. Pepitone, and Vicki Abt, eds. *Advances in Field Theory.* Thousand Oaks: Sage, 1991. Print.

Anthony R. Pratkanis and Marlene E. Turner

See Also: Achievement motivation; Cognitive dissonance; Cooperation, competition, and negotiation; Group decision making; Groups; Lewin, Kurt; Motivation; Prejudice reduction; Thought: Inferential.

Fight-or-flight response

Type of psychology: Biological bases of behavior; Emotion; Stress

The fight-or-flight response describes a physiological reaction that occurs when one is confronted with a stimulus that is perceived as threatening. It may be considered the alarm phase of the body's reaction to a stressor. It is an adaptive response and becomes pathological only if it occurs when there is no obvious threatening stimulus or when it continues over a long period of time..

Key Concepts

- Adrenal glands
- Autonomic nervous system
- Homeostasis
- Hypothalamus
- Parasympathetic nervous system
- Stress
- Sympathetic nervous system

INTRODUCTION

In his classic book *The Wisdom of the Body* (1932), American physiologist Walter Bradford Cannon introduced the term fight-or-flight to describe the physiological (or bodily) reaction that occurs when humans or animals are confronted with something that they see as threatening. He was also the first person to use the word stress,

Perhaps the best way to illustrate the fight-or-flight response is to look at common animals. It can be seen in cats or dogs: the hair on the back of their necks stands up, and they may take a position that indicates they are ready to fight. Cats may take the "Halloween cat" stance, with the back arched and hair standing on end, and tend to spit, hiss, and otherwise attempt to look threatening; dogs may growl and keep their heads lowered, eyes narrowed, and feet planted wide, ready to take on the enemy. Alternatively, the animal simply runs. This is fight-or-flight at its most obvious.

In humans, the fight-or-flight response is usually less obvious, but it contains most, if not all, of the same physiological reactions. The heart pounds, the blood rushes to the muscles to prepare to fight or run, sweating begins, and the bowels may actually loosen. Maxims referring to persons being so frightened that they wet themselves actually describe part of the physiological reaction that occurs during the fight-or-flight response. Further, one may feel a strange feeling on the back of one's neck. This is piloerection, which is the scientific name for the hair on the back of the neck standing up. If one is unaware of what is causing the sensation, it can make what is already stressful even more so.

BASIC BIOLOGY

To understand the fight-or-flight response, it is necessary to review some of the basic biology of the nervous system. In the nineteenth century, French physiologist Claude Bernard first proposed the idea that there was a need for a stable internal environment even as external conditions change. Cannon further developed this idea in his book The Wisdom of the Body, proposing the concept of negative feedback as the mechanism for maintaining homeostasis (which means same-staying, or physiological equilibrium) in the body.

The nervous system of all vertebrates is composed of two major divisions: the central nervous system (CNS) and the peripheral nervous system (PNS). The CNS consists of the brain and spinal corde —everything encased in bone. The PNS is everything else—all the motor and sensory nerves in the body outside the brain and spinal cord. The PNS is further divided into two parts: the skeletal (also called somatic) system, which controls voluntary muscle movement for the most part, and the autonomic nervous system, which for the most part mediates involuntary activity in the body. The autonomic nervous system is divided further into the parasympathetic division, which is what maintains homeostasis, operating to keep the body, including internal organs, in a mode that allows it to rest and digest, terms introduced by Cannon at the same time as he introduced fight-or-flight. The parasympathetic nervous system maintains the basal heart rate, respiration, and metabolism under normal conditions. This is the opposite of the sympathetic nervous system, which reacts to anything perceived as stressful or threatening and is responsible for getting the body ready to stand or run, fight or flee.

The body needs to be able to react to changes in the internal or external environment. These changes include blood loss from an accident or injury, running a marathon, changes in temperature, emotional stress, an earthquake, or hearing an unexplained noise in the night. In fact, although people sometimes say that they wish they did not react to stress, it has been demonstrated experimentally that animals that lack stress responses require special care to stay alive. The fight-or-flight response is, therefore, a very adaptive reaction and becomes pathological only when it goes on for long periods of time or when it happens when there is nothing to precipitate it.

Cannon first recognized that the sympathetic and parasympathetic nervous divisions had different functions, although the two divisions actually work together most of the time. It may seem as if they are pulling in opposite directions, but there is a balance between the two systems resulting from an interaction between what is going on inside the body and what is going on in the environment. The body needs a certain amount of tension between the two systems to maintain the correct balance of arousal and relaxation (homeostasis) under normal circumstances.

A good example of how the two systems work together, and how one can be more active than the other at any given time, is the situation of a person sitting quietly in the living room, reading a book after eating dinner. During this time, the parasympathetic nerves have slowed the heart rate and the digestive system has become active. The nerves mediating the sympathetic nervous system are not inactive, but the parasympathetic is "in control." If the motion sensor–controlled light outside the house were suddenly to come on and the person in the living room were to see a figure standing outside the window, the sympathetic nervous system would react within one or two seconds. The digestion would slow down, the heart rate would increase, and the blood would be diverted from the skin and digestive organs and rush to the muscles and brain. The person would begin to breathe harder to make more oxygen available, the mouth would get dry, the pupils of the eyes would dilate (letting more light in for better sight), and the sweat glands would become more active, getting ready to cool the body during its coming activity—either fighting or running. When the figure turns and the person realizes it is a neighbor retrieving a wayward cat, the parasympathetic system resumes control. Heart rate slows and pupils return to normal size.

BRAIN ACTIVITY

The fight-or-flight response is mediated by the hypothalamus, which is a very small (about only 4 grams of the approximately 1,400 grams a normal adult brain weighs) but a very important group of nuclei (groups of nerve cells, or neurons, that are functionally related) deep in the brain. The hypothalamus integrates the functions of the autonomic nervous system, both the parasympathetic and the sympathetic divisions, via the pituitary gland and ascending and descending fibers that pass through it, connecting the brain with the rest of the body, including the internal organs.

When the brain perceives a threatening stimulus, whether it is something that one assesses cognitively (such as realizing that one is being attacked verbally) or something that suddenly appears and to which one reacts reflexively (such as being confronted by a bear or a snake in the wild), a cascade of events begins. It may be that by the time the actual physiological reaction takes place, one would have already started to respond, protecting oneself from the bear, for instance, or confronting the person who is attacking. There are hierarchical neural pathways from the sensory receptors that send messages to the brain. Some messages travel through the thalamus—an important area deep within the brain for sending and receiving messages between the brain and the environment—and up to the cortex so appropriate action can be taken. Simultaneously, messages are also sent via the thalamus to the hypothalamus (which contains many nuclei that actually control the autonomic nervous system) and the frontal cortex, passing through the amygdala (a part of the brain important in remembering emotional responses to previous occurrences) and the hippocampus (a part of the brain known to be important in forming memories).

If these brain systems concur that there is a threatening stimulus, the hypothalamus initiates a cascade of events that activates the sympathetic portion of the autonomic nervous system, and the fight-or-flight response begins within one or two seconds. Thus, the hypothalamus sends a chemical signal to the pituitary gland, causing it to release adrenocorticotropic hormone (ACTH), and also activates the adrenal glands (a set of glands, one of which sits on top of each kidney). Before a person can even begin cognitively processing what has happened, the adrenal medulla, the center of the adrenal gland, has begun to secrete epinephrine (also known as adrenaline), norepinephrine, and steroid stress hormones called glucocorticoids. The substances secreted by the pituitary and adrenal medulla are distributed systemically, which means they are blood-borne. They take longer to reach their destinations than messages traveling along neural pathways, which explains why people can slam on their brakes at the sight of an oncoming car within seconds and then notice that they are shaking and their heart is pounding minutes later.

PATHOLOGICAL MANIFESTATIONS

Although the fight-or-flight response is an appropriate reaction to many threatening stimuli, there are times when people report all the symptoms of the fight-or-flight response when there are no threatening stimuli. People who describe panic attacks will often describe all the physiological signs of fight-or-flight, including racing heart, dry mouth, disturbed bowel function, and increased breathing (sometimes even hyperventilation). Panic attacks can be unnerving. People who experience them are usually unaware of what is causing the feelings they are experiencing and may think they are having a heart attack. Evidence suggests that panic attacks have a genetic component, with family history suggesting it is carried on a single dominant gene.

The fight-or-flight response may be considered to correspond to the first, or alarm, phase of the general adaptation syndrome described by Hans Selye in 1956. When the fight-or-flight response (or alarm phase) is not quickly resolved so that the body is returned to homeostasis, with the parasympathetic division of the autonomic nervous system regaining control, the body then progresses into the second, or resistance, phase and then on to exhaustion. The long-term release of corticosteroids can be harmful to the body because every cell in the body has receptors for them. This is good in the short run, during the fight-or-flight or alarm phase, because these hormones help the body to use glucose for energy more efficiently, among other effects. However, continued production of corticosteroids has been associated with disruption of the immune system, high blood pressure, and other cardiovascular illnesses.

BIBLIOGRAPHY

Bloom, Floyd E., and Arlyn Lazerson. *Brain, Mind, and Behavior*. 3rd ed. New York: Worth, 2001. Print.

"Brain Basics." *National Institute of Mental Health*. Natl. Inst. of Health, n.d. Web. 13 May 2014.

Carlson, Neil R. Physiology of Behavior. 10th ed. Boston: Allyn, 2009. Print.

Jackson, Mark. *The Age of Stress: Science and the Search for Stability*. New York: Oxford UP, 2014. Print.

Kandel, Eric R., James H. Schwartz, and Thomas M. Jessell, eds. *Principles of Neural Science*. East Norwalk: Appleton, 2006. Print.

Kolb, Bryan, and Ian Q. Whishaw. *An Introduction to Brain and Behavior.* 2nd ed. New York: Worth, 2006. Print.

"Understanding the Stress Response." *Harvard Health Publications*. Harvard Medical School, Mar. 2011. Web. 13 May 2014.

Gayle L. Brosnan-Watters

See Also: Adrenal gland; Aggression; Behaviorism; Brain structure; Cannon, Walter Bradford; Fear; General adaptation syndrome; Selye, Hans; Stress: Physiological responses.

Flying phobia

Types of Psychology: Clinical; Counseling; Psychopathology; Psychotherapy.

An intense fear of flying can have many impacts on one's life from cccepting jobs or promotions to positions in the airline industry to visiting family and friends and going on vacation. Flying phobia hinders lifestyle. The phobia has four components: possibility of a crash (although statistically flying commercial airplanes is safer than nearly every other mode of transportation), confinement, heights, and turbulence. Evidenced-based psychotherapy offers short-term treatment to overcome fear of flying.

Key concepts

- Areophobia
- Autonomic nervous system
- Exposure therapy
- Intense fear of flying
- Panic
- Systematic desensitization
- Virtual reality

INTRODUCTION

Specific phobias are among the most common psychological problems, ranging from 10% to 30% of the population experiencing some form and varying with individuals' learning history of and exposure to sources of phobia.

Fear of flying, or aerophobia, is a situational phobia. It is an emotional and mental anxiety, worry, or preoccupation which is out of proportion to the rationale, objective danger of taking an airplane. This can involve extreme anxiety any time before the flight, even before arriving at the airport, during the flight, and it may not abate until after landing. This fear leads to maladaptive behaviors subject to the autonomous nervous system and treatment requires regulation of these responses.

According to the fifth edition of the Diagnostic and Statistical Manual (DSM-5), fear of flying is characterized by three symptoms: 1) marked fear of airplanes, 2) avoidance of airplanes, and 3) impairment in flying.

The fear reaction occurs upon encountering the feared stimulus, fixed or rotary wing aircraft, and may escalate the anxiety into a full-fledged panic attack. Psychologists and allied health professionals who treat flying phobia distinguish when the anxiety is excessive and irrational and whether sufferers' anxiety is fear of crashing while flying or anticipated fear of having a panic attack during a flight.

CAUSES

Past personal experiences and a learning history including observing others' anxiety over the same situation or informational learning after reading or hearing about dangerous situations in flying are among the most common reasons flying phobia develops. Often, those who suffer with flying phobia have histories of struggling with anxiety which predate their fear of flying. Aerophobia frequently exists with other anxiety disorders. Competent treatment requires a thorough understanding of diagnostic criteria and potential sources of diagnostic error are required to establish an accurate assessment and focused treatment plan.

Psychotherapy based on empirical evidence suggests that behavioral and cognitive psychotherapy, or some variation of them, are the most effective approaches. They are common sense procedures that usually make immediate sense to those in treatment. These approaches prioritize results, demystify the patient-therapist relationship, assign homework, and usually include these basic areas of evaluation:

List of urgent and realistic problems. A structured interview evaluates the biographic history and thereon remains in the here and now using Microsoft excel charts which are individualized using specific questionnaires.

Strategies for intervention. Even though psychologists use manuals, intervention is tailored for each symptom and each individual.

Progress evaluation. Every session records the progress. Sub-goals are useful to accelerate behavior change. Efficacy is more important than etiology; effectiveness and relief are more important than causes and explanations.

Behavior and cognitive psychotherapy are both approaches that utilize case formulation based in hypotheses about the patients' problems. The formulation aids in the development of a plan in order to treat this emotionally painful and socially embarrassing psychological disorder. It is mandatory to monitor the psychotherapeutic process on a regular basis.

Photo: iStock

A CASE EXAMPLE

A case of flying phobia might be treated as follows: a 40-year-old woman describes her problem as "every time I am going to fly I stay at home with my suitcase." She related that when she last booked travel to Europe with her husband some years ago, she had to return home from the airport. The following year, she tried again, this time flying to Mexico, but was unable to surmount her fear. Her aerophobia started 20 years earlier during her honeymoon. Last year, when her husband was flying to Europe for business and invited her to come along, she remained too anxious, and she knew that if she declined, he would simply travel alone.

BEHAVIORAL ANALYSIS

In a structured interview, factors that may facilitate or complicate treatment are identified. In this case the patient was prompted to travel as soon as possible. She embraced the belief that she must insist to herself that she has to travel and that she will be successful this time. A positive and hopeful belief helps deal with her specific fears, and unlearning the maladaptive fear is the main focus behavioral and cognitive behavioral approaches take.

QUESTIONNAIRES

Frequently, questionnaires are used to engage patients or clients in this treatment while helping the psychologist better assess the source, frequency, and intensity of the fear. The Fear Survey Schedule of two researchers, Wolpe and Lang, asks clients to rate the intensity of their distress associated with fear using 108 items. Huag and colleagues developed their Fear of Flying Scale which uses 21 items to assess levels of fear associated with different aspects of flying. In 1966, researchers produced the widely used Subjective Units of Distress Scale, commonly referred to as SUDS. This scale asks people to subjectively rate the intensity of their fear using a verbal rating on a 10-point scale, where 10 represents the worst fear one can imagine, and 0 represents no fear at all.

ASSESSMENT

Assessment begins by emphasizing that the goal is not to completely eliminate anxiety but rather to minimize the distress and avoidance of the source of the anxiety through systematically confronting the fear of flying.

The result of the structured interview might be an anxiety hierarchy that looks something like this:

- Fear of boarding the airplane 10 SUDS
- Walk up the steps to the aircraft 9 SUDS
- Taking the bus to the airplane 8 SUDS
- In the line for the flight check-in 7 SUDS
- See the airplanes from a terrace 4 SUDS

WHAT TREATMENT MIGHT LOOK LIKE: EXPOSURE THERAPY

Systematic desensitization is a form of behavior therapy which has evolved into what is today called exposure therapy and is based on the theory that maladaptive emotional responses are learned and can also be unlearned through re-education. The treating clinician gradually exposes the person in small, incremental steps that must be taken in order to fly: thinking about taking a flight, purchasing tickets, driving to the airport, checking in, waiting for boarding, boarding itself, settling in and buckling the seat belt, take-off, achieving cruising altitude, flying, descent, and landing.

PROCESS

(The numbers are SUDS from 0 to 10)

Session I (45 minutes) Exposure in Imagination

Scene 1: "Imagine driving to the airport and observing airplanes in the sky flying over the ocean," might be presented three times with the patient reporting SUDS ratings of 3 than 2 than 1 on the third presentation.

Scene 2: "Look at these four photos of airplanes," is the presentation of external visual stimuli, again presented three times. The patient might report an initial SUDS of 9. After exposure to the pictures of the anxiety-provoking stimulus (airplanes) in the safe environment of a psychologist's office, the patient may report gradually lessened anxiety, ending with a SUDS of 6 on the third presentation.

Session II (45 minutes) Exposure in Imagination

Scene 1: "Imagine that the flight is being announced for departure." The patient is asked to hold that image imaging herself present in the airport. She might be given the same instruction two additional times with a resulting decrease in her anxiety reaction. It would be common for a patient to begin with a SUDS of 7 and end with a SUDS of 4 or 5 by the third presentation.

Session III (45 minutes) Exposure in Vivo

Scene 1: "Imagine yourself traveling to just visit the airport; you are not going to try to board a flight. You are simply and safely going to visit the airport." This session might end with the homework assignment of actually traveling to the airport and spending an hour there while practicing a relaxed breathing technique. Commonly, aerophobic patients will end this exposure with a SUDS rating of 3 or 4.

Session IV (45-minutes) Exposure in Imagination

Scene 1: "Imagine that you are flying in 15 days." This image might be presented three or four times, with the patient visualizing what her life would really be like if she were actually flying in 15 days. SUDS scores of 4 and 3 would be usual.

Scene 2: (If session time allows.) "Imagine that you are flying tomorrow," would be followed by at least two presentations. The typical patient might have an initial SUDS of 4 or 5 at that prospect with gradual reduction in anxiety as the presentations continued.

Session V (45 minutes) Instructions for Self-monitoring

At this point in treatment, the patient would be given a list to record her SUDS ratings while traveling: traveling to airport, checking in at the airline counter, arriving and waiting at the gate, going on the entryway ramp, entering the airplane, finding her seat, going through the preflight checklist, taxiing, taking off, reaching cruising altitude,assessing each hour during the flight, and landing.

DISCUSSION OF TREATMENT

The goal of psychotherapy in this situation is to monitor the progress of each session and, if progress is made, continue stepwise until the problem, here debilitating anxiety, is resolved. When progress is insufficient to move forward, the psychologist will re-evaluate the patient's anxiety hierarchy, develop an alternative hypothesis, and offer another plan of treatment. The psychologist usually does not push the patient beyond her level of comfort, and pacing and time until resolution will vary with each patient. Generally, except for short-term, occasional use, pharmacotherapy is not necessary for the treatment of specific phobias. Also, when there is more than one problem, the clinician-patient collaboration will address the more urgent problem first. The method described here utilized patients' precise conceptualization of what and which characteristics of flying are anxiety triggers for them. Patients' conceptualization includes knowing the triggers and cues, anticipating the consequences of their avoidance, and recognizing objective safety behaviors.

APPLIED RELAXATION

Fear of flying may include physical symptoms such as changes in brain activity, the release of cortisol, insulin, and growth hormone, and increases in blood pressure and heart rate. Among other symptoms are unsteadiness, dizziness and lightheadedness, nausea, sweating, shortness of breath, trembling or shaking, upset stomach, and irregular bowel movements.

For this therapy to work, it was believed for many years that patients had to be relaxed and many psychologists and allied behavioral health professionals utilized a technique known as progressive muscle relaxation to promote a physically relaxed state. However, empirical evidence has shown that while effective, attaining deep relaxation is not necessary. It is sufficient for patients to simply be calm through diaphragmatic breathing and visualization of pleasing scenes. Being in a calm state is neuropsychologically antagonistic to being in an anxious state. Human neurology and more specifically the autonomic nervous system does not permit being anxious and breathing slowly to co-exist at the same time.

Progressive muscle relaxation is directed to five group of muscles, arms and shoulders, face (forehead, eyes, nose, tongue, and neck), thorax and lower back, diaphragmatic breathing, and legs and feet. Patients are instructed to practice these exercises at a minimum of twice a week. Progressive muscle relaxation is an auxiliary tool for reducing discomfort and stress. Its goal is not to promote relaxation per se, but for the patient to let go of physiological tensions in her body.

VIRTUAL REALITY (VR) AND COMPUTER-ASSISTED EXPOSURE THERAPY

Other forms of treatment are a variation of exposure therapy. To counteract the physiological symptoms associated with the fear of flying, VR software has been produced that includes four sessions of anxiety management training followed by exposure to a virtual airplane or an actual airplane at the airport. This treatment protocol involves follow-up at six and 12 months and boasts a 70% success rate.

CONCLUSION

Patient confidence in psychological treatments and their benefit is enhanced by promoting the scientific value of existing and future empirical research guides for treatment decisions. Scientific understanding, assessment, prevention, and treatment of human problems are the road to advance public health. Psychological clinical science is an applied science. As such, it is concerned with generating new knowledge regarding the nature of psychological problems, and with translating that knowledge into applications that improve the human condition.

BIBLIOGRAPHY

Bourne, E., & MacKay, M. (1980). *Overcoming Specific Phobia Client Manual*. Newharbinger.

Brown, D. (2009). *Flying Without Fear.* Newharbinger. This is an updated version of a widely-used program tailed for aerophobia. It now includes information about terrorism and airport security in the wake of September 11. The book details the sights, sounds, and sensations associated with flying. Provides step-by-step instructions for self-management of flying phobia.

Jacobson, E. (1938). *Progressive Relaxation*. Chicago, IL: Chicago University Press.

Haug, T., Brenne, L., Johnsen, B. H., Berntzen, D., Gotestam, K. G., & Hugdahl, K. (1987). "The Three-Systems Analysis of Fear of Flying: A Comparison of a Consonant vs. a Non-Consonant Treatment Method". *Behaviour Research and Therapy*, 25, 187–194.

Öst, L. G., Fellenius, J., & Sterner, U. (1991). "Applied Tension, Exposure In Vivo, and Tension Only In The Treatment of Blood Phobia". *Behaviour Research and Therapy,* 29, 561–574.

Ost, L. G., Brandberg, M., & Alm, T. (1997). "One Versus Five Sessions of Exposure In The Treatment of Flying Phobia". *Behavior Research and Therapy*, 35(11), 987-996.

Nussbaum, A. (2013). "The Pocket Guide To The DSM-5 Diagnostic Exam", *American Psychiatric*. Rothbaum,

B., Anderson, P., Zimand, E., Hodges, L., Lang, D., & Wilson, J. (2006). *Behavior Therapy* 37 pp 80-90 Elsevier Ltd.

Wolpe, J., & Lazarus, A. A. (1966). *Behavior Therapy Techniques: A Guide To The Treatment of Neuroses.* New York, NY: Pergamon Press.

Wolpe, J., & Lang, P. J. (1977). *Manual For The Fear Survey Schedule* (revised). San Diego, CA: Educational and Industrial Testing Service.

Felicitas Kort

See Also: Anxiety; Exposure therapy; Fear; Phobia; Systematic desensitization therapy.

Forensic psychology

Type of psychology: Motivation; Personality; Psychological methodologies

Forensic psychology is the study of psychology pertaining to the law. It specifically examines issues of competency, deviant and criminal behavior, courtroom practices, prediction of future criminal behavior, psychological profiling of criminal offenders, and correctional practices of rehabilitation.

Key Concepts

- Competency
- Correctional practices of rehabilitation
- Courtroom practices
- Criminal behavior
- Prediction of future criminal behavior
- Profiling of criminal offenders

INTRODUCTION

Forensic psychology is the practice of psychology as it pertains to aspects of the law. The specific functions of forensic psychology are multifaceted; however, they are dominated by participation in the criminal justice system. The legislative process of the proposal and passage of laws acknowledges and identifies behavior that society has determined to be inappropriate. Persons who choose to perform behavior that falls outside societally determined parameters are considered deviant and commonly criminal. It is this set of behaviors and the persons who commit the behaviors that are the subject of the study of forensic psychology. Specific activities and concerns of this field of study include competency, the prediction of future behavior of convicted criminals, and the profiling of the unknown criminal offender.

COMPETENCY

Prior to the recognition of forensic psychology as a specific discipline of psychology, the determination of competency, mental was a criminal justice activity of psychologists and psychiatrists. Historically, psychologists and psychiatrists have been utilized by the courts to issue professional opinions pertaining to the competency of persons brought before the court. The earliest determinations of competency were associated with persons whose mental capacities to make rational decisions were impaired by age, disability, or injury. To determine the validity of claims that a person was incompetent to make rational decisions for himself or herself and was in need of assistance and guardianship in decision making, the courts referred these individuals for examination and determination to psychologists and psychiatrists. On a determination of incompetence, the court would appoint a relative to serve as a guardian of the incompetent person. This guardian would assume legal responsibility for the estate and person of the individual deemed incompetent. Forensic psychologists and psychiatrists continue to perform these types of competency determinations today and are critical to the activities of juvenile and probate courts.

Forensic psychologists and psychiatrists also perform critical competency functions for the criminal courts. Since the M'Naghten decision in the 1800's in England, the courts have struggled with determining whether individuals afflicted with mental health disorders and intelligence deficiencies should be held accountable for their criminal behavior. Defense attorneys argue that their clients afflicted with deficiencies in mental health and intelligence should not be held accountable for their alleged criminal conduct. Persons afflicted with certain mental illnessesMental illnesslegal issues do not have a reality perspective that allows them the ability to discriminate between lawful and unlawful behavior. Individuals who have reduced intellectual capacity do not possess the ability to distinguish right from wrong and cannot appreciate the consequences of their actions. Attorneys also argue (and the law recognizes) that children cannot be compared with adults and consequently cannot completely appreciate the consequences of their behavior and should not be held accountable in the same ways that adults are held accountable for their behaviors.

The Sixth Amendment to the U.S. Constitution guarantees the rights of due process, which include the right to assist in one's own defense. Persons may not, because of age, mental illness, or diminished intellectual capacity, be capable of assisting in their own defense, and consequently, their defense counsels argue that they should not be prosecuted. Numerous challenges to this amendment have resulted in appellate decisions that have influenced judicial procedure. The judicial system is administrated by attorneys who are not clinically trained or qualified to make determinations regarding whether or not a defendant was competent at the time of the offense or at the time of the trial. Courts appoint forensic psychologists and psychiatrists to determine whether the defendant was competent at the time of the offense and whether the defendant is competent to stand trial.

If an individual is determined to have been competent at the time of the offense, an insanity defense is not acceptable to the court. If an individual is determined to be competent at the time of the trial, then the court will proceed with the trial. If the individual is determined to be incompetent at the time of the trial and incapable of assisting in his or her own defense, then the defendant is remanded to a psychiatric facility until it is determined that he or she is sufficiently competent to assist in the defense, at which time the trial will commence.

John W. Hinckley, Jr., was found to be incompetent at the time of his attempted assassination of President Ronald Reagan in 1981, and consequently he was acquitted of the charge and remanded to a psychiatric facility until the point in time that he was found to be sane. The Hinckley determination of incompetence initiated a national legislative movement to modify the state statutes pertaining to findings of "not guilty by reason of insanity." As of 2002, most states had modified their laws pertaining to competency, and at least two states have completely abolished the insanity defense.

Appellate courts are inundated with appeals of convictions and sentences by defendants who have been found to be too young, too old, or too intellectually deficient to understand the consequences of their acts. Several states have determined that persons determined to be clinically retarded cannot be executed because of their inability to understand the relationship between their criminal behavior and the consequence of execution, a position affirmed by the U.S. Supreme Court in 2002. Competency is a contemporary criminal justice issue that requires the involvement of forensic psychology.

PREDICTION OF FUTURE CRIMINAL BEHAVIOR

Following the initial utilization of forensic psychology in determinations of competency, the next step was the prediction of future Criminal behaviorrisk assessmentcriminal behavior. Forensic psychologists and psychiatrists have been utilized in the process of making parole decisions as long as parole boards have been determining the early release of inmates.

The length of incarceration for a crime, established in states' criminal codes, is commonly a range of years with a minimum and a maximum. Judges and prosecutors utilize this range of years in plea bargaining and in consideration of mitigating circumstances. Prior to sentencing to a term of incarceration, a pre-sentence investigation is conducted on the convicted defendant. Pre-sentence investigations commonly include psychological evaluations performed by forensic psychologists and psychiatrists. These evaluations contain recommendations for therapeutic interventions and predictions of future criminal behavior.

Similarly, forensic psychologists and psychiatrists conduct evaluations on incarcerated inmates who have met their minimum lengths of sentence. These evaluations are intended to ascertain the effectiveness of the period of incarceration and whether it is safe to release the inmate back to the community. If the evaluator recommends early release, then a list of parole conditions intended to assist in success on parole is commonly attached to the recommendation.

Forensic psychologists have conducted empirical research that has successfully precipitated the development of statistically reliable recidivism prediction instruments that are utilized in sentencing and diversion.

PROFILING UNKNOWN CRIMINAL OFFENDERS

The Federal Bureau of Investigation (FBI) initiated the Violent Criminal Apprehension Program (ViCAP)Violent Criminal Apprehension Program in the mid-1980's with the objective of collecting demographic, personal, and behavioral data on violent offenses and offenders. Profiling Prior to the ViCAP initiative, there was no central depository of data on violent offenses committed in the United States; consequently, it was impossible for law-enforcement agencies to share information. Persons committing violent crimes in different jurisdictions and particularly in different states had the advantage over law-enforcement agencies because of the lack of a central depository. Shortly after the FBI began to serve as the central depository, law-enforcement agencies began to contact ViCAP personnel, asking them to search the database for crimes committed in other jurisdictions that were similar to ones committed in their jurisdictions.

In response to these inquiries, the FBI special agents in charge of ViCAP began to consult with law-enforcement agencies with unsolved violent crimes. These consulting activities resulted in the formal formation of the Behavioral Sciences Unit of the FBI as a consulting agency on unsolved violent crimes. The Behavioral Sciences Unit of the FBI achieved national notoriety with the release of the movie *Silence of the Lambs* (1991), which depicts the FBI's involvement in the identification and apprehension of a serial killer. The psychological aspects of criminal investigation were clearly exposed in this movie, which was the single most significant contribution to society's infatuation with the forensic sciences and particularly forensic psychology.

There is a significant relationship between criminal investigation and psychology. This relationship is easy to understand because criminal behavior is behavior first and criminal second. If one considers that behavior is learned, or precipitated by a stimulus or a motive, then crime can be evaluated like any other behavior. It has been empirically demonstrated that no one variable is directly correlated with criminal behavior, but rather criminal behavior is caused by many variables, and that individuals commit crime because of their unique relationship to the precipitating variables. Consequently, the physical evidence procured at a crime scene provides criminal investigators not only with fingerprints, deoxyribonucleic acid (DNA), and modus operandi but also with clues to the psychological profile of the offender. Individuals afflicted with clinically different personality disorders and mental illnesses may commit the same legally classified crime, but the manner in which they perform the crime will differ and the physical evidence will demonstrate these differences. Persons who commit sexual assaults do so in a fashion that meets their own dysfunctional needs. The characteristics of the victim as well as the manner in which the assault was inflicted are indicative of the perpetrator's psychological disturbances. Analysis of the physical evidence for psychological clues assists criminal investigators in delineating the suspect group.

OTHER FORENSIC PSYCHOLOGY FUNCTIONS

Forensic psychology is utilized in a variety of other functions pertaining to the law. Forensic psychologists conduct interviews and evaluations pertaining to the abuse and neglect of dependent children, adoptions, and domestic violence. Forensic psychologists are also retained by lawyers to assist in the selection of jurors for jury trials, preparation of witnesses, and proper and influential courtroom decorum.

BIBLIOGRAPHY

American Psychiatric Association. *Diagnostic and Statistical Manual of Mental Disorders: DSM-IV-TR*. Rev. 4th ed. Washington, D.C.: Author, 2000. The DSM-IV-TR is the most comprehensive and authoritative description of mental health and personality disorders.

Bartol, Curt R. *Criminal Behavior: A Psychosocial Approach*. 8th ed. Upper Saddle River, N.J.: Pearson, 2008. The author summarizes the theories, concepts, and practices of forensic psychology.

Bartol, Curt R., and Anne M. Bartol, eds. *Current Perspectives in Forensic Psychology and Criminal Behavior*. 2d ed. Los Angeles: Sage Publications, 2008. This resource provides information on criminal behavior, forensic psychology, and psychology and law. It includes commentaries by forensics experts.

Dobbert, Duane, ed. *Forensic Psychology*. Columbus, Ohio: McGraw-Hill Primus, 1996. The editor compiles significant contributions from distinguished authors on a variety of topics pertaining to forensic psychology.

Goode, Erich. *Deviant Behavior*. 8th ed. Upper Saddle River, N.J.: Prentice Hall, 2008. The author provides an excellent description of deviant behavior.

Wrightsman, Lawrence. *Forensic Psychology*. 3d ed. Belmont, Calif.: Wadsworth, 2009. This undergraduate/graduate-level textbook offers a comprehensive discussion of the practice of forensic psychology.

Duane L. Dobbert

SEE ALSO: Abnormality: Legal Models; Confidentiality; Cultural competence; Eyewitness testimony; Incompetency; Insanity defense; Law and psychology; Psychology: Fields of specialization.

Forgetting and forgetfulness

TYPE OF PSYCHOLOGY: Memory

Forgetting is one of the many puzzling aspects of memory, and various theories have tried to explain it in different ways; among the proposed theories are the concepts of memory decay, interference, and purposeful forgetting. One approach describes different types of forgetting as byproducts of otherwise desirable, adaptive features of memory. Although memory is especially important for students and courtroom witnesses, forgetfulness is a particular concern of older adults. At the same time, victims and witnesses of traumatic events might prefer not to remember.

KEY CONCEPTS

- Absentmindedness
- Bias
- Blocking
- Decay
- Encoding
- Interference
- Misattribution
- Persistence
- Purposeful, or intentional, forgetting
- Retrieval
- Suggestibility
- Tip-of-the-tongue phenomenon
- Transience

INTRODUCTION

The mysteries of remembering and forgetting have fascinated humankind for hundreds, even thousands of years. In the late nineteenth century, memory was one of the areas of interest to early psychologists such as Hermann Ebbinghaus and William James. Ebbinghaus conducted an experiment in 1885 in which he tested his own memory, and he then graphed a forgetting curve, which illustrated how much information on a particular list he forgot over time. James wrote about the tip-of-the-tongue phenomenon in 1890, evocatively describing the gap that exists in the place of a name one is trying to recall as "intensely active" and containing the "wraith of the name" beckoning within it.

Though often reliable—and, at times, astoundingly accurate—human memory is fallible. Daniel Schacter, a prominent cognitive psychologist, has referred to this duality as "memory's fragile power." During the twentieth century, scientists who studied artificial intelligence occasionally clashed with neuroscientists on the relative merits of machine-based models of memory. Later, scientists uncovered the deleterious effects of some pharmaceutical compounds on memory, which suggests that drugs may help trauma victims reduce or erase their recollection of events, thereby lowering the risk of posttraumatic stress disorder (PTSD) or facilitating the treatment of PTSD.

Memory's power is evident in what it makes possible in everyday life: a sense of personal history, knowledge of countless facts and subtle concepts, learning and mastery of complex skills, and even personal identity. The fragile side of memory is also quite apparent in both mundane and dramatic ways. Most people struggle to remember the names of others they have just met or of those they have not seen for some time. People forget events rapidly or gradually; even wonderful memories seem to fade in time. The past is distorted with sometimes surprising results that belie strongly held beliefs or deep-seated feelings.

PHYSICAL CAUSES

Research on the causes of memory failure has examined the range of forgetting, from the more normal tip-of-the-tongue phenomenon to total amnesia. Memory loss as a result of brain damage caused by disease and injury has also been the focus of research. Head injuries, for example, can cause difficulties remembering certain information. In cases of brain tumor, in which certain parts of the brain are removed, aspects of memory may be irreparably lost. Alcoholics who drink heavily for many years frequently encounter difficulties remembering; this condition is sometimes termed Wernicke-Korsakoff syndrome. Those who use drugs may also experience memory impairment; actual brain damage may occur in such cases. Strokes or internal injuries can also cause memory loss, as can epilepsy; during an epileptic seizure, oxygen is not getting to the brain, a condition that may result in brain damage and memory loss.

Older people with Alzheimer's disease or other types of dementia have trouble remembering. For years, many believed that the hormonal changes associated with menopause produced memory impairment, but the evidence has not supported this as a causal factor. Aging itself seems to affect memory retrieval in a phenomenon once known as benign senescent forgetfulness, but later referred to as age-associated memory impairment (AAMI). The reasons for this fairly common condition are not completely understood but may include changes in brain physiology and diminished care, concern, or motivation. With the aging of the population, concern over the extent and social cost of Alzheimer's disease has risen. Perhaps as a result, new medications known as cholinesterase inhibitors have been developed and marketed. Although these drugs do not cure or reverse the course of the disease, there is reliable evidence of their capacity to slow its associated declines.

It is not known exactly how people learn or why they remember or forget. Some psychologists posit that the brain's chemical makeup and activity (particularly involving those substances known as neurotransmitters) are central to learning and remembering; others contend that the brain's electrical activity is crucial in determining one's memory. If there is either a chemical or an electrical abnormality in the brain, people may have difficulties in learning or in recalling information and events. With modern methodologies for brain scanning, including such noninvasive procedures as nuclear magnetic resonance (NMRI) spectroscopy, positron emission tomography (PET) scanning, and computed tomography (CT) scanning, researchers may be better able to probe various physiological reasons for forgetting. With functional magnetic resonance imaging (fMRI), it is possible to track changes in brain activity as someone, for example, attempts to remember a past event.

THEORIES OF NORMAL FORGETTING

One theory of forgetting holds that "forgotten" material was never learned in the first place. In other words, the information was never encoded. Another possibility is that such little importance was attached to the material that it was poorly learned—or encoded—and was subsequently forgotten. Sometimes people are overwhelmed by the sheer amount of information they must learn and are simply incapable of remembering the massive amount of material.

Another theory about forgetting suggests that material is never really forgotten; rather, people cannot find the key to retrieve the information from the brain's filing system—its long-term memory. Nearly everyone has experienced the tip-of-the-tongue phenomenon (seeing someone at a party, for example, but being unable to remember the person's name). Sometimes concentration aids memory retrieval; often association helps the process. At the same time, anxiety and depression can interfere with recall. Psychologists have also noted primacy and recency effects regarding memory; that is, people remember what is learned first and what is learned last most efficiently. Material that is presented in the middle tends to be more easily forgotten.

In William James's "booming, buzzing confusion," people frequently are unable to process adequately all the information encountered; forgetting some information is necessary. Moreover, people must often replace existing information with new information, as when a friend or family member relocates and acquires a new address and telephone number. Research on directed forgetting has shown that people are able to deal more effectively with large amounts of information by following instructions to treat some of the information as "to be forgotten." In this way, interference is reduced and people are able to devote all of their resources to the remaining to-be-remembered information.

Other theories of normal forgetting attempt to explain the ways in which various types of interference affect people's ability to remember material. If a student is taking classes at nine, ten, and eleven in the morning, for example, that person may have difficulty remembering material because the information from each of the three classes interferes with that of the other classes; this will be especially true if the subject matter is similar. This same process can affect memories of everything from movies to events in people's own lives. The greater the number of similar films or events (such as dinners in the same type of restaurant) there have been, the more interference there may be. There are two types of interference, retroactive and proactive interference. In proactive interference, occurrences that come before an event or learning situation interfere with the ability to learn or remember; in retroactive interference, the occurrence that interferes with remembering comes after the event or learning situation.

People's mental state, according to many psychologists, has much to do with the ability to learn, retain, and recall information. If people are suffering from depression, grief, or loss, the ability to remember will be severely impaired. Children who are abused often have difficulties learning and remembering because they are preoccupied with the worries and concerns caused by their traumatic home situation. People suffering from depression also may have problems remembering. Counseling or therapy will sometimes alleviate people's emotional concerns and therefore result in better recall. Emotional problems that may be helped in this way include depression, anxiety, and fear of failure.

Psychologists have debated whether information stored in long-term memory is stored there permanently. Some memory theorists believe that a decay or fading factor is at work when people forget information. That is, memory traces naturally fade away and are lost simply because of the passage of time. If a person is a freshman in college, that student may remember many members of his or her high school senior class very well. In another ten years, however, that individual may be less able to remember high school classmates and may have forgotten some of those who were not close friends. In twenty years, more information will fade unless the person actively tries to rehearse or review the people who were in the class. For example, if people took out their high school yearbook every June for twenty years and reminisced about the people in it, they would be better able to recall the names at a twenty-fifth high school reunion.

Some theorists believe that if people can link or associate people, places, or events with other things, they may be able to recall past people or events more effectively. This theory holds that people's minds normally tend to associate one thing with another. These "associationistic" theories are based on the idea that bonds are formed in the brain between places or bits of information. If the bonds are inadequately or poorly formed, then forgetting may occur; bonds must periodically be reformed to guard against forgetting.

The psychoanalytic (or Freudian) perspective on forgetting emphasizes the idea that people "forget" events that are emotionally traumatic. This is motivated, or purposeful, forgetting; the Freudian term for it is "repression." An example would be a woman who, as a six-year-old girl, had been sexually molested by her father or another relative and who has since forgotten the incident. Interestingly, repression has been known to occur in both victims and perpetrators of violent crimes.

FORGETTING AS A BY-PRODUCT OF AN ADAPTIVE SYSTEM

In *The Seven Sins of Memory: How the Mind Forgets and Remembers* (2001), Daniel Schacter presents a framework for classifying the various ways memory fails. He reviews decades of research evidence from social, cognitive, and clinical psychology, as well as later work using imaging methods that make it possible, for example, to observe changes in brain activity as someone retrieves previously learned information. Schacter suggests that like the biblical seven deadly sins—pride, anger, envy, greed, gluttony, lust, and sloth—the seven sins of memory occur frequently in everyday life.

Memory's seven sins are transience, absentmindedness, blocking, misattribution, suggestibility, bias, and persistence. The first three are different types of forgetting. Transience involves decreasing accessibility of information, with recent evidence indicating that forgetting over time is best described mathematically as a power function; that is, the rate of forgetting slows down with the passage of time. Absentmindedness results from inattentive or shallow processing of information that in turn causes weak memories of ongoing events, such as forgetting where one recently placed an object. When absentminded lapses involve forgetting to carry out a planned action at some time in the future, such as picking up the dry cleaning on the way home from work, they are referred to as failures of prospective memory. Blocking refers to the temporary inaccessibility of information that is stored in memory. The tip-of-the-tongue phenomenon is a commonly experienced example of blocking; the incidence of this type of blocking appears to increase with aging.

The next three sins involve distortion or inaccuracy of memory. Misattribution occurs when a person attributes a recollection or idea to the wrong source, such as recalling having read something in the newspaper when, in fact, the person heard it on the radio. Another type of misattribution occurs when people falsely recall or recognize items or events that never happened. Suggestibility refers to memories that are implanted, for example, as a result of leading questions during attempts to elicit recall of past events. This phenomenon is closely related to the controversy concerning false and recovered memories of childhood sexual abuse. Bias occurs when memories of previous experiences are influenced or distorted by current knowledge, beliefs, or expectations, or by present mood and emotional states. A number of studies have identified a consistency bias in retrospection: People's recollections tend to exaggerate the degree of similarity between their past and present feelings, attitudes, or beliefs.

The final sin, persistence, refers to intrusive recollections of traumatic events or obsessional thinking about negative symptoms and events or chronic fears. In other words, these are memories that people wish they could forget but cannot. Just as current feelings can distort recollections of past events or emotions, they can also increase the likelihood of persistence; for instance, memories whose affective tone matches a person's current mood are more accessible.

Schacter asserts that it is wrong to view the seven sins as flaws in the design of the human memory system. Rather, they should be thought of as by-products of what he calls "otherwise adaptive features of memory." Consider, for example, what would happen without blocking, the sin whereby information is temporarily inaccessible because of some inhibitory process. In a system without blocking, all information that is potentially relevant to what is sought would invariably and rapidly come to mind. The likely result would be massive confusion.

WAYS TO MINIMIZE FORGETTING

Two different types of tests are used to assess memory and learning; one type tests recognition, while the other tests recall. A multiple-choice test assesses the first type of memory, because in this type of test one needs to recognize the correct answer when one sees it. An essay examination tests recall—all the responsibility is on the learner to recall as much relevant information as possible.

Research on memory and forgetting can be applied in both academic and nonacademic settings. There are a number of things people can do to aid learning and protect against forgetting. Overlearning is one tactic that ensures that people have learned material and will remember it later. In this technique, students repeat the material by rehearsing it in their head to ensure later recall. If they need to learn a formula, they may repeat it over and over—perhaps writing it a hundred times. This can be tedious, which undoubtedly spurred the search for other options to learn and remember more effectively. Constant review is another strategy. In spaced practice, students study materials to be learned for one hour each night before the test. These students seem to remember the material better than those who spend eight hours studying the material the night before the test. (That type of study—"cramming"—is called massed practice.) For some students, cramming does work, but the material is easily forgotten immediately after the cramming session. Cramming also creates anxiety and fatigue, which may interfere with optimal performance. Some students with poor organizational skills need to expend extra effort to organize the material they have learned. They may employ index cards, for example, to help group and link relevant materials. Mnemonics are memory tricks or devices that help people recall information. The rhyme that begins "Thirty days have September, April, June, and November," for example, helps people remember the number of days in each month. The word "homes" is frequently used as an acronym for the names of the Great Lakes: Huron, Ontario, Michigan, Erie, and Superior.

Note taking is one way to minimize forgetting; reviewing notes can help people prepare for an examination. For this to be most effective, however, people must be able to discriminate between useful and unimportant information at the time of writing the material down. The same holds true for underlining or highlighting material in books or notes. Recording lectures for later review is particularly useful in cases in which a lecturer speaks very rapidly, making effective note taking difficult.

Concentration is an important part of learning and remembering, and people often do not spend enough time concentrating intensely. It has been said that thirty minutes of concentrated, uninterrupted study is better than two hours of haphazard study. The minimizing of outside stimuli is also important; people should study in a quiet place with few distractions. Studying in the same place (and at the same time) every night is also thought to be important for optimal results. Learning should be active to minimize forgetting. Making decisions regarding material to be learned is a useful tool for facilitating learning; students may ask themselves questions about topics or subjects to learn or review. Students should be prompted to think about their own learning styles and to allot the necessary time to learn a given amount of material. Many people have their own preferred learning style. Some people learn better by seeing data and information; others assimilate information better by hearing it. Ideally, students should find and maximize their preferred mode. There are tests designed to determine a person's preferred mode of learning.

If people are trying to assimilate too much information in too short a time, they may experience information overload. Students taking summer classes in which a semester's worth of information is compressed into a few weeks experience this overload, as may those taking eighteen or more hours of classes in a semester. Overload may also affect someone beginning a new job that involves mastering a large amount of information or technical material. Material that is meaningful to the learner has been found to be easier to remember and recall.

FORGETTING IN THE COURTROOM

Forgetting is especially problematic when eyewitnesses are required to testify in courtroom settings. Some argue that given extensive trial preparation, the likelihood of false memories being implanted or the corruption of recall is significant. This has been a concern when prosecution is delayed, as in holocaust and war crimes. The seven sins of memory have particular relevance in this setting and have been helpful to forensic psychologists seeking to enhance the accuracy of courtroom testimony.

BIBLIOGRAPHY

Alexandrov, Arseni K., and Lazar M. Fedoseev. *Long-Term Memory: Mechanism, Types, and Disorders.* New York: Nova Science, 2012. Print.

Bjork, Elizabeth Ligon, and Robert A. Bjork, eds. *Memory.* 2nd ed. San Diego: Academic P, 1998. Print.

Brainerd, C. *The Science of False Memory.* New York: Oxford UP, 2005. Print.

Byster, Mike. *The Power of Forgetting: Six Essential Skills to Clear Out Brain Clutter and Become the Sharpest, Smartest You.* New York: Random House, 2014. Print

Golding, Jonathan M., and Colin M. MacLeod, eds. *Intentional Forgetting.* Mahwah: Lawrence Erlbaum, 1997. Print.

Naveh-Benjamin, Moshe, and Nobuo Ohta. *Memory and Aging: Current Issues and Future Directions.* New York: Psychology P, 2012. Print.

Schacter, Daniel L. *The Seven Sins of Memory: How the Mind Forgets and Remembers.* Boston: Houghton Mifflin, 2001. Print.

Thompson, Charles P., et al., eds. *Autobiographical Memory: Theoretical and Applied Perspectives.* Mahwah: Lawrence Erlbaum, 1997. Print.

Thompson, Charles P., et al., eds. *Eyewitness Memory: Theoretical and Applied Perspectives.* Mahwah: Lawrence Erlbaum, 1997. Print.

Michael F. Shaughnessy; updated by Allyson Washburn

See Also: Alzheimer's disease; Aphasias; Brain damage; Brain structure; Encoding; Long-term memory; Memory; Memory: Animal research; Memory: Empirical studies; Memory: Physiology; Memory: Sensory; Memory storage; Short-term memory.

Forgiveness

Date: 1980's forward

Type of psychology: Emotion; Motivation; Personality; Psychotherapy; Social psychology

Forgiveness theory is a fairly new social psychology term, so much so that even its definition is still a matter of issue in the psychological community. Although most research supports the fact that a forgiving nature leads to a better quality of life, academicians and clinicians argue about the overall value of forgiveness, as well as its potentially negative effects.

Key Concepts

- Apology
- Dispositional forgiveness
- Interpersonal relationships
- Religiosity
- Victimization

INTRODUCTION

Perhaps the most prevalent issue in forgiveness research is the definition of the concept itself. Everett L. Worthington, Jr., observed that there seems to be a scholarly consensus on what forgiveness is not, yet researchers are nowhere near an agreement on exactly what constitutes forgiveness. The *de facto* consensus is that the verb "forgiving" is not synonymous with the verbs "pardoning," "condoning," "excusing," "forgetting," "denying," or "reconciling," although these actions may result; nonetheless, some of the literature reflects the reality that clinicians are well aware of the possibility that any focus on forgiveness, even for personal or spiritual growth, may unintentionally translate as pardoning or as condoning, regardless of attempts to distinguish between these motivations, as with situations of domestic violence, where fear of losing a relationship may play a role.

Michael E. McCullough, Kenneth I. Pargament, and Carl E. Thoresen raise interesting questions about the relationship between forgiveness and the idea of apology, identifying elements common to theorists' diverse definitions. These common elements include the idea of an interpersonal context and an action that may lead to prosocial change toward a perceived transgressor. In addition, McCullough and his associates posit that forgiveness must be viewed through the lens of a specific context. Similar to the discourse used with the concept of apology, forgiveness theory uses the terms "injury," "wrongdoer," "transgressor," "offender," "injured party," and "victim." Because forgiveness can occur in the absence of reconciliation (with the wrongdoer), it is viewed primarily as an intrapersonal process. In other words, when victims forgive an offender, they have completed the process of internally changing for the better how they view the offender (and possibly the offense), without necessarily reconciling the relationship. By the same token, transgressors can also forgive themselves through an internal process of coming to terms with their role in transgressions.

METHODOLOGIES

Overall, forgiveness can be viewed as being one of two types: Decisional forgiveness has to do with behavioral changes, and emotional forgiveness hinges on a difference in feelings toward the wrongdoer or situation. The literature identifies three responses to transgressions: cognitive, affective, and motivational. Cognitive responses include attributions of blame and ruminative thoughts; affective responses include feelings such as hostility, sadness, or fear; and motivational responses include desires for revenge or avoidance. Traditionally, definitions of forgiveness have hinged on whether the process involved only a reduction in the victim's experiences or whether it also led to a corresponding movement toward a positive experience toward the offender. In other words, definitions of the concept emphasize either the reduction of negative emotions, motivations, behaviors, and cognition, or both a reduction and a resulting tendency toward amelioration of the offender. Both schools of thought agree that forgiveness occurs within an individual, and most theorists agree that people who forgive are emotionally and physically healthier. Forgiveness myths include the belief that forgiving is the same as condoning, that forgiving solves all problems and does not involve lamenting, and that forgiveness is an isolated moment in time rather than a process.

HISTORY

According to McCullough, forgiveness theory is a fairly new field in the social sciences. The concept itself was never mentioned by Sigmund Freud, and left untouched by most other great psychologists, perhaps because of its usual association with religion and spirituality. In the social sciences, the beginnings of forgiveness theory can be traced to the 1930s and 1940s, with Jean Piaget, among others, sometimes examining its significance. The 1950s saw a movement toward forgiveness as being part of religiosity, as pastoral counselors theorized that forgiveness could be an important antidote to pathology. In the 1960s, James G. Emerson posited a relationship between forgiveness and well-being and developed a crude measuring method that was loosely related to the Rokeach Value Survey. Articles on forgiveness began to appear in trade books, such as Lewis B. Smedes's *Forgive and Forget: Healing the Hurts We Don't Deserve* (1984) and in clinical journals during the 1980s and 1990s, and eventual strategies for using forgiveness in counseling and psychotherapy became popular in the latter decade. There is some argument that the University of Wisconsin-Madison's Robert Enright, founder of the International Forgiveness Institute, should be credited with calling attention to forgiveness as an important psychological concept.

INTERPERSONAL VERSUS INTRAPERSONAL FORGIVENESS

Forgiveness has been conceptualized as both an interpersonal process and an intrapersonal process. Interpersonal models that incorporate forgiveness focus on an expression of forgiveness toward the offender and can include models based on reconciliation, evolutionary processes, and the interdependence theory. Intrapersonal models include decision-based and cognitive models, in which case the process emphasizes cognition, affect, and behavior. Other possibilities include emotion-focused models, change-over-time measures, attributional models, and stress and coping models. Regardless of which model is used, the question of how to measure forgiveness continues to vex theorists, because most forgiveness ratings will suffer from rater biases since many measurements are based on self-ratings. In addition, rating systems must take into account the roles of culture, geography, ethnography, and age because these factors have been shown to influence and even determine forgiveness beliefs and practices. Various measurement constructs are being examined, such as offense-related scales, dyadic or tendency (toward forgiveness) measures, and dispositional measures. Each of these takes into account self-reporting, partner reporting, observer reporting, and behavioral methods of measuring.

CONTROVERSIES

According to psychiatry professor Karl Tomm, one of the big problems with forgiveness-based therapy is that counselors find it easier to work with victims; wrongdoers, in fact, are unlikely to seek help of their own volition. In cases in which the wrongdoer is forced into therapy, the person is likely to act defensively. In couples therapy, the need for forgiveness is sometimes viewed as the underlying problem, and it then becomes the focus of therapy. Most models of forgiveness involve structured psychoeducational methods for use with groups, and their aim is to facilitate forgiveness independently of responsibility, apology, or atonement. In these cases the focus is on dealing with the problem by letting go of the desire for vengeance and the recollections of wrongdoing. In such interventions, forgiveness is considered a therapeutic goal. Other aspects of the forgiveness process, such as identifying responsibility, receiving an apology from the transgressor, and reaching a level of atonement, may come to be viewed as unnecessary steps in the process. This does not mean that the transgressor's responsibility is ignored; it is simply de-emphasized. Some theorists argue against this de-emphasis and state that it undermines the wrongdoer's responsibility and may give the message to victims that they should again trust the transgressor. In other words, therapy that emphasizes forgiveness alone defeats the idea of accountability.

USES AND LIMITATIONS IN FAMILY THERAPY

Although these models assume that forgiveness is healthy and a worthwhile goal of intervention, there are exceptions such as in family therapy literature concerned with abuse and trauma. Here the emphasis is on protecting the victims and not expecting the victims to forgive. The focus in not on the offenders' accountability. Authors who focus on child abuse or domestic violence are more likely to emphasize such responsibility. Forgiving is also considered questionable when there is a likelihood of further transgressions, as in interpersonal environments characterized by hostility and mistrust. Therefore, encouraging someone to forgive a wrong without an assessment of the relationship may be inviting further injury. Another limitation with this type of therapy is that victims who are unable to forgive (despite undergoing the processes) may judge themselves lacking, which may then perhaps lead to feelings of self-blame that compound the original transgression. A number of studies have elaborated on the forgiveness process in relation to extramarital affairs, particularly using the decision-based forgiveness treatment approach, while other couple-based studies focus on apology (and forgiveness/reconciliation) as a method of overcoming insult, devaluation, irreconcilability, and emotional distancing. One of the claims of current forgiveness theory is that the ability, and perhaps even the propensity, to forgive is integral to an individual's health and well-being. Some theorists view the act of forgiving, especially when combined with a sincere eschewal of resentment, as indicative of a more enlightened and desirable personality, particularly if the alternative is the polar opposite: holding grudges and carrying unresolved anger. Discussions of forgiveness imply that the ability or willingness of a victim to forgive is a salient personality characteristic; often this tendency is portrayed as a virtue or as a positive personality trait.

RESEARCH

The idea that one can be predisposed to forgive has piqued the curiosity of forgiveness researchers. Some have examined the neuropsychological possibilities, positing that forgiveness may be tied to three factors: a victim's sense of self, perception of beneficence or injury, and ability to recollect the cause-and-effect behavior by the perpetrator. Forgiveness research on nonhuman primates indicates that there may be a neurological function at play, as studies have found that feelings of reconciliation and consolation occur among various primates and that reconciliation aims to restore the most valuable tribal relationships. In family therapy literature, there has been increasing interest in the area of forgiveness and apology. Family therapists use face-to-face interaction in what is called a forgiveness intervention. In this planned session, family members (after each meets privately with the therapist) admit whatever wrongdoings they have committed and do so with the understanding that they will seek and give forgiveness to others. Contextual family therapy addresses issues such as intergenerational problems and violations of trust and emphasizes forgiveness as a significant component of healing. Some therapy methods encourage the wrongdoer to validate the victim's experience, acknowledge the transgression, and offer restitution or compensation. As with most forgiveness therapy, the onus is placed on the injured party to acknowledge efforts on the part of the wrongdoer.

To date, forgiveness researchers have tended to examine responses to wrongs that people have experienced directly, what might be called firsthand forgiveness. Ryan P. Brown, Michael J. A. Wohl, and Julie Juola Exline, by studying Americans' reactions to the September 11, 2001, terrorist attacks, examine the experience of forgiveness among people who have not been wronged directly. Secondhand forgiveness research looks at indirect victims who experience antipathy toward offenders, leading to a dynamic similar to that experienced by firsthand victims. In secondhand forgiveness, social identification is important, and the effects of apologies are moderated by the level of identification with the wronged group.

Another recent trend in forgiveness theory is the exploration of the extent to which religious belief and being forgiving are related, which is a notion referred to as the religiosity-forgiveness link. Such research examines both specific and dispositional forgiveness measures (dispositional forgiveness, also referred to as forgiveness dispositions, refers to the stable tendency to forgive transgressions across time and situations). Because dispositional forgiveness is associated with a number of long-term mental and physical health benefits such as less psychological distress and greater life satisfaction, theorists view the concept as worthy of further investigation. The literature discusses three types of forgiveness dispositions: attitudinal, behavioral, and projective forgiveness. Respectively, these refer to general attitudes toward forgiveness, the tendency to forgive transgressions, and the likelihood of forgiving in the future. Theorists interested in forgiveness have at their disposal a vast array of literature.

BIBLIOGRAPHY

Alford, C. Fred. *Trauma and Forgiveness: Consequences and Communities*. New York: Oxford UP, 2013. Print.

Brown, Ryan P., Michael J. A. Wohl, and Julie Juola Exline. "Taking Up Offenses: Secondhand Forgiveness and Group Identification." *Personality and Social Psychology Bulletin* 34.10 (2008): 1406–19. Print.

Enright, Robert D. *Forgiveness Is a Choice: A Step-by-Step Process for Resolving Anger and Restoring Hope*. Washington: American Psychological Association, 2006. Print.

Holmgren, Margaret R. *Forgiveness and Retribution: Responding to Wrongdoing*. New York: Cambridge UP, 2012. Print.

McCullough, Michael E., Kenneth I. Pargament, and Carl E. Thoresen. *Forgiveness: Theory, Research, and Practice*. New York: Guilford, 2001. Print.

Pettigrove, Glen. *Forgiveness and Love*. Oxford: Oxford UP, 2012. Print.

Smedes, Lewis B. *The Art of Forgiving: When You Need to Forgive and Don't Know How*. New York: Ballantine, 1997. Print.

Worthington, Everett L., Jr., ed. *Handbook of Forgiveness*. New York: Routledge, 2005. Print.

Anthony J. Fonseca

Also: Attitude formation and change; Child abuse; Domestic violence; Piaget, Jean; Religion and psychology; Religiosity: Measurement; Spirituality and mental health.

Freud, Anna

Born: December 3, 1895, in Vienna, Austria
Died: October 9, 1982, in London, England
Identity: Jewish Austrian psychoanalyst and child psychologist
Type of psychology: Developmental psychology; psychological methodologies

Freud was the founder of child psychoanalysis and a contributor to the development of ego psychology.

Anna Freud was born in Vienna, Austria, daughter of Sigmund Freud, the founder of psychoanalysis, and the only one of his six children to follow in his footsteps. She learned psychoanalysis from her father and in turn helped him to develop many of his theories, including those on repression and other defense mechanisms. Anna Freud was a gifted teacher, a skill she later put to use to further the interests of psychoanalysis.

Despite being plagued by ill health, Anna Freud maintained a rigorous work schedule and a lively interest in many topics. Her teaching work and volunteer work with Jewish children orphaned or homeless due to World War I nurtured her interest in child psychology and development. Around this same period, 1918-1922, her father psychoanalyzed her, and in 1922 she became a member of the International Psychoanalytic Congress. In 1925, she became a member of the executive board of the Vienna Psychoanalytic Institute. In the same year, she began a career as a training analyst and assumed control of the psychoanalytic publication Verlag.

In her first book, *Einführung in die Technik der Kinderanalyse* (1927; *Introduction to the Technique of Child Analysis*, 1928), she brought together her ideas on the new field of child psychoanalysis, later applying these ideas in her teaching. Her techniques with children differed from those of her father with adults, and Sigmund Freud delighted in her initiative even when she refuted his findings in the case of "Little Hans." Her book *Einführung in die Psychoanalyse für Pädagogen* (1929; *Psychoanalysis for Teachers and Parents*, 1935) demonstrated her continued desire to move psychoanalysis to the forefront in the care of working-class people and away from its elite concerns. She became increasingly involved in the upheaval of Europe's financial decline and the rise of dictator Adolf Hitler, running the Vienna Psychoanalytic Association and aiding those seeking refuge from Hitler's Germany. She found time to write *Ich und die Abwehrmechanismen* (1936; *The Ego and Mechanisms of Defense*, 1946), moving her child psychology into the study of adolescence and arguing that the id, ego, and superego each deserve equal attention in the study of human development. Fleeing Nazis in 1938, she accompanied her father to England. After Sigmund Freud's death in 1939, Anna Freud's own contribution to psychoanalysis became clearer. In 1947, for example, she and a friend, Kate Fridländer, established the Hampstead Child Therapy Courses. In 1952, they added a children's clinic. Additionally, Anna Freud published a number of books in which she contributed to the study of child and ego psychology.

Anna Freud became a British subject; she received the Order of the British Empire in 1967, adding it to her long list of honors, including an honorary doctorate from Clark University in Massachusetts. She often visited the United States, teaching in various places, including Yale Law School, where she collaborated with Joseph Goldstein and Albert Solnit on *Beyond the Best Interests of the Child* (1973). Her collected works were published between 1968 and 1983. She died in 1982 in London, and in 1986 her home became the Freud Museum.

BIBLIOGRAPHY

Dreher, Anna Ursula. *Foundations for Conceptual Research in Psychoanalysis.* Reprint. Madison, Conn.: International Universities Press, 2000. The contributions of Anna Freud to the field of psychoanalysis are placed in the context of the field's overall development.

Peters, Uwe Henrik. *Anna Freud: A Life Dedicated to Children.* New York: Schocken Books, 1984. A biography that focuses on what Anna Freud considered the essence of her life's work.

Young-Bruehl, Elisabeth. *Anna Freud: A Biography.* 2d ed. New Haven, Conn.: Yale University Press, 2008. An overall view of a remarkable life.

Frank A. Salamone

See also: Defense mechanisms; Ego defense mechanisms; Ego, superego, and id; Freud, Sigmund; Freudian psychology; Play therapy; Psychotherapy: Children.

Freud, Sigmund

Born: May 6, 1856, in Freiberg, Moravia, Austrian Empire (now Příbor, Czech Republic)
Died: September 23, 1939, in London, England
Identity: Jewish Austrian psychoanalyst
Type of psychology: Personality; Psychotherapy

Freud was a pioneer in psychoanalytic theory and therapy.

Sigmund Freud was born in Freiberg, a small town in Moravia, which is now part of the Czech Republic. His family moved to Vienna when he was four years old, and he lived there for most of his life. When he entered the University of Vienna at the age of seventeen, his initial interest was the study of law. After deciding to become a medical student, he earned his degree as a doctor of medicine in 1881. During his medical studies, Freud was most influenced by Ernest Brucke, a noted physiologist who viewed humans as being controlled by dynamic physiological forces.

Freud's initial work was in theory and research in the field of neurology. For financial reasons, he soon left the physiological laboratory and began a private practice. In 1886 he married Martha Bernays and had six children within a period of nine years. Just prior to his marriage, Freud spent about six months with Jean-Martin Charcot, a famous French neurologist, who was treating neurotic patients with hypnosis, and began his specialization in nervous disorders and therapeutic treatment.

In the 1890's, Freud tried several techniques for the treatment of nervous disorders, including hypnosis, concentration techniques, catharsis (releasing emotions by talking), and free association (saying whatever comes to mind without censorship). He coined the term "psychoanalysis" in 1896. Although Freud had been rooted thoroughly in physiological interpretations of mental events, he began exploring psychological explanations of human behavior. Freud's work in the late nineteenth century culminated in the completion of one of his key books, *Die Traumdeutung* (1900; *The Interpretation of Dreams*, 1913), explaining his theory of the mind and dream Freudian psychology analysis.

During the next twenty years, Freud published extensively, writing about such varied subjects as sexuality, jokes, religion, creativity, and psychoanalytic techniques. His increasing fame led to an invitation in 1909, from G. Stanley Hall, to give a series of lectures at Clark University. His increased recognition also brought ridicule and forceful criticism.

World War I served to darken his view of human nature. He expressed his changing views by writing of the significance of aggression and the death instinct (a wish to die) in *Jenseits des Lustprinzips* (1920; *Beyond the Pleasure Principle*, 1922). Freud continued to write and revise his ideas throughout the 1920's and 1930's. He was persecuted as a Jew by the Nazis and in 1938 was persuaded to leave Vienna for England. Freud had been quite ill from cancer of the jaw and mouth, enduring much pain from his illness, which required thirty-three operations. Freud died in London on September 23, 1939, at the age of eighty-three.

BIBLIOGRAPHY

Bettelheim, Bruno. *Freud and Man's Soul.* New York: Vintage Books, 1984. Succinctly outlines Freud's key concepts and carefully examines translation issues influencing a proper understanding of Freud's ideas.

Edmundson, Mark. *The Death of Sigmund Freud: The Legacy of His Last Days.* New York: Bloomsbury USA, 2008. This resource focuses on the last years of Freud's life, which occurred at the same time as the rise of Adolf Hitler. The writer shows how these two dramatic lives intertwined, especially in Freud's provocative book Moses and Monotheism (1939).

Freud, Sigmund. *An Autobiographical Study*. New York: W. W. Norton, 1963. Freud writes about his life and psychoanalytic concepts.

Gay, Peter. *Freud: A Life for Our Time.* 1988. Reprint. New York: W. W. Norton, 2006. Comprehensive study of Freud's life. Includes a bibliographical essay.

Jones, Ernest. *The Life and Work of Sigmund Freud.* New York: Basic Books, 1981. Biographical analysis detailing Freud's life experiences and their relevance to his ideas.

Joanne Hedgespeth

See Also: Breuer, Josef; Dreams; Ego, superego, and id; Freud, Anna; Freudian psychology; Hypnosis; Hypochondriasis, conversion, and somatization; Hysteria; Oedipus complex; Penis envy; Personality theory; Psychoanalysis; Psychoanalytic psychology; Psychoanalytic psychology and personality: Sigmund Freud; Psychosexual development; Psychosomatic disorders; Women's psychology: Sigmund Freud.

Freudian psychology

Date: 1900 forward

Type of psychology: Personality; Psychopathology; Psychotherapy

Freudian psychology maintains that each individual experiences painful inner conflicts between impulses (id) and internalized ideals (superego) that the conscious self (ego) tries to keep out of awareness by using defense mechanisms that distort reality. Psychoanalytic therapy helps the patient gain insight into these unconscious conflicts. Such Freudian emphases as childhood attachments, intrapsychic conflict, and unconscious processes continue to be important in psychology.

Key concepts

- Attachment
- Cognitive unconscious
- Ego
- Id
- Intrapsychic conflict
- Mechanisms of defense
- Oedipal conflict
- Psychoanalytic therapy
- Superego
- Unconscious

INTRODUCTION

Freudian psychology refers to the psychological system that was developed by Austrian neurologist Sigmund Freud between 1900 and 1939 and continues to be used by psychoanalysts who look to the Freudian tradition. Basically, Freudian psychology holds that personality results from the clash between instinctual drives such as sex and aggression (the id) and internalized self-imposed controls (superego). These conflicting motives may be unconscious, and they are transformed through the stages of childhood experience. Such unconscious intrapsychic conflicts, unresolved in childhood, can result in painful anxiety. The conscious self (ego) temporarily tries to reduce this anxiety by using defense mechanisms, misconstruing the situation in a way that keeps the conflict out of conscious awareness. This sequence can be understood by first looking at Freud's ideas about personality structure, the system of motives within a person. Second, the Freudian view of dynamics, the adjustments that occur when an individual deals with stress, must be examined. According to Freud, both structure and dynamics are much influenced by childhood experiences.

PERSONALITY STRUCTURE AND DYNAMICS

Freud divided the structure of personality into three parts: the ego, the id, and the superego. The ego, or conscious self, is what people recognize as themselves and would describe to others. It is the consciousness that people know and can summon to mind to see events realistically and solve problems logically. The id and the superego are mostly unconscious in the sense that people are unaware of their contents. The id is the locus of instincts, such as sex and aggression, which demand immediate and total release. In its rawest form, the id is entirely unconscious. Socialized residues of these impulses arise into consciousness in a modified form, allowing them to be expressed appropriately. The superego consists of the moralistic ideals and restraints of conscience that are internalized from parental figures during maturation. Pressures from the superego can block spontaneous impulses in an arbitrary way. The individual may feel pressure from unrealistic ideals or be afflicted with irrational guilt. In a well-adjusted adult, the ego should be sufficiently strong to counter irrational superego and id pressures and to permit realistic decisions. When functioning is optimal, both id impulses ("I want sex now") and superego restraints ("Sexual thoughts are naughty") may never become conscious. An ego dominated, socially acceptable compromise usually prevails ("Let's get together for dinner tonight").

Conflicts that persist can lead to anxiety, a painful state of physiological arousal that feels similar to fear. To Freud, anxiety is unlike fear because it lacks an object. The anxious person does not know the reason for the anxiety because the conflict is unconscious. The individual may try to keep the conflict unconscious or defend the ego by the use of defense mechanisms. These are ways of interpreting events that allow the person to deny the unacceptable impulse or conflict. One important defense mechanism is repression, simply keeping the conflict out of awareness. To help keep the conflict out of awareness, more complicated strategies may be used. One such strategy is reaction formation, or acting in a direction that is the opposite of the disowned feeling. Denied sexual feelings, for example, may be reacted against by joining a religious order demanding celibacy. Alternatively, the conflict may be handled by projection, or attributing the unacceptable feeling and blame to another. An individual might project sexual interest by thinking "This person is trying to seduce me." Any pointless behavior that emerges as the result of an inner conflict may also be rationalized by giving a seemingly sensible reason for an irrational behavior. Such defense mechanisms temporarily reduce anxiety but at the price of distorting perception and keeping people from dealing with a persisting conflict.

NEUROSIS AND ITS ORIGINS

Everyone is vulnerable to anxiety, as conflict is inevitable. The most persistent conflicts, however, are those that replay the unresolved conflicts of childhood. Freud saw development as occurring in a series of stages, each defined by the part of the body yielding sensual (psychosexual) pleasure. In the oral stage, the nursing infant is totally dependent on a mothering person for security. In the anal stage, the toddler being toilet trained first experiences the demands of others and explores independence from their control. In the phallic stage, the three- or fouryear- old first experiences pleasure from the genitals. Freud paid great attention to the conflicts of the phallic stage. He concluded that the child's emerging genital sensitivity became linked to an eroticized love for the opposite-sex parent, jealousy of the samesex parent, and fears of retaliation from the same-sex parent. This Oedipal conflict is resolved only, Freud speculated, by the process of identifying with the same-sex parent, imagining oneself as that parent, and thereby incorporating the ideals of the parent and of the culture. According to Freud, the child also acquires appropriate gender-related behavior through identification with the same-sex parent.

Freud theorized that neurosis occurs when a person becomes arrested in one of these immature stages. A neurotic man might, for example, seek to relive Oedipal fantasies by seeking out a mother-like mate. Neurosis develops when an adult faces a toostrong impulse or conscience and a too-weak ego. Vulnerable to continual conflict and anxiety, as well as defense mechanisms that distort the real situation, neurotics suffer further complications in their lives. Neurotics can gain insight into these unconscious conflicts through psychoanalytic therapy. A truly well-integrated person, in contrast, is one who works through developmental crises successfully and can perceive the real world accurately, unimpeded by childish conflicts and the consequent anxiety.

ORIGIN AND HISTORY

Although such concepts as unconscious conflicts and human instincts had been suggested by earlier writers, Freudian psychology—as a theory applied to the dynamics and treatment of emotional disturbance— came from the observations and speculation of one man, Sigmund Freud. Freud began an innovative treatment program by applying hypnosis (a technique of using powerful suggestion to create disconnected states of mind) to patients who experienced severe physical distress without signs of concomitant physical disease. He had some success in getting patients to talk about deep and forbidden subjects. He soon learned that it was not hypnosis alone but talking about painful memories that helped the patient. He found that the release of painful memories could be facilitated in other ways, including eliciting spontaneous associations, paying attention to seemingly accidental behavior, and discussing the dreams of his patients. Freud was struck by how often such dreams involved sexual themes, with recurring accounts of the seduction of the patient in childhood by the child's opposite-sex parent, a theme he summarized as the Oedipus complex. By the time Freud wrote *Die Traumdeutung* (1900; The *Interpretation of Dreams*, 1913), much of psychoanalysis was already in place: the significance of the unconscious, the power of sexual energy (the libido), the pervasiveness of the Oedipal complex, and psychoanalytic techniques of exploring the unconscious.

Freud's early writings were sometimes denounced as bizarre or immoral. Nevertheless, he began attracting physician followers, formed a local analytic society, and was invited to address eminent American psychologists at Clark University in 1909. His ideas gradually became respectable.

At the same time, professional criticism arose among the ranks of his psychoanalytic followers, who questioned the basis of his theory. Critics of Freud within the psychoanalytic community especially objected to the emphasis Freud placed on the libido, or sexual energy. Austrian psychoanalyst Alfred Adler, once one of Freud's followers, viewed the basic source of internal conflict as compensation for inferiority rather than libido; Austrian psychoanalyst Otto Rank viewed as fundamental the struggle between the fear of independence and separation from stable relationships (the life fear) and the fear of losing one's independence in relationships (the death fear). Freud argued that the analyses of these critics were superficial.

In his later writings, Freud broadened his concept of instincts to include that of destructive aggression, which he termed the "death instinct," and revised his concept of libido as a more general "life instinct." He also extended the implications of psychoanalysis to human society, which he saw as forever doomed by the unstable repression of the impulses of sex and blind aggression.

After World War II, psychoanalysis reached a new pinnacle in the number and enthusiasm of followers in the United States. Many psychoanalysts who had fled Nazi Germany came to America. American psychiatrists sought psychoanalytic training as never before. Some of these psychoanalysts accepted the writings of Freud without question. However, the main stream of Freudian psychology shifted in two ways to expand the Freudian concept of motivation. First, some psychoanalysts reemphasized the ego as itself a source of motivation. They thought that motives related to ego development—such as curiosity and the desire to exercise one's talents—were as ingrained as sex and aggression. A second expansion of the motivation concept was championed by psychoanalysts known as object-relations theorists. By objects, these analysts meant significant relationships. They emphasized the importance of relationships, especially relationships with the significant people of childhood such as mother and father figures. For example, the American psychoanalyst Erik H. Erikson argued that the important feature of the oral stage of early infancy was not the sexual sucking pleasure but rather the existence of consistent, stable, warm mothering that encouraged a basic trust in the benevolence of the world.

Many analysts in the latter part of the twentieth century expanded the Freudian concept of motivation to include both such positive ego motives such as self-development and a built-in desire for relationships. To these analysts, conflicts related to the desire for autonomy as opposed to the desire for close relationships were as basic as those concerning sex or aggression.

A LITTLE PERSPECTIVE

Freud was privy to lengthy, detailed spontaneous ruminations of patients, the like of which had seldom before been heard. He was a brilliant and creative observer. Nevertheless, Freud's concepts, imprecisely stated and obviously subject to possible observer biases, required validation from the experience of other psychotherapists and from the objective methods of experimental science. Several decades of such research since Freud's death offer some perspective on his ideas.

It has become clear that Freud's original motivational theory based on sex and aggression was far too narrow. These motives and their control pose major developmental tasks, but the child's moving from an immature dependent state to a mature interdependent state is even more basic. Almost all observers agree that sexual conflicts, important as they are, were overemphasized by Freud, probably because he observed mostly middle-class female patients in early twentieth century Vienna, where sexual taboos were unusually prevalent. Especially criticized is Freud's concept of penis envy, the suggestion that female jealousy of male privileges is biologically rooted and universal because of female jealousy of the supposedly superior male organ. That unconscious female jealousy of male privileges detected by Freud was culturally rooted in the subordinate social position of women in Vienna in the 1900's. Psychoanalytic descendants of Freud pay explicit attention to issues of affection, dependence, and autonomy, a welcome expansion of Freud's view.

According to one view, Freudian psychoanalysis is a sort of archaeological expedition into the distant past of the patient, and this past is revealed with pristine clarity in recovered memories. The view that accurate, detailed infantile memories are recovered in therapy is based on a theory of memory as a sort of mental photograph album of the past. Most modern memory research suggests an alternative view. This research suggests that memory is a reconstructive process in which fragments of the past are incorporated into present themes influenced by one's present values and concerns. American psychologist Elizabeth F. Loftus demonstrated in experiments that memories of early childhood experiences accepted as valid can actually be implanted by recent suggestions. Memories are notoriously fragmentary and vulnerable to suggestion. Apparent memories of childhood experiences dredged from psychotherapy can reveal ongoing conflicts and concerns, but such memories cannot be trusted to reveal accurate factual information about a person's childhood.

TIME-TESTED CONCEPTS

Major Freudian concepts have endured the test of time and have been validated by research and the experience of practicing psychologists. Specifically, concepts of Freud that continue to inform psychological science include talking therapy, with the goal of attaining insight; continuities between patterns of behavior in childhood and corresponding patterns in adulthood; the importance of inner conflict; the ego's mechanisms of defense; and the unconscious.

Talking therapy, with the goal of attaining insight, has become a major enterprise of psychology. Psychoanalytic therapy is not as popular as it was in the 1950's because of the widespread use of effective pharmacological treatments for mental illness. However, more than ten thousand therapists within the United States still view their major therapeutic approach as psychoanalytic. Multitudes of other therapists who use eclectic approaches borrow on occasion from Freud's uncovering techniques to penetrate defensive postures or to understand at a deeper level the meaning of symptoms. Talking therapy itself began with Freud.

Freud's belief in the importance of the nature and quality of the relationship between the child and the primary caretakers—his hypothesis that stable, warm mothering encourages basic trust in the benevolence of the world—remains viable. If caretakers are rejecting or inconsistent, such trust may never be established. Modern researchers in child psychology explore patterns of attachment between children and caretakers. These researchers find secure and insecure attachment styles continue to influence subsequent relationships even into adulthood, much as Freud predicted.

Inner conflict, to Freud, is both pervasive and important. People can both love and hate the same person. People want the freedom to explore new horizons and grow, yet they also yearn to return to the security of home and stable relationships. Ambivalence is an inevitable part of close human relationships and is an inevitable part of all decisions. From conflict comes anxiety. Studies in the twentieth century and beyond have found that the degree of stress people experience is highly correlated with the abruptness and extent of life transitions. Also correlated with degrees of stress is vulnerability to physical and mental disease. Such research attests to the continuing importance of research based on hypotheses about conflict.

The concept of defense mechanisms is another example of an idea originating in the writings of Freud that has become important in several areas of psychology. Such mechanisms are often listed in general articles on how people deal with stress. In abnormal psychology texts, the thought patterns that define categories of abnormality are described in terms of the exaggerated use of particular defense mechanisms. Paranoia, for example, is viewed as the exaggerated use of projection. Irrational strategies researched by social psychologists as social cognition are highly similar to defense mechanisms. Studies of cognitive dissonance, for example, document instances of people who have made a foolish decision expending a great deal of energy in the pursuit of a mistaken goal, simply to avoid admitting their mistake to themselves. People speak of winning at any cost or throwing good money after bad. Most examples of cognitive dissonance could as well be considered examples of the defense mechanism of rationalization.

The unconscious is another Freudian concept that continues to be important to psychology. Freud's unconscious is a motivated unconscious. Freudian therapists feel that the relief experienced by patients who have achieved insights in therapy validates their theory. Experimental psychologists have explored the unconscious in well-controlled experiments. Several researchers have implanted unconscious motivation by conditioning words, pictures, or phrases to emotional states. It has been shown that these stimuli can later bring back the emotional state without the awareness of the conditioned person. Other psychologists have demonstrated that fantasy productions such as imaginative stories rated for power themes can predict such specified criteria as attention-seeking behavior. Also cognitive psychologists have expanded the range of what they call the cognitive unconscious to include the many skills and procedures that are performed automatically by people who cannot explain the skill to themselves or to others. Beginning in the 1990's, the exploration of areas of thought unavailable to introspective analysis has become a major topic within psychology. The existence of unconscious processes is seldom doubted.

Although not all Freud's ideas have withstood the test of time, psychoanalysis still flourishes. Important ideas first given serious attention by Freud have become part of mainstream psychology. Sad clowns and vulnerable tough guys are common in drama and literature. Most of all, the notion that human life is riddled with conflict, that human passions and hatreds are often irrational, subtle, and unrecognized, has become the prevailing wisdom. This view of human existence was pioneered by Freud.

BIBLIOGRAPHY

Adler, Joseph. "Freud in Our Midst." *Newsweek*, March 27, 2006, 42-49. This article probes the paradox that Freud is frequently maligned, yet such major Freudian themes as "unconscious conflict" are taken for granted in contemporary thought. A convenient glossary of Freudian concepts is included.

Bornstein, Robert F., and Joseph M. Masling, eds. *Empirical Perspectives on the Psychoanalytic Unconscious.* Washington D.C.: American Psychological Association, 1998. This work includes a series of articles on major research within psychology that, it is argued, clearly establishes the existence of unconscious processes.

Epstein, S. "Integration of the Cognitive and Psychodynamic Unconscious." *American Psychologist* 49 (1994): 709-724. Here the unconscious processes explored by cognitive psychology are integrated with the psychoanalytic unconscious into an experiential information processing system contrasted with the conscious rational system.

Freud, Sigmund. *The Interpretation of Dreams*. Translated by Joyce Crick, edited by Ritchie Robertson. New York: Oxford University Press, 2000. Freud herein outlines the major tenets of the theory that became psychoanalysis. Freud considered this his greatest work.

Gay, Peter. *Freud: A Life for Our Time*. 1988. Reprint. New York: W. W. Norton, 2006. An excellent biography of Freud that benefits from access to personal papers and from earlier biographies. Freud's controversial ideas are discussed in the context of his life and personal relationships.

Nye, Robert D. *Three Psychologies: Perspectives from Freud, Skinner, and Rogers*. 6th ed. Pacific Grove, Calif.: Brooks/Cole, 2000. Outlines Freud's basic concepts and includes practical examples, real world applications, and commentaries.

Westen, D. "The Scientific Legacy of Freud: Toward a Psychodynamically Informed Psychological Science." *Psychological Bulletin* 124 (1998): 333-371. A detailed description of those Freudian concepts, such as the unconscious and conflict, that are still important in science and psychotherapy. The author supports his viewpoint by references to research.

Thomas E. DeWolfe

See also: Adler, Alfred; Aggression; Consciousness; Defense mechanisms; Dreams; Drives; Ego defense mechanisms; Ego psychology: Erik H. Erikson; Ego, superego, and id; Erikson, Erik H.; Hypnosis; Jung, Carl; Jungian psychology; Memory; Mother-child relationship; Motivation; Motivation: Intrinsic and extrinsic; Oedipus complex; Penis envy; Personality theory; Psychoanalysis; Psychoanalytic psychology; Psychoanalytic psychology and personality: Sigmund Freud; Psychotherapy: Historical approaches; Repressed memories; Self; Sexual behavior patterns.

Fromm, Erich

Born: March 23, 1900, in Frankfurt am Main, Germany
Died: March 18, 1980, in Muralto, Switzerland
Identity: German American psychoanalyst
Type of psychology: Personality; Psychotherapy

Fromm practiced and taught a social psychoanalysis and a socialist humanistic philosophy.

Erich Fromm was born in 1900, the only child of a middle-class, German, Orthodox Jewish family in Frankfurt, Germany. Influenced by the rabbinical tradition of study and by his readings in the Old Testament and in Karl Marx, coauthor with Friedrich Engels of the *Manifest der Kommunistischen Partei* (1848; *The Communist Manifesto,* 1850), Fromm became a committed socialist humanist. He received a Ph.D. from Heidelberg in 1922, joining the Frankfurt School for Social Research, which sought to integrate history with the ideas of Marx and with Freudian psychoanalysis under the rubric of critical theory. After training in psychology and psychiatry at Munich, he became a psychoanalyst, graduating from the Berlin Psychoanalytic Institute in 1931. In 1934, Fromm emigrated to America, where he, Karen Horney, Harry Stack Sullivan, and Clara Thompson collaborated in creating a psychoanalytic theory and practice that was oriented to social and cultural factors, arousing the ire of the traditional Freudian psychoanalytical associations.

In 1941, Fromm published his most important work, *Escape from Freedom,* which presented a historical explanation of social character development, the idea that the needs and pressures of a particular society require a particular adaptation by the members of a society. Because of the historical changes that have occurred since the medieval period, which include the Protestant revolution and capitalism, the Western person has been freed from the shackles and also the security of that preindividualistic period. The contemporary person who does not find productive love and work defends the self from this freedom by creating character traits that favor authoritarianism or submissiveness, leading to the political choice of fascism. *The Sane Society* (1955) continued this argument and suggested socialistic humanism as a solution to psychological alienation and destructive political options.

Fromm was a prolific and popular writer. Other examples are *The Art of Loving* (1956), which defined love as active caring for the life and growth of the other, and *The Anatomy of Human Destructiveness* (1973), which offers Fromm's humanistic psychoanalysis as a preferred mode of explanation to purely instinctual or environmental approaches.

Through his adult life, Fromm studied and practiced a form of Zen Buddhism and worked for the international peace movement, cofounding the National Committee for a Sane Nuclear Policy (SANE) in 1957. He taught at many institutions in the United States and Mexico, influencing other academics in the arts and sciences with his philosophy. In 1974, he and his third wife made their home in Switzerland, where he died in 1980.

BIBLIOGRAPHY

Evans, Richard I. *Dialogue with Erich Fromm.* New York: Praeger, 1981. A personal interview reveals Fromm's important ideas.

Funk, Rainer. *Erich Fromm: The Courage to Be Human.* New York: Continuum, 2003. A thorough presentation of Fromm's ideas and their early development. Includes a detailed bibliography of Fromm's work and of books written about him.

Landis, Bernard, and Edward S. Tauber, eds. *In the Name of Life: Essays in Honor of Erich Fromm.* New York: Holt, Rinehart and Winston, 1971. A festschrift written by younger and distinguished scholars attesting to Fromm's significance.

Everett J. Delahanty, Jr.

See Also: Horney, Karen; Humanistic psychology; Personality theory; Social psychological models: Erich Fromm; Sullivan, Harry Stack.

Frontotemporal dementia (Pick's Disease)

Type of psychology: Biological bases of human behavior, Clinical, Counseling, Geriatric, Neuropsychology

Also known as lobar sclerosis, circumscribed brain atrophy, focal cerebral atrophy, semantic dementia, and primary progressive aphasia, frontotemporal dementia (FTD) is a brain disease that causes dysregulation and shrinkage of tissue in discrete areas (focal lesions) in the frontal and temporal anterior brain lobes. As these areas shrink, they reduce abilities in verbal reasoning and speech production. Frontotemporal dementia (FTD) is similar to, but much rarer than, Alzheimer's disease. The current designation of the syndrome groups Pick's disease, primary progressive aphasia, and semantic dementia together. Some medical researchers propose adding "corticobasal degeneration" and "progressive supranuclear palsy" to FTD and calling the whole group, the "Pick Complex," but this has yet to gain wide acceptance. The differing terms reflect different theoretical models of what the disease is exactly. Specialists are likely to continue to debate these models.

Key Terms

- Anterior brain lobes
- Autosomal gene
- Frontotemporal lobe

CAUSES

In only 10 to 20 percent of cases is a specific cause even speculated: An autosomal dominant genetic trait. In these cases, there is a family history of someone showing symptoms of a frontal lobe dementia. In 60 to 90 percent of cases, there is no evident family (genetic) history and the cause is unknown. FTD is usually not inherited.

SYMPTOMS

Onset is slow and insidious. Tissues shrink (atrophy) in the frontal and temporal brain lobes. FTD also causes some brain cells to develop abnormal fibers that are called "Pick's bodies." The cells in these bodies have an abnormal amount of a protein called tau. Tau appears throughout the body's cells, but exists in abnormally high amounts in Pick's bodies and in Pick cells that exist inside normal brain cells (neurons). These form elsewhere in the brain and are not limited to the frontotemporal regions. These fibers are generally straight and single as compared to Alzheimer's neurofibrillary tangles that tend to be paired and helical.

Though Pick's disease varies greatly in how it affects individuals, it has a common core or clusters of symptoms. Some or all may be present at different stages of the disease. Since the frontal lobes involve emotional and social functioning, the first notable cluster usually cause behavioral and affective changes like impulsivity, compulsive overeating or only eating one type of food, drinking alcohol to excess (when not a prior problem), rudeness, impatience, aggressiveness, social withdrawal, poor social interaction, inability to hold a job, inattention to personal hygiene, sexual exhibitionism, promiscuity, abrupt mood changes, emotional aloofness, environmental indifference, marked distractibility, decreased interest in daily activities, and being unaware of these changes (lack of insight). Deterioration in personality usually occurs before dementia itself is evident, that is, before there is evident memory deficits and loss in judgment. This is one way specialists diagnose it as distinct from Alzheimer's disease in which the early symptoms primarily involve memory loss.

Changes in physical mobility and coordination (apraxia) can also present as early symptoms. These can include increased muscle rigidity or stiffness, difficulty getting around, worsening coordination, generalized weakness, and urinary incontinence.

Another characteristic cluster relates to worsening language. Speech can be reduced in quality, shrinking vocabulary, word-finding problems, difficulty understanding (receptive aphasia) or producing understandable speech (expressive aphasia), repeating words and phrases others use (echolalia), progressive loss of reading and writing, and possibly complete loss of speech (mutism).

TREATMENT

There are no medications that can effectively treat FTD though there are several that can help treat many of its symptoms. Medications used in Alzheimer's disease are not routinely prescribed because they often increase aggression in FTD patients.

Maximizing quality of life is the key treatment and many of the more disturbing behaviors respond well to medication, including aggression and agitation. In addition to adding medications for symptom control, discontinuation of medications that promote confusion or that are not essential to the care of the person may improve cognitive function. It is common for anticholinergics, analgesics, and central nervous system depressants to be discontinued.

Because many of the functions FTD affects are also affected by low levels of thiamine, thiamine supplementation is often recommended. In addition, good nursing and caregiving, guided occupation activities and participation in support groups all can improve the management of this type of dementia. It is also important that families of FTD patients get support to help them cope with a disease that is likely to have a prolonged, ever-demanding course.

Sensory functions, often overlooked, should be evaluated and augmented as needed: hearing-aids, eye glasses, cataract surgery, and the like.

Behavior modification is often the treatment of choice in controlling unacceptable or dangerous behaviors. Rewarding and reinforcing appropriate, positive behaviors while ignoring inappropriate, negative behaviors (within the bounds of safety), can significantly influence how patients act and interact. Formal psychotherapy is seldom effective because it overloads patients' progressively limited cognitive resources. Reality orientation, with repeated reinforcement of environmental and other cues, can reduce disorientation and agitation. Family counseling and family psychoeducation often goes a long way in fostering adaptive changes that are necessary to care for patients at home.

Visiting nurses or aides, volunteer services, homemakers, adult protective services, and other community resources may be helpful in caring for the person. In some communities, there may be access to support groups (such as the Alzheimer' support group, elder care support group, or others).

Legal advice may be appropriate early in the course of the disorder. Advance directives, power of attorney, health care proxy, and do not resuscitate orders can make dealing with the later stages of the disease easier.

THE FUTURE

Pick's disease affects about 1 out of 100,000 people, accounting for 0.4% to 2% of all cases of dementia. More common in women then men, it typically onsets between ages 40 and 60 with a modal age of 54, but has been known to affect patients as young as 20. A family history of FTD is considered a risk factor though, as noted before, most Pick's patients have no family history of the disease.

The first description of the disease was published in 1892 by Arnold Pick. Until recently it was thought that Pick's disease could not be distinguished from Alzheimer's disease during life. In accordance with major research criteria of German neuropsychiatry, Pick's atrophy was constructed as a full-blown disease entity in the 1920s. This concept gained acceptance in the German and Anglo-American scientific community and was the starting point for further investigations in the 1950s and 1960s.

Initial diagnosis is mostly based on history and symptoms, signs, and tests, and by ruling out other causes of dementia, especially those due to metabolic causes. The development of neuropsychological assessment procedures, use of electroencephalograms (EEGs), computerized tomography (CT scans), magnetic resonance imaging (MRI) techniques are generally necessary in the pre-diagnostic work-up of the disease. Functional brain imaging, such as single-photon emission computed tomography ([SPECT) scans or physiologic imaging with positron emission tomography (PET) scans are often appropriate in some patients.

Patients with FTD or Pick's disease will show a progressive decline. Rapid progressing forms may take two years; slower forms may take ten. The cause of death is often opportunistic infection or, less commonly, the general failure of total body systems.

Recent identification of pathogenic mutations in Alzheimer's disease and frontotemporal dementia has improved understanding of these dementias and is guiding the investigations that use animal and tissue culture models. Eventually, it is hoped that this research will result in developing medications that can treat, stop and reverse these diseases.

BIBLIOGRAPHY

Regrettably, there are no lay-focused readings that are readily accessible even in this internet age. Likely, the relative rarity of the disease contributes to leaving it in the field of professional to professional communication. Of some accessibility for lay readers are these:

Frederick, Justin, "Pick Disease: A Brief Overview," *Archives of Pathology and Laboratory Medicine*, 130 (July 2006): 1063—1066. Just as it's titled, this is a clear abbreviated overview of the disease. It is somewhat technically demanding on the reader as it presumes a basic understanding of neuroanatomy.

Kertesz, Andrew, and David G. Munoz, "Frontotemporal Dementia," *The Medical Clinics of North America*, 86 (2002): 501—518. This series, Medical Clinics, is a continuing education review for health professionals. Nonetheless, the authors provide a guide for what is happening in the field.

Mayo Clinic Staff, "Non-Alzheimer's Forms of Dementia," *In The Mayo Clinic Guide to Alzheimer's Disease: The Essential Resource for Treatment, Coping, and Caregiving,* edited by Ronald Peterson, Rochester, MN: Mayo Clinic, 2002. A user-friendly review for those who have to cope with the presence of the disease in their and their loved-ones' lives.

National Institute of Neurological Disorders and Stroke, "Frontotemporal Dementia," Bethesda, MD: National Institutes of Health, 2006. Admittedly more technical than casual, this National Institute review captures the singular features of this disease and its attendant processes.

Paul Moglia

See Also: Aging; Aphasia; Dementia; Language; Memory; Neuropsychology; Temporal lobe.

G

Gambling

DATE: 2000 forward

TYPE OF PSYCHOLOGY: Psychopathology

Gambling can be a recreational activity, a profession, or a psychopathology. Pathological gambling is an impulse-control disorder that often produces depression and anxiety as secondary conditions and also disrupts marital and family relationships. Psychopharmacological, behavioral, and twelve-step treatments are helpful.

KEY CONCEPTS

- Antisocial personality disorder
- Gamblers Anonymous
- Mania
- Neurotransmitters
- South Oaks Gambling Screen (SOGS)

INTRODUCTION

A gambler is a person who risks something of value based on an uncertain outcome for the possibility of reward: Typically, money is bet in the hope of making more money. Gamblers are classified as recreational, professional, or pathological. Recreational gambling is an enjoyable activity that has no evident adverse effects and may have possible mental-health benefits among certain groups, such as the elderly. A few individuals are professional gamblers, making their living by playing games of chance that involve some level of skill. Pathological gambling has a long history in the psychiatric literature, but it was not defined as a medical problem until 1980, when it was added to the diagnostic nomenclature. It is an impulse-control disorder and tends to lead to increasingly adverse consequences for individuals, their families, and others.

A diagnosis of pathological gambling requires the presence of five out of ten criteria:

1. becoming preoccupied with gambling,
2. exhibiting tolerance and withdrawal,
3. escaping from moods and life's problems,
4. chasing losses with more gambling,
5. lying about gambling,
6. losing control over the reduction of betting,
7. becoming irritable when trying to stop gambling,
8. committing illegal acts to obtain funds,
9. risking interpersonal relationships and vocation to gamble, and
10. seeking bailouts, such as turning to others for financial assistance. Mania must be ruled out when diagnosing pathological gambling.

PREVALENCE, RISK FACTORS, AND THEORIES

Most people who gamble in a given year are recreational gamblers. In the United States, only about 1 percent of adults (2.4 million people in 2012) become pathological gamblers—about the same percentage as are diagnosed with schizophrenia. Another 2 to 3 percent are considered problem gamblers, who experience detrimental consequences as a result of their betting but meet fewer than five of the diagnostic criteria. Slightly higher rates of pathological and problem gambling are found among adolescents.

Risk factors for developing pathological gambling include a parental history of gambling problems, alcohol and tobacco use, and membership in a minority. Males are more likely to be pathological gamblers than females. The most common comorbid conditions with pathological gambling are a personality disorder, which occurs in about half of those diagnosed (antisocial personality disorder is the most frequently found), and substance abuse, which is found in about one-third of pathological gamblers. Whether as a cause or a consequence, anxiety and depressive disorders are often diagnosed as well. When pathological gambling becomes chronic, a major depressive disorder may be present. Pathological gambling invariably affects the spouse and family of the gambler, making marital and family counseling necessary.

Theories explaining the development of pathological gambling are multivariate and address a range of factors, including biological, environmental, and parental. Studies during the first decade of the twenty-first century suggest a biological foundation for pathological gambling. The neurotransmitters serotonin and dopamine are implicated, as are endorphins. For example, some patients treated for Parkinson's disease with a dopamine agonist spontaneously developed urges to gamble and, in some instances, progressed to problem and pathological gambling. The urges remitted with cessation of medication.

Pathological gamblers show impulsivity, an inability to delay gratification, and higher levels of physiological arousal, such as increased heart rate, during gambling activity. There may be fundamental physiological differences in the neurological makeup of people who gamble to excess compared with those who can gamble in moderation.

Also associated with gambling are elaborate contingencies of reinforcement to create and sustain the behavior. The modern casino is a technological wonder designed to produce only one outcome: sustained gambling. In the 1970s, when the American gaming industry discovered that marketing to the middle class could significantly increase the pool of gamblers, industry members sought to increase the number of states in which gambling was legal. Eventually, gambling was legalized in some form in every state except Hawaii and Utah. The availability of gaming opportunities has led to an increase in pathological gamblers, which the industry has addressed with programs promoting responsible gambling. States that introduced lotteries have established programs to educate citizens about the dangers of gambling in excess.

TREATMENT AND PREVENTION

A treatment program for pathological gambling begins with a comprehensive assessment that examines the individual's gambling frequency and duration, the extent of negative consequences, personality type, and psychological context. Common assessment tools include the South Oaks Gambling Screen (SOGS), a general psychiatric symptoms checklist, and careful questioning about substance abuse.

Treatment for pathological gambling can take a variety of forms. One effective method is cognitive behavior therapy, which focuses on changing patterns of thought and cognition related to gambling impulses. Another is Gamblers Anonymous, founded in 1957 and patterned after Alcoholics Anonymous, which provides a free twelve-step program with strong peer support. Daily meetings are held in many cities in the United States, and Gamblers Anonymous offers support and education for spouses, family, and friends of gamblers. Psychopharmacological treatments for gambling—including selective serotonin reuptake inhibitors (SSRIs), opioid antagonists, and mood stabilizers—also have shown some promise.

Many states have websites that guide those who might have a problem with gambling to treatment locations. These sites also provide educational information and self-assessments. The National Council on Problem Gambling also provides educational information. Programs to prevent pathological gambling include state-mandated informational cards and plaques placed in casinos, state-supported television and billboard advertisements warning of the consequences of excessive gambling, and educational curricula designed to enlighten adolescents about the dangers of gambling.

BIBLIOGRAPHY

Ariyabuddhiphongs, Vanchai. "Problem Gambling Prevention: Before, During, and After Measures." *International Journal of Mental Health and Addiction* 11.5 (2013): 568–82. Print.

Brewerton, Timothy D., and Amy Baker Dennis, eds. *Eating Disorders, Addictions and Substance Use Disorders*. Heidelberg: Springer, 2014. Print.

Castellani, Brian. *Pathological Gambling: The Making of a Medical Problem*. Albany: State U of New York P, 2000. Print.

Grant, Jon E., and Mark N. Potenza. *Pathological Gambling: A Clinical Guide to Treatment*. Arlington: Amer. Psychiatric, 2004. Print.

Knapp, Terry J., and Edward W. Crossman. "Pathways to Betting: Childhood, Adolescent, and Underage Gambling." *Gambling: Behavior Theory, Research, and Application*. Ed. Patrick M. Ghezzi et al. Reno: Context, 2006. 207–30. Print.

Koot, S., et al. "Compromised Decision-Making and Increased Gambling Proneness following Dietary Serotonin Depletion in Rats." *Neuropharmacology* 62.4 (2012): 1640–50. Print

Lesieur, Henry R., and Sheila B. Blume. "The South Oaks Gambling Screen (SOGS): A New Instrument for the Identification of Pathological Gamblers." *American Journal of Psychiatry* 144.9 (1987): 1184–89. Print.

Perkinson, Robert R., Arthur E. Jongsma Jr., and Timothy J. Bruce. *The Addiction Treatment Planner.* 5th ed. Hoboken: Wiley, 2014. Print.

Petry, Nancy M. *Pathological Gambling: Etiology, Comorbidity, and Treatment*. Washington: APA, 2004. Print.

Whelan, James P., Timothy A. Steenbergh, and Andrew W. Meyers. *Problem and Pathological Gambling*. Cambridge: Hogrefe, 2007. Print.

Terry J. Knapp

See Also: Addictive personality and behaviors; Alcohol dependence and abuse; Behavior therapy; Cognitive behavior therapy; Games and mental health; Impulse control disorders; Substance use disorders.

Games and mental health

Type of psychology: Cognition; Developmental psychology; Emotion; Intelligence and intelligence testing; Language; Learning; Memory; Motivation; Psychopathology; Psychotherapy; Stress

Play is an essential activity in all phases of human development, and games are an important part of play. Game-related behavior can reflect and facilitate normative development as well as provide important clues to disruptions in development.

Key Concepts

- Addiction
- Identity development
- Intrinsic motivation
- Learning styles
- Moral development
- Play behavior
- Play therapy
- Role play
- Symbolic play

INTRODUCTION

Games are mental and physical activities engaged in for learning, leisure, or other social reasons. They are a recognized type of play behavior, in that they are motivating by virtue of their pleasure. Play is a voluntary activity that is intrinsically motivating, suggesting that it is sustained for its meaning or pleasure. It is a normal part of human development that reflects that development, helps it advance, and provides a window into understanding any developing problems.

Play first evidences in childhood and continues throughout the life cycle. It serves many functions, including simple expression and expressions of individuality. It is also part of cognitive development, problem solving, and creative thinking and can be done with language and behavior or with thinking and imagery. It can be done in solitude or with others. As such, it may affect language, intellectual, social, emotional, motor, or other physical development. Furthermore, because play often has rules, it is related to moral development and can affect abilities to learn, recognize, respond to, obey, circumvent, or transcend rules.

PLAY AND GAMES IN DEVELOPMENT AND HEALING

Play and games are influenced by culture, family patterns, and physical and mental capacities of individuals. First play experiences are typically with parents. Thus, the extent to which parents do or do not interact with their child or have play experiences to draw on affects what the child learns. Different cultures have different games based on their resources and history, a fact that affects the content and amount of play.

As infants progress to early childhood, they engage in symbolic play via activities involving imagined or substituted objects. Symbolic play may be done alone or with a group. As children age, they typically move from solitary to social play. In early social play, children may be in parallel or near to each other without necessarily engaging each other. As development advances, social engagement, such as playing together using imagination, occurs more frequently. For example, a little girl might first pretend to be talking on the phone by talking into a block of wood. Later, the girl and another girl may sit side by side doing the same thing but not talking to each other. Eventually, this will evolve into a conversation between the two through the make-believe phones.

As children age, they typically become involved in formal games such as sports, board games, puzzles, storytelling, and role-playing. Adults play games similar to those played by children but often with more complex rules. Also, games for adults often involve more adult content and behavior, such as use of money, as in gambling or card games, or complex roles, as in multiple role-player and sexual games.

Games as a form of play serve many purposes and shift in form and function to mirror the developmental level of individuals. However, despite these shifts, games and play behaviors continue to function as expressions of feelings, wishes, fears, and experiences and are the basis for forming and developing relationships with others. They also affect identity development, the process by which one comes to define and recognize oneself.

Thus, play and gaming are normative and healthy. They are activities that provide opportunities for learning, growth, stress reduction, social bonding, general well-being, and, therefore, good mental health. In fact, play and gaming are also useful as therapeutic strategies for mental health treatment. Play therapy, the use of play for treating mental health disorders in children, often helps children deal with traumatic events or other psychopathology. Similarly, role-playing, which entails acting out new behaviors, personae, or past or future experiences, is a helpful strategy for adolescents and adults to work on mental health problems.

Games are also used for educational purposes. Teachers use games as a way to engage different learning styles. Regular classroom teaching might involve writing on a chalkboard, reading, and taking notes. Games allow for social collaboration, competition, and tactile and kinesthetic involvement, each of which enhances learning because of the engagement of different learning styles. Teachers may also use games to help students learn rules and problem solving or to develop different ways of remembering information through the use of rhymes, songs, stories, or dances. Role-playing can also be used by teachers, even advanced professionals, to learn new skills. Finally, video and computer games can be valuable teaching aids for facilitating skills related to dexterity, hand-eye coordination, and strategy. In military applications, for example, the use of flight and war games helps in these ways and may mirror what trainees experienced earlier while playing games for different reasons.

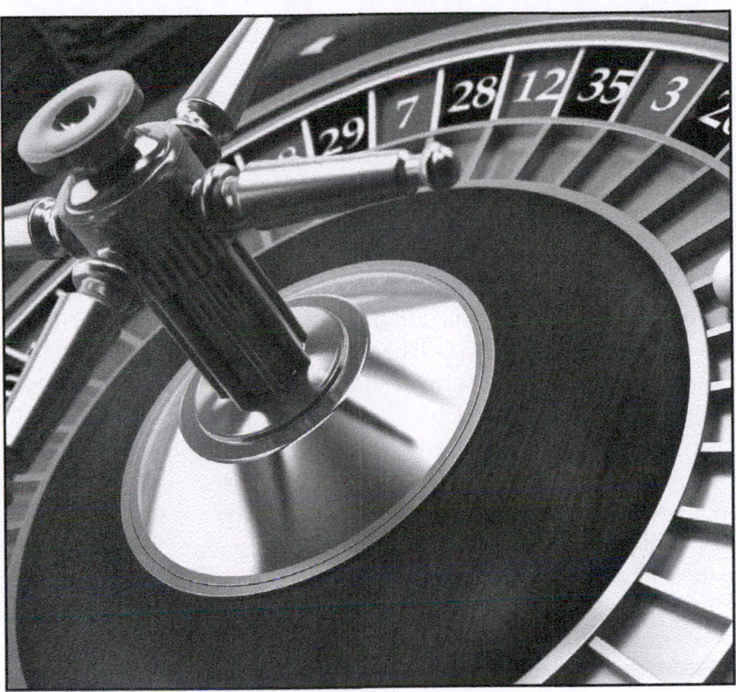

Photo: iStock

DISORDERS RELATED TO GAMES

Games involving violence and aggression are controversial and often a cause for concern. The risks of encouraging expression of aggressive feelings and behaviors—such as is found in some contemporary video games that feature reckless driving, weaponry, or hand-to-hand combat with virtual opponents—are balanced against any benefits in terms of stress relief, physical coordination, or strategic thought. While in a computer- or Internet-based game, one can hit a reset button, but in real life, expression of aggressive or destructive behavior can have dire consequences.

Even in competitive games, reckless competition can be dangerous and have impact. For instance, in virtual role-playing games, the reckless killing of a character whose identity and skills had been developed over many years can trigger a real-world emotional impact in the person who created the character. Because the individual's personal identity development or psychological health was related to that character's existence, the character's termination may have a profound impact. Social combat between characters resulting in virtual death may also have social and psychological implications for the victor. In the worst case, such gaming behavior can lead to conditions such as depression and anxiety in losers and potential patterns of socially aggressive behavior in victors.

Extraordinary competition or excessive participation in gaming can become an obsession. Individuals may experience such problems with almost any game, including online or face-to-face gambling, multiple role-player games, board games, solitary- or social-play games that may involve cards or other props, and sexual play. For some individuals, high levels of involvement with a game may become all consuming, isolating the person from others and interfering with everyday roles and obligations in real life. For children, adolescents, and young adults, this can take the form of interfering with important social or emotional developmental tasks.

Personal resources also may become diverted to support the gaming activity. For instance, in the case of pathological gambling, individuals may spend such large amounts of money on gaming that they cannot pay their regular living expenses. In such cases, the gaming activity has become an addiction. The person may also feel inescapably compelled to participate in the behavior, as in a compulsion. People in such situations may feel depressed, anxious, and out of control or perceive actual damage done to their lives and be unable to meet basic living needs. Often, the losses related to the behavior may be hidden or concealed until the problem has escalated beyond repair. In addition to suffering feelings of isolation, the compulsive individual may later lose relationships and social support, leaving the victim alone and even more emotionally vulnerable to the gaming behavior. Furthermore, many individuals participate in gaming activities while also using substances and therefore may develop unhealthy habits of both behaviors. Different forms of excessive gaming are often tied to problems with alcohol, nicotine, sleep aids, painkillers, or other substances. In such cases, violence against others or the self, in the form of suicide, may be potential dangers as the situation deteriorates.

For some individuals, these other conditions may only follow the onset of pathological gaming. Conditions such as anxiety, depression, or social isolation may be risk factors that leave individuals vulnerable to the reinforcing nature of gaming activities, and treatment for such problems must take this into account. In general, gaming and play are developmental and healthy aspects of youth and adulthood. While these activities can create problems for some, for most they are vital to good mental health and development.

BIBLIOGRAPHY

Brack, Greg, et al. "Individual Psychology on the Virtual Frontier: Massive Multiplayer Online Role-Playing Gaming." *Journal of Individual Psychology* 69.1 (2013): 24–40. Print.

Brotchie, Alastair, and Mel Cooding. *A Book of Surrealist Games: Including the Little Surrealist Dictionary.* Boston: Shambhala, 1995. Print.

Brown, Stuart, and Christopher Vaughan. *Play: How It Shapes the Brain, Opens the Imagination, and Invigorates the Soul.* New York: Avery, 2009. Print.

Cheung, Monit. *Therapeutic Games and Guided Imagery: Tools for Mental Health and School Professionals Working with Children, Adolescents, and Their Families.* Chicago: Lyceum, 2006. Print.

Cheung, Monit. *Therapeutic Games and Guided Imagery: Tools for Professionals Working with Children and Adolescents with Specific Needs and in Multicultural Settings.* Vol. 2. Chicago: Lyceum, 2014. Print

Dibbell, Julian. *Play Money; or, How I Quit My Day Job and Made Millions Trading Virtual Loot.* New York: Basic, 2007. Print.

Elkind, David. *The Power of Play: Learning What Comes Naturally.* New York: Da Capo, 2007. Print.

Ferguson, Christopher, and Cheryl Olson. "Video Game Violence Use among 'Vulnerable' Populations: The Impact of Violent Games on Delinquency and Bullying among Children with Clinically Elevated Depression or Attention Deficit Symptoms." *Journal of Youth and Adolescence* 43.1 (2014): 127–36. Print.

Gobet, Fernand, Alexander de Voogt, and Jean Retschitzki. *Moves in Mind: The Psychology of Board Games.* New York: Psychology, 2004. Print.

Gussin Paley, Vivian. *A Child's Work: The Importance of Fantasy Play.* Chicago: U of Chicago P, 2005. Print.

Scholes-Balog, Kirsty E., and Sheryl A. Hemphill. "Relationships between Online Gambling, Mental Health, and Substance Use: A Review." *Cyberpsychology, Behavior, and Social Networking* 15.12 (2012): 688–92. Print.

Wetzel, Kathryn C., and Kathleen Harmeyer. *Mind Games: The Aging Brain and How to Keep It Healthy.* Albany: Delmar, 2000. Print.

Williams, Patrick J., Sean Q. Hendricks, and W. Keith Winkler, eds. *Gaming as Culture: Essays on Reality, Identity, and Experience in Fantasy Games.* Jefferson: McFarland, 2006. Print.

Young, Kimberly S. *Caught in the Net: How to Recognize the Signs of Internet Addiction—and a Winning Strategy for Recovery.* New York: Wiley, 1998. Print.

Nancy A. Piotrowski

See Also: Addictive personality and behaviors; Aggression; Computer and Internet use and mental health; Creativity and intelligence; Development; Exercise and mental health; Gambling; Internet psychology; Music, dance, and theater therapy; Play therapy; Sports psychology; Virtual reality.

Gay, lesbian, bisexual, and transgender mental health

Type of psychology: Multicultural psychology; Psychopathology; Psychotherapy

Homosexuality was once considered a psychological disorder, but it was removed from the American Psychiatric Association's manual of disorders in 1973. Society's views of sexual orientation are varied, with some people seeing homosexuality as a choice and others as an inborn trait. Many of the psychological issues faced by gay and lesbian people are directly correlated with the prejudice and discrimination they face. The study of homosexuality and mental health has been influenced by negative and stereotypical views of homosexuals.

Key Concepts

- Bisexual
- Coming out
- Gay
- Gender identity
- GLBT
- Homosexual
- Lesbian
- Sexual orientation
- Transgender
- Transsexual

INTRODUCTION

Sexual orientation is frequently defined as a person's emotional, romantic, or sexual attraction to another person. Sexual orientation can be viewed on a continuum, with heterosexuality at one end, homosexuality at the other end, and bisexuality in the middle. Individuals who are attracted to same-sex partners are generally referred to as gay, lesbian, or homosexual. Individuals who are attracted to opposite-sex partners are considered heterosexual, and individuals who are attracted to both men and women are referred to as bisexual. Sexual orientation can be a source of psychological and cultural identity for some individuals. For example, individuals who openly identify themselves as gay may consider this identity to be an important part of who they are. Lesbian, gay, bisexual, and transgender (LGBT) individuals are often grouped together and referred to as the gay community.

Sexual orientation is different from gender identity. Whereas sexual orientation refers to romantic or sexual attraction, gender identity refers to roles society views as being appropriate for men or women. Gender identity is influenced by culture and socialization processes that change over time. It includes attitudes, cognitions, belief systems, gender roles, and norms for men and women as determined by culture and society. It is not directly related to sexual orientation.

The term "homosexual" was once used as a clinical term that defined same-sex attraction as a mental illness. The American Psychiatric Association's *Diagnostic and Statistical Manual of Mental Disorders* (2d ed., 1968, DSM-II) used this term to describe a mental illness, although the association changed its position on homosexuality in 1973. Homosexuality was determined to be a normal sexual variant and not a mental illness, and the term was removed from further editions of the association's manual.

HISTORICAL OVERVIEW

Historically, homosexuality has been accepted and rejected within different cultural groups at various points in history. In ancient Greece, homosexual acts between adult men and adolescent boys were considered acceptable. Judaism and Christianity viewed sodomy as a "crime against nature" and sinful behavior punishable by law. Like the ancient Greeks, some American Indians had a more flexible view of sexual orientation. Among some tribes, homosexual people were viewed as members of a "third gender" and were accepted. These tribes believed gay and lesbian people to have both male and female spirits. Evidence suggests that throughout history homosexuality has existed in various cultures around the world, including pre-Columbian tribes in Latin America, some tribes in Africa, and groups in China, Rome, Persia, the Middle East, South Asia, and Central Asia.

In societies in which homosexuality was considered an abomination, individuals who were suspected of engaging in homosexual acts were publicly ridiculed, socially ostracized, and even murdered. For example, in Nazi Germany, homosexuals were placed in concentration camps, subjected to painful medical experiments without anesthesia, and murdered. The Nazis believed that homosexuals could not contribute to the "master race" because they did not reproduce.

Homosexuality was not studied empirically until the twentieth century. Alfred Kinsey, a human sexuality researcher, developed a scale (later known as the Kinsey scale) that measured sexual orientation on a continuum from 0 (exclusively heterosexual) to 6 (exclusively homosexual). He felt that there were many individuals who could not be classified as exclusively heterosexual or homosexual. Kinsey and his associates' large-scale surveys were the first source of information about the prevalence of homosexuality in the United States in the 1950s. Kinsey's studies and subsequent research have highlighted the number of individuals who have had same-sex sexual experiences but do not consider themselves to be homosexual.

Because gay and lesbian people have a history of being discriminated against, many hide their sexual orientation. The term "coming out" or "coming out of the closet" describes a voluntary process by which gay or lesbian people publicly reveal their sexual orientation. Coming out is both a risk and a challenge because gay and lesbian people can face discrimination and rejection by their families and communities.

CONTROVERSY

American society is conflicted about the origin of sexual orientation. Some people believe that sexual orientation is determined by nature or biology from birth, while others believe that it is a choice. Historically, American society viewed homosexual acts as amoral and sinful, and some Americans still hold this view. Not surprisingly, the study of sexual orientation has often been influenced by the investigators' personal beliefs. Subjective studies by those opposed to homosexuality were often used to justify violence and hatred against gay, lesbian, bisexual, and transgender individuals. Science suggests that sexual orientation is not determined by a single cause. Identical twin studies show that these genetically identical individuals tend to have the same sexual orientation, suggesting a strong genetic influence for this trait. However, it is generally accepted by the scientific community that biological, social, psychological, and cultural influences interact to produce sexual orientation. Scientists disagree about which of these factors most strongly influence sexual orientation.

BISEXUALITY

Bisexual people have rarely been studied as a group with a distinct sexual orientation, separate from homosexuals. As a result, there are many misconceptions about bisexuality. Many view bisexual men as gay men who have not yet come out of the closet; bisexual people are also viewed as sexually promiscuous because of their attraction to both men and women. The limited research on bisexuality finds that bisexual individuals do not have to be attracted equally to men and women. Some bisexual individuals are more attracted to one sex than the other but still maintain an attraction to both. Bisexual individuals continue to be viewed with confusion and hostility from both the homosexual and heterosexual populations because bisexual people are often able to "fit in" with either community and hide their sexual orientation if they so choose.

TRANSGENDER

Gender or gender identity is a culturally and socially influenced concept that shapes an individual's behavior, gender roles, and psychological identity as being male or female. Sex has often been narrowly defined as being male (XY chromosomes) or female (XX chromosomes). Individuals who are born with ambiguous genitalia are often referred to as intersexed or intersexual.

Transgender individuals have a gender identity that is inconsistent with their biological sex. These people have normal genitalia yet feel that they are actually a member of the opposite sex. They feel as if they are "trapped" in the wrong body and frequently seek gender identification with the opposite sex. The Diagnostic and Statistical Manual of Mental Disorders: DSM-V (rev. 5th ed., 2013) defines this condition as gender dysphoria ; this marks a change from the previous edition, in which the diagnosis was gender identity disorder. It can be seen in childhood, although individuals may not express their dysphoria openly until adulthood. The nonclinical term for this condition embraced by many individuals with gender dysphoria is transsexual. The criteria for this disorder are behaviors that indicate identification with the opposite gender and behaviors that indicate discomfort with one's own anatomy and gender roles.

One of the treatments for gender dysphoria is sex reassignment surgery and hormone therapy; however, not all transgender individuals seek this treatment.

RATES OF MENTAL ILLNESS

Those in the LGBT community have higher rates of suicide, depression, eating disorders, and substance abuse than do people in the general population. This is often attributed to the pressures of being gay or lesbian in a society that continues to actively discriminate against homosexuals. Coming out is a lifelong process because gay and lesbian individuals continually must determine if it is safe to reveal their sexual orientation in the environments in which they find themselves. Many LGBT people have lost social and familial relationships as a result of coming out, and this population continues to be frequent victims of hate crimes. Among young gay men, the use of "party drugs" such as cocaine and ecstasy is more common than in the general population. Gay men with the human immunodeficiency virus (HIV) or acquired immunodeficiency syndrome (AIDS) often experience higher rates of depression and anxiety and substance abuse disorders than do their noninfected peers. Lesbians tend to have higher rates of alcohol use than their heterosexual counterparts. A disproportionate number of LGBT people use mental health services. Most report using mental health services to cope with how society stigmatizes them and the strain this has on their relationships.

One controversial treatment for homosexuals is conversion therapy, which is aimed at changing an individual's sexual orientation from homosexual to heterosexual. The assumption underlying treatment is that homosexuality is an individual choice, or a mental illness that needs to be treated. The American Psychological Association does not support this treatment; however, it respects psychotherapy clients' rights to seek this treatment from practitioners willing to provide it.

BIBLIOGRAPHY

Alyson Almanac: *The Fact Book of the Lesbian and Gay Community*. Los Angeles: Alyson, 1993.

Bieschke, Kathleen J., Ruperto M. Perez, and Kurt A. DeBord, eds. *Handbook of Counseling and Psychotherapy with Lesbian, Gay, Bisexual, and Transgender Clients*. 2d ed. Washington, DC: American Psychological Assn., 2007. Print.

Clarke, Victoria, Sonja J. Ellis, Elizabeth Peel, and Damien W. Riggs. *Lesbian, Gay, Bisexual, Trans, and Queer Psychology: An Introduction*. Cambridge: Cambridge UP, 2010. Print.

Das Nair, Roshan, and Catherine Butler. *Intersectionality, Sexuality, and Psychological Therapies: Working with Lesbian, Gay, and Bisexual Diversity.* Chichester: BPS Blackwell, 2012. Print.

Dynes, Wayne, ed. *Encyclopedia of Homosexuality*. 2 vols. New York: Garland, 1990. Print.

Faderman, Lillian, Yolanda Retter, and Horacio Roque Ramírez, eds. *Great Events from History: Gay, Lesbian, Bisexual, and Transgender Events*. Pasadena: Salem, 2006. Print.

Gates, Gary J., and Jason Ost. *The Gay Atlas*. Washington, DC: Urban Inst., 2004. Print.

Levounis, Petros, Jack Drescher, and Mary E. Barber. *The LGBT Casebook*. Washington, DC: American Psychiatric, 2012. Print.

Katherine M. Helm

See Also: Abnormality: Biomedical models; Abnormality: Psychologcial models; Adolescence: Sexuality; Attraction theories; Aversion therapy; Gender differences; Gender identity disorder; Gender identity formation; Gender roles and gender role conflicts; Hate crimes: Psychological causes and effects; Homosexuality; Kinsey, Alfred; Prejudice; Psychosexual development; Sexism; Sexual behavior patterns; Sexual dysfunction; Sexual variants and paraphilias; Transvestism.

Gender differences

Type of psychology: Psychopathology; Psychotherapy; Social psychology; Stress

Gender differences in mental health exist in the prevalence of various diagnoses, help-seeking behaviors, and severity of impairment. Biological, psychosocial, and sociocultural explanations account for disparities in mental health between men and women.

Key Concepts

- Biological differences
- Differential patterns of diagnosis
- Double standard
- Psychosocial explanations
- Sociocultural theories

INTRODUCTION

Gender and other social factors influence popular conceptions of mental health. Overall, the prevalence rates of most mental health disorders are almost identical for men and women; however, gender differences occur in the rates of the most common mental disorders, particularly depression, anxiety, and somatic complaints, which are more prevalent in women. Socially constructed differences between men and women regarding role responsibilities, status, and power interact with biological differences, creating variations in mental health problems, help-seeking behavior, and the response of the mental health community.

THE DOUBLE STANDARD

In 1970, Inge Broverman and her colleagues used an adjective checklist to demonstrate that clinicians defined characteristics of mental health differently based on the sex of the person being described. Mental health professionals were asked to describe the characteristics of a healthy, mature, and socially competent man, woman, or "adult person." A normal, healthy adult of unspecified gender was described with similar adjectives as a healthy man, with adjectives such as independent, adventurous, objective, and decisive. By contrast, a normal, healthy woman was described as noncompetitive, passive, emotional, and dependent—adjectives that the mental health professionals more readily ascribed to "unhealthy" individuals.

These descriptions of mature, competent men and women revealed a double standard concerning mental health. Stereotypical male behavior was shown to serve as the norm to identify good mental health overall; however, many of the characteristics viewed as positive in terms of mental health in general were seen by these professionals as being negative in women. Consequently, if women demonstrated the characteristics that these mental health professionals attributed to healthy and socially competent women, they would be labeled abnormal (having masculine traits). This study demonstrated that the behaviors and characteristics judged by clinicians to reflect an ideal standard of mental health resembled the characteristics and behaviors deemed to be healthy for men but not for women.

Broverman and her colleagues pioneered the study of sex role stereotypes and their impact on mental health services for both men and women.

DIAGNOSES AND DISTRIBUTION PATTERNS

Research shows that some of the most common mental health disorders (such as depression, anxiety, and anorexia nervosa) are more prevalent in women. On the other hand, mental health problems such as alcohol addiction, substance abuse, and antisocial personality disorder are more common in men. Other disorders that affect less than 2 percent of the world's population (such as schizophrenia and borderline personality disorder) are equally prevalent in both genders. Multiple diagnoses, especially the presence of three or more conditions, are more common in women than in men.

The rates of depression in surveys of both clinical patients and the general population are higher in women than in men. More than twice as many women as men report a major depressive episode in any given year. The gender disparity in rates of depression is one of the strongest findings in epidemiological psychiatry. Depression persists longer in women, and women are more likely to relapse than men.

Depression rates vary by country. According to the World Health Organization, depression is the leading cause of disease burden for women worldwide. Depressive disorders account for approximately 41 percent of the disability from neuropsychiatric disorders among women compared to 29 percent among men.

Furthermore, postpartum depression affects 10 to 15 percent of mothers worldwide, presenting a significant public health problem for women and their families. However, clinicians are more likely to diagnose women with depression than men, even when men have similar scores on standardized measures of depression or present identical symptoms, indicating an ongoing gender bias in the assessment of mental health disorders.

Anxiety diagnoses, including panic disorder, posttraumatic stress disorder, generalized anxiety disorder, and phobias, are nearly twice as common among women than men.

The National Comorbidity Survey Replication surveyed the general population of the United States and found that 23 percent of women reported suffering from an anxiety disorder in the last twelve months compared to 14 percent of men. Social anxiety disorder and obsessive-compulsive disorder, by contrast, are equally prevalent in men and women. Generalized anxiety disorder affects about 6.6 percent of women and 3.6 percent of men during their lives. Anxiety disorders are also associated with a greater illness burden in women than in men, indicating that anxiety disorders are not only more prevalent in women but also tend to have a more severe impact. The lifetime prevalence rate of violence against women ranges from 16 to 50 percent worldwide, and at least one in five women suffer sexual assault or rape in their lifetimes; the psychological impact of experiencing physical and sexual violence is thought to contribute to the higher rates of anxiety disorders among women. Furthermore, women are more frequently diagnosed with somatic symptom disorder, in which mental factors such as stress cause debilitating physical symptoms. Eating disorders, including anorexia and bulimia, are more prevalent in women than in men. Women are more likely to evaluate their self-worth in terms of appearance, largely due to sociocultural expectations that highly value women's attractiveness. Furthermore, women report higher rates of discrimination related to being overweight or obese than men.

Men are more likely than women to drink in public, to drink alone, and to engage in episodic binge drinking. Men are more likely to use alcohol to manage stress and are more likely than women to become dependent on it. Twelve-month prevalence rates of alcohol abuse are nearly three times higher among men than women. One in five men as compared with one in twelve women develop an alcohol problem over the course of their lives.

Furthermore, men are more likely than women to abuse drugs other than alcohol; however, rates of prescription drug abuse are nearly identical across genders. About twice as many men as women report illicit drug use. Additionally, men and women continue to use drugs for different reasons: men for thrill seeking and pleasure, and women for self-medication of abuse or trauma.

Men are more likely than women to be diagnosed with neurodevelopmental disorders such as autism spectrum disorder, intellectual disability, and attention-deficit hyperactivity disorder. About four times more men than women receive diagnoses of autism spectrum disorder. However, women with autism tend to have more severe symptoms and greater cognitive impairment than men with autism. Although schizophrenia affects men and women equally, clinicians identify the onset of symptoms in men with schizophrenia earlier (late teens or early twenties) than in women with schizophrenia (late twenties or early thirties). In contrast to autism, schizophrenia is typically more disabling in men, and symptoms more commonly found in men are harder to treat. Four times as many men as women die by suicide, even though women attempt suicide at two to three times the rate at which men do. Most successful suicides among both men and women are related to a diagnosed mental disorder, typically depression or substance abuse.

TREATMENT DISPARITIES

Overall, women are more likely than men to seek out and make use of mental health services. Women are more likely to disclose mental health issues to general practitioners, while men are more likely to ignore mental problems in their early stages and prefer to deal with mental health specialists. Women are also more ikely than men to seek psychological help, particularly regarding anxiety and depression. After admitting mental health problems, men and women are equally likely to accept help, but women are overrepresented in mental health statistics.

The problem lies in men's reluctance to admit to mental health disorders and professionals' frequent failure to diagnose them in men. Professionals are less likely to perceive men's problems as psychological. Cultural patterns of male stoicism and a reluctance to ask for help may cause lower diagnosis and treatment rates in men.

More women than men use outpatient care; however, men are more likely than women to be involuntarily committed. Apparently, many men wait to seek help until a later stage of disease, when the symptoms are more severe and hospitalization more necessary. However, women are almost twice as likely to be prescribed psychotropic drugs, regardless of social class, physical health status, and type of diagnosis, and most are prescribed by a general practitioner, internist, obstetrician, or gynecologist.

Men's mental health symptoms tend to be more severe and difficult to treat. Onset of many mental disorders in women occurs at older ages than in men, and consequently women may have a better established base of social skills and cognitive functioning, allowing them to better cope with symptoms of the disorder than younger men with the same diagnosis.

EXPLANATIONS FOR VARIATIONS

Gender differences in patterns of diagnosis and treatment of mental illnesses have been studied since at least the 1970s. Explanations for these differences have been both biological and social.

Many scientists suggest that biology and reproductive functions may account for gender differences in mental health. Different levels of hormones between men and women are related to some diagnoses. Scientists know that estrogen reacts with serotonin, a neurotransmitter associated with mood, and some studies suggest estrogen may protect against schizophrenia. Biological reactions to stress in general, and specifically biological changes associated with motherhood, help explain higher levels of depression and anxiety in women. Though biological factors, especially hormones, play a role in mental health, social class, cultural values, and family relationships also significantly affect mental health.

Psychosocial theorists point to the fact that girls experience greater levels of violence than boys do and that their responses to this violence lead to higher rates of mental disorders in adult women. Child abuse creates long-term changes in brain circuitry and thus increases the likelihood of anxiety disorders. Rates of depression in adult women are three to four times higher for women exposed to childhood violence than for those without this exposure. A particularly strong connection between sexual abuse and posttraumatic stress disorder (PTSD) has been established. The severity of and length of exposure to violence is positively correlated with being diagnosed with a mental illness.

Sociocultural explanations focus on the dominance of a masculine model of mental health. Definitions of normality are often based on culturally determined gender roles. A social constructionist explanation of mental health differences by gender focuses on how conceptions of proper male and female behavior and characteristics are embedded into diagnostic categories of mental disorders.

GENDER STEREOTYPING

Early socialization of children into gender-appropriate behavior may teach girls to internalize distress and boys to act out. Consequently, when subjected to stressors, women tend to experience depression and anxiety as internal responses, whereas men tend to take more external action by abusing substances, engaging in antisocial behavior, and committing suicide.

Worldwide, women's social roles and positions in society may make them more vulnerable than men to mental health disorders. Traditional gender roles for women offer fewer personal choices and lower life satisfaction. Positive psychological health is linked to a greater number and increased diversity of social roles. A variety of roles gives an individual a stronger sense of identity, leading to fewer mental health problems.

Furthermore, gender affects control of socioeconomic determinants of mental health. Women's greater exposure to poverty, combined with low social standing, job insecurity, and housing uncertainties, leads to more chronic stressors and increases the severity of mental health problems. Depression, anxiety, and somatic symptoms are highly related to social status and responsibility for the care of others.

The relationship between mental health and gender is complicated by issues of class, age, race, and ethnicity. Gender differences in mental health have been examined more in industrialized countries than in less developed countries, and adult women and men have been studied more than children and adolescents. Although the rates of most mental disorder diagnoses are similar for men and women, there are definite patterns regarding the types of problems men and women experience.

Future research needs to consider gender discrepancies in more detail, and professionals need to consider gender disparities in planning, implementing, and evaluating mental health programs. Mental health professionals must be aware of gender stereotypes in the diagnosis and treatment of mental disorders, as these stereotypes can present a significant barrier to the accurate identification and treatment of psychological disorders in both men and women.

BIBLIOGRAPHY

Fine, Cordelia. *Delusions of Gender: How Our Minds, Society, and Neurosexism Create Difference*. New York: Norton, 2010. Print.

Freeman, Daniel, and Jason Freeman. *The Stressed Sex: Uncovering the Truth about Men, Women, and Mental Health*. Oxford: Oxford UP, 2013. Print.

Maclean, Alice, Kate Hunt, and Helen Sweeting. "Symptoms of Mental Health Problems: Children's and Adolescents' Understandings and Implications for Gender Differences in Help Seeking." *Children and Society* 27.3 (2013): 161–73. Print.

McGeown, Sarah. *Psychology of Gender Differences*. New York: Nova Science, 2012. Print.

Narrow, William D., et al., eds. *Age and Gender Considerations in Psychiatric Diagnosis*. Arlington: American Psychiatric Association, 2007. Print.

National Institute of Mental Health. "The Numbers Count: Mental Disorders in America." Washington: Author, 2007. Print.

Nydegger, Rudy. "Gender and Mental Health: Incidence and Treatment Issues." *The Psychology of Gender*. Ed. Michele A. Paludi. Westport: Praeger, 2004. Print.

Prior, Pauline M. *Gender and Mental Health*. New York: New York UP, 1999. Print.

Sachs-Ericsson, Natalie. "Gender, Social Roles, and Mental Health: An Epidemiological Perspective." *Sex Roles: A Journal of Research* 43.9/10 (2000): 605–28. Print.

Barbara E. Johnson

SEE ALSO: Alcohol dependence and abuse; Anxiety disorders; Asperger syndrome; Autism; Borderline personality disorder; Child abuse; Depression; Femininity; Gender identity disorder; Gender identity formation; Gender roles and gender role conflicts; Masculinity.

Gender identity disorder

DATE: 1980 forward

TYPE OF PSYCHOLOGY: Psychopathology

Gender identity disorder is the diagnosis for individuals who are highly uncomfortable with the sex of their bodies and who wish to behave, think, and be members of the opposite sex. This diagnosis is the subject of considerable controversy among psychiatrists. The causes for this disorder remain speculative, and treatment typically aims to diminish associated symptoms of anxiety, depression, or other social interactional difficulties. In severe cases, psychiatrists may recommend sex changes.

KEY CONCEPTS

- Cross-dressing
- Gender
- Homosexuality

- Transgender
- Transsexual

INTRODUCTION

Gender identity disorder is an artifact of psychiatric politics in the 1970's and 1980's. To understand this diagnosis and contemporary debates, some awareness of the past is essential. The American Psychiatric Association (APA), one of the major professional organizations for medical practitioners and therapists dealing with mental health, was the obvious organizational choice when there was a need to create a list of mental illnesses to provide some unity of medical diagnoses across the United States. The early *Diagnostic and Statistical Manual of Mental Disorders* (1952, DSM) and the second edition, published in 1968, provided brief definitions of psychiatric ailments, although they typically lacked clear diagnostic criteria, posing dilemmas for practitioners.

During the 1950's and 1960's, American psychiatrists were strongly influenced by the Austrian psychologist Sigmund Freud, who popularized psychoanalysis. Freud's work encouraged the view that adult mental maladies often were the result of stunted or misdirected sexual desires in childhood. This emphasis on the importance of sexuality meant that psychiatrists paid a tremendous amount of attention to activities in the nation's bedrooms, although little research data supported many contentions about sexual practices.

One of the early outcomes of this history was that the first edition of the manual listed homosexuality as a sociopathic personality disturbance and the second edition moved it into the category of nonpsychotic mental ailments, including a variety of other supposedly unhealthy sexual practices. Some psychiatrists argue that this inclusion of homosexuality paved the way for the later conceptualized gender identity disorder, while others would dispute this contention. Certainly, many of the same objections to the earlier inclusion of homosexuality as a mental illness also plague later supporters of gender identity disorder. For this reason, it is important to revisit some of this early history.

During the 1950's and 1960's, research evidence provided some challenges to the view that homosexuality was a mental illness. Sexual researcher Alfred Kinsey of Indiana University demonstrated that homosexual behavior was more common in the general population than typically recognized. Evelyn Hooker, who conducted research in the psychology department at the University of California, Los Angeles, and worked with homosexual individuals from outside therapeutic groups, showed that they displayed the same range of mental health issues as members of the general nonhomosexual population. In addition, cross-cultural anthropologists wrote about other societies with very different understandings of mental illness and sexuality, casting doubt on the universality and applicability of American beliefs and norms about mental well-being and sexual behaviors. These findings suggested that homosexuality might not be a mental illness, in direct opposition to the information published by the APA. Increasingly, organization members were challenged on this issue, and several association annual conferences in the early 1970's were disrupted by protests, fueled by the growth of civil rights and gay rights activism. By this time, the Association of Gay and Lesbian Psychiatrists (AGLP), informally founded in the late 1960's, was also active within the ranks of the APA, contributing to the impetus for change. Eventually after considerable internal dispute and political maneuvering, in 1973, the Board of Trustees of the APA (followed by the full membership in 1974) agreed to remove homosexuality from the list of mental illnesses in the next edition of the DSM. This history assists in understanding contemporary disputes about gender identity disorder.

CAUSES AND DIAGNOSTIC CRITERIA

The term "gender identity disorder" was first included in the DSM-III (1980) and appeared in the fourth edition in 1994 and the fourth revised edition in 2000, with its operational definition. An individual suffering from gender identity disorder was a person who felt strongly that he or she was living in an incorrectly sexed body. For example, boys or men would feel their gender, behavior, and feelings were feminine, and their physique should be female to reflect this identity, while girls or women would feel the opposite.

Despite the fact that gender identity disorder has been considered to be a problem for both adults and children for several decades, there are limited data about causation. It has been suggested that biology may play a role, with possible proposals including intrauterine development of the fetus and hormonal influences. Other hypotheses uphold cultural influences, with parental behavior, socialization by peers, or the presence of other social norms providing a causal link. Most likely, the answer lies in some combination of these or other factors.

Although the causes of gender identity disorder remain unclear, distinct diagnostic criteria are presented in the fourth revised edition of the manual. The diagnosis

DSM-IV-TR CRITERIA FOR GENDER IDENTITY DISORDER

Strong and persistent cross-gender identification, not merely a desire for any perceived cultural advantages of being the other sex

In children, disturbance manifested by four or more of the following:

- repeatedly stated desire to be, or insistence that he or she is, the other sex
- in boys, preference for cross-dressing or simulating female attire; in girls, insistence on wearing only stereotypically masculine clothing
- strong and persistent preferences for cross-sex roles in make-believe play or persistent fantasies of being the other sex
- intense desire to participate in the stereotypical games and pastimes of the other sex
- strong preference for playmates of the other sex; in adolescents and adults, symptoms such as stated desire to be the other sex, frequent passing as the other sex, desire to live or be treated as the other sex, conviction that he or she has the typical feelings and reactions of the other sex

Persistent discomfort with his or her sex or sense of inappropriateness in the gender role of that sex

In children, disturbance manifested by any of the following:

- in boys, assertion that his penis or testes are disgusting or will disappear or assertion that it would be better not to have a penis, or aversion toward rough-and-tumble play and rejection of male stereotypical toys, games, and activities
- in girls, rejection of urinating in a sitting position, assertion that she has or will grow a penis, or assertion that she does not want to grow breasts or menstruate, or marked aversion toward normative feminine clothing

In adolescents and adults, disturbance manifested by symptoms such as preoccupation with getting rid of primary and secondary sex characteristics (request for hormones, surgery, or other procedures to physically alter sexual characteristics to simulate the other sex) or belief that he or she was born the wrong sex

Disturbance not concurrent with a physical intersex condition

Disturbance causes clinically significant distress or impairment in social, occupational, or other important areas of functioning

DSM code based on current age:

- Gender Identity Disorder in Children (DSM code 302.6)
- Gender Identity Disorder in Adolescents or Adults (DSM code 302.85)

For sexually mature individuals, specify if Sexually Attracted to Males, Sexually Attracted to Females, Sexually Attracted to Both, or Sexually Attracted to Neither

requires the presence of a minimum of four behaviors or beliefs, all of which must be strongly expressed on a variety of occasions over some time period. The criteria include identification with a different sex, cross-dressing, occupying cross-sex roles while playing or daydreaming, stating the strongly expressed goal to perform as the other sex, and expressing the desire to play or interact with members of the different sex, or live as a member of the opposite sex. In addition, individuals are distressed by the presence of their female or male external genitalia and secondary sexual characteristics, such as breasts. Generally, they do not want to behave according to the norms of their socially ascribed gender, and their reactions are not simply based on awareness of gender inequities in society, but on strong feelings of revulsion for the sex of their bodies. These individuals are not physically intersexed, and their sense of distress is so strong that they function poorly in their daily lives.

PROBLEMS WITH THE DIAGNOSIS AND TREATMENT OPTIONS

Several different concerns have been expressed about applying a diagnosis of gender identity disorder. Culturegender identity disorderOne issue is that gender identity disorder is not diagnosed in the same manner internationally, and if it is assumed that all human minds operate in a similar manner, this is problematic. In addition, the history of the APA and the battles over homosexuality foreshadow many of the current debates over gender identity disorder. Certainly, the pathologization of cross-dressing, transgender, and transsexual community members is in striking opposition to greater knowledge about gender and sexual diversity around the world, the relaxing of sexual norms in the United States, and an increasingly activist and rights-conscious society. For these reasons, the diagnosis of gender identity disorder and its inclusion in the APA's manual is not accepted by all of the association's members, mental health workers, or members of the general public.

Additional questions surround the practice of applying the diagnosis of gender identity disorder to Childrengender identity disorderchildren. One issue is that some individuals may be diagnosed as gender identity disordered when in fact they are merely expressing their dissatisfaction with contemporary gender inequities, and desiring to behave and be treated in the manner accorded to the more dominant sex. This issue would most likely pertain more to girls. Another development is that girls seem to be diagnosed with gender identity disorder at lower rates than boys, and the underlying reason is unclear. It may relate to hormonal or other factors of the ailment, or it may relate to social comfort with girls cross-dressing and demonstrating "tough boy" behavior. This gender difference in the disorder has been used by some social scientists to argue that gender identity disorder is more a function of American culture rather than a real mental illness.

People who are comfortable with their experiences cross-dressing orTransgendered peopletransgendering, and who live in locations where others are comfortable with their identities are unlikely to seek help from psychiatrists. It is those adults who are uncomfortable with their cross-gender identities and their inability to fit social expectations who often feel depression or anxiety, and consequently may seek treatment at clinical outpatient facilities. Gender identity disorder can feel overwhelmingly difficult for people. In these cases, initially, the accompanying anxiety or depression may be treated, possibly by pharmaceutical interventions in combination with talk therapies. The type of treatment will vary depending on the patient's symptoms. A similar treatment trajectory is often experienced by children or adolescents, although in their cases, parental intervention may play a greater role in moving them into treatment.

Once some of the accompanying issues are under control, individuals may then become more comfortable with their sex and gender disjunction. If this does not occur, people may request psychiatric and medical assistance in changing their bodies and becoming transsexuals. This is a slow process, with individuals first living as the opposite sex for a period of time, often with hormonal prescriptions helping them look more like their desired sex. Ultimately, with medical approval, they may be offered sex change surgeries of various kinds, which allow them to live permanently as the opposite sex.

BIBLIOGRAPHY

Bartlett, Nancy H., et al. "Is Gender Identity Disorder in Children a Mental Disorder?" *Sex Roles* 43, nos. 11/12 (December, 2000): 753-785. Consideration of gender identity disorder and its diagnosis in children.

Bayer, Ronald. *Homosexuality and American Psychiatry: The Politics of Diagnosis.* Princeton, N.J.: Princeton University Press, 1987. Discussion of the 1970's disputes among members of the American Psychiatric Association, which can be argued to underlie the creation of the diagnosis of gender identity disorder in DSM-III.

Besnier, Niko. "Polynesian Gender Liminality Through Time and Space." *In Third Sex, Third Gender: Beyond Sexual Dimorphism in Culture and History,* edited by Gilbert Herdt. New York: Zone Books, 1993. Provides cross-cultural data on gender and sexuality that suggests that the diagnosis of gender identity disorder may be a product of specific cultural, geographic, and temporal conditions, rather than a psychiatric illness identifiable in all social groups. Other chapters in the volume contribute to this theme.

Giordano, Simona. "Gender Atypical Organization in Children and Adolescents: Ethico-Legal Issues and a Proposal for New Guidelines." *International Journal of Children's Rights* 15, nos. 3/4 (July, 2007): 365-390. Consideration of gender identity disorder in youth, ethics, legal rights, and a comparison of the situation in the United Kingdom with the United States.

McHugh, Paul R., et al. *The Perspectives of Psychiatry.* 2d ed. Baltimore: Johns Hopkins University Press, 1998. History of psychiatry, with information about how disorders are conceptualized and researched.

Wilson, Mitchell. "DSM-III and the Transformation of American Psychiatry: A History." *American Journal of*

Psychiatry 150, no. 3 (March, 1993): 399-410. History of the DSM and the conceptualizations underlying new editions.

Zucker, Kenneth J. "Commentary on Langer and Martin's 2004 'How Dresses Can Make You Mentally Ill: Examining Gender Identity Disorder in Children.'" *Child and Adolescent Social Work Journal* 23, nos. 5/6 (December, 2006): 533-555. Detailed discussion about gender differences in the diagnosis of gender identity disorder, including the history of the disorder.

Susan J. Wurtzburg

SEE ALSO: Abnormality: Biomedical models; Abnormality: Psychological models; Gay, lesbian, bisexual, and transgender mental health; Gender identity formation; Gender roles and gender role conflicts; Homosexuality; Sexual variants and paraphilias; Transvestism

Gender identity formation

TYPE OF PSYCHOLOGY: Developmental psychology

Gender identity formation refers to the complex processes through which young children come to incorporate their sex and gender into their behavior, attitudes, and self-understanding. This includes the development of an inner sense of one's femaleness or maleness, the acquisition of knowledge about cultural expectations for women and men, and the development of attitudes, interests, and behavior that reflect these sociocultural expectations.

KEY CONCEPTS

- Gender constancy
- Gender identity
- Gender schema
- Sex role
- Sex-role socialization
- Sex typing

INTRODUCTION

The first question that is usually asked about a newborn baby is whether the child is a boy or a girl. The single fact of the child's biological sex has enormous implications for the course of the baby's entire life. Gender identity formation refers to the complex processes through which children incorporate the biological and social fact of their sex and gender into their behavior, attitudes, and self-understanding. This area includes ideas about two major interrelated processes: gender identity development and sex typing. The term "gender identity development," used in its narrower sense, refers to the process through which children come to label themselves as boys or girls and to have an inner sense of themselves as male or female. "Sex typing," also called gender role acquisition or gender socialization, refers to the processes through which children learn what is expected of members of their gender and come to exhibit those personality traits, behaviors, interests, and attitudes.

CULTURAL CONTEXTS

Social-learning theorists such as Walter Mischel, Walter have described mechanisms of learning through which children come to exhibit sex-typed behavior. Boys and girls often behave differently because they are rewarded and punished for different behaviors. In other words, they receive different conditioning. In addition, children's behavior becomes sex typed because children observe other male and female individuals regularly behaving differently according to their gender, and they imitate or model this behavior.

Parents are especially important in the process of learning a gender role because they act both as models for gender-appropriate behavior and as sources of rewards or reinforcement. Because parents become associated with positive experiences (such as being praised or comforted) early in life, children learn to look to them and other adults for rewards. Parents and other adults such as teachers often react differentially to gender-typed behaviors, rewarding gender-appropriate behavior (for example, by giving praise or attention) and punishing gender-inappropriate behavior (for example, by frowning, ignoring, or reprimanding).

As children become more involved with their peers, they begin to influence one another's behavior, often strongly reinforcing traditional gender roles. The fact that children are usually given different toys and different areas in which to play based on their gender is also important. Girls are given opportunities to learn different behaviors from those of boys (for example, girls may learn nurturing behavior through playing with dolls) because they are exposed to different experiences.

Using a cognitive developmental perspective, Lawrence Kohlberg described developmental changes in children's understanding of gender concepts. These changes parallel the broad developmental changes in the way children's thinking is organized, first described by Jean Piaget and Barbel Inhelder. Children mature naturally through stages of increasingly complex cognitive organization. In the area of understanding gender, the first stage is the acquisition of a rudimentary gender identity, the ability to categorize oneself correctly as a boy or a girl.

Children are able to apply correct gender labels to themselves by about age two. At this stage, young children base gender labeling on differences in easily observable characteristics such as hairstyle and clothing, and they do not grasp the importance of biological differences in determining gender. As children's thinking about the physical world becomes more complex, so does their understanding of gender. Gradually, between the ages of five and seven, children enter a second stage and acquire the concept known as gender constancy.

GENDER CONSTANCY

Gender constancy refers to the understanding that gender is a stable characteristic that cannot change over time and that is not altered by superficial physical transformations such as wearing a dress or cutting one's hair. As children come to see gender as a stable, important characteristic of themselves and other people, they begin to use the concept consistently to organize social information. They learn societal expectations for members of each gender by watching the actions of the people around them.

Kohlberg proposed that children use their developing knowledge of cultural gender expectations to teach themselves to adopt culturally defined gender roles (self-socialization). He argued that children acquire a strong motive to conform to gender roles because of their need for self-consistency and self-esteem.

Children hold rigid gender stereotypes before they acquire gender constancy; once gender constancy is achieved, they become more flexible in their adherence to gender roles. As children enter adolescence, their thinking about the world again enters a new stage of development, becoming even more complex and less rigid. As a result, they may be able to achieve what Joseph Pleck has called "sex-role transcendence" and to choose their interests and behaviors somewhat independently of cultural gender role expectations.

GENDER SCHEMA

Gender schema theory is a way of explaining gender identity formation, which is closely related to the cognitive developmental approach. The concept of a schema or a general knowledge framework comes from the field of cognitive psychology. Sandra Bem proposed that each person develops a set of gender-linked associations, or a gender schema, as part of a personal knowledge structure. This filters and interprets new information, and as a result, people have a basic predisposition to process information on the basis of gender. People tend to dichotomize objects and attributes on the basis of gender, even qualities such as color, which has no relevance to biological sex.

Bem proposed that sex typing develops as children learn the content of society's gender schemas and as they begin to link those schemas to their self-concept or view of themselves. Individuals vary in the degree to which the gender schema is central to their self-concept; it is more central to the self-concept of highly sex-typed individuals (traditionally masculine men or traditionally feminine women).

GENDER DYSPHORIA

Ideas about gender identity formation have important implications for child rearing and education. Most parents want to help their children identify with and feel positive about their own gender. Those few children who feel a marked difference between their expressed or experienced gender and the gender assigned to them by others may be diagnosed with gender dysphoria if the condition causes them serious distress or impairment in social, occupational, or other areas of functioning. It is important to note that gender nonconformity is not a mental disorder; instead, gender dysphoria is characterized by the presence of clinically significant distress associated with the condition.

According to the fifth edition of the American Psychiatric Association's *Diagnostic and Statistical Manual of Mental Disorders* (DSM-5, 2013), gender dysphoria is characterized by clinically significant distress or impairment arising from marked differences between one's assigned gender and one's perceived or experienced gender identity. With the DSM-5, gender dysphoria replaced the diagnostic name "gender identity disorder," which was previously defined by a strong and persistent cross-gender identification. However, by establishing the diagnostic term gender dysphoria, the American Psychiatric Association sought to emphasize that gender nonconformity is not in itself a mental disorder, and the diagnostic criteria for gender dysphoria focus only on the distress and impairment caused by such a condition.

Individuals who experience gender dysphoria for more than six months have a number of a treatment options, including counseling, hormonal treatments, gender reassignment surgery, or social and legal transition to the desired gender. The diagnosis of gender dysphoria protects individuals' access to care and ensures their ability to receive insurance coverage for the related medical treatments.

GENDER EQUALITY

Often, parents and educators want to help children avoid becoming strongly sex typed. They do not want children's options for activities, interests, and aspirations to be limited to those traditionally associated with their gender.

Considerable research has focused on whether and how socializing agents, including parents, teachers, peers, and media such as children's books and television, reinforce gender stereotypes and teach children to exhibit sex-typed behaviors. Researchers have been concerned both with how gender roles are modeled for children and with how sex-typed behavior is rewarded. Parents often report that they try to treat their children the same regardless of their gender, and indeed studies show that there are no gender-based differences in the amount of attention or affection that parents give to their sons and daughters. However, studies have shown that parents' styles of interaction with male and female children are consistently different. Furthermore, parents' standards and expectations may be markedly different for their sons and daughters, thereby reinforcing gender stereotypes. A number of studies in which the gender of infants and young children was hidden from observers revealed that adults often perceive identical behavior in boys and girls differently, based solely on the child's presumed gender, and these different perceptions shape how adults treat and interact with young boys and girls, thereby reinforcing sex-typed behaviors.

Children's peers also play an important role in sex-role socialization. Particularly in early childhood, when children's gender concepts tend to be far more rigid than those of adults, peers may be a source of misinformation (for example, "boys can't play with dolls" or "girls can't play football") and of strong sanctions against behavior that is inconsistent with one's gender role.

Laboratory studies have also shown that exposure to gender stereotypes in books and on television tends to have a measurable effect on children's sex-typed behavior. In addition, these media may be important in the development of a child's gender schema because they provide a rich network of information and associations related to gender. Research indicates that children who are heavy viewers of television tend to have more rigid gender stereotypes than children who watch less television. The influence of media is also highlighted in studies showing that children who watch shows or read books in which the main characters go against traditional gender roles (for example, a female firefighter who saves lives) have less rigid gender stereotypes than children who are not exposed to these sorts of egalitarian gender models.

BIOLOGICAL BASES OF GENDERED BEHAVIOR

Research on gender identity formation in the 1970s through the 1990s tended to focus on the social forces leading to children's sense of themselves as male or female. However, researchers have turned their attention to the biological bases of gendered behavior. For example, brain imaging studies indicate that male and female brains differ in their structural organization; in particular, male brains are more strongly lateralized, meaning that specific cognitive functions tend to be located on one side of the brain or the other, whereas in female brains, there is more widespread activity across the left and right hemispheres.

Studies with young infants indicate that there are differences in boys' and girls' behavior and interests as early as the first few months of life. For example, newborn girls are more likely to imitate the facial and hand movements of other people during face-to-face interactions. Furthermore, when offered two videos to watch, one portraying a social event such as two people talking together and another portraying a mechanical event such as racing automobiles, one-year-old girls prefer to watch the people, but one-year-old boys generally prefer to watch the cars. These studies suggest that there are differences in the ways that boys and girls approach the world that are evident before gender identity development or sex typing has occurred. However, a significant number of the identified differences between male and female brains become more pronounced in adulthood, indicating that these innate differences in brain structure may be reinforced through social learning and the plasticity of the brain. A challenge for the twenty-first century will be to understand how biological and social forces interact in the formation of gender identity.

BIBLIOGRAPHY

Baron-Cohen, Simon. *The Essential Difference: Male and Female Brains and the Truth About Autism*. London: Penguin, 2004. Print.

Blakemore, Judith E. Owen, Sheri A. Berenbaum, and Lynn S. Liben. *Gender Development*. New York: Psychology, 2008. Print.

Bussey, K., and A. Bandura. "Social Cognitive Theory of Gender Development and Differentiation." *Psychological Review* 106.4 (1999): 676–713. Print.

Farris, Demetrea Nicole, Mary Ann Davis, and D'Lane R. Compton. *Illuminating How Identities Stereotypes, and Inequalities Matter through Gender Studies*. New York: Springer, 2014. Print.

Foss, Sonja K., Mary E. Domenico. and Karen A. Foss. *Gender Stories: Negotiating Identity in a Binary World*. Long Grove: Waveland, 2013. Print.

Kimmel, Michael. *The Gendered Society*. New York: Oxford UP, 2001. Print.

Kreukels, Baudewijntje P. C., Thomas D. Steensma, and Annelou L. C. de Vries, eds. *Gender Dysphoria and Disorders of Sex Development: Progress in Care and Knowledge*. New York: Springer, 2013. Print.

Pauletti, Rachel E., Patrick J. Cooper, and David G. Perry. "Influences of Gender Identity on Children's Maltreatment of Gender-Nonconforming Peers." *Journal of Personality and Social Psychology* 106.5 (2014): 843–66. Print.

Unger, Rhoda K., ed. *Handbook of the Psychology of Women and Gender*. New York: Wiley, 2001. Print.

Lesley A. Slavin; updated by Virginia Slaughter

See Also: Children's mental health; Cognitive ability: Gender differences; Developmental psychology; Freud, Sigmund; Freudian psychology; Gender identity disorder; Gender roles and gender role conflicts; Genetics and mental health; Hormones and behavior; Horney, Karen; Kohlberg, Lawrence; Personality theory; Piaget, Jean; Psychoanalytic psychology and personality: Sigmund Freud; Sexism; Sexual variants and paraphilias; Women's psychology: Karen Horney; Women's psychology: Sigmund Freud.

Gender roles and gender role conflicts

Type of psychology: Cognition

Gender roles, or people's perceptions of what it is to be a man or woman, are psychosocial constructions. Unlike sex, gender roles are based not on biology but rather on learned cultural norms or roles. These roles affect the course of people's lives, influencing the areas of socialization, communication, family life, household responsibilities, occupations, hobbies, and education.

Key Concepts

- Gender roles
- Left-brained
- Right-brained
- Stereotype
- Underachievement

INTRODUCTION

Although many people hold certain beliefs about gender and its impact on men and women's capabilities, these perceived truths are actually evolved psychosocial constructions called gender roles. Although the sex of a person is based in biology, gender roles are learned social norms. Although there are significant biological differences between the sexes, gender is largely viewed as a social construction that affects individuals' psychosocial development. Therefore, gender roles are subject to change over time, and there are significant differences in cross-cultural perspectives on gender and gender roles.

FAMILY LIFE

Researchers have found that the gender roles of married couples tend to become more clearly defined following the birth of a child. Often the woman assumes the primary responsibility for child care and the greater part of the housework. Some people see these family gender roles and the unequal distribution of familial responsibility as unfair and claim that each parent should take equal responsibility. They argue that placing too much stress on one parent is not good for the family. In most countries, even women who work outside the home complete a majority of the housework involved in raising their children and maintaining their homes. Researchers have found that these working mothers have fragmented leisure time because their off-work hours are consumed by household and child-care chores. Since the 1970s, when the women's rights movement began gaining traction, men's participation in housework in the United States has nearly doubled, and their time spent on child care has tripled. However, women still complete the majority of household chores and child care responsibilities, in accordance with traditional concepts of gender roles, even in families in which women work equivalent or longer hours outside the home and earn salaries that are equal to or higher than their husbands. On the other hand, men are more likely to work longer hours outside the home than women, and surveys have indicated that a majority of men would prefer to have more time to dedicate to raising their children.

The household structure in which a person is raised has been shown to correlate with the degree to which the person as an adult believes in and follows traditional gender roles. It makes sense logically that family members become used to a structure they have lived with for all or most of their lives and interpret it as the norm, especially if they have not experienced any other family situation. Members of such a family may not even be aware of the existence of other functional family structures. Kelly found that a significantly higher number of girls than boys participated in household cleanup, a chore traditionally associated with women: according to researcher Alison Kelly, 72 percent of eleven-year-old girls as compared with 29 percent of eleven-year-old boys participated in household chores. Such childhood experiences are likely to produce adults who tend to follow traditional gender roles.

OCCUPATION

Occupation is another area in which gender stereotypes abound, and gender roles can have a significant impact on men's and women's career trajectories and lifetime earnings. Common gender stereotypes hold that men are better at so-called "left-brained" skills such as logic mathematics and that women are better at "right-brained" skills such as language and communication. Kelly found that parents had a tendency to guide their children toward certain occupations and interests based on the child's gender. According to Kelly's research, the jobs of nurse, social worker, and teacher were traditionally seen as more fitting for women, and manual jobs such as electrician and engineer were considered more suitable for men. However, Kelly noted that parents did not link all professions with a specific gender: Jobs such as doctor, manager, and computer operator were not viewed as being more suitable for either men or women. Kelly concluded that women business professionals may gain acceptance more easily than women who choose to work in a trade or craft. Furthermore, social-science research indicates that the lack of same-gender role models and mentors in traditionally gendered fields—particularly science, technology, engineering, and mathematics (STEM) careers for women and care-giving careers such as nursing for men—have a significant impact on dissuading individuals from pursuing their interest in a particular career.

Salaries and wages are also affected by traditional concepts of gender roles. According to the Organisation for Economic Co-operation and Development (OECD), women across the developed world earn approximately 16 percent less than men employed in similar full-time jobs and with similar skill and experience levels. This wage discrepancy becomes even larger for women with children, particularly in countries that do not ensure paid maternity and/or paternity leave following the birth of a child. The pay gap becomes even larger when comparing all working mothers, not just full-time employees, as many women opt to return to work part time following the birth of a child, particularly when they do not have access to maternity leave or affordable child care. This phenomenon, dubbed "the mommy penalty," relates directly to women's traditional gender role as the primary caregivers to their children. Women who take time away from their jobs to have and raise children are often penalized for their absence with lower wages and fewer opportunities for advancement.

One of Kelly's major findings is that most of parents interviewed believed in equality of education and occupational opportunities for both genders, but with limitations. The parents' formal commitment to equality coexisted with other attitudes that might make equality difficult or even impossible, such as a belief that women have the right to work but only if their work does not interfere with their roles as mothers. Many parents were idealistic about equality of education and work, but they saw equality as an ideal rather than as a practical, reachable goal. Therefore, in essence, these parents exhibited a subtle but real sexism that likely shaped their children's perceptions of gender and gender roles.

EDUCATION

The behavior of boys and girls at school differs, according to researchers Susan Jones and Debra Myhill of Exeter University. Boys may underachieve because they feel that they are supposed to be "macho" or "tough," and they may view sitting in a classroom, quietly doing written work, as "wimpy" or "compliant" and therefore undesirable behavior. Another possible cause of underachievement in boys is that they typically have weaker hearing than girls; therefore,if they are placed in the back of the classroom, they may strain to hear the teacher's words and will find it harder to follow along and accomplish the assigned tasks.

Similarly, Jones notes that girls were once viewed as struggling in a male-dominated classroom and suffering from low self-esteem and poor self-confidence as a result. People often repeat the notion that girls are inferior at math and science, although this attitude is slowly growing less common. Research has shown that the gender achievement gap in math and science closes in countries that have high levels of gender equity. In countries with the highest levels of gender equality, both boys and girls perform better on standardized mathematics tests. Several researchers have explored the concept of stereotype threat, which holds that when individuals are aware of negative stereotypes about their group (and most children are aware of their culture's sex stereotypes at a young age), they are likely to conform to those negative or positive expectations.

In a 2001 study by N. Ambady and colleagues, Asian American girls in kindergarten through the eighth grade were presented with tasks intended to highlight either their female identity, their Asian identity, or neither identity, and the girls then completed a grade-level-appropriate standardized math test. Compared to the group of girls who were not primed to consider either their racial or sexual identity, girls whose gender had been emphasized performed worse (conforming to the stereotype that girls are not good at math) while those girls whose race had been emphasized performed better (conforming to the stereotype that Asians are good at math). Stereotype threat may also explain boys' relative underachievement in language arts, as children may not be motivated to try in certain subjects if they believe they have a particular gender deficit in that area. Ultimately, long-standing educational gender stereotypes have the potential to become self-fulfilling prophecies when it comes to overall achievement in school or in specific subjects, to the detriment of both girls' and boys' academic performance.

The stereotypes that portray girls as compliant and boys as challenging also affect the kind of attention that teachers give to each student. Jones argued that the stereotype of girls as more compliant may make it harder for teachers to identify underachieving girls than underachieving boys. If teachers do not see these girls' performances as problematic, they are not likely to intervene and help them do better. This results in teachers paying greater attention to underachieving boys than to underachieving girls, thereby affecting the quality of the education that the children receive.

IMPLICATIONS

Gender roles have both positive and negative influences on society. One task for researchers is to find ways, beginning in childhood, to minimize or alter the negative effects that gender roles have on psychological and intellectual development. Society may be difficult to change, but gradual alterations in the definitions of gender roles could help. Another way to minimize negative effects is to eliminate the inferiority associated with various gender traits.

BIBLIOGRAPHY

Bonvillain, Nancy. *Women and Men: Cultural Constructs of Gender.* 4th ed. Upper Saddle River: Pearson, 2007. Print.

Buchanan, Tom. "The Influence of Gender Role Attitudes on Perceptions of Women's Work Performance and the Importance of Fair Pay." *Sociological Spectrum* 34.3 (2014): 203–21. Print.

Jones, Susan, and Debra Myhill. "'Troublesome Boys' and 'Compliant Girls': Gender Identity and Perceptions of Achievement and Underachievement." *British Journal of Sociology of Education* 25.5 (2004): 547–61. Print.

Kelly, Alison, et al. "Gender Roles at Home and School." *British Journal of Sociology of Education* 3.3 (1982): 281–95. Print.

Lindsey, Linda A. *Gender Roles: A Sociological Perspective.* 5th ed. Boston: Pearson, 2010. Print.

Miville, Marie L. *Multicultural Gender Roles: Applications for Mental Health and Education.* Hoboken: Wiley, 2013. Print.

OECD. *Closing the Gender Gap: Act Now.* N.p.: OECD, 2012. PDF file.

Patten, Eileen, and Kim Parker. "A Gender Reversal on Career Aspirations." *Pew Research Social and Demographic Trends.* Pew Research Center, 19 Apr. 2012. Web. 31 July 2014.

Perrone-McGovern, Kristin M., Stephen L. Wright, Desiree S. Howell, and Emily L. Barnum. "Contextual Influences on Work and Family Roles: Gender, Culture, and Socioeconomic Factors." *Career Development Quarterly* 62.1 (2014): 21–28. Print.

Rampell, Catherine. "The 'Mommy Penalty,' around the World." Economix. New York Times, 17 Dec. 2012. Web. 31 July 2014.

Smoreda, Zbigniew, and Christian Licoppe. "Gender-Specific Use of the Domestic Telephone." *Social Psychology Quarterly* 63 (2000): 238–52. Print.

Stone, Pamela. *Opting Out? Why Women Really Quit Careers and Head Home.* Berkeley: U of California P, 2008. Print.

Walker, Alexis. "Couples Watching Television: Gender, Power, and the Remote Control." *Journal of Marriage and the Family* 58.4 (1996): 813–23. Print.

Elyssa Pearlstein

See Also: Adolescence: Sexuality; Aggression; Attitude formation and change; Children's mental health; Family life: Adult issues; Family life: Children's issues; Femininity; Gender differences; Gender identity disorder; Gender identity formation; Hormones and behavior; Masculinity; Teenagers' mental health.

General adaptation syndrome (GAS)

Type of psychology: Stress

General adaptation syndrome is the name given to the manifestations of the state of stress in a body. Stress is the most active specific conditioning factor in the human organism. Psychosomatic medicine had its beginnings with the discovery of this syndrome.

Key Concepts

- Adaptation
- Adrenal glands
- Alarm reaction
- Conditioning factors
- Glucocorticoids
- Lymphatic tissue
- Mineralocorticoids
- Stage of exhaustion
- Stage of resistance
- Thymus gland

INTRODUCTION

Stress is the rate of wear and tear, in particular the strain on the nervous system, in an organism. It is the sum of all adaptive reactions in the body and manifests itself by a specific syndrome that consists of all the nonspecifically induced changes within the individual.

Adaptive reactions, or adaptation, are the processes by which the organism adjusts itself to changed circumstances. A syndrome is a group of symptoms usually appearing together in a disease. Nonspecific changes are those that involve many organs of the body and can be induced by a variety of causal factors. Nevertheless, the form in which these changes appear is quite specific: It is the general adaptation syndrome (GAS), first described by Hans Selye in the 1950's. The explanation of this seeming contradiction lies in the fact that stress produces two kinds of change: one that is nonspecifically caused and appears in a nonspecific form, called the primary change; and one that, although nonspecifically caused, is specific in form, the secondary change called general adaptation syndrome.

STAGES

The general adaptation syndrome is composed of three stages. The first is the alarm reaction, in which the body arms itself for defense against an aggression (such as a bacterial or viral infection, physical damage, or a strong nervous stimulus) but has had no time to adjust itself to the new condition. The second is the stage of resistance, in which the body succeeds in adapting itself to the condition. The third is the stage of exhaustion, in which the body's resistance breaks down with the loss of its adaptive response, a development that can lead to death.

There are three main signs of the first (alarm reaction) stage: an enlargement of the cortex (outer layer) of the adrenal glands; a degeneration of the thymus gland (located in the front of the chest, playing an important role in defense against infections) and the lymphatic system (the vessels that carry the lymph, or white blood, and the lymph nodes, including the spleen and tonsils); and the appearance of gastrointestinal (stomach and gut) ulcers.

In the second (resistance) stage, the body is at its highest level of adaptation, above the normal range, and the body organs return to their normal state. The adrenals, which in the first stage completely discharged their hormones, again accumulate large amounts of hormones. In the last (exhaustion) stage, the adrenals again lose their secretions and the other organs degenerate even more; the body's resistance drops to below-normal levels. Although the third stage can lead to death, this is not necessarily the outcome. Often a person undergoes all three stages only to recuperate at the end. A marathon runner goes through all stages of the general adaptation syndrome and, although completely exhausted at the end of the race, regains strength after only a few hours of rest.

The adrenal glands have an important role in the general adaptation syndrome. These are two little glands, each sitting on top of one of the kidneys. The gland is composed of an outer part, or cortex, and a core, or medulla. The cortex is subdivided into layers, one of which manufactures the so-called mineralocorticoids, aldosterone and desoxycorticosterone (DOCA), which have a role in electrolyte (salt) metabolism and have a proinflammatory effect in the body; the second layer secretes the glucocorticoids, cortisol and cortisone, which play a role in sugar metabolism and have an anti-inflammatory effect. Inflammation is a local defense mechanism of the body; the anti-inflammatory hormones suppress this defensive weapon. They also promote the spread of infections and the formation of gastrointestinal ulcers. In spite of this apparent antagonism between the two types of cortical hormones, their effects are absolutely necessary for the body to resist aggression. If the adrenal glands are damaged to a degree that they can no longer produce these hormones, then, without treatment, death is inevitable. In contrast, the hormones secreted by the medullary part of the adrenal gland, epinephrine (also known as adrenaline) and norepinephrine, are not absolutely necessary for survival because they are also produced by nerve endings in other parts of the body.

AGENTS AND EFFECTS

Any agent that attacks the body will induce both specific and nonspecific effects. These are direct effects, such as a burn wound, and indirect effects, which are of two kinds: one that triggers the proinflammatory mechanism, inducing it to fight the damage, and one that triggers the anti-inflammatory mechanism, which limits the extent of the damage. The system is actually a bit more complex than this; another component, the so-called conditioning factors, must be taken into account.

Conditioning factors are agents or situations that themselves have no independent effects; however, they can modify the response to a particular stimulus. There are external and internal conditioning factors. The external ones comprise, for example, geographical, social, and nutritional factors, whereas the internal conditioning factors are those determined by genetics and previous experiences.

Based on this information, the sequence of events that occurs when a stressor (a stress inducer) acts on an individual may be summarized as follows: The brain senses the stimulus and sends messages to the adrenal medulla, inducing it to release epinephrine, and to the pituitary gland, inducing it to release adrenocorticotropic hormone (ACTH). Epinephrine has two effects: It acts on the pituitary gland, increasing the secretion of ACTH, and it acts on most of the body tissues, increasing their rate of activity. The heart rate, breathing rate, and blood pressure are increased, as well as the blood sugar level. All these changes prepare the organism for fight or flight. ACTH, in the meantime, reaches the adrenal cortex and induces the secretion of anti-inflammatory hormones. Simultaneously, proinflammatory hormones are released. Both types act on the tissues affected directly by the stressor and also have a systemic effect on the whole body, inducing the general adaptation syndrome. The particular type and degree of response are modulated by the conditioning factors.

STRESS AND DISEASE

Disease could be defined as an alteration, as a result of a changed environment, of the structure and function of tissues that interferes with their ability to survive. To produce a disease, two types of factors are necessary: environmental, or external, factors; and the response of the organism, or internal factors. The discovery that stress elicits a specific response, the general adaptation syndrome, made it possible to apply exact measurements to the state of stress and its consequences (stress-induced diseases). Although the general adaptation syndrome has a defensive purpose in the body because it promotes adaptation to new conditions, an excess of adaptive hormones can induce untoward symptoms, that is, cause disease. This aspect of stress, that adaptive reactions can themselves become harmful, is one of the most important characteristics of the phenomenon. It made physicians realize that there are many diseases that are not caused by specific agents such as microorganisms, toxic chemicals, or injuries, but rather by the response of tissues to these aggressors (stressors). An example of this type of disease is an allergy such as hay fever or hives. It was found that the inflammation of the nasal passages, eyes, or skin is caused by the tissues reacting against chemicals contained in pollen or in some foods. The body fights these reactions with glucocorticoids (anti-inflammatory hormones) secreted by the adrenal cortex. This discovery, that adrenal glucocorticoids have anti-inflammatory and antiallergic effects, was immediately applied in clinical medicine to treat very grave diseases such as arthritis and asthma. The glucocorticoids proved to be lifesaving in these cases.

As the phenomenon of stress is primarily produced by a strain on the nervous system, it seemed reasonable to look into the role of the general adaptation syndrome in nervous and mental diseases. It became clear that what is called maladaptation can be the cause of a nervous breakdown or even outright mental disease. This realization led physicians to search for the connection between psychological maladjustments and bodily diseases. The result was the foundation of the medical specialty called psychosomatic medicine. It is known that what is called "executive disease"—that is, gastrointestinal ulcers and high blood pressure, sometimes accompanied by a nervous breakdown—is induced by the inability to adjust to a new situation, by an exceptionally heavy workload, or by fear of responsibility and an inability to make decisions. Psychosomatic medicine attempts to elucidate the way in which maladaptation causes disease as well as the way in which it influences aging and the degenerative diseases of old age, in particular, coronary heart disease and cancer. It is known that chronological age is not the same as physiological age. That is, a fifty-year-old person, from the point of view of tissue integrity and function, may be much older than a seventy-year-old person whose tissues are still in good functioning order. The underlying causes of these individual differences are based in an individual's differential response to stressful situations.

As an outgrowth of the study of stress and the GAS, two subfields of research opened up: the psychology of stress and psychophysiology. The study of stress psychology implies that human behavior is affected by biological mechanisms that appear to be a common heritage of all mammals. The aim of the study would be to enable people to control their emotions and, thus, their behavior. This would be of obvious benefit in the rehabilitation of persons who come in conflict with the law because of their violent behavior and, possibly, would allow society to reduce violent crimes. Psychophysiology, which was founded as a separate branch of psychology in 1960, studies psychological or behavioral variables with their respective physiological responses. For example, one of the major preoccupations of psychophysiology is the study of biofeedback, or the control by subjects of their own heart rates or brain function. There is great interest in biofeedback studies, because it is hoped that psychosomatic disturbances could be treated successfully by this technique. In 1949, researchers studied two groups of patients: one group that had recurring head and neck pains, and another that complained of cardiovascular (heart) symptoms. When the researchers administered painful stimuli to the two groups, the members of each group reported an increased intensity in its particular symptoms, although they had been well before the test. The researchers concluded that psychosomatic disorders are caused by the exaggerated response of a particular physiological system, characteristic for the individual. This phenomenon has been named symptom specificity.

HISTORY OF STRESS RESEARCH

In ancient Greece, the father of medicine, Hippocrates, taught that in every diseased body there is a natural force that fights the disease from within. Later, in eighteenth century England, John Hunter stated that every injury has the tendency to produce the means for a cure. That is, the concept of being sick includes a battle between the aggressor and the defense mechanisms of the body. Rufus of Ephesus, a Greek physician, around the year 100 c.e. discovered that high fever had a beneficial effect on the progression of many illnesses. This fact was rediscovered by a nineteenth century Viennese psychiatrist, Julius Wagner von Jauregg, who tried to alleviate the mental disease of patients in the last stage of syphilis. In 1883, he observed that the symptoms improved markedly when the patients contracted typhoid fever. Subsequently, he introduced the treatment with malaria and achieved spectacular results, but without knowing the reason for the cure.

The great French physiologist Claude Bernard, in the nineteenth century, taught that a characteristic of living organisms is their ability to maintain a constant internal environment in spite of significant fluctuations in the external conditions in which they live. Walter Bradford Cannon, at Harvard University, gave this phenomenon the name " homeostasis." He also coined the term "emergency reaction" to describe the immediate functional changes occurring in the body as a consequence of stressful stimuli. When the homeostatic mechanisms of the body fail to maintain the constancy of the internal medium, disease and eventually death ensue. Although all these findings converged in the treatment of disease by nonspecific means, it was a Viennese physician, Selye, who formulated a scientific theory of the "syndrome of being sick," or, in other words, the concept of stress and of the general adaptation syndrome.

Selye, who was born in Vienna but immigrated to Canada, discovered in 1936 that the physical response to stress could cause disease and even death. He detected the effects of stress when he injected ovarian extracts into laboratory rats. He found that the extract induced enlargement of the adrenal cortex, shrinkage of the thymus gland, and gastric ulcers. Selye realized that it was the stress caused by the impurities in the extract that induced the characteristic changes. He extrapolated his findings to humans and stated that stress could initiate disease and cause death. In 1950, he published *The Physiology and Pathology of Exposure to Stress*, in which he gave a detailed description of the general adaptation syndrome concept.

In the beginning, the medical establishment was reluctant to accept the idea that hormones could have a role in the causation of nonspecific aspects of disease; until that time, hormones were known to act only on specific target tissues. They caused disease either by too little or too much of a particular hormone. For example, a lack of growth hormone resulted in dwarfism, whereas too much of the same created a giant. Selye, however, postulated general hormonal effects that transcended their known immediate action on target tissues. Another, unjustified, criticism of his theory was that he attributed too great a role to the hormonal system, neglecting the part played by the nervous system. These criticisms did not hold up in the long run, and Selye's teachings on stress and the general adaptation syndrome were in the end accepted by medical and physiological researchers.

BIBLIOGRAPHY

Kahn, Ada P., ed. *The Encyclopedia of Stress and Stress-Related Diseases*. 2d ed. New York: Facts On File, 2005. Print.

Khazan, Inna Z. *The Clinical Handbook of Biofeedback: A Step by Step Guide for Training and Practice with Mindfulness.* Chichester: Wiley-Blackwell, 2013. Print.

Marks, David, Michael Murray, Brian Evans, and Emee Vida Estacio. *Health Psychology: Theory Research, and Practice*. 3rd ed. London: Sage, 2011. Print.

Romas, John A., and Manoj Sharma. *Practical Stress Management: A Comprehensive Workbook for Managing Change and Promoting Health*. 5th ed. San Francisco: Pearson, 2009. Print.

Sapolsky, Robert. *Why Zebras Don't Get Ulcers: An Updated Guide to Stress, Stress-Related Diseases, and Coping*. New York: Freeman, 1998. Print.

Seaward, Brian L. *Managing Stress: Principles and Strategies for Health and Well-being*. 7th ed. Sudbury: Jones, 2012. Print.

Selye, Hans. *The Stress of Life*. Rev. ed. New York: McGraw-Hill, 1978. Print.

Wulsin, Lawson R. *Treating the Aching Heart: A Guide to Depression, Stress, and Heart Disease*. Nashville: Vanderbilt UP, 2007. Print.

René R. Roth

See Also: Adrenal gland; Cannon, Walter Bradford; Endocrine system; Fear; Fight-or-flight response; Hormones and behavior; Nervous system; Selye, Hans; Stress: Behavioral and psychological responses; Stress: Physiological responses; Stress related diseases; Stress: Theories.

General aptitude test battery (GATB)

Date: 1947 onward

Type of psychology: Intelligence and intelligence testing; Personality; Social psychology

The General Aptitude Test Battery is a vocational aptitude test that takes about three hours to complete and includes both physical tests, such as manipulating objects, and paper-and-pencil questions.

Key Concepts

- Aptitude tests
- Job satisfaction
- Race norming

INTRODUCTION

Developed by the US Employment Service, the General Aptitude Test Battery (GATB) can identify aptitudes for different occupations. It has been used by state employment services as well as other agencies and organizations, such as the US Employment Service and the Employment Security Commission.

The GATB comprises twelve timed subtests: vocabulary, arithmetic, computation, mark making, assembling, disassembling, turning, placing, name comparison, tool matching, form matching, and three-dimensional space. These twelve subtests correspond to nine aptitudes: intelligence, verbal, numerical, spatial, form perception, clerical perception, motor coordination, finger dexterity, and manual dexterity. These nine aptitudes in turn can be divided into three composite aptitudes: cognitive, perceptual, and psychomotor.

The entire test takes about two to three hours to complete. About one-half of the test deals with psychomotor tasks, such as manipulating small objects with the fingers; the other half consists of paper-and-pencil questions. In some cases, an examiner might administer only selected tests of the battery as a measure of aptitude for a specific line of work. Scores for each aptitude test are based on the total number of correct answers. Raw scores are converted to norm-referenced aptitude scores.

Its average is 100; its standard deviation is 20. Anyone of working age can take the GATB. Most people complete fewer than half of the items, but people who are familiar with timed tests may be able to increase their scores by quickly completing all the items.

USES AND LIMITATIONS

The GATB can be used to help job seekers or employers. Typically, job seekers who take the GATB receive counseling on their scores for each of the nine aptitudes. Their pattern of scores can be compared with the patterns deemed necessary for different occupations. Employers might use the GATB in their efforts to hire qualified employees. Also, the GATB has been used in research, such as exploring the differences in abilities of different groups or assessing the impact of various training programs or work experience.

The GATB has been translated into several languages and has been used in many different countries, including Australia, Brazil, Canada, China, Colombia, France, India, Italy, Portugal, and Switzerland, as well as in the United States. There is also a completely computerized version.

As is true of other tests, the GATB has limitations. In the late 1980s, the GATB became a center of controversy when people discovered that it had been race normed. Subsequently, the National Academy of Sciences studied the situation and concluded that race norming was reasonable, because it corrected for test bias. In a controversial move, the National Academy of Sciences recommended to continue the practice of race norming. In July 1990, the Department of Labor (DOL) proposed a two-year suspension of the GATB to study whether it worked well enough to continue to be used. The question became moot in 1991, however, when Congress passed the Civil Rights Act of 1991, a law that outlawed the practice of race norming. Consequently, reports are no longer race normed. Instead, raw scores of people from all racial and ethnic groups are converted to standard scores using the same norms.

As a result of the controversy and federal suspension of the GATB, the US federal government, as well as many state governments and other employers, have discontinued it in favor of other, more up-to-date multiple-aptitude test batteries or more specific ability and skill assessments. The DOL's O*NET Ability Profiler tool, which indicates percentile ranks of each aptitude needed for a specific occupation, is based on forms of the GATB and has largely replaced the traditional GATB. Where it is still used, the GATB can be useful in predicting who will be the most successful person on the job, but it is not considered strong enough to be the sole determinant in selection. For instance, in Canada, the GATB is frequently used for vocational counseling purposes.

BIBLIOGRAPHY

Baydoun, Ramzi B., and George A. Neuman. "The Future of the General Aptitude Test Battery (GATB) for Use in Public and Private Testing." *Journal of Business and Psychology* 7 (1992): 81–91. Print.

"General Aptitude Test Battery (GATB): An Occupationally-Oriented Multiple-Aptitude Test." *Nelson Education*. Nelson Education, 1 July 2013. Web. 15 May 2014.

Gottfredson, L. S. "The Science and Politics of Race-Norming." *American Psychologist* 49 (1994): 955–63. Print.

Leahy, Michael J. "Assessment of Vocational Interests and Aptitudes in Rehabilitation Settings." *Psychological Assessment in Medical Rehabilitation*. Ed. Laura A. Cushman and Marcia J. Scherer. Washington: Amer. Psychological Assn., 1999. Print.

Lock, Robert D. *Taking Charge of Your Career Direction: Career Planning Guide*. Belmont: Thomson Brooks/Cole, 2005. Print.

McIntire, Sandra A., and Leslie A. Miller. *Foundations of Psychological Testing: A Practical Approach*. 2nd ed. Thousand Oaks: Sage, 2007. Print.

Savickas, Mark L., and Arnold R. Spokane, eds. *Vocational Interests: Meaning, Measurement, and Counseling Use*. Palo Alto: Consulting Psychologists P, 1999. Print.

Schmidt, Frank L., and John E. Hunter. "The Validity and Utility of Selection Methods in Personnel Psychology: Practical and Theoretical Implications of Eighty-five Years of Research Findings." *Psychological Bulletin* 124 (1998): 262–74. Print.

Thomas, Jay C. *Specialty Competencies in Organizational and Business Consulting Psychology*. Oxford: Oxford UP, 2010. Print.

Wigdor, Alexandra K., and Paul R. Sackett. "Employment Testing and Public Policy: The Case of the General Aptitude Test Battery." *Personnel Selection and Assessment: Individual and Organizational Perspectives*. Ed. Heinz Schuler, James L. Farr, and Mike Smith. Hillsdale: Lawrence Erlbaum, 1993. Print.

Lillian M. Range

SEE ALSO: Ability tests; Assessment; Career and personnel testing; Career Occupational Preference System (COPS); College entrance examinations; Creativity: Assessment; Human resource training and development; Intelligence tests; Interest inventories; Kuder Occupational Interest Survey (KOIS); Peabody Individual Achievement Test (PIAT); Race and intelligence; Scientific methods; Stanford-Binet test; Strong Interest Inventory (SII); Testing: Historical perspectives; Wechsler Intelligence Scale for Children-Third Edition (WISC-III).

Generalized anxiety disorder (GAD)

DATE: 1980 forward
TYPE OF PSYCHOLOGY: Psychopathology

Generalized anxiety disorder (GAD) is a mental disorder in which the person worries excessively about a number of topics. These worries occur daily, continue over a period of six or more months, and typically diminish the person's quality of life. GAD is treated with medications, cognitive behavior therapy, or both. The medications used are antidepressants and antianxiety medications.

KEY CONCEPTS
- Amygdala
- Azapirone derivatives
- Benzodiazepines
- Cognitive behavior therapy
- Dopamine
- Gamma-aminobutyric acid (GABA)
- Norepinephrine
- Selective serotonin reuptake inhibitors (SSRIs)
- Serotonin-norepinephrine reuptake inhibitors (SNRIs)
- Tricyclic antidepressants

INTRODUCTION

Generalized anxiety disorder (GAD) is characterized by excessive worry about a variety of topics. This anxiety occurs every day, over a period of at least six months. The worries tend to be difficult to control and to diminish the person's quality of life. Signs and symptoms of GAD include restlessness, difficulty concentrating, fatigue, irritability, impatience, being easily distracted, muscle tension, trouble falling asleep or staying asleep, excessive sweating or hot flashes, shortness of breath, diarrhea, headache, stomachache, having trouble swallowing, feeling light-headed, and having to go to the bathroom frequently.

POSSIBLE CAUSES

The cause of generalized anxiety disorder is not known, although there are a number of theories as to its cause. There may be a hereditary tendency to develop GAD. Some of the causative theories are based on experiences in the person's life, such as traumatic events occurring in childhood, serious illness, and stressful life experiences. Anxiety may be an inherent part of the person's personality. Some medications and medical conditions can cause GAD. It is also theorized that persons with GAD may produce low levels of brain chemicals such as serotonin, gamma-aminobutyric acid (GABA), norepinephrine, and dopamine, which are thought to improve mood. It is thought that the amygdala, a small structure within the brain, is a depository for memories of frightening and other highly emotional events. Persons with GAD may have an overly sensitive amygdala that tends to react to situations that are not actually threatening. Questions remain as to whether physical changes in the brain lead to anxiety or whether stressful situations and the resulting anxiety lead to changes in the brain.

DIAGNOSIS

In 1980, the American Psychiatric Association split the diagnosis of anxiety neurosis into two diagnoses: panic disorder and general anxiety disorder.

The diagnosis of GAD is a subjective one, based on the patient's reporting of excessive worrying about a variety of topics that has lasted more than six continuous months. GAD can develop in people of all ages, including children. However, all anxiety disorders, including GAD, are more common in women and in older persons.

TREATMENT OPTIONS

The treatment for GAD is antianxiety medications, cognitive behavior therapy(CBT), or both. Antianxiety medications used to treat GAD include benzodiazepines, selective serotonin reuptake inhibitors (SSRIs), serotonin-norepinephrine reuptake inhibitors (SNRIs), tricyclic antidepressants, and an azpirone derivative.

Benzodiazepines are the first medications prescribed for GAD. They cause mental and physical relaxation by increasing levels of GABA in the brain. They include alprazolam (Xanax), lorazepam (Ativan), clonazepam (Klonopin), and diazepam (Valium).

SSRIs are drugs, developed in the 1990's, that interfere with the reabsorption (reuptake) of serotonin in the brain, leading to higher levels of serotonin in the body. These medications are less habit-forming than the benzodiazepines and have fewer side effects than older antidepressant medications. SSRIs include fluoxetine (Prozac), paroxetine(Paxil), citalopram (Celexa), sertraline (Zoloft), and escitalopram (Lexapro).

Serotonin-norepinephrine reuptake inhibitors (SNRIs) interfere with the reabsorption of both serotonin and norepinephrine in the brain. There are two drugs in this group: venlafaxine (Effexor) and duloxetine (Cymbalta).

Tricyclic antidepressants (TCAs), which were developed in the 1970's, interfere with the reabsorption of serotonin and norepinephrine in the brain, and they increase the sensitivity of the serotonin and norepinephrine receptors. TCAs have more side effects and more serious side effects than SSRIs, including altering the rhythm of the heart. TCAs include amitriptyline (Elavil), clomipramine (Anafranil), and imipramine (Tofranil).

There is only one azapirone derivative, buspirone (BuSpar). Buspirone increases the activity of serotonin and decreases the activity of dopamine. It accomplishes this by binding to the serotonin and dopamine receptors in the brain. Buspirone has few side effects compared with other drugs used to treat GAD.

Cognitive behavior therapy increases the levels of serotonin and norepinephrine in the body by changing the negative thought patterns of the patient. Persons with anxiety disorders, including GAD, tend to get caught up in their excessive reactions to stressful situations. Cognitive behavior therapy teaches them to stop these negative thoughts and to evaluate the validity of their fears.

BIBLIOGRAPHY

Bourne, Edmund J., and Lorna Garano. *Coping with Anxiety: Ten Simple Ways to Relieve Anxiety, Fear, and Worry.* Oakland, Calif.: New Harbinger, 2003. This book discusses ways to deal constructively with anxiety so that it does not control a person's life.

Dugas, Michel J., and Melisa Robichaud. *Cognitive-Behavioral Treatment for Generalized Anxiety Disorder: From Science to Practice.* New York: Routledge, 2007. This guide for clinicians provides the etiology, assessment, and treatment of this disorder, focusing on the cognitive behavior approach.

Gliatto, Michael F. "Generalized Anxiety Disorder." *American Family Physician* 62 (2000): 1509-1600, 1602. This article provides an in-depth description of how GAD is diagnosed and treated. In addition, it discusses the difficulties that can arise in diagnosing GAD.

Mufson, Michael, et al., eds. *Coping with Anxiety and Phobias.* Boston: Harvard Medical School, 2002. One in a series of medical reports, this work discusses the causes of anxiety, the types of anxiety disorders, and how anxiety is diagnosed and treated. It also describes how people can assist with their own treatment.

Rugh, Jayne L., and William C. Sanderson. *Treating Generalized Anxiety Disorder: Evidence-Based Strategies, Tools, and Techniques.* New York: Guilford Press, 2004. Examines the disorder and its treatments, with emphasis on how they are applied and how they work.

Christine M. Carroll

See Also: Antianxiety medications; Antidepressant medications; Anxiety disorders; Behavior therapy; Cognitive therapy; Drug therapies; Psychopharmacology.

Genetics and mental health

Date: 1930s onward

Type of psychology: Psychological methodologies; Psychotherapy; Stress

Mental health is influenced by proper functioning of myriad genes. Many of these genes and their interactions among themselves and with environmental factors have been identified. Research has been facilitated by the cracking of the genetic code and the availability of affordable tools for genetic testing. However, therapeutic interventions based on this knowledge are still limited.

Key Concepts

- Association studies
- Family studies
- Linkage analysis
- Mutations
- Structure of genes
- Twin studies

INTRODUCTION

The idea that genes can influence mental health has been entertained from the early part of the twentieth century. Several studies have shown positive association of genetic components with various mental disorders such as schizophrenia and bipolar disorder. Although a plethora of evidence suggests that many mental and psychiatric diseases have tremendously influential genetic components, solid evidence pointing to specific genes or gene variations as the direct cause of particular diseases is still lacking. Mental disorders are fairly complicated, because in most cases, diagnosis is based on self-reported symptoms (which could be subjective and overlap with other disorders) or clinical observations (which are hampered by the lack of sophisticated diagnostic and screening tools). Most mental disorders are complex in nature, with varying degrees of manifestations, onset times, and symptoms. Determining a genetic basis for such complex mental disorders becomes even more challenging because a disorder can be polygenic (more than one gene is responsible for the symptoms) or multifactorial in nature (both genetic and environmental factors are responsible), the genes may not adhere to Mendelian patterns of inheritance (the segregation of genes into the following generations is complex), and the loci of the risk alleles is heterogeneous in nature. Some researchers suspect that genes merely mediate some disorders rather than determine them. As more information emerges about the role of genes and their variations in mental illnesses, researchers are hopeful that methods for detecting mental illnesses will improve, that better, more tailored treatments will become available, and that prevention may even be possible, if environmental exposures and other risk factors can be mitigated for those with genetic susceptibility.

STRUCTURE OF GENES

Knowledge of the structure and functioning of genes provides a better understanding of how complex diseases can have a genetic basis. Genes are made up of deoxyribonucleic acid (DNA), which consists of bases called "nucleotides." Numerous nucleotides (called "polynucleotides"), interspersed with sugar molecules, are bound together through chemical bonds to form helical strands. Each DNA has two polynucleotide strands forming a double helical structure. Four bases have been identified—adenine (A), guanine (G), thiamine (T), and cytosine (C)—each of which has specific binding partners (A binds with T, and G binds with C).

Chromosomes consist of uninterrupted stretches of DNA molecules. During cell division, these DNA molecules get shuffled, and the resultant cells acquire a new combination of genes that are unique to an individual. This process is called "recombination of DNA." Recombination occurs through independent segregation and assortment of genes so that the unique combination of genes in the offspring has a fair mixture of the parents' DNA. In some cases, however, genes that are located in close proximity to each other stay together and do not segregate during cell division. These genes are said to be linked together, and the process of inheritance of a group of genes together is called "linkage." Linkage aids enormously in studying the genetic basis of many phenomena, including the occurrence of diseases. Traits or characters that are expressed together are of particular interest to linkage studies. If the gene responsible for one of these traits has been characterized, it can be used as a biological marker to study the putative genes that are responsible for the other linked trait.

Epigenetic markers are special chemical "tags" that become attached to DNA and affect which genes are activated under certain environmental conditions. These markers are also heritable. The study of epigenetics is a growing area of mental health research.

MUTATIONS

Alterations to the DNA sequences (called "mutations") can result in drastic changes, sometimes even changing a cell from a normal to a diseased state. Mutations can be at the level of one base pair (for example, A can mutate to G, which when copied will bind with C, instead of T), and this one base pair change (called a "point mutation") changes the code to a different amino acid, which can result in a malfunctioning or nonfunctional protein. Proper functioning of specific proteins is key for a normal or healthy state, and a point mutation can very well change that state of a cell. Mutations can also be insertions or deletions, in which a few additional nucleotides are added or deleted. All these can lead to drastic changes in the physiology of the cell.

In addition, mutations can also occur at the level of whole chromosomes. Chromosomal aberrations—deletions, duplications, inversions, insertions, or translocations—alter a whole array of genes, resulting in significant abnormalities. A common example of this is Down syndrome, in which the affected individual possesses either an extra copy of chromosome 21 or an additional piece attached to that chromosome because of a translocation event. The translocation of chromosomes that could be related to schizophrenia was first observed between chromosomes 1 and 11 in a large Scottish family study. Genes that elicited considerable interest in this region are *DISC1* (*Disrupted in Schizophrenia 1*) and *DISC2*. In the genome of patients with schizophrenia, either one or both of these genes is disrupted.

PENETRANCE AND EXPRESSIVITY

The extent to which a certain gene mutation results in symptoms varies between and within specific diseases. Some mutations lead to a distinctly altered physical manifestation (phenotype) or symptoms, and all individuals carrying a certain genetic composition (genotype) manifest those symptoms. Such mutations are called "penetrant," and the state is called "complete penetrance." Penetrance directly indicates the onset of an illness, which is the point at which the affected individual begins to show enough symptoms that a diagnosis can be made. If a certain illness affects the succeeding generation earlier than it did the previous one (a phenomenon called "early onset" or "anticipation"), the gene is said to be more penetrant. Early onset can somewhat simplify the identification of genes involved in mental disorders, but many individuals with the disease genes do not develop the disease until a later stage or do not develop the disease at all. Such incomplete penetrations pose serious problems, especially when conducting large family studies.

The degree of manifestation of the symptoms may range from mild to serious. This is referred to as the "expressivity" of the gene. Factors such as penetrance and expressivity complicate the understanding of the genetic bases of most diseases.

TYPES OF GENETIC ANALYSES

Many types of genetic analyses are performed to identify the genes involved and to decipher their roles in mental illnesses. Chief among them are linkage analysis, family studies, association studies, twin studies, and the candidate gene approach.

Linkage analysis. Linkage analysis is a powerful statistical tool that bases its findings on linkage maps and deduces the combination of alleles that are inherited together from multiple loci (haplotypes). It uses the location of commonly known markers (such as color blindness) and attempts to map potential genes of interest in the chromosome. Linkage mapping helps reduce the number of genes that need to be studied in a certain chromosome. A variety of associated biomarker tests help in narrowing down the genes associated with illnesses. Data are mostly collected from large families with multiple members, consisting of cases and probands (the first member of the family who reported the disease). Data from large samples are pooled in meta-analyses, and statistical tests are applied to deduce the probability of certain genes being linked and cosegregated and to exhibit certain disease phenotypes (called the "logarithm-of-odds ratio," or "lod score"). Most diseases that have a high degree of penetration use linkage studies for determining the relevant genes. Linkage studies, however, are limited by the number of genetic recombinations occurring within the specific set of chromosomes and sometimes (as in major mental illnesses such as schizophrenia and bipolar diseases) by the heterogeneous nature of specific loci in chromosomes.

Several studies identified strong linkage associations to chromosome 13 (13q) with schizophrenia. Other studies pointed to chromosomes 8 (8p), 22 (22q) and 1. Chromosomes 13 (13q) and 22q showed significant linkage to both schizophrenia and bipolar disease in a meta-analysis. However, much of the data on schizophrenia could not be replicated or yielded disappointing results. More consistent results have been obtained for autism, showing strong and reproducible linkages to chromosomes 2q, 7q, 15q, and 16p. Chromosomes 6 and 8 have strong genome-wide significance for bipolar disorder.

Family Studies. Family studies have proved to be valuable in studies investigating the genetic basis of various mental illnesses. They are usually performed on the affected individual and the two parents (called a "trio") and siblings (first-degree relatives). Both bipolar disease and schizophrenia have about a 5 to 10 percent occurrence rate for siblings and parents. Large populations of individuals need to be studied to gain further insight. The linkage of schizophrenia to chromosomes 13 and 1 was derived from a few family studies involving a large Canadian population. This study concluded that schizophrenia is manifested in three to four generations in this family. Another family study involving a large and isolated Finnish population, consisting of eighteen thousand individuals, revealed a linkage of schizophrenia to chromosome 1. However, many family studies cannot be replicated or are not followed up as rigorously as they should be. Some family studies on autism have identified a linkage to the gene *WNT2*, and this result has been consistent and repeatable.

Association Studies. A closely related approach is to study associations among genes in different chromosomes. Association studies use linkage disequilibrium maps, in which tightly linked alleles from one or more chromosomes are mapped and identified. A test that is commonly used in linkage disequilibrium studies is the transmission disequilibrium test (TDT), which provides a ratio of transmitted versus nontransmitted alleles from both parents. Linkage and association studies are used in tandem to deduce the genes potentially involved in mental illnesses. After the decoding of the human genome, approaches have come to involve genome-wide tracking of associated genes. Genome-wide association studies (GWASs) have added value to association studies by increasing the number of genes studied 1,000- to 10,000-fold and making high-throughput genotyping possible. GWASs are able to circumvent the impediments posed by the sheer number of samples involved in several meta-analyses and have yielded valuable information about many mental illnesses. One GWAS, which pooled the results from a large number of studies, showed a significant genome-wide linkage of chromosomes 6 and 8 to bipolar disorder.

A technique called "positional cloning" is used to amplify the genes of interest and to identify those that are mutated in the patients compared with the control subjects. Several genes of interest have been cloned from the chromosomal regions that have been identified from linkage, family, and association studies. In recent years, specific variations (polymorphisms) occurring on single nucleotides, called "single nucleotide polymorphisms," or SNPs, have been paid serious consideration. Some particularly interesting genes have emerged for bipolar disorder and schizophrenia. The gene *DISC1*, whose linkage to schizophrenia is based on evidence converging from multiple approaches and studies, is the first gene that has been reported as a causative gene for a mental disorder. Strong linkage association of *DISC1* is reported with schizophrenia and to different forms of biopolar disorders. Genome-wide analysis of SNPs for schizophrenia recently identified strong association with the *CSF2RA* (*colony stimulating factor 2 receptor, type A*) gene. G72 is another gene that exhibits robust association with bipolar disorder and depression. In addition, a few genes, such as *dysbindin* (*DTNBP1*), *DISC1*, *COMT*, and *BDNF*, have been implicated in rendering individuals susceptible to both schizophrenia and bipolar disease. Some hypothesize that both bipolar disorder and schizophrenia are modulated by clusters of genes that overlap with each other.

Twin Studies. Twin studies are conducted by comparing twins who share a certain mental illness or share the risks of developing one by having affected members in the family. Twins could be either monozygotic (from the same zygote, share identical genotypes) or dizygotic (from two zygotes, share 50 percent of genes). Both schizophrenia and bipolar disorder have shown a concordance rate of about 10 percent for dizygotic and 50 percent for monozygotic twins. In autism, the concordance rate for monozygotic twins is 60 percent. The influence of environment on these disorders is studied through adoption studies, using twins who were separated at a very early stage. Data from adoption studies have strengthened the genetic basis of various mental disorders by demonstrating that even if twins are separated at very early stages, the individual twin still carries the same amount of risk.

Candidate Gene Approach. In this method, specific candidate genes (genes that are suspected of causing a particular mental illness) are studied. Genes involved in the dopaminergic system (involving the common neurotransmitter dopamine, its receptors, and transporters in the brain) are the most widely studied in relation to a variety of mental illnesses. An impaired dopaminergic system is responsible for many mental illnesses. Among the candidate genes, those encoding the serotonin transporter (*5-HTT*), monoamine oxidase A (*MOA*), dopamine transporter (*DAT*), and the precursor enzyme tryptophan hydroxylase have received some evidence supporting their linkage to bipolar disorder. Genes involved in the glutamatergic system (involving another excitatory neurotransmitter, glutamate) are also of great interest. The gene encoding for the mGlu2/3 receptor showed so much promise that agonists of these receptors have been developed as drugs for schizophrenia. *Neuregulin 1* is another gene that exhibits strong linkage associations with schizophrenia. It is also surmised that the interaction of both dopaminergic and glutamatergic systems may influence the pathophysiology of schizophrenia.

Genes that are crucial in the circadian rhythm pathway, such as *BMAL1*, *Timeless*, and *Period 3* (*PER3*) are found to have some association with bipolar disorder. *PER3*, *Timeless*, and another circadian gene, *CLOCK*, have been found to have linkage associations for schizophrenia. Circadian rhythm gene changes have also been found in postmortem studies on patients with Alzheimer disease.

Most mental disorders are influenced by not just one gene, but rather by a cluster of genes exerting their influence independently, making individuals vulnerable to a certain disorder. Identification of the genes influencing mental health is just the first step. For these studies to culminate in a treatment therapy, several studies, involving multifarious approaches, need to be performed. First, the fact that alteration of these genes results in altered protein function needs to be confirmed. Often, there are compensatory mechanisms for the loss or modifications of important proteins by induction or suppression of gene expression. Several studies using animal models have been undertaken to confirm this. Next, the fact that such alterations actually result in biologically significant and diagnosable symptoms should be confirmed. This would give a correlation between the genotypes and the phenotypes. For complex mental disorders, with all the limitations of diagnostics, requirements, and variabilities, these validations still require a lot more work and time. However, it is also true that there is a clear genetic component in most mental disorders, however complicated they are, and that the risk rate for families with affected individuals is in fact higher than for those without affected individuals. With genome-wide screening becoming increasingly available and affordable, with the knowledge of the entire human genome, and with more investigators focusing on the genetic aspects of mental health, the prospects for finding the genetic basis for mental health and eventually developing it into a therapy that can be administered are much higher.

BIBLIOGRAPHY

A.D.A.M. Medical Encyclopedia. "Genetics." *Medline Plus*. US Dept. of Health and Human Services, National Institutes of Health, 16 May 2012. Web. 21 May 2014.

Andreasen, Nancy. *Brave New Brain: Conquering Mental Illness in the Era of the Genome*. New York: Oxford UP, 2001. Print.

Collier, D. A., and T. Li. "The Genetics of Schizophrenia: Glutamate Not Dopamine?" *European Journal of Pharmacology* 480.1–3 (2003): 177–84. Print.

Cowan, W. M., et al. "The Human Genome Project and Its Impact on Psychiatry." *Annual Review of Neuroscience* 25 (2002): 1–50.

Detera-Wadleigh, S. D., and F. J. McMahon. "Genetic Association Studies in Mood Disorders: Issues and Promise." *International Review of Psychiatry* 16.4 (2004): 301–10. Print.

Lakhan, S. E., and A. Kramer. "Schizophrenia Genomics and Proteomics: Are We Any Closer to Biomarker Discovery?" *Behavioral and Brain Functions* 5.2 (2009): 1–9. Print.

Lin, P. I., and B. D. Mitchell. "Approaches for Unraveling the Joint Genetic Determinants of Schizophrenia and Bipolar Disorder." *Schizophrenia Bulletin* 34.4 (2008): 791–97. Print.

"Looking at My Genes: What Can They Tell Me?" *National Institute of Mental Health*. US Dept. of Health and Human Services, National Institutes of Health, n.d. Web. 21 May 2014.

Losh, M., P. F. Sullivan, D. Trembath, and J. Piven. "Current Developments in the Genetics of Autism: From Phenome to Genome." *Journal of Neuropathology and Experimental Neurology* 67.9 (2008): 829–37. Print.

Reilly, Philip R. *Is It in Your Genes? The Influence of Genes on Common Disorders and Diseases That Affect You and Your Family.* Cold Spring Harbor: Cold Spring Harbor Laboratory P, 2004. Print.

Stahl, Rebecca J. "Genetics and Mental Health." *Health Library.* EBSCO, 4 Feb. 2014. Web. 21 May 2014.

Weir, Kirsten. "The Roots of Mental Illness." *Monitor on Psychology* 43.6 (2012): 30. Print.

Geetha Yadav

See Also: Abnormality: Biomedical models; Alzheimer's disease; Asperger syndrome; Autism; Bipolar disorder; Schizophrenia: Background, types, and symptoms; Schizophrenia: Theoretical explanations.

Geriatric psychological disorders

Type of psychology: Biological bases of human behavior; Clinical; Counseling; Developmental; Family; Geriatric; Psychopathology; Psychotherapy

In 2013 the population of people in the U.S. older than 65 was 14%, an increase from 11% 30 years ago. This number is expected to soar to 20%, or 90 million people, within the next 30 years. The sheer amount of resources that will be spent on the care of older persons makes it imperative for those in the medical industry to find effective, efficient, and holistic mechanisms to support the mental and psychological health of aged persons. There can be some optimism as the majority of mental health disorders that older persons face can be prevented or delayed with simple and straightforward lifestyle changes.

Key Concepts
- Psychology and aging
- Behavioral and mental health in the elderly
- Aging and behavioral and mental health

INTRODUCTION

The diagnosis and treatment of mental health problems in older persons is more difficult than that of young people for three reasons. First, there is a greater number of elderly people than ever before. The result is more cases of certain disorders that previously went unnoticed in the elderly. Second, the lack of previous data on these disorders makes effectively treating them more difficult. Care must be taken to account for physical differences in the aged body and mind. Diagnostic tools and treatments that are used for young people may not be appropriate for older patients. Third, many mental health problems in older persons stem from physical problems. Psychologists and caregivers may face a "chicken and egg problem" when diagnosing mental health disorders in older persons. That is, did mental decline begin first or did physical impairment lead to cognitive impairment? In addition, mental health disorders may change over time symptomatically or may not emerge until one is of advanced age. Care must be taken to properly diagnose and treat the root cause of a mental health disorder in an elderly person.

DEMENTIA, DEPRESSION, AND ANXIETY: THE BIG THREE

Older people may suffer from the same psychological disorders as younger people. However, there are several conditions that normally do not begin until old age. The most common of these is dementia, but older persons may also develop depression and/or anxiety. A survey of U.S. nursing home residents revealed that a staggering 89% suffered from dementia or the behavioral and psychological symptoms associated with dementia, 36% showed signs of depression, and 12% suffered from anxiety disorders.

ALZHEIMER'S AND DEMENTIA

Dementia is the most common mental disorder affecting older persons, and it negatively impacts memory, thinking, and reasoning abilities. Simple chores such as driving from one place to another are affected. The behavioral and psychological symptoms of dementia include non-cognitive aspects such as agitation, sleep disturbances, elation, and hallucinations.

Alzheimer's disease is the most common cause of dementia in older persons. It involves the slow and irreversible degeneration of brain tissue due to structural abnormalities or the loss of connections between nerve cells. Initial stages may go undetected but as the disease progresses cognitive function gradually declines and worsens to the point of interfering with one's ability to function normally. Those who suffer from the disease ultimately become completely incapable of caring for themselves. Death typically occurs three to 10 years after initial diagnosis.

Changes in the blood supply to the brain may also cause dementia. This is known as vascular dementia and is sometimes the result of one or more strokes that block arteries and reduce blood flow to parts of the brain. Vascular dementia can also be the result of chronically damaged brain blood vessels. Much like other blood vessels in the body, brain blood vessels may be damaged from high blood pressure, diabetes, hardening of the arteries, or the wear and tear associated with aging. Older persons sometimes experience dementia-like symptoms without suffering from the disease for other medical reasons including chronic alcoholism, brain tumors or infections, vitamin deficiency, and thyroid, kidney, or liver disorders.

There is no known cure for Alzheimer's disease or dementia. Symptoms, however, can be managed with medicines that increase neuronal activity in the brain. Behavioral and psychological symptoms of the disease can be treated with prescriptions for sleep disturbances, depressed mood, anxiety/restlessness, and hallucinations.

DELIRIUM

Delirium is a temporary condition similar to dementia that causes patients to be disoriented and inattentive and and experience an overall cognitive dysfunction. Side effects from certain medications, physical immobility, malnutrition, sleep deprivation, and chronic conditions such as renal disease, stroke, and hearing or vision loss all increase one's risk for developing delirium. Many delirium cases can be prevented altogether with adequate nutrition, hydration, and rest and by maintaining a patient's orientation to surroundings. Physical restraints should be avoided if an episode does occur and the patient should not experience frequent changes in rooms or staff. Sleep is an important factor in treating delirium patients; a quiet, low light setting should be provided at night.

DEPRESSION

Depression is a mood disorder that causes persistent feelings of sadness and loss of interest in normal daily activities. For those who suffer from the disease it affects how they feel, think, and behave. Depression in older individuals is sometimes characterized by physical symptoms like agitation, hypochondriasis, and gastrointestinal malfunction. They may also experience confusion, social withdrawal, and delusions and hallucinations. The long-term prognosis is poor for older depressed persons because they tend to have higher relapse rates. Older individuals are also more likely to have concurrent medical problems that exacerbate their conditions such as cognitive impairment.

Older persons who have had a major surgery, heart attack or stroke, or hearing or vision loss are at increased risk for developing depression. Those who are isolated, have lost loved ones, and are lacking in a supportive social network are also more susceptible to depression. Women are more likely to become depressed than men in the general population, a difference that increases later in life because of the hormonal changes associated with aging. Psychotherapy and mood-improving medications are both effective in treating depression in older persons. Once the patient's mood has improved subsequent lifestyle changes should be made to increase social contact and support. Some form of pharmacological maintenance is also in order because of the chronic nature of depression in older adults.

ANXIETY

Anxiety is frequent and intense fear and worry about normal situations, sometimes including panic. The feelings of fear are difficult to control and are out of proportion to the actual danger. Generalized anxiety disorder is the most common anxiety disorder in older persons and is characterized by persistent, excessive, and unrealistic worry about everyday things. Like depression, older persons often develop anxiety because of a traumatic event such as developing an illness. Older persons also fear crime, further illness, and financial stress. Limited mobility is an important factor; many older persons have a fear of falling which can be so severe they avoid physical activities, leading to further disability. This interferes with daily activities such as shopping and bathing and reduces their overall quality of life. Once an older person has been diagnosed with anxiety, a prescription regimen, sessions with psychotherapist, or the combination of the two can be quite effective at treatment.

Dementia, depression, and anxiety are the most common psychological disorders in older persons and much of the mental health resources dedicated to the elderly are expended to address these issues. However, there are other mental health issues that persist from young and middle adulthood into old age or sometimes develop in old age.

OTHER MENTAL HEALTH DISORDERS

Alcohol and substance abuse. One-third of money spent on prescription drugs in the U.S. is from elderly patients, and many of these purchased drugs have the potential to be abused. In this category fall benzodiazepines, opiate analgesics, and medicines for pain and insomnia which, by misuse and overuse, can lead to substance abuse and addiction. It is estimated that 12-15% of older adults abuse prescription drugs. Alcoholism is another issue affecting aged persons; by some estimates 11% of adults aged 50–64 years and 6.7% of adults older than 65 report alcohol abuse or dependence. These statistics indicate that alcohol and substance abuse are the fourth most common mental health issue for older adults following dementia, depression, and anxiety.

Most alcohol and prescription drug abusers begin abuse prior to age 65. These are considered early onset abusers and comprise two-thirds of the population of elderly persons that are alcoholic. Because of the extended period of abuse, these individuals tend to have greater physical and psychiatric problems. It is challenging to diagnose late onset abusers because they do not fit the profile of younger abusers and their symptoms are often attributed to other causes.

Substance abuse in the aged increases the possibility of other mental health conditions like cognitive impairment. Psychotherapy and/or various medicines proven to work in younger populations are viable treatment options.

Bipolar disorder. Bipolar disorder, also known as manic depression, is a chronic, debilitating condition characterized by major shifts in mood and energy levels. In manic states patients may feel constantly overjoyed, need very little sleep, and have rapid flights of ideas. In depressive states patients feel sad and hopeless, experience changes in appetite and sleep, and have suicidal thoughts. Bipolar disorder is commonly diagnosed in young people and is highly treatable using mood-stabilizing drugs. Without medical treatment, however, those with the disease have trouble carrying out their normal daily activities. Until recently it was believed that bipolar disorder "burnt out" in older adults whose symptoms often appear to go into remission. However, symptoms may present differently in older patients who experience agitation and irritability during a manic phase rather than feeling "high" or on top of the world.

Some patients do not develop bipolar disorder until late in life. This is far less common but in fact 10% of patients are diagnosed with the disorder after age 50. Diagnosing bipolar disorder in older persons is difficult as symptoms may be confused with other possible disorders. Once diagnosed, aged sufferers of bipolar disorder can also benefit from mood-stabilizing drugs.

Schizophrenia. Schizophrenia is a serious and chronic mental disorder that affects 1% of the adult population world-wide. The disorder manifests itself in delusions, auditory hallucinations, confused thinking, erratic behavior, and a pervasively abnormal interpretation of reality. Patients are normally diagnosed with a sub-type of the disorder in young adulthood although any diagnosis prior to age 45 is considered early or normal in onset.

A fascinating component of the disease is that in some cases it may develop later in life so that individuals who were previously symptom free are diagnosed between the ages of 45 and 65 (late onset) or with a very late onset schizophrenia-like psychosis (older than 65). Most that are diagnosed with the disorder in young adulthood are males who have otherwise structurally sound brain matter. In contrast, those diagnosed with very late onset schizophrenia-like psychosis are usually women who have marked brain structure abnormalities and progressive cognitive deterioration. Estrogen may play some protective role in preventing schizophrenia early in life, a protection that disappears after menopause is reached. Treatment-wise, newer, atypical antipsychotic medicines are recommended for older patients as they have fewer possible side effects that the elderly, who are especially susceptible, might experience.

Personality disorders. Personality disorders are characterized by rigid, unhealthy, and inaccurate patterns of thinking and behaving. Those with a personality disorder commonly have difficulty relating to people or functioning in normal situations. There are multiple sub-types of personality disorders; these usually begin in young adulthood and can change symptomatically with age. Generally speaking, extreme symptoms such as aggression decrease with age. However, some traits such as passive-aggressiveness, hypochondriasis, and depression increase with age. Like bipolar disorder it was commonly held that personality disorders declined with advanced age. However, it may simply be the case that those aspects of personality disorders that require a certain amount of energy, sexuality, and social interaction only appear to decrease when in fact they simply have fewer opportunities for expression in later life.

Healthcare workers can more accurately diagnose personality disorders when the more stable psychological factors are taken into greater consideration and when there is correspondingly less emphasis on the more dramatic features of particular disorders. Once diagnosed, some psychotherapeutic treatments that specifically focus on current behaviors and relationships are most effective for older adults.

TREATMENT FOR AND PREVENTION OF BEHAVIORAL HEALTH DISORDERS IN GERIATRIC PATIENTS

When treating mental health disorders of any type in the elderly, extreme caution is advised. It is important for healthcare workers to use diagnostic tools that rule out other medical conditions such as stroke, brain abnormalities, or medicinal side effects. Pharmacological approaches to treat mental health disorders in older persons should be avoided at all costs as they can further compromise the patient's mental state and make it difficult to monitor the patient's condition. When medicine is prescribed appropriate dosages must be carefully managed as absorption and efficacy can be different for the aged. Furthermore, concurrent medicines may negatively interact with drugs used to treat psychological disorders. Generally speaking, older patients often require much smaller doses because of physical changes associated with aging that affect the metabolism of medicine in the body.

Many mental health disorders persist from young adulthood. However, the big three, dementia, depression, and anxiety, often begin with advanced age, and, thus, can largely be prevented. Certain lifestyle changes such as being mentally active while aging, having frequent social contact, and remaining physically active can significantly decrease an older person's likelihood of developing one or more of the common disorders associated with aging. Returning to the chicken and egg problem, the number of older persons is increasing at an unprecedented rate, and the bulk of resources spent addressing these issues may be more wisely, and more effectively, spent in measures of prevention. While the aging process cannot be stopped there are actions that communities and individuals can take to help older persons maintain their health and independence.

BIBLIOGRAPHY

Anxiety and Depression Association of America http://www.adaa.org/living-with-anxiety/older-adults. A general resource on the topic that is very informative and written in a plain and understandable fashion. Information is also well-formatted with a number of links that allow the reader to explore related topics.

Kennedy, G. (2008, January 1). *Bipolar disorder in late life: Mania*. Retrieved February 13, 2015, from Primary Psychiatry website: http://primarypsychiatry.com/ bipolar-disorder-in-late-life-mania/ A straightforward and somewhat technical article describing diagnoses and treatment of bipolar disorder that occurs in later life.

Mayo Clinic. http://www.mayoclinic.org/disease-conditions/dementia/basics/definition/con-20034399. A basic and comprehensive source of information on Alzheimer's disease, it provides the reader with information including disorder recognition, prevention, management, and treatment.

National Alliance on Mental Illness. http://www.nami.org/Template.cfm?Section=By_Illness&template=/ContentManagement/ContentDisplay.cfm&ContentID=7515 A fact sheet on depression in older persons written in plain English.

National Institute on Aging. http://www.nia.nih.gov/alzheimers/topics/alxheimers-basics. A great place for extensive information on the biological and neurological components of Alzheimer's disease; a short but comprehensive video is included.

Jacquelyn H. Berry

See Also: Aging; Alzheimer's disease; Aphasia; Dementia; Depression; Memory; Mood disorders.

Gesell, Arnold

Born: June 21, 1880, in Alma, Wisconsin

Died: May 29, 1961, in New Haven, Connecticut

Identity: American pediatrician and developmental psychologist

Type of psychology: Developmental psychology

Gesell was a pioneer in the study of the physical and mental development of children.

Arnold Gesell was born in a village on the Mississippi River. He received a scholarship to Clark University in Worcester, Massachusetts, where he studied under such scholars as psychologist G. Stanley Hall and where he earned his Ph.D. in 1906. Lewis Terman, an innovator in intelligence testing, invited him to teach at Los Angeles State College, where Gesell met and married colleague Beatrice Chandler in 1909. Gesell returned to Wisconsin and studied medicine and anatomy. He was appointed assistant professor of education at Yale University, where he earned his M.D. in 1915.

Gesell helped organize the Yale Clinic of Child Development, providing laboratories and playrooms where mothers brought their infants for observation and testing. In 1930, a grant from the Laura Spelman Rockefeller Memorial allowed Gesell to build a homelike studio to film babies' daily activities: sleeping, walking, feeding, and playing. The Yale Clinic added a nursery school, allowing the staff to follow children from infancy through adolescence to adulthood.

These studies were the basis of Gesell's most important work: *Infant Behavior: Its Genesis and Growth* (1934), with Helen Thompson and Catherine Amatrude. The three joined Burton Castner in writing the two-volume *Biographies of Child Development: The Mental Growth Careers of Eighty-four Infants and Children* (1939), which discussed the differences in physical and mental development among normal, superior, atypical, and premature infants.

Gesell stressed that the growth characteristics of children are determined primarily by hereditary factors but that these factors do not operate independently of environmental influences. Every individual has a distinctive complex of growth, but each infant goes through the same fundamental sequences. Developmental norms are useful for comparison and diagnosis but not as a unit of absolute measurement.

Gesell wrote books reassuring parents and challenging them to stimulate their children's development. *Infant and Child in the Culture of Today*, written with Frances Ilg, went through seventeen editions in the United States between 1943 and 1974. Gesell and Ilg also published *The Child from Five to Ten* (1946), providing further norms for growing children and recommending books, records, and games. He, Ilg, and Louise Ames concluded their child development studies with *Youth: The Years from Ten to Sixteen* (1956).

In 1948, Gesell retired from Yale but continued to work in his field. He died in 1961, leaving a legacy of studies showing the importance of prenatal and infant care.

BIBLIOGRAPHY

Ames, Louise Bates. *Arnold Gesell: Themes of His Work*. New York: Human Sciences Press, 1990. An expert in adolescent and child psychology, Ames has also coauthored a book with Gesell. Includes an index and extensive bibliography.

Cravens, Hamilton. "Child-Saving in the Age of Professionalism, 1915-1930." *In American Childhood: A Research Guide and Historical Handbook,* edited by Joseph M. Hawes and N. Ray Hiner. Westport, Conn.: Greenwood Press, 1985. An evaluation of Gesell and such contemporaries as Henry Herbert Goddard, Lawrence K. Frank, and John Dewey.

Bernard Mergen

See Also: Adolescence: Cognitive skills; Attachment and bonding in infancy and childhood; Birth: Effects on physical development; Development; Developmental disabilities; Developmental psychology; Learning; Reflexes in newborns.

Gestalt therapy

Type of psychology: Psychotherapy

Gestalt therapy, founded by Fritz Perls, is an outgrowth of the existential-humanistic approach to psychotherapy. It focuses on nonverbal behaviors, dreams, and current thoughts and emotions; as clients become more aware of denied feelings, their innate healing powers are activated.

Key Concepts

- Dreamwork
- Empty-chair technique
- Existential-humanistic psychotherapy
- Here and now
- Hot seat

INTRODUCTION

Gestalt therapy emerged during the 1960s as a powerful alternative to the two main available therapeutic techniques: psychoanalysis and behavioral therapy. This approach to therapy, founded by Fritz Perls, attempts to integrate clients' thoughts, feelings, and actions into a unified whole; Gestalt, in fact, is the German word for "whole." Gestalt therapists believe that emotional problems and some of the dissatisfactions experienced by ordinary individuals are attributable to a lack of recognition and understanding of one's feelings. The fast pace of technological society and the general loss of purpose in individuals' lives has led to a numbing of emotions. Gestaltists believe that many people deny or lose parts of themselves when they are faced with the overwhelming task of coping in society; for example, a person may deny anger toward a loved one.

The role for the Gestalt therapist is to help the client become more aware of the split-off emotions. The therapist takes an active role by requiring the patient to talk about current experiences and feelings. The patient is neither allowed to look for explanations or problems from the past nor expected to talk about future plans. Gestaltists believe that anxiety is the result of an excessive focus on the future. The client is expected to attend to current feelings and experiences—to stay in the here and now.

Gestalt therapy arose from existential psychology and humanistic psychology. Prior schools had portrayed individuals rather pessimistically, believing that human beings are relatively evil creatures whose actions are determined by forces outside their control (such as instincts or the environment). People were seen as adaptive hedonists trying to receive the greatest amount of pleasure for the least amount of effort. The existential-humanistic school of psychology portrays individuals more optimistically, believing people innately strive to achieve their fullest human potential. Failure to do so is not the result of an evil nature but rather the fault of obstacles on this path to perfection. Gestalt therapists agree with the existential-humanistic focus on individual responsibility. One freely chooses one's actions and therefore is responsible for them. There is no provision for blaming a past situation or one's current environment. Gestalt therapists encourage independence and uniqueness in their clients. They push them to be themselves rather than adopting the "shoulds" and "oughts" recommended by society. Perls emphasized this focus on independence and responsibility by stating that the process of maturation is moving from environmental support to self-support.

Probably the greatest contribution of the Gestalt style of therapy has been the techniques it developed to increase individual self-awareness. These techniques are consistent with the belief that emotional problems stem from avoidance of or failure to recognize one's feelings. The Gestalt therapist is very active and confrontational during the therapy session (in fact, in a group setting, talking to the therapist is called "taking the hot seat") and frequently interprets and questions the client's statements. The goal is a genuine relationship between two individuals, free of normal social conventions, in which a free exchange of thoughts and feelings can take place.

THERAPEUTIC TECHNIQUES

In one technique of Gestalt therapy, called the "dreamwork," the client reports a recent dream. The Gestalt school believes that the events in a dream represent fragmented and denied parts of the personality. Rather than search for explanations in one's childhood, as in the technique of dream analysis originated by Sigmund Freud, clients are encouraged to bring the dream into the present by acting out different parts of the dream. Rather than saying "There was a train in my dream," the person is required to act out the part of the train. He or she might say, "I am a train. I am very powerful and useful as long as I stay on track." This moves the focus of the dream into the here and now.

Another therapeutic technique used by Gestalt therapists involves a focus on and exaggeration of nonverbal behaviors. Gestaltists believe that much denied information is accessible through body language. For example, a client may state that she is happy and content in a relationship, while she is scowling and keeping her arms and legs crossed in a tight and tense fashion. Gestalt therapists help their clients become aware of these feelings by getting them to exaggerate their actions. A man who is talking about his wife while clenching his hand in a fist and tapping it on the table may be told to clench his fist tighter and bang it hard on the table. This exaggeration of nonverbal behavior would be to make him acutely aware of his anger toward his wife.

Another well-known procedure developed by the Gestalt school of psychotherapy is the empty-chair technique. This strategy is employed to bring past conflicts into the here and now, where feelings can be reexperienced. The client often will relate to the therapist a disagreement with some significant other. Rather than ask for details of the encounter (a procedure that keeps the focus in the past), the therapist will encourage the client to address an empty chair in the office as though that person were sitting in it. The client must role-play the relevant situation. The therapist may also get the client to play the part of the significant other in the empty chair. This switching back and forth of chairs and roles is a powerful technique to foster empathy, understanding, and a clarification of feelings. This technique can be used not only for conflicts between individuals but also for discrepant feelings within one person.

GESTALT IN PRACTICE

The Gestalt approach to psychotherapy is best explained by examples. A student once reported a dream in which she remembered a gum wrapper being dropped outside a nearby church. Rather than search for a meaning of the dream's symbols in her childhood, her friend, a clinical psychologist, asked her to become the elements in the dream. She initially chose the gum wrapper. She stated that as a gum wrapper she concealed something very good and appealing and that most people took the good part from inside her and then threw her away. She stated that she felt like trash littered on a beautiful lawn and that eventually some caring person would come and throw her away.

The student then began to play the role of the church in the dream. She stated that as a church she was a beautiful building constructed by caring hands. She indicated that good things happened inside her but that she was used too infrequently. Many people were afraid of or disliked coming to her, she said, and most of the time she was empty inside. The student was surprised as she completed this description of the dream. She talked about the similarity of her explanations of the two elements in the dream. When asked if she felt this way, she stated that this idea at first surprised her somewhat; however, as she continued to elaborate, she became more aware of her feelings of emptiness and loneliness. She had become aware of denied aspects of her emotions.

Gestalt therapy's active focus on nonverbal behavior and denied portions of the personality often can be quite dramatic. The judicious use of these techniques may allow insights into dynamics that are not available through ordinary interpersonal interactions. In one case, a family was being seen by cotherapists in family therapy. The family consisted of a mother, father, son, and daughter. The son was identified as the troublemaker in the family, and he demonstrated a wide range of symptoms that caused the family much pain and suffering. During the course of therapy, it became apparent that the mother was an unwitting conspirator in these troubles. She often would rescue her son from his precarious and often dangerous situation and restore matters to normal.

This served the function of ensuring her role as a "good mother," while providing the son with the reassurance that he was loved by her. Whenever she threatened not to rescue him, he accused her of not caring for him. She inevitably crumbled and provided for his needs. The father and daughter had their own alliance in the family, and although they complained, they did not interfere in this dysfunctional family pattern that frequently ended in severe problems.

The two therapists hypothesized the pathological nature of this interaction and periodically attempted to present it to the family; however, the pattern was so important and so entrenched in the family's style of interaction that any mention of it led to vehement protests and denials that it was an issue of importance. During a therapy session, one of the therapists noticed the pattern in which the family members usually seated themselves. The mother and son sat close to each other on one side of the therapy room, while the father and daughter sat near each other across from them. The two therapists sat across from each other on the other sides of the room. One therapist, taking a cue from the Gestalt emphasis on the importance of nonverbal behaviors, moved his chair and sat in the small space between the mother and son. A stunned silence ensued. The mother and son began to show agitation, while the father and daughter, from across the room, became increasingly amused at the nature of this interaction.

The therapists elicited the reactions and analyses of the family to this new seating arrangement. The mother and son continued to display uncertainty and bewilderment, while the father and daughter immediately recognized that someone had dared to come between "Mom and her boy." This led to a more open discussion of the pathological nature of the family interactions. The father and daughter could see that they had allowed this damaging pattern to continue. The mother and son, while not quite as open to this discovery because of the threatening nature of the disclosure, could not deny the emotions that were aroused by someone physically invading their territory. The insights that resulted from this simple Gestalt technique moved therapy along much more quickly than had previous verbal interactions. It demonstrates the Gestalt tenet that a focus on nonverbal patterns of communication may allow clients to become aware of previously denied aspects of their personalities.

EXISTENTIAL-HUMANISTIC PSYCHOLOGY

Gestalt therapy emerged during a period of increased popularity for the existential-humanistic position in psychology. This approach, sometimes known as the "third force" in psychology, came from opposition to the earlier forces of psychoanalysis and behaviorism. Existential-humanistic proponents objected to the pessimistic psychoanalytic view of humans as vile creatures held captive by primitive, unconscious desires. They also differed from the environmental determinism, set forth by the behavioral school, that people are simply products of past punishments and rewards. The existential-humanistic therapists focused on the human freedom to choose one's actions (regardless of unconscious desires and past consequences), the relative goodness of the human species, and people's innate desire to reach their fullest potential. This approach fit well with the period of great social upheaval and change following World War II.

The Gestalt approach often is compared to the person-centered (or client-centered) therapy of Carl R. Rogers. Both types of psychotherapy endorse the basic assumptions of the existential-humanistic school; however, they differ considerably in their approach and techniques. In person-centered therapy, the client is encouraged to express his or her thoughts and feelings about a situation. The therapist remains relatively passive, giving minimal verbal prompts or paraphrasing the client's statements. The client is responsible for the direction and content of the therapy session; the therapist provides only a clarification of unclear statements or feelings. The idea behind this approach is that the therapist is providing an atmosphere of unconditional acceptance in which the client can explore his or her emotional issues. Eventually, the client's innate curative ability will take over. The Gestalt therapist, in contrast, is much more confrontational in interpreting statements and asking questions. The Gestalt approach places a greater emphasis on the interpretation of nonverbal behaviors and the usefulness of dreams. Although different in technique, both approaches point to the freedom to choose, the innate goodness of the client, and the strength of the therapeutic relationship as curative factors.

The influence of the Gestalt approach to psychotherapy diminished with the death of Perls in 1970. He was the emotional and spiritual leader of the group, and his charisma was not replaced easily. Gestalt therapy is not considered a mainstream psychotherapy; however, it does have numerous enthusiastic followers. The greatest contribution of the Gestalt orientation has been the techniques developed to assist clients in becoming more aware of hidden thoughts and emotions. Therapists with a wide variety of orientations have adapted and applied these procedures within their own theoretical framework. The impact of dreamwork, the hot seat, nonverbal interpretations, and the empty-chair techniques seems to have outlasted the theory from which they came.

BIBLIOGRAPHY

Clarkson, Petruska, and Simon Cavicchia. *Gestalt Counseling in Action*. 4th ed. Thousand Oaks: Sage, 2013. Print.

Ivey, Allen E., Michael D'Andrea, and Mary Bradford Ivey. *Theories of Counseling and Psychotherapy: A Multicultural Perspective*. 7th ed. Thousand Oaks: Sage, 2012. Print.

Kring, Ann M., Sheri L. Johnson, Gerald Davison, and John M. Neale. *Abnormal Psychology*. 12th ed. New York: Wiley, 2012. Print.

O'Leary, Eleanor, ed. *Gestalt Therapy around the World*. Malden: Wiley-Blackwell, 2013. Print.

Perls, Frederick S. *The Gestalt Approach and Eye Witness to Therapy*. New York: Bantam, 1978. Print.

Tønnesvang, Jan, et al. "Gestalt Therapy and Cognitive Therapy—Contrasts Or Complementarities?." *Psychotherapy: Theory, Research, Practice, Training* 47.4 (2010): 586–602. Print.

Brett L. Beck

See Also: Abnormality: Psychological models; Dreams; Existential psychology; Family systems theory; Group therapy; Humanistic psychology; Personcentered therapy; Self-actualization.

Giftedness

Type of psychology: Developmental psychology; Intelligence and intelligence testing

Giftedness refers to a capability for high performance in one or more areas of accomplishment. The focus on giftedness as a human capability has led to efforts to identify giftedness early in life, to develop special programs of instruction for gifted children and adolescents, and to design counseling interventions to help gifted learners realize their potential.

Key Concepts
- Gifted education program
- Intelligence test scores
- Marland definition
- Precociousness
- Standardized test scores
- Talent

INTRODUCTION

Modern studies of giftedness have their origin in the work of Lewis Madison Terman at Stanford University, who in the 1920s used intelligence test scores to identify intellectually gifted children. His minimal standard for giftedness was an intelligence quotient (IQ) of 140 on the Stanford-Binet test, a number at or above which only 1 percent of children are expected to score. (The average IQ score is 100.) Terman and his associates identified more than fifteen hundred children in California as gifted, and follow-up studies on the Terman gifted group were conducted throughout their adult lives. Although individuals in the gifted group tended to achieve highly in school and in their careers, they were not greatly different from average scorers in other ways. Terman's research dispelled the myths that high scorers on IQ tests were, as a group, socially maladjusted or "burned out" in adulthood. They were high achievers and yet normal in the sense that their social relationships were similar to those of the general population.

By the time the Terman gifted group reached retirement age, it was clear that the study had not realized the hope of identifying eminence. None of the children selected had, as adults, won the Nobel Prize, although two children who were rejected for the study later did so (physicist Luis Alvarez and engineer William Shockley). Nor did high IQ scores seem to be characteristic of artistic ability. Apparently, an IQ score of 140 or above as a criterion for giftedness in children was not able to predict creative accomplishments in later life.

Studies conducted in the 1950s under the direction of Donald MacKinnon at the University of California, Berkeley, tended to confirm this conclusion. Panels of experts submitted the names of whomever they believed to be the most creative architects, mathematicians, and research scientists in the United States; then these individuals were invited to take part in assessments, including measurement of their intelligence through the Wechsler Adult Intelligence Scale. The IQ scores of these highly creative individuals ranged from 114 to 145, averaging around 130, significantly below Terman's criterion for giftedness. No one knows how these adults would have scored on the Stanford-Binet as children or how creative adults in other domains would have scored, but the results confirmed that a score of 140 on an intelligence test is not a prerequisite for outstanding creative accomplishment.

More recent studies have cast light on the importance of nurture in the development of a broader range of talent. A team of researchers at the University of Chicago headed by Benjamin Bloom investigated the lives of 120 talented adults in six fields: concert piano, sculpture, swimming, tennis, mathematics, and research neurology. They found that in most cases, accomplishments on a national or international level by the age of forty had their origin not in a prodigious gift, but in child-centered homes. The child's early experiences of the field were playful, rewarding, and supported by parents. Rapid progress was due to a work ethic instilled by parents ("always do your best") and by increasingly expert and selective teachers, whom parents sought out. Bloom's findings did not exactly contradict those of Terman (no testing was done), but they suggested to the researchers that nurture and motivation play the lead and supporting roles in the development of a wide range of talent.

Just what general ability IQ tests measure remains uncertain, but increasingly, psychologists and educators have conceptualized giftedness as a function of specialized capabilities and potential for performance in specific fields such as mathematics, biology, dance, or visual arts. A definition of giftedness first offered in a 1971 report to the Congress of the United States by Sidney P. Marland, then commissioner of education, indicates a much broader concept of giftedness than high IQ scores have been found to measure. "Gifted and talented children are those identified by professionally qualified persons who, by virtue of outstanding abilities, are capable of high performance." He defined gifted children as those with demonstrated achievement or potential ability in the following areas, singly or in combination: general intellectual ability, specific academic aptitude, creative or productive thinking, leadership ability, visual or performing arts, and psychomotor ability. This definition of giftedness, known as the Marland definition, does not distinguish giftedness from talent and includes performance capabilities that are sometimes related only distantly to performance on an IQ test. Nevertheless, the legacy of the Terman study of giftedness is that high IQ test scores remain one among several ways for psychologists and educators to identify intellectual giftedness among children in the general population. Giftedness in academic, creative, leadership, artistic, and psychomotor domains, however, is generally identified in other ways.

IDENTIFICATION OF GIFTEDNESS

Different percentages of the general population have been identified as gifted, depending on the definition of giftedness. Terman's use of IQ scores of 140 or above identified 1 percent of scorers as gifted. The common, contemporary indicator of intellectual giftedness is a score of 130 or above on a standardized, individually administered intelligence test, which is achieved by the top 2.5 percent of scorers. By the broader Marland definition, some form of which has been enacted through legislation by most states that have mandated gifted education programs, a minimum of 3 to 5 percent of school children are estimated to be gifted. Other definitions would identify as many as 10 to 15 percent of schoolchildren as gifted or as many as 15 to 25 percent in a talent pool. Gifted and talented students receiving services in schools in the United States constitute about 6 percent of all children who are enrolled.

By almost any definition, giftedness is very difficult to identify during infancy. Most researchers would agree that giftedness has a biological foundation, but whether this foundation exists as a general or a specific capability is unknown. One of the earliest indicators of many forms of giftedness is precociousness, or unusually early development or maturity. During preschool years, precociousness can generalize across several domains, such as the use of logic with an extensive vocabulary, or it can be more specialized, such as drawing realistic pictures of animals or objects or picking out a tune by ear on a musical instrument. Development does not seem to proceed in all areas at the same pace, however, so a young child may develop early in one or two areas but still behave in many ways like other children of the same age. Because of such asynchronous development, parents should not assume that a child who can master the moves of checkers at four years old, for example, will accept losing a game any better than the average four-year-old.

There has been debate regarding whether giftedness is the result of intense practice. Children with talents in specific areas, such as math or tennis, are seen to practice these skills very often and intensely. Often, giftedness in a specific domain is identified after much practice has occurred.

A surprising number of gifted children are their parents' only children or first-borns, but this fact reveals only that their precocious development is due, at least in part, to learning from the models in their early environment, who are adults rather than age-mates. As Bloom's study suggested, parents or other adult caretakers provide opportunities, resources, and encouragement to learn. Whatever reading ability a child may have, for example, can be nurtured by adults who read both to and around the child, who provide appropriate materials to read, and who show interest in the child's spontaneous efforts to read.

A child who is developing a talent early often will tend to rehearse it spontaneously or call for repeated performance or for explanation by the parent (or other model) to review or understand what the child wants to learn. The products and performances of gifted children in elementary school are often similar to the products and performances of skilled but less gifted adolescents. For this reason, gifted children are often bored when instruction is designed for their age level rather than for an advanced level and rapid pace of learning.

By the school years, children's giftedness can be assessed reliably in ways other than observation of precociousness. Assessment usually begins with nomination by a teacher, parent, or school social worker. Teacher nominations cannot be the sole indicator of who is gifted, however, because studies have shown them to miss about half of all gifted children. Nominations by teachers and others are often supported by academic marks during the previous year, often supplemented by standardized test scores. These scores can result from individual or group assessments of intelligence, school ability, cognitive abilities, academic aptitudes or achievements, and creative or productive thinking abilities. Since tests themselves have been found to identify only half of all gifted children, test scores are sometimes supplemented by scores from other types of instruments (such as checklists), ratings of portfolios or performances, or interviews to complete the assessment process. No single assessment technique or instrument has been found to satisfactorily identify all types of giftedness outlined in the Marland definition. Underrepresentation of African American, Latino, and Native American children in gifted education programs in the United States is largely a problem of identification. Some gifted children do not meet cutoff scores yet still have exceptional abilities. Other gifted children have poor test-taking skills, which highlights the need for multiple methods of identification of gifted children.

INSTRUCTION OF GIFTED CHILDREN AND ADOLESCENTS

Eligibility for a gifted education program may be decided as a result of the process of identification, but the design of a program of instruction for each child is often a separate set of decisions, sometimes requiring further assessments. It must be decided whether a child who is nearing the end of first grade but who has performed at the seventh-grade level on a standardized achievement test should be promoted to a much higher grade level the next year. An adolescent who is writing commercial music and who is successfully performing it on weekends might be allowed to leave school during the day to make a recording. The programming decisions to be made are as diverse as the talents of the children themselves.

It is not surprising, then, that no single strategy for teaching the gifted child has been found to be the best. Rather, broad strategies of intervention can be classified as modifications in curriculum content or skills and modifications in school environment. Modifications in curriculum content for gifted students might include content acceleration (such as early admission, grade skipping, or telescoping two years into one), content enrichment (materials to elaborate on basic concepts in standard programs), content sophistication (more abstract or fundamental considerations of basic concepts), and content novelty (such as units on highly specialized topics). Modifications in skills include training in component skills of problem solving, various forms of problem solving (such as creative, cooperative, or competitive), and development of creativity. A program for the first-grader who is performing on achievement tests at the seventh-grade level, for example, might call for placement in a higher grade level (grade skipping), although which grade level is appropriate for placement would have to be determined using teacher observations, interview results, and diagnostic tests.

Possible modifications in the school environment include provisions for enrichment in the regular classroom (such as access to special equipment), a consultant teacher (who helps the classroom teacher develop lessons), a resource room (or "pullout" program), mentoring (often by a professional in the community), independent study (often a special project), special-interest classes (such as creative writing), special classes (such as advanced placement biology), and special schools (such as a statewide math and science school). A program for the musically creative adolescent might incorporate mentoring by a music professional, who would report to the school on a regular basis about work completed by the adolescent at a recording studio or while otherwise away from school during school hours.

LEGAL ASPECTS

No federally accepted definition of giftedness exists within the United States and Canada. In the United States, definitions of giftedness are left up to individual states and most gifted programming is left to individual school districts. This has created wide variance in services. Although the No Child Left Behind and Race to the Top legislation both mandated support to help struggling students, there is no mandate to support gifted children. Moreover, the extra support for struggling students often comes at the expense of gifted students. Although children who are labeled as learning disabled or developmentally delayed are entitled to extra resources, gifted students are often neglected. Likewise, while Common Core State Standards are being implemented in many states to improve the rigorousness of general education course, they specifically do not outline options for gifted students.

Most states require that children identified as gifted, just like those identified as delayed, have an individualized education plan (IEP) in place. This plan outlines how the gifted child is to be educated during the following year and is typically constructed and agreed on by teachers in conjunction with the parents of the gifted student and sometimes also with the gifted student.

COUNSELING GIFTED LEARNERS

Beginning in the 1920s, Leta Anna Stetter Hollingworth at Columbia University investigated characteristics of children who scored over 180 on the Stanford-Binet test. Her study of twelve children (eight boys and four girls) suggested that despite their overall adjustment, children who were highly intellectually gifted tended to encounter three challenges not encountered by most other children. The first was a failure to develop work habits at school because of a curriculum paced for much less capable learners. The second was difficulty in finding satisfying companionship because of their advanced interests and abilities in relation to their age-mates. The third was vulnerability to frustration and depression because of a capacity to understand information on an adult level without sufficient experience to know how to respond to it.

Hollingworth suggested that the problem of work habits could be addressed by a combination of acceleration and enrichment. The problem of loneliness could be solved by training gifted children in social games—such as checkers or chess—that could be played by people of any age, and the problems of frustration and depression by careful adult supervision and patience. Research has tended to confirm that the problems Hollingworth identified often need to be addressed not only in cases of extreme precociousness but also, to a lesser extent, in the lives of many people identified as gifted.

If underachievement by a gifted child has its source in an unchallenging or otherwise inappropriate educational program, the recommended action is to assess strengths and weaknesses (a learning disability may be the problem), then design a more appropriate program or place the child in one that already exists. If the source of underachievement is low self-esteem, the home environment may be unlike that found by Bloom to nurture talent. In this case, family counseling can often reverse underachievement.

To help a gifted child with peer relations, group therapy with other gifted children can be particularly beneficial. Group members not only can share their experiences of being gifted but also can establish and maintain friendships with those who have similar (or sometimes quite different) exceptional abilities. Group counseling sessions can be both therapeutic and developmental.

At least some of the emotional challenges facing gifted children develop from their emotional sensitivity and excitability. Because parents and siblings often share these characteristics, the stage is set for conflict. What is surprising is that conflict does not create unhappiness more often. In the main, gifted people report satisfaction with their home lives. If tensions in the home arise more often than in the average home, the parents of gifted children and the children themselves may need to develop more effective conflict resolution strategies and higher levels of self-understanding. Developmental counseling can assist parents and children in making these changes. Research has shown that gifted children do not have a higher level of psychopathology than do nongifted children. However, it is often assumed that because of their abilities, these children can find their way on their own.

It has been suggested that modern psychology could have much to offer the field of giftedness. Steven Pfeiffer of the Talent Identification Program at Duke University conducted a study to identify how the field of psychology could contribute to the study of giftedness and to gifted individuals. Psychologists could help build consensus around a definition of giftedness. After almost a century of work and research in giftedness, there is still no single definition to which all practitioners can turn. Although many schools use standardized intelligence tests to identify gifted students, there is considerable debate regarding the best way to test and measure giftedness. A considerable problem exists, especially in the identification of gifted minorities, who remain underrepresented in the gifted population. Psychologists could become more involved in the debate concerning how to identify all children who are gifted, regardless of race, gender, and ethnic background. Finally, there are still problems addressing the needs of gifted students within the classroom setting. Most teachers are unprepared by their schooling to meet the needs of gifted children. It is not merely a matter of giving gifted students more work, but different work that uniquely suits their abilities.

BIBLIOGRAPHY

Colangelo, Nicholas, and Gary A. Davis, eds. *Handbook of Gifted Education*. 3rd ed. Boston: Allyn, 2002. Print.

"Common Core State Standards and Gifted Education." *National Association for Gifted Children*. National Assn. for Gifted Children, 2008. Web. 20 May 2014.

Gallagher, James, and Shelagh Gallagher. *Teaching the Gifted Child*. 4th ed. Boston: Allyn, 1994. Print.

Gavin, Mary L. "Gifted Education." *KidsHealth.org*. Nemours Foundation, Apr. 2014. Web. 15 May 2014.

MacKinnon, Donald W. *In Search of Human Effectiveness*. Buffalo: Creative Education Foundation, 1978. Print.

Marland, Sidney P. *Education of the Gifted and Talented*. Washington: GPO, 1971. Print.

Mendaglio, Sal, and Jean Sunde Peterson. *Models of Counseling Gifted Children, Adolescents, and Young Adults*. Waco: Prufrock, 2006. Print.

Morrissey, Annie-Marie, and Anne Grant. "Making a Difference for Young Gifted and Talented Children." *Education.vic.gov.au*. Dept. of Education and Early Childhood Development, State Government of Victoria, 21 Mar. 2014. Web. 15 May 2014.

Pfeiffer, S. "Professional Psychology and the Gifted: Emerging Practice Opportunities." *Professional Psychology: Research and Practice* 32.2 (2001): 175–80. Print.

Rivero, Lisa. "Many Ages at Once." *Psychology Today*. Sussex Publishers, 24 Jan. 2012. Web. 15 May 2014.

Sawyer, R. Keith. *Explaining Creativity: The Science of Human Innovation*. 2nd ed. New York: Oxford UP, 2012. Print.

Shurkin, Joel N. *Terman's Kids: The Groundbreaking Study of How the Gifted Grow Up*. Boston: Little, Brown, 1992. Print.

Winner, Ellen. *Gifted Children: Myths and Realities*. New York: Basic, 1996. Print.

John F. Wakefield;
updated by Ayn Embar-Seddon O'Reilly
and Allan D. Pass

See Also: Children's mental health; Emotional intelligence; Intelligence; Intelligence quotient (IQ); Intelligence tests; Learning; Multiple intelligences; Stanford-Binet test.

Gilligan, Carol

Born: November 28, 1936
Birthplace: New York, New York
Identity: American psychologist
Type of psychology: Developmental psychology

Gilligan theorized that there are differences between men and women in values and views when confronted with ethical dilemmas.

Carol Gilligan grew up in the 1940s in the Upper West Side of Manhattan. After completing a highest honors degree in English at Swarthmore College in 1958 and earning a doctorate in clinical psychology at Harvard University in 1964, she began teaching at Harvard during the late 1960s.

While researching moral and personality development, Gilligan became convinced that the study of psychology was based primarily on studies of men and lacked women's voices. Although a collaborator of developmental psychologist Lawrence Kohlberg, she has argued that Kohlberg's stages of moral development explain the "moral voice" of only boys and young men.

Gilligan is best known for her book *In a Different Voice* (1982), which presents a conceptual framework for two different "themes" or "voices." Her theory of moral development contrasts the masculine ethic of justice, as presented by Kohlberg, with the feminine ethic of care. She explains these gender differences in moral perspective as caused by contrasting images of self. The ethic of care stresses the connectedness or relatedness of persons. The ethic of justice or ethic of rights is based on separateness or distinctiveness of the self. Individuals stand alone and independently make moral decisions.

Gilligan does not argue for the superiority of either the interpersonal theme of women or the formal rule-bound morality of men. Instead, she insists that male and female moral orientations should be considered apart from each other and that development within each should be studied according to the unique facets of each. Her own studies have also included boys and their development into manhood.

Critics note a lack of empirical research to support Gilligan's argument that women score lower than men on Kohlberg's scale. Nevertheless, Gilligan's work is accepted as having created an appreciation of women's voices, resulting in a new interest in female developmental psychology and an abundance of literature on feminist ethics.

Gilligan was selected by *Time* magazine as one of the twenty-five most influential people in 1996. In 1997, she became the first holder of a chair on gender studies at the Harvard Graduate School of Education. Five years later, in 2002, she began teaching at New York University. She has also taught at the University of Cambridge in England and the University of Brussels in Belgium.

Collaborative publications include *Making Connections* (1990), *Mapping the Moral Domain* (1990), *Women's Psychology and Girls' Development* (1992), *Meeting at the Crossroads* (1993), *Between Voice and Silence* (1997), and *The Deepening Darkness: Patriarchy, Resistance, and Democracy's Future* (2009). In addition, Gilligan has independently authored *The Birth of Pleasure* (2002) and *Joining the Resistance* (2011).

BIBLIOGRAPHY

Aldridge, Jerry, and Lois McFadyen Christensen. "Carol Gilligan." *Stealing from the Mother: The Marginalization of Women in Education and Psychology from 1900-2010*. Lanham: Rowman, 2013. 125–30. Digital file.

Ball, Laura. "Carol Gilligan." *Feminist Voices*. Psychology's Feminist Voices Multimedia Internet Archive, 2010. Web. 27 Feb. 2014.

Berube, Maurice R. *Eminent Educators, Studies in Intellectual Influence*. Westport: Greenwood, 2000. Print.

Fite, Kathleen E., and Jovita M. Ross-Gordon. "Carol Gilligan." *A Critical Pedagogy of Resistance*. Ed. James D. Kirylo. London: Springer, 2013. 57–59. Print.

Gilligan, Carol. " 'Mommy, I Know You': A Feminist Scholar Explains How the Study of Girls Can Teach Us about Boys." *Newsweek* 30 Jan. 2006: 53. Print.

Hekman, Susan J. *Moral Voices, Moral Selves: Carol Gilligan and Feminist Moral Theory.* University Park: Pennsylvania State UP, 1995. Print.

Puka, Bill. *Caring Voices and Women's Frames: Gilligan's View.* Vol. 6 of Moral Development: A Compendium. New York: Garland, 1994. Print.

Lillian J. Breckenridge

See Also: Development; Developmental psychology; Feminist psychotherapy; Kohlberg, Lawrence; Moral development; Women's psychology: Carol Gilligan.

Gonads

Type of psychology: Biological bases of behavior

The gonads are the mammalian male testes and female ovaries, which secrete sex hormones. These hormones determine sex differences in reproductive structures and functions and have been strongly implicated in the expression of sexual, aggressive, and maternal behaviors.

Key Concepts

- Activational effects
- Adrenogenital syndrome
- Androgen insensitivity syndrome
- Androgenization
- Androgens
- Estradiol
- H-Y antigen
- Organizational effects
- Ovaries
- Progesterone
- Testes
- Turner's syndrome

INTRODUCTION

The gonads are endocrine glands that secrete sex hormones in all mammalian species. In males, the gonads are the testes, which secrete sex hormones called androgens; in the female, the gonads are the ovaries, which secrete estradiol and progesterone. These sex hormones, which are released into the bloodstream, have effects on the formation of both internal and external reproductive organs during prenatal development; later, they have important behavioral effects, particularly in the expression of sexual behaviors. They are also implicated in maternal and aggressive behaviors.

PRENATAL DEVELOPMENT

In the prenatal period, as the embryo is developing, the gonads are the first sex organs to differentiate into male and female organs. Prior to the seventh week of human gestation, the gonads are identical for the two sexes. If the embryo is genetically male, the gonads differentiate into male testes at the seventh or eighth week of development. If the embryo is female, the gonads differentiate into ovaries at around the tenth or eleventh week. This differentiation is controlled by a protein called the sex-determining region Y (SRY) protein, which is encoded by a gene on the Y chromosome known as the SRY gene. When the SRY protein is present, it will stimulate the formation of testes. If it is absent, ovaries will automatically develop several weeks later.

Once the sexual differentiation of the gonads has occurred, a sequence of events takes place that will determine the sexual dimorphism of both the internal and the external reproductive organs, and therefore the sex of the individual. This is known as the organizational effect of the gonads. If the gonads have differentiated into testes, the testes will begin to secrete androgens, primarily testosterone, which have a masculinizing effect and cause the development of internal male structures such as the prostate, the vas deferens, and the epididymis. If there is an absence of androgens, the female uterus, fallopian tubes, and inner two-thirds of the vagina will develop instead. A genetic disorder called Turner syndrome illustrates how the absence of androgens results in the development of female structures. In this disorder, the individual has only one X chromosome, which prevents the development of functioning ovaries, and no Y chromosome, which precludes the secretion of androgens; in their absence, the individual's other internal female sexual organs develop normally.

The external or visible genitalia develop in much the same way, governed by the presence or absence of androgens. The embryos of both sexes begin with undifferentiated genitals that are capable of becoming characteristically male or female, depending on androgen exposure. If there is androgen exposure, the primordial phallus will differentiate into the glans or head of the penis, the genital swelling will become the scrotum (into which the testes will eventually descend from the abdominal cavity), and the genital tubercle will differentiate into the shaft or main body of the penis. If there is no androgen exposure, then the primordial phallus will become the clitoris, the genital swelling will become the labia majora, and the genital tubercle will become the labia minora and the outer one-third of the vagina. Again, regardless of the genetic sex of the embryo, the absence of stimulation of primordial genital tissue by androgens will result in female structures. The presence of androgens is required for masculine development. In the example of Turner syndrome, the external genitalia are those of a normal female even though she lacks ovaries.

PUBERTY

At birth, the infant has his or her primary sex characteristics: testes or ovaries and both internal and external sexual organs characteristic of males or females. It is not until puberty that an individual's gonadal hormones begin to determine further development. Puberty begins with the secretion of hormones by the hypothalamus and the pituitary, located in the brain; the hormones travel via the bloodstream to the testes or ovaries, causing the production of the gonadal hormones that will direct the development of sexual maturation and the emergence of secondary sexual characteristics. The ovaries begin to produce estradiol, while the testes secrete testosterone. Estradiol causes enlargement of the breasts, growth in the lining of the uterus, widening of the hips, changes in the deposition of fat, and maturation of the female genitalia. Testosterone is responsible for growth of facial hair, deepening of the voice, masculine muscular development, and growth of the male genitalia.

Estradiol secretion in the female is also responsible for the onset of the first menstrual cycle. The cycle begins when an ovarian follicle is stimulated by hormones from the pituitary and thereby matures. It then secretes estradiol, which causes growth in the lining of the uterus in preparation for implantation of a fertilized ovum. It also causes ovulation, in which the follicle ruptures, releasing an ovum. During the second half of the cycle, the follicle itself becomes the corpus luteum, which produces both estradiol and progesterone. The latter hormone is responsible for maintaining the lining of the uterus during pregnancy. If the ovum is not fertilized, the production of both estradiol and progesterone decreases and the uterine lining is sloughed off in menstruation.

ROLE IN SEXUAL BEHAVIOR

The influence of gonadal hormones has been studied in relation to the activation of sexual, maternal, and aggressive behaviors. The effects of gonadal hormones on behavior can be subdivided into organizational and activational influences, with the former occurring during prenatal development and the latter occurring after puberty.

Psychologists have studied the ways in which prenatal exposure or insensitivity to androgens organizes sexual behavior. In adrenogenital syndrome, the adrenal glands secrete unusually high levels of androgens, to which the developing embryo is exposed. If the embryo is male, normal development will occur. If the embryo is female, masculinization will occur, with enlargement of the clitoris and possibly fused labia. Researchers at the Johns Hopkins University studied thirty young women with adrenogenital syndrome to determine whether androgenization (exposure of the developing embryo to male sex hormones) affected their sexual orientation. The women described themselves as homosexual or bisexual at approximately four times the rate that occurs naturally in random populations of women. This hints that exposure of the developing female fetus to androgens may affect sexual orientation, possibly by altering the organization of the brain in ways that are not yet understood. A similar finding has occurred in primate research. When androgens were injected into monkeys pregnant with female fetuses, these androgenized infants became significantly different from their nonandrogenized peers in displaying more malelike behaviors, such as engaging in attempted mountings of other females.

Androgen insensitivity syndrome prevents male fetuses from being androgenized properly. These genetically male individuals will develop female genitalia and, if reared as females, will easily assume female sexual identities and overwhelmingly prefer male sexual partners. There is some possibility, then, that prenatal androgenization encourages a preference for female sexual partners, while lack of such exposure results in a preference for male sexual partners, regardless of genetic sex. It should be remembered, however, that this remains quite speculative, and conclusive research has not yet been conducted.

The activational effects of gonadal hormones on adult sexual behavior have also been of interest to psychologists. While estradiol and progesterone strongly influence the sexual behaviors of lower animals, these hormones do not seem to influence human female sexual behavior. For example, while both estrogen and progesterone levels fluctuate considerably over the menstrual cycle, women can become aroused at any time in the cycle and are not more easily aroused when these hormones are especially high or low. Further, when a woman's ovaries are surgically removed or cease to produce hormones after menopause, sexual activity and interest are not affected.

There is some evidence that androgens, either present in small amounts secreted by the adrenal glands or ingested in the form of synthetic male hormones, will cause greater sexual desire in females and more frequent instigation of sexual activity but will have no effect on an already-established sexual orientation. The influence of androgens on male animals is direct: All male mammals respond to the presence of testosterone with increased sexual desire. Without testosterone, sperm production and copulatory ability cease.

ROLE IN AGGRESSIVE BEHAVIOR

Much aggressive behavior among animals takes place within the context of reproductive behavior. It comes as no surprise, then, that aggressive behaviors in both sexes are also strongly influenced by gonadal hormones, particularly androgens. Male offensive attacks and competitive behaviors, as well as interfemale aggressiveness and maternal aggression, are increased by exposure to androgens in most mammals.

One of the most stable behavioral differences between males and females is aggression; males display higher levels of aggression at all ages and in all forms. Because this sex difference has been observed in toddlers, before strong socialization influences have had their impact, it is speculated that prenatal exposure to androgens is partly responsible for these behavioral differences. This same relationship holds for all other mammalian species: the greater the prenatal androgenization, the more aggressive the subsequent behavior.

The relationship between aggressive behavior and testosterone levels has been studied in a variety of ways. One avenue of research has been to examine the testosterone levels of males who display different levels of aggressive behavior. For example, the testosterone levels of male prisoners with histories of violent crime have been compared with the frequency of their violent behavior while incarcerated. No relationship between the androgen levels and current aggressive expression has been found; however, androgen levels have been positively correlated with the frequency of these prisoners' aggressive behaviors in adolescence. Perhaps by adulthood, learning had intervened to modulate this relationship, with some high-testosterone males able to exert control over their aggressive impulses while some men with lower testosterone levels have learned to vent their aggressiveness.

MATERNAL BEHAVIOR AND GENDER IDENTITY

With regard to the effects of gonadal hormones on maternal behavior, the findings are clear in most lower animals. In laboratory rats, for example, sequences of progesterone followed by estradiol will facilitate nest-building behaviors. No such relationship, however, seems to hold for humans. It seems that maternal behavior is determined largely by learning and by an early bonding between mother and infant and that caretaking behaviors are not influenced by hormonal activation.

Research concerning the effects of gonadal hormones on behavior is one of the many avenues of investigation into the development of gender identity, an individual's sense of being a man or a woman. There are many determinants of such identity: one's genetic makeup, prenatal sex hormone exposure, one's internal and external genitalia, the gender to which one is assigned at birth, and socialization—learning about culturally appropriate gender behaviors through interaction with parents and peers. Most often, these determinants are consistent with one another, and the individual develops a clear, stable sense of gender identity. When this is not the case, such inconsistencies may lead to an individual experiencing gender dysphoria.

RESEARCH DIRECTIONS

Future research concerning gonadal hormones will continue in two major directions: the effects of gonadal hormones on the sexual differentiation of the brain and the interaction between sex hormones and adult sexual behaviors. Most research on sexual differentiation of the brain has been conducted with nonhuman species. For example, it has been found that testosterone "masculinizes" the brains of birds to produce typical male birdsong and produces male or female sexual behaviors in laboratory animals. The way in which this masculinization occurs is somewhat paradoxical: Inside the brain of the male embryo, testosterone is converted to estrogen, the hormone that actually produces the masculinization. In females, on the other hand, a protein exists in the neurons of the brain that prevents estrogen from effecting such masculinization.

In humans, it is known that the absence of prenatal androgen exposure sets the brain in a female pattern, which causes the pituitary to function in a cyclical manner, thus creating the menstrual cycle. Some interesting initial research with humans suggests that as a result of prenatal hormone exposure, there is greater lateralization of male brains than of female brains. Therefore, there is more specialization of the two cerebral hemispheres in males and more crossover of functions across the two hemispheres in females. This observation remains speculative and will be subject to considerable scrutiny.

Research interest will continue to be directed toward discovering the role of gonadal hormones in adult sexual behavior. More recent areas of study concern the question of prenatal hormonal determinants of sexual orientation. Studies will also continue to be focused on the question of sexual motivation in general to determine the levels and kinds of sex hormones that either enhance or depress sexual interest.

BIBLIOGRAPHY

Beyer, Carlos, ed. *Endocrine Control of Sexual Behavior.* New York: Raven, 1979. Print.

Blakemore, Judith E. Owen, Sheri A. Berenbaum, and Lynn S. Liben. *Gender Development*. New York: Psychology, 2008. Print.

Constantinescu, Mihaela, and Melissa Hines. "Relating Prenatal Testosterone Exposure to Postnatal Behavior in Typically Developing Children: Methods and Findings." *Child Development Perspectives* 6.4 (2012): 407–13. Print.

Drickamer, Lee C., Stephen H. Vessey, and Elizabeth Jakob. *Animal Behavior: Mechanisms, Ecology, Evolution.* 5th ed. New York: McGraw, 2002. Print.

Graham, Robert B. *Physiological Psychology.* Belmont: Wadsworth, 1990. Print.

Money, John, and Anke A. Ehrhardt. *Man and Woman, Boy and Girl*. 1972. Northvale: Aronson, 1996. Print.

Unger, Rhoda K. *Female and Male: Psychological Perspectives.* New York: Harper, 1979. Print.

Visvanathan, Nalini, et al., eds. *The Women, Gender and Development Reader.* 2nd ed. New York: Zed, 2011. Print.

Zambrano, Elena, et al. "Fetal Programming of Sexual Development and Reproductive Function." *Molecular and Cellular Endocrinology* 382.1 (2014): 538–49. Print.

Barbara E. Brackney

See Also: Adolescence: Sexuality; Endocrine system; Gay, lesbian, bisexual, and transgender mental health; Gender identity formation; Hormones and behavior; Pituitary gland; Prenatal physical development; Sex hormones and motivation; Sexual behavior patterns.

Gossip

Type of psychology: Counseling; Clinical; Social

Gossip is defined as talk or rumor, typically about other people's personal matters. Gossip can be a key part to forming meaningful relationships. By creating a bond over shared information, people are able to feel closer and ultimately develop closer relationships. However, gossip is not always good. When people are on the receiving end of negative or embarrassing gossip about themselves, they often feel angry and upset.

Key Concepts

- Bonding
- Cyberbullying
- Gossip
- Rumor

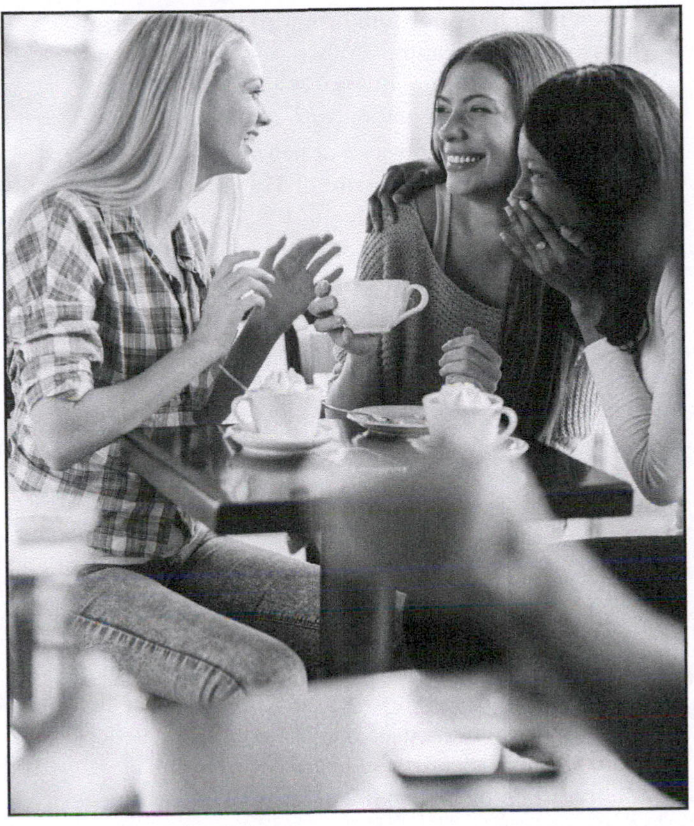

Photo: iStock

INTRODUCTION

Gossip is ubiquitous. Anthropologists, along with other social scientists, have found that gossip occurs around the world and in both men and women. However, there are gender differences between the content of male and female gossip. Gossiping across genders allows men and women to form bonds and during this bonding activity, gossip loses its negative connotation. Instead, gossip is seen as helping people form and deepen bonds with others. However, when a person is on the receiving end of negative gossip about him-or herself, that person often feels dejected, upset, and hurt about the negative message communicated. Currently, because of technology and online access, gossip can quickly be spread and accessed.

Cyberbullying is one of the many harmful effects of gossip and because it leads to profound shame and embarrassment, it has even been linked to suicides among youth. Prior to the rise of the Internet, negative gossip spread about young people would be able to be left at school or a similarly restrictive environment. With instant and constant access to social media sites, people are able to continuously bully by spreading derogatory information about others in a context that does not allow easy rebuttal or explanation. This article will explore the benefits and harmful effects of gossip, gender differences, and the future of gossip.

DEFINING GOSSIP

We all have an idea of what gossip is, but developing a concrete definition for the purpose of research has become challenging. At a very general level, researchers define gossip as idle talk or "chit chat" about daily life (Dunbar, 2004). In feminist criticism, gossip is "girl talk" (Eckert, 1990). In an attempt to define gossip more narrowly for the purpose of this article, gossip refers to any instance of information being discussed without the third party (whom the information is about) being present or giving assent.

THE POSITIVES AND NEGATIVES OF GOSSIP

In the field of communications there is a term called communication privacy management theory which centers on how people make decisions about revealing and concealing private information. When a person decides to share information with another, it is usually after he or she weighs the potential benefits and harm of disclosing to the other person. If a person chooses to tell another some kind of personal, private information, the informed person now owns the information with the informant.

This ownership obligates him or her to act according to the informant's expectations. When this obligation is not fulfilled, boundary turbulence occurs, and the informant is unlikely to share information with that person again.

While gossip can be positive or negative, it does seem abundant. In a 2001 University of Pennsylvania study, Eric Foster concluded that about 70% of our conversations involve gossip, and it is nearly impossible to be a non-participant. Gossip can be valuable, because people need to know information about those around them. It is impossible for people to be everywhere, all the time, making gossip an important way to give others insight into our lives who might otherwise not get a chance to know much about us. When gossip is used to inform and does not break any preset boundaries, it is beneficial, but when boundary turbulence occurs and a person shares more than he or she is supposed to, gossip becomes hurtful.

Given the potential for individual harm, societal mores usually dissuade people from participating. In the Bible, Leviticus commands religious followers to "Be not a talebearer." Today, parents, teachers, and other adults in authority may simply dissuade children from participating in this behavior. These warnings stem from feelings of hurt when people do not agree with our actions.

PROS

As mentioned, gossip can be beneficial. As the gossiper we are able to give information about others that is not our own. Additionally, we are able to disclose something personal without putting anything about ourselves on the line. By talking about others we no longer have the fear of rejection which allows us to be more open and talk freely about topics we otherwise would not discuss. For example, if we hear that a colleague is going through a divorce we might talk to another colleague about the divorce. In this scenario we would be able to disclose our own opinions as to why the divorce is happening or if we think the couple should or should not be getting a divorce. We can talk about this without having any intention of harming the person getting the divorce. Rather we are disclosing his or her private information to someone else to form a bond with him or her. It is natural to want to have deep and meaningful bonds with other people and we often use gossip as a way of doing this. We have less at stake when we talk about others, but we are still able to share something meaningful and gauge how the other person reacts to the information before we disclose anything personal about ourselves.

While we are able to form meaningful bonds with people in social settings by gossiping, current research also suggests that gossiping at work can lead to a more efficient workplace. People are able to know who is and is not getting work done, meeting deadlines, and fulfilling their responsibilities. This information can be insightful to those in higher positions since they are often too removed from the day to day work to recognize those who are key to successful operations.

CONS

While gossip can be used to deepen relationships and form meaningful bonds , gossip can also be hurtful. Gossip is often information not meant to be shared with others which leads to the person who originally shared the information feeling ashamed, embarrassed, and even angry at the informant. Gossip can also be untrue. In these instances, gossip can become a false rumor which, in the most serious of cases, ends up defaming a person's character. Additionally, by gossiping, the bonds that people form are not built on disclosed information about the people who are forming the bond. If the people in the relationship do not connect about personal information, the relationship will either remain superficial or will end.

GENDER DIFFERENCES AND GOSSIP

While mentioned previously that both men and women gossip, there are important differences that must be accounted for. For instance, women are more likely to gossip about personal or relational issues whereas men are inclined to disclose competitive gossip. An example of competitive gossip would be when a man talks about his baseball team losing a game because a team member was going through a difficult time and was not playing well. While this is arguably similar to relational gossip, it is different because the intent of the gossip is to justify the loss of the game. In general, men tend to gossip about shared activities, mirroring how men bond by doing things together whereas women bond by talking. Research also suggests that women tend to gossip about physical appearances more than men which can be detrimental to their mental state. By constantly comparing themselves to others, whether it is their friends or media figures, they are inadvertently putting pressure on themselves to obtain unachievable goals or standards. Sometimes, when the relationship is based on talking about other people's appearances, it can endanger the friendship by being in constant competition, whereas, with males, their friendships thrive.

TECHNOLOGY AND GOSSIP

While there are numerous benefits to technology, one of the biggest issues surrounding the increase of social media websites is cyberbullying among youth. Cyberbullying is bullying that takes place through social networking sites, texting, and other types of electronic communication. Often, cyberbullying begins with a rumor started at school, and the rumor then rapidly spreads through the use of technology. Cyberbullying can be incredibly detrimental to a young person and in some instances has led to suicide. While many argue that bullying and spreading rumors have always been part of society's fabric, it has not historically filtered back into the home. In today's world, bullying goes beyond school and potentially anywhere in the world. Children can now be bullied without reprieve, resulting in them not feeling safe anywhere. In cyberbullying, technology has created a negative space for gossip and has allowed the information to be spread to many people at a rapid pace. According to the U.S. government's website stopbullying.gov, children and teens who are cyberbullied tend to skip school, experience bullying in real life, have low self-esteem, earn poor grades, and have more health problems. Since this is clearly detrimental to a child's overall well-being, it further proves the negative impact technology has on gossip.

BIBLIOGRAPHY

Beersma, B., & Van Kleef, G. (2011). How the grapevine keeps you in line. *Social Psychological and Personality Science,* 2(6), 642-649. Retrieved from http://spp.sagepub.com/content/2/6/642 Workplace gossip and its many benefits.

Dunbar, R. I. M. (2004). Gossip in evolutionary perspective. *Review of General Psychology,* 8,100-110. An overview of gossip's evolution.

Eckert, P. (1990). Cooperative competition in adolescent "girl talk." *Discourse Processes,* 13, 91-122. Gossip is no longer just for girls.

Foster, E. (2004). "Research On Gossip: Taxonomy, Methods, and Future Directions. *Review of General Psychology,* 8(2), 78-99. Discusses the current state of gossip and how it has evolved over time and gives insight into the future of gossip.

Furnham, A. (2013, November 9). "Gossip Is Good For You". *Psychology Today*. Retrieved from https://www.psychologytoday.com/blog/sideways-view/201311/gossip-is-good-you?tr=HdrQuote Discusses the positive aspect of gossip helping people form meaningful bonds.

Kennedy-Moore, E. (2014, January 7). "Why do girls gossip?" *Psychology Today.* Retrieved from http://www.psychologytoday.com/blog/growing-friendships/201401/why-do-girls-gossip Explores why young girls gossip, shows how gossip can be detrimental, and provides suggestion about teaching young girls how to make gossip work in their favor rather than using it to hurt others.

Watson, D. (2014). "Gender Differences In Gossip and Friendship". *Sex Roles,* 67, 494-502. Men are more likely to benefit from gossip than women given men's competitive nature.

What is Cyberbullying? (n.d.). Retrieved October 24, 2014, from http://www.stopbullying.gov/cyberbullying/ A government website that thoroughly explains cyberbullying and gives in-depth explanations of what it is, how it is done, and how to prevent it. There are also many links to other sources and statistics on cyberbullying.

Lauren Ruvo

See Also: Adolescents; Aggression; Bullying; Group dynamics; Interpersonal communcation; Social interaction; Social perception.

Grammar and speech

Type of psychology: Language

Grammar and speech are the building blocks of the human communication systems known as languages. The study of language structure has enhanced growth in a number of areas in psychology, including language acquisition, the biological basis for language, and the relationship between language and thought..

Key Concepts

- Critical period
- Generative grammar
- Morpheme
- Morphology
- Phonology
- Suffix
- Syntax

INTRODUCTION

Human beings everywhere, despite differences in geography, culture, and ethnicity, have a capacity for language, a system of communication primarily involving a patterned, rule-governed sequence of oral sounds. The rules that human beings implicitly use to produce and understand such communication are collectively known as grammar, and the vocalizations that serve as the vehicle of the communication are called speech.

When people think of grammar, they usually think of a set of arbitrary rules learned in school about correct and incorrect ways of speaking or writing. Indeed, such rules do constitute a grammar of sorts, one that prescribes standards of appropriate style. Grammar, however, has a wider and more important meaning, because without a grammar, no language is possible. In fact, every speaker of a language knows the rules of the grammar of that language without being explicitly taught them. Grammar, in its most important sense, is the set of rules that each language has and that each native speaker of that language knows even before going to school; it determines what the basic building blocks of the language are (the words, the morphemes, and the sounds) and specifies the rules for combining those basic elements into meaningful utterances. Grammar is simply the structure of that unique human behavior called language.

LANGUAGE SUBSYSTEMS

Language scientists generally subdivide language into a set of structural subsystems, each of which has its own set of rules, or regular patterns. When discovered, these rules can be seen to operate in every utterance of that language. Each of these subsystems—syntax, morphology, and phonology—therefore is a grammar, although the term "grammar" in its everyday use is usually associated only with syntax.

The syntax of a language is the set of rules that govern how meaningful elements, the words, are combined into the permissible sequences known as sentences. Syntax also dictates how sentences can be combined with other sentences to form more complex utterances and how elements within sentences can be rearranged to change the focus of a sentence without changing its meaning. For example, speakers of English know that the sequence of words "the dog chased the cat" means that an instigator of an action, a dog, behaved in such a way to affect the second participant mentioned in the string of words, the cat. Moreover, they know that the word "the" must precede and never follow words such as "cat" and "dog." Finally, they know that the sequence "the cat was chased by the dog" is merely a paraphrase, a restatement, of the original string and not a contradiction of it.

The morphology of a language, the second subsystem, defines the basic set of elements that operate in the formation of words. Each of these basic elements is called a morpheme. Many morphemes may be words in a language, but some morphemes are less than an entire word. For example, the English suffix-s attached to a word such as "cup" states that there is more than one cup; it is apparent to any speaker of English that this suffix (ending) is considerably less than a word. Nevertheless, the -s is a meaningful element in the English language and constitutes a morpheme, or minimal meaningful unit, of the language. The way words are constructed is governed by rules and is therefore a kind of grammar; for example, the -s that signals "more than one" is always attached to the end of the word, not to the beginning of it, and it cannot be inserted in the middle. This fact about English is predictable. If English speakers encounter a new word that designates some object, they know that talking about more than one of these objects usually requires the addition of the-s suffix to the new word. This implicit knowledge is a kind of grammar known as morphology.

The third important structural subsystem of language is phonology, or the sound system of a language. Each of the world's languages uses only some of the vocal sounds, or phonemes, that human beings are capable of producing, and this limited set is further constrained regarding what sounds may follow one another at the beginnings, middles, and ends of words. For example, the English language has both /t/ and /l/ as sounds that may be used in words, and though /l/ may follow /t/ in the middle of words such as "antler" and "butler," there are no English words beginning with this sequence of sounds, nor are there likely to be any. The sequence tl simply does not occur at the beginning of English words, although there is no physiological reason that it cannot. Human beings are perfectly capable of producing such a sound combination, and it does exist at the beginning of words in other languages. It is the grammar of the sound system of English—its phonology—that prohibits such a possibility.

UNIQUE GRAMMAR OF LANGUAGES

These subsystems of language are found in every one of the world's languages, even though each subsystem's particulars and importance are unique for each language. As an example, languages such as modern English can be compared to classical Latin, the ancestor language of French, Italian, and Spanish. In English, the ordering of words is of paramount importance. A sentence such as "The boy loved the girl" has only one meaning, and changing the sequencing of words would drastically change that meaning. That is, if the words "boy" and "girl" were interchanged, the resulting sentence, "The girl loved the boy," would mean something entirely different: the initiator of the state of love is now the girl, not the boy. Thus, in English, the critical information of who is doing what to whom is given in the syntax, in the ordering of words. In Latin, on the other hand, although there is surely word sequencing, since words can be expressed only one at a time, the word order—the syntax—does not indicate relationships as it does in English. Instead, the matter of who is doing what to whom is given by morphology, by suffixes attached to the ends of words. The sentence "The boy loved the girl" could be expressed by any of the following: puer puellam amabat, puellam puer amabat, amabat puer puellam, puellam amabat puer, and so on. The arrangement of words has little effect on meaning; the endings on the words tell speakers of Latin who does what. The-m at the end of the word for "girl" (puella) signals that the girl is affected by the action and is not the initiator of it. These facts about the two languages show that word order is more important to English than it is to Latin and that endings on words are more important to Latin, even though English continues to make use of endings to some degree (the -ed on "love" indicates, for example, that an action or state occurred at some past time).

The fact that all languages have a grammar, a predictable pattern underlying every utterance, allows human languages to be unique among all the communication systems found in nature. Grammar allows people to talk about new things, about events that occurred in the past, about events that might possibly occur in the future, and even about things that can never be. A grammar allows people to produce an infinite number of possible sentences because words can be combined and recombined in many ways to generate many different meanings. This possibility makes language qualitatively different from the songs and calls of birds, which are rigidly structured to allow only a limited number of meanings; from the dances of bees, which have the single function of indicating the location of nectar; and even from the gestures of the apes, which can indicate only a limited set of communications.

LANGUAGE ACQUISITION

The complexity and variation in systems of grammar have led to a number of speculations about the nature of the human mind in particular, about the relationship between language and thought, and about how such complex systems could be achieved by human children before they are capable of logical thought. The first of these two areas is also known as linguistic relativity. The second, the possibility that at base all languages are essentially the same because they are constructed by human beings who have an innate capacity for language, has been proposed by linguist Noam Chomsky, the founder of the field of syntactic inquiry known as generative grammar. Generative grammar can be defined as a grammar that projects the structure of a potentially infinite number of sentences, including both those already produced and those yet to be uttered.

Examining the complexity of the syntax of English, Chomsky suggested that the capacity for language must be innate, that human beings have an inborn language-acquisition device that enables them to determine the grammar of the language spoken by the people who rear them. Chomsky explained that much of what young children hear must be full of errors and false starts, and yet, before age five, most children speak their native language with a high degree of accuracy. He suggested that the language-acquisition device must act as a kind of analyzer that assigns a structure to the incoming stream of speech. The resulting analysis then becomes the foundation of the grammar that permits children to produce new, original sentences in the language they hear all around them.

This speculation fueled much research during the 1960s and 1970s, and the result is that most language scientists—linguists and psychologists alike—agree that indeed the capacity for language acquisition is innate; the actual nature of the innate capacity, however, remains uncertain. Research has generally found that parents and other caregivers tend to be extremely careful in the kinds of speech they address to children; that is, they tend to speak without the errors and the false starts Chomsky had supposed. Moreover, they tend to pause and change the pitch of their voices at precisely those places in an utterance where the grammar would assign an important boundary. In many ways, then, the speech addressed to children seems an ideal teaching device, and so Chomsky's hypothesis that children formulate a grammar on the basis of fragmentary and poorly structured input has been disconfirmed. It also has been found that even very young infants tend to prefer the sound of human voices to other sounds and are capable of telling the difference between very similar but distinct speech sounds. Thus, it is clear that human beings are predisposed to acquire language.

CRITICAL PERIOD HYPOTHESIS

Other evidence supports the notion that there is a biological predisposition to language. In his book *Biological Foundations of Language* (1967), Eric Lenneberg proposed that there is a critical period for language acquisition, an age beyond which the acquisition of a first language would not be possible. That is, Lenneberg contended that a child deprived of the opportunity to acquire a language—any language at all—would never be able to do so if the deprivation continued past the onset of puberty. Supporting evidence for this hypothesis suggested a discontinuity in language abilities at adolescence. Children who suffer trauma to the parts of the brain where language is processed, for example, tend to recover if the injury occurs before puberty but typically do not recover their language abilities if the injury occurs in their mid-teen years. In addition, children who are exposed to a second language during childhood seem to acquire that language with little difficulty when compared with adults facing the same task. This, too, seems to support the hypothesis of a critical period for language acquisition. Moreover, case studies of feral children raised without language by nurturing animals such as wolves have indicated that these children failed to acquire language when introduced into civilization.

These kinds of evidence provide only partial (and debatable) support for the critical-period hypothesis. For example, no two injuries are exactly alike, so the successful recovery of one patient from a brain injury compared to the failure of another may stem from a number of causes. The facility of children compared to the difficulty for adults with respect to second-language acquisition may result from children's lack of self-consciousness. Finally, children raised by wolves during the last several centuries may have been abandoned by their parents because they had some apparent disability; perhaps the children lacked the cognitive or speech skills necessary to acquire language.

THE "GENIE" CASE STUDY

In 1970, a thirteen-year-old girl suffering from severe neglect was found. The child of a psychotic father and an abused and half-blind mother, "Genie," as she came to be called, had been locked in a darkened room since infancy and deprived of all genuine human contact. She was absolutely devoid of any language skills, although her hearing was found to be normal. Since medical records indicated normal development during infancy, save for a hip defect, and since she was clearly past puberty, Genie provided a test case for the critical-period hypothesis. Removed from her abusive environment and given the attention of caring adults, Genie made remarkable progress. At first, she seemed able to acquire language after all, and reports of her linguistic achievements were thought to herald the demise of the critical-period hypothesis. It soon became evident, however, that although Genie was making excellent progress with social and cognitive skills, her development of syntax and morphology lagged far behind. She was able to acquire a vocabulary of some size—a word list—but she failed to put words together in the ways that were typical of children acquiring language during the usual developmental period. She also had difficulty with those English morphemes that show relationships between elements in a sentence. In short, although Genie could understand words and word meanings, she was having considerable difficulty mastering grammar. Genie's case provides partial support for the critical-period hypothesis; after puberty, parts of language may still be acquired, but a full elaboration of the grammatical patterns that underlie a language will not be achieved. The importance of the early childhood years to the acquisition of language skills is clearly demonstrated by this case.

Genie's progress with language acquisition—or lack of it—could not be mapped without a knowledge of the parts of language, an understanding of syntax and morphology. Similarly, the accomplishments of young children with respect to language acquisition could not be appreciated without a knowledge of the structures underlying grammar and speech. The field of language acquisition is an entire area of study that crucially depends on knowledge of the structure of language. To study acquisition requires a knowledge of what is being acquired.

EVOLUTION OF LANGUAGE RESEARCH

Although interest in language is as old as language itself, prior to the nineteenth century investigations were philosophical and speculative. Questions about language were likely to concern the origins of language or the identity of the oldest language. During the early part of the nineteenth century, newly discovered relationships between languages fueled interest in a field of study now called comparative linguistics, which attempted to ascertain which languages derived from the same prehistoric ancestor language. Late in that century, however, interest began to turn away from the comparison of languages and toward an investigation of languages on their own terms. In the early part of the twentieth century, the scientific study of language was encouraged by the great American linguists Edward Sapir and Leonard Bloomfield.

Both Sapir and Bloomfield were spurred by the study of the indigenous languages of the United States, the languages spoken by the peoples often called American Indians. These languages were unwritten, so recording them involved a detailed investigation of their phonology, morphology, and syntax. The languages of Europe were also subjected to this new, rigorous scientific study, now called linguistics.

At first, scientific linguistics dealt mainly with phonology and morphology and studied syntax only as an afterthought. The publication of Chomsky's *Syntactic Structures* (1957), however, revolutionized the field. This small book redistributed the rankings of the various subfields of language by showing the formal relationships among apparently diverse structures in syntax; what had previously been backgrounded in the study of language, the syntax, was now seen as the central focus of linguistic inquiry. In fact, syntax became so important within linguistics that Chomsky and his colleagues argued for an autonomous syntax, a system of structural relations that has an existence apart from sound and meaning. In the last decades of the twentieth century, many linguists abandoned this notion and opted instead for a pragmatic analysis of language, a description based on how particular words, syntactic structures, phonological features, and other patterns of discourse such as overlaps and interruptions among participants in a conversation are used to achieve certain effects in the real world. This approach has the effect of integrating the subsystems of language so that the focus is on the basic circumstance of communication: people talking.

BIBLIOGRAPHY

Arbib, Michael A. *How the Brain Got Language*. New York: Oxford UP, 2012. Print.

Baker, Mark C. *The Atoms of Language: The Mind's Hidden Rules of Grammar.* New York: Oxford UP, 2002. Print.

Carroll, David W. *Psychology of Language*. 5th ed. Belmont: Thomson, 2008. Print.

Chomsky, Noam. *Aspects of the Theory of Syntax.* Cambridge: MIT P, 1965. Print.

Crain, Stephen. *The Emergence of Meaning*. New York: Cambridge UP, 2012. Print.

Harley, Trevor A. *The Psychology of Language: From Data to Theory*. 4thd ed. Washington: Psychology, 2014. Print.

Jackendorff, Ray. *Foundations of Language: Brain, Meaning, Grammar, Evolution.* New York: Oxford UP, 2004. Print.

Karmiloff, Kyra, and Annette Karmiloff-Smith. *Pathways to Language: From Fetus to Adolescent*. Cambridge: Harvard UP, 2002. Print.

Loritz, Donald. *How the Brain Evolved Language*. New York: Oxford UP, 2002. Print.

Sanz, Montserrat, Itziar Laka, and Michael K. Tanenhaus, eds. *Language down the Garden Path: The Cognitive and Biological Basis for Linguistic Structures*. Oxford: Oxford UP, 2013. Print.

Sapir, Edward. *Language: An Introduction to the Study of Speech*. 1921. Mineola: Dover, 2004. Print.

Yule, George. *The Study of Language*. 5th ed. New York: Cambridge UP, 2014. Print.

Marilyn N. Silva

See Also: Analytic psychology: Jacques Lacan; Artificial intelligence; Bilingualism; Concept formation; Lacan, Jacques; Language; Linguistics.

Gratitude

Type of psychology: Biological bases of human behavior; Consulting; Clinical; Counseling; Developmental; Personality; Psychotherapy

Gratitude is a positive emotion that can flood our bodies with hormones that make us feel good. Gratitude can be scientifically measured and, through practice and use, an attitude of gratitude can help us feel more joy and happiness, lower our blood pressure, and improve our immune system. Further, it can enhance interpersonal relationships as well as intrapersonal insight.

Key concepts

- Appreciation
- Coherence
- Gratitude
- Incoherence

INTRODUCTION

Research shows that grateful thoughts flood our bodies with endorphins which are hormones that make us feel good, and it seems that some people are born with the gift of expressing gratitude. Some learn this from parents while others glean it from significant influences such as teachers or religious and spiritual sources. Fortunately, it is a quality and state of being that anyone can cultivate. The attainment of gratitude is most often associated with emotional maturity.

Gratitude is a positive emotion, an affirmation of goodness, a virtuous quality, and a gracious way of being. Gratitude requires admiration and a readiness to show appreciation for the giving or returning of a kindness that has enhanced someone's life in a positive and uplifting way. Expressing gratitude helps people feel positive emotions, deal with adversity, improve relationships, and improve health. It is often heard that one should develop "an attitude of gratitude" in order to put his or her life in perspective.

THE BIOCHEMISTRY OF GRATITUDE

Self-evoked, sincere feelings of gratitude and appreciation produce favorable changes in the body's biochemistry. Hormonal balance improves, there is an increase in the production of DHEA (dehydroepiandrosterone, often called the "anti-aging" hormone), and IgA (immunoglobulin A). These antibodies are also our first line of defense against pathogens. Those same feelings can decrease anxiety and depression, lower blood pressure, and lower heart rate.

Research has demonstrated that true feelings of gratitude, appreciation, and other positive emotions can synchronize the brain and heart rhythms, create a shift throughout the whole body, and create a scientifically measurable mind state called coherence. Sensitive instruments can measure the level of coherence during feelings of gratitude and appreciation. It can also be measured by the heart-rate variability (HRV) recorded during an electrocardiogram (ECG). Measuring coherence can accurately show how the heart, brain, and nervous system interactions are sensitive to changes in emotions. During an ECG, while a person is experiencing true, sincere feelings of gratitude and other positive emotions, the heart rhythm appears as a smooth wavelike pattern on an HRV graph. Incoherence, the opposite of coherence, is created by negative emotions such as frustration and anger. Such emotions disrupt the synchronization of the body's systems resulting in jagged, chaotic patterns of the heart rhythm on an HRV graph.

RESEARCH

Scientists are interested in understanding gratitude and the circumstances in which it either flourishes or diminishes. Some research initiatives are aimed at promoting evidence-based practices of gratitude for use in medical facilities, universities, schools, homes, communities, and workplaces. Other studies are interested in researching the effect of gratitude practices on the well-being of personal and professional relationships.

Over the last 10 years, hundreds of research studies have documented the psychological, physical, and social benefits of gratitude. One of the research-based reasons for practicing gratitude is that it is one of the most reliable methods for increasing happiness and life satisfaction. Another reason is that gratitude reduces depression and anxiety. Often, one can change one's perspective on his or her difficulties when an intervention assists with gratitude. One sage proverb that is often repeated is "I was upset because I had no shoes. And then I met a man who had no feet." It is not clear who the original speaker was, but the emphasis on gratitude for what one has is discernible and therapeutic.

Overall, studies have concluded that being grateful helps people sleep better. They may also recover more quickly from trauma and become more resilient. Being grateful as a way of being promotes forgiveness and strengthens relationships. Grateful people are more altruistic, compassionate, and connected to their community.

GRATITUDE PRACTICES

The mental state of gratitude grows stronger with use and practice. Various exercises and activities used to enhance and sustain feelings of gratitude help people refocus on what they have instead of what they do not have and on what works instead of what does not work. Numerous studies have found the following practices as highly effective in cultivating the mental and physical state of gratitude. Some of the practices and exercises are used by the U.S. military to help individuals and families develop resilience after deployment.

Write a Gratitude Letter – Identify a person to whom you are grateful for his or her presence in your life. The person does not have to be in your life now. Express your gratitude for his or her presence in your life or the actions that person took on your behalf that affected your life. The letter can be mailed or kept as a reminder of your gratitude.

Mentally thank someone – Think of someone who has been nice or kind to you in some way.

Imagine thanking that person for all they have done for you. Go to another person you want to thank. Keep finding new people to mentally thank. Some people simply pray for others.

Look for opportunities to be grateful – Notice when things seem to appear in your favor such as gifts that are not owed you. Examples could include someone letting you into traffic, an unexpected big smile from someone, or someone showing a random act of kindness toward you. Notice the beauty in nature, beautiful music, children's faces, and laughter.

Meditate – Mindfulness meditation involves focusing on a word such as peace or something for which you are grateful. Many CDs are available through the Internet with guided exercises in practicing gratitude.

If you have children in your life – Make it a practice to discuss gratitude on a daily basis as a tool to teach your children how to choose gratitude no matter what circumstances they face.

Write a heart-felt thank-you note – A great way to nurture your relationship with another person is by writing a thank-you note that expresses your gratitude for the positive and inspiring effect he or she has on your life. It could be a brief note after spending time with a friend or after having dinner at someone's home.

Pray – Many people use prayer with intention to cultivate gratitude which means to think carefully about what you want to communicate through prayer.

Keep a gratitude journal – Writing down each day about the things you are grateful for can help you practice generating the mind state of gratitude.

Counting your blessings – Counting your blessings can help you remember and recreate the sensations you felt when good things happened to and for you. You can write them down or share with someone.

BENEFITS OF PRACTICING GRATITUDE

Researchers have found that people who practice gratitude consistently report many significant benefits from their practice. They report feeling more joy, optimism, and happiness. They have noticeably higher levels of positive emotions. They act with more compassion and generosity and report feeling less lonely and isolated than before they began practicing gratitude. On a biological level, tests indicate that they have lower blood pressure and stronger immune systems.

Through the sustained practice of feelings of appreciation and gratitude, it becomes easier to feel those feelings because the repeated experiencing of those emotions and the corresponding biochemical effects in the brain, heart, and nervous system reinforce neural pathways in the body and mind for those emotions. Gratitude is then easier to recreate due to the accumulated effect of feeling those emotions repeatedly through practice.

BIBLIOGRAPHY

Goulston, M. (2010). *Just listen*. New York, NY: American Management Association.

http://www.psychologytoday.com/blog/the-mindful-self-express/201111/the-seven-best-gratitude-quotes

Michael Shaughnessy and June Shepherd

See Also: Positive emotion.

Grieving

Type of psychology: Emotion; Psychopathology; Stress

Grieving is the usual, expected reaction to loss. After a loss, a normal process occurs in grieving, involving feelings such as anger and sadness, followed by reassessment and reorganization of oneself and one's perspective. Some bereaved individuals experience prolonged or extreme grief reactions, commonly referred to as "complicated grief." In these cases, grief may be associated with depression, physical illness, and heightened risk of mortality. Some losses, such as miscarriage or loss of a lover, are not widely recognized, leading to an experience known as "disenfranchised grief."

Key Concepts

- Anger
- Denial
- Depression
- Loss
- Mourning
- Realization
- Reassessment
- Sadness
- Stress

INTRODUCTION

Much of life depends on successful adaptation to change. When that change is experienced as a loss, the emotional and cognitive reactions are properly referred to as "grief." When the specific loss is acknowledged by a person's culture, the loss is often met with rituals, behaviors that follow a certain pattern, sanctioned and choreographed within the culture. The term "bereavement" is applied to the loss of a significant person (such as a spouse, parent, child, or close relative or friend). In this case the grief and the sanctioned rituals are referred to as "mourning," although some writers use the terms "mourning" and "grieving" as synonyms.

Reaction to a loss often depends on whether the loss is experienced as central as opposed to peripheral to the self, with more central losses exerting greater impact on the people's ability to function. People who have experienced an important loss may experience obsessive thoughts about who or what was lost, a sense of unreality, a conviction that they were personally responsible for the loss, a sense that there is no help or hope, a belief that they are bad people, and a sense that they are not able to concentrate and remember. Searching for and even perceiving the lost person (often in a dream) are not uncommon.

People's emotional response may at first be engrossing. Shock, anger, sadness, guilt, anxiety, or even numbness are all possible reactions. Crying, fatigue, agitation, or even withdrawal are not unusual. Some people find it difficult to accept or absorb the reality of the loss in a reaction known as "denial." Depending on cultural, family, and individual traditions, some people suppress, repress, and deny part of their awareness, grief reaction, or both.

The centrality of loss within the self is also related to its circumstances. If people are prepared for the loss, they have made themselves less vulnerable to the loss of that person, place, or object in a process known as "anticipatory grief." This is experienced, for example, by those caring for terminally ill patients, as well as by the patients themselves. Although some argue that grief that is anticipated may be less challenging than that following an unexpected loss, the experience of grieving for someone and caring for that person at the same time can be extremely challenging.

HISTORY OF GRIEF STUDIES

The study of grief as a scholarly concern was started by an essay, "Mourning and Melancholia," written in 1917 by the Austrian founder of psychoanalysis, Sigmund Freud. In it, Freud proposed that hysteria (a disorder of emotional instability and dissociation) and melancholia are symptoms of pathological grief. He indicated that painful dejection, loss of the ability to love, inhibition of activity, and decrease in self-esteem that continue beyond the normal time are what distinguish melancholia from mourning (the pathological from the normal). In melancholia, it is the ego (or self) that becomes poor and impoverished. In the pathological case, the damage to self is becoming permanent instead of being a temporary and reversible deprivation.

The study of grief as a normal process of loss evolved over two-and-a-half decades. It was not until 1944 that psychiatrist Erich Lindemann published a study based mostly on interviews with relatives of victims of the Cocoanut Grove nightclub fire in Boston in 1942. He characterized five different aspects of the grief reaction. Each of the five was believed by Lindemann to be normal. Each would give way as the individual readjusted to the environment without the deceased, formed new relationships, and released the ties of connection with the deceased. Morbid or pathological grief reactions were seen as distortions of the normal patterns. A common distortion had to do with delay in reacting to the death.

In these cases, the person would either deny the death or continue to maintain composure and show little or no reaction to the death's occurrence. Other forms of distorted reactions were overactivity, acquisition of symptoms associated with the deceased, social isolation, repression of emotions, and activities that were detrimental to the person's social status and economic well-being. Examples of such detrimental activities might be getting drunk, being promiscuous, giving away all one's money, and quitting one's job.

In the early 1950s, British psychoanalyst and physician John Bowlby began to study loss in childhood, usually with children who were separated from their mothers. His early generalization summarized the child's response in a threefold way: protest, despair, and detachment. From his later work, which included adult mourning, he came to the conclusion that mourning follows a similar pattern whether it takes place in childhood, adolescence, or adulthood. In his later work, he specified wide time frames for the first and second phases and expanded his threefold description of the process to identify four phases of mourning. All four phases overlap, and people may go back for a while to a previous phase. These phases were numbing, which may last from a few hours to a week and may be interrupted by episodes of intense distress or anger; yearning and searching for the lost figure, which may last for months and even for years; disorganization and despair; and reorganization to a greater or lesser degree.

What was new and interesting about the fourth phase is Bowlby's introduction of a positive ending to the grieving process. This is the idea of reorganization, a positive restructuring of the person and the individual's perceptual field. This is a striking advance beyond Lindemann's notion that for the healthy person, the negative aspects of grieving would be dissipated in time.

Meanwhile, in the mid-1960s, quite independently of Bowlby, Swiss-born psychiatrist Elisabeth Kübler-Ross was interviewing terminally ill patients in Chicago. She observed closely, listened sensitively, and reported on their experiences in an important book, *On Death and Dying* (1969). Her work focused on the experiences of the terminally ill.

Kübler-Ross was there as patients first refused to believe the prognosis, as they got angry at themselves and at others around them, as they attempted to argue their way out (to make a deal with God or whoever might have the power to change the reality), as they faced their own sadness and depression, and finally as they came to a sense of acceptance about their fate. (Her idea of acceptance is similar to Bowlby's concept of reorganization.) From her interviews, she abstracted a five-stage process in which terminally ill patients came to deal with the loss of their own lives: denial and isolation, anger, bargaining (prayer is an example), depression, and acceptance.

THE PROCESS

The grief process is complex and highly individualized. It is seldom as predictable and orderly as the stages presented by Bowlby and Kübler-Ross might imply. Studies conducted by psychologist Janice Genevro in 2003 and Yale University researchers in 2007, as well as a survey of Canadian hospices in 2008, contradict the stage theory of grief altogether and suggest that grief is actually a complex mix of recurring emotions and symptoms that eventually alleviate. The duration of intense grief is quite variable, which can be a source of frustration to bereaved individuals who just want to know when their intense grief will end. Some people take a while to fully realize their loss. In a process known as "denial" or "disbelief," the grieving itself may be delayed. In a normal grief process, bereaved people eventually reach acceptance and accomplish reassessment and reorganization of their lives.

Grieving is the psychological, biological, and behavioral way of dealing with the stress created when a significant part of the self or prop for the self is taken away. Austrian endocrinologist Hans Selye made a vigorous career defining stress and considering the positive and negative effects that it may have on a person. He defined stress as "the nonspecific response of the body to any demand made upon it." Clearly any significant change calls for adjustment and thus involves stress. Selye indicated that what counts is the severity of the demand, and this depends on the perception of the person involved.

COMPLICATED GRIEF OR DEPRESSION?

Researchers and practitioners are beginning to understand the antecedents and consequences of complicated grief. To some extent, the likelihood of complicated grief depends on the nature of the loss. Losses that are unexpected and those involving sudden or violent death or suicide are especially problematic, as are those associated with childhood abuse or neglect. Individuals who are socially isolated, who were abused or neglected as children, who had a difficult emotional relationship with the deceased, or who lack resilience are particularly vulnerable to complicated grief. Prior history of mental illness, religion, gender, age, and social support are other factors. Between 10 and 20 percent of individuals experiencing a loss exhibit complicated grief reactions. Apart from its negative emotional attributes, this type of grief reaction is associated with higher rates of illness and suicide. In 2013, the American Cancer Society estimated that major clinical depression develops in up to 20 percent of bereaved persons, diagnosable after two months of extreme symptoms such as delusions, hallucinations, feelings of worthlessness, or dramatic weight loss.

Clinical trials suggest that cognitive behavioral therapy or complicated grief treatment may be helpful for those experiencing complicated grief. There is also limited evidence for using antidepressant medications for treating complicated grief, though the outcomes were not as good as those for people with clinical major depression unrelated to grief.

The Diagnostic Statistical Manual of Mental Disorders (*DSM*) long stated that clinicians should rule out grief due to a recent loss (within the first few weeks after the death) before making a diagnosis of depression or an adjustment disorder. The fifth edition (DSM-5), published in 2013, eliminates this "bereavement exclusion," generating a great deal of controversy. The American Psychiatric Association states that the reasons for the change are that bereavement often lasts one to two years, not less than two months, and that major depression can be triggered by bereavement, particularly in those who have personal or family histories of depression. Proponents argue that bereavement is merely another stressor like unemployment or divorce and therefore should be considered similarly in diagnosing a patient. Many critics warn that normal grief reactions will be pathologized and patients given unnecessary treatment, particularly antidepressants.

CULTURAL AND SOCIAL INFLUENCES

Because loss is such a regular part of life, a person's reaction to it is likely to be regulated by family and cultural influences. Religious and cultural practices have developed to govern the expected and acceptable ways of responding to loss. Many of these practices provide both permission for and boundaries to the expression of grief. They provide both an opportunity to express feelings and a limit to their expression. Often a religion or culture will stipulate the rituals that must be observed, how soon they must be concluded, how long they must be extended, what kind of clothing is appropriate, and what kinds of expressions are permissible and fitting. They also provide a cognitive framework in which the loss may be understood and, perhaps, better accepted—for example, framing the loss as God's will.

The funeral home industry has been subject to criticism for profiting from the ubiquity of death. In part as a result, several organizations have sprung up to deliver affordable alternatives to traditional funeral arrangements, such as cremation, home-based funeral services, and green (environmentally sensitive) burials.

Toward the end of the twentieth century, professional interest in grief and grief counseling began to grow. The Association for Death Education and Counseling was founded in 1976 to provide a forum for educators and clinicians addressing this concern. Major journals such as Omega and Death Studies provide sources for research on grief and loss.

BIBLIOGRAPHY

American Cancer Society. *Coping with the Loss of a Loved One*. Atlanta: American Cancer Society, 4 Feb. 2013. PDF file.

Bowlby, John. *Loss: Sadness and Depression*. London: Tavistock Inst., 1980. Print.

Doka, Kenneth J. "Grief and the DSM: A Brief Q&A." *HuffPost Healthy Living*. TheHuffingtonPost.com, 29 May 2013. Web. 21 May 2014.

Freud, Sigmund. "Mourning and Melancholia." *Collected Papers*. Vol. 4. London: Hogarth, 1956. Print.

"Grief, Bereavement, and Coping with Loss." *National Cancer Institute*. US Dept. of Health and Human Services, National Institutes of Health, 6 Mar. 2013. Web. 21 May 2014.

Harvey, John H., ed. *Perspectives on Loss: A Sourcebook*. Philadelphia: Taylor, 1998. Print.

Konisberg, Ruth Davis. "New Ways to Think about Grief." *Time*. Time, 29 Jan. 2011. Web. 21 May 2014.

Lindemann, Erich. "Symptomatology and Management of Acute Grief." *American Journal of Psychiatry* 101 (1944): 141–48. Print.

Marrone, Robert. *Death, Mourning, and Caring*. Pacific Grove: Brooks/Cole, 1997. Print.

Mitford, Jessica. *The American Way of Death Revisited*. Rev. ed. New York: Knopf, 1998. Print.

Parkes, Colin Murray, and Holly G. Prigerson. *Bereavement: Studies of Grief in Adult Life*. 4th ed. New York: Routledge, 2010. Print.

Worden, M. *Grief Counseling and Grief Therapy: A Handbook for Mental Health Professionals*. 3rd ed. New York: Springer, 2008. Print.

Everett J. Delahanty, Jr.; updated by Allyson Washburn

SEE ALSO: Coping: Social support; Coping: Terminal illness; Death and dying; Denial; Depression; Emotions; Kübler-Ross, Elisabeth; Post-traumatic stress disorder; Self-help groups; Support groups.

Group decision making

TYPE OF PSYCHOLOGY: Social psychology

Group decision making is one of the oldest areas of inquiry in social psychology. Research has shown that groups have profound effects on the behavior of their individual members; the decisions that people make in groups can be quite different from those that they make on their own.

KEY CONCEPTS

- Choice shift
- Group confidence
- Heterogeneity
- Informational influence
- Normative influence

- Process loss
- Social decision scheme

INTRODUCTION

Important societal, business, medical, legal, and personal decisions are often made by more than one person. Psychologists in the field of group decision making have attempted to describe the processes through which such decisions are made. The process by which a set of individual group members' decisions becomes transformed into a single group decision can be described by a "social decision scheme." Research by James H. Davis and his colleagues at the University of Illinois has shown the conditions under which groups use various decision-making rules, such as adopting the preference of the majority or that of the member who has the best answer.

VARIABLES IN GROUP TASKS

The nature of the decision problem facing a group must be considered in an evaluation of the group's decision process. Psychologist Ivan Steiner pioneered the analysis of the group's task in his book *Group Process and Productivity* (1972). Steiner identified three characteristics of group tasks that should be considered in analyzing group decision making. The first is the ability to subdivide the task into subtasks that members can perform individually. For example, a group can plan a meal by making one member responsible for selecting a meat dish, another for choosing a vegetarian entrée, another for choosing desserts, and so forth. Other tasks, in which division of labor is not feasible, are said to be "unitary." In general, the more important the decision, the more difficult it is to divide it among group members. Yet it is often precisely because a decision task is important that it is given to a group rather than an individual. Therefore, even if some aspect of the task (such as gathering information) can be done individually, final responsibility for the decision rests with a set of people.

Another variable in group tasks is the nature of the goal. In many cases, there is no "best" or "right" decision; the process is simply a matter of determining the group preference. Other decision tasks were called "optimizing" by Steiner because it was assumed that some optimal decision exists. The group's task is to find it. Most important group-decision tasks are not only unitary but also optimizing. Finally, Steiner noted that the rules governing the group's decision-making activities were a critical feature of the task. If the group members are not constrained to particular procedures, the task is "discretionary."

CHOICE SHIFT

Important insights about decision process and quality in unitary, optimizing, and discretionary tasks have been gained by comparing the decision-making behavior of individuals acting alone to that of persons in groups. It is apparent that the way people behave in groups is different from the way they behave alone. As a consequence, decisions made in groups can differ radically from those made by the same persons acting alone. It is not uncommon for group decisions to be more extreme than an average of members' individual decisions.

Such a "choice shift" (the difference between the decision of a group and the average decision of group members as individuals) can lead to group decisions that are better than—or not as good as—the average member's decision. The average group member's judgment or choice provides one standard against which group decision quality can be compared. Another is the quality of the best decision from an individual member. Steiner called any decrease in quality from the decision of the best member, acting alone, to the group decision "process loss." Reviews of group-decision research typically conclude that an average group performs above the level of its average member but below that of its best member. It is possible, however, for groups to reach better decisions than can any of their members alone.

NORMATIVE AND INFORMATIONAL INFLUENCES

Social psychologists recognize two types of influence that can cause group decisions to differ from those of individual group members: normative and informational. Normative influence comes merely from knowledge of the positions of others. One may come to doubt the quality of the alternative that one has selected simply by learning that everyone else believes that another alternative is superior. Confidence in a belief is difficult to maintain in the face of others who are in consensus about a contrary belief. The second type of influence, informational influence, results from logic or argument concerning the relative merits of various choice alternatives. Both types of influence usually operate in group decision making. Through normative or informational influence, individual group members can shift their positions.

Since groups usually make decisions under conditions of uncertainty, it can be difficult to evaluate the actual quality of a group decision. For this reason, the study of "group confidence" has become increasingly important. In general, groups exhibit greater confidence about the quality of their decisions than do individuals. This can be a desirable outcome if commitment to the group decision is necessary. As Irving Janis has shown in his analyses of political and managerial decision making, however, groups can be highly confident even while making disastrous decisions. Proper evaluation of the quality and confidence of the group decision requires an ability to evaluate objectively the decision outcome. This has been done in a number of laboratory studies.

TASK ACCURACY AND CONFIDENCE

Experiments on group judgment by Janet A. Sniezek and her colleagues show how different group and individual decision making can be. These studies examine two aspects of group performance in judgment tasks. The first, accuracy, refers to the proximity of the consensus group judgment of some unknown value to the actual value. The other performance measure is one of confidence. Results show that consensus group judgments are typically far more accurate, and somewhat more confident, than the independent judgments of two or more comparable individuals.

Two factors appear to be related to an increase in judgment accuracy in groups. One is the tendency of some groups to develop group judgments that are quite different from the members' individual judgments. A representative study asked students to judge various risks by estimating the annual frequency of deaths in the United States from each of several causes. A minority of group judgments were either higher or lower than all the members' individual estimates. For example, individual members' estimates for a given cause of death were 300, 500, and 650, but the consensus of these persons as a group was 200. This phenomenon is often associated with great gains in group judgment accuracy, but unfortunately, such radical shifts in judgment as a result of grouping can also lead to extreme process loss. Some groups become far more inaccurate than their average members by going out of the range of individual estimates.

The second factor that is related to improvements in the accuracy of group judgment is heterogeneity (variety in a group) within the group. On the whole, groups that begin with a wide variety of judgments improve more in comparison to their average members than groups that begin with more homogeneity. This supports the creation of groups with members from different ethnic, racial, religious, or educational backgrounds. Such differences are likely to promote heterogeneity because the members of the group will have different sources of information and varying perspectives. Groups that lack sufficient heterogeneity face the danger of merely averaging their individual contributions. The result of averaging is to fail to improve appreciably in comparison to the level of quality of the average member.

TECHNIQUES

There have been many efforts to identify procedures that are better than discretionary procedures in improving the quality of group decisions for optimizing tasks. Many group techniques have been developed in an attempt to eliminate factors that are thought to contribute to process loss. The most popular techniques are designed to alter group discussion. Some inhibit normative influence by restricting the extent to which group members can reveal their preferences. Instead, group discussion is limited—at least initially—to a thorough evaluation of all options.

Other techniques for enhancing group decision making are designed to suppress the extent to which members are influenced by irrelevant factors. For example, status effects can operate in groups, causing the person with the highest status to exert a greater influence on the group decision than other members. This is undesirable if the high-status person's judgments are no more accurate—or even less accurate—than those of other group members. Other factors that have been shown to be irrelevant include the amount of participation in group discussion and self-confidence. Perhaps the most well-known technique developed to maximize informational influence and minimize irrelevant influences is the Delphi technique. This procedure prevents any potential problems of noninformational influence by not allowing face-to-face interaction. Instead, group members are given periodic anonymous feedback about the current positions of other group members. Often, group members provide information and logic to support their positions. More advanced technology, such as that available with computerized group-decision support systems, has greatly expanded the ability to control group decision-making processes.

In addition to the goal of improving the quality of group decision making, some theorists have stressed the importance of increasing group members' satisfaction with their decisions. This objective remains somewhat controversial, because it is not always the case that people are more satisfied with better decisions and less satisfied with inferior ones. Ironically, people appear to be most satisfied when given the opportunity for group discussion—though this is precisely what is often eliminated in the hope of improving group decision quality.

Nevertheless, high group confidence can be an important end in itself. Presumably, groups with more confidence in their decisions are more committed to implementing them successfully. The increasing use of groups for decision making in organizations is based in part on this principle. Confidence in decision making can be increased by encouraging the participation of employees from various segments and levels of the organization. With such participative decision making, not only is confidence increased, but also the number of organizational members who support the decision.

SOCIAL IMPLICATIONS

Historically, scientific interest in group phenomena in general has been linked to social movements. Group research seems to thrive in the "we" decades, compared with the "me" decades. Interest specifically in group decision making, however, has tended to be stimulated by political and economic events.

Janis carefully analyzed decision making by groups in President John F. Kennedy's administration. He diagnosed numerous problems regarding the way in which the Bay of Pigs Invasion of 1961 was handled during group meetings. Collectively, the symptoms represent "groupthink," a narrow-minded approach to decision making that is caused primarily by a strong attachment of the group to its prevailing viewpoints. Janis shows how Kennedy altered the group decision process to accommodate and stimulate diverse perspectives during meetings about the Cuban Missile Crisis one-and-a-half years later.

For many reasons, the study of decision making by groups is likely to become increasingly important to psychologists. As a result of the collectivist nature of most cultures, the discipline of psychology will need to become less individualistic as it grows in non-Western societies and as social psychology expands to encompass more cultures. In addition, the growing interdependence of nations means that more and more global decisions are being made by groups of leaders, not by individual leaders.

Events within the United States can also be expected to create further demand for scientific investigation of group decision making. American organizations are using groups to a larger extent than ever before. For example, the group meeting is the most common approach to forecasting within organizations. The movement toward group decision making has been influenced in part by the apparent success of groups in Japanese firms. The desire to provide greater representation of workers in decisions should result in the increased use of groups for decision making.

While group decision-making research and applications are encouraged by national and global changes, these are insufficient to bring about a genuine revolution in the making of decisions. There must also be an increase in the capacity to use groups. Here, too, it is reasonable to expect developments that support the use of groups in decision making. Major advances in communications allow more people to participate in the decision process in a timely fashion. These advances also have the potential for creating techniques that lead to higher-quality decision making than can be provided by traditional meetings.

BIBLIOGRAPHY

Alter, Adam. "The Folly of Crowds." *Psychology Today.* Sussex, 22 Aug. 2011. Web. 20 May 2014.

"Are Six Heads as Good as Twelve?" *American Psychological Association*. American Psychological Assn., 28 May 2004. Web. 20 May 2014.

Ariely, Dan. *Predictably Irrational: The Hidden Forces That Shape Our Decisions.* New York: Harper, 2010. Print.

Cannon-Bowers, Janis, and Eduardo Sales, eds. *Making Decisions under Stress: Implications for Individual and Team Training*. Washington: Amer. Psychological Soc., 2000. Print.

Davis, James H. "Social Interaction as a Combinatorial Process in Group Decision." *Group Decision Making*. Ed. H. Brandstatter, James H. Davis, and Gisela Stocker-Kreichgauer. London: Academic, 1982. Print.

Guzzo, Richard A., ed. *Improving Group Decision Making in Organizations.* New York: Academic, 1982. Print.

Hastie, Reid. "Experimental Evidence on Group Accuracy." *Decision Research*. Vol. 2. Ed. B. Grofman and G. Owen. Greenwich: JAI, 1986. Print.

Janis, Irving Lester. *Victims of Groupthink*. Boston: Houghton, 1972. Print.

Laughlin, Patrick R. *Group Problem Solving*. Princeton: Princeton UP, 2011. Print.

McGrath, Joseph Edward. *Groups: Interaction and Performance*. Englewood Cliffs: Prentice, 1984. Print.

Parks, Craig D., and Lawrence J. Sanna. *Group Performance and Interaction*. Boulder: Westview, 1999. Print.

Sniezek, Janet A., and Rebecca A. Henry. "Accuracy and Confidence in Group Judgment." *Organizational Behavior and Human Decision Processes* 43 (1989): 1–28. Print.

Steiner, Ivan Dale. *Group Process and Productivity*. New York: Academic, 1972. Print.

Surowiecki, James. *The Wisdom of Crowds*. New York: Anchor, 2005. Print.

Witte, Erich H., and James H. Davis, eds. *Understanding Group Behavior: Consensual Action by Small Groups*. Vol. 1. New York: Psychology, 2014. Print.

Janet A. Sniezek

SEE ALSO: Behavioral economics; Consumer psychology; Cooperation, competition, and negotiation; Crowd behavior; Decision making; Groups; Leadership; Organizational behavior and consulting.

Group therapy

TYPE OF PSYCHOLOGY: Psychotherapy

Group therapy allows individuals to enter into the therapeutic process with others who have the same or similar problems. This gives an individual much more freedom of expression as well as the support of others from within the group.

KEY CONCEPTS

- Disclosure
- Group dynamic
- Group leader
- Session
- Therapeutic process

INTRODUCTION

Society to a greater or lesser degree always forms itself into groupings, whether they are for economic stability, religious expression, educational endeavor, or simply a sense of belonging. Within the field of psychotherapy, many theories and practices have been developed that deal with specific problems facing individuals as they try to relate to their environment as a whole and to become valuable members of society. Available approaches range from psychoanalysis to transpersonal therapy. Taking advantage of the natural tendency for people to form groups, therapists, since the years following World War II, have developed various forms of group therapy. Therapy groups, although they do not form "naturally," are most frequently composed of people with similar problems.

Immediately after World War II, the demand for therapeutic help was so great that the only way to cope with the need was to create therapeutic groups. Group therapy did not boast any one particular founder at that time, although among the first counseling theorists to embrace group therapy actively were Joseph Pratt, Alfred Adler, Jacob Moreno, Trigant Burrow, and Cody Marsh. Psychoanalysis, so firmly placed within the schools for individual psychotherapy, nevertheless became one of the first therapeutic approaches to be applied to group therapy. Gestalt psychology and transactional analysis have proved extremely successful when applied to the group dynamic. Fritz Perls was quick to apply his Gestalt theories to group therapy work, although he usually worked with one member of the group at a time. Gestalt group therapists aim as part of their treatment to try to break down the numerous denial systems that, once overcome, will bring the individual to a new and more unified understanding of life. Eric Berne, the founder of transactional analysis, postulated that the group setting is the ideal therapeutic setting.

TYPES AND ADVANTAGES OF GROUP COUNSELING

Among the different types of group counseling available are those that focus on preventive and developmental aspects of living. Preventive group counseling deals with enhancing the individual's understanding of a specific aspect of life. These aspects range from simple job-seeking skills to more complex studies of career changes in midlife. Developmental groups are composed of well-adjusted people who seek to enhance their social and emotional skills through personal growth and transformation. Conversely, group therapy is concerned with remedial help. The majority of people entering group therapy are aware that they have dysfunctional components in their life; they are seeking group work as a possible way of resolving those problems. The size of most groups ranges from five to fifteen participants. Sometimes all the members in the group belong to one family and the group becomes a specialized one with the emphasis on family therapy. Treating the problems of one family member in the larger context of the whole family has proved successful.

There are as many approaches to therapy as there are therapists; thus, the direction that any given group takes will be dependent on the group leader. Group leadership is probably the one factor that is vital in enabling a group to succeed in reaching both individual and group goals. A leader is typically a qualified and trained therapist whose work is to lead the group through the therapeutic process. Often there will be two therapists involved with the one group, the second therapist sometimes being an intern or trainee.

There are definite advantages, both economic and therapeutic, to group therapy. The economic burden of paying for therapy does not fall solely on one person's shoulders; moreover, the therapist can use his or her time economically, helping a larger number of people. More important, group work may be much more beneficial than individual therapy for certain people. For some, it can be less intimidating than the one-on-one interaction that characterizes individual therapy. Often, the group setting will produce conditions similar to those the member faces in real life and can thus offer an opportunity to face and correct the problem.

STAGES OF GROUP SESSIONS

In group therapy, a "session" consists of a number of meetings; the number is specific and is usually determined at the beginning by the group leader. Flexibility is a key concept in counseling, however, and if a group requires more time and all the participants agree, then the number of sessions can usually be extended. In closed groups, all members start the session together whereas in open group therapy, new participants can join whenever. Therapists have generally come to accept five stages as being necessary for a group to complete a therapy session. These five stages do not have definite boundaries; indeed, if a group experiences problems at any stage, it may return to earlier stages.

Orientation is a necessary first step in establishing a sense of well-being and trust among the group's members. A therapy group does not choose its own members; it is a random and arbitrary gathering of different people. Each member will assess the group critically as to whether this group will benefit him or her. One way for participants to discover the sincerity of the membership of the group is to reveal something of the problem that brought them to the group in the first place, without going into a full disclosure (the point at which a member of a group will share private feelings and concerns). An individual can then assess from the responses of the other members of the group whether they are going to be empathetic or critical. After the orientation stage comes the transitional stage, in which more self-revelation is required on the part of the individual members. This is usually a time of anxiety for members of the therapy group. Yet despite this anxiety, each member must make a commitment to the group and must further define the problem that has brought him or her to the group in the first place.

When the transitional stage has proved successful, the group will be able to begin the third stage, which involves a greater sense of cohesiveness and openness. This sense of belonging is a necessary and important aspect of group therapy. Without this feeling, the subsequent work of resolving problems cannot be fully addressed. By this time, each member of the group will have disclosed some very personal and troubling part of their lives. Once a group cohesiveness has been achieved, the fourth stage—actually wanting to work on certain behavior-modifying skills—becomes dominant. At this point in the therapeutic continuum, the group leader will play a less significant role in what is said or the direction taken. This seeming withdrawal on the part of the leader allows the group participants to take the primary role in creating changes that will affect them on a permanent basis.

As with all therapeutic methods and procedures, regardless of school or persuasion, a completion or summation stage is vital. The personal commitment to the group must be seen in the larger context of life and one's need to become a part of the greater fabric of living. By consciously creating a finale to the therapy sessions, members avoid being limited in their personal growth through dependence on the group. This symbolic act of stepping away from the group reaffirms all that the group work achieved during the third and fourth stages of the therapeutic process.

GROUP DYNAMICS

Group work offers participants an opportunity to express their feelings and fears in the hope that behavioral change will take place. Group therapy takes on significance and meaning only when the individual members of the group want to change their old behavioral patterns and learn a new behavioral repertoire. Most individuals come from a background in which they have experienced difficulties with members of their immediate family. Whether the problem has been a spousal difficulty or a parental problem, those who enter into therapy are desperately looking for answers. The very fact that there is more than one person within the group who can understand and sympathize with another's problem begins the process of acceptance and change. The group dynamic is thus defined as the commonality of purpose that unites a group of people and their desire to succeed.

A group will very quickly become close, intimate, and in some ways self-guarding and self-preserving. Through continually meeting with one another in an intense emotional environment, members begin to look on the group as a very important part of their lives. When one member does not come to a meeting, it can create anxiety in others, for the group works as a whole; for one person not to be present undermines the confidence of those who already lack self-esteem. There are also those who come to group meetings and express very little of what is actually bothering them. While even coming into the therapeutic process is one large step, to disclose anything about themselves is too painful. For those who remain aloof and detached, believing that they are the best judge of their own problems, the group experience will be a superficial one.

EMOTIONAL INVOLVEMENT AND COHESIVENESS

According to Irvin D. Yalom, therapy is "an emotional and a corrective experience." The corrective aspect of therapy takes on a new meaning when placed in a group setting. There is general agreement that a person who seeks help from a therapist will eventually reveal what is truly troubling him or her. This may take weeks or even months of talking—generally talking around the problem. This is equally true of group participants. Since many difficulties experienced by the participants will be of an interpersonal nature, the group acts as a perfect setting for creating the conditions in which those behavioral problems will manifest. One major advantage that the group therapist has over a therapist involved in individual therapy is that the conditions that trigger the response can also be observed.

For those people who believe that their particular problem inhibits them from caring or even thinking about others, particularly those with a narcissistic or schizoid personality disorder, seeing the distress of others in the group often evokes strong sympathy and caring. The ability to be able to offer some kind of help to another person often acts as a catalyst for a person to see that there is an opportunity to become a whole and useful member of the greater community. For all of its limitations, the group reflects, to some degree, the real-life situations that each of its members experiences every day.

The acknowledgment of another member's life predicament creates a cohesiveness among the members of the group, as each participant grapples with his or her own problems and with those of the others in the group. As each member becomes supportive of all other members, a climate of trust and understanding comes into being. This is a prerequisite for all group discovery, and it eventually leads to the defining of problems and thus to seeking help for particular problems shared by members. Respecting each member's right to confidentiality is another important component to building and maintaining trust. When the individual members of a group begin to care and respond to the needs of the other members, a meaningful relationship exists that allows healing to take place. Compassion, tempered by understanding and acceptance, will eventually prove the ingredients of success for participating members.

ASSESSING EFFECTIVENESS

Group therapy has not been fully accepted in all quarters of the therapeutic professions. Advocates of group therapy have attempted to show, through research and studies, that group therapy is equally effective as individual therapy, but this claim has not settled all arguments. In fact, what has been shown is that if the group leader shows the necessary warmth, understanding, and empathy with the members, then success is generally assured. If, however, the group leader is more on the offensive—even taking on an attacking position—then the effects are anything but positive.

Group therapy continues to play an important role within the field of professional care. There is increasing systematized study and research into the effectiveness of group therapy, especially as far as feedback from the participants of the group therapy experience is concerned. The findings of such studies may led psychologists and counselors to assess more closely the type of therapy that is being offered.

BIBLIOGRAPHY

Black, Bethanne. "Group Therapy: Can It Help You?" *Health Library.* EBSCO, 13 Sept. 2013. Web. 20 May 2014.

Corey, Gerald, Marianne Schneider Corey, and Cindy Corey. *Groups: Process and Practice*. 9th ed. Belmont: Brooks/Cole, 2014. Print.

Donigian, Jeremiah, and Richard Malnati. *Critical*

Incidents in Group Therapy. 2nd ed. Belmont: Brooks/Cole-Wadsworth, 1999. Print.

Fehr, Scott Simon. *101 Interventions in Group Therapy*. Rev. ed. New York: Routledge, 2010. Print.

Howes, Ryan. "What about Group Therapy?" *Psychology Today*. Sussex, 30 May 2013. Web. 20 May 2014.

Peterson, Vincent, and Bernard Nisenholz. "Group Work." *Orientation to Counseling*. 4th ed. Boston: Allyn, 1999. Print.

"Psychotherapy: Understanding Group Therapy." *American Psychological Association*. American Psychological Assn., 2014. Web. 20 May 2014.

Rogers, Carl R. *On Becoming a Person*. Boston: Houghton, 1995. Print.

Rutan, J. Scott, Walter N. Stone, and Joseph Shay. *Psychodynamic Group Psychotherapy*. 5th ed. New York: Guilford, 2014. Print.

Tomasulo, Daniel J. "Shhh! Confidentiality in Group Therapy: It's No Joke." *Psychology Today*. Sussex, 27 Jan. 2011. Web. 20 May 2014.

Yalom, Irvin D. *The Theory and Practice of Group Psychotherapy*. 5th ed. New York: Basic, 2005. Print.

Richard G. Cormack

SEE ALSO: Behavioral family therapy; Brief therapy; Community psychology; Couples therapy; Group decision making; Groups; Person-centered therapy; Psychotherapy: Goals and techniques; Self-actualization; Self-help groups; Social support and mental health; Strategic family therapy; Support groups; Yalom, Irvin D.

Groups

TYPE OF PSYCHOLOGY: Social psychology

The structure and function of groups have stimulated a large quantity of research over the years. What groups are, how groups form, and the positive and negative effects of groups on individuals are the primary areas of research that have provided insights into social behavior.

KEY CONCEPTS

- Deindividuation
- Density
- Group formation
- Identity
- Self-attention
- Social support

INTRODUCTION

In any newspaper, one is likely to find several captivating stories that highlight the powerful negative influence that groups can exert on individuals. For example, one may recall the tragic violence exhibited by rival Egyptian sports fans during a post–soccer match riot in Port Said in early 2012, resulting in seventy-three deaths.

There are equally dramatic instances of the powerful positive influences of groups. In September 2011, when a car crashed into young motorcyclist Brandon Wright of Utah University, setting his bike ablaze and pinning him beneath, a dozen or so bystanders lifted the car, despite the risk that it might explode. A few years later, in March 2014, bystanders and lifeguards rushed to the aid of a woman and her three children when their minivan plunged into the ocean off Daytona Beach, Florida, and began to sink. This type of bystander intervention, or lack thereof, has been the subject of much psychological study, particularly following the brutal stabbing death of Kitty Genovese within hearing of her neighbors in 1964.

These real-life events are noteworthy because they illustrate the universality of groups and the various ways that groups influence individual behavior. Although everyone can attest the prevalence of groups and the power that they can wield over individuals, several characteristics of groups are not as well defined. Several questions remain as to what groups are, how groups form, what groups look like, and the disadvantages and advantages of group membership. In spite of these questions, psychologists have come to understand many aspects of groups and the ways in which they influence individual behavior.

DEFINITION AND FORMATION OF GROUPS

The members of Congress who compose the House of Representatives of the United States are a group. The urban committee deciding how to allocate budgetary resources for unwed mothers in a particular city is a group. The members of a carpool sharing a ride to the train station every day are a group. The family seated around the dinner table at home in the evening is a group. The acting troupe performing a Shakespearean play is a group. There are other examples of groups, however, that may be a little less obvious. All the unwed mothers in an urban area might be considered a group. A line of people waiting to buy tickets to a Broadway show might be thought of as a group. People eating dinner at the same time in a diner might even be considered a group. The people in the audience who are watching an acting troupe perform could behave as a group.

There are several ways in which people come to join the groups to which they belong. People are born into some groups. Several types of groupings are influenced in large part by birth: family, socioeconomic status, class, race, and religion. Other groups are formed largely by happenstance: for example, a line of the same people waiting for the 8:05 ferry every day. Some groups, however, are determined more clearly by intentional, goal-oriented factors. For example, a group of people at work who share a common concern for well-being, health, and fitness may decide to form an exercise and nutrition group. Students interested in putting on a concert might decide to form a committee to organize bake sales, car washes, and fund drives to raise the money needed to achieve this goal. Finally, group memberships are sometimes created or changed as an effort toward self-definition or self-validation. For example, one can try to change one's religion, political orientation, professional associations, friendships, or family in an effort to enhance how one feels about oneself—or how others feel about one. An individual searching for a positive self-definition may join a country club, for example, to benefit from the social status acquired from such group membership.

STAGES OF GROUP DEVELOPMENT

Although there are countless underlying reasons for someone's membership in a given group, the work of Bruce Tuckman suggests that groups progress through a relatively consistent series of stages or phases—forming, storming, norming, performing, and adjourning—in their development. "Forming" refers to a phase of coming together and orientation. Group members become acquainted with one another and define the requirements of group membership as well as the tasks to be performed. "Storming" refers to a phase of polarization and conflict. During this phase, group members deal with disagreements, compete for attractive positions within the group, and may become dissatisfied with other group members or with the group as a whole. "Norming" refers to a phase when conflicts are solved and group members arrive at agreements regarding definitions of tasks and the requirements of group membership. "Performing" refers to the phase when group members concentrate on achieving their major task and strive toward shared goals. Finally, for some groups, "adjourning" refers to the disbanding or dissolution of the group after task completion.

For example, consider a special task force created to search for a missing child. During the forming stage, the members of this group will volunteer for, or be appointed to, the group. Although the general goals and definition of the group may have been established with the decision to implement such a task force, a storming phase would occur that would lead the group members into the sometimes difficult task of defining specific procedures of operation, responsibilities of particular task force members, a functional hierarchy, and so on. The norming phase would represent the resolution of the polarizations that emerged during the storming phase, as the committee proceeded to establish an agenda, a decision structure, and a means of implementing decisions. During the performing phase, the task force would actually perform the tasks agreed on during the norming phase. Having finished its task, the group would then be adjourned.

GROUP TOPOGRAPHY

The topography of a group refers to its physical features. This includes such elements as the size of the group, the composition of the group, and the relationships among the various members of the group. These topographical features of groups have been the focus of countless studies.

One obvious physical feature that could vary from one group to another is size. Some scholars have categorized group types in terms of size. For example, some researchers have found it useful to distinguish between small primary groups (from two to twenty group members), small nonprimary groups (from three to a hundred members), large groups (one thousand to ten thousand members), and largest groups (ten thousand-plus members). While such classifications may be interesting, the realities of everyday groups are typically more modest than such grand schemes would suggest. In a large number of settings, naturally occurring, free-forming groups typically range in size from two to seven persons, with a mean of about three. There are certainly exceptions to this rule of thumb; for example, most audiences watching theater troupes are considerably larger than three people. Nevertheless, most of the groups in which people interact on a day-to-day basis are relatively small. The size of a group tends to set the stage for many other topographical features of group life.

VARIATIONS IN GROUP COMPOSITION

The number of relationships possible in a group, according to James H. S. Bosard, is a direct consequence of the size of the group: the larger the group, the larger the number of possible relationships the individual might find within the group. It is possible to express the precise mathematical function relating the number of possible relationships between individuals in a group and group size (n): this function is represented by the formula (n2 – n)/2. For example, if the group is made of Tom and Dick, there is only one possible relationship between members of the group (Tom-Dick). If the group is made up of the three people (Tom, Dick, and Harry), there are three possible relationships (Tom-Dick, Tom-Harry, and Dick-Harry). If the group is made up of seven people, there are twenty-one possible relationships between individuals; if there are ten people in the group, there are forty-five possible relationships between individuals.

Thus, groups have the potential to become increasingly complex as the number of people in the group increases. There are many possible consequences of this increasing complexity. For one thing, it becomes increasingly harder to pay an equal amount of attention to everyone in the group as it increases in size. Brian Mullen and colleagues state that the person in the group who talks the most is paid the most attention and in turn is most likely to emerge as the leader of the group; this effect (sometimes referred to as the "blabbermouth" theory of leadership) increases as the size of the group increases. It also becomes increasingly difficult to get to know everyone in the group and to spend equal amounts of time with everyone in the group as the group increases in size.

SIMPLIFYING GROUP COMPLEXITY

People in groups may tend toward a convenient simplification of this inevitable complexity. Scholars have long recognized the tendency for group members to divide other group members into groups of "us" and "them," ingroups and outgroups, rather than to perceive each person as a distinct entity. Groups can often be divided into perceptually distinct, smaller groups. For example, a committee might be composed predominantly of elderly members, with only one or a few young members. The general tendency is for people to focus their attention on the smaller group. The reason for this is that the smaller group seems to "stand out" as a perceptual figure against the background of the larger group. Thus, the youthful member of an otherwise elderly committee is likely to attract a disproportionate amount of attention from the committee members.

Not only will the members of the larger group pay more attention to the smaller group, but the members of the smaller group will do so as well. Thus, the members of the smaller group will become more self-attentive, more aware of themselves and their behavior. On the other hand, the members of the larger group become less self-attentive, or, as Ed Diener contends, more deindividuated—less aware of themselves and their behavior. For example, the single female in a group of mechanical engineers that is otherwise male will quickly stand out. The male mechanical engineers may tend to think of that one distinct individual in terms of her status as a female. Moreover, the lone female may become more sensitive than usual about her behavioral transgressions of the norms guiding sexual roles in an all-male working environment.

IMPLICATIONS FOR SOCIAL BEHAVIOR

Thus, group composition has been demonstrated to predict the extent to which people pay attention to, and are aware of, themselves and specific facets of themselves and to predict a variety of social behaviors, including participation in religious groups, bystander intervention in emergencies, worker productivity, stuttering in front of an audience, and conformity.

For example, an analysis of the participation of congregation members in their religious groups documented the powerful effect of group composition on behavior of group members. As the size of the congregation increased relative to the number of ministers, the congregation members were less likely to participate in the group (in terms of activities such as attending worship services, becoming lay ministers, or "inquiring for Christ"). In this instance, becoming "lost in the crowd" impaired the normal self-regulation behaviors necessary for participation. Alternatively, analysis of the behavior of stutterers in front of an audience also documented the powerful effects of group composition on the behavior of group members. As the size of the audience increased relative to the number of stutterers speaking, the verbal disfluencies (stuttering and stammering) of the speakers increased. In this instance, becoming the center of attention exaggerated the normal self-regulation behaviors necessary for speech, to the point of interfering with those behaviors. Another potential outcome of being "lost in the crowd" is the bystander effect, or the diffusion of responsibility in a group setting. In a large group, each individual believes that another has taken or will take responsibility, which can lead to inaction. Group composition's effects of making the individual lost in the crowd or the center of attention are not inherently good or bad; positive or negative effects depend on the context.

GROUP DENSITY

Another facet of the topography of the group that is related to group size is density. Density refers to the amount of space per person in the group (the less space per person, the higher the density). Doubling the number of people in the group meeting in a room of a given size will decrease by one-half the amount of space available for each member of the group. Alternatively, halving the number of people in the group will double the amount of space available per person. Thus, in a room of a given size, density is directly linked to the size of the group. This particular approach to density is called "social density," because it involves a change in density by manipulation of the social dimension (group size). One could also manipulate the physical dimension (room size), rendering a change in what is called "spatial density." Thus, halving the size of the room will halve the amount of space available to each group member.

Density has been demonstrated to influence a variety of social behaviors. People have been found to report feeling more anxious, more aggressive, more unpleasant, and, understandably, more crowded as a function of density. An analysis of the effects of "tripling" in college dormitories illustrates these types of effects. As a cost-cutting measure, colleges and universities will often house three students in a dormitory room that was initially constructed for two (hence, tripling). Tripling has been demonstrated to lead to an increase in arguments among the roommates, increased visits to the student health center, decreased grades, and increased overall dissatisfaction.

ROLE IN BEHAVIOR AND IDENTITY

Groups exert sometimes dramatic, sometimes subtle influences on behavior. These influences are sometimes beneficial and sometimes detrimental. An understanding of the effect of groups on the individual sets the stage for a deeper understanding of many facets of social life. One of the reasons for the formation or joining of groups is the definition of the self. On a commonly used questionnaire that requires a person to respond twenty times to the question "Who am I?," people tend to respond with references to some sort of group membership, be it family, occupation, hobby, school, ethnic, religious, or neighborhood. Groups help establish one's identity, both for one's own benefit and for the benefit of others with whom one interacts.

COSTS OF GROUP MEMBERSHIP

Belonging to groups has its price, however; as discussed at length by Christian Buys, one's very membership in a group may carry with it hidden costs, risks, or sacrifices. A more complete understanding of groups requires a consideration of this aspect of membership in a group. Attaining certain types of rewards may be incompatible with belonging to a group. For example, the goal of completing a difficult and complicated task may be facilitated by belonging to a group of coworkers who bring the varied skills and knowledge required for successful task completion. Yet one group member's goal of always being the center of attention, or of needing to feel special and unique, may have to be subverted if the group is to perform the task for which it formed. What the individual wants or needs may sometimes be displaced by what the group needs.

Moreover, the deindividuation (an individual's loss of self-awareness, resulting in a breakdown in the capacity to self-regulate) fostered by groups breaks down the individual's ability to self-regulate. Research has demonstrated the state of deindividuation to increase the simulated electric shocks people will deliver to other people in experiments, to increase the use of profanity, and to increase stealing among Halloween trick-or-treaters. The paradigmatic illustration of the negative effects of deindividuation is the lynch mob. An analysis of newspaper accounts, conducted by Brian Mullen, of lynch-mob atrocities committed in the United States over a sixty-year period showed that the savagery and atrocity of the mob toward its victim(s) increased as the size of the mob increased relative to the number of its victims.

GROUP MEMBERSHIP BENEFITS

Yet, as discussed by Lynn Anderson, just as there are costs involved in belonging to a group, there are also benefits that accrue from group membership. Although the negative aspects of group membership may capture one's attention more forcefully, the positive aspects are no less common or important. A complete understanding of the purpose of groups requires a consideration of the positive side of belonging to a group. A considerable amount of evidence has documented the physiological, attitudinal, and health effects of social support. For example, people who belong to a varied and tight social support network have been found to be in better physical health and to be better able to resist stress than those lacking such support. As examples, one might consider the effects of such popular support groups as Alcoholics Anonymous and

Mothers Against Drunk Driving as well as less popular support groups that deal with specific issues such as loss and bereavement. These groups provide the imperative psychological function of allowing their members a new avenue for coping with their problems.

Perhaps the most notable effects of the group on self-definition and identity are observed when these taken-for-granted benefits are taken away. The woman who has defined herself in terms of her marital status can find herself in the midst of an identity crisis after a divorce. Similarly, foreign-exchange students often report dislocation or disorientation of identity immediately on their return home. After months or years of trying to establish a new identity based on new friends, new social contexts, or new groups, that new identity is now inappropriate and out of place in the old social context.

BIBLIOGRAPHY

"Biker Pulled from Fiery Wreck Thanks 'Heroes.'" *CBS News*. CBS Interactive, 15 Sept. 2011. Web. 20 May 2014.

Brown, Rupert, ed. *Group Processes: Dynamics within and between Groups*. 2nd rev. ed. New York: Basil Blackwell, 2007. Print.

Canetti, Elias. *Crowds and Power.* Trans. Carol Stewart. 1962. New York: Noonday, 1998. Print.

"Florida Mom, Three Kids Rescued after Minivan Sinks into the Ocean." *Good Morning America*. ABC News, 5 Mar. 2014. Web. 20 May 2014.

Forsyth, *Donalson R. Group Dynamics*. 6th ed. Belmont: Wadsworth, 2014. Print.

Kirkpatrick, David D. "Egyptian Soccer Riot Kills More than 70, and Many Blame Military." *New York Times* 2 Feb. 2012: A10. Print.

Kirst-Ashman, Karen K. *Human Behavior in the Macro Social Environment: An Empowerment Approach to Understanding Communities, Organizations, and Groups*. 4th ed. Belmont: Brooks/Cole, 2014. Print.

Mullen, Brian, and George R. Goethals, eds. *Theories of Group Behavior.* New York: Springer-Verlag, 1987. Print.

Turner, John C., et al. *Rediscovering the Social Group: A Self-Categorization Theory.* New York: Basil Blackwell, 1988. Print.

Tara Anthony and Brian Mullen

See Also: Affiliation and friendship; Affiliation motive; Bystander intervention; Cooperation, competition, and negotiation; Crowd behavior; Group decision making; Group therapy; Leadership; Organizational behavior and consulting; Prejudice; Prejudice reduction; Self-help groups; Social identity theory; Social networks; Social support and mental health; Support groups.

Guilt

Type of psychology: Emotion

The psychoanalytic and psychological concept of guilt has received extensive attention. Guilt, the feeling of tension when violating a moral code, is one of the significant ideas in psychoanalytic theory. Its psychological understanding has changed over time and continues to evolve..

Key Concepts

- Ambivalent feelings
- Conscience
- Neurotic guilt
- Oedipus complex
- Superego
- Unconscious guilt

INTRODUCTION

The concept of guilt has played an important role in the development of human behavior and culture since the early days of civilization. More recently, there has been a focus on the psychological understanding of guilt. One of the first people to write extensively about the psychological meaning of guilt was the Austrian founder of psychoanalysis, Sigmund Freud. His writings from the 1890s to the 1930s provide the basic foundation of the contemporary understanding of guilt. Guilt is the feeling of tension when one feels that one has violated a moral code by thought, action, or nonaction. It is considered to be a type of anxiety. The unpleasant feeling of guilt usually prompts the guilty person to take some type of action to relieve the tension.

Freud believed that guilt starts in early childhood as a result of the child's fear of being punished or of losing the love of the parent through misbehavior. Freud stressed that the most significant event in establishing guilt is the Oedipus complex. At the age of four or five, Freud hypothesized, the male child wants to kill his father and have sex with his mother. In the counterpart to this, sometimes called the Electra complex, the female child wants to kill her mother and have sex with her father. The child becomes anxious with these thoughts and attempts to put them out of his or her consciousness. As a result of the Oedipus complex, the child develops a conscience, which represents inner control and morality. There is the ability to recognize right from wrong and to act on the right and refrain from doing wrong. Freud would later use the concept of the superego to explain conscience. The superego represents the parental thoughts and wishes that have been internalized in the child. Now the internal superego can monitor the morality of the child, and guilt can be generated when the superego is displeased.

An important distinction is to be made between normal guilt and neurotic guilt. Normal guilt is experienced when one has acted in such a way as to violate one's moral code. A person then usually takes some action to relieve the guilt. Neurotic guilt relates to thoughts or wishes that are unacceptable and cause anxiety. These thoughts are pushed out of consciousness, so that the person feels guilt-ridden but is not aware of the source of the guilt. There is no relief from the guilt. In neurotic guilt, the thought is equated with the deed.

ORIGIN

The origin of guilt can be traced back to childhood. In human development there is a long period in which the baby is dependent on the parent. The young baby cannot survive without someone providing for its care. As the baby begins to individuate and separate from the parent, ambivalent feelings are generated. Ambivalent feelings are opposing feelings, typically love and hate, felt for the same person. The child begins to worry that these hateful feelings will cause the parents to punish him or her or remove their love. With this fear of parental retaliation, the child becomes guilty when thinking or acting in a way that might displease the parents.

The Oedipus complex dramatically changes this situation. The dynamics of this complex are based on the play by the Greek playwright Sophocles, in which Oedipus murders his father and takes his mother as his wife, unaware that they are his parents. When Oedipus finds out the truth, he blinds himself and goes into exile. Freud believed the Oedipal situation to be a common theme in literature. He also discussed the play *Hamlet* (1603) by the English playwright William Shakespeare. At the beginning of the play, Hamlet's uncle has killed Hamlet's father and married Hamlet's mother. There is the question as to why Hamlet hesitates in killing his uncle, and Freud attributed this indecision to Hamlet's Oedipus complex. Freud argued that Hamlet had thoughts of killing his father and having sex with his mother, and Hamlet's uncle only put into action what Hamlet had thought. Hamlet's guilty desires prevent him from taking any action. Freud believed that the Oedipus complex can exist throughout one's life. People can feel guilty about separating from their parents or achieving more than their parents, as this can unconsciously represent killing them off.

Freud's examination of neurotic guilt led him to the concept of unconscious guilt. Neurotics experience guilt but are not sure what they are guilty about. Freud first noticed this attitude in obsessive patients. These patients tended to be perfectionistic and overly conscientious, and yet they were wracked by guilt. Freud believed them to be feeling guilty about thoughts and wishes they had pushed out of consciousness, that is, Oedipal wishes. Freud observed the paradox that the more virtuous a person, the more the person experiences self-reproach and guilt as temptations increase.

Freud's final writings on guilt highlighted its importance for civilization. He wrote that guilt enabled people to get along with others and form groups, institutions, and nations. Without the ability to curb impulses, particularly aggression, society would suffer. Freud did feel that humans pay a price for this advance in civilization, in that there is a loss of personal happiness due to the heightening of the sense of guilt.

HISTORY

Writing in the 1930s, child psychoanalyst Melanie Klein argued that the Oedipus complex started much earlier in the child's development than Freud had suggested. She believed that it started toward the end of the first year of life and centered primarily on the mother. The baby hates the mother for withdrawing the breast during feeding. The baby then feels guilty and worries that the mother will no longer breast-feed. Klein felt that the baby would want to relieve its guilt by making amends to the mother, causing it to show concern and care for the mother. Klein felt that this was the most crucial step in human development, the capacity to show concern for someone else. Guilt is thus seen as a critical ingredient in the ability to love.

The psychoanalyst Franz Alexander further advanced understanding of guilt. He wrote that feeling guilty can interfere with healthy assertiveness. The guilty person may need excessive reassurance from other people. When the guilty person is assertive, he or she fears retaliation from others. Alexander also wrote about the concept of guilt projection. This term refers to situations in which people who tend to be overly critical induce guilt in other people.

The psychoanalyst Erik H. Erikson also wrote on the theme of guilt interfering with assertiveness. He formulated a theory of eight stages of human development, focusing primarily on early development. The fourth stage of development, around the age of four to five, is called guilt/initiative. The child must successfully repress Oedipal wishes to avoid feeling excessive guilt. The child can then proceed with normal initiative.

Another perspective on guilt is the concept of existential guilt, discussed by American psychiatrist James Knight. Existential guilt is the failure to live up to one's expectations and potentialities. It can lead to questioning one's existence and to states of despair until personal meaning can be established.

Erich Fromm expanded the concept of guilt in order to better understand group psychology. He wrote that there are essentially two types of conscience: authoritarian and humanistic. Authoritarian conscience is the voice of internalized external authority. It is based on fear and danger. It is afraid of displeasing authority and actively seeks to please authority. Authoritarian conscience can lead to immoral acts committed as the individual conscience is given over to this higher authority. Humanistic conscience is one's own voice expressing one's own true self. It is the essence of one's moral experience in life. It includes integrity and self-awareness.

CURRENT STATUS

Since 1960, there has been a significant change in the views of psychoanalytic theory on guilt. The psychoanalyst Hans Loewald wrote extensively about guilt. He considered that guilt does not necessarily lead to punishment; sometimes punishment is sought to evade guilt. Bearing the burden of guilt makes it possible to master guilt by achieving a reconciliation of conflicting feelings. Guilt is thus seen not as a troublesome feeling but as one of the driving forces in the organization of the self. Guilt plays a critical part in developing self-responsibility and integrity.

The American psychoanalyst Stephen Mitchell, writing in 2000, expanded on Loewald's ideas. Mitchell concerned himself with the concept of genuine guilt. He believes it is important to tolerate, accept, and use this feeling. People need to take responsibility for the suffering they have caused others and themselves. People particularly hurt those they love, but by taking personal responsibility for their behavior, they can repair and deepen their love.

GUILT AND SHAME

Throughout the 1990s, there were a number of writings about the concept of shame and its relation to guilt. Shame is experienced as a feeling of inadequacy in the self. There can be physical, psychological, or emotional shame.

The American psychoanalyst Helen Lewis wrote extensively about this topic. She believed that shame includes dishonor, ridicule, humiliation, and embarrassment, while guilt includes duty, obligation, responsibility, and culpability. A person can feel both guilt and shame.

BIBLIOGRAPHY

Akhtar, Salman, ed. *Guilt: Origins, Manifestations, and Management*. Lanham: Aronson, 2013. Print.

Carveth, Donald L. *The Still Small Voice: Psychoanalytic Reflections on Guilt and Conscience*. London: Karnac, 2013. Print.

Freeman, Lucy, and Herbert S. Strean. *Understanding and Letting Go of Guilt*. Northvale: Aronson, 1995. Print.

Joseph, Fernando. "The Borrowed Sense of Guilt." *International Journal of Psychoanalysis* 81.3 (2000): 499–512. Print.

Lewis, Michael. *The Rise of Consciousness and the Development of Emotional Life*. New York: Guilford, 2014. Print.

Piers, Gerhart, and Milton B. Singer. *Shame and Guilt: A Psychoanalytic and a Cultural Study*. New York: Norton, 1971. Print.

Reilly, Patrick. *The Literature of Guilt: From Gulliver to Golding*. Iowa City: U of Iowa P, 1988. Print.

Rodogno, Raffaele. "Gender and Shame: A Philosophical Perspective." *Gender and Emotion*. Ed. Ioana Latu, Marianne Schmid Mast, and Susanne Kaiser. Bern: Lang, 2013. 155–70. Print.

Tangney, June Price, and Ronda L. Dearing. *Shame and Guilt*. New York: Guilford, 2004. Print.

Tournier, Paul. *Guilt and Grace: A Psychological Study*. San Francisco: Harper, 1983. Print.

Daniel Heimowitz

See Also: Anger; Ego, superego, and id; Emotional expression; Emotions; Freud, Sigmund; Freudian psychology; Grieving; Hysteria; Jealousy; Love; Moral development; Neurotic disorders; Oedipus complex; Post-traumatic stress disorder; Psychoanalytic psychology; Psychoanalytic psychology and personality: Sigmund Freud; Self-esteem.

H

Habituation and sensitization

Type of psychology: Learning

Habituation is a decrease in behavioral response that results from repeated exposure to a stimulus, whereas sensitization is a heightened behavioral response that results from a stronger stimulus. These two processes differ physiologically and are the most fundamental and widespread forms of learning in the animal kingdom..

Key Concepts

- Adaptation
- Innate
- Learning
- Neuron
- Neurotransmitter
- Opponent process theory
- Stimulus
- Synapse

INTRODUCTION

Habituation and sensitization are the two most fundamental and widespread forms of learning in the animal kingdom. According to ethologists, learning is any modification in behavior that results from previous experience, in some way involves the nervous system, and is not caused by development, fatigue, or injury. More advanced forms of learning include association, perceptual or programmed learning, and insight; the two simplest (nonassociative) forms are habituation and sensitization. These two processes can be characterized as behavioral modifications that result from repeated presentation of simple environmental stimuli.

Habituation is a decrease in response to repeated presentation of a stimulus—an environmental cue that can potentially modify an animal's behavior via its nervous system. One of the most widely cited examples of this kind of learning involves the startle response exhibited by nestling birds in response to potential predators such as hawks. A young duck, for example, will exhibit an innate startle response whenever a hawk-shaped model or silhouette is passed overhead. With repeated presentation of the model, however, the intensity of the bird's response will decline as the animal becomes habituated, or learns that the stimulus bears no immediate significance.

Common throughout the animal kingdom and even among some groups of protozoans, habituation is important for preventing repeated responses to irrelevant environmental stimuli that could otherwise overwhelm an organism's senses and interfere with other critical tasks. In the case of a nestling bird, there is a clear advantage to an alarm response in the presence of a potential predator; however, a continued fixed response would result in an unnecessary expenditure of energy and distraction from other important activities, such as feeding.

In identifying a habituation response, it is necessary to distinguish between true habituation and sensory adaptation and fatigue. These latter two phenomena involve a waning in responsiveness that is caused by temporary insensitivity of sense organs or by muscle fatigue and thus are not considered forms of learning. In contrast, habituation results in a drop in responsiveness even though the nervous system is fully capable of detecting a signal and eliciting a muscle response.

In contrast to habituation, sensitization is the heightened sensitivity (or hypersensitivity) that results from initial or repeated exposure to a strong stimulus. Examples of sensitization include the increased sensitivity of humans to soft sounds following exposure to a loud, startling noise such as a gunshot and the increased responsiveness and sensitivity of a laboratory animal to mild (usually irrelevant) tactile stimulation after an electric shock. Sensitization increases an organism's awareness and responsiveness to a variety of environmental stimuli, thereby preparing it for potentially dangerous situations.

COMPARISON OF RESPONSES

At first glance, habituation and sensitization seem to be opposite behavioral responses—one a decrease in responsiveness and the other an increase—but in fact, they are physiologically different processes, each with its own set of unique characteristics.

At the physiological level, the two responses are determined by contrasting neurological processes that take place in different parts of the nervous system. Habituation is thought to take place primarily in the reflex arc (or SR) system, which consists of short neuronal circuits between sense organs and muscles. In contrast, sensitization is assumed to occur in the state system, or that part of the nervous system that regulates an organism's state of responsiveness. The SR system controls specific responses, while the state system determines an organism's general level of readiness to respond. The interaction between habituation and sensitization and these systems determines the exact outcome of a response. At the cellular level, habituated sensory neurons produce fewer neurotransmitters on the postsynaptic membrane, while sensitized neurons are stimulated by other neurons to increase neurotransmitter production and hence responsiveness of the nerves. Thus, while their ultimate neurological effects seem linked, the mechanisms by which such effects are achieved are quite different.

Other important differences between habituation and sensitization include contrasting recovery times, opposite patterns of stimulus specificity, and differences in responsiveness to stimulus intensity. Sensitization is generally characterized by a short-term or spontaneous recovery, as are some cases of habituation. In certain situations, however, recovery from habituation may take several days, and even then it may result in incomplete or less intense responses.

Habituation is usually elicited by very specific sign stimuli, such as certain colors, shapes, or sounds. Thus, even after complete habituation to one stimulus, the organism will still respond fully to a second stimulus. Sensitization, on the other hand, can be characterized as a more generalized response, one in which a single stimulus will result in complete sensitization to a variety of stimuli. Such fundamental differences between these two learning processes reflect differences in their function and survival value. It is a clear advantage to an organism to increase its general awareness of a variety of stimuli, as occurs in sensitization, once it is alarmed. A similar generalized pattern of habituation, however, would shut down the organism's sensitivity to many important stimuli and possibly put the organism in danger.

A final important difference between habituation and sensitization is the manner in which the two processes are affected by stimulus strength. Habituation is more likely to occur if the repeated stimulus is weak, while sensitization will occur when the stimulus is strong.

These various characteristics have important survival implications, especially for species that rely on stereotypic responses to avoid predation and other life-threatening situations. They ensure that the response is elicited in a timely fashion, that the animal is returned to a normal state in a relatively short period of time, and that the animal is not overwhelmed with sensory input.

APLYSIA RESEARCH

Habituation and sensitization have been studied in a variety of contexts and in a number of organisms, from simple protozoans, such as the genus Stentor, to human subjects. Such studies have focused on the adaptive significance of these simple learning processes, their neurological control, and the range of behavioral responses that result from interaction between these two forms of learning.

One particular organism in which the neurological basis of habituation and sensitization has been extensively studied is the *Aplysia* genus of marine slugs. Eric Kandel and his associates at Columbia University showed that when the mantle of this organism is prodded, the slug quickly withdraws its gills into a central cavity; but after repeated prodding, it learns to ignore the stimulus—that is, it becomes habituated. Conversely, when the slug is stimulated with an electric shock, its sensitivity to prodding increases greatly, and it withdraws its gills in response to even the slightest tactile stimulation—that is, it becomes sensitized.

Because *Aplysia* possesses only a few large neurons, it is an excellent organism in which to study the physiological basis of learning. Capitalizing on its unique system, Kandel and his colleagues have been able to establish the neurological changes that accompany simple forms of learning. In the case of habituation, they have shown that repeated stimulation interferes with calcium-ion channels in the nerve that, under normal circumstances, causes synaptic vesicles to release neurotransmitters, which in turn relay a nervous impulse between two neurons. Thus, habituation results in a blocking of the chemical signals between nerves and thereby prevents gill withdrawal. When *Aplysia* is stimulated (or sensitized) by an electric shock, on the other hand, an interneuron (a closed nerve circuit contained within one part of the nervous system) stimulates the sensory neuron by opening calcium-ion channels, increasing neurotransmitter production, and promoting gill withdrawal. Thus, the proximate neurological changes that take place during sensitization and habituation are nearly opposite, but they are achieved by very different neurological circuits.

STUDIES OF THE SUCKING REFLEX

A second area in which habituation and sensitization responses have been the subject of extensive investigation is the sucking reflex exhibited by human infants. When the cheeks or lips of a young child are touched with a nipple or finger, the infant will automatically begin sucking. In a study designed to explore how various stimuli affect this reflex, it was shown that babies respond much more vigorously to a bottle nipple than to the end of a piece of rubber tubing. In addition, repeated presentation of a bottle nipple causes an increase in sucking response, whereas repeated stimulation with rubber tubing causes a decrease in sucking. The sensitized or elevated response to a rubber nipple is a result of activation of the state system, which increases the baby's awareness and readiness to respond. Sensitization, however, does not occur when the baby is stimulated with rubber tubing, and instead the child habituates to this stimulus.

ROLE IN EMOTIONAL REACTIONS

In addition to influencing simple innate behaviors such as sucking reflexes and withdrawal responses, habituation is believed to be responsible for a number of more complex emotional reactions in humans. Explanations for the effects of habituation on emotions are derived primarily from the opponent process theory of motivation.

The opponent process theory holds that each emotional stimulation, or primary process, initiated by an environmental stimulus is opposed by an internal process in the organism. The emotional changes that actually occur in the organism are predicted to result from the net effect of these two processes. The opponent process detracts from the primary process, and summation of the two yields a particular emotional response. It is hypothesized that when the organism is repeatedly stimulated, the primary process is unaffected but the opponent process is strengthened, which results in a net reduction in the overall emotional response. In other words, repeated presentation of an emotion-arousing stimulus results in habituation in the emotional response, primarily as a result of the elevated opponent response.

An increase in drug tolerance, which results from repeated usage of a drug, is best explained by this kind of habituation. Habitual users of alcohol, caffeine, nicotine, and various opiate derivatives must consume greater quantities of such drugs each time they are ingested to achieve the same emotional stimulation. Thus, with repeated usage, there is a decline in the overall emotional response. This decline in the euphoric effects of a drug is primarily the result of an increase in the opponent process, which can be characterized as the negative effects of the drug. This is presumably why habitual users experience more severe physiological problems, such as headaches or delirium tremens, on termination of a drug.

Similar patterns of habituation have also been suggested to explain the human emotional responses associated with love and attachment and the extreme feelings of euphoria derived from various thrill-seeking activities such as skydiving. Thus, while habituation and sensitization are simple forms of learning, they may be involved in a variety of more complex behaviors and emotions as well.

INTERACTION OF LEARNING AND INSTINCT

Studies of habituation and sensitization have been especially helpful in clarifying the physiological and genetic mechanisms that control various forms of learning. Such investigations have also shown that habituation and sensitization are widespread phenomena with tremendous adaptive significance throughout the animal kingdom.

Ethologists, in marked contrast to psychologists (especially behaviorist psychologists), historically have emphasized the importance of underlying physiological mechanisms in the regulation of various behavioral phenomena. Traditionally, they argued that many forms of behavior are not only genetically determined, or innate, but also further constrained by the physiological hardware of the organism. They held that psychologists completely ignored these factors by focusing only on the input and output of experiments. Psychologists, on the other hand, have maintained that nearly all forms of behavior are influenced in some way by learning. These contrasting views, which developed largely as a result of different experimental approaches, eventually gave way to a more modern and unified picture of behavior.

One area of research that greatly facilitated this unification was the study of habituation and sensitization. By discovering the chemical and neurological changes that take place during these simple forms of learning, neurobiologists succeeded in demonstrating how the physiological environment is modified during the learning process and that such modifications are remarkably similar throughout the animal kingdom. Thus, it became quite clear that an understanding of proximate physiological mechanisms is central to the study of behavior and learning.

Other studies on sensitization and habituation also helped establish the generality of these processes among various groups of animals. They showed that simple forms of learning can occur in nearly all major animal phyla and that these learning processes often result in modification of simple innate behaviors as well as a variety of more complex responses. From these and other studies, it was soon evident that learning and instinct are not mutually exclusive events but rather two processes that work together to provide animals with maximum adaptability to their environment. The kind of learning that occurs during habituation and sensitization allows animals to modify simple, fixed behaviors in response to repeated exposure to environmental stimuli. Habituation allows an organism to filter irrelevant background stimuli, preventing sensory overload and interference of normal activities critical to its survival, while sensitization helps increase an organism's awareness of stimuli in the face of potentially dangerous situations.

These two forms of learning represent important behavioral adaptations with tremendous generality in the animal kingdom. Even in humans, a variety of seemingly complex behaviors can be attributed to interactions between sensitization and habituation and the simple neurological changes that accompany them.

BIBLIOGRAPHY

Domjan, Michael. *The Principles of Learning and Behavior*. 6th ed. Belmont: Wadsworth, 2010. Print.

Eichenbaum, Howard. *The Cognitive Neuroscience of Memory: An Introduction*. 2nd ed. New York: Oxford UP, 2012. Print.

Grier, James W. *Biology of Animal Behavior*. 3rd ed. New York: McGraw, 1999. Print.

Klein, Stephen B. *Learning: Principles and Applications*. 7th ed. Thousand Oaks: Sage, 2015. Print.

McFarland, David, ed. *The Oxford Companion to Animal Behavior*. Rev. and enl. ed. New York: Oxford UP, 1987. Print.

Manning, Aubrey, and Marian Stamp Dawkins. *An Introduction to Animal Behaviour*. 6th ed. Cambridge: Cambridge UP, 2012. Print.

Raven, Peter H., et al. *Biology*. 10th ed. New York: McGraw, 2014. Print.

Shepherd, Gordon Murray. *Neurobiology*. 3rd ed. New York: Oxford UP, 1994. Print.

Michael A. Steele

See Also: Aversion therapy; Conditioning; Emotional intelligence; Ethology; Learning; Motivation; Neurotransmitters; Operant conditioning therapies; Pavlovian conditioning; Reflexes; Systematic desensitization.

Hall, G. Stanley

Born: February 1, 1844
Died: April 24, 1924
Birthplace: Ashfield, Massachusetts
Place of death: Worcester, Massachusetts
Identity: American psychologist, journal editor, and university president
Type of psychology: Developmental psychology

Hall was a pioneer in the study of adolescent psychology and, through the professional journals that he edited, in introducing Freudian psychoanalysis to the United States.

Much of the credit for introducing the academic study of psychology to the United States belongs to G. Stanley Hall, who began his career as a student of theology. His academic interests turned to philosophy and later to psychology, a pursuit that consumed him after reading some of Wilhelm Wundt's seminal writing in psychology. Although he wanted to go to Germany immediately to study with Wundt, his major professor at Harvard University, William James, persuaded him to remain at Harvard to complete one of the first American doctorates in psychology.

After receiving his degree in 1878, Hall fulfilled his dream of studying with Wundt, going to Leipzig, Germany, to undertake postdoctoral work with Wundt and other notable European psychologists. After returning to the United States, he taught briefly at Harvard before moving to Johns Hopkins University in 1881, where he established an outstanding American psychology laboratory. In 1887, he founded the *American Journal of Psychology*.

In 1888, he became the founding president of Clark University in Worcester, Massachusetts, where he remained until his retirement in 1920. His tenure at Clark was often troubled and was clouded by the accidental deaths of his wife and daughter in 1890. Nevertheless, in 1909, he brought Sigmund Freud and Carl Jung to the dicennial conference that he organized at Clark, thereby introducing them to American audiences.

By 1893, Hall had supervised the doctoral studies of eleven of the fourteen Americans holding doctorates in psychology. By 1898, thirty of the fifty-four American doctorates in psychology had been earned under Hall's supervision. Hall died in 1924 and left his entire estate to Clark University.

BIBLIOGRAPHY

Hothersall, David. *History of Psychology*. 4th ed. New York: McGraw-Hill, 2004.

Hulse, Stewart H., and Bert F. Green, eds. *One Hundred Years of Psychological Research in America: G. Stanley Hall and the Johns Hopkins Tradition*. Baltimore: Johns Hopkins UP, 1986.

Rosenzweig, Saul. *Freud, Jung, and Hall, the King-Maker: The Historic Expedition to America* (1909) and G. Stanley Hall as Host. St. Louis: Rana House, 1992.

Ross, Dorothy. *G. Stanley Hall: The Psychologist as Prophet*. Chicago: U of Chicago P, 1972.

R. Baird Shuman

See Also: Adolescence: Cognitive skills; Developmental psychology; Freud, Sigmund; Freudian psychology; Jung, Carl; Jungian psychology; Teenagers' mental health.

Hallucinations

Type of psychology: Consciousness; Psychopathology

Hallucinations are unusual perceptual phenomena that cause a person to experience imaginary perceptions as reality. There are several different types of hallucinations, and they can result from several different causes..

Key Concepts

- Atypical antipsychotic medications
- Delusions
- Hallucinogens
- Phenothiazines
- Schizophrenia

INTRODUCTION

Hallucinations are defined as sensory experiences that occur in the absence of sensory stimulation. Hallucinations, therefore, are false perceptions. There are five major types of hallucinations, which correspond with the five senses. Visual hallucinations occur when a person sees something that is not there, such as a person whom others do not see. They usually involve the false perception that one sees God, the devil, or a meaningful person in one's life. Visual hallucinations are usually reported to appear in black and white. They can be very frightening for the individual experiencing them. An individual initially may be reluctant to tell others about these visual phenomena. Auditory hallucinations are more common than visual hallucinations and refer to the phenomenon of hearing things that others do not hear, such as voices that seem to be coming from the person's own mind. Tactile hallucinations correlate with the sense of touch and involve the perception of feeling things that are actually not present. The mistaken perception that bugs are crawling down one's arm is an example of a tactile hallucination. The insistence that one feels two strands of hair in one's eye is another example of a tactile hallucination. Gustatory hallucinations involve the false perception of tasting things that are not present, such as experiencing an imaginary metallic taste in one's mouth. Olfactory hallucinations involve smelling things in the absence of stimuli to create such smells, such as the smell of burning flesh.

A hallucination is a perceptual experience that differs from the occasional mistaken perception, such as the belief that one's name has been called or that one has seen a friend or acquaintance across the street. Instead, a hallucination is believed by the person to be real, in spite of repeated evidence to the contrary. Individuals experiencing hallucinations will insist vehemently on the existence of such stimuli and will reject explanations that suggest they are mistakenly perceiving something. (If an individual experiences a hallucination but recognizes that it is not real, it is called a pseudohallucination instead.) Hallucinatory behavior is often recurrent.

Hallucinations are altered states of consciousness or awareness and can result from several different causes. They may be caused by changes in neurological stimulation, such as a high fever, delirium, or epileptic seizure. Different somatic, or bodily, states may foster the development of hallucinations. For example, the effects of starvation, oxygen deprivation, sleep deprivation, or a heightened state of awareness can increase the likelihood of hallucinating. Hallucinations also may be a symptom of a psychological disorder such as schizophrenia or major depression. Hallucinations may be induced with psychoactive substances, such as hallucinogenic drugs.

SCHIZOPHRENIC HALLUCINATIONS

Schizophrenia is a mental disorder characterized by a loss of contact with reality and the presence of psychotic behaviors, including hallucinations and delusions.

Symptoms of schizophrenia are classified as positive or negative; positive symptoms of schizophrenia refer to behavioral excesses, whereas negative symptoms refer to behavioral deficits. Examples of positive symptoms of schizophrenia include hallucinations, delusions, and disorganized speech. Negative symptoms include the neglect of one's hygiene, social withdrawal, and a flattening of one's emotions.

The most commonly experienced hallucinations among schizophrenic patients are auditory hallucinations. Schizophrenic patients will report that they hear voices commenting on their behavior. Others will report hearing voices that are arguing with each other. Some with schizophrenia state that the voices they hear are insulting and antagonistic toward them. The voices may be of either gender. Command hallucinations are hallucinations that involve voices that order one to do something, such as cause harm to oneself or others. Research has suggested that individuals with command hallucinations are more likely to obey a command hallucination if they recognize the "voice" issuing the command. These perceptual experiences can be very distressing to the person experiencing them. A person suffering from schizophrenia may feel plagued by the voices that are heard. An individual experiencing chronic auditory hallucinations may wear headphones in a desperate attempt to stop the perceived voices. It is common for the individual experiencing auditory hallucinations to experience depression.

Schizophrenia is also characterized by the presence of delusions, or false beliefs that persist in spite of contrary evidence. Delusions might involve the false and persistent belief that one is being followed or poisoned or that one's thoughts are being broadcast for others to hear. They often develop due to an effort by the individual to explain his or her hallucinations. Individuals who experience frequent auditory hallucinations may develop the delusion that others are plotting against them and are lying when they say that they do not hear the hallucinatory voices.

The auditory areas in the temporal lobes of the brain are associated with hearing ability. Stimulation of these parts can create the false perception of sound. Magnetic resonance imaging (MRI) scans of the brains of schizophrenics who experience auditory hallucinations reveal activity in the auditory centers of the brain even when no external sound has stimulated that brain region. Research has suggested that patients who claim to be hearing voices may actually be unable to distinguish their internal thoughts from external stimuli. Therefore, an individual experiencing auditory hallucinations may be attributing internally generated thought processes to an external source. This research, however, fails to offer plausible explanations for the occurrence of visual, tactile, olfactory, or gustatory hallucinations.

Schizophrenic patients are often treated with antipsychotic medications to alleviate the psychotic symptoms they experience. In the 1930s and 1940s, French chemists developed a group of medications called phenothiazines. The phenothiazines were found to be effective for decreasing positive symptoms among schizophrenic patients, such as hallucinations and delusions, but they also carried the risk of serious side effects. In the 1980s, new antipsychotic drugs known as atypical antipsychotics were found to be effective in treating both the positive and the negative symptoms of schizophrenia with fewer side effects than phenothiazines. Clozapine, risperidone, and olanzapine are some of the atypical antipsychotics that became increasingly popular in the 1990s. These drugs have been especially successful in treating schizophrenia symptoms such as hallucinatory experiences. Research studies have suggested that cognitive behavior therapy (CBT) is effective in treating schizophrenic patients who experience hallucinations and delusions.

DRUG-INDUCED HALLUCINATIONS AND DELIRIUM

Certain psychoactive drugs (substances that affect the brain's functioning) can induce hallucinatory experiences. Hallucinogens are the class of psychoactive substances that include lysergic acid diethylamide (LSD), psilocybin, ecstasy, and mescaline. All these drugs are powerful and potentially dangerous substances that have proved harmful to many who have ingested them in a recreational context.

LSD gained notoriety during the 1960s. Harvard University professor Timothy Leary was an influential advocate for the use of LSD, touting its ability to induce a greater self-awareness. LSD is a powerful hallucinogen that is odorless and tasteless. After using the drug, the individual will experience about eight hours of altered perception, accompanied by mood changes and other symptoms. Psilocybin, another hallucinogen, is found in certain types of mushrooms. Psilocybin is a less potent hallucinogen than LSD and has for centuries been considered sacred by the Aztecs in Mexico and Central America. Methylenedioxymethamphetamine (MDMA), more commonly known as ecstasy, stimulates the central nervous system, resulting in hallucinogenic experiences.

Mescaline is a hallucinogen derived from a cactus plant called the peyote. For hundreds of years, Native Americans have used peyote during religious ceremonies to facilitate and intensify spiritual experiences.

Much of what is known about the hallucinatory experiences of people who use hallucinogens is derived from their first-person reports. Hallucinogens usually induce colorful, vivid images in the initial stages of use. These hallucinations may include images of places, scenes, people, or animals. Some hallucinatory experiences are reported to be pleasant, and sometimes inspiring, perceptual experiences. Individuals who use hallucinogens are frequently searching for a spiritual transcendence. Others who have used these substances report a "bad trip," or a hallucinatory experience that was unpleasant or frightening and could lead to panic attacks and heightened anxiety. Heavy use of stimulant drugs, such as cocaine and amphetamines, can cause frightening hallucinations and delusions. Marijuana may produce mild hallucinatory effects, as sensory experiences are enhanced by the effects of the substance. Hallucinations can also be a part of the withdrawal symptoms from alcohol dependence.

Delirium is a mental state characterized by a clouding of consciousness in which a person may seem confused and disorganized. The symptoms of delirium have a rapid onset and include a difficulty in maintaining or shifting attention, disorientation, and at times the presence of visual and tactile hallucinations. There are many possible causes of delirium, including metabolic disease, infection, endocrine disease, and side effects of certain medications, and treatment involves identifying and then treating the source.

Sleep deprivation seems to alter people's perceptions of their surroundings and can also produce mild hallucinations. Research suggests that hallucinations have been reported among subjects who were deprived of sleep for sixty hours.

BIBLIOGRAPHY

Aleman, André, and Frank Larøi. *Hallucinations: The Science of Idiosyncratic Perception*. Washington: APA, 2008. Print.

Caballo, Vincent E., ed. *International Handbook of Cognitive and Behavioural Treatments for Psychological Disorders*. Oxford: Elsevier, 1998. Print.

Hagen, Roger, et al., eds. *CBT for Psychosis: A Symptom-Based Approach*. New York: Routledge, 2011. Print

Heinrichs, R. Walter. *In Search of Madness: Schizophrenia and Neuroscience*. New York: Oxford UP, 2001. Print.

Jardri, Renaud, et al., eds. *The Neuroscience of Hallucinations*. New York: Springer, 2013. Print.

Jung, John. *Psychology of Alcohol and Other Drugs: A Research Perspective*. Thousand Oaks: Sage, 2001. Print.

Leudar, Ivan, and Anthony David. "Is Hearing Voices a Sign of Mental Illness?" *Psychologist* 14.5 (2001): 256–59. Print.

McCarthy-Jones, Simon. *Hearing Voices: The Histories, Causes and Meanings of Auditory Verbal Hallucinations*. New York: Cambridge UP, 2012. Print.

Meaden, Alan, et al. *Cognitive Therapy for Command Hallucinations: An Advanced Practical Companion*. New York: Routledge, 2013. Print.

Sacks, Oliver. *Hallucinations*. New York: Knopf, 2012. Print.

Smith, Daniel B. *Muses, Madmen, and Prophets: Rethinking the History, Science, and Meaning of Auditory Hallucination*. New York: Penguin, 2008. Print.

Tarrier, Nicholas, et al. "Are Some Types of Psychotic Symptoms More Responsive to Cognitive-Behavior Therapy?" *Behavioral and Cognitive Psychotherapy* 20.1 (2001): 45–55. Print.

Janine T. Ogden

See Also: Antipsychotic medications; Consciousness; Consciousness: Altered states; Hearing; Schizophrenia: Background, types, and symptoms; Schizophrenia: Theoretical explanations; Sensation and perception; Smell and taste; Synesthesia; Touch and pressure; Visual system.

Hate crimes
Psychological causes and effects

Type of psychology: Learning; Psychopathology; Social psychology

Hate crimes are criminal offenses, such as murder, assault, arson, or vandalism, that are motivated by the offenders' bias against the race, nationality, religion, ethnicity, disability, or sexual orientation of the targeted person. The motives for these crimes are rooted in learned behaviors and discrimination that may have been present for generations.

Key Concepts

- Antisocial personality
- Bias
- Offenders
- Prejudice
- Victims

INTRODUCTION

The term "hate crime" is a relatively new term, though bias-motivated crime has a much longer history. Advocates who were addressing violent crime in the United States that targeted African Americans, Asian Americans, and Jewish Americans in the 1980s are believed to have coined the term. Since the coining of the term, federal and state governments, as well as social scientists, have made efforts to formally define hate crimes for the purposes of collecting statistics and improving law-enforcement and prevention efforts.

The Federal Bureau of Investigation (FBI) defines a hate crime as a "a criminal offense against a person, property or property motivated in whole or in part by the offender's bias against a race, religion, disability, sexual orientation, or ethnicity/national origin." However, complete agreement on what constitutes a hate crime has not been reached.

In the past, although these criminal acts could be prosecuted, the punishment did not include a consideration of the bias motivating the crime. Thus, painting a swastika on the door of a Jewish person's home was considered a crime because the graffiti defaced property and a law existed against vandalism, but not because the act was done to intimidate the resident. Hate crime laws allow the psychological harm done to a victim to be factored into the determination of whether any special sanctions should occur. Research has suggested that the victim of a hate crime experiences more harm than does the victim of a similar crime not motivated by bias or hate. In 2009, the United States Congress passed the Matthew Shepard and James Byrd Jr. Hate Crimes Prevention Act, which provides federal funding and assistance to state, local, and tribal jurisdictions to assist in the investigation and prosecution of hate crimes. The law also created a new federal criminal law that criminalizes causing bodily injury when the crime was committed because of the actual or perceived race, color, religion, or national origin of any person, or when the crime was committed because of the actual or perceived religion, national origin, gender, sexual orientation, gender identity, or disability of any person and the crime affected interstate or foreign commerce or occurred with federal special maritime and territorial jurisdictions. The law removed the requirement that the victim be engaged in a federally protected activity, such as voting or attending a public school, at the time of the crime.

The law is named after Matthew Shepard and James Byrd Jr., who were both victims of violent hate crimes in 1998 in US states that had no existing hate crime laws at the time.

CAUSES

The central cause of these crimes is hate, which most often is the result of fear, anger, and ignorance. Hate crimes are acts of bias, bigotry, and intolerance toward an identified group. Though individuals and small groups may be the actual victims, the ultimate target of the perpetrators is the group to which the victims belong. For example, a hate crime offender may target and beat a black man in order to intimidate all African Americans in the community. Perpetrators of hate crimes seek to terrorize the larger group by criminal acts against its members.

The beliefs and prejudices held by hate crime offenders are learned and can go back for generations. Perpetrators develop an "us-versus-them" outlook, in which they hold that their own group is superior and correct in its view and that the other group is inferior. The other group's members may be seen as interlopers. In addition, they may be made the scapegoats for what is perceived to be wrong in a society. In this way, the other group is made responsible for economic problems, crime, and the other ills of society. Often when an identifiable group migrates into an area (community, state, or country), the resident group sees the immigrants as a drain on—or competitor for—the available resources and views their removal as the only solution. Research indicates that some of the most extreme biased responses are sparked by a perceived threat to the cultural integrity of the perpetrators' ingroup by members of an outgroup. Typically, a hate group or hate crime perpetrator does not know much about the identified group. In fact, the less people know about an identified outgroup, the stronger their prejudices will be. Social psychology research has identified a phenomenon known as the "outgroup homogeneity effect," by which people tend to see members of groups that they are not apart of as more homogenous than members of their own group, empowering stereotypes and leading to deindividuation of outgroup members.

Researchers Jack McDevitt, Jack Levin, and Susan Bennett, in a 2002 study published in the *Journal of Social Issues,* classified hate time offenders into four categories based on the psychological and situational factors that led to hate crimes: thrill-seeking perpetrators are motivated by a desire for excitement and power; defensive perpetrators are motivated by protecting their community from perceived outsiders; retaliatory perpetrators commit violence in response to a real or perceived hate crime against their own group by members of the target group; and missionary perpetrators are typically members of hate groups who are deeply motivated by bigotry and see it as their "mission" to intimidate or eliminate the other group. These categories are widely used by law enforcement officers in the investigation and identification of hate crimes. Thrill-seeking is thought to be the most common motivation for hate crime offenders.

VICTIMS AND OFFENDERS

Potential hate crime victims are those who are or are thought to be members of an identifiable group. These victims differ from victims of random crimes in that hate crime victims are specifically selected as a crime target due to their race, ethnicity, nationality, religion, sexual orientation, gender identity, or disability. They were not victimized for what they were doing or what they had in their possession, but for what and who they are. Consequently, these victims cannot alter their behaviors to protect themselves from possible future ttacks.

While all violent crime puts victims at risk for psychological distress, victims of violent hate crimes are even more likely to suffer from depression, anxiety, anger, and posttraumatic stress disorder than victims of comparable violent crimes that are not motivated by bias and hate. Furthermore, hate crimes send a message to all members of a given group that their neighborhood, school, workplace, or community is hostile and dangerous to them. Hate crimes victimize not only the targeted individuals but members of their group at large. Members of the targeted group may experience psychological distress, heightened anxiety, and lowered self-esteem.

In the United States, the most frequent profile of a hate crime offender is a young white man, usually one who has low self-esteem and is socially isolated. Research demonstrates that the perpetrators of hate crimes also demonstrate above-average levels of aggression and antisocial behavior. However, most offenders do not have a diagnosable psychopathology. Alcohol and drug use can contribute to their behavior. Other characteristics of offenders include a history of abuse and of witnessing violence used as a coping method.

These hate crime offenders hold stereotypical beliefs that cause them to view the entire identified group as a threat. Out of their need for belonging, they may be attracted to hate groups, where people share their beliefs. Though less than 10 percent of the reported hate crimes are committed by members of organized hate groups, these groups can produce splinter groups or influence individuals who come in contact with them. Areas where there are high levels of hate-group activity and membership typically report higher numbers of hate crimes.

Offenders may plan their crimes over a period of time or act spontaneously on finding a target. However, there is a strong premeditated component to hate crimes compared to other criminal offenses. People who commit hate crimes are more likely to deliberate on and plan their attacks than the perpetrators of nonbias-related crimes, and some may even travel long distances to seek out members of their targeted group. Though their crimes may appear irrational to most people, the perpetrators see them as logical and defensible, the natural result of the cultural climate that fostered the hate ideology.

HATE CRIME STATISTICS

According to FBI statistics, there were 5,796 reported hate crime incidents involving 6,718 criminal offenses in the United States in 2012. Approximately 49 percent of these hate crimes were racially motivated, with 66 percent of racially motivated hate crimes involving anti-black bias, 22 percent involving anti-white bias, 4 percent involving anti-Asian/Pacific Islander bias, and 3 percent involving anti–American Indian bias. The next most common types of hate crimes, in descending order, were motivated by bias against sexual orientation (19 percent), religion (19 percent), ethnicity or nationality (12 percent), and disability (1.5 percent). Nearly 60 percent of all hate crimes motivated by ethnicity or nationality bias targeted Hispanic and Latino individuals. Of the 6,718 hate crime offenses reported in 2012, nearly 60 percent involved crimes against persons and 38 percent involved crimes against property.

Approximately 28 percent of all reported hate crime offenses in 2012 involved property damages and vandalism, 23 percent involved simple assault, 22 percent involved intimidation, and 12 percent involved aggravated assault.

Of the 5,331 hate crime offenders whose race was reported in 2012, approximately 55 percent were white, 23 percent were black, 9 percent were groups made up of individuals of various races, 0.9 percent were Asian or Pacific Islander, and 0.9 percent were American Indian.

The majority of victims of antireligious hate crimes were Jewish (62 percent), followed by Muslims (12 percent), Catholics (6 percent), Protestants (3 percent), and atheists or agnostics (0.9 percent). Of the individuals targeted due the offender's bias against disability, approximately 80 percent were targeted due to mental disability and 20 percent were targeted due to physical disability.

HATE CRIME VERSUS TERRORISM

When compared, hate crimes and terrorist acts share many of the same characteristics. They are acts of intimidation, acts against an identifiable group, and attempts to send a message of hostility and induce fear. However, terrorism tends to be national or international in scope and to be better organized and planned than most hate crimes. Terrorists tend to seek large gatherings with many potential victims, partly because of the greater expected media coverage. Terrorists also tend to have political motives and often seek the removal of the targeted group, particularly if it is a government group or occupying force. Some theorists have argued that terrorism is an "upward crime," in which a perpetrator of lower social standing targets members of the majority or the dominant group in society, whereas hate crimes are largely committed by members of the dominant group against members of minority groups.

BIBLIOGRAPHY

Cheng, Wen, William Ickes, and Jared B. Kenworthy. "The Phenomenon of Hate Crimes in the United States." *Journal of Applied Social Psychology* 43.4 (2013): 761–94. Print.

Deloughery, Kathleen, Ryan D. King, and Victor Asal. "Close Cousins or Distant Relatives: The Relationship between Terrorism and Hate Crime." *Crime and Delinquency* 58.5 (2012): 663–88. Print.

Gerstenfeld, Phyllis B. *Hate Crimes: Causes, Controls, and Controversies.* 3rd ed. Los Angeles: Sage, 2013. Print.

King, Ryan D., and Gretchen M. Sutton. "High Times for Hate Crimes: Explaining the Temporal Clustering of Hate-Motivated Offending." *Criminology* 51.4 (2013): 871–94. Print.

Mason-Bish, Hannah, and Alan Roulstone. *Disability, Heat Crime and Violence.* London: Routledge, 2013. Print.

McDevitt, J., J. Levin, and S. Bennett. "Hate Crime Offenders: An Expanded Typology." *Journal of Social Issues* 58.2 (2002): 303–17. Print.

Merino, Noël, ed. *Hate Crimes.* Detroit: Greenhaven, 2009. Print.

Paulson, Lawrence N. *Hate Crimes: Legal Issues and Legislation.* New York: Nova Science, 2008. Print.

Post, Jerrold M., Cody McGinnis, and Kristen Moody. "The Changing Face of Terrorism in the 21st Century: The Communications Revolution and the Virtual Community of Hatred." *Behavioral Sciences and the Law* 32.3 (2014): 306–34. Print.

Schafer, J., and J. Navarro. "The Seven-Stage Hate Model: The Psychopathology of Hate Groups." *FBI Law Enforcement Bulletin* 72.3 (2003): 1–8. Print.

Shively, Michael, and Carrie F. Mulford. "Hate Crime in America: The Debate Continues." *National Institute of Justice Journal* 257 (2007): 8–13. Print.

Richard L. McWhorter

See Also: Aggression; Anger; Antisocial personality disorder; Group decision making; Groups; Homosexuality; Racism; Violence: Psychological causes and effects.

Health insurance

Type of psychology: Developmental psychology; Psychopathology; Stress

Health insurance is a type of insurance designed to help defray the costs of medical treatment. A wide variety of public and private health insurance plans have been developed and differ dramatically in what they pay for and how they function.

Key Concepts

- Co-pay
- Deductible
- Fee-for-service insurance
- Health maintenance organizations (HMOs)
- Long-term care insurance
- Managed care plans
- Medicaid
- Medicare
- Professional provider organizations (PPOs)
- Universal health insurance

INTRODUCTION

The first modern private health insurance plans were developed in the United States in 1929, and since then, they have taken a wide variety of forms. One of the first successful plans was created in 1932 by Blue Cross/Blue Shield, which contracted with physicians and hospitals to obtain discounted health care for its members. In the 1940's and 1950's, employer-sponsored health insurance became increasingly common.

The U.S. government became involved in sponsoring health insurance in the 1960's, introducing MedicareMedicare and Medicaid in 1965. Medicare, which supplies health insurance for people aged sixty-five and over and for disabled people who have paid into the Social Security system, is a federally funded and operated program. Medicaid, which provided health insurance for low-income people, is federally and state funded and state operated. When these two forms of health insurance were developed, they accounted for 25 percent of all health care costs. By the twenty-first century, Medicare and Medicaid accounted for nearly 50 percent of all health care costs.

Individuals on Medicare can purchase Medigap insurance, which is private insurance that supplements Medicare coverage by paying co-pays and deductibles. Co-pays are the flat fees that individuals must pay each time they receive a service. Deductibles are the amount that individuals must pay for health care each year before insurance begins to cover the costs. Many Americans receive health coverage through their employers, as part of their compensation packages. If they cease to be employed, their health benefits terminate, but they do have the right to continue to be covered through their employers' plans for eighteen months through the Consolidated Omnibus Budget Reconciliation Act of 1985 (COBRA).

TYPES OF HEALTH INSURANCE

Traditional (standard) health insurance offered fee-for-service plans. Under these types of plans, patients could use whatever physician or hospital they chose. They paid the deductible and any co-pays, and the insurer paid the rest. However, by the end of the twentieth century, to cut costs, insurers had moved toward offering more cost-effective managed care plans. These plans consist of networks of providers and hospitals who provide care to plan members at reduced costs. These managed care plans include Health maintenance organizationshealth maintenance organizations (HMOs) and preferred provider organizations (PPOs). In HMOs, patients must get all their care from participating providers, and must receive referrals from their primary care provider to see specialists. In PPOs, clients may choose to see either in-network or out-of-network providers but will pay less if they see those who belong to the network of providers and hospitals affiliated with their plans.

Because people have been living longer, health care costs have been rising exponentially, particularly in the latter part of life. Many people find themselves in need of long-term health care during the last years of their lives. Many types of private and government health insurance do not cover long-term treatment, so the insurance industry developed plans to meet this need. Long-term care insurance covers the costs of long-term home health care or extended care in an assisted living facility or a nursing home.

The United States is one of the only industrialized nations that does not have universal health care, although the administration of President Bill Clinton proposed a plan for such health care in the 1990's. Basically, universal health care would provide all Americans with health insurance through the federal government. Many nations with universal health care also have a single-payer system, whereby a single insurance agency (public or private) provides health insurance to everyone. As of the beginning of the twenty-first century, about 46 million Americans did not have health insurance. Providing accessible health care to all Americans, and practicing primary prevention could dramatically improve the health of the nation.

MENTAL HEALTH COVERAGE

Regardless of the type of health insurance, historically, benefits for mental health have not been as extensive as those for medical or surgical services and have varied from state to state. The Mental Health Parity Act (1996) Mental Health Parity Act of 1996 required insurers that offered Mental health servicesparitymental health coverage to set lifetime dollar limits equivalent to limits for medical and surgical benefits, but it did not require insurers to offer coverage for mental problems. In 2008, Congress passed a law stipulating the Medicare co-pays for mental health were to be reduced from 50 percent to 20 percent, the same as for most doctors' services, over a six-year period. In October, 2008, the Paul Wellstone and Pete Domenici Mental Health Parity and Addiction Equity Act (2008) Mental Health Parity and Addiction Equity Act required that coverage for treatment for addiction and mental illness be on a par with that for medical and surgical services for employer and group health plans in companies with more than fifty employees. The law would take effect on January 1, 2010.Insurance, health

BIBLIOGRAPHY

Agency for Healthcare Research and Quality. *Questions and Answers About Health Insurance: A Consumer Guide*. Washington, D.C.: U.S. Department of Health and Human Services, 2008. This guide to health insurance available in the United States was developed by the federal government to make consumers aware of the various options available to them. It guides their decision-making process by providing answers to commonly asked questions.

Franks, P., C. M. Clancy, M. R. Gold, and C. M. Franks. "Health Insurance and Mortality: Evidence from a National Cohort." *Journal of the American Medical Association* 270 (1993): 737-741. This article looks at the relationship between health insurance (or lack thereof) and illness and death. It highlights the importance of insurance to overall health.

Pear, Robert. "Bailout Provides More Mental Health Coverage." *The New York Times*, October 5, 2008. Describes the mental health parity law that was passed along with the financial security law and its effects on mental health coverage by insurance companies.

Pilzer, P. Z. *The New Health Insurance Solution*. San Francisco: Wiley Interscience, 2005. This popular book explains the different types of health insurance available in the United States. It describes options that may be available to those who do not have health insurance through their employers, highlighting the advantages and disadvantages of each.

Shelton, P. *Long-Term Care: Your Financial Planning Guide*. New York: Kensington, 2003. This book explains the importance of long-term care insurance. It focuses both on the nature and potential costs of long-term care, indicating why it is becoming an essential part of financial planning.

Stevens, W. S. *Health Insurance: Current Issues and Background*. Hauppauge, N.Y.: Nova, 2003. This book focuses on major issues and controversies dealing with health insurance in the United States. It includes a discussion of problems facing the uninsured and the underinsured.

Robin Kamienny Montvilo

SEE ALSO: Confidentiality; Health maintenance organizations; Hospice; Mental health parity.

Health maintenance organizations (HMOs)

DATE: Twentieth century forward
TYPE OF PSYCHOLOGY: Psychopathology

Health maintenance organizations (HMOs) are a type of managed care health insurance plan that bring together a wide range of health services into one organization and provide health care to subscribers for a fixed, prepaid fee.

KEY CONCEPTS

- Cost containment
- Health care
- Member
- Network
- Prepaid
- Primary care provider

INTRODUCTION

From the early part of the twentieth century until the 1960s, many employers provided prepaid, limited health insurance plans. Their popularity waned considerably in the late 1960s, however, when health care costs soared and pressure grew for the government to intervene. In 1973, as part of a health care cost containment initiative, the US Congress passed the Health Maintenance Organization Act in an effort to improve the efficiency of the national health care system. This act provided grants and loans to establish or expand on federally certified HMOs and removed legal barriers that had previously inhibited their development. It required employers with twenty-five or more employees to offer federally certified HMO plans. In the 1980s, the number of HMOs in the United States doubled. By 1996, almost 25 percent of the US populace was enrolled in an HMO, and by 2001 this number had peaked at almost 30 percent. By 2010, rates of HMO enrollment in the United States varied widely between geographic regions, with higher enrollment in the West (33 percent) and Northeast (26 percent) and lower enrollment in the South (12 percent) and Midwest (11 percent), where a majority of covered workers are enrolled in preferred provider organizations (PPOs).

HMOs contract with health care providers who become part of a network that provides health services to HMO patient members at a fixed, prepaid fee regardless of actual medical costs or the number of times they are seen in the office. In return, the HMO ensures a steady flow of patients to the providers. The major goal of HMOs is to provide quality health care while reducing health care costs and administrative complexities. The premise is that because of the reduction of out-of-pocket expenses, HMO patient members will seek medical treatment more routinely. As such, a focus on preventive care will identify health problems before they worsen and their treatment becomes more unmanageable and expensive.

Additionally, utilization management controls, such as requiring referrals from a primary care provider for medical procedures and care by a medical specialist, reduce the number of specialists required and limit unnecessary tests and procedures. HMOs were largely designed to replace fee-for-service medical care, which many believed incentivized doctors to order and perform unnecessary tests and procedures.

HMO subscribers must receive health care services from doctors, hospitals, and other health care professionals that are within the HMO network. Because managed care does not allow free choice in selecting health care providers that are not within a given network, however, the system is looked upon by some as limiting access to specialized care and treatment at the cost of patient well-being.

Patient members choose a primary care provider (PCP) from the HMO member providers. The PCP provides basic medical care, authorizes access to other medical services, and refers patients to health care specialists. Patient members also pay a nominal copayment for office visits. Some HMOs do not require a referral before seeing a specialist. There is usually no lifetime limit on benefits as there are with other types of medical insurance. Experimental and nonnecessary elective treatments are rarely covered by HMOs.

MENTAL HEALTH CARE

Outpatient mental health services are often limited in HMO plans. In fact, many provisions for long-term mental health needs are minimal. Many HMO plans increase a patient's copay for extended mental health treatment. For example, a plan may require no copay for the first five mental health visits, a five-dollar copay for mental health visits six through ten, and a fifteen-dollar copay for additional visits. There may be no copay, however, for inpatient mental health treatment because such treatment often focuses on crisis intervention and short-term therapy. In addition, many HMOs depend on the primary care provider to treat mental health disorders instead of referring patients to licensed mental health care providers or psychiatrists. Treatment for addiction or substance abuse services is also limited.

The Mental Health Parity Act of 1996 began the process of ending the practice of providing less insurance coverage for mental than for medical illnesses or surgical procedures. However, it only pertained to plans that already covered mental health care, and although mental illnesses were covered, it did not include coverage of treatment for substance abuse or addiction. The Mental Health Parity and Addiction Equity Act of 2008 requires that mental health and addiction treatment copayments and treatment limitations could not be any more restrictive than medical treatment copayments and treatment limitations. This legislation also incorporates methods of oversight to evaluate for discrimination against specific conditions. The Patient Protection and Affordable Care Act of 2010 (PPACA) required insurance providers to include certain treatment services for mental health and substanceabuse disorders in their benefits packages; created incentives to coordinate primary care, mental health, and addiction services through federal grants; and prohibited insurers from denying coverage to subscribers with preexisting conditions, including chronic mental health conditions such as schizophrenia.

BIBLIOGRAPHY

Culyer, A. J. *Encyclopedia of Health Economics*. Burlington: Elsevier Science, 2014. Print.

Kongstvedt, Peter. *Managed Care: What It Is and How It Works*. Sudsbury: Jones, 2008. Print.

Marcinko, David, and Hope Hedico. *Dictionary of Health Insurance and Managed Care*. New York: Springer, 2006. Print.

Pearlman, S. A. "The Patient Protection and Affordable Care Act: Impact on Mental Health Services Demand and Provider Availability." *Journal of the American Psychiatric Nurses Association* 19.6 (2013): 327–34. Print.

Sederer, Lloyd I. *Family Guide to Mental Health Care*. New York: Norton, 2013. Print.

Sharon Wallace Stark

See Also: Health insurance; Law and mental health; Mental health parity.

Health psychology

DATE: Late 1970's forward
TYPE OF PSYCHOLOGY: Stress

Health psychology studies the biological, psychological, and social interactions of health, illness, recovery from illness, and the impact of health care systems and treatments. It encompasses the maintenance and promotion of health, the treatment and prevention of illness, and the development of health policy.

KEY CONCEPTS

- Behavioral components of chronic disease
- Biomedical model
- Biopsychosocial model
- Cost of health care
- Dispositional optimism
- Perceptions of control
- Positive psychology
- Psychoneuroimmunology
- Salutogenic focus

INTRODUCTION

Health psychology is concerned with the psychdiaological components of promoting and maintaining health, treating and preventing illnesses, improving health care services, and developing health care policy. Health psychology seeks to generate new knowledge about people's health beliefs and practices and to apply existing knowledge to improve health and well-being. Psychologists interested in health psychology generally adhere to the belief that health cannot be understood exclusively by focusing on the physical condition of the body. The psychological side—the state of the mind—must be considered as well.

THE BIOPSYCHOSOCIAL MODEL

The relationship between mind and body and its impact on health are best understood by using what has been labeled the biopsychosocial model. This model assumes that one's health state is based on the often-complicated interactions of three sets of factors: biological factors, psychological factors, and social factors. Biological factors include genetic or inherited influences that may predispose some individuals to be more susceptible than average to certain maladies such as heart disease. Examples of psychological factors could include the amount of stress an individual experiences, a personality trait such as optimism, or the degree of belief in control over one's own health. Support and empathy one receives from family, friends, or colleagues constitute social factors. Such social support can come in the form of emotional, informational, or even tangible resources such as financial assistance. Other social factors that play roles in health and illness are cultural, ethnic, and gender differences.

Thus, the biopsychosocial model assumes that health is based on more than the absence of illness; it is also based on attaining physical, social, and mental well-being. Indeed, this model highlights the role of psychosocial variables. Psychosocial variables can be internal mental states, such as depression, or external situational factors, such as the quality of social support one receives. The important point is that psychosocial factors should be examined in combination with, not independent of, biological influences.

Although this model's biological aspects are readily accepted as important to understanding health, the psychosocial components are controversial in some areas in which the biomedical model is heavily relied on. This more traditional model assumes that disease or illness is exclusively biological in nature, so that diagnosis and subsequent treatment are focused on the state of the body as distinct from the mind. The controversy concerning the biopsychosocial model is relatively minor, however, because there is a recognition among many researchers and health professionals that psychosocial variables often add more to knowledge concerning health, illness, and disease than do biological factors alone.

THE RISE OF LIFESTYLE DISEASES

The rise in interest concerning psychosocial variables specifically, and health psychology generally, can be attributed in part to the changing conditions of health problems. Because of advances in disease prevention, vaccination, and other biomedical treatments, many of the primary health problems are no longer major infectious diseases, such as polio, smallpox, or rubella. (Acquired immunodeficiency syndrome, AIDS, is one important exception.) The threat of these acute diseases has been successfully eliminated through vaccination programs, which resulted in a doubled life expectancy within the twentieth century. This increased life span, however, has a price. A collection of more chronic and age-related diseases, including cancer, heart disease, and stroke, are increasingly prevalent health problems worldwide. Unlike infectious diseases, these threats cannot be treated through vaccination because they are largely caused by people's lifestyles or aging.

The intriguing aspect of these modern lifestyle diseases is that they have a significant behavioral component and may be preventable. Ironically, most people are probably aware of ways they could reduce their susceptibility to these diseases, yet they choose not to change their lifestyles. To decrease the risk of lung cancer, for example, people who smoke should pursue smoking cessation treatments. Heart disease can be controlled through improved diet and a moderate amount of exercise. Alcohol consumption should be moderate, and recreational drugs should be avoided altogether. Making people aware of the origins of these lifestyle diseases is no longer the key problem. It has been replaced by the problem of how to alter negative behaviors affecting health. Many of these negative behaviors, such as binge drinking, have rewarding short-term consequences that increase these negative behaviors more effectively than delayed punishment, such as a hangover, can decrease them. Health psychologists are interested in researching motivation, coping strategies, and other behavioral modification techniques and therapies that promote health and well-being.

Some advances in dealing with the problems of lifestyle and behavior have been made. There has been a downward trend in smoking; more people are aware that exercise and eating healthier food improves the quality and quantity of life. However, people in industrialized countries are showing alarming increases in obesity and decreases in physical activity. Finding ways to alter health behaviors is one of the major contributions health psychologists can provide, one that relies on an understanding of biological as well as psychosocial factors in health.

The changing nature of illness, related in complex ways to biology and behavior, must be understood in relation to broader issues in health psychology, such as the expansion and development of adequate health care services. Preventable illness account for the bulk of health care costs in the United States. In 2012, *Forbes* magazine reported that obesity accounted for a staggering $190 billion in annual national health care costs, exceeding only smoking in terms of health care costs. A 2012 study published in the *Journal of Health Economics* estimated that obese men account for an additional $1,152 annual in medical spending, predominantly due to hospitalizations and prescription drugs, and obese women account for an additional $3,613 per year. This money supports escalating health expenses such as health care, health care workers' jobs, and health-related research. Health psychology seeks to address these issues as well as make recommendations concerning future directions for health care.

OPTIMISM AND HEART SURGERY

Because health psychology encompasses both theoretical and applied elements, researchers work in both laboratory and field settings. Given the variety of research efforts that potentially fall within the bounds of health psychology, only a brief review of representative pieces of research is possible. This review will be highly selective, focusing on two studies that explicitly link psychosocial variables to health-related issues: recovery following coronary artery bypass surgery and adjustment to a nursing care facility.

Heart disease is an important topic within health psychology because it accounts for more deaths annually in the United States than all other diseases combined. Each year, many persons require life-saving cardiac surgery to increase blood flow to the heart, thereby decreasing the risk of subsequent heart attack. The surgery itself, however, can be a stressful and physically and emotionally draining experience. It is useful for medical professionals to be able to predict which patients will cope better with the coronary artery bypass operation and show more rapid rates of recovery.

Michael F. Scheier and Charles S. Carver have argued that a personality trait they call "dispositional optimism" can lead to more effective coping with a threatening event such as heart surgery. Dispositional optimism refers to a person's general belief that positive outcomes will occur in the future. If individuals can envision good things happening in the future, then these expectations might allow them both to cope effectively with and to recover more quickly from the surgery. Pessimists, those who anticipate relatively negative outcomes, might show a slower rate of recovery and poorer adjustment to the surgery.

In an article published in the *Journal of Personality and Social Psychology* in 1989, Scheier, Carver, and their colleagues assessed the optimism of a group of middle-aged men one day before their coronary artery bypass surgeries. As expected, following surgery the optimists showed earlier signs of physical recovery, such as walking around their hospital rooms, than did the pessimists. They were also judged by the medical staff to have demonstrated faster recovery rates. After six months, optimists were more likely to have resumed their normal routines of work, exercise, and social activity and to have done so more quickly than the pessimists. Furthermore, there is accumulating evidence that even mild depression, which is related to pessimism, increases the chances of death from a future heart attack.

Clearly, a more optimistic orientation can lead some people to deal effectively with adverse health problems. It may be that dispositional optimism promotes a reliance on useful coping strategies, such as making future plans or setting goals. In turn, these strategies affect one's adjustment to the physical illness. Further research has shown that optimism leads people to seek social support and to focus on the positive aspects of stressful events. As a psychosocial variable, then, dispositional optimism has important implications for adjusting to physical problems related to disease. Health psychologists are interested in studying and reinforcing positive coping strategies for individuals with chronic illnesses or terminal diseases.

CONTROL IN THE NURSING HOME

Other psychosocial variables are relevant to adequate adjustment to health problems posed by particular environments. Many older adults may need to live in nursing care facilities because of health or economic difficulties. Such facilities provide adequate shelter and health care, but they frequently operate under fixed financial resources which limit the individualized activities and freedoms enjoyed by their residents.

Writing in the *Journal of Personality and Social Psychology* in 1976, Ellen J. Langer and Judith Rodin argued that such institutional environments unwittingly reduce morale and health by gradually taking away the patients' perceptions of control over daily events. As a psychosocial variable, the perception of control is the belief that one can influence outcomes. Nursing home residents may lack such perceptions of control in nursing homes where almost no aspect of their environment is their responsibility. Practically all decisions, from hygiene to entertainment, are made for them by staff members.

Langer and Rodin reasoned that by creating opportunities for patients living in nursing homes to perceive even relatively small amounts of control and autonomy, their health and well-being might improve. To test this idea, these researchers gave one floor of patients in a nursing home plants to care for and then asked them to make some decisions regarding participation in recreational activities in the facility. Patients on a comparison floor also received plants but were told that the nursing staff would be responsible for their care. This group also participated in the same recreational activities but made no decisions about them. Several weeks later, staff observations and comments made by the patients showed that those individuals who perceived control were more physically active and had a stronger sense of well-being. One year later, those patients who were made to feel responsible for events in their environment were still physically and psychologically healthier, even exhibiting a lower mortality rate than those who did not perceive control.

Perceived control is only one psychosocial variable that can be linked to environmental effects on health and well-being, just as nursing home residents represent only one group who may benefit from interventions of this sort. Based on these results, however, a few conclusions can be drawn. Perceived control can be engendered in fairly simple ways with profound effects on people's physical and mental health. The adverse effects of some environments, such as institutions that care for patients with chronic health problems, can also be reduced. Finally, some health interventions can be implemented in a cost-effective manner. Many applications of the biopsychosocial model are clearly possible.

EVOLUTION OF THE FIELD

The belief that a sound mind leads to a sound body is by no means novel. The medical and psychological communities have long operated under the assumption that mental and physical states affect one another, though active cooperation between professionals in these two fields was limited. Psychiatry, for example, served as one of the bridges for communication between these groups. Within psychology itself, there have always been scholars whose research focused on health and medical issues, although they tended to identify themselves with areas such as clinical, social, or physiological psychology.

In the late 1970s, there was growing recognition that a distinct subdiscipline of psychology relating to health matters was coalescing. Various names for this subdiscipline, such as behavioral medicine, medical psychology, and behavioral health, became more common, as did specialized journals, texts, symposia, and organizations. A division of health psychology became an official part of the American Psychological Association in 1978. Health psychology has since become more formalized, articulating its goals, defining its scientific and professional orientations, and evaluating the training needs of students drawn to it. One prominent health psychologist,

Shelley E. Taylor, has described the field as a "maturing discipline."

Because philosophers have always speculated about the association between mind and body, the philosophical roots of health psychology can be located in antiquity and traced forward to modern times. Psychology's interest and experimental approaches are more recent developments. From the 1930s to the 1950s, researchers such as Flanders Dunbar and Harold Wolff attempted to link personality variables and psychosocial stressors to specific diseases. In the early 1960s, Stanley Schachter and Jerome E. Singer examined the role of cognitive and physiological processes in the perception of emotional states. In related work during the same period, Richard S. Lazarus pioneered the study of stress and coping.

In the twenty-first century, diseases with strong behavioral components such as type 2 diabetes, heart disease, and various types of cancer will continue to be major concerns. The human genome will provide new insights into interplay of genes and behavior in the development of health and illness. The developing field of psychoneuroimmunology, which is the study of the complex interplay of behavior, the nervous system, the endocrine system, and the immune system, will take on more significance. For example, psychoneuroimmunological research is progressing rapidly on the effects of social stress on upper respiratory infections and speed of wound healing. Finally, the new discipline of positive psychology will become infused into health psychology. Martin E. P. Seligman and Mihaly Csikszentmihalyi wrote in *American Psychologist* in 2000 that scientific study of the development and fostering of positive traits in humans and their institutions will eliminate many of the mental and physical maladies that affect the human condition. Scientific research in the twenty-first century will help to develop and foster traits such as hope, wisdom, creativity, courage, and perseverance and will determine how these traits can positively influence health and allow individuals and social groups to thrive.

Because of this growing interest in health threats, health psychology may increasingly adopt a salutogenic rather than a pathogenic focus. A salutogenic focus seeks to understand the origins of health by attending to those factors that promote people's health and psychological well-being. Healthy people behave in ways that keep them healthy, and researchers attempt to uncover the aspects of healthy and happy lifestyles that may aid individuals suffering from illness or disease. In contrast, a pathogenic focus highlights the causes of illness and disease and is less prevention-oriented. This is not to say that the cause of illness is a secondary concern. Rather, the onset of illness should be understood in relation to behaviors and psychological factors that maintain good health.

Health psychology promises to continue as an important arena for interdisciplinary research on health. Basic and applied approaches to understanding health will develop by examining the interplay of biological, psychological, and social factors. As a growing subdiscipline of the field of psychology, health psychology will yield intriguing insights regarding the relationship between mind and body.

BIBLIOGRAPHY

Antonovsky, Aaron. *Unraveling the Mystery of Health: How People Manage Stress and Stay Well.* San Francisco: Jossey-Bass, 1988. Print.

Brannon, Linda, Jess Feist, and John Updegraff. *Health Psychology: An Introduction to Behavior and Health.* 8th ed. Belmont: Wadsworth, 2014. Print.

Jones, Fiona, and Jim Bright. *Stress: Myth, Theory, and Research.* Upper Saddle River: Prentice Hall, 2001. Print.

Murray, Michael. "Social History of Health Psychology: Context and Textbooks." *Health Psychology Review* 8.2 (2014): 215–37. Print.

Peterson, Christopher, and Lisa M. Bossio. *Health and Optimism.* New York: Free, 1991. Print.

Rodin, Judith, and P. Salovey. "Health Psychology." *Annual Review of Psychology.* Vol. 40. Stanford: Annual Reviews, 1989. Print.

Sanderson, Catherine A. *Health Psychology.* 2nd ed. Hoboken: Wiley, 2012. Print.

Sarafino, Edward P. *Health Psychology: Biopsychosocial Interactions.* Hoboken: Wiley, 2008. Print.

Seligman, Martin E. P., and Mihaly Csikszentmihalyi. "Positive Psychology: An Introduction." *American Psychologist* 55 (2000): 5–14. Print.

Taylor, Shelley E. *Health Psychology.* 9th ed. New York: McGraw-Hill, 2014. Print.

Dana S. Dunn; updated by William M. Miley

See Also: Assisted living; Biofeedback and relaxation; Coping: Chronic illness; Coping: Social support; Coping: Strategies; Coping: Terminal illness; Elders' mental health; Emotions; Environmental psychology; Health insurance; Health maintenance organizations; Hope and mental health; Intervention;

Meditation and relaxation; Positive psychology; Seligman, Martin E. P.; Stress: Behavioral and psychological responses; Stress: Physiological responses; Stress-related diseases; Stress: Theories.